ETHICS
Revised Edition

Ethics
Revised Edition

Volume 1
Abelard, Peter — Genocide, frustration-aggression theory of

Edited by

JOHN K. ROTH
Claremont McKenna College
Department of Philosophy and Religious Studies

SALEM PRESS, INC.
PASADENA, CALIFORNIA   HACKENSACK, NEW JERSEY

Editor in Chief: Dawn P. Dawson
Managing Editor: Christina J. Moose
Project Editor: R. Kent Rasmussen
Assistant Editor: Andrea Miller
Acquisitions Editor: Mark Rehn
Photograph Editor: Philip Bader
Research Assistant: Andy Perry
Production Editor: Kathy Hix
Graphics and Design: James Hutson
Layout: William Zimmerman

Library of Congress Cataloging-in-Publication Data

Ethics / edited by John Roth.— Rev. Ed.
    p. cm.
  Includes bibliographical references and index.
   ISBN 1-58765-170-X (set : alk. paper) — ISBN 1-58765-171-8 (vol. 1 : alk. paper) — ISBN 1-58765-172-6 (vol. 2 : alk. paper) — ISBN 1-58765-173-4 (vol. 3 : alk. paper)
  1. Ethics—Encyclopedias. I. Roth, John K.
  BJ63.E54 2004
  170'.3—dc22

2004021797

First Printing

CONTENTS

PUBLISHER'S NOTE

Ethics, Revised Edition, is the first revision of Salem Press's well-received *Ethics*, which was published in 1994. This new edition adds more than 200 completely new articles to the set, raising the total to 1,007 essays and 6 appendices. This edition also updates and expands many of the original essays and adds other new features. The main thrust of this edition is on applied ethics, with particular emphasis on current issues.

Ethics, in one form or another, has been a central issue in history since the earliest human beings began living together in communities. Throughout human history, people have always wondered whether they were being held accountable for their actions by a higher power or powers. Those believing that such higher powers exist have needed to know what their relationships with those powers are and what they are required to do or not to do. Those lacking such beliefs have needed to believe that their lives have meaning; they, in turn, have wondered how they should act and what they should do. In addition, all people need to know what other people expect of them and what the limits of their freedom of action are. All these questions are essentially ethical matters.

ISSUES IN ETHICS

Many of the basic ethical issues with which early human societies wrestled still confront modern societies. However, early societies did not confront the vast variety of complex ethical issues that modern societies face. As societies have grown larger and more complex, and as human knowledge and technological ability have increased, the numbers and varieties of ethical issues that human beings face have also increased. For example, the twentieth century development of computer technology introduced knotty problems regarding privacy rights, the replacement of human workers by robots, and the possibility of artificially created intelligent beings. Along with the modern medical technologies that have extended human life spans have come complex bioethical questions such as balancing the needs of the productive young and the nonproductive old. Recent advances in biotechnology have raised a host of new ethical questions about genetic engineering and other matters that members of earlier societies could never have imagined.

Recent decades have seen unprecedented concerns about gross inequities in the worldwide distribution of food, resources, and power. These questions become more glaring as the world becomes more crowded and more interdependent and as the gaps between the rich and the poor and the powerful and the weak grow larger. These changes are raising questions about how much responsibility those who have the means to prosper should take for promoting the welfare of those who lack the resources to survive.

Religion is another field in which new ethical questions are being posed. Throughout much of the world, traditional attitudes toward religion have changed, and many societies have seen growing numbers of their members reject the old ethical and moral codes of the religions into which they were born, while not finding other codes to replace them. At the same, many religious leaders, politicians, and other public figures have demonstrated that their own personal codes of ethics will not bear scrutiny. These developments and others have led many people to focus more attention on secular ethics. As a consequence, governments, professional organizations, industries, and individual businesses have adopted codes of ethics in attempts to improve their images, and many educational institutions have added ethics classes and programs to their curricula.

EXPANDED COVERAGE IN THIS EDITION

As the world enters the twenty-first century, new questions are being asked about political, economic, social, and scientific ethics. Examples of topics new to this edition range from the etiquette of cell-phone use and the pirating of digital media to the permissible limits of stem-cell research and the role of religion in world terrorism. As Dr. John K. Roth points out in his Introduction to this revised edition, the past decade alone has raised ethics questions that were not imagined when the first edition of *Ethics* was published.

Before the appearance of the first edition of *Ethics* in 1994, students interested in learning more about ethics had to consult many separate, specialized studies to gain a general knowledge of applied ethics. Salem Press created *Ethics* in its Ready Reference series to provide the first comprehensive reference work examining all aspects of applied ethics as well as the more traditional ethical areas of religion and philosophy. *Ethics, Revised Edition*, expands the earlier work's coverage by addressing many ethics issues that have come to prominence over the past decade. These include such religious topics as church-state separation, faith healers, Islamic ethics, the jihad concept, religion and violence, the Roman Catholic priests sexual abuse scandal, Scientology, and televangelists.

Ethics, Revised Edition, also gives particular attention to business and labor ethics, with new articles on such topics as advertising, several aspects of computer misuse, corporate compensation, professional athlete incomes, downsizing and outsourcing, and the tobacco industry. New topics relating to political and economic issues include Congress, distributive justice, famine as an instrument of oppression, care of the homeless, lobbying, lotteries, minimum wage laws, and the fairness of taxes. Personal and social ethics issues are the subject of a similar number of new essays, which include topics ranging from cell-phone etiquette and workplace dress codes to premarital sex and professional resumes.

The revised edition's increased emphasis on applied ethics can also be seen in the new essays on contemporary newsmakers whose ethical behavior—whether positive or negative—has been in the news. These people include William Bennett, Bill Clinton, Louis Farrakhan, Saddam Hussein, Jesse Jackson, Martha Stewart, and Desmond Tutu.

Some of the most important topics of the new essays concern the burgeoning field of bioethics. New topics in this field include biometrics, assisted suicide, cloning, genetic engineering, and stem-cell research. International relations is another field that is constantly raising new ethics questions. Among the topics covered in new essays in this field are the Bosnia conflict; globalization; Iraq; and terrorism. New topics dealing with ethics questions relating to more purely military issues include biological warfare and bioterrorism, child soldiers, the just war theory, mercenary soldiers, peacekeeping missions, and war crimes trials.

FORMATTING OF ARTICLES

Every article is written to emphasize the relevance of ethics to its subject. To that end, each essay begins with ready-reference top matter providing such information as dates and places of birth and death for important personages; dates of important events; a line identifying the most relevant type of ethics to which the topic relates; and a summary statement of the subject's significance in the field of ethics. In addition, at the end of every entry, a list of cross-references to other articles is provided to help guide readers to related subjects covered in the set. Within the main body of each article, clear subheads are provided to help guide readers.

More than half the articles in the set—all those 500 or more words in length—include bibliographies. The bibliographies of all the original articles in the set have been updated through mid-2004. Additional bibliographical information is provided in an appendix in volume 3.

SPECIAL FEATURES

The essays in *Ethics, Revised Edition*, are illustrated by 180 photographs and more than 200 maps, graphs, charts, and textual sidebars. The set's attention to current ethical concerns can be seen in the selection of photographs—more than one third of which were created after the publication of the first edition of *Ethics*.

The 6 appendices in volume 3 include an annotated list of organizations and Web sites devoted to ethics issues, with addresses and Web site information; a comprehensive and categorized bibliography; a glossary of basic ethics terminology; a biographical directory of people mentioned in the essays; a list of Nobel Peace Prize winners through 2004; and a Time Line of Primary Works in Moral and Ethical Philosophy

The set's three indexes include a categorized list of essay topics arranged by types of ethics, an index of personages, and a detailed subject index.

ACKNOWLEDGMENTS

Reference works of this kind would not be possible without the generous support of many scholars. Salem Press would like to thank the 366 writers who contributed essays to the original and revised editions. We are especially grateful to contributors who responded to our call for updates of original articles. We are also grateful to Professor John K. Roth, of Southern California's Claremont McKenna College, who has served as consultant for both editions of *Ethics*.

INTRODUCTION: OLD AND NEW IN ETHICS

Ethics is at once as old as human existence and as new as today's dilemmas and tomorrow's possibilities. It is thus both the same and different as experience unfolds and history develops. Considering how and why those claims make sense may help to introduce this revised and expanded edition of *Ethics*.

Among the defining characteristics of human life are the abilities to think, make judgments, and remember. Human beings are also identified by webs of social relationships. They are members of families and societies; they have networks of friends, neighbors, and associates. As history has unfolded, human beings have participated in political and religious traditions and have become members of communities and citizens of nation-states. Enriched and complicated by human memories of past actions and their consequences, these characteristics and relationships require human beings to make evaluations. With the structure of human life and our environments forcing people to make choices and to live or die with the consequences of their decisions, human existence is unavoidably inseparable from distinctions between what is right and wrong, just and unjust, good and evil.

As human beings, we all deal constantly with factual matters. However, we also make value judgments, issue prescriptive statements, and formulate normative appraisals. In short, we try to figure out what we ought to do. Few of us are always and entirely content with the ways in which the events that surround us unfold. Often, we ask, How *should* events turn out? There is nothing new about these realities. They have been with humanity from its beginnings.

Whenever concepts such as *justice* vs. *injustice*, *right* vs. *wrong*, *good* vs. *evil* are employed, ethics comes into play. However, what it means to say this requires close examination. Many factors enter into the evaluations that we as human beings make. These factors include our different cultural backgrounds, religious training or lack of it, and the influences of our families, teachers, and friends. Ethics may refer simply to the value judgments that people make and to the beliefs that people hold—individually and collectively—about what is right or wrong, good or evil, precious or worthless, beautiful or ugly, and sacred or profane. Value judgments affect everything we do: from the ways that we spend our money to the interests that our nations defend. Taken in this sense, it may be argued that every person, community, and nation is ethical. All persons, communities, and nations have normative beliefs and make evaluative judgments. However, to understand ethics adequately, a sharper focus is needed.

THE SCOPE OF ETHICS

Ethics involves much more than a primarily descriptive use of the term suggests. For example, ethics also refers to the study of value judgments and the ways in which such judgments influence—and are influenced by—institutions. The study of value judgments has historical dimensions; it may concentrate, for example, on how a society's values have changed or developed over time. In one way or another, work of this sort has also been going on for centuries. Its roots are in the earliest human awareness that groups and persons are not identical, that they think and act differently.

How important is wealth? Is religion desirable? What kinds of education should the young receive? Versions of questions such as these are ancient, and responses to them both reflect and depend upon the value commitments that people make. Historically, people have taken varied positions on ethical issues, even as they have exhibited persistent continuity about some fundamental convictions such as those, for instance, that condemn murder. If ethics is inseparable from human existence, however, the manifestations of that fact are many and varied. Arguably, comparative study of ethical beliefs and practices throughout human history is likely to confirm that their variety is more pronounced than their commonality.

Ethics does not end with either descriptions or studies of human beliefs and actions. The core of ethics, in fact, lies elsewhere. People make value judgments when they say, for example, that abortion is wrong or that the death penalty is right. Does the variety of values, and especially the arguments that conflicting value judgments can produce, mean that value judgments are culturally relative and even personally subjective? Or, are some value judgments objectively grounded and true for everyone? For centuries, philosophers and religious teachers have debated such questions, which are crucial parts of ethics as normative inquiry.

Although agreement about how to answer these questions is not universal, ethics would not be *ethics* if it failed to emphasize the importance of critical inquiry about the values that people hold. For example, much can be learned by asking, "Is this value judgment true, and, if so, why?" Much can also be learned by asking, "What makes some values positive—for example, courage, honesty, and trust? Why are other values negative—for instance, hatred, selfishness, and infidelity?"

In the form of critical inquiry about values, ethics contends that nothing is truly good or right simply because someone desires or values it. In fact, to say that something is good or right simply because someone values it would contradict one of the most fundamental experiences of human beings; differences between what is valuable and what is not depend on more than an individual's feelings or a culture's preferences. We know this because our value judgments can be mistaken. We often criticize, change, or even reject our judgments because we learn that they are wrong. Thus, while people may not agree about values, the questions that critical inquiry raises—for example, how should we evaluate the values we hold, and which values matter most?—are at the heart of ethics. Again, such insights are not new. Buddha, Confucius, Moses, Jesus, Socrates, and Plato brought them to life thousands of years ago, and even those ethical pioneers had predecessors in earlier history.

THE ETHICAL FAILINGS OF HUMAN BEINGS

Ethics is as old as human existence itself. Its basic questions, concerns, and fundamental vocabulary have exhibited considerable continuity amid the accompanying diversity. One of the reasons is that another feature of human life also remains deeply entrenched, namely, that human beings so often make bad judgments, inflict harm, lay waste to things that are good, treat each other brutally, rob, rape, and kill. Ethics attempts to check and correct those tendencies by urging all people to make human life more caring and humane and by showing how it can be more just and promising. Such work is an indispensable part of ethics.

Unfortunately, human abuses of human life are often so great that ethics seems too fragile and weak to achieve what we hope—at least in our better moments—that it can accomplish. Ethical theory and teaching have a long history, but it hard to say with clarity and confidence that humankind has made steady moral progress. The twentieth century, after all, was arguably the most murderous in human history. Moreover, there is no assurance that the twenty-first will be an improvement, despite the fact that there may be more talk than ever about the need for ethics. Human life is full of discouragement, cynicism, and despair produced by human folly, miscalculation, and wrongdoing. Undeniably, the importance of ethics looms large because the core issue remains: Will human beings ever take their ethical responsibilities seriously enough?

Concerns of this kind have led philosophers to offer new approaches to ethical reflection. French philosopher Emmanuel Levinas is a case in point. After losing much of his family to Nazi butchery during the Holocaust of World War II, Levinas argued that ethical theory had failed to concentrate on something as obvious and profound as the human face. By paying close and careful attention to the face of the other person, he suggested, there could be a reorientation not only of ethics but also of human life itself, for our seeing of the other person's face would drive home how closely human beings are connected and how much the existence of the other person confers responsibility upon us.

Working in a different but related way, the late twentieth century American philosopher John Rawls proposed a form of ethical deliberation that could make human life more just. He suggested that we consider ourselves behind what he called a "veil of ignorance." In that position, we would not know our exact status or role in the world, but we would be able to deliberate constructively about the rights and rules that we would all find reasonable to implement. Rawls thought that such deliberation would place a high priority on liberty and equality. Much of his work in *A Theory of Justice* (1971) and other influential writings was devoted to considering how those values could best be mutually supportive. Rawls did not conclude that deliberation behind the veil of ignorance would lead reasonable persons to expect that everyone should be treated exactly alike. Inequality of the right kind could be beneficial for everyone, but for that condition to hold, caring attention would always have to be paid to those who are the least well-off.

Levinas and Rawls are by no means the only recent innovators in ethical theory. This edition of *Ethics* covers many thinkers who have contributed to contemporary ethical thought. Nor is it true that Levinas, Rawls, and their most recent peers have developed their ideas independently of previous traditions in ethics. Levinas, for example, took seriously the ancient Jewish teaching that human beings are created in the image of God. The face of the other person, therefore, has at least traces of the divine within it and deserves respect accordingly. Rawls reinvented the idea of the social contract, which thinkers such as Thomas Hobbes, John Locke, and Jean-Jacques Rousseau developed in the seventeenth and eighteenth centuries. Levinas, Rawls, and their twenty-first century counterparts build upon and move beyond previous theories, trying to help humankind to respond to the ethical dilemmas of our time.

CHANGING PERSPECTIVES

Ethical theory is not only a historical matter. It goes on and on, partly because the seminal thinkers of the past keep provoking reflection on the questions they raised and partly because human experience requires ethics to break new ground. The first edition of this encyclopedia appeared in 1994. As the twentieth century drew to its close, it became clear that humanity faced ethical issues that had not existed a hundred or even fifty years earlier. For example, although the world knew nothing of nuclear weapons in 1894, their threat shadowed the world in 1994. In 1944, World War II and the Holocaust raged, but it was only during that year that Raphael Lemkin coined the term *genocide*. The grim reality denoted by that term erupted again in Rwanda in 1994, but too late to receive attention in the first edition of *Ethics*.

The Internet was coming into widespread use during the early 1990's, but only one decade later it is affecting our lives—and our ethics—in ways that would scarcely have been imaginable in 1994. Stem-cell research was not a household word in 1994; however, as the twenty-first century unfolds, the issues surrounding it are contested in national political debates. "Nine Eleven" meant nothing in 1994, but the attacks on the World Trade Center and the Pentagon on September 11, 2001, made the devastation of terrorism all too real and ignited a new kind of war, one that has no clear end in sight.

Human experience and ethical dilemmas go hand in hand. As some problems appear to be resolved or eliminated, new ones rise up or old ones reappear in different and even novel forms. Hunger, poverty, and crime, for example, are age-old, but their shapes and sizes and the resources for dealing with them change with developments in politics, economics, technology, religion, and even ethics itself. Arguably critical ethical reflection would not exist—there would be no need for it—if human beings knew everything, understood all the consequences of their actions, never made mistakes, always agreed with one another about what to do, and put exactly the right policies into practice. Human experience, however, is neither that clear nor that simple. Our knowledge is incomplete. We do make mistakes; we do disagree. Often, human life is full of conflict because different people do not see eye to eye about what is true and right. Thus, human life simmers, boils, and at times erupts in controversies, debates, and disputes. All too often, issues intensify and escalate into violence, war, and even genocide.

Fortunately, those destructive responses are not the only ones that human beings can make. Ethical reflection may prove insufficient to save the day; nevertheless it remains crucial, and it is ignored at our peril. Done well, ethical thinking can focus a community's attention helpfully and stimulate constructive activity—education, cooperation, better understanding, caring, and beneficial political and economic action. Human experience will keep moving so that third, fourth, and fifth editions of this encyclopedia will be necessary. Meanwhile the contributors to this second edition have written with the hope that their scholarship can assist people to understand contemporary life better and to make their own thoughtful responses to the ethical issues that require attention both now and in the future.

John K. Roth
Claremont McKenna College

CONTRIBUTING SCHOLARS

Norman Abeles
Michigan State University

Steven C. Abell
Marquette University

Bland Addison
Worcester Polytechic Institute

Joseph K. Adjaye
University of Pittsburgh

Richard Adler
University of Michigan, Dearborn

Olusoji A. Akomolafe
Le Moyne-Owen College

Thomas M. Alexander
Southern Illinois University at Carbondale

L. Dean Allen
Andover Newton Theological School

Majid Amini
Virginia State University

James August Anderson
Bellarmine College

Stanley Archer
Texas A&M University

Anne Freire Ashbaugh
Colgate University

Betty Attaway-Fink
Southeastern Louisiana University

Bryan C. Auday
Gordon College

Michael W. Austin
University of Colorado, Boulder

James V. Bachman
Valparaiso University

Philip Bader
Independent Scholar

James A. Baer
Northern Virginia Community College

Charles F. Bahmueller
Center for Civic Education

Bruce E. Bailey
Stephen F. Austin State University

Daniel G. Baker
Ocean County College

Robert Baker
Union College

Carl L. Bankston III
Tulane University

Russell J. Barber
California State University, San Bernardino

Evelyn M. Barker
University of Maryland, Baltimore County

Stephen F. Barker
Johns Hopkins University

Dan Barnett
California State University, Chico
Butte College

Charles A. Bartocci
Dabney S. Lancaster Community College

Rose Ann Bast
Mount Mary College

Erving E. Beauregard
University of Dayton

Tanja Bekhuis
TCB Research

Jeff Bell
University of Southwestern Louisiana

Raymond Angelo Belliotti
State University of New York, Fredonia

Alvin K. Benson
Utah Valley State College

George C. S. Benson
Claremont McKenna College

Richard P. Benton
Trinity College

S. Carol Berg
College of St. Benedict

Milton Berman
University of Rochester

Cynthia A. Bily
Adrian College

Amy Bloom
Harris Corporation
University of Central Florida

George P. Blum
University of the Pacific

Warren J. Blumenfeld
Independent Scholar

Paul R. Boehlke
Dr. Martin Luther College

David Boersema
Pacific University

Howard Bromberg
Ave Maria School of Law

M. Leann Brown
University of Florida

Dallas L. Browne
Southern Illinois University at Edwardsville

Anthony R. Brunello
Eckerd College

Thomas W. Buchanan
Ancilla College

Michael H. Burchett
Limestone College

Tonya S. Butler
Independent Scholar

Joseph P. Byrne
Belmont University

Malcolm B. Campbell
Bowling Green State University

Edmund J. Campion
University of Tennessee

Michael R. Candelaria
California State University, Bakersfield

Byron D. Cannon
University of Utah

Richard K. Caputo
Yeshiva University

David Carleton
Middle Tennessee State University

E. L. Cerroni-Long
Eastern Michigan University

Paul J. Chara, Jr.
Northwestern College

Weihang Chen
Hampshire College

Sandra L. Christensen
Eastern Washington University

Ron Christenson
Gustavus Adolphus College

Maria Cimitile
Grand Valley State University

Douglas Clouatre
Mid Plains Community College

Bonnidell Clouse
Indiana State University

Robert G. Clouse
Indiana State University

George Connell
Concordia College

Michael L. Coulter
Grove City College

Arlene R. Courtney
Western Oregon State College

D. Kirk Davidson
Mount Saint Mary's College

Edwin R. Davis
Independent Scholar

Robert C. Davis
Pikeville College

Scott A. Davison
University of Notre Dame

James M. Dawsey
Auburn University

Richard A. Dello Buono
Rosary College

Margaret B. Denning
Slippery Rock University of Pennsylvania

James D'Entremont
Independent Scholar

Fritz Detwiler
Adrian College

Robert E. Dewhirst
Northwest Missouri State University

Gordon Neal Diem
ADVANCE Education and Development Institute

Ileana Dominguez-Urban
Southern Illinois University at Carbondale School of Law

David R. Dow
University of Houston Law Center

Ted William Dreier
Portland State University

Margaret Duggan
South Dakota State University

William V. Dunlap
Quinnipiac University School of Law

John M. Dunn
Independent Scholar

Calvin Henry Easterling
Oral Roberts University

Jennifer Eastman
Independent Scholar

Craig M. Eckert
Eastern Illinois University

Robert P. Ellis
Independent Scholar

Kevin Eyster
Madonna University

Susan A. Farrell
Kingsborough Community College

Anne-Marie E. Ferngren
Covenant College

Gary B. Ferngren
Oregon State University

Aaron Fichtelberg
University of North Carolina, Wilmington

John W. Fiero
University of Southwestern Louisiana

David Marc Fischer
Independent Scholar

Cheri Vail Fisk
Oregon State University

Dale L. Flesher
University of Mississippi

Michael J. Fontenot
Southern University, Baton Rouge

Barbara Forrest
Southeastern Louisiana University

Donald R. Franceschetti
Memphis State University

Catherine Francis
Independent Scholar

Carol Franks
Portland State University

Norris Frederick
Queens University of Charlotte

Gregory Freeland
California Lutheran University

Lawrence Friedman
Harvard Law School

C. George Fry
*Lutheran College of Health
Professions*

Patricia H. Fulbright
Portland Community College

David M. Gallagher
Catholic University of America

Paul Gallagher
Assumption College

Eric H. Gampel
California State University, Chico

Zev Garber
Los Angeles Valley College

Thomas Gaskill
*Southern Illinois University at
Carbondale*

R. Douglas Geivett
Biola University

Mitchel Gerber
Southeast Missouri State University

Phyllis B. Gerstenfeld
*California State University,
Stanislaus*

Sheldon Goldfarb
University of British Columbia

Sanford Golin
University of Pittsburgh

Myrna L. Goodman
Sonoma State University

Robert F. Gorman
Texas State University

Roy Neil Graves
University of Tennessee, Martin

Lloyd J. Graybar
Eastern Kentucky University

Noreen A. Grice
Boston Museum of Science

Michael Haas
Independent Scholar

Peter J. Haas
Vanderbilt University

Don A. Habibi
*University of North Carolina,
Wilmington*

Jacqueline Haessly
*Peacemaking Associates
Cardinal Stritch College*

Irwin Halfond
McKendree College

Timothy L. Hall
University of Mississippi

Robert Halliday
Utica College of Syracuse University

Craig L. Hanson
Muskingum College

Robin G. Hanson
Muskingum College

Claude Hargrove
Fayetteville State University

Keith Harper
Mississippi College

Fred R. van Hartesveldt
Fort Valley State College

Sterling Harwood
*California State University,
San Jose*

David Haugen
Western Illinois University

Margaret Hawthorne
Independent Scholar

Robert M. Hawthorne, Jr.
Independent Scholar

James L. Hayward
Andrews University

Maria Heim
Amherst College

Ruth B. Heizer
Georgetown College

Mary A. Hendrickson
Wilson College

Stuart Henry
Wayne State University

Howard M. Hensel
U.S. Air Force, Air War College

Stephen R. C. Hicks
Rockford College

Rita C. Hinton
Mississippi State University

Carl W. Hoagstrom
Ohio Northern University

Kimberley M. Holloway
*King College
East Tennessee State University*

Gregory D. Horn
*Southwest Virginia Community
College*

William L. Howard
Chicago State University

John L. Howland
Bowdoin College

Vanessa B. Howle
Grand Valley State University

Diane White Husic
East Stroudsburg University

Charles C. Jackson
Northern Kentucky University

Robert Jacobs
Central Washington University

Dale Jacquette
Pennsylvania State University

Bruce E. Johansen
University of Nebraska at Omaha

Edward Johnson
University of New Orleans

Mary Johnson
University of South Florida
Hillsborough Community College

David W. Jones
Southeastern Baptist Theological
Seminary

Joe Frank Jones III
Barton College

Marcella Joy
Independent Scholar

Richard C. Kagan
Hamline University

Charles L. Kammer III
The College of Wooster

Laura Duhan Kaplan
University of North Carolina at
Charlotte

Robin Bradley Kar
University of Michigan

T. E. Katen
Community College of Philadelphia

William E. Kelly
Auburn University

Mara Kelly-Zukowski
Felician College

Terry J. Knapp
University of Nevada, Las Vegas

Nathan R. Kollar
St. John Fisher College

Abraham D. Kriegel
Memphis State University

Todd M. Krist
Rockford College

Robert B. Kruschwitz
Georgetown College

Rosalind Ekman Ladd
Wheaton College

Ralph L. Langenheim, Jr.
University of Illinois at Urbana-
Champaign

Ron Large
Gonzaga University

Michael M. Laskier
Sephardic Educational Center
University of Chicago

William F. Lawhead
University of Mississippi

Richard M. Leeson
Fort Hays State University

Lisa Soleymani Lehmann
Harvard Medical School

Thomas Tandy Lewis
Anoka-Ramsey Community College

Harry van der Linden
Butler University

Victor Lindsey
East Central University

Ronnie Littlejohn
Belmont University

Corinne R. Livesay
Bryan College

Stephen D. Livesay
Bryan College

Ronald W. Long
West Virginia Institute of Technology

Martha O. Loustaunau
New Mexico State University

Adele Lubell
Independent Scholar

David W. Lutz
University of Notre Dame

Richard D. McAnulty
University of North Carolina at
Charlotte

John A. McClung
Westchester Medical Center

Nancy E. Macdonald
University of South Carolina,
Sumter

F. Scott McElreath
Peace College

Erin McKenna
Pacific Lutheran University

Voula Tsouna McKirahan
Independent Scholar

Marguerite McKnight
Slippery Rock University of
Pennsylvania

Paul Madden
Hardin-Simmons University

Paul D. Mageli
Independent Scholar

Philip Magnier
Independent Scholar

Cynthia Keppley Mahmood
University of Maine

Khalid N. Mahmood
Maine Science and Technology
Commission

Jon Mahoney
Auburn University

Edward W. Maine
California State University,
Fullerton

Krishna Mallick
Bentley College

Robin Sakina Mama
Monmouth University

Bill Manikas
Gaston College

Jonathan Hugh Mann
B.E.S.T., Business Ethics Strategies

Coleman C. Markham
Barton College

Jill S. Marts
Independent Scholar

Lisa Maruca
Wayne State University

Thomas D. Matijasic
Prestonsburg Community College

David M. May
*Midwestern Baptist Theological
  Seminary*

S. M. Mayo
Charleston Southern University

Linda Mealey
College of St. Benedict

Gregory F. Mellema
Calvin College

Michael W. Messmer
*Virginia Commonwealth
  University*

Andrea Miller
Independent Scholar

Laurence Miller
Western Washington University

Roman J. Miller
Eastern Mennonite University

Randall L. Milstein
Oregon State University

Eli C. Minkoff
Bates College

William V. Moore
College of Charleston

Mario Morelli
Western Illinois University

Brian K. Morley
The Master's College

Rodney C. Mowbray
University of Wisconsin, La Crosse

Mark William Muesse
Rhodes College

Jay Mullin
Queensborough Community College

Turhon A. Murad
California State University, Chico

Tod Charles Murphy
Independent Scholar

D. Gosselin Nakeeb
Pace University

Steve Neiheisel
St. Mary's University

Peimin Ni
Grand Valley State University

Steve A. Nida
Franklin University

Joseph L. Nogee
University of Houston

Norma Corigliano Noonan
Independent Scholar

Kathleen O'Brien
Independent Scholar

Daniel W. O'Bryan
Sierra Nevada College

O. A. Ogunseitan
University of California, Irvine

Patrick M. O'Neil
Broome Community College

Sharon K. O'Roke
*Oklahoma City University School
  of Law*

Amy J. Orr
Linfield College

Lisa Paddock
Independent Scholar

Robert L. Palmer
*George Washington University
  School of Law*

W. Jackson Parham, Jr.
Hillsdale College

Paul Plenge Parker
Elmhurst College

Judith A. Parsons
Sul Ross State University

Garrett E. Paul
Gustavus Adolphus College

Tinaz Pavri
Spelman College

Cheryl Pawlowski
University of Northern Colorado

Thomas R. Peake
King College

William A. Pelz
DePaul University

Andy Perry
Independent Scholar

Mark Stephen Pestana
Grand Valley State University

Nis Petersen
Jersey City State College

James M. Petrik
Ohio University

Frank J. Prerost
Midwestern University

Marc Georges Pufong
Valdosta State University

Kathleen D. Purdy
Basic Business Strategies

Howard B. Radest
Independent Scholar

Habibeh Rahim
Hofstra University

Lillian M. Range
University of Southern Mississippi

John David Rausch, Jr.
West Texas A&M University

Paul L. Redditt
Georgetown College

Thomas Renna
Saginaw Valley State University

Paul August Rentz
South Dakota State University

Gregory P. Rich
Fayetteville State University

John E. Richardson
Pepperdine University

Edward A. Riedinger
Ohio State University Libraries

Janice G. Rienerth
Appalachian State University

John R. Rink
University of Wisconsin, Platteville

John L. Rittenhouse
Eastern Mennonite College

Carl Rollyson
Baruch College, City University of New York

John K. Roth
Claremont McKenna College

Robert Rubinson
University of Baltimore School of Law

Joseph R. Rudolph, Jr.
Towson University

Frank Louis Rusciano
Rider College

Sunil K. Sahu
DePauw University

Frank A. Salamone
Iona College

Hilel B. Salomon
University of South Carolina

Steven M. Sanders
Bridgewater State College

John Santelli
Fairleigh Dickinson University

Joseph C. Santora
Independent Scholar

John Santore
Pratt Institute

Daniel C. Scavone
University of Southern Indiana

F. Scott Scribner
University of Hartford

John H. Serembus
Widener University

Lynda Sexson
Montana State University

Manoj Sharma
University of Nebraska at Omaha

Elizabeth Algren Shaw
Kitchen, Deery & Barnhouse

John M. Shaw
Education Systems

Martha Sherwood-Pike
University of Oregon

R. Baird Shuman
University of Illinois at Urbana-Champaign

Julius Simon
University of Texas at El Paso

Sanford S. Singer
University of Dayton

Andrew C. Skinner
Brigham Young University

Jane A. Slezak
Fulton-Montgomery Community College

Genevieve Slomski
Independent Scholar

Robert W. Small
Massasoit Community College

James Smallwood
Oklahoma State University

Christopher E. Smith
University of Akron

Nick Smith
University of New Hampshire

Roger Smith
Independent Scholar

Ira Smolensky
Monmouth College

Marjorie Smolensky
Carl Sandburg College

A. J. Sobczak
Independent Scholar

J. Michael Spector
Armstrong Laboratory

Shaun B. Spencer
Harvard Law School

Richard A. Spinello
Boston College

C. Fitzhugh Spragins
Arkansas College

Barry M. Stentiford
Grambling State University

Charles E. Sutphen
Blackburn College

Roy Arthur Swanson
University of Wisconsin, Milwaukee

Leland C. Swenson
Loyola Marymount University

Glenn L. Swygart
Tennessee Temple University

Larry N. Sypolt
West Virginia University

Robert D. Talbott
University of Northern Iowa

Harold D. Tallant
Georgetown College

Stephen C. Taylor
Delaware State University

Nancy Conn Terjesen
Kent State University

David R. Teske
Russell C. Davis Planetarium

Nicholas C. Thomas
Auburn University, Montgomery

Susan L. Thomas
Hollins University

Leslie V. Tischauser
Prairie State College

Evelyn Toft
Fort Hays State University

Paul B. Trescott
Southern Illinois University

David Treviño
Donna Klein Jewish Academy

Mfanya D. Tryman
Mississippi State University

Mary S. Tyler
University of Maine

I. Peter Ukpokodu
University of Kansas

Mary Moore Vandendorpe
Lewis University

Harry van der Linden
Butler University

Diane C. Van Noord
Western Michigan University

Gary E. Varner
Texas A&M University

Suzanne Araas Vesely
Fort Hays State University

Theodore M. Vestal
Oklahoma State University

Mary E. Virginia
Independent Scholar

Paul R. Waibel
Liberty University

Randolph Meade Walker
Le Moyne-Owen College

William T. Walker
Chestnut Hill College

T. Steuart Watson
Mississippi State University

Donald A. Watt
Southern Arkansas University

William L. Waugh, Jr.
Georgia State University

Donald V. Weatherman
Arkansas College

Marcia J. Weiss
Point Park University

Robert Whealey
Ohio University

Winifred Whelan
St. Bonaventure University

Alisa White
University of Texas at Arlington

Carol Wayne White
Bucknell University

Robert Whitman
University of Connecticut School of Law

Gloria A. Whittico
Hampton University

Richard Whitworth
Ball State University

Joel Wilcox
Providence College

Clifford Williams
Trinity College, Deerfield

Robert A. Willingham
Independent Scholar

Richard L. Wilson
University of Tennessee at Chattanooga

Michael Witkoski
University of South Carolina

Shawn Woodyard
Independent Scholar

Linda M. Woolf
Webster University

Kerrie Workman
Hamline University

Michael J. Wreen
Marquette University

Keith E. Yandell
University of Wisconsin, Madison

Regina Howard Yaroch
Independent Scholar

Clifton K. Yearley
State University of New York at Buffalo

Tung Yin
University of Iowa College of Law

Kristen L. Zacharias
Albright College

Mara Kelly Zukowski
Iona College

COMPLETE LIST OF CONTENTS

Volume 1

Volume II

Complete List of Contents

Volume III

ETHICS
Revised Edition

A

Abelard, Peter

IDENTIFICATION: French theologian and philosopher
BORN: c. 1079, Le Pallet, Brittany
DIED: April 21, 1142, Chalon-sur-Saône, Burgundy
TYPE OF ETHICS: Medieval history
SIGNIFICANCE: Abelard was one of the earliest schoolmen to advance the study of dialectics (logic) and applied it to theology and moral philosophy; his later famous theory of intention was considered too radical at the time. He authored numerous works on theology, philosophy, logic, ethics, and biblical exegesis.

In his autobiographical *The Story of My Misfortunes* (*Historia calamitatum*, c. 1132), Abelard describes his rise to fame as a philosopher and theologian. His love affair with Héloïse—attested in their correspondence—compelled him to leave the cathedral school of Paris and become a monk at St. Denis. Later, Abelard became the leader of a hermitage, the Paraclete, which he gave to Héloïse and her nuns. He remained a wandering maverick because of his dialectics and his sharp criticism of monasticism. His *Sic et non* (c. 1123) used the new methods of the schools, which consisted of posing problems and resolving them by means of logic and close textual analysis. Older methods of teaching and writing consisted of the presentation of texts and commentaries on those texts.

Because Abelard's writings were twice condemned by the Church, his influence is difficult to gauge. As an ethical thinker, Abelard viewed himself as a monastic reformer who sought to restore the eremitic spirit to religious practice. Unlike his contemporaries, he believed that some monks should use the new dialectical methods to intensify the monastic life. As an admirer of the ancient pagan philosophers, he tried to reconcile natural law ethics with Christian morality and doctrine. Abelard defined sin as consenting to an evil will (concupiscence) rather than as performing evil actions. He believed that actions were, in themselves, morally neutral.

Thomas Renna

SEE ALSO: Christian ethics; Natural law; Post-Enlightenment ethics; Religion.

Abolition

DEFINITION: Movement to abolish slavery in the United States based upon moral, rather than practical, considerations
DATE: Mid-eighteenth century to 1865
TYPE OF ETHICS: Race and ethnicity
SIGNIFICANCE: The abolition movement attempted to apply the concepts of Christian brotherhood and democratic egalitarianism to race relations; it helped to end slavery in the United States.

The most prolonged social struggles within the United States have been in the area of race relations. Although the nation was founded upon the principle that "all men are created equal," American citizens continued to hold large numbers of African Americans in bondage until 1865. Those who participated in the abolitionist movement called Americans to a higher ethical standard. They demanded that both slaveholder and nonslaveholder take responsibility for the institution of slavery and take immediate measures to liberate their fellow countrymen.

HISTORY

Antislavery sentiment predates the American Revolution. By the mid-eighteenth century, American Quakers such as John Woolman and Benjamin Lay were denouncing slavery as un-Christian. The rationalism of the Enlightenment, with its stress upon natural law, added ammunition to the arsenal of critics of slavery.

The egalitarian rhetoric of the Revolutionary era

1

Time Line of Abolition in the U.S. States

Year	State	Year	State
1777	Vermont	1862	Washington, D.C.
1780	Pennsylvania		Western Territories
1783	Maine	1863	West Virginia
	Massachusetts	1864	Louisiana
	New Hampshire		Maryland
1784	Connecticut	1865	Delaware
	Rhode Island		Kentucky
1787	Illinois		Missouri
	Indiana		Tennessee
	Michigan		Alabama
	Ohio		Arkansas
	Wisconsin		Florida
1799	New York		Georgia
1804	New Jersey		Mississippi
1820	Iowa		North Carolina
1846	Oregon		South Carolina
1850	California		Texas
1858	Minnesota		Virginia
1861	Kansas	1866	Oklahoma

illustrated the irony of slaveholders fighting for liberty. As a result, most northern states abolished slavery by 1784. New York and New Jersey did so afterward. Southern whites believed that they could not afford to abolish slavery, yet they felt the need to justify the institution on ethical grounds. They concentrated on humanizing the institution and argued that it was a "necessary evil."

Antislavery feeling receded after 1793 because of fear of slave revolts, the increasing profitability of slavery following the invention of the cotton gin, and new scientific theories that reinforced racism. The leading antislavery organization during the early nineteenth century was the American Colonization Society (ACS). The ACS attempted to resettle free blacks in Africa and encouraged voluntary emancipation without challenging the right to own human property. The colonization plan allowed liberal slaveholders and moderate members of the clergy to rationalize their guilt over slavery.

In 1825, a great Protestant religious revival swept the northeastern region of the country. Ministers such as Charles Grandison Finney preached a new perfec-

tionist theology that sought to counter the growing worldliness of Americans. This revival sparked a host of humanitarian crusades designed to protect the rights of the disadvantaged and to cleanse American institutions of contamination.

By the early 1830's, many evangelical reformers began to view slavery and racism as sinful because racism violated the Christian ethic of equality. Known as immediate abolitionists, they demanded the immediate and unqualified liberation of slaves and an end to racial discrimination. With the formation of the American Anti-Slavery Society in 1833, abolitionist speakers toured the northern states attempting to rally support for their cause. Abolitionists were frequently attacked by angry mobs, and their literature was destroyed in southern post offices.

The abolition movement failed to end racism in the North. It did, however, spark antisouthern feelings, which led to increased controversy within the national government. This conflict led directly to the Civil War. During the war, abolitionists pressured the federal government to transform the conflict from a war to preserve the Union into a war to end slavery. Abolition advocates were disappointed by the Emancipation Proclamation because it was based upon military necessity rather than moral principle, but they accomplished their central purpose with the passage of the Thirteenth Amendment, which ended slavery in the United States.

GARRISONIAN ETHICS

One major faction within the abolition movement was led by editor William Lloyd Garrison. In a real sense, the publication of the first issue of the *Liberator* on January 1, 1831, established Garrison as the foremost abolitionist in the country. Garrison's harsh attacks upon slaveholders and colonizationists caused a national sensation even though the circulation of his newspaper never exceeded three thousand. Like most abolitionists, Garrison demanded that everyone recognize a personal responsibility to improve society. The three major tenets of his ethical philosophy were human liberation, moral suasion, and no compromise with evil.

Because of his devotion to human liberation, Garrison actively campaigned on behalf of legal equality for African Americans, temperance, and equality for women. His strong stand in behalf of women's rights helped to cause a major split in the abolition movement in 1840. Garrison rejected force and violence in human affairs. He sought the moral reformation of slave owners, not their destruction. He never advocated slave revolts, and he wanted the northern states to allow the South to secede during the crisis of 1860-1861.

Garrison sincerely believed in all that he advocated, and he would not compromise his principles. He rejected any solution to the issue of slavery that involved a program that would delay emancipation. He also demanded that his followers reject participation in the American political system because the Constitution was a proslavery document. The American political system was based on compromise, making it inherently corrupt. Other abolitionists, such as Gerrit Smith and James Birney, attempted to use the political system as a way to gain publicity for the cause of abolition.

AFRICAN AMERICAN ABOLITIONISM

In a sense, there were two abolition movements. The white-led movement was based on a moral abstraction. African Americans were forced to confront the everyday realities of racism in nineteenth century America. Frederick Douglass emerged as the major spokesman for African Americans during the antebellum period. Douglass self-consciously attempted to use his life as an example to repudiate racist stereotypes. Because of his eloquence, Douglass gained an international reputation as a public speaker, and in doing so, he proved the humanity of African Americans.

Like Garrison, Douglass strongly supported temperance and women's rights. He was, however, willing to use any means to achieve the liberation of slaves, including violence and political action. He approved of John Brown's idea of using the southern Appalachians as an armed sanctuary for runaways. He also supported the Free Soil and Republican Parties even though neither advocated the emancipation of southern slaves. He justified his positions as

part of a larger struggle to advance the cause of racial equality in America. For Douglass, as for other African Americans involved in the cause of abolition, equality was the only acceptable ethical standard for a free society.

Thomas D. Matijasic

FURTHER READING

Barnes, Gilbert Hobbs. *The Antislavery Impulse, 1830-1844.* New York: Harcourt, Brace & World, 1964.

Duberman, Martin, ed. *The Antislavery Vanguard: New Essays on the Abolitionists.* Princeton, N.J.: Princeton University Press, 1965.

Huggins, Nathan Irvin. *Slave and Citizen: The Life of Frederick Douglass.* Boston: Little Brown, 1980.

McKivigan, John R., ed. *Abolitionism and American Reform.* New York: Garland, 1999.

Newman, Richard S. *The Transformation of American Abolitionism: Fighting Slavery in the Early Republic.* Chapel Hill: University of North Carolina Press, 2002.

Nye, Russel B. *William Lloyd Garrison and the Humanitarian Reformers.* Boston: Little Brown, 1955.

Sorin, Gerald. *Abolitionism: A New Perspective.* New York: Praeger, 1972.

Stewart, James Brewer. *Holy Warriors: The Abolitionists and American Slavery.* New York: Hill & Wang, 1976.

Tyler, Alice Felt. *Freedom's Ferment: Phases of American Social History to 1860.* Freeport, N.Y.: Books for Libraries Press, 1970.

SEE ALSO: Emancipation Proclamation; Racial prejudice; Racism; *Scott v. Sandford*; Slavery; *Uncle Tom's Cabin*.

Abortion

DEFINITION: Technique of removing a developing embryo or fetus from the maternal uterus for the purpose of preventing its birth

TYPE OF ETHICS: Bioethics

SIGNIFICANCE: The practice of abortion raises the question of the morality of terminating a prenatal human life in response to the desire of others who would be adversely affected by the birth. The subject has become one of the most emotionally and hotly debated social issues in modern America.

Childbirth should be a happy occasion; however, other influences often prevent that ideal from being realized. During the first years of the twenty-first century, worldwide estimates suggested that thirty to fifty million women were undergoing abortions each year, almost half of which are performed illegally. In the United States, about 1.5 million women were terminating their pregnancies each year, resulting in the statistic that about one pregnancy in four was being ended with an induced abortion. Statistics on U.S. women who have undergone abortions have shown that about 26 percent of the women are under nineteen years of age, 58 percent are under twenty-five years of age, and a little more than half of them are unmarried. The nonwhite abortion rate is 57 per 1,000 women, compared to 21 per 1,000 white women.

STATISTICS

Since the 1973 U.S. Supreme Court decision, *Roe v. Wade*, that made abortion legal, this medical procedure has been in popular use and has generated a sharp controversy between those who advocate a woman's right to have an abortion (pro-choice) and those who oppose abortions (pro-life). The arguments have encompassed moral and medical issues as well as legal and social issues. Churches and religious denominations as well as politicians and political parties have been separated by the intense emotions of persons who oppose or defend abortion.

Abortions can be classified into two types: spontaneous and induced. Spontaneous abortions, commonly called miscarriages, are those that occur before the time of viability. Viability, the time when the developing fetus can potentially survive outside the uterus, is set at about the twenty-sixth week of development. Spontaneous abortions that result from unknown reasons are attributed to natural causes. Estimates suggest that among normal, healthy women, more than half of fertilized embryos never implant and are spontaneously aborted. Furthermore, it is thought that about 10 to 15 percent of the implanted embryos spontaneously abort.

Spontaneous abortions after the time of viability are typically called preterm deliveries or stillbirths.

Induced abortions are those that result from medical procedures designed to terminate development. As the word "abortion" is most commonly used, it refers primarily to induced abortions. In the United States, 90 percent of induced abortions take place earlier than the twelfth week of pregnancy; about 10 percent take place between the twelfth and twentieth weeks of pregnancy, and less than 1 percent take place after the twentieth week of pregnancy.

HISTORICAL BACKGROUND

Abortions have been performed on women for centuries. The ancient Greeks advocated abortion as a method of birth control. Plato advocated that women after age forty should be compelled to have abortions. Early Roman law proclaimed that a "child in the belly of its mother" is not a person. Thus, abortion and even infanticide were permitted and practiced. Roman physicians described the use of abortifacient drugs in their treatment of patients.

Early Christians during the first centuries C.E. largely prohibited the practice of abortion for their adherents, unlike the Greeks and Romans. The early Christian Church objected to some abortions on the basis of ensoulment or animation, the point at which the soul entered the body. It was thought that the soul entered the developing embryo about forty days after conception in the case of the male and eighty days after conception in the case of the female. Thus, abortions after ensoulment were considered as murder, but abortions before ensoulment were merely considered to be serious sins.

In North America during the seventeenth and eighteenth centuries, abortions were neither prohibited by written laws nor prosecuted under common law. Abortion was regarded as immoral if it occurred after the time of quickening, when the mother first perceived fetal movements. Abortion become so widespread in the nineteenth century that the fertility rate of American women decreased by half, returning to what it had been in the previous century.

Three significant events occurred toward the end of the nineteenth century. Most states enacted antiabortion statutes; the American Medical Association developed an antiabortion committee to raise public awareness; and the Roman Catholic Church began to lay the ideological groundwork for its subsequent ban on abortion. Late in the nineteenth century, considering abortion to be a violation of natural law, the

Catholic Church took a restrictive stance against abortion and prohibited it at any time of pregnancy, beginning from the time of conception. However, modern Catholic teaching permits indirect abortion, when an embryo or fetus is lost as a side effect of a medical treatment that is given to save the mother's life.

In modern times, societal and religious groups are strongly divided regarding the acceptability of abortion. Many religious denominations have struggled in attempts to denounce or condone abortion as a women's rights issue. In many cases, opposing voices that presented the other side of the issue have moderated such attempts. Globally, about fifty-three countries with populations greater than 1 million (totaling 25 percent of the world's population) prohibit abortions except to save the life of the mother. However most nations permit abortion to save the life of the mother.

Laws restricting abortion are most prominent in countries found in Central Asia, Latin America, and Africa. Another twenty-three countries (40 percent of the world's population) permit abortions on the request of the woman. These countries include China,

Russia, the United States, and about half of the countries in Europe. Most of the remaining countries of the world (35 percent of the world's population) permit abortion on broad medical grounds or for extreme situations such as rape. Some of these countries, such as Australia, Finland, Great Britain, Japan, and Taiwan, include "adverse social conditions" as justification for abortion. The World Health Organization's 1997 report revealed that 70,000 women died from unsafe abortions; 69,000 of those deaths occurred in Asia, Latin America, and Africa.

PERSONHOOD

Some people have suggested that controversies over abortion are actually controversies on the view of the embryo/fetus. Is the developing fetus a mere piece of tissue or is it a person? Those who view the developing fetus as a "conceptus," or piece of tissue, tend to place value and base their ethical arguments on the needs and rights of the mother. In most cases, they freely advocate abortion on demand in the attempt to support the pregnant mother's wishes. Individuals who view the embryo/fetus as a person (a baby), however, maintain a responsibility to protect

---

Countries with the Least Restrictive Abortion Laws

In 2003, the fifty-four countries listed below did not require women seeking abortion to provide any reasons, with the exception that China and Nepal did not permit abortion for the purpose of selecting a child's sex. All fifty-four countries imposed gestational limits of at least twelve weeks, and limits in some countries ranged up to twenty-four weeks. Countries marked (PA) required minors to obtain parental authorization; Turkey required spousal authorization.

Albania	Croatia (PA)	Latvia	Slovakia (PA)
Armenia	Cuba (PA)	Lithuania	Slovenia (PA)
Austria	Czech Republic (PA)	Macedonia (PA)	South Africa
Azerbaijan	Denmark (PA)	Moldova	Sweden
Bahrain	Estonia	Mongolia	Switzerland
Belarus	France	Nepal	Tajikistan
Belgium	Georgia	Netherlands	Tunisia
Bosnia and	Germany	North Korea	Turkey (PA)
Herzegovina (PA)	Greece (PA)	Norway (PA)	Turkmenistan
Bulgaria	Guyana	Romania	Ukraine
Cambodia	Hungary	Russia	United States (PA)
Canada	Italy (PA)	Serbia and	Uzbekistan
Cape Verde	Kazakhstan	Montenegro (PA)	Vietnam
China	Kyrgyzstan	Singapore	

Source: Center for Reproductive Rights, September, 2003.

the developing fetus. In that situation, abortion is viewed as a heinous crime that violently snuffs out the life of an innocent, defenseless, living person.

In the middle of the controversy stand a group of persons who are often uncomfortably changing their position and ethic. On one hand, they recognize the emotional and psychological pain that an unwanted pregnancy can elicit. On the other hand, they believe that the developing embryo minimally bears the potential of personhood and thus has intrinsic value. A fetus is not a mere piece of tissue that can be harmlessly trimmed away for the sake of convenience.

Personhood is a fundamental issue in the abortion debate, and a cultural ethic colors attitudes toward personhood. For example, in some societies, personhood begins at a birth ceremony that is celebrated shortly after the birth event. The ceremony confers status and protection on the newly born child. Within such a view, abortion or infanticide that occurs after birthing but before the birth ceremony is considered to be a legitimate means of birth control. Others see personhood as a developmental process that occurs in the uterus. Thus, aborting a third-trimester fetus may have moral consequences, while an early first-trimester abortion may be acceptable. Some mark the advent of conception as the origination of the person. In this view, all abortion is immoral and the embryo and fetus must be protected in the same way that a newborn baby is protected.

BEGINNING OF LIFE

Frequently, the abortion debate centers on the question of when life begins. Historically, that moment has been placed at one of three points: the moment of conception; the time of "quickening," when the mother can first feel the fetal movements; or the time of birth itself. From a biological perspective, however, life does not begin; instead, life is a continuum in which a living sperm fertilizes a living egg to form the unique first cell, the zygote.

The distinctiveness of the zygote is based on the reality that it contains a unique assortment of genes on its chromosomes that are a product of the specific genes carried by the fertilized egg and sperm. In the hours and days that follow fertilization, the zygote divides to form multiple cells that give rise to the mass of cells that will form the embryo as well as the tissues that will form the placental attachments of the

embryo to the uterine wall. By the third week of development, the embryonic heart begins to beat and brain tissue is differentiating and forming. Early neural responses can be detected late in the first trimester; these responses become more sophisticated and complex as development progresses in the second and third trimester. Fetal behavior is an area of research that investigates the effects of environmental conditions—light, sound, maternal voice, temperature, and so forth—on fetal responses and subsequent developmental patterns. Research in this area indicates that postnatal behavior patterns are significantly affected by prenatal influences and that the fetus learns certain behaviors while it is developing in the uterus.

According to this understanding, a unique individual is formed at the point of conception that developmentally obtains the characteristics of personhood. Therefore, the embryo and fetus have intrinsic value because of their individuality and personhood. Thus, abortion becomes a moral issue when one considers the possibility of destroying a person or, at the very least, a potential person.

MEDICAL ASPECTS

Numerous studies indicate that within societies in which abortions are illegal, the percentages of women who die from the illegal abortions are about ten times greater than those in societies in which abortions are legal and are regulated by medical practice. Nearly two-thirds of the world's women live in countries in which abortion is available on request for social reasons.

Normally, a fertilized ovum or zygote, which forms a developing embryo, implants in the mother's uterus about ten days after conception. Early abortions are designed to prevent this implantation step in the development process. Such abortion procedures include the use of RU-486 (the so-called "abortion pill," an abortive drug first developed in France in 1988), intrauterine devices (IUD) placed in the uterus by a physician, or the administration of the drug DES (often called the "morning after pill").

If abortion is desired between two and seven weeks after conception, a simple vacuum extraction is frequently used. The embryo at this time is less than three centimeters in length and can be removed easily from the uterus wall. After seven weeks until about the fifteenth week, the uterus is dilated before

Antiabortion protestors gather outside the Supreme Court building in Washington, D.C., on January 22, 2004—the thirty-first anniversary of the Court's decision in Roe v. Wade. *(AP/Wide World Photos)*

vacuum extraction is used. Following the fifteenth week of development, abortions generally consist of an induced labor that results from uterine injections of concentrated salt solutions (hypertonic saline) or prostaglandins (hormones that stimulate uterine contractions). In the United States, the use of hypertonic saline has been largely discontinued due to the negative side effects of large amounts of salt experienced by the mother.

Late-term abortions, also called "partial birth" abortions, are done during the third trimester of pregnancy and make up a very small percentage of the induced abortions. Medically, a late-term abortion is initiated by injecting prostaglandins to induce labor.

Then a breech delivery is initiated with a forceps that results in the torso and legs passing through the cervix, while the head is retained within the uterus. The fetal skull is then punctured and its contents removed, causing the skull to collapse with the fetus's death and a subsequent delivery of the remaining portion. This particular abortion procedure has resulted in extensive legislative actions in the United States, with many states banning the procedure. Abortion opponents see this procedure as a gruesome act that must be outlawed, since the fetus is subjected to extensive pain and discomfort. Abortion proponents emphasize that this procedure is sometimes needed for the health of the mother and to outlaw this method of abortion will lead to further abortion restrictions. Thus the debate continues.

Complications of abortions may vary greatly, depending upon the timing of the abortion, the particular technique used, the skill of the abortionist, and the unique physiology of the woman involved in the procedure. For many women, only minor symptoms such as slight bleeding or cramps occur. For others, complications may include severe hemorrhage, infection from contaminated instruments, uterine perforation, cervical injury, or an incomplete abortion in which the fetal remains may induce infection. Some cases of psychosocial and emotional disturbances of women who have had abortions have been documented, although the percentage of women thus affected is not high.

FETAL RESEARCH

An ethical issue related to abortion is fetal research. If abortions occur, what should be done with the aborted fetuses? Should they be buried, or might some of them be used for medical research and medical treatment? Legally, the fetus is not a protected entity, yet it is a growing human, which is why it is prized as a source for tissue and organ transplantation in humans. Such a valuable commodity brings in the issues of ownership and economics that frame additional ethical dilemmas. Does the mother who has undergone the abortion own the aborted fetus and thereby have the right to sell the remains to the highest bidder? What are the ethics of buying and selling body parts?

Experimental efforts to transplant fetal cells into Parkinson's patients have been very successful in alleviating this debilitating disease. This technology paves the way for transplanting fetal tissues in attempts to control diabetes, Alzheimer's disease, and Huntington's disease, as well as other diseases. Ethically, on one hand it seems wasteful to discard embryos whose tissues could be used improve the quality of life for another person. On the other hand, the danger exists that women might become pregnant so that valuable fetal tissues could be "harvested" from their bodies for the medical treatment of a parent or loved one, or even for sale for profit. The current controversy in the United States centers on the possibility of using aborted embryos as sources

---

Pro-Abortion Rights Marchers Converge on Washington, D.C.

On April 25, 2004, an estimated 800,000 pro-choice activists gathered in Washington, D.C.'s National Mall to protest the abortion policies of President George W. Bush's administration. The marchers charged that reproductive liberties were being eroded in the United States and that the Bush administration's foreign polices were endangering women around the globe. Marchers chanted and carried signs with slogans such as "It's Your Choice, Not Theirs!" and "My Body Is Not Public Property!" Francis Kissling of the Catholics for a Free Choice organization addressed her comments directly to legislators when she stated "You will hear our pro-choice voices ringing in your ears until such time that you permit all women to make our own reproductive choices." During the last major pro-abortion march in Washington in 1992, an estimated 500,000 people participated.

---

of stem cells for research or for therapeutic techniques.

BIOTECHNOLOGY

Biotechnology has developed abortive techniques that are minimally traumatic to the mother. One example is the use of the aborticide drug RU-486, also called mifepristone. This drug works by preventing a fertilized egg or early embryo from implanting into the uterine wall. RU-486, an antiprogestin, breaks the fertilized egg's bond to the uterus wall and thus induces a miscarriage. Tests of this drug on thousands of women show that it is about 97 percent effective in terminating early pregnancies. The drug can be administered in the privacy of a doctor's office and therefore avoids the woman's stigmatization of going to an abortion clinic. That fact alone arouses strong responses both from advocates and opponents of the drug.

With sophisticated embryo screening techniques such as ultrasound and amniocentesis, it is possible to determine the gender of an embryo. By using genetic screening, one can also determine specific genes that the developing embryo may have that are beneficial or undesirable. One of the ethical dilemmas of the use of this technology is that abortion may become a means for obtaining a child of preferred genotype and gender, while discouraging the attitude of accepting all prenatal embryos as unique human beings who are intrinsically valuable, regardless of their gene makeup or gender.

SUMMARY

Two absolute moral positions directly oppose each other and prevent an easy resolution to the abortion controversy. One position maintains that abortion is the killing of human beings. The other position declares that a woman has the right to control her own body. For many who hold one position or the other, there can be no compromise. In the face of such irreconcilable attitudes, public policy about abortion must be formed. For such policy to endure, it must compromise both positions. Two areas of compromise have been seen historically and are continuing: to allow abortion only for certain specific reasons, such as to save the life of the mother or in the situation of rape or incest; and to permit early abortions but to forbid or strongly regulate mid-term or late-term abortions. Many abortion laws in various states of the United States and in other countries recognize and attempt to integrate some aspects of these two compromises in their structure. Trends indicate that public policy may move more deliberately toward these compromises, which carve out a middle ground between two absolutist postures.

Roman J. Miller

FURTHER READING

Costa, Marie. *Abortion: A Reference Handbook.* Santa Barbara, Calif.: ABC-Clio, 1991. Informative handbook on various aspects of abortion. Contains facts and statistics, a chronology of historical and political events, biographical sketches of persons involved, and organizations and resources relating to abortion, listed in a very objective fashion.

Fowler, Paul B. *Abortion: Toward an Evangelical Consensus.* Portland, Oreg.: Multnomah Press, 1978. Popular paperback that illustrates the divided opinions of one group of Christians, the evangelicals, over the issue of abortion. The author describes the basis for the differences in thought and points to a possible resolution of this controversy.

Hull, N. E. H., and Peter Charles Hoffer. *"Roe v. Wade": The Abortion Rights Controversy in American History.* Lawrence: University Press of Kansas, 2001. Historical sketch of the legal and social influences surrounding the early criminalization of abortion in the nineteenth century, the landmark U.S. Supreme Court decision in 1973 legalizing abortion, and the continuing controversy since that time. Well-written and balanced account that will be of interest to high school and college students.

Larsen, William J. *Human Embryology.* 3d ed. New York: Churchill Livingstone, 2001. Well-written text on human development that is clearly illustrated with colored diagrams and superb photographs. Larson presents the normal biological development of the embryo and fetus and provides references to clinical cases.

Miller, Roman J., and Beryl H. Brubaker, eds. *Bioethics and the Beginning of Life.* Scottdale, Pa.: Herald Press, 1990. Collection of writings attempting to demonstrate the complexity that biotechnology has brought to issues at the beginning of life, including abortion. Chapters cover such perspectives as biological, ethical, theological, legal, historical, psychological, maternal, sociological, and others, framed within a Christian communal consensus.

Pojman, Louis P., and Francis J. Beckwith. *The Abortion Controversy: Twenty-five Years After "Roe v. Wade": A Reader.* Belmont, Calif.: Wadsworth, 1998. After summarizing the Supreme Court's *Roe v. Wade* decision, this anthology with more than twenty authors discusses the ongoing controversy by presenting a wide range of philosophical, legal, religious, and cultural arguments that relate to the abortion issue.

Rodman, Hyman, Betty Sarvis, and Joy Walker Bonar. *The Abortion Question.* New York: Columbia University Press, 1987. The authors attempt to present the bases of the controversy over the abortion issue by describing the moral positions of the contending sides within the context of their historical development. While the authors acknowledge their pro-choice position, they attempt to present each side objectively, without embellishment or bias.

SEE ALSO: Homicide; Infanticide; Privacy; Prochoice movement; Pro-life movement; Right to life; *Roe v. Wade.*

Absolutism

DEFINITION: Any ethical theory that claims there is only one correct ethical standard applicable to everyone everywhere, or any theory that claims there are ethical values or principles that hold for all humans regardless of their society, culture, or religion

TYPE OF ETHICS: Theory of ethics

SIGNIFICANCE: Absolutism is one of the three mutually exclusive positions that one may adopt concerning the nature of ethical principles and values; the others are relativism, which claims that ethical principles and values vary from culture to culture and that no one is better than any other, and perspectivism or pluralism, which holds that, while some ethical systems are superior to others, there will always be at least two different such systems that are equally valid.

As the definition of absolutism implies, any absolutist theory will acknowledge the existence of ethical absolutes. These will be values or principles that absolutists believe should be embraced by every moral agent. Part of the absolutist's task is to convince people that the values or principles are in fact objective and universally binding. The issue of absolutism versus relativism has existed since the beginnings of ethics. One could make the argument that ethics as a branch of philosophy got its start with the development of the absolutist ethical theory of Socrates in the fifth century B.C.E. It may be best, then, to explain absolutism from a historical perspective.

HISTORY

Socrates lived during a period that exhibited moral skepticism. A group of itinerant teachers known as sophists were advocating various versions of relativism claiming that right and wrong were ultimately determined by, and thus relative to, the individual. It is against this position that Socrates offered his account of right and wrong, which turns out to be the first major version of absolutism. What is interesting is that he relied on a grand metaphysical scheme to supply the justification for his absolutist claim. Socrates believed that human beings are composed of two radically different kinds of substance: bodies and souls, with the soul, because it is the seat of reason, being more important. In addition, reality is also a fundamental dichotomy.

One part of that dichotomy is the world of appearance; the other, the world of form. For Socrates, the world of appearance is an imperfect copy and, hence, less real than the world of form. If one focused on the world of appearance, the ever-changing world of daily experience, the world the body is in, it is easy to believe that relativism is the case. The one constant is that there are no constants. Everything is transitory. The world of form, however, is timeless, changeless, and eternal. It is a world with which the soul is acquainted. Everything is permanent and stable. It is the world that supplies both knowledge and absolute moral values and principles, to which humans have access and which they recognize as absolutely binding in virtue of their rationality.

With a few minor exceptions, the issue of absolutism versus relativism did not pose a major problem to the Western intellectual tradition until well into the nineteenth century. This is so, in part, because of the dominant role that Roman Catholicism played in this tradition. According to Catholicism, there are moral absolutes and there is one correct ethical theory that is applicable to everyone everywhere. Right and wrong are simply a matter of what God commands. What is of moral value is simply a matter of what God deems valuable.

With the coming of the Enlightenment came a rejection of the above-described theory of ethics but not a rejection of absolutism. Christian ethics were replaced with other absolutist theories that appealed to human reason instead of God. One example is the utilitarianism of Jeremy Bentham, which claims that defining right and wrong is simply a matter of calculating which action would produce the greatest good for the greatest number. This so-called "principle of utility" is applicable to everyone everywhere. Another example is the deontological ethics of Immanuel Kant. For him, right and wrong is a matter of whatever reason determines through use of the categorical imperative, which, again, is applicable to everyone everywhere.

MODERN CHALLENGES TO ABSOLUTISM

The most recent challenge to absolutism comes from the social sciences—in particular, cultural anthropology. Cultural anthropology is the study, observation, and description of the customs and mores of various cultures and societies. Cultural anthropologists have gone to all parts of the globe to study, observe, and describe the cultures they have found. They have also gone into the historical record to do the same for cultures past. If absolutism were true, one would expect that there would be some common values or principles. When the gathered data are compared, however, what strikes the observer is the great diversity of values and principles. Given an action one culture sanctions as right, one would have little difficulty finding a different culture that would claim the same action wrong. It seems that all the empirical evidence supports relativism. There is no universal agreement. Values and principles vary from culture to culture.

ABSOLUTIST REPLY

The absolutists have a three-part reply to the claims of the cultural relativists. First, it is shown that the data do not support what relativists claim but rather something weaker. All the data show is that, at best, there is not now one correct ethical theory. It does not rule out, logically, the possibility that the one correct standard may be discovered in the future. Second, there may be less disagreement than there seems. This disagreement among cultures may be the result of differing physical circumstances or factual beliefs and not necessarily the result of differing values. In other words, there may be absolute values that are implemented in different ways. Finally, there may well be absolute values and principles; namely, those necessary for the preservation and continuation of the society or culture. For example, all societies have some rules that protect children. This will ensure that the culture or society will continue into the future.

John H. Serembus

FURTHER READING

Brink, David. *Moral Realism and the Foundations of Ethics*. Cambridge, England: Cambridge University Press, 1989.

Kane, Robert. *Through the Moral Maze: Searching for Absolute Values in a Pluralistic World*. New York: Paragon House, 1994. Reprint. Armonk, N.Y.: North Castle Books, 1996.

Mackie, J. L. *Ethics: Inventing Right and Wrong.* New York: Penguin Books, 1977.

Pojman, Louis P. *Ethics: Discovering Right and Wrong*. 2d ed. Belmont, Calif.: Wadsworth, 1995.

Rachels, James. *The Elements of Moral Philosophy.* 3d ed. Boston: McGraw-Hill, 1999.

Williams, Bernard. *Ethics and the Limits of Philosophy*. Cambridge, Mass.: Harvard University Press, 1985.

SEE ALSO: Anthropological ethics; Diversity; Pluralism; Relativism; Situational ethics; Socrates; Truth.

The Absurd

DEFINITION: That which points toward the ultimately meaningless character of human life

TYPE OF ETHICS: Modern history

SIGNIFICANCE: In the view of French philosopher and novelist Albert Camus, the absurd presents philosophy with its most fundamental problem: justifying the value of human existence.

Owing largely to World War II and its aftermath, it seemed to Albert Camus that traditional values and ways of life had collapsed. He dramatized that situation in novels such as *The Stranger* (1942) and *The Plague* (1947) and reflected on it philosophically in essays such as *The Myth of Sisyphus* (1942). Especially in the latter work, Camus explained that absurdity arises from the confrontation between "human need and the unreasonable silence of the world." The absurd exists partly because human beings ask "Why?," but that is only part of the story. The other key component is that answers to the question "Why?"—at least ones that are complete, final, and convincing to all—never appear. The collision between the questioning human consciousness and "the unreasonable silence of the world" brings the absurd into existence.

Camus could see no way to overcome the absurd and its "total absence of hope." He did not, however, conclude that the absurd dictated nihilism and death. On the contrary, he argued that humanity's task was to rebel against the absurd by making life as good as it can possibly be.

SEE ALSO: Camus, Albert; Evil; Existentialism; Sartre, Jean-Paul; Value.

Abū Bakr

IDENTIFICATION: Early Arab caliph
BORN: c. 573, Mecca, Arabia (now in Saudi Arabia)
DIED: August 23, 634, Medina, Arabia (now in Saudi Arabia)
TYPE OF ETHICS: Religious ethics
SIGNIFICANCE: Abū Bakr succeeded the Prophet Muḥammad as the first caliph and expanded the nascent Muslim empire by conquering neighboring states.

One of the first persons to convert to Islam, Abū Bakr lent much-needed credibility to the cause of Prophet Muḥammad during the early days of Islam. He belonged to a rich trading family and was a crucial figure in providing moral and financial support to sustain Muḥammad in Mecca at the time that Muḥammad declared his prophethood. The close relationship between the two men was further strengthened by marital relations. Abū Bakr gave two of his daughters in marriage to Muḥammad. One of them, Khadīja, was only thirteen years of age when she married Muḥammad.

Muḥammad gave Abū Bakr the title *Siddiq*, one who always speaks truth, because he became a disciple of Muḥammad at a time when it was not safe for Muslims to reveal their allegiance openly. Abū Bakr is supposed to have accompanied Muḥammad at the time of their flight from Mecca to the city of Medina, which provided a safe haven to Muḥammad and his followers. Abū Bakr remained close to the Prophet in Mecca as well as in Medina and assisted him in becoming established in Medina. Abū Bakr negotiated on behalf of the Prophet with other clans in and around Medina whose support was crucial in the struggle against the Meccans. The Quraish tribe of Mecca tried to march on Medina to destroy Muḥammad's forces three times but failed. After the death of Muḥammad, Abū Bakr was chosen to lead the Muslims. He assumed the title caliph, or successor.

Khalid N. Mahmood

SEE ALSO: ʿAlī ibn Abī Ṭālib; Holy war; Ḥusayn; Islamic ethics; Muḥammad; Shīʿa.

Abū Ḥanīfah

IDENTIFICATION: Muslim theologian and jurist
BORN: c. 699, al-Kufa, Iraq
DIED: 767, Baghdad, Iraq
TYPE OF ETHICS: Religious ethics
SIGNIFICANCE: As a theologian, Abū Ḥanīfah founded the first of the four orthodox schools of law in Sunnī Islam. As a legal scholar, he was among the earliest to formulate judicial doctrines relating to questions that might arise in the future of the Islamic community.

Born to a family of non-Arab converts to Islam, Abū Ḥanīfah was originally attracted to theology but soon turned to Islamic law. His principal teacher was Hammad ibn Abī Sulayman, the foremost representative of the Iraqi school of legal thought.

Following the death of his mentor in 737, Abū Ḥanīfah was acknowledged as the head of the school. Throughout his career, he declined offers of governmental positions under the Umayyad and Abbasid dynasties, and there are indications that he harbored antigovernment sympathies. Indeed, he seems to have been imprisoned from 762 because of his support for an Alid revolt. As a theologian, Abū Ḥanīfah vigorously opposed the Khariji rigorist doctrine that sin rendered one an unbeliever. He declared that faith was the ultimate determinant of a person's membership in Islam. It was this doctrine that ultimately became the orthodox position in Islam. As a jurist, Abū Ḥanīfah spent many years reviewing the corpus of Islamic law; formulating new, systematic legal doctrines based on religious tradition and judicial precedent; and, most important, proposing legal responses to hypothetical situations that might arise later in the Islamic community.

Craig L. Hanson

SEE ALSO: Islamic ethics; Qurʾān; Sunnīs.

Abuse

DEFINITION: Acts of physical or psychological violence or neglect that are designed to cause emotional trauma, usually to a person who is in a subordinate power relationship to the abuser

TYPE OF ETHICS: Personal and social ethics

SIGNIFICANCE: Because it often generates feelings of shame or guilt in its victims that prevent them from resisting or reporting it, abuse is one of the most insidious of all ethical violations and one of the most difficult to combat effectively.

Physical abuse, which is nonaccidental injury to another person, includes actions that physically damage another person, such as pushing, shoving, hitting, slapping, and throwing things. The consequences of physical abuse can be minor, such as a bruise, or major, such as death. Physically abusive actions are fairly stable, so that a person who is physically abusive early in life usually stays that way. Young adults (under age thirty) are more likely to engage in domestic violence than are older adults.

Because ordinary physical punishment is widely accepted as an appropriate form of discipline in the United States, it is typically excluded from definitions of physical abuse. Physical abuse is, however, often difficult to distinguish from physical punishment. When does spanking become abuse? One guiding principle in distinguishing physical punishment from physical abuse is the leaving of bruises. Physical punishment that leaves bruises on a child is often considered physical abuse. Parents who endorse physical punishment are more likely than are others to physically abuse their children. Physical abuse is widespread.

Sexual abuse includes any sexual behaviors that are forced upon a person. Sexual abuse includes any type of sexual fondling, touching, or other such behaviors of a sexual nature (such as being exposed involuntarily to someone's genitals); rape (involuntary sexual intercourse); and incest (sexual activity between close relatives).

Sexual abuse may be the result of physical force, threat, or intimidation. Sexual abuse violates community norms in an extreme way; therefore, it is typically viewed with abhorrence and is often punished with imprisonment. Nevertheless, some form of sexual abuse has been reported by between 19 percent and 38 percent of adult American women, and by between 5 percent and 30 percent of adult men. Thus, even though sexual abuse is not condoned in society, it is experienced by a significant percentage of women and men.

Many adults who have been molested as children report feeling guilt, anger, depression, disordered sexual behavior, poor self-esteem, feelings of isolation and stigma, self-destructive behavior, difficulties trusting others, substance abuse, and a tendency toward revictimization.

Sustained physical or sexual abuse is thought to be a primary culprit in the development of multiple personality, a psychological disorder in which a person has two or more distinctly different personalities, each of which has a unique way of thinking and behaving. Not all people who were physically or sexually abused as children, however, develop multiple personalities as adults.

Psychological abuse, which is also called emotional or mental abuse, includes actions that damage a person's behavioral, cognitive, emotional, or physical functioning. Psychologically abusive behaviors are those that ridicule, belittle, degrade, exploit, intimidate, and so forth. Psychological abuse may be the most prevalent form of child abuse, and it is also a widespread form of adult abuse. Often occurring in conjunction with other forms of abuse, psychological abuse may exist independently of other types of abuse.

Because its consequences are often invisible, psychological abuse is seldom reported. Despite this fact, many experts believe that psychological abuse is the most damaging of all forms of abuse. It lowers a person's self-image, distorts his or her relationships with others, and leads to increased fear, anxiety, helplessness, aggression, and self-destructive behavior.

In a comprehensive overview of domestic violence, Donald Dutton suggested a nested ecological explanation of domestic violence that includes at least four factors. First, the cultural values of the individuals involved may contribute to abuse. For example, are men and women considered to be equal? Is hitting one's wife considered to be an indication of affection? Second, the social situation may contribute to abuse. For example, are the individuals involved unemployed? Are they under severe economic or other stress? Third, the family unit may contribute to domestic abuse. For example, do the individuals communicate as a couple? Do the parents typically use physical punishment? Fourth, the level of individual development may contribute to domestic abuse. For example, does the couple excuse violence? Have they witnessed family violence in the past? The nested ecological approach suggests multiple levels of causes, with the importance of each level differing in each assault case.

Lillian Range

FURTHER READING

Bonnie, Richard J., and Robert B. Wallace, eds. *Elder Mistreatment: Abuse, Neglect, and Exploitation in an Aging America.* Washington, D.C.: National Academies Press, 2003.

Dutton, Donald G. *The Domestic Assault of Women.* Boston: Allyn & Bacon, 1988.

McCabe, Kimberly A. *Child Abuse and the Criminal Justice System.* New York: Peter Lang, 2003.

National Committee for the Prevention of Child Abuse. *Child Abuse and Neglect Statistics.* Chicago: Author, 1992.

Russell, Diana E. H. *Sexual Exploitation: Rape, Child Sexual Abuse, and Workplace Harassment.* Beverly Hills, Calif.: Sage, 1984.

Van Hasselt, Vincent B., et al. eds. *Handbook of Family Violence.* New York: Plenum Press, 1988.

Zorza, Joan, ed. *Violence Against Women: Law, Prevention, Protection, Enforcement, Treatment, Health.* Kingston, N.J.: Civic Research Institute, 2002.

SEE ALSO: Ageism; Child abuse; Drug abuse; Exploitation; Police brutality; Rape; Roman Catholic priests scandal; Sexual abuse and harassment; Torture; Violence.

Academic freedom

DEFINITION: State in which teachers are free to discuss their subjects in the classroom, to conduct research, and to publish the results of that research, without fear of repercussions

TYPE OF ETHICS: Beliefs and practices

SIGNIFICANCE: Academic freedom makes it possible for both teachers and students to question the status quo and to arrive at conclusions other than those endorsed by the majority or supported by dominant structures of power. It increases the likelihood that academic inquiry will be motivated by truth rather than politics.

The freedom of teachers to instruct and to do research is fundamental for civilization. The discovery and dissemination of knowledge form the basis for positive dialogue. Such dialogue can lead to consensus, which can serve to motivate people both individually and collectively to take action that can bring moral order. Such an ethical dynamic makes it possible for new ideas to be advanced and new, positive action to be taken on an ethical and moral level.

Academic freedom is inextricably intertwined with conflict. Socrates' incessant probing in search of the truth led to his execution on the charge of corrupting the youth of Athens. During the Middle Ages in Europe, academic freedom began its relationship with institutions of higher learning.

The medieval era displayed contradiction concerning academic freedom. The Roman Catholic Church preached and insisted on a single system of truth that was anchored in God. Most medieval scholars accepted this central body of authority, but some rejected the idea that the hierarchy represented the true Church. In the thirteenth and fourteenth centuries, the ecclesiastical authorities, through condemnations and censures, greatly hindered philosophical and theological inquiry. Nevertheless, scholars fought back in the pursuit of truth that would outlast and even reverse condemnations.

Italian thinkers enjoyed a remarkable degree of academic freedom during the Renaissance. For example, Professor Pietro Pompanazzi published a book questioning the immortality of the soul and also attacked the clergy. Far from being censured, Pompanazzi was protected by Pope Leo X, and his salary was increased.

During the Reformation, Protestantism both impeded and advanced academic freedom. Rigorous orthodox Calvinism held that freedom of thought was an obstacle to ethics. Arminianism brought a latitudinarian thrust. The Dutch city of Leiden was the home of the first European university to follow an intentional and consistent policy of academic freedom.

In seventeenth century England, the Act of Uniformity led to ejections from academic institutions. Those who were purged founded academies noted for liberality in thought. The graduates of these academies contributed to the American Enlightenment, which supported secularism in ethics. Academic freedom has had a precarious life in the United

States. Seventeenth century colleges demanded religious conformity from its faculty. In 1654, Harvard University dismissed its first president, the Reverend Henry Dunster, for heresy.

The eighteenth century displayed a mixed tableau. The secularization of colleges introduced skepticism and inquiry into ethics. Between 1740 and 1766, however, Yale University experienced illiberalism under the Reverend President Thomas Clap, who promoted orthodox Calvinist ethics. Nevertheless, the Reverend Edward Wigglesworth, the first person in American collegiate education to hold a major professorship, enjoyed notable academic freedom as Harvard's Hollis Professor of Divinity from 1722 to 1765. Wigglesworth's namesake son, who was Hollis Professor between 1765 and 1791, advanced the cause of liberal ethics. In 1756, the University of Pennsylvania acquitted the Reverend Provost William Smith of the charge of teaching irreligious ethics.

Pre-Civil War America experienced various notable situations regarding academic freedom. For example, the Unitarian reverend president Horace Holley, who raised Transylvania University to distinction, resigned because of Presbyterian charges that he had made that institution infidel. President Thomas Cooper of South Carolina College, a materialist ethicist, put forward the boldest and most advanced argument for academic freedom.

Later nineteenth century America made significant strides in academic freedom. Despite opposition, the teaching of evolution and attacks on transcendental ethics entered institutions. At Yale, Professor William Graham Sumner ably defended his rigid ethic of self-reliance. The introduction of the German concept of *Lehrfreiheit*—freedom of teaching and freedom of inquiry for the university professor—was profoundly significant.

Between 1890 and 1900, a number of academic freedom incidents occurred in which a professor was summarily dismissed after espousing reform or criticizing the social order. Such cases involved Richard T. Ely (University of Wisconsin), Edward W. Bemis (University of Chicago in 1895 and Kansas State Agricultural College in 1899), E. Benjamin Andrews (Brown University), Frank Parsons (Kansas State Agricultural College), and Edward A. Ross (Stanford University). Ross's views had antagonized Mrs. Leland Stanford, Sr.

In 1913, the dismissal of Professor John M. Mecklin, a professor of philosophy and psychology at Lafayette College, proved to be noteworthy. President Ethelbert D. Warfield detested Mecklin's philosophical relativism, his interest in pragmatism, and his teaching of evolution. The American Philosophical and American Psychological Associations failed to obtain justice for Mecklin. A body representing the entire professorate was needed to protect academic freedom.

That organization appeared in the form of the American Association of University Professors (AAUP). Founded in 1915, its principal promoter was Arthur O. Lovejoy of Johns Hopkins University. By 2003, the organization's *1940 Statement of Principles on Academic Freedom and Tenure* had been been endorsed by 175 educational and scholarly organizations. Meanwhile, however, AAUP's national office was growing weak. During World War I, it chose not to defend academic freedom. Between 1949 and 1955, the AAUP general secretary Ralph Himstead gave no help to victims of Congress's House Committee on Un-American Activities and neglected more than a hundred casualties of Senator Joseph R. McCarthy's misguided witch-hunts in search of communists.

Later twentieth century America experienced attacks against academic freedom. Both secular institutions, public and private, and religious organizations, Jewish, Protestant, and Roman Catholic, have stifled or attempted to stifle professors. The Catholic University of America, for example, dismissed Father Charles E. Curran because of his views on ethics.

The battle over academic freedom has continued in the twenty-first century, and there is no indication that it will be resolved in the foreseeable future.

Erving E. Beauregard

FURTHER READING

Beale, Howard K. *A History of Freedom of Teaching in American Schools.* New York: Octagon Books, 1966.

Beauregard, Erving E. *History of Academic Freedom in Ohio.* New York: Peter Lang, 1988.

Glenn, Charles, and Jan de Groof. *Finding the Right Balance: Freedom, Autonomy, and Accountability in Education.* Utrecht, the Netherlands: Lemma, 2002.

Gruber, Carol S. *Mars and Minerva: World War I and*

15

the Uses of the Higher Learning in America. Baton Rouge: Louisiana State University, 1975.

Hofstadter, Richard, and Walter P. Metzger. *The Development of Academic Freedom in the United States.* New York: Columbia University Press, 1956.

Schrecker, Ellen W. *No Ivory Tower: McCarthyism and the Universities.* New York: Oxford University, 1986.

SEE ALSO: American Civil Liberties Union; Book banning; Censorship; Cold War; College applications; Communism; Loyalty oaths; Sedition; Truth.

Accountability

DEFINITION: State of being responsible, liable, or answerable for one's thoughts or actions

TYPE OF ETHICS: Theory of ethics

SIGNIFICANCE: Systems of morality generally require accountability, either individual or collective, before ethical evaluations can assign praise or blame.

Accountability can be either individual or collective, but the latter has been much more controversial (for example, the alleged collective responsibility of Germans for Nazi atrocities). Ethicists usually believe that individual accountability applies to any free or voluntary act. Accountability is thus a key concept in morality and metaphysics.

A key doctrine that is related to accountability is compatibilism, the view that the causal determination of actions is consistent with moral responsibility for those actions. For example, a compatibilist holds that one would still be accountable for one's actions even if a scientist or a god could predict all those actions in detail. Compatibilism is a metaphysical doctrine that is relevant to ethics. Incompatibilists claim that the causal determination of one's acts would prevent one from having the freedom necessary for having moral accountability for one's acts. Metaphysical libertarianism (which is completely distinct from political libertarianism) endorses incompatibilism but allows for accountability by denying that acts are causally determined.

Another key doctrine here is the idea that "ought"

implies "can," which denies that an agent can be accountable for failing to do the impossible. Accountability assumes that there is a duty (that is, a responsibility or obligation) that one is to discharge. One can generally be held to account for failure to do one's duty. As Joseph F. Newton wrote, "A duty dodged is like a debt unpaid; it is only deferred, and we must come back and settle the account at last."

Accountability is a key concept in law, where ethical issues are often discussed in terms of liability. Strict liability implies that one is responsible even if one is not at fault. Thus, strict liability seems to be inconsistent with the doctrine that ought implies can. Vicarious liability is responsibility for harm done by another (for example, one's child). Product liability is a field of law that holds manufacturers and merchants accountable for defective goods that they sell. Legal liability is the most general term for exposure to being held to account by a court or other legal institution. To be legally liable is to be subject to punishment or to an order to provide compensation to at least help make up for one's infraction.

Accountability is a key concept in politics. The Left (liberals, socialists, and communists) often calls for increased social responsibility for corporations and social elites, and often criticizes the allegedly unaccountable power that corporations and elites wield. The Right (conservatives, traditionalists, and fascists) often calls for people to take more responsibility for their own actions, and often criticizes individuals for allegedly shirking their duties by claiming to be victims of circumstance or of society. The importance of accountability is thus something about which the political moralities of the Left and the Right seem to agree.

Some people argue that corporations cannot be accountable, because, first, they are not persons or agents that are distinct from corporate employees, and, second, praise and blame can apply only to distinct agents. Others argue that corporations are agents, since they have internal decision-making structures, which arguably provide enough of a chain of command for ethicists to attribute acts to corporations as distinct from merely attributing the acts to some individual or some subset of the corporation's employees. Some argue that the whole is greater than the sum of its parts in this case. Even if no single employee were held accountable for a bad result, for example, the corporation could still be held accountable. Synergistic effects of individual acts of employees can produce corporate accountability for an immoral outcome. To deny this possibility would seem to be to commit the fallacy of composition, which assumes that whatever is true of each part of a whole (in this case, unaccountability) must be true of the whole as well.

Sterling Harwood

FURTHER READING

Adkins, Arthur W. H. *Merit and Responsibility: A Study in Greek Values.* New York: Oxford University Press, 1960. Reprint. Chicago: University of Chicago Press, 1975.

Allen, Anita L. *Why Privacy Isn't Everything: Feminist Reflections on Personal Accountability.* Lanham, Md.: Rowman & Littlefield, 2003.

French, Peter A. *Collective and Corporate Responsibility.* New York: Columbia University Press, 1984.

_____, ed. *Individual and Collective Responsibility: Massacre at My Lai.* Cambridge, Mass.: Schenkman, 1972.

_____. *The Spectrum of Responsibility.* New York: St. Martin's Press, 1991.

Gorr, Michael J., and Sterling Harwood, eds. *Controversies in Criminal Law: Philosophical Essays on Liability and Procedure.* Boulder, Colo.: Westview Press, 1992.

Hart, Herbert L. *Punishment and Responsibility: Essays in the Philosophy of Law.* New York: Oxford University Press, 1968.

May, Larry, and Stacey Hoffman, eds. *Collective Responsibility: Five Decades of Debate in Theoretical and Applied Ethics.* Savage, Md.: Rowman & Littlefield, 1991.

Muirhead, Sophia A., et al. *Corporate Citizenship in the New Century: Accountability, Transparency, and Global Stakeholder Engagement.* New York: Conference Board, 2002.

Nadel, Mark V. *Corporations and Political Accountability.* Lexington, Mass.: D. C. Heath, 1976.

Pritchard, David, ed. *Holding the Media Accountable: Citizens, Ethics, and the Law.* Bloomington: Indiana University Press, 2000.

SEE ALSO: Bad faith; Corporate responsibility; Duty; Libertarianism; Moral responsibility; Negligence; Responsibility; Social justice and responsibility.

Accuracy in Media

IDENTIFICATION: Politically conservative nonprofit watchdog group that critiques news media coverage of political, social, legal, and economic issues
DATE: Founded in 1969
TYPE OF ETHICS: Media ethics

Examples of Accuracy in Media News Stories

News stories posted on accuracyinmedia.org in May, 2004

"Clinton, Character, and 9/11" (February 26, 2004)

"Fine Print of 'Stem Cell' Bill Goes Unreported" (January 9, 2004)

"Why Marriage Is Worth Defending" (December 26, 2003)

"How Bush Can Use the Media to Sink Kerry" (Apr 29, 2004)

"Big Media Back Kerry" (Apr 16, 2004)

"Media Admit Anti-Bush Bias" (March 31, 2004)

"How to Slant the News: NBC's Andrea Mitchell Distorts CIA Testimony to Benefit Democrats" (March 19, 2004)

"George W.: What You Didn't See on *Meet The Press*" (March 8, 2004)

"Ralph Nader Cannot Be Bought" (March 4, 2004)

"Pandora's Welfare Box: Do Not Open" (February 27, 2004)

"Vietnam Vets Mobilize Against John Kerry" (February 26, 2004)

"John Kerry Waffles Over Gay Marriage" (February 20, 2004)

"The Media's Credibility Gap" (February 17, 2004)

"Punishing Bush May Punish the Country" (February 10, 2004)

"The Media's Rush to Distort" (January 20, 2004)

"Fox News Fair and Balanced?" (November 6, 2003)

"Putting Words in the President's Mouth" (November 4, 2003)

"Media Bias Killing Our Troops" (September 29, 2003)

"Hillary Clinton's Biggest Cover-Ups" (August 11, 2003)

SIGNIFICANCE: One of the best-known American news media pressure groups, Accuracy in Media has been criticized for being more biased than the liberal news media that it criticizes.

Accuracy in Media (AIM) raises the issue of defining ethical news coverage of public issues. It has been financed through donations and dues paid by members and major conservative donors, such as billionaire Richard Mellon Scaife. AIM's staff and supporters monitor daily media coverage and provide news outlets immediate criticism of what they regard as instances of biased or otherwise unethical reporting. Staff members also solicit and regularly receive citizen complaints about perceived biased news coverage. The organization's nationwide activities include providing media guides, holding conferences, providing books and tapes to members, maintaining an intern program, and maintaining an information site on the World Wide Web (www.accuracyinmedia.org).

AIM publishes a twice-monthly newsletter, the *AIM Report*. It also broadcasts a daily news commentary program, *Media Monitor*, over more than 150 radio stations throughout the United States; publishes a syndicated weekly newspaper column; and supports a speaker's bureau. AIM members are encouraged to attend the annual shareholder meetings of large media organizations and initiate mass letter-writing campaigns to newsrooms to complain about specific acts of biased or incomplete news coverage.

The organization also presents annual awards for what members judge to be outstanding examples of fair and accurate news coverage. Criticisms of AIM, often from activists on the political Left, charge the organization with being more biased and less accurate than the media they monitor. In part in response to AIM, political liberals established a rival media monitoring organization, Fairness and Accuracy in Reporting (FAIR), in 1986.

Robert E. Dewhirst

SEE ALSO: American Society of Newspaper Editors; Fairness and Accuracy in Reporting; Journalistic ethics; Media ownership; News sources; Photojournalism.

Accused, rights of

DEFINITION: Procedural and substantive legal rights possessed by persons who have been formally accused of criminal acts
TYPE OF ETHICS: Legal and judicial ethics
SIGNIFICANCE: In the U.S. criminal justice system, persons accused of wrongdoing are presumed innocent until proven guilty and are entitled to certain rights, including fair trials. Balancing the rights of the accused against society's goal of bringing criminals to justice can create serious ethical dilemmas.

The American criminal justice system encounters significant ethical dilemmas when it attempts to balance the competing interests of the participants in its processes. On one hand, there are those people who have been accused of criminal acts. Even after they have been accused, they are supposed to be presumed innocent of the crimes until they have been duly convicted. Moreover, they are entitled to fair trials. This right is guaranteed by the Fourth and Fifteenth Amendments to the U.S. Constitution, which state that a person cannot be deprived of life, liberty, or property without due process of law. The U.S. Constitution does not specify, however, what constitutes "due process."

On the other hand, there is the right of society to punish those who violate its laws. In some cases, the welfare of victims must be considered as well. In addition, certain high-profile cases involve the media's First Amendment rights, as well as the public's right to be informed. It is often quite difficult to balance the rights the accused with those of society.

A specific situation that poses significant ethical issues is when one person is accused of sexually assaulting another and claims that the encounter was consensual. An example of such a case arose in 2003-2004, when basketball star Kobe Bryant was accused of raping a Colorado hotel worker. Bryant admitted having engaged in sexual intercourse with the woman but claimed the encounter was mutually consensual. In such situations, defendants often wish to present evidence of their alleged victims' sexual histories—just as Bryant's defense team did. From the defense standpoint, such evidence may be essential to proving that the alleged victims actually consented to the acts. However, if the crimes did actually occur, the public presentation of such evidence may unfairly humiliate the victims. Courts frequently struggle with how to protect the defendants' rights to fair trials in such situations, without further harming victims.

Ethical difficulties are sometimes also evoked when criminal defendants appear to be mentally ill and consequently incompetent to stand trial. Prosecutors may wish to require them to take medications to treat their mental illness; otherwise, their trials might have to be postponed indefinitely. However, such defendants may invoke the right to make their own decisions about their medical treatment, especially as the medications they take may have significant side effects. Moreover, the defense teams may believe that forced medication will hinder their clients' rights to fair trials when the defendants plan insanity pleas, as the medications may alter a jury's perceptions of the defendants.

Even quite ordinary criminal cases raise ethical issues. For example, what means may be used to interrogate suspects, and what limits are to be placed on interrogations? What kinds of evidence may be admitted, and what excluded? What procedures ought to be used to ensure juries that are fair and that represent cross-sections of their communities? Some sorts of balance must always be made between the interests of people accused of crimes and the interests of those who may be harmed by criminal acts, and such balance is often difficult to achieve.

Phyllis B. Gerstenfeld

FURTHER READING

Bodenhamer, David J. *Fair Trial: Rights of the Accused in American History.* New York: Oxford University Press, 1991.

Hall, Timothy L. *The U.S. Legal System.* Pasadena, Calif.: Salem Press, 2004.

Ramen, Fred. *Rights of the Accused.* New York: Rosen Publishing, 2001.

SEE ALSO: American Civil Liberties Union; Arrest records; Erroneous convictions; *Gideon v. Wainwright*; Homeland defense; Jury system; Mental illness; Victims' rights.

Acquired immunodeficiency syndrome (AIDS)

DEFINITION: Commonly known as AIDS, a physical condition believed to be caused by a virus of indeterminate origin that invades and seriously damages the body's immune system, leaving it vulnerable to a number of opportunistic infections and rare cancers

DATE: Discovered in 1981

TYPE OF ETHICS: Bioethics

SIGNIFICANCE: The worldwide AIDS pandemic has highlighted a host of crucial policy issues including civil and human rights, confidentiality and privacy, accessibility to medical and social services, the drug trial and approval process, prisoners' rights, substance-abuse treatment, school-based sex education, equitable distribution of scarce resources, and international cooperation.

Acquired immunodeficiency syndrome, or AIDS, is a term given to a collection of life-threatening medical conditions that result from acquisition of the human immunodeficiency virus (HIV). Before 1981 the virus was unknown, and it is unknown how many cases of this disease occurred. In early 1981 eight cases of a rare, relatively benign tumor that affected older men, Kaposi's sarcoma, suddenly appeared in New York City. At the same time in New York and California, cases of a rare pneumonia caused by *pneumocystis carinii* were reported. Soon the Centers for Disease Control and Prevention (CDC) created a task force to study the situation. Many of the earlier cases occurred in gay men, and therefore the disease was initially dubbed the "gay compromise syndrome" or "gay-related immune deficiency (GRID)." Later the virus was also found among heterosexuals, and the syndrome's name was changed to acquired immunodeficiency syndrome, or AIDS. In 1984 the causative virus was isolated. By the first years of the twenty-first century, HIV disease was a worldwide pandemic.

THE WORLD PANDEMIC

By the beginning of 2003, 42 million cases of AIDS had been reported around the world, with 816,149 cases in the United States. From the beginning of the epidemic in 1981 until December, 2002,

467,910 deaths attributed to AIDS had occurred in the United States alone, while at least 3.1 million deaths had occurred elsewhere in the world. During the mid- to late 1990's, the rate of progression from HIV to AIDS slowed in the United States, due to advances in treatment. The result was that increasing numbers of people were living with HIV. By 2003, it was estimated that there were 800,000 to 900,000 people with HIV living in the United States, with 40,000 new cases reported each year. Worldwide in 2002, 5 million new cases of HIV were identified, and the epidemic showed no signs of decline.

ISSUES OF LIABILITY

HIV is most commonly transmitted from one person to another through physical sexual contact. The second-most common method of transmission is blood-to-blood contact, followed by contacts between infected mothers and their children. Before 1985, HIV was transmitted through infected blood supplies and accidental needle pricks in health-care workplaces. Such accidents raise several issues of liability. First, a person suffering from the disease may indulge in behaviors that purposely transmit the virus to others, leading to criminal liability. Any of three types of criminal laws may be applied in such cases: traditional (such as attempted murder, aggravated assault, assault with a deadly weapon, or attempted manslaughter); criminal violations of public health statutes; and AIDS-specific criminal statutes.

Criminal prosecutions often pose ethical challenges by being essentially punitive acts directed toward victims of HIV/AIDs that do little or nothing for public health. Several issues pertain to civil liability. Tort law is the area of law that governs harms allegedly caused by a private individual or group of individuals against other private individuals. Tort laws vary from state to state and are usually based on previous cases or precedents. Civil liability for transmitting HIV/AIDS may occur for any of four reasons: negligence or lack of use of reasonable care to avoid harm to others, battery involving unwanted touching or infliction of injury on other persons, intentional infliction of emotional distress, and fraud.

ISSUES OF DISCRIMINATION

HIV/AIDS raises a number of issues relating to discrimination. At the societal level, it is a disease that has a great stigma attached to it. That stigma is enhanced by the popular association of AIDS with homosexuals—a fact that also enhances negative images of gay people.

People carrying the HIV virus have also been discriminated against when they have sought health care. However, the federal Americans with Disabilities Acts (ADA) of 1990 bans discrimination against HIV-infected persons at any stage of their disease. In addition various professional codes such as the American Nurses Association Code also encourage respect for human dignity and prohibit discrimination against carriers of HIV. Nevertheless, there is evidence that many health care workers so fear HIV/AIDS that they prefer not to care for persons with the disease.

Discrimination against people with HIV/AIDS has also been an issue in public accommodations, including hotels, restaurants, theaters, and nursing homes. Title III of the ADA protects HIV carries from such discrimination; however, violations of the law have been common. An even more serious issue is employment discrimination, which is also covered by the ADA. HIV infection is considered a disability, and employers are obligated to provide reasonable accommodations for persons carrying the virus. Another controversial issue is the placing of limits or caps by employers on the amount of health insurance coverage provided to HIV sufferers.

Housing discrimination is also an issue. Despite the fact that HIV cannot be transmitted through casual physical contact, people with HIV have been discriminated against in housing allotments. This, too, violates federal laws. For example, the Fair Housing Act of 1968 is designed to prevent landlords and real estate agents from discriminating against potential tenants on the basis of race, color, religion, sex, family status, national origin, or handicap. AIDS is considered a handicap under section 504 of the Rehabilitation Act of 1973. In addition there are state and local laws that prohibit housing discrimination due to HIV/AIDS.

INDIVIDUAL LIBERTIES

The U.S. Constitution has many provisions protecting the rights of citizens to pursue their goals without restraints from others. Confidentiality and privacy are important ethical considerations within the broader framework of liberty. Health care professionals are ethically obligated to protect confidential information about their patients. Professionals who provide counseling before and after HIV testing procedures are also expected to maintain complete confidentiality of the results. However, diagnoses that turn up positive results can pose serious ethical dilemmas. The fact that health care professionals are expected to protect the privacy and confidentiality of their patients leaves open the question of who is ethically responsible for alerting the sexual partners of persons who test positive for HIV.

In HIV/AIDS, as for any medical condition, health care providers cannot perform examinations, conduct treatments, or even touch patients without their consent. This doctrine of informed consent is grounded under the overall principle of autonomy and respect for people. *Autonomy* is a Greek word that means self-governance or self-rule. Health care professionals are obligated to provide to their patients details of treatment and medical procedures to be performed, accurate descriptions of the potential risks and benefits of the procedures, explanations of alternative treatments or procedures, and assessments of the likelihood of success. After receiving this information, patients who decide they do not want the procedures or treatments to be performed may choose to reject them. All adults with decision-making capacity who suffer from HIV/AIDS have the right to self-determination in their medical treatments and care.

The increasing numbers of women diagnosed with HIV/AIDS, many of whom become pregnant, raise additional ethical questions. For example, should legal restrictions on abortion be loosened for pregnant women?

EDUCATION AND RESEARCH

Efforts to educate the public on the dangers of AIDS often collide with other public-education goals. For example, encouraging young people to practice safer sex and to use condoms is seen by some as condoning adolescent sexual activity. Providing drug users with free hypodermic needles to reduce the transmission of diseases may be seen as condoning illegal drug use.

Medical ethics require that researchers obtain the informed consent of their subjects. However, since no complete cures of HIV infection are know, persons carrying the virus may be inclined to accept unsafe risks in the hope of finding a cure. Researchers

must be sensitive to that fact in evaluating their subjects' understanding of the risks they may take.

In any society there are some that have easy access to resources while others do not. Despite the illegality of discrimination in access to care, poor persons find it very hard to have access to enough resources. This disparity is even more glaring at the global level. Some of the poorer nations in Africa have a higher burden of this disease and very scarce resources to cope with the problem.

Manoj Sharma

FURTHER READING

Adams, William E., et al. *AIDS Cases and Materials.* 3d ed. Durham, N.C.: Carolina Academic Press, 2002. Collection of case studies on legal and ethical issues relating to HIV/AIDS.

Ahmed, Paul I. *Living and Dying with AIDS.* New York: Plenum Press, 1992. Study of issues of coping with AIDS, including ethical and legal issues and the effects of AIDS on families and adolescents,.

Almond, Brenda. *AIDS—A Moral Issue: The Ethical, Legal and Social Aspects.* London: Macmillan, 1990. Study of medical issues relating to AIDS and its effect on communities.

Dickson, Donald T. *HIV, AIDS, and the Law: Legal Issues for Social Work Practice and Policy.* New York: Aldine de Gruyter, 2001. Integrated approach to legal and social aspects of HIV/AIDS, with special attention to ethical issues..

Huber, Joan, and Beth E. Schneider. *The Social Context of AIDS.* Newbury Park, Calif.: Sage Publications, 1992. Overview of the directions that sociological research on AIDS has taken. Chapters are organized in three sections, which examine medical aspects of the disease, risky behaviors, and treatment.

Rubenstein, William B., Ruth Eisenberg, and Lawrence O. Gostin. *The Rights of People Who Are HIV Positive.* Carbondale: Southern Illinois University Press, 1996. Authoritative guide to the rights of people living with HIV or AIDS.

Stein, Theodore J. *The Social Welfare of Women and Children with HIV and AIDS: Legal Protections, Policy, and Programs.* New York: Oxford University Press, 1998. Ethical issues specific to women and children with HIV/AIDS are discussed.

SEE ALSO: Americans with Disabilities Act; Health care allocation; Homosexuality; Medical ethics; Medical research; National Gay and Lesbian Task Force; Promiscuity; Sexually transmitted diseases.

Adultery

DEFINITION: Sexual relations by a married person with someone other than the person's own spouse
TYPE OF ETHICS: Personal and social ethics; religious ethics
SIGNIFICANCE: Adultery is widely perceived as a practice that undermines the basic social institution, the family, causing both innocent spouses and children to suffer trauma.

Taboos, or at least prohibitions, against adultery exist in virtually every society, both past and present—the taboo is about as common as marriage itself. Under Mosaic law, a married man who had intercourse with a single woman was deemed not to have committed adultery, but a married woman who had sex with someone other than her spouse *was* deemed guilty. Furthermore, punishment varied according to time and place, with women usually receiving harsher "discipline" than the male. Under the ancient Babylonian Code of Hammurabi punishment for adultery was death by drowning.

In ancient Greece and Rome, men were not harshly dealt with, but offending female spouses could be punished by death. Likewise, in the Old Testament and in the Qurʾān, offending women were killed, while punishment for men was much less severe. Under ancient Hindu law, marriage was so sacrosanct that even a wife's adultery was *not* grounds for ending a legal union. At the time of Oliver Cromwell in mid-seventeenth century England, authorities put adulterers to death, but afterward, under English common law, adultery was held to be a private wrong, not an indictable offense.

Among the Senoufo and Bambara peoples of West Africa, a man may kill his adulterous wife and her lover, but among the Kaka in Cameroon, a man may freely have sex with the wives of certain relatives without punishment. Among many Pacific islanders, as among certain Pueblo Indians, nonincestuous adultery is common and is tolerated if the actors are discreet and secretive. Wife "lending" is a common practice among the Eskimos.

ADULTERY IN THE UNITED STATES

Although "reform" laws passed by enlightened state legislators have "softened" legal punishments for adultery, in most states the practice is still grounds for divorce, especially when combined with the "general breakdown" charge or the "mental cruelty" charge. Until recently, Virginia fined adulterers twenty dollars for the first offense, while repeat offenders could be sentenced to prison for terms of from six months up to one year. Vermont's legal code once held adultery to be a felony punishable by up to five years in prison—for both offenders. Various other states, such as Oklahoma, once had "alienation of affection" codes (that is, an innocent spouse could sue and collect money damages from the guilty spouse's companion, who presumedly caused such "alienation of affection"); such laws amounted to a "seduction" code for all would-be seducers of married people. Most states, however, have repealed many of the old punishments; unfortunately, incidents of adultery in the United States seem to have skyrocketed—or at least the reporting of such behavior is now more widespread than was the case previously.

EXTENT OF AND EFFECTS OF ADULTERY

Many authorities in the United States agree that approximately 50 percent of all married persons commit adultery. In addition, more commit "infidelities" that may well stop short of intercourse. Such escapades include "flirting" (done in front of the spouse to make him or her insecure and upset) and "psychic infidelity" (a man telling his mate about the beautiful secretary whom he has just hired; a woman telling her spouse about the handsome young man who is her new tennis coach).

Although most people seem to cope well with psychic infidelity, others become jealous. Jealousy leads to more and more suspicions and may also lead to vitriolic quarrels, with the result that a marriage may be permanently undermined; when the adultery is "real," the strain on a marriage becomes even more pronounced. It is, then, no surprise that the modern American divorce rate is close to 50 percent, the same percentage as that of adultery. In the case of a parent who commits adultery, the children may suffer most by having to cope with a broken home and by living in a poisoned atmosphere created by the adulterer.

EXCEPTIONS

In some cases, adultery—as it narrowly defined—may be sanctioned by certain spouses. For example, some married women (and men) become prostitutes with the approval or at least the toleration of their husbands. Sometimes, married "swingers" engage in mate swapping or group orgies. Likewise, psychologists have reported cases wherein heterosexual couples allow each other to take on homosexual lovers, because they believe that no "real" sex with such partners can take place. Indeed, enough mutual adultery apparently occurs that psychologists and other therapists exempt such cases from the "body count" of adultery.

ADULTERY AND ETHICS

Clearly, adultery often destroys families, leaving spouses and children in disaster's wake. Certainly, the practice contributes to social disorganization in the United States and elsewhere. Many analysts hold, however, that adultery does not solve the problems of the adulterer (whatever they might be); to solve those problems likely would involve hours of counseling and a look at the previous life of the perpetrator. Adultery is a moral and medical problem of the first magnitude that most people believe society should examine more closely.

James Smallwood

FURTHER READING

Boylan, Brian Richard. *Infidelity.* Englewood Cliffs, N.J.: Prentice-Hall, 1971.

Brown, Emily M. *Patterns of Infidelity and Their Treatment.* 2d ed. Philadelphia: Brunner-Routledge, 2001.

Caprio, Frank S. *Marital Infidelity.* New York: Citadel Press, 1953.

Edwards, John N. *Sex and Society.* Chicago: Markham, 1972.

Gross, Leonard. *Sexual Issues in Marriage: A Contemporary Perspective.* New York: Spectrum, 1975.

Levitt, Shelley. "Why Men Cheat." *New Woman* 20 (October, 1990): 74.

Mason, Georgia. "Female Infidelity: May the Best Sperm Win." *New Scientist* 129 (January 19, 1991): 29.

Pittman, Frank S. *Private Lies: Infidelity and the Betrayal of Intimacy.* New York: Norton, 1990.

SEE ALSO: Clinton, Bill; Divorce; Loyalty; Marriage; Premarital sex; Promiscuity; Prostitution; Sexual abuse and harassment; Sexual revolution; Sexuality and sexual ethics; Sexually transmitted diseases.

Adversary system

DEFINITION: System of law in which opposing parties appear before a neutral tribunal; the parties have equal rights to present evidence, examine witnesses, and compel the attendance of witnesses

TYPE OF ETHICS: Legal and judicial ethics

SIGNIFICANCE: The adversary system rests on the judgment that a neutral tribunal is more likely to be fair in both criminal and civil cases than a panel of judges or other government officials would be; this is a much debated proposition, since administrative law systems exist nearly everywhere in the world other than the English-speaking countries.

In the adversary system of justice, a neutral, independent judge presides over a criminal trial. The judge is said to be independent because his or her tenure does not depend on executive or legislative officials. Federal judges in the United States are appointed for life; state judges are either elected or appointed for life or for other long terms. In trials of serious crimes, moreover, defendants have the right to have the facts determined by an impartial jury of laypeople. Both the prosecution and the defense have the right to present evidence, cross-examine witnesses brought by the other side, and argue their side of the case to the fact finders. Defendants need not testify in such trials if they do not wish to. In the United States and England, this form of trial is believed to be the most just.

Robert Jacobs

SEE ALSO: Arbitration; Attorney-client privilege; Divorce; Due process; Jurisprudence; Jury system; Law; Lawyer for the situation; Perjury.

Advertising

DEFINITION: Public promotion of goods or services designed to increase their sales, directly or indirectly

TYPE OF ETHICS: Media ethics

SIGNIFICANCE: Advertisers have a financial stake in crafting their messages in ways that persuade consumers to buy their products. At the same time, they also have a responsibility to craft their messages in ways that do not take unfair advantage of prospective consumers or competitors, or negatively influence vulnerable populations, such as children.

The ethics of advertising are professional ethics, not theoretical ethics. They operate to serve various loyalties, to clients, advertising agencies, consumers, and society in general. Often, the identified constituents have different—and conflicting—needs that must be balanced. Moreover, advertising is ubiquitous, pervasive, and influential, so its potential effects should be considered when determining what level of corresponding responsibility should accompany it.

ADVERTISING AS COMMUNICATION

Advertising is one of the oldest forms of mass communication. Since the days of the European town crier, advertising has carried messages of people who things to sell to people who might want to buy those things. The modern American advertising industry is a multibillion-dollar business, and advertising messages are inescapable. In addition to advertising's role in providing information to potential consumers, it may be argued that advertising can have a profound influence on societal values and norms.

Advertising influences the target audience's worldview. Consumers who routinely see stereotypical images and unrealistic depictions of physiques and relationships in radio and television commercials, magazine ads, and other forms of advertising may blur the lines between reality and fantasy. Advertising can promote materialism by keeping images of bigger, better, new, advanced, and the latest "must haves" in front of consumers. Advertising can also influence the self-images of people who receive its messages. Advertisements usually depict beautiful, young people enjoying life with the help of such products as the right toothpastes, the right shampoos, the right clothes, and the right cars, and against the glamour of the people using those products in advertisements, the average person rarely measures up.

ADVERTISING AS BUSINESS

Advertising supports the free market. Businesses attempt to increase their profits by increasing sales, and advertising can place sales messages in front of the audiences who are most likely to respond. Increased sales of products can lead to lower prices, and that in turn can aid consumers. It is thus clear that both marketers and consumers both can benefit from advertising.

According to social contract theory, businesses exist not only for their own profit but also for the benefit of their consumers, and they are thus accountable to their consumers. In addition, much advertising is the product of advertising agencies, and advertising agencies expect practitioners to be loyal to the agencies, which are also businesses that operate for profit in their own right.

PROFESSIONAL CODES OF ETHICS

The advertising industry has several professional organizations that publish codes of ethics as industry guidelines. These organizations include the American Association of Advertising Agencies, the American Advertising Federation, the Promotional Products Association International, and the Outdoor Advertising Association of America. Professional journalism organizations also publish guidelines on advertising as well. Guidelines may be stated as "action-guides," moral statements that are prescriptive, are normative, and direct people toward particular actions while keeping them from other actions.

The American Association of Advertising Agencies developed a creative code to support healthy competition. Specifically, the code stipulates that association members should not knowingly create false, misleading, or exaggerated claims; dishonest testimonials; misleading price claims; unsupported claims; or content offensive to decency or members of minority groups. The code also stipulates that comparative advertising be truthful, substantiated, and tasteful. Ads that compare an advertiser's products and services with those of the competition may be helpful to consumers but must be handled fairly. Dishonest testimonials are from people who do not actually use the products that they tout or who have hidden conflicts of interest.

The American Advertising Federation created "The Advertising Principles of American Business," a document that cautions members in eight areas. It stipulates that advertisers should be truthful, be prepared to substantiate claims, avoid untruthful comparisons, refrain from bait-and-switch advertising, offer specific information about guarantees and warranties, avoid false or misleading price claims, limit testimonials to real and competent witnesses, and avoid content that is offensive or indecent. Substantiation is a legal consideration as well, and advertisers are expected to have prior proof before making claims in advertising.

The Promotional Products Association International, a specialty advertising trade group, focuses its guidelines on customer service. It asks its members to offer quality products and services and to work toward complete customer satisfaction. The Outdoor Advertising Association of America is an organization of owners and operators of standardized outdoor advertising displays. Its code focuses on the responsibility of advertisers to ensure that outdoor displays do not detract from their surroundings. It specifically stipulates that members refrain from placing advertising displays in areas of natural scenic beauty, parks, or historical monuments and requires that members follow regulations and zoning laws. Members may erect advertising displays only on properties that they lease or own, and the displays must be truthful, attractive, and consistent with high moral standards.

Sweepstakes competitions are often attention-getting promotions used by advertisers, and the Magazine Publishers of America even has a code for ethical sweepstakes promotions. Critics have charged that the advertising industry has marketed sweepstakes in ways that are confusing to consumers. The guidelines outline specific components of contest solicitations and state that each component should be easy to read and understand, that the individual's chances of winning should not be overstated, and that recipients of the promotions should not be duped into ordering or extending their magazine subscriptions by being

led to believe that doing so will enhance their changes of winning the competitions.

TWENTY-FIRST CENTURY ISSUES

The codes of ethics outline valuable lists of do's and don'ts for advertising professionals. However, as society has evolved, additional ethical issues have emerged. For example, only during the late twentieth century did the advertising industry begin to make a large-scale effort to depict members of racial minorities in advertisements targeting the general population. Minorities had long been token representatives

Long before he entered politics, future president Ronald Reagan was one of many film stars who used his celebrity to help make smoking appear glamorous. Another Chesterfield advertisement of the period showed Reagan wrapping cartons of cigarettes as Christmas gifts to all his friends. (AP/Wide World Photos)

those that distort opponents' records. Subliminal messages have also been criticized, although it is unclear whether or not subliminal messages have any impact on the audience. During the 2000 election, the George W. Bush presidential campaign pulled a Republican National Committee ad that criticized opponent Al Gore's plan on prescription drugs and used subliminal messages to tell television viewers that the opponents were the "bureaucRATS."

Another controversial issue is the manner in which advertisers target vulnerable populations, particularly children. Advertisers have been criticized for targeting children through ads promoting movies they are too young to view and through ads promoting cigarettes to children too young to buy tobacco products legally. RJ Reynolds's Joe Camel campaign ended because of the cartoon character's popularity with the younger set. Young children spend a lot of time watching television and, in some cases, listening to the radio. Many advertisers are cognizant of their younger audience members and refrain from exposing them to vulgar, age-inappropriate content.

Some debate has centered on advertising to older persons and members of minority groups. Direct mail, in particular, has been used to get the attention of older people who are in the habit of opening official-looking envelopes and who may confuse advertising materials with official business documents. On the other hand, because older persons are not children, many people would argue that they should not need to be protected from advertisers.

Another controversial type of advertising is "advertorials"—advertisements packaged to look like news. Advertorials blur the lines between advertising and news and can confuse people who are exposed to a diverse variety of nontraditional sources of news. For example, audiences who are accustomed to network news, cable news channels, entertainment news, and other sources may not readily distinguish advertorial programming from genuine news programs because the presentations are similar. To avoid confusion, most advertorials, or "infomercials," include disclaimers. In addition, many news departments have guidelines designed to protect the editorial process from the influence of the advertising department.

Ethics Challenges for Advertisers

The Better Business Bureau is a nationwide network of businesses that was founded in 1912 for the purpose of improving ethical relationships businesses and the public. To that end, it has posed these questions to advertisers:

- Does your advertising make your customers satisfied they do business with you?

- Are you avoiding impossible promises and guarantees?

- Is your advertised merchandise readily available?

- Do you mean to sell what you advertise?

- Do your ads avoid misleading inferences?

- Do your advertised terms agree with the facts?

- Is your advertising easy to understand without asterisks and fine print?

- Do you believe your own comparatives?

- Would you be attracted by what your ad says?

Source: Better Business Bureau (http://www.bbb.org/bizethics/tips.asp)

---

in popular media, but the failure to include them in general interest advertisements projected narrow views of American society.

Ads also long employed stereotypes to make points. For example, the Frito-Lay Corporation once used a character called the "Frito Bandito" to advertise its corn chips. The Frito Bandito provided an attention-getting and easily remembered product icon, but at the cost of reinforcing negative stereotypes of Mexican Americans as criminals. Advertisements that objectify women and men are common. For example, ads may depict human bodies without heads or show a satiny-smooth human shoulder and arm that are not connected to the rest of a body. Critics charge that such ads are destructive in that they promote the practice of viewing individuals as body parts rather than as whole people.

Political advertising has its own issues. Political advertising plays an important role in society and can directly influence political outcomes. Political ads that commonly receive criticism are those that rely only on emotional appeals rather than providing information that can be evaluated by the receiver and

Unusual situations may develop when advertisers try to get audience attention with shock tactics. People for the Ethical Treatment of Animals (PETA) once produced an advertising campaign called "The Holocaust on Your Plate," which showed pictures of naked concentration camp inmates alongside pictures of abused animals. Its caption read, "To animals, all people are Nazis." The ad succeeded in attracting attention but offended many people, especially Jews, who thought that it trivialized the Holocaust. PETA supporters maintained that people are animals, too, and that animals should get similar protection.

The terrorist attacks of September 11, 2001, negatively affected many businesses in America. After the attacks, many corporations ran ads to offer condolences for the victims of the attacks and to express hope for the future of the country. However, some of these advertisements also tied into commercial pitches that critics saw as attempts to capitalize on tragedy. For example, General Motors ran a "Keep America Rolling" campaign that offered consumers zero percent financing on new vehicles. The ad attempted to link buying a new American car with being patriotic, but the link was weak.

Pharmaceutical companies have long advertised their products to doctors and other medical professionals. During the mid-1990's, the industry began greatly increasing direct advertising appeals to consumers. This trend spurred a debate in the medical community, because some say that direct-to-consumer advertising puts incomplete information in the hands of people with medical problems who may not be trained to interpret it. Other observers, however, have said that it is valuable for patients to know their medical options and to be able to ask their doctors about advertised medications that may help them.

Finally, Internet advertising has opened up a new way for advertisers to reach audiences, and a new set of issues has arisen. Unsolicited e-mail, or spam, clogs the in-boxes of millions of Internet users daily, and companies are devising ways to help users filter out unwanted messages. Opt-in options give users the opportunity to ask to be added to e-mail mailing list. Opt-out options give the user the opportunity to ask to be deleted or unsubscribed from e-mail lists, but they assume tacit approval unless the messages are received. Opt-out options require users to take steps to avoid receiving unsolicited e-mail.

LEGAL CONSIDERATIONS

The Federal Trade Commission regulates the American advertising industry and has the power to constrain and punish advertisers who create ads that are deceptive, fraudulent, or misleading. In addition to ethical considerations, advertisers must consider legal ramifications of their advertising. Many consumers are suspicious of advertisers who have financial stakes in their buying decisions; however, ethical advertising can serve needed functions for businesses and consumers alike.

Alisa White

FURTHER READING

Bivens, T., ed. *Mixed Media: Moral Distinctions in Journalism, Advertising, and Public Relations.* Mahwah, N.J.: Lawrence Erlbaum, 2004. Examines ethical issues in the mass media in view of social responsibility, truth, and harm.

Day, L. A. *Ethics in Media Communications.* Belmont, Calif.: Wadsworth, 2000. Provides an ethical decision-making model to help readers decide how to resolve moral dilemmas presented in hypothetical cases and in real life. Also covers ethical theories and includes the ethics codes of the American Advertising Federation and other professional organizations.

Donaldson, Thomas. *Corporations and Morality.* Englewood Cliffs, N.J.: Prentice-Hall, 1982. Sets forth a social contract theory for corporations based on loyalties to consumers and society as a whole.

Fink, Conrad C. *Media Ethics: In the Newsroom and Beyond.* New York: McGraw-Hill, 1988. Case studies and examples of moral dilemmas that arise in journalism and other media professions. Offers a framework whereby readers can make moral decisions.

Jamieson, K. H., and K. K. Campbell. *The Interplay of Influence: News, Advertising, Politics and the Mass Media.* 5th ed. Belmont, Calif.: Wadsworth, 2000. Examines the relationship among media outlets and the influence the messages they carry have on the public.

Leslie, L. *Mass Communication Ethics: Decision Making in Postmodern Culture.* Boston: Houghton Mifflin, 2000. Establishes an ethical framework in theory and philosophy, and discusses cases in cultural context.

Rotzell, K. B. "Persuasion in Advertising." In *Media Ethics: Cases and Moral Reasoning*, edited by C. Christians et al. 6th ed. New York: Longman, 2001. Considers moral dilemmas that confront media practitioners through the framework of the Potter Box, a four-step ethical decision-making model that asks subjects to define dilemmas and identify values, principles, and loyalties before making decisions.

SEE ALSO: Applied ethics; Business ethics; Children's television; Choice; Consumerism; Electronic mail; Infomercials; Journalistic ethics; Marketing; Sales ethics; Tobacco industry.

Advice columnists

DEFINITION: Journalists who offer advice on wide-ranging topics in columns that are typically syndicated in many newspapers and magazines
DATE: The first advice column appeared in 1901
TYPE OF ETHICS: Media ethics
SIGNIFICANCE: Influential columnists can profoundly affect the attitudes and behavior of their readers, even though the columnists may lack expertise in their subjects or exhibit bias.

In 1901, the *New York Journal* began publishing the first nationally recognized advice column, "Dorothy Dix Talks." For fifty years, Dix dispensed advice to lovelorn, confused, and worried readers. For the most part, she avoided difficult and taboo subjects. However, by the 1950's, when Ann Landers and her twin sister, Abigail Van Buren, began their long careers as advice columnists, America had changed. Landers and Van Buren were able to take on more sensitive issues than Dix ever discussed, such as homosexuality, abortion, abusive parenting, and premarital sex. The two women enjoyed immense success, but not without criticism. While nei-

ther Landers nor Van Buren had any formal training in psychology or counseling, their status as widely syndicated and respected columnists gave them the appearance of authority. Their popularity alarmed many mental health professionals, who often disagreed with the advice the columnists provided. For example, Landers initially regarded homosexuality as an illness, even though the American Psychiatric Association had concluded otherwise. Landers later softened her stance on that subject, but only after homosexuality began to gain wider acceptance in America.

Twenty-first century advice columns are more popular than ever; they also tend to be more specialized. Readers want specific advice from experts in health, the law, technology, investing, and other subjects. Even personal advice columns—the successors of Dix, Landers, and Van Buren—have become more narrowly focused, targeting limited demographic groups. This has raised new issues. Columnists, unlike other journalists, deal in opinions as well as facts. However, while facts may be checked, opinions are easily subjected to manipulation. With the proliferation of specialized and technical columns, it has become more difficult for newspaper and maga-

Advice columnists Ann Landers (left) and her twin sister, Pauline, better known Abigail Van Buren of "Dear Abby" fame, at their fiftieth high school reunion in 1986. (AP/Wide World Photos)

zine editors to "backstop" their columnists, challenging assertions and rooting out bias.

Columnists are particularly prone to conflicts of interest. Lawyers writing columns on law may suggest that home buyers should hire lawyers to review their sales documents, knowing full well that this may bring new business to their own law firms. However, this relatively benign form of conflict of interest pales in comparison to scandals in the securities industry, where investment columnists have touted specific stocks that they themselves, or their employers, own and from which they hope to profit from future eventual sales.

Technology is providing a sea change for advice columnists. With the Internet, anyone can claim to be an expert and give advice. In consequence, ethical constraints on advice columnists will be further eroded.

Robert L. Palmer

FURTHER READING

Fink, Conrad C. *Media Ethics*. Boston: Allyn and Bacon, 1995.

Grossvogel, David I. *Dear Ann Landers: Our Intimate and Changing Dialogue with America's Best-Loved Confidante*. Chicago: Contemporary Books, 1987.

Paul, Pamela. "Dear Reader, Get a Life." *Psychology Today* 36, no. 4 (2003): 56-71.

Winans, Foster R. *Trading Secrets: An Insider's Account of the Scandal at the "Wall Street Journal."* New York: St. Martin's Press, 1986.

Zaslow, Jeffrey. *Tell Me About It: A Personal Look at the Advice Business*. New York: William Morrow, 1990.

SEE ALSO: Cohen, Randy; Confidentiality; Ethical Principles of Psychologists; Homosexuality; Insider trading; Journalistic ethics; Tabloid journalism.

Affirmative action

DEFINITION: Aspect of government programs designed to increase the participation of statistically underrepresented groups in education, employment, and public works

DATE: Concept developed during the mid-1960's

TYPE OF ETHICS: Civil rights

SIGNIFICANCE: Affirmative action programs have promoted cultural diversity and reduced invidious discrimination against women and members of particular racial minorities; however, other persons frequently feel threatened by the programs.

The federal Civil Rights Act of 1964 and similar laws of the states prohibit employers and educational institutions from discriminating against individuals on the basis of race, national origin, or sex. Initially, the term "affirmative action" referred simply to employment policies designed to enforce these laws and ensure equal opportunities for members of groups that had historically encountered prejudicial attitudes and discriminatory practices. However, as these groups, especially African Americans, continued to experience subtle forms of discrimination, regulatory agencies and courts began to consult statistical data when assessing compliance with the laws.

By the early 1970's, the term "affirmative action" was being applied to aggressive programs of recruitment that could be evaluated on the basis of quantitative results. Most programs included racial and gender preferences, and some utilized "quotas" or "goals and timetables." Arguing that the programs contradicted the principle of equal opportunity, white men often claimed to be victims of "reverse discrimination."

MORAL ARGUMENTS

Almost all modern ethicists endorse the ultimate goal of an equality of opportunity for every individual, without regard to characteristics such as sex, ethnicity, or religion, except in special situations in which such characteristics are relevant. Because of the pernicious consequences of past discrimination, however, defenders of affirmative action policies argue that some preferences will be necessary for a limited period of time in order to level the playing field. In contrast, opponents insist that discriminatory practices are inherently unjust, even when used as a means toward a just goal.

Proponents tend to believe that racism and sexism are profoundly entrenched in American beliefs, practices, and attitudes. Believing that white males are beneficiaries of unacknowledged privileges, moreover, they typically assume that women and minorities, except for invidious discrimination, would occupy prestigious positions in rough proportion to their numbers. Some radical proponents justify affirmative action as atonement for past discrimination and argue that justice demands "equality of results" rather than "equality of opportunity."

Opponents, in contrast, usually argue that the relative successes of various groups are more influenced by culture than by invidious discrimination. As an example, they point to the conspicuous achievements of Jewish Americans and Asian Americans in the liberal professions, in spite of continuing discrimination. Believing that some groups will always excel in particular endeavors, the opponents conclude that preferential treatment, once begun, will continue indefinitely. From their perspective, it is wrong to penalize an individual person because of membership in a group judged to be excessively successful.

Many libertarians view affirmative action as a pernicious example of "social engineering" that denigrates individual freedom, and they insist that the value of liberty is more basic than equality. Persons committed to the idea of meritocracy usually concede that government has a legitimate interest in promoting equal opportunity, but they strongly oppose the notion that government should decide on the statistical representation of groups in various professions. A basketball team, for instance, is more likely to win if it recruits its players strictly on the basis of their ability to play basketball.

Moral debates about affirmative action frequently deal with questions about which persons should be beneficiaries. One problem is that racial classifications are socially defined and constantly changing. Another problem is that affirmative action tends to limit the opportunities of white males raised in poverty, while preferences sometimes go to women and minorities from relatively higher socioeconomic backgrounds. Proponents insist that race and socioeconomic class are closely correlated and that, in any case, discrimination has significantly limited the opportunities of women and minorities of all classes. One suggested compromise is to base affirmative action programs primarily on socioeconomic status rather than race or sex.

LEGAL CONTROVERSIES

The literal words of the "equal protection" requirement of the U.S. Constitution and almost all civil rights laws appear to require race neutrality and to extend equal rights to all citizens, including white men—who are generally regarded as the least disadvantaged people in the society. Proponents of affirmative action, however, argue that these legal documents must be interpreted in accordance with their primary objective, which is to achieve equality for African Americans and other victims of longstanding discrimination. Proponents emphasize that affirmative action programs, in contrast to earlier Jim Crow discrimination, do not totally exclude any persons or deny their full human dignity.

During the late 1970's, the U.S. Supreme Court approved several aggressive programs of affirmation action. In *Regents of the University of California v. Bakke* (1978), the Court examined a competitive medical school's policy of reserving a fixed percentage of admissions to members of disadvantaged minorities, even if those applicants' qualifications were less impressive than those of some white applicants who are denied admission. Although the Court disallowed the use of specific quotas, it endorsed admissions policies that gave some consideration to race in an attempt to promote a diverse enrollment. In *United Steelworkers v. Weber* (1979), the Court allowed a private employer to utilize a racial quota rather than seniority in order to achieve a minimum number of skilled African American workers.

By the 1990's, there was a strong public backlash against affirmative action programs. In 1996, California voters approved Proposition 209, which prohibits state institutions, including universities, from giving any preferences based on race, ethnicity, or sex. Likewise, the U.S. Supreme Court held that a number of affirmative action programs were discriminatory. In *Adarand Constructors v. Peña* (1995), the Court ruled that all race preferences were inherently suspect and must be narrowly designed to further compelling governmental objectives. For several years it appeared that the Court might strike down all race-based preferences. In *Grutter v. Bollinger* (2003), however, it allowed educational institutions to take race into account as a "plus" factor in order to obtain a "critical mass" of minorities. However, it also prohibited rigid quotas, required individualized evaluation of each applicant, and called for the end of all preferences in twenty-five years.

Thomas Tandy Lewis

FURTHER READING

Beckwith, Francis, and Todd Jones, ed. *Affirmative Action: Social Justice or Reverse Discrimination?* New York: Prometheus Books, 1997.

Cahn, Stephen, ed. *The Affirmative Action Debate.* New York: Routledge, 2002.

Eastland, Terry. *Ending Affirmative Action: The Case for Colorblind Justice.* New York: Basic Books, 1997.

Kranz, Rachel. *Affirmative Action.* New York: Facts On File, 2002.

Leiter, Samuel, and William Leiter. *Affirmative Action in Anti-Discrimination Law and Policy: An Overview and Synthesis.* Albany: State University of New York Press, 2002.

Rosenfeld, Michel. *Affirmative Action and Justice: A Philosophical and Constitutional Inquiry.* New Haven, Conn.: Yale University Press, 1993.

Skrenty, John. *The Ironies of Affirmative Action: Politics, Culture and Justice in America.* Chicago: University of Chicago Press, 1996.

SEE ALSO: Americans with Disabilities Act; Disability rights; Discrimination; Inequality; Integration; Political correctness; Reverse racism; Supreme Court, U.S.; Title IX.

African ethics

DEFINITION: Traditional, indigenous African views of the natural and supernatural worlds and their effect on morality and practices

TYPE OF ETHICS: Beliefs and practices; religious ethics

SIGNIFICANCE: The traditional African approach to ethics has grown out of religious, philosophical, and cultural beliefs shared by a significant percentage of the world's population.

Although Africa is made up of many countries and societies, a common thread runs through most of its peoples' indigenous religious and philosophical concepts. It is in putting these concepts into practice that each society establishes its distinguishing mark.

Africa is the continent on which humanity originated, and religious and philosophical ethics in Africa date back to as early as 4000 B.C.E., when the priests and inhabitants of the Nile Valley reasoned that the best way to inculcate religion and morality in the minds of the people was through drama. The priests wrote hieroglyphic texts that established the existence of gods and goddesses and pondered the moral question of human mortality by viewing death as the ascent of the soul of the dead to immortality, and by posing the possibility of the physical resurrection of the dead. That belief that the dead live has continued through the ages in various African traditional and cultural practices, including deification, reincarnation, divination, prayers, ancestral masquerades, and the cult of the living dead. Although most African civilizations did not develop writing until after they interacted with Muslim and Christian travelers, traders, and missionaries, religious and ethical ideas were passed down orally and through practice and observance from one generation to another by parents, guardians, elders, age-groups, and socioreligious institutions.

CHAIN OF EXISTENCE

In 1977, the second World Black and African Festival of Arts and Culture was held in Lagos, Nigeria. As part of that festival, a colloquium on "Black Civilization and Religion" was held. Its report was published among the proceedings of the *Colloquium on Black Civilization and Education* (1977). Among other things, the report determined that belief in a universe where everything is living and strong, in the existence of two worlds of which one is visible and the other invisible, and in the interdependence of being and a fundamentally vital unity in spite of the existence of hierarchy are essential elements of doctrine in African traditional religion. It also pointed out that the sacred, invisible world is made up of a Supreme Being, spirits, ancestors, and cosmic forces. This makes possible the creation of a chain of being in the level-belief system that stretches hierarchically from the highest—that of the Supreme Being (God)—through the supernatural world of spirits (divinities, spirits per se), ancestors, and cosmic or earth forces to the mundane world of humanity and animate and inanimate beings.

The Supreme Being, who is omniscient, omnipotent, omnipresent, and immortal, is the ultimate creator of humanity and of everything in existence. He created male and female, and the colors of people's skins are explained by the colors of clay that

31

Africa

the Supreme Being used in fashioning them. To ask about the Supreme Being's origin is deemed foolish and disrespectful, and it is fundamentally assumed, not argued, that he created the universe. Because the universe is the Supreme Being's by virtue of his creating it, it is a religious universe, and no strict separation is made between sacred and secular affairs. The seal of the Supreme Being is found in the most secular and the most sacred, as is seen, for example, in the person of the monarch, who is both secular (political figure) and sacred (divine deputy with religious rights).

Next to the Supreme Being are the spirits, who are referred to as divinities, deities, or simply gods. They are the Supreme Being's associates and ministers. Some of them are dead national heros or heroines and legendary figures who have been defined and are associated with aspects of nature and of cultural life. For example, Sango (or Shango) of the Yoruba people of Nigeria is the god of thunder and lightning, who represents the Supreme Being's wrath, while the Zulu of Southern Africa have a goddess described as the queen of Heaven, from whom emanates the beauty of the rainbow. The queen of Heaven taught women the culinary arts, feminine responsibility, and gracefulness.

The members of another category of spirits, next in hierarchy to the divinities, are generally called spirits. They are superhuman beings that were created to assist the deities. Some of them are human ancestors who have lost touch with their earthly lineage over the ages and have risen to the spirit status, which is higher than that of the ancestors. There are myriad spirits, some of whom inhabit trees, animals, rivers, and mountains and are generally referred to as nature spirits. Spirits can possess human beings and do possess mediums when solicited. Although invisible, they can appear to humans, especially priests, diviners, and shamans,

Ancestral spirits (simply called ancestors or the living dead) are deceased family elders who are still fondly remembered by name and deed and are honored with libations and prayers by the living. From their spiritual abode, they participate in the affairs of their descendants. They are revered as part of the family; they protect it and are called upon as guardians of morality and as witnesses at important events such as marriages and the resolutions of family feuds. They are humanity's closest links to the supernatural world, and they demonstrate in the African tradition that there is life after death.

Usually, human beings are next in the hierarchical structure, followed by animals, plants, earth, and water. There is some fluidity here, because when animate and inanimate objects are occupied by spirits or "cosmic powers," they assume a higher position than that occupied by humanity. In ordinary life, however, human beings rank higher. A child that is being formed in the womb is considered a human being; Banyarwanda women of Rwanda believe that the Supreme Being "shapes children" in the mother's womb. The chain of being is rounded out by rain, the sun, the moon, stars, and other natural objects and phenomena.

Each element of the chain of being is very important to the whole, because it helps to sustain harmony. This is underscored by the fact that what brings up the rear in the chain is linked to the Supreme Being directly. The Akan people of Ghana, the Galla of Ethiopia, the Nandi of Kenya, and the Ovambo of Namibia are among the peoples who see the sun, moon, and stars as the eyes of the Supreme Being, while the Shona of Zimbabwe view the cotton softness of the cloud as his bed.

Irreligious, immoral, and antisocial activities such as murder, ritual impurity, incestuous relationships, adultery, wanton destruction of nature, irresponsible acts, and disrespect to older people could create disharmony in the chain of existence. This could cause epidemics, droughts, deaths, and natural disasters if not detected and corrected. Priests and priestesses, who may combine their vocation with rainmaking, divining, mediumship, and medicine, often function to restore harmony.

THE ORDERLY UNIVERSE

John S. Mbiti has shown that Africans view the universe as one of harmony, order, and logic and that this orderliness comes from and is maintained by the Supreme Being. Natural laws govern everything. Among human beings there are moral and religious orders. It is believed that the Supreme Being instituted the moral order. The Zulu, Nuer, Ila, Lugbara, Nuba, Etsako, and Edo peoples believe that the Supreme Being established their customs, laws, and regulations so that people could live in harmony with one another and know what is right and wrong as they live a dutiful and responsible life.

Because the universe is created by the Supreme Being, it is necessarily imbued with a religious order. It is directly or indirectly (through social institutions, sanctions, and natural law) controlled by him. Through prayers, ceremonies, rituals, blessings, sacred places, objects, and personages, humanity actively engages the religious order of the universe.

Africans also believe that there is a mystical order or power that is closely linked to the religious order of the universe because it comes from the Supreme Being; it can be tapped into by spirits and by some human beings. The order shows itself in the ability of some Africans to predict events accurately, to perform miracles and wonders, to be telepathic, and to ward off evil. It can also be negatively used to bring misfortune and harm to people and property. Africans believe in the reality of witches and sorcerers, and especially in their power to bring illness, infertility, suffering, failure, death, and general calamity. Their power comes from tapping into the mystical force of the universe and directing that energy toward evil deeds.

Although humanity is at the center of the African concept of the universe, human beings are not seen as the masters of nature. They are simply nature's friends and the recipients of its riches, which they must use judiciously. Humans are required to live harmoniously with the universe by obeying its natural, moral, and mystical laws. Humankind suffers when this harmony is upset.

CORPORATE VALUES

African religious and ethical behavior seems to be guided by the following philosophy: "I am because we are, and since we are, therefore I am." The individual does not exist except in a corporate manner. Each person exists because of other people, including that person's family and people of past and contemporary generations. Being a part of the whole, the individual is a product of the community and necessarily depends on it. In no better way is this corporate nature of the African society depicted than in rites of passage that are communally observed as one goes through birth, initiation (maturity), marriage, old age, and death. These changes that an individual goes through are regarded as challenging, upsetting, and at times dangerous to social and individual life. African rites of passage help to "cushion the disturbance," to ease the pains and difficulties that occur in the society's or the individual's transition from one status to another. Initiation rites provide an excellent example.

Among the Akamba people of Kenya, the first stage of initiation rites involves circumcision for boys and clitoridectomy for girls: The foreskin of the penis and a tiny portion of the clitoris are excised. As a group act, the rites are performed the same day in the same place. The activity symbolizes separation from childhood, just as the ritual cutting and disposal of the umbilical cord at birth symbolize mother-baby separation and the acknowledgment that the child belongs to the corporate society represented then by the family, and not only to the mother's family. Anyone who does not go through this first stage of initiation rites, even after attaining maturity, age, and position, is communally despised and regarded as a baby in most, if not all, African societies.

It is the belief among the Akamba that ritually cutting the skin from one's sexual organ moves the individual from the state of sexual dormancy and ignorance to one of action and knowledge, and therefore to the crucial stage of sexual reproduction, which keeps the lineage and society going. The blood shed on Earth during the excision mystically forms a bond of unity between the initiates and the ancestors. The

accompanying pains prepare the initiates for the pain, suffering, and difficulty they will inevitably encounter. They are encouraged to endure such discomforts and to overcome them instead of despairing. The reason that the initiation is a group act is to encourage the participants to seek help and solace from others when they encounter difficult times.

Human beings can bear much suffering when they realize there are other people who will help them. The initiates are then given presents—an introduction to keeping and owning property. There is general merriment and dancing to emphasize communal solidarity. The initiates, for the first time in their lives, are officially allowed to join in public dances.

The second stage of initiation, which follows years later, is meant to help the initiates as they approach full maturity. The ceremony lasts about a week, during which time the initiates are sequestered in huts built outside the village and away from public interaction. Accompanied by watchful older people, the youths are taught all they need to know concerning womanhood and manhood. The process is referred to as "brooding over the initiates." They learn educational songs, are tested for bravery, and are taught the roles they are expected to play as adults and as future married people and parents. They are taught dances that symbolically imitate the performance of sexual acts. They also learn moral and corporate responsibilities, and are reminded of their religious obligations. They have full access to the wisdom of the elders and the secrets of their society. When they emerge from their seclusion on the last day, they are recognized in the society as people who may legally and morally establish families, and who are capable of protecting themselves, their dependents, and their society. A new generation capable of carrying on the life of the community thus comes into being, and the community is assured of immortality.

The maturity of those who emerge from the Akamba initiation rites helps to prevent the unhappy syndrome of "babies producing babies." When they eventually marry, they are responsibly fulfilling an African corporate requirement that ties marriage to procreation. To the African, marriage without procreation is incomplete. Humanity, through marriage and procreation, tries to recapture the lost gift of immortality, since husband and wife reproduce themselves in their children and by so doing perpetuate not only their family lineage but also the chain of humanity. In *African Religions and Philosophy* (1990), Mbiti hits the mark when he points out that marriage is viewed in the African society as a "rhythm of life" that involves everyone. Anyone ignoring participation in it is a "curse to the community" and a rebellious lawbreaker. It is an immoral act to reject the society, and society is bound in turn to reject the person who does so.

The importance of marriage is underscored by the fact that it involves the entire family, all of whose members must give support and approval. Female virginity at the time of marriage is highly prized and rewarded. Monogamy and polygamy—especially polygyny—are legitimate; a widow may be remarried to a male adult member of the family of the deceased husband, who then assumes full responsibility for her and the children she brings along. Bride price and dowry are important parts of the custom: They symbolize the value and importance placed on the women as a person and as a wife, and they are a constant reminder that the bride and the groom are together under some mutual agreement between their families. They cannot simply terminate their marriage on their own, because people other than themselves are involved.

TRADITIONAL ENFORCEMENT OF MORALITY

In African societies in which traditions and customs have not been replaced by Christian and Islamic customs, people owe allegiance to a common founding ancestor and are bound by common hopes and fears and by destiny. The social structure helps in the formulation and enforcement of moral ideals and ethical standards. Factors that determine morality in such a society include religious beliefs; practices and taboos; the desire for communal solidarity; the influence of proverbs, folk stories, and wise sayings; and the experiences, common sense, and conscience of the individual and of the group. Although each person regards himself or herself in some form of relationship to the other, human passions and interests do come into conflict, leading some members of the society to flout established norms. The enforcement of morality then becomes important. The examples listed have come from the religious and social methods used by the Ga and Adangme of Ghana, though similar methods are found among the Etsako, Ishan, Edo, and Yoruba peoples of Nigeria.

J. N. Kudadjie of the University of Ghana, Legon,

points out that people's beliefs about the Supreme Being, the divinities, the spirits, and the ancestors are used to enforce morality. "The promise and expectation, coupled with actual experience, of the blessing and protection of the Supreme God and the other spirit-powers for those who kept the moral code, on the one hand, and the fear and threat, coupled with actual experience, of punishment and desertion by the spirit-powers kept people doing what was right and avoiding what was wrong." The practice of the religious and magical "cursing" of an offender in which supernatural agencies bring harm, misfortune, or even strange death to the culprit or his or her family keeps people on the right path.

Even marital infidelity is checked through the curse, whose punishments for adulterers include barrenness and impotence, the inability to leave the scene of adultery or to disengage the sexual organs, insanity, incurable physical illness, and sudden death. In entrances to farms and homes, magical objects are buried, hung, or displayed to warn people that they will not go undetected and unpunished for any crime they may commit when the owner of the property is not present: The gods, spirits, ancestors, and mystical forces are ever-present law-enforcement agents.

Positive social sanctions such as parental gifts to a good, reliable, and well-behaved child; admission of the young to the presence of elders where they are given secret knowledge of herbs, spiritual powers, and activities well beyond their age; and the award of honors, chieftaincy, titles, and property are used by the society to reward people who have distinguished themselves. These sanctions are meant to "encourage and give incentive to the good life."

There are also negative sanctions that are meant to discourage unethical behavior. A family may hold a special meeting to correct a notoriously wayward member. If the person persists in bad behavior, the family severs all ties with him or her, including such family occasions as marriage, birth, and death. A family may even disinherit a member who brings material and spiritual disgrace to it. Initiates are made to swear oaths regarding specific things they should or should not do; the ancestors are invoked as witnesses.

Other social sanctions include invoking a parental curse banning a disobedient and immoral child from attending the parent's funeral; ostracizing sorcerers, witches, hardened criminals, and morally perverse individuals from the society or excluding them from social intercourse; publicly disgracing a person by having his or her bad deeds announced or sung at public festivals and social gatherings; and finally, in extreme cases, causing those considered destroyers of society to disappear. At least once a year, in some societies, a day is set aside in which the traditional ruler is publicly insulted for various acts of inefficiency; the idea is to make him correct his mistakes and be a better leader. Formerly, in some African societies, such as the Banyoro, Shona, Luvedu, Amhara, and Yoruba, a bad ruler was ritually killed, usually through poisoning. In traditional African societies, it is not so much the physical punishments that keep people observing the moral codes as it is the threat of disgrace to one's self, family, relatives, friends, future and present offspring, and ancestors.

CHANGING AFRICA

Colonialism, Christianity, and Islam have also had an impact on Africa, contributing to new forms of religious and philosophical ethics. In the cities where these religions are most successful, traditional African ethics have been undermined and are practiced secretly. One interesting phenomenon is the emergence of new Christian and Islamic religious movements founded by Africans that merge aspects of the imported religions with aspects of African belief and cultural systems to form new distinctly syncretist African religious and philosophical ethics. Among such movements are the Falasha (Beta Israel) movement of Ethiopia, the Mahdist movement of Sudan, the Mourides (Islamic Brotherhood) movement of Senegal, the Kimbanguist movement of the Congo (later Zaire), the Zulu Zionist movement of South Africa, the Aladura movement of Nigeria, and the Eden Revival movement of Ghana. Behind these movements is an undying respect and a yearning for the traditional African moral universe, and in them the old gods and spirits are revitalized, not displaced, by the new ones. It is a dynamic universe.

I. Peter Ukpokodu

FURTHER READING

Adegbola, E. A. Ade, ed. *Traditional Religion in West Africa.* Ibadan, Nigeria: Daystar Press, 1983. An illustrated collection of essays on religious personalities, rites of passage, festivals, morality, mythology, and the concepts of humanity and God. Some comparison with world religions.

Bujo, Bénézet. *Foundations of an African Ethic: Beyond the Universal Claims of Western Morality.* Translated by Brian McNeil. New York: Crossroad, 2001. Simultaneously uses traditional African ethics to critique Western morality and synthesizes a new, distinctively African theory of ethics.

Chidester, David. *Religions of South Africa.* London: Routledge, 1992. A comparative study of different religions in South Africa; particularly rich in its treatment of independent churches and their relationship to traditional religious practices.

Joint Symposium of Philosophers from Africa and from the Netherlands. *I, We, and Body.* Edited by Heinz Kimmerle. Amsterdam: Verlag B. R. Grunner, 1989. Various scholars of African philosophy, anthropology, and theology discuss the individual and the community in African thought, the perception of reality, and the notion of time, among other things. Examples are drawn from many African peoples: Dogon, Lingala, Akan, Turkana, Massai, Yoruba, Kikuyu, and Nuer.

Jules-Rosette, Bennetta, ed. *The New Religions of Africa.* Norwood, N.J.: Ablex, 1979. Various academic essays discuss the role of African religions in cultural transformation and the relationships between men and women in them; important in its treatment of newer religions that are usually left out of other works.

Kamalu, Chukwunyere. *Foundations of African Thought.* London: Karnak House, 1990. A well-documented, illustrated book that discusses numerous aspects of African thought from the earliest times. Origins; being; ethics; arts and sciences; and ancient Egyptian, Dogon, and Bambara cosmology are among the many topics treated.

Kasenene, Peter. *Religious Ethics in Africa.* Kampala, Uganda: Fountain, 1998. Comparative study of African and other world religions' responses to specific moral issues. Recommends that Africans embrace their traditional values, while still taking into account the values of other religions.

King, Noel Q. *African Cosmos.* Belmont, Calif.: Wadsworth, 1986. Presents some of "Africa's deepest wisdom" as an attempt to know the world better. The religious worlds of various African peoples—Dinka, Acholi, Nubia, Yoruba, Akan, and the Bantu-language groups—are presented along with Christianity and Islam.

Mbiti, John S. *African Religions and Philosophy.* 2d rev. ed. Portsmouth, N.H.: Heinemann, 1990. A comprehensive study of traditional religion in Africa and its supporting philosophy. African cosmology, rites of passage, witchcraft, ethics, sacred officials, and the presence of Judaism, Christianity, and Islam in Africa are among the topics examined. A valuable book that should be read by scholars and laypersons alike.

Parrinder, Edward Geoffrey. *African Traditional Religion.* 3d ed. London: Sheldon Press, 1974. A valuable, accessible book that shows, by describing and analyzing religious pantheons, social groups, and spiritual forces, that knowing about African religion is essential to understanding the motive forces of African life.

Wiredu, Kwasi. *Philosophy and an African Culture.* Cambridge, England: Cambridge University Press, 1980. Using Ghanaian traditional culture, Wiredu's philosophical analysis tries to distinguish those aspects of African traditional culture that are worth preserving from those that should be discarded; also examines African philosophy vis-à-vis Western thought.

SEE ALSO: Colonialism and imperialism; Mandela, Nelson; Multiculturalism; Pan-Africanism; Pantheism; Religion; Rwanda genocide; Taboos; Tutu, Desmond; *Wretched of the Earth, The.*

Ageism

DEFINITION: Prejudice or discrimination against a particular age group and the promotion of false stereotypes about the members of that group

DATE: Expression coined in 1969

TYPE OF ETHICS: Civil rights

SIGNIFICANCE: Ageism, or age discrimination, inhibits the fair and accurate determination of each person's true potential.

Although certain age groups have always been subjected to unfair treatment, the concept of ageism, or age discrimination, is a relatively recent one. Robert Butler, the first director of the National Institute on Aging, introduced the term "ageism" in 1969. Butler used this term to describe systematic prejudice or discrimination against older people. Butler believed that a pervasive youth culture had developed in the United States in which old people were frequently devalued and denigrated. Although the term "ageism" was still being used during the early twenty-first century, primarily to describe society's negative view of older people, most social scientists had come to believe that other age groups, such as young children, can also be subject to forms of ageism. Most modern social ethicists define ageism as prejudice or discrimination against any group of individuals on the basis of chronological age.

DISCRIMINATION AGAINST OLDER PEOPLE

Although any age group can be subject to unfair treatment, prejudice against older people appears to be the strongest form of ageism in the United States. Many researchers have discovered pervasive but erroneous beliefs that all old people are senile, cranky, physically unattractive, weak, and without sexual desire. Erdman Palmore, a sociologist and authority on aging, has suggested that many Americans have stereotyped views that see older people as useless individuals who place both emotional and financial burdens on the rest of society. Palmore believes that the numerous derogatory terms that are used to describe older people, such as " coot," "geezer," "old hag," "old buzzard," and "over the hill," merely reflect the negative views that many Americans have toward older people.

Such terms fly in the face of research conducted by gerontologists, who study aging and the needs of older people. In a review of research on the aged, psychologist David Myers concluded in 1992 that many older people are physically healthy, socially active, and mentally alert. Although most individuals experience some decline in mental and physical abilities with advancing age, the vast majority of older Americans remain capable of living happy and productive lives. Stereotypical beliefs about frail and lonely old people are often based on worst-case scenarios and should not be applied to the whole population of aged individuals.

PRACTICAL CONCERNS

In addition to developing a poor self-image because of the negative social stereotypes that abound in American society, many older people experience discrimination in practical matters as well. Perhaps the most blatant example of this is the traditional practice of mandatory retirement at age sixty-five, which forces many older adults to stop working when they are still competent and talented. While many organizations have questioned this practice, it has remained common for healthy individuals to be forced from their professions simply because of their chronological age.

In the past, many older people have suffered not only from forced retirement but also from poverty and poor medical care. By joining forces, senior citizens have made significant progress in overcoming these difficulties. Groups such as the American Association of Retired Persons, the National Council of Senior Citizens, and the more radical Gray Panthers have lobbied to improve the fate of older adults. A number of factors, such as the Social Security Act of 1935, subsequent cost-of-living increases in Social Security benefits, and the accumulation of individual assets through home mortgages have gradually improved the economic status of older Americans. Senior citizens no longer constitute the poorest age group in American society.

In addition to financial gains, older Americans have benefited from programs such as the Medicare Act of 1965, which provided basic medical care for all older Americans. However, this act did not extend medical benefits to other members of the population. Some theorists, such as gerontologist Richard Kalish, have argued that special programs for older people create a "new ageism." Kalish believes that programs such as Medicare, which provide older people with special benefits, promote a new ageism by reinforcing the notion that old people are weak and ineffective and need the rest of society to care for them.

DISCRIMINATION AGAINST CHILDREN

Other theorists have also suggested that society must redefine the standard notion of ageism to include any age group that lives in a disadvantaged position. In particular, scholars concerned with social justice have pointed out that young children now constitute the poorest age group in the United States, with approximately one-fifth living below the federal poverty level. Many children lack basic necessities such as adequate nutrition and proper medical care.

Social critics such as Marian Wright Edelman, the director of the Children's Defense Fund, have argued that society devalues children and considers them to be unimportant because they are young.

Whether ageism affects children or older people, this form of discrimination always causes an ethical dilemma. Ageism contradicts America's democratic ideals of fairness and equal treatment for all. A society that strives to promote justice must treat people in an equitable fashion, regardless of their chronological age.

Steven C. Abell

FURTHER READING

Barrow, Georgia, and Paula Smith. *Aging, Ageism, and Society.* St. Paul, Minn.: West, 1979.
Butler, Robert. *Why Survive? Being Old in America.* New York: Harper & Row, 1975.
Friedan, Betty. *The Fountain of Age.* New York: Simon & Schuster, 1993.
Levin, Jack, and William C. Levin. *Ageism: Prejudice and Discrimination Against the Elderly.* Belmont, Calif.: Wadsworth, 1980.
Nelson, Todd D., ed. *Ageism: Stereotyping and Prejudice Against Older Persons.* Cambridge, Mass.: MIT Press, 2002.
Palmore, Erdman. *Ageism: Negative and Positive.* New York: Springer, 1990.
Rosenthal, Evelyn R., ed. *Women, Aging, and Ageism.* Binghamton, N.Y.: Haworth Press, 1990.

SEE ALSO: Abuse; American Association of Retired Persons; Discrimination; Ecofeminism; Equality; Gray Panthers; Retirement funds; Sexual stereotypes.

Aggression

DEFINITION: Any behavior that is intended to harm someone, either physically or verbally
TYPE OF ETHICS: Theory of ethics
SIGNIFICANCE: Aggression in Western society is an intractable social ill; there have been as many as 685,000 violent assaults and 18,000 killings in the United States in a single year.

Hostile aggression is intended solely to hurt another person. Instrumental aggression is intended to achieve some goal. Aggression generally declines with age, and it changes in form as it does so. Younger children display more instrumental aggression; older children, more hostile aggression. With age, aggression tends to become less physical and more verbal.

Instinct theories are proposed as one cause of aggression. The Viennese psychoanalyst Sigmund Freud proposed that aggression is an instinct that gradually builds. He thought that the drive to return to an inanimate, lifeless state conflicted with the pleasure drive and was satisfied by being turned outward. The result was aggression toward others. If this drive turned inward for some reason, the person would become suicidal.

Another proponent of an instinctive theory of aggression, ethologist Konrad Lorenz, argued that aggression is adaptive for animals, so it is the natural product of evolution. Although all animals, including humans, have an aggressive instinct, most have "built-in safety devices" such as exposing their throats to signal submission. Unlike Freud, however, Lorenz suggested that an environmental stimulus must be present in addition to the genetic predisposition. Studies of identical twins support the theory that there is a genetic or instinctive component to aggression. For example, identical twins are more similar to each other than fraternal twins are to each other in terms of measures of aggression.

Biological theories seek to identify the biological structures or processes responsible for the expression of aggression. Numerous areas of the brain influence aggression. Lesions of the septum, hypothalamus, amygdala, and related areas in lower animals are followed by defensive aggression. Mild electrical stimulation of a specific region of the hypothalamus produces aggressive, even deadly, behavior in animals. Hormones also influence aggression. Injections of the masculine hormone testosterone increase aggression in animals, and criminals with higher testosterone levels commit crimes that are more violent than those committed by criminals with lower levels of testosterone. Neurotransmitters play a role in aggression as well. Aggression is associated with high levels of adrenaline and noradrenaline and low levels of serotonin. Thus, experimental evidence supports biological theories of aggression.

Learning theories explain aggression in terms of learning principles, noting that in two specific ways learning shapes aggression. First, aggression is learned by watching others (modeling). For example, in classic experiments with children and Bobo dolls, Albert Bandura and his colleagues found that the amount of violent content watched on television by eight-year-olds predicts aggressiveness in these children even ten years later. Further, children will imitate the behavior of live models, filmed humans, and cartoon characters all to about the same degree. Second, aggression depends greatly on the pattern of rewards and punishments that a person has received. People become more aggressive when they are positively reinforced for aggression and less aggressive when they are punished for it. Experimental support exists for learning theories of aggression, just as it does for instinctive and biological theories.

Emotional factors exist in aggression. One such emotional factor is frustration. John Dollard's 1939 frustration-aggression hypothesis proposed that whenever a person's effort to reach any goal is blocked, an aggressive drive is induced that motivates behavior that is intended to injure the obstacle (person or object) that causes the frustration. Thus, frustration causes aggression and aggression is always a consequence of frustration.

Leonard Berkowitz's 1981 modification of the hypothesis proposed that frustration produces a readiness toward aggression. Then, cues in the environment that are associated with aggression often lead a frustrated person toward aggression. Also, unexpected failure at some task creates a more intense reaction than does expected failure, and intentional attempts to annoy a person are more provocative than are unintentional acts. Research has supported Berkowitz's modification of the frustration-aggression hypothesis and the learning theory of aggression.

Another emotional factor in aggression is arousal. Transferred excitation is arousal from one experience that is carried over to an independent situation. For example, a person who remains excited after riding a Ferris wheel would probably be more aggressive when struck than a person who is bored after reading an article about gardening is apt to be. Generalized arousal alone does not lead to aggression. Rather, aggression occurs when the situation contains some reason, opportunity, or target for aggression.

Situational factors influence aggression. One situational factor is aggression itself. Participating in aggressive activities either increases aggression or maintains it at the same levels. For example, individuals who are given repeated opportunities to shock another person who cannot retaliate become more and more aggressive. Those who are angry react even more strongly. Thus, aggression breeds aggression rather than dissipating it, which provides an argument against catharsis as a value of watching television violence.

Other situational factors that influence aggression are temperature, noise, exposure to erotic stimuli, the presence of weapons, and deindividuation (loss of all concern for oneself as an individual and a focus instead on the present environment with little thought of past or future). When people are exposed to high temperatures, noisy environments, weapons, or erotic stimuli, they as a rule become more aggressive. As they become deindividuated by being lost in crowds, for example, they exhibit behaviors—such as aggression—that they would ordinarily inhibit. This principle explains the tendency for crowds to yell "Jump!" to a suicidal person on a high ledge. Overall, aggression has instinctive, biological, learning, emotional, and situational components.

Gender also influences aggression. Boys are generally more aggressive than girls and are more affected by violence than girls. Boys who are low achievers and are unpopular at school are more likely than other boys to imitate aggression on television. Young males, who have the highest levels of testosterone, are most likely to be violent. Women behave as aggressively as men, however, when they are alone or when urged on by another person.

Lillian Range

FURTHER READING

Deffenbacher, Jerry L., et al. "Cognitive-Relaxation and Social Skills Interventions in the Treatment of General Anger." *Journal of Counseling Psychology* 34, no. 2 (April, 1987): 171-176.

Goldstein, Arthur P. *The Psychology of Group Aggression.* New York: J. Wiley, 2002.

Grobel, Jo, and Robert A. Hinde, eds. *Aggression and War: Their Biological and Social Bases.* New York: Cambridge University Press, 1989.

Robbins, Paul R. *Anger, Aggression, and Violence: An Interdisciplinary Approach.* Jefferson, N.C.: McFarland, 2000.

Tavris, Carol. *Anger: The Misunderstood Emotion.* New York: Simon & Schuster, 1982.

Wood, Wendy, Frank Y. Wong, and Gregory J. Chachere. "Effects of Media Violence on Viewers' Aggression in Unconstrained Social Interaction." *Psychological Bulletin* 109, no. 3 (May, 1991): 371-383.

SEE ALSO: Abuse; Anger; Child abuse; Genocide and democide; Milgram experiment; Sexual abuse and harassment.

Agreement for the Suppression of White Slave Traffic

DEFINITION: International treaty that committed thirteen nations, including the United States, to investigate and halt prostitution

DATE: Ratified in 1904

TYPE OF ETHICS: Sex and gender issues

SIGNIFICANCE: This agreement, the first international accord on the issue of prostitution, marked the first time that men in power viewed prostitutes as potential victims.

In most European countries, prostitution has long been considered a social evil; however, it was nevertheless generally tolerated through the nineteenth century. The early twentieth century brought a dramatic increase in young women migrating from one country to another to work as prostitutes. Many of them were brought to prostitution through deceptive offers for employment, or kidnapping, or even sale by their parents. These women became known as "white slaves."

Government officials came to believe that the only way to stop the exploitation of young girls and women was to stop prostitution altogether. In 1904, France invited other nations to a conference at which the International Agreement for the Suppression of White Slave Traffic was signed by thirteen nations. The signatory nations agreed to stop prostitution on their own soil and to share information with other countries. Late twentieth century critics of this and other antiprostitution legislation have argued that these laws do not take into account that many prostitutes—like their clients—have chosen their careers freely and should have an ethical right to do so.

Cynthia A. Bily

SEE ALSO: Prostitution; Sexuality and sexual ethics; Slavery; Vice.

Agribusiness

DEFINITION: Term applied to the increasing integration of the world's food production—and consumption—into the processes of modern big business

TYPE OF ETHICS: Business and labor ethics

SIGNIFICANCE: The rationalization and coordination of agricultural production and distribution and their subordination to the requirements of global investment practices have combined with technological developments to transform the ethics of the world food supply.

According to its advocates, agribusiness methods have been vindicated by past successes and offer the only hope of being the world's continued ability to feed its people, as supplies of land and water dwindle while human population increases. The first Green Revolution may have confounded prophets of mass starvation, such as the early nineteenth century political economist Thomas Malthus, but new techniques are required if human lives, and particularly high-consumption lifestyles, are to survive.

Critics of agribusiness view its tactics as predatory and contrary to the long-term stability and well-being of human society. They view global agribusiness as disrupting local ecologies and economies, and restructuring and subordinating them according to the vicissitudes of high finance. Developing world famines are due, such critics claim, to inequities of distribution as international markets are manipulated to maximize profits. Apart from the impact on the hungry, critics have also focused attention on the effect of global corporate agricultural development on the prospects of the traditional family farm.

ETHICAL DEBATES

Broadly, the ethical debates about agribusiness can be seen as falling into four overlapping areas:

business, international relations, environmental ethics, and biotechnology.

As a form of business, agribusiness involves the routine issues of business ethics, such as fairness in relation to employees, integrity in dealing with competitors, honesty toward customers, and decency in relation to society. This includes concerns about the working conditions of farm and factory laborers.

In the light of its importance and worldwide impact, agribusiness is also part of the ethics of international relations, particularly the debate over globalization. Critics question whether the opportunities that agribusiness opens up in countries outweigh new distortions introduced into local economies.

As an enterprise based on the cultivation of domesticated fauna and flora, agribusiness represents one of humanity's most significant impacts on the natural environment. As such, agribusiness is deeply enmeshed in issues of environmental ethics, such as crop selection, soil depletion, and rain-forest reduction. Critics question whether agribusiness decisions lead to sustainable development or merely quick profits. Factory farming is particularly subject to criticism.

Agribusiness is also becoming increasingly embroiled in the ethical quandaries of biotechnology, particularly vigorous debates about genetic engineering, such as cloning issues. Other issues include risk estimation, risk and benefit distribution, concerns about extending human control across "natural" boundaries, and the impact of human design and decision making on the diversity of the gene pool.

Edward Johnson

FURTHER READING

Berry, Wendell. *The Unsettling of America: Culture and Agriculture.* San Francisco: Sierra Club Books, 1977.

Charles, Daniel. *Lords of the Harvest: Biotech, Big Money, and the Future of Food.* Cambridge, Mass.: Perseus Publishing, 2001.

Manning, Richard. *Food's Frontier: The Next Green Revolution.* New York: North Point Press, 2000.

SEE ALSO: Animal rights; Biotechnology; Business ethics; Developing world; Ecology; Famine; Genetically modified foods; Globalization; Hunger; Lifeboat ethics; Multinational corporations.

Ahiṁsā

DEFINITION: Doctrine of nonkilling or noninjury to living beings

DATE: Attested in Chāndogya Upaniṣad, tenth to fifth century B.C.E.

TYPE OF ETHICS: Religious ethics

SIGNIFICANCE: A basic principle in Indian thought, ahiṁsā has influenced such behavior as vegetarian diet and pacifism; it served as the foundation for Mohandas K. Gandhi's view of nonviolent resistance.

The idea of noninjury appeared first in the Chāndogya Upaniṣad, which described the enlightened person as one who was nonviolent toward all things except the victim; that is, the victim of the Vedic sacrifice. The contradiction between noninjury and sacrifice led Hinduism to abandon such rituals in favor of knowledge. Noninjury also influenced Hindu thinking about warfare. The *Bhagavadgītā* argued that since fighting belonged to the duties of the warrior caste, warriors could not avoid killing; however, they should fight without malice or desire.

During the early twentieth century, Gandhi reinterpreted noninjury by incorporating it into his political program of nonviolent resistance in India. In Buddhism, the concept of ahiṁsā constitutes the first of five precepts or vows taken by both laypeople and monks, which is to abstain from taking life. That view precluded the devout Buddhist's eating meat or engaging in violent occupations. Jainism also demanded noninjury as the first of its Five Great Vows and extended it to preclude even unintentional injury to insects by accidentally swallowing or stepping on them.

Paul L. Redditt

SEE ALSO: Buddhist ethics; Five precepts of Buddhism; Ḥallāṛ, al-; Jain ethics; Karma; Nirvana; Pacifism; Upaniṣads.

Akbar the Great

IDENTIFICATION: Mogul emperor

BORN: October 15, 1542, Umarkot, Sind (now in Pakistan)

DIED: October 16, 1605, Āgra, India

TYPE OF ETHICS: Religious ethics

SIGNIFICANCE: Akbar solidified the Mogul Empire in the Indian subcontinent and introduced a new religion of his own invention that combined elements of Hinduism and Islam.

The longest-reigning Mogul emperor of India, Akbar, also known as Akbar the Great, was a man of great talent. He became the emperor of India at the age of fourteen. Despite the fact that he did not receive any formal education, Akbar acquired knowledge by having books read to him and through discussions among scholars belonging to different religions, including Christians, Zoroastrians, Hindus, and Jains. He hosted several religious scholars belonging to different religions to acquire knowledge of these religions, and he held debates with them. He invited Portuguese Jesuit missionaries to his court and discussed Roman Catholicism at length with them.

Although Akbar became disillusioned by Islam and is said to have renounced it completely, he did not formally join any other religion. One of his concerns was to create harmony among the majority Hindu populations of India and the Muslims, who formed a small minority. One of the most important steps that he took in this regard was to repeal a religious tax called jizya, which all non-Muslims paid in exchange for protection. He also married into prominent Hindu families to forge close ties with the Hindus. Finally, he introduced his own religion, "Din-e-Ilahi," which sought to combine elements of the various religions to which he had been introduced over time. The divinity of the king was central to this new religion. Other important milestones of his reign were introduction of an elaborate revenue system, the introduction of land rights, and the creation of a civil bureaucracy to run the government.

Khalid N. Mahmood

SEE ALSO: Aśoka; Hindu ethics; Jain ethics; Zoroastrian ethics.

ʿAlī ibn Abī Ṭālib

IDENTIFICATION: Early Arab caliph
BORN: 600, Mecca, Arabia (now in Saudi Arabia)
DIED: 661, al-Kufa, Iraq
TYPE OF ETHICS: Religious ethics
SIGNIFICANCE: One of the first converts to Islam, ʿAlī was the last of the four caliphs after the death of the Prophet Muḥammad. Shīʿites contend that ʿAlī should have been chosen as the first caliph.

ʿAlī, a first cousin of Muḥammad and later his son-in-law, was the youngest of the first three persons to convert to Islam. When ʿAlī's father, Abū Ṭālib, became unable to care for his son because of ill health and poverty, Muḥammad allowed ʿAlī to live with him. Muḥammad was returning a favor to Abū Ṭālib, who had taken care of Muḥammad after the death of Muḥammad's grandfather, with whom Muḥammad had lived in his youth. Alī was only ten years old when Muḥammad declared his prophecy.

Followers of the Shīʿite sect of Islam believe that ʿAlī was the first person to convert to Islam. Sunnīs, however, believe that Khadīja, Muḥammad's first wife, was the first Islamic convert and that Abū Bakr was the second. During the difficult early period of Islamic history, ʿAlī stayed by Muḥammad's side as he struggled to spread the new religion.

ʿAlī is considered to be one of the most important persons in early Islamic history, because of his qualities as a warrior, a statesman, and a person with immense knowledge of Islam as a result of his close association with Muḥammad. Muḥammad entrusted ʿAlī with many important missions; for example, he used ʿAlī as a decoy when he escaped to Medina. It is popularly believed that Muḥammad occasionally asked ʿAlī to take charge of battles when no one else could bring victory to the Islamic forces. ʿAlī is said to have possessed a magical sword given to him by Muḥammad that he used in battle and to have been able to subdue many warriors single-handedly.

ʿAlī is also revered for his patronage of the arts and sciences and for his alleged special insight and knowledge that ordinary humans did not possess. In the South Asian subcontinent, Sufis seek endorsement from ʿAlī for their beliefs. His wisdom was valued greatly by the first three caliphs, who sought advice from him regarding both religion and politics. Muḥammad is believed to have said that he himself was the city of knowledge and that ʿAlī was the door to the city.

ʿAlī was chosen as caliph after ʿUthmān, the third caliph, was assassinated by those who claimed that ʿUthmān was guilty of favoritism toward his Banu Umayya clan. Rebellious forces from Egypt attacked and killed ʿUthmān. After ʿAlī became caliph, a rebellion against him was led by Aʿisha, the widow of the Prophet Muḥammad, who demanded swift punishment for those who had killed ʿUthmān. ʿAlī defeated Aʿisha and her followers, but his authority was seriously challenged by Amir Muʿawiyya, a relative of ʿUthmān and governor of Syria. Muʿawiyya said that he would not recognize ʿAlī as caliph until those who killed ʿUthmān were punished. In fact, Muʿawiyya wished to lead the Muslim community himself.

A battle between the two ensued, and although ʿAlī's forces were superior to his opponent's, Muʿawiyya tricked ʿAlī into accepting a truce. At that time, some of ʿAlī's followers deserted him and elected their own leader, which weakened ʿAlī's position. ʿAlī was assassinated in the year 661. Muʿawiyya foiled all attempts by ʿAlī's followers to appoint ʿAlī's son Ḥasan to lead the Muslim community. Muʿawiyya established himself as the leader of the Muslim community but never officially received the title of caliph.

After Muʿawiyya's death, his son Yazid became the leader of the Muslims. At that time, ʿAlī's second and best-known son, Ḥusayn, challenged Yazid's authority. Ḥusayn's followers believed that he was the rightful heir to the seat that had belonged to ʿAlī, but Ḥusayn was defeated and killed in a battle with Yazid's forces near Karbala in present-day Iraq. This incident had a major impact on the subsequent history of Islam. Those who belong to the Shīʿa sect revere Ḥusayn as a martyr and a true hero of Islam. The death of Ḥusayn precipitated the schism between Sunnī and Shīʿa Muslims, who came to have distinctly different interpretations of Islam and the teachings of Muḥammad. The death of Ḥusayn in Karbala is commemorated each year for ten days throughout the Muslim world, particularly in areas where the Shīʿites are in the majority.

ʿALĪ'S LEGACY

Shīʿites believe that ʿAlī and his family were the rightful successors of the Prophet Muḥammad and that the first three caliphs conspired to deny ʿAlī the caliphate. The Sunnîs claim, however, that those caliphs took power because of their personal ability and their knowledge of Islam. ʿAlī actually had no desire to become caliph; he was too busy making arrangements for Muḥammad's burial to attend the assembly at which the successor was chosen. During ʿAlī's rule as caliph, clan rivalries began that pitted the Banu Umayya against the Banu Hashim, Muḥammad's clan, leading ultimately to ʿAlī's assassination and the victory of the Banu Umayya.

ʿAlī and, later, his sons Ḥasan and Ḥusayn commanded a large, faithful group of followers, whose cause ultimately led to the emergence of the Shīʿite sect. Shīʿites believe that God sent imams to lead the Muslim community after the deaths of Muḥammad and ʿAlī. They believe that Ḥasan, ʿAlī's son, was the first imam. The last imam, it is believed, vanished at the age of three and will return again as the savior who will rescue the world and restore the glory of God and Islam.

Khalid N. Mahmood

FURTHER READING

Cole, Juan. *Sacred Space and Holy War: The Politics, Culture, and History of Shiʿite Islam.* London: I. B. Tauris, 2002.

Momen, Moojan. *An Introduction to Shiʿi Islam: The History and Doctrines of Twelver Shiʿism.* New Haven, Conn.: Yale University Press, 1985.

Muir, William. *The Caliphate: Its Rise, Decline, and Fall.* Beirut, Lebanon: Khayats, 1963.

Nasr, Seyyed Hossein Hamid Dabashi, and Seyyed Vali Reza Nasr, eds. *Shiʿism: Doctrines, Thought, and Spirituality.* Albany: State University of New York Press, 1988.

Pinault, David. *The Shiites: Ritual and Popular Piety in a Muslim Community.* New York: St. Martin's Press, 1992.

Shah, S. Afsar Ali. *The Lion of Allah: Hazrat Ali-ul-Murtaza.* Lahore, Pakistan: Intikhab-e-Jadeed Press, 1999.

SEE ALSO: Abū Bakr; Muḥammad; Shīʿa; Sunnīs.

Alienation

DEFINITION: Separation of the self from itself, or an inability of the self to be at home in the world

TYPE OF ETHICS: Personal and social ethics

SIGNIFICANCE: Alienation raises questions about the fundamental nature of human beings and the relationship that ought to exist between the self and society. Traditionally, social critics have seen the prevalence of alienation within a given society as a basis for the moral condemnation of that society.

Semantically considered, alienation may be understood as a sense of loss, separation, estrangement, or self-denial. Metaphysically, alienation refers to a state of affairs in which the self suffers either from an internal split in the psyche or from an external separation from society. There are, therefore, two fundamental forms of alienation. Its corollary term, "de-alienation," refers to the process by which alienation is overcome. Jean-Jacques Rousseau, Georg Wilhelm Friedrich Hegel, and Karl Marx understood alienation, fundamentally, as an external split between the self and society. De-alienation, implied in this point of view, would consist of a social transformation resulting in an accord between self-determination and social conformity. Sigmund Freud, however, described alienation as an internal split. Following this line of thought, de-alienation would primarily consist of a pyschological process of restoring wholeness to the self.

SOCIAL CONTRACT THEORY AND HEGELIANISM

Jean-Jacques Rousseau employed the term "alienation" in *On the Social Contract* (1762). Rousseau contended that society corrupted human beings by separating them from their natural state. He is widely remembered for his most famous epigram: "Man is born free but everywhere he is in chains."

Georg Wilhelm Friedrich Hegel gave alienation a prominent place in his writings. In *The Philosophy of History* (1822), he depicted alienation as the separation between the idea of freedom in itself and its realization or actualization in world history. In *The Phenomenology of Spirit* (1807), Hegel employed the concept of alienation to articulate the failure of human consciousness to recognize itself in the external world of nature and culture. Culture, the world of produced objects and human actions, represents the process of the transformation of the natural human being into the social being. Thus, culture alienates the socialized self from the naturalized self. Estrangement results from the split occurring in intellectual life. For example, law, a product of culture, divides the self into the legal person, from whom the law demands social conformity, and the self-conscious person who values freedom. De-alienation would result from the union of personal freedom and the objective rule of the state.

MARXISM

Karl Marx applied alienation to politics and economics. In *On the Jewish Question* (1843), Marx denounced the split existence of human beings in modern societies. In civil society, people function as egoistic, private, self-interested individuals. In the political community of the state, however, people are regarded as abstract citizens. Human emancipation, or de-alienation, requires the unification of the communal being and the real individual.

In the *Economic and Philosophical Manuscripts* (1844), Marx specified four forms of alienation in the section entitled "Alienated Labor." The first form of alienation is the separation between the laborer and the product of labor. Alienation occurs because the object, as the realization of the life activity of the worker under capitalism, does not belong to labor. Therefore, the loss of the object represents the loss of reality to the worker.

If it is the case that the worker is alienated from the product, then it logically follows that the worker is also alienated in the act of production. If the result of production is alienation, then the process is also alienating. In productive activity, the worker becomes self-alienated because labor is the life-activity of the worker. Rather than becoming self-affirming activity, work becomes self-denying activity. Rather than becoming the satisfaction of a need for human self-fulfillment, work becomes only a means to satisfy the basic needs of human survival.

The third form of alienation is that of alienation from species-being (society, social consciousness). Because labor serves only to further basic survival, workers exist only as egoistic individuals and not as social beings; that is, they think egoistically, not communally.

The last form of alienation is the estrangement between the self and the other. Each person is equally estranged from his or her true human essence. Self-estrangement therefore manifests itself in estrangement with others. Under capitalism, the estrangement between the self and the other finds expression in the alienation between labor and capital. De-alienation therefore entails the emancipation of the worker by abolishing private property. Private property is both the presupposition and the result of alienated labor.

FREUD

Sigmund Freud posited alienation as the fundamental human condition. The self is split between the ego and the ego ideal. The latter, a social and conditioning factor, becomes a repressive mechanism. The conflict between the ego and the ego-ideal is alienation. Repression is the agency of alienation to the extent that it keeps away from consciousness those elements that are not approved by the superego.

Several questions relating to alienation remain open. If there is such a universal phenomenon as self-alienation, is it necessary to presuppose a universal human nature? If alienation is not universal, is it relative to history and culture? If alienation is universal, de-alienation must be considered a psychological fantasy or a social utopia. If it is psychologically relative, its psychological causes must be discovered so that wholeness can be restored. If it is sociologically relative, then its social causes must be revealed so that they can be transformed.

Michael R. Candelaria

FURTHER READING

Feuerbach, Ludwig. *The Essence of Christianity.* Translated by George Eliot. New York: Harper & Row, 1957.

Freud, Sigmund. *The Ego and the Id.* Edited by James Strachey. Translated by Joan Riviere. New York: W. W. Norton, 1962.

Geyer, Felix. *Alienation, Ethnicity, and Postmodernism.* Westport, Conn.: Greenwood Press, 1996.

_____, and Walter R. Heinz, eds. *Alienation, Society, and the Individual: Continuity and Change in Theory and Research.* New Brunswick, N.J.: Transaction, 1992.

Hegel, Georg Wilhelm Friedrich. *The Phenomenology of Spirit.* Translated by A. V. Miller. Oxford, England: Oxford University Press, 1977.

Marx, Karl. *Selected Writings.* Edited by David Mc-

Lellan. 2d ed. New York: Oxford University Press, 2000.

Meszaros, Istvan. *Marx's Theory of Alienation.* New York: Harper & Row, 1972.

Morris, Warren Frederick. *Escaping Alienation: A Philosophy of Alienation and Dealienation.* Lanham, Md.: University Press of America, 2002.

SEE ALSO: Durkheim, Émile; Existentialism; Freud, Sigmund; Hegel, Georg Wilhelm Friedrich; Marx, Karl; Rousseau, Jean-Jacques.

Altruism

DEFINITION: Behavior meant to benefit others rather than, or at the expense of, oneself.

TYPE OF ETHICS: Theory of ethics

SIGNIFICANCE: While absent in ancient ethical work, the concept of altruism has been crucial to modern thought about morality and virtue.

The concept of altruism can be developed in at least two different ways. It may be looked at historically, beginning with the opposition of altruism to egoism by Thomas Hobbes and moving primarily forward, or it may be looked at with a view toward simple definition. The meaning of altruism, or, vaguely, other-directed behavior in ethics, is not as clear as it might be, as Lawrence Blum and others have noted. Simple definitional concerns will be taken first.

If the term "altruism" is taken to mean action that benefits others, immediately the problem arises that such behavior can quite easily be part of a scheme that is ultimately selfish. If, for example, creatures from an advanced civilization were to land on Earth; quell all international, civil, and family strife; and institute a plan of resource management, child-rearing, and government that ensured peace, tranquillity, and the development of learning for all, that behavior would have to be construed as altruistic according to this initial definition, whether the aliens were raising people for food or not.

To avoid this problem, one might consider some restriction regarding motivation. The word "altruism" applies to actions intended to benefit others. This definitional amendment raises the question of who decides what is of benefit to whom. A mother may consider it a benefit to her son to quash a relationship in which he is involved. The son may disagree. If she succeeds, then she does what she intended to do and may well continue to defend her action as beneficial to her son. Who is correct?

Since the mother seems to be serving her own interests, one might propose an amendment that altruism applies to behavior that is intended to benefit others and places the interest of others ahead of one's own interest. This, however, makes the definition worse. According to this definition, a morally altruistic woman who had been raped and beaten should not bring charges against the man responsible, because it is would not be in his best interest. Any other reason for not bringing charges would be more palatable than this one.

There are also general objections to placing restrictions regarding motivation in the definition of altruism. Psychologists state that people are often not aware of their own real motivations. For example, when alcoholics begin to deal with their alcoholism, their spouses often sabotage their efforts by offering them drinks. If one asks why, they may give one of any number of reasons, such as giving the alcoholics a break from feeling bad about their childhoods. These reasons all have in common that they are focused on the alcoholics. In truth, however, according to psychology, the mates' own identities may be dependent upon helping the alcoholics with their problem, and these identities are threatened when the alcoholics begin to get better. Therefore, other-directed behavior according to the mates' perceptions turns out to be self-directed behavior according to the psychologists.

Indeed, those who have paid any attention to their own decisions have found it difficult to know whether their motivations are simply self-serving or take others properly into account, particularly when there is disagreement with someone else on the issues. This inability to isolate motivation accurately dims enthusiasm for restrictions regarding motivation in a functional definition of altruism.

Sociobiologists E. O. Wilson and Richard Dawkins offer a different reason for the inability to isolate and be certain of motivation. Their conjecture, based on the behavior of certain animals, is that people are genetically programmed to act in such a way as to bring about the greatest survival rate for their own genes. One might, then, sacrifice oneself for one's progeny much more quickly than for one's spouse or strangers. This action is not the result of a decision. It is the decision of the gene pool, according to the law of perpetuation of the species. If motivation cannot be determined, however, what are the ramifications for the definition of altruism?

At this point, one is foundering on the impossibility of deciding whether altruistic acts should all be reinterpreted as egoistic. What is peculiar here has to do with egoism as a theory of motivation. Any piece of behavior can be seen as egoistic. No human behavior can fail to be explained as motivated by self-interest. This fact makes the modern project of discovering an altruistic ethic in an egoistic human nature hopeless. The next step is to inspect historical uses of the word "altruism" in the hope of illumination.

THOMAS HOBBES

The place to begin is with is the seventeenth century British philosopher Thomas Hobbes, though he is not the earliest philosopher to be considered. Hobbes's view of the state of nature, in which life is "nasty, brutish, and short," is consistent with his belief that human beings are motivated only by fear of death and desire for dominance. According to this view, altruistic behavior is always a screen for egoistic behavior. This seems the point at which the modern problem in ethics mentioned above arises: finding a place for altruistic behavior in an egoistic human nature.

The strength of this position is not that Hobbes's premises concerning motivation are persuasive. One can easily reject the contention that persons are exclusively motivated by fear of death and desire for dominance by positing, for example, the independent power of compassion as a motivator of human behavior, as does Arthur Schopenhauer. Much of modern ethical philosophy can be seen as either affirming Hobbes's position concerning the impossibility of altruism or hypothesizing some independent, altruistic motivation as part of human nature. Examples of those who opt for some altruistic principle are, in addition to Schopenhauer, Søren Kierkegaard; the third earl of Shaftesbury, called simply "Shaftesbury"; Anthony Ashley Cooper; Francis Hutcheson; the later David Hume; and Henry Sidgwick. Among those who opt for self-interest alone, in addition to Hobbes, are Bernard Mandeville, John Grote, and, with a twist, the theologian William Paley.

The twist with Paley is that he considered benevolence to be in a person's long-term self-interest rather than short-term self-interest. According to Paley, all persons are egoistic, but God has arranged that the only way to secure eternal happiness is to obey the fundamental (and, for Paley, utilitarian) moral rule. In this way, he makes the transition between egoistic human nature and altruistic moral behavior.

One thinker who perhaps deserves separate mention is Friedrich Nietzsche, who attacked altruism as a moral mistake.

NIETZSCHE

It was noted above that a definition of altruism that included a restriction on motivation to the effect that one should always place others' interests ahead of one's own is inadequate. Nietzsche thought so, too, but recognized large groups of persons who in fact upheld this definition in what he called a "slave morality." Nietzsche was passionately opposed to such morality, which glorified suffering as meaningful. His primary target was Christianity, though he also sideswiped Judaism and Greek ethics. He was apparently not, however, the virulent anti-Semite that some have made him out to be. Nietzsche saw the Judeo-Christian values of humility, passivity, and dependence as necessarily grounded in a value system built on fear, guilt, and a distortion of the will to power. Master morality, however, extolled the proper virtues of courage and self-grounded spiritual strength. Thus, altruism was condemned by Nietzsche as unworthy of highly evolved individuals.

Concern for others need not be a sign of poor self-esteem or any sort of escape from higher values. Such concern for others might well exist in very strong persons who need no rhetoric of a master mentality to know their worth, attending to the needs of others with utter confidence in their capacity to care also for themselves. Still, there is such a thing as the pathology of low self-esteem, a suppression or devaluing of the self, and it is correct to eschew such an attitude. This eschewing does not require the adoption of an attitude that demands individual dominance, however, as Nietzsche recommends. It is this recommendation of individual dominance, however, that made Nietzsche useless to the Third Reich until he was edited. Ethnic group dominance is not the same thing as individual dominance, even if both are misguided.

The total of all the developments since Hobbes

does not seem to advance the problem significantly. There are exceptions, notably Joseph Butler, who takes a different direction. Even today, however, many ethicists presuppose the opposition between altruism and egoism as the fulcrum for allegedly historically informed discussions of ethical thinking and behavior. This is the case with, for example, Richard Norman's popular textbook *The Moral Philosophers: An Introduction to Ethics* (1983). Much of value is said in this intelligent book, but it ends without closure concerning its central tension: the problem of egoism and altruism. Ethics interpreted in terms of this narrow, insoluble problem cannot satisfy the desire to understand.

JOSEPH BUTLER

The significance of Joseph Butler, an Anglican clergyman, is that he reintroduced a larger model for ethical reflection than can be used if one limits oneself to issues of altruism and egoism. This broader model is presented primarily in Butler's "Three Sermons on Human Nature" (1726). It is a common claim among philosophers that Butler's sermons are the closest thing in English to Aristotle's ethical thought. A larger model was standard during Classical times and in the thought of Thomas Aquinas during medieval times.

Thomism, as Thomas Aquinas's thinking is called, is also a reintroduction of Aristotle's thinking into the Christian, European world, made possible by the Islamic scholars Averroës and Avicenna and the Jewish scholar Moses Maimonides. Maimonides set forth, in his *Guide of the Perplexed* (1190), discussions of Aristotle's thinking that were especially influential on Thomas Aquinas and other medieval Scholastics. Aristotle had been lost to Europe at the close of the Classical Age and was regained through these Islamic and Jewish scholars, primarily via paths between Moorish Spain and the rest of Europe.

The primary idea reintroduced by Butler is that self-love and benevolence, or egoism and altruism, are part of a larger motivational whole. It is not that Butler transcended his age without connection to it. He took himself to be looking, along with most other seventeenth and eighteenth century writers, for a foundation for morals that was independent of the divine will. He found it in the divine creation. Although Butler's ethical thinking is similar to Aristotle's, it should not be forgotten that he wrote as a Christian.

In the divine creation, Butler found human nature. As a creation of God, human nature could not be depraved, as John Calvin, Martin Luther, and perhaps even Immanuel Kant held. Rather, human nature is a reasonable guide to the way in which God would have human beings behave. Furthermore, what human beings desire, or what motivates them, is a reasonable guide to what they should want, or that by which they should be motivated. The claim that what people actually want, overall, is a happy life is not necessarily egoism—at least not egoism as opposed to altruism.

Consider a happy life as one that involves trusting relationships, friendship, and cooperative endeavors. Persons possessing a desire for this kind of life could not separate their interests and others' interests according to different motives. Allowing self-interests to outweigh others' interests, and vice versa, will both be involved in a life in which decisions produce, overall, trusting relationships, friendship, and cooperative endeavors. Therefore, to allow the distinction between altruism and egoism to occupy a central place in ethical discussion or to consider that egoism might be an all-encompassing motivation is to narrow one's perspective on ethical behavior to a small class of conflict situations. This leaves behind both common sense and common life.

If what is good is what is desired by natural persons, then pursuing trusting relationships, friendship, and cooperative endeavors as a means to a happy life is good. The good of this kind of life is not good for a self only, except in the trivial sense that a self desires and pursues it. The good of this kind of life includes the good of other lives. Therefore, the model wherein two person's goals conflict and each person's goals connect to self-interest alone covers only a small area even of human conflict, and certainly not the entire arena of human ethical behavior. This small area is not qualified to serve as a model for ethics, and Butler understands this fact.

When challenged, Butler had recourse to his own experience. He claimed, and urged others to agree, that the vast majority of persons are motivated completely by neither self-interest nor benevolence. Exceptional individuals, such as conscienceless businessmen or servants with no detectable personal wishes, should be ignored in such an assessment. Furthermore, self-regard and other-regard exist side by side in the same person, most of the time without conflict, and even reinforce each other. Most people are much more integrated than the opposition between altruism and egoism would lead one to believe. This integration involves not only altruism and egoism, which have no relationship of priority of one over the other, but also many other affections or goal-oriented motivations.

A full analysis of the problems of modern ethics that contrasts Butler's point of view, called an ethic of "virtue," with the modern presupposition that altruism and egoism are foundational to ethical discussions is available in Alasdair MacIntyre's *After Virtue* (1981). Butler himself traces his views to Epictetus, not Aristotle. As far as the present analysis goes to this point, he and Aristotle are agreed. Aristotle offers the more complete virtue ethic, so it will be instructive to discuss Aristotle at this point.

ARISTOTLE

The first thing to understand about Aristotle's view of happiness is that it applies only to a whole life. A happy life is a whole life well lived. A life well lived is a life lived according to virtue and accompanied by the blessings of good fortune. Good fortune, which is a matter of luck, is necessary. The best overview of the function of luck in Greek philosophy and literature is available in Martha Nussbaum's *The Fragility of Goodness* (1986).

A virtuous person who meets a bad end, such as Socrates, cannot properly be called happy according to Aristotle. Aristotle took steps once to ensure that Athens did not have the opportunity to treat him as it had treated Socrates, and no doubt would have explained this behavior as pursuing a happy life.

This "happy life" is not to be experienced or enjoyed at any particular moment, but functions as a goal for the sake of which everything else works. The virtues, such as courage, temperance, prudence, and justice, are functional means toward the end of living a good life. Altruism is not taken into account by Aristotle, and it is not clear whether altruism should be treated as a virtue. Modern ethicists consider that only altruistic behavior can properly be called ethical. Aristotle considers that behavior in accordance with the virtues is a means to the unique, practical goal of all persons, happiness, offering a broader goal for virtuous activity than either the good of self or that of others, either egoism or altruism.

Aristotle was aware that not all persons pursue the same ultimate good, but he was convinced that the real goods that people naturally desire, which meet human needs, are the same for everyone. Some persons mistakenly acquire desires for goods that are not real goods. This explains why the word "good" is used differently by different persons, even when all admit happiness as the name for that which is always pursued as an end and never as a means.

Aristotle's works offer a flexible absolutism. He claims that a whole life is made good, or happiness is achieved, by the cumulative attainment of all real goods in the period of that whole life. Real goods are those to which natural desires lead. These natural desires are the same for all in view of their identical natures and needs as human beings. Individualistic relativism is rejected by Aristotle.

Such a complete view of ethics is difficult even to compare with modern, truncated discussions of altruism and egoism. It is very tempting to endorse MacIntyre's suggestion that one should move toward an integration of modern law and a virtue ethic in the postmodern predicament, whether one agrees with MacIntyre's particular attempt to construct such an ethic or not.

Joe Frank Jones III

FURTHER READING

Blum, Lawrence. "Altruism." In *Encyclopedia of Ethics*, edited by Lawrence C. Becker and Charlotte B. Becker. New York: Garland, 1992. A first-rate article overall, and with interesting material on Anna Freud's work with not-really-altruistic mental patients.

Butler, Joseph. *Fifteen Sermons Preached at the Rolls Chapel and A Dissertation upon the Nature of Virtue*. London: G. Bell, 1964. This book, the best text available, contains useful introductory material.

Cooper, John M. "Aristotle on the Goods of Fortune." *Philosophical Review* 94 (April, 1985): 173-196. This article explains the essential role of luck in Greek ethics.

Hobbes, Thomas. *Man and Citizen: "De Homine" and "De Cive."* Edited and introduction by Bernard Gert. Indianapolis: Hackett, 1991. The text is accurate, and the introduction by Gert is excellent.

MacIntyre, Alasdair. *After Virtue: A Study in Moral Theory*. 2d ed. Notre Dame, Ind.: University of Notre Dame Press, 1984. Reviews and critiques Western moral theory thus far, structuring it as a debate between Aristotle and Nietzsche. Creates a new moral theory, based upon social practices, which overcomes the weaknesses of his predecessors.

_____. "Egoism and Altruism." In *The Encyclopedia of Philosophy*, edited by Paul Edwards. New York: Macmillan, 1972. This extended discussion, historically informed, is an excellent place to begin.

Maimonides, Moses. *The Guide of the Perplexed.* Translated by Shlomo Pines. Chicago: University of Chicago Press, 1963. This difficult work benefits from both an introduction by the translator, Pines, and an introductory essay by Leo Strauss.

Nussbaum, Martha C. *The Fragility of Goodness: Luck and Ethics in Greek Tragedy and Philosophy.* New York: Cambridge University Press, 1986. An insightful, scholarly look at the notion of luck in ancient literature and philosophy. The next step after Cooper's article concerning "fortune" in Aristotle.

Post, Stephen G., et al., eds. *Altruism and Altruistic Love: Science, Philosophy, and Religion in Dialogue.* New York: Oxford University Press, 2002. A multidisciplinary examination of altruism by philosophers, religious scholars, scientists, and social scientists. Somewhat weak on the religious perspective.

Ridley, Matt. *The Origins of Virtue: Human Instincts and the Evolution of Cooperation.* New York: Penguin, 1998. A scientific and sociological account of altruism as an evolved behavior which benefits the human species.

SEE ALSO: Aristotelian ethics; Charity; Egoism; Generosity; Good, the; Hobbes, Thomas; Human nature; Kierkegaard, Søren; *Nicomachean Ethics*; Public interest; Self-interest; Service to others.

American Association of Retired Persons

IDENTIFICATION: Lobbying organization claiming more than 35 million members that advances the ethical principle of equal treatment for older persons

DATE: Founded in 1958

Challenges to AARP's Own Ethics

Despite its reputation as a champion of the rights of older people, AARP itself is occasionally criticized for its own ethics. In November, 2003, for example, dozens of AARP members demonstrated in front of AARP's Washington, D.C., headquarters to protest the organization's endorsement of the Republican Party's Medicare bill. Unhappy with the proposed law's provision for prescription drug benefits, the protesters destroyed their AARP membership cards. Meanwhile, Democratic leaders in Congress charged that AARP had unethical ties with Republican leaders and might even have had a financial stake in the Medicare legislation.

TYPE OF ETHICS: Politico-economic ethics

SIGNIFICANCE: Best known by its acronym, AARP is the world's most successful organization in promoting the rights of older people.

In 1947, when private health insurance was denied to most older Americans, Dr. Ethel Percy Andrus founded the National Retired Teachers Association (NRTA) to promote the ethical principle of productive aging and, more practically, to have an organization large enough to attract companies to provide health insurance and discount mail-order pharmacy services. In 1958, Andrus founded the AARP to cover all persons fifty years of age and over, whether retired or not, to establish the ethical principle that senior citizens should live with dignity and independence. In 1998, the organization changed its name to its acronym, "AARP."

AARP advances the ethical principle that retired persons—people who have given so much to society—should at least be entitled to affordable health care. In 1965, the U.S. Congress responded by enacting the Medicare program, which provides health insurance to Americans aged sixty-five and older for physician and hospital care. In 2003, AARP successfully lobbied Congress to add a prescription drug plan.

In 1965, Congress also passed the Older Americans Act to fund programs for those over sixty years of age in all states. A decade later, in 1975, when AARP complained that the quality of such programs was uneven, Congress passed the Age Discrimination Act, which established the ethical principle that all older persons must be provided equal benefits from federally funded programs.

Congress again responded to AARP in 1967 by passing the Age Discrimination in Employment Act, to establish the ethical principle of nondiscrimination against those over the age of forty. Soon, thanks to AARP lawsuits, courts ruled that employers cannot force employees to retire without just cause or compensation.

By the early twenty-first century, AARP was offering its members a wide variety of low-cost programs while exposing such forms of elder abuse as unethical practices of advertisers, telemarketers, and others who take advantage of older people.

Michael Haas

SEE ALSO: Ageism; Congress; Equality; Gray Panthers; Lobbying; Medical insurance.

American Civil Liberties Union

IDENTIFICATION: Nonpartisan organization created to defend and protect the individual rights and freedoms guaranteed all persons in the United States by the Constitution and statutes

DATE: Founded in 1920

TYPE OF ETHICS: Civil liberties

SIGNIFICANCE: The American Civil Liberties Union (ACLU) adheres to the principle that everyone in the United States should have the same basic rights regardless of their backgrounds, their beliefs, or any crimes with which they may be accused. A nonpartisan organization, the ACLU does not limit itself to the defense of particular groups.

The ACLU was founded by Roger Baldwin and other social activists in 1920. It was an outgrowth of the American Union Against Militarism, an organization formed during World War I that advocated amnesty for conscientious objectors who refused to participate in military combat for moral reasons. Throughout its existence, the mission of the ACLU has been to preserve the individual rights and guarantees stated in the Bill of Rights and other amendments to the U.S. Constitution. These include free speech, free press, right of assembly, religious freedoms, and the separation of church and state, as well as equal protection under the law, due process, fair treatment by the government, and the right to privacy or freedom from government intrusion into one's private affairs.

ACLU members believe that a government does not have the right to insulate itself against ideas with which it disagrees. The organization's representation of unpopular groups and causes is based on the principle that if government has the power to violate one person's rights, such power could be extended to everyone. The ACLU occasionally defends the right to freedom of speech of controversial and unpopular groups without endorsing the beliefs of such groups, and it defends the right of accused criminals to fair trials, regardless of the acts committed by such persons or whether the accused criminals are guilty or innocent. Such stances have often subjected the ACLU to strong public condemnation.

EVOLVING MISSION

During its early years, the ACLU opposed the federal government's attempt to deport politically radical immigrants and worked to secure the release of activists who were jailed for antiwar activities, arguing that they too had the right to freedom of speech. In 1925, the ACLU defended Tennessee high school teacher John T. Scopes's right to freedom of speech after he violated a state law by teaching the theory of evolution in his classes. During the 1930's, the ACLU strongly opposed censorship and defended the rights of American Nazi groups. In the 1940's, it provided legal assistance to Japanese Americans who were forcibly interned in government relocation centers. During the 1940's and 1950's, it opposed anticommunist measures taken by federal and state governments. During the 1960's and 1970's, it defended the First Amendment rights of Nazis and members of both the Ku Klux Klan and the Nation of Islam.

During the 1960's, the mission of the ACLU expanded to include other groups that had traditionally been denied equal protection, including women, children, prisoners, the mentally ill, persons with disabilities, and gays and lesbians. The organization also advocated the abolition of criminal abortion laws under the constitutional right to privacy. In later years, it supported affirmative action, education reform, voting rights, and the rights of individuals with acquired immunodeficiency syndrome (AIDS).

Because of its defense of unpopular causes and groups, the ACLU has been accused by its detractors as being radical and un-American. Some also criticize the organization for its absolutist definition of civil liberties. The ACLU, however, has consistently adhered to the principle that everyone has the same basic rights and has continued to defend individuals and groups regardless of their beliefs.

William V. Moore

FURTHER READING

Garey, Diane. *Defending Everybody: A History of the American Civil Liberties Union*. New York: TV Books, 1998.

Walker, Samuel. *In Defense of American Liberties: A History of the ACLU*. Carbondale: Southern Illinois University Press, 1999.

SEE ALSO: Academic freedom; Bill of Rights, U.S.; Book banning; Church-state separation; Civil rights and liberties; Constitution, U.S.; First Amendment; Ku Klux Klan; Nation of Islam.

American Federation of Labor

IDENTIFICATION: First permanent national-international federation of skilled trades
DATE: Founded on December 8, 1886
TYPE OF ETHICS: Business and labor ethics
SIGNIFICANCE: The American Federation of Labor (AFL) asserted the rights of workers to organize on their own behalf and upheld the dignity of labor against the impositions of the business community.

A successor to the Federation of Organized Trades and Labor Unions, which was established in November of 1881 in Pittsburgh, Pennsylvania, the American Federation of Labor (AFL) became the first permanent American trade union federation. Earlier American national labor organizations, such as the National Labor Union (established in 1866) and the Knights of Labor (established in 1871), had been loosely structured industrial unions with polyglot memberships and broad economic and political pro-

grams. Despite some limited successes, they ultimately failed because of internal divisions, the dispersion of their energy, and the hostility of the public and the business community.

The AFL was founded largely through the efforts of Samuel Gompers and Adolf Strasser, both of whom were immigrant cigar makers and socialists. A pragmatic organization, it was tailored to American workers' lack of class consciousness and emphasized the improvement of wages, hours, and working conditions—that is, bread-and-butter unionism. Its constituent organizations—carpenters, coal miners, building tradespeople, and railroad workers—enjoyed almost complete autonomy and enlisted skilled workers almost exclusively.

The relatively high wages of skilled workers made it possible for the organization to accumulate substantial strike funds. AFL membership rapidly grew to two million by 1910 and more than tripled by 1950. Publicly, the AFL sought the mediation of labor disputes, the enactment of labor legislation, limits on immigration, protection from technological unemployment, and, whenever possible, collaboration with employers. The AFL's merger with its rival, the Congress of Industrial Organizations, in 1955 (founding the AFL-CIO) created the free world's largest labor union. The merger also resulted in diminished autonomy and the acceptance of industrial unionism and political action.

Clifton K. Yearley

SEE ALSO: International Labour Organisation; Knights of Labor; Labor-Management Relations Act; National Labor Union; Work.

American Inns of Court

IDENTIFICATION: Voluntary legal organization comprising judges, lawyers, law professors, and students
TYPE OF ETHICS: Legal and judicial ethics
SIGNIFICANCE: Chapters of the American Inns of Court seek to foster excellence in professionalism, ethics, civility, and legal skills.

The American Inns of Court was organized in the early 1980's at the suggestion of Chief Justice Warren Burger. Patterned after the English Inns of Court, this organization consists of an association of local chapters devoted to improving the legal profession. Each chapter unites judges, lawyers, law teachers, and third-year law students in a focus on professionalism, legal ethics, civility, and a variety of legal skills. Members, who gather monthly for educational programs, may engage in mock trials, demonstrate appellate arguments, or simply discuss their ideas and experiences on various topics.

Chapters of the American Inns of Court limit themselves to no more than eighty active members to encourage the kind of mentoring and support relationships rooted in close contact. The organization attempts to foster relationships among students, lawyers, and other legal professionals with a broad range of experience. The four categories of membership illustrate this range. Masters of the bench are experienced lawyers, judges, and law professors. Barristers are practicing attorneys with three to five years of experience, and associates are lawyers who have been practicing less than three years. Finally, pupils are third-year law students.

Timothy L. Hall

SEE ALSO: Attorney-client privilege; Code of Professional Responsibility; Codes of civility; Judicial conduct code; Jurisprudence; Law; Legal ethics; Mentoring; Professional ethics.

American Medical Association

IDENTIFICATION: National professional organization of licensed physicians
DATE: Founded in 1847
TYPE OF ETHICS: Bioethics
SIGNIFICANCE: The stated purpose of the American Medical Association (AMA) is to improve the quality of medical services provided to Americans and to maintain high standards of ethical behavior within the medical profession.

The AMA held its first official meeting in Philadelphia in 1847. The delegates to the meeting established a Code of Medical Ethics and set minimum requirements for medical education and training. To reflect changing times and conditions, major revi-

sions were made to the Code of Medical Ethics in 1903, 1912, 1947, and 1994. The preamble, and primary component, of the code is known as the Principles of Medical Ethics. It contains nine fundamental ethical principles that have been applied to nearly two hundred different ethical issues in medicine, ranging from genetic testing to family abuse. Two other components of the Code of Medical Ethics are the Current Opinions with Annotations of the Council on Ethical and Judicial Affairs, which interprets the Principles of Medical Ethics, and the Reports of the Council on Ethical and Judicial Affairs. Together, the three components of the Code of Medical Ethics determine the AMA's overall position on ethical issues.

The Principles of Medical Ethics establish general rules of ethical conduct among doctors, between doctors and their patients, and between doctors and society at large. They require doctors to maintain secrecy within the requirements of the law, temperance, delicacy, punctuality, and respect for the rights of others. Physicians are requested to keep abreast of important medical developments that may benefit their patients, share relevant medical information with their patients, and consult and work with other medical professionals as necessary. The ethical behavior of physicians is determined by the overall content of the Principles of Medical Ethics. Although ethical values and legal principles are typically interrelated, the AMA advocates that ethical obligations of a physician usually supersede legal obligations.

Alvin K. Benson

SEE ALSO: Bioethics; Diagnosis; Ethical codes of organizations; Hippocrates; Medical bills of rights; Medical ethics; Medical research; *Principles of Medical Ethics*.

American Society of Newspaper Editors

IDENTIFICATION: Organization that encourages newspaper editors to concern themselves with the ethics, quality, and history of editorial and news policy
DATE: Founded in 1922
TYPE OF ETHICS: Media ethics

SIGNIFICANCE: Of the many groups monitoring the news media for fairness and accuracy, the American Society of Newspaper Editors is among the most influential because it is made up of editors themselves.

At the beginning of the twenty-first century, the American Society of Newspaper Editors (ASNE) had more than one thousand members. Its members are the directing editors who determine editorial and news policy on daily newspapers across the country. The organization has several goals: to improve the quality of journalism education and of newspaper writing and editing, to help newspaper managers work more effectively with employees, to encourage adequate minority representation on newspaper staffs, and to protect First Amendment rights and freedom of information. To achieve these goals, ASNE publishes several periodicals for editors, educators, and others, and presents awards for excellence in editing and writing.

ASNE monitors its own members to see how newspapers are responding to various needs. This often leads to controversy. During the late 1980's, ASNE began surveying daily newspapers to determine whether gay and lesbian journalists were being given fair treatment in hiring and promotion, and whether the AIDS epidemic was receiving fair and adequate coverage. During the same period, ASNE researched the hiring and promotion of members of racial and ethnic minorities, and debated whether to publicize the names of newspapers with poor minority-hiring records.

Cynthia A. Bily

SEE ALSO: Accuracy in Media; Journalistic entrapment; Journalistic ethics; Media ownership; News sources; Photojournalism; Tabloid journalism.

Americans with Disabilities Act

DEFINITION: Federal civil rights law enacted to protect people with disabilities from discrimination
DATE: Passed on July 26, 1990
TYPE OF ETHICS: Civil rights
SIGNIFICANCE: Prior to the passage of the Americans with Disabilities Act (ADA), the civil rights of the

disabled community were not protected; the ADA strictly prohibits discrimination against people with disabilities.

The Civil Rights Act of 1964 did not prohibit discrimination against people with disabilities. The Rehabilitation Act of 1973 required that increased opportunities be made available for people with disabilities, but discrimination against the disabled continued to be evident until the passage of the Americans with Disabilities Act in 1990. The Americans with Disabilities Act stands as a comprehensive civil rights law for people with disabilities.

The ADA states that no individual shall be discriminated against on the basis of a disability in seeking employment, receiving state and local government services, or having full and equal enjoyment of public accommodations. Title I of the ADA prohibits discrimination against hiring a "qualified applicant" only on the basis of the applicant having a disability. The ADA public accommodation provisions, known as Title III, which became effective on January 26, 1992, require accessible wheelchair routes and signage identifying special services for the disabled. Such services may include braille materials and assistive listening devices. The effect of the passage of the ADA has been increased accessibility for people with disabilities and an increased awareness of disability civil rights.

Noreen A. Grice

SEE ALSO: Civil Rights Act of 1964; Disability rights; Keller, Helen; United Nations Declaration on the Rights of Disabled Persons; Veterans' rights.

Amnesty International

DEFINITION: International organization that seeks to protect human rights throughout the world
DATE: Founded in 1961
TYPE OF ETHICS: Human rights
SIGNIFICANCE: By monitoring the state of human rights throughout the world, publicizing violations, and seeking to correct errors, Amnesty International has raised the consciousness of people everywhere about the need to protect and defend people's rights. In 1977 the organization was

awarded the Nobel Peace Prize for its work in aiding political prisoners throughout the world.

Amnesty International is an international agency that seeks enforcement of the Universal Declaration of Human Rights (1948). Working to ensure these rights for all people in all countries of the world, it uses research and action to focus on preventing violations of human rights; ending severe abuses of all types of human rights, including physical, mental, freedom of conscience, and expression; and protecting people from all types of discrimination,

English human rights activist Peter Bennenson founded Amnesty International in 1961, building on an organization named Justice that he and other British lawyers had founded in 1959. Justice sought adherence to the Universal Declaration of Human Rights.

The immediate occasion for the founding of Amnesty International was the arrest by the Portuguese dictatorship of two students in November, 1960. The students' alleged crime was toasting freedom in public. For that offense Portugal's rigged courts sentenced the students to seven years in prison. On May 28, 1961, Bennenson published on article in the *London Observer* titled "The Forgotten Prisoners." The article evoked a large response.

THE ORGANIZATION'S MISSION

To achieve its mission of protecting human rights, Amnesty International has remained officially independent of any ideology except the protection of human rights. By the early twenty-first century it claimed more than 1,500,000 members in more than 150 countries and remained independent of any government organizations in its governance and fundraising.

Toward its goal of respect for universal human rights, Amnesty International conducts research and action geared toward the prevention and elimination of serious abuses of human rights in all guises, physical and psychological. Its overriding ethic has been to promote and work for freedom throughout the inhabited world, and it has played a major role in bringing the world's attention to the importance of human rights on the international scene. Among its accomplishments has been the publication of a code of medical ethics for professionals that prohibits torture. It has worked for international business ethics, opposing child labor and other forms of exploitation. The standards of Amnesty International have influenced numerous world leaders, especially President Jimmy Carter, who made human rights a key factor during his political career and afterward and won a Nobel Peace Prize in 2002 for his work.

Frank A. Salamone

FURTHER READING

"Amnesty International Sees Pervasive Violations; Human Rights Casualty in War on Terrorism, Group Says." *Washington Times*, May 29, 2002, p. A10.

Roht-Arriaza, N. "Institutions of International Justice." *Journal of International Affairs* 52, no. 2 (1999): 473.

Tolley, H. B. *The International Commission of Jurists: Global Advocates for Human Rights*. Philadelphia: University of Pennsylvania Press, 1994.

SEE ALSO: American Civil Liberties Union; Capital punishment; Child soldiers; Human rights; Human Rights Watch; Nobel Peace Prizes; South Africa's Truth and Reconciliation Commission; Torture; Universal Declaration of Human Rights.

Anarchy

DEFINITION: Political theory holding that individual freedom has been destroyed by the coercive power of the state and seeking to replace the state with voluntary associations

TYPE OF ETHICS: Politico-economic ethics

SIGNIFICANCE: As a belief in the importance of individual freedom over the values of the state, anarchy questions virtually all traditional models of government, including social contract theories of democracy.

Anarchy, as the word is commonly used, refers to chaos that results from an absence of authority. The term has its roots in Greek and means, literally, leaderless. As a political philosophy, however, anarchy seeks to liberate the individual from the coercion of the state and to create a society of voluntary participation. This dual nature of anarchy—disorder and individual freedom—is reflected in the approaches taken by anarchists since its inception as a political philosophy in the nineteenth century.

HISTORY

Pierre-Joseph Proudhon, a French writer and social theorist, came from a lower-class background. "What is property?" he asked in his most famous work, with that title (1840). His answer, "Property is theft," is one of the intellectual foundations of modern anarchism. Proudhon believed that one's labor was the basis of value in society. Property, in the form of capital or land, whose owners were supported by the state, denied workers their fair shares. This emphasis on the economic foundation of the state would be appropriated by syndicalist labor unions at the beginning of the twentieth century, and it provided the justification for revolutionary general strikes aimed at destroying the state.

Anarchism was popular among workers because it promised action. Revolutionaries, such as the Russian Mikhail Bakunin and the Italian Enrico Malatesta, worked for the revolution that, sparked by an act of violence, would bring about the new society. At the end of the nineteenth century and the beginning of the twentieth, some anarchists engaged in terrorism, which they called "propaganda of the deed." They thought that one dramatic act of violence, especially the assassination of a major political leader,

would bring about the long-awaited revolution. President William McKinley of the United States; Antonio Cánovas del Castillo, the premier of Spain; and Umberto I, king of Italy, all died at the hands of anarchist assassins. Assassinations and bomb-throwing attacks led to the image of anarchists as violent criminals plotting to destroy society.

The Russian-born American anarchist Emma Goldman was a symbol of this terror in the minds of many Americans. Children were threatened with capture by "Red" Emma, and their fate was left to the imagination. Emma Goldman's life, however, was a testament to the ethics of anarchy as a way of life. She believed in her rights as a woman to work, to practice birth control, and to love without the bonds of marriage. She supported labor unions and openly opposed the entry of the United States into World War I.

Goldman was deported back to Russia in 1917 but became disillusioned by the authoritarian nature of the revolutionary Bolshevik regime. Instead, she favored the anarchist revolution that occurred in Spain at the outbreak of the Spanish Civil War in 1936. In Barcelona, workers took over factories and set up committees to oversee production. Factory committees then elected representatives to regional industry councils in an attempt to organize an economy and a society without exploitation. This worker control ended when the military, under Francisco Franco, defeated the Republican government and set up a dictatorship in Spain.

ETHICAL PRINCIPLES

Another and more intellectual approach to anarchy focused less on the destruction of the state and more on the freedom of the individual. Several Russian intellectuals, among them Leo Tolstoy and Peter Kropotkin, used the peasant village as an example of individual cooperation and moral authority. Kropotkin was an advocate of mutual aid, believing that individuals would spontaneously create groups for their mutual benefit and join voluntarily. The state existed to coerce individuals to conform to moral

In September, 1901, U.S. president William McKinley was shot by an anarchist named Leon Czolgosz, who was executed for murder only six weeks after McKinley died. (Library of Congress)

standards and economic organization that benefited those who controlled that state.

The ethics of anarchy is more than a protest against a particular state or society or economic organization: It is an expression of complete faith in the individual. In the twentieth century, the legacy of anarchy has influenced both violent demonstrations and scholarship. The worldwide student uprisings of the late 1960's owed much to the anarchist belief in direct action and mistrust of the state. In Chicago, Paris, and Mexico City, students battled police to protest government policies.

Herbert Read, an English writer, has sought to explain the ideals of freedom through anarchy. Read addresses the differences between individual freedom and the concept of liberty. Liberty, according to Read, is a doctrine that depends on the relationship of the individual to the state. Liberty is a civil right; freedom is a personal attribute. One is granted liberty but possesses freedom. Anarchy, according to Read, recognizes that freedom is innate and leaves the individual unfettered.

Paul Goodman was an American scholar who wrote about education, society, and urban living. Goodman's human perspective envisaged educational communities, not mammoth universities, and cities on a human scale, designed around the individual rather than around a system of production and transportation.

Anarchy is not a system, and its adherents often exhibit contradictory behavior and ideas. It accepts spontaneity and variety as attributes of freedom, and it welcomes diversity. Anarchy opposes uniformity enforced by dictatorships or elected governments and supports the freedom of each individual. It is this respect for the value of the individual that marks the ethics of anarchy.

James A. Baer

FURTHER READING

Adem, Seifudein. *Anarchy, Order, and Power in World Politics: A Comparative Analysis.* Burlington, Vt.: Ashgate, 2002.

Avrich, Paul. *Anarchist Portraits.* Princeton, N.J.: Princeton University Press, 1988.

Bakunin, Mikhail Aleksandrovich. *Bakunin on Anarchism.* Edited and translated by Sam Dolgoff. New York: Black Rose Books, 2002.

Drinnon, Richard. *Rebel in Paradise: A Biography of Emma Goldman.* Chicago: University of Chicago Press, 1982.

Goldman, Emma. *Anarchism, and Other Essays.* 1917. Reprint. New York: Dover, 1969.

Horowitz, Irving L. *The Anarchists.* New York: Dell, 1964.

Joll, James. *The Anarchists.* 2d ed. Cambridge, Mass.: Harvard University Press, 1980.

Read, Herbert. *Anarchy and Order: Essays in Politics.* Boston: Beacon Press, 1971.

SEE ALSO: Assassination; Class struggle; Communism; Freedom and liberty; Nihilism; Politics; Revolution; Social contract theory.

Anger

DEFINITION: Primary, reactive emotion characteristic of both humans and animals
TYPE OF ETHICS: Personal and social ethics
SIGNIFICANCE: Often thought of as a base or dark emotion, anger may motivate unethical or illegal acts. Its fundamental biological nature, however, may also indicate that it is a necessary survival mechanism.

Modern psychology and psychoanalysis have to some measure removed the onus that medieval Christianity attached to anger when identifying it as one of the seven cardinal, or deadly, sins. It is now viewed as a natural, reactive, even mature emotion experienced by all humans at some time in their lives, as unavoidable as other primary emotions such as fear, sadness, and joy. However, orthodox moral philosophers knew that unabated anger, or wrath, could be destructive, particularly in the guise of vengeful fury, and argued that in that form it should be God's prerogative alone. As the fourth century Greek theologian Saint Basil proclaimed, in mortals it was viewed as a reprehensible "temporary madness."

THE HUMORS THEORY

The primitive, physiological "humors" theory that persisted from antiquity through the Renaissance and explained emotions as "passions" should have called into question the idea that anger per se could be deemed sinful. After all, if a person was disposed to choler because of an imbalance in body chemistry, an excess, specifically, of yellow bile, anger could arise without permission of the will, making sin a moot concept. Morality must hinge on both the cognitive distinction between good and evil and a voluntary choice between them—that is, free will.

The implications of the pseudo-scientific idea of the humors simply remained as remote from moral philosophy as modern physiological study is likely to remain. Knowing, for example, that under stress, as in an angry condition, there is a decrease of lymphocytes in the blood but an elevation of free fatty acid avails the moralist nothing. Knowing that anger can contribute to destructive behavior, however, provides some food for ethical thought. Moral principles based on emotions must therefore focus on their effects rather than on the emotions themselves.

HEALTHY EMOTION VS. DESTRUCTIVE POTENTIAL

Anger is engendered by some sort of stimulus, usually in the present but possibly recalled from memory. It is normally a conscious feeling accompanied by physical discomfort and tension, and may be outwardly expressed by glaring, gritting of teeth, clenching of the fists, or even quaking of the bodily frame, depending on its intensity. Most psychologists believe that it is a realistic, healthy emotion, unlike hostility, which is based in immature fear. It is, however, a delimited emotion, and unless it subsides or finds outlet in expression, it can yield to more destructive reactions such as anxiety, depression, and aggression. When sublimated through creative energy, however, it can lead to positive behavior, such as efforts to ameliorate social injustice.

Anger tends to become dangerous when it is suppressed, repressed, or displaced. Both suppression and repression work to deny its expression an outlet, while displacement, common in dreams, redirects the expression of anger from the actual stimulus to a surrogate or scapegoat. Repressed, seething anger may find sudden, explosive release, as it did in the 1992 riot in Los Angeles, which was prompted by the acquittal of the police officers in the Rodney King beating trial. The violence erupted because the demands of a collective anger aroused by the beating were not satisfied by the jury's verdict. The anger was then displaced as violence against persons and property that had no rational link to the King affair.

The widespread deflection of anger away from its actual cause toward a scapegoat has affected even whole nations. A prime example is Nazi Germany, in which Jews were blamed for the economic ills of the nation and displaced anger gradually gave way to hatred and murderous, genocidal aggression. How that could have happened in such a highly developed culture remains something of a mystery, but the basic model of hatred arising from anger joined to frustration is clear enough.

The vestiges of the idea of anger as a sort of madness persist in law, as, for example, in the "temporary insanity" defense, or as a mitigating factor in sentencing in "crimes of passion." Moreover, the cumulative effect of long-suppressed anger has increasingly been used as a defense in court, when, for example, a battered wife has killed her spouse under circumstances that would otherwise preclude a plea of self-defense. For some theorists, that defense has opened a legal version of Pandora's box.

Furthermore, as the Rodney King case revealed, the legal process is a potential hostage to collective anger. The videotape of King's beating, repeatedly aired by the media, aroused great public indignation, which could have intimidated and suborned the jury. It did not, but the lawlessness that followed in the wake of that jury's verdict may weigh heavily on some future jury.

Although modern psychologists can agree on the symptomatic behavior and physiological phenomena accompanying anger, they can provide no definitive conclusions regarding what it is or even where, anatomically, it resides. Practical ethics must take anger and other emotions into account, but using them as primary building blocks of moral principles is at best subjective and very risky.

John W. Fiero

FURTHER READING

Averill, James R. *Anger and Aggression: An Essay on Emotion.* New York: Springer-Verlag, 1982.

Beck, Aaron T. *Prisoners of Hate: The Cognitive Basis of Anger, Hostility, and Violence.* New York: Perennial, 2000.

Callwood, June. *Emotions: What They Are and How They Affect Us.* Garden City, N.Y.: Doubleday, 1986.

Eigen, Michael. *Rage.* Middletown, Conn.: Wesleyan University Press, 2002.

Gaylin, Willard. *The Rage Within: Anger in Modern Life.* New York: Simon & Schuster, 1984.

Izard, Carroll E., Jerome Kagan, and Robert B. Zajon C., eds. *Emotions, Cognition, and Behavior.* New York: Cambridge University Press, 1984.

Sontag, Frederick. *Emotion: Its Role in Understanding and Decision.* New York: Peter Lang, 1989.

Stearns, Frederic R. *Anger: Psychology, Physiology, Pathology.* Springfield, Ill.: Charles C Thomas, 1972.

SEE ALSO: Aggression; Darwin, Charles; Freud, Sigmund; James, William; Passions and emotions; Violence.

Animal consciousness

DEFINITION: Argument that animals may experience thought processes, self-awareness, and emotions similar to, though simpler than, those of humans

TYPE OF ETHICS: Animal rights

SIGNIFICANCE: Representations of animal consciousness are used to argue for the ethical treatment of animals.

Early in the twentieth century, in response to exaggerated claims for mental abilities in animals, the behaviorist tradition came to dominate psychology and animal behavior. Behaviorists claimed that animals are probably not conscious of themselves or of their behavior; that if they were, the knowledge would not be important to them; and that this consciousness would be impossible for humans to measure, analyze, or understand. Through the following decades, behavioral scientists assumed that animals were incapable of thought, emotions, and self-awareness. Animals were treated almost as machines in behavioral studies.

Later in the century, some ethologists (people who study animal behavior under conditions as nearly natural as possible) began to question the assumptions of behaviorism. One of these was Donald R. Griffin, who was impressed by the number of animal capabilities that were initially considered to be preposterous by behavioral scientists but were later clearly demonstrated. His own discovery (with Robert Galambos) that bats use a sonarlike system for spatial orientation and insect capture is an example of such a capability. Griffin thought that animals might also have greater mental ability than behaviorists believed.

Karl von Frisch had already described an elaborate dance of honeybees, with which scout bees direct their coworkers to sources of nectar. The dance uses symbolic representations for the direction, distance, and quality of the nectar source. Other examples of animal mental accomplishments ranged from navigation in birds to evidence of learning and language use in apes, monkeys, dolphins, sea lions, and parrots.

Griffin wrote *The Question of Animal Awareness* in 1976 to explore the possibility that reason and consciousness might exist in animals. The question of animal awareness has actually been in existence since people became conscious. Animal thought and awareness were assumed to exist by many scientists and most laypersons before the establishment of behaviorism. Griffin's book, supported by his impeccable scientific reputation, brought the idea back for serious consideration among behavioral scientists and initiated a new science: cognitive ethology.

Griffin argued that animals do many things that can be most easily explained if animals are assumed to have at least a limited ability to think and plan. Also, given the fact that human anatomy and physiology—including the anatomy and physiology of the nervous system, the center of thought and consciousness—are very similar to those of animals, there is good reason to assume that human mental processes are also similar to those of animals. Further, he proposed that the ability to reason, even in a very rudimentary fashion, should be of value to animals, as it is to humans, and so should be favored by natural selection. He suggested that there is no more evidence demonstrating animals' inability to think and feel than there is demonstrating their ability to do so, and that it is foolish to assume they lack such abilities without evidence.

Griffin did not say that animal reason is on the same level as that of humans. Although whales and apes, especially chimpanzees, have been assigned near-human abilities by some investigators, these claims have always shown lack of support when carefully investigated. Griffin argued that awareness and thinking ability are far greater in humans than in animals, but that the essential processes supporting consciousness are the same in the two groups. In other words, there are great quantitative differences, but no qualitative differences.

In some people's minds, the ethical treatment of animals hinges on the question of animal consciousness. If animals are aware of fear and pain, ethical consideration requires that any human use of an animal be designed to minimize the animal's distress. Assuming that animal consciousness exists, animal rights extremists argue that animals should not be used by humans in any way. Instead, as sentient beings, they should be given the same rights and respect as humans. Organisms that are not aware of their pain and fear, however, need not be so carefully treated. The most extreme animal use proponents assume that there is no animal consciousness and argue that unfeeling beasts can be used in any way humans see fit. Most cognitive ethologists agree that humans have a right to use animals, since all species use others in natural ecological interactions such as predation. Animal use should, however, be carried out with the animal's potential awareness in mind, and pain or discomfort should be minimized.

Animal awareness might also prove to be of importance to the study of ethics. Ethics, like consciousness, has been assumed to be the exclusive concern of humans. Some animals, however, appear to use deception to manipulate their fellows intentionally. If such behavior occurs widely among animals, the evolution of ethical systems might be profitably studied using these primitive systems. A problem with this prospect, and with the question of animal consciousness in general, is the difficulty of understanding what is going on in another species' mind. Behaviorist assumptions are still prevalent in psychology and animal behavior. Not everyone is convinced that animals think or are aware of themselves and their actions, let alone that they make conscious ethical (or unethical) decisions.

Carl W. Hoagstrom

FURTHER READING

Cheney, Dorothy L., and Robert M. Seyfarth. *How Monkeys See the World: Inside the Mind of Another Species*. Chicago: University of Chicago Press, 1990.

Griffin, Donald R. *Animal Minds: Beyond Cognition to Consciousness*. Chicago: University of Chicago Press, 2001.

Linden, Eugene. "Can Animals Think?" *Time* 141 (March 22, 1993): 54-61.

Ristau, C. A., ed. *Cognitive Ethology*. Hillsdale, N.J.: Lawrence Erlbaum, 1991.

Sorabji, Richard. *Animal Minds and Human Morals: The Origins of the Western Debate*. Ithaca, N.Y.: Cornell University Press, 1995.

Waal, F. B. M. de. *Chimpanzee Politics: Power and Sex Among Apes*. Baltimore: Johns Hopkins University Press, 1989.

SEE ALSO: Animal research; Animal rights; Cruelty to animals; Moral status of animals; People for the Ethical Treatment of Animals; Sentience; Singer, Peter; Vivisection.

Animal research

DEFINITION: Use of animals in research for the purpose of education, product testing, or acquiring new knowledge that might benefit humankind

TYPE OF ETHICS: Animal rights

SIGNIFICANCE: Research conducted on animals raises questions regarding the moral acceptability of subjecting animals to pain, suffering, and sometimes death for the benefit of people.

Using animals for purposes of research (closely allied to vivisection) has been practiced since the beginning of scientific medicine, when it was practiced by the ancient Greeks. The field of medicine benefited from the study of living organisms, and the fields of experimental physiology, biology, and comparative anatomy could not have emerged as independent disciplines without the knowledge gained from animal laboratory research.

Through the seventeenth century, the scientific community had no moral, legal, or religious objection to vivisection. As Nicolaas Rupke, a scientific historian, points out in his book *Vivisection in Historical Perspective* (1987), it was not until the nineteenth century that vivisection became the focus of public controversy. This controversy grew out of the animal welfare movement of the 1820's and eventually led to the introduction in Great Britain of the Cruelty to Animals Act of 1876, which was the first law enacted to regulate animal research.

Arguments for and Against the Use of Animals in Research

Pro	*Con*
Since animals are less complex organisms (both biologically and psychologically), they provide a good beginning point for exploratory research.	Animal research has no value or efficacy for understanding human processes or disorders.
Animals have shorter life spans, which facilitates the study of genetically transmitted traits.	Most animal research serves no beneficial purpose for humans and is unnecessary.
Scientists are able to control an animal's environment effectively, reducing the number of confounding variables that plague research.	In many cases the costs of harming animals outweigh the benefits to human society.
Animals can be used for experiments that would be considered unethical to perform on humans.	Animals have intrinsic worth and deserve to live freely, unrestricted by selfish motives of another species.

The public debate over vivisection continued into the twentieth century, and the publication of *Animal Liberation* (1975) by animal rights activist Peter Singer fueled and revived the antivivisection movement. Singer's book contained the most powerful arguments to date against the use of animals in research. He used the term "speciesism" to encapsulate the notion that it is morally indefensible for one particular species (humans) to dominate and abrogate the rights of another species for its own interests. One of the first books published by a member of the scientific community to rebut the antivivisection arguments was William Paton's *Man and Mouse: Animals in Medical Research* (1984).

THE EXTENT OF ANIMAL RESEARCH

Animals are frequently used for research in such biomedical fields as pharmacology, bacteriology, and toxicology and in such social sciences as psychology. Although estimates are difficult to make, the National Research Council has indicated that as many as 17 million animals may be used for research every year in the United States alone. The majority of these animals, roughly 85 to 90 percent, are laboratory rats and mice. Primates appear to account for less than 7 percent of research animals. In comparison, the American Humane Association reports that approximately 12 million animals are killed in shelters each year.

ARGUMENTS

Many views exist concerning the moral acceptability of using animals in research. On one end of the continuum, a minority of scientists advocates the unrestricted use of animals for experimental research, teaching purposes, or product testing, regardless of the value of that research for improving the welfare of the human condition. On the other end of the continuum, a minority of animal activists, such as Tom Regan of the Animal Liberation Movement, promotes the total elimination of the use of animals for science. Most scientists and activists hold positions in between these extremes.

Advocates of vivisection maintain that animal research has unlocked mysteries in the fields of physiology, biochemistry, neuroscience, and pathology, among others, which have allowed discoveries to be made that have led to the elimination or reduction of human pain and suffering for generations of people to come. These advocates point to progress in mental illness, neurological disorders, genetic disorders, pain management, vaccinations, and many other areas, all made possible by animal research. Antivivisectionists argue, primarily on moral or ideological grounds, that inflicting pain on another species is cruel and immoral. Many activists state that humans do not have the authority to usurp the rights of another species for their own purposes, holding that animals possess intrinsic worth and should be able to live freely, without restrictions imposed by an intellectually superior species. Singer asks: Is speciesism merely another form of blatant racism? Those who support animal research counter with the argument that animals are not morally equal to humans.

Most animal rights groups do not want to see all animal research abolished. However, they want to see the institution of more responsible research practices. Philosopher Michael A. Fox, the author of *The Case for Animal Experimentation* (1986), states that animal rights groups have accused the scientific community of being reluctant to use humane research methods that are intended to reduce the number of animals being used and minimize or eliminate the pain or suffering that they experience. In addition, the animal rights groups maintain that much research serves no valuable purpose. Fox agrees that pain and suffering should be minimized whenever possible but points out that in some instances, it may not be possible. Also, it is difficult to predict how valuable research is going to be before it is conducted.

REGULATIONS

Guidelines created by a number of scientific organizations, along with state and federal laws, exist to help regulate the use of animals in research. Many of these documents address the humane treatment of animals, including the concern for the animals' comfort and health. The guidelines typically stress the need to reduce pain and discomfort by using anesthesia or analgesics and to use particularly invasive techniques only when no other alternatives can be found.

Bryan C. Auday

FURTHER READING

Cothran, Helen, ed. *Animal Experimentation: Opposing Viewpoints*. San Diego, Calif.: Greenhaven Press, 2002.

Fox, Michael A. *The Case for Animal Experimentation: An Evolutionary and Ethical Perspective*. Berkeley: University of California Press, 1986.

Gluck, John P., Tony DiPasquale, and F. Barbara Orlans, eds. *Applied Ethics in Animal Research: Philosophy, Regulation, and Laboratory Applications*. West Lafayette, Ind.: Purdue University Press, 2002.

Linzey, Andrew. *Christianity and the Rights of Animals*. New York: Crossroad, 1987.

Paton, William D. *Man and Mouse: Animals in Medical Research*. Oxford, England: Oxford University Press, 1984.

Rollin, Bernard. *Animal Rights and Human Morality*. Buffalo, N.Y.: Prometheus Books, 1981.

Rupke, Nicolaas, A., ed. *Vivisection in Historical Perspective*. New York: Croom Helm, 1987.

Singer, Peter. *Animal Liberation*. New York: Ecco, 2002.

SEE ALSO: Animal consciousness; Animal rights; Cruelty to animals; Experimentation; Mean/ends distinction; Moral status of animals; National Anti-Vivisection Society; People for the Ethical Treatment of Animals; Singer, Peter; Vivisection.

Animal rights

DEFINITION: Extension of rights-based ethical theories to nonhuman animals

TYPE OF ETHICS: Animal rights

SIGNIFICANCE: Animal rights have been advocated by a political movement with philosophical foundations in both the utilitarian and rights-based traditions in ethical theory. This movement raises the issues of the basis of human rights and the grounds upon which such rights should or should not be extended to other living beings.

The animal rights groups that became a potent and pervasive political force in the United States and Europe during the last quarter of the twentieth century were distinguished from earlier, more moderate animal protection groups by their rights-based rhetoric, but they also drew freely on the thinking of utilitarian ethicist Peter Singer.

HISTORY

The older "animal protection" groups, such as the American Society for the Prevention of Cruelty to Animals (ASPCA) and the Humane Society of the United States (HSUS), had as their primary focus the prevention of blatant mistreatment of work and companion animals. In 1975, the Australian philosopher Peter Singer published *Animal Liberation*, which subsequently became the bible of the animal rights movement, and during the early 1980's, a number of professional philosophers began devoting serious attention to the ethics of the treatment of nonhuman animals. The new animal rights groups, such as People for the Ethical Treatment of Animals (PETA), the Fund for Animals, and the Farm Animal Reform Movement (FARM), used ideas that emerged from the philosophical debate to question the very use of animals, especially in agriculture and science.

While some groups, such as the Animal Legal Defense Fund, worked within the system, the best-known groups emphasized confrontation and "direct action," especially the clandestine Animal Liberation Front (ALF), which devoted itself solely to illegal actions such as stealing ("liberating") lab animals and destroying scientific equipment and data. In 1981 Alex Pacheco, who later founded PETA along with Ingrid Newkirk, volunteered as an assistant to Edward Taub, who was doing research on nerve damage using monkeys at Silver Spring, Maryland. Pacheco documented violations of state cruelty laws, and Taub was convicted on six counts. Then, in 1984, the ALF provided PETA with videotapes stolen from a laboratory at the University of Pennsylvania that was using baboons to study head injuries. The footage, which had been shot by the scientists themselves, showed researchers joking about the animals, which were being subjected to severe, brain-damaging whiplash, and showed what appeared to be inadequately anesthetized baboons left unattended. PETA edited the footage into a widely distributed video, *Unnecessary Fuss*, and the resulting publicity forced the closure of the lab.

Although Taub's conviction was subsequently overturned on the grounds that the state cruelty laws in question did not govern federally funded research, groups such as PETA capitalized on the publicity from such cases to become a potent political force. In 1985, the federal Animal Welfare Act of 1966 was amended to require all universities accepting federal funds to have an Institutional Animal Care and Use Committee (IACUC), and by the late 1980's there were persistent calls, from a number of scientists and in proposed legislation, for "The Three R's": *replacement* of animals with nonanimal models, *refinement* of experimental protocols to eliminate animal suffering, and *reduction* of the number of animals used.

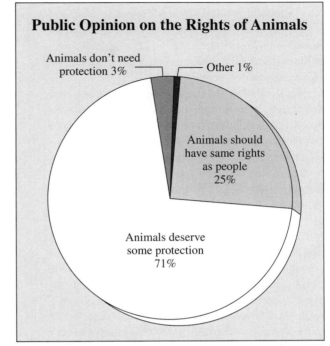

Public Opinion on the Rights of Animals

Animals don't need protection 3%

Other 1%

Animals should have same rights as people 25%

Animals deserve some protection 71%

Source: Gallup Poll, May 5-7, 2003. Figures reflect responses from 1,005 adults throughout the United States.

The political success of animal rights groups was reflected in the birth of groups defending the use of animals, such as the Animal Industry Foundation, the Incurably Ill for Animal Research, and the Foundation for Biomedical Research (FBR). The FBR produced a response to *Unnecessary Fuss* called *Will I Be Alright Doctor?* featuring children whose lives had been saved with medical procedures first developed on animals, and it took out ads with photos of animal rights protesters captioned: "Thanks to animal research, they'll be able to protest 20.8 years longer."

Although most philosophers writing on the subject concluded that animal rights and environmental ethics are based on incompatible foundations (concern for individuals versus concern for ecological wholes) and environmental groups such as the Sierra Club and the Audubon Society took steps to distance themselves from animal rights groups during the late 1980's and early 1990's, some animal rights activists sought to forge coalitions with environmental concerns. From its founding in 1967, the Fund for Animals merged concerns for animals and endangered species in its campaigns against hunting and trapping. Similarly, Animal Rights Mobilization (founded in 1981 as Trans-Species Unlimited) conducted an annual "Fur-Free Friday" the day after Thanksgiving in more than 100 cities, in an effort to meld animal rights and environmental ethics.

While emphasizing action and sometimes even disparaging philosophical reflection as a frivolous distraction, animal rights activists borrowed two notions from philosophers studying the ethics of the human treatment of nonhuman animals: Peter Singer's principle of equal consideration of interests and Tom Regan's analysis of the concept of moral rights. Although most activists read Singer's popular *Animal Liberation*, few read his more philosophical book *Practical Ethics* (1979) or Regan's lengthy and rigorous *The Case for Animal Rights* (1983). Yet it is in these latter two books that Singer and Regan provide careful analyses of the concepts that animal rights activists commonly invoked, and, in particular, Regan's book—not Singer's—is the source of the analysis of moral rights that activists used to question the very use of animals.

PRINCIPLE OF EQUAL CONSIDERATION OF INTERESTS

Singer wrote *Animal Liberation* for popular consumption, and in it he spoke loosely of animals having moral rights. In later, more philosophically rigorous work (summarized in *Practical Ethics*), however, he explicitly adopts a utilitarian stance and eschews talk of rights. Utilitarianism is the view that right actions maximize aggregate happiness. In principle, nothing is inherently or intrinsically wrong, according to a utilitarian; any action could be justified under some possible circumstances. One way of characterizing rights views in ethics, by contrast, is that there are some things that, regardless of the consequences, are simply wrong to do to individuals, and that moral rights single out these things. To defend the moral rights of animals would be to claim that certain ways of treating animals cannot be justified on utilitarian grounds.

As a utilitarian, however, Singer does not oppose all uses of animals. If the benefits to humans of scientific experimentation or animal agriculture sufficiently outweighed the harms to animals, then they would be justified in utilitarian terms. What Singer insists on is equal consideration of interests. Singer argues that what makes racism and sexism morally objectionable is that the racist does not give equal weight to the similar interests of members of different races and the sexist does not give equal weight to the similar interests of men and women. Borrowing a term from Richard Ryder, he defines a speciesist as one who ignores or gives different weights to the similar interests of humans and animals.

To insist on equal consideration of animals' interests is not to claim that animals have all the same interests as human beings or that animals ought to be treated in the same way as humans. Singer illustrates these points with the following example. Because a pig has no interests that would be served by an education, whereas a child does, equal consideration for the interests of a pig and a child will lead to very different treatment.

What a child and a pig do have in common, however, is an interest in avoiding suffering. Singer argues that sentience, the capacity for suffering, is a necessary and sufficient condition for moral standing. Arguing that if a being suffers, there can be no excuse for refusing to take its suffering into account, Singer concludes that sentience is sufficient for moral standing. Arguing that if a being is incapable of suffering, there is no individual welfare to be taken into account, he concludes that sentience is a necessary condition for moral standing. Singer speculates that sentience may have vanished from the phylogenetic "scale" by the level of clams, oysters, and scallops, because these organisms' nervous systems and behaviors are so simple that they probably are not conscious at all.

Singer argues that the status quo in science and in agriculture is based on violations of the principle of equal consideration of interests. He argues that one would not subject a human being to the amount of pain routinely inflicted on sentient animals for the kind of results usually obtained. Similarly, he argues, one would not subject any human being to the pain and stress routinely inflicted on farm animals for the sake of nutritionally unnecessary meat.

Singer's *Animal Liberation* became the bible of the animal rights movement. PETA distributed it to new members, and many who read it were inspired to political activism and vegetarianism. To the extent that the animal rights activists opposed all use of animals, however, Singer's utilitarian stance was not the philosophical foundation of their cause. As a utilitarian, Singer could countenance some uses of animals under some conditions, as he himself admitted in his later, more philosophical book *Practical Ethics*.

There he argues that if a happy animal is slaughtered painlessly and replaced with an equally happy animal, then the world is no worse off, in utilitarian terms. Singer denies, however, that this "replaceability argument" can be used to defend large-scale, intensive animal agriculture, for two reasons. First, he claims that the humaneness of living conditions, handling, and slaughter is inversely proportional to the scale of animal agriculture, so that the argument would apply only to an idealized, small-scale animal agriculture. Second, Singer argues that "self-conscious individuals, leading their own lives and wanting to go on living," are not replaceable, because when such an individual dies, its desires go unsatisfied even if another individual's desires are satisfied in its stead. Arguing that a case can be made that all mammals are self-conscious, Singer concludes that the replaceability argument would not apply to most types of farm animals (although he admits that it applies to both fowl and fish, which he thinks are not self-conscious).

Still, Singer's utilitarian position does not imply blanket, exceptionless opposition to animal agriculture. This is all the more clear in the case of medical research, where—at least sometimes—it is not only culinary taste but also the health and lives of self-conscious beings that are at stake. An animal rights activist adhering carefully to Singer's utilitarian position could endorse *some* types of experimentation under *some* circumstances.

REGAN'S ANALYSIS OF "HAVING MORAL RIGHTS"

In *The Case for Animal Rights*, Tom Regan claims, for this reason, that it is his "rights view," rather than Singer's utilitarianism, which is the philosophical basis of the animal rights movement. Regan argues that respecting animals' moral rights would imply not only improving the conditions under which they are kept but also the total abolition of animal agriculture and experimentation.

Although there is controversy as to the specifics, there is general agreement among ethicists about what it means to "have moral rights": To attribute moral rights to an individual is to assert that the individual has some kind of special moral dignity, the value of which is that there are certain things that cannot justifiably be done to him or her (or it) for the sake of benefit to others. For this reason, moral rights have been characterized as "trump cards" against utilitarian arguments. In *The Case for Animal Rights*, Regan explores the implications of recognizing moral rights so conceived in at least all normal mammals one year old or older.

Regan argues that in order to possess moral rights, an individual must be not merely sentient but also a "subject of a life," with self-consciousness, beliefs, memories, desires, and a sense of its future. Just as Singer argues that probably all mammals are self-conscious, Regan argues that at least all normal mammals one year old or older have these capacities. He argues that birds, reptiles, amphibians, and fish ought all to be treated *as if* they have rights, out of a spirit of moral caution (they *may* be subjects of a life, but the case for saying that they are is weaker than the case for saying that mammals are).

According to Regan, all subjects of a life have basically one moral right: the right not to be harmed on the grounds that doing so benefits others. Recognizing this right would, he argues, imply the total dissolution of animal agriculture and animal experimentation. If animals have moral rights, then the slaughter of an animal cannot be justified in terms of the benefits accruing to humans. Even experimentation calculated to save human lives cannot, Regan argues, be justified. If animals have moral rights, then humans are not justified in harming them for the sake of benefits to humans, no matter how great those benefits may be. Human beings can knowingly waive their rights and accept the suffering or additional risks involved in experimentation, but animals cannot. Regan's view is that the only permissible experiments on animals are those that impose no new risks on the animals involved, such as trials of new drugs on animals already suffering from currently incurable diseases.

INFLUENCE OF PHILOSOPHY ON PRACTICE

In practice, the animal rights activists of the late twentieth century drew freely on the ideas of both Singer and Regan. They often invoked the concept of moral rights, but they also commonly invoked Singer's principle of equal consideration of interests and claimed his *Animal Liberation* as their philosophical inspiration.

Although both philosophers opposed the status

quo in agriculture and science, their professional philosophical writings dramatically illustrate the distinction between rights-based and utilitarian theories of ethics and the degree to which animal rights activists could differ over specific issues. An activist thinking in utilitarian terms might endorse animal experimentation that is likely to save lives, whereas one thinking in terms of animals' rights might oppose all research, no matter how beneficial to humans. An activist thinking in utilitarian terms might endorse the humane slaughter of some animals, whereas one thinking in terms of animals' rights might oppose slaughter under all circumstances.

THE PHILOSOPHICAL RESPONSE

Just as the political successes of animal rights groups inspired the formation of groups defending various uses of animals, the attention given Singer's and Regan's work on the subject inspired opposing philosophical work. Two philosophers' works are especially noteworthy in this regard.

In 1980, Canadian philosopher Michael A. Fox published *The Case for Animal Experimentation*, the first book-length defense of animal experimentation by a philosopher. Fox's defense of experimentation turns on an anthropocentric conception of ethics. Fox argues that rights and duties apply only among individuals capable of recognizing reciprocal obligations, and that only humans are capable of this. He concludes that only human beings are full-fledged members of the moral community and that we have no duties directly to animals. He nevertheless opposes cruelty (deliberately inflicting unnecessary pain) because doing so makes us more likely to wrong our fellow human beings. Fox subsequently recanted his central argument, but his book nevertheless represents a systematic development of an argument commonly used by defenders of animal research.

A more persistent critic of animal rights philosophies was American philosopher Raymond G. Frey. In *Interests and Rights: The Case Against Animals* (1980), Frey expresses skepticism about the very usefulness of "rights" as a moral concept (Frey, like Singer, is a utilitarian), but for the sake of argument he accepts the view of rights theorists like Regan that having rights implies having desires. Frey's central argument in the book is that animals cannot have rights because they are incapable of having desires.

In defense of this claim, Frey offers a subtle, original analysis of what it means to have desires. He argues that, in order to have desires, one must be capable of entertaining various beliefs, because what distinguishes conscious desires from mere needs is their sensitivity to the individual's beliefs.

Frey argues that animals that lack language lack beliefs, because it is only sentences that can be true or false, and only creatures with language can think about a sentence being true or false. Therefore, only creatures endowed with language can have desires, and hence, only they can have moral rights. Frey concludes that neither vegetarian nor antivivisectionist conclusions can follow from a rights-based philosophy. Frey's later *Rights, Killing, and Suffering: Moral Vegetarianism and Applied Ethics* (1983) is focused specifically on moral arguments for vegetarianism, and while less original, philosophically, than his earlier book, it probably contains a version of every argument ever offered in response to ethical arguments in favor of vegetarianism, including utilitarian arguments such as Singer's.

Gary E. Varner

FURTHER READING

Fox, Michael A. "Animal Experimentation: A Philosopher's Changing Views." *Between the Species* 3, no. 2 (Spring, 1987): 55-82. Fox's recantation of his earlier argument and a sketch of the direction in which his views were evolving.

_____. *The Case for Animal Experimentation: An Evolutionary and Ethical Perspective.* Berkeley: University of California Press, 1986. A systematic defense of animal experimentation, based on an anthropocentric conception of ethics.

Frey, R. G. *Interests and Rights: The Case Against Animals.* Oxford, England: Clarendon Press, 1980. A rigorous and original analysis of key concepts leading to the conclusion that animals cannot have rights because they have no interests.

_____. *Rights, Killing, and Suffering: Moral Vegetarianism and Applied Ethics.* Oxford, England: Basil Blackwell, 1983. An eclectic critique of all the main moral arguments for vegetarianism, including both rights-based and utilitarian arguments.

Regan, Tom. *The Case for Animal Rights.* Berkeley: University of California Press, 1983. A philosophically rigorous defense of the claim that animals have moral rights, with applications to experimentation and agriculture.

Scully, Matthew. *Dominion: The Power of Man, the Suffering of Animals, and the Call to Mercy*. New York: St. Martin's Press, 2002. Defense of animal welfare; argues that assigning rights to animals is less important than simply treating them decently.

Singer, Peter. *Animal Liberation*. New York: Ecco, 2002. The bible of the animal rights movement.

_____. *Practical Ethics*. 2d ed. New York: Cambridge University Press, 1993. A rigorous introduction to applied ethics and the definitive statement of Singer's position on ethics and animals.

SEE ALSO: Animal consciousness; Animal research; Cruelty to animals; Humane Society of the United States; Moral status of animals; People for the Ethical Treatment of Animals; Sentience; Singer, Peter; Vegetarianism; Vivisection; World Society for the Protection of Animals.

Anthropological ethics

DEFINITION: Study of the moral issues raised in the course of conducting fieldwork in anthropology

TYPE OF ETHICS: Scientific ethics

SIGNIFICANCE: An ethical approach to anthropology that tries to minimize negative effects of the anthropologist's presence and behavior upon the peoples being studied.

Anthropology studies human culture and behavior primarily through the observation of participants living intimately with and observing a community. Anthropologists risk negatively affecting a community or individuals within it by their presence, actions, or reportage of information.

Anthropology originated only during the mid-nineteenth century, and its early practice betrayed its colonialist roots. Field anthropologists often were government agents sent on espionage expeditions to colonies or territories, informants typically were misled regarding the uses to which information would be put, and concern for informants often was sorely lacking. As early as 1916, Franz Boas and other prominent anthropologists had decried these abuses in print.

World War II proved to be a watershed in terms of concern about ethics in anthropology. The second half of the twentieth century saw the development of formal ethical codes for most of the major anthropological organizations, including the American Anthropological Association, the Society for Applied Anthropology, and the Association of Social Anthropologists of the Commonwealth. These codes contain a core of generally accepted principles, though controversy flourishes regarding other issues.

CORE PRINCIPLES

Formal ethical codes in anthropology emphasize the obligations of the anthropologist to the people under study, the discipline, and the sponsors of the research.

The anthropologist's greatest responsibility is to the people under study. These people are critical to the study and can be hurt by it. Furthermore, in some cases, cultural differences make people unlikely to understand fully the possible ramifications of their participation. Consequently, anthropologists must use extreme care to protect their informant-hosts.

Knowledge of the political or social structure of a community, even if it is divorced from the specifics of individual officeholders, can be used by governments and others to control, terrorize, or punish a community, and individuals should be aware of what level of risk they are taking by providing that information to anthropologists. Only if the informants find these conditions acceptable should the research continue.

The anthropologists must be prepared to withhold information if necessary to protect the people under study. Many ethnographic reports use pseudonyms or nonspecific reporting in attempts to disguise informant and community identities. Recognizing the trust placed in them, anthropologists should be very sensitive to issues of confidentiality and reveal nothing that is likely to harm the study community or its individual members.

Ethical obligations to the discipline revolve around publication. Anthropologists are obligated to publish the results of their studies, lest they become mere self-indulgent "custom collectors." In order to achieve the greater goals of anthropology, the broadest possible corpus of evidence is necessary. Clearly, falsification and distortion are intolerable.

Sponsors of ethnographic fieldwork vary greatly. Academic funding agencies sponsor much research, and they typically are sympathetic to anthropological ethics. Other funding, however, may come from private foundations or government agencies that may be unfamiliar with ethical standards or even antagonistic toward them. Project Camelot, for example, was sponsored by the Special Operations Research Office of the U.S. Army between 1964 and 1967. As described in the prospectus, which was mailed to many anthropologists and other social scientists, the goal of this project was "to predict and influence politically significant aspects of social change in the developing nations of the world," particularly Latin America. This kind of a project can place an anthropologist in an untenable position, since it may require providing information that will harm (in the anthropologist's judgment) the people under study.

While many anthropologists argue that anthropologists should never accept funding from agencies with questionable motives, ethical codes typically are less dogmatic. They stress the need for a clear agreement regarding what information is to be made available to the sponsor. Obviously, the anthropologist should reject funding if agreement cannot be reached. If agreement is reached, the anthropologist has an obligation to provide accurate, though not necessarily complete, reporting.

INTERVENTION VS. SCHOLARLY NEUTRALITY

Under the leadership of Franz Boas, early twentieth century anthropology was committed to preserving information about "traditional" societies before they were transformed by the spread of Western civilization. This led to a nonintervention ethic maintaining that anthropology should dispassionately describe and analyze societies but not try to change them.

The twentieth century, however, showed that these societies were changing in response to Western civilization and would continue to do so. An emerging cadre of applied anthropologists argued that anthropology properly should help direct this change in the manner least damaging to these societies.

Not all anthropologists, however, have accepted the tenets of applied anthropology, and critics argue that anthropological understanding is too rudimentary to permit control of cultural change. Further concern derives from the fact that most funding for applied anthropological research comes from governments that may not be particularly concerned about the welfare of the people under study; pressure placed on an anthropologist by such a sponsor can be considerable.

ISSUES OF RELATIVISM AND CULTURAL CONFLICT

In response to ethnocentrism in early anthropology, Boas and others argued for cultural relativism, the recognition that all cultures are equally valid and worthy of respect. Cultural relativism remains entrenched in anthropology, but twentieth century ethnogenocide and human rights violations have led some anthropologists to reconsider, arguing that cultures advocating these and other unaccept-

---

Preamble to the American Anthropological Association Code of Ethics

Anthropological researchers, teachers and practitioners are members of many different communities, each with its own moral rules or codes of ethics. Anthropologists have moral obligations as members of other groups, such as the family, religion, and community, as well as the profession. They also have obligations to the scholarly discipline, to the wider society and culture, and to the human species, other species, and the environment. Furthermore, fieldworkers may develop close relationships with persons or animals with whom they work, generating an additional level of ethical considerations

In a field of such complex involvements and obligations, it is inevitable that misunderstandings, conflicts, and the need to make choices among apparently incompatible values will arise. Anthropologists are responsible for grappling with such difficulties and struggling to resolve them in ways compatible with the principles stated here. The purpose of this Code is to foster discussion and education. The American Anthropological Association (AAA) does not adjudicate claims for unethical behavior.

The principles and guidelines in this Code provide the anthropologist with tools to engage in developing and maintaining an ethical framework for all anthropological work.

Source: http://www.aaanet.org/committees/ethics/ethcode.htm

able practices are not compatible with world values and must change.

Another related issue occasionally arises. The ethics of anthropology are culture-bound, closely tied to Western precepts, and they may conflict with the ethics of another society. When living in and studying a society whose ethics are very different, should anthropologists cling to their own culture's ethical standards?

"THE DELICATE BALANCE OF GOOD"

The ethical perspectives discussed above are full of contradictions. Obligations to the discipline require that studies be published fully; obligations to the people studied require that sensitive information be withheld. These and other conflicts should be resolved by reference to what Erve Chambers calls "the delicate balance of good." The anthropologist must examine the likely results of actions, assess their impact on all parties concerned, and follow the path that is most likely to lead to the best overall outcome.

Russell J. Barber

FURTHER READING

Beals, Ralph. *Politics of Social Research.* Chicago: Aldine, 1969.

Cassell, Joan. "Ethical Principles for Conducting Fieldwork." *American Anthropologist* 82 (March, 1980): 28-41.

Fluehr-Lobban, Carolyn, ed. *Ethics and the Profession of Anthropology: Dialogue for Ethically Conscious Practice.* 2d ed. Walnut Creek, Calif.: AltaMira Press, 2003.

MacClancy, Jeremy, ed. *Exotic No More: Anthropology on the Front Lines.* Chicago: University of Chicago Press, 2002.

Murphy, Michael Dean, and Agneta Johannsen. "Ethical Obligations and Federal Regulations in Ethnographic Research and Anthropological Education." *Human Organization* 49 (Summer, 1990): 127-138.

Rynkiewich, Michael, and James Spradley. *Ethics and Anthropology.* New York: John Wiley & Sons, 1976.

SEE ALSO: Colonialism and imperialism; Custom; Durkheim, Émile; Ethnocentrism; Professional ethics; Relativism; Social Darwinism; Sociobiology; Taboos.

Anthropomorphism of the divine

DEFINITION: Description of God or gods in terms of properties that are typical of human beings

TYPE OF ETHICS: Beliefs and practices

SIGNIFICANCE: The extent to which God is conceived to be similar to human beings may influence the way in which people relate to God and to one another, providing a basis for ethical systems.

Anthropomorphism is the attribution of human characteristics or properties to nonhuman beings or objects. One form of anthropomorphism that raises philosophical and ethical issues is the attribution of such features to divine beings. These may include physical properties, such as having eyes and hands; psychological properties, such as feeling sadness or anger; or cognitive or intellectual properties, such as possessing knowledge or power.

Insofar as anthropomorphic descriptions imply defects or limitations, monotheistic traditions (unlike polytheistic traditions) treat such descriptions figuratively. For example, physical properties are almost always taken to imply defects or limitations; therefore, references to "God's strong right arm" are typically taken to refer to divine power rather than divine right-handedness. Insofar as anthropomorphic descriptions do not imply defects or limitations, they are typically regarded as being literally true. Human beings typically possess some knowledge and power.

Likewise, in monotheistic traditions, God is held to be omnipotent and omniscient. Being omnipotent entails having power and being omniscient entails having knowledge, so describing God in these terms is anthropomorphic in that it ascribes knowledge and power to God. Because the terms "omnipotent" and "omniscient" mean that there is no limit to God's power and knowledge, these concepts are taken literally. Typically, having psychological properties is thought to involve limitations and defects, either directly or by way of implication that having psychological properties also means that one has physical properties, although this implication is sometimes denied. Unless it is denied, descriptions of God as having psychological properties are also taken figuratively. The fact that having psychological properties also implies having intellectual or cognitive properties typically is not taken to imply any defect or limitation.

Keith E. Yandell
Updated by the editors

SEE ALSO: Animal consciousness; Divine command theory; Ethical monotheism; God.

Anti-Semitism

DEFINITION: Hostility and ill-feeling directed toward Jews

TYPE OF ETHICS: Race and ethnicity

SIGNIFICANCE: Anti-Semitism raises questions about ethical justifications for discrimination, arguments of moral responsibility posed by non-Jews to Jews in the aftermath of the Holocaust, and ethical demands made by Jews.

Prejudice against Jews goes back to antiquity. It was widespread in Europe during the early Christian era, during the Middle Ages in Spain, during the early modern and modern eras in Europe, in the Islamic Arab world, and in the modern Americas. As Christianity emerged as the official religion of the Roman Empire, accusations that Jews murdered Christians to obtain blood for ritual purposes intensified, as did their portrayal as the "executioners of Jesus." Jews were gradually excluded from society.

In regions under Islamic rulers, Jews, like Christians, were often treated as second-class subjects. Nevertheless, they were regarded by the Qurʾān as "people of the book," as they possessed scriptures of their own. Because Islam spread by physical conquest, rather than by spiritual propaganda, it did not seek, initially at least, to conquer souls as early Christianity had done. At first, it displayed greater tolerance for practitioners of other monotheistic religions.

EUROPEAN ANTI-SEMITISM

Anti-Semitism was prevalent in Europe throughout the Middle Ages. It surfaced in the form of expulsions, inquisitions, and massacres. In addition, the catechism taught to Christian children instilled in their minds negative attitudes toward the "execution-

ers of Christ." The Enlightenment, on the other hand, offered mixed signals to the Jews. That era's philosophers did not constitute a cohesive and unified force in their attitudes toward anti-Semitism. An important segment of philosophers denounced Christianity in the name of deism (natural religion) and promoted secularism and tolerance toward members of ethnic minorities. This view made deists natural allies of Jews, who were victims of Christian intolerance. However, while prominent philosophers such as Gotthold Ephraim Lessing, Jean-Jacques Rousseau, and Montesquieu advocated tolerance of Jews, other philosophers, equally influential albeit secular, did not hesitate to criticize "Jewish particularisms."

Although the French Revolution of 1789 gave Jews political rights through emancipation, France did not remain devoid of anti-Semitic manifestations. During the 1880's, Edouard Drumont, the anti-Semitic author of a best-selling book on Jews in France; clerical-royalist right-wingers; and socialists perpetuated the myth that the Jews secretly controlled world governments and international money markets. The Dreyfus affair of the 1890's—in which Alfred Dreyfus, a Jewish French army officer, was falsely accused of spying for Germany—revealed the extent of French Jewry's vulnerability to prejudice. The trials and legal battles that finally led to Dreyfus's vindication nearly destroyed France's Third Republic.

Anti-Semitism was strongest in Eastern Europe, especially in the Russian Empire before World War I. There were violent pogroms in Odessa during the 1880's and in Kishinev during the early 1900's. After the creation of the Soviet Union, Joseph Stalin's regime both practiced and condoned anti-Semitism, from the 1930's through the early 1950's.

Anti-Semitism reached its peak under Germany's Third Reich, which lasted from 1933 until the end of World War II, in 1945. Under Adolf Hitler, Jews were depicted as the corrupters of society and blamed for Germany's misfortunes after World War I. Coupled with the ascendance of European fascism and aryanization policies, these trends culminated in the Holocaust. The application of racial anti-Semitism and the laws limiting the representation of Jews in the professions in Germany, Italy, France, and North Africa revealed anti-Semitism at its worst.

Zionism was a movement that emerged during the 1890's and contributed to the creation of a Jewish national home in Palestine and, eventually, the state of Israel. Anti-Semitism and anti-Zionism gained momentum in the Arab world during the 1930's and 1940's. After Israel became an independent nation in 1948, each war that Israel fought with neighboring Arab countries was followed by anti-Jewish and anti-Zionist backlashes in the Arab nations and expulsions of Jewish communities, pogroms, and allegations that Jews controlled Western governments, using Zionism and Israel to realize its own colonialist goals.

ETHICAL PRINCIPLES

According to Wendy Stallard Flory, the legitimation of anti-Semitism (and racism in general) may be the result of a selfish attempt to inflate one's self-worth, and often to compensate for one's feelings of inadequacy, by choosing to treat differentness as though it were a moral failing. For example, any attempt to identify specific personality traits of Jews as "reasons" for prejudice is an attempt to rationalize the real motive: a narrowmindedness and defensive refusal to allow others the fundamental human right to be judged as individuals. Anti-Semitism, then, does not necessarily begin with hatred, but with selfish impulses to reinforce one's sense of worth at the expense of others.

After World War II, there emerged the "sense of guilt" phenomenon, evinced by Europeans. This was especially evident in France and Germany. During the war, while France was divided into a German-occupied zone and a French-ruled zone based at Vichy, the French police who collaborated with the Germans rounded up tens of thousands of Jews and had them transferred them to Nazi concentration camps. Following the liberation of France in 1944, a sense of guilt struck the French people. It has been argued that although during the postwar years French Jews were the targets of anti-Semitic activity, the perpetrators were punished and their organizations forced to disband. This is in marked contrast to the political climate and ethos of the 1930's and 1940's, when anti-Semitism was embraced by the state or disregarded.

The German sense of postwar guilt was even more pronounced. The German Federal Republic, under Konrad Adenauer's leadership, sought to convince the world that Germany was stepping out of Adolf Hitler's shadow. During the 1950's, Germany

moved from the one extreme of depicting the Jews as morally and physically inferior to the other extreme of philo-Semitism. This tendency included idolizing all things Jewish. Every Jewish child, it seemed, was a genius, and every Jewish woman seemed to be regarded as a beautiful "Jewess."

Offering German financial and material reparations to Israel, to Holocaust survivors and their families, and to Jewish institutions was reciprocated with moral restitution. In the case of the latter, the Germans were eager to promote the image of the "new" Germany.

As time passed, however, the notion that the Jews and the Germans shared a collective memory of the Holocaust began to fade. Furthermore, a new generation of Germans that emerged in the 1960's and 1970's included elements that equated Israel's policies toward the Palestinian Arabs with pre-1945 Germany's treatment of its own Jewish citizens. Gradually, latent German anti-Semitism was transformed into overt political anti-Zionism.

As a Third World/Soviet bloc-sponsored United Nations resolution equating Zionism with racism in 1974 won the approval of young leftist Germans, the denial of the realities of the Holocaust by right-wing forces during the 1980's and 1990's began penetrating academic circles in parts of the Western world. To Jewish thinkers and scholars, the Holocaust and Zionism are the two central reasons for the emergence of the state of Israel, which is seen as the cradle for Jews in need of refuge. Israeli scholars in particular are profoundly concerned with what they regard as a growing myth of "German innocence" about the Holocaust. The fear was that these developments could set the stage for the rise, legitimation, and institutionalization of large-scale anti-Semitism in the future.

ANTI-SEMITISM IN THE TWENTY-FIRST CENTURY

At the beginning of the new millennium, a rise in anti-Semitic sentiment was evident throughout the world, but particularly in Europe. In 2003 Nathan Sharansky argued that anti-Semitism was reaching heights not seen since the Holocaust. Anti-Semitic propaganda and horrific acts of violence toward Jews and Israeli supporters were becoming common in many European countries. Terrorism, although a problem through the previous several decades, was taking on a new face, caring not for the identity of its victims, while citing Israeli policy toward Palestinians in the Middle East as its justification.

Although most terrorist attacks against Jews are committed inside Israel, countries elsewhere have fallen prey to the onslaught of violence. Israel's Deputy Foreign Minister Rabbi Michael Melchior pointed out that during 2000 and 2001 nearly two hundred anti-Semitic incidents occurred in France alone and that the situation was growing serious in Belgium as well. Meanwhile, the governments of these countries were generally downplaying the seriousness of anti-Semitism within their borders.

Vandalism of synagogues and Jewish schools along with assaults of Jewish people were becoming commonplace throughout the world. One of the most horrific acts of modern terrorism was the attack on the World Trade Center in New York City on September 11, 2001. Once the instinctual, anti-Semitic attempt to blame the Jews for the attacks had subsided, much of the world held the United States responsible because of its foreign policies, particularly its support of Israel, whose treatment of Palestinians is commonly known through Europe as the "modern Nazism."

Michael M. Laskier
Updated by Robert Whitman

FURTHER READING

Birnbaum, Pierre. *Jewish Destinies: Citizenship, State, and Community in Modern France.* New York: Hill & Wang, 2000. Examination of issues concerning minority communities in France and their place in society.

Goldhagen, Daniel Jonah. *A Moral Reckoning: The Role of the Catholic Church in the Holocaust and Its Unfulfilled Duty of Repair.* New York: Random House, 2002. Study of the role that the Roman Catholic Church played in the Holocaust.

Reuter Ltd. *The Israeli-Palestinian Conflict: Crisis in the Middle East.* Upper Saddle River, N.J.: Prentice Hall, 2003. Examination of the modern Middle East conflict by a team of journalists.

Sharansky, Nathan. "Fighting the Same Battle from Europe to the Mideast." *Jerusalem Post* (August, 2003).

Weiss, John. *The Politics of Hate: Anti-Semitism, History, and the Holocaust in Modern Europe.* Chicago: Ivan R. Dee, 2003. History of anti-Semitism throughout Europe offering comparisons of the anti-Semitic views that ultimately led to the Holocaust.

Wistrich, Robert S. *Anti-Semitism: The Longest Hatred.* New York: Pantheon Books, 1991. History of anti-Semitism, from its earliest historical roots through the twentieth century, by a distinguished historian. Wistrich also edited *Anti-Zionism and Antisemitism in the Contemporary World.* (New York: New York University Press, 1990).

SEE ALSO: Genocide, cultural; Genocide, frustration-aggression theory of; Genocide and democide; Hate crime and hate speech; Hitler, Adolf; Holocaust; Israeli-Palestinian conflict; Jackson, Jesse; Jewish ethics; Nazism; Pogroms; Racial prejudice.

Antitrust legislation

DEFINITION: Federal laws that define certain actions of large companies, or combinations of companies, as illegal because they give the actors too much power in the marketplace

TYPE OF ETHICS: Business and labor ethics

SIGNIFICANCE: Antitrust laws attempt to create marketplace conditions that are fair to all buyers and sellers.

Federal antitrust legislation regulates the behavior of American businesses, in particular large businesses and business combinations. The combinations that are regulated can take the form of agreements, formal contracts, and legally identified organizations such as trusts and holding companies. Through antitrust legislation, governments attempt to balance the goal of business, which is to control the market to earn profits, with the goal of providing all marketplace actors, including both buyers and sellers, with the opportunity to compete. By definition, noncapitalist societies do not have antitrust laws, since firms are owned and operated by the state rather than competing independently.

Federal law generally recognizes that size confers benefits on firms and can be beneficial to society, as in the case of "economies of scale." A firm with economies of scale can produce its product at a lower cost per unit the more it produces. The law also recognizes, however, that the existence of a large firm may make operation more difficult for smaller firms and that consumers generally benefit from having a choice among sellers. These considerations prompt the drafting of antitrust legislation.

HISTORY

One of the earliest pieces of antitrust legislation was the Statute of Monopolies, which was enacted in England in 1623. It stated that monopolies, or single firms producing a given product in a certain market, were not allowed. That law had many exceptions but did set the precedent for later antitrust legislation.

The United States developed the most comprehensive antitrust legislation in the world. The Sherman Antitrust Act of 1890 represented the first clear statement that the U.S. government disapproved of abuse of market power by large firms. That law led to an era of "trust busting" over the next thirty years, particularly under the administration of Theodore Roosevelt. The Sherman Antitrust Act was somewhat vague in its prohibitions. The Clayton Antitrust Act of 1914 clarified the actions that would be subject to antitrust prosecution.

Two major cases in 1911 clarified judicial thinking on antitrust policy. The U.S. Supreme Court ordered the breakup of Standard Oil and of the American Tobacco Company. The Court established the "rule of reason" approach, whereby the law proscribed only actions that were "unreasonable" restraints of trade. The Court ruled that largeness of a company was not necessarily an offense but that both of those companies had used the power associated with their size in "unreasonable" ways.

ANTITRUST ISSUES

The history of antitrust legislation, both in the United States and elsewhere in the world, has been uneven. Actions prohibited at one time have later been allowed, and actions that were legal have been prohibited. In general, the law has come to specify particular actions that are not allowed and has clarified the conditions under which various actions are allowed.

In the United States, the Robinson-Patman Act of 1936 specified types of price discrimination that are illegal. Price discrimination consists of setting different prices for different customers when those differences are not justified by differences in the cost of serving customers. Price discrimination prevents each customer from being offered the best price on a product.

Other laws and regulations concern tie-in sales, in which a consumer has to buy one product before being allowed to buy another; resale price maintenance, whereby a manufacturer forces distributors to charge a minimum price; and base-point pricing, under which competitors agree to set prices as if their products were delivered from a given "base point," thereby not using a location that allows lower transportation costs to offer lower prices to customers. The law covers both "horizontal" business combinations (those at the same stage of production or sale, such as a retailer forming a contract with or acquiring another retailer) and "vertical" combinations (those at different stages of production, such as a manufacturer buying a retail outlet for its product).

ETHICAL PRINCIPLES

The most basic goal of antitrust legislation is to create a marketplace that produces the best results for society. Economists define an "efficient" marketplace as one that produces a given product at the least cost. In this sense of "good" results, a large firm can benefit society if it operates under economies of scale. A firm that has control over its customers because it is the only seller (or only one of a few sellers), however, may not pass those cost advantages on to customers. Antitrust legislation attempts to prevent that possibility. Some firms with economies of scale are allowed to operate under regulation by the government. Examples include telephone companies, cable television operators, and electric companies.

Most market economies respect freedom. Freedoms, however, can conflict. The freedom of businesses to get together and agree to charge the same price conflicts with the freedom of consumers to shop around to find the lowest price. Most governments that have consciously considered the issue have ruled in favor of the consumer, to at least some extent. The Sherman Antitrust Act, for example, outlaws every "contract, combination . . . or conspiracy" in restraint of trade. That means that firms are not allowed to hinder competition among themselves. Antitrust legislation seeks to clarify which actions constitute hindrances of competition.

A. J. Sobczak

FURTHER READING

Armentano, Dominick T. *Antitrust and Monopoly: Anatomy of a Policy Failure.* New York: Wiley, 1982.

Hahn, Robert W., ed. *High-Stakes Antitrust: The Last Hurrah?* Washington, D.C.: AEI-Brookings Joint Center for Regulatory Studies, 2003.

Howard, Marshall C. *Antitrust and Trade Regulation: Selected Issues and Case Studies.* Englewood Cliffs, N.J.: Prentice-Hall, 1983.

Kintner, Earl W., and Mark R. Joelson. *An International Antitrust Primer.* New York: Macmillan, 1974.

Low, Richard E. *Modern Economic Organization.* Homewood, Ill.: Richard D. Irwin, 1970.

Posner, Richard A. *Antitrust Law: An Economic Perspective.* Chicago: University of Chicago Press, 1976.

Sherman, Roger. *Antitrust Policies and Issues.* Reading, Mass.: Addison-Wesley, 1978.

Wells, Wyatt. *Antitrust and the Formation of the Postwar World.* New York: Columbia University Press, 2002.

Whitney, Simon N. *Antitrust Policies: American Experience in Twenty Industries.* New York: Twentieth Century Fund, 1958.

SEE ALSO: Business ethics; Capitalism; Communism; Economics; Monopoly; Price fixing; Profit economy.

Apartheid

DEFINITION: Policy of racial segregation nurtured by political and economic discrimination against non-European groups in the Republic of South Africa

DATE: 1948-1991

TYPE OF ETHICS: Race and ethnicity

SIGNIFICANCE: South Africa's apartheid system promoted racial discrimination and segregation based on the color of one's skin.

An Afrikaans word, *apartheid* means "apartness" or "separateness." It was the core of a political, economic, and social system in which nonwhite citizens of South Africa were denied power and control over their lives by the country's white minority, through an elaborate network of legislation and custom. From 1948 to 1991, successive national governments created a closed, compartmentalized society in which each racial group had prescribed living areas, kinds of work, levels of wages, and distinctive educational systems.

In order to enforce the segregation policies of the government after the Afrikaner-dominated National Party came to power in 1949, various major apartheid laws were put into place. Among others, the Prohibition of Mixed Marriages Act (1949) and the Immorality Act (1950) made all marriages and sexual relations between whites and other races illegal, and the Group Areas Act (1950) set aside specific areas for the exclusive occupancy of each racial group, with powers to forcibly remove African tenants (most of whom were confined to the so-called "homelands") from specified areas. In addition, all Africans over age sixteen were required to be fingerprinted and to carry a passbook. Opposition to any of these laws was crushed by means of the Suppression of Communism Act (1950) and the Internal Security Act (1982), both of which were enforced by a ruthless police force and an omnipresent secret police.

MORAL ISSUES

While cases of racial discrimination occur in other parts of the world, it was the systematic, official, and legalistic character of apartheid that made South Africa unique. South Africa was divided hierarchically into four major population groups, based primarily on shades of skin color. White South Africa (15.6 percent) occupied the top rank, followed by mixed-race "Coloureds" (9.7 percent) and Asians (2.7 percent) in the middle, and black Africans (72 percent) at the bottom. As the figures indicate, apartheid was imposed by a minority on the majority, which questioned the legitimacy of its authority. According to the political philosophy of the French philosopher Jean-Jacques Rousseau, governments should derive their just powers from the consent of the governed. Thus, from Rousseau's perspective, a minority government without the consent of the majority of the governed would be difficult to justify through moral laws. Besides, as the most inclusive form of government, majority rule is more likely to have regard for the rights and best interests of most people than is a minority government. In the light of

Apartheid Time Line

Time	Event
1652	Dutch expedition founds Cape Town, establishing the first permanent white settlement in South Africa.
1820	Five thousand British colonists arrive at Port Elisabeth.
1836	To escape from British rule, thousands of Afrikaner (Boer) farmers move inland from the Cape during the Great Trek, spreading throughout what would become the nation of South Africa.
1899-1902	Great Britain defeats the Afrikaner republics in the South African (Boer) War.
1910	Union of South Africa is created, merging British colonies with the former Afrikaner republics, form one country for the first time.
1912	First major African nationalist movement, the African National Congress (ANC), is founded.
1948	Predominantly Afrikaner Nationalist Party is elected to power and makes the segregation policy of apartheid the official policy of the Union.
1958	Some African nationalists break away from the ANC to form the Pan-African Congress (PAC).
1960	Sharpeville massacre leaves sixty-nine Africans dead and many wounded during a nonviolent protest against government pass laws. Government bans the ANC and PAC, and African nationalists begin taking up the tactics of sabotage and guerilla war.
1961	South Africa becomes a republic and withdraws from the British Commonwealth of Nations. African nationalist leader Albert John Luthuli wins the Nobel Peace Prize.
1964	Nelson Mandela, a prominent ANC leader, is sentenced to life imprisonment.
1976	Government police kill a number of young demonstrators in Soweto during a protest begun by schoolchildren against the imposition of Afrikaans as a medium of expression.
1983	United Democratic Front (UDF), a multiracial anti-apartheid movement, is formed.
1984	Constitutional reform establishes a three-parliament system that allows for token participation of Indians and Coloureds (mixed-race South Africans) in decision making but excludes blacks. Bishop Desmond Tutu wins the Nobel Peace Prize.
1991	Government releases Mandela from prison and lifts ban on nationalist movements.
1993	Africans are allowed to participate in the voting process for the first time in South African history.
1994	South Africa's first fully democratic election lifts the ANC to power and makes Mandela president of the republic.

these precepts, the South African system of apartheid may be described as both illegal and immoral—a view held by much of the outside world.

Over the years apartheid was in effect, supporters and detractors of this system existed both within and without South Africa. Black resistance to the policy was championed by such nationalist movements as the African National Congress (ANC), the Pan-African Congress (PAC), the United Democratic Front (UDF), the Azania Peoples Organization (AZAPO), and the Black Consciousness Movement, whose leader, Stephen Biko, died in detention under suspicious circumstances and was later shown to have been murdered by government agents.

Despite the government's cruelty, immorality, and absurdity, the Afrikaner-dominated Dutch Re-

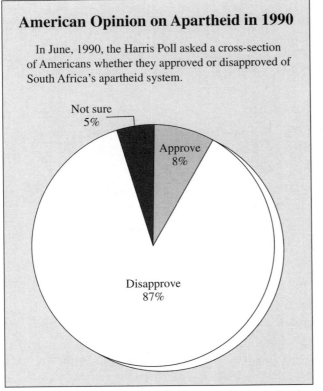

American Opinion on Apartheid in 1990

In June, 1990, the Harris Poll asked a cross-section of Americans whether they approved or disapproved of South Africa's apartheid system.

Not sure
5%

Approve
8%

Disapprove
87%

Source: Roper Center for Public Opinion Research. Figures are based on responses of 1,254 adults.

formed Church of South Africa, to a large extent, supported the government and condoned its policies. The church's theological position was that equality between blacks and whites involves a misapprehension of the fact that God made people into different races and nations. The more liberal English-speaking churches and prominent African nationalist leaders were at various times victims of the wrath of the government, which was expressed through bannings, withdrawal of passports or visas, deportations, and often imprisonment. Nelson Mandela, one of the leading members of the ANC and South Africa's first postapartheid president, was incarcerated for almost three decades as a political prisoner.

Over the course of the 1990s, apartheid was gradually dismantled. The last Afrikaner president, Frederick W. de Klerk, repealed much of the social legislation underpinning the apartheid system in 1990-1991. In April of 1994, elections open to all races were held for the first time. A new constitution went into effect, and Mandela and the ANC were placed in power. The social and economic damage done by apartheid had still to be addressed, but the formal legal system of discrimination and racial inequality was utterly dissolved.

Olusoji A. Akomolafe
Updated by the editors

FURTHER READING

Davis, Hunt R., Jr., ed. *Apartheid Unravels.* Gainesville: University of Florida Press, 1991.

Grundy, Kenneth W. *South Africa: Domestic Crisis and Global Challenge.* Boulder, Colo.: Westview Press, 1991.

McCuen, Gary E. *The Apartheid Reader.* Hudson, Wis.: Author, 1986.

Mandela, Nelson. *No Easy Walk to Freedom.* Edited and introduction by Ato Quayson. Foreword by Oliver Tambo. New York: Penguin, 2002.

Motlhabi, Mokgethi B. G. *Challenge to Apartheid: Toward a Morally Defensible Strategy.* Grand Rapids, Mich.: Wm. B. Eerdmans, 1988.

Terreblanche, Sampie. *A History of Inequality in South Africa, 1652-2002.* Pietermaritzburg, South Africa: University of Natal Press, 2002.

Walshe, Peter. *The Rise of African Nationalism in South Africa: The African National Congress, 1912-1952.* Berkeley: University of California Press, 1971.

SEE ALSO: Freedom of expression; Mandela, Nelson; Racism; Segregation; South Africa's Truth and Reconciliation Commission; Tutu, Desmond.

Apologizing for past wrongs

DEFINITION: Statements of regret and responsibility made defined groups of people for historical wrong-doing

TYPE OF ETHICS: Race and ethnicity

SIGNIFICANCE: Throughout history, some races and nations have dominated and exploited other races and nations, and many people have argued that groups of those who have suffered at the hands of other groups deserve apologies.

The issue of ethical obligations to apologize to groups of people is an exceptionally complicated one. In cases such as the historical enslavement of African Americans or the past colonizing of many parts of the world by Western European nations, the supposed wrongdoers are not individual persons but groups or governments. In the case of groups, such as racial or national groups, it is not clear that any individual members can act as representatives in order to make apologies.

The ethical responsibilities of governments are somewhat more securely based on reason than are the responsibilities of nations or races. In 1988, when the United States government apologized to Japanese Americans for interning them during World War II, it was expressing responsibility and regret for its own past actions. Similarly, claims that the United States should apologize for slavery are not based on the idea that all Americans or any particular group of Americans created or maintained slavery, but on the government's official acceptance of the institution in judicial and legislative actions. Nevertheless, governmental apologies pose both practical and philosophical difficulties.

Modern governments represent their citizens and act in the names of their citizens. If a majority of citizens do not feel responsibility and regret, their political leaders will be reluctant to make an unpopular apology. Moreover, any apology a government were to make in such a situation might have little meaning. Further, even though an apology does not necessarily lead to compensation, it is an admission of responsibility and may be a first step toward payment of damages. Political activist Jesse Jackson has argued, along these lines, that an apology for slavery would not be meaningful unless it were followed by efforts

In August, 1988, U.S. president Ronald Reagan signed into law the Civil Liberties Act, which authorized the payment of cash reparations to Japanese Americans who had been interned during World War II. (Ronald Reagan Library)

to repair the social damage of the heritage of slavery. The issue of apologies, to groups such as African Americans or Native Americans, is therefore linked to the issue of reparations. Some, such as Jackson and author Roy L. Brooks, oppose apologies for historical wrongs unless these also involve some form of payment of reparations. Others oppose apologies precisely because they believe that these will open the way for redistribution of wealth or services to groups that have been historically victimized.

Finally, it may be debatable exactly who the victims are in many cases of historical injustice. When the U.S. government apologized to Japanese Americans interned during World War II, most of the internees themselves were still alive. The situation of African Americans is less clear. Many commentators argue that the direct victims of slavery have long been dead. In response, authors such as sociologist Joe Feagin maintain that living African Americans are nevertheless victims of slavery because they continue to suffer social disadvantages created by it.

Carl L. Bankston III

FURTHER READING

Feagin, Joe R. *Racist America: Roots, Current Realities, and Future Reparations.* New York: Routledge, 2000.

Robinson, Randall. *The Debt: What America Owes to Blacks.* New York: Dutton, 2000.

SEE ALSO: Collective guilt; Developing world; Jackson, Jesse; Japanese American internment; Racism; Reparations for past social wrongs; Slavery; South Africa's Truth and Reconciliation Commission.

Apology

IDENTIFICATION: Book by Plato (c. 427-347 B.C.E.)
DATE: *Apologia Sōkratous*, wr. between 399 and 390 B.C.E.
TYPE OF ETHICS: Politico-economic ethics
SIGNIFICANCE: In his account of his mentor Socrates' decision to accept an unjust judicial verdict, Plato's book portrays a conflict between personal ethical values and the judicial system of the Western world's first democracy.

It is important to understand two things about the *Apology*. First, it is Plato's dramatic, eyewitness account of the apology of his friend and teacher. Second, this apology is not an expression of regret for an error but a defense of Socrates' conduct and whole way of life.

In 399 B.C.E., the seventy-year-old Athenian citizen Socrates went on trial for allegedly disrespecting the gods and corrupting the youth of Athens. It is clear both from the text of the *Apology* itself and from external evidence that Socrates' real "crime" was severely embarrassing important people in the Greek city-state by his habit of questioning them in public places with respect to matters about which they claimed expertise, exposing their true ignorance, and providing amusement to the onlookers who gathered to see the supposed experts confounded. Socrates regularly insisted that he was merely an earnest philosophical inquirer after truth asking those who presumably knew. In this insistence he was only half sincere. He was pursuing the truth, but he knew that his shallow interlocutors would fall victim to his superior logical and rhetorical skill. He chose the questioning method as an effective way of developing and presenting his own philosophy—a method later adopted in written form by Plato.

SOCRATES' DEFENSE

Plato's account, the first literary "courtroom drama," purports to be a verbatim record of Socrates' defense. Far from corrupting youth by promoting atheism or belief in strange gods (for his accusers have vacillated on this point), Socrates explains that he philosophizes in obedience to a divine command. Since he has carried out his divine mission in a quasi-public way, Socrates feels obliged to explain why he has never made an effort to serve the state as an adviser, since the state would seem to need all the wisdom it can find. Here, he raises an ethical issue with which many later thinkers have struggled, including, notably, Sir Thomas More in his *Utopia* (1516).

Socrates has proclaimed himself a loyal Athenian. Why should not a loyal citizen use his primary talent for the benefit of the state? He argues that if he had gone into political life he would have long since "perished." The struggle for the right in his mind required "a private station and not a public one." He once held the office of senator and discovered that his efforts at promoting justice were futile and in fact on one occasion nearly cost him his life. He did not fear death, he explains, but realized that neither he "nor any other man" could effectively fight for the right in a political position. He could do Athens the greatest good in a private effort to inquire into virtue and wisdom. The state would profit most from citizens schooled in this sort of inquiry. He closes his defense by leaving the decision to the jury and to God.

SOCRATES' RESPONSE

According to the rules of an Athenian trial, the jury of 501 men must decide his guilt or innocence by majority vote. Socrates' opponents have taken every advantage possible of the prevailing prejudice against him as a "clever" intellectual skilled in "making the weaker case appear stronger." Such prejudice no doubt contributed substantially to what seems in retrospect a misguided verdict. Having been found guilty in a close vote, Socrates exercises his right to propose an alternative to the death penalty requested by the prosecution as a preliminary to the jury's choice of one of the two proposed punishments. When asked for his counter-sentence, Socrates banteringly suggests that he should be honored, not punished, but finally proposes a token fine that he then raises somewhat at the urging of his friends, whose expressions of dismay actually interrupt the proceedings. They realize that he is in effect condemning himself to death, but Socrates considers that as an unjustly convicted man he should not be punished at all.

To have offered the kind of alternative his enemies undoubtedly expected—exile—would have amounted to a repudiation of his vocation. He is aware that nowhere else would he be free to exercise this vocation as he has been doing in Athens for years before his enemies' conspiracy to silence him. To save his own life by leaving Athens or by accepting some other compromise such as agreeing to cease philosophizing would contradict the values that he has spent that life to date elucidating. Were he to compromise those values, he would give his shabby accusers a moral victory. Instead, he guarantees that his memory will be revered and—what surely is more important to him—that his work in pursuit of the truth will endure, thanks especially to Plato's decision to publish it. (Socrates himself never transcribed his dialogues.)

After the jury's inevitable vote in favor of the prosecution's request for the death penalty, Socrates rebukes his judges as men more interested in escaping the pressure of the accusers than in giving an account of their own lives. He believes that he is going to "another world where they do not put a man to death for asking questions." He does have a final request of them, however: that they punish his own still young sons if they show more interest in riches or anything else than in virtue. In this way, the judges can still do him and his sons justice.

Robert P. Ellis

FURTHER READING

Friedlander, Paul. *Plato.* Translated by Hans Meyerhoff. New York: Harper & Row, 1964.

Plato. "Apology." In *The Collected Dialogues of Plato*, edited by Edith Hamilton and Huntington Cairns. 1961. Reprint. Princeton, N.J.: Princeton University Press, 1984.

Reeve, C. D. C. *Socrates in the "Apology": An Essay on Plato's Apology of Socrates.* Indianapolis: Hackett, 1989.

Shorey, Paul. *What Plato Said.* Chicago: University of Chicago Press, 1978.

Strycker, E. de. *Plato's Apology of Socrates: A Literary and Philosophical Study with a Running Commentary.* Edited by S. R. Slings. New York: E. J. Brill, 1994.

Taylor, A. E. *Plato: The Man and His Work.* New York: Dover, 2001.

SEE ALSO: Capital punishment; Democracy; Freedom of expression; Justice; Plato; Platonic ethics; Socrates.

Applied ethics

DEFINITION: Application of ethical and moral principles to particular disciplines and situations

TYPE OF ETHICS: Theory of ethics

SIGNIFICANCE: The ways in which ethics are applied in a society help to determine the nature of that society.

There is no consensus regarding the meaning of the term "applied ethics." Some people hold that applied ethics involves methods of enforcing ethics. Others view it as a kind of ethics that is used up over a period of time. In academic circles, however, there is an increasing tendency to view applied ethics as the large body of codes that define desirable action and are required to conduct normal human affairs. These codes may produce rules that come to be regarded as formal, legal ethics.

Every kind of ethics has been applied at one time or another. A prehistoric cave dweller, for example, who hit his wife or child with a club and afterward felt sorry and vowed to refrain from beating members of his family was developing an applied ethic. Such a rule remained in the realm of applied ethics until some prophet wrote it down or until a chieftain or legislative body adopted it as a law.

Many varieties of ethics have developed by themselves. As modern civilization developed, new applied ethics were developed for specific vocations or specific households. When Harriet Beecher Stowe wrote *Uncle Tom's Cabin*, she helped many men and women to understand that slavery was unethical because of its effects on men, women, and children; in doing so, she introduced an applied ethic. Later, a constitutional amendment changed this applied ethic to a permanent, legal ethic.

In the United States, many professional and vocational groups have established rules for conducting business. The rules that they devised probably grew out of applied ethics. Groups endeavor to secure in their work certain rules that initially do not have the force of law but can certainly be described as applied ethics. These ethics are used as the basis for determining which rules should become rules of law.

PUBLISHED ETHICAL CODES

There are many published codes of applied ethical rules. Of these, one of the most important to the business and financial world is the code of the American Institute of Certified Public Accountants. This code requires members of the institute to exercise "professional and verbal judgments" in all accounting activities. In addition, they are told to maintain the "public trust" and "professionalism." They are also required to maintain "integrity and objectivity" and to avoid discreditable acts and advertising. Unfortunately, however, these rules have been violated fairly frequently. Suits brought chiefly by shareholders who found that their clients' stocks had been overvalued by auditors have resulted in multimillion-dollar fines being levied against auditing firms. The federal government and some state governments have at times tried to support rules of accounting ethics.

The American Association of Advertising Agencies created its own applied ethics banning false or exaggerated statements, recognizing an obligation to clients and the public. The standards also forbid unfair competition practices, disclaiming "suggestions or pictures offensive to public decency." Advertising agencies "should not knowingly fail to fulfill all lawful contracted commitments with media."

It should be noted that industry efforts to inculcate standards of applied ethics in the areas of accounting and advertising have not been fully realized. Governmental efforts have helped to move these applied ethics closer to the status of formal ethics.

The Direct Marketing Association enjoins its members to use applied ethics in advertising, solicitations, and special offers. The association may be moving toward developing an ethical code.

The American Institute of Architects has a code that has probably had some effect on the field of architecture. This code includes general obligations regarding knowledge and skill as well as specific obligations to the public, including involvement in civic activities and public interest service. Obligations to clients, to the profession, and to colleagues are fully outlined.

OTHER PROFESSIONAL CODES

Applied ethics have not yet taken an adequate step toward genuine ethical values in the business world. New efforts are being made, however, to institute better ethics in business management. The federal government and the Business Roundtable, a thoughtful group of chief executive officers of large corporations, have recommended that corporations adopt written codes of conduct and well-defined corporate policies regarding executive compensation, fair play for employees, freedom of expression, and product quality. Corporate codes may do more than any other single policy to humanize business ethics.

The American Association of Engineering Societies has prepared a Model Guide for Professional Conduct that includes a number of applied ethics. Engineers are to be honest and truthful in presenting information and to consider the consequences of their work and the social issues that are pertinent to it. They should let affected parties know about potential conflicts of interest.

The American Society for Public Administration has prepared a code for its members to use. This code is not now actively promoted by the association, however, and for that reason the likelihood of developing new ethics is slim.

Bar associations have worked hard to enforce ethical considerations; Bar examinations include ethical questions, and law schools, some of them reluctantly, offer courses in legal ethics. State officials who regulate legal practice, however, note that ethical violations still occur all too often. A former worker on the staff of the Los Angeles County Bar Association, for example, has observed that there seems to be a trend toward light treatment of unethical behavior.

Similar problems arise in medical practice, and efforts to enforce ethical standards are sometimes hampered by problems of short staffing of local medical associations. Most physicians are relatively committed to following ethical standards, particularly because medical students are required, upon graduation, to take the Hippocratic oath, which dates from the fifth century B.C.E., a period during which the Greeks were greatly interested in ethics.

BANKING

Banking is so basic in modern capitalist democracies that one would expect to see a host of applied ethics studies in the field. Banking has been so much a creation of politics, however, that there has been little discussion of banking ethics. President Andrew Jackson probably made a basic ethical mistake when he killed the Second National Bank and its equalizing rules. President Woodrow Wilson tried to remedy Jackson's mistake with the establishment of the Federal Reserve System in 1914.

Clearly, banks that hold deposits of public funds should invest those funds carefully and pay interest to depositors. Some banks have maintained adequate resources, but many others have sought growth by endangering depositors' funds. Government regulators have tried to establish ethics of safe banking but have been unsuccessful in developing applied ethics.

The American Bankers Association has had a tough job outlining applied ethical demands on an industry that at times has helped to improve American economic life and at other times has caused the bankrupting of innocent citizens. The Revised Code of Ethics of 1985 lists basic ethical values that are needed in banking as well as a number of practices that should help to ensure the safety of depositors' money. It is unlikely, however, that the code places sufficient emphasis on establishing ethics that relate to maintaining bank safety. A more appropriate system of banking ethics must be developed, and this is particularly true of the savings and loan branch of the banking industry.

George C. S. Benson

FURTHER READING

Chadwick, Ruth, ed. *Encyclopedia of Applied Ethics*. 4 vols. San Diego, Calif.: Academic Press, 1998.

Chadwick, Ruth, and Doris Schroeder, eds. *Applied Ethics: Critical Concepts in Philosophy*. New York: Routledge, 2002.

Demarco, Joseph P., and Richard M. Fox, eds. *New Directions in Ethics: The Challenge of Applied Ethics*. London: Routledge & Kegan Paul, 1986.

Gorlin, Rena. *Codes of Professional Responsibility*. Washington, D.C.: Bureau of National Affairs, 1986.

Olen, Jeffrey, and Vincent Barry. *Applying Ethics: A Text with Readings*. 4th ed. Belmont, Calif.: Wadsworth, 1992.

Rachels, James, ed. *Moral Problems: A Collection of Philosophical Essays*. 3d ed. New York: Harper & Row, 1979.

Singer, Peter, ed. *Applied Ethics*. Oxford, England: Oxford University Press, 1986.

SEE ALSO: Business ethics; Cohen, Randy; Ethical codes of organizations; Ethics; Honor systems and codes; Law; Marketing; Medical ethics; Professional ethics; Sales ethics; Theory and practice.

Arbitration

DEFINITION: Mechanism for dispute resolution—often employed as an alternative to litigation—to which parties to a given controversy voluntarily submit

TYPE OF ETHICS: Legal and judicial ethics

SIGNIFICANCE: Arbitration is part of a self-regulating process in that disputants agree to submit their disagreements to a mutually acceptable disinterested third party for settlement, rather than go through court proceedings.

Although arbitration agreements were not traditionally favored in common, or judge-made, law, in modern times arbitration has come to be viewed as an expedient, less-expensive alternative to litigation that—not incidentally—helps to ease court docket congestion. Indeed, agreements to arbitrate are now protected by statute, at both state and federal levels. Contracts, or other written agreements between parties, often include an arbitration clause, and arbitration is used to settle disputes in such contexts as labor, insurance, and commerce. Because the rules of arbitration are not legally mandated but are set by the parties concerned, the process of settling disputes by this means is more informal than that of court proceedings. Arbitration does, however, proceed in accordance with rules agreed upon in advance—often those of the American Arbitration Association, founded in 1926—and unlike less-formal proceedings, its outcome is final and is enforceable in a court of law.

Lisa Paddock

SEE ALSO: Adversary system; Jury system; National Labor Relations Act.

Hannah Arendt. (Library of Congress)

Arendt, Hannah

IDENTIFICATION: German philosopher
BORN: October 14, 1906, Hannover, Germany
DIED: December 4, 1975, New York, New York
TYPE OF ETHICS: Politico-economic ethics
SIGNIFICANCE: Hannah Arendt analyzed twentieth century totalitarianism and posited the essential conditions of a genuine political order in such works as *The Origins of Totalitarianism* (1951), *The Human Condition* (1958), *Eichmann in Jerusalem* (1963), and *On Revolution* (1963).

A student of philosophers Karl Jaspers and Martin Heidegger, Arendt, a German Jew, fled Europe for the United States in 1941. She taught at the New School for Social Research in New York City and at the University of Chicago.

Arendt claimed that, beginning with Plato, the Western tradition has tended to denigrate human action by misconstruing it as production—that is, as something fabricated by a craftsman—and by valorizing the solitary life of contemplation rather than the plural realm of interaction. As a result, the political realm of human interaction is not given intrinsic value and is misconstrued as the mere execution of rules dictated by a "master," as in the workshop of the craftsman. Ethically speaking, Arendt claimed that those who are reliable are *not* those who "hold fast" to ethical codes or formulae but those who engage in critical self-examination and dialogue. Twentieth century totalitarianism rendered individuals "superfluous" and attempted to replace critical debate with abstract ideologies. What interested Arendt were the conditions that make political life possible or impossible.

Vanessa B. Howle

SEE ALSO: Collective guilt; Dictatorship; Heidegger, Martin; Human nature; Orwell, George; Tyranny.

Aristotelian ethics

DEFINITION: Ethical system put forward by, or modeled after that of, Aristotle, primarily concerned with determining what the good life is and how to go about living it

DATE: Formulated in the fourth century B.C.E.

TYPE OF ETHICS: Theory of ethics

SIGNIFICANCE: Aristotelian ethics emphasize the moral analysis of one's overall character rather than that of particular actions one may perform. They center on the concepts of the golden mean and natural law, as well as stressing the importance of moral education.

Aristotle's ethical theory is contained in two works: the *Nicomachean Ethics* (*Ethica Nicomachea*) and the *Eudemian Ethics*. The *Nicomachean Ethics* is later and more comprehensive than the *Eudemian Ethics*, and it has been studied far more. A third book sometimes attributed to Aristotle, the *Magna Moralia*, is probably not authentic.

Aristotle's ethical theory was conditioned by his training as a biologist. He observed that every living thing tends to develop into a mature specimen of its kind that may be either healthy and flourishing or somehow stunted. His ethical theory is an attempt to describe the healthy, flourishing way of life for human beings (the "good life"). His motivation was political, since he believed that an understanding of the good life should guide lawmakers. He believed that since human beings are naturally social beings, a normal person whose natural inclinations are properly cultivated will be virtuous; hence, wrongdoing is a function of stunted development. In basing ethical behavior upon human nature (the essence of human beings), Aristotle largely founded natural law theory.

THE GOOD LIFE

Aristotle followed Greek practice in calling the good life *eudaimonia*, often translated as "happiness." He observed that people agree that happiness is an intrinsic good and that attaining happiness is the guiding directive of life; however, they disagree concerning the nature or content of the happy life.

Aristotle criticized three popular candidates (then and now) for the happy life: sensual pleasure, pursuit of honors and recognition, and money-making. He assumed that human happiness must be unique to human beings. Hence, a life of sensual pleasure cannot be happiness, since sensual pleasures derive from behaviors—eating, drinking, sex—that animals also display; that is, they are not based upon human nature. He also assumed that happiness must be achievable through one's own efforts. Hence, receiving honors cannot be happiness, since merit is not necessarily recognized; it is not "up to us." Moreover, recognition is pursued as a warrant of excellence; therefore, excellence is valued more highly than recognition even by those who esteem recognition. Aristotle dismissed the life of money-making on the ground that money is essentially a tool and therefore cannot be an end in itself.

Aristotle recognized sensual pleasure, honors, and money as concomitants of the good life but held that genuine happiness is "an activity of the soul in accordance with excellence": Happiness consists in self-development, or the positive, habitual expression or realization of potentials inherent in human nature. Since human beings are both social and rational, they possess basic potentials for moral goodness and intellectual goodness (wisdom). Aristotle held that intellectual goodness is produced by training and moral goodness by habituation. Therefore, all persons are morally and intellectually neutral at birth and are subsequently shaped by their experiences and education. Modern criticisms that media violence leads to violence in society agree with Aristotle that character is shaped rather than inborn. In this view, the notion of education is expanded to include all character-determining experiences, moral education becomes the foundation for society, and censorship may seem attractive.

Moral goodness consists of possession of the virtues, which include courage, temperance, generosity, "greatness of soul," magnanimity, response toward small honors, mildness, friendliness, truthfulness, wit, "shame," and justice. Some commentators allege that this list specifies an ideal of the Greek upper class, so that Aristotle's ethics is relativistic. Aristotle believed, however, that he had grounded his theory upon human nature, and his intent was not relativistic.

VIRTUE

A virtue is a trained disposition to express a particular emotion, through behavior, to a degree that is neither deficient nor excessive relative to a given agent in a given situation. For example, a generous rich person will donate more money than will a generous poor person. Aristotle coined the phrase "golden mean" to denote the midpoint between excess and deficiency to which virtuous actions conform. He probably arrived at this idea by analogy with Greek medical theory, according to which bodily health consists of a balance between opposite bodily states.

Aristotle held that character is fixed by repeated actions: One becomes like what done does. Hence, every virtue results from repetition of acts of the relevant sort, which train their corresponding emotions. For example, one becomes generous by, in effect, practicing to be generous through repeated instances of giving. Moral education consists in training persons to experience pleasure in doing virtuous acts and displeasure in doing vicious acts. Hence, a virtuous person will enjoy behaving well. The tie between virtuous behavior and pleasure solves the problem of motivation ("Why be moral?") to which more rationality-based theories tend to be subject, but it also invites the criticism that Aristotle's ethical theory is egoistic.

Intellectual goodness is of two kinds: practical and theoretical. Practical wisdom is knowledge for the sake of action. It enables one to discern the golden mean in particular situations. Doing so is a complex process that cannot be reduced to rules; it requires experience. The rejection of a definite method for determining right actions distances Aristotle's theory from rule-based theories as varied as Kantianism and utilitarianism. Theoretical wisdom is knowledge of basic truths of philosophy and science solely for the sake of knowledge. Aristotle held that theoretical wisdom is the noblest part of life and that the happiest life is a life of moral goodness with a large admixture of study and learning. Critics respond that study tends to isolate one from society.

Joel Wilcox

FURTHER READING

Aristotle. *Nicomachean Ethics*. Translated and edited by Roger Crisp. New York: Cambridge University Press, 2000.

Heinaman, Robert, ed. *Plato and Aristotle's Ethics*. Burlington, Vt.: Ashgate, 2003.

Hughes, Gerard J. *Routledge Philosophy Guidebook to Aristotle on Ethics*. New York: Routledge, 2001.

Kenny, Anthony. *Essays on the Aristotelian Tradition*. New York: Oxford University Press, 2001.

MacIntyre, Alasdair. *After Virtue: A Study in Moral Theory*. 2d ed. Notre Dame, Ind.: University of Notre Dame Press, 1984.

Rorty, Amélie O., ed. *Essays on Aristotle's Ethics*. Berkeley: University of California Press, 1980.

Sherman, Nancy. *The Fabric of Character*. New York: Oxford University Press, 1989.

_____, ed. *Aristotle's "Ethics": Critical Essays*. Lanham, Md.: Rowman & Littlefield, 1999.

Urmson, J. O. *Aristotle's Ethics*. New York: Basil Blackwell, 1988.

SEE ALSO: Aristotle; Character; Excellence; Golden mean; Kantian ethics; Moral education; Natural law; *Nicomachean Ethics*; Platonic ethics; Stoic ethics; Wisdom.

Aristotle

IDENTIFICATION: Greek philosopher
BORN: 384 B.C.E., Stagirus, Chalcidice, Greece
DIED: 322 B.C.E., Chalcis, Euboea, Greece
TYPE OF ETHICS: Classical history
SIGNIFICANCE: Aristotle wrote the *Nicomachean Ethics* (*Ethica Nicomachea*), the first systematic treatment of ethics in Western civilization. His definition of virtue, which combines fulfillment of function, striving for a mean between extremes, and rational control of the appetites, has influenced ethical theory for over two thousand years.

A philosopher with encyclopedic knowledge, Aristotle wrote on numerous topics, including physics, metaphysics, logic, ethics, politics, poetics, and rhetoric. In the area of ethics, his major works are the *Nicomachean Ethics*, the *Eudemian Ethics*, and the *Politics* (all written between 335 and 323 B.C.E.). He claims that the purpose of the state is to provide for the intellectual and moral development of its citizens. The *Nicomachean Ethics* is considered to contain Aristotle's mature moral theory.

THE GOOD

Aristotle begins the *Nicomachean Ethics* by claiming, "Every art and every inquiry, and similarly every action and pursuit, is thought to aim at some good; and for this reason the good has rightly been declared to be that at which all things aim." The good is what human beings are seeking. The Greek word for this goal is *eudaimonia*, which can be roughly translated as "happiness." *Eudaimonia* means much more, however, than mere transitory happiness. *Eudaimonia* can be equated with having a good spirit or with the fulfillment of function. Humans have many goals, but *eudaimonia* is that goal that is final, self-sufficient, and attainable.

Aristotle discusses the fulfillment of function in terms of a member of a species doing what is distinctive to that species. Other species share with human beings the ability to live and to experience sensation. Neither of these capabilities is unique to the human species. No other species, however, is able to reason. Therefore, when a human being is performing his distinctive function, he is using reason. Aristotle remarks that the human is potentially a rational animal. He attains *eudaimonia* only when he is actually engaged in activity according to reason. (The use of the masculine pronoun is necessary for the above discussion, since Aristotle was referring specifically to the male of the species.)

STRUCTURE OF THE SOUL

Aristotle claims that the human soul has two parts: a rational element and an irrational element. The irrational part of the soul may also be divided into two parts: the part concerned with nutrition and growth, which is shared with other living species, and the appetites, which are shared with other animal species. The rational part of the soul likewise has two divisions: One part is concerned with pure contemplation, while the other part is occupied with control of the appetites.

There are proper virtues, or excellences, which belong to each of the rational divisions of the soul. A virtue is the performing of a proper function. Intellectual virtues, such as wisdom, belong to the contemplative part of the soul; moral virtues, such as courage, belong to the part of the soul that is concerned with control of the appetites. Intellectual virtues are attained through education, whereas moral virtues are a matter of habit. One becomes courageous by repeatedly behaving courageously. According to Aristotle, it is important to behave in such a way as to develop the moral virtues.

Aristotle. (Library of Congress)

VIRTUE AS A MEAN BETWEEN EXTREMES

Aristotle claims that for many activities and ways of behavior there is an excess and a deficiency. Reason shows that the proper way of acting or being is to strive for a midpoint between these extremes. For example, cowardice is a deficiency of courage. There is also an excess of courage that may be termed rashness or foolhardiness. This is a jump-before-you-think way of behaving. Courage, the mean, is having the right amount of fearlessness so that one is neither a coward nor a fool. Reason determines midpoints such as this. These means are the virtues.

Virtue, however, is not an absolute mean. It is relative, varying from individual to individual and from time to time. Courage for one person might be cowardice for another. What one must do as a moral individual is to strive for behavior that is somewhere near the mean between the two extremes of excess and deficiency. This is often done by realizing to which extreme one is closer and aiming for the opposite extreme. This will result in the individual being closer to the mean.

RESPONSIBILITY

Aristotle claims that one is responsible for one's voluntary actions. These are actions that are not committed out of ignorance. The individual is not externally compelled and is not acting to avoid a greater evil. Therefore, if an individual, with full knowledge, freely chooses an action, he may be held morally responsible for that action. Aristotle is here departing from the Socratic/Platonic position that to know the good is to do it. Knowledge is important, but so is making the right choice. Making the right choice is an activity of the soul that is in accord with reason. Reason controls the appetites and adds to the fulfillment of man's function by choosing rightly. Furthermore, this right choice will be a mean between extremes. For the moral individual, this will become habitual behavior.

Rita C. Hinton

FURTHER READING

Aristotle. *Nicomachean Ethics.* Translated and edited by Roger Crisp. New York: Cambridge University Press, 2000.

_____. *The Politics.* Translated by Ernest Barker. Rev. ed. Introduction by R. F. Stalley. New York: Oxford University Press, 1995.

Hardie, William. *Aristotle's Ethical Theory.* 2d ed. New York: Oxford University Press, 1980.

Heinaman, Robert, ed. *Plato and Aristotle's Ethics.* Burlington, Vt.: Ashgate, 2003.

Hughes, Gerard J. *Routledge Philosophy Guidebook to Aristotle on Ethics.* New York: Routledge, 2001.

Joachim, H. H. *Aristotle: The Nicomachean Ethics: A Commentary.* Edited by D. A. Rees. Oxford, England: Clarendon Press, 1951.

MacIntyre, Alasdair. *After Virtue: A Study in Moral Theory.* 2d ed. Notre Dame, Ind.: University of Notre Dame Press, 1984.

Ross, William D. *Aristotle.* 6th ed. Introduction by John L. Ackrill. New York: Routledge, 1995.

Smith, Thomas W. *Revaluing Ethics: Aristotle's Dialectical Pedagogy.* Albany: State University of New York Press, 2001.

Urmson, J. O. *Aristotle's Ethics.* New York: Basil Blackwell, 1988.

SEE ALSO: Aristotelian ethics; Golden mean; *Nicomachean Ethics*; Responsibility; Virtue; Virtue ethics.

Arrest records

DEFINITION: Documents recording the arrests of persons charged with crimes for which they may or may not eventually be convicted

TYPE OF ETHICS: Legal and judicial ethics

SIGNIFICANCE: Having a record of prior arrests generates a strong and possibly misleading inference that a person has a propensity toward criminal behavior, so the use of such records raises independent ethical concerns that have led to restrictions on how such records can be used.

Under American criminal procedure, the level of evidence needed before an arrest can constitutionally take place is not nearly as high as that required for a criminal conviction. These distinct standards have led to different conclusions dependent on circumstance about the ethics of how arrest records are used. For example, the rules of evidence rarely allow the admission of a defendant's prior arrest records at a trial. This principle is well established, as the admission of an arrest record would be intensely prejudicial to an accused person. Indeed, the law even places significant restrictions on the admissibility of a defendant's prior convictions at trial. However, the records of some convictions are admissible when a court determines that the value of admitting such evidence outweighs its prejudicial effect to the accused.

The retention and use of arrest records by law enforcement agencies, however, is often viewed as ethical as an aid to law enforcement. This may sometimes be true even when a charge against an accused is dismissed or even if the accused is subsequently exonerated of wrongdoing at trial. A conclusion reached in these circumstances is that a legal arrest, while rarely rising to evidence admissible at trial, may be useful to authorities investigating similar crimes, and material gathered as a result of the arrest, including photographs of the accused, can be shown to subsequent victims of a crime as a means of investigating the crime.

Despite these legal restrictions, prior arrests may still impair the ability of arrestees to obtain professional licenses or apply for employment. Some applications for admission to the bar, for example, require that applicant disclose any prior arrests. This raises independent ethical concerns because arrested persons retain the presumption of innocence under

American law. Moreover, it is well established that certain ethnic groups are subject to a disproportionate number of unjust arrests, and the use of such arrests in other contexts perpetuates and intensifies the consequences of such arrests.

Robert Rubinson

FURTHER READING

Leipold, Andrew D. "The Problem of the Innocent, Acquitted Defendant." *Northwestern University Law Review* 94 (2000): 1297-1356.

Park, Roger C., David P. Leonard, and Stephen H. Goldberg. *Evidence Law: A Student's Guide to the Law of Evidence as Applied in American Trials*. St. Paul, Minn.: West Publishing, 1998.

SEE ALSO: Accused, rights of; Attorney-client privilege; Erroneous convictions; Information access; *Miranda v. Arizona*; Police brutality; Scottsboro case; Three-strikes laws.

Art

DEFINITION: Human creative expression

TYPE OF ETHICS: Arts and censorship

SIGNIFICANCE: Issues of censorship and artistic freedom are raised by artistic production in virtually all human societies. In addition, some philosophers and artists believe that aesthetic creation is in itself a profoundly moral activity.

The earliest discussion of the relationship of art and ethics goes back to the Greek classical period, when philosophers such as Socrates, Plato, and Aristotle considered art and its goodness and importance in relationship to the search for truth and virtue in human life. Socrates believed that the beautiful is that which both serves a good purpose and is useful, therefore uniting the beautiful and the good. He viewed the arts as being only incidental to other concerns, however, not of primary importance. Plato considered the relationship of art to nature and truth, and its resulting ethical function, which led him to reject art. Art was imitation and therefore was not good because imitations were untrue. Plato loved beauty but hated painting. Aristotle separated ethics and art by describing goodness as present in human conduct and beauty as existing in a motionless state. He saw moral good and aesthetic value as separate considerations.

In the modern understanding, art—specifically, the fine arts of drawing and painting, sculpting, dance, music, theater, photography, and creative writing—is the act and process of creating. Works of art are the creations of the artistic process. It is the contact of the artist's work—the painting, dance, musical composition, and so forth—with the lives of other people that creates an ethical responsibility for the artist. Such contact invites participation by persons other than the artist in the artistic product, and it is this participation that implies an ethical responsibility.

ARTISTIC FREEDOM

Artistic freedom is publicly determined by ethical values; art as a creative act is independent of morality, but the artist as a human being is not. By making artwork public, artists involve themselves in the lives of others, necessarily resulting in accountability for the contributions they are making to their lives. While artists are not responsible for every effect their work may have, tension can exist between their aesthetic interests and the moral interests of the community.

The relationship of art and ethics is different from the relationship of art and aesthetics in that ethics deals with the concepts of what is good or bad, while aesthetics deals with the concepts of what is beautiful or ugly. These relationships are different yet closely related, because ethics raises questions of morality and propriety and aesthetics helps judge the aims and values of art: Is the end product beneficial for human life? Does it elevate the human spirit? Does the work of art respect the common good in intellect and conscience?

Answers to these questions involve the public in the role of censor when ethical standards are violated by the artist. Public censorship and self-censorship can determine the success or failure of a work of art but not the success or failure of the artistic process.

It is generally not subject matter but the manner of its treatment that causes art to be subject to moral ethical considerations. The very nature of art requires complete artistic freedom for the artist in order to "create," to bring about something new that is highly personal and unique. To impose limits on the creative process often stymies the goal of the process. Many people believe that art in itself is amoral, that the process cannot be subjected to ethical judgment because of its very nature. It is, however, the result of this process, the creative work of art, that is subject to ethical judgment. Moral value is judged by its contribution to the richness of human experience. Is it honest and fair-minded as well as aesthetically pleasing? Does it elevate the human spirit?

The issues of artistic freedom and artistic responsibility and the subordination of one to the other are at the heart of art and ethics. Using sensitivity, imagination, and inspiration, it is the responsibility of the artist to nourish the human spirit and express human emotion. Certain types of subject matter, such as nudity, cultural social taboos, religious concepts, and sexual perversion, can be difficult for the general public to accept. Art that utilizes such subjects is often subject to ethical examination and/or censorship.

The issues of forgery, plagiarism, and honest business practices are also important to the relationship of art and ethics. Professional artistic standards in the modern world require that works of art be original if presented as such and that ethical business standards apply to the marketing of works of art.

The relationship of art and ethics touches the lives of all artists who share their work with others. The artist is often on the edge of cultural and societal changes, supporting as well as challenging traditional and modern ethical standards, broadening and enriching the human experience.

Diane Van Noord

FURTHER READING

Barasch, Moshe. *Theories of Art: From Plato to Winckelman.* New York: New York University Press, 1985.

Benjamin, Walter. "The Work of Art in the Age of Mechanical Reproduction." In *Illuminations*, edited by Hannah Arendt. Translated by Harry Zorn. London: Pimlico, 1999.

Eldridge, Richard. *The Persistence of Romanticism: Essays in Philosophy and Literature.* New York: Cambridge University Press, 2001.

Haapala, Arto, and Oiva Kuisma, eds. *Aesthetic Experience and the Ethical Dimension: Essays on Moral Problems in Aesthetics.* Helsinki: Philosophical Society of Finland, 2003.

Hygen, Johan B. *Morality and the Muses.* Translated by Harris E. Kaasa. Minneapolis, Minn.: Augsburg, 1965.

McMahon, A. Philip. *Preface to an American Philosophy of Art.* Port Washington, N.Y.: Kennikat Press, 1968.

Marcuse, Herbert. *The Aesthetic Dimension: Toward a Critique of Marxist Aesthetics.* Boston: Beacon Press, 1978.

Maritain, Jacques. *The Responsibility of the Artist.* New York: Scribner, 1960.

Taylor, Harold. *Art and the Intellect.* Garden City, N.Y.: Doubleday, 1960.

Tolstoy, Leo. *What Is Art?* Translated by Aylmer Maude. Introduction by Vincent Tomas. Indianapolis: Hackett, 1996.

SEE ALSO: Art and public policy; Book banning; Censorship; Christian ethics; Golden mean; *Index librorum prohibitorum*; Mapplethorpe, Robert; Plagiarism.

Art and public policy

DEFINITION: Relationship between artistic freedom of expression and governmental and public policies and attitudes

TYPE OF ETHICS: Arts and censorship

SIGNIFICANCE: Public funding of the arts raises issues of freedom of speech, cultural bias, and appropriate uses of taxpayer money.

The legislation creating the National Endowment for the Arts (NEA) and the National Endowment for the Humanities (NEH), passed by the U.S. Congress in 1965, maintained that "it is necessary and appropriate for the federal government to help create and sustain not only a climate encouraging freedom of thought, imagination, and inquiry, but also the material conditions facilitating the release of this creative talent." In a speech at Amherst two years earlier, President John F. Kennedy had pledged support for artistic achievement, stating, "I look forward to an America which commands respect not only for its strength but for its civilization as well."

THE ARTS AND AMERICAN CULTURE

During the 1960's, there was widespread agreement across the United States that the time had come for federal, state, and local governments to subsidize the arts; however, the notion that public funds could properly be spent on art was never universally embraced. Traditionally, in the fabric of American life, the arts were considered marginal. Puritan contempt for artistry outlived colonial times. Among the grievances held against the British by Boston patriots during the 1770's was that the soldiers of King George III staged plays. The antiobscenity campaigns of Anthony Comstock and others in the nineteenth century masked profound mistrust of artists, art, and free expression. Until Franklin D. Roosevelt's Works Progress Administration created programs to get artists off the relief roles, government support for the arts was restricted to funding for military bands, statuary in public spaces, and adornment of public buildings.

The National Endowment for the Arts, resulting from years of lobbying by arts organizations, was hailed as a wise first step toward cultural democracy. The endowment immediately contributed to a flowering of the arts at the local level, nudging state arts councils into being and fostering unprecedented attention to arts education. After President Richard M. Nixon came to power in 1969, however, his NEA Chairperson Nancy Hanks set about increasing the endowment's funding by favoring well-heeled elitist institutions such as symphony orchestras and large urban museums. The endowment began to back away from individual artists and small arts organizations. By 1981, when President Ronald Reagan took office, there was a serious movement to relegate funding for the arts to the private sector. This was thwarted by pressure from major arts institutions, and the endowment survived with some cuts.

CULTURE WARS

During Reagan's administration, powerful forces began to use the "immorality" of the arts as a rallying point for fund-raising and political gain. The failure of any meaningful public arts education ensured that much contemporary art would remain incomprehensible to the masses and that isolated examples of publicly supported art works that were difficult, heterodox, or sexually explicit could offend people whose previous exposure to art was minimal. The propaganda of the religious right exploited the belief that art was at best a frill and at worst a cause of moral turpitude and treason. A typical advertisement from Pat Robertson's Christian Coalition asked members of Congress: "Do you want to face the voters with the charge that you are wasting their hard-earned money to promote sodomy, child pornography, and attacks on Jesus Christ?"

Within the U.S. Congress, the most powerful adversary of the arts was North Carolina senator Jesse Helms, a former television personality who was given to taking the University of North Carolina to task for the teaching of such "filth" as Andrew Marvell's 1650 poem "To His Coy Mistress." In 1989, outraged by an NEA-supported exhibit of Robert Mapplethorpe's occasionally homoerotic photographs, Helms, a conservative Republican, attached to NEA funding legislation an amendment forbidding the funding of "obscene or indecent materials," work that "denigrates the objects or beliefs of a particular religion or nonreligion," or work that denigrates particular persons "on the basis of race, creed, sex, handicap, age, or national origin."

This Helms Amendment was stripped away from the appropriations bill by the House of Representatives, but its language was reflected in a pledge the NEA began to require of its grantees, who were asked to sign statements promising not to use NEA money to create anything obscene. Interpreted as a loyalty oath that exercised prior restraint on artistic expression, the antiobscenity pledge sparked an uproar. More than thirty grant recipients, including Joseph Papp of the New York Shakespeare Festival, refused to sign; some artists sued. The pledge was quietly retired at the end of the 1990 fiscal year. Congress, however, soon augmented the agency's enabling legislation with a clause stating that NEA-supported art must reflect "general standards of decency and respect for the diverse beliefs and values of the American public." Although blandly worded, the clause cast a wide net and had an insidious effect on grant-making policy.

From 1989 through the 1990's, a succession of subsidized artists and arts organizations were effectively demonized by right-wing activists, both secular and religious. In response, President George Bush's appointee as NEA chairman, John Frohnmayer, and his successor, Anne-Imelda Radice, preemptively vetoed a number of grants that had been approved by peer panels. The artists most typically affected were gay men, lesbians, feminists, AIDS activists, and members of racial minorities: Robert Mapplethorpe, Andres Serrano, David Wojnarowicz, Todd Haynes, Mel Chin, Marlon Riggs, Kiki Smith, and many others. At the heart of this cultural strife was enmity between those who saw the NEA as custodian to a Eurocentrist tradition and those who believed that the NEA should nurture art at the grassroots level, acknowledging the diverse cultures that constitute the United States. The real issue was a clash of incompatible American dreams. In this context, concern for "your hard-earned tax dollars" was disingenuous.

Defunded performance artists Karen Finley, Tim Miller, Holly Hughes, and John Fleck—the "NEA Four," whose concerns included sexual issues—fought back by suing to reclaim their fellowships. After receiving out-of-court restitution of grant money in 1993, the NEA Four continued litigation in order to challenge the arts agency's "decency and respect" clause, which they viewed as an unconstitutionally vague measure that facilitated viewpoint discrimination.

In 1993, when Democratic president Bill Clinton selected Jane Alexander to replace Radice as chair of the NEA, many believed the public-funding debate was over. A respected actress, Alexander was the first working artist to head the NEA; it was assumed that she would bring vision and integrity to the role of NEA chair. However, during Alexander's tenure, the Republican-dominated 104th Congress, led by House Speaker Newt Gingrich, sought aggressively to eliminate "socialistic" government services. In 1994, threatened with draconian cuts or extinction, the NEA's governing body, the National Council on the Arts, began preemptively vetoing grants awarded by peer panels in various disciplines, targeting anything conservatives could use as propaganda.

When Alexander resigned in 1997, the NEA's budget had been reduced to $99.5 million from its 1993 appropriation of $176 million. The agency's spending power had dipped below its late 1970's lev-

Anticensorship demonstrators march in Cincinnati to protest the trial of the city's Contemporary Arts Center directors, who were charged with obscenity for staging an exhibition of Robert Mapplethorpe's homoerotic photographs in 1989. (AP/Wide World Photos)

els. Awards to individual artists had been eliminated in all but a few literary categories. The NEA had been restructured in a way that placed more emphasis on its administrative role in funding state, jurisdictional, and regional cultural agencies.

Meanwhile, the NEA Four's legal initiative, *Finley v. National Endowment for the Arts*, made its way through the judicial system. When lower courts ruled in favor of the artists, the Clinton administration appealed the case at every turn. In 1998, it reached the U.S. Supreme Court. To the dismay of many arts professionals and First Amendment advocates, the William Rehnquist court upheld the NEA's "decency and respect" clause. Writing for the majority, Justice Sandra Day O'Connor interpreted the clause as "merely hortatory" language that "stops well short of an absolute restriction."

In a rigorous dissent, Justice David Souter said the proviso "should be struck down on its face." He declared its language "substantially overbroad," with "significant power to chill artistic production." Souter noted that the high court was, in effect, giving the NEA permission to practice viewpoint discrimination, and he asserted that "the government has wholly failed to explain why the statute should be afforded an exemption from the fundamental rule of the First Amendment that viewpoint discrimination in the exercise of public authority over expressive activity is unconstitutional. . . . "

Once the decency clause had obtained the Supreme Court's imprimatur, oversight of artistic content by public officials became more overt. Following the *Finley v. National Endowment for the Arts* ruling, the best-known local censorship imbroglio took place in New York City in 1999. That year, Mayor Rudolph Giuliani targeted the Brooklyn Museum over an exhibit including Anglo-Nigerian artist Chris Ofili's iridescent, stylized painting of an African "Holy Virgin Mary." The work involved a lump of elephant dung, an African symbol of fertility and renewal that Giuliani interpreted as blasphemous. Failing to obtain court approval for shutting down the show or freezing the museum's city funding, the mayor eventually revived New York's dormant Cultural Advisory Commission and redirected its mission toward decency issues.

Most arts advocates consider such machinations superfluous. Institutions dependent in part upon government subsidy almost always play it safe. In the case of the NEA, its yearly per capita expenditure on "controversial" art was, in fact, infinitesimal. In 1992, when the agency was near its budgetary peak, the combined budgets of the National Endowments for the Arts and Humanities added up to about 0.024 percent of the total federal budget. In 2002, thanks to his skill at distancing the NEA from creation of art, the new chairman, William J. Ivey of the Country Music Foundation, who succeeded Jane Alexander, managed to obtain an NEA budget of $115.7 million—far below its appropriations during the first Bush administration. At the beginning of the twenty-first century, the United States government continued to spend less on the arts than any other Western industrialized nation.

At the start of the new century, the future of public arts funding hinged on whose vision of the United States will prevail, and on the availability of arts education. Former arts administrator Edward Arian had assessed the struggle in his 1989 book, *The Unfulfilled Promise*: "The stakes in the contest are high. The right to artistic experience cannot be separated from the quality of life for every citizen, the opportunity for full self-development for every citizen, and the creation of the open and tolerant personality that constitutes the underpinning of a democratic society."

James D'Entremont

FURTHER READING

Alexander, Jane. *Command Performance: An Actress in the Theater of Politics*. New York: Da Capo Press, 2001.

Arian, Edward. *The Unfulfilled Promise: Public Subsidy of the Arts in America*. Philadelphia: Temple University Press, 1989.

Binkiewicz, Donna M. *Federalizing the Muse: United States Arts Policy and the National Endowment for the Arts, 1965-1980*. Chapel Hill: University of North Carolina Press, 2004.

Bolton, Richard, ed. *Culture Wars: Documents from Recent Controversies in the Arts*. New York: New Press, 1992.

Dowley, Jennifer, and Nancy Princenthal. *A Creative Legacy: A History of the National Endowment for the Arts Visual Artists' Fellowship Program*. Introduction by Bill Ivey. New York: Harry N. Abrams, 2001.

Frohnmayer, John. *Leaving Town Alive: Confessions*

of an Arts Warrior. Boston: Houghton Mifflin, 1993.

Heins, Marjorie. *Sex, Sin, and Blasphemy: A Guide to America's Censorship War.* New York: New Press, 1993.

Zeigler, Joseph Wesley. *Arts in Crisis: The National Endowment for the Arts Versus America.* Chicago: Chicago Review Press, 1994.

SEE ALSO: Art; Censorship; Mapplethorpe, Robert; Motion picture ratings systems; Song lyrics.

The Art of War

IDENTIFICATION: Book attributed to Sunzi (fl. c. 500 B.C.E.)

DATE: *Sunzi Bingfa*, c. 500 B.C.E.; English translation, 1910

TYPE OF ETHICS: Military ethics

SIGNIFICANCE: *The Art of War* provided the theoretical and strategic basis for the way in which war was waged by East Asian countries for many centuries.

According to Sunzi (also known as Sun Tzu), a state should not begin a war unless definite advantages are foreseen; indeed, aggressive war should be avoided unless the situation is absolutely critical and no alternative exists. In determining whether war should be waged, questions should be raised regarding not only its moral basis but also season and weather, the kind of terrain to be traversed, the qualities necessary to a competent commander, and army organization and discipline. Success also depends on the internal harmony (dao) of the state; without such harmony, the state's efforts in war will fail. One should never engage in a protracted war, which is likely to result in military defeat and heavy financial deficit.

In waging war, deception is the key to success and attacks should always be conducted according to a coherent strategy. Indeed, supreme military excellence consists of breaking the enemy's resistance without fighting. The best tactics involve blocking the enemy's plans. The worst tactics involve besieging walled cities and fighting in mountains. The best strategy is always a balancing of the possibilities for victory. The good commander places himself in an invulnerable position and then watches for a favorable opportunity to defeat the enemy. Good tactics involve varying the concentration and division of forces. No one should attempt to wage war without knowing the topography of the territory involved. Above all, if a general fails to acquaint himself with the character of the enemy, whatever he does will lead to ruin. What enables a general to employ stratagems and deception is his knowledge of the enemy. Such information can be obtained only by means of espionage. Captured spies should be well treated and should be turned into defectors and double agents.

SEE ALSO: Just war theory; Limited war; Military ethics; War.

Artificial intelligence

DEFINITION: Electronic processes that simulate human thinking

DATE: Earliest developments began around 1945

TYPE OF ETHICS: Scientific ethics

SIGNIFICANCE: Artificial intelligence research is creating increasingly complex, computer-generated processes that are increasingly affecting the lives of humans. Because of this development, human beings must address the ethical behavior of such machines and the possible ethical treatment of future thinking machines.

Secret research in British and U.S. military labs during World War II spawned the age of modern digital computers. The house-sized machines of that era performed vast number of computations at speeds no human could match. Soon, however, researchers sought to build machines that did more than compute numbers. Their goal was to create artificial intelligence (AI), electronic processes that simulate human thought patterns.

During the late 1940's, the English mathematician and computer pioneer Alan Turing was the first scientist to suggest that the key to creating artificial intelligence lay in developing advanced software, not more advanced hardware. From that moment, computer labs around the world began investing increasing resources in software development. As a result, AI software is everywhere. Online shopping, voice recognition systems, robotic probes that search Mars for sign of life, automated climate-controlled "intelligent" buildings, and "smart" credit cards are all made possible by advances in artificial intelligence. Researchers have also developed "expert systems," or software programs that replicate human decision-making processes to aid corporations in marketing, research, costing, management, and billing operations. AI systems work quickly and consistently, and they eliminate much of the tedium and drudgery of modern work. Coupled with the power of the Internet, they also give human beings astounding personal power in the privacy of their own homes.

BEHAVIOR OF ARTIFICIAL INTELLIGENCE MACHINES

Artificial intelligence is, however, also provoking concern. Critics argue that too little research is going into addressing the question of how the machines themselves should behave. Some ethicists argue that AI systems that function automatically and independently of human control pose great dangers. Because AI systems lack the ability to emulate human empathy, compassion, and wisdom, they have no ability to use discretion over when to act. Also troubling to ethicists are AI systems programmed with malicious intent that can release confidential information, steal from bank accounts, and disrupt communication and transportation systems. Virulent computer viruses—a malicious form of artificial intelligence—already create havoc on the Internet worldwide. Artificial intelligence offers such tantalizing prospects in weaponry that by the early twenty-first century military organizations were pouring billions of dollars into creating software designed to disrupt the daily operations of modern nations and cause widespread misery, deprivation, and death.

Many ethical questions arise over the use of modern "smart weapons." By 2004, several nations possessed a host of AI-based missiles, bombs, and electronic monitoring systems, programmed to detect enemy targets and automatically attack them, often without human intervention. Enabling machines, and not humans, to decide whether to inflict death upon human beings strikes many thinkers as morally and ethically repugnant. By distancing humans from the killing, artificial intelligence may also entice them to ignore their moral responsibilities. Moreover, argue critics, when human beings are fighting in a war, they

often experience profound abhorrence over killing other human beings and may thus be moved to stop further bloodshed. By contrast, AI weaponry may be programmed to continue killing with cold, mechanical efficiency, without compunctions.

In addition, the absence of human beings from the decision making of waging war might trigger the loss of innocent lives when a smart weapon errs. Such was the case in July, 1988, when an American warship, the USS *Vincennes*, destroyed an Iranian passenger jet flying over the Persian Gulf and killed 290 civilians. The mishap occurred when the ship's electronic detection system on the *Vincennes* incorrectly profiled the Iranian aircraft as a warplane and alerted its crew to launch a missile attack.

WHEN ARTIFICIAL INTELLIGENCE BECOMES SELF-AWARE

Smart weapons and similar forms of rules-following technologies are often called "soft" artificial intelligence, as they are not truly independent, intelligent agents capable of reason or any form of true human thought. Some researchers, however, believe it is simply a matter of time until researchers produce "hard" artificial intelligence—artificial intelligence that is truly alive, or at least appears to be. Computer entities already exist that imitate biologic systems. They move, reproduce, consume other computer-generated entities, and react to external stimuli. Advanced synthetic thinking systems also exit. Deep Blue—an advanced AI system—now plays chess well enough to defeat a human world-class master.

Some researchers also predict that before the middle of the twenty-first century advanced AI systems will be more than high-tech problem solvers. They may also become conscious, or semi-conscious, of their own mental states. If and when that develop occurs, will such machines be entitled to ethical treatment from humans? Will artificial beings deserve civil rights or due process of law? Who should decide such questions? Will AI systems themselves be designed to evaluate ethical questions? Some ethicists suggest that if machines ever do become aware of their own existence, they should be included in the growing rights movement, which bestows rights on animals and other living things that are not conscious, such as plants and ecosystems.

Skeptics, such as philosopher John Searle of the University of California, dismiss such concerns.

They argue that there is a marked difference between machines that appear to think and machines that really do create intelligence. Machines may be programmed to respond in human ways, but only actual human beings can reflect intelligently on what they are experiencing. Some critics also suggest that emotion is a necessary ingredient of intelligence—something that artificial intelligence lacks. Moreover, they ask, does artificial intelligence have needs? A psyche?

Nonetheless, some ethicists envision a near future when AI systems will interact with human brains. Some speculate that nanotechnology will make possible electronic replicas of human brains. In such an event, it could be theoretically possible to implant a memory chip with an electronic copy of the mind of a deceased person into the consciousness of a living person and create an after-death existence. Some observers believe that AI systems may one day even surpass human beings in intelligence. In fact, philosopher Nick Bostron at Oxford University believes that super-intelligent machines will be the last invention humans ever need to make.

ETHICAL PRECAUTIONS

Although ethicists can only speculate about the future of artificial intelligence, they do offer some practical suggestions. Ethical safeguards, for example, might be programmed in soft AI systems to protect privacy and reduce automated decision making. Hard AI systems, however, would require more complex programs that impart a deep, universal understanding of ethics that benefit both human and machines. Otherwise, as some futurists warn, the possibility of a super-intelligent sociopathic machine may someday be realized. Other ethicists wonder if artificial intelligence should be allowed to evolve its own ethics, as humans have done. Perhaps, they suggest, artificial intelligence could develop ethics superior to those of humans.

Finally, some thinkers wonder if humans ought to be creating life at all, and whether Earth really needs another highly developed intelligence. They also point out that if super-intelligent artificial intelligence ever emerges, it may be so profoundly different from what is predicted that all ethical questions now being asked will become irrelevant.

John M. Dunn

FURTHER READING

Bentley, Peter J. *Digital Biology: How Nature Is Transforming Our Technology and Our Lives.* New York: Simon & Schuster, 2001.

Gershenfeld, Neil. *When Things Start to Think.* New York: Henry Holt, 1999.

Grand, Steve. *Creation: Life and How to Make It.* Cambridge, Mass.: Harvard University Press, 2000.

Hogan, James P. *Mind Matters: Exploring the World of Artificial Intelligence.* New York: Ballantine, 1997.

Kurzweil, Ray. *The Age of Spiritual Machines: When Computers Exceed Human Intelligence.* New York: Viking, 1999.

Menzel, Peter, and Faith D'Alvisio. *Robosapiens: Evolution of a New Species.* Cambridge, Mass.: MIT Press, 2000.

Mulhall, Douglas. *Our Molecular Future: How Nanotechnology, Robotics, Genetics, and Artificial Intelligence Will Transform Our World.* Amherst, N.Y.: Prometheus Books. 2002.

SEE ALSO: Computer misuse; Computer technology; Exploitation; Robotics; Sentience; Technology.

Asceticism

DEFINITION: The theory and practice of using self-discipline to gain self-mastery, usually in order to fulfill religious or spiritual ideals

TYPE OF ETHICS: Religious ethics

SIGNIFICANCE: Ascetical practices include the cultivation of virtue and the performance of good works. In addition, increased virtue and ethical conduct contribute to greater mastery of self, the immediate objective of ascetical practice.

Although popularly associated with extreme forms of bodily penance such as the wearing of hair shirts or self-flagellation, asceticism in its broadest sense refers to practices of self-discipline designed to benefit body and mind and to gain self-mastery. Even today, people modify their lifestyles and make use of practices to care for body, mind, and spirit. Physical exercise routines, special diets, meditation, and relaxation techniques are examples of modern ascetical practices.

Traditionally, ascetical practices have been linked to religious or spiritual goals. Ascetical self-mastery has been sought in order to achieve salvation, expiate individual or communal guilt, or imitate the example of a divine figure. In its positive expression, asceticism has taken the form of the practice of virtues—such as patience, forgiveness, or generosity—to benefit others. Ascetical practices remove personal limitations so that a person is less egoistic and better able to serve others.

Asceticism is a feature of the major religious and philosophical traditions. The term "asceticism" is derived from the Greek word *askesis*, meaning "athleticism" or "athletic training." The Christian apostle Paul of Tarsus likens the renunciation that Christians practice to gain eternal life to the discipline that prepares athletes to win a perishable trophy. The earliest records of ascetical thought are found in the Upaniṣads, written between 800-400 B.C.E. in India. They urge the wise person to practice austerities, or *tapas*, in order to apprehend the Cosmic Self, the unmanifest source and ground of creation.

JUDAISM, CHRISTIANITY, AND ISLAM

The earliest Jewish thought valued asceticism little, limiting ascetical practices to the fasting and sexual abstinence required by the divine commandments. In later Jewish thought, an awareness of individual and communal guilt led believers to acts of penance and expiation for sin. In the aftermath of the expulsion of the Jews from Spain in 1492, ethical and ascetical practice fused with mystical thought. This fusion continues to influence Jewish ethical teaching. It can be summarized as follows: Every action in accord with the divine commandments and every ethical deed provides a way for each Jew to help bring redemption to the Jewish nation and the world.

Christian asceticism takes the example of Jesus' life as its model for ascetical practice. Jesus did the will of his Heavenly Father in his life of teaching and service and in his death by crucifixion. Christians follow his example by crucifying their selfish desires and sinful inclinations. They accept suffering in imitation of Jesus' suffering. Leaders of the Protestant Reformation attacked asceticism because salvation is God's free gift and cannot be merited by good works. In response Catholic teaching maintains that although salvation is a gift, the good Christian freely chooses to grow in unity with Jesus by trying to live and die as he did.

Muḥammad, the founder of Islam in the seventh century, stressed the need for asceticism. Prayer and fasting are two of the Five Pillars of the Faith central to Islamic teaching. Many ascetical practices are associated with Sufism, the mystical movement in Islam. These include cleansing one's heart through the constant remembrance of God and through restraining the breath in the recitation of one's prayers. A clean heart brings conformity to the will of God, the basis of right action in Islam.

HINDUISM AND BUDDHISM

The traditional structure of Hindu life sets aside the last two of four stages in life for ascetical practices and spiritual development. While the individual is engaged in worldly affairs, the performance of social duties is emphasized and every aspect of life is governed by elaborate codes of behavior. After supporting a family, serving the community, and accomplishing the worldly aims of life, the householder is freed from those responsibilities to devote the rest of life to gaining *moksha*, or liberation, union with the transcendental Ground of Being. By setting aside a certain time in life for spiritual development, Hinduism makes asceticism an established part of life while guaranteeing that the needs of family and society are also met.

Buddha advocated moderation in ascetical practice. The Eightfold Path of Buddhism sets forth the ethical conduct and ascetical practices necessary to gain nirvana, a state of absolute consciousness. Buddhist asceticism demands discipline, psychological control, and selflessness in order to develop compassion, the supreme virtue according to the Buddhist tradition. Certain livelihoods, such as the manufacture of weapons and the butchering and sale of meat, are considered illegitimate in Buddhist societies because they violate the rule of compassion.

MODERN ASCETICISM

Asceticism has fallen out of favor because of its association in the past with philosophies that condemned the body and matter. The forms of physical torture some ascetics chose to discipline their bodies disgust most modern people. Asceticism has come to be advocated on much more positive grounds. Discipline can aid in gathering and focusing personal energy in a culture that distracts its members in countless ways. Quiet reflection can help a person locate negative cultural conditioning in order to confront it. Spiritual discipline can intensify and concentrate awareness in order to help one make sound choices in life. Asceticism means having the power to choose. Choice is essential for ethical conduct. Bodily and spiritual discipline not only benefit body and mind but also contribute to ethical decision making by increasing a person's options.

Evelyn Toft

FURTHER READING

Dan, Joseph. *Jewish Mysticism and Jewish Ethics.* Seattle: University of Washington Press, 1986.

Huxley, Aldous. *The Perennial Philosophy.* London: Triad Grafton, 1985.

Miles, Margaret R. *Fullness of Life: Historical Foundations for a New Asceticism.* Philadelphia: Westminster Press, 1981.

Nietzsche, Friedrich. *On the Genealogy of Morals.* Edited and translated by Walter Kaufmann. New York: Vintage Books, 1967.

Valiuddin, Mir. *Contemplative Disciplines in Sufism.* London: East-West Publications, 1980.

Wimbush, Vincent L., and Richard Valantasis, eds. *Asceticism.* New York: Oxford University Press, 2002.

SEE ALSO: Buddha; Jesus Christ; Mysticism; Schopenhauer, Arthur.

Aśoka

IDENTIFICATION: Early Indian emperor
BORN: c. 302 B.C.E., India
DIED: c. 230 B.C.E., India
TYPE OF ETHICS: Religious ethics
SIGNIFICANCE: Aśoka unified India and promoted the spread of Buddhism. He redefined Buddhist ethics as they relate to statecraft.

The emperor of India from approximately 270 to 230 B.C.E., Aśoka is known to posterity through the rock and pillar inscriptions that he left across the Indian subcontinent and through various Buddhist chronicles. Aśoka, who was the grandson of Chandragupta, was the third monarch of the Maurya Dynasty. From his capital at Pataliputra (modern Patna), he governed the largest Indian empire that had existed up to that time.

Aśoka converted to Buddhism after a particularly bloody campaign to win the territory of Kalinga (modern Orissa). He is said to have been so distraught over the sufferings caused by war that he renounced violence as a tool of statecraft. The central concept in his political philosophy was *dhamma* (Pali; Sanskrit, dharma), a Buddhist and Hindu concept that, in one of its meanings, referred to a kind of civic morality.

Aśokan reforms, which have been valorized by Buddhists throughout history, included social services such as free medical aid and the development of rest houses for travelers. He also promoted vegetarianism, enacting laws that restricted animal sacrifices and limited butchering and hunting.

Although Aśoka was said to have given up military imperialism, the expansion of his influence continued, this time through *dhamma-vijaya*, or "moral conquest." This idea of winning over one's enemies by dint of sheer moral superiority is echoed in Mohandas K. Gandhi's twentieth century notion of *satyagraha*, or the "victory of truth."

Although much about Aśoka is wrapped up in legend, it is clear that he attempted to rule in a way that no other Indian ruler had attempted. He developed a concept of citizenship that was broader than those of the caste and local loyalties to which people had adhered before his rule. The modern symbol of India, four lions facing the four directions, is derived from the capital of one of Aśoka's famous pillars.

Cynthia Keppley Mahmood

SEE ALSO: Akbar the Great; Buddhist ethics; Citizenship; Hindu ethics.

Assassination

DEFINITION: Killing, often by stealth, of persons prominent in government, religion, or culture, usually for the purpose of effecting political or social change
TYPE OF ETHICS: Politico-economic ethics
SIGNIFICANCE: Whether and under what circumstances assassination is ever morally justified has

perplexed ethicists for centuries, as has the search for practical and morally permissible methods of combating terroristic assassination.

Assassination, which is as old as history, arose at least in part from the lack of mechanisms for the removal of rulers in antiquity and also from the need of subjects to protect themselves from oppression. The Bible relates numerous acts of assassination, many of which receive the approval of Holy Writ. For example, in Judges, the prophet Ehad stabbed Eglon, King of Moab. Jael slew the retreating Canaanite general Sisera, and Judith decapitated general Holofernes. The tyrannical judge-king Abimelech died when a woman dropped a millstone on him. Under the monarchies of Israel and Judea, many tyrants were killed, including Nadab, Elah, Jehoram, Ahaziah, Jezebel, Zechariah, Jobesh, and Pekah.

In the ancient world, Hipparchus, a tyrant of Athens, was fatally stabbed by Harmodius and Aristogiton. That these tyrannicides acted more from personal motives than from love of political liberty

Notable Assassinations in History

Year	Place	Person
514 B.C.E.	Athens	Hipparchus
44 B.C.E.	Rome	Julius Caesar
661 C.E.	Mecca	Caliph ʿAli ibn Abi Talib
1170	England	Thomas Becket, archbishop of Canterbury
1192	Tyre	Conrad of Montferrat, king of Jerusalem
1327	England	King Edward II
1400	England	King Richard II
1610	France	King Henry IV
1762	Russia	Emperor Peter III
1792	Sweden	King Gustav III
1801	Russia	Emperor Paul I
1828	South Africa	King Shaka of the Zulu
1865	United States	President Abraham Lincoln
1881	United States	President James A. Garfield
1900	Italy	King Umberto I
1901	United States	President William McKinley
1914	Bosnia	Archduke Francis Ferdinand of Austria-Hungary
1922	Ireland	Prime Minister Michael Collins
1934	Austria	Chancellor Engelbert Dollfuss
1935	United States	Louisiana governor Huey Long
1940	Mexico	Soviet exile Leon Trotsky
1948	India	Nationalist leader Mohandas K. Gandhi
1948	Palestine	U.N. observer Count Folke Bernadotte
1956	Nicaragua	President Anastasio Somoza Garcia
1958	Iraq	King Faisal II
1961	Democratic Republic of the Congo	Premier Patrice Lumumba
1961	Dominican Republic	President Rafael Trujillo *(continued)*

Notable Assassinations in History — continued

Year	Place	Person
1963	Iraq	Abdul Kareem Kassem
1963	South Vietnam	President Ngo Dinh Diem
1963	United States	Civil rights leader Medgar Evers
1963	United States	President John F. Kennedy
1965	United States	Black nationalist leader Malcolm X
1966	South Africa	Prime Minister Hendrik Verwoerd
1968	United States	Civil rights leader Martin Luther King, Jr.
1968	United States	Senator Robert F. Kennedy
1973	Chile	President Salvador Allende Gossens
1975	Bangladesh	President Mujibur Rahman
1975	Saudi Arabia	Faisal ibn al-Saud
1978	United States	San Francisco mayor George Moscone and Supervisor Harvey Milk
1979	Ireland	Louis, First Earl Mountbatten
1979	South Korea	President Park Chung Hee
1981	Bangladesh	President Ziaur Rahman
1981	Egypt	President Anwar el-Sadat
1983	Philippines	Opposition leader Benigno Aquino, Jr.
1984	India	Prime Minister Indira Gandhi
1986	Sweden	Prime Minister Olof Palme
1992	Algeria	President Mohammed Boudiaf
1994	Mexico	Presidential candidate Luis Donaldo Colosio
1994	Rwanda	President Juvenal Habyarimana
1995	Israel	Prime Minister Yitzak Rabin
2001	Democratic Republic of the Congo	President Laurent-Désiré Kabila
2002	Afghanistan	Vice President Abdul Qadir
2003	Serbia	Prime Minister Zoran Djindjic

did not cloud their godlike status in antiquity.

From the experiences of the Roman Empire, the West absorbed a deep ambivalence about assassination, since many targets were vicious tyrants, such as Caligula, Domitian, Commodius, Caracalla, and Heliogabalus, but the heroic reformer emperor Julius Caesar was also a victim.

THE MIDDLE AGES

Ambivalence toward assassination carried over to the Middle Ages, when Scholastic theologians struggled with the divergent traditions of Christianity. Its early pacifism had evaporated, but the tradition of obedience to authority and of suffering evils meekly remained. Yet Old Testament support for assassination and the natural law tradition's support for a right of rebellion against wickedly unjust rule created support for the practice.

John of Salisbury, the English medieval theologian, held that any subject might kill an oppressive tyrant for the common good, but Saint Thomas Aquinas, like many later figures, retreated from the full implications of that view. Thomas Aquinas introduced the *melior pars* doctrine, which placed responsibility for elimination of a tyrant upon those in society who enjoy office, wealth, or rank.

A vital distinction drawn by the medieval schoolmen was between a tyrant by usurpation (*tyrannus in titulo*) and a tyrant by oppression (*tyrannus in regimine*). The former is one who has no legal right to rule but seizes power. The latter is one who rules unjustly. Thomas Aquinas, Francisco Suarez, and others maintained that private individuals had a tacit mandate from legitimate authority to kill a usurper to benefit the community.

REFORMATION AND RENAISSANCE

During the Reformation, most Protestant reformers endorsed tyrannicide: Martin Luther held that the whole community could condemn a tyrant to death, Philipp Melanchthon called tyrannicide the most agreeable offering man could make to God, and John Calvin endorsed the *melior pars* doctrine. The Jesuit Juan de Mariana condemned usurpers and praised slayers of princes "who hold law and holy religion in contempt."

Renaissance drama often centered upon assassination; for example, Christopher Marlowe's *Edward II* and much of William Shakespeare concentrated upon the morality of it—in historical plays such as *Richard II*, *Henry VI* (in three parts), and *Richard III*, and also in *Macbeth*, *Hamlet*, and *Julius Caesar*. Julius Caesar was a tyrant by usurpation against the corrupt Roman Republic, but he ruled well. King Claudius in *Hamlet* was a tyrant by usurpation and oppression, as was Macbeth. A constant Renaissance theme involved the motivation for the tyrannicidal act. In *Julius Caesar*, all the assassins except Brutus have motives of jealousy, and Hamlet must struggle within himself, since he desires to kill the king because of private hatred rather than justice.

In the East, religion was often the motive, as with the Order of the Assassins in Muslim Syria in the

On November 24, 1963, two days after the assassination of President John F. Kennedy in Dallas, Texas, suspected assassin Lee Harvey Oswald was himself assassinated when Dallas nightclub owner Jack Ruby shot him on live television while police were escorting him out of a building. (Library of Congress)

twelfth and thirteenth centuries, and the Thuggees in India strangled travelers to honor the goddess Kalī until the British suppressed the cult during the 1830's.

THE MODERN ERA

In the modern era following the French Revolution, the main sources of assassinations have been nationalism, political ideology, and madness. Daniel McNaughtan, a Scot who killed the secretary of British prime minister Sir Robert Peel, represents an entire class of assassins. Because of McNaughtan's manifest insanity, the House of Lords created the McNaughtan Rule, which set the standard for the insanity plea in criminal law.

Nationalism motivated assassinations from the Phoenix Park murders in Ireland in 1882 and the calamitous slaying of Austrian archduke Francis Ferdinand in 1914 to the killing of Indian premier Indira Gandhi by Sikhs in 1984. Finally, political ideologies, especially anarchism, claimed many victims, such as Russian prime minister Peter Stolypin and U.S. president William McKinley.

With both extreme nationalism and radical political ideologies, the moral arguments about assassination have tended to be focused upon the practical question of the effects of assassination rather than upon its abstract moral nature. V. I. Lenin, the founder of the Soviet Union, condemned assassinations of political figures and other terroristic acts as tactically inopportune and inexpedient.

In the twenty-first century, international terrorism has used random assassination as a tool to disrupt society by putting pressure upon targeted governments in order to alter policies, as when the president of Chechyna was assassinated in May, 2004.

ETHICAL ISSUES

Similar to personal self-defense, capital punishment, and just war, assassination raises general issues of whether homicide can ever be justified. Beyond this, there are special issues raised by the particular nature of assassination. Can the private citizen be trusted to wield the power of life and death, especially over his or her own magistrates?

Ethicists see assassination as destructive of the trust and loyalty that ought to exist between subject and ruler, and they dislike the fact that even when used upon vicious tyrants, it necessarily involves circumventing judicial forms, though the guilt of the tyrant may be manifest.

Practically speaking, attempted assassinations, like abortive revolts, may intensify the repression of a tyrannical regime. Additionally, it is notorious that democratic and even authoritarian rulers are more susceptible to assassination than are truly totalitarian despots.

Patrick M. O'Neil

FURTHER READING

Ben-Yehuda, Nachman. *Political Assassinations by Jews: A Rhetorical Device for Justice.* Albany, N.Y.: SUNY Press, 1992.

Ford, Franklin L. *Political Murder: From Tyrannicide to Terrorism.* Cambridge, Mass.: Harvard University Press, 1985.

Hudson, Miles. *Assassination.* Stroud, Gloucestershire, England: Sutton, 2000.

Lentz, Harris M. *Assassinations and Executions: An Encyclopedia of Political Violence, 1865-1986.* Jefferson, N.C.: McFarland, 1988.

Sifakis, Carl. *Encyclopedia of Assassinations.* New York: Facts On File, 1991.

SEE ALSO: Anarchy; Covert action; Evers, Medgar; Homicide; International law; Lincoln, Abraham; Tyranny.

Atatürk

IDENTIFICATION: First president of Turkey
BORN: Mustafa Kemal; May 19, 1881, Salonika, Ottoman Empire (now Thessaloniki, Greece)
DIED: November 10, 1938; Istanbul, Turkey
TYPE OF ETHICS: Modern history
SIGNIFICANCE: Between 1921 and 1923, Atatürk successfully drove the Greeks out of Turkey, thwarted postwar partition by the allies, and established the modern nation of Turkey. As the founder and first president of that nation, Atatürk aggressively initiated a reform movement designed to Westernize and modernize Turkish law and social customs.

The son of an Ottoman bureaucrat, the young Mustafa Kemal (Atatürk, meaning "father of the Turks," was added to his name in 1934) was educated at the Istanbul military academy, where, like many other youths, he participated in subversive organizations. While initially allied with the Young Turk revolution, Atatürk in 1919 founded the rival Turkish Nationalist Party and was elected its president. His military acumen and leadership, best illustrated by his engineering of the World War I victory over the British at Gallipoli, earned him a substantial and loyal following.

After his masterful ousting of the Greeks in 1923, Atatürk, as head of the Nationalist Party, declared Turkish independence and was subsequently elected Turkey's first president. While serving for fifteen years as a virtual dictator, Atatürk initiated a program of modernization that fundamentally altered Turkish society. His reforms included the disestablishment of Islam, the abolition of the sultanate, the banning of polygamy, the institution of compulsory civil marriage, the enfranchisement of women, the replacement of Arabic script with the Latin alphabet, and compulsory literacy training for adults under age forty.

Atatürk also introduced economic reforms, including a policy of self-sufficiency and refusal of foreign loans.

Mary E. Virginia

SEE ALSO: Constitutional government; Dictatorship; Islamic ethics.

Atheism

DEFINITIONS: Unbelief in supreme beings, religion, or the supernatural
TYPE OF ETHICS: Beliefs and practices
SIGNIFICANCE: Although ethical systems in Western cultures have traditionally been grounded in religions, unbelievers also have their own value systems and seek to know and practice what is good and right.

Although some ethicists find unbelief incompatible with ethics, many ethical views and practices grow from atheism. Because atheism is not institutionalized or codified in the same way that religions are, generalizations about the "ethics of atheists" are risky.

Paul Roubiczek restates three main ethical ques-

tions: How should people act? What does "good" mean? Are people able to do what they should? A fourth question, raised by G. E. Moore in *Principia Ethica* (1903), is "What kind of things ought to exist for their own sake?" Atheists, like believers, struggle to answer these hard questions.

ATHEISTS

The term "atheism" was first used in 1571 to define an ideology "without theism." Many atheists do not deny the existence of a god; instead, they find the term "god" itself meaningless. Atheists constitute a small minority in modern society: In 1989, only 10 percent of American adults reported having "no religious preference." This figure also includes agnostics and people without clear ideas about religion.

Unbelief places atheists outside the mainstream, because even in modern, secularized societies, most people have some sort of religion to guide them. Religions often prescribe traditional codes of conduct, such as the Ten Commandments of the Old Testament or the New Testament teachings of Jesus Christ. Atheists lack such institutionalized ethical codes. Atheists tend to be well educated and trained in the humanities or sciences; they usually entertain scientific, not supernatural, theories about cosmic and human origins.

To religious believers, the term "atheist" may trigger the negative stereotype of one who is "against" something good and sacred; "atheist" may even suggest "demonically inspired," though "devil worship" is inconsistent with unbelief. The public image of modern atheists has been shaped by abrasive activists such as Madalyn Murray O'Hair, a highly publicized crusader against Bible readings and prayer in American public schools, and author Ayn Rand, founder of a unique conservative ideology: objectivism.

HISTORY

Religious unbelief has a long history. One of the early figures to question religious orthodoxy and customs was Hecataeus, who ridiculed the Greek myths in the sixth century B.C.E. Herodotus and, later, the Sophists were also critical of justifying Greek customs as "the will of the gods." Socrates was sentenced to death in 399 B.C.E. partly for being "impious." Epicurus—still popularly associated with an "eat, drink, and be merry" ethic—denied the gods' supernatural power and doubted the afterlife.

James Thrower traces the historic stages of unbelief: the breakdown of classical myths; the rise of science in the Renaissance; the rationalism of the Enlightenment, when such philosophers as Immanuel Kant and David Hume attacked the "reasonable" bases of religion; and later movements such as Marxism and existentialism. The moralist Friedrich Nietzsche, who died in 1900, declared, "God is dead," inaugurating what some call the "post-Christian" era.

VARIETIES OF ATHEISM

Confusingly, modern atheists call themselves skeptics, utilitarians, objectivists, self-realizers, emotivists, relativists, Marxists, pragmatists, intuitionists, materialists, naturalists, empiricists, positivists, nihilists, libertarians, rationalists, hedonists, secularists, humanists, and existentialists. The principles of each ideology have ethical implications—but not easily predictable ones. Existentialism and ethical humanism are among the best-known atheistic philosophies.

Mary Warnock, who surveys nonreligious ethical theories, says that modern ethicists have not built large metaphysical systems but have focused, instead, on human nature, social interaction, and language. According to existentialists such as Jean-Paul Sartre, individuals confront isolation, impermanence, and the "burden of choice" in a stark, incomprehensible world. As Warnock notes, that view is not a helpful ethical guide. However, existentialist Albert Camus has urged humans not to give up the quest for right action in an absurd world.

Paul Kurtz says that the flexible ethics of modern humanism stands on basic principles: tolerance, courage, freedom from fear, respect for individuals, social justice, happiness and self-fulfillment, and the ideal of a world community. Kurtz believes that ethical conduct is possible without religious belief because certain "human decencies" are almost universally accepted: telling the truth; dealing fairly with others; being kind, sincere, honest, considerate, thoughtful, helpful, and cooperative; having friends; seeking justice; not misusing others; and not being cruel, arrogant, vindictive, or unforgiving.

Most modern philosophies and ethical theories leave humans free to make subjective, contingent, and relativistic choices; thus, students searching for specific, practical guides to personal morality may find modern writings theoretical, complex, and in-

conclusive. Ross Poole says, pessimistically, "The modern world calls into existence certain conceptions of morality, but also destroys the grounds for taking them seriously. Modernity both needs morality, and makes it impossible." John Casey, however, affirms the persistent relevance of "pagan" virtues: courage, temperance, practical wisdom, justice, and respect for the personhood of all people. Such time-proven guides encourage honor, humanistic achievement, and proper kinds of pride and self-assertion.

Roy Neil Graves

FURTHER READING

Baggini, Julian. *Atheism: A Very Short Introduction.* New York: Oxford University Press, 2003.

Casey, John. *Pagan Virtue: An Essay in Ethics.* Oxford, England: Clarendon Press, 1991.

Kurtz, Paul. *In Defense of Secular Humanism.* Buffalo, N.Y.: Prometheus Books, 1983.

Martin, Michael. *Atheism, Morality, and Meaning.* Amherst, N.Y.: Prometheus Books, 2002.

Poole, Ross. *Morality and Modernity.* London: Routledge, 1991.

Roubiczek, Paul. *Ethical Values in the Age of Science.* London: Cambridge University Press, 1969.

Smith, George H. *Atheism, Ayn Rand, and Other Heresies.* Buffalo, N.Y.: Prometheus Books, 1991.

Stein, Gordon, ed. *The Encyclopedia of Unbelief.* 2 vols. Buffalo, N.Y.: Prometheus Books, 1985.

Thrower, James. *A Short History of Western Atheism.* London: Pemberton Books, 1971.

Warnock, Mary. *Ethics Since 1900.* 3d ed. New York: Oxford University Press, 1978.

SEE ALSO: Camus, Albert; Epicurus; Existentialism; God; Humanism; Marxism; Nietzsche, Friedrich; Nihilism; Postmodernism; Religion; Secular ethics.

Atom bomb

THE EVENT: Creation of an extremely powerful bomb utilizing the process of nuclear fission

DATE: 1939-1945

TYPE OF ETHICS: Scientific ethics

SIGNIFICANCE: Scientists ordinarily prefer to regard themselves as members of an international brotherhood devoted to the expansion of knowledge;

however, the race to create an atom bomb during World War II highlighted the fact that scientific knowledge also has direct nationalist and military applications.

Among those caught in the ferment of World War I were members of the international scientific community. Early in the war, scientists in the United States were shocked to find that distinguished Germans such as Wilhelm Roentgen had signed a manifesto justifying the destruction of the famed library at Louvain, Belgium, by German armed forces. Soon, however, the imperatives of the war effort placed greater and more direct demands upon scientists, who generally were eager to use their abilities to advance the causes of their respective nations.

Although chemists bore the moral burden most directly, thanks to their essential role in the development of increasingly lethal poison gases, physicists also shared in the war efforts of the various belligerents, making significant contributions to the development of acoustic devices for detecting enemy submarines and of flash-ranging and acoustic apparatuses for ascertaining the location of enemy artillery positions.

DEMANDS OF WORLD WAR II

World War II demanded still more of scientists, and physicists in particular, for several of the war's most far-reaching new technologies demanded their expertise: the proximity fuze, radar, and the atom bomb. "Almost overnight," a scientist at a midwestern state university remarked, "physicists have been promoted from semi-obscurity to membership in that select group of rarities which include rubber, sugar and coffee." Colleges and universities readily made their facilities available for various wartime endeavors, weapons research among them. In wartime, ethical distinctions between defensive and offensive weaponry can easily be blurred, for physicists who entered radar work labored over devices ranging from microwave apparatuses used to detect enemy submarines and approaching aircraft to equipment designed to enable Allied bombers to drop their bombs with greater accuracy.

At all stages of the conflict, ethical concerns about the war and its weapons were revealed in the

Characteristic "mushroom" cloud created by the explosion of an atom bomb over Nagasaki. (National Archives)

thinking of various groups and individuals, including military personnel. Before the war and early in it, air force officers preferred to think of strategic bombing as so precise that only targets of direct military value such as the submarine pens at Wilhelmshaven, Germany, or the ball-bearing plants at Schweinfurt would be attacked. Precision bombing was much more difficult to accomplish than prewar theorists had argued, however, and area bombing, in which not only the plants but also the surrounding communities were designated as target areas, was increasingly used. It was only a matter of time until the communities themselves became targets. Japan's great distance from Allied bases meant that sustained bombing of Japanese targets could not even be undertaken until well into 1944, by which time American forces had had more than a year of experience in the air war against Germany. Area bombing therefore played an especially large role in the air war against Japan. Would the use of an atom bomb represent something altogether different or would it simply expand the still uncertain boundaries of area bombing?

Almost as soon as the discovery of nuclear fission was revealed in 1939, physicists began to discuss an atom bomb. Such a bomb would be a weapon of enormous destructive potential, and using it would claim the lives of many thousands of individuals. First it had to be asked whether an atom bomb could be developed. American physicists and their émigré colleagues rallied to the war effort, nearly five hundred going to the Radiation Lab at the Massachusetts Institute of Technology and many others entering the Manhattan Project (organized in 1942 to coordinate and push forward ongoing fission research) and its various facilities: Among these were the Metallurgical Lab at Chicago, where a controlled chain reaction was first achieved; Oak Ridge, Tennessee, where weapons-grade uranium was processed; and Los Alamos, New Mexico, where work on the bomb itself—it was innocuously called "the gadget" for security reasons—was undertaken. Even when their own efforts seemed disappointing, Manhattan Project scientists could not know whether their German counterparts, such as Nobel laureate Werner Heisenberg, had achieved an insight that had eluded them and had therefore put the atom bomb into Adolf Hitler's hands.

Preoccupied with the work before them, these scientists rarely took time to reflect upon what they were doing. The surrender of Germany in the spring of 1945 was the occasion when scientists should have paused to ask themselves whether work on the atom bomb should continue. A young physicist at Los Alamos did raise the question of resigning from atom bomb work en masse, only to be told by a senior colleague that if work were suspended it would be easy for another Hitler to pick up where they had left off.

At the Met Lab, where work was nearly done by 1945, scientists did join in issuing the Franck Report, which asked that a demonstration of the new weapon be made on an uninhabited area before any use of it was made against Japan. Some half dozen of the most eminent scientists involved in war work, however—those with access to policymakers in Washington—rejected such a recommendation. A direct use of the atom bomb against a Japanese city would be far more likely to bring the war to a prompt conclusion and to increase the likelihood of maintaining peace afterward, they reasoned. Although many scientists involved in the Manhattan Project did at one time or another speculate upon the ethical questions that the development of an atom bomb posed, their concern that Hitler might secure prior access to this weapon sufficed to keep their efforts focused on developing the atom bomb. Moreover, mastering the physics involved in creating an atom bomb was an immensely challenging and absorbing scientific and technological problem. "For most of them," Michael Sherry has observed, "destruction was something they produced, not something they did," an attitude that helps explain the wagers these scientists made on the magnitude of the explosive yield of the bomb used in the July, 1945, Trinity test.

GERMAN SCIENTISTS

Ironically, some German physicists might have pondered the ethical dimensions of the atom bomb more keenly than had their Allied counterparts. Unlike the Manhattan Project scientists, the Germans knew that their own research could give Hitler the atom bomb. After the war had ended, scientists were more likely to step back and ask what the atom bomb meant and whether international control of it or further development of nuclear weapons should take precedence.

Among those who went on to develop a far more devastating weapon, the hydrogen bomb, the fear of Joseph Stalin and the Soviet Union provided the ethical justification that the thought of a Nazi atom bomb had provided for their Manhattan Project colleagues. By the same token, however, as historian Daniel Kevles put it, "To maintain their scientific, political, and moral integrity, the Los Alamos generation on the whole declared . . . that scientists could 'no longer disclaim direct responsibility for the uses to which mankind . . .put their disinterested discoveries.'"

Lloyd J. Graybar

FURTHER READING

Batchelder, Robert C. *The Irreversible Decision, 1939-1950.* Boston: Houghton Mifflin, 1961.

Boyer, Paul. *By the Bomb's Early Light: American Thought and Culture at the Dawn of the Atomic Age.* Chapel Hill: University of North Carolina Press, 1994.

Powers, Thomas. *Heisenberg's War*. New York: Knopf, 1993.

Rhodes, Richard. *The Making of the Atom Bomb*. New York: Simon & Schuster, 1986.

Rigden, John S. *Rabi: Scientist and Citizen*. New York: Basic Books, 1987.

Schaffer, Ronald. *Wings of Judgment: American Bombing in World War II*. New York: Oxford University Press, 1985.

Schweber, S. S. *In the Shadow of the Bomb: Bethe, Oppenheimer, and the Moral Responsibility of the Scientist*. Princeton, N.J.: Princeton University Press, 2000.

Serber, Robert. *The Los Alamos Primer: The First Lectures on How to Build an Atomic Bomb*. Berkeley: University of California Press, 1992.

Smith, Alice Kimball. *A Peril and a Hope: The Scientists' Movement in America, 1945-47*. Chicago: University of Chicago Press, 1965.

VanDeMark, Brian. *Pandora's Keepers: Nine Men and the Atomic Bomb*. Boston: Little, Brown, 2003.

SEE ALSO: Biochemical weapons; Hiroshima and Nagasaki bombings; Manhattan Project; Military ethics; Mutually Assured Destruction; Nazi science; Nuclear arms race; Nuclear energy; Union of Concerned Scientists; Weapons research.

known. Furthermore, advocates of military applications of nuclear energy insisted on continuing development and testing of atomic weapons.

In this atmosphere, the Atomic Energy Act of 1946 was signed into law. It provided for the formation of a presidentially appointed commission, with separate military and civilian committees under it. The AEC devoted much attention to military weaponry in its early years, but the Atomic Energy Act of 1954 provided for civilian industrial participation in the research and manufacture of atomic materials and in the construction of atomic power installations, licensed by the AEC.

In 1974, the AEC was disbanded, and in 1975 two new organizations took up changed functions: the Nuclear Regulatory Commission, charged with the investigation and licensing of all uses of atomic energy—medical, industrial, and power, as well as the health aspects connected with these uses; and the Energy Research and Development Administration, which later became the Department of Energy, with the narrower function implied by its name. The weapons applications have been less prominent since then.

Robert M. Hawthorne, Jr.

SEE ALSO: Hiroshima and Nagasaki bombings; Nuclear energy; Nuclear Regulatory Commission; Union of Concerned Scientists; Weapons research.

Atomic Energy Commission

IDENTIFICATION: Federal government agency established to provide joint military and civilian supervision of nuclear power

DATE: Founded in 1946; superseded 1974-1975

TYPE OF ETHICS: Scientific ethics

SIGNIFICANCE: After World War II, it became clear that nuclear energy called for special regulation, and the Atomic Energy Commission (AEC) was created to provide it.

When World War II was ended by the atom bombs that were dropped on Hiroshima and Nagasaki, nearly all that the general public knew about nuclear energy was that it could be devastatingly destructive. The many medical and industrial uses of the atom lay mostly in the future, and only its horrific power was

Attorney-client privilege

DEFINITION: Testimonial privilege that permits clients and their attorneys to refuse to disclose or to prohibit others from disclosing certain confidential communications between them

TYPE OF ETHICS: Legal and judicial ethics

SIGNIFICANCE: Although the disclosure of certain sorts of information that is exchanged between attorney and client is relevant to legal proceedings, the rules of attorney-client privilege are designed to ensure the confidentiality of this relationship.

In the U.S. legal system, the following rules apply to the attorney-client privilege. First, in order for a communication to be covered by the attorney-client privilege, an attorney-client relationship in which the client or the client's representative has retained or is seeking the professional services of the attorney must exist at the time of the communication. Second, only communications that are intended to be confidential—that is, those that are not intended to be disclosed to third parties other than those who are involved in rendering the legal services—are protected by the privilege. Third, the privilege cannot be invoked by either the plaintiff or the defendant in a lawsuit when both are represented by the same attorney in the transaction that is at issue. Either party may, however, invoke the privilege against third parties. Fourth, the client holds the power to invoke or waive the privilege.

No privilege can be invoked in any of the following circumstances: when the attorney's services have been sought in connection with planning or executing a future wrongdoing, when the adversaries in a lawsuit make their respective claims through the same deceased client, or when the communication concerns a breach of duty between lawyer and client, such as attorney malpractice or client failure to pay legal fees.

Lisa Paddock

SEE ALSO: Adversary system; Arrest records; Attorney misconduct; Code of Professional Responsibility; Codes of civility; Confidentiality; Jurisprudence; Legal ethics; Personal injury attorneys; Privacy.

Attorney misconduct

DEFINITION: Illegal or unethical behavior of attorneys that relates to their professional work
TYPE OF ETHICS: Legal and judicial ethics
SIGNIFICANCE: Attorneys who act inappropriately may be punished by the bar associations or supreme courts of the states in which they practice law.

In the United States admission to the practice of law and oversight of attorney conduct are matters supervised generally by the each state's supreme court. In most states the supreme court remains the final authority in regulating admissions and attorney conduct, although the court may rely in part on the assistance of state bar associations. In practice, however,

complaints concerning the conduct of lawyers should normally be directed to the state or local bar association, which generally plays the most important role in the initial investigation of and decisions concerning complaints.

Sanctions against attorneys for unethical conduct should be distinguished from other means of redress for inappropriate attorney behavior. The chief alternative avenues for such redress are criminal proceedings and civil lawsuits. Attorneys who violate the law in connection with their legal practice can find themselves subject to criminal sanctions. Similarly, attorneys who violate legal obligations owed to clients and other third parties can be sued for legal malpractice or a variety of other legal claims.

VARIETIES OF SANCTIONS

The sanctions available to disciplinary authorities who regulate the conduct of lawyers vary from private reprimands to disbarment. For a relatively minor infraction disciplinary authorities may simply censure an attorney privately, informing him or her of the bar's verdict and warning against repeating the infraction. This private reprimand remains in the attorney's file, however, and might have a bearing on the severity of sanctions in future cases should further transgressions occur. For more serious cases, disciplinary authorities may move to a public reprimand, which informs other lawyers of the offending lawyer's ethical misconduct, generally by mentioning it in a legal publication such as the state bar association's monthly periodical. The next level of sanction is a suspension from the practice of law for some period of time, generally ranging from three months to five years. Finally, disciplinary authorities deal with the most severe ethical lapses by disbarring the offending attorney. Disbarment strips the attorney of the right to practice law in the state in question. In some cases, attorneys so disbarred may seek reinstatement to the bar after a period of time, normally specified in the original disbarment order. Reinstatement depends on whether the attorney demonstrates that the offending conduct is not likely to be repeated.

In the late twentieth century the traditional sanctions of reprimand, suspension, and disbarment were supplemented with other sanctions designed to educate offending lawyers. For example, disciplinary authorities sometimes dismiss complaints against lawyers for relatively minor infractions if the lawyers agree to attend a continuing legal education program on the subject of attorney ethics. Sometimes the right to undertake the practice of law again after a suspension or disbarment is linked to this kind of requirement. In addition, disciplinary authorities may occasionally make readmission to the bar after disbarment contingent on an erring lawyer's passing all or part of the state bar examination.

ETHICAL RULES

Beginning early in the twentieth century national and state bar associations attempted to set forth principles of legal ethics that would guide the conduct of lawyers and provide a basis for disciplining wayward attorneys. In 1983 the American Bar Association (ABA) proposed a set of ethical rules called the Model Rules of Professional Conduct. Since the ABA does not itself have authority to establish standards for legal ethics in each state, the Model Rules were simply a uniform collection of ethical principles proposed for adoption by the various state supreme courts. In fact, most states subsequently enacted some version of the Model Rules as their own, although many states modified them in some respects. A few states still operate under a predecessor set of ethics rules proposed by the ABA in the 1970's called the Model Code of Professional Responsibility.

Rules of legal ethics, whether the Model Rules or the older Model Code, attempt to set forth ethical principles to guide lawyers in dealing with the various ethical problems that occur in the practice of law. They define the various obligations that lawyers owe their clients, the courts, and third parties. Violation of these rules, which touch on matters as various as the kinds of fees lawyers may charge and their obligation to disclose the misconduct of their fellow lawyers, is the chief basis for sanctions against lawyers.

SANCTIONS FOR OTHER TYPES OF UNETHICAL CONDUCT

In the main, lawyers receive sanctions for unethical conduct committed in their role as attorneys. Occasionally, however, disciplinary authorities sanction lawyers for ethical infractions that are not com-

mitted in the context of legal practice. For example, a lawyer might be sanctioned after being convicted of embezzlement or tax evasion. Lawyers may also be sanctioned for unethical business conduct, even if the conduct does not occur in connection with their practice of law.

The modern view—reflected, for example, in the ABA's Model Rules of Professional Conduct—is that lawyers should be disciplined for conduct outside the scope of their practice only under certain circumstances. According to the ABA's Model Rules, some kinds of illegal or unethical conduct may not reflect adversely on lawyers' fitness to practice law. Thus, even though private moral infractions, such as adultery, might be a crime in particular jurisdictions, this infraction does not necessarily mean that an attorney who engages in this conduct lacks the characteristics necessary to practice law. On the other hand, criminal offenses involving violence, dishonesty, or interference with the administration of justice would reflect adversely on a lawyer's fitness to practice law.

Timothy L. Hall

FURTHER READING

Applbaum, Arthur Isak. *Ethics for Adversaries: The Morality of Roles in Public and Professional Life.* Princeton, N.J.: Princeton University Press, 1999.

Rhode, Deborah L. *In the Interests of Justice: Reforming the Legal Profession.* New York: Oxford University Press, 2001.

Rhode, Deborah L., ed. *Ethics in Practice Lawyers' Roles, Responsibilities, and Regulation.* New York: Oxford University Press, 2000.

Salkin, Patricia E., ed. *Ethical Standards in the Public Sector: A Guide for Government Lawyers, Clients, and Public Officials.* Chicago: Section of State and Local Government Law, American Bar Association, 1999.

Simon, William H. *The Practice of Justice: A Theory of Lawyers' Ethics.* Cambridge, Mass.: Harvard University Press, 1998.

SEE ALSO: Attorney-client privilege; Code of Professional Responsibility; Codes of civility; Ethical codes of organizations; Legal ethics.

Augustine, Saint

IDENTIFICATION: North African theologian and philosopher

BORN: Aurelius Augustinus; November 13, 354, Tagaste, Numidia (now Souk-Ahras, Algeria)

DIED: August 28, 430, Hippo Regius, Numidia (now Annaba, Algeria)

TYPE OF ETHICS: Religious ethics

SIGNIFICANCE: Augustine's most influential works were *Confessions* (*Confessiones*, 397-400) and *The City of God* (*De civitate Dei*, 413-427). His abiding importance rests on his unique understanding and interpretations of salvation history, human psychology, and Christian moral imperatives.

For centuries, the immense influence of Augustine of Hippo has been felt in the life of the Christian Church in the West. Theologians, preachers, ecclesiastical officials, and laity alike have been guided by, or forced to respond to, the power of his ideas and ethical teachings. Thomas Aquinas, Martin Luther, and John Calvin, to name only a few, formulated their own theological positions with special reference to Augustinian thought. A prolific and brilliant writer whose works range from spiritual autobiography to biblical interpretation, Augustine was also a man of the people and a man of action.

Born of a pagan father and a Christian mother, he received a first-rate education in Rome's North African province of Numidia and later became a teacher of rhetoric in Italy. Reconverted to Christianity in 386, Augustine went on to become bishop of Hippo Regius, in what is now Algeria, in 395/396 and served in that capacity until his death.

As with any great thinker, Augustine's ideas developed and changed somewhat over the years, but there is also a remarkable consistency to much of his thought, especially in the area of ethics. Augustine's views on ethics were conditioned by his own powerful, personal experiences as well as by the theological and ecclesiastical controversies that erupted during his period of service in the Church. Although he had some knowledge of the ethical theories of both Plato and Aristotle, his familiarity was derived at second hand from his reading of Cicero, Plotinus, and others. Nevertheless, his high regard for Platonic thought can be seen in his attempts to reconcile Christian ideals and Platonic teachings.

GOD, LOVE, AND DESIRE

On the general issues of human conduct and human destiny, Augustine's thinking was naturally conditioned by the New Testament and by Church tradition. Human beings, he states, are truly blessed or happy when all their actions are in harmony with reason and Christian truth. Blessedness, accordingly, does not mean simply the satisfaction of every desire. Indeed, the satisfaction of evil or wrong desires provides no ultimate happiness: "No one is happy unless he has all he wants and wants nothing that is evil." Central to Augustine's understanding here is his emphasis on God and love. Indeed, for Augustine, virtue can be defined as "rightly ordered love." Throughout his writings, he stresses that for the Christian an action or work can have value and be worthy only if it proceeds from the motive of Christian love, that is, love of God. Augustine's famous and often-misunderstood injunction "Love, and do what you will" is to be understood in this context.

For Augustine, there exists in humans a conflict of wills, a struggle between original human goodness and the later, inherited desire for lesser things. Although, as he states, "the guilt of this desire is remitted by baptism," nevertheless "there remains the weakness against which, until he is cured, every faithful man who advances in the right direction struggles most earnestly." In time, as a person matures in the Christian faith, the struggle lessens. As long as humans allow God to govern them and sustain their spirits, they can control their lower natures and desires, and advance on the Christian path. As the concluding prayer of *On the Trinity* (*De Trinitate* c. 419) puts it: "Lord, may I be mindful of you, understand you, love you. Increase these gifts in me until you have entirely reformed me."

SIN, MORAL CONDUCT, AND SOCIETY

According to Augustine, the essential task of humans is to attempt the restoration of the image of God within themselves through prayer, meditation on Scripture, worship, and moral conduct. Sin, by its very nature, obscures and imprisons this image. Especially dangerous to people is the sin of pride, which opens the soul to other vices such as earthly desire and curiosity. Each is destructive of the human soul as well as of human society. A properly ordered moral life not only marks a person's individual movement toward God but also contributes to the improvement of earthly society.

Although Augustine believed that humans are social animals by nature and that human potential can be realized only within such an environment, he did not agree that the machinery of political organization is natural. Rather, government institutions are at most a necessary check on the worst excesses of human behavior following the fall of Adam and Eve. The best government is one that provides a peaceful, stable environment in which people can work out their own salvation. For Augustine, as for other early Christian teachers, humans are earthly pilgrims in search of a final resting place. God is both the goal and the means of attaining such: "By means of him we tend towards him, by means of knowledge we tend towards wisdom, all the same without departing from one and the same Christ."

Craig L. Hanson

FURTHER READING

Augustine, Saint. *The City of God Against the Pagans.* Edited and translated by R. W. Dyson. New York: Cambridge University Press, 1998.

_____. *The Confessions.* Translated and edited by Philip Burton. Introduction by Robin Lane Fox. New York: A. A. Knopf, 2001.

Babcock, William S., ed. *The Ethics of St. Augustine.* Atlanta: Scholars Press, 1991.

Banner, William Augustus. *The Path of St. Augustine.* Lanham, Md.: Rowman & Littlefield, 1996.

Bourke, Vernon. *Joy in Augustine's Ethics.* Villanova, Pa.: Villanova University Press, 1979.

Burnaby, John. *Amor Dei: A Study of the Religion of Saint Augustine.* London: Hodder & Stoughton, 1938. Reprint. Foreword by Oliver O'Donovan. Norwich, England: Canterbury Press, 1991.

Connolly, William E. *The Augustinian Imperative: A Reflection on the Politics of Morality.* New ed. Lanham, Md.: Rowman & Littlefield, 2002.

Deane, Herbert. *The Political and Social Ideas of St. Augustine.* New York: Columbia University Press, 1963.

Gilson, Étienne. *The Christian Philosophy of Saint Augustine.* Translated by L. Lynch. New York: Random House, 1960.

O'Connell, Robert. *St. Augustine's Early Theory of Man, A.D. 386-391.* Cambridge, Mass.: Harvard University Press, 1968.

Portalié, Eugene. *A Guide to the Thought of Saint Augustine.* Translated by R. J. Bastian. Chicago: H. Regnery, 1960.

SEE ALSO: Christian ethics; Dignity; Evil; Just war theory; Lying; Manichaeanism; Natural law; Self-love; Violence; Virtue.

Aurobindo, Sri

IDENTIFICATION: Indian philosopher
BORN: August 15, 1872, Calcutta, India
DIED: December 5, 1950, Pondicherry, India
TYPE OF ETHICS: Religious ethics
SIGNIFICANCE: Sri Aurobindo, one of the foremost religious thinkers of twentieth century India, helped to revitalize India both politically and spiritually. He is the author of *The Life Divine* (1914-1919) and *Synthesis of Yoga* (1948).

After being educated in England from the age of seven until he was twenty-one, Sri Aurobindo returned to India in 1893. He soon became involved in the nationalistic movement in India, and he was imprisoned for his activities in 1908. Realizing through visionary experience that real human liberation went far beyond the political liberation of India, he withdrew from the world and established an ashram, or retreat, in Pondicherry, India.

Aurobindo was very much influenced by the Western philosopher Henri Bergson, and he created a synthesis of Bergson's evolutionary view and the Upaniṣads. According to Aurobindo, no evolution is

---

The Three Steps of Integral Yoga

1. Surrender oneself totally to God.

2. Recognize that one's progress is a result of the śakti energy working within oneself.

3. Have the divine vision of the deity in all things.

---

possible without involution, which entails the descent of the divine to the world of matter. The Eternal Spirit is beyond all description, but it descends into the lower realms of being and then by evolution ascends until it returns to its source. This transition from the Eternal Spirit to the multiplicity of the phenomenal world is what Aurobindo calls Supermind. Although matter is the lowest level of being, it is nevertheless a low form of the Supreme. The practice of integral yoga, which consists of three steps, awakens the potentiality of self-perfection that exists in each person.

Krishna Mallick

SEE ALSO: Bergson, Henri; Śaṅkara; Upaniṣads; Vedānta.

Authenticity

DEFINITION: Individual's autonomy in making moral choices that are not bound by society's norms
TYPE OF ETHICS: Modern history
SIGNIFICANCE: Authenticity is opposed to conformity. Adherence to an ethic of authenticity shifts the basis of moral judgment from the shared values of society to the personal values of each individual.

Lionel Trilling, who wrote *Sincerity and Authenticity* (1971), concurs with French philosopher Jean-Jacques Rousseau that society thwarts authenticity. Trilling analyzes the relationship between sincerity, which he defines as the similarity of what one says and what one feels, and authenticity, which is the essence of that person revealed. He finds that society often rejects authenticity when it conflicts with prevailing standards. Authentic individuals may find it difficult to remain true to themselves and still meet with social acceptance. Such alienation could lead to a form of madness—either clinical madness, as Sigmund Freud suggested could occur when one's ego is unable to reconcile primitive desires with social norms; or a spiritual form of madness-as-truth of the type suggested by Michel Foucault.

The authentic person acts from a sense of innate principles and does not depend on social acceptance for his or her standards of ethics. This emphasis on the individual has led some critics to claim that authenticity tends toward situation ethics. Jean-Paul Sartre has suggested, however, that the actions of the individual are not completely separate but link him or her with society, and Simone de Beauvoir believed that genuine authenticity requires a sustained commitment by the individual within a community.

James A. Baer

SEE ALSO: Autonomy; Bad faith; Existentialism; Relativism; Sartre, Jean-Paul; Situational ethics.

Autonomy

DEFINITION: Absence of external constraint plus a positive power of self-determination
TYPE OF ETHICS: Theory of ethics
SIGNIFICANCE: Moral autonomy is considered by many philosophers to be both a prerequisite for moral accountability and a basis for moral dignity. It is a fundamental feature of the more traditional Western models of personhood.

There are many levels at which autonomy can be said to operate. For example, nations can be said to be autonomous if they formulate and enforce their own laws and policies. (The original use of the word "autonomy," in ancient Greek political thought, designated the independence of city-states that created their own laws instead of having them imposed from without by other political powers.) Similarly, other groups of people can be said to be autonomous, including companies, universities, religious institutions, and even families.

INDIVIDUAL AUTONOMY

The most important level at which autonomy is believed to be operative, however, is probably the level of the individual person. In Western thought, the ideal of individual autonomy has become enormously important for the evaluation of various political arrangements and for moral reasoning in general (at both the theoretical level and the level of practice). For example, the idea of a totalitarian state is often criticized by political philosophers because of the failure of such an arrangement to respect the autonomy of individual citizens.

In a similar way, at the level of particular moral practices, people often appeal to individual autonomy in order to justify or criticize specific ways of behaving. For example, many people argue that in order to respect the autonomy of individual patients, medical professionals are typically obligated to obtain some kind of informed consent from patients before treating them. The notion of individual moral autonomy also plays a very significant role in modern moral theory; for example, many theorists insist that the morality of particular actions depends in part upon the self-determined moral outlook of the person acting, and others claim that some kind of individual autonomy in action is necessary in order for persons to be morally responsible agents.

In order to explore the notion of individual autonomy, it will be helpful to consider in some detail what it involves and to examine briefly the influential views of Immanuel Kant concerning individual moral autonomy.

The notion of individual autonomy is often applied to the actions of individual people; in this sense, people are said to act autonomously to the extent that they determine for themselves what to do, independently of external influences (including the wishes of other people). This individual autonomy with respect to action is often viewed as essential for attributing actions to people as their own and for holding people morally responsible for what they do. It is a matter of great controversy, however, just how much independence a person must have from external influences in order to act autonomously. Some people claim that the actions of persons cannot be determined by environmental factors that are beyond their control if they are to act autonomously, whereas others claim that such independence is not necessary for individual autonomous action.

It is important to realize that the notion of individual autonomy is not applied only to the actions that people perform; it is also applied to the formation of individual beliefs, desires, and preferences, as well as of individual moral principles and motives for acting. Since Immanuel Kant's influential views concerning moral autonomy involve individual autonomy with respect to moral principles and motives for acting, perhaps it would be wise to consider his views at this point.

For Kant, people are distinctive because they are sources of value or ends in themselves, rather than mere means to ends. (In this respect, people are different from other things, such as tables and chairs, which can be treated only as means to other ends, not as ends in themselves.) People are autonomous, self-determining moral agents who are capable of adopting different principles of action. According to Kant, one ought to adopt only those principles that are universalizable; that is, principles that could be willed rationally to become universal laws of conduct for anyone, anywhere, at any time. (Such principles must be completely impartial and make no reference to any particular person's preferences, values, or circumstances.)

The following principle expresses one version of Kant's universally binding moral principle (or categorical imperative): One should always act so as to treat persons as ends in themselves, and never merely as means to ends. This principle reflects the emphasis upon respect for individual moral autonomy in Kant's moral philosophy, an emphasis that has had considerable influence upon later moral philosophers.

The idea of autonomy plays a crucial role in political and moral philosophy. Although other notions of autonomy are important, Kant's account of individual moral autonomy has probably been the most influential, and it has served to focus the attention of many moral philosophers upon notions of individual autonomy.

Scott A. Davison

FURTHER READING

Descartes, Rene. *Meditations on First Philosophy: In Which the Existence of God and the Distinction of the Soul from the Body Are Demonstrated.* Translated by Donald A. Cress. 3d ed. Indianapolis: Hackett, 1993.

Dworkin, Gerald. *The Theory and Practice of Autonomy.* Cambridge, England: Cambridge University Press, 1988.

Groarke, Louis. *The Good Rebel: Understanding Freedom and Morality.* Madison, N.J.: Fairleigh Dickinson University Press, 2002.

Kant, Immanuel. *Critique of Practical Reason.* Edited and translated by Lewis W. Beck. 3d ed. New York: Maxwell Macmillan, 1993.

_____. *Critique of Pure Reason.* Translated by Norman Kemp Smith. Introduction by Howard Caygill. Rev. 2d ed. New York: Bedford/St. Martins, 2003.

_____. *Groundwork for the Metaphysics of Morals*. Edited and translated by Allen W. Wood. New Haven, Conn.: Yale University Press, 2002.

_____. *The Metaphysics of Morals*. Translated by Mary Gregor. New York: Cambridge University Press, 1991.

Lindley, Richard. *Autonomy*. Atlantic Highlands, N.J.: Humanities Press, 1986.

Mill, John Stuart. *"Utilitarianism"; "On Liberty"; "Considerations on Representative Government"; "Remarks on Bentham's Philosophy."* Edited by Geraint Williams. London: Dent, 1993.

Santoro, Emilio. *Autonomy, Freedom, and Rights: A Critique of Liberal Subjectivity*. Boston: Kluwer Academic, 2003.

SEE ALSO: Accountability; Choice; Coercion; Determinism and freedom; Freedom and liberty; Impartiality; Individualism; Kant, Immanuel; Moral responsibility.

Avalokiteśvara

DEFINITION: Personification of wisdom and compassion understood as a bodhisattva (an enlightened being who postpones entrance into nirvana to help people achieve salvation)

DATE: Depicted in art and literature in India by the third century

TYPE OF ETHICS: Religious ethics

SIGNIFICANCE: A bodhisattva who destroys false views and passions, Avalokiteśvara is an important figure in the Buddhist religion.

Avalokiteśvara is the bodhisattva of compassion par excellence, who preaches the way to Buddhahood, saves people from suffering and death, and leads them to safety and even enlightenment. The Sanskrit name perhaps meant "the Lord who looks in each direction"; hence, he is sometimes depicted iconographically as a being with eleven or more heads. He is believed to dwell on a mountain, from which he hears the cries of suffering people and brings them aid. In the *Pure Land* sūtras (scriptures), he is one of two bodhisattvas associated with the Buddha Amitābha, who dwells in the Western Paradise and saves those who call upon him. Avalokiteśvara es-

corts believers from their deathbeds to the Western Paradise.

The *Avalokiteśvara Sūtra* teaches that he will intervene directly in human affairs to make fires burn out, enemies become kind, curses fail, and fierce animals calm. Originally conceived of as masculine, Avalokiteśvara could take feminine forms to teach. In addition, believers thought that the bodhisattva could fulfill wishes, including the wish to bear children.

By the fifth century, some Buddhists in China had begun to view Avalokiteśvara (in Chinese, Kuan Yin) as primarily feminine, although this view did not predominate until the twelfth century. Even then, some held that the bodhisattva had transcended sexual identity altogether, and many representations of Avalokiteśvara combine both masculine and feminine features in order to denote this transcendence. In Japan, the bodhisattva is known as Kannon, a feminine figure; in Tibet, the bodhisattva is known as the male figure Chenrezig.

Paul L. Redditt

SEE ALSO: Bodhisattva ideal; Buddhist ethics; Shinran.

Averroës

IDENTIFICATION: Arab philosopher

BORN: Abū al-Walīd Muḥammad ibn Aḥmad ibn Muḥammad ibn Rushd; 1126, Córdoba, Spain

DIED: 1198, Marrakech, Almohad Empire (now in Morocco)

TYPE OF ETHICS: Religious ethics

SIGNIFICANCE: Averroës' philosophical innovations and interpretations of Aristotle were important as far east as the Levant, and his European followers challenged Roman Catholic orthodoxy.

The most scrupulously Aristotelian of the medieval Islamicate philosophers, Averroës nevertheless introduced some significant innovations in his interpretation of Aristotle. His *The Incoherence of the Incoherence* (*Tahāfut al-tahāfut*, 1180) responded to al-Ghazālī's attacks on demonstrative philosophy, which, Averroës argued, is independent of revelation and even is necessary for correct interpretation of revelation. Religion is useful for the masses, who can attain only a modicum of practical moral virtue at best, whereas philosophy is for the few who can attain intellectual contemplation of immaterial substance.

Agreeing with Aristotle that only the intellectual part of the soul is immaterial, Averroës argued that the bliss of the soul is in its conjoining (*ittiṣāl*) with the (Neoplatonic) Active Intellect, returning the individual intellectual soul to the source from which it emanated. This apparent denial of the individual immortality of the soul was championed by Latin Averroists (such as Siger of Brabant), whose challenge to Roman Catholic orthodoxy was so persistent that it was the professed target of René Descartes in his *Meditations* (1680).

Thomas Gaskill

SEE ALSO: Altruism; Avicenna; Ghazālī, al-.

Avicenna

IDENTIFICATION: Medieval Persian philosopher
BORN: Abū ʿAli al-Ḥusayn ibn ʿAbd Allāh ibn Sīnā; 980, Afshena, Transoxiana Province of Bukhara, Persian Empire (now in Uzbekistan)
DIED: 1037, Hamadhan, Persia (now in Iran)
TYPE OF ETHICS: Religious ethics
SIGNIFICANCE: The author of *The Book of Healing* (early eleventh century) among numerous other works, Avicenna is arguably the most widely discussed philosopher in the Islamic world. In medieval Europe, his early works contributed to the understanding of Aristotle and the framing of twelfth through fourteenth century philosophical controversies.

Avicenna happily acknowledged his debt to Aristotle and al-Fārābī, but he was also an original thinker. His distinctive ethical concern with the relation between individual beings and Pure Being (which was to become important for Thomas Aquinas, John Duns Scotus, and others) focused on the fate of the soul after bodily death. The being of individual things is utterly dependent on Pure Being, from which one came and to which, if one is to attain bliss, one returns. That return is ensured only by rigorous study, which over-

Avicenna. (Library of Congress)

comes attachment to this world of change and purifies the soul so that it can be immersed in the Light of Being.

Although he was sometimes a commentator on Aristotle (frequently, in *The Book of Healing*), Avicenna also wrote mystical allegories and poetry that suggest a strong affinity with his Sufi contemporaries.

Thomas Gaskill

SEE ALSO: Altruism; Averroës; Fārābī, al-; Ghazālī, al-.

Ayer, A. J.

IDENTIFICATION: English philosopher
BORN: October 29, 1910, London, England
DIED: June 27, 1989, London, England
TYPE OF ETHICS: Modern history
SIGNIFICANCE: In *Language, Truth, and Logic* (1936), Ayer combined the principles of Austrian logical positivism with the tradition of British empiri-

cism to argue for a noncognitivist (emotivist) view of ethics.

Ayer was Wykeham professor of logic at Oxford, where he completed his education in 1932. Through his early association with the Austrian group of philosophers known as the Vienna Circle, he became a logical positivist. In 1936, he published his best-known book *Language, Truth, and Logic*, one of the most influential philosophical essays of the twentieth century.

Ayer's book defended the logical positivist doctrine known as the verification principle, which states that the meaning of any statement is its method of verification. According to this view, which was adopted in order to eliminate all metaphysics, a statement is meaningful if and only if it is either analytic or verifiable by empirical means. Thus, many utterances are pseudo-statements, since they do not express any matter of fact even though they have the grammatical appearance of doing so. Such utterances are therefore neither true nor false. Moral utterances conform to this analysis. So-called "judgments of value" of the form "*x* is good" are not factual judgments at all; instead, they are emotional judgments (reports) meaning "*x* is pleasant" or "*x* is desired." This view of the nature of moral judgments came to be called "emotivism." For Ayer, who was an atheist, moral philosophy is reducible to the metaethical analysis of the meaning of ethical terms.

R. Douglas Geivett

SEE ALSO: Atheism; Cognitivism; Comte, Auguste; Emotivist ethics; Epistemological ethics; Metaethics.

B

Bacon, Francis

IDENTIFICATION: English philosopher
BORN: January 22, 1561, London, England
DIED: April 9, 1626, London, England
TYPE OF ETHICS: Renaissance and Restoration history
SIGNIFICANCE: Bacon inaugurated the naturalistic approach to ethics that came to dominate British moral philosophy into the twentieth century.

Francis Bacon's chief contribution to modern philosophy was his effort to reconstruct completely the conception and practice of science. His own novel method of induction figures prominently in his reconstruction, which helped to launch the modern period of philosophy. His approach, however, was quickly surpassed by better accounts of scientific methodology.

In ethics, the *Essayes* was Bacon's main work. These essays were published in three editions (1597, 1612, 1625), the second one an enlargement upon the first, and the third a completion of the whole. No systematic moral theory is presented; Bacon's style is more aphoristic than philosophical. The *Essayes* offers practical advice on moral and social questions. Bacon's major preoccupation as a philosopher was to point the way in which individuals could be restored to a position of superiority over nature. His views about ethics exhibit a hint of this same spirit. Thomas Hobbes, who is best known for his own elaborate political and moral philosophy, was Bacon's apprentice for a time. His emphasis on overcoming the state of nature may have been reinforced by his association with Bacon.

On a personal note, Bacon pleaded guilty in 1621 to charges of political corruption. For this offense, he paid a fine, was imprisoned in the notorious Tower of London for a brief time, and was permanently banned from political office. Although his particular actions clearly were illegal, the morality of a law that would impugn them has been disputed. As a happy consequence of the leisure thus afforded him, Bacon composed most of his writings during the last five years of his life.

R. Douglas Geivett

SEE ALSO: Enlightenment ethics; Hobbes, Thomas; Power; Science; Technology; Theory and practice.

Bad faith

DEFINITION: Existentialist form of self-deceit in which one accepts as true that which one knows, on some level, to be false
TYPE OF ETHICS: Theory of ethics
SIGNIFICANCE: Bad faith results from the natural human tendency to avoid the sense of responsibility that truly free human beings feel for the consequences of their actions. As authenticity is the ultimate result of complete freedom, moral, social, and political constructs in a free society must discourage bad faith.

The notion of bad faith was introduced by existentialist philosopher Jean-Paul Sartre in his book *L'Être et le néant* (1943; *Being and Nothingness*, 1956). Sartre was known for his theory that humans are not born with an essential nature but have complete freedom to create their essence as individuals. He saw bad faith, or self-deception, as one's denial of one's freedom. When acting in bad faith, individuals willingly accept as true what they know on some level is actually false. It is the acceptance of nonpersuasive, or faulty, evidence about the object of one's deception.

A modern example of society's effort to discourage bad faith is the legal doctrine allowing extracontractual damages for bad faith breach of contract. Under ordinary legal doctrine, damages for breach of contract are limited to those that will put the parties in the same positions they would have been had the contract been performed. In the early 1980's, courts began to award damages beyond this in cases in which contracts were breached in bad faith, that is, with the knowledge that there was no real question as to the existence and extent of the breaching party's obligation.

Sharon K. O'Roke

SEE ALSO: Accountability; Authenticity; Beauvoir, Simone de; *Being and Nothingness*; Conscience; Existentialism; Responsibility.

Baḥya ben Joseph ibn Paḳuda

IDENTIFICATION: Arab philosopher
LIVED: Second half of eleventh century
TYPE OF ETHICS: Religious ethics
SIGNIFICANCE: Baḥya ibn Paḳuda's *Duties of the Heart* (c. 1080) is a classic statement of the inner response necessary for a true commitment of self to the service of God.

Despite Arab and Islamic influence (notably, Muslim Sufism and Arabic Neoplatonism), the cosmological, ethical, and eschatological discourses of Baḥya ben Joseph ibn Paḳuda's *Duties of the Heart* are essentially Jewish in both content and character. Indeed, although written originally in Arabic as *al-Hidāya ilā farāʿid al-gulūb*, *Duties of the Heart* was first popularized in a Hebrew translation of questionable accuracy (*Ḥovot ha-levavot*, 1161).

The introduction distinguishes between overt ceremonial rituals and commandments performed by organs and limbs of the body ("duties of the limbs")—such as prayer, charity, fasting, and so forth—and inward belief, intention, attitude, and feeling, which are accomplished by the human conscience. Each of the ten sections that follow highlights a specific duty of the heart, which serves as a gate through which the soul must ascend if it is to attain spiritual perfection. The ten gates are divine unity, divine wisdom and goodness as the foundation of creation and nature, divine worship, trust in God, unification of and sincerity in purpose and action in serving God, humility, repentance, self-examination, abstinence, and the love of God. Each duty of the heart is illustrated by both positive and negative precepts (for example, to attain

nearness to God, to love those who love him and to hate those who hate him).

All duties of the heart are informed by revealed Torah, tradition, and—especially—reason. Philosophical proofs are offered for the unity and incorporeality of God and for the creation of the world, including teleology and *creatio ex nihilo*. Total separation from the pleasures of the world is not encouraged; the recommended asceticism involves living in society and directing societal obligations toward the service of God.

In summation, the communion of humanity and God is made possible by the duties of the limbs, but the further union of the soul of humanity with the "divine light" of God is by the synthesis of virtues gained by the duties of the heart. Baḥya's theological work, which is considered the most popular moral-religious work of the medieval period, has left an indelible mark on subsequent generations of Jewish ethical and pietistic writing.

Zev Garber

SEE ALSO: God; Jewish ethics; Sufism; Teleological ethics; Torah.

Beauvoir, Simone de

IDENTIFICATION: French philosopher and novelist
BORN: January 9, 1908, Paris, France
DIED: April 14, 1986, Paris, France
TYPE OF ETHICS: Modern history
SIGNIFICANCE: An important voice of both existentialism and feminism, Beauvoir defended existentialist ethics as optimistic, identified ethics with politics, upheld the value of authentic individualism, and propounded the concept that meaning (function, essence) is never fixed. She is author of *The Second Sex* (*Le Deuxième Sexe*, 1949), and other works.

Like Jean-Paul Sartre, her partner in philosophy and in life, Simone de Beauvoir maintained the existentialist point of view that individuals are free from every principle of authority save that which they consciously choose and that they are ineluctably free in a meaningless existence to determine the meaning, or essence, that their lives are to have. She insisted that one's individual existence is authentic to the extent that it is defined by oneself in relation to, but never as prescribed by, others (or the Other).

ETHICS AND AMBIGUITY

According to Beauvoir's 1947 book, *The Ethics of Ambiguity* (*Pour une morale de l'ambiguïté*), the difference between absurdity and ambiguity, as ethical directions, is that absurdity denies the possibility of any meaning, while ambiguity allows that existence, although it has no absolute meaning and no meaning that can achieve permanence, can be given meanings by individuals who do not deceive themselves about the arbitrariness of meaning: Those who do deceive themselves are inauthentic and in "bad faith" (*mauvaise foi*).

Beauvoir illustrated "bad faith" by identifying eight types of man (*l'homme*: Beauvoir always used the generic masculine): the "sub-man," who limits himself to facticity and makes no move toward ethical freedom; the "serious man," who claims to subordinate his freedom to a movement or cause, the values of which he takes as the valorization of himself; the "demoniacal man," who rigidly adheres to the values of his childhood, a society, or a religious institution in order to be able to ridicule them; the "nihilist," who, in wanting to be nothing, rejects, as a corollary to rejecting his own existence, the existences of others, which confirm his own; the "adventurer," who is interested only in the process of his conquest and is indifferent to his goal once it is attained; the "passionate man," who sets up an absolute, such as a work of art or a beloved woman, that he assumes only he is capable of appreciating; the "critic," who defines himself as the mind's independence; and "artists and writers," who transcend existence by eternalizing it. In her categorization, authenticity, which is the self's full awareness and acceptance of its own responsibility for what it is and what it does, can be generated in the movements of only the last two types, each of whom accepts existence as a constant and recognizes the inconstancy of meanings; each is susceptible, however, to the self-deception that characterizes the other six types.

In *Pyrrhus et Cinéas* (1944) Beauvoir had argued the ambiguity of ends: Every goal attained or every end reached becomes no more than a means to still another end, but not to act in the face of nonfinality is to deceive oneself about human reality. Life is incon-

clusive action, and action is one's relationship to the Other and to existence.

The existentialist ethics of ambiguity is individualistic in its opposition to conventional principles of authority, but Beauvoir insisted that it is not solipsistic, since the individual defines himself in relation to others. It is an ethics of freedom but not, she asserted, of anarchy, since the individual discovers his law by being free, not from discipline, but for constructive self-discipline.

EXISTENTIALISM AND CONVENTIONAL WISDOM

The nonsolipsistic character of existentialism is presented with broader scope in the collection of four essays originally written for *Les Temps modernes* during 1945 and 1946. The title essay—literally, "Existentialism and the Wisdom of Nations"—condemns conventional wisdom as resignation. Phrased in commonplaces such as "Possession kills love" and "Human nature will never change," it amounts, in Beauvoir's opinion, to a shirking of the responsibility of challenging the sources of pessimism. She contrasted it with existentialism, which is the directing of one's individual freedom toward the mastery of one's fate, along with the willingness to risk one's own existence in striving to improve the conditions of all existence.

The other three essays in this volume carry ethical risk to levels of abstraction, idealism, and metaphysics (for example, literature should "evoke in its living unity and its fundamental living ambiguity this destiny which is ours and which is inscribed in both time and eternity") from which she retreated in her next three essays.

Must We Burn Sade? (*Privilèges*, 1955) "Right-Wing Thinking Today" attacks bourgeois idealism and conservative ideology in favor of Marxist realism. "Merleau-Ponty and Pseudo-Sartrism" defends Sartre's Marxist philosophy against Maurice Merleau-Ponty's utopian reading of Marxism. Both essays revert to Beauvoir's identification of ethics with politics. The most challenging of the essays in *Must We Burn Sade?* is the title essay, which reemphasizes individualist ethics, self-definition in relation to others without being dictated to by the Other. Beauvoir defended the eighteenth century aristocrat, from whose name the word "sadism" was coined, as one who fashioned a consistent ethics apart from a conventional moral system and in keeping with his self-identifying choice. She applauded neither his actions nor his fictional wish-fulfillments, but she saw his defiant flouting of conventional morality and his exercise of choice as prerequisites for authentic individualism.

Beauvoir elaborated the existentialist concepts of living both for oneself and with others, accepting no situation or moral system that one does not make one's own, acting in commitment, being realistic about human limitations, and eschewing all modes of self-deception.

Roy Arthur Swanson

FURTHER READING

Appignanesi, Lisa. *Simone de Beauvoir.* New York: Penguin Books, 1988.

Arp, Kristana. *The Bonds of Freedom: Simone de Beauvoir's Existentialist Ethics.* Chicago: Open Court, 2001.

Bair, Deirdre. *Simone de Beauvoir: A Biography.* New York: Summit Books, 1990.

Beauvoir, Simone de. *The Ethics of Ambiguity.* Translated by Bernard Frechtman. Secaucus, N.J.: Carol, 1996.

Brosman, Catharine Savage. *Simone de Beauvoir Revisited.* Boston: Twayne, 1991.

Hypatia 14, no. 4 (Fall, 1999). Special issue on "The Philosophy of Simone de Beauvoir," edited by Margaret A. Simons.

Keefe, Terry. *Simone de Beauvoir: A Study of Her Writings.* London: Harrap, 1983.

Whitmarsh, Anne. *Simone de Beauvoir and the Limits of Commitment.* New York: Cambridge University Press, 1981.

SEE ALSO: *Being and Nothingness*; Existentialism; Humanism; Individualism; Sartre, Jean-Paul; *Second Sex, The.*

Behavior therapy

DEFINITION: Collection of procedures for changing behavior based upon principles of learning

DATE: Developed during the early 1950's

TYPE OF ETHICS: Bioethics

SIGNIFICANCE: Because behavior therapy techniques often involve extensive control of patients' environments and can include aversive procedures, they raise ethical concerns about manipulation, denial of rights, and the dehumanization of people.

Behavior therapy describes a set of specific procedures, such as systematic desensitization and contingency management, which began to appear during the early 1950's based on the work of Joseph Wolpe, a South African psychiatrist; Hans Eysenck, a British psychologist; and the American experimental psychologist and radical behaviorist B. F. Skinner. The procedures of behavior therapy are based upon principles of learning and emphasize the careful measurement of undesired behavior and the setting of objective goals. By the 1960's, behavior therapy and behavior-modification procedures were widely taught in colleges and universities and practiced in schools, prisons, hospitals, homes for the developmentally disabled, businesses, and in private practice offices. By the early 1970's, the ethical and legal status of behavior therapy was being challenged from several sources.

ETHICAL CHALLENGES TO BEHAVIOR THERAPY

Behavior therapy techniques have associated with them the same concerns raised by any form of psychotherapy; namely, that informed consent be obtained from the patient, that the patient play the central role in the selecting of therapy goals, that the patient be primary even when a third party may be paying for or requiring the services, and that the least restrictive means (those that least restrict the freedom of the patient) be employed.

Behavior therapy procedures have been challenged on a variety of ethical grounds. Humanistic psychologists, most notably the late Carl Rogers, argued that behavior modification as practiced by the followers of Skinner led to treating people as objects to be manipulated by contrived rewards and denied patients the opportunity to find solutions to their problems through their own resources. Behavior modifiers reply that contrived reinforcers are already a part of our culture, that the learning of self-control techniques increases the client's or patient's freedom, that the patient or client is already controlled by the current environmental consequences, and that the client can select the desired goals of the behavior modification program.

Behavior therapy procedures that involve deprivation (withholding of desired objects and events) or aversive conditioning have come under special criticism. Aversive procedures (such as contingent electric shock) have been employed most often to lessen physically self-abusive behavior in the developmentally disabled and, during the 1970's, in attempts to change the behavior of persons with lengthy histories of sexual deviance. Time-out (a procedure in which a person is removed from all sources of reinforcement for a brief period of time) has also received criticism. Its use by school districts has been restricted in some states.

Legal authorities at two levels have singled out behavior therapy for regulation (again, nearly always techniques that involve aversive procedures or depriving a patient in some manner). Federal courts in several decisions have restricted the kinds of reinforcers (rewards) that may be withheld from patients and have required that in all circumstances the "least restrictive alternative" be employed in treating a patient. In addition, state legislatures and state divisions of mental health have established regulations limiting the use of aversive procedures and requiring review committees for certain behavior-modification techniques.

The Association for the Advancement of Behavior Therapy has developed a set of ethical guidelines for behavior therapists and has, along with the Association for Behavior Analysis, assisted states in developing appropriate regulations that ensure that patients have the right to effective treatment and the right to decline treatment. The associations have also been concerned that persons instituting behavior modification and therapy programs in fact have the requisite training to do so. Standards for claiming expertise in the field have been developed.

One of the unique aspects of behavior analysis and therapy is the attempt to develop ethical principles based upon theories of behaviorism and behavior analyses of the situations in which ethical constraints are necessary. For the most part, these efforts have been undertaken by followers of B. F. Skinner, who have tried to develop his ethical ideas.

Terry Knapp

FURTHER READING

Barker, Philip J., and Steve Baldwin, eds. *Ethical Issues in Mental Health*. London: Chapman & Hall, 1991.
Bellack, Alan S., Michel Herson, and Alan E.
Kazdin, eds. *International Handbook of Behavior Modification and Therapy*. 2d ed. New York: Plenum Press, 1990.
Keith-Spiegel, Patricia, and Gerald P. Koocher. *Ethics in Psychology: Professional Standards and Cases*. New York: McGraw-Hill, 1985.
Scotti, Joseph R., and Luanna H. Meyer, eds. *Behavioral Intervention: Principles, Models, and Practices*. Baltimore: Paul H. Brookes, 1999.
Stolz, Stephanie B. *Ethical Issues in Behavior Modification*. San Francisco: Jossey-Bass, 1978.
Van Hoose, William H., and Jeffery A. Kottler. *Ethical and Legal Issues in Counseling and Psychotherapy*. 2d ed. San Francisco: Jossey-Bass, 1985.

SEE ALSO: Behaviorism; Family therapy; Group therapy; Psychology; Therapist-patient relationship.

Behaviorism

DEFINITION: Systematic study of how environmental factors affect behavior
DATE: Developed during the early twentieth century
TYPE OF ETHICS: Personal and social ethics
SIGNIFICANCE: Behaviorism holds that traditional ethics should be replaced by an objective science of behavior and that such a science should be applied to correct the ills of society and foster moral behavior in individuals.

As a psychological theory, behaviorism can be distinguished from behaviorism as an ethical theory. Psychological behaviorism is a loosely knit collection of theories and doctrines concerning the nature of science and the study of humankind woven around the central idea that psychology should model itself on the objective methods of natural science. In particular, psychology should restrict itself to descriptions of observable behavior, the situations in which it occurs, and its consequences. Such descriptions should make clear, among other things, whether particular environmental conditions tend to positively reinforce (make more likely) or negatively reinforce (make less likely) certain behaviors.

Behaviorism in that sense aims not so much at *explaining* behavior as it does *predicting* and *control-*

ling it. The methodological precept of psychological behaviorism is that this is *all* that a scientific psychology should study. Behaviorism as an ethical theory builds upon the prescriptions and insights of psychological behaviorism and argues that the only effective means of solving individual and social problems is by implementing environmental conditions that systematically encourage "desirable" behaviors and discourage "undesirable" ones. In what follows, the term "behaviorism" will refer both to the methodology of psychological behaviorism and to the goals and procedures of ethical behaviorism.

THEORY OF HUMAN NATURE

The late Harvard psychologist B. F. Skinner is primarily responsible for the development of modern behaviorism. According to Skinner, much of what is called "human nature" refers not to inborn propensities (such as aggression or altruism), but to the effects of environmental variables on behavior. Like other behaviorists, Skinner is little concerned with innate determinants; for, if they exist at all (for example, as part of the genetic endowment), then they, too, can be traced back to the environment through our evolutionary history. The basic qualities of human nature, therefore, are neither good nor bad; they are merely the results of complex environmental interactions. Perhaps more important, what is called an individual's "personality" consists of nothing more than his or her overall behavior repertoire, which is itself a function of the individual's idiosyncratic history of reinforcement.

The behaviorist makes two important assumptions regarding the study of human nature and personality. First, the behaviorist assumes that all behavior is lawful and determined; that is, that behavior is governed by scientific laws of some kind or other. Call this the assumption of universal determinism. Second, the behaviorist assumes that these scientific laws relate environmental causes to behavioral effects. These so-called stimulus-response relations state causal connections that a properly scientific psychology will discover and exploit in the prediction and control of behavior. Call this the assumption of environmentalism. (Environmentalism is as important for what it *denies* as for what it *asserts*. In particular, environmentalism denies that internal mental or physiological processes play an important role in the production of behavior.)

SOCIAL POLICY

The behaviorist's optimism in shaping human behavior by the manipulation of environmental variables is nowhere more evident than in J. B. Watson's famous claim that if he were given a dozen healthy infants, he could guarantee to take any one at random and train the child to become a doctor, lawyer, beggar-man, or thief. This optimistic (and extreme) version of environmentalism forms the basis of behaviorism as a social policy.

Skinner has repeatedly made the argument that the inescapable fact of the matter is that behavior is controlled either by factors that lie outside human knowledge and thereby intelligent control and manipulation or by factors that people create and can thereby direct toward ends of their choosing. The choice is *not* between actions that are "free" and actions that are "determined," as perhaps a traditional ethicist might insist, for *all* human actions (behaviors) are under the control of the environment. Rather, Skinner insists, the choice is to allow arbitrary and unknown factors to shape behavior or to manipulate the environment in order to create the best possible humans.

Behaviorists are vague about how one should go about manipulating the environment, though a few steps immediately suggest themselves. First, science must elucidate the processes and factors that control behavior. Why is it, for example, that Peter becomes a doctor and Paul becomes a thief? Second, this knowledge must be utilized by governments, educators, parents, and so on to develop more productive and socially beneficial behaviors. Parenting and social policy must work in tandem in this (as yet unspecified) process.

Behaviorists are even more vague about what should count as desirable behaviors and who should decide them. To say that people ought to be "happy and productive" is platitudinous, and it hardly guarantees respect for human rights or democratic forms of government. Skinner claims that objective science can settle the matter of what should count as socially beneficial behavior, and he states that totalitarian societies would be inimical to the flourishing of human potential. The fact remains, however, that what is good for the individual may not be what is good for society, and neither may be what is good for the long-term survival of the species. How these competing conceptions of the good might be resolved by science is far from clear.

ANALYSIS

Psychological behaviorism has been used with much success in behavior modification therapy, educational and industrial settings, prisons, and even advertising. Few would disagree that the behavioral sciences have made great progress in predicting and controlling behavior. The question of whether the principles and methods of behaviorism can be extended to deal with problems of enormous magnitude and complexity, however, is far from answered.

Even if such principles and methods can be extended, one is still left with the question of whether they should be. Moreover, many philosophers and psychologists doubt either universal determinism or environmentalism, or both. Long-standing beliefs regarding human freedom and volition contradict the assumption of universal determinism, and modern cognitive science is committed to the view that internal mental processes are not incidental to intelligent behavior—that they are, in fact, essential to it. On either account, behaviorism may be deeply flawed. Even so, behaviorism's vision of a happier and more rational human order based upon the tenets of natural science and human reason remains the hope of many.

James A. Anderson

FURTHER READING

Nye, Robert D. *Three Psychologies: Perspectives from Freud, Skinner, and Rogers.* 6th ed. Pacific Grove, Calif.: Brooks/Cole, 2000.

Skinner, B. F. *Science and Human Behavior.* New York: Free Press, 1965.

_____. *Walden Two.* 2d ed. New York: Macmillan, 1990.

Staddon, John. *The New Behaviorism: Mind, Mechanism, and Society.* Philadelphia: Psychology Press, 2001.

Stevenson, Leslie, and David L. Haberman. *Ten Theories of Human Nature.* 3d ed. New York: Oxford University Press, 1998.

Watson, J. B. *Behaviorism.* New York: W. W. Norton, 1970.

SEE ALSO: Animal consciousness; Behavior therapy; Choice; Human nature; Motivation; Psychology.

Being and Nothingness

IDENTIFICATION: Book by Jean-Paul Sartre (1905-1980)

DATE: *L'Être et le néant*, 1943 (English translation, 1956)

TYPE OF ETHICS: Modern history

SIGNIFICANCE: According to *Being and Nothingness*, human beings are free, but freedom is given within the limits of historical existence; interhuman relationships are threatened by each person's ability to objectify others.

For Jean-Paul Sartre, human existence is conscious being, "being-for-itself" (*pour-soi*). Human existence as "being-for-itself" is temporal—always in some present, always on the way from some past toward some future. Another characteristic of human existence is its dependence on things. Things have a fundamentally different mode of existence: "being-in-itself" (*en-soi*). They have no consciousness, no possibilities, no freedom. Their being is complete as it is.

One danger for human existence is that it may be falsely reduced from free "being-for-itself" to unfree "being-in-itself." This threat may come from others or from oneself. One may intentionally avoid freedom and the anxiety of conscious decision making by convincing oneself that one has no options, but this is to reduce oneself to an object, to use freedom to deny freedom, to live in "bad faith" (*mauvaise foi*).

The existence of "the others" (*autrui*) is a fundamental fact of human existence. In Sartre's view, however, the constant factor in interpersonal relationships is not potential harmony, but inevitable alienation. Lovers, in his analysis, cannot avoid the objectifying will to possess, which denies freedom and reduces the loved one from "being-for-itself" to "being-in-itself."

SEE ALSO: Bad faith; Beauvoir, Simone de; Cruelty; Existentialism; Lifestyles; Love; Other, the; Personal relationships; Sartre, Jean-Paul.

Benevolence

DEFINITION: Motivation to act sympathetically and altruistically

TYPE OF ETHICS: Theory of ethics

SIGNIFICANCE: Benevolence is a source of controversy in ethics. For some theorists, the central task of ethics is to encourage benevolence; for others, benevolence is unethical.

Thomas Aquinas, David Hume, and many others consider benevolence or altruism a key virtue. As Michael W. Martin acutely observes, "Hume makes [benevolence] the supreme virtue, and of all virtue ethicists Hume most deserves to be called the philosopher of benevolence." Jonathan Edwards considers benevolence the supreme virtue in Christianity. Hume believes that benevolent acts are natural products of two features of human nature: sympathy and imagination. Sympathy generates altruistic desires, while imagination enables one to see oneself in the shoes of others in need and conclude, "There but for the grace of God or good fortune go I."

Charity is a virtue that involves benevolence. Martin reported some hard data on charity. He found that rich people and wealthy foundations account for only 10 percent of private donations. The remaining 90 percent comes from individuals, half of whom are in families whose income is under $39,000 a year. Also about half of Americans older than thirteen volunteer an average of 3.5 hours of their time each week. Horace Mann used the concept of benevolence to try to distinguish between the ethical value of generosity during the prime of life (for example, teenage volunteers) and deathbed generosity. He said, "Generosity during life is a very different thing from generosity in the hour of death; one proceeds from genuine liberality and benevolence, the other from pride or fear."

In law, mortmain statutes forbid deathbed gifts, apparently out of concern that the gift may be motivated by desperate fear rather than genuine benevolence. Law often encourages benevolence by providing tax deductions for charitable donations, but traditional Anglo-American law (unlike Islamic law, for example) imposes no general duty to rescue strangers and thus fails to require much benevolence.

Regarding political and business ethics, some people argue that the welfare state institutionalizes benevolence and charity. They contend that welfare state programs such as those that mandate minimum wages and relief payments smooth some of the rough edges of laissez-faire capitalism, which is notorious for its cutthroat competition. The alternative of relying on private donations to charity, they believe, will tend to fail precisely when charity is needed most, during an economic recession or depression. During such hard times, people will have less to give for charity and will be less willing to give what they do have as a result of economic insecurity. These trends will intensify as the number of charity cases grows and the need for charitable giving grows with them.

In political ethics and in debates on sex and gender issues, benevolence plays a crucial role. While many feminists try to debunk stereotypes of women as the more emotional and illogical sex, other feminists support the idea that women have a special ethical outlook called care ethics. The latter feminists follow Carol Gilligan in suggesting that women are generally more cooperative and less confrontational than men.

Care ethics claims that women are generally less interested in dealing with abstract rules and impersonal ideals such as justice and impartiality and are more interested in nurturing personal relationships by attending to the specifics of the backgrounds or surroundings of particular people. This view seems self-contradictory, however, since so much of the specific backgrounds of particular people consists of rules, which care ethics was designed to deemphasize. Such contradictions do not deter some feminists, who openly embrace inconsistency while criticizing traditional ethics for being male-dominated and logocentric. Unfortunately, aside from its obvious illogic, this view has the defect of playing into the hands of those who would stereotype women as more prone to hysteria and inconsistent mood swings between emotional extremes (for example, the view that it is a woman's prerogative to change her mind). Some feminists thus regard care ethics as making a retrograde step in the women's movement.

Ethical egoism and the thinking of Friedrich Nietzsche condemn benevolence. Ethical egoists, such as Ayn Rand, think that each person should always act only in his or her self-interest. In contrast, Johann Friedrich Herbart argued that benevolence involves the harmonization of one's will with others' wills. Nietzsche's concept of the will to power rejects such harmony between wills. One's will to power involves one's domination of the weak.

In conclusion, it would be appropriate to ponder Walter Bagehot's view that "The most melancholy of human reflections, perhaps, is that, on the whole, it is a question whether the benevolence of mankind does most good or harm."

Sterling Harwood

FURTHER READING

Bartkowski, John P., and Helen A. Regis. *Charitable Choices: Religion, Race, and Poverty in the Post Welfare Era.* New York: New York University, 2003.

Gauthier, David P., ed. *Morality and Rational Self-interest.* Englewood Cliffs, N.J.: Prentice-Hall, 1970.

Gilligan, Carol. *In a Different Voice: Psychological Theory and Women's Development.* Cambridge, Mass.: Harvard University Press, 1982.

Kaufmann, Harry. *Aggression and Altruism.* New York: Holt, Rinehart and Winston, 1970.

Martin, Michael W. *Everyday Morality: An Introduction to Applied Ethics.* Belmont, Calif.: Wadsworth, 1989.

Nagel, Thomas. *The Possibility of Altruism.* Oxford, England: Clarendon Press, 1970.

Post, Stephen G., et al., eds. *Altruism and Altruistic Love: Science, Philosophy, and Religion in Dialogue.* New York: Oxford University Press, 2002.

Rand, Ayn. *The Virtue of Selfishness: A New Concept of Egoism.* New York: New American Library, 1964.

Rescher, Nicholas. *Unselfishness: The Role of the Vicarious Affects in Moral Philosophy and Social Theory.* Pittsburgh: University of Pittsburgh Press, 1975.

Singer, Peter. *The Expanding Circle: Ethics and Sociobiology.* New York: Farrar, Straus & Giroux, 1981.

Wilson, Edward O. *On Human Nature.* Cambridge, Mass.: Harvard University Press, 1978.

SEE ALSO: Altruism; Christian ethics; Edwards, Jonathan; Hume, David; Nietzsche, Friedrich; Rand, Ayn; Thomas Aquinas; Virtue ethics.

Bennett, William

IDENTIFICATION: Official in two Republican presidential administrations, popular speaker, and author

BORN: July 31, 1943, Brooklyn, New York

TYPE OF ETHICS: Personal and social ethics

SIGNIFICANCE: The public's discovery of Bennett's gambling habit seemed to some observers inconsistent with his well-known stances on moral issues.

William J. Bennett spent most of the 1980's in prominent political posts, beginning with his tenures as chairman of the National Endowment for the Humanities and as secretary of education under President Ronald Reagan, and continuing as President George Bush's director of drug policy (for which he was dubbed the "drug czar") from 1989 to 1990. Bennett afterward earned a reputation as a champion for traditional moral values, especially through his publication in 1993 of *The Book of Virtues: A Treasury of Great Moral Stories.* This collection of stories and other readings was designed to provide readers with examples of virtues around which they might anchor their own moral lives. Bennett followed this best-selling volume with *The Book of Virtues for Young People: A Treasury of Great Moral Stories* (1996) and *The Children's Book of Heroes* (1997), books specifically targeted at younger readers.

Bennett's reputation as a kind of "czar" of virtue suffered a severe setback in 2003, upon the public's discovery that he was a high-stakes gambler and a preferred customer at several Las Vegas and Atlantic City casinos. By at least some accounts, his gambling losses over the previous decade had amounted to millions of dollars. Bennett's initial response to these revelations was to insist that he had never jeopardized his family's financial security through his gambling and that he had broken no laws. Although some critics accused him of hypocrisy, Bennett insisted that he had never publicly assailed gambling as a vice. However, he subsequently announced to the public that he believed his gambling to have been a sin and that he planned to give it up.

Timothy L. Hall

SEE ALSO: Conscience; Ethics/morality distinction; Family values; Hypocrisy; Value; Values clarification.

Bentham, Jeremy

IDENTIFICATION: English philosopher and economist
BORN: February 15, 1748, London, England
DIED: June 6, 1832, London, England
TYPE OF ETHICS: Modern history
SIGNIFICANCE: Bentham was a founder of English utilitarianism. In such works as *A Fragment on Government* (1776), *An Introduction to the Principles of Morals and Legislation* (1789), *The Rationale of Reward* (1825), and *The Rationale of Punishment* (1830), he systematically developed a social theory and an ethics based upon the goal of the "greatest happiness for the greatest number" of people.

Frustrated by his inability to pursue a career in politics and law, Jeremy Bentham developed a radical philosophy based upon the notion of the "greatest happiness principle." He argued that humankind by nature seeks pleasure and the avoidance of pain and that this principle should be the dominant value in society. Society should seek to promote the "greatest happiness for the greatest number." Furthermore, Bentham contended that the law should be based upon this ethical principle. The level of "evil" that results from a crime should be the basis for appropriate punishment; the motivation for the crime is fundamentally insignificant.

Bentham maintained that some alleged crimes, such as homosexuality, were not criminal actions because they did not cause harm to anyone. The greatest happiness principle would be realized through an effective government that would be focused on four major concerns: subsistence, abundance, security, and equality. Bentham and John Stuart Mill were the founders of English utilitarianism, which was a philosophic elaboration of the greatest happiness principle.

William T. Walker

SEE ALSO: Consequentialism; Criminal punishment; Distributive justice; Good, the; Hedonism; Mill, John Stuart; Teleological ethics; Utilitarianism.

Berdyayev, Nikolay

IDENTIFICATION: Russian philosopher
BORN: March 6, 1874, Kiev, Ukraine, Russian Empire
DIED: March 24, 1948, Clamart, France
TYPE OF ETHICS: Modern history
SIGNIFICANCE: Berdyayev's Christian existentialism explored the role of freedom in the improvement of humankind. He was author of *The Origin of Russian Communism* (1937) and editor of the journal *Put'* (path).

A Marxist in his youth, Nikolay Berdyayev moved steadily toward religious idealism. After failed attempts to revitalize Russian spirituality by reconciling the intelligentsia with the Russian Orthodox Church, he distanced himself from the main socialist and liberal reform movements and investigated teleological and eschatological approaches. While retaining traces of his early Marxism, he combined mystical elements taken from early Christian theology, the Reformation theologian Jacob Boehme, and the Moscow philosopher Vladimir S. Solovyov with the idealistic philosophy of Immanuel Kant to develop a Christian existentialist philosophy.

In numerous writings, Berdyayev criticized the materialism and spiritual impoverishment of the Russian intelligentsia; promoted intuitive, mystical modes of investigation; and rejected logic and rationality. To Berdyayev, the value of humanity lay in its capacity for creation. The act of creation illuminated truth and helped to bridge the gap between God and human beings, Creator and created. The key element in Berdyayev's God/human relationship was the way in which freedom was used. If it was used in the service of enlarged awareness and capacity, God and humanity became co-creators in a continually progressing universe; if it was turned toward material products instead of being, humanity and society remained in turmoil and confusion.

Michael J. Fontenot

SEE ALSO: Christian ethics; Determinism and freedom; Existentialism.

Bergson, Henri

IDENTIFICATION: French philosopher
BORN October 18, 1859, Paris, France
DIED: January 4, 1941, Paris, France
TYPE OF ETHICS: Modern history
SIGNIFICANCE: The first person to advance a "process philosophy," Bergson emphasized the primacy of personal actions within the context of evolutionary processes. He wrote several important philosophical treatises, the most famous of which was *Matter and Memory* (*Matière et mémoire: Essai sur la relation du corps à l'esprit,* 1896).

Throughout his professional life, Henri Bergson maintained that ethical questions, which are affected by myriad external factors, were fundamentally personal issues. During the latter part of his life, Bergson became absorbed in mysticism and religious thought. In *The Two Sources of Morality and Religion* (*Les Deux Sources de la morale et de la religion*, 1932), he argued that human progress—including the ethical dimension—would be advanced by those few who gained intuitive insight into the mind of God. These "enlightened" individuals would contribute to the continuing progressive evolution of humanity by providing direction and leadership.

Thus, Bergson moved in the direction of the authoritarianism of the Christian tradition in which mystics assume an obligation to control society and direct it toward the realization of its fullest potential (the good) in the evolutionary process. He noted that this process would be impeded by the seemingly endless effort to provide the requirements for sustaining physical life. Bergson's philosophy opposed "radical finalism"; in the ethical aspect as in all others, it supported a "progression," or "fulfillment," predicated upon the direction of overriding principles.

William T. Walker

SEE ALSO: Aurobindo, Sri; Christian ethics; Mysticism; Whitehead, Alfred North.

Betting on sports

DEFINITION: Legalized gambling on the outcome of sporting events that is sanctioned by, and sometimes promoted by, governmental bodies
TYPE OF ETHICS: Personal and social ethics
SIGNIFICANCE: Although sometimes defended as a way of discouraging organized crime from dominating gambling, legalized betting on sports has created other ethical problems.

Wagering on sporting events has existed at least since the time of the ancient Greek Olympic Games, but it now pervades many parts of the world. In the early twentieth century, the influence of organized crime resulted in scandals in both professional and amateur sports and led to greater vigilance by governmental bodies. The sanctioning or tacit approval of betting on sports events by the media has reduced the involvement of organized crime but has undoubtedly made betting on sports more popular than ever.

The question of the advisability of allowing betting to flourish legally is part of the larger question of whether gambling should be permitted at all. In a society of religious diversity and widespread religious skepticism, prohibitions based on specific religious doctrines do not command widespread allegiance. In a country such as the United States, such prohibitions are likely to be condemned as violating the separation of church and state as well as being constitutional affronts to personal freedom. Important arguments remain, however, to the effect that betting on sports events is harmful both to the bettors and to the sports on which they bet.

Although liberal moralists are likely to argue that the follies of weak individuals may be addressed without impinging on the freedoms of others, gambling may be objected to as leading to personal dissolution and the neglect of family and other social responsibilities. Regardless of whether a given behavior is intrinsically wrong, however, it becomes a legitimate concern of citizens and lawmakers if it leads to criminal behavior that is costly or destructive to society. Compulsive betting, like addiction to drugs, may lead participants into levels of financial ruin that in turn offer strong temptations to commit actual crimes, such as larceny, to sustain the addiction.

With specific reference to sports betting, oppo-

In 1989, former baseball star Pete Rose was banned for life from Major League Baseball, apparently for having gambled on baseball games while managing a team. Fifteen years later he published a memoir, My Prison Without Bars, *in an evident attempt to win reinstatement in time to be admitted into the Baseball Hall of Fame.* (AP/ Wide World Photos)

nents of the routine modern publication of point spreads and betting odds on games in the sports pages of daily newspapers see these practices as encouragements to more widespread wagering than would otherwise be the case, thus increasing the numbers of bettors. Published point spreads offer inducements to bettors and sports participants alike. An individual athlete urged to shave the margin of victory may conclude that merely winning by a closer margin than expected is not as serious as "throwing" a game; however, such behavior poses a threat to the integrity of games such as basketball and football in which spreads are widely publicized and discussed.

A final objection to legalized betting is that emphasizing the importance of betting odds tends to persuade sports devotees of the dubious proposition that the most important measure of the worth of sport is the money that can be made, whether by playing or gaming.

Robert P. Ellis

FURTHER READING

Pavalko, Ronald M. *Risky Business: America's Fascination with Gambling.* New York: Wadsworth, 1999.

Walker, Michael B. *The Psychology of Gambling.* New York: Pergamon Press, 1997.

SEE ALSO: Family values; Lotteries; Medical ethics; Native American casinos; Relativism; Responsibility; Vice.

Beyond Good and Evil

IDENTIFICATION: Book by Friedrich Nietzsche (1844-1900)

DATE: *Jenseits von Gut und Böse: Vorspiel einer Philosophie der Zukunft*, 1886 (English translation, 1907)

TYPE OF ETHICS: Modern history

SIGNIFICANCE: The first of his two major treatises on morality, Nietzsche's *Beyond Good and Evil* argues against the unquestioning acceptance of universal value systems or seemingly absolute values such as good or truth. It advocates instead a critical, pragmatic approach to values in which each individual subscribes to those values that are best suited to the individual's own life and experience.

Friedrich Nietzsche disputed the long-unexamined notion that morality was an absolute. He believed that morality was relative to the condition in which one finds oneself. In *Beyond Good and Evil*, he defined two moralities. The "master morality" encouraged strength, power, freedom, and achievement, while the "slave morality" valued sympathy, charity, forgiveness, and humility. Those qualities that the master morality deemed "good," such as strength and power, were a source of fear to the slave morality and were thus deemed "evil." Nietzsche believed that each person was motivated by the "will to power," the essential driving force behind human behavior, and that exploitation of the weak by the strong was the very nature of life. Reform movements such as democracy and Christianity, which he associated with the slave morality, tried to negate this basic life function and were thus "antilife."

Nietzsche feared that Western society had been unduly influenced by the slave morality's resentment and fear of the life-affirming qualities of the master type. Because the achievements of the master class were necessary to human progress, the overall effect was a weakening of the human race. To solve the problem, *Beyond Good and Evil* suggested that the master class's will to power should be encouraged and that members of this class should be freed from the debilitating value system of the oppressed so that they could rise above the paradigm of the slave morality; that is, "beyond good and evil." Thus freed, they could metamorphose into a higher level of existence, which Nietzsche termed "the overman."

William L. Howard

SEE ALSO: Elitism; Evil; Maximal vs. minimal ethics; Nietzsche, Friedrich; Police brutality; Power.

Bhagavadgītā

IDENTIFICATION: Central text of Hinduism

DATE: Written between c. 200 B.C.E. and 200 C.E

TYPE OF ETHICS: Religious ethics

SIGNIFICANCE: Taken from the Vedic tradition, the *Bhagavadgītā* contains practical guidelines for ethical living, acknowledging standard moral values but emphasizing that the particular situation determines the right course of action.

The *Bhagavadgītā* is the crown jewel of Vedic literature and has had a profound influence on Hindu thought, ethics, and practices. A short eighteen chapters in the epic *Mahābhārata*, the Gita consists of a dialogue between Lord Kṛṣṇa (an incarnation of the god Viṣṇu) and Arjuṅa, a great warrior. A battle between the Pavas—Arjuṅa and his brothers—against the evil Kauravas is imminent, but Arjuṅa is suddenly transfixed when he realizes that he must wage war against relatives and close friends. He asks for Kṛṣṇa's guidance.

Kṛṣṇa's reply to this and subsequent questions constitutes the text of the *Bhagavadgītā*, whose title translates literally as "divine song."

Kṛṣṇa begins by addressing Arjuṅa's problem, stressing that nothing with a soul really dies. People are immortal. Furthermore, Arjuṅa's duty as a warrior is to fight in a righteous battle. With these instructions, Kṛṣṇa reveals his relativistic ethics—right action must be appropriate to the specific situation.

CENTRAL MESSAGE OF THE GITA

Kṛṣṇa continues by revealing the central message of the Gita: be without the three *guṇas*, the basic forces of nature that bind people to the temporal world. The first, *sattva*, or light, binds people to happiness and lower knowledge. The second, *rajas*, or fire, binds people to action with strong desires. The third, *tamas*, or darkness, binds people to sleepy dullness. In transcending the everyday world of the senses to gain a direct perception of God, or ultimate reality, one must resist being overcome by these forces. By working toward this transcendence, one can achieve liberation from the cycle of death and rebirth and live in eternal bliss consciousness.

At first, Kṛṣṇa describes two basic ways to transcend the three *guṇas*: Jñāna Yoga and Karma Yoga. Jñāna Yoga is the way of monks or renunciants—the path of wisdom on which one studies the sacred texts and lives life away from the pleasures of the world. Karma Yoga is the way of the householder—the path of action on which one is active in the world, meditates, and follows one's dharma, or duty. In terms of talent and temperament, people are suited to different roles in society; therefore, everyone has a duty that, however lowly, should always be followed. In later epochs of Indian history, this key concept gave rise to a rigid caste system.

Later, Kṛṣṇa talks about a third path, that of Bhakti Yoga, or the path of devotion, on which one practices Vedic rituals or simply offers anything one does to Kṛṣṇa or some lesser god. Kṛṣṇa emphasizes that everyone should practice all three Yogas, although one Yoga will tend to predominate in one's life.

Philip Magnier

SEE ALSO: Ahiṁsā; Caste system, Hindu; Gandhi, Mohandas K.; Ḥallāṛ, al-; Hindu ethics; Karma; Narrative ethics; Nonviolence; Religion.

Bigotry

DEFINITION: Obstinate and unreasonable attachment to one's own opinions and prejudices
TYPE OF ETHICS: Race and ethnicity
SIGNIFICANCE: Bigotry causes innumerable personal and social problems, raising many issues in ethics.

Bigotry is the obstinate and unreasonable attachment to one's own opinions or beliefs. A bigot is intolerant of beliefs that oppose his or her own. This is the state of mind of a prejudiced person. Often, such a person is very emotional and may become stubbornly intolerant or even hostile toward others who differ with him or her regarding religion, race, sexual orientation, or other issues. This state of mind encourages stereotyping, overgeneralization, and other errors that suggest the absence of critical thinking.

Bigoted attitudes can be culturally transmitted as part of the education of children or adults. Bigotry is a learned prejudice that is founded on inaccurate and inflexible overgeneralizations. Bigots may believe, for example, that all black people are thieves, despite the fact that they have no experience on which to base

such a belief. They may even know scrupulously honest black people. In such cases, the bigots will state that such black people are the exceptions to the rule or that they have yet to reveal their truly degenerate characters by being caught stealing. When confronted with new information that contradicts their beliefs, bigots are unwilling to change. Instead, they typically grow excited and emotional when their prejudices are threatened.

Bigoted attitudes are learned from the social environment. Some people believe that economic competition creates conflict between groups and that this scenario may create hostility and prejudices. The probability of conflict increases if two groups differ in easily identifiable ways. Thus, those who pose the greatest threat to people's jobs or security become the targets of those people's prejudice and bigotry. For example, when Vietnamese immigrants to the United States bought fishing boats and began successfully to fish off the coast of Texas, many Texan fishermen called them names, threatened them, and physically attacked them. The immigrants' fishing boats were burned by Texan bigots who feared being displaced because they could not compete with the Vietnamese. Bigotry and unfair tactics were used to eliminate competition and reward inefficient fishermen.

OTHER FORMS OF BIGOTRY

Bigotry is not confined to race. Some bigots dislike fat people, redheads, or older people and discriminate against these populations without cause. It should not be forgotten that, in addition to persecuting African Americans, the Ku Klux Klan targeted Roman Catholics and Jews as objects of their hatred.

In societies such as the old American South or the white minority-ruled apartheid regime of South Africa, where racial prejudice was legally sanctioned and socially rewarded, people often manifested both prejudice and discrimination as a means of conforming to prevailing social norms, values, and beliefs. It was against the law for black South Africans to become bosses or managers because it would have given them authority over white workers, which was unthinkable to white South Africans. To them, a person's biological inheritance set limits upon that person's current position and what he or she would be allowed to achieve. Where social reward and reinforcement for such ethically reprehensible behavior are absent, bigotry and prejudice are likely to be exhibited by people who suffer from personal insecurity or psychological problems.

Bigotry is not immutable behavior. Social policy can be used to influence bigots in positive ways. Teaching bigots to avoid overgeneralizations and to think critically can provide a good beginning.

Dallas L. Browne

SEE ALSO: Anti-Semitism; Apartheid; Civil rights and liberties; Discrimination; Ethnocentrism; Hate crime and hate speech; Racial prejudice; Racism; Segregation; Sexual stereotypes.

Bilingual education

DEFINITION: Educational policy developed in late twentieth century America for the purpose of instructing young immigrant and ethnic minority children in their native or home languages and in English at the same time
TYPE OF ETHICS: Children's rights
SIGNIFICANCE: Educating non-English-speaking children to acquire English-language skills that will enable them to succeed in the classroom and become self-reliant, productive citizens is a generally accepted goal. However, the question of whether achieving this goal through bilingual education is ethical remains debatable.

Political and philosophical differences and debates over educational direction have resulted in sharp disagreements among those involved regarding the purpose and value of bilingual education. Some educators have argued that non-English-speaking children should be mainstreamed into English-medium classes in what has been dubbed the "immersion," "transitional," or "English-only" method. Others have argued that successful immersion experiences seldom occur and that "developmental" or "dual language" bilingual education remains the most effective way.

As part of the Title VII Elementary and Secondary Education Act, the Bilingual Education Act became federal law in 1968. The Bilingual Education Act was based on three points: Many immigrant children have limited ability to speak or write English; many come from ethnically diverse, non-English-speaking backgrounds; and native languages and cul-

ture affect a child's learning. Based on these points, Congress reached a decision that many children in the United States need to be educated through programs in bilingual education. Since 1968, amendments to Title VII in 1974, 1978, 1984, 1988, 1994, and 2002 resulted in policy changes promoting or opposing bilingual education methods. For example, in 1999, the Educational Excellence for All Children Act was implemented, mandating English-language standards for all children, regardless of their backgrounds. The No Child Left Behind Act of 2001 included a provision supporting the "preservation and maintenance" of Native American languages only. In 1998, California's Proposition 227 mandated abolishing bilingual education practices altogether in that state. In 2000, Arizona followed suit.

CONTROVERSY

One perspective places greater emphasis on attaining more successful integration and assimilation of immigrant and ethnic minority children. The expected outcomes mostly have to do with English-language acquisition. Accelerated assimilation of all non-English-speaking children into an English-speaking society remains the central goal of many parents, educators, and politicians. Many people believe that bilingual-education practices promote diversity to the detriment of national unity.

Others argue in favor of sustaining a child's home language and culture, contributing to the overall development of the child. Sociocultural, academic, cognitive, and linguistic factors become interdependent and—some parents, educators, and politicians assert—should not be overlooked. For bilingual education to become effective, the active involvement of parents, the relationships between schools and communities, and financial and material resources all come into play.

Bilingual education persists as a deeply divisive issue on educational as well as political grounds. Because desired means to ends are varied, bilingual education is likely to remain a political issue.

Kevin Eyster

FURTHER READING
Bull, Barry L., Royal T. Fruehling, and Virgie Chattergy. *The Ethics of Multicultural and Bilingual Education.* New York: Teachers College Press, 1992.

Cutri, Ramona Maile, and Scott Ferrin. "Moral Dimensions of Bilingual Education." *Bilingual Research Journal* 22, no. 1 (Winter 1998): 31-44.

Midobuche, Eva. "Respect in the Classroom." *Educational Leadership* 56, no. 7 (1999): 80-82.

SEE ALSO: Child psychology; Children; Diversity; Head Start; Intelligence testing; Multiculturalism.

Bill of Rights, U.S.

IDENTIFICATION: Collective name for the first ten amendments to the U.S. Constitution

DATE: Adopted on December 15, 1791

TYPE OF ETHICS: Civil rights

SIGNIFICANCE: The Bill of Rights provides legal and civil rights and liberties to all citizens of the United States and places limits upon the powers of the federal government.

The Bill of Rights, which comprises the first ten amendments to the U.S. Constitution, is the legal basis for the protection of the civil and legal rights and liberties of the people of the United States. Protection of those rights and liberties was not included in the Constitution itself because the majority of the framers did not feel it was necessary. The federal government was a government of limited powers and therefore could not violate the rights of the citizens. It was at the state level that protection was necessary, and most state constitutions included bills of rights.

When the U.S. Constitution was submitted to the states for adoption, however, objections centered on its lack of a bill of rights. Its proponents agreed to submit amendments after the adoption was completed. James Madison led the effort and persuaded the first House of Representatives and the Senate to submit twelve amendments to the states. Ten of the amendments were approved between 1789 and 1791. In December, 1791, the ten amendments were adopted and became known as the Bill of Rights.

PROTECTIONS OFFERED BY THE BILL

The first eight amendments enumerate rights that cannot be abridged by Congress. Freedom of speech, press, assembly, petition, and religion are included in the First Amendment. The right to keep and bear arms is in the Second Amendment. The Third Amendment prohibits the quartering of troops in private homes. The Fourth Amendment provides for persons to be secure in their person, homes, and papers against unreasonable search and seizure, and sets limits for search warrants. The Fifth Amendment rights are concerned with procedural guarantees. Indictment by a grand jury in criminal cases, a ban on double jeopardy, and a ban on self-incrimination are included in the Fifth Amendment. It also mandates that persons cannot be deprived of life, liberty, or property except by due process of law and that private property cannot be taken for public use without just compensation.

The Sixth Amendment ensures the right to a speedy and public trial by an impartial jury in the state and district where a crime was committed and in a court previously established by law. The accused shall be informed of the charge, be confronted with the witnesses, and shall have subpoena power and council. The right of trial by jury is included in the Seventh Amendment. The Eighth Amendment prohibits excessive bail and cruel and unusual punishment. The Ninth and Tenth Amendments were added to ensure that the Bill of Rights would not be used to deprive the people or the states of their implied rights or reserved powers. The Ninth Amendment says that the enumeration of rights does not mean that others not included are denied. Powers not delegated to the federal government or denied to the states are reserved to the states or to the people by the Tenth Amendment.

Initially, the Bill of Rights was not tested in the federal courts. Even the Alien and Sedition Acts, passed by the Federalists in 1798, were not taken into court, because people believed that the Supreme Court, staffed by Federalists in 1798, would not declare them unconstitutional.

The Supreme Court accepted cases involving the Bill of Rights during the 1830's. Chief Justice John Marshall's decision in *Barron v. Baltimore* in 1833 established the principle that the Bill of Rights did not apply to the states. This view dominated Court decisions, with only a couple of isolated exceptions, until the 1930's. In 1897, the due process clause of the Fourteenth Amendment was used to apply the Fifth Amendment right of protection of property to the states, and in 1925 in *Gitlow v. United States*, the Supreme Court held that freedom of speech and press

The Bill of Rights

ARTICLE I

Congress shall make no law respecting an establishment of religion, or prohibiting the free exercise thereof; or abridging the freedom of speech, or of the press; or the right of the people peaceably to assemble, and to petition the Government for a redress of grievances.

ARTICLE II

A well regulated Militia, being necessary to the security of a free State, the right of the people to keep and bear Arms, shall not be infringed.

ARTICLE III

No Soldier shall, in time of peace be quartered in any house, without the consent of the Owner, nor in time of war, but in a manner to be prescribed by law.

ARTICLE IV

The right of the people to be secure in their persons, houses, papers, and effects, against unreasonable searches and seizures, shall not be violated, and no Warrants shall issue, but upon probable cause, supported by Oath or affirmation, and particularly describing the place to be searched, and the persons or things to be seized.

ARTICLE V

No person shall be held to answer for a capital, or otherwise infamous crime, unless on a presentment or indictment of a Grand Jury, except in cases arising in the land or naval forces, or in the Militia, when in actual service in time of War or public danger; nor shall any person be subject for the same offence to be twice put in jeopardy of life or limb; nor shall be compelled in any criminal case to be a witness against himself, nor be deprived of life, liberty, or property, without due process of law; nor shall private property be taken for public use without just compensation.

ARTICLE VI

In all criminal prosecutions, the accused shall enjoy the right to a speedy and public trial, by an impartial jury of the State and district wherein the crime shall have been committed, which district shall have been previously ascertained by law, and to be informed of the nature and cause of the accusation; to be confronted with the witnesses against him; to have compulsory process for obtaining Witnesses in his favor, and to have the assistance of counsel for his defence.

ARTICLE VII

In Suits at common law, where the value in controversy shall exceed twenty dollars, the right of trial by jury shall be preserved, and no fact tried by a jury, shall be otherwise reexamined in any Court of the United States, than according to the rules of the common law.

ARTICLE VIII

Excessive bail shall not be required, nor excessive fines imposed, nor cruel and unusual punishments inflicted.

ARTICLE IX

The enumeration in the Constitution, of certain rights, shall not be construed to deny or disparage others retained by the people.

ARTICLE X

The powers not delegated to the United States by the Constitution, nor prohibited by it to the States, are reserved to the States respectively, or to the people.

are among the fundamental liberties protected by the due process clause of the Fourteenth Amendment from impairment by the states.

During the 1930's, the Supreme Court began the "modernization" of the Bill of Rights by incorporating the Bill of Rights into the Fourteenth Amendment. The Court applied the federal guarantees to the states. The judicial principle used in *Palko v. Connecticut* (1937) became the basis for fully incorporating the First Amendment rights of freedom of speech, press, assembly, and religion in the due process clause of the Fourteenth Amendment. During World War II and the Cold War era, however, some restrictions upon these rights were permitted in the interest of security; for example, federal and state loyalty programs.

The Court's incorporation of rights accelerated after 1950. In a series of cases, the Court said that part of the Fourteenth Amendment that reads "no state shall . . . deprive any person of life, liberty, or property without due process of law" provides a guarantee of the fundamental liberties in the Bill of Rights that state governments must protect to the same extent as does the federal government.

By 1991, all the rights included in the first eight amendments were protected from state encroachment except the Second Amendment right to keep and bear arms, the Fifth Amendment right to a grand jury indictment, the Sixth Amendment requirement of twelve jurors in a criminal trial, and the Seventh Amendment right to a civil jury. The Supreme Court has held that state procedures are adequate to protect the values inherent in those Bill of Rights guarantees.

Robert D. Talbott

FURTHER READING

Alderman, Ellen, and Caroline Kennedy. *In Our Defense: The Bill of Rights in Action*. New York: Morrow, 1991.

Brand, Irving. *The Bill of Rights: Its Origin and Meaning*. Indianapolis: Bobbs-Merrill, 1965.

Bryner, Gary C., and A. D. Sorensen, eds. *The Bill of Rights: A Bicentennial Assessment*. Albany, N.Y.: State University Press, 1993.

Cortner, Richard C. *The Supreme Court and The Bill of Rights: The Fourteenth Amendment and the Nationalization of Civil Liberties*. Madison: University of Wisconsin Press, 1981.

Douglas, William O. *A Living Bill of Rights*. Garden City, N.Y.: Doubleday, 1961.

Goldwin, Robert, and William A. Schambra, eds. *How Does the Constitution Secure Rights?* Washington, D.C.: American Enterprise Institute for Public Policy Research, 1985.

SEE ALSO: American Civil Liberties Union; Civil Rights Act of 1964; Constitution, U.S.; Declaration of Independence; Due process; English Bill of Rights; First Amendment; Freedom of expression; Human rights; Magna Carta; Supreme Court, U.S.

Biochemical weapons

DEFINITION: Living organisms, or infected materials derived from them, used as weapons for the hostile purpose of causing disease or death among humans, animals, and plants

TYPE OF ETHICS: Military ethics

SIGNIFICANCE: The use of biological agents by military combatants or terrorists is generally regarded as inhumane and a violation of human rights.

After the terrorist attacks on the United States on September 11, 2001, grave concern arose about the threat of biological warfare. Biological weapons that cannot be controlled or focused solely on military targets have long been condemned as being particularly heinous. Even though 144 nations ratified the international Biological Weapons Convention (1972) that banned deployment and use of the weapons and ordered the destruction of existing stores, some governments and terrorist groups have been accused of continuing to develop such pathogens as well as toxins (deadly biological agents that are produced by living organisms such as bacteria, plants, or animals) and chemical agents (chemicals intended to kill, injure, or incapacitate because of their physiological effects). By 2004, not all the world's nations had ratified the convention, and terrorists, by definition, continued to flout internationally accepted norms of behavior.

The Geneva Protocol of 1925 sought to prevent the use of such agents in war on the grounds that they were justly condemned by the general opinion of the civilized world and were an inhumane violation of

Time Line of Biochemical Weapons

Time	Event
Chemical Weapons	
1500-1855	Toxic smoke weapons include arsenical compounds.
1845-1920	Asphyxiating gas weapons include the industrial-scale production of chlorine and phosgene.
1920-1960	Nerve gases, such as tabun and sarin, are developed to inhibit nerve function, leading to respiratory paralysis or asphyxia.
1959-1970	Psychoactive chemical weapons are developed to produce hallucinations in exposed individuals.
1970-present	Binary chemical weapons, stored and shipped in their component parts, are developed to increase quantities that can be safely transported to deployment sites.
Biological Weapons	
300 B.C.E.-1763 C.E.	During the miasma-contagion phase, environments are deliberately polluted with diseased carcasses and corpses.
1763-1925	During the fomites phase, specific disease agents and contaminated utensils are introduced as weapons, with smallpox, cholera, and the bubonic plague as popular agents.
1925-1940	During the cell culture phase, biological weapons are mass-produced and stockpiled; Japan's research program includes direct experimentation on humans.
1940-1969	During the vaccine development and stockpiling phase, there are open-air tests of biological dispersal in urban environments in the United States.
1969-present	During the genetic engineering phase, recombinant DNA biotechnology opens new frontiers in the design and production of biological weapons.

human rights. Nevertheless, Western nations, including the United States, Great Britain, Canada, and the Soviet Union had biological research programs for both offensive and defensive purposes. Several other nations were known or thought to have such programs. Iraq's possible development of biological agents as weapons of mass destruction was one of the reasons cited for coalition forces' invasion of that country in 2003.

Although biological warfare had been used only on a small scale by the early years of the twenty-first century, the experience of military operations influenced by the introduction of disease by combatants provides a grim preview of what could happen if biological agents were intentionally used against a targeted population. Dispersion under optimum conditions of even a small volume of biological warfare agents might cause high morbidity and mortality that might be intensified by public panic and social disruption.

Biological warfare agents are well suited for use in bioterrorism or by poorer nations against richer ones because they are inexpensive and are relatively easy to obtain and disperse. Indeed, biological and chemical agents have euphemistically been called the poor man's atom bomb. Equipment and technology used for research on biological weapons are no different from those used in legitimate biomedical research and hence are difficult to detect. The ingredients are available on the open marketplace or in nature, and the necessary formulas can be found on the Internet or in other public sources. However, their full-scale use as weapons is difficult. Anyone attempting to disperse biological agents in a manner that will actually cause widespread casualties faces formidable technical obstacles involving advanced skills and technologies for the drying, milling, and delivery of the agents.

TYPES OF BIOCHEMICAL WEAPONS

Biological agents that are potential weapons are classified by the Centers for Disease Control according to their clinical characteristics and impact on public health. Clinical effects vary from high mortality (due to smallpox, anthrax, plague, botulism, tularemia, and viral hemorrhagic fevers such as Ebola) to prolonged incapacity (for example, from Q fever, brucellosis, and viral encephalitis).

Many biochemical agents can be transmitted from animals to humans and could have powerful effects on agriculture as well as on human health. Early symptoms of diseases induced by a biological agent may be nonspecific or difficult to recognize. Genetic engineering of biological agents can alter the manner of development of diseases, their incubation periods, or even their clinical symptoms. The threat of the use of biological agents, which potentially could be disseminated on a large-scale and produce mass casualties, requires broad-based public health preparedness efforts.

The mere threat of the use of biological weapons in a military setting can impair the effectiveness of opposing troops. When the U.S.-led alliance invaded Iraq in early 2003, its troops wore cumbersome full-protective suits in high temperatures. In civilian settings, the disruption of logistic support and the economy and long-lasting psychological effects on the general public may have a greater impact than the direct medial effects of a deliberate attack, as exemplified by terrorist releases of anthrax in the United States in late 2001.

Biological weapons can be delivered by aerosol generators mounted on trucks, cars, or boats and from missiles and planes equipped with tanks and spray nozzles. Weather factors, such as wind velocity and direction, humidity, degree of cloud protection

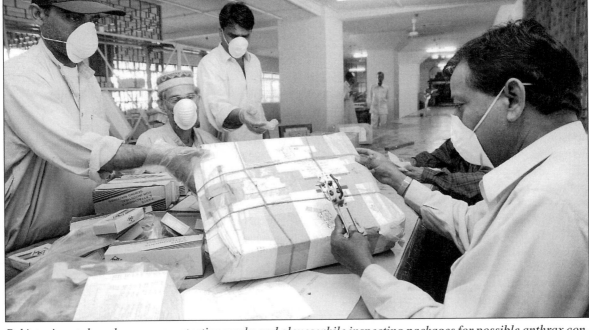

Pakistani postal workers wear protective masks and gloves while inspecting packages for possible anthrax contamination shortly after the September 11, 2001, terrorist attacks on the United States. (AP/Wide World Photos)

from direct sunlight, and rainfall, may affect the efficiency of such delivery methods. Terrorists might deliver biological agents—such as salmonella or cholera germs—directly into food and water supplies, through ventilation or air-conditioning systems, or by letter or parcels. Suicide attacks also might be used to disseminate pathogens.

HISTORY

Germ and chemical warfare predate the twentieth century. During Europe's Middle Ages, for example, human bodies infected with plague were sometimes catapulted into enemy fortifications, and poisons were dumped into wells of cities under siege—long before the nature of contagion was even understood. The original inhabitants of the New World were ravaged by smallpox, measles, and other Old World diseases that explorers and conquerors began introducing in the sixteenth century. Indeed, Old World diseases often made it possible for small forces to conquer numerically superior combatants. In pre-Revolutionary America, British forces used blankets contaminated with smallpox to infect North American Indians, a tactic later used by the U.S. military on the frontier.

However, it was not until World War I that biochemical weapons were widely used in modern warfare. Both the Allies and the Central Powers used choking and mustard gases that killed almost 100,000 people and injured more than a million. Postwar public opinion turned against the use of chemical and biological agents in battle, and in 1925 the Geneva Protocol banned the military use of such weapons. However, the lack of enforcement provisions in the protocol provided industrial nations an opportunity to develop lethal chemicals such as nerve gas.

In 1935, Benito Mussolini's Italian Fascists employed poison gas during their invasion of Ethiopia, and during the 1930's and 1940's, the Japanese used chemical agents and released fleas infected with plague in Chinese cities—the only known use of biological weapons during World War II. Although both the Allies and the Nazis possessed chemical and biological weapons throughout the war, neither side was willing to use them in fear of retaliation by the other—a unique deterrence during war. At the conclusion of the Korean War, North Korea charged that the United States had attempted to spread disease among its people, but the charges were not substanti-

ated. In the Vietnam War, U.S. forces sprayed Agent Orange, a defoliant, over jungle hiding places of the Viet Cong, and some veterans of that war suffered health problems they maintained were related to exposure to that agent.

THE MODERN SITUATION

Throughout the Cold War, both the United States and the Soviet Union developed massive biochemical weapons programs. Some of the weapons were made available to military forces of East Bloc nations and developing world countries friendly to the Soviets. In 1969, President Richard M. Nixon declared that the United States would not retaliate in kind against an enemy attack using biological or chemical weapons and unilaterally ended the development, production, stockpiling, and use of biological warfare agents. Toxins were added to the biological weapons ban in 1970. The U.S. Department of Defense is required to dispose of existing biological weapons and scale down the program to include research only for defensive measures.

In 1972, more than one hundred countries, including the United States and the Soviet Union, signed the Biological and Toxin Weapons Convention banning the possession of lethal biological agents except for research into vaccine development and other defensive programs. An outbreak of anthrax in Russia in 1979, however, indicated that the Soviet Union had continued its own biological weapons program in violation of the convention. It was not until 1992 that Russian president Boris Yeltsin announced that Russia would halt its biological weapons program.

Both Iraq and Iran used chemical weapons during the war between those nations from 1983 to 1988. Subsequently, President Saddam Hussein used poison gas and possibly anthrax to kill Kurdish civilians in northern Iraq. In the 1990-1991 Gulf War, some U.S. forces probably were exposed to biochemical agents that produced "Gulf War Syndrome," a malady still under investigation. In 1993, the Chemical Weapons Convention (CWC), with extensive provisions for monitoring compliance, was ratified by 145 nations. CWC prohibits the development, production, acquisition, stockpiling, retention, transfer, and use of chemical weapons and is the most significant agreement to stem the proliferation of weapons of mass destruction since the 1968 Nuclear Nonproliferation Treaty.

Terrorists pose the greatest threat of using bio-chemical weapons, and as the Japanese cult Aum Shinrikyo proved, the technical hurdles can be scaled. In 1995, Aum Shinrikyo released the nerve gas sarin in a crowded Tokyo subway, killing twelve people and injuring more than five thousand people.

Aside from product-tampering cases, the sole large-scale attempt to inflict mass casualties with a biochemical agent in the United States was the 1985 Rajneesh cult salmonella salad bar poisoning in Dalles, Oregon, where nearly one thousand people suffered from food poisoning. Even the modest success of these biochemical attacks served notice that certain doomsday cults, religious fanatics, racial supremacists, and state-sponsored terrorists may be determined enough and desperate enough to use such weapons against civilian targets.

IMPLICATIONS FOR ETHICAL CONDUCT

Scientific development of biochemical agents has outpaced society's ability to deal effectively with the complex issues raised by such weapons. Research in genetic engineering and molecular biology raises ethical issues about science manipulating nature without clear societal controls. Bioengineered organisms of plant and animal origin may have dangerous effects on the environment. The use of human embryonic tissue in research and the control, storage, and access of genetic information pose new ethical dilemmas.

The military use of biochemical weapons infringes upon the long respected ideas that unnecessary suffering should be avoided and that civilians should not be attacked. Thus, specific military knowledge of genetic defects or vulnerabilities of humans and the ability to modify microorganisms or toxins that would increase disease or death take on added concern.

Medical doctors and researchers involved with biological weapons violate their professional ethics as laid down in the Hippocratic oath. Biotechnology provides opportunities to modify existing organisms so that they gain specific characteristics such as increased virulence, infectivity, or stability. Biological research has made possible the inexpensive production of large quantities of replicating microorganisms and the possibility of creating "new" agents for future warfare that surpass present means of prevention or treatment. This could be accomplished in secret programs in apparently open biomedical research in pharmaceutical firms or government laboratories. Although such programs might produce dreaded pathogens, the same research could contribute to the development of new medical countermeasures, such as new vaccines, drugs, and diagnostic tests.

At the beginning of the twenty-first century, international agreements designed to limit the use of biological warfare agents needed strengthening. In particular, methods of verification analogous to those used for verifying compliance with chemical weapon treaties remained to be negotiated.

Theodore M. Vestal

FURTHER READING

Alibek, Ken, and Stephen Handelman. *Biohazard: The Chilling True Story of the Largest Covert Biological Weapons Program in the World*. New York: Random House, 1999. Alibek, once a top scientist in the Soviet Union's biological weapons program, describes the extent of the program and how its deadly agents have gone missing.

Falkenrath, Richard A., Robert D. Newman, and Bradley A. Thayer. *America's Achilles' Heel: Nuclear, Biological, and Chemical Terrorism and Covert Attack*. Cambridge, Mass.: MIT Press, 1998. An analysis of the threat posed by nuclear, biological, and chemical weapons being delivered covertly by terrorists or hostile governments into the United States or other countries.

Garwin, Richard L. "The Many Threats of Terror." *The New York Review of Books*, November 1, 2001: 16-19. Describes potential catastrophic attacks on the United States by terrorists.

Miller, Judith, William Broad, and Stephen Engelberg. *Germs, Biological Weapons and America's Secret War*. New York: Simon & Schuster, 2001. Three *New York Times* reporters survey the history of biological weapons and conclude that while a biological attack against the United States is not necessarily inevitable, the danger is too real to be ignored.

Smithson, Amy E. *Ataxia: The Chemical and Biological Terrorism Threat and the U.S. Response*. Henry L. Stimson Center, 2002. Assesses effectiveness of federal, state, and local preparedness to deal with biochemical attacks.

Tucker, Jonathan B., ed. *Toxic Terror: Assessing Terrorist Use of Chemical and Biological Weapons*.

Cambridge, Mass.: MIT Press, 2000. Case studies of twelve terrorist groups and individuals who, from 1946 to 1998, allegedly acquired or employed CBW agents; identifies characteristic motivations and patterns of behavior associated with CBW terrorism.

SEE ALSO: Atom bomb; Bioethics; Chemical warfare; Homeland defense; Hussein, Saddam; Iraq; Military ethics; Native American genocide; War.

Biodiversity

DEFINITION: Genetic diversity of all forms of life on Earth, measured in terms of both numbers of species and genetic variability within species
TYPE OF ETHICS: Environmental ethics
SIGNIFICANCE: An ethical mandate for the preservation of biodiversity can be derived either from the potential usefulness of the organisms to human beings or from the viewpoint that humans are stewards of the earth's resources and have no moral right to destroy a unique biological species.

The importance of conserving biodiversity is an idea that attracted increasing international attention during the 1980's; previously, conservationists had concentrated their efforts on preservation of conspicuous and economically important organisms. The 1992 United Nations Conference on Environment and Development ("Earth Summit") arrived at a convention on biodiversity with protocols for protecting endangered species and international cooperation on biotechnology.

Species are undoubtedly becoming extinct at a rapid rate because of pollution, habitat destruction, deforestation, overexploitation, and other human activities. The approximately seven hundred extinctions that have been recorded in the last three hundred years are only a small fraction of the total, which is estimated by some scientists to be approaching fifty thousand species per year. Much of the world's genetic biodiversity is concentrated in inconspicuous insects, fungi, aquatic invertebrates, and herbaceous plants that have never been fully described.

Efforts to conserve biodiversity involve balancing known present needs with projected future needs and balancing the conflicting demands of local, national, and international agencies. Frequently, corporate and national policy have favored overexploitation. The well-being of the indigenous population of an area is an important consideration. Resource management by stable traditional societies, which is more sophisticated than is commonly realized, favors biodiversity, but global upheaval and the population explosion have destroyed the delicate balance between society and the biosphere in much of the developed and developing world.

The rise of genetic engineering has served to highlight the economic value of biodiversity and raise the question of ownership. Historically, species have been regarded as common property, but advocates for the rights of indigenous peoples have suggested that something akin to patent rights should belong to the group of people on whose territory an economically important organism is discovered.

Martha Sherwood-Pike

SEE ALSO: Conservation; Deforestation; Dominion over nature, human; Earth and humanity; Ecology; Endangered species; Environmental ethics.

Bioethics

DEFINITION: Multidisciplinary study of ethical problems of humanity arising from scientific advances in medicine and technology
TYPE OF ETHICS: Bioethics
SIGNIFICANCE: As a discipline, bioethics seeks to develop a set of guidelines for moral decision making utilizing the resources of medicine, biology, law, philosophy, theology, and social sciences.

While the rudiments of bioethics are ancient in origin, modern bioethics—medical, scientific, and environmental—is a relatively young field, which emerged around 1970. Its growth has been necessitated by increasingly complex dilemmas brought about by sophisticated technological knowledge and capabilities. Bioethics deals with questions of moral dimension and professional responsibility involving all forms of life: issues of medical decision making, living and dying, withdrawing and withholding medical care, conducting research on human subjects, allocating scarce resources, transferring cells from one or several organisms to produce another with particular characteristics ("cloning"), and preserving natural resources by efficient use of energy to protect the atmosphere and counteract the deleterious effect of pollutants.

These are issues for which no single clear-cut or mechanical answers are possible. Proposed solutions involve reviewing the parameters of various options and selecting the most beneficial. Superimposed on that seemingly facile solution are overriding considerations such as the identity of the decision maker, his or her values, legal capacity, and priorities. Bioscience is based on principles of natural science and risk assessment, while bioethics is based on moral principles developed and applied in the context of professional ethics.

HISTORICAL BACKGROUND

Ethical medical guidelines are rooted in the writings of the Greek physician Hippocrates, who was born about 460 B.C.E. The Hippocratic oath taken by physicians reflects the traditional notions of paternalism of the medical profession, which regard the physician as the primary decision maker for the patient and the person best able to decide what course of action is in the patient's best interest. The oath requires physicians to act to benefit the sick and keep them from harm ("*primum non nocere*"). It also admonishes physicians to refrain from assisting patients in suicide or abortion. Most of the codes of ethics adopted by the American Medical Association (AMA) in 1847 and revised in 1903, 1912, 1947, 1955, and 1980 use a similar approach. In 1957, the AMA adopted *Principles of Medical Ethics*, a set of ten principles outlining the ethical mandate of the physician and requiring the medical profession to use its expertise to serve humanity. In 1973, the American Hospital Association adopted a "Patient's Bill of Rights," which ensures patient privacy and confidentiality.

Lectures on the Duties and Qualifications of a Physician, written by John Gregory, professor of medicine at the University of Edinburgh, was published in 1772. The book emphasized the virtues and dignity of the physician and further defined his responsibilities and duties. In 1803, Thomas Percival, an English physician, wrote *Medical Ethics*. Pragmatic in approach, it stressed the professional con-

duct of the physician, and his relationships with hospitals, medical charities, apothecaries, and attorneys. Percival encouraged physicians to act to maximize patients' welfare. His influence is reflected in the AMA codes of 1847 and 1957.

A changed focus from a theological approach to a growing secularization of bioethics began with Episcopalian theologian Joseph Fletcher's *Medicine and Morals* (1954), which introduced "situation ethics," emphasizing the uniqueness of moral choice. Protestant theologian Paul Ramsey's *The Patient as Person* (1970) examined the emerging moral issues.

Environmentalism is derived from conservation and ecology. The former concept originated with forester Gifford Pinchot during the administration of President Theodore Roosevelt in the early twentieth century. At that time, the populace first became aware of conservation, but only in the context of how to manage natural resources; the consequences of the wasteful use of property were not considered. The term "ecology" was invented by Ernst Haeckel, a biologist and philosopher, and introduced in his 1866 book *General Morphology of Organisms*. Use of the term spread throughout the life sciences. Charles Elton, a founder of scientific ecology, explained that primitive men and women are actually ecologists who interpreted their surroundings. Therefore, environmentalism may be said to equate to primitivism. Ecology became a household word during the 1960's, when a public outcry arose concerning abuses of the environment.

Biotechnology evolved from biblical times. Noah's drunkenness, described in the Book of Genesis, indicates a requisite familiarity with the process of fermentation, which must have been used to produce the alcohol that Noah imbibed. Used in leavened bread, cheese, and pickling, the fermentation process was later utilized to isolate organisms capable of producing acetone and butanol and, in 1928, penicillin and streptomycin.

During the late 1940's, the study of deoxyribonucleic acid (DNA) began, for scientists recognized that every inherited characteristic has its origin somewhere in the code of each person's DNA. The structure of DNA was discovered during the early 1950's. Viewed as one of the major scientific accomplishments of the twentieth century, the study of DNA has significantly widened the horizons of biotechnology.

PRINCIPLES OF BIOMEDICAL ETHICS ILLUSTRATED

The U.S. Constitution guarantees persons the right to exercise their liberty and independence and the power to determine their own destinies and courses of action. Autonomy is legally grounded in the right to privacy, guaranteed as a "penumbra," or emanation, of several amendments of the U.S. Bill of Rights. The philosophical origins of autonomy stem from John Locke's *Two Treatises of Government* (1690), Immanuel Kant's *Grundlegen Zur Metaphysik deu Sitten* (1785; *Groundwork for the Metaphysics of Morals*), and John Stuart Mill's *On Liberty* (1989).

There is an inherent tension at the core of biomedical ethics, which springs from the need to balance the rights of patients to act in their own best interests without constraint from others (autonomy) and the obligation of health care professionals to act to promote the ultimate good of the patients, prevent harm, or supplant harm (beneficence). A conflict between patient autonomy and beneficence may arise in the context of medical treatment, acute care, or chronic care.

Acting in the patient's best interest may dictate a certain course of conduct that is medically indicated but whose result is unacceptable to the patient in terms of limitations in lifestyle. The President's Commission for the Study of Ethical Problems in Medicine and Biomedical and Behavioral Research (1983) declared that where conflicts between patients' self-interest and well-being remain unresolved, respect for autonomy becomes paramount. A weighing or balancing of the benefits against the burdens must be considered in order to arrive at an acceptable solution. Often, notions of paternalism are raised.

The principle of nonmaleficence, or the noninfliction of harm or evil on the patient, may conflict with obligations to promote the good of the patient, because many medical courses of action may involve certain undesirable consequences yet result in an ultimate benefit. (An example is inflicting a negligible surgical wound to avoid death). In other circumstances, such as the continued futile treatment of seriously ill newborns, pointless treatment for the irreversibly comatose patient, or a decision to withdraw artificial nutrition or hydration from a patient in a persistent vegetative state, there must be a weighing of potential benefit versus potential harm. Quality of life considerations may influence the outcome of the analysis.

The principle of justice seeks a scheme whereby scarce resources may be allocated fairly and uniform criteria may be developed to determine, for example, an order for the allocation of organs for transplantation, space in intensive care units, participation as clinical research subjects, and access to health care for those who lack health insurance. Governed by a cost-benefit analysis, distributive justice issues arose as pressures for health care cost containment that emerged during the 1980's escalated during the 1990's.

INFORMED CONSENT

The most concrete example of autonomous decision making is contained in the doctrine of informed consent: an explanation of the patient's condition; an explanation of the procedures to be used, along with their risks and benefits; a description of available alternatives or options, if any; and reasonable opportunity for the patient to change his or her mind, withdraw consent, or refuse consent. Informed consent free from coercion or deception must be obtained before procedures that invade the body can be performed. In the normal setting absent an emergency, if proper consent is not obtained, a legal action for battery may ensue.

In the partnership model that characterizes the physician-patient relationship in pluralist Western society, variables may act as obstacles to the true exercise of autonomy. Individual circumstances and cultural, familial, and religious differences may color a person's moral judgment and influence that person's decision-making capacity. Because of patients' limited understanding of their medical conditions, they may make decisions that are ambivalent, contradictory, or detrimental to their own health. At the same time, they may be harmed by the fears and anxieties induced by a more accurate understanding of the risks and options they face. The health care professional may be required to make a determination about the extent of disclosure and the degree of assimilation of the information conveyed.

The most controversial exception to informed consent is the therapeutic privilege, which permits medical personnel to withhold information intentionally if in the exercise of sound medical judgment it is determined that divulging certain information would be harmful to the patient. The use of placebos for the welfare of the patient is an extension of the therapeutic privilege. Another instance of intentional nondisclosure or limited disclosure occurs in the context of clinical research, where "adequate" disclosure for purposes of consent does not necessitate "complete" disclosure. Resolution of these and other dilemmas of this nature are the subject of debate in this area.

ENVIRONMENTAL ETHICS

The steadily developing global environmental crisis is serving as a catalyst for the reexamination of human values and ethical concerns about moral responsibility for the common good. Questions of environmental concern include the propriety of exposing workers to substances whose toxicity is unknown or discharging pollutants into the air, the role of the government in preventing adverse activity, a determination of the steps to be taken to halt or slow the erosion of biological diversity, and the fair and equitable allocation of material resources.

Examples of serious environmental problems that threaten the earth and its inhabitants are overpopulation, an inadequate food supply, the threat of global warming or climate change caused by the release of greenhouse gases and the destruction of the ozone layer, deforestation, loss of biodiversity, threats of water and air pollution, and the depletion of mineral and energy resources. Wastes and poisons are threatening land, water, and air quality as well as mineral and energy resources. Soil erosion is the greatest threat to farmland. Chemical fertilization, once thought to provide a solution to the problem of the billions of tons of topsoil that are lost in runoff, is costly and does not accomplish its goal effectively. Worldwide dumping of litter has caused the loss of millions of sea birds and animals and contamination from crude oil residue. Freshwater lakes have become polluted from bacteria, sewage, groundwater contamination, and hazardous waste; drinking water has remained unprotected.

Acid rain is a damaging form of air pollution. Wind may cause acid rain to rise high in the air and travel many miles. A product of combustion, acid rain kills fish in lakes, destroys crops, corrodes pipes carrying lake water, and releases toxic metals from soil compounds into groundwater. The main sources of contaminants in acid rain are combustion fumes from industry and automobile and truck exhausts. Environmentalists have warned of a "greenhouse effect"—that is, a trend toward global warming—resulting from the buildup of carbon monoxide and other gases in the atmosphere. These climatic changes are expected to melt glaciers and ice caps, causing sea levels to rise, flooding cities and coastal areas. The decline in rainfall could potentially cause mass starvation and the extinction of plant and animal life unable to adapt to changed conditions. Depletion of the earth's ozone layer would permit potentially carcinogenic ultraviolet rays to escape into the atmosphere. Because of the worldwide deforesting of acres of trees, the earth's ability to reabsorb carbon dioxide has been reduced.

A general increase in energy efficiency is the fastest and cheapest solution to the problem. Energy efficiency reduces fuel consumption, thereby reducing the output of gases into the atmosphere. The development of automobiles that run on clean-burning natural gas or methanol will reduce emissions into the atmosphere. Using solar power, tidal power, and geothermal energy (natural steam produced by heat within the earth itself) as alternative energy sources have also been proposed as solutions. The use of atomic energy has also been debated.

In 1993, U.S. president Bill Clinton signed an international biodiversity treaty designed to protect plants and animals, committing the nation to reduce emissions of greenhouse gases to their 1990 levels by the year 2000. Earth Day, celebrated on April 22 of each year since 1970, calls attention to environmental problems. Community groups have instituted recycling programs. Activist groups such as the Sierra Club and Greenpeace and organizations such as Earthwatch and the Worldwatch Institute have flourished, alerting policy makers and the general public to emerging trends and the availability and management of resources.

The Environmental Protection Agency (EPA) is the federal governmental agency with the responsibility to enforce compliance with environmental standards through monitoring programs and inspections. Those who knowingly violate environmental laws may be subject to criminal sanctions. Under the Clean Water Act of 1972, negligent acts can also be construed as criminal violations (felonies or misdemeanors punishable by fine, imprisonment, or both).

BIOMEDICAL TECHNOLOGY

The use of new technological powers brings challenges to traditional notions of preserving human dignity, individual freedom, and bodily integrity. Scientific ability to prolong life through the use of respirators, pacemakers, and artificial organs; to conquer infertility and gestation through in vitro fertilization and fetal monitoring; and to practice birth control through abortion and techniques for reducing fertility make it possible to manipulate life. Genetic engineering and human genetic manipulation have unlimited potential. Overriding ethical considerations concerning problems of abuse and misuse of technological powers, must, however, be addressed.

GENETIC ENGINEERING

Ethical and social questions about experimenting on the unborn and the possible misuse and abuse of power have been raised since genetic engineering (also known as gene splicing, genetic manipulation, gene cloning, and recombinant DNA research) sparked the revolution in biotechnology. The debate was especially intense during the mid-1970's, when fear about the wisdom of interfering with nature in a fundamental way was thought to outweigh the possible benefits in biological and medical research. It was feared that genetic accidents could occur when someone with expertise deliberately constructed an organism with the potential to threaten human health. There was also the fear that gene therapy might be used to alter human attributes such as intelligence or physical appearance. As scientists demonstrated evidence of precautions and federal government guidelines regulating genetic engineering research and banning certain types of experiments were drafted, a majority of biologists concluded that the risks were negligible.

The industry most affected by biotechnology is the pharmaceutical industry. In September, 1982, insulin from bacteria became the first of many genetically engineered materials licensed for human consumption. The potential is enormous as better and cheaper antibiotics are developed, improved methods for matching organs for transplantation are found, and techniques for correcting body chemistry emerge. Transferring genes from one organism to another would reduce the cost and increase the supply of materials used in medicine, agriculture, and industry. Far-reaching benefits from the bioindustrial revo-

lution include better health, more food, renewable sources of energy, more efficient industrial processes, and reduced pollution.

GENETIC SCREENING AND THE HUMAN GENOME PROJECT

The genome, or combination of genes acquired from one's biological parents, is central to a person's development. The three-billion-dollar, fifteen-year Human Genome Project, initiated during the 1990's to map human DNA, aims to study the total genetic endowment in the chromosomes, identify new markers for traits and diseases believed to have a genetic basis, and develop diagnostic tests to screen for hereditary diseases. Advances in human gene therapy could lead to the prevention of hereditary diseases and the alteration of inherited characteristics. Prenatal screening through amniocentesis or chorionic villus sampling makes possible informed choices about childbearing and alleviates the anxiety of noncarriers of diseases such as sickle-cell anemia and Tay-Sachs disease. Ethical issues and public policy dilemmas in this area involve the right to experiment, accessibility to organ and fetal transplants, and the imposition of controls in genetic testing.

Marcia J. Weiss

FURTHER READING

Beauchamp, Tom L., and James F. Childress. *Principles of Biomedical Ethics*. 5th ed. New York: Oxford University Press, 2001. An important textbook and central resource in the study of bioethical theory.

Engelhardt, H. Tristram, Jr. *The Foundations of Bioethics*. New York: Oxford University Press, 1986. A critique of theoretical bioethics and a cogent issue-oriented explanation of the role of theories and values in the concepts of health and disease.

Gore, Albert. *Earth in the Balance: Ecology and the Human Spirit*. Boston: Houghton Mifflin, 1992. The former vice president of the United States discusses the environmental crisis on a global scale and alleges that every aspect of society, including political leaders, is involved in its consequences.

Holland, Stephen. *Bioethics: A Philosophical Introduction*. Malden, Mass.: Blackwell, 2003. This indispensable introduction to contemporary bioethical issues includes discussions of the moral status of biological tissue, the effects of biotechnology upon personal identity, and the natural or unnatural status of genetic modification, as well as the more traditional issues of life, death, and euthanasia.

Kass, Leon R. *Toward a More Natural Science: Biology and Human Affairs*. New York: Free Press, 1985. An issue-oriented discussion of the relationship between science and ethics in the light of new technologies and traditional democratic values.

Kogan, Barry S., ed. *A Time to Be Born and a Time to Die: The Ethics of Choice*. Hawthorne, N.Y.: Aldine De Gruyter, 1991. Proceedings of a thought-provoking conference dealing with the impact of current medical and technological advances on the ethics of controversies concerned with the beginning and the end of life from philosophical, religious, medical, and legal perspectives.

Olson, Steve. *Biotechnology: An Industry Comes of Age*. Washington, D.C.: National Academy Press, 1986. A basic book on the advances in biotechnology and their implications.

Pierce, Jessica, and Andrew Jameton. *The Ethics of Environmentally Responsible Health Care*. New York: Oxford University Press, 2004. This original and important text draws connections between bioethics and environmental ethics. Not only does it advocate environmentally responsible medicine, but it also argues that environmental degradation is making people sick and increasing the burden on the health care system.

Prentis, Steve. *Biotechnology: A New Industrial Revolution*. New York: George Braziller, 1984. A detailed book with diagrams and illustrations explaining basic concepts in biotechnology and their uses in medicine, agriculture, and industry.

Scheffer, Victor B. *The Shaping of Environmentalism in America*. Seattle: University of Washington Press, 1991. Explores the roots of environmentalism and examines progress in education, law, and politics in dealing with areas of concern.

SEE ALSO: Biometrics; Biotechnology; Birth defects; Cloning; Eugenics; Euthanasia; Genetic engineering; Genetic testing; Global warming; Hippocrates; Human Genome Project; Stem cell research.

Biofeedback

DEFINITION: Discipline that trains people to regulate physical functions of their bodies that are under involuntary control or are no longer under voluntary control

DATE: Established during the early 1960's

TYPE OF ETHICS: Bioethics

SIGNIFICANCE: Biofeedback provides an alternative to painful and more extreme treatments for health problems, but it poses ethical questions in areas of human and other animal research.

Biofeedback has been used to treat a variety of health problems and to help people perform well. Among the health problems treated with biofeedback are gastrointestinal cramping, fecal incontinence, frequency and severity of epileptic seizures, high blood pressure, migraine headaches, tics, insomnia, bronchial asthma, bruxism (clenching and grinding of the teeth), sexual dysfunction, masticatory pain and dysfunction (MPD), temporomandibular joint (TMJ) syndrome, and Raynaud's disease (a functional disorder of the cardiovascular system characterized by poor blood circulation to the hands, feet, and face).

Biofeedback has also been used to treat patients whose muscles are no longer under voluntary control because of a stroke or an injury. Among the uses of biofeedback to improve performance are controlling test anxiety, improving athletic performance, controlling motion sickness in Air Force pilots, and reducing space adaptation syndrome (SAS) for astronauts. Biofeedback has also been used to help people quit smoking and to help people lose weight.

Biofeedback trains people to regulate physical functions of their bodies. It provides continuous information about physiological responses so that individuals can learn to regulate these responses. Three types of biofeedback are integrated electromyographic feedback (EMG), electrodermal response (EDR), and electroencephalographic response (EEG). EMG, in which muscular activity is recorded, is used for treatment of muscles and migraine headache. EDR, which records perspiration responses on the palms, is more often used for weight control, managing stress, or improved athletic performance. EEG biofeedback helps individuals gain voluntary control of their alpha rhythms.

Biofeedback is based on operant, rather than classical, conditioning. (In operant conditioning, desired behavior is rewarded with a stimulus; in classical conditioning, a conditioned stimulus precedes an unconditioned stimulus—for example, Pavlov's class heard the sound of the bell and then were shown food—until the conditional stimulus alone can elicit the desired behavior.) During the process of biofeedback, machines record physiological functions such as muscle movement, alpha waves, heart rate, blood pressure, or body temperature. The machines feed this information back to the patient in the form of numbers, gauges on a meter, lights, or sounds. Through this process, the patient learns to focus attention on controlling physical responses. The result, in part, is training of alpha waves that results in the calming effects of meditation.

RESEARCH AND EXPERIMENTATION

In the United States, experiments with operant conditioning of heart rate began in 1962. The first biofeedback studies of controlling blood pressure in humans were reported at Harvard in 1969. Such studies mark the early stages of biofeedback. Even though biofeedback, by historical standards, was first explored in the United States quite recently, Asian spiritual practitioners have, for centuries, been practicing conscious control of involuntary functions though meditation. Today, in clinics throughout the United States, biofeedback techniques are being taught to patients in as few as five to ten sessions.

According to Dr. Lilian Rosenbaum, in her 1989 book *Biofeedback Frontiers*, biofeedback research has moved into applications for diabetes, cancer, acquired immunodeficiency syndrome (AIDS), physical rehabilitation, education, vision disorders, improving performance in space, and developing superior athletes. Biofeedback is also being used to treat social disorders in criminals who voluntarily participate in the experiments. As researchers move into new areas, the machines that record the individuals' responses become more sophisticated. Among the most sophisticated of these machines is the computerized automated psychophysiological scan (Capscan), developed by Charles Stroebel and his colleagues. The Capscan "combines advances in computers, computerized electroencephalography (brain-wave measurements) and biofeedback, according to Rosenbaum.

Concerning the ethics of biofeedback, it is rele-

vant that much of the data on biofeedback comes from those who practice biofeedback and believe in its effectiveness. Several researchers, however, are exploring the ethical concerns in biofeedback research. Much of their concern focuses on the need for human subjects, since human consciousness is involved in the control of muscle responses that are usually regarded as involuntary. Testing the validity of biofeedback involves, in part, establishing control groups so that researchers can determine whether biofeedback or a placebo effect of psychotherapy is responsible for the results. Researcher Martin T. Orne observes that not only drugs but also treatment procedures themselves have "placebo components" that have "powerful effects on their own."

In summarizing the effects of biofeedback, Orne concludes that the effects of biofeedback are similar to the effects of relaxation therapy, self-hypnosis, or meditation. Nevertheless, he concludes, each of these techniques shows "considerable therapeutic effect" for various individuals, and such approaches "have been overlooked for many years, at least in this country."

Another ethical issue in biofeedback research involves the use of animal subjects. Research in biofeedback has often involved animal experimentation, especially with curarized animals—that is, animals in a state of drug-induced immobility. Some of the first studies with curarized animals involved rats that responded to stimulation of the pleasure center in the brain to slow down or speed up involuntary body functions. When the pleasure centers in the brain were stimulated, some of the rats responded by slowing down involuntary responses so much that death resulted. Other animal studies involved learning visceral and glandular (autonomic) responses. Additional animal studies have involved mice, golden hamsters, and baboons in Kenya.

Modern researchers have posed a number of complex ethical questions related to research in biofeedback, particularly questions involving the "justification for withholding therapy for research purposes." John P. Hatch, in his discussion of ethics, lists a number of concrete ethical questions related to placebo therapy, fees for service, random selection of subjects, acceptable control treatment, and effects of biofeedback research on patients. He concludes that the "central ethical question is whether current knowledge allows a preferred treatment to be chosen, and whether the relative risk to a patient would be greater as a result of assigning treatments randomly versus basing treatment assignments on clinical judgment."

Carol Franks

FURTHER READING

Hatch, John P., Johnnie G. Fisher, and John D. Rugh, eds. *Biofeedback: Studies in Clinical Efficacy.* New York: Plenum Press, 1987.

Lattal, Kennon A., and Michael Perone, eds. *Handbook of Research Methods in Human Operant Behavior.* New York: Plenum, 1998.

Rosenbaum, Lilian. *Biofeedback Frontiers.* Vol. 15 in *Stress in Modern Society.* New York: AMS Press, 1989.

Schwartz, Mark Stephen, and Frank Andrasik. *Biofeedback: A Practitioner's Guide.* 3d ed. New York: Guilford Press, 2003.

Van Hoose, William H., and Jeffrey A. Kottler. *Ethical and Legal Issues in Counseling and Psychotherapy.* 2d ed. San Francisco: Jossey-Bass, 1985.

White, Leonard, and Bernard Tursky, eds. *Clinical Biofeedback: Efficacy and Mechanisms.* New York: Guilford Press, 1982.

SEE ALSO: American Medical Association; Bioethics; Biotechnology; Ethical Principles of Psychologists; Holistic medicine; Hypnosis; *Principles of Medical Ethics.*

Biometrics

DEFINITION: Scientific techniques of measuring human biological data for purposes of identification

TYPE OF ETHICS: Bioethics

SIGNIFICANCE: Identifying people through biometrics reduces the incidence of false identifica-

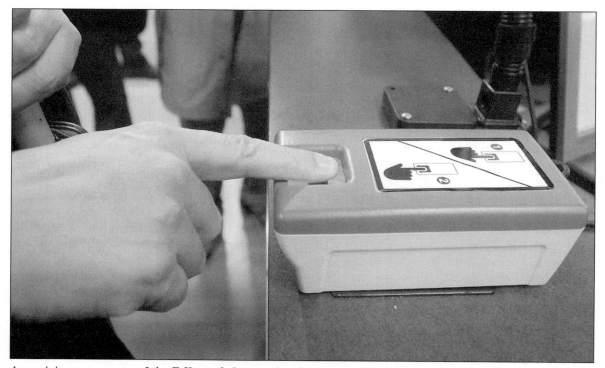

An arriving passenger at John F. Kennedy International Airport in New York uses an inkless fingerprint scanner, which instantly checks the print against a national database for evidence of criminal backgrounds or for names included on terrorist watch lists. Airport authorities began using the scanner and photographing travelers on Monday, January 3, 2003, as part of a new program initiated by the Department of Homeland Security. (AP/Wide World Photos)

Principles of the International Biometric Industry Association

Members of the International Biometric Industry Association (IBIA) pledge to observe a code of ethics based on these principles:

Public safeguards	Biometric technologies should be used solely for legal, ethical, and nondiscriminatory purposes and must be protected by the highest standards of systems integrity and database security.
Respect for competitive technologies	Competitors in the biometric industry should be treated with courtesy and civility in all discourse, including marketing and advertising.
Market accountability	Members' claims about their products must be accurate and lend themselves to independent verification by competent authorities.
Marketplace legitimacy	IBIA membership is open only to biometric developers, manufacturers, integrators, and end-users who have proven their biometric technologies and applications to be safe, accurate, and effective.
Free trade	Members are committed to the principles of free trade and open competition in the worldwide biometric marketplace.

tion but at the same time poses ethical questions about how to protect such data from error and irresponsible dissemination.

As modern society grows more ever more complex, new questions of identification loom, especially for organizations that, for security reasons, must control access to their facilities and databanks. However, using biological data for human identification is not a new idea. In the late seventeenth century, a British physician noted that each human being has fingerprints that are wholly unique. Fingerprinting was perhaps the earliest form of biometrics but was not widely used by law enforcement and other agencies until the mid-nineteenth century. By the early twentieth century, fingerprinting was well entrenched as a means of identifying people, particularly those who left incriminating marks behind at the scenes of their crimes. Eventually, police departments began routinely fingerprinting suspects and building files of their prints. By the 1920's, such agencies as the Federal Bureau of Investigation (FBI) had extensive fingerprint files. Local police departments could match prints they took from recently arrested prisoners against those collected in the huge FBI fingerprint archive.

BIOMETRIC FUNDAMENTALS

The word "biometrics" is derived from two Greek roots, *bio-*, for life, and *metrein*, for "to measure." The science of biometrics rests on the supposition that no two living entities are wholly identical. Every living entity has physical and behavioral characteristics that distinguish it from every other living entity, including members of its own species. Underlying the implementation of biometrics to human beings is the presumption that every person, or at least the vast majority of people, share common characteristics, like fingers or eyes. Obviously, some people lack body parts for various reasons; however, because the vast majority of people have all the basic parts, reasonably accurate biological measurements involving these features have been devised.

Biometrics is ineffective unless elements of entities' features are unique to those entities, such as the whorls of individual fingerprints or specific characteristics of hands, eyes, or faces. These characteristics must be relatively constant. Characteristics that change over time often yield false readings if biometric measures are applied to them. Moreover, the physical features or behaviors being measured, such as handwriting or speech patterns, must be measurable by reliable devices.

Common Uses of Biometrics

Devices that can verify the identity of people have obvious practical uses. A device that can scan eyes, faces, or hands of people and identify them accurately in mere seconds, provides a more foolproof safeguard against identity theft and related problems than such measures as passwords, keys, and entry cards. As security has been increasingly necessary because of widespread international terrorism, those entrusted with protecting the national welfare have accelerated the use of biometrics to screen people in many contexts, most notably in airports and at border crossings.

Business corporations employ biometric devices to permit quick and easy entry of authorized personnel into restricted facilities. One simple practical application is employee time clocks that identify people by having them insert their hands into slots to have their identities confirmed. Employees who arrive late or leave their jobs early thus cannot have friends punch in or out for them, as was sometimes done in the past.

Ethical Concerns

Because some biometric processes are conducted without the knowledge and consent of those being scrutinized, significant ethical questions arise. For example, a supermarket chain might gather information about its customers' shopping habits by identifying otherwise anonymous customers through eye scans—something it could do without its customers' knowledge. One might therefore justifiably ask how such information would be used and to whom and under what circumstances the information might be disseminated.

Similar concerns are voiced about medical records that may in time come to haunt a person whose eye scans reveal, as they surely might, some health conditions, such as diabetes or hypertension, that could keeping them from getting jobs or insurance coverage. Questions regarding the individual privacy of people raise both ethical and constitutional concerns when biometric procedures make it possible for databases to be developed that might, if broadly available to employers or organizations, jeopardize individual rights to privacy.

As societies grow in complexity, trade-offs be-

tween individual rights and the protection of society often seem justifiable. When such trade-offs stay within bounds, many people accept them. The question arises, however, of whether some zealous officials might allow anticipated ends to justify the means of achieving them, perhaps for purely political reasons. In situations in which employers require employees to sign out by putting their hands into a scanner that will identify them, presumably unerringly, one can reasonably argue that employers have the right to verify that their employees are giving them the full measure of time for which they are being paid. Even if the use of scanners for this purpose appears to infringe on individual privacy, most people will realize the validity of such measures and will not strongly object to them.

Mark Twain and Biometrics

Although Mark Twain never knew the word "biometrics," he might fairly be credited with introducing that science to fiction in *Pudd'nhead Wilson* (1894)—the first novel to use fingerprint evidence as a plot device. The title character of the novel, David Wilson, mystifies and amuses the simple people of Dawson's Landing, Missouri, by collecting their fingerprints on glass slides. For years, the villagers dismiss him as a "puddingheaded" fool—until the final chapter, when he displays his legal brilliance in a murder trial. Wilson creates a sensation by using his slides to prove the innocence of the murder suspect he is defending. However, that revelation is minor compared to his second use of fingerprint evidence at the trial. Drawing on glass slides he has collected over more than two decades, he proves that the culprit in the murder case is a man who was born a slave and somehow got switched with the infant son of his master in infancy. The theme of switched identities that are sorted out by fingerprint evidence gives the novel a strong claim to be called the first application of biometrics in fiction.

However, if biometric devices gather and store data about individuals, the situation becomes more questionable. Even when safeguards are in place to protect the privacy of individuals, many people fear that such safeguards at some future point might be relaxed in ways that would compromise individual privacy rights. Those who use biometric devices for purposes of identification may vow that they will make no unethical uses of the information they gather, but a danger lurks in the minds of many people that public and private attitudes toward the inviolability of such information will eventually weaken, and that harmful information may become accessible to those who can justify their need for it in the name of assuring the national security or some vague greater good.

R. Baird Shuman

FURTHER READING

Smith, Richard E. *Authentication: From Passwords to Public Keys.* Boston: Addison-Wesley, 2002.

Tocci, Salvatore. *High-Tech IDs: From Finger Scans to Voice Patterns.* New York: Franklin Watts, 2000.

Vacca, John R. *Identity Theft.* Upper Saddle River, N.J.: Prentice-Hall PTR, 2003.

Woodward, John D., Jr., Nicholas M. Orlans, and Peter T. Higgins. *Biometrics.* Boston: New York: McGraw-Hill/Osborne, 2003.

Zhang, David. *Automated Biometrics: Technologies and Systems.* Boston: Kluwer Academic Publishers, 2000.

SEE ALSO: Bioethics; Biotechnology; Business ethics; Drug testing; Employee safety and treatment; Hiring practices; Identity theft; Invasion of privacy; Privacy.

Biotechnology

DEFINITION: Application of science to the biological realm; the term is often used synonymously with genetic engineering, the artificial modification of the genetic codes of living organisms

DATE: Concept first emerged during the 1960's

TYPE OF ETHICS: Bioethics

SIGNIFICANCE: Because of the great potential for changes that may have social, economic, political and environmental consequences, ethical principles must guide biotechnological choices.

A host of issues are subsumed under the rubric "biotechnology," including human and animal reproductive technologies such as cloning, the creation of genetically modified organisms and products, including food, xenotransplantation (the cross transplantation of human and animal genes and organs), human genetic testing and therapies, and stem cell research. As with most novel and highly complex technologies, no consensus obtains regarding the relevant ethical principles.

THE BASES FOR ETHICAL JUDGMENTS

The utilitarian principle posits that when the potential exists for good and harm, the ratio of good to harm must be considered when developing, employing, and regulating technologies. Debates then may arise as to how benefits and risks should be prioritized. The "precautionary principle" would lead decision-makers to act with caution in advance of scientific proof of harm, to place the onus of proof on those who propose new technologies, and to promote intrinsic natural rights. Calculating potential benefits and harm is a formidable task given the novelty of these technologies, high levels of scientific uncertainty, the interconnected character of all natural phenomena, and the multiple economic, political, and social issues involved. Some fear that development of some biotechnologies increases moral hazard (or represents a "slippery slope") in that it increases the likelihood that humankind will cross fundamental thresholds with potential significant negative consequences for humankind.

The Human Genome Project well illustrates the potential benefits, risks, and moral hazards of biotechnology. This large research effort, funded by the United States and other governments, has now decoded the human deoxyribonucleic acid (DNA) sequence. This knowledge will ultimately allow scientists to understand diseases such as cystic fibrosis and conditions such as intelligence and aggression and to create drug therapies for specific genetic abnormalities. However, the success of the project raises the prospect of genetic profiling, which creates the possibility that employers may discriminate against applicants on the basis of their genetic profiles, or that corporations may adjust medical insurance rates to reflect policyholders' genetic predispositions. A potential moral hazard associated with this technology is that once an individual is classified by genotype, it is but a step to justify death for undesirable genetic traits.

JUSTICE AND FREEDOM

Universal principles of justice and autonomy may also serve as the bases for evaluating biotechnol-

Reflecting a growing public uneasiness with modern biotechnology, protestors greeted scientists attending Bio 2004, the biotechnology industry's annual international conference, in San Francisco, in June, 2004. Of particular concern to protestors was the issue of genetically modified foods.(AP/Wide World Photos)

ogies. When combined with utilitarian considerations, principles of distributive justice would dictate that the issue of potential benefit and harm be considered. It is important that the benefits of biotechnologies are distributed equitably: Potential risks should not fall disproportionately on those already burdened with various forms of discrimination, and powerful individuals, corporations, and states should not benefit disproportionately from development and use of these technologies. Moreover, the technologies' consequences for those without strong voices must be taken into account. Justice would also mandate careful consideration of who can legitimately make decisions about the development and regulation of biotechnologies. For example, what should be the role of the scientific community and profit-driven corporations relative to other stakeholders in deciding which technologies are developed?

The principle of autonomy recognizes that the right to self-determination and freedom from coercion as an inalienable right. This logic would allow individuals to consent or decline, to participate in the biotechnology research, or to consume bioengineered products. Openness and honesty are required if people are to understand the implications of their choices and exercise their freedom, so it is incumbent on all actors involved in creating, marketing, and regulating biotechnologies to educate the public as to the potential consequences of various biotechnologies and to ensure that political decision making be transparent and democratic. Concerns about freedom and autonomy are complicated when the rights of embryos, the gravely ill, or future generations are taken into account.

"HUMAN" THRESHOLDS

Biotechnologies may raise philosophical concerns about what it means to be human in that they may change or breach thresholds associated with bisexual reproduction, social entities and roles such as the family and child rearing, and taboos against homicide. While many boundaries serve vested interests and are not essential to human well-being, some thresholds may preserve the essence of "humanness," including the actualization of individual identity and beneficent communal interaction.

Physical attributes, such as genetic makeup and intelligence, and the assignment of dignity to life also distinguish human beings from other species. Xenotransplantation clearly blurs barriers between humans and other organisms. The medical advances achieved by the year 2100 are expected to allow physicians to transplant human heads. By the early twenty-first century, reproductive technologies were already allowing humans to select the genetic makeup of their offspring, create new organisms, and create embryos for reproduction and other medical and scientific research. Many people worry that the commonplace creation, manipulation, and destruction of life portend changes in what it means to be "human" and reduce respect for the dignity of humankind and life.

Ethical biotechnologies demand that individuals and groups most affected by their advances be invited to participate in the discourse and decision making about which biotechnologies are developed and how they will be regulated. Science and technology are not ethically neutral; human beings can reflect upon and assume responsibility for ethical choice among biotechnologies.

M. Leann Brown

FURTHER READING

Charles, Daniel. *Lords of the Harvest: Biotech, Big Money, and the Future of Food.* Cambridge, Mass.: Perseus Publishing, 2001.

Fukuyama, Francis. *Our Posthuman Future.* New York: Picador, 2002.

Kristol, William, and Eric Cohen, eds. *The Future Is Now.* Lanham, Md.: Rowman & Littlefield, 2002.

Sherlock, Richard, and John D. Morrey. *Ethical Issues in Biotechnology.* Lanham, Md.: Rowman & Littlefield, 2002.

Stock, Gregory. *Redesigning Humans.* Boston: Houghton Mifflin, 2002.

SEE ALSO: Bioethics; Biofeedback; Biometrics; Cloning; Genetic testing; Genetically modified foods; Human Genome Project; Medical research; Stem cell research; Technology.

Birth control

DEFINITION: Methods of contraception by physical, surgical, or chemical means

TYPE OF ETHICS: Bioethics

SIGNIFICANCE: The decision to use birth control is affected by one's views of the moral status of sexuality and of potential human life and by one's ethical obligations to society and to the human species.

Questions about birth control have faced humanity throughout history. In the modern world, overpopulation and Malthusian doctrine loom ever larger, making birth control a must. Consequently, equitable and ethical solutions to the problem are essential. Modern birth control consists of and combines physical methods, chemical methods, and surgical intervention that must be applied with good ethical judgment to provide results that prevent both overpopulation and the exploitation of individual population sectors.

METHODOLOGY

Among modern methods of birth control are coitus interruptus; the rhythm method; pessaries, condoms, diaphragms, and intrauterine devices (IUDs); chemical intervention via birth control pills; and surgical vasectomy or tubal ligation. Least satisfactory are coitus interruptus and rhythm methods, which involve male withdrawal prior to climax and intercourse during safe portions of the menstrual cycle. The difficulties here are adequate self-control and variation of the fertile period of the cycle. The problems associated with pessary, condom, diaphragm, and IUD use are mechanical faults and incomplete understanding of the proper usage of these devices. Birth control pills have the disadvantages of causing health problems in some users and of often being used incorrectly. Surgical interventions via tubal ligation and vasectomy are usually irreversible, which often makes them psychologically inappropriate.

HISTORY

Birth control techniques go back at least as far as the nineteenth century B.C.E. At that time, a wide range of methods—including incantations, crude chemical preparations (for example, animal dung, plant products, and crude spermicide salves), and pessaries—

were used with questionable results. Such methodologies flourished until the Hippocratic school of medicine realized that there were nonfertile times during the menstrual cycle that could be utilized for birth control.

During the following historical period, however, contraception was frowned upon by many people. Relatively flexible Judaic theological doctrine proposed that "no man or woman among you shall be childless" but allowed birth control. In the Greek and Roman milieus, birth control was practiced but was controversial because high population went hand in hand with political security. A powerful ethical judgement against its use was made by the Greek Stoics, who believed that sexual intercourse was intended solely for the purpose of procreation and that all forms of birth control were wrong.

With the rise of Christianity, birth control practices were denounced as sinful, and practitioners of birth control were classed with murderers. The view of Christian ethics was that even coitus interruptus was wrong and that marital intercourse had to be procreative. In time, Christianity was to become the strongest ethical movement against birth control. In contrast, Islamic culture did not actively condemn birth control. In fact, the eleventh century Arab physician Avicenna described many ways to prevent pregnancy in an encyclopedic medical work.

The dichotomy of attitudes toward birth control continued until the end of the eighteenth century, despite the development of Protestantism and the doctrine of rationalism. Religious movements condemned birth control thunderously from the pulpit as opposed to Christian ethical principles, and the rationalists did not advocate it as rational behavior. One useful development during this period was the invention of the condom.

The beginning of the advocacy of birth control can be traced to the development of the Malthusian doctrine by Thomas Malthus, who proposed that famine and war would come to the world unless population growth was curbed. Malthus favored postponement of marriage, not birth control via contraceptives. Others advocated the use of birth control methods, however, despite unrelenting opposition from Christian churches and most governments. For example, the America Comstock Act of 1873 made the importation of contraceptives illegal, and many state governments forbade their sale.

The climate had begun to change, however, and by the 1920's, many favored birth control. Particularly important was the American nurse Margaret Sanger, one of the strongest advocates of birth control. Furthermore, scientific and medical endeavors caused changes of opinion in the intellectual and biomedical community. This development was aided by the invention of diaphragms and birth control pills. Furthermore, the realization of pending overpopulation and possible apocalypse quickly led to the widely held view that it was unethical to oppose birth control measures.

By the 1970's, American laws fostered the development of family planning research, and the Population Council had brought the technology of birth control to the world. Europe concurred, and while the responses of various countries in the less-developed areas of the world varied, birth control was generally accepted. In addition, the world's major religions began to endorse birth control practices to various extents. In response to the change in the ethical climate, techniques of voluntary sterilization by vasectomy and tubal ligation developed further, new contraceptive preparations were discovered, and state-endorsed birth control programs developed in many countries. During the 1980's and 1990's, further progress along these lines occurred.

CONCLUSIONS

The ethical issue that has long caused disharmony concerning birth control is whether it is ever appropriate to prevent the occurrence of a human life. In part, the idea that it is never appropriate to do so was based on the fact that in an underpopulated world, the more humans in a society or religion, the safer that sociopolitical entity would be. A radically changed ethical model now supports birth control procedures.

Other negative ethical issues, however, remain. These issues include the ethical choice of individuals who will practice birth control, especially in instances in which a nation implements policies that lead to inequities (for example, limitation of birth control to the less-advantaged classes). In addition, there is the question of the ethics of irreversible birth control and informed consent, the understanding of which governs individual freedom when a choice of sterilization is made under duress and may be regretted later. Finally, there is the ethical question of whether birth control will diminish family ties, causing future societal and individual problems. Surely, answers to these ethical problems will come and new problems will arise when the paradigm changes again.

Sanford S. Singer

FURTHER READING

Baulieu, Etienne-Emile, and Mort Rosemblum. *The Abortion Pill.* New York: Simon & Schuster, 1991.

Lammers, Stephen E., and Allen Verhey, eds. *On Moral Medicine: Theological Perspectives in Medical Ethics.* Grand Rapids, Mich.: W. B. Eerdmans, 1987.

Maguire, Daniel C., ed. *Sacred Rights: The Case for Contraception and Abortion in World Religions.* New York: Oxford University Press 2003.

Silber, Sherman J. *How Not to Get Pregnant.* New York: Charles Scribner's Sons, 1987.

Veatch, Robert M. *The Patient as Partner: A Theory of Human-Experimentation Ethics.* Bloomington: Indiana University Press, 1987.

_____. *A Theory of Medical Ethics.* New York: Basic Books, 1981.

SEE ALSO: Bioethics; Birth defects; Cesarean sections; Family; Future-oriented ethics; *Griswold v. Connecticut*; Parenting; Population control; Pro-choice movement; Sterilization of women.

Birth defects

DEFINITION: Malformation of body structures present at birth

TYPE OF ETHICS: Bioethics

SIGNIFICANCE: Birth defects raise serious questions of prevention, responsibility, and treatment for the medical community and society as a whole.

Birth defects are the primary cause of death of children under one year of age. Estimates of occurrence vary depending on what is classed as a defect, ranging from 2 percent to 15 percent of live births. Many defects result in spontaneous abortion or stillbirth and therefore are not included in these statistics. In most cases, the causes of malformation are unknown. After the 1960's, however, enormous advances were made in the determination of factors that affect fetal growth. Of those cases in which etiology has been discovered, the anomalies are the results of genetic causes, environmental causes, or a combination of the two.

Genetic causes include mutation and abnormality of chromosomal material as well as inherited traits. Environmental factors range from maternal nutrition or disease to exposure of the fetus to toxic substances. These factors include certain drugs, such as alcohol; chemicals, such as mercury and lead; radiation, such as radon and X rays; maternal illness, such as diabetes or rubella (German measles); intrauterine infection, such as cytomegalovirus; and parasites, as in toxoplasmosis. Some of these environmental factors act by causing genetic anomalies, resulting in multifactorial defects. Also included as birth defects are birth injuries and low birth weight.

ETHICS OF PREVENTION

The ethical issues involved in birth defects can be divided into three major areas: prevention, treatment, and responsibility.

In those cases in which the cause is known, there is a societal obligation to minimize the possibility of the occurrence of a particular defect. The question is, however: How far does this obligation extend? Does it supersede the rights of the mother, a competent autonomous adult? Consider this example: Hydantoin and phenobarbital are drugs commonly used to treat epileptic seizures. Hydantoin has been shown to cause mental deficiencies and abnormal body structures. Phenobarbital causes defects in laboratory animals, but it is not clear whether it does so in humans, although some studies have found a correlation. Ninety percent of women with epilepsy have as many or more seizures during pregnancy as they did before they became pregnant. Is it ethical to treat the mother with anticonvulsants that may endanger the fetus? Is it ethical to set the possibility of fetal problems above the actuality of maternal illness and not treat the disease?

Certain birth defects, such as Tay-Sachs disease and sickle-cell anemia, follow the strict laws of genetic inheritance. Genetic testing and counseling is generally available now for potential parents who carry the genes for these traits. These parents must make the decision to risk having an affected child or to not have children. What is an acceptable risk in these cases? Is it ethical to ask a couple not to have children when this violates their religious beliefs or personal aspirations?

Many abnormalities, including spina bifida and Down syndrome, can be detected as early as the fourth month of pregnancy. In these cases, the parents must decide whether to continue the pregnancy or to abort the fetus. If they choose to carry the fetus to term, who is financially responsible for treatment, the cost of which can go far beyond most individuals' abilities to pay?

ETHICS OF RESPONSIBILITY

Abnormalities caused by environmental factors raise the question of societal and maternal responsi-

bility. One of the earliest recognized causes of birth defects was exposure to lead. Does society have an obligation to eradicate the presence of lead where any pregnant woman might be exposed to it? Is it possible, physically and economically, to completely eliminate exposure to teratogenic agents (agents that cause birth defects)? Does this elimination of possible teratogenic exposure extend to the prohibition of pregnant women from jobs that might endanger the fetus? If so, is this ethical if a consequence is unemployment resulting in the woman being unable to obtain adequate prenatal care and nutrition? Should

Human-Made Causes of Birth Defects

Year recognized	Defect or defects	Cause
1952	Growth retardation, distinctive facial defects, shortened limbs, mental retardation	Aminopterin
1957	Intrauterine growth retardation, low birth weight	Cigarette smoking
1961	Severe physical malformations, especially of limbs	Thalidomide
1963	Mental retardation, microcephaly	Radiation, including X rays
1968	Fetal Alcohol Syndrome, which may include mental retardation, fine motor dysfunction, irritability or hyperactivity, malformed hearts and brains, and abnormal facial features	Alcohol
1968	Heart defects, microcephaly, growth and mental retardation, chromosomal abnormalities	Anticonvulsants
1968	Growth retardation, microcephaly, deafness, blindness	Mercury, often in fish
1970	Malformations, growth and mental retardation	Lead
1973	Addicted babies, growth impairment, respiratory disorders	Heroin
1977	Uterine lesions, increased susceptibility to immune disorders	Female sex hormones, especially diethylstilbestrol
1982	Vitamin A toxicity, which may cause various malformations, especially of the face, heart, central nervous system, and lungs	Overuse of vitamin A, especially in Accutane
1987	Growth retardation, defects of heart, skull, and central nervous system	Cocaine
1990	Reye's Syndrome	Aspirin
2002	Miscellaneous defects	Herbal supplements
2003	Toxoplasmosis, which may cause blindness, deafness, seizures, and mental retardation	Parasite found in cats feces and undercooked meat
2004	Anencephaly, spina bifida, and other potentially fatal defects	Fumonisin in corn tortillas

the prohibition extend to all women of childbearing age?

Maternal drug use is becoming more of a problem all the time. Fetal alcohol syndrome, low birth weight caused by cigarette smoking, and cocaine- and heroin-addicted babies are all common problems. What legal responsibilities does the mother have during pregnancy? What responsibilities does society have to the children of these mothers? Should custody be rescinded at birth? Should these women be detained during pregnancy and be forced to conform to certain specifications of acceptable maternal behavior? Should they be prosecuted for child abuse?

ETHICS OF TREATMENT

When a baby is born with severe defects, issues arise regarding whether to treat the defect or to allow the child to die. Considerations include the quality and length of life the child will have if allowed to live and the ability and desire of the parents to care for the defective child. If nontreatment is chosen, the question of active euthanasia (infanticide, or withdrawal of all life support including feeding) versus passive euthanasia (nontreatment but continuation of feeding) arises. Furthermore, who makes these decisions is a question that is becoming more prominent. Should the parents have the final word? Should the physician, who has more medical knowledge? Should a "disinterested party," such as a hospital ethics committee, make such a decision?

The ethical dilemmas regarding birth defects are endless. As medicine advances in its ability to diagnose and treat these problems, more issues will arise. One of the few things upon which most people agree is that prevention is preferable to treatment, whenever possible.

Margaret Hawthorne

FURTHER READING

Arras, John D., and Bonnie Steinbock, eds. *Ethical Issues in Modern Medicine.* 5th ed. Mountain View, Calif.: Mayfield, 1999.

Capron, Alexander Morgan. "Fetal Alcohol and Felony." *Hastings Center Report* 22 (May/June, 1992): 28-29.

Persaud, T. V. N. *Environmental Causes of Human Birth Defects.* Springfield, Ill.: Charles C Thomas, 1990.

Schardein, James L. *Chemically Induced Birth Defects.* 3d ed, rev. and expanded. New York: Marcel Dekker, 2000.

Smith, David W. *Smith's Recognizable Patterns of Human Malformation.* Edited by Kenneth L. Jones. 5th ed. Philadelphia: Saunders, 1997.

Wynbrandt, James, and Mark D. Ludman. *The Encyclopedia of Genetic Disorders and Birth Defects.* 2d ed. New York: Facts On File, 2000.

SEE ALSO: Bioethics; Birth control; Cesarean sections; Euthanasia; Genetic counseling; Genetic engineering; Infanticide; Life and death; Toxic waste.

Bodhidharma

IDENTIFICATION: Buddhist monk
BORN: Fifth century, southern India
DIED: Sixth century, place unknown
TYPE OF ETHICS: Religious ethics
SIGNIFICANCE: Bodhidharma founded Chinese Chan Buddhism and taught that ethical living depends upon understanding and believing that there is no individual self.

The legendary founder of the Chan (Japanese: Zen) school of Buddhism in China, Bodhidharma brought Indian meditation practices to China. His life and teachings have been reworked and expanded by later Buddhists to the point that certainty about either is impossible. A saying attributed to him, though almost certainly from a latter period, may nevertheless capture one aspect of Bodhidharma's thinking:

> A special tradition outside the scriptures;
> No dependence upon words and letters;
> Direct pointing at the soul of man;
> Seeing into one's own nature, and the attainment of Buddhahood.

This passage links Bodhidharma to the Zen Buddhist practice of meditation leading to enlightenment. He seems also to have treasured particular sutras, or scriptures, that emphasized the unity of all things. Furthermore, ethical thinking that probably goes back to him is found in a text called *Two Entrances and Four Acts.* In "Entrance by Conduct" into the path of enlightenment, he emphasized that karma (consequences adhering to deeds) causes adversity, pain and pleasure are the result of previous actions, escape from karma is possible by avoiding attachment to anything, and that the mind of enlightenment is above such attachments.

Paul L. Redditt

See also: Buddhist ethics; Dōgen; Karma; Zen.

Bodhisattva ideal

Definition: Postponement of personal enlightenment in favor of remaining in the world of suffering to work for the enlightenment of all beings
Type of ethics: Religious ethics
Significance: The primacy of the bodhisattva ideal in Mahāyāna Buddhism serves to refute the commonly held misconception that Buddhism is a religion of withdrawal from the everyday world; there is no higher ideal in Buddhism than that of working for the enlightenment of all sentient beings.

The Sanskrit word *bodhisattva* means "enlightenment being." The bodhisattva ideal is the highest ideal to which a Buddhist practitioner can aspire, the ultimate expression of the ethical tradition of Buddhism. The historical Buddha, Śākyamuni, or Siddhārtha Gautama, the founder of Buddhism, is the ultimate bodhisattva. After he realized his own enlightenment, he could have enjoyed the great bliss of the enlightened state and had nothing further to do with his fellow beings. Instead, however, he chose to remain in the world to teach what he had learned. He made the choice to teach others the tenets of the religion that came to be called Buddhism out of a tremendous sense of compassion for all beings, whose existence is characterized by suffering of various kinds.

When Buddhists say that all life involves suffering, they do not mean that there is no pleasure to be experienced in ordinary existence. It is emphasized, however, that all pleasure is fleeting. No joy or sorrow lasts forever. All happiness must end, and therefore it is a mistake to make the search for happiness one's primary goal in life. All that is born must die, and everything that comes together must sooner or later come apart. It is possible, however, to live in such a way that one sees and understands the processes that operate in life. When one lives in this way, one gives up the vain search for worldly happiness and begins to see more clearly the way things really are.

All major schools of Buddhism recognize the importance of the bodhisattva ideal, which involves the commitment to work to bring all sentient beings to enlightenment, thereby ending the suffering that they experience in the fruitless search for happiness. In the Theravāda tradition, a tradition that is much like the Buddhism of the earliest followers of the Buddha, it is believed that to aspire to be a bodhisattva is beyond the capabilities of men and women. It is thought that the Buddha is the only bodhisattva and that only by first aspiring to less lofty goals can Buddhist practitioners proceed on the Buddhist path toward ultimate enlightenment. Theravādins typically work toward the goal of individual liberation, of becoming *arhats*, who have conquered ignorance and desire and see reality as it truly is.

In the Mahāyāna Buddhist tradition, however, it is believed that to aspire to become an *arhat* is inherently selfish, not realistic, and ultimately harmful to the practitioner who has such an aspiration. Mahāyāna means "great vehicle," and Mahāyānists use the term to differentiate themselves from the Theravādins, whom they call practitioners of the Hīnayāna, or "lesser vehicle." It should be clearly understood, however, that this simple differentiation is ultimately unfair to the Theravāda tradition. The Mahāyāna approach was developed at least partly in response to the selfish approaches and practices of early Buddhist splinter groups whose members did not practice Buddhism in a way that sincere Theravādins would recognize as true Buddhist practice.

There are three main stages of the path of the bodhisattva. The first is *anuttara-pūjā*, or supreme worship, which consists of various devotional practices that are intended to break down the practitioner's sense of self (Buddhism holds that no self truly exists) and prepare him or her for the later stages of the path. Supreme worship involves, among other things, obeisance before the image of the Buddha; the taking of refuge (the placing of one's faith) in the Buddha, the dharma (the teachings of Buddhism), and the sangha (the community of Buddhist practitioners); the confession of one's sins; and the act of rejoicing because of the spiritual attainments of others.

The Six Pāramitās (Perfections)

	English	Sanskrit	Description
1.	Giving	Dāna	Physical and spiritual generosity
2.	Morality	Śila	Refraining from doing harm to oneself or others
3.	Patience	Ksānti	Accepting things as they are and having confidence in Buddhism
4.	Effort	Vīrya	Continuing one's spiritual practice without losing enthusiasm
5.	Meditation	Dhyāna	Seeing clearly and maintaining spiritual stability
6.	Understanding	Prajñā	Directly perceiving the truth of emptiness

The second stage of the bodhisattva path is *bodhicitta-utpāda*, the generation of the thought of enlightenment. It is during this stage that the practitioner truly becomes a bodhisattva, vowing to save all sentient beings. This stage does not entail a simple wish to become enlightened but represents the point at which the desire to realize enlightenment becomes so powerful that the practitioner is, psychologically, completely altered by it. The generation of *bodhicitta* necessarily involves an awareness of the suffering of all beings. Indeed, the bodhisattva feels that when any being suffers, he or she suffers as well. At this point, the bodhisattva has given up the illusion of self, the illusion that there is any such thing as an individual being. Although beings do not exist in any ultimate sense, however, beings do experience suffering, and it is the bodhisattva's aspiration to alleviate that suffering.

The third stage of the bodhisattva path involves the practice of the four *caryās*, or modes of conduct. These four are *bodhipakṣya-caryā*, or the practice of the constituents of enlightenment; *abhijñā-caryā*, the practice of the knowledges; *pāramitā-caryā*, the practice of the perfections; and *sattvaparipāka-caryā*, the practice of teaching sentient beings. Of these four modes of conduct, the practice of the perfections is the most important.

In large part, the practice of the bodhisattva is the practice of the six *pāramitās*, or perfections.

The first perfection is *dāna*, or giving. Giving does not simply mean giving alms to the needy or clothing to the unclothed, although such actions are certainly aspects of the first perfection. It can also mean sheltering a person from fear, thereby giving that person a sense of security. It can also mean helping a person to develop spiritual awareness.

The second perfection is that of *śila*, or morality. In essence, Buddhist morality involves refraining from doing harm to oneself or others. It also includes promoting goodness and being helpful to others.

The third perfection is *kṣānti*, or patience, which entails keeping one's mental balance in the face of difficulties, tolerating the way things are. It also involves having confidence in the Buddhist path.

The fourth perfection is *vīrya*, or effort, which means continuing one's spiritual practice without losing enthusiasm.

The fifth perfection is *dhyāna*, or meditation, the practice of which enables one to see more clearly and to gain spiritual stability, without which one's practice will degenerate.

The sixth perfection is *prajñā*, or understanding. In addition to ordinary understanding, the sixth perfection entails the direct perception of the truth of emptiness, the truth that nothing exists in an ultimate sense.

By practicing the six perfections and the other practices that are part of the bodhisattva's path, the Buddhist practitioner who has raised the thought of enlightenment and taken the vow to work for the enlightenment of all beings travels through ten *bhumis*, or levels, of development, ultimately realizing buddhahood, which is complete enlightenment.

Shawn Woodyard

FURTHER READING

Dharmasiri, Gunapala. "The Bodhisattva Ideal." In *Fundamentals of Buddhist Ethics*. Antioch, Calif.: Golden Leaves, 1989.

Gyatso, Geshe Kelsang. *Meaningful to Behold: A Commentary Guide to Shantideva's "Guide to the Bodhisattva's Way of Life."* London: Tharpa, 1989.

Sangharakshita. *The Bodhisattva Ideal: Wisdom and Compassion in Buddhism.* Birmingham, England: Windhorse, 1999.

Shantideva. *A Guide to the Bodhisattva's Way of Life.* Dharamsala, India: Library of Tibetan Works and Archives, 1979.

Snelling, John. *The Buddhist Handbook: A Complete Guide to Buddhist Schools, Teaching, Practice, and History.* Rochester, Vt.: Inner Traditions, 1991.

SEE ALSO: Buddha; Buddhist ethics; Five precepts of Buddhism; Four noble truths; Mādhyamaka; Nirvana.

Boethius

IDENTIFICATION: Early Roman philosopher
BORN: c. 480, Rome (now in Italy)
DIED: 524, Pavia (now in Italy)
TYPE OF ETHICS: Classical history
SIGNIFICANCE: In *The Consolation of Philosophy* (*De consolatione philosophiae*, 523), Boethius combined classical philosophical traditions with Christian morality and theology.

A member of the Roman upper classes and a seminal Christian philosopher, Boethius served as a transition between the pagan classical world and the Christian one. An educated man, Boethius was among the first Western Christian writers to be well acquainted with classical Greek philosophical and ethical thought, including Aristotle's *Nicomachean Ethics*.

Boethius was also influenced by Platonic thought and by the ethical views of the Stoics. Boethius combined these views with Christian morality to create a practical guide for living a moral life. Knowledge, according to Boethius, is based upon self-evident axioms revealed by God; building upon these axioms, humans can discover additional truths that bring them, ultimately, to the greatest good of all, which is God.

Michael Witkoski

SEE ALSO: Aristotelian ethics; Aristotle; Christian ethics; *Nicomachean Ethics*.

Bonhoeffer, Dietrich

IDENTIFICATION: German theologian
BORN: February 4, 1906, Breslau, Germany (now Wrocław, Poland)
DIED: April 9, 1945, Flossenburg concentration camp, Germany
TYPE OF ETHICS: Religious ethics
SIGNIFICANCE: Bonhoeffer believed that ethical conduct is to be judged not by absolute principles nor by the demands of changing conditions and situations, but rather by their consequences for the future. His key works include *The Cost of Discipleship* (*Nachfolge*, 1937), *Ethics* (*Ethik*, 1949), and *Letters and Papers from Prison* (*Widerstand und Ergebung: Briefe und Aufzeichnungen aus der Haft*, 1951, revised, 1964, 1970).

Dietrich Bonhoeffer's ethical thought was forged in the furnace of Nazi Germany. As one of the founders of the Confessing Church, which refused to submit to Nazi ideology, and a member of the resistance movement inside Germany, Bonhoeffer was compelled by the conviction that Christian ethics consist not of trying to do good but of assuming responsibility for the future. His ethical theology is, therefore, "teleological" or "consequentialist." The focus is not upon motives (for example, adhering to some set of moral rules labeled "Christian") but upon living in light of the reality that in Jesus Christ, God has reconciled the world to himself. By rooting ethics in the person of Jesus Christ, the Christian is freed from the need to conform to the world's standards and is thus free to conform to Jesus Christ as Jesus Christ takes form in him or her. The individual, like the church, is then free to participate in the suffering of Christ in the life of the world.

In focusing on the resurrected Jesus Christ as the ultimate reality, Bonhoeffer is able to avoid legalism and moralism. If there is a moral or ethical code, a pattern of behavior, that can be labeled "Christian," then living a Christian life can be separated from Jesus Christ. It then becomes only a lifestyle, a universal moralism, which can be followed by anyone who is attracted to it, whether or not that person is conforming to Jesus Christ.

Bonhoeffer also avoids the dangers inherent in the traditional Lutheran doctrine of the two realms (or spheres). As originally formulated by the sixteenth century reformer Martin Luther, the doctrine states that God rules in both realms, the holy (the church) and the profane (the state). What was meant by Luther to be a duality (God ruling in both realms) became instead a dualism or dichotomy in which the state became autonomous. What is in fact one reality, "the reality of God, which has become manifest in Christ in the reality of the world," was split into two realities.

Once split off from the world, the church becomes merely a "religious society" having only spiritual authority, while individual Christians pursue lives of personal piety. Bonhoeffer saw this development as a reversal of God's intent. Rightly understood, the church is the world redeemed by God through Jesus Christ. It exists to serve the world by witnessing to Jesus Christ. When the two spheres (church and state) become autonomous, as happened in Germany, the church abdicates its responsibility for the fallen world, while the state is free to become idolatrous.

Bonhoeffer saw a similar danger in the traditional Protestant orders of creation concept. In Protestant writings on ethics, the orders of creation serve a role similar to that of natural law in Roman Catholicism. Whatever the particular version of the concept, the orders always include church, state, and family. The danger latent in the orders concept became all too clear in its exploitation by the pro-Nazi "German Christian" movement. Referring to Romans 13:1, "the powers that be are ordained by God," the German Christians argued that Christians were obliged to support the Third Reich.

In their "Guiding Principles" of June 6, 1932, the German Christians declared that "race, folk, and nation" were "orders of existence granted and entrusted to us by God," which Christians were obligated by God's law to preserve. The danger in their argument, as Bonhoeffer saw it, was that almost any existing order could be defended by it, even a positively demoniac one such as the Third Reich.

Bonhoeffer argued that the fallen nature of creation precludes the concept of orders from being used to discern the will of God for today. The central fact of the fall means that "each human order is an order of the fallen world, and not an order of creation." As an alternative to the orders of creation, Bonhoeffer developed his concept of the "divine mandates" in *Ethics*, which was written between 1940 and 1943. These divine mandates are social relationships, or structures, by means of which God brings order out of the chaos of the fallen world. The mandates include the church, family, labor, and government.

ULTIMATE REALITY OF JESUS CHRIST

In the social relationships of the divine mandates, the individual Christian lives as a member of a community. There in the real world where God meets fallen humanity in the person of Jesus Christ, the individual is conformed to the image of Jesus Christ. By living responsibly as a Christian upon whose heart is written the law of God, the individual Christian becomes the means by which "the reality of Christ with us and in our world" is manifested. In focusing on the ultimate reality of Jesus Christ, the individual Christian finds both freedom and responsibility. He or she becomes free to live in obedience to God's commands, even though that may bring him or her into conflict with human laws. The individual must seek and do the will of God in the historic, space-time world, while living as a responsible member of the community though the divine mandates.

The Christian is free to live as a disciple of Christ in the world, but that discipleship can be costly. Sharing Christ's suffering for the lost always places the Christian on the side of justice. Like Jesus Christ, his Lord, the Christian becomes the advocate of the weak. By choice, he or she takes up the cross and follows Christ, even when, as in the case of Bonhoeffer, it leads to a martyr's death in a concentration camp.

Paul R. Waibel

FURTHER READING

Bonhoeffer, Dietrich. *The Cost of Discipleship*. Translated by R. H. Fuller. New York: Macmillan, 1963.

———. *Ethics*. Edited by Eberhard Bethge. Translated by Neville H. Smith. London: SCM Press, 1971.

———. *Letters and Papers from Prison*. Enl. ed. Edited by Eberhard Bethge. Translated by R. H. Fuller. New York: Macmillan, 1972.

Burtness, James. *Shaping the Future: The Ethics of Dietrich Bonhoeffer*. Philadelphia: Fortress Press, 1985.

Hamilton, Kenneth. *Life in One's Stride: A Short Study in Dietrich Bonhoeffer*. Grand Rapids, Mich.: W. B. Eerdmans, 1968.

Huntemann, Georg. *The Other Bonhoeffer.* Grand Rapids, Mich.: Baker Book House, 1993.

Kelly, Geffrey B., and F. Burton Nelson. *The Cost of Moral Leadership: The Spirituality of Dietrich Bonhoeffer.* Grand Rapids, Mich.: W. B. Eerdmans, 2003.

Klassen, A. J., ed. *A Bonhoeffer Legacy: Essays in Understanding.* Grand Rapids, Mich.: W. B. Eerdmans, 1981.

Nickson, Ann L. *Bonhoeffer on Freedom: Courageously Grasping Reality.* Burlington, Vt.: Ashgate, 2002.

SEE ALSO: Christian ethics; Consequentialism; Deontological ethics; Jesus Christ; Natural law; Niebuhr, Reinhold; Religion; Situational ethics.

Book banning

DEFINITION: Suppression of literary works deemed to be politically or socially unacceptable or otherwise threatening

TYPE OF ETHICS: Arts and censorship

SIGNIFICANCE: Books are generally banned when their contents are judged to be immoral; however, to many people, book banning itself is immoral. As a result, it is an inherently controversial practice.

Book banning is an ancient activity practiced throughout history and the world. The first recorded book banning occurred in Western civilization in 387 B.C.E., when Plato recommended that Homer be expurgated for immature readers. Four hundred years later, the Roman emperor Caligula tried to ban Homer's *Odyssey* (c. 800 B.C.E.) because he feared that the book's strong theme of freedom and liberty would arouse the citizenry against his autocratic rule. In 1559, Pope Paul IV issued a list of prohibited books, the *Index librorum prohibitorum.*

BOOK BANNING IN THE UNITED STATES

In the United States, the First Amendment to the Constitution seems unequivocally and absolutely to guarantee freedom of speech, no matter how that speech is expressed, without interference by the government. The First Amendment states in part that "Congress shall make no law . . . abridging the freedom of speech." In fact, however, this freedom is by no means absolute or unfettered. Donna E. Demac correctly points out that the history of freedom of expression in the United States is a complex mixture of a commitment to personal rights and intolerance of ideas deemed subversive, dissident, or obscene.

Certain books, by the very nature of their subject matter or writing style, will offend the values and attitudes of certain individuals or groups. As Kenneth Donelsen has observed: "Any book or idea or teaching method is potentially censorable by someone, somewhere, sometime, for some reason." A book's ideas may be disliked, the book may be perceived to ridicule certain individuals or to ignore others; or the book may be judged to be dangerous or offensive. If these parties believe the book has transgressed the bounds of acceptability, they may take action to have the book banned.

Book banning is in fact a common and everyday occurrence in the United States. More than a thousand incidents are recorded each year, and no doubt many other incidents go unrecorded or unrecognized. William Noble called book banning "a pervasive ethic" and noted that banning incidents arise throughout the country and in many forums—school board meetings, public libraries, legislative hearings, ad hoc parental complaints, governmental committees, private groups assessments, open court and even commercial publishing decisions. "Book banning is as much a part of our lives as the morning newspaper or . . . television; its cultural influence is strong enough to affect the way we think and the way we communicate."

Four Primary Reasons Behind Banning a Book

1. The book is deemed to be obscene.

2. The book promotes secular humanism or is antireligious.

3. Self-censorship in the publishing business or government.

4. Subordination of individuals belonging to a particular racial or sexual group.

OBSCENITY

The first antiobscenity law passed in the United States was in 1712 by the colony of Massachusetts. The "composing, writing, printing, or publishing of any filthy, obscene, or profane song, pamphlet, libel or mock sermon" was prohibited. The first obscenity case in America occurred in 1821 in Massachusetts, when Peter Holmes was found guilty for publishing and circulating a "lewd and obscene" book, John Cleland's *Memoirs of a Woman of Pleasure*. The federal government effected its first antiobscenity statute in 1842, and in 1865 Congress passed a law prohibiting the sending of obscene materials by mail.

The modern era of book censorship and book banning commenced after the U.S. Civil War, a period of urban upheaval, rootlessness, loosening of moral controls, and widespread circulation of graphic erotica. The most notable milestones of this era were the passage of the Comstock Act by Congress in 1873 and the passage of antiobscenity legislation by most states by 1900. The Comstock Act prohibited using the U.S. mails to send any "obscene, lewd, or lascivious, indecent, filthy or vile book" through the mails and was responsible for the seizure and destruction of thousands of tons of books and court prosecutions.

The 1920's marked the end of an era for the book banners. The liberalizing influences of 1920's American culture resulted in a change in attitudes and values among the population and judiciary toward what had been formerly considered obscene. Three landmark court decisions occurred between 1933 and 1973. In 1933, James Joyce's *Ulysses* (1922) was declared to be a work of art that was not written for the purpose of exploiting obscenity. Also, in determining whether a book was obscene, the entire book now had to be considered, whereas previously obscenity charges could be based on a single page or paragraph. In 1957 in *Roth v. United States*, the Supreme Court specifically defined what constituted obscenity: "Obscenity is utterly without redeeming social importance." This definition was further refined in 1973 when the Supreme Court established three criteria to be used to determine if material is obscene:

(1) [The] average person, applying modern community standards would find that the work, taken as a whole, appeals to the prurient interest; (2) whether the work depicts or describes, in a patently offensive way, sexual conduct specifically defined by the applicable state law; and (3) whether the work, taken as a whole, lacks serious literary, artistic, political or scientific value.

These rulings had the effect of making it much more difficult to prove a work was obscene. Old bans were overturned (*Lady Chatterley's Lover* in 1959, *Memoirs of a Woman of Pleasure* in 1966), and although attempts at censorship and book banning continued to occur with frequent regularity, the early twenty-first century era is characterized by greater tolerance and openness in artistic and personal expression. To an extent, this greater tolerance and openness fostered by the judicial process can be circumvented by the political process. For example, a bill that prohibited the use of federal money for any work of art deemed obscene was passed by Congress and signed into law by President Ronald Reagan.

SECULAR HUMANISM AND ANTI-RELIGIONISM

Secular humanism has been characterized by an attorney as "a godless religion which rejects any notion of the supernatural or a divine purpose for the world" and which also "rejects any objective or absolute moral standards and embraces a subjective 'anything goes' approach to morals based on personal needs and desires." According to plaintiffs, secular humanism has been advocated in public school textbooks. Since secular humanism is a religion, it violates the constitutionally mandated separation of church and state, and therefore the books should be banned. Plaintiffs were upheld in a court case in 1987, but this decision was reversed by the Court of Appeals.

A much broader and more widespread attack on school textbooks has been instituted by various watchdog groups that believe that a number of textbooks are antireligious. For example, Beverly LaHay of Concerned Women for America expressed the necessity "to preserve, protect, and promote traditional and Judeo-Christian values through education, legal defense. . . . The sad fact is that educational systems in most American schools has already removed any reference to God or teaching of Judeo-Christian values that is the most important information a child can learn." In a famous case, LaHay's group supported seven families in Hawkins County, Tennessee, who were attempting to ban a series of textbooks. Purportedly, the books contained passages about witchcraft, astrology, pacifism, feminism, and evolution, while ignoring religion and creationism.

The trial judge agreed that the textbooks interfered with the parents' free exercise of religion, that the children were exposed to offensive religious beliefs that interfered with practice of their own religion and that put Tennessee in the position of favoring one religion over another. Ten months later, however, the court of appeals reversed this decision, stating that the Constitution was not violated and that exposure to offensive religious beliefs is not identical to requiring them to be accepted.

SELF-CENSORSHIP BY PUBLISHERS AND GOVERNMENT

William Noble has observed that the absorption of many independent publishing houses into conglomerates has produced more reluctance to stir up controversy or to offend, resulting in self-censorship of what is published. Unlike the previously discussed situations, the publisher may be the only one who knows what has happened. Self-censorship takes several forms. Probably the mildest form occurs when an author is asked (not ordered) to change or eliminate some text. For example, Judy Blume removed text at her publisher's request in her young-adult book *Tiger Eyes*: "There was just one line in the book [about masturbation], but my publishers said it would make the book controversial and limit the book's audience. I took it out but I wish I hadn't."

Similar to Judy Blume's encounter with self-censorship is bowdlerism, named for Thomas Bowdler, a nineteenth century British physician who excised text from William Shakespeare's plays. These "bowdlerized" versions can still be found in schools, and in 1980 Harcourt Brace Jovanovich published an edition of William Shakespeare's *Romeo and Juliet* minus about 10 percent of the text. About two-thirds of the omitted passages had sexual connotations.

A more severe form of self-censorship is to fail to publish a book or to withdraw it from publication under pressure once it has been published. Deborah Davis's unflattering 1980 biography of Katharine Graham, owner of the *Washington Post*, was pulled from circulation after Graham and the *Post*'s executive director, Ben Bradlee, protested in private to the publisher. When the Ayatollah Khomeini of Iran issued a

death warrant on Salman Rushdie for his authorship of his "blasphemous" *The Satanic Verses* in 1989, worldwide book bannings and burnings occurred. In the United States, three of the largest book chains—Waldenbooks, B. Dalton, and Barnes and Noble—removed all copies of *The Satanic Verses* from open display (the book could still be bought by request). This action was justified in terms of protecting the safety and welfare of employees and patrons.

Frank W. Snepp, a former Central Intelligence Agency (CIA) agent, wrote a critical book (*Decent Interval*) about the CIA's involvement in the Vietnam War. The book was published in 1977 without prior CIA approval, to which Snepp had previously agreed in writing. In federal district court, Snepp's attorney argued that since no classified information was revealed in the book, the government was violating Snepp's rights under the First Amendment. The CIA argued that finding Snepp innocent would create a dangerous precedent and that the CIA would lose control and be unable to enforce the guarantee. Snepp was found guilty, but the decision was reversed in appeals court on the grounds that since no classified information was revealed, Snepp was protected by the First Amendment. The Supreme Court upheld the district court decision, however, stating that Snepp's book had "irreparably harmed the United States government," and Snepp was ordered to hand over more than $200,000 in royalties to the Department of Justice.

RACIAL AND SEXUAL SUBORDINATION

Mark Twain's *Adventures of Huckleberry Finn* (1884) was considered to be racist by the National Association for the Advancement of Colored People, which sought to have it banned from New York City Schools in 1957. The book was said to demean African Americans but not whites, resulting in a loss of respect by the reader for African Americans. The book continued to be attacked. In 1984, an African American alderman in Illinois succeeded in having it removed from a high school reading list for its use of offensive language. Similarly, the British novelist William Golding's *Lord of the Flies* (1954) was branded as racist by the Toronto School Board for using the term "nigger" and for demeaning African Americans and was banned from schools.

Radical feminist writer Andrea Dworkin and lawyer Catharine MacKinnon attempted to regulate por-

Notable Book Bannings

Year	Book (Author)	Censor	Stated reason
387 B.C.E.	*The Odyssey* (Homer)	Plato	Harmfulness to immature readers
35 C.E.	*The Odyssey* (Homer)	Caligula	Anti-autocratic content
1525-1526	New Testament	Church of England	Irreligious content
1922	*Ulysses* (James Joyce)	U.S. Post Office	Obscenity
1927	*Elmer Gantry* (Sinclair Lewis)	Boston local officials	Obscene depiction of religious hero
1929	*Lady Chatterley's Lover* (D. H. Lawrence)	U.S. Customs	Obscenity
1931	*The Merchant of Venice* (William Shakespeare)	New York Jewish organizations	Fostering of intolerance
1934	*Tropic of Cancer* (Henry Miller)	U.S. Customs	Obscenity
1939	*The Grapes of Wrath* (John Steinbeck)	St. Louis public library	Vulgarity
1941	*Tobacco Road* (Erskine Caldwell)	U.S. Post Office	Obscenity
1948	*Sanctuary* (William Faulkner)	Philadelphia vice squad	Obscenity
1955	*From Here to Eternity* (James Jones)	U.S. Post Office	Obscenity
1955-	*The Catcher in the Rye* (J. D. Salinger)	Various schools	Obscenity
1957	*Ten North Frederick* (John O'Hara)	Detroit police commissioner	Obscenity
1960	*The Sun Also Rises* (Ernest Hemingway)	San Jose and Riverside, Calif., public libraries	Obscenity
1965	*The Naked Lunch* (William Burroughs)	Boston Superior Court	Obscenity
1972	*Catch 22* (Joseph Heller)	Strongsville, Ohio, schools	Obscenity
1989	*The Satanic Verses* (Salman Rushdie)	Iran's Ayatollah Khomeini	Offensiveness to Muslims

nographic literature on the grounds that it discriminated against women and therefore was under the jurisdiction of civil rights laws. According to Dworkin, pornography produced "bigotry and hostility and aggression toward all women," and promoted the idea that "the hurting of women is . . . basic to the sexual pleasure of men." Legislation intended to allow a woman who perceived herself to be hurt by

pornography to sue the bookstore owner for civil damage and have the materials banned was proposed in three cities but was never put into law. In Indianapolis, the case was appealed to the Supreme Court, which upheld a lower court's ruling that "to deny free speech in order to engineer social change in the name of accomplishing a greater good for one sector of our society erodes the freedoms of all and, as such, threatens tyranny and injustice for those subjected to the rule of such laws."

THE CASE AGAINST BOOK BANNING

Some Americans have interpreted the First Amendment literally to mean that book banning or censorship is not justifiable or permissible under any circumstances. The Supreme Court justices William O. Douglas and Hugo L. Black and the American Civil Liberties Union (ACLU) stated that the First Amendment protected all publications, without qualification, against either civil or criminal regulation at any level of government. Douglas tolerated "no exceptions . . . not even for obscenity." To Douglas, the First Amendment can have meaning and significance only if it allows protests even against the moral code that is the standard in the community. The ACLU declared that all published material is protected by the First Amendment unless it creates a "clear and present danger" of causing antisocial behavior.

George Elliot stated the case for removing all censorship for pornography: (1) No law can be stated clearly enough to guide unequivocally those who decide censorship cases. The ACLU has called such laws "vague and unworkable." The Supreme Court has for years grappled with defining obscenity and pornography with considerable disagreement among justices and changes in definition over the years. (2) There is no clear and unequivocal evidence that in fact pornography does severely injure many people, even adolescents. (3) The less power government has the better. As Justice Hugo L. Black wrote in 1966: "Criminal punishment by government, although universally recognized, is an exercise of one of government's most awesome and dangerous powers. Consequently, wise and good governments make all possible efforts to hedge this dangerous power by restricting it within easily identifiable boundaries."

The essence of the belief that reading materials should not be banned under any circumstance rests on the assumption that the citizenry has free will and is intelligent. Therefore, each citizen is free and able to reject material that he or she finds personally offensive, but no person has the right to define what is personally offensive for anyone else or to limit anyone else's access to that material. To do so is, to paraphrase the words of federal judge Sarah Backer, to erode freedom for the entire citizenry and threaten

tyranny and injustice for those at whom the laws are directed.

THE CASE FOR BOOK BANNING

An editorial in the April 2, 1966, issue of *The New Republic* commented on Justice William O. Douglas's position: "It would be nice if we could have a society in which nothing that others sold or displayed made anyone fear for the future of his children. But we are not that society, and it is hard to protect Mishkin's [a convicted pornographer] freedom to make a profit any way he likes, when his particular way is a stench in the nostrils of his community, even though the community would perhaps be better advised to ignore him." The editorial advocated permitting Mishkin to cater to those who seek his product but not allowing him to display it in public.

That editorial represented the stance of most of the pro-censorship articles that have been published, as well as the position of the courts. It is a middle-of-the-road position. Censorship itself and the power vested in agencies to enforce it should be approached warily. Pornography does exist; however, many consider it to be a social evil that needs to be controlled. When material is perceived to destroy or subvert social and moral laws, undermine community standards, or offend decency without aesthetic justification, it may be banned.

The two situations of most concern are materials available to or directed at minors and material that is publicly displayed and available that is indecent and offensive to community standards. If such material is made unavailable to minors and kept from public view, it may be permissible to offer it to those who desire it. A more extreme and minority position is that the ban on pornography should be total, and the material should not be made available to anybody.

Most of the debate about censorship and the banning of books has focused on pornography and obscenity. The other areas of book banning (self-censorship, religion, and sexual and racial subordination), however, would no doubt find adherents to each of the above positions. Probably the only area of censorship that comes close to finding a consensus is the revelation of classified material that would endanger lives or national security. Most people support the censorship and banning of such material.

Defining what kinds of books and other reading materials should be banned and the subject of banning itself are slippery issues. The reason is, as George Elliott noted, that these issues are not amenable to scientific analysis. They cannot be numerically defined or objectively measured. They are ambiguous matters of personal preference and consensus opinion. Censorship and book banning are psychological, aesthetic, and political phenomena.

Laurence Miller

FURTHER READING

Demac, Donna A. *Liberty Denied*. New Brunswick, N.J.: Rutgers University Press, 1990. An excellent discussion of the different kinds of censorship and book banning and their effect on the authors and on society. Takes a strong anticensorship position.

Haight, Anne Lyon, and Chandler B. Grannis. *Banned Books, 387 B.C. to 1978 A.D.* 4th ed. New York: R. R. Bowker, 1978. A comprehensive list of book banning and related incidents through the years and in various countries.

Kravitz, Nancy. *Censorship and the School Library Media Center*. Westport, Conn.: Libraries Unlimited, 2002. An exhaustive study of censorship and book banning in schools, including historical background, a survey of contemporary pressures upon school libraries, and analysis of current laws and court decisions.

McClellan, Grant S., ed. *Censorship in the United States*. New York: H. W. Wilson, 1967. An excellent collection of magazine and newspaper articles that argue the pros and cons of censorship.

Noble, William. *Bookbanning in America*. Middlebury, Vt.: Paul S. Erickson, 1990. Highly recommended. A lively, very readable, thorough, and thoughtful discussion of the various forms of censorship. Takes a strong anticensorship position.

Rauch, Jonathan. *Kindly Inquisitors: The New Attacks on Free Thought*. Chicago: University of Chicago Press, 1993. A leisurely and very personal but insightful essay on the evils of censorship.

Woods, L. B. *A Decade of Censorship in America: The Threat to Classrooms and Libraries, 1966-1975*. Metuchen, N.J.: Scarecrow Press, 1979. A detailed and thorough presentation of the censorship wars as fought in public schools and libraries. Presents both pro- and anticensorship points of view.

SEE ALSO: Academic freedom; Art; Art and public policy; Censorship; First Amendment; Freedom of expression; *Index librorum prohibitorum*; Library Bill of Rights; Song lyrics.

Bosnia

IDENTIFICATION: Balkan nation whose separation from Yugoslavia during the early 1990's quickly led to the first major post-World War II ethno-nationalist conflict in Europe

DATE: Became independent in 1992

TYPE OF ETHICS: Human rights

SIGNIFICANCE: The conflict in Bosnia represented a major challenge to the world, to address issues of nationalism, separatism and human rights in Europe, raising issues of ethnic cleansing and the ethics underlying the role of United Nations peacekeeping forces there.

When the Soviet Union fell in 1990, its repercussions were felt all over the world, but particularly in the former Soviet satellite states of Eastern Europe. As one state after another unraveled, the world watched the creation of new sovereign states arise, often along ethnic and nationalist lines. Bosnia, a former republic of Yugoslavia, was one such nation that declared its independence. A civil war ensued between the Bosnian Muslims and the Serbs that was eventually settled through the intervention of the United Nations and the signing of peace accords through U.S. mediation.

THE FORMER YUGOSLAVIA

The Balkan nation of Yugoslavia was formed after World War I, assembled by the great European powers. It was made up of six republics: Serbia, Croatia, Bosnia-Herzegovina, Slovenia, Macedonia, and Montenegro. While many ethnic groups coexisted in these republics, Serbia was primarily dominated by its Orthodox Christian Serbian majority, Slovenia and Croatia were primarily Roman Catholic, and Bosnia-Herzegovina had a Muslim majority and a sizable Serb minority.

Historical grievances had long plagued relations among Yugoslavia's diverse peoples. For instance, the Croats had turned against the Serbs during Germany's wartime occupation of Yugoslavia. After World War II, however, Yugoslavia appeared to be on the way to solving its historical nationalist problems. Josip Broz Tito, the country's dominant postwar leader, was a powerful, charismatic figure who held the country together and touted a special Yugoslav brand of socialism as the path to prosperity. Along with India's Jawaharlal Nehru and Egypt's Gamal Abdel Nasser, Tito spearheaded the Non-Aligned Movement, bringing international respect to Yugoslavia.

BLOODSHED IN BOSNIA

After Tito's death in early 1980, old ethnic hatreds and nationalistic fervor came to the fore. The morality of his strategy—papering over ethnic differences in an effort to hold together the state—came into question. Serbs who had felt diminished under Tito asserted their identity and came under the influence of Slobodan Milošević, a hard-line Serb nationalist. In 1990, the Serb army crushed Kosovo, which had been a partly autonomous unit within Tito's Yugoslavia, as it pressed for independence and fought against Slovenia's declaration of independence before finally being forced to accept it.

When Bosnia-Herzegovina voted for independence in 1992 and was recognized by the United States and members of the European Community, the Serbs refused to accept the change. The Serbian army was accused of committing grave atrocities against the Bosnian Muslims and of trying to force them from large areas in order to form a solid Serbian belt in Bosnia. Images of Bosnian Muslim men being rounded up, held, and exterminated in camps recalled the concentration camps of the World War II Holocaust. At the end of the Bosnian war, the number dead was estimated to be around 100,000, with some reports citing higher or lower figures. In addition, around 20,000 people remained missing.

SETTLEMENT IN BOSNIA

The international community intervened with U.N. peacekeeping forces; however, these forces were accused of standing by while the Serbs continued their campaign against the Bosnians. U.N. peacekeepers traditionally serve as neutral reminders to conflicting parties to resolve their conflict in nonviolent ways. Peacekeepers do not use force except in self-defence. In traditional conflicts, this neutrality has served the forces well. However, in the case of Bosnia, they were often reduced to standing by as Serbian forces rounded up Bosnian Muslim men to forcibly take them to concentration camps. In other cases, they failed to intervene as brutal killings took place during their watch.

The ethical and moral questions raised by U.N. peacekeepers maintaining neutrality in the face of Serb aggression was still being debated a decade later. In 1995, after much bloodshed, the Dayton Peace Agreement was signed in Dayton, Ohio, by representatives of the Republic of Bosnia and Herzegovina, the Republic of Croatia, and the Federal Republic of Yugoslavia. Un-

der this framework agreement, all sides agreed to work toward a peaceful settlement. By 2004, progress had been made toward the various ethnic communities living harmoniously side by side, although tensions and unresolved issues remained.

Tinaz Pavri

FURTHER READING

Clark, Wesley K. *Waging Modern War: Bosnia, Kosovo, and the Future of Conflict.* New York: Public Affairs, 2001.

Malcolm, Noel. *Bosnia: A Short History.* New York: New York University Press, 1999.

Sacco, Joe. *Safe Area Gorazde: The War in Eastern Bosnia, 1992-1995.* Seattle: Fantagraphics Press, 2000.

SEE ALSO: Concentration camps; Ethnic cleansing; Islamic ethics; Kosovo; North Atlantic Treaty Organization; Peacekeeping missions; Rwanda genocide; United Nations.

A Bosnian man walks past a poster in Sarajevo showing the candidates of a Muslim party running in the nation's October, 2002, general elections. (AP/Wide World Photos)

Boycotts

DEFINITION: Organized attempts to achieve certain goals by convincing consumers not to buy specific products or not to buy products from specific stores

TYPE OF ETHICS: Politico-economic ethics

SIGNIFICANCE: Boycotts are attempts to realize certain consumer or civil rights or to correct perceived imbalances of political or economic power among individuals and organizations.

Boycotts—which take their name from Charles Boycott, a notoriously unfair Irish landlord—have been a recognized form of protest at least since the Boston Tea Party, which signaled the beginning of the American Revolutionary War. However, boycotts did not become common until the late 1960's. Since that time, more and more groups have used boycotts to achieve increasingly diverse goals. By the 1990's,

more than one hundred local or national consumer protests were in progress throughout the United States at any given time.

Some boycotts are organized by groups for their own benefit; for example, customers stop shopping at certain stores that they believe are charging unfair prices. Other boycotts are aimed at gaining benefits for third parties; for example, consumers in the United States refused to buy Nestlé products until that company changed its infant formula marketing practices in developing countries. Still other boycotts have been called against one company to put economic or social pressure on a different company, as when the United Farm Workers and their supporters boycotted stores that sold table grapes until the growers recognized the union. Organizations now use boycotts to achieve such wide-ranging political goals as animal rights, environmental protection, and the rights of women and minority groups. Nor are boycotts the exclusive province of progressive groups and agendas. In 1997, the Southern Baptist Convention organized a boycott of the Walt Disney Corporation, largely in response to Disney's willingness to host gay and lesbian groups at its theme parks.

D. Kirk Davidson
Updated by the editors

SEE ALSO: Business ethics; Civil disobedience; Civil Rights movement; Coercion; Consumerism; Economics; Jackson, Jesse; Marketing.

Bradley, F. H.

IDENTIFICATION: English philosopher
BORN: January 30, 1846, Clapham, Surrey, England
DIED: September 18, 1924, Oxford, England
TYPE OF ETHICS: Modern history
SIGNIFICANCE: F. H. Bradley stressed the significance of ideas, especially spiritual ideas, as the fundamental reality, and he criticized the utilitarian concept that happiness is the goal of ethical behavior. His works include *The Presuppositions of Critical History* (1874), *Ethical Studies* (1876), *Principles of Logic* (1883), and *Appearance and Reality: A Metaphysical Essay* (1893).

Francis Herbert Bradley was a nineteenth century British philosopher whose career spanned more than five decades at Oxford University, where he was first elected to a fellowship in 1870. His writing eventually earned him Britain's Order of Merit.

Bradley's keen critical analysis of the dialectic between the importance of spirituality and that of reality stood in opposition to utilitarian thought, whose advocates, such as John Stuart Mill, wrote that the goal of humankind should be to do that which would bring the greatest good to the greatest number of individuals.

Bradley's own work was based on the ideals of Georg Wilhelm Friedrich Hegel, which stressed the social nature of morality and held that one's ethics was determined by one's place in society. Since Bradley focused on the place of the individual within society, some of his critics have suggested that his ideas led to moral relativism. Bradley's most famous work, *Appearance and Reality: A Metaphysical Essay*, appeared in 1893. Although this book spoke of

the spiritual nature of reality, Bradley recognized that the existence of that spiritual nature was impossible to prove intellectually because of the limitations of the human intellect.

James A. Baer

SEE ALSO: Bentham, Jeremy; Hegel, Georg Wilhelm Friedrich; Idealist ethics; Mill, John Stuart; Utilitarianism.

Brain death

DEFINITION: Cessation of the organic functions of the human brain
TYPE OF ETHICS: Bioethics
SIGNIFICANCE: New definitions of what constitutes human death are integrally tied to ethical decisions relating to decisions about efforts to sustain life and the possibility of organ transplantation.

Throughout most of history, human death was defined in terms of cessation of the heart and lungs. Human beings were considered to be dead only after their hearts and lungs permanently ceased functioning. Those criteria sufficed until modern advances in medical technology required reconsideration of how death should be defined. The invention of the iron lung and artificial stimulation of hearts has made continued respiration and circulation possible long after hearts and lungs lose their normal functional capacities. Death has consequently come to be understood in terms of functional activity associated with the organs, not the organs themselves.

A greater challenge to the traditional definition of death came to the fore during the 1960's. New medical technology made it possible for the first time to maintain the cardiopulmonary functions of patients whose entire brains—or at least large portions of them—were effectively dead. Since that time, brain-dead patients have never been able to regain consciousness, but their bodies have been maintained for long periods of time, sometimes years or even decades, in an unconscious state. Another important advance during the 1960's was the beginning of successful transplants of complex organs, including the heart.

DEVELOPMENT

Maintaining patients in a permanent vegetative state is expensive and a drain on human personnel and medical resources. In addition, because of continued respiration and blood flow, the organs of such patients do not necessarily degrade if blood pressure and essential plasma and blood gas components are properly regulated. Medically speaking, the organs of such patients frequently are prime candidates for successful transplantation. The high costs of keeping comatose patients alive and the growing need for organs for transplants place a new urgency on the need to reconsider traditional definitions of death.

Over the course of about ten years, many ethical, legal, and medical authorities explicitly rejected a definition based on cessation of the lungs and heart and embraced a brain-oriented definition of death. During the first years of the twenty-first century, the prevailing view was a brain-death definition: A human being is dead when and only when the brain has permanently ceased functioning.

Despite the popularity of the new brain-oriented definition, two opposing schools of thought have arisen. One group advocates a whole-brain definition. This view holds that a human being is dead when and only when the entire brain, including the cerebrum (the outer shell of which is the cortex), the cerebellum, and the brain stem (which includes the mid-brain, the pons, and the medulla oblongata), permanently stops functioning.

The other group advocates a higher-brain definition. According to their view, a human being is dead when and only when the cerebrum (or cortex) permanently stops functioning. The latter view is the more radical of the two. The difference between the two views is important: A patient considered dead on a higher-brain definition might still be considered alive on a whole-brain definition. In some cases, brain stem function, for example, can continue in the absence of cortical activity. A patient with such a condition might even exhibit spontaneous respiration and heartbeat.

CONTROVERSY

Although brain death definitions have largely superseded the heart-lung definition, controversy still surrounds them. Advocates of a heart-lung definition argue that brain-death definitions represent no new or deeper insights into the nature of human death. They further charge that those definitions are motivated by attempts to redefine costly and inconvenient patients out of existence, coupled with medical opportunism on the part of transplant surgeons and potential organ recipients.

Even within the brain death camp there are disagreements. Advocates of the whole-brain definition have argued that the higher-brain view confuses the idea of a human being ceasing to be a person—permanent loss of consciousness, associated with permanent loss of cerebral function—with the idea of a human being ceasing to be alive—permanent loss of governing organic function, associated with permanent loss of all brain functions. On the other hand, advocates of a higher-brain definition have argued that once the heart-lung definition has been abandoned, there is tacit recognition that what human death really concerns is the loss of what is essentially significant to human existence—consciousness—and not mere organic function. Thus, brain stem function, as not intrinsically associated with consciousness, is no more relevant to the determination of human death than kidney function.

Michael J. Wreen

FURTHER READING

Lamb, David. *Death, Brain Death and Ethics*. London: Croon Helm, 1985.

Potts, Michael, Paul A. Byrne, and Richard G. Nilges. *Beyond Brain Death: The Case Against Brain-Based Criteria for Human Death*. Boston: Kluwer Academic Publishers, 2000.

President's Commission for the Study of Ethical Problems in Medicine and Biomedical Behavioral Research. *Defining Death*. Washington, D.C.: U.S. Superintendent of Documents, 1981.

Youngner, Stuart J., ed. *The Definition of Death: Contemporary Controversies*. Baltimore: Johns Hopkins University Press, 1999.

SEE ALSO: Bioethics; Life and death; Medical bills of rights; Medical ethics; "Playing god" in medical decision making; Right to die; Sentience; Stem cell research.

Brandeis, Louis D.

IDENTIFICATION: U.S. Supreme Court justice
BORN: November 13, 1856, Louisville, Kentucky
DIED: October 5, 1941, Washington, D.C.
TYPE OF ETHICS: Legal and judicial ethics
SIGNIFICANCE: One of the leading progressives of the
   early twentieth century, Brandeis sat on the U.S.
   Supreme Court from 1916 to 1939 and was an important leader of the American Zionist movement. He espoused an environmental view of law
   known as sociological jurisprudence whereby
   law is guided by reason.

From 1916 until his retirement in 1939, Louis D.
Brandeis served as an associate Supreme Court Justice. His progressivism on the Court was manifested
by his use of the power of government to protect the
interests of all Americans. Brandeis translated controversies in court into universal moral terms and incorporated those moral values into the framework of
law. His leadership in the World Zionist Organization, as on the Supreme Court, demonstrated his consuming passion to create a just democracy for all individuals and to use every avenue of government to
perfect and preserve a genuine equality.

Brandeis wrote that democracy "demands continuous sacrifice by the individual and more exigent
obedience to the moral law than any other form of
government . . ." Deciding each case on the basis of
moral rectitude within a democracy, he wrote opinions that were detailed, were intended to instruct, and
reflected his beliefs in the maintenance of the federal
system of government. He was willing to attempt social experimentation within the structure of the government to achieve a democratic equality and preserve the liberties of speech, press, and assembly—
all of which are requisites for the maintenance of a
free society.

Stephen D. Livesay

SEE ALSO: Jurisprudence; Progressivism; Supreme
Court, U.S.; Supreme Court Justice selection;
Zionism.

Bribery

DEFINITION: Illegally or improperly obtaining favors
   in exchange for money or other items of value
TYPE OF ETHICS: Personal and social ethics
SIGNIFICANCE: The concept of bribery focuses attention upon the relationship of special duties to general moral obligations.

Bribery involves paying somebody else in money or
other things of value, whether objects or favors, to violate a special obligation or duty. Payments to violate
general ethical duties, such as to refrain from murder
or robbery, would not ordinarily be classified as bribery. Very often, however, general ethical duties and
special obligations may be linked. For example, a
prosecutor who through bribery is induced falsely to
prosecute the briber's political opponent is violating
both general and special obligations.

It might be tempting to analyze bribery in terms
of extrinsic morality, in which a morally neutral act
is made wrong (or obligatory) by some just authority for the common good. Modern industrial societies have found bribery to be inconsistent with efficiency and have, therefore, outlawed bribery. Most
ethicists, however, see true bribery as a violation
of intrinsic morality—a wrong in itself—because it
aims at luring persons to neglect or to trespass the
obligations they have taken upon themselves by acceptance of public or private office with inherent
duties.

The moral impermissibility of bribery arises out
of two primary considerations: First, the bribers induce the bribees to violate their special duties, and
second, evil consequences may flow from the actions
undertaken for the bribes. Consider the employment
manager of a corporation who accepts a bribe to hire
a particular candidate for a job. Even if the candidate
is fully qualified, if the bribe causes the choice of a
less-than-best candidate, that manager makes his
company slightly less competitive in the free market,
potentially costing jobs, profits, and even the future
existence of the enterprise. In the case of a scrupulous
bribee, who will accept a bribe only from the candidate he considers best qualified for the position, the
evil of the bribe rests on the violation of the duty
alone, or that violation plus a kind of fraud against the
briber (although the latter is problematical).

Problems still arise, however, for the right to re-

When Taking Bribes May Be Honorable

The ethics of bribery become more complicated when one considers the actions of officials of illegal or immoral organizations. During World War II, would an SS officer who took bribes from Jews to help them escape from Nazi persecution and extermination have acted unethically? Certainly, that officer would have been in technical violation of his official duties, both to his specific organization and to his national government, Adolf Hitler's Nazi government. However, there can be no morally binding special obligation to a thoroughly immoral organization, for one cannot morally bind oneself to do that which is ethically wrong.

quire payments for doing a good act remains uncertain. If the good deed is morally obligatory, it would seem that demanding payment for it would not be right unless the payment were actually necessary to carry on the good work. If, on the contrary, the good act were supererogatory, then perhaps a requirement of payment might be justifiable.

BRIBERY VS. EXTORTION

Another area of concern in regard to bribery involves payments made in response to demands by persons in authority (or otherwise influential) to prevent the conduct of business or to inflict other harms. Moral philosophers have established a useful distinction between bribery and extortion. Demands of payment to prevent harm are, properly speaking, extortion, and the theoretical considerations involved in such payments are extremely complex. Clearly, refusing to pay extortion must usually be regarded as praiseworthy, but under many circumstances such a principled approach must be judged to be supererogatory.

The customs of many regions and nations support the making of moderate payments to public officials to perform their ordinary tasks. Persons seeking permits, licenses, visas, passage through customs, and so forth, may be required to pay small "bribes" to the appropriate officials, but where sanctioned by long-standing custom (even though technically illegal),

such payments are more akin to tips than to bribes. In much of the world, furthermore, such practices may be accepted on account of the unrealistically low salaries of officials, which necessitate the supplementation of pay. In addition, gift giving to public officials has the beneficial effect of giving an incentive for the performance of duty when civic virtue does not suffice.

The offering of bribes, whether accepted or not, may be assumed to be morally reprehensible in circumstances in which the taking of bribes would be blameworthy. In a situation in which taking a bribe would be morally blameless, such as making nominal payments to public servants where custom sanctions it, the offering of such bribes must be held innocent.

In Plato's *Crito*, Socrates refused to allow his friends to bribe his guards in order that he escape into exile, avoiding his execution. Socrates had numerous reasons for his principled stance, and among these was that bribery would cause the guards to fail in the duties they owed by virtue of their office. Simply stated, the moral maxim would be that nobody ought to induce (or attempt to induce) another to do wrong—that is, to violate his or her special obligations and duties.

The federal Foreign Corrupt Practices Act of 1977 was enacted by Congress to restrict both the payment of bribes and extortion by U.S. corporations operating overseas. Some ethicists praise the act as holding American corporations to the highest ethical standards, but others see it as an unrealistic imposition upon American businesses, damaging their competitiveness.

Patrick O'Neil

FURTHER READING

Carson, Thomas L. "Bribery and Implicit Agreements." *Journal of Business Ethics* 6 (February, 1987): 123-125.

Noonan, John T. "Bribery, Extortion, and 'The Foreign Corrupt Practices Act.'" *Philosophy and Public Affairs* 14 (Winter, 1985): 66-90.

_____. *Bribes*. New York: Macmillan, 1984.

Philips, Michael. "Bribery." *Ethics* 94 (July, 1984): 621-636.

_____. "Bribery, Consent, and *Prima Facie* Duty: A Rejoinder to Carson." *Journal of Business Ethics* 6 (July, 1987): 361-364.

Vincke, François, Fritz Heimann, and Ron Katz, eds. *Fighting Bribery: A Corporate Practices Manual*. Paris: ICC, 1999.

SEE ALSO: Business ethics; Cheating; Duty; Hiring practices; Inside information; Lobbying; Politics; Professional ethics; Sales ethics.

Brown v. Board of Education

THE EVENT: U.S. Supreme Court decision that overturned the principle of separate-but-equal segregation in public schools

DATE: Ruling made on May 17, 1954

TYPE OF ETHICS: Race and ethnicity

SIGNIFICANCE: The Court found in *Brown* that segregated public schools were not "equal," could not be made "equal," and had a psychologically detrimental effect on African American children.

Racially segregated public schools dominated education for African Americans until 1954, when the U.S. Supreme Court decision *Brown v. Board of Education*, rejected its earlier *Plessy v. Ferguson* (1896) decision, which had established the segregation principle of "separate but equal." *Brown v. Board of Education* inspired several years of struggle by African Americans, the courts, and supporters of equal rights to force its implementation. In the years preceding *Brown*, education throughout the South had constituted an effective means of discrimination.

HISTORY

Until the 1950's, *Plessy v. Ferguson* continued to justify all segregation, including school segregation. In *Plessy*, the Supreme Court upheld a Louisiana law requiring equal but separate accommodations for "white" and "colored" railroad passengers. The Court assumed that legislation was powerless to eradicate racial dispositions or abolish distinctions based upon physical differences, and that any attempts to do so could only complicate the issue. Laws requiring the separation of African Americans and whites in areas of potential interaction did not imply the inferiority of either race, according to the Court.

Besides the fact that racism was inherent in *Plessy*, it was clear by the 1950's that the separate schools,

transportation, and public facilities that were provided for African Americans were not equal to those provided for whites. Oliver Brown, whose daughter Linda was denied entrance to a white school three blocks from their home and ended up at an African American school twenty-one blocks away, questioned the constitutionality of the Topeka board of education's policies. Authorities, citing state laws permitting racial segregation, denied Linda Brown admission to the white school.

In *Brown*, a district court found segregation to have a detrimental effect on African American children; however, African American and white schools were found to be substantially equal. The plaintiff took the case to the U.S. Supreme Court, arguing that segregated public schools were not equal and that they constituted denial of equal protection of the laws. The Fourteenth Amendment (1868) grants equal protection, stating, "no state shall deprive any person of life, liberty, or property, without due process of the law; nor deny to any person within its jurisdiction the equal protection of the laws."

In the first cases following the adoption of the Fourteenth Amendment, the Supreme Court interpreted it as proscribing all state-imposed discriminations against African Americans. The Court, led by Chief Justice Earl Warren, chose this perspective in handling the *Brown* case. In deliberations, the Court focused on the effect of segregation, not on whether the schools were considered equal.

ETHICAL PRINCIPLES AND ISSUES

The Supreme Court detailed the importance of education and posited education as the foundation of good citizenship. Thurgood Marshall (who later became a U.S. Supreme Court justice himself), the National Association for the Advancement of Colored People's chief counsel for *Brown*, argued on the basis of the inequalities of segregation, noting the findings of social scientists on segregation's negative effects. Chief Justice Warren's majority opinion expressed doubt that any child could reasonably be expected to succeed in life when denied educational opportunity, and further, that such an opportunity, where the state has undertaken to provide it, is a right that must be made available to all on equal terms. The Court found that the doctrine of "separate but equal" has no place in the field of public education.

The Court's decision to take a substantive look at

the *Brown* case, along with the procedural approach, led to a 9-0 decision in favor of Brown. Arguments alluding to the negative psychological impact of segregation on African American children keyed the decision. A public school system that was erected for the betterment of all citizens but denied certain segments of the citizenry access to the system's best public education was held to be unethical. The *Brown* decision, (which says, in effect, that no matter how equal the physical qualities of separate schools or any other public facilities may be, their segregated nature has negative effects on the psyche of African American children, hindering their ability to learn and consequently to become productive citizens), provided the Court with a precedent on which to build and ensured that public education would be conducted on an ethical basis at least in theory.

AFTER BROWN V. BOARD OF EDUCATION

Implementing and enforcing the *Brown* decision proved to be infinitely more difficult than arriving

at the decision itself had been. Public officials, especially in the South, openly, aggressively, and consistently defied the Court. This reaction did not, however, prevent the Court from ruling on a desegregation order. Thus, on May 31, 1955, the Court, in *Brown v. Board of Education II*, ruled that school authorities have the primary responsibility for dismantling segregationist policies. Courts were given the responsibility of considering whether the actions of school authorities constituted good-faith implementation of the governing constitutional principles. The Court required that desegregation be carried out "with all deliberate speed."

The intention of "deliberate speed" was to assist school authorities in making smooth transitions from segregation to integration; however, school officials throughout the South interpreted it to mean little or no action. Several southern school districts closed down public schools rather than integrate, while others, such as the Little Rock, Arkansas, district, were forced to deploy armed soldiers to ensure success-

President George W. Bush with members of a Birmingham, Alabama, choir, after speaking in Topeka, Kansas, on May 17, 2004—the fiftieth anniversary of the Brown v. Board of Education *decision.* (AP/Wide World Photos)

ful integration. By the late 1960's, most southern schools settled into a pattern of integration. After the *Brown* cases, the Supreme Court dealt little with desegregation, allowing the lower courts to handle such cases.

The *Brown v. Board of Education* decision had an influence that reached well beyond the desegregation of public schools. It inspired court cases involving the segregation of public transportation, hotel accommodations, restaurants, and other public facilities. Although the *Brown* decision did not explicitly outlaw racial discrimination in areas other than education, the decision influenced the rulings of lower court judges in other discrimination cases. The impact of *Brown v. Board of Education* on the lives of African Americans, and all Americans, cannot be overemphasized.

Gregory Freeland

FURTHER READING

Atkinson, Pansye. *Brown vs. Topeka, an African American's View: Desegregation and Miseducation.* Chicago: African American Images, 1993. Analysis of the legacy of *Brown* and its effects upon education for African Americans.

Cottrol, Robert J., Raymond T. Diamond, and Leland B. Ware. *"Brown v. Board of Education": Caste, Culture, and the Constitution.* Lawrence: University Press of Kansas, 2003. Places the decision in its broad historical context, while also discussing the specific institutions and individuals at the heart of the case.

Lagemann, Ellen Condliffe, and LaMar P. Miller, eds. *"Brown v. Board of Education": The Challenge for Today's Schools.* New York: Teachers College Press, 1996. A collection of essays by educators, first published in a special issue of *Teachers College Record.*

Nieman, Donald G. *Promises to Keep: African Americans and the Constitutional Order, 1776 to the Present.* New York: Oxford University Press, 1991. A concise book on the history and effects of critical court rulings affecting African Americans.

Patterson, James T. *"Brown v. Board of Education": A Civil Rights Milestone and Its Troubled Legacy.* New York: Oxford University Press, 2001. This historical and legal analysis of *Brown* also delves into the issue of the limits of the courts' abilities to bring about social change.

Sarat, Austin, ed. *Race, Law, and Culture: Reflections on "Brown v. Board of Education."* New York: Oxford University Press, 1997. A diverse and useful collection of lectures delivered at the Amherst College conference on the fortieth anniversary of *Brown.*

SEE ALSO: Bigotry; Civil Rights movement; Evers, Medgar; King, Martin Luther, Jr.; *Plessy v. Ferguson*; Racial prejudice; Racism; Segregation; Supreme Court, U.S.

Buber, Martin

IDENTIFICATION: Austrian philosopher
BORN: February 8, 1878, Vienna, Austro-Hungarian Empire (now in Austria)
DIED: June 13, 1965, Jerusalem, Israel
TYPE OF ETHICS: Religious ethics
SIGNIFICANCE: In *I and Thou* (*Ich und Du*, 1923), Buber interpreted the foundation of ethics and morality as the personal "I-Thou" (as opposed to the impersonal "I-It") relationship of people to one another, to existence, and to God.

For Martin Buber, the two primary ways in which people relate to their world are characterized by the words "I-It" and "I-Thou (or You)." The "I-It" way of seeing life is one in which people objectify the reality they see and deal with as *things*—mere objects to be used, understood, manipulated, and controlled. In such a way of relating to life, perhaps characterized best by the business or scientific approach to exisistence, there is little opportunity for a true personal connection between the individual and the rest of reality. Instead, life is spent trying to attain goals, analyze and control others, and organize reality into something that can be used or consumed.

While the "I-It" approach to reality might be necessary to conduct the everyday affairs of life or create intellectual circumstances for technological advancement, Buber believed that its aggressive domination of modern culture had created a painful and pitiful climate that fostered human isolation. As a result, people had become alienated from their fellow human beings, their world at large, and their God. To

Buber, such a life was not authentic, not genuine, and not fully human.

The "I-Thou" attitude is characterized in terms of an honest and open "dialogue" between the "I" and the "Thou." A mutual and dynamic, though intimately personal, connection ensues in the "I-Thou" mode, in which there is a marrying of the subjective "I" and the objective other, which is now no longer a dominated "It" but instead a responsive partner in a profoundly communicative and respectful meeting of the two: "I-It" becomes "I-Thou."

In Buber's "I-Thou" relationship, people are relieved of their isolation and alienation from those around them and the world at large because they no longer relate to what is not themselves as merely means to purposes or goals ("Its"), but instead as respected and appreciated ends in and of themselves ("Thous"). People no longer live life as detached and solitary but are connected and "whole" with everything in the realm of their "I-Thou" encounter.

The most basic example of the "I-Thou" relationship for Buber is that between two people in honest, dialogic communication in which both encounter the essential integrity and *being* of the other. Yet Buber also believes that this relationship can exist between humans and nature. A tree, for example, is no longer a commodity to be made into lumber for a house; it is, in the "I-Thou" relationship, a significant object with which, perhaps as a thing of beauty or simply as a "being" itself, one can have an intimate connection. In the same way, an artist can have such a relationship with those things that become objects in the artist's works.

SOCIAL IMPLICATIONS

Buber's perspective also has social implications. If a community of people is to succeed, it must be based on an "I-Thou" dialogue that nurtures a humanizing, unselfish climate of respect for individuals and the common good. In this regard, Buber was an advocate of utopian social models such as the Israeli *kibbutz*, which promoted mutual cooperation among all members of the community at every level of life.

Finally, there are the religious dimensions of Buber's thought. For him, every "I-Thou" relationship brings individuals in touch with the eternal "Thou," or God. In fact, Buber asserts that it is impossible to relate to God in a manipulative "I-It" mode. He believed that it was only through the direct,

dialogic encounter with the otherness of objective existence in the respectful "I-Thou" mode that the qualities and presence of God became actual in the world. It is only in such personal, and finally mysterious, circumstances (so alien to traditional theologies that seek to make God an "It" by explaining and dogmatizing) that the living God can be discovered.

ETHICAL IMPLICATIONS

Buber's philosophy demands that people take the risk of opening themselves up to "I-Thou" relationships, no matter how fleeting they may be. It is only in the experience of such profoundly personal relationships with their fellow human beings, the world at large, and God that humans, even momentarily, become able to escape the propensity to transform everything into an object of "I-It" use and scrutiny. It is only through the "I-Thou" dialogue that human beings can move out of a life of lonely impersonality and into a mode of existence that keeps them personally involved with the uniqueness of their fellow human beings, communities, and God. Without such an "I-Thou" foundation, there is no possibility for a moral life of meaning and purpose.

Richard M. Leeson

FURTHER READING

Arnett, Ronald C. *Communication and Community: Implications of Martin Buber's Dialogue.* Carbondale: Southern Illinois University Press, 1986.

Buber, Martin. *I and Thou.* Translated by Ronald Gregor Smith. 1958. Reprint. New York: Scribner, 2000.

Diamond, Malcolm L. *Martin Buber: Jewish Existentialist.* New York: Oxford University Press, 1960.

Friedman, Maurice S. *Martin Buber and the Eternal.* New York: Human Sciences Press, 1986.

_____. *Martin Buber: The Life of Dialogue.* 4th ed., rev. and expanded. New York: Routledge, 2002.

Manheim, Werner. *Martin Buber.* New York: Twayne, 1974.

Mendes-Flohr, Paul, ed. *Martin Buber: A Contemporary Perspective.* Syracuse, N.Y.: Syracuse University Press, 2002.

Ross, Dennis S. *God in Our Relationships: Spirituality Between People from the Teachings of Martin Buber.* Woodstock, Vt.: Jewish Lights, 2003.

Silberstein, Laurence J. *Martin Buber's Social and Religious Thought: Alienation and the Quest for Meaning.* New York: New York University Press, 1989.

Smith, Ronald G. *Martin Buber.* Richmond, Va.: John Knox Press, 1967.

SEE ALSO: Existentialism; Hasidism; *I and Thou*; Jewish ethics; Tillich, Paul.

Buddha

IDENTIFICATION: Indian religious leader
BORN: Siddhārtha Gautama, c. 566 B.C.E., Lumbinī, (now Rummindei, Nepal)
DIED: c. 486 B.C.E., Kuśinagara, India
TYPE OF ETHICS: Religious ethics
SIGNIFICANCE: The Buddha founded one of the world's major religious and ethical systems. Buddhism provides a comprehensive moral discipline designed to liberate humankind from an existence characterized by impermanence, suffering, and delusion.

The son of a chief of the warrior clan of the śakyas, Siddhārtha Gautama was born in approximately 566 B.C.E. at the edge of the Himalayas, in what is now Nepal. His father, Śuddhodana, although not the king he was once thought to be, nevertheless provided Gautama with all of the elements necessary for a comfortable, luxurious existence. Legend and myth cloud much of the surviving information regarding Gautama's early years, but at approximately the age of nineteen, he was married to his cousin Yaśodharā, by whom he had one child, Rāhula.

At the age of twenty-nine, according to some accounts, he was exposed to the basic realities of existence. While being driven around his father's estate in his chariot, he saw four things that would ultimately change his life: a man suffering from disease, a man weakened and reduced by age, a corpse, and a wandering ascetic. Questioning his charioteer about these sights, he learned that although no one can escape disease, age, and death, asceticism might at least offer some sort of alternative.

Having realized the fate of all living things, Gau-

tama resolved to leave the luxurious life of his youth in order to seek the cause of the horrors of human existence and, if possible, to discover a solution. In this homeless, wandering existence, Gautama sought instruction from adepts in the art of meditation, but finding little of real value there, he began to practice the most extreme forms of asceticism for the next six years, almost starving himself to death in the process. At last, seeing the inadequacy of this approach, he decided to abandon asceticism and, by the pure force of will, achieve his goal.

At Bodh Gayā, Gautama sat down at the foot of a tree, resolving not to leave until he had achieved enlightenment. Passing beyond all previously attained meditative states and conquering manifold temptations in the process, he at last attained complete liberation and found the answers that he had sought. He was thirty-five years old.

Having resolved to proclaim his message of enlightenment to the world, Gautama, now the Buddha, or Enlightened One, spent the next forty-five years teaching his doctrine up and down the Ganges and establishing his monastic order, or *sangha*, of Buddhist monks and nuns. At the age of eighty, the Buddha died at Kuśinārā, India, in approximately 486 B.C.E.

After his enlightenment at the age of thirty-five, the Buddha proposed both a diagnosis of the human condition and a response to it. The human condition is characterized by impermanence, suffering, and false consciousness. Throughout his career, the Buddha claimed to teach but two things: suffering and the end of suffering.

THE NATURE OF EXISTENCE

With systematic, scientific rigor, the Buddha began his analysis of existence by citing three of its basic characteristics: impermanence (*anitya*), suffering (*duḥkha*), and the lack of an abiding self (*anātman*). Why is existence bound up with suffering and impermanence? The Buddha saw life in terms of a "chain of dependent origination" (*pratītya-samutpāda*). This chain begins with ignorance (*avidyā*), which leads to choices both negative and positive (*saṃskāra*), which in turn result in a will to live. This will takes the form of consciousness (*vijñāna*), and consciousness is followed by a material mind and body (*nāma-rūpa*). Mind and body connect with the external world through the sense organs (*ṣaḍāyatana*), the most prominent of which is touch (*sparśa*).

Fifth century C.E. statue of the Buddha in Saranath, India. (Library of Congress)

Once the consciousness is active, feelings (*vedanā*) that are associated with sensations follow, giving the impression of pleasure, pain, or neutrality. The combination of these feelings produces desire (*tṛṣṇā*) and attachment (*upādāna*), finally resulting in becoming (*bhava*). Becoming, in turn, inevitably results in birth (*jāti*) and decay (*jāra*).

The Buddha employed the Hindu concept of karma, the law of cause and effect following both thought and action, to explain the cycle of life. Through many lifetimes and many rebirths, positive and negative thoughts and actions have karmic reverberations, either shortening or prolonging the round of rebirths (*saṃsāra*). The practical aim of moving beyond karma is to free oneself from the round of *saṃsāra* and all of its suffering. Once this liberation is achieved, nirvana (Sanskrit, *nirvāṇa*), the cessation of desire, of karmic residue, and of a sense of self ensues. Although it is not extinction, nirvana is clearly a transcendental, unconditioned, and ineffable state—the final goal of Buddhism.

THE MORAL LIFE

With this analysis of existence, the Buddha developed a comprehensive moral code intended to bring about happiness and liberation. He began his moral superstructure with the four noble truths: (1) all is suffering (*duḥkha*); (2) suffering has a cause, which is desire, or craving (*tṛṣṇā*); (3) suffering has an end (*duḥkha-nirodha*); (4) the end of suffering is achieved by means of the noble eightfold path (*ārya-aṣṭāṅga-mārga*).

The noble eightfold path consists of (1) right understanding (*samyag-dṛṣṭi*), (2) right aspiration (*samyak-saṃkalpa*), (3) right speech (*samyag-vācā*), (4) right action (*samyak-karmanta*), (5) right livelihood (*samyag-ājīva*), (6) right effort (*samyag-vyāyāma*), (7) right mindfulness (*samyak-smṛti*), and (8) right concentration (*samyak-samādhi*).

The Buddha's emphasis on systematic, cause-and-effect analysis makes practical morality the core of Buddhist doctrine. In order to follow the advice given in the Dhammapada—"Cease to do evil,/ Learn to do good,/ Purify your mind"—one must begin with a series of freely adopted precepts to address the grosser physical defilements of life. The five precepts (*pañca-śila*), once internalized, set the stage for more advanced levels of endeavor. They exhort one to:

1. Refrain from taking life
2. Refrain from taking what is not given
3. Refrain from engaging in sexual misconduct
4. Refrain from telling lies
5. Refrain from taking intoxicants

The five precepts apply to all who consider themselves to be Buddhists. The list of precepts is expanded and applied more rigorously to Buddhist monks and nuns.

In Buddhism, a virtuous or proper ethical action is simultaneously a rational action. Rationality, or wisdom, is directly connected to morality, and the one generates the other.

According to Maurice Walshe's translation of the *Digha Nikāya,*

For wisdom is purified by morality, and morality is purified by wisdom; where one is, the other is, the moral man has wisdom and the wise man has morality, and the combination of morality and wisdom is called the highest thing in the world. Just as one hand washes the other, or one foot the other, so wisdom is purified by morality and this is the highest thing in the world.

Once the negative dimensions of life have been addressed in an honest attempt to cease to do evil, a positive reconstruction can begin and one can learn to do good. This positive reconstruction will take such forms as generosity (*dāna*), loving kindness (*maitri*), compassion (*karunā*), sympathetic joy (*mudita*), and equanimity (*upeksā*).

THERAVĀDA AND MAHĀYĀNA

In time, Buddhist ethics developed the different ideals of the *arhat*, the accomplished individual of the older Theravāda tradition, and the *bodhisattva*, the heroic world-savior of the later Mahāyāna tradition. For the *arhat*, individual salvation culminating in nirvana is primary; for the *bodhisattva*, the salvation of all beings is foremost. With its wider focus (all of suffering existence), the Mahāyāna tradition has tended to be less strictly concerned with specific precepts, occasionally permitting the transgression of certain rules to attain the final goal. The *bodhisattva* ideal represents the most extreme extension of Buddhist compassion, integrating all existence into its perspective.

In those countries in which Buddhism is a living social and religious tradition, a practical ethics has developed over time in which sincere practitioners may, through careful attention to the four noble truths, the eightfold path, and the five precepts, attain a morally pure and productive state in this life with at least the hope of ultimate liberation.

Daniel W. O'Bryan

FURTHER READING

Buddha. *The Dhammapada.* London: Oxford University Press, 1950.

_____. *Thus Have I Heard, The Long Discourses of the Buddha Digha Nikaya.* Translated by Maurice Walshe. London: Wisdom Publications, 1987.

Conze, Edward. *Buddhism: Its Essence and Development.* Preface by Arthur Waley. New York: Harper & Row, 1975.

Harvey, Peter. *An Introduction to Buddhist Ethics: Foundations, Values, and Issues.* New York: Cambridge University Press, 2000.

Keown, Damien. *The Nature of Buddhist Ethics.* New York: St. Martin's Press, 1992.

King, Winston L. *In the Hope of Nibbana: An Essay on Theravada Buddhist Ethics.* Lasalle, Ill.: Open Court, 1964.

Rahula, Walpola. *What the Buddha Taught.* Rev. ed. New York: Grove Press, 1974.

Saddhatissa, H. *Buddhist Ethics: Essence of Buddhism.* London: Allen & Unwin, 1970.

SEE ALSO: Asceticism; Bodhisattva ideal; Buddhist ethics; Dōgen; Five precepts of Buddhism; Four noble truths; Karma; Kūkai; Mādhyamaka; Nāgārjuna.

Buddhist ethics

DEFINITION: Diverse sets of beliefs or opinions about behavior that have grown out of the teachings of Siddhārtha Gautama, the Buddha

TYPE OF ETHICS: Religious ethics

SIGNIFICANCE: As one of the world's major religions, Buddhism provides one of the most widely accepted frameworks for ethical thought and behavior.

Moral teachings of Buddhists can be understood as extensions of the insights of Siddhārtha Gautama, the Buddha (d. c. 486 B.C.E.). The heart of his teachings as handed down by Buddhist tradition includes the four noble truths: (1) Life is suffering; (2) Suffering has a cause; (3) That cause is self-seeking desire; (4) There is a way of escape, the eightfold path (the path of escape), and the five (or ten) precepts. Buddhists have developed these teachings in terms of proper behavior for both the laity and the monks, basic virtues, and social ethics.

RULES FOR PROPER BEHAVIOR

The first two steps on the eightfold path involve right knowledge and right aspiration; that is, recognition of the four noble truths and the will to relinquish anything that interferes with gaining liberation. The third step requires right speech—saying the correct things in accordance with the other steps. The fourth step, right behavior, includes the basic ethical teachings for the laity known as the five precepts. (1) Abstain from taking life. This precept goes beyond a prohibition against killing fellow humans to include taking the life of any sentient being. As a result, most Buddhists are vegetarians. (2) Abstain from taking what is not given, and practice charity instead. (3) Do not engage in sexual misconduct but practice self-control. (4) Practice right speech (step 3 on the eight-fold path) by refraining not only from lying but also from gossip and back-biting. (5) Abstain from intoxicating drinks and drugs. The fifth step on the eightfold path is right livelihood. For the layperson, this meant following no occupation precluded by these precepts.

A monk would be held to an even stricter application of these rules. In connection with the second precept, for example, he would own nothing but the robes, toilet articles, and begging bowl given him at ordination. In addition, the monk would agree to as many as five more precepts: to eat moderately and not at all after noon, to refrain from attending dramatic performances, to refrain from self-decoration, to refrain from luxurious living, and to refrain from handling money. The rules derived from these precepts, along with the rules for monasteries, eventually numbered 227. The normative collection of these rules is called, in Pali, the *Patimokkha*.

Buddhists analyzed behavior carefully to determine when the precepts were violated. In connection with the injunction against taking life, for example, the following five conditions had to be present: (1) the thing destroyed must have actually been alive; (2) the Buddhist must have known that the thing was alive; (3) the person must have intended to kill the thing; (4) the person must have acted to carry out that intention; and (5) death must have resulted from the act. Hence, Buddhism was concerned both about the facts of the deed and the motives behind it.

BASIC VIRTUES

Theravāda Buddhism emphasized four "cardinal" virtues: love, compassion, joy, and equanimity (defined as the absence of greed, hatred, and envy). All these virtues derived from the basic Buddhist insight that there is no underlying self, so self-seeking is inevitably futile. Later, Mahāyāna Buddhism enjoined several basic virtues, including generosity, righteousness, patience, and wisdom. The Mahā-

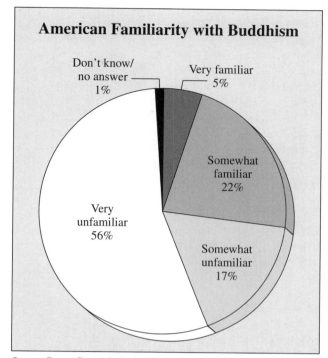

American Familiarity with Buddhism

Don't know/ no answer 1%

Very familiar 5%

Somewhat familiar 22%

Very unfamiliar 56%

Somewhat unfamiliar 17%

Source: Roper Center for Public Opinion Research. Religion & Ethics Newsweekly, U.S. News & World Report survey. March 26–April 4, 2002. Figures based on responses of 2,002 adults throughout the United States.

yānist virtue par excellence, however, is compassion, which is embodied in the bodhisattva, the enlightened being who postpones entrance into the bliss of nirvana in order to help other beings reach salvation.

SOCIAL OBLIGATIONS

Wherever one finds Buddhism, one finds monks. Even in Shin Buddhism, which allows monks to marry, the distinctions between monks and laypeople are only minimized, not eliminated. For many Buddhist laypeople, therefore, the first social obligation is to feed and otherwise support the monks. A layperson can also build a pagoda or perform other meritorious acts that benefit the larger Buddhist community. At the same time, the monks have the responsibility to share with the laity the results of their study and meditation through teaching and to officiate at various public ceremonies.

Over the years, Buddhism has addressed other areas of social responsibility. Two examples must suffice. First, one of the early figures to address social responsibility was King Aśoka, who became king of Magadha, which dominated the Indian subcontinent. Penitent over suffering caused by his wars, he looked to Buddhism for help in ruling. His inscriptions advocated living peacefully, and he sent Buddhist missionaries to a number of other countries.

The second example comes from 1946, when the Buddhist monks of Sri Lanka joined ongoing efforts to free their country from British rule, thus injecting themselves into political dispute, if not revolt. The monks distributed seeds and vegetables, settled disputes that would otherwise have gone to court, gave out medicines, supported the arts, and helped fuel Sinhalese nationalism. Although not all Buddhists (even in Sri Lanka) have agreed that such behavior is appropriate for monks, it shows how seriously they take social ethics.

ETHICS AND ENLIGHTENMENT

The ultimate goal of Buddhist teachings is to lead people to enlightenment, not to define ethical behavior. Both Theravāda and Mahāyāna Buddhism portray the enlightened person as one beyond the categories of right and wrong, moral and immoral. This is so because such persons have achieved a level of equanimity and insight at which calculations such as those discussed above are left behind. The person who sees that there is no abiding self and who sees the suffering that will result from selfish behavior will naturally feel no inclination to act in such a destructive fashion. Those who have not yet achieved such a state, however, benefit from ethical rules.

Paul L. Redditt

FURTHER READING

Davids, T. W. Rhys, ed. *The Questions of King Milinda*. Sacred Books of the East 35-36. New York: Dover, 1963.

Harvey, Peter. *An Introduction to Buddhist Ethics: Foundations, Values, and Issues*. New York: Cambridge University Press, 2000.

King, Winston L. *In the Hope of Nibbana: An Essay on Theravada Buddhist Ethics*. LaSalle, Ill.: Open Court, 1964.

Rahula, Walpola. *The Heritage of the Bhikku*. Translated by K. P. G. Wijayasurendra. New York: Grove Press, 1974.

Saddhatissa, H. *Buddhist Ethics: Essence of Buddhism*. London: Allen & Unwin, 1970.

Tachibana, Shundo. *The Ethics of Buddhism*. London: Oxford University Press, 1926. Reprint. Richmond, Surrey, England: Curzon Press, 1992.

SEE ALSO: Asceticism; Aśoka; Avalokiteśvara; Bodhisattva ideal; Buddha; Dalai Lama; Daoist ethics; Five precepts of Buddhism; Huineng; Karma; Mādhyamaka.

al-Būkhārī

IDENTIFICATION: Islamic scholar
BORN: July 19, 810, Bukhara, Central Asia (now in Uzbekistan)
DIED: August 3, 870, Khartank, near Samarkand (now in Uzbekistan)
TYPE OF ETHICS: Religious ethics
SIGNIFICANCE: Al-Būkhārī compiled *al-Jāmiʾ al-Ṣaḥīḥ* (the authentic collection), the second most revered book in Islam. It is a compendium of sayings and traditions, or *Ḥadīth*, from the life of Muḥammad.

From an early age, al-Būkhārī took an interest in the study of oral and written traditions harking back to the days of the first Muslims. By his late teens, he had traveled extensively in the Near East and had made a pilgrimage, or *hajj*, to Mecca and Medina. Because of the pressing need in contemporary Muslim society for explicit ethical and legal precepts that could be said to derive from Muḥammad's teachings and actions, it was vital that the historicity and accuracy of popular *Ḥadīth* be determined. It is to al-Būkhārī's credit as a painstaking scholar and devoted traveler that he is said to have examined more than 600,000 *Ḥadīth* during his lifetime. Of these, he designed 2,602 as authentic (*ṣaḥīḥ*). *Al-Jāmiʾ al-Ṣaḥīḥ* was intended to provide future generations of Muslims with verified historical, legal, and ethical material from which their societies could draw in times of need. This work still stands as the most respected collection of *Ḥadīth* in the Islamic world.

Craig L. Hanson

SEE ALSO: *Ḥadīth*; Islamic ethics; Muḥammad; Qurʾān.

Burke, Edmund

IDENTIFICATION: English journalist and politician
BORN: January 12, 1729, Dublin, Ireland
DIED: July 9, 1797, Beaconsfield,
    Buckinghamshire, England
TYPE OF ETHICS: Politico-economic ethics
SIGNIFICANCE: The author of *Reflections on the Revolution in France* (1790), Burke put forward a pragmatic organic model for the development of citizen's rights that became a pillar of modern conservatism.

Edmund Burke's career, which began in 1759, was devoted to politics and journalism. He rose to prominence as a member of the marquis of Rockingham's political faction, but his real fame was the result of his becoming the spokesman for the new Whig Party view of the constitution. Burke drew from England's Glorious Revolution of 1688 a conception of the rights of citizens that was based on a combination of tradition and evolution. The natural order, set by God, would inevitably have inequalities, but the need to unify the nation led to rules that evolved into rights and privileges. Those with better situations were obligated by their privileges to act in the public interest, with respect for traditional rights.

Burke's seemingly contradictory support for the rights of the Americans and the Irish and his savage denunciation of the French Revolution become quite consistent in view of his ideas of rights. The Crown, the power of which Burke was always eager to reduce, was infringing on traditional rights in America and Ireland, whereas the revolutionaries in France were attempting to create a wholly new society based on a utopian rationalistic model that, like all such models, could never exist in practice. In such a case, the existing good would be destroyed in pursuit of a pipe dream. It should be allowed to evolve over time in the natural order. Burke's *Reflections on the Revolution in France* was read all over Europe, provoking opposition to the Revolution and giving his ideas a wide audience.

Fred R. van Hartesveldt

SEE ALSO: Conservatism; Human rights; Revolution.

Edmund Burke. (Library of Congress)

Bushido

DEFINITION: Japanese military code meaning "way of the warrior" that incorporates strict ethical responsibilities with a code of physical sacrifice
DATE: Developed in the seventeenth century
TYPE OF ETHICS: Military ethics
SIGNIFICANCE: Bushido requires systematic training of mind and body, emphasizing absolute loyalty, spontaneity, collective responsibility, and personal sacrifice; this training has been adapted to business and religious practices.

Bushido, or the Japanse way of the warrior, derives from three early sources. First, the ancient animistic belief of the Japanese, known as Shintōism (the Way of the Gods) emphasized naturalness, sincerity, and the spirituality of all things Japanese. This tradition suffused bushido with the sense of a sacred link to one's peers, the soil, and the mission of Japan.

Second, during the twelfth century, a warrior class (*bushi*) emerged near present-day Tokyo. The *bushi* usurped power from the aristocratic elite in the capital of Kyoto, and conquered new territory in eastern Japan. Some of these bands gave allegiance to their lords through total self-renunciation and personal loyalty; others constantly shifted their allegiance for materialistic gain. Gradually, a code of ethics developed that stressed the samurai's unconditional willingness to die for his master. By the mid-seventeenth century, this code supported an attitude toward death that idealized and romanticized the warrior who was honor-bound to die for his lord, or even to commit ritualistic suicide (*seppuku*).

Third, the major religious influence on the warrior class was Zen Buddhism, which teaches that the goal of life is personal enlightenment through ascetic selflessness, rigorous discipline, and repetitive effort. Religious discipline must not, however, become lost in the drudgery of the rituals. Enlightenment is achieved through spontaneous, intuitive revelations, or single acts of self-awareness that can erupt from toilsome tasks. Enlightenment is not a consequence of rational judgment, but of sudden personal discovery.

PRINCIPLES OF BUSHIDO

Yamaga Soko synthesized the thinking of the various religious and military schools to describe what became known as the way of the warrior. Yamaga related the traditional values of sincerity, loyalty, self-discipline, and self-sacrifice to the Chinese values of a sage. To be a real warrior, one needs to be cultivated in humanistic arts—that is, poetry, painting, calligraphy, and music—while in service to the master. The true sage combines the virtues of "wisdom, humanity, and valor" to perform his service to his lord's government.

During Japan's peaceful Tokugawa era (1602-1868), the ethics of bushido prevented the military from becoming a warlike and oppressive elite. Rather, the samurai became administrators, accountants, artists, scholars, and entrepreneurs. Miyamoto Musashi combined the roles of warrior, artist, and intellectual. In 1643, he wrote a classic work on military strategy, *A Book of Five Rings*. As an artist, he became noted for the intensity of his extraordinary monochromatic ink paintings. Other samurai such as Uragami Gyokudo renounced or neglected their military role and concentrated on the humanistic arts of music, painting, and literature. The Mitsui Company,

one of Japan's largest business enterprises, was one of many Tokugawa businesses operated by a samurai family. These contributions to civil society helped Japan to develop economically and intellectually into the twentieth century.

There was also a non-Chinese or indigenous influence. The samurai classic *Hagakure* (1716), by Yamamoto Tsunetomo, provided the famous aphorism "bushido is a way of dying." Contrary to Yamaga's emphasis on public service or the balance between the military and civic role of the samurai, Yamamoto idealized and spiritualized the role of death. The loyal and self-abnegating samurai is expected to give his life spontaneously and unquestioningly for his master. A life that ends in death on the battlefield with unswerving hard work and dedication, or in ritualistic suicide, is glorious.

Yamaga and Yamamoto agreed that only through action could one pursue truth and self-enlightenment. The way of the warrior emphasized human performance, intuition, and spontaneity. Training in the martial arts (*bujutsu*) was an important technique to promote group cohesiveness and self-awareness. Through *bujutsu* the samurai discovers and overcomes his spiritual and physical weaknesses, thereby deepening his self-awareness and ultimately preparing himself for a life of service and a readiness to sacrifice.

The abolition of feudalism and the samurai class in 1872 did not also end the appeal of bushido. The rise of militant nationalism and Imperial Shintōism created a militaristic bushido. The publication of *Fundamentals of Our National Polity* by Japan's ministry of education in 1937 declared in unequivocable terms that bushido was the "outstanding characteristic of our national morality." The new bushido "shed itself of an outdated feudalism . . . [and] became the Way of loyalty and patriotism, and has evolved before us as the spirit of the imperial forces." The Japanese soldier was called upon to sacrifice his life for the emperor. A strong central government and a fascist military system forcefully made the new bushido a significant part of Japan's imperialist expansion.

LEGACIES

After World War II, bushido ceased to be a military force in Japan. The vainglorious attempt by the writer Yukio Mishima to revive the martial spirit of

Japan ended in his brutal and meaningless act of *seppuku*. Bushido's ethical foundations are, however, still part of Japanese culture and society. Bushido's stress on loyalty to the head of a group is still evident in the strong sense of loyalty workers have to their employers, students to their teachers, and apprentices to their masters. Corporate groups imitate the samurai system by dovetailing the personal values of their members with common group and public goals. Ethical training camps (a direct legacy of Zen martial arts training) for workers are weeklong intensive seminars combining physical exertion with a type of group therapy. These consciousness-raising exercises are designed to create a loyal, harmonious, and ethical workforce.

The term *bushido* invokes images of Japanese soldiers dashing off into suicidal missions against the enemy and committing atrocities of every kind. Since World War II, cartoons have depicted Japanese businessmen as samurai warriors in business suits. The relationship of bushido with the military nationalism of World War II and its alleged association with Japan's postwar economic expansion have obscured its ethical contributions of loyalty, frugality, and dedication to Japanese society and culture.

Richard C. Kagan

FURTHER READING

Addiss, Stephen, and Cameron Hurst III. *Samurai Painters*. Tokyo: Kodansha, 1983.

De Bary, Theodore, with Ryusaku Tsunoda and Donald Keene. *Sources of Japanese Tradition*. New York: Columbia University Press. 1958.

Leggett, Trevor. *The Spirit of Budo: Old Traditions for Present-Day Life*. New York: Kegan Paul International, 1998.

Lowry, Dave. *Moving Toward Stillness: Lessons in Daily Life from the Martial Ways of Japan*. Boston: Tuttle, 2000.

Mishima, Yukio. *Way of the Samurai: Yukio Mishima on Hagakure in Modern Life*. Translated by Kathryn Sparling. New York: Basic Books, 1977.

Yamamoto, Tsunetomo. *Hagakure: The Book of the Samurai*. Tokyo: Kodansha, 1983.

SEE ALSO: Honor; Military ethics; Wang Yangming; Zen; Zhuangzi.

Business ethics

DEFINITION: Moral behavior of individuals and organizations in the performance of their business activities

TYPE OF ETHICS: Business and labor ethics

SIGNIFICANCE: Because the conduct of business has become such a pervasive part of human existence and because business organizations have grown so large and powerful, a study of ethical behavior in this dimension of the social fabric has become increasingly important.

The study of business ethics has a long history. Questions regarding the need for honest dealings between buyers and sellers, for example, have stirred ethical deliberation for every generation in all cultures. The Old Testament, from the fifteenth century B.C.E., states that when buying from or selling to one another, "ye shall not oppress one another" (Leviticus 25:14) and that one must use "a perfect and just [weight] and measure," in one's business dealings (Deuteronomy 25:13-15).

As civilizations have evolved from pastoral and agrarian to highly industrialized societies and as humans have become increasingly interdependent, concerns about the proper way in which to conduct business have become more pressing. Especially since the Industrial Revolution, as business units have become huge corporate entities and as rapid changes in technology have led to extremely complex products and processes for producing them, imbalances in power between buyers and sellers, between employees and employers, and between businesses and the communities in which they operate have focused increased attention on business ethics.

During the late 1960's and early 1970's, American society began increasingly to question established institutions' business ethics. At the same time, the concept of corporate social responsibility started assuming ever-greater importance by business critics. Discussion of these subjects became more common in business school curricula and inside corporate boardrooms. As consumerism, feminism, environmentalism, and the Civil Rights movement gained strength, it was only natural that society would examine the extent to which members of the business community had been exacerbating the problems of consumer deception and harm, unequal treatment of women in the workplace, environmental degradation, and racial discrimination. More pressure began to be applied to encourage businesses to become a part of the solution to these social problems.

FRAMEWORKS OF ANALYSIS

Ethicists have generally used a number of different concepts—such as utility, rights, justice, virtue—to analyze and judge the morality of business behavior. Utilitarianism focuses on the results or consequences of any business decision. It requires managers first to identify all the costs and benefits to all of society of a given set of alternative business actions and to choose the alternative that will result in the greatest net benefit to society. An important aspect of this framework is that it requires business managers to consider not only the consequences for their businesses, that is, the effects on company profits, but also the consequences to the greater society. An advantage of the utilitarian approach is that it corresponds closely with cost-benefit analyses so common to business decision making. There are, however, some decided disadvantages. It is difficult for managers to identify all costs and benefits to society. Moreover, it is difficult to measure certain social benefits such as improvements in the general level of health, aesthetic improvements, or greater enjoyment of life. Finally, utilitarianism ignores questions of rights, duties, fairness, and justice.

Using rights as the framework for analyzing business decisions requires that managers identify what stakeholders—that is, affected individuals or groups—will be involved in a particular decision, and then ask what rights those individuals or groups may have and what obligations the business may have to those stakeholders. As the late eighteenth century German philosopher Immanuel Kant stressed, people must be considered as ends in themselves and not merely as means toward some other end. This is especially problematic for business managers who have traditionally thought of their employees as a "means of production" and of their customers as the ultimate source of their profits. Furthermore, this deontological framework of ethical analysis creates difficulties when managers must attempt to weigh and prioritize the rights of various competing stakeholder groups: for example, employees who feel they have a right to more generous health care plans versus their companies' owners and shareholders, who

would like to see those funds distributed in the form of dividends.

A third framework for assessing the appropriateness or morality of business decisions involves focusing on justice or fairness. Justice requires an equitable distribution of life's benefits and burdens. The twentieth century American philosopher John Rawls was a leading proponent of this school. Using this approach, managers would be required to ask which of their alternative courses of action would be the most fair to all affected parties. The advantage here is that justice and fairness are widely accepted as desirable goals. The disadvantage is that there is little agreement on how to define them. A free, democratic, capitalistic system that prizes individualism, free choice, and the sanctity of private property allows its individual citizens—and its corporate citizens—to pursue their economic goals, that is, acquire wealth, according to their individual and differing abilities. This necessarily leads to unequal distribution of income and assets, and therefore, of benefits and burdens. There are no commonly accepted standards regarding what degree of inequality can still pass the justice and fairness test.

The issue of executive compensation vis-à-vis the average worker's pay is an interesting and contentious example of the concerns raised by this framework. Some business critics—and even a few socially conscious firms—have held that chief executive officers' compensation should be no more than seven times that of the average "shop floor" worker. Before the 1990's, the average chief executive officer of a U.S. firm was likely to earn forty times the salary of an average employee. However, by the beginning of the twenty-first century, that ratio had grown to a factor of four hundred times. There are partial explanations, such as the deferred compensation through stock options and the necessity of a major corporation to pay what the market demands for top-flight leaders. Nevertheless, this enormous differential in pay, especially when combined with poor corporate performance and layoffs of thousands of workers, strikes many as patently unfair and, therefore, unethical.

Another approach to analyzing ethical dilemmas—the virtue ethics framework—entails identifying certain principles or virtues that are universally accepted as worthy behavior. Among those usually accepted are honesty, loyalty, integrity, making good on commitments, steadfastness, and the like. Viewed through this perspective, managers are called upon to act—to choose those alternatives—which reinforce and are in harmony with these virtues, regardless of the consequences.

There is no agreement among business ethicists or business managers that any one of these frameworks is superior to the others. Each has its merits; each has its advantages and disadvantages. Managers need to be familiar with all these approaches and may need to analyze a given ethical dilemma through all these different lenses to arrive at the "best" decision.

LEVELS OF ANALYSIS

Scholars and managers can analyze business ethics problems on four different levels. First, at the individual level, unethical acts are seen as the results of individuals who make unethical decisions. If this is the case, corporation need only rid itself of its "bad apples" and do a better job of training and supervising its managers and employees. The second level is the corporation or organization, which allows for the possibility that a firm—such as Enron—may develop a culture that condones or perhaps even encourages unethical behavior. The third level is the industry. Some would argue that certain industries are, by the very nature of the products they produce, unethical. Examples might include the tobacco industry, the munitions industry, and perhaps even the fast-food industry—which has come under increasing criticism for fostering poor eating habits and contributing to obesity and associated health problems. Finally, there is the systemic level, which holds that there are fundamental flaws in the entire capitalistic, free-enterprise system that inevitably lead to unethical behavior of one form or another.

RELEVANT ISSUES

The field of business ethics is often organized around specific issues, and these issues may be grouped according to the stakeholders that are most affected: employees, customers, shareholders, the environment, communities, and so forth. Managers faced with making decisions regarding one of these issues must ask themselves what the nature is of the relationship between the organization and a particular stakeholder group. What responsibilities does the organization have? What rights do these stakeholders enjoy? How best can competing claims or rights be resolved?

Due to changes in the social, technological, or political environments, new issues may appear and old issues may disappear. For example, because of the rapid growth of use of the Internet, the subject of intellectual property and the rights of musicians, film producers, and computer software creators became an important issue in the early years of the twenty-first century.

A company's employees constitute one of the company's most important stakeholder groups, and many ethical issues involve employees. For example, discrimination in all of its many forms is one of the most common. Since the pas-

---

How Businesses Can Avoid Ethics Problems

In the wake of highly publicized corporate scandals in 2002, the Better Business Bureau offered these broad recommendations to companies wishing to avoid having ethics problems of their own.

- Lead by example by demonstrating high ethical standards of behavior toward customers, suppliers, shareholders, employees, and communities in which you do business. Be honest in all dealings.

- Create an ethics policy that starts at the top level so that management sets an example for all employees.

- Set up a system that encourages employees to express concerns directly to top management if they suspect wrongdoing or are uncomfortable with company practices.

- Treat all employees with respect and fairness.

- Reward employees for their ethical decisions and actions.

- Cultivate the highest possible standards of reporting and accounting.

- Monitor what is going on in your company; communicate with employees directly; get a feel for what they are doing and be accessible and interested.

Source: Better Business Bureau (http://www.bbb.org/bizethics/tips.asp)

sage of the federal Civil Rights Act of 1964, along with subsequent related legislation, American employers have been forbidden by law from discriminating on the basis of sex, race, national origin, age, religion, or disability in their employment policies: hiring, pay, promotion, benefits, or termination. Decisions in these matters must be made on each individual's ability to perform on the job, with only a minimum number of exceptions, such as seniority. From an ethical perspective, this is seen as necessary to satisfy society's view of fairness and to protect each individual's right to equal opportunity. The issue is complicated, however, by affirmative action programs that may lead to reverse discrimination against majority groups. The growing number of different minority groups as well as the growth of the overall minority population in the United States, the so-called glass ceiling that prevents women from achieving top management positions in numbers equivalent to their prevalence in the workforce, and discrimination against workers on the basis of sexual preference all continue to be important ethical issues for employers to address in the twenty-first century.

Employer-employee issues also include employees' right to privacy; relationships and responsibilities to union organizations; whistle-blowing; advance notice of large-scale layoffs or plant closings; the question of whether employers have the obligation to provide a minimum level of health insurance, child care, pension plans, and other benefits; and the question of whether workers have some right to participate in management decisions that affect their jobs. In all these issues, managers face questions about how far beyond minimum legal requirements they must go to satisfy prevailing social expectations.

CUSTOMER RELATIONSHIPS

Customers represent another vital stakeholder group for any organization, and the organization's relationship with them has its own set of complex ethical issues. One of the most enduring issues is the question of product liability: To what extent should manufacturers be held responsible for harm caused by their products or services? Caveat emptor (let the buyer beware) is no longer the guiding principle in transactions between buyers and sellers or between manufacturers and their customers. The courts and some state laws have moved steadily in the direction of placing on the manufacturer more and more of the liability for harm done by its products. Under the concept of strict liability, it is no longer necessary to prove that a manufacturer has been negligent in the production or the design of a product. Courts routinely expect manufacturers to anticipate any potential problems and have increasingly held producers responsible even though state-of-the-art scientific knowledge at the time of production could not have predicted the ensuing problems.

The asbestos industry has, in effect, ceased to exist in the United States. Virtually all the major asbestos producers have disappeared, often into bankruptcy, because of massive class-action lawsuits against them. During the 1990's, the tobacco industry came under severe legal and social pressure from a broad coalition of state governments, health associations, and advocacy groups. Cigarette manufacturers have been accused of conspiring to hide from their customers and from the public what they have known about the addictiveness and other harmful—often deadly—effects of smoking. While cigarettes have continued to be legal products, the tobacco companies have agreed to pay massive sums to the states in reimbursement for costs to the state health care systems. They have also agreed to serious restrictions in the way they market their products. Alleged ethical violations cover a wide range of subjects including the falsifying of information regarding the effects of smoking on health and inappropriately targeting children with cigarette advertising, especially in the use of icons such as "Joe Camel" and the Marlboro Man. Once deemed invulnerable, the tobacco industry was being forced to accept responsibility for the harm caused by its products during the first years of the twenty-first century.

Emboldened by developments in the tobacco industry, other advocacy groups have moved against the firearms industry in an attempt to hold gun manufacturers, especially handgun makers, responsible for deaths and accidents resulting from the use of their products. By the year 2004, moves against the firearms industry have had little success in the courts, but the ethical questions continued to be debated.

Other advocacy groups have started claiming that the fast-food industry bears some of the responsibility for the growing problem of obesity in the United States. They have urged McDonald's and the rest of the industry to acknowledge and accept their ethical responsibilities by offering wider selections of healthy menu items and by providing more information to the public about the fat content of their hamburgers and french fries.

ADVERTISING

Another major category of ethical problems associated with the buyer-seller relationship stems from the advertising and other promotional tactics that sellers employ. Advertisers are often tempted to make claims about their products and services that are either blatantly fraudulent or that can be easily misconstrued by the public. Such claims are unethical because they do not respect the rights of customers to be fully and properly informed, and they do not measure up to societal expectations that business dealings be conducted in an honest (virtuous) manner. Various governmental agencies, such as the Food and Drug Administration and the Federal Trade Commission, have the statutory responsibility for protecting against dishonest advertising, while nongovernmental groups such as Better Business Bureaus and the American Association of Advertising Agencies provide a modest level of self-policing.

As the persuasive power of advertising messages has become more subtle, some businesses have been accused of exploiting certain "vulnerable" groups. Targeting children, especially for products such as breakfast cereals and violent video games, has been criticized frequently. The argument is made that children lack the experience and the maturity to evaluate advertising messages, especially when manufacturers blur the lines between commercials and entertainment programs. Cigarette, alcoholic beverage, and handgun advertisers have also been sharply criticized, notably when they have targeted women and racial minorities.

Heavily criticized for promoting its cigarettes with a cartoon character highly appealing to children, the RJ Reynolds Tobacco Company announced in 1997 that it was abandoning its "Joe Camel" advertising campaign. (AP/Wide World Photos)

OTHER ISSUES

Another major category of business ethics problems is related to environmental concerns. By the early twenty-first century, it was widely reported and understood that business, in its normal functions of manufacturing and transporting products, contributes to environmental problems around the world: air pollution, water pollution, solid and toxic wastes, and so on. A number of ethical questions are then posed: What responsibilities must business assume for the clean-up of polluted water and dump sites?

185

What responsibilities does the business community have to redesign its products and processes to reduce waste and consume fewer natural resources? To what extent must business protect endangered species and respect the rights of animals, for example, in testing the safety of pharmaceuticals and personal care products?

In the early years of the twenty-first century, the United States was rocked with a series of highly publicized business ethics scandals involving such corporations as Enron, Arthur Anderson, WorldCom, and Tyco. These situations tended to fall into the subject of accounting issues or into the subject of governance, which involves the role of the board of directors and its relationship to management. In the former category, ethical issues were raised when information was either withheld or falsified by internal or external auditors to the point that shareholders and the investing public could not use the accounting information available to them to make sound judgments about the company. In the latter category, it was becoming apparent that the boards of directors in a large number of publicly held companies were not exercising independent judgment in monitoring and evaluating the work of management.

TRANSNATIONAL PROBLEMS

As the globalization of business has continued to grow in importance, so too have the business ethics issues related specifically to doing business in and with other countries. One set of ethical problems derives from the old maxim, "When in Rome, do as the Romans do." This may be fine advice under most circumstances for business managers venturing out into other countries and other cultures, but does it, or should it apply, to ethical matters?

Bribery—under all its different names and different forms—has been the most often debated issue. Since the passage of the Foreign Corrupt Practices Act in 1977, it has been illegal under United States law to offer bribes to foreign officials in return for business contracts or other favors. However, the law specifically condones "facilitating payments," and so managers are called on to distinguish such payments from outright bribes. At the heart of this debate, however, is this question: If an act is deemed to be wrong—that is, absolutely immoral—in this country, why should it be considered acceptable to perform the same act in a different country or culture?

A quite different set of questions is raised when companies from developed countries do business in developing nations. Do such firms have special obligations and responsibilities? Nestlé was widely criticized during the late 1970's for the tactics it used to market its infant formula in developing countries. A variation of this issue regards the responsibility of manufacturers and retailers for the working conditions and wages in the factories of its suppliers. Nike and Wal-Mart are examples of large international firms that have been criticized for using developing world suppliers who employ child labor, pay wages so low that they cannot provide even the bare essentials of food and shelter, and where the working conditions and treatment by supervisors is inhumane. Under these circumstances manufacturers and retailers are called upon to be responsible not only for their own employees but for the employees of their suppliers and contractors as well.

The early twenty-first century also witnessed a growing world debate over the responsibility of pharmaceutical companies to make their patented drugs for acquired immunodeficiency syndrome (AIDS) and other life-threatening diseases available to poor African and Asian nations at greatly reduced prices.

ATTENTION TO ETHICAL ISSUES

Interest in business ethics in the academic community began increasing during the mid-1980's. Since then, colleges and universities have incorporated growing numbers of ethics courses and modules into their graduate and undergraduate business curricula. A number of professional academic societies such as the Society for Business Ethics, the International Association for Business and Society, the Social Issues in Management division of the Academy of Management, and the Marketing in Society division of the American Marketing Association hold annual meetings and encourage the writing and publication of scholarly papers. The Center for Business Ethics at Bentley College has sponsored a series of national conferences on the subject.

Within the business community itself, there has also been a marked increase in the recognition of ethical problems. A number of companies have created the new position of "ethics officer." Most large companies have adopted "codes of conduct," programs that are designed to clarify their policies regarding ethical behavior, and systematically inculcate their managers and employees at all levels with these policies. Johnson & Johnson credits the company-wide understanding of and respect for its Credo with helping the organization through its Tylenol crisis in 1982, still regarded as one of the great exemplars of ethical corporate behavior.

Throughout the economic history of the United States there have been periods of corporate misconduct followed by periods of heightened concern for business ethics and government regulation. There is no reason to think that this wavelike pattern of scandal and ethical reform will not continue.

D. Kirk Davidson

FURTHER READING

Acton, H. B. *The Morals of Markets: An Ethical Exploration.* Harlow, England: Longmans, 1971. This work covers the systemic level of business ethics in presenting a defense of capitalism, especially as it has developed in the United States.

De George, Richard T. *Business Ethics.* 5th ed. Englewood Cliffs, N.J.: Prentice Hall, 1999. An exposition on moral reasoning in business that includes good coverage of the important issues by a widely respected professor in the field.

Donaldson, Thomas. *The Ethics of International Business.* New York: Oxford University Press, 1989. Donaldson is one of the leading business ethicists in the United States. This work focuses only on international issues and defends the position that there are certain absolute standards or "hyper-norms" that transcend all countries and all cultures.

Donaldson, Thomas, Margaret Cording, and Patricia Werhane, eds. *Ethical Issues in Business: A Philosophical Approach.* 7th ed. Englewood Cliffs, N.J.: Prentice Hall, 2001. This book includes an excellent group of case studies and sets forth an analysis of the most important ethical issues facing businesses today.

Donaldson, Thomas, and Thomas W. Dunfee. *The Ties That Bind: A Social Contract Approach to Business Ethics.* Boston: Harvard University Business School Press, 1999. An important work from two noted scholars at the University of Pennsylvania grounding business ethics in a broader ethics concept.

Smith, N. Craig, and John A. Quelch. *Ethics in Marketing.* Homewood, Ill.: Richard D. Irwin, 1993. A very good collection of business case studies and articles from business periodicals on all aspects of marketing ethics: advertising, pricing, product policy, research, and so forth.

Velasquez, Manuel G. *Business Ethics: Concepts and Cases.* 5th ed. Englewood Cliffs, N.J.: Prentice Hall, 2002. An excellent all-purpose text on the subject. Explains in readable, straightforward language the various frameworks for analyzing business behavior and uses those frameworks to analyze the most important ethical issues such as honesty in advertising and insider trading.

SEE ALSO: Advertising; Antitrust legislation; Corporate compensation; Corporate responsibility; Corporate scandal; Downsizing; Ethical codes of organizations; Marketing; Multinational corporations; Sales ethics; Wage discrimination; Whistleblowing.

Butler, Joseph

IDENTIFICATION: English cleric
BORN: May 18, 1692, Wantage, Berkshire, England
DIED: June 16, 1752, Bath, Somerset, England
TYPE OF ETHICS: Religious ethics
SIGNIFICANCE: A pastor and bishop in the Church of England, Butler stressed the complexity of human nature and moral life and the importance of the conscience in decision making, most notably in his *Fifteen Sermons Preached at the Rolls Chapel* (1726).

In his Anglican sermons, Joseph Butler focused on various topics, including human nature and the love of one's neighbor. Humans and animals both have instincts, but humans also have a conscience, a inner sense of direction that holds authority over all other principles. Indeed, human government is possible only because people have this moral nature. One's conscience will direct one toward behavior that is most appropriate in the long run. It is possible, Butler conceded, to violate one's conscience in favor of some passion, but such behavior that gratifies the appetites at the expense of the conscience is unnatural. Conversely, acting in one's long-term self-interest is both rational and natural.

Likewise, Butler contended, the conscience urges one to act benevolently toward other people, since such behavior is also in one's long-term best interest. Thus, love of one's neighbors is as natural as love of oneself. Virtues such as temperance and sobriety are traceable to the exercise of benevolence, and vices to ignoring it. Butler disagreed with Francis Hutcheson, however, that benevolence is the sum of virtue in human beings, though he thought it to be so in God. In humans, conscience dictates that one should never approve on the grounds of benevolence such acts as falsehood, violence, and injustice.

Paul L. Redditt

SEE ALSO: Altruism; Christian ethics; Compassion; Conscience; Moral-sense theories; Self-love.

Bystanders

DEFINITION: Individuals who fail to take action to stop or relieve wrongdoing that they witness
TYPE OF ETHICS: Personal and social ethics
SIGNIFICANCE: The inaction of bystanders makes it easier for wrongdoers to harm their victims and raises questions about the ethics of those who remain passive in times of crisis.

Everyday life is filled with incidents in which bystanders watch events unfold without getting involved themselves. In most situations, such inaction is benign. However, ethical questions arise when bystanders passively observe wrongdoing or fail to act in emergency situations in which they might provide help to victims of crime or accidents, A particularly famous case of bystander inaction involved the murder of a young New York woman named Kitty Genovese. While walking home from work one evening in 1964, she was attacked and repeatedly stabbed by a stranger over a period of thirty-five minutes. At least thirty-eight neighbors witnessed her killing, but not one came to her assistance or even called the police to report the crime.

Such incidents raise questions as to why individuals fail to take action when another human being is in distress. Research has demonstrated two primary reasons for inaction. First, individuals in emergency situations tend to look to others for clues as to what they should do themselves. If they see no one else seemingly concerned, they assume that no action is needed. Additionally, when many bystanders are involved, a diffusion of responsibility develops. Each person tends to assume that taking action is someone else's responsibility. Once individuals choose not to become involved in a situation, the possibility of taking action later grows more difficult. To move from inaction to action requires individuals to confront the moral and ethic choices for passivity they make initially. Initial inaction also leads individuals to accept a "just world" position. In other words, to rationalize their lack of involvement, they may decide that victims somehow deserve their misfortunes.

Bystanders include not only individual human beings but also groups and nations. During the late nineteenth and early twentieth centuries, for example, many law enforcement agencies turned a blind eye to the lynching of African Americans in the American South. During World War II and the period leading up to it, much of the world stood by passively in the face of the Holocaust. Such inaction, particularly by groups, creates an atmosphere of impunity that may embolden perpetrators. Thus, passive bystanders can essentially serve to fuel wrongdoing and atrocity.

Linda M. Woolf

SEE ALSO: Duty; "Everyone does it"; Genocide and democide; Guilt and shame; Holocaust; Lynching; Nussbaum, Martha; Police brutality.

C

Calvin, John

IDENTIFICATION: Swiss theologian
BORN: July 10, 1509, Noyon, Picardy, France
DIED: May 27, 1564, Geneva, Switzerland
TYPE OF ETHICS: Religious ethics
SIGNIFICANCE: Calvin led the Swiss Reformed branch of the Protestant Reformation. His doctrine of the "elect" emphasized the sovereignty of God, seeing the ultimate fate of all humans as determined in advance.

John Calvin studied theology, law, and classics, and he wrote his *Commentary on Lucius Anneas Seneca's Two Books on Clemency* (1532) by the age of twenty-three. His sympathies with emerging Protestant thinking caused him to flee Paris in 1534. He wrote the first edition of his *Institutes of the Christian Religion* in 1536 in Basel, Switzerland. That same year, he settled in Geneva, where he acted as both its civil and its religious leader. His own conversion experience gave him a sense of God's direct dealings with people.

Calvin emphasized the sovereignty of God. He believed that knowledge of God came only through revealed scriptures, not through unaided human reason. Humans were created morally upright, but through Adam's sin human nature became "totally depraved"; that is, all human faculties have been corrupted, and as a result humans are incapable of any act that God would deem good. Salvation is thus necessary but is wholly the act of God. Jesus died to effect the salvation of those God elects, and even the faith to accept salvation is God's irresistible gift. God alone chooses who will and who will not receive the faith to accept forgiveness. Further, those whom God saves, God preserves. The responsibility of the Christian is to lead a moral, temperate life.

The German sociologist Max Weber (*The Protestant Ethic and the Rise of Capitalism*, 1904-1905) has argued that Calvinism has given rise to a work ethic and capitalism, although that conclusion is debated.

Paul L. Redditt

SEE ALSO: Christian ethics; Determinism and freedom; Edwards, Jonathan; Fatalism; God; Work.

Campaign finance reform

DEFINITION: Efforts to improve the procedures through which political candidates collect and spend money in their efforts to win elections
TYPE OF ETHICS: Politico-economic ethics
SIGNIFICANCE: Advocates of campaign finance reform argue that increased regulation of campaign finance would lead to greater political fairness and decreased corruption in politics; opponents argue that new regulation would unduly limit the freedom that individuals should have when participating in elections.

Campaign finance reform became a hotly contested issue in American politics during the last several decades of the twentieth century. Proponents of reform have argued that allowing large campaign contributions undermines equality in a liberal democracy by giving undue influence to small groups who can demand favors from the candidates who receive their contributions. Reform advocates also argue that limitations on campaign spending for candidates, individuals, and groups makes it possible to have a more level playing field for those seeking public office.

Critics of campaign finance reform counter that limitations on making and receiving contributions limits freedom of citizens who desire to participate in the political process. They also argue that limiting contributions would lead to less-informed voters.

EARLY FEDERAL CAMPAIGN FINANCE LAW

From the founding of the American Republic until 1971, there were relatively few restrictions on the financing of political campaigns. The Civil Service Reform Act of 1883 prohibited candidates for federal offices from collecting contributions on federal property. This regulation was primarily aimed at protecting federal employees, rather than at protecting or restoring the integrity of federal elections.

Because persons holding positions in the federal government had previously contributed large portions of the money spent on early federal campaigns, candidates and parties looked to other sources after passage of the reform act. Powerful corporations associated with manufacturing, railroads, and natural resources provided significant contributions to both major political parties during the finals years of the nineteenth century. The criticism of the economic power of large corporations not only led to antitrust legislation, but also led to the Tillman Act of 1907 that prohibited corporations from making direct contributions to candidates for federal office.

In 1910 the Federal Corrupt Practices Act passed. It required disclosure of donors and for a short time established limitations on campaign spending. Neither that act nor its revisions established an independent enforcement agency, a fact that made the law's provisions largely ineffectual. The argument for disclosure was that the public should be able to know the identities of people attempting to influence political candidates. The law assumed that voters would be able to determine when office seekers were considering the interests of their district or the interests of their donors.

MODERN CAMPAIGN FINANCE REFORM

Significant campaign finance reform began in 1971. The modern reforms have been driven, in large part, by concerns about political fairness and the integrity of political campaigns. In 1971 the Federal Election Campaign Act (FECA) established a comprehensive reform of campaign finance. The act required regular disclosure of campaign contributions and expenditures. It established limits on the amounts of money that candidates and their own families could contribute to their campaigns and set restrictions on advertising expenditures. A related act passed that same year provided limited tax deductions and credits for small contributions to political campaigns.

The purpose of that law was to encourage more individuals to participate in political campaigns.

In the wake of very large contributions made to President Richard M. Nixon's campaign for reelection in 1972 and increasing concern about corruption in government, Congress amended FECA in 1974. The changes that year included spending limits for presidential and congressional elections, a one-thousand-dollar contribution limit for individuals, a five-thousand-dollar limit for political action committees (PACs), and additional restrictions on how much individuals could spend on campaigns. The revision created the Federal Election Commission as a agency for enforcing the new regulations. The act also established a system of matching funds for candidates in presidential elections. Partial public funding of presidential campaigns was initiated as a means to provide fairness for candidates seeking the presidency and to limit candidates' reliance on private contributors.

In its *Buckley v. Valeo* (1976) decision, the U.S. Supreme Court struck down the spending limits for campaigns, limits on what individuals could spend on their own campaigns, and limits on what independent groups could spend to influence elections as violations of the First Amendment. The court did uphold disclosure requirements and limits on contributions.

In 2002 a major addition to campaign finance regulation was the Bipartisan Campaign Finance Reform Act. That act changed the system of campaign finance in many ways, but most significantly it prohibited political parties from raising and spending so-called "soft money"—large contributions given to parties and originally intended support general party activities. These large contributions were often used to influence particular elections. The act also prohibited independent organizations from broadcasting "electioneering communications" to defeat or elect candidates in close proximity to elections. Defenders of the bill saw it as removing the corrosive effects of large contributions. Critics asserted that the bill restricted the free speech of candidates.

VALUES AND CAMPAIGN FINANCE REFORM

One side in the debate over campaign finance reform argues that the right of free speech should be the preeminent political value. It is an argument made by both conservative Republicans and the American Civil Liberties Union. Those who favor increased regulation and greater public funding of campaigns assert that money greatly contributes to the corruption of both candidates and the democratic system and that increased regulation would lead to greater fairness. John Gardner, founder of Common Cause, summarized this sentiment stating that "there is nothing in our political system that creates more mischief, more alienation, and distrust on the part of the public than does our system of financing elections." In *Political Liberalism* (1996), political philosopher John Rawls sided with proponents of reform. He argued that "political speech may be regulated in order to preserve the fair value of the political [system]."

Michael L. Coulter

Albert Camus (center) on his arrival with his wife (left) in Sweden to accept his Nobel Prize in literature in 1957. (AP/Wide World Photos)

FURTHER READING

Clawson, Dan, Alan Newustadtl, and Denise Scott. *Money Talks: Corporate PAC's and Political Influence.* New York: HarperCollins, 1992.

Drew, Elizabeth. *Politics and Money.* New York: MacMillan, 1983.

Luna, Christopher, ed. *Campaign Finance Reform.* H. W. Wilson, 2001.

Rawls, John. *Political Liberalism.* New York: Columbia University Press, 1996.

Smith, Bradley. *Unfree Speech: The Folly of Campaign Finance Reform.* Princeton, N.J.: Princeton University Press, 2001.

SEE ALSO: Democracy; Ethics in Government Act; League of Women Voters; Liberalism; Politics; Suffrage; Voting fraud.

Camus, Albert

IDENTIFICATION: French Algerian journalist and author

BORN: November 7, 1913, Mondovi, Algeria

DIED: January 4, 1960, near Villeblevin, France

TYPE OF ETHICS: Modern history

SIGNIFICANCE: One of the most important voices of existentialism, Camus was an opponent of totalitarianism in any form and a proponent of the individual. His many works include *The Stranger* (*L'Étranger*, 1942), *The Myth of Sisyphus* (*Le Mythe de Sisyphe*, 1942), *The Plague* (*La Peste*, 1947), *The Rebel* (*L'Homme révolté*, 1951), and *The Fall* (*La Chute*, 1956).

After growing up in Algeria, Albert Camus went to Paris in 1940 to work as a journalist. In 1943, he became a reader for the publishing firm Gallimard. He worked there until the end of his life to subsidize his writing. His writings may be divided into three periods: first, the period of the absurd or the antihero; second, the period of man in revolt, or the hero; and finally, the period of man on the earth.

During the period of the absurd, which is best exemplified by the novel *The Stranger,* man kills and is killed in turn by the state in a relatively senseless existence. During the second period, characters who are larger than life defy the world's absurdity and find meaning in life. In both *The Plague* and *The Rebel,* heroic men fight to overcome the evils of totalitarianism. The struggle reveals possibilities of goodness and principled existence hitherto not present in

Camus's work. During the final period, Camus often portrays characters who are wounded by their existence in the world. Yet these characters are often able to find some measure of human happiness and redemption in everyday life.

Camus received the Nobel Prize in Literature in 1957. He died in an automobile accident in 1960.

Jennifer Eastman

SEE ALSO: Absurd, the; Atheism; Common good; Existentialism; Human rights; Life, meaning of; Moral realism; Moral responsibility; Other, the.

Cannibalism in the Twenty-first Century

In January, 2004, a German court sentenced a forty-two-year-old man to eight and one-half years in prison for killing, dismembering, and eating another man. The cannibal's victim had allegedly submitted to being killed voluntarily, after replying to an Internet advertisement seeking a man for "slaughter and consumption." Outraged by the comparative leniency of the court's sentence, prosecutors planned to appeal the verdict, calling the murderer a "human butcher" who wanted to "satisfy a sexual impulse." However, the judge in the case stated that he did not believe the man had acted with cruel intent when he killed his victim, suggesting that his motive was a wish to "make another man part of himself"—a goal he achieved by eating his victim.

Cannibalism

DEFINITION: Consumption of human flesh by human beings
TYPE OF ETHICS: Beliefs and practices
SIGNIFICANCE: The morality of the practice of cannibalism is a matter of some controversy, especially because of the broad range of diverse circumstances in which it might occur.

When considering the morality of cannibalism, it is important to keep in mind several crucial distinctions. First and most important, there is the distinction between lethal cannibalism, which involves killing the person whose flesh is eaten by the cannibal, and nonlethal cannibalism, which does not involve killing a person whose flesh is eaten by the cannibal. Clearly enough, since it involves killing a person, lethal cannibalism is nearly always morally wrong. (Cases of morally permissible lethal cannibalism would be cases involving some special circumstance that justified killing another person; although this is very controversial, there may be cases in which lethal cannibalism is justified as a form of self-defense.)

Whereas it seems clear that lethal cannibalism is nearly always morally wrong, the moral status of nonlethal cannibalism is less clear. How might nonlethal cannibalism occur? One kind of case involves people who are stuck in places without food and are forced to consume the flesh of other people, with or without permission.

Thinking about this possibility (or about cannibalism in general) probably causes disgust or revulsion in many people. It is important, however, to recognize the distinction between what people find disgusting or repulsive and what people sense to be morally wrong. Many things are disgusting although they are not morally wrong (for example, the consumption of human waste). One must be careful not to infer that nonlethal cannibalism is morally wrong merely because one finds it disgusting or repulsive.

What should one say about the morality of nonlethal cannibalism? Perhaps what one should say here depends in part upon one's view of the relationship between human beings and their bodies. For example, if people are really nonphysical souls that are "attached" to physical bodies until the moment of death (when souls "leave" their bodies), then nonlethal cannibalism might seem to be morally permissible after death. After the soul has left the body, in this view, the dead person's body is very similar to the dead body of an animal, and it seems morally permissible to many people to consume dead animals.

However, that argument could be reversed. If one believed that it was morally impermissible to consume dead animals, then one could draw the same conclusion about dead persons. There are interesting similarities between arguments concerning nonlethal cannibalism and arguments concerning the consumption of animals; it is important in both cases to observe the lethal/nonlethal distinction.

A similar argument is suggested by the very different view that persons are physical creatures without nonphysical souls. In this view, death involves the cessation of bodily function. While a person is alive, she is identical to her body; once she has died, however, she ceases to exist and her body becomes a physical object much like the body of a dead animal. As previously mentioned above, if it is morally permissible to consume the flesh of a dead animal, then it might seem morally permissible to consume the flesh of a dead person.

Another consideration that suggests this conclusion is the fact that, typically, the bodies of dead persons naturally decompose and become changed into other organic substances. Sometimes these same bits of matter eventually become parts of new plants or animals, which are consumed by human persons in morally permissible ways. At what point in this transition does it become morally permissible to consume the matter in question? It seems hard to offer a nonarbitrary answer, which suggests that it is morally permissible to ingest the matter in question at any stage in the process, even when it is still recognizable as part of a dead person's body.

That argument, too, could be reversed: One might conclude instead that it is morally impermissible to ingest the matter in question at any stage in the process.

There are other considerations, however, that must be weighed against these arguments on behalf of the moral permissibility of nonlethal cannibalism. For example, it might be suggested that unless the lives of other people are at stake, respect for dead people requires that their bodies not be ingested by others. It also might be argued that religious prescriptions concerning the treatment of dead persons' bodies make nonlethal cannibalism morally impermissible. Finally, it might be unwise to permit nonlethal cannibalism because such a policy might encourage lethal cannibalism, which is almost always morally wrong.

Because of the arguments on both sides and the controversial issues that surround them, it is very difficult to settle the dispute over the morality of nonlethal cannibalism in a brief article such as this one. Hence, people should consider carefully the arguments on both sides in order to arrive at a well-informed opinion.

Scott A. Davison

FURTHER READING

Goldman, Laurence R., ed. *The Anthropology of Cannibalism.* Westport, Conn.: Bergin & Garvey: 1999.

Hogg, Garry. *Cannibalism and Human Sacrifice.* New York: Citadel Press, 1966.

Read, Piers Paul. *Alive: The Story of the Andes Survivors.* Philadelphia: Lippincott, 1974.

Sanday, Peggy Reeves. *Divine Hunger.* Cambridge: Cambridge University Press, 1986.

Simpson, A. W. Brian. *Cannibalism and the Common Law: A Victorian Yachting Tragedy.* 1984. Reprint. Rio Grande, Ohio: Hambledon Press, 1994.

Tannahill, Reay. *Flesh and Blood.* New York: Stein and Day, 1975.

SEE ALSO: Animal rights; Death and dying; Dominion over nature, human; Homicide; Immortality; Life and death; Moral status of animals; Morality; Permissible acts; Taboos.

Capital punishment

DEFINITION: Punishment that takes away the life of a convicted wrongdoer; also known as the death penalty

TYPE OF ETHICS: Legal and judicial ethics

SIGNIFICANCE: Capital punishment is an ethical and legal life-and-death issue that may be seen in the contexts of justice, deterrence, and the progress of society.

Laws calling for capital punishment can be found in the earliest criminal codes, and the death penalty is probably as old as civilization itself. During the eighteenth century B.C.E., Hammurabi's code provided for capital punishment in Babylon for a number of offenses, including murder, putting death spells on people, lying in capital trials, and adultery. During the Industrial Revolution, Great Britain applied death penalties to more than two hundred offenses, including certain cases of cutting down trees and picking pockets. Throughout history, capital punishment has been applied most readily to the lowest economic and social classes.

The history of capital punishment raises questions about cruel and unusual punishment. Executions of human beings have been carried out by such savage methods as boiling, burning, choking, dismembering, impaling, disemboweling, crucifixion, hanging, stoning, and burying alive. Modern gas chambers, electric chairs, and lethal injections are seen by many as humane advances; others respond that the guillotine—used to chop off heads efficiently—was also once seen as humane.

Because of constitutional challenges carried to the U.S. Supreme Court, no executions took place in the United States between 1967 and 1977. In 1972, the Court ruled, in *Furman v. Georgia*, that capital punishment violated the Eighth Amendment's prohibition against cruel and unusual punishment because the penalty was often administered in an "arbitrary and capricious manner." After that Court ruling, many states began to redraft their statutes on capital punishment. Four years later, in *Gregg v. Georgia*, the Supreme Court ruled that capital punishment was not unconstitutional, so long as the punishment was administered within systems designed to prevent ju-

ries from imposing the death penalties in an arbitrary or capricious manner.

After executions were resumed in the United States in 1977, convicts who were executed were those found guilty of either murder or of committing acts that led to the deaths of other persons. Some state statutes also allowed capital punishment for treason, aircraft piracy, and train-wrecking.

RETRIBUTIVE JUSTICE

One argument for capital punishment appeals to the desire for retribution to fit the offense, as expressed by the saying "an eye for an eye, and a tooth for a tooth." The argument was articulated most eloquently by Immanuel Kant during the eighteenth century. He argued that the only fitting repayment for murder is the life of the murderer, for to inflict any lesser punishment would be to devalue the unconditional worth of human life. Kant took the unusual tack of arguing that it also would be an offense to murderers themselves not to take their lives, for not to do so would imply that the murderers were not re-

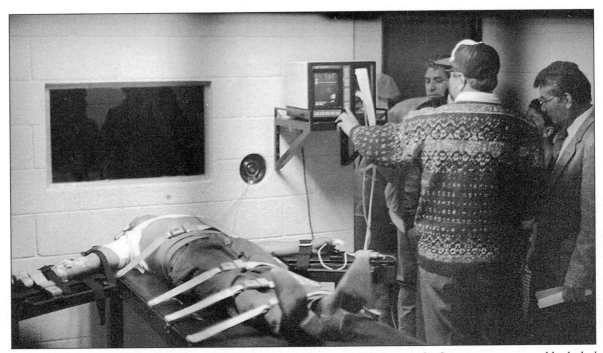

Technicians check for vital signs in the body of a confessed mass-murderer—the first person executed by lethal injection in Guatemala, in 1998. All previous executions in the Central American nation had been by firing squad. By the early twenty-first century, lethal injection was the preferred form of execution in virtually every U.S. state and in many other nations. (AP/Wide World Photos)

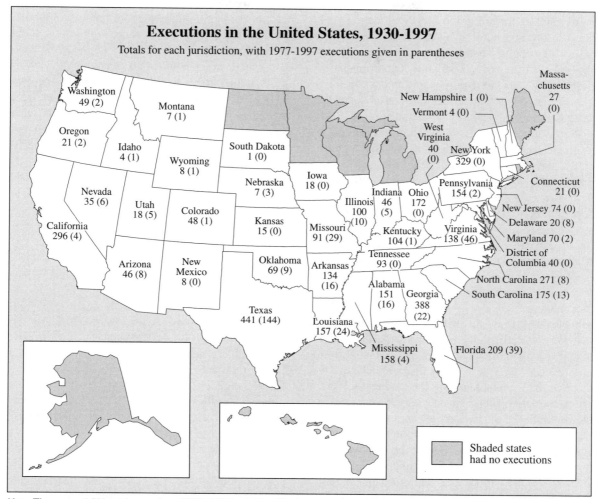

Executions in the United States, 1930-1997
Totals for each jurisdiction, with 1977-1997 executions given in parentheses

Washington 49 (2)
Oregon 21 (2)
Montana 7 (1)
Idaho 4 (1)
South Dakota 1 (0)
Wyoming 8 (1)
Iowa 18 (0)
Nevada 35 (6)
Utah 18 (5)
Colorado 48 (1)
Nebraska 7 (3)
Kansas 15 (0)
California 296 (4)
Arizona 46 (8)
New Mexico 8 (0)
Oklahoma 69 (9)
Missouri 91 (29)
Arkansas 134 (16)
Texas 441 (144)
Louisiana 157 (24)
Illinois 100 (10)
Indiana 46 (5)
Ohio 172 (0)
Kentucky 104 (1)
Tennessee 93 (0)
Alabama 151 (16)
Georgia 388 (22)
Mississippi 158 (4)
Florida 209 (39)

New Hampshire 1 (0)
Vermont 4 (0)
West Virginia 40 (0)
New York 329 (0)
Massachusetts 27 (0)
Pennsylvania 154 (2)
Connecticut 21 (0)
New Jersey 74 (0)
Delaware 20 (8)
Maryland 70 (2)
District of Columbia 40 (0)
Virginia 138 (46)
North Carolina 271 (8)
South Carolina 175 (13)

Shaded states had no executions

Note: There were 4,291 total executions, 1930-1997, including 33 prisoners executed in the federal system. The total for 1977-1997 of 432 prisoners executed includes no federal executions.

Source: U.S. Department of Justice, Bureau of Justice Statistics, *Capital Punishment 1997* (December, 1998).

sponsible for their actions and were therefore not human beings.

Several objections can be made to the retributive justice arguments. First, it may be argued that on Kant's own grounds of the unconditional worth and dignity of the individual, execution should not take place, for surely the concept of unconditional worth applies even to a murderer. Second, many social scientists would argue that two centuries of empirical investigation since Kant's time have shown that murderers often are not responsible for their own actions. Third, it is clear that by Kant's insistence that murderers not be maltreated in their deaths, he is saying that justice requires not an identical act as retribution,

but one of likeness or proportion. Therefore, would not a life sentence without the possibility of parole be proportionate, and in addition allow for the reversal of erroneous verdicts?

DETERRENCE

Reform movements of the eighteenth and nineteenth centuries, led intellectually in Great Britain by the utilitarians Jeremy Bentham and John Stuart Mill, questioned the logic behind the widely varying punishments set forth in the legal codes. The utilitarians questioned the authority of religion and tradition, pointing to the often inhumane results of such reasoning by authority. Instead of basing legal penalties on retribution, the utilitarian agenda of maximizing the pleasure and minimizing the pain of a society called for penalties based on deterrence: Penalties should be only as harsh as necessary to prevent undesirable acts from occurring again, and no harsher. This utilitarian argument has been used to make cases both for and against capital punishment.

Some argue that capital punishment is necessary as a deterrent against further murders. Surely, they reason, having one's life taken is the greatest fear that a person should have, and a swift and just application of the death penalty would prevent many future murders from occurring. Execution would obviously deter convicted murderers from committing later offenses, and would also deter potential murderers who would fear the consequences.

Numerous objections have been raised to the deterrence argument. First, while deterrence seems to be a modern, progressive view that is far more reasonable than an "eye for an eye," opponents point out that society is still engaging in the barbaric practice of taking human life. In addition, the argument from progress can well be used against capital punishment, as the United States was the only major Western country that still practiced capital punishment at the beginning of the twenty-first century. South Africa also had capital punishment until 1995, when its supreme court unanimously ruled the death penalty unconstitutional. Progressivists also point out that in 2001 only three nations executed more people than did the United States: China, Iran, and Saudi Arabia.

Another argument against the principle of deterrence is that it is not intuitively clear that a would-be murderer would fear a relatively painless death, as by lethal injection, more than the prospect of unending days in prison. Also, there is great question about the empirical claim that the death penalty actually does deter potential murderers. Opponents argue that of the many studies done, none has ever showed convincing evidence that the death penalty is an effective deterrent. Many murders are crimes of passion in which the murderers do not rationally assess the penalties they may face if they are caught.

Others argue that the death penalty continues to be cruel and unusual punishment because it is imposed disproportionately on members of minority groups and poor people. Several studies have concluded that a prime factor in determining whether the death penalty will be imposed in a murder case is the race of the victim. Regardless of the race of the defendant, the death penalty is imposed far more often if the victim is white. Between 1977 and 2002, African Americans constituted 46 percent of the victims of homicides in the United States, but only 14 percent of executions were in cases in which victims were African Americans. On the other hand, during that same period, white Americans constituted 51 percent of the victims of homicides, but 81 percent of executions were in cases where whites were victims.

Another type of disproportion is regional. Fifteen southern states accounted for more than 80 percent of the executions in the United States after 1977. Moreover, within any given state, different counties may have widely differing execution rates.

The disproportions by race and economic class, along with cases of exonerations of dozens of persons on death row, have led a number of organizations to call for a moratorium on the death penalty until justice can be more certainly established. In 1997, the American Bar Association began calling on each state that practiced capital punishment to enact a moratorium until it could show that its policies were fair and impartial and minimize the risk of executing innocent persons. However, by 2003, Illinois was the only state that had imposed such a moratorium, which it adopted in 2000.

Despite the arguments about the injustice of the death penalty, support for the death penalty in public opinion polls actually grew substantially through the quarter-century following the restoration of executions in 1977. However, as is always the case in public opinion polls, the ways in which questions are asked may influence the responses. For example, when respondents to polls are given the option of choosing life in prison without the possibility of parole for offenders, their support for capital punishment tends to lessen substantially.

Norris Frederick

FURTHER READING

Amnesty International. *Fatal Flaws: Innocence and the Death Penalty*. London: Author, 1999.

Banner, Stuart. *The Death Penalty: An American History*. Cambridge, Mass.: Harvard University Press, 2002.

Bedau, Hugo Adam, ed. *The Death Penalty in America: Current Controversies*. New York: Oxford University Press, 1998.

Berns, Walter. *For Capital Punishment*. New York: Basic Books, 1979. Reprint. Washington D.C.: University Press of America, 1991.

Currie, Elliott. *Crime and Punishment in America*. New York: Henry Holt, 1998.

Gray, Mike. *The Death Game: Capital Punishment and the Luck of the Draw*. Monroe, Maine: Common Courage Press, 2003.

Prejean, Sister Helen. *Dead Man Walking: An Eyewitness Account of the Death Penalty in the United States*. New York: Random House, 1993.

Zorea, Aharon W. *In the Image of God: A Christian Response to Capital Punishment*. Lanham, Md.: University Press of America, 2000.

SEE ALSO: American Civil Liberties Union; Amnesty International; Criminal punishment; Deterrence; Erroneous convictions; Hammurabi's code; Homicide; Punishment; Supreme Court, U.S.; War crimes trials.

Capitalism

DEFINITION: Economic system based on the private ownership of capital and the distribution of commodities through a free market

TYPE OF ETHICS: Politico-economic ethics

SIGNIFICANCE: On an economic level, capitalism creates the opportunity for each individual to improve his or her standard of living, while simultaneously ensuring that a minority of the citizens will always control a majority of the wealth. On the level of ethics, capitalism encourages the development of personal freedom rather than social justice, and of individual rights rather than interpersonal responsibilities.

An economic system is a set of arrangements by means of which people living in a relatively large group, generally a country, make decisions about how they will produce, distribute, and consume goods and services. Broadly speaking, those decisions can be made by means of either central planning by the government or consumer choices in a free market.

The existence of the capitalist economic system that prevails in the United States is made possible by the political system, which is based on the idea of the highest possible level of individual freedom and re-

sponsibility. Capitalism emphasizes three principles: the private ownership of property, including the means of production; the dominance of the consumer, who is free to buy or not, as he or she pleases; and individual rewards for those producers whose products please the consumer.

A FRAME OF REFERENCE

In every field of human activity, ethics involves determining what types of human behavior are right, good, and to be encouraged, and what types are wrong, bad, and to be avoided. In order to make such determinations, there must be standards against which to judge specific actions and sets of rules that are used to guide the personal decision-making process.

The most appropriate ethical system by which to judge capitalism is, as it happens, also the ethical system that has exerted the most influence over the past several hundred years: utilitarianism. Developed during the nineteenth century by John Stuart Mill, utilitarianism has as its *summum bonum*, its highest good, the principle of the greatest good for the greatest number, which, Mill said, "holds that actions are right in proportion as they tend to promote happiness, wrong as they tend to produce the reverse of happiness." (Each ethical system has its own *summum bonum*. What has been described here applies specifically to Mill's utilitarianism.)

Matters of human happiness and well-being generally bring to mind conditions that are measured by degrees of political liberty and freedom from oppression. If people in a society are enjoying political freedom and democratic government, if they are not living under a military dictatorship or in a police state, and if they have elections that are fair and honest, the spectrum of activities in which day-to-day freedom is a major factor would seem to be covered. Yet that may not be the case. In a democracy, it is true that the majority rules, and that would appear to be consistent with the principle of the greatest happiness for the greatest number.

A closer look at capitalism gives rise to a question: How is the minority represented? Consider, for example, that, even with the greatest degree of political freedom, an individual voter generally is faced with only two choices. An issue passes or fails. A candidate wins or loses. It is a fact that, although the supporters of an unsuccessful issue or candidate may not be completely ignored, they are not represented in the same way that the majority is. To say this is, to be sure, not to disparage democratic freedoms or personal liberties or free elections. It is simply to state that, by their very nature, political (government-developed) responses to human needs usually have one great limitation: They provide a single or a very limited selection. That limitation applies also to government-developed responses to economic questions involving the production, distribution, and consumption of goods and services, to the arrangements for the actual day-to-day business of providing for oneself. It affects the standard of living and the quality of life.

CONSUMER HAPPINESS

Capitalism, however, once established as an economic system within a free political system, can offer the individual consumer, who is voting with dollars at the cash register with each purchase, a huge number of choices. Free entry into markets brings out multiple producers, all of whom offer their wares and are able to satisfy, together, virtually all consumers by satisfying separately a large number of very small markets, producing in the end the greatest happiness for the greatest number and achieving the *summum bonum* of Mill's utilitarianism.

The incentive for producers to enter any market in a capitalist system is to try to satisfy as many people as possible in order to make a profit, which comes to a producer as the result of sufficient voluntary patronage by free consumers. That tangible reward for producers induces them to put forth their best efforts, to produce the best product, and to attempt to capture the largest share of their market. The principal beneficiary of profit, therefore, is not the producer but the consumer. Building a better mousetrap will certainly make the producer prosperous, but the real payoff for society at large is that the better mousetrap will catch everyone's mice, and in that way everyone will be better off. In other words, the *summum bonum*, the greatest happiness, is achieved.

Nevertheless, it is still often said that capitalism, with its emphasis on the profit incentive, has no ethics or principles. That view misunderstands, however, the real and fundamental nature of profit as it relates to the consumer. Profit is a means of communication from consumer to producer. It is the consumer's voice and the producer's ears. Because it is communication that cannot be ignored by the pro-

ducer, who wants to stay in business, it is a device that enables the control of the producer by the consumer. Profit exists only when a sufficiently large segment of a producer's market has chosen to buy the product being offered for sale. If customers are not happy, they do not buy, and there is no profit. Profit is a real-time indicator of the degree to which a producer is serving the greatest-happiness principle.

THE REAL TEST

The true test of any economic system, however, asks but one question: How well are those who are using it able to provide for themselves and their families? Even a cursory glance around the world will reveal at once that capitalism has proved itself best able to improve the human condition. When the question of the unequal distribution of wealth in a capitalist society is raised, it should be noted that people in noncapitalist states are working very hard indeed to establish capitalism. Capitalism is the economic system of choice when people are free to choose their own economic system.

John Shaw

FURTHER READING

Beaud, Michel. *A History of Capitalism, 1500-1980*. Translated by Tom Dickman and Anny LeFebvre. New York: Monthly Review Press, 1983.

Dunning, John H., ed. *Making Globalization Good: The Moral Challenges of Global Capitalism*. New York: Oxford University Press, 2003.

Friedman, Milton, with Rose D. Friedman. *Capitalism and Freedom*. Chicago: University of Chicago Press, 1962.

Heilbroner, Robert L. *The Nature and Logic of Capitalism*. New York: Norton, 1985.

Muller, Jerry Z. *The Mind and the Market: Capitalism in Modern European Thought*. New York: Alfred A. Knopf, 2002.

Rand, Ayn. *Capitalism: The Unknown Ideal*. New York: New American Library, 1966.

Smith, Adam. *An Inquiry into the Nature and Causes of the Wealth of Nations: A Selected Edition*. Edited by Kathryn Sutherland. New York: Oxford University Press, 1998.

Stripling, Scott R. *Capitalism, Democracy, and Morality*. Acton, Mass.: Copley, 1994.

Williams, D. T. *Capitalism, Socialism, Christianity, and Poverty*. Cape Town: J. L. van Schaik, 1998.

Zsolnai, László, and Wojciech W. Gasparski, eds. *Ethics and the Future of Capitalism*. New Brunswick, N.J.: Transaction, 2002.

SEE ALSO: Choice; Communism; Distributive justice; Economics; Free enterprise; Individualism; Marketing; Marxism; Profit economy; Smith, Adam; Socialism.

Caste system, Hindu

DEFINITION: Social order indigenous to India in which society is divided into hierarchically ranked, occupationally specialized, endogamous groups

DATE: First millennium B.C.E. to present

TYPE OF ETHICS: Beliefs and practices

SIGNIFICANCE: The caste system was founded on the principle that ethics are not universal but are relative to one's niche in society.

The Hindu caste system is one of the oldest recorded forms of social organization in the world. It is based on the conception of society as an organic whole in which each group serves a particular function. The social order of caste emphasized hierarchy and interdependence rather than equality and independence. Although the idea of caste is most fully elaborated and justified in the Hindu religious tradition, elements of caste organization have permeated South Asian society generally. The caste system is being eroded by urbanization, industrialization, and the increasing influence of Western ideas.

CHARACTERISTICS OF CASTE

From a sociological viewpoint, the caste system can be defined as a form of social stratification based on hierarchically ranked, occupationally specialized, endogamous (in-marrying) groups. Caste is an ascribed rather than an achieved status, meaning that an individual is born into the caste niche that he or she will occupy throughout life.

There are four basic caste levels, or *varna* in the Hindu system. The highest ranked level is that of the *Brāhmin*, traditionally associated with the priesthood. The second level is that of the *Kṣatriya*, warriors and rulers, and the third is that of the *Vaiśya* or merchants. The bottom level is that of the *Śūdra*, the commoners. Beneath the four major *varna* of the system are the outcastes, or untouchables.

Within the *varna* categories of Hindu society are numerous smaller groupings called *jāti*. (The English word "caste" is used, somewhat confusingly, to refer to both *varna* and *jāti*.) Like the *varna* themselves, *jāti* are also ranked strictly in terms of social prestige. Intricate rules govern the interactions of the *jāti* in daily life; for example, some groups may not accept food from other groups, some groups have access to sacred scriptures and some do not, and some groups must indicate humility and subservience before other groups. In addition to rules that divide and separate people, however, there is another principle that unites them: *jajmani*, or the exchange of services. Through a *jajmani* relationship, a *jāti* of shoemakers might exchange services with a *jāti* of potters, for example, however separate they may be in other areas of social life.

HISTORY OF CASTE

Although some scholars search for the roots of India's caste system in the ancient civilization of the subcontinent, the Indus Valley or Harappan civilization, the earliest clear evidence for caste is found in the texts of Indo-European groups who migrated into the area in several waves beginning about 1500 B.C.E. These texts, collectively called the Vedas, or books of knowledge, which became the sacred texts of the Hindu religion, describe three classes of society roughly corresponding to the top three *varna* of the later system. Although archaeological and historical evidence for this ancient period is scanty, most people believe that the fourth, or *Śūdra varna* was added to the three Indo-European classes as these immigrants moved into the subcontinent, encountering indigenous people who were pushed to the lowest position in the social hierarchy. Supporting this scenario is the fact that the top three *varna* are called *ārya*, or "pure" (from "Aryan," another name for the Indo-Europeans), while the *Śūdra varna* is *anārya*, "impure" (un-Aryan). The untouchable stratum, with its particularly despised status, would have been added to the system as the migration southward forced the Indo-Europeans into contact with even more remote indigenous peoples.

Buddhism and Jainism, which arose during the fifth century B.C.E., were in part rebellions against Vedic society with its unequal social divisions. Both

Members of India's lower castes light candles in a peaceful plea for equal rights and nondiscrimination during the World Social Forum held in Bombay, India, in January, 2004. Delegates to the convention also called for non-discrimination against other oppressed minorities throughout the world. (AP/Wide World Photos)

religions renounced the institution of caste, and Buddhism became particularly popular in India by about the third century B.C.E. Afterward, however, there was a revival of Vedic tradition with its attendant social order, which became codified in legal treatises such as the Code of Manu. While it is unclear whether the rules prescribed for caste behavior in such texts were enforced, certainly the conception of what caste meant and how a caste system should function was solidified by the middle of the first millennium C.E. The religious tradition of Hinduism, which arose out of a synthesis of Vedicism, Buddhism, Jainism, and other strands of thought and culture, developed an intricate philosophical justification for caste that remains valid for many Hindus today.

RELIGIOUS JUSTIFICATION FOR CASTE

The Hindu understanding of caste is tied to the notion of reincarnation, an eschatology that sees souls as being reborn after death in an endless cycle. Dependent on the karma that people accumulate during their lifetimes, they might be reborn at higher or lower levels than during their previous lives. One implication of this vision is that the respect that one owes to high-caste individuals has been earned by them in previous lifetimes, and that the scorn heaped upon those of low birth is deserved because of similar past deeds.

Linked to this understanding of karma is the notion of dharma, or duty, meaning in the Hindu sense duty to one's caste niche. "One's own duty imperfectly performed is better than another's duty perfectly performed," is the wisdom offered by the *Bhagavadgītā*, a text holy to many Hindus. In one scene in this text, a *Kṣatriya* prince named Arjuna hesitates on the eve of battle out of an ethical concern for killing, and is advised by his charioteer Kṛṣṇa that since he is of *Kṣatriya*, or warrior, status, his dharma is to kill. The highest ethic for him is to do what he was born to do (that is, to fight), which will then accrue positive rather than negative karma. Another's dharma, and hence his or her karma, would be different. This is the particularism of Hinduism's ethical tradition, which leads to an unwillingness to generalize about rights and wrongs of human action in the universalist way familiar to most Westerners.

Another component of Hinduism's conceptualization of caste involves the traditional cosmogony in which the various levels of society were created out of the primordial cosmic being, the *Brāhmin* arising from his mouth, the *Kṣatriya* from his arms, the *Vaiśya* from his thighs, and the *Śūdra* from his feet. This vision of the divine spirit being equivalent to the social order itself leads to a sense of division and difference as themselves holy. Combined with the notion of a moral duty to accept one's caste position as discussed above, this image contributes to a deep resistance to change in the caste system.

Although caste has been legally abolished in modern India, it continues to function on many levels of social life. In recent years, there has been some attempt on the part of the government of India to uplift those of lower-caste backgrounds through preferential admissions and hiring policies, but caste conflict remains a potent force in Indian politics.

INTERPRETATIONS OF CASTE

Among many perspectives on the caste system, two general trends can be discerned. Some prefer to emphasize the consensus that is implicit in the conceptualization of society as an organic whole, contrasting this with the individualist and competitive character of social relations in Western societies. Others focus on the degree of conflict that is inherent in the caste model, which privileges some groups and subordinates others. The first of these is most common in the Indian Hindu community and is favored by many Indian and Western social scientists, while the second is expressed most vociferously by non-Hindu minorities and by Marxist scholars.

Western interpretations of caste are tied into the notion of cultural relativism—the idea that other cultures have to be understood in their own terms and not in those imposed by the West. While this concept leads many to respect caste as an indigenous form of social organization, others believe that it needs to be circumscribed by a cross-cultural commitment to hu-

man rights and basic equality. The caste system of India therefore provides an entry point to some of the key issues facing those who are interested in the study of other cultures.

Cynthia Keppley Mahmood

FURTHER READING

Das, Veena. *Structure and Cognition: Aspects of Hindu Caste and Ritual.* 2d ed. Delhi, India: Oxford University Press, 1990.

Dumont, Louis. *Homo Hierarchicus: The Caste System and Its Implications.* Translated by Mark Sainsbury, Louis Dumont, and Basia Gulati. Chicago: University of Chicago Press, 1980.

Freeman, James M. *Untouchable: An Indian Life History.* Stanford, Calif.: Stanford University Press, 1979.

Gupta, Dipankar. *Interrogating Caste: Understanding Hierarchy and Difference in Indian Society.* New York: Penguin Books, 2000.

Joshi, Barbara, ed. *Untouchable! Voices of the Dalit Liberation Movement.* London: Zed Books, 1986.

Kolenda, Pauline. *Caste in Contemporary India: Beyond Organic Solidarity.* Menlo Park, Calif.: Benjamin/Cummings, 1978.

McGilvray, Dennis B., ed. *Caste Ideology and Interaction.* New York: Cambridge University Press, 1982.

Naipaul, V. S. *India: A Million Mutinies Now.* London: Heinemann, 1990.

SEE ALSO: *Bhagavadgītā*; Discrimination; Hindu ethics; Inequality; Karma; Laozi; Poona Pact; Segregation; Sikh ethics.

Casuistry

DEFINITION: Method of resolving ethical dilemmas through the analysis and comparison of individual cases of decision making

TYPE OF ETHICS: Theory of ethics

SIGNIFICANCE: For millennia, casuistry was an influential method in Judaic and Christian ethics; it reemerged during the 1970's as a dominant approach in professional ethics and especially in bioethics.

Casuistry focuses on cases of decision making in which agreed-upon moral principles do not provide obvious answers about what would be the right action. The method involves comparing a difficult case with settled cases and using these comparisons, along with agreed-upon principles, to debate what should be done in the difficult case.

Casuistry is a natural method that is employed by nearly every human culture. It was self-consciously developed and taught in Greco-Roman rhetoric and in Judaism, and it was dominant in Christianity from 1200 to 1650. Casuistry decreased in influence thereafter, partly as a result of its abuse by some medieval authors to justify whatever decision they preferred, and partly as a result of the rise of systematic moral theory. Since a consensus on moral theory did not develop, however, and modernity brought new moral problems, casuistry continued to be employed. It has been especially prominent since the 1970's in professional ethics.

SEE ALSO: Applied ethics; Conscience; Dilemmas, moral; Intuitionist ethics; Medical ethics; Pascal, Blaise; Situational ethics.

Cell-phone etiquette

DEFINITION: Proper and improper use of cell phones in public places

TYPE OF ETHICS: Personal and social ethics

SIGNIFICANCE: The rapid growth of cell phones that began in the late 1980's has led to public debate on the ethics of using such in public.

Almost since the time that the first cell phones were introduced to the public in 1977, questions have been raised concerning the proper way to conduct cell-phone conversations in public places. By the middle to late 1980's, the cell-phone industry and the number of cell-phone customers was growing rapidly, and the early years of the twenty-first century users in North America numbered more than sixty million. The widespread use of cell phones has led to what many people consider misuse of cell phones. Some of the main grievances concerning inappropriate use of this relatively new industry include people talking on their phones in restaurants, theaters, checkout lines in stores, and their cars. In addition, interruptions due to cell-phone calls often disrupt classrooms and business meetings.

A 2003 survey conducted by the web site LetsTalk.com found that only 57 percent of cell-phone users turn off their ringers while in movie theaters and even fewer—43 percent—turn off their phones while in restaurants. This behavior is considered by many people to be unacceptable and has raised the issue of the need to curb cell-phone use in public places. In 2004, many Americans cities and states were considering legislation to ban cell phones from public places such as restaurants, theaters, and public transportation.

A more important consideration in cell-phone use is public safety. Using cell phones while driving vehicles is believed by many people to be more than simply ethically wrong; it is also seen as a safety issue. In response to this concern, New York became, in June 2001, the first state to require motorists to use hands-free devices to talk on cell phones while driving. Mean-

A driver entering the New Jersey Turnpike in early 2004 talks on his cell phone on the first day that a New Jersey law outlawed the use of hand-held cell phones by people driving vehicles. Some studies have shown that the rates of accidents involving drivers using cell phones are similar to those of accidents involving drunk drivers. (AP/Wide World Photos)

An Embarrassing Moment

Actor Brian Dennehy has developed a dislike of cell phones because of the disruptions they have caused in theaters in which he has performed. He had a particularly bad moment while starring in the Arthur Miller play *Death of a Salesman*, when a cell phone went off in the audience during the second act.

As he later recalled, the incident happened during a "very beautiful scene, heartbreaking scene, and this thing went off, and it went off, and it went off, and it went off." He finally simply said, "'Alright, let's stop. We'll wait while you find your phone and turn it off, have your conversation, whatever it is, but we'll just wait.' Well of course the guy was mortified and ran out of the theater."

while, as the cell-phone industry continues its rapid expansion, so too, does the debate over the need for legislation concerning the ethical uses of cell phones.

Kimberley M. Holloway

SEE ALSO: Computer technology; Confidentiality; Electronic mail; Electronic surveillance; Etiquette; Gossip; Invasion of privacy; Privacy.

Censorship

DEFINITION: Official scrutiny and consequent suppression or alteration of publications, performances, or art forms that fail to meet institutional standards

TYPE OF ETHICS: Arts and censorship

SIGNIFICANCE: Justification of censorship in virtually all cultures is founded upon policies concerning public welfare and morals; arguments against censorship center on the moral values of free expression and the open exchange of ideas. The strength of ethical convictions on both sides of the issue continues to fuel controversy.

Since classical times, proponents of censorship have invoked religion or government to promote the repression of material that purportedly threatened pub-

lic morals or controlling institutions. In this context, artistic expression has been targeted as potentially harmful by ancient philosophers, religious organizations, special-interest groups, and governmental bodies. Throughout the ages, the basic arguments for and against freedom of expression have remained remarkably consistent.

HISTORY

Plato was among the earliest proponents of censorship of the arts. His *Laws* (360 B.C.E.) argued for strict censorship of the literary and visual arts, particularly poetic metaphor, which he claimed interfered with achieving pure, conceptual truth.

Early Christianity took a similar position concerning mythology and art. The Roman Catholic Church eventually utilized censorship to control philosophical, artistic, and religious belief generally. In 1521, Holy Roman emperor Charles V issued the Edict of Worms, which prohibited the printing, dissemination, or reading of Martin Luther's work. The *Index librorum prohibitorum* (1564), which was published by the Vatican, condemned specific books. The *Index* eventually included such works as Galileo Galilei's *Dialogue Concerning the Two Chief World Systems* (1632); Galileo was subsequently prosecuted for heresy during the Inquisition.

The scope of governmental censorship in Europe changed with the separation of powers between the church and state. When church courts were abolished and religious beliefs and mores were no longer subject to government control, censorship laws focused on political speech and writing. Works criticizing government practices ran the risk of prosecution for seditious libel in England; in France, Napoleon censored newspapers, publications, theatrical productions, and even private correspondence at will.

Politically motivated censorship became common in countries with totalitarian governments, from communism to fascism. *The Communist Manifesto* (1848) of Karl Marx and Friedrich Engels was banned throughout Europe, yet subsequently communist leaders from V. I. Lenin to Mao Zedong to Fidel Castro routinely practiced political censorship. In the Soviet Union, political censorship targeted the arts when it imposed the doctrine of Socialist Realism in 1932. The following year in Germany, Adolf Hitler organized nationwide book burnings in the name of the National Socialist government.

Soviet-bloc writers, artists, and scientists have been imprisoned, exiled, and have had their work confiscated, when it has been deemed ideologically impure. Aleksandr Solzhenitsyn was arrested in 1945 for a pejorative remark about Joseph Stalin, spent eleven years in prison, and was finally exiled in 1974. In Muslim fundamentalist countries, religious censorship is the norm. For example, the publication of Salman Rushdie's *The Satanic Verses* (1989) prompted Iran's Ayatollah Khomeini to pronounce a *fatwa*, calling for Rushdie's death and forcing the author into seclusion.

Public political debate was given constitutional protection in some jurisdictions. Article 5 of the Basic Law of West Germany (1949) and Article 10 of the European Convention on Human Rights and Fundamental Freedoms (1953) specifically provided for free speech rights. The First Amendment to the U.S. Constitution, ratified in 1791, expressly prohibited Congress from making any law that abridged freedom of speech, press, religion, assembly, or the right to petition the government for redress of grievances. This right to free speech was not, however, absolute. The First Amendment has generated an enormous amount of litigation over its interpretation, particularly when it has collided with other rights in American society.

The degree to which the principle of free speech has been extended to the arts has been a matter of case law in all jurisdictions in which censorship has been scrutinized. Most troublesome for the courts has been the issue of the protection of allegedly obscene or pornographic material.

When free expression has come into conflict with potentially overriding public policy concerns, the courts have engaged in complex legal reasoning, often guided by philosophical and political arguments, in order to determine which interests dominate. Despite the evolution of cultural values, vestiges of several arguments remain common to most court deliberations of the free speech principle.

The argument from truth (also referred to as the libertarian argument) has been associated with the works of John Stuart Mill, but it was also articulated by John Milton two hundred years earlier. It emphasizes the importance of open discussion to the discovery of truth as a fundamental good and invaluable to the development of society. To some extent, this philosophy has been utilized by the U.S. Supreme

Court, first in Justice Oliver Wendell Holmes's now-famous dissent, in *United States v. Abrams* (1919), although its application is limited to speech with political, moral, aesthetic, or social content.

The argument from democracy views freedom of speech as a necessary component of any democratic society, in which public discussion is a political duty. Alexander Meiklejohn is one of its leading proponents, and similar theories are found in the works of Immanuel Kant, Baruch Spinoza, and David Hume. The constitutional scholar Alexander Meiklejohn considered the First Amendment a protection of the right of all citizens to discuss political issues and participate in government. Similarly, the German Constitutional Court and the European Court have recognized the importance of public debate on political questions. The argument from democracy has had little success in cases involving nonpolitical speech.

By contrast, the argument from individuality is rights-based rather than consequentialist, recognizing the interest of the speaker, rather than society, as being paramount. It asserts that there is an individual right to freedom of speech, even though its exercise may conflict with the welfare of society. A free expression rationale based solely on individual fulfillment has raised philosophical and legal quandaries when it has come into conflict with other equally important liberties.

The argument from the paradox justifies censorship in cases in which freedom of speech is exercised by those who would use it to eliminate the free speech principle itself. For example, in England, it was used to set regulations restricting the activities of the National Front. In the United States, those seeking to prohibit the marching of the Nazi Party in Skokie, Illinois, a predominantly Jewish suburb of Chicago, relied on this argument without success. The European Convention on Human Rights employed it as a fundamental consideration in Article 10, and it has been cited as authority for outlawing the German Communist Party.

The utilitarian argument suggests that the speech in question should be weighed for the balance of pleasure and pain. Its value is limited in assessing the extent of free speech protection contemplated by the U.S. Constitution, or other legislation with similar provisions.

The contractualist argument is a rights-based conception that excludes certain rights from state power, particularly the right to conscience. This argument asserts that the government violates this right when it superimposes its own value judgment on the speech at issue.

Censorship and the Arts in Europe

Artistic freedom is protected in Europe in all countries adhering to the European Convention of Human Rights and Fundamental Freedoms. Article 10 guarantees everyone the right to freedom of expression. Any prior restraints on publication must be justified as necessary in a democratic society in order to constitute permissible restraints on the free expression principle.

Germany's Basic Law, Article 5, provides for freedom of expression rights, specifically designating art, science, research, and teaching. This freedom of expression is, however, subject to a fundamental right to dignity and is limited by the provisions of the general laws. As a result, the German Constitutional Court has balanced the interests of free expression and other specific laws in a manner similar to that used by the U.S. Supreme Court.

Great Britain does not constitutionally protect speech; instead, it relies upon common law and administrative agencies to resolve issues involving free expression. Courts often articulate a common law principle of freedom of speech to limit the scope of other rules that impinge on this freedom. Prior restraint by licensing of the press was abolished in 1694, but films remain subject to scrutiny under the Video Recordings Act of 1985.

In 1979, a special committee, popularly known as "The Williams Committee," presented to the government its report containing studies and policies on obscenity and film censorship. Its findings, which recommended the restriction of material that is offensive to reasonable people, are frequently cited by the courts as well as by legal scholars.

Obscenity is prosecuted under the Obscene Publications Act of 1959, provided that the work is not justified as being for the public good or in the interest of science, literature, art, learning, or any other area of general concern. This exception to the obscenity law bears a strong resemblance to the balancing of interests tests utilized by American Supreme Court justices.

Censorship and the Arts in the United States

The constitutional guarantee of free speech was articulated in one simple phrase, yet its interpretation has been a matter of intricate, strenuous legal debate since its inception. When state laws are challenged as unconstitutional restraints on free speech, the ultimate determination of their legality rests with the U.S. Supreme Court. This court has established, on a case-by-case basis, both the scope and limitations of the free speech doctrine as well as its applicability to the states through the Fourteenth Amendment.

It has been argued that the drafters of the First Amendment contemplated only the protection of political speech. The path that the Supreme Court took in extending the free speech principle to the arts was long, arduous, and occasionally winding. Most instances of repression of the literary and visual arts have occurred under the guise of preservation of moral standards, pertaining to blasphemy and obscenity. Antivice movements and groups have operated on the premise that society needed protection from exposure to material that those movements and groups considered threatening to public morals. Although not necessarily acting under the color of state law, organizations such as the Legion of Decency, the New England Watch and Ward Society, and various independent groups constituting what became known as the "moral majority" have pressured municipalities and businesses into tacitly censoring material deemed offensive.

The U.S. Supreme Court began to address the extension of First Amendment protection beyond political speech during the 1940's. Blasphemy prosecutions are all but obsolete in the United States, but it was not until 1952 that the Supreme Court ruled that a film (*The Miracle*) could not be censored for sacrilegious content. The Court also ruled that motion pictures were included within the free speech and press guarantee of the First and Fourteenth Amendments; the importance of films as organs of public opinion was not lessened by the fact that they were designed to entertain as well as inform.

Literary and visual arts in the form of erotica have been afforded the least First Amendment protection. Obscenity has always been criminally sanctioned and subjected to prior restraints in the United States, based on numerous policy considerations: that it corrupts the individual, that it leads to sex-related crime and illegal sexual activity, that it serves no socially redeeming purpose, and that it is lacking in any solid element of the search for truth.

Until 1934, American courts relied on the English common law Hicklin test when determining whether a given work was to be considered illegally obscene. *Regina v. Hicklin* (1868) defined the test of obscenity as whether the tendency of the matter is to deprave and corrupt those whose minds are open to such immoral influences and into whose hands a publication of this sort may fall. Thus, a publication was judged obscene if any isolated passage within it could corrupt the most susceptible person.

The Hicklin rule was replaced by the "Ulysses standard," first articulated in *United States v. One Book Entitled Ulysses* (1934), which required that the entire work, rather than an isolated passage, be evaluated for its libidinous effect. The Supreme Court continued to proclaim in *Chaplinsky v. New Hampshire* (1942) that there were certain well-defined and narrowly limited classes of speech that are of such slight social value as to be clearly outweighed by the social interest in order and morality. Such classes of speech included the lewd and obscene, the profane, the libelous, and insulting words that by their utterance inflict injury.

The first landmark case setting forth a standard for determining whether a work was to be considered obscene, and therefore undeserving of First Amendment protection, was *Roth v. United States* (1957). The Court, in upholding convictions for violations of California and federal obscenity statutes, found that the statutes did not violate constitutional standards. The Court stated that the test for obscenity was whether the average person, applying contemporary community standards, would find that the dominant theme of the material, taken as a whole, appealed to prurient interest.

Three years later, the Supreme Court found that a Chicago city ordinance requiring submission of film for examination as a prerequisite to obtaining a permit for public exhibition was not void as a prior restraint under the First Amendment. In *Times Film Corp. v. City of Chicago* (1961), the Court indicated that there is no complete and absolute freedom to exhibit, even once, any and every kind of motion picture. The Court limited the scope of the First Amendment, based on the overriding societal interest in preserving the decency of the community, as-

suming that the ordinance was directed at obscenity.

In applying the "*Roth* standard" in *Jacobellis v. Ohio* (1964), the Court found the motion picture *Les Amants* not to be obscene and overturned the prosecution of a theater manager who had exhibited the film. The court stated that obscenity is excluded from constitutional protection only because it is utterly without redeeming social importance, and that the portrayal of sex in art, literature, and scientific works is not in itself sufficient reason to deny material the constitutional protection of freedom of speech and press.

In 1970, a presidential commission appointed to study the statistical correlation, if any, between crime and pornography published its conclusions, finding that there was no direct correlation. There was, however, considerable dissension among the members of the committee, who sought to lodge their conclusions separately.

In 1973, *Miller v. California* was decided, again refining an earlier standard set in *Memoirs v. Massachusetts* (1966). The test for obscenity established three standards that must be independently met in order for a work to be removed from the umbrella of First Amendment protection: whether the average person, applying contemporary community standards, would find that the work, taken as a whole, appeals to prurient interest; whether the work depicts or describes, in a patently offensive way, sexual conduct specifically defined by the applicable state law; and whether the work, taken as a whole, lacks serious literary, artistic, political, or scientific value.

Consequently, a work that had political value was protected, regardless of its prurient appeal and offensive depiction of sexual activities. Sexually explicit art was immune if it demonstrated serious artistic value. Subsequent cases have made it clear that works found by a reasonable person to have serious artistic value are protected from censorship, regardless of whether the government or a majority approve of the ideas these works represent.

A companion case to *Miller v. California, Paris Adult Theater I et al. v. Slaton*, held that a state could prohibit hard-core pornographic films. Although there were extensive dissenting opinions, the majority categorically disapproved the theory that obscene, pornographic films acquire constitutional immunity from state regulation simply because they are exhibited for consenting adults; they stated further that the states have a legitimate interest in regulating the use of obscene material in local commerce and in all places of public accommodation. The Court concluded that a legislature could quite reasonably determine that a connection between antisocial behavior and obscene material does or might exist.

In October of 1989, the "*Miller* standard" of obscenity became controversial outside the courts. A censorious bill proposed by Senator Jesse Helms, which sought to restrict and punish the National Endowment for the Arts (NEA) for allegedly funding "obscene" art, was defeated. Congressional critics had assailed the NEA for funding two controversial projects: a photography exhibit by Robert Mapplethorpe that included homoerotic images and an exhibit by Andres Serrano entitled "Piss Christ," which was criticized as sacrilegious. Congress passed instead a compromise bill that removed most penalties against specific artists and institutions but required that the NEA observe legal bans on obscenity by employing standards reminiscent of the language in *Miller v. California*. Further, grant recipients were required to sign a nonobscenity oath.

Subsequently, many organizations and artists refused to sign the oath, and several initiated lawsuits against the NEA. *Bella Lewitzky Dance Foundation v. Frohnmayer et al.* (1991) held that the nonobscenity oath requirement was unconstitutional. Artists and legal scholars alike voiced strenuous objections to the *Miller*-style decency standards of the legislation, particularly because the determination of obscenity was made by NEA panelists and administrators rather than by peer review, and because the standards ignored the nature and purpose of postmodern art, which rejects the previous definition that art must be "serious."

In June, 1992, a United States District Court heard the suit of *Karen Finley et al. v. National Endowment for the Arts and John Frohnmayer*, in which four performance artists whose grant applications were denied by the NEA brought suit alleging improper denial of the grant applications. The governing statute as amended in 1990 provided that artistic merit was to be judged taking into consideration general standards of decency and respect for the diverse beliefs and values of the American public. The Court found that the decency provision violated the Fifth Amendment's due process requirement. It further held that the public funding of art is entitled to First Amendment protection and that the decency clause on its face violates the First Amendment on the basis of overbreadth.

The influence of ethical arguments throughout the constitutional case law concerning censorship and the arts is unmistakable. Throughout the twentieth century, the Supreme Court has labored to give contemporary meaning to the terms of the First Amendment, affording broad freedom of expression to the arts while balancing various community values and shifting interests in a pluralistic society.

Kathleen O'Brien

FURTHER READING

Barendt, Eric. *Freedom of Speech*. Oxford, England: Clarendon Press, 1985. A comparative treatment of the protection afforded speech and other forms of expression in the United States, the United Kingdom, Germany, and countries adhering to the European Convention.

Egendorf, Laura K., ed. *Censorship*. San Diego, Calif.: Greenhaven Press, 2001. An anthology of opposing viewpoint essays arguing each side of controversial issues in censorship. Issues covered include the role of government in regulating popular culture, the existence of censorship in the educational system, and whether to censor speech or pornography.

Gerber, Albert B. *Sex, Pornography, and Justice*. New York: Lyle Stuart, 1965. A complete study of the topic from the Middle Ages to the twentieth century, including exhibits of the items that came before the courts. Updated supplements are available.

Hurwitz, Leon. *Historical Dictionary of Censorship in the United States*. Westport, Conn.: Greenwood Press, 1985. An overview of the types of expression subjected to repression in the United States, with cases, concepts, terms, and events listed alphabetically with brief summaries. An extensive bibliography and a table of cases make the book a useful reference tool.

Richards, David A. J. *Toleration and the Constitution*. New York: Oxford University Press, 1986. Provides a contractualist account of U.S. constitutional law regarding religious liberty, free speech, and constitutional protection of privacy.

Schauer, Frederick. *Free Speech: A Philosophical Enquiry*. Cambridge, England: Cambridge University Press, 1982. Draws extensively on legal rules and examples to present the author's political philosophy as well as his analysis of the right to free speech principle and the variety of communication that it includes.

SEE ALSO: Academic freedom; Art; Art and public policy; Book banning; First Amendment; Freedom of expression; *Index librorum prohibitorum*; Library Bill of Rights; Mapplethorpe, Robert; Pentagon Papers; Political correctness.

Cesarean sections

DEFINITION: Surgical delivery of a viable fetus through an incision in the uterus
DATE: First documented procedure on a living woman in 1610; routine use began during the 1960's
TYPE OF ETHICS: Bioethics
SIGNIFICANCE: Obstetricians claim that the cesarean section is a life-saving procedure, but its opponents claim that it is dangerous major surgery and that 80 percent of its use is for the convenience of physicians.

In Roman times, cesarean sections (C-sections) were legally required if a pregnant mother was dead or dying. In the modern United States, C-sections are necessary to save the life of mother and baby when a baby cannot be born vaginally. This happens in a total of 5 percent of births. In the United States, however, C-sections are performed in 30 percent of births. Obstetricians defend the high rate by saying that it is better to have an unnecessary C-section than to risk losing a baby and that a C-section can end the pain of a long and difficult labor.

Opponents of C-sections, such as the Cesarean Prevention Movement, attribute the high rate to obstetricians' fear of lawsuits, poor training in managing the natural process of birth, lack of patience for the variations in and length of normal labor and birth; and naive enthusiasm for using the latest technological interventions. As a result of these deficiencies, opponents allege, obstetricians subject mothers to

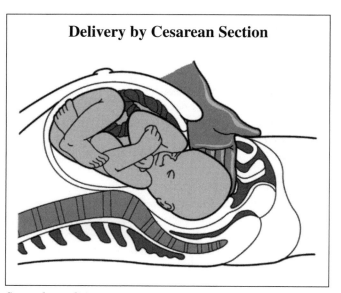

Delivery by Cesarean Section

Several conditions may necessitate the delivery of a baby through an incision in the lower abdomen instead of through the birth canal, including fetal distress or the inability of the baby's head to fit through the mother's pelvis

unnecessary surgery, including unnecessary pain, recovery time, scarring, and financial expense, as well as the risk of infection, adhesions, and bad reactions to anesthesia.

Laura Duhan Kaplan

SEE ALSO: Bioethics; Birth control; Birth defects; Medical ethics; Parenting.

Character

DEFINITION: Person's pattern of behavior related to the moral qualities of self-discipline and social responsibility
TYPE OF ETHICS: Theory of ethics
SIGNIFICANCE: Consideration of a person's character is a common method for evaluating the person's level of moral and ethical development.

The terms "character" and "personality" are sometimes used interchangeably, although character is more apt to be associated with behavioral and attitudinal characteristics that are consistent with the ethical standards of a community. It is thought that a wholesome character is not inherited but begins to form during the early years of the child's life and continues to form into adulthood.

During the mid-1920's, Hugh Hartshorne and Mark May were funded by the Institute of Social and Religious Research to conduct a study that came to be known as the Character Education Project. The purpose of the project was to ascertain the effect of character education programs on the ethical behavior of children. The study took five years and produced three volumes, all published under the title, *Studies in the Nature of Character.* Almost 11,000 children, ages eleven through sixteen, in both private and public schools were tested for behaviors that could be labeled "character."

Tests included situations in which the children had opportunities to cheat by copying answers, situations in which they had the opportunity to lie by answering in the affirmative such questions as "I always obey my parents cheerfully" and "I always smile when things go wrong," and situations in which it was possible for them to steal by taking money out of a coin box on their desk. More than 17,000 tests were given. The purpose was not to counter any student regarding his or her behavior but rather to determine for the group as a whole the variables that correlate with good character.

It was found that almost all children were dishonest under some circumstances but not under others. Moral behavior tended to be specific to the situation. Age and gender were not relevant. Furthermore, children who participated in organized programs of religious education or other programs emphasizing character development were not more honest than children without this training. What did make a difference was that children who were less apt to cheat or lie or steal were more intelligent and came from homes that were better off socioeconomically. Siblings also tended to resemble each other, showing the influence of the family.

The Hartshorne and May study has been used to discredit organized programs in character education. Simply telling the child what is right and what is wrong was not sufficient to produce good character. Methods other than direct instruction would need to be implemented. Moral educators came to believe that children must understand why it is important to be honest or brave or kind. Children also need to be actively involved in learning how they can show

these favorable characteristics in their day-to-day dealings with others. Participatory decision making and opportunities to practice the desired character traits are essential.

CHARACTER EDUCATION

The American Institute for Character Education, which developed the Character Education Curriculum in 1970, based its program on "a worldwide study of value systems" and identified fifteen basic values "shared by all major cultures and world religions." These values are courage, conviction, generosity, kindness, helpfulness, honesty, honor, justice, tolerance, the sound use of time and talents, freedom of choice, freedom of speech, good citizenship, the right to be an individual, and the right of equal opportunity.

Almost all character education programs list individual character traits. Boston University's Character Education program emphasizes such basic virtues as honesty, courage, persistence, loyalty, and kindness, which students learn from studying the lessons of history and reading good literature. The Heartwood Project in the Pittsburgh Public Schools has seven universal values developed for children at the elementary grades. Courage, loyalty, justice, respect, hope, honesty, and love are learned through stories, songs, art, and saying the seven virtue words in another language. The development of character comes not only from knowing what society expects of its members but also from a desire to incorporate that expectation into one's daily life.

Thomas Lickona writes that good character consists of knowing the good, desiring the good, and doing the good—habits of the mind, habits of the heart, and habits of action. His integrated approach to character development consists of fifteen components. Moral knowing is composed of awareness, values, perspective-taking, reasoning, decision making, and self-knowledge; moral feeling includes conscience, self-esteem, empathy, loving the good, self-control, and humility; and moral action incorporates competence, will, and habit. For each of these fifteen components, illustrations are given and suggestions are offered as to how they can be taught to children.

There have always been persons in every society who are so deficient in their moral makeup that they are said to have a "character disorder." Many of these persons are average or above average in intelligence, are neither neurotic nor psychotic, and can verbalize the rules of society. Yet they seem unable to understand why they should obey the rules or conform to the expectations of others. Sometimes called "sociopathic," they tend to project blame onto others, taking no responsibility for their own failures. They act impulsively, are unconcerned about the rights and privileges of others, are pathological liars, are unable to form deep attachments to other persons, display poor judgment and planning, and lack emotional control. The prognosis for such persons who are in therapy is poor, since they experience little anxiety or distress because of their social maladjustment and are unwilling or unable to see why they should change.

Bonnidell Clouse

FURTHER READING

Axtell, Guy, ed. *Knowledge, Belief, and Character: Readings in Virtue Epistemology.* Lanham, Md.: Rowman & Littlefield, 2000.

Clouse, Bonnidell. *Teaching for Moral Growth: A Guide for the Christian Community.* Wheaton, Ill.: Victor Press, 1993.

Doris, John M. *Lack of Character: Personality and Moral Behavior.* New York: Cambridge University Press, 2002.

Hartshorne, Hugh, and M. A. May. *Studies in Deceit.* Studies in the Nature of Character 1. New York: Macmillan, 1928. Reprint. New York: Arno, 1975.

Hartshorne, Hugh, M. A. May, and J. B Maller. *Studies in Service and Self-Control.* Studies in the Nature of Character 2. New York: Macmillan, 1928-1930.

Hartshorne, Hugh, M. A. May, and F. K. Shuttleworth. *Studies in the Organization of Character.* Studies in the Nature of Character 3. New York: Macmillan, 1930.

Lickona, Thomas. *Educating for Character: How Our Schools Can Teach Respect and Responsibility.* New York: Bantam Books, 1991.

Pritchard, Ivor. *Moral Education and Character.* Washington, D.C.: U.S. Department of Education, 1988.

SEE ALSO: Dignity; Godparents; Integrity; Loyalty; Personal relationships; Pride; Responsibility; Self-control; Self-respect; Self-righteousness.

Charity

DEFINITION: Propensity to share one's property and person with others in order to alleviate their wants

TYPE OF ETHICS: Theory of ethics

SIGNIFICANCE: Charity is grounded in a recognition of the interdependence of humans and an ethical imperative to act based upon recognition of the needs of others. When a society institutes benefits designed to motivate charity, such as tax deductions, the needy benefit, even as the authenticity of the charitable act may be called into question.

Every culture and religion recognizes the necessity of charity to healthy social and personal living. The unconditioned giving of oneself and one's possessions to alleviate the basic needs of others is the foundation of a good society.

The experience of receiving an unexpected gift is one that is enjoyed by most people. The experience of giving an unsolicited gift has been known by many people. These experiences of giving and receiving are fundamental to being charitable, since charity is both the act of giving and the act of receiving the basic necessities of life. Sharing is always a mutual action.

Modern Western culture is ambivalent about the place of such gift-giving in personal and social affairs. To clarify the reasons for this ambivalence, it is necessary first to review the etymology of the word "charity" and the history of the practice of charity in Western culture. Then it is possible to review the paradoxical nature of charity in modern American culture.

ETYMOLOGY AND HISTORY

The word "charity" comes from the old French *charité* and the Latin *caritas*. The Latin word is a translation of the Greek New Testament word *agape*. Most modern translators of the Bible translate *agape* as love. Love of one's neighbor and charity toward one's neighbor originally, and until recently, meant the same thing. Charitable acts such as feeding the hungry, giving water to the thirsty, providing homes for the homeless, educating the ignorant, giving medicine to the sick, burying the dead, and visiting those in prison were seen as acts of love to those in need. These acts of love were performed in imitation of the God who freely gave humans life.

In Western cultures, the concept of charity is closely associated with Christianity. The following of Jesus Christ's command to love, or be charitable to others, was institutionalized by placing some Church officials, deacons, in charge of these institutional acts of charity/love and by establishing institutional means, such as collecting food, to aid those in need. Every Christian had the obligation to love his or her neighbor. The community of Christians, the Church, understood love of neighbor as essential to its mission. During the Middle Ages (500-1500), groups of men and women, religious orders, organized themselves to continue this mission of the Church and thus dedicated themselves to educating the ignorant, feeding the hungry, clothing the unclothed, caring for the slaves and imprisoned, healing the sick, and caring for orphans.

With the advent of the modern Western state in the eighteenth century and that of the social sciences in the nineteenth century, the questions of who should care for the needy, how to train those who cared for the needy, and whether to care for the needy arose. In general, the care of the needy began to be seen in Europe as an obligation of the state in the eighteenth century and gradually began to be accepted as a governmental obligation by many people during the first quarter of the twentieth century in the United States. The obligation to love or be charitable toward one's neighbor continued to be recognized as an essential ingredient of an individual's life—and certainly of the Church's existence—but the means for fulfilling this command gradually became part of the government and came under the control of professionals.

WEALTH AND POVERTY

The evolving social sciences and the ideologies that supported them developed a different view of gaining and possessing wealth. Before the mid-nineteenth century, the possession of great wealth was seen as a danger to the individual and society. Wealth was for sharing. The poor were acknowledged and cared for because, it was understood, anyone could become poor. Life, riches, and personal abilities were all gifts from God that could easily be lost. Thus, both rich and poor acknowledged the tenuousness of their position. With the advent of entrepreneurial capitalism and Social Darwinism, everyone began to be seen as destined to be rich and to possess the goods of this earth. The poor were seen as poor because they

did not work hard enough or had bad habits or genes or some other fault. It was their own fault that the poor were poor, it was claimed. The rich were rich because of their own initiative and work.

Since being in need was perceived as being one's own fault, the poor should not be rewarded by being given the basic necessities of life. They needed a stimulus for work. That stimulus was poverty. If, for whatever reason, the state did help individuals with the basic necessities of life, the state should never deprive the rich of the wealth that they had gained through their hard work. The command to love and the command to share was replaced by the demand for the ideological means to reduce one's guilt in the face of the starving, unclothed, and homeless. Institutions were developed in order to professionalize and economize the care of the needy. Thus, the needy were gradually segregated into institutions according to their specific needs: hospitals, orphanages, schools, and prisons. One result of such institutionalization was the invisibility of those in need. Charity became professionalized, love eroticized, and the possession of wealth individualized. Consequently, the original command to love one's neighbor through acts of charity/love lost all meaning, and with it the sense of community and self changed. Charity was no longer the sharing of one's goods with those in need, but rather the giving of one's leftovers to those who had failed.

COMPETITION AND SELF-SACRIFICE

The goal of competition is to win. Life, as competition, results in winners and losers. What part does charity play when one wins or loses? Should one accept the necessities of life from the winner? Should one provide the loser with the necessities of life, knowing that these provisions may enable that person to challenge one again? If one never aids the losers, what kind of a human being is one? If everyone always and everywhere acts only out of selfishness, what becomes of community?

Some modern authors argue that humans always act out of selfishness. Even at one's most giving moments, it is claimed, one is actually seeking self-gratification. This psychological claim is reflected in philosophical studies that make a distinction between *agape*, or disinterested love, and *eros*, or sensual love. True charity is then disinterested charity, something no human can do on his or her own. Only

God can provide the ability to act out of *agape*. Followers of these contemporary authors are left with a cynical distrust of anyone who does good.

Actually, love can be both gratifying and sacrificial. It is paradoxical but nevertheless true that people act against every obvious self-interest in performing such heroic acts as jumping in front of a speeding car to save a child and jumping on a live hand grenade to save the lives of fellow soldiers. To risk death or to die for others may be interpreted as inherently pleasurable to the risk taker or the dead hero, but these theories seem to be held in the face of obvious contradiction. Even if true, they should not be used to destroy all charity, if only because of the obvious result: A world without love and charity would be a world devoid of humanity as people now know it.

Nathan R. Kollar

FURTHER READING

Bartkowski, John P., and Helen A. Regis. *Charitable Choices: Religion, Race, and Poverty in the Post Welfare Era*. New York: New York University, 2003.

Friedman, Lawrence J., and Mark D. McGarvie, eds. *Charity, Philanthropy, and Civility in American History*. New York: Cambridge University Press, 2003.

Gaylin, Willard, et al. *Doing Good: The Limits of Benevolence*. New York: Pantheon Books, 1978.

Outka, Gene. *Agape: An Ethical Analysis*. New Haven, Conn.: Yale University Press, 1972.

SEE ALSO: Altruism; Benevolence; Christian ethics; Greed; Homeless care; Service to others; Welfare rights.

Cheating

DEFINITION: Willful violation of rules with the intent to benefit oneself
TYPE OF ETHICS: Personal and social ethics
SIGNIFICANCE: As an ethical violation for personal gain, cheating is one of the central issues addressed by any system of personal ethics.

Broadly speaking, cheating can be taken to mean any violation of known social norms, therefore encompassing all deliberate deception and lawbreaking. A narrower interpretation restricts cheating only to situations in which an individual has voluntarily agreed to behave according to a set of rules and willfully violates those rules for personal gain. Examples of such cases are games and marketplace behavior. In the former, rules are usually explicit; in the latter, rules may be implicit—taking the form of customs—or may be explicit or even established by law. Often, the punishment for cheating is limited to expulsion from the activity. Cheating is similar to breaking a personal promise in that a person willfully breaks an expected standard of behavior; it differs in that the standard was set socially rather than individually.

FORMS OF CHEATING

All immoral action can be taken to constitute cheating, but most disc.ussions limit cheating to several broad areas. Cheating is taken to mean willful breaking of rules. The breaking of formal established rules, such as laws, most often falls outside discussions of cheating. The innocent violation of rules is not considered to be cheating; even though "ignorance of the law is no excuse," a person is not said to have cheated by violating a rule of which he or she was unaware. Cheating is deliberate behavior.

The clearest cases of cheating are those in which individuals deliberately violate rules that they have willingly agreed to follow. Games provide some examples. By participating in a game, a player agrees to follow the rules of the game. Cheating takes place when a player violates the rules with the intention of winning. This behavior takes advantage of other players who follow the rules. Clearly, if everyone cheated, games would cease to have any meaning and would cease to exist. This would deprive people of any enjoyment they derive from playing games.

Societies have rules in the forms of laws and social conventions. Lawbreaking is usually, but not always, a clear violation of social norms. The exceptions occur in cases in which there is a perception that the law is widely violated or is irrelevant to the situation. Such cases include speeding, jaywalking, and cheating on taxes. Even though all of those behaviors are violations of laws, many people do not believe themselves to have behaved unethically by performing those behaviors, since "everyone does it." Unwritten social conventions include positive reinforcement for helping those in need and prohibitions against eavesdropping, spreading gossip, and skipping ahead in lines, to name only a few.

Ethical issues arise when people argue that they do not enter into social contracts voluntarily and thus are not bound by those contracts. Examples include taxpayers who argue that they did not vote for the tax

---

Forms That Cheating May Take

Criminal
- Forgery
- Bribery of officials
- Tax fraud
- Tax evasion
- Misrepresentation on tax forms

Games and gambling
- Marking cards
- Stacking decks
- Altering dice
- Bribing athletes to underperform
- Drugging animals
- Using steroids or other banned substances
- Illegally signaling gaming partners

Marriage
- Infidelity

Employment
- Lying on resumes or employment applications
- Submitting false expense accounts
- Claiming hours not worked
- Taking credit for work done by others

Schoolwork
- Stealing examinations
- Copying from other students' work
- Having someone else do one's homework
- Plagiarism

Driving
- Speeding
- Rolling stops through intersections
- Parking in restricted areas

Shopping
- Purchasing mislabeled items at prices known to be too low
- Requesting unauthorized discounts

Self-discipline
- Dieting or other regimens
- Cheating at solitaire

---

laws and students who state that they are in school against their will and thus are not subject to its rules. As in games, when people violate social contracts, even those entered into implicitly (through citizenship in society) or against individuals' will, those contracts become meaningless and people become less certain of what they can expect of others. Behavior becomes less cooperative and more self-serving and protective.

MISREPRESENTATION

Misrepresentation, or lying, is a particular case of violation of rules. One of the most basic social conventions is that people should tell the truth. In some cases, as in courts of law or on legal documents, that convention is enforced by threat of legal sanction. In many cases, people simply rely on each other to tell the truth.

In the United States, laws specifically cover many types of misrepresentation, including that in many sales contracts, employment contracts, and even the marriage contract. Cheating behavior involving any of these contracts gives the damaged party the right to dissolve the contract and possibly to claim damages. Other countries that rely less on the legal system to settle disputes have not codified prohibitions against misrepresentation to the same extent, instead relying on social conventions and social sanctions against those found to misrepresent themselves.

ETHICAL IMPLICATIONS

Cheating involves taking advantage of a situation to gain an unfair advantage. In competitions of all sorts, the objective is to win, but winning carries less meaning when the rules of the game are violated. A student who cheats on a test, for example, appears to have proved attainment of knowledge but instead has proved only the ability to defeat any monitoring system. To the extent that cheating is successful, it punishes those who behave ethically and honestly by giving rewards to those who cheat. This harm to society is one reason that many social conventions have been codified into law. The same reasoning helps to explain why payment of taxes is not voluntary and is subject to rules, with punishment for violation. Individuals would believe themselves to be gaining by violating any voluntary system of taxation, but the society as a whole would lose because there would be insufficient money to allow the government to provide goods for the benefit of everyone. In cases where conventions are important to society, governments tend to mandate behavior through laws rather than relying on people to behave ethically.

A. J. Sobczak

FURTHER READING

Brandt, Richard B. *A Theory of the Good and the Right*. Foreword by Peter Singer. Rev. ed. Amherst, N.Y.: Prometheus Books, 1998.

Callahan, David. *The Cheating Culture: Why More Americans Are Doing Wrong to Get Ahead*. Orlando, Fla.: Harcourt, 2004.

Gert, Bernard. *The Moral Rules: A New Rational Foundation for Morality*. New York: Harper & Row, 1970.

Harman, Gilbert. *The Nature of Morality: An Introduction to Ethics*. New York: Oxford University Press, 1977.

Lande, Nathaniel, and Afton Slade. *Stages: Understanding How You Make Your Moral Decisions*. San Francisco: Harper & Row, 1979.

Langone, John. *Thorny Issues: How Ethics and Morality Affect the Way We Live*. Boston: Little, Brown, 1981.

Shermer, Michael. *The Science of Good and Evil: Why People Cheat, Gossip, Care, Share, and Follow the Golden Rule*. New York: Times Books, 2004.

Weiss, Paul, and Jonathan Weiss. *Right and Wrong: A Philosophical Dialogue Between Father and Son*. New York: Basic Books, 1967.

SEE ALSO: College applications; Conscience; Fairness; Fraud; Integrity; Lying; Moral education; Resumes; Taxes; Temptation; Universalizability.

Chemical warfare

DEFINITION: Use of chemical substances as military weapons

TYPE OF ETHICS: Military ethics

SIGNIFICANCE: Chemical agents, along with biological and nuclear agents, are categorized as nonconventional weapons; the nature of the damage they cause to their targets, the increased collateral damage associated with them, and the history of their use against nonmilitary targets all raise special ethical issues.

A nation engaged in military aggression inevitably causes human casualties on the opposing side, but the development of toxic chemical agents against an enemy poses special moral problems for a nation. Chemical weapons can be effective in a variety of military situations. When used against unprotected individuals, they cause painful, lingering death and injuries.

HISTORY

The use of toxic chemical substances in warfare dates to ancient times. This includes the use of toxic substances to poison soldiers' drinking water and the production of poisonous clouds of sulfur dioxide by burning sulfur and pitch during battles. Condemnation of these primitive forms of chemical warfare also dates from these early times, as reflected in an ancient Roman quotation: "War is waged with weapons, not with poison."

Modern chemical warfare began during World War I. Germany released deadly chlorine gas from thousands of cylinders against French and British troops at Ypres in Belgium in 1915. As a result, more than 5,000 men were killed in the attack. Later, Germany also employed phosgene and mustard gas. By the end of the war, both sides had used chemical weapons, causing more than 1.25 million casualties, including 90,000 deaths. After the war, families and friends of veterans exposed to chemical weapons were shocked to see their effect—coughing and gasping for breath and horrible scars on the victims. Public outrage sparked a worldwide drive to eliminate the use of these weapons in future conflicts, leading to the Geneva Protocol of 1925 prohibiting the use of poison gas in warfare. This agreement was signed by all the world's major powers except the United States and Japan.

Although they were never used in combat, highly toxic nerve agents were developed by Germany during World War II. With the surrender of Germany, the United States army came into possession of one such substance, sarin, an incredibly lethal compound; one drop could kill fifty men. Since the end of World War II, some countries, including the United States, have continued to manufacture and store chemical weapons, but they have been employed in only a few of the more than two hundred wars fought since

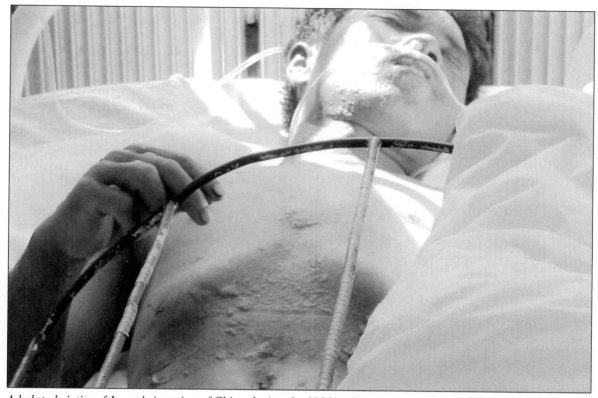

A belated victim of Japan's invasion of China during the 1930's, this man was severely burned in August, 2003, by the contents of a mustard gas canister left by Japanese troops in northern China decades earlier. (AP/Wide World Photos)

World War II. They were used by Italy in Ethiopia and by Japan in China during the 1930's and 1940's, in Yemen during the 1960's, and in the Iran-Iraq conflict during the 1980's. Although chemical weapons were not used in the Persian Gulf War of 1991 or the U.S.-led coalition invasion of Iraq in 2003, military units fought in chemical protective clothing as a preventative measure.

In 1995, Aum Shinrikyo, a Japanese religious cult, released the chemical agent Sarin in the Tokyo subway system and planned other attacks with chemical weapons in Japan. Eight people were killed and hundreds were injured. This incident proved how dangerous chemical weapons could be and how real a threat they posed if they were to fall into the hands of terrorist organizations. After terrorist attacks on New York City and Washington, D.C., in September, 2001, many nations expanded their defenses against weapons of mass destruction, including chemical agents.

The international community reacted diplomatically to the continuing threat of chemical weapons. In April, 1997, the Chemical Weapons Convention (CWC) was ratified by eighty-seven countries and formally established in the United Nations. The CWC included extensive provisions for monitoring compliance with a goal of destroying all stockpiles of chemical weapons by the year 2007. By 2004, 158 countries had signed the convention.

ETHICAL PRINCIPLES

The ethics of using chemical weapons focus on several important issues. Proponents of chemical weapons cite several arguments justifying the use of these weapons: First, military strength is a deterrent to a nation or state contemplating aggression toward another nation. If the types of weapons potentially available for use are restricted, this may reduce the deterrent factor. Therefore, all kinds of weapons—conventional, nuclear, chemical, and biological—

should be available for use. Second, while chemical weapons produce human casualties, they do not, like conventional weapons, destroy inanimate objects such as roads, houses, hospitals, and bridges. Reconstruction of cities devastated by chemical weapons is therefore likely to be quicker and less costly.

A third issue is that chemical weapons can be effective in a variety of situations. For example, they can be used against concentrated or dispersed troops, against troops that are above or below ground, or against concealed troops. Fourth, if an enemy is believed to possess a chemical weapon capability, it forces soldiers to wear cumbersome protective devices that may hinder their effectiveness. The fear of chemical weapons may also affect the morale of soldiers. Fifth, unlike biological weapons, which are impossible to contain, the application and control of chemical weapons are relatively easy to maintain. Sixth, injuries inflicted by chemical weapons are not necessarily more terrible than those inflicted by the weapons of conventional warfare. Flying fragments of hot metal from conventional weapons can produce horrible injuries comparable in severity to those caused by chemical weapons.

By contrast to the above arguments, opponents of chemical weapon use cite the following arguments. First, many political and military leaders have had an aversion to employing chemical warfare because of the insidious nature of these substances and their effects on humans. In the case of nerve gases, they produce intense sweating; the filling of bronchial passages with mucus; decreased vision; uncontrollable vomiting, defecation, and convulsions; and eventual paralysis and respiratory failure leading to death. Other less lethal agents can produce painful blisters and blindness. In addition, the long-term effect of exposure to some chemical weapons is difficult to quantify. Second, while chemical weapons are effective when used against unprotected individuals, they have minimal effect against soldiers wearing gas masks and protective clothing. Third, although chemical weapons are more predictable than biological weapons, weather conditions and human error may still result in chemical weapons reaching unprotected nonmilitary targets. Fourth, compared to conventional weapons, chemical weapons are somewhat easier and cheaper to obtain and manufacture. Consequently, they are more likely to be used in conflicts within Third World countries. This was the case in the Iran-Iraq conflict in the 1980's, in which Iraq employed chemical weapons not only against Iran but also within its own border on the civilian Kurdish population.

Demonstration of an airport security device on the opening day of the Milipol 2003 exposition at Le Bourget airport near Paris, France. As the woman stands inside the General Electric Ion Track EntryScan3 portal, fans blow air past her that is then scanned for microscopic particles of explosives and drugs. The GE Ion Track is an example of new technology being developed in the ongoing struggle against biochemical warfare. (AP/Wide World Photos)

Military operations—whether they involve conventional or chemical weapons—that cause the widespread injury and death of civilians are condemned by most nations. For the reasons outlined above, most nations possessing chemical weapons could justify their use only in retaliation if they themselves were subject to a chemical weapons attack. Because of the many problems of chemical weapons, including their safe manufacture, storage, transportation, and disposal, most nations are reluctant to acquire these weapons of destruction, let alone use them. Terrorist organizations, although restrained by these same factors, may be less reluctant to use chemical weapons in the future. Hence governments have to be prepared to react to the use of chemical weapons upon civilian populations.

Nicholas C. Thomas
Theodore M. Vestal

FURTHER READING

Cole, Leonard A. *The Eleventh Plague: The Politics of Biological and Chemical Warfare.* New York: W. H. Freeman, 1997.

Croddy, Eric, Clarisa Perez-Armendariz, and John Hart. *Chemical and Biological Warfare: A Comprehensive Survey for the Concerned Citizen.* New York: Copernicus Books, 2002.

Laqueur, Walter. *No End to War: Terrorism in the Twenty-first Century.* New York: Continuum International Publishing, 2003.

Lavoy, Peter R., ed. *Planning the Unthinkable: How New Powers Will Use Nuclear, Biological, and Chemical Weapons.* Ithaca, N.Y.: Cornell University Press, 2000.

Mauroni, Albert J. *Chemical and Biological Warfare: A Reference Handbook.* Santa Barbara, Calif.: ABC-CLIO, 2003.

_____. *Chemical Demilitarization: Public Policy Aspects.* Westport, Conn.: Praeger, 2003.

Solomon, Brian, ed. *Chemical and Biological Warfare.* New York: H. W. Wilson, 1999.

Vogel, Frederick J. *The Chemical Weapons Convention: Strategic Implications for the United States.* Carlisle Barracks, Pa.: Strategic Studies Institutes, U.S. Army War College, 1997.

SEE ALSO: Atom bomb; Biochemical weapons; Bioethics; Geneva conventions; Homeland defense; Iraq; Military ethics; War.

Child abuse

DEFINITION: Physical or psychological violence against or neglect of a child
TYPE OF ETHICS: Children's rights
SIGNIFICANCE: Children are commonly thought of as both innocent and powerless. As a result, acts which harm or traumatize them are often considered to be among the most egregious moral transgressions.

In 1988, the National Center on Child Abuse and Neglect estimated that 500,000 children are physically abused each year in the United States. The American Humane Society estimated that 2.2 million children were abused or neglected in 1986. The incidence of reported child abuse tends to be highest in the lower socioeconomic groups, where opportunities are most limited and stress is greatest. Between 1976 and 1986, reported child abuse tripled, indicating an increased willingness to report mistreatment, an increased incidence of mistreatment, or both.

Most child abuse occurs in the home. Although parents may abuse their children at any age, abused and neglected children are most often younger than age three. Signs of sexual abuse include extreme changes in behavior, such as loss of appetite; sleep disturbance or nightmares; regression to bed-wetting, thumb-sucking, or frequent crying; torn or stained underclothes; vaginal or rectal bleeding or discharge; vaginal or throat infection; painful, itching, or swollen genitals; unusual interest in or knowledge of sexual matters; and fear or dislike of being left in a certain place or with a certain person. Abuse is most traumatic if a nonabusive parent is unsupportive on hearing of the abuse, if the child is removed from the home, and if the child suffered from more than one type of abuse (for example, physical and sexual).

Explanations for child abuse include personality and behavioral characteristics of the parents, stresses on the parents, personality and behavioral characteristics of the child, and cultural values and institutions. Personality traits of parents that contribute to increased likelihood of abuse include low self-esteem, frustrated dependence needs, low family satisfaction, low need to give nurturance, and low ability to recognize or admit feelings of rejection of the child. Behaviorally, parents who abuse their children are more likely than nonabusing parents to be young and poorly

"Mary Ellen" and the Society for the Prevention of Cruelty to Children

The very concept of child abuse was largely unheard of, and certainly had no legal recognition, in America until the 1870's. Child welfare laws were passed first in New York City in 1875, thanks to the efforts of the newly formed New York Society for the Prevention of Cruelty to Children (NYSPCC). The NYSPCC was founded, and the laws were passed, largely in response to the case of "Mary Ellen," a nine-year-old girl who was neglected, tied up, and beaten by her foster parents. When concerned neighbors became aware of her situation in 1874, they reported the case to the authorities, only to discover that no legal provisions for removing abused children from foster care existed. The New York police and district attorney lacked the statutory authority to help Mary Ellen. The neighbors then approached the Society for the Prevention of Cruelty to Animals (SPCA) and persuaded it to use its legal resources to help Mary Ellen. SPCA lawyers succeeded in having Mary Ellen removed from her abusive situation, and the activists, recognizing the need for an organization devoted to the rights of human children, formed the NYSPCC the following year. The Society's purview eventually became national, and by 1895 its name had been changed to the American Society for the Prevention of Cruelty to Children, or, more simply, the Society for the Prevention of Cruelty to Children.

educated, and they are often grossly ignorant of normal child development. For example, they may expect their children to be neat or toilet-trained at an unrealistically early age.

Stresses on the parents that contribute to increased likelihood of child abuse include unemployment or other chronic financial hardships, marital difficulties, social isolation, large families, poor living conditions, being isolated from the child at birth, and having been abused as children themselves. Approximately 30 percent of abused children actually become abusive parents.

A personality characteristic of children that contributes to increased likelihood of child abuse is difficult temperament (fussy, irritable, dependent). Behaviorally, children who are abused are more likely than nonabused children to be premature or low-birth-weight, to have colic, to have a serious illness during their first year of life, to have a mental or physical handicap, to be hyperactive, to have other behavioral abnormalities, and to be unattractive in appearance.

Cultural values and institutions that contribute to increased likelihood of child abuse include acceptance of violence, approval of physical punishment and power assertion as methods of discipline, high levels of social stress, isolation, and absence of community support systems for individuals and families.

Abuse is a complex phenomenon that results from an interaction between the child's problematic traits, the parents' personality problems and social stresses, and cultural values and institutions. Compensatory factors that can prevent an abused child from repeating the abuse as a parent include having a history of positive attachment to a caregiver, resolving not to repeat the abuse, having an awareness of one's early abusive experiences and being openly angry about them, experiencing fewer stressful life events than the abusing parents did, being aware of one's own inner needs, and having a supportive spouse or committed relationship or social network.

PREVENTION

At the individual level, child abuse prevention programs, which involve some combination of personal therapy and behavioral modification, have proved to be relatively successful in decreasing child abuse. Abusive parents need help in learning about and developing social relationships, including relationships with their own children. They also need training in caregiving, including learning how to meet the physical, social, and emotional needs of their children. Abusive parents are less likely than nonabusive ones to smile, praise, and touch their children, and they are more likely than nonabusive parents to threaten, disapprove, and show anger toward their children. Treatment includes helping the parent identify specific situations that trigger abuse, modeling how to reward appropriate behaviors, using time-out periods instead of physical punishment and threats, and learning how to settle problems and arguments through negotiation rather than violence.

At the community level, child abuse prevention programs involve identifying high-stress families and high-risk infants, providing crisis services and home support assistance, providing social support networks (such as Parents Anonymous), and offering public education. Also, people who are arrested for family violence are less likely to continue the maltreatment than are those who are not arrested. Many social agencies offer free services to those in need of help and/or counseling about child abuse.

Lillian M. Range

FURTHER READING

Bergman, A. B., R. M. Larsen, and B. A. Mueller. "Changing Spectrum of Serious Child Abuse." *Pediatrics* 77 (January, 1986): 113-116.

Browne, Angela, and David Finkelhor. "Impact of Child Sexual Abuse: A Review of the Research." *Psychological Bulletin* 99 (January, 1986): 66-77.

Cicchetti, Dante, and Vicki Carlson, eds. *Child Maltreatment: Theory and Research on the Causes and Consequences of Child Abuse and Neglect.* Cambridge, England: Cambridge University Press, 1989.

McCabe, Kimberly A. *Child Abuse and the Criminal Justice System.* New York: Peter Lang, 2003.

Schwartz-Kenney, Beth M., Michelle McCauley, and Michelle A. Epstein, eds. *Child Abuse: A Global View.* Westport, Conn.: Greenwood Press, 2001.

Wolfe, D. A. "Child-Abusive Parents: An Empirical Review and Analysis." *Psychological Bulletin* 97 (May, 1985): 462-482.

SEE ALSO: Abuse; Child labor legislation; Child soldiers; Children; Children's Bureau; Children's rights; Incest; Parenting; Roman Catholic priests scandal; Sexual abuse and harassment.

Child labor legislation

DEFINITION: Laws designed to protect children from exploitative and dangerous conditions of employment

DATE: Early nineteenth century to present

TYPE OF ETHICS: Children's rights

SIGNIFICANCE: Attention to children's rights, in the workplace or elsewhere in the social system, in-volves the ethical issue of protecting the defenseless or most vulnerable members of society.

By the end of the twentieth century, nearly all countries in the world had developed some form of legislative protection to guard against the abuse of child labor in the workplace. General (but clearly not complete) acceptance of the role of the International Labor Office of the United Nations in establishing guidelines for international standards of child labor legislation, however, can be considered the result of more than a century of reform efforts that originated in only a few Western countries.

One aspect of transition from the latter stages of what is called the Agrarian Age to the Industrial Age was the movement of large segments of the rural population into more concentrated wage-earning zones, either in cities or in areas where raw materials for newly established industries, especially coal and minerals from mines, were produced. Other sites that typically attracted cheap wage labor from economically depressed agricultural hinterland zones as the eighteenth century gave way to the nineteenth century were processing mills, especially in the textile manufacturing sector.

PRECEDENTS IN WESTERN COUNTRIES

The most notable examples of countries that were first to address child labor in legislation include those areas that first experienced industrialization on a significant scale, particularly Great Britain, France, and the United States.

The issue of child labor in Great Britain was the object of several legislative reform efforts in the nineteenth century. Robert Oastler was one of the earliest reformers to denounce what he called "Yorkshire slavery" in 1830. He charged that children were being "sacrificed at the shrine of avarice . . . compelled to work as long as the necessity of needy parents may require, or the cold-blooded avarice of . . . worse than barbarian masters may demand!" Responding to claims of inhumanity in conditions of work in 1833, Parliament banned children between the ages of nine and thirteen from factory labor, limited working hours for those between thirteen and eighteen, and required that all child workers must receive two hours of schooling each day. From this point, reformers drew attention not only to near-slave-level pay, long hours, and harsh physical conditions and standards of hygiene, but also to one of the things that became generally recognized as a harmful social effect of child labor: deprivation of minimal opportunities for education.

This factor was visible in Great Britain's 1844 Child Labor Act (which called for certificates proving a half-time education schedule daily) and especially the Education Acts of 1870, 1876, and 1891. The latter, soon backed up by a law making twelve the universal minimum age for leaving school, provided free elementary education for all children for the first time. The main motivation in this combination of child labor and education reform legislation

Liberated child laborers in India are symbolically bound in a protest against child labor in New Delhi on December 2, 2003—a date proclaimed the International Day for the Abolition of Slavery. The International Labour Organisation estimated that between 11 and 23 million children in India were then working in forced labor. (AP/Wide World Photos)

was to provide what otherwise would be a totally ignorant youthful labor force with basic knowledge that could protect young workers from being dependent on exploitative offers coming from the lowest levels of the employment market.

FRENCH LEGISLATION

In France, the second country to pioneer child labor legislation, information on actual conditions in factories and mines after 1837 had to be gathered by governmental authorities from local chambers of commerce and appointed labor arbitration boards, who encountered a clear unwillingness on the part of private employers to reveal what could only be described as exploitative conditions. Some even claimed that if harm was occurring to children who came to work in factories or mines, it came from unhealthy home environments. Basing this judgment partially on considerations of how children get into the situation of having to seek work, even under the worst conditions, child labor reformers in France during the rest of the century sought to legislate better general social and family environmental laws.

Examples of French laws that would be copied by other European countries and that were even assumed to be applicable in France's foreign colonies include the Child Labor Laws of 1841, 1851, and 1874. These laws carried varied emphases. The law of 1841 mandated a maximum eight-hour work shift for children between eight and twelve and required proof of school attendance until the age of twelve. Certain factories were prevented from hiring any laborers under sixteen.

The 1851 law defined conditions of apprenticeship, obligating mutual commitments. Children worked under predefined conditions in return for a guarantee of training that would eventually allow "full" integration, under agreed-upon conditions, into the "adult" trained labor ranks. The law of 1874 banned child labor for wages before the age of twelve unless guarantees of continued schooling apply. Fifteen state inspectorates were established to oversee application of proper standards of work for children and to report to a national "High Commission" in the Ministry of Commerce to judge and penalize employers when complaints arise.

ATTEMPTS TO INTERNATIONALIZE LEGISLATIVE MODELS

Eventual legislative reactions to the exploitation of child workers in most Western countries represent an uneven record even where nineteenth century laws existed and were updated to try to meet twentieth century expectations; conditions in less developed countries would constantly lag far behind. In some cases there could be a claim of "double standards." In what came to be called a "neocolonial" situation following generations of actual colonial domination of many Asian and African countries, Western consumer markets for items produced under deplorable physical and near-slave labor conditions of child labor in other countries might have abandoned responsibility for obvious inequities had it not been for certain twentieth century humanitarian-inspired international agencies.

One of these agencies, the International Labor Office (ILO), originally under the League of Nations, later under the United Nations, has attempted since 1919 to obtain acceptance by member states of a number of international conventions on child labor. The formal reports of literally dozens of ILO conferences contain descriptions of key industrial and commercial activities throughout the world in which problem cases can be identified. In order to obtain a degree of international moral authority to "shame" potentially negligent countries into accepting general standards (regarding age, schooling, safety standards, and so forth), the ILO circulates questions to all member nations, who are expected to vote openly, giving their reasons for either accepting or rejecting suggested amendments (where needed) to individual country law codes with respect to child labor.

Byron D. Cannon

FURTHER READING

Assefa Bequele. *Child Labor: Law and Practice.* Geneva: International Labor Office, 1991.

Bennett, Alan. *A Working Life: Child Labor through the Nineteenth Century.* Dorset, England: Waterfront, 1991.

Gollan, John. *Youth in British Industry.* London: Victor Gollancz, 1937.

Hindman, Hugh D. *Child Labor: An American History.* Armonk, N.Y.: M. E. Sharpe, 2002.

International Labor Office. *Minimum Age for Admission to Employment: Fourth Item on the Agenda.* Geneva, Switzerland: Author, 1972.

Mendelievich, Elias, ed. *Children at Work.* Geneva, Switzerland: Author, 1979.

Weissbach, Lee S. *Child Labor Reform in Nineteenth Century France.* Baton Rouge: Louisiana State University Press, 1989.

SEE ALSO: Child abuse; Child soldiers; Children; Children's Bureau; Children's rights; Fair Labor Standards Act; Minimum-wage laws; United Nations Declaration of the Rights of the Child; Work.

Child psychology

DEFINITION: Diagnosis and treatment of children with mental, emotional, or behavioral disorders

TYPE OF ETHICS: Bioethics

SIGNIFICANCE: The practice of child psychology raises ethical questions about consent; confidentiality; values conflicts among parents, child, and therapist; guidelines for research, and the role of the professional in court cases.

Because persons under the age of eighteen (minors) are considered by American law to be incompetent to make decisions for themselves, proxy consent from parents or guardians is required for medical treatment. Involving the child in the decision when possible respects the child as a person and has the practical advantage of giving the child information and enlisting his or her cooperation, which may be very important for the success of the treatment. Parents may commit children to hospitalization against their will, however, and still have the admission labeled as "voluntary."

While the law seems to assume that parents always decide in the best interest of the child, ethical dilemmas may arise when parents refuse consent for treatment of children deemed in need by school officials or others. This raises the question of whether children have a right to needed treatment. Exceptions to the parental consent requirement may be made in cases of older adolescents who are legally emancipated minors—that is, living independently of parents, married, or in the armed services—or who are considered by the therapist to be mature minors and thus able to decide for themselves.

CONFIDENTIALITY

The maintenance of confidentiality between therapists and adult patients is recognized as an important ethical rule, and there are many reasons why confidentiality should be respected for children as well. Much of the material that becomes known to the therapist is very personal and may involve issues that are sensitive for the child or family. Pledges to honor confidentiality can enhance trust between children and their therapists.

Also, harm may be done to children by "labeling." Revealing past status as psychiatric patients can be a factor in denying later educational or job opportunities. Despite the importance of confidentiality, parents often think that they have a right to know everything, and sometimes a therapist may have to break confidentiality to protect the child or others. A therapist should be honest and state ground rules before beginning treatment and inform the child or family before revealing information.

CONFLICTS IN VALUES

Who should set the goals for psychiatric or behavioral therapy for a child? Parents may have unrealistic expectations for their children or want help in making them conform to cultural ideals of behavior that are different from societal norms or that the therapist may find inappropriate for a particular child. The therapist must decide whether to accept the family's values and help the child adapt to them or to help the child develop the strength to stand against parental pressures. Even using the best interest of the child as the standard, this can be a difficult decision. It is the right of parents to make decisions for their children and to bring them up as they see fit, and many child-rearing practices and behavioral expectations are accepted in a pluralistic society. Although society does set limits and require that certain basic needs be met, and has legal standards of abuse or neglect, therapists must be careful not to impose their own personal values on families.

RESEARCH

Research in child psychology and psychiatry can run from totally nonintrusive observation of normal children in public places to surveys by questionnaire and interviews all the way to trials of new behavior modification techniques or clinical trials of psychotropic drugs. The use of children as research subjects presents ethical problems because as minors they cannot legally volunteer and because in many studies it is very difficult to assess potential risk. Thus, some questions are virtually unexplored and data about causes and effective treatment are lacking. The picture is improving, however, since in 1991 Congress approved a national initiative for increased research on child and adolescent mental health.

Ethical guidelines for medical research with children were adopted as federal regulations in 1983, and they provide that research be well-designed in order to give valid, nontrivial results, that trials be made on animals and adults rather than on children when possible, that risks be outweighed by expected benefits, and that informed consent of parents or guardian be given. It is recommended that children older than age seven be asked for their assent, as well. Nontherapeutic research, whose main goal is to obtain scientific information, has stricter standards than does therapeutic research, whose primary goal is to benefit the child-subject. Despite parental consent, in nontherapeutic research any child over age seven may refuse assent and veto participation, any child may withdraw from the research at any time for any reason, and except under very special conditions, no child may be subjected to anything greater than "minimal" risk, defined as the sort of experience likely to be encountered in everyday activities.

FORENSIC ISSUES

Courts often depend on the professional evaluations of psychiatrists or psychologists to determine the "best interest of the child" in custody or adoption suits, the reliability of child witnesses, or the competency of juvenile offenders to stand trial as adults. One must beware of potential bias or conflict of interest in such cases, since the professional may be hired by one party and be expected to give favorable testimony. There is no general agreement on the age or standards of competency that apply to adolescents or tests to determine the truthful reporting of young children; thus, professionals may offer conflicting judgments, and there may be no clear way to resolve the conflict.

Rosalind Ekman Ladd

FURTHER READING

Forman, Edwin N., and Rosalind Ekman Ladd. *Ethical Dilemmas in Pediatrics*. New York: Springer-Verlag, 1991.

Graham, Philip. "Ethics and Child Psychiatry." In *Psychiatric Ethics*, edited by Sidney Bloch and Paul Chodoff. Oxford, England: Oxford University Press, 1981.

Hoagwood, Kimberly, Peter S. Jensen, and Celia B. Fisher, eds. *Ethical Issues in Mental Health Research with Children and Adolescents*. Mahwah, N.J.: Lawrence Erlbaum Associates, 1996.

Koocher, Gerald P., ed. *Children's Rights and the Mental Health Professions*. New York: Wiley, 1976.

Koocher, Gerald P., and Patricia C. Keith-Spiegel. *Children, Ethics, and the Law*. Lincoln: University of Nebraska Press, 1990.

Melton, Gary B., G. P. Koocher, and M. J. Saks, eds. *Children's Competence to Consent*. New York: Plenum, 1983.

Stein, Ronald. *Ethical Issues in Counseling*. Buffalo, N.Y.: Prometheus, 1990.

SEE ALSO: Child abuse; Child soldiers; Children; Children's rights; Confidentiality; Medical ethics; Psychology; Psychopharmacology; Therapist-patient relationship.

A thirteen-year-old Myanmar government soldier, armed with an M-79 rocket launcher, guards a jungle camp near the Thai border in late 2003. Thousands of child soldiers have been forced to fight on both sides of Myanmar's long-standing civil war. (AP/Wide World Photos)

Child soldiers

DEFINITION: Children under the age of eighteen recruited or conscripted into military and armed groups

TYPE OF ETHICS: Military ethics

SIGNIFICANCE: Using children as soldiers cruelly exploits the children, distorts the nature of the combat in which they serve, and creates a class of citizens who may threaten the long-term stability of their societies.

In 2003, an estimated 500,000 children under eighteen years of age served in the government armed forces, paramilitary forces, civil militia, and armed groups of more than eighty-five nations, and another 300,000 children were active in armed combat in more than thirty countries. Some of the children were as young as seven years of age.

Many child soldiers are volunteers seeking to avenge harm done to family members, seeking refuge from social and economic desperation, or seeking parental surrogates or group membership. Others are conscripts captured, kidnapped, drafted, or otherwise forced or threatened into service. Many are abandoned or orphaned children found wandering the countryside.

Child soldiers are prized because their youth and physical vulnerability makes them obedient and easily intimidated into undertaking dangerous and undesirable tasks and providing personal services for adult soldiers. Many child soldiers are incompletely socialized, lack moral foundations, and lack full understandings of pain and death; they are often more willing than adults to commit atrocities and acts of terror. They are also generally more willing to undertake dangerous missions as spies, lookouts, messengers, suicide fighters, and human mine detectors. Drugs, threats, and brainwashing are used to overcome any fear or reluctance to fight. Developmental learning theory suggests that, until about the age of fifteen, children cannot critically evaluate the merits of the causes for which they fight.

Child soldiers are denied their childhood and appropriate socialization and enculturation. They often suffer trauma and psychological damage from exposure to danger, violence, and carnage. Most never receive education or training beyond that required for combat. Many are physically maimed, permanently handicapped, and become addicted to drugs. Most are social outcasts once armed conflict ends, either because of their actions and injuries in combat or because of society's rejection of the sexual exploitation most, especially female child soldiers, experience within their armed units. This underclass enters adulthood with little prospect for employment, marriage, or acceptance by society. They become constant threats to social and political stability within their countries.

The 1949 Geneva Convention and 1977 Additional Protocols, 1989 Convention on the Rights of the Child (CRC), and 1998 International Criminal Court set fifteen as the minimum age for soldiers. An Optional Protocol to the CRC, adopted by the United Nations in the year 2000, raised the age to eighteen. Child soldiers remain in spite of these efforts.

Gordon Neal Diem

FURTHER READING

Amnesty International. *Child Soldiers: One of the Worst Abuses of Child Labor.* London: Author, 1999.

Brett, Rachel, and Margaret McCallin. *The Invisible Soldiers.* Stockholm: Raedda Barnen, 1998.

Coalition to Stop the Use of Child Soldiers. *Global Report.* London: Author, 2001.

Goodwin-Gill, Guy, and Ilene Cohn. *Child Soldiers: The Role of Children in Armed Conflicts.* Oxford, England: Clarendon Press, 1994.

SEE ALSO: Child abuse; Child labor legislation; Children; Children's rights; International Criminal Court; Land mines; Limited war; Mercenary soldiers; Military ethics; United Nations Declaration of the Rights of the Child; War.

Child support

DEFINITION: Regular financial contributions to help raise, educate, and maintain a child, paid by a divorced or otherwise absent parent to the primary caregiver of the child

TYPE OF ETHICS: Children's rights

SIGNIFICANCE: Laws mandating the payment of child support seek to protect minor children from the financial consequences of family disruptions.

Children have a legitimate expectation of protection and nurturance from adults. As society became increasingly complex during the twentieth century, that responsibility grew to cover a longer period of time and a wider range of obligations. Traditionally, the adults responsible for providing this nurturance have been the child's parents. While there have always been children who have not had two parents, owing to death, divorce, and out-of-wedlock childbirth, the number of children in single-parent households grew significantly during the late twentieth century. Simultaneously, changes in gender roles challenged traditional assumptions about the delegation of moral and legal obligations to children. The consequence was the nonsupport of many children and the insufficient support of far more.

HISTORY

Common law assumed that the physical care of children was the responsibility of the mother, while the financial support of the children (and, in support of that end, the mother) was the responsibility of the father. Courts adjudicated divorces and child support awards with this assumption until the 1960's. Two related trends altered this longstanding approach.

California passed the first "no-fault" divorce law in 1970. The intent was to minimize acrimony in divorce proceedings, with the anticipated consequence of alleviating the financial and emotional disruptions to children, as well as adults, imposed by an adversarial system. Cultural changes in gender role expectations led to additional changes in the division of responsibility between parents. These changes were reflected in the courts in the initiation of "joint custody" arrangements and an increase in contested custody.

Research by Ron Haskins showed that noncustodial fathers continued during the 1980's to recognize a moral responsibility to support their children. Nevertheless, critics such as Lenore J. Weitzman, in *The Divorce Revolution* (1985), and Ruth Sidel, in *Women and Children Last* (1986), argued that changes in the application of divorce law in fact had the unanticipated effect of impoverishing women and children. First, "no-fault" laws made divorce easier to obtain. Second, growing legal assumptions of gender equality led to equal divisions of property, even when the mother had neither the education nor the job history to allow her to earn an equal income. Child support awards were based not only on unjustified assumptions about the mother's earning potential but also on the implicit assumption that she would continue the traditional role of sole physical care while assuming half of the financial responsibility. As noted, the law also changed to allow for joint custody. In practice, however, this applied to a tiny fraction of children during the 1980's.

The situation was further exacerbated by a trend of noncompliance with legally adjudicated child support. Recognition of social responsibility to the involved children was embodied in national legislation, notably the Child Support Enforcement Act, which passed in 1975. Nevertheless, critics charged that enforcement of child support payments remained insufficient.

These social changes created a situation that has been called the "feminization of poverty." While the term refers to adult women impoverished by circumstances such as divorce, in fact, the largest growing segment of the population trapped in poverty during the 1980's were children, in particular the children of these women. These children were effectively denied their right to appropriate nurturance in the form of proper nutrition, medical care, and education.

AREAS OF CONTENTION

There were several specific areas that created disputes among lawyers and social policy analysts, as well as among the involved parties. The legal determination of the appropriate amount of child support weighed a number of complex factors, including the ability to pay and previous lifestyle. Many of these issues were determined from the perspective of the adult's concerns rather than from that of the child's rights. When that perspective was included, additional issues arose. Appropriate support included medical care; in practice, this entailed paying for health insurance. Educational needs were frequently a point of controversy, particularly since the age of majority usually determined the extent of legal child support obligation. In 1972, California changed that age from 21 to 18, with tremendous consequences for the support of college-age children.

Other disputes centered on how best to encourage noncustodial parents to meet their responsibilities. Legally, during the 1990's, there was no link between visitation arrangements and child support, but research by Mavis Hetherington suggested that fathers retained a greater sense of responsibility to their children when visitation was more frequent and/or extended. The organization Equal Rights for Fathers developed as a goal the greater enforcement of visitation and other policies to enhance visitation.

Most social policy analysts during the 1980's and 1990's focused efforts on enforcement of child support awards. Methods included attachment of wages, attachment of income tax refunds, and public humiliation of the worst offenders. Child advocates also noted that the size of awards at that time needed to be increased substantially to meet the real needs of children. Additionally, Ruth Sidel argued, in *Women and Children Last* (1986), that social policies needed to be designed to enable custodial parents to meet the obligations they could neither escape nor fulfill. Programs such as job training and childcare, and an end to wage discrimination against women, were deemed critical to that end.

The United States during the late twentieth century confronted a major ethical dilemma. Those who had reached adulthood had to find a way to meet their obligations to those who had not.

Nancy E. Macdonald

FURTHER READING

Cassetty, Judith, ed. *The Parental Child-Support Obligation: Research, Practice, and Social Policy.* Lexington, Mass.: Lexington Books, 1983.

Crowley, Jocelyn Elise. *The Politics of Child Support in America.* New York: Cambridge University Press, 2003.

Garfinkel, Irwin. *Assuring Child Support: An Extension of Social Security.* New York: Russell Sage Foundation, 1992.

Kahn, Alfred J., and Sheila B. Kamerman, eds. *Child Support: From Debt Collection to Social Policy.* Newbury Park, Calif.: Sage, 1988.

Sidel, Ruth. *Women and Children Last: The Plight of Poor Women in Affluent America.* New York: Penguin Books, 1987.

Weitzman, Lenore J. *The Divorce Revolution: The Unexpected Social and Economic Consequences for Women and Children in America.* New York: Free Press, 1985.

SEE ALSO: Children; Children's rights; Divorce; Family; Family values; Parenting; Welfare programs.

Children

DEFINITION: People who have not yet come of age; youths lacking the full rights and privileges of adults.

TYPE OF ETHICS: Children's rights

SIGNIFICANCE: Because "childhood" is itself a constantly evolving social creation, the ethical views and practices that prevail toward children within particular societies provide substantial insight into the historical development of moral values both within and across those societies.

How adults treat children differs discernibly from culture to culture and has continually changed throughout history, as have general attitudes toward childhood. The social status of "childhood" is culturally defined and cannot be precisely identified through strictly biological or any other type of universal criteria. All culturally accepted conventions are, ultimately, arbitrary, so they gain their normative or legal validity only by social fiat.

Despite the commonsensical understanding of children as a "biologically immature" adults, it is the social recognition of this "immaturity" that defines children's status. For example, while the achievement of childbearing age may signify full maturity and thus adulthood among females of certain indigenous peoples of South America, it emphatically does not among industrialized North American societies.

Indeed, the very fact that many modern states legally specify a certain age to define childhood/adulthood contradicts the biological fact that human beings "mature" (however that is socially defined) at significantly different ages.

CHILDREN'S ETHICS

In moral terms, the norms of "acceptable" treatment of those people socially recognized as "children" are equally subject to historical and culturally relative criteria. The most common ethical issues that arise relate either to the extent to which full social obligations can be placed upon children or to the moral responsibilities of adults toward children, including the respective legal rights of both parties.

The ethical content of child status versus adult status can attain a profound social significance, determining the eligibility of people to perform certain types of work, consume alcoholic beverages, exercise control over their own health treatment, fight in wars, engage in sexual activity, vote in elections, and so on. In modern criminal law codes, the recognition of child status usually determines the extent to which one is legally punishable or even culpable for criminal behavior.

HISTORICAL ATTITUDES

The specification of "childhood" as a special social category is relatively recent in human history. As a legally recognized status, it is only a few hundred years old. The apparent social indifference toward young people prior to this specification is thought by some experts to be related to their high mortality rate. Until the seventeenth century, more than half of the twenty-one-year-old and younger population died before entering what many modern societies now define as "adulthood." In such societies, it is reasoned, there was no strong argument for becoming too interested in members of a population who could not be expected to survive. Comparative perspectives call these assertions into question, however, citing evidence from non-Western cultures that challenge the universality of these historical stereotypes.

Most experts agree that the general unifying characteristic from ancient times up to the sixteenth century, at least in European societies, was the virtual absence of societal institutions aimed specifically at children. In short, Western societies were "adult centered" for centuries, and children simply grappled with society by mixing with adults and eventually learning how to function as adults. Up into the eighteenth century, childhood in the contemporary sense essentially referred to pre-five-year-olds. Those individuals who were older became immersed in the normal work responsibilities of the household, though stratified by gender.

The origin of the social status of childhood as defined in Western societies is most frequently attributed to the eighteenth century Enlightenment. The Enlightenment weakened many of the most traditional religious notions that had governed human self-understanding, including the presumption of an inherent "evil" that resided in people as described in the biblical metaphor of "after the fall." With the rise of social "progress" theories that would in turn lead to the development of the social sciences, more sanguine images of human nature began to trickle down into the Western mind-set, and notions of the perfectibility of the human race became widely disseminated.

Philippe Aries' seminal work on the history of childhood, *Centuries of Childhood: A Social History of Family Life* (1962), chronicles how social attitudes toward children began to change during this period. Using content analysis of portraits, early writings on pedagogy and pediatric medical care, and other cultural artifacts, Aries uncovered the various ways in which the developmental phases of childhood and the passage into adulthood became reconceptualized.

Examining the affluent classes of European societies, Aries shows how portraits began to appear as early as the sixteenth and seventeenth centuries in which children were depicted as having a distinct and "innocent" character and were no longer made to look like miniature adults. This notion of childhood innocence became one of the defining features of children in the post-Enlightenment period, which in turn helped fuel a shift in social attitudes. Children became increasingly thought of as "pure" and "good" people who needed protection from rude, dangerous, and immoral social processes that could harm their development. Social attention turned decisively toward child upbringing and the need to instill morality into children under the protection of adults. Activities formerly common among young people as well as adults, such as cursing, drinking alcoholic beverages, and sexual activities, all became increasingly

regarded as antithetical to childhood and became socially prohibited among children.

Greater emphasis on structured childrearing gradually became the norm among the middle classes during this period. During the seventeenth century, the apprentice system routinely took young males and females between the ages of ten and fifteen out of the household, whereupon they became members of another in order to learn a trade from a skilled artisan. The apprentice earned his or her keep but remained under the strict control of the master. This was viewed socially as a means by which parental coddling could be defeated, since children completed the rearing process under the more detached supervision of an unrelated master. The apprentice system was ultimately dismantled by the onset of the Industrial Revolution and had largely disappeared by the nineteenth century.

CHILD WELFARE IN THE UNITED STATES

In the United States, social attitudes became more child-centered following the rise of the factory system during the early nineteenth century. Once seen as little more than the waiting period before becoming an adult, childhood became more idealized and regarded as an end in itself, an object of increasing social attention.

New social institutions designed to address the special needs and characteristics of children began to proliferate and expand in importance during the nineteenth century, with the most important being formal education. The eventual rise in popularity of kindergartens previsioned the subsequent social concern with progressive educational reform that aimed to nurture the spontaneity and creativeness of children rather than repress it. All such trends provide evidence of the continuous evolution in American attitudes toward recognition and respect of a "child's world."

Of equal ethical importance was the creation of social agencies aimed at dealing with child deviance. With deviant acts committed by children becoming increasingly regarded as a reflection on the social environment rather than as evidence of the "evil" lurking in the young person's soul, social forces arose to intervene in the lives of failed or defunct families so as to "rescue" children from their defective environment. "Houses of refuge" were opened for children throughout the United States during the 1820's, becoming the first generation of "child-saving" institutions that would later culminate in the expansion of state child protection services during the twentieth century.

Child refuges attempted to create a "properly structured environment" in which the negative influences of poverty, neglectful parents, and/or a syndrome of poor behavior on the part of the child could be corrected through military-like discipline and the learning of model social roles. The state was frequently called upon by charitable institutions to facilitate their child-saving activities by granting them legal rights of supervision over the children, a process that gradually drew the state into greater involvement in child welfare.

After the U.S. Civil War, social reformers began to criticize the prison-like model of child refuge centers, calling instead for more humanistic interventions that aimed to restore family life settings and to focus on teaching skills to errant children. With child saving emerging as a major ethical concern in the late nineteenth century, many feminists began to enter into the child advocacy movement, emphasizing child welfare over child punishment.

Largely because of child welfare reformers, the juvenile court system was formed during the turn of the century, with the first court instituted in Illinois in 1899. Within three decades, virtually every state had a juvenile court system that typically exercised its jurisdiction over children "in trouble" under the age of sixteen. Invoking the principle of *parens patriae*, a notion dating back to feudal times that asserts that the state is the ultimate parent to children, the juvenile courts established the power of the state to designate as "wards of the state" those children who had broken laws, been improperly treated by their parents, or had engaged in behavior considered immoral for children, and to thus assume full legal responsibility for their welfare.

Many experts argue that the juvenile justice system as it developed acted primarily to address the concerns of the middle and upper classes by enabling the state to intervene in the lives of poor families. While the overarching ideology governing the court was child welfare through therapeutic action rather than a punishment ethic, critics over the years argued that the court routinely violated the civil rights of children, particularly those of the lower classes. The 1967 U.S. Supreme Court decision *In re Gault* reaffirmed the constitutional impropriety that pervaded the juvenile justice system in practice, its good intentions notwithstanding, and ruled that juveniles were entitled to the full legal protection of the due process enjoyed by adults.

Along with the increasing specialization of the legal system designed to differentiate children from adults, the social sciences gradually developed specialized research traditions in the area of juvenile delinquency. Institutes for the study of juvenile delinquency were formed and became influential in consulting with the state on the expansion of state social welfare agencies. By the early twentieth century, children received a variety of public services, usually for their material support in cases in which a need was recognized. State-sponsored foster homes and a variety of residential facilities were created to offer child care and child protection. The eventual creation of specialized state child protection agencies led to the development of comprehensive systems of family welfare, with intervention into child abuse and neglect cases, emerging as systems that would coexist with legal and medical authorities.

ETHICS OF CHILD MALTREATMENT

The social recognition of child maltreatment and the "discovery" of child abuse provide a dramatic example of changing social attitudes toward children and their proper ethical treatment. In Ancient Rome, the principle of *patria potestas* established the complete control of fathers over their children, including decisions concerning their right to live, regardless of age. Infanticide was widely practiced there, as it was in virtually all ancient societies, including ancient Egypt and Greece. Often, a particular ritual was practiced that established the social expectation that a particular child was to be raised to maturity. Prior to the event, unwanted children could in most cases be disposed of without social sanction. Among the most common situations in which infanticide was practiced were cases of birth deformities and cases of children who were "illegitimate," conceived by incest, or considered likely to become a drain on the state in the absence of a conducive family setting.

During the Middle Ages, the Christian doctrine of parental love tempered somewhat the brutality latent in the absolute authority it granted parents over children in cultures where it predominated. Nevertheless, severe corporal punishment remained a norm in most Christian cultures. For example, historical data show that when French Jesuits first encountered the Eskimo societies of North America during the seventeenth century, they observed with horror that the aborigines refused to hit their children for any reason. To the French missionaries, the taboo on child beating was evidence of the primitive and paganistic ways of the Eskimos. Once the conversion to Christianity began, the Catholic missionaries placed special emphasis on preaching the necessity of beating children so that they would "learn to fear God."

In no way unique to France, the physical punishment of children, often in an extreme form, was considered fully legitimate in Western societies until the late nineteenth century. During the 1870's, the Society for the Prevention of Cruelty to Children (SPCC) was formed to advocate for legislation in the United States designed to protect children from abusive employers and surrogate caretakers. While the success of the SPCC and other child-saving institutions is shown by the formation of the juvenile justice system, it was the parallel development of social welfare agencies that pioneered the emphasis on direct intervention within conflictual families. Child protective services (CPS) exhibit a paternalistic and therapeutic model of intervention.

With their legislative authority based in juvenile and criminal court statutes, CPS bureaucracies are firmly controlled by government agencies, primarily at the state level. The Child Abuse and Prevention Act of 1974 mandated that state CPS agencies follow certain federal guidelines with respect to creating open channels of reporting child maltreatment.

The expansion of CPS during the 1970's and 1980's emphasized the provision by social caseworkers of services that could repair and restore the family, with removal into state foster homes as a last recourse; this contrasted with the early child-saving movement, which emphasized removal and the creation of alternative arenas of socialization.

MEDICALIZATION AND CHILD ETHICS

Another important shift in social attitudes toward children grew out of changes in the medical establishment. The early development of pediatric medicine had paralleled the increasing social recognition of childhood. During the 1960's, the discovery of the "battered child syndrome" by pediatric radiologists helped fuel social concern about child abuse. During the same decade, an explosion of pediatric medical

research occurred concerning the phenomenon of child hyperactivity, providing another example of the impact that modern medicine has had on social attitudes and the treatment of children.

Hyperactive children have a long history of being socially defined in adverse terms, either as "possessed" by the devil or other "evil spirits," or as malicious, disorderly, rebellious, and so on. Nurtured by the specialized study of children among psychiatric researchers, medical research in the second half of the twentieth century began to discover various biological factors that influence child hyperactivity, along with an array of pharmacological treatments that proved to be effective in controlling it. This led to the clinical designation of child hyperactivity as an illness known as "hyperkinesis."

The "medicalization" or general social recognition of hyperactive child behavior as an illness constituted a qualitative break from earlier conceptions. From a moral category of "bad" or "evil" activity, the medical profession has largely succeeded in shifting the larger social understanding of a whole set of aberrant child behaviors into the more neutral terrain of a "sick" condition that rests outside the control of the afflicted child. The medicalization of this form of child deviance helps to illustrate the continuing erosion of traditional conceptions of children and child care as much as it demonstrates the power of the medical community to alter the perceptions and ethical standards of child treatment.

The celebrated child-rearing manual of Benjamin Spock, *Common Sense Book of Baby and Child Care* (1946 and many revisions), provides yet another example of the direct impact that medical authorities have had upon attitudes toward and the treatment of children. Spock's instructive emphasis on preserving happiness in childhood socialization helped contribute to the social recognition of a science of parenting, initiating a trend in which adults look to medical experts for advice on the optimal technique for raising their children.

PERSISTENT ETHICAL DILEMMAS

The ethical issues that surround the social attitudes and treatment of children must be continually reexamined and considered in their overarching complexity. At all levels, the socially acknowledged rights and obligations accorded to children as well as the transgressions against them have historically been stratified by social class, race, and gender. Young females are sexually abused at a rate six times that of young males. The rate of physical neglect of impoverished children is invariably higher and unlikely to improve merely through therapeutic means of treatment.

Just as maltreatment exhibits its social biases, so too do the various institutions that are involved in the professional treatment of children. If sociohistorians have shown how child savers of the nineteenth century enacted reforms that disproportionately affected poorer families, modern child protection agencies can likewise be seen to enforce white, middle-class standards in their practices at the expense of poor women and people of color. Any perspective that claims to grasp the tremendous complexity of child ethics must continually and critically evaluate how childhood is intertwined with the dynamics of social class, gender, and racial inequalities.

Richard A. Dello Buono

FURTHER READING

Archard, David, and Colin M. Macleod, eds. *The Moral and Political Status of Children*. New York: Oxford University Press, 2002. An anthology of essays by moral and political theorists covering such issues as the existence or nonexistence of children's rights, education, familial duties, and distributive justice.

Aries, Philippe. *Centuries of Childhood: A Social History of Family Life*. Translated by Robert Baldick. New York: Knopf, 1962. A classic work on the history of childhood. The author attempts to make a comprehensive study of social attitudes toward children throughout the entire span of recorded history.

Bernard, Thomas J. *The Cycle of Juvenile Justice*. New York: Oxford University Press, 1992. A very readable review of the changing historical conceptions of justice and legal rights regarding children. The author shows how the breakdown of traditional social controls led to the social creation of "juvenile delinquency."

Binder, Arnold, Gilbert Geis, and Dickson Bruce. *Juvenile Delinquency: Historical, Cultural and Legal Perspectives*. New York: Macmillan, 1988. A well-written text that provides useful information on the historical conceptions of children and the social construction of "child deviance." The his-

torical background of virtually all of the principal social institutions that affect children are considered.

Platt, Anthony. *The Child Savers*. Chicago: The University of Chicago Press, 1969. An excellent empirical study of the changing social definitions of child deviance and how the label of "juvenile delinquent" is unevenly applied to different social classes. Considerable historical information is presented on the "child savers movement" of the nineteenth century.

Rabb, Theodore K., and Robert I. Rotberg, eds. *The Family in History: Interdisciplinary Essays*. New York: Harper & Row, 1971. An extremely useful collection of interdisciplinary essays that includes several in-depth chapters on the changing conceptions of children and a bibliographic note on the literature concerning the history of childhood.

Rosenheim, Margaret K., et al., eds. *A Century of Juvenile Justice*. Chicago: University of Chicago Press, 2002. A comprehensive and broad-ranging collection of essays on the history of juvenile justice. The majority of the volume focuses on twentieth century U.S. history, but individual essays also treat the nineteenth century, Japan, and Great Britain.

SEE ALSO: Child abuse; Child labor legislation; Child psychology; Child support; Children's Bureau; Children's rights; Children's television; Family; Family values; Moral education; Parenting.

Children's Bureau

IDENTIFICATION: Federal agency charged with investigating and reporting on "all matters pertaining to the welfare of children"

DATE: Founded in 1912

TYPE OF ETHICS: Children's rights

SIGNIFICANCE: The establishment of the Children's Bureau was the first U.S. institutional recognition of children as individuals—not property—with their own rights and needs.

During the late nineteenth century, children's health became an issue in the United States. Child mortality rates were high, largely because neither parents nor physicians knew much about the specific needs of children. Doctors had begun to understand that simply providing adult treatments in smaller doses was not adequate. Gradually, new thinking about child psychology and development spread.

In 1912, the U.S. Congress established the Children's Bureau to deal with infant mortality, preventive medicine, orphanages, the juvenile justice system, and child labor. The bureau quickly became a strong force for the improvement of children's lives. It established national birth registration to make possible the first useful study of infant mortality. The bureau produced two booklets, *Prenatal Care* (1913) and *Infant Care* (1914), which were updated and distributed for decades. For the first time, mothers had access to sound advice. By disseminating information and training new professionals, the bureau greatly expanded public health services for mothers and children.

After the passage of the Social Security Act in 1935, the bureau added services for new populations, including disabled, abandoned, and delinquent children, the mentally retarded, and specific minority groups.

Cynthia A. Bily

SEE ALSO: Child abuse; Child labor legislation; Child support; Children; Children's rights; United Nations Declaration of the Rights of the Child.

Children's rights

DEFINITION: Area of legislation, social work, and activism that seeks to protect children from discriminatory or abusive practices
TYPE OF ETHICS: Children's rights
SIGNIFICANCE: Distinctive, child-specific forms of exploitation exist in modern mass society, so there is an ethical imperative to institute equally distinctive safeguards to protect children against exploitation.

When the Universal Declaration of Human Rights was passed by the United Nations General Assembly in 1948, the wording of Article 2 provided for the protection of rights "without distinction of any kind, such as race, color, sex, language, religion, political

or other opinion, national or social origin, property, birth or other status." Thus, as in the famous French Revolutionary Declaration of the Rights of Man and the Citizen (1789), formulators of identifiable categories of persons with unalienable rights omitted specific mention of age (either old age or youth). Such omissions may have stemmed from a general assumption that children are automatically an essential component of any population. Historical experiences before those famous declarations, however, and many key social developments, particularly in the second half of the twentieth century, suggest that there should be a specific sphere of concern for the rights of children in all regions of the world.

HISTORICAL PRECEDENTS

It was the spreading mid-nineteenth century impact of the Industrial Revolution that brought a desire by mine and factory owners to cut unskilled labor costs and, in the process, ushered in an entire era of employer exploitation of child workers. In several countries where such exploitation (long hours, very low pay, hazardous work conditions) became the object of public and political outrage, special child labor legislation acts were passed. An important part of such legislation in Great Britain and in France was to oblige employers to guarantee that working children could receive enough education to "free" them from the bonds of ignorance (and therefore near slavery in the unskilled workplace). In most cases, the question of whether the wider social and family environment in which disadvantaged children had to live could be addressed and resolved by laws was hardly posed in this era of early child labor legislation.

CHILDHOOD VS. ADULTHOOD

Various societies have defined "rights" or "rites" of passage from childhood in different ways. In some traditional tribal settings, for example, important cultural distinctions have been made between what constitutes becoming a man and what constitutes becoming a woman. These tend in general to be linked with puberty and "qualification" for marriage and family responsibilities. In modern Western societies, however, passage from adolescence to early adulthood tends to relate to a number of legal rights. Characteristic rights here might be the right to make legally binding decisions (including marriage and the establishment of a separate place of residence) without necessary parental consent, the right to vote, and the right to purchase controlled substances such as alcohol or tobacco. In addition to such rights, there may also be certain obligations attached to the attainment of a certain age. These include, according to the country in question, obligatory military service and the right to be tried in court according to the same conditions that apply to persons of full adult status.

In the United States, a legal division between juvenile and adult criminal jurisdictions has existed only since about 1900. The juvenile court system was

established on the assumption that children are more likely to reform themselves if instructed rather than punished to the full limits of penal law. Because the juvenile system functions according to procedures quite different from those of the regular courts (notably in its emphasis on the judge's role, with less attention given to formal representation of the accused by an attorney), critics from the 1960's forward have called for its reform. In addition, some specialized agencies, including the National Legal Resource Center for Child Advocacy and Protection in Wash-

Turning Points in the History of Children's Rights

Date	Event	Impact
1833	British Parliamentary Act	Ages and hours limited for children in factories
1844	British Child Labor Act	Requires guarantee of minimal education for working children
1851	French Child Labor Law	Defines rights of apprentices
1874	French Inspectorates placed over employers of children	Provides for fines when minimal standards not met
1890's	Education Curriculum Reforms passed in United States	Emphasizes social democratization of all classes of pupils
1900-1910	Juvenile Court System introduced	Establishes different courts, procedures, and punishments
1912	U.S. Children's Bureau established	First federal agency devoted to monitoring the welfare of children
1950's-1960's	U.S. Aid to Families with Dependent Children introduced	Provided for tangible government welfare aid to needy children
1959	United Nations Declaration of the Rights of the Child	Recognized the ethical responsibility of national governments to look after the welfare of children
1960's-1970's	Child Welfare System created	Public assignment to foster homes to protect children's rights
1990	Convention on the Rights of the Child ratified	Enumerated thirty-eight specific rights of children that all nations must respect
1998	Establishment of the permanent International Criminal Court	Measures included defining the use of child soldiers as a punishable war crime.
1999	International Labour Organisation's Convention Concerning the Prohibition and Immediate Action for the Elimination of the Worst Forms of Child Labour	Designed to protect children from working in unsafe and unhealthful environments

ington, D.C., and the National Center for Youth Law in San Francisco, have taken it upon themselves to serve as watchdogs to assure that juvenile justice, while remaining separate, provides adequate guarantees of equality of rights within the total penal system.

CHILDREN'S RIGHTS IN MODERN MASS SOCIETIES

The concerns of lawmakers and courts over the phenomenon of child abuse in many modern countries have had many historical precedents. Extreme cases of systematic infanticide can be found in a number of historical cultures. One example only among others appears in the Islamic Qur'ān itself, in passages exhorting Arab tribes living in ignorance of God's ways to abandon the custom of preferring male over female infants, some of whom might be killed at birth. The physical abuse of children, ranging from beatings by one or both parents to sexual exploitation either in the family (the object of anti-incest laws) or commercially (the object of special laws against child prostitution or pornography) has existed in one form or another from antiquity to the present. The compounded negative effects of mass societies, however, combined with the increasingly intensive examination of such problems by the media, seem to have focused more attention in the second half of the twentieth century than in any other period on the need to address protective rights for children.

After experiencing rather distressing early campaigns for special legislation to protect children's "external" rights in the workplace and in the penal justice system, modern society seems to have identified a general ethical need to look more closely at the internal functioning of the family to determine whether one of the key contributors to the eventual "external" abuse of children's rights is the home (or the absence of a real home).

In cases in which children do not receive the nurturing experience of a nuclear family (orphans, for example, or those who are assigned by public authorities to foster homes), there may be less difficulty in establishing certain objective criteria for determining whether children's rights are being respected: Specific legislation exists in most modern countries that defines exact procedures for meeting required standards of care for dependent children who do not live with their own families. If shortcomings are dis-

covered, these same laws provide for terminating a foster care contract, for example, or even for closing down specialized childcare institutions, be they orphanages or part-time day-care centers.

Determining whether children are fully safe within their own families, however, is a very different matter. Here, the legal rights of privacy stand as protective barriers intended to keep the public authority of the state from infringing on personal freedoms (guaranteed, in the United States, under the Bill of Rights). Certain forms of legislation have been passed that, on the surface, at least, aim at protecting children living in families experiencing deprivation.

Perhaps the best known (and most controversial) packet of social legislation targeting children was the Aid to Families with Dependent Children (AFDC) program, also referred to as welfare. Although AFDC did not speak directly to questions of children's rights in ethical terms, it was the only government cash-disbursing program in the United States that assumed that the primary beneficiaries of special assistance are children who would otherwise have gone without many essentials. Part of the process of determining the effectiveness of AFDC aid involved social workers' intervention in determining how families managed the funds they received. In extreme cases, such intervention took forms that were resisted by families who, although desperate for aid, resented interference in the private sphere of family-child relations. In 1997, AFDC was superseded by the Temporary Assistance for Needy Families (TANF) Program created by the Welfare Reform Law of 1996.

A second agency that is meant to serve as a watchdog over children's rights is the child welfare system. Its responsibility is to remove children from family situations that may be detrimental to their personal development and even personal safety. As the main authority referring children to foster homes, the child welfare system comes closest to executing public responsibility to protect the private rights of children despite the will of their own families.

Until the mid-1980's and into the 1990's, the assumed typical dilemmas of child deprivation or abuse (alcoholism, drugs, dysfunctional families also confronted with poverty-level existence, and so forth) seemed to lend themselves to the programmatic actions provided for in the child welfare system. By the 1990's, however, a series of quite different issues began to attract the attention of the media and the court system. The most controversial involved recognition that children themselves might, under particular circumstances, exercise the legal right to "divorce" their parents. This issue promised to invite a critical turning point, since it implied transfer of the decision-making process in children's rights from the public to the individual private sphere.

Byron D. Cannon

FURTHER READING

Alaimo, Kathleen, and Brian Klug, eds. *Children as Equals: Exploring the Rights of the Child.* Lanham, Md.: University Press of America, 2002.

Boulding, Elise. *Children's Rights and the Wheel of Life.* New Brunswick, N.J.: Transaction Books, 1979.

Cohen, Howard. *Equal Rights for Children.* Totowa, N.J.: Rowman and Littlefield, 1980.

De Lone, Richard. *Small Futures.* New York: Harcourt Brace Jovanovich, 1979.

Vittachi, Anuradha. *Stolen Childhood.* Cambridge, England: Polity Press, 1989.

White House Conference on Children. *Report to the President.* Washington, D.C.: Author, 1970.

SEE ALSO: Child abuse; Child labor legislation; Child soldiers; Child support; Children; Head Start; Infanticide; United Nations Declaration of the Rights of the Child.

Children's television

DEFINITION: Television programming and advertisements designed specifically for children

TYPE OF ETHICS: Media ethics

SIGNIFICANCE: Numerous studies have indicated that children are particularly vulnerable to being influenced by messages contained in television programs and advertisements; for this reason, broadcasters of children's programming have a special ethical responsibility.

By the age of eighteen, most North American children have spent more than two solid years of their lives watching television—more time than many of them have spent in school. Studies dating back to the 1960's indicate that television programming and ad-

---

V-chips

Developed during the early 1990's, V-chips are devices built into television sets that permit owners of the sets to block designated categories of programs, based on their ratings. Their purpose is to allow parents to limit their children's viewing of programs with what they consider to be excessive amounts of violence, sexual content, or other objectionable material. In 2001 the Federal Communications Commission (FCC) adopted a rule requiring all new television sets with thirteen-inch or larger screens to be equipped with V-chip technology. The television industry itself established a system for rating the content of programs and coding those ratings into the signals that stations broadcast so that V-chips can read the ratings.

Also known as TV Parental Guidelines, the program-rating system was established by the National Association of Broadcasters, the National Cable Television Association, and the Motion Picture Association of America.

---

vertisements can have a strong influence on children, who are frequent viewers. Further, television and media violence, gender and race portrayals, and advertisements have been linked to a variety of adverse behaviors, including violence in later life, aggressive attitudes, and obesity.

Although children's television in the United States has been bound by few ethical codes beyond the broad mandate that broadcasters serve the "public interest, convenience, and necessity," two key pieces of U.S. congressional legislation have attempted to codify that directive. The Children's Television Act of 1990 required programming that met the educational and informational needs of children. The Telecommunications Act of 1996 mandated a program-rating system similar to that used by the film industry and also required manufacturers to install computer devices called V-chips on all new televisions. V-chips read ratings embedded in programs and allow owners of the sets—such as parents—to block shows with specific ratings. In addition, the 1996 law called for broadcasters to air a minimum of three hours of children's educational programming per week.

Although V-chip technology was widely publicized, the device was slow to catch on. By 2004, it was estimated that less than 20 percent of Americans who owned V-chip-equipped televisions were using the device. Further research suggested that broadcasters may not be providing enough information via the rating system, and the definition of educational television remained murky, at best.

VIOLENCE

More than one thousand studies have identified links between childhood exposure to television violence and real-life violent behaviors. Some studies have suggested that exposure to television violence, including the make-believe, or fantasy, violence associated with cartoons, may not only desensitize children to acts of real violence but also change their opinions about what constitutes right and wrong behavior. Several studies have found that childhood exposure to media violence predicts aggressive behavior in both male and female adults.

Saturday-morning television programming, typically consisting of cartoons and other shows targeting children, has been found to average twenty-five acts of violence per hour. In addition to programming content, more than a third of commercials airing on children's shows contain aggressive acts, and many advertisements linked to adult-related programming target children. For example, World Wrestling Entertainment, which produces such shows as *SmackDown* and *Raw*, also licenses a series of action figures modeled after wrestling stars.

GENDER ROLES

Although many children's shows reflect changing modern gender expectations, most programs continue to portray male and female characters with stereotypical traits. For example, male figures appear more frequently in cartoons than do female figures and are generally more action-oriented. Male characters are also more likely to use physical aggression, and female characters are more likely to demonstrate fear, romantic behavior, and supportive gestures. On the other hand, when female characters are portrayed in action roles, they often behave as violently as their male counterparts.

Advertisements targeting children showed similar characteristics. Boys typically appear more often and are placed in contexts in which they have traits of power, control, action, competition, and destruction. The content of commercials targeting girls generally emphasizes more limited physical activity, as well as feelings and nurturing.

EDUCATIONAL TELEVISION

Although U.S. federal law requires broadcast television stations to air at least three hours per week of educational programming, the Federal Communications Commission's definition of educational television is vague: "any television programming that furthers the educational and informational needs of children." Broadcasters have frequently pointed to their own studies, which indicate that their educational programming has increased 100 percent since 1990—more than complying with the federal law. However, by the broadcasters' definitions, their educational programming has included such shows as *NBA: Inside Stuff*, *G.I. Joe*, *America's Funniest Home Videos*, *The Flintstones*, *The Jetsons*, and *Teenage Mutant Ninja Turtles*. At one point, ABC-TV even attempted to depict its program *Tales from the Crypt*, based on HBO's adult horror series, as a way to teach children a "wonder-filled morality lesson."

More traditional forms of educational television often appear on Public Broadcasting System (PBS) including *Sesame Street*, *Barney*, and *Wishbone*. Research studies have suggested that these shows do, indeed, provide young viewers with educational experiences. For example, children who watch *Sesame Street* generally know and understand more words, have a better grasp of mathematics, and are better prepared for school than children who watch only cartoons and general programming on commercial television.

ADVERTISING

In 1750 B.C.E., Hammurabi's code made it a crime punishable by death to engage in commerce with a child without first obtaining the permission of a parent. Historically most societies have implicitly understood the ethical questions raised by selling goods to children. Sweden has banned all advertising directed at children under twelve, and in Greece, commercials for toys are banned before 10 P.M.

In North America, however, children represent an exceptionally ripe demographic market. By the early twenty-first century advertisers were spending more than two billion dollars per year on commercials targeting children alone. Numerous studies have suggested that young children are typically unable to understand the intent of advertisements and frequently accept advertising claims as literally true. Many parents also voice concerns that advertising makes children too materialistic and encourages youths to define their self-worth by their possessions.

HEALTH IMPLICATIONS

Around the turn of the twenty-first century, the number of overweight children in North America was double what it had been two decades earlier. Some authorities believed that television was at least partly to blame. Beyond promoting physical inactivity, food advertisements were a regular part of children's television. On Saturday-morning television, for example, 61 percent of commercials were for food, and more than 90 percent of those advertise-

ments were for sugared cereals, fast foods, and other nutritionally questionable foods. Numerous studies have now documented that such advertising is very effective in increasing children's requests for junk food and fast food, and in changing their fundamental views of healthy nutrition.

Cheryl Pawlowski

FURTHER READING

American Academy of Pediatrics: "Media Education." *Pediatrics* 104 (1999): 341-343.

Macklin, M. C., and L. Carlson, eds. *Advertising to Children: Concepts and Controversies*. Thousand Oaks, Calif.: Sage, 1999.

Robinson, T. N. "Does Television Cause Childhood Obesity?" *Journal of the American Medical Association* 279 (1998): 959-960.

Strasburger, V. C., and B. Wilson. *Children, Adoles-*

Sesame Street characters Elmo (left) and Dani (center) talk to a doctor about Dani's asthma condition in an instructional video titled Sesame Street "A" Is for Asthma. *Released in 1998, the video was part of a Children's Television Workshop series designed to capitalize on the popularity of familiar television characters to educate children about a medical condition that affects millions of young Americans.* (AP/Wide World Photos)

cents, and the Media: Medical and Psychological Impact*. Thousand Oaks, Calif.: Sage, 2002.

Villani, S. "Impact of Media on Children and Adolescents." *Journal of the American Academy of Child and Adolescent Psychiatry* 40, no. 4 (2001): 392-401.

Walsh, D. *Selling Out America's Children*. Minneapolis: Fairview Press, 1995.

SEE ALSO: Advertising; Censorship; Child psychology; Children; Head Start; Moral education; Reality television; Song lyrics; Violence.

Chivalry

DEFINITION: Medieval code of conduct that stressed loyalty, wisdom, courage, generosity, religious fidelity, and the virtues of courtly love

DATE: Influential from the eleventh century to the end of the fourteenth century

TYPE OF ETHICS: Medieval history

SIGNIFICANCE: Forms of chivalry helped to stabilize the power structure of the nobility, contributing to feudal Europe's social coherence for several centuries.

The dissolution of the Carolingian empire in the ninth century completed the decentralization of political authority in western Europe. Although there would soon be signs of newly evolving nation-states, nearly four hundred years passed before strong central monarchies were again dominant in France, Spain, and England. During the intervening years, a complex network of local authorities arose to maintain small subsistence economies and to secure them against attacks and invasions. Never a "system," these local arrangements, based on varying personal and contractual agreements, loosely described western European feudalism. It was in this context that, between the ninth century and the eleventh century, codes of chivalry evolved, reaching their refinement in the thirteenth and fourteenth centuries.

Whatever the immediate intent of chivalry codes, over time they set ethical standards for both personal conduct and social relationships. They applied only to nobles, most of whom at some point in life fulfilled their chief social functions as warriors. (For maximum military effectiveness and to bear the weight of his armor, each noble warrior required a horse. The French word *cheval*, which means "horse," is the source of the English word "chivalry.") Consequently, among the nobility, most chivalric standards derived from military obligations. Others especially concerned the conduct of lords, knights, and their vassals in relation to the ideals or needs of Europe's remaining universal institution, the Roman Catholic Church. Additional rules of behavior, which developed later, pertained to courtly, or romantic, love. Chivalry affected the lives of peasants only indirectly, although peasants were by far the largest segment of Europe's population.

MILITARY CHIVALRY

Feudal society generally was based on a division of labor that was essential for life because of the scarce resources available during the middle Ages. A handful of nobles thus devoted themselves to providing security for the peasants, who, in turn, furnished the means to feed, arm, and maintain the nobles. Chivalry therefore reflected the centrality of the warrior in feudal society and warrior virtues—loyalty above all, but also courage, wisdom, physical skill, individual prowess in battle, and a longing for glory.

Chivalric behavior was also pragmatic, however, and was intended to make the warrior's tasks easier. For example, knights were armored—over time, more and more heavily. Armor was cumbersome, uncomfortable, and hot. Few nobles chose to wear it at all times. Accordingly, an armored knight was forbidden to ambush an unarmored one; ambush was permissible, but the armorless victim had to be allowed to suit up before battle legitimately could begin. Then, too, since the purpose of taking prisoners was to ransom them, and since the prospect of any captor—including a king—becoming a captive himself was good, knights began to treat their captives as honored guests.

By the thirteenth century, if captive nobles were unable to raise ransoms, their captors frequently released them and accepted their children or other relatives as hostages. On other occasions, if captives were unable to meet their ransoms, they were released after a simple pledge to return if they were unable to secure the sums demanded. An example of this was the voluntary return of France's Jean I to captivity in England when his countrymen failed to raise his ransom.

Military chivalry reached polished forms in tournaments, which were arranged mock battles. Their original goals were to maintain knightly skills and to profit from the capture of those who were defeated in jousts. The principal objective of the participants, however, soon became the achievement of glory; for example, to win admiring attention from higher nobles, to charm ladies, to bear the flags or colors of noble houses into jousts with panache, or to distinguish themselves by means of various gallantries. The English word "gallant," in fact, derives from the French *galant*, a thirteenth century word associated with chivalric dash and spiritedness.

RELIGIOUS CHIVALRY

The Roman Catholic Church persistently sought to mitigate the perpetual violence of European aristocracies by diverting knightly energies to more peaceful or more obviously religious ends. Gradually, the Church's sermons and literature sketched out fresh knightly ideals. The ideal knight should become the ideal Christian. If fight he must, he should fight for God, not for personal aggrandizement, land, or booty. He should observe Church-decreed periods of truce. He should serve the Church and his secular lords faithfully. He should suppress crime and bring order to his realms. He should also care for the weak and helpless. Scholars have noted that medieval Church-sponsored Crusades against infidels were partially attempts to steer knightly energies toward religious goals and divert them from self-destruction and the disruption of daily life.

CHIVALRY AND COURTLY LOVE

The songs and poems of French and Spanish troubadours during the thirteenth century successfully celebrated the notion that the leading nobility could derive great benefit by conducting themselves in ways that led ladies to admire and adore them. Thus, incentives were provided for the cultivation of gentler manners, for elevating the status of women, and for making them the center of the actions of such figures as Richard the Lion Hearted, Roland, or Galahad. In addition, the troubadours, whose livelihoods depended on lordly patrons, did much to exalt generosity by making it a cardinal virtue in their lengthy songs and poems.

Clifton K. Yearley

FURTHER READING

Campbell, Joseph. *Creative Mythology*. Vol. 4 in *The Masks of God*. New York: Penguin Books, 1976.

Keen, Maurice. *Origins of the English Gentleman: Heraldry, Chivalry, and Gentility in Medieval England, c. 1300-c. 1500*. Stroud, Gloucestershire, England: Tempus, 2002.

Painter, Sidney. *French Chivalry*. Ithaca, N.Y.: Cornell University Press, 1957.

_____. *Medieval Society*. Ithaca, N.Y.: Cornell University Press, 1968.

Stephenson, Carl. *Medieval Feudalism*. Ithaca, N.Y.: Cornell University Press, 1967.

SEE ALSO: Bushido; Etiquette; Generosity; Honor; Loyalty; Mercy.

Choice

DEFINITION: Ability to do one thing rather than another

TYPE OF ETHICS: Theory of ethics

SIGNIFICANCE: Choice is fundamental to any ethical discussion; an act becomes one's act, whether right or wrong, when one chooses to do it. Moreover, within modern, liberal, capitalist societies, personal choice is celebrated as a good in itself. Less individualist societies, on the other hand, resist the valorization of choice over such other ethical principles as tradition or the good of the community.

When one congratulates others for jobs well done or punishes them for harming others, one does so because what they have done is their action. They chose to act this way rather than that way and, as a consequence of that choice, they accepted the responsibility of that action—it became their act. Legal, ethical, and everyday culture are founded on the responsibilities that are the consequences of free choice. At the same time, one is surrounded by those who wish to control one's choices to achieve their ends. Modern free choice must always be considered within the context of personal responsibility and communal control. As a result, in any discussion of choice in its ethical context, it is necessary to consider the nature of choice itself, its freedom, and the various theoretical and practical attempts to destroy or control this freedom of choice.

THE NATURE OF CHOOSING

Almost every living thing moves: Birds fly, dogs bark, wasps build nests, and bees sting. Within a certain range of activity, living things move in a purposeful manner: There is a pattern to their movement and a selection from among possible movements. Living things seem to do this action rather than that action because of some inner purpose. The human observer easily projects onto all living things both human feelings and thought. When one sees the dog bark, the bee sting, the bird fly, one may presuppose that the dog, bee, and bird are doing things similar to what one does oneself—they choose to bark, sting, or fly. Such a projection upon the surrounding world is part of those magic years of childhood when the child talks to the doll and listens to its answer. It is part of primitive tribal life, in which the whole world is viewed as being animistic and filled with life.

Some modern scientific methods reverse this common experience by suggesting that human actions are like animal actions. Behaviorism, a type of determinism, suggests that all living things act as a consequence of the causes that surround them. There is no such thing as free choice; everything is already determined by forces outside of one's control. Religious determinists claim that God determines what humans do, psychological determinists claim that mental and emotional makeup determine what people do, and sociological determinists claim that society determines what people do. For determinists, human free choice is purposeful activity performed as a result of the inanimate forces that surround people.

Although these deterministic theories are favored by many in the social sciences, modern culture is based on an entirely different principle. The prison, education, legal, and political systems are based on the principle of responsible free choice. Culture demands an answer to various questions: Whose fault is it? Who performed such a wonderful job? The answers determine reward and/or punishment. The system of rewards and punishment is based on the presupposition that people, not circumstances, are responsible for actions. Ethical theory has the same presupposition.

All ethical theory is based upon responsible free choice. People act as a consequence of freely chosen goals and purpose. Culture, as well as ethical theory, recognizes that humans can do things that are unexpected and different, things that are beyond scientific systems and attempts to explain. There is something about the human being that enables him or her to say no when everyone expects a yes and yes when everyone expects a no. There is something about human beings that enables them to create something new. People have not made their homes the same way throughout time because they have freely chosen to do otherwise. Activity by animals and humans is not the same: People choose to act. Somehow, people can take what is outside them, bring it inside them, and, because of certain ideas, choose to change what is outside them.

CHOICE AS ACTION AND AS INTENDED ACTION

Choice is not only internal, it is also an action—what one does. Choosing and doing are internally linked. Certainly, people think about things, reflect upon things, imagine things. Choosing, however, is an intimate link between one's personal, internal goals, principles, and habits and how one affects the world around one by operationalizing and creating one's own world through choosing what will make it up.

What one chooses to do is purposeful—one wants to do it. It is not necessary that one have the intention of doing something every time one does it. Many choices are not intentional in terms of the here and now. Most choices are part of a more extensive intentionality of wanting, for example, to be a good person, a generous person, or an industrious person. In the light of these general intentions, people build habits of goodness or virtue, and these good intentions constitute the intention for specific actions.

Because ethical individuals make choices based on such general intentions, their lives have a consistency to them such that one can say "This is a good person" and expect a consistency of ethical actions.

ETHICAL CHOICE IS FREE ACTION FREELY INTENDED

Freedom is the possibility and ability of making choices. Such a definition of freedom is easy to read but difficult to apply. Certainly one is not more free the more choices one has or makes. It is not possible to quantify freedom. A blind person does not have to wait for sight to live freely. Those who are surrounded by the constant attempt to control their political, economic, educational, food, drink, and dress choices through advertising should not say that they were forced to vote for a U.S. senator or drink a soft drink because advertising dominated the air waves and limited their choices.

At the same time, people should realize that there is a great deal of subtle manipulation of choices. Advertising is sold on the basis of the claim that consumers' choices can be manipulated by the advertiser. In modern technological consumer culture, choice is never had without someone trying to influence it. Most of the social sciences, which began as disinterested attempts to understand human behavior, are now used to attempt to control human behavior for economic or ideological purposes. One must develop a strong character in order to choose freely in the modern world. When one accepts the necessity and the possibility of free choice in modern society, one also accepts the responsibility that accompanies it. Ethical life is not freedom alone or choice alone, but free choices that result in acceptance of responsibility for one's actions. A free choice may be a bad choice or a good choice.

Nathan R. Kollar

FURTHER READING

Brewer, Talbot. *The Bounds of Choice: Unchosen Virtues, Unchosen Commitments.* New York: Garland, 2000.

Farrer, A. M. *The Freedom of Will.* London: A. & C. Black, 1958.

Feinberg, Joel. "Freedom and Behavior Control." In *The Encyclopedia of Bioethics*, edited by Warren T. Reich. Rev. ed. Vol. 2. New York: Macmillan, 1995.

Hume, David. *Enquiries Concerning Human Understanding and Concerning the Principles of Morals.* 3d ed. Oxford, England: Clarendon Press, 1975.

Kane, Robert, ed. *The Oxford Handbook of Free Will.* New York: Oxford University Press, 2002.

Kant, Immanuel. *Critique of Practical Reason.* Edited and translated by Lewis W. Beck. 3d ed. New York: Maxwell Macmillan, 1993.

Macmurray, John. *The Self as Agent.* Atlantic Highlands, N.J.: Humanities Press, 1991.

Neville, Robert. "Behavior Control and Ethical Analysis." In *The Encyclopedia of Bioethics*, edited by Warren T. Reich. Rev. ed. Vol. 1. New York: Macmillan, 1995.

Oldenquist, Andrew. "Choosing, Deciding, and Doing." In *The Encyclopedia of Philosophy*, edited by Paul Edwards. New York: Macmillan, 1972.

SEE ALSO: Behaviorism; Choiceless choices; Cost-benefit analysis; Determinism and freedom; Dilemmas, moral; *Either/Or*; Ethics/morality distinction; Incommensurability; Motivation; Stoic ethics.

Choiceless choices

DEFINITION: Ethical concept articulated by Lawrence Langer describing a situation in which all choices facing an actor are equally unacceptable or immoral

TYPE OF ETHICS: Human rights

SIGNIFICANCE: The concept of choiceless choices offers a rationale for behavior that may offend the ethics of others but for which there is no moral alternative available to the actor.

The "choiceless choice" is a false choice, or a nonchoice, between one form of abnormal response and one or more other abnormal responses, all imposed by situations that are not of the actor's own choosing. Persons in such situations cannot select the lesser of two evils, because *all* the available choices are equally unacceptable. Immoral choices must thus be made in the absence of morally acceptable alternatives. The concept provides solace and succor to those seeking to understand the apparent immoral and incomprehensible behavior of others, or their own behavior, in times of extraordinary stress.

The decisions people make when faced with choiceless choices are often not conscious ones, but decisions made automatically, motivated by rules ingrained inside the actors' heads. An example of one such rule is that of physical survival. A person may act to survive physically, but in doing so may have to pay a moral price that leaves the person facing self-loathing and spiritual death. In the absence of choices that support one's personal integrity, self-worth and self-esteem, one has no alternative but to act in ways that are destructive of one's own sense of self, even as the actions allow for physical survival.

Examples of Choiceless Choices

- Cooperating with enemy captors in order to stay alive

- Undergoing dangerous and unproven treatments when conventional medical treatments are unlikely to cure a terminal disease

- Committing suicide rather than facing the dishonor of surrendering to an enemy

- Tossing a defenseless person from a crowded lifeboat to avoid the risk of having everyone on the boat drown

- Killing one's own children to spare them from lives of slavery or abuse

- Committing a crime oneself in order to expose a crime committed by others

- Eating human flesh to avoid starvation

- Amputating one's own limb to escape a death trap

In some societies, a common rule impressed into the minds of members is the importance of avoiding dishonor. In such societies, people faced with choiceless choices may choose death over dishonor, to the astonishment of persons outside the culture.

Lawrence Langer developed the concept of choiceless choices to describe behavior of Jewish concentration camp prisoners who collaborated with Nazi camp officials during the Holocaust. In some camps, Jewish prisoners were put in charge of other Jewish prisoners. These prisoners policed the camps, operated the crematoria in which the bodies of executed prisoners were burned, and scavenged the remains of the dead for their gold teeth and other valuables. Langer contends that people who did such horrendous things were not true "collaborators" but victims who faced a lack of alternatives. The choiceless choice concept also explains the immoral acts of conquered peoples during wartime, such as the collaboration of the Vichy French authorities with the German occupiers of France during World War II.

Gordon Neal Diem

FURTHER READING

Langer, Lawrence. *Versions of Survival: The Holocaust and the Human Spirit.* Albany: State University of New York Press, 1982.

Strom, Margot, and William Parsons. *Holocaust and Human Behavior.* Brookline, Mass.: Facing History and Ourselves National Foundation, 1994.

SEE ALSO: Choice; Concentration camps; Dilemmas, moral; *Either/Or*; Genocide, frustration-aggression theory of; Holocaust; Honor; Nazism.

Christian ethics

DEFINITION: Ethical systems put forward and endorsed by various forms of Christianity
TYPE OF ETHICS: Religious ethics
SIGNIFICANCE: Christianity and Christian ethical values, in both religious and secularized form, have shaped Western and global thinking about morality for almost two thousand years.

A rich and complex religion, Christianity takes many divergent and occasionally even contradictory forms. It draws upon many resources: the Jewish scriptures, Jesus of Nazareth (whom Christians call Christ), Zoroastrianism, Stoicism, and Neoplatonism.

JESUS OF NAZARETH

The whole of Christian ethics (called moral theology in Roman Catholicism) can be seen as a series of footnotes to the Sermon on the Mount (Matthew 5-7). In this collection of sayings attributed to Jesus, Jesus calls upon his followers to reject the dominant values of their culture and to live according to a different vision. Calling them "the salt of the earth" and "the light of the world," he urges them to trust in God rather than money, to pray in secret and not to broadcast their piety before others. He condemns not only murder but hatred as well; not only adultery but also lust. In one of the most famous moral sayings of all time, he instructs his disciples to "turn the other cheek" to those who strike them, to "repay evil with good," to "love your enemies," and to "pray for those who persecute you."

It is commonplace to say that Christian ethics is an ethics of love—love of God, love of neighbor, and love of self. When asked to summarize the Law, Jesus quoted the Jewish scriptures: "You shall love the Lord your God with all your heart, soul, mind, and strength, and your neighbor as yourself." This is not the same love as desire (*eros*) or kinship (*philia*); it is a self-giving love (*agape*) that creates and finds fulfillment in the other.

Even more important than Jesus' teachings, however, are what he did and what happened to him—his life, death, and resurrection. His life, characterized by healing, power, suffering, forgiveness, obedience, and ultimate submission to a humiliating death by crucifixion—followed by the ultimate triumph of resurrection—has been taken by countless Christians as the pattern for their own lives.

PRIMACY OF GOD AND UNIVERSALITY OF SIN

A pious Jew, Jesus took for granted Judaism's belief in one powerful, just, and merciful God who was God of all the world even if all the world did not acknowledge him. This included a belief in the primacy of divine action over human action—the belief that human beings are neither self-made nor accidents of nature but creatures of the God before whom the nations of the world are mere drops in a bucket. The God of Jesus is active and enmeshed in the world and all human history, even though still above it.

One of the most controversial of all Christian teachings is the universality of sin, which is sometimes described as Original Sin. Broadly speaking, it is the belief that everything that human beings do—and particularly the good that they do—is infected by an evil for which they are responsible but over which they have little control. Hence all human actions fall short of the good; although some are clearly worse than others, none is wholly good.

CONFLICT WITH CULTURE

These beliefs and teachings have put Christians in conflict with both their cultures and themselves. Most cultures value self-preservation and self-assertion, and use violence and coercion to achieve justice and maintain order; but the Sermon on the Mount is in profound contradiction to such a view, as was Jesus' refusal to resist the Roman soldiers who arrested him. Christianity seems to require the impossible: Who can avoid hating some people and lusting after others? The inner tension between the

commandment to love one's enemies and normal tendencies toward self-preservation is equally profound. How can a soldier, a judge, or a ruler, all of whom must make use of violence, be a Christian?

Thus, Christianity finds itself in the midst of overwhelming contradictions and tensions between religion and culture, tensions mirrored in its own history. The new religion grew from a persecuted and illegal sect (c. 30 to 300 C.E.) into a rich and powerful church that dominated European culture and politics (c. 300 to 1800 C.E.), only then to find itself bitterly criticized, put on the defensive, and transformed into one voice among many in a pluralist world (c. 1800 C.E. to present). How has Christianity responded to these tensions?

Christian ethics seems to have taken one of three basic responses to these tensions. It can take the path of cooperation and compromise, becoming part of the power structure and working through the culture, as have medieval Roman Catholicism and nineteenth century American Protestantism. It can take the path of withdrawal, separation and purity, removing itself into separate communities and then either criticizing the surrounding culture (as the Jehovah's Witnesses do) or ignoring it (as the Amish do). Finally, it can take the path of inner withdrawal into the self, as medieval mystics and modern intellectuals who emphasize personal spirituality have done.

In technical terms, these three approaches are called the church, the sect, and mysticism. All three of these "types" are authentically Christian, all have great strengths, and all have weaknesses. The church engages the world and society but tends toward hierarchy, conservatism, and compromise with the great evils of the age (slavery, for example); the sect usually appeals to oppressed members of society and tends toward purity and radicalism (sometimes liberal, sometimes conservative), but at the cost of self-righteousness and fanaticism; and the mystic can combine a tremendous inner liberation with profound tolerance of others but often becomes an utter relativist, profoundly indifferent to most serious moral questions. For the past two or three hundred years, the church type has been in relative decline, while the sect type and mysticism have increased.

PRESENT AND FUTURE DEBATES

Although confident predictions of religion's demise have clearly failed, Christian ethics is nevertheless undergoing massive changes. Christian ethics is no longer identical with the ethics of Western civilization, in two senses: Western civilization no longer regards itself as Christian, and the majority of Christians were living in the developing world at the beginning of the twenty-first century. Two hundred years earlier, Christianity was criticized for being too pessimistic. By the twenty-first century, it was being criticized for being too optimistic. Several vigorous debates arising from these and other changes should both enliven and frustrate Christian ethics for the foreseeable future.

The growth in the number of developing world Christians and the worldwide increase in minority populations in the developed world will fuel continuing debates over the extent to which salvation entails liberation from economic and social oppression. Does God clearly side with the poor, as liberation theology insists? What does that mean? At the same time, the rapid growth in charismatic and conservative Christianity, particularly in South America and in the nations of the former Soviet Union, require reevaluation of an ethics that emphasizes personal morality and responsibility over social change (which it nevertheless unintentionally produces). The growing importance of women in culture and religious institutions will intensify debates over gender and oppression, as can be seen in the growth of feminist liberation theology.

New debates have also arisen over the role of love and suffering in the Christian life. Christian love has often been described as self-sacrificial, and human suffering has been viewed as an opportunity to share in Christ's suffering; but now many question whether Christianity should be in the business of prescribing self-sacrifice and suffering for women and the poor. Nevertheless, it is impossible to remove all suffering from human life; everyone must suffer and die. Must we resist all pain and suffering at all costs? Are there times when they should be accepted and even embraced? These questions are also relevant to the euthanasia debate and to the growing cost of health care.

Concern over Christian teachings regarding the environment will also grow, as the Christian ethic of Earth stewardship wrestles with various forms of biocentrism and recent attempts to revive some pagan religions.

Finally, one may continue to look for debates over the primacy and power of God's involvement in nature and history, apart from which it will be impossible to sustain Christian ethics.

Garrett E. Paul

FURTHER READING

Boff, Leonardo, and Clodovis Boff. *Introducing Liberation Theology.* Translated by Paul Burns. Maryknoll, N.Y.: Orbis Books, 1987.

Gutierrez, Gustavo. *We Drink from Our Own Wells.* Translated by Matthew J. O'Connell. Maryknoll, N.Y.: Orbis Books, 1984.

Hauerwas, Stanley. *The Peaceable Kingdom: A Primer in Christian Ethics.* Notre Dame, Ind.: University of Notre Dame Press, 1983.

Kirkpatrick, Frank G. *A Moral Ontology for a Theistic Ethic: Gathering the Nations in Love and Justice.* Burlington, Vt.: Ashgate, 2003.

McFaul, Thomas R. *Transformation Ethics: Developing the Christian Moral Imagination.* Lanham, Md.: University Press of America, 2003.

Niebuhr, H. Richard. *Christ and Culture.* New York: Harper & Row, 1975.

Niebuhr, Reinhold. *An Interpretation of Christian Ethics.* New York: Meridian Books, 1956.

Ruether, Rosemary. *Gaia and God: An Ecofeminist Theology of Earth Healing.* San Francisco: HarperSanFrancisco, 1992.

Tillich, Paul. *Love, Power, and Justice: Ontological Analyses and Ethical Applications.* New York: Oxford University Press, 1972.

SEE ALSO: Augustine, Saint; Calvin, John; Ethical monotheism; Islamic ethics; Jesus Christ; Jewish ethics; Luther, Martin; Religion; Sin; Televangelists; Thomas Aquinas.

Church-state separation

DEFINITION: Issues arising from the U.S. Constitution's First Amendment, which prohibit laws "respecting an establishment of religion," and comparable state constitutional provisions,

TYPE OF ETHICS: Religious ethics

SIGNIFICANCE: Most accounts of church-state separation insist that involvement by government in religious affairs infringes upon rights of citizens to be free from compulsion in religious matters and to be treated with equal respect without regard to their religious beliefs.

The notion of church-state separation, often associated with the establishment clause of the U.S. Constitution's First Amendment, is not specifically referred to in that document. Nevertheless, during the course of the twentieth century, courts relied on the establishment clause—and comparable provisions in state constitutions—to prohibit close alliances between government and religion. Disestablishment is generally understood to protect individuals from compulsion in matters regarding religion and to safeguard their standing as citizens without respect to their religious beliefs.

PROTECTION FROM COMPULSION

In the American experience, the principle of church-state separation springs from a commitment to religious liberty. A variety of colonial and state religious establishments existed during the seventeenth and eighteenth centuries. Some of these—such as the establishment of the Congregational Church in Massachusetts—did not collapse until the early decades of the nineteenth century. However, all of these establishments eventually came to be viewed as encroachments on the religious freedom of individuals because they exerted the force of law to compel support for particular religious traditions. Rhode Island founder Roger Williams, for example, complained bitterly against official support for religion, insisting that "forced worship stinks in God's nostrils."

Thomas Jefferson joined those who opposed a tax scheme in Virginia that would have contributed financial support to a variety of Christian churches. In the "Bill for Establishing Religious Freedom," which Jefferson wrote and which Virginia ultimately passed, he declared that forcing individuals to contribute to the propagation of opinions in which they did not believe was "sinful and tyrannical." Eventually, the Constitution was amended to include the religion clauses of the First Amendment. Although the free exercise clause most directly limits the power of government to exercise compulsion in religious matters, the establishment clause is generally understood as erecting a barrier against even indirect forms of compulsion.

EQUAL RESPECT AS CITIZENS

Church-state separation also secures a measure of respect for citizens without regard to whatever religious beliefs they do or do not hold. In North American colonies with established religions, membership in a colony's official church was often a prerequisite to holding public office or enjoying other benefits. Article VI of the U.S. Constitution specifically prohibits religious tests for office and thus dethroned this kind of religious favoritism, at least as applied to federal political positions.

More recently, the U.S. Supreme Court has interpreted the establishment clause, as well, as preventing government from endorsing particular religious traditions. In so holding, the Court has argued that such endorsements impermissibly make the possession of certain religious beliefs relevant to one's standing as a citizen. Thus, the Court has held that publicly sponsored displays of religious symbols designed to endorse particular religions are forbidden by the establishment clause. In *County of Allegheny v. American Civil Liberties Union* (1989), the Court declared unconstitutional the display of a nativity scene—depicting the birth of Jesus Christ—during the Christmas season, when the scene was not accompanied by other holiday symbols. Although the Court had previously upheld the display of a nativity scene in conjunction with other Christmas symbols in *Lynch v. Donnelly* (1984), it ruled in *County of Allegheny v. ACLU* that the solitary display of the nativity scene amounted to an impermissible endorsement of Christianity.

SUPPORT FOR RELIGIOUS ACTIVITIES

Throughout most of the twentieth century, the Supreme Court interpreted the establishment clause to forbid most public aid to religious organizations or institutions. This interpretation of church-state separation was often justified as preventing citizens from being compelled to support religions to which they did not adhere. By the end of the twentieth century, however, the Court had focused attention on whether it was appropriate that religious believers be disqualified from receiving certain generally available benefits, especially those that facilitated freedom of speech. Eventually, the Court read the First Amendment's free speech clause to require governments to make available to religious speakers opportunities comparable to those provided other speakers.

This, the Court reasoned, was made necessary by the free speech clause's general requirement that government not favor particular speakers over others. By the beginning of the twenty-first century, the Court had not yet dissolved its longstanding ban on direct aid by governments to religious institutions. Nevertheless, by focusing on the equal rights of religious speakers, the Court had retreated from vigorous notions of church-state separation that had prevailed only fifty years earlier.

As is often the case in constitutional law, competing ethical principles each claim a harbor within the First Amendment's establishment clause. On the one hand, the principle of preventing compulsion in religious matters might justify a sturdy wall of separation between church and state. On the other hand, the principle of equality has made it increasingly difficult for the Supreme Court to justify excluding religious believers from access to many public benefits that are available to their fellow citizens. The Court is still reluctant to countenance direct public aid to religious institutions, but it has become more willing to guarantee—at a minimum—that religious citizens have equal free speech rights.

Timothy L. Hall

FURTHER READING

Adams, Arlin M., and Charles J. Emmerich. *A Nation Dedicated to Religious Liberty: The Constitutional Heritage of the Religion Clauses.* Philadelphia: University of Pennsylvania Press, 1990.

Curry, Thomas J. *The First Freedoms: Church and State in America to the Passage of the First Amendment.* New York: Oxford University Press, 1986.

Hamburger, Philip. *Separation of Church and State.* Cambridge, Mass.: Harvard University Press, 2002.

Levy, Leonard W. *The Establishment Clause: Religion and the First Amendment.* 2d rev. ed. Chapel Hill: University of North Carolina Press, 1994.

Noonan, John T., Jr. *The Lustre of Our Country: The American Experience of Religious Freedom.* Berkeley: University of California Press, 1998.

SEE ALSO: American Civil Liberties Union; Bill of Rights, U.S.; Bonhoeffer, Dietrich; Christian ethics; First Amendment; Holy war; Jefferson, Thomas; Religion; Religion and violence; Secular ethics.

Cicero

IDENTIFICATION: Roman orator and politician
BORN: June 3, 106 B.C.E., Arpinum, Latium (now Arpino, Italy)
DIED: December 7, 43 B.C.E., Formiae, Latium (now Formia, Italy)
TYPE OF ETHICS: Classical history
SIGNIFICANCE: A leading figure in the tumultuous final days of the Roman Republic, Cicero articulated and attempted to practice his belief that the good man gives himself to unselfish public service. His many treatises include *On the Republic* (*De republica*, 52 B.C.E.), *On the Laws* (*De legibus*, 52 B.C.E.), *On Fate* (*De fato*, 45 B.C.E.), *Tusculan Disputations* (*Tusculanae disputationes*, 44 B.C.E.), and *On Duties* (*De officiis*, 44 B.C.E.).

The author and orator Cicero was one of the most eloquent exponents in the Roman world of the Stoic belief that there is an inherent natural order in the universe and that this order requires human beings, as rational creatures, to follow natural law. This natural law, which can be apprehended through a calm and philosophical survey of the world, clearly indicates that humans are morally obliged to conform to the universal rule of reason. This is particularly true in social relationships, since Cicero shared the Greek belief in the natural brotherhood and equality of man; this belief makes serving the common good of humanity the highest duty of every individual. For Cicero, enlightened patriotism was an ethical as well as a political duty.

Michael Witkoski

SEE ALSO: Children; Common good; Duty; Just war theory; Natural law; Parenting.

Citizenship

DEFINITION: Status held by individuals born or naturalized into a community or state that confers upon the individual certain rights and duties in relationship to other members of the community and to the community itself
TYPE OF ETHICS: Politico-economic ethics
SIGNIFICANCE: Citizens are both empowered by, and beholden to, the states in which they enjoy citi-

zenship. The rights and obligations of citizenship provide the framework for some of the oldest reflections upon ethical life and moral duty in the Western canon.

The idea of citizenship is central to any conception of ethics. Human beings, by necessity, live in or rely on social and political communities. To avoid conflict and promote cooperation in these communities, it is necessary that individual members of it learn how to accommodate their own interests and needs with those of the collective whole. The earliest systematic treatment of politics and the ethical comportment of citizens in political contexts undertaken by the ancient Greeks recognized that necessity drove individuals into the social context and held that duty was the primary content of citizenship.

To Greeks and Romans, citizens enjoyed certain privileges or rights denied to outsiders, but the notion of an individual right, a natural right inhering in the individual, as opposed to a positive customary or statutory right that might be granted or withdrawn by the state, was not conceived until the seventeenth century. Political and ethical theory now posits that rights are inherent in the individual as individual, and one of the rights now affirmed is the right to citizenship itself. If rights have become the primary focus of much thinking about modern citizenship, however, there can be little doubt that duty must remain a significant feature of citizenship if the concept is to have any genuine content, since rights have no meaning if no one has a duty to respect the rights of others.

HISTORY

The earliest conceptions of citizenship stressed the importance of the individual's duty to the state. Not all persons were considered citizens in the fullest sense of the term, even in the most democratic of states, such as Athens in the fifth century B.C.E., where active citizenship was limited to propertied men. With the privileges of citizenship came responsibilities: to participate in assemblies, to hold office, to defend the city from external enemies, to serve in the army or navy, to pay taxes, to outfit a naval vessel, or to subsidize a public festival. In the intimate confines of the Greek polis the citizen might enjoy certain privileges, but above all the citizen was duty bound to the state. Still the Greeks, as evidenced in Sophocles' story *Antigone* (c. 441 B.C.E.) and in

Plato's accounts of the trial and death of Socrates, were alive to the contradictions that citizens might face in honoring civic duty on one hand and the dictates of individual conscience on the other.

In Rome, a more extensive body of rights was enjoyed by its citizens, although, as in Greece, citizenship carried with it certain duties, such as paying taxes and serving in the legions or navy. Moreover, the rights of Roman citizens were not conceived as natural or human rights, but rather were rooted in the custom or statutes of the city, and could be revoked. As Rome expanded beyond a republic to an empire, its conception of citizenship also enlarged, and under Caracalla in 212 C.E., citizenship was extended to all the empire's inhabitants.

By that time, the rights of the citizen had been substantially diluted. The coming of Christianity created new tensions for the citizen. In general, Christianity taught that the good Christian should obey and serve the political ruler except in matters that called for the Christian to violate fundamental tenets of faith or scruples of conscience. In these circumstances, passive disobedience and the acceptance of punishment for such disobedience was counseled. Violent rebellion was considered wrong. Christians were urged to respect the need for political authority and civil order. Duty, as in the classical ages, still dominated thinking about the individual citizen's relationship with the state. Not until the Religious Wars of the seventeenth and eighteenth centuries did philosophers (such as Thomas Hobbes and John Locke) posit the notion that individuals had inherent human rights that no state in principle should violate. Not until after World War II, however, did governments begin to adopt human rights treaties stipulating what those rights were or how they might be guaranteed.

MODERN ISSUES

Modern issues concerning the ethical content of citizenship include the nature of citizenship as a human right, the problem of civil disobedience, the scope of freedom in which citizens may act in face of the community's need for order, and the problem of citizens and outsiders. Modern human rights treaties suggest that individuals have a right to citizenship. No state, however, has a duty to extend citizenship to any particular person, which leaves many people, including refugees, in precarious situations.

States also have the power to take away citizenship. Citizenship, then, is still governed by sovereign states and has only a tenuous claim to status as a human right. Within democratic systems, however, citizens are guaranteed civil rights and individual freedoms in domestic law. Even aliens are guaranteed individual freedoms by most governments, although civil rights, such as the right to vote and hold office, are reserved for citizens alone. Citizens also have duties, such as supporting the state, serving in its defense, and obeying its laws. On occasion, the individual's religious beliefs or personal conscience come into conflict with the law. This may lead an individual into acts of protest or civil disobedience. Modern examples of movements that espouse civil disobedience include the Civil Rights movement, the sanctuary movement, and some factions of the pro-life movement. Citizens practicing civil disobedience risk punishment for violation of the law.

The tendency in many democratic countries has been for citizens to claim an expanding body of rights and personal freedoms. This overemphasis on rights has often ignored the importance of duties to others and to the community as a whole. A perpetual clash of rights without a sense of corresponding duties can lead to disorder and eventually to the endangerment of rights. An increasingly important ethical question for modern democratic societies, then, is how to ensure a balance between rights and duties.

Finally, what duties do the citizens of a society have toward aliens, illegal immigrants, refugees, or asylum seekers? In an era of substantial migration, questions about how to deal with outsiders—whether to grant them admission or citizenship or to exclude or deport them—become increasingly important. Decisions about who should or should not be admitted raise ethical issues for public policymakers regarding the needs and rights of the existing citizen body and the predicament of asylum seekers and prospective immigrants who wish to become members of it.

Robert F. Gorman

FURTHER READING

Allman, Dwight D., and Michael D. Beaty, eds. *Cultivating Citizens: Soulcraft and Citizens in Contemporary America.* Lanham, Md.: Lexington Books, 2002.

Aristotle. *The Politics.* Translated by Ernest Barker. Rev. ed. Introduction by R. F. Stalley. New York: Oxford University Press, 1995.

Augustine, Saint. *The Political Writings of St. Augustine.* Edited by Henry Paolucci. Chicago: Gateway Editions, 1987.

Beiner, Ronald. *Liberalism, Nationalism, Citizenship: Essays on the Problem of Political Community.* Vancouver: UBC Press, 2003.

Lister, Ruth. *Citizenship: Feminist Perspectives.* 2d ed. Washington Square, N.Y.: New York University Press, 2003.

Paine, Thomas. *"Common Sense" and "The Rights of Man."* Edited and foreword by Tony Benn. London: Phoenix, 2000.

Plato. *The Collected Dialogues of Plato.* Edited by Edith Hamilton and Huntington Cairns. 1961. Reprint. Princeton, N.J.: Princeton University Press, 1984.

Rousseau, Jean-Jacques. *"The Social Contract" and "The First and Second Discourses,"* edited by Susan Dunn. New Haven, Conn.: Yale University Press, 2002.

Thoreau, Henry David. *"Walden" and "Civil Disobedience": Complete Texts with Introduction, Historical Contexts, Critical Essays.* Edited by Paul Lauter. Boston: Houghton Mifflin, 2000.

Von Glahn, Gerhard. *Law Among Nations: An Introduction to Public International Law.* 7th ed. Boston: Allyn and Bacon, 1996.

SEE ALSO: *Apology*; Aśoka; Conscientious objection; Democracy; Duty; Human rights; *Leviathan*; *Nicomachean Ethics*; Patriotism; Rights and obligations.

Civil disobedience

DEFINITION: Nonviolent form of social protest in which protesters defy the law with the aim of changing the law or effecting social change

TYPE OF ETHICS: Civil rights

SIGNIFICANCE: Civil disobedience is closely associated with an ethical commitment to nonviolent resistance to the infractions of a government. It is therefore significant both as a means of effecting social change, and as an expression of the moral belief that such change should be brought about through peaceful means.

Major Events in the History of Civil Disobedience

1849	Henry David Thoreau publishes "Resistance to Civil Government" (later known as "Civil Disobedience").
1906	Mohandas K. Gandhi urges Indians in South Africa to go to jail rather than accept racist policies, beginning his *satyagraha* campaign.
1919	Gandhi leads nationwide closing of businesses in India to protest discriminatory legislation.
1928	Gandhi organizes on behalf of indigo workers in Bihar, India, and initiates fasting as a form of *satyagraha*.
1920-1922	Gandhi leads boycott of courts and councils in India and develops noncooperation strategies.
1932-1933	Gandhi engages in fasts to protest untouchability.
1942	Gandhi arrested for *satyagraha* activities.
1955	Martin Luther King, Jr., leads boycott of transit company in Montgomery, Alabama.
1956-1960	King leads protest demonstrations throughout the American South.
1963	King leads March on Washington for civil rights.
1965	King leads "Freedom March" from Selma to Montgomery and organizes voter registration drive.
1968	King initiates a "Poor People's Campaign" but is assassinated before it can be carried out.

Most civil disobedience movements have been nonviolent, hence the term "civil" (disobedience to the law in a civil, or nonviolent, manner). Civil disobedience has been used by people in various societies as a vehicle to seek changes in the laws considered unjust by those participating in these movements.

The resistance by the state to such protests is based on the moral and political legitimacy claimed by the rulers in the name of the people. The fundamental philosophical issue here is that although the rule of law must be maintained in order for the society to function and to protect life and property, civil disobedience movements represent a challenge to the legitimacy of that rule of law. Participants in actions of civil disobedience recognize a higher moral au-

thority than that of the state, asserting that the laws do not reflect the ethical norms of the people. They believe that it is therefore justifiable to disobey the law.

PHILOSOPHICAL BACKGROUND

Political philosophers since Socrates have discussed and debated the rule of law and the legitimacy sought by the state in demanding obedience to its laws from its citizens. Socrates was accused of corrupting the minds of young people by preaching atheism. He thought it was his moral duty to disobey laws that he thought were immoral. Thomas Hobbes considered it the prerogative of the sovereign to institute laws that must be obeyed. He considered all laws to be just laws. John Locke, however, considered that the citizens did not completely surrender their right to resist a law they considered unjust. Henry David Thoreau advocated the right of citizens to resist laws they considered immoral or laws that forced people to commit injustice to others. Thoreau is considered the pioneer in the United States in advocating civil disobedience on moral grounds.

An important element of civil disobedience is conscientious objection. Conscientious objectors defy laws that they consider repugnant to their moral principles. Unlike civil disobedience, in which the participants are seeking to change laws, in conscientious objection, objectors seek exemption from laws only for themselves. For example, many individuals have refused to pay portions of their federal taxes that would be used for defense expenditures. An important distinction here is the fact that these people are disobeying the law to pay taxes but they are not necessarily urging others to do the same.

CIVIL DISOBEDIENCE IN INDIA

A key civil disobedience movement in modern history was led by Mohandas K. Gandhi of India, popularly known as Mahatma Gandhi. He led protest movements in South Africa during the early twentieth century to challenge laws of racial discrimination by the whites against the indigenous peoples and non-whites of South Africa. The technique he developed, based on ancient Indian philosophical ideas, focused on the notion of *satyagraha,* or "moral victory." According to this concept, the protesters would win their campaigns because they stood on higher ethical ground than did the laws they chose to disobey.

After winning many legal battles in South Africa, Gandhi returned to India to take part in the movement for national independence from the British. This is where he perfected the art of nonviolent civil disobedience. He soon realized that the most effective way of hurting the British was to deny them the revenue they earned by selling products manufactured in Britain to Indians. Gandhi launched a movement to boycott goods made in Britain. Two important milestones in Gandhi's civil disobedience movement were the boycott of British-made cloth, which Gandhi reinforced by encouraging Indians to weave their own cotton, and the second was the defiance of the ban on making salt from saltwater. These two movements mobilized millions of people in boycotting British-made goods and defying British laws in a nonviolent manner.

CIVIL DISOBEDIENCE IN THE UNITED STATES

The civil disobedience movement in the United States was essentially the struggle of African Americans to gain equal rights. An important milestone in the Civil Rights movement in the United States was the refusal of Rosa Parks to vacate her bus seat to a white passenger in Montgomery, Alabama. This act

Rosa Parks is fingerprinted after being arrested in December, 1955, for refusing to give up her seat to a white man in the nonwhite section of a Montgomery, Alabama, bus. (Library of Congress)

of civil disobedience led to widespread agitation in the southern United States. Martin Luther King, Jr., who organized and led the protests, is considered the father of the civil disobedience movement in the United States. King adopted Gandhi's idea of nonviolent noncooperation. He led protesters in challenging segregation laws that separated whites and nonwhites in education, public facilities, and other arenas. This civil disobedience movement led to the dismantling of most of the racially discriminatory laws in the United States and the passage of the Civil Rights Act in 1964.

Another important civil disobedience movement in the United States was the opposition to the United States' involvement in the Vietnam War. Many young people refused to join the armed forces. There were protests all over the country, mainly in educational institutions, demanding the withdrawal of U.S. troops from Vietnam. Resistance to the draft was a key form of civil disobedience in this era.

The civil disobedience movement poses a serious challenge to the authority and the claim of the state for total compliance of laws by its citizens in the name of maintaining peace and order in society. By defying laws considered morally repugnant, civil disobedience movements have played a key role in changing numerous unjust laws in the United States and abroad.

Khalid N. Mahmood

FURTHER READING

Fullinwider, Robert K., and Claudia Mills, eds. *The Moral Foundations of Civil Rights*. Totowa, N.J.: Rowman & Littlefield, 1986.

Gandhi, Mohandas K. *An Autobiography: The Story of My Experiments with Truth*. Translated by Mahadev Desai. Foreword by Sissela Bok. Boston: Beacon, 1993.

Gans, Chaim. *Philosophical Anarchism and Political Disobedience*. New York: Cambridge University Press, 1992.

Haksar, Vinit. *Rights, Communities, and Disobedience: Liberalism and Gandhi*. New York: Oxford University Press, 2001.

Thoreau, Henry David. *"Walden" and "Civil Disobedience": Complete Texts with Introduction, Historical Contexts, Critical Essays*. Edited by Paul Lauter. Boston: Houghton Mifflin, 2000.

Williams, Juan. *Eyes on the Prize: America's Civil Rights Years, 1954-1965*. New York: Viking, 1987.

SEE ALSO: Boycotts; Conscience; Conscientious objection; Gandhi, Mohandas K.; King, Martin Luther, Jr.; Nonviolence; Revolution; Taxes; Thoreau, Henry David.

Civil Rights Act of 1964

IDENTIFICATION: Federal law outlawing racial, religious, and ethnic discrimination in places of public accommodation

DATE: Became law on July 2, 1964

TYPE OF ETHICS: Civil rights

SIGNIFICANCE: Passage of the Civil Rights Act signaled that the American public had accepted that racial discrimination and the "Jim Crow" system were evils that should be eliminated; the statute and its successor acts set American race relations on a new course.

The first true civil rights law in the United States since Reconstruction, the Civil Rights Act of 1964 passed after decades of southern resistance to any new civil rights laws. Public opinion in the United States had changed as a result of violent southern resistance to demonstrations such as the sit-ins and freedom rides of the Civil Rights movement.

The assassination of President John F. Kennedy and the murders of several civil rights activists strengthened the public sense that it was time to reform American race relations. The bill was powerfully pressed by President Lyndon B. Johnson, who, as a southerner, was able to generate a great deal of support for it. The law prohibited discrimination on account of race, color, religion, or national origin in access to places of public accommodation such as hotels, restaurants, shops, and theaters. Later amendments to the law added age, gender, and disability as forbidden grounds for discrimination; employment and education were later added as protected activities.

Robert Jacobs

SEE ALSO: *Brown v. Board of Education*; Civil rights and liberties; Civil Rights movement; Commission on Civil Rights, U.S.; Congress.

Civil rights and liberties

DEFINITION: Legally codified private rights and duties granted to citizens by their governments

TYPE OF ETHICS: Civil rights

SIGNIFICANCE: The system of civil rights and civil liberties is intended to permit every member of a polity to seek liberty, property, and happiness, free of interference from others or from the government.

Civil rights and liberties, in the broadest sense, permit citizens to live their lives free of fear of being victimized by other members of their communities or by the government. Thus, laws that establish and protect property and personal rights are an important part of civil liberty. The common usage of the terms, however, encompasses both the rights and liberties of individuals in relationship to government and those rights that are enforceable in courts. In this sense, there are two types of rights: substantive and procedural.

SUBSTANTIVE RIGHTS

Substantive rights are those things that one can do as a matter of right without interference from the government or public officials. In the United States, there is constitutional and customary protection for many of the most basic aspects of life; for example, the rights to citizenship, to own property, to choose one's spouse, to choose an occupation, to be protected by laws, and to make and enforce lawful contracts. There is additional constitutional protection for other substantive rights. Most of the limits on government are found in the U.S. Bill of Rights. The First Amendment freedom of speech, press, and assembly and the right to the free exercise of one's religion protect the individual's conscience and allow him or her to associate with whomever he or she chooses.

The Fourth Amendment, which has both procedural and substantive aspects, forbids agents of the government to enter one's home or other places where one can reasonably expect privacy, except under narrowly defined circumstances. The First and Fourth Amendments combined establish additional rights of privacy that protect access to birth control information, access to abortion for a pregnant woman in the first trimester of pregnancy, privacy in the choice of one's reading matter, and privacy in intimate marital matters. Under the Second Amendment, there is still a limited private right to keep and bear arms.

There are also substantive political rights in the United States. In general, political rights are conferred only on citizens; most of the other substantive rights discussed above are conferred on citizens and noncitizens alike. Political rights include citizenship itself, the right to vote, and the right to hold public office or to participate in other ways in the administration of government.

PROCEDURAL RIGHTS

Procedural rights are those procedures that the government must afford an individual whose life, liberty, or property it proposes to take. The foremost expression of procedural rights is found in the due process clause of the Fifth Amendment, which promises that no "person will be deprived of life, liberty, or property without due process of law." At a minimum, then, the government must afford the individual a fair hearing before imposing any kind of punishment or deprivation.

The U.S. Constitution is full of provisions that specify the contents of fair procedure. An arrested person must be brought before a magistrate soon after arrest and, except under certain narrowly defined circumstances, is entitled to be released on bail while awaiting trial. The defendant in a criminal case is entitled to a trial by an impartial jury; the government may not force him to stand trial away from the area in which the crime occurred. No one can be forced to incriminate himself or herself either before a tribunal or during a police interrogation. A defendant has the right to confront and cross-examine opposing witnesses as well as the right to have illegally seized evidence excluded from consideration at trial, thus making good the procedural side of the Fourth Amendment. Hearsay evidence is inadmissible in court. A defendant cannot be tried twice for the same crime if acquitted and cannot be subjected to cruel or unusual punishment. An indigent defendant has the right to representation by court-appointed counsel at public expense.

The crime of treason is narrowly defined by the Constitution, thus preventing the government from using treason charges against its political opponents. The writ of habeas corpus, which is the main procedural safeguard against unlawful arrest, may not be suspended by the government except in time of war or other emergency.

CONCLUSION

The guarantees discussed above reflect centuries of ethical thought and also incorporate the legal and political wisdom of bench and bar over the years. The fundamental principles that emerge are that people should be allowed to do and think as they see fit so long as they do not injure public peace or order, that only the guilty should be punished, that the powers of the government should never be used to injure people who are not guilty of crimes, and that fair evidentiary rules must be applied in the search for the truth when someone is accused of a crime.

Robert Jacobs

FURTHER READING

Abraham, Henry J., and Barbara A. Perry. *Freedom and the Court: Civil Rights and Liberties in the United States.* 8th ed. Lawrence: University of Kansas Press, 2003.

Alexy, Robert. *A Theory of Constitutional Rights.* Translated by Julian Rivers. New York: Oxford University Press, 2002.

The Declaration of Independence and the Constitution of the United States. Scarsdale, N.Y.: Lion Books, 1987.

Locke, John. *Two Treatises of Government.* Edited by Peter Laslett. New York: Cambridge University Press, 1988.

McLaughlin, Andrew C. *A Constitutional History of the United States.* New York: Appleton-Century-Crofts, 1935.

Mendenhall, Michael J., ed. *The Constitution of the United States of America: The Definitive Edition.* Monterey, Calif.: Institute for Constitutional Research, 1991.

Mill, John Stuart. *Utilitarianism, Liberty, and Representative Government.* New York: E. P. Dutton, 1951.

Smith, Goldwin. *A Constitutional and Legal History of England.* New York: Charles Scribner's Sons, 1955.

SEE ALSO: Bill of Rights, U.S.; Citizenship; Civil Rights movement; Commission on Civil Rights, U.S.; Constitution, U.S.; English Bill of Rights; First Amendment; Freedom of expression; International Covenant on Civil and Political Rights; Magna Carta; Rights and obligations.

Civil Rights movement

THE EVENT: Historical movement dedicated to bringing substantive civil rights to all American citizens by dismantling legally sanctioned systems of racial prejudice in the United States.

DATE: 1950's-1960's

TYPE OF ETHICS: Civil rights

SIGNIFICANCE: The Civil Rights movement changed the status of race relations in the United States, especially between African Americans and whites, and formed a model for other struggles for equality during the late twentieth and early twenty-first centuries.

The Civil Rights movement in the United States represents a broad and protracted struggle in the effort to establish constitutional liberties for African Americans and members of other historically disadvantaged groups. A liberal interpretation of the movement's history suggests that it could be dated as far back as the Emancipation Proclamation of 1863. Some scholars maintain that the Montgomery bus boycott of 1955 represents the genesis of the Civil Rights movement. Yet this assessment tends to ignore the contributions of many individual activists, such as W. E. B. Du Bois and A. Philip Randolph, and organizations such as the National Association for the Advancement of Colored People (NAACP) and the National Urban League (NUL) that took place prior to 1955. These and other initiatives gave rise to countless efforts over the next twenty years or so by African Americans and their supporters.

HISTORY

The U.S. Supreme Court's *Brown v. Board of Education* decision in 1954 augured a dramatic shift in the status of race relations in America. "Separate but equal" had been declared unconstitutional in education. The system of segregated education in the South was ordered to be dismantled.

The *Brown* decision did not go unchallenged. In 1956, the White Citizens Council of America was

Ronald Martin, Robert Patterson, and Mark Martin were among the first civil rights activists to stage peaceful sit-ins at the Woolworth store lunch counter in Greensboro, North Carolina, in 1960. (Library of Congress)

formed. Its expressed purpose was to provide "massive resistance" against the desegregation effort in the South. The organization was successful in pressuring school boards, business leaders, and politicians to maintain a hard line against the desegregation effort. In 1957, massive resistance emboldened Arkansas governor Orval Faubus to use the National Guard to prevent African American students from integrating Central High School in Little Rock, Arkansas. As the civil rights effort broadened in scope, so did the violence caused by some whites. Freedom riders were sometimes brutally beaten; peaceful demonstrators were frequently attacked by local police with dogs and blasted with high-pressure water hoses; some demonstrators were jailed for marching and sit-ins; and some civil rights leaders were physically abused, while others had their homes bombed.

The 1955 Montgomery bus boycott, however, appeared to have begun a spirit of social activism that could not be easily deterred. The refusal of Rosa Parks, an African American seamstress, to give up her seat to a white passenger sparked a protest that lasted more than a year, paralyzing the city buses. The significance of the bus boycott was that it kept the Supreme Court involved in the desegregation debate, gave national prominence to Martin Luther King, Jr., and demonstrated that direct action could bring about desired change.

The movement appeared to have gained momentum following the Montgomery bus boycott. Soon after, challenges to Jim Crow began to spring up in various places throughout the South. In Greensboro, North Carolina, in 1960, four African American college students sat at a lunch counter, challenging Woolworth's policy of serving only white customers. The sit-in became a powerful weapon of nonviolent direct action that was employed by the Congress of Racial Equality (CORE), the Student Nonviolent Coordinating Committee (SNCC, pronounced "snick"), the Southern Christian Leadership Conference (SCLC), and other nonviolent activist groups and organizations fighting discriminatory practices.

Also during this time, CORE began the "freedom rides," while the SCLC began organizing a major voter rights drive (Voter Education Project), both in the South. All such efforts were met with resistance from whites who were determined to hold on to the advantages that racial discrimination afforded and to the traditions of segregation.

Some significant legislation supporting the civil rights effort was passed by Congress. The 1964 Civil Rights Act and the 1965 Voting Rights Act are often viewed as the most important legislation of the period. Together, they enhanced the Fourteenth and Fifteenth Amendments to the Constitution, guaranteeing equal protection of the law and the right to vote. Legislation did not, however, readily translate into a more open society. Frustration over the lack of opportunity for jobs, better housing, and greater educational opportunity resulted in a series of riots from 1965 to 1967. In 1968, the Kerner Commission (National Advisory Commission on Civil Disorders) concluded that white racism was responsible for the conditions leading up to the riots.

RETRENCHMENT

Some observers suggest that the Civil Rights movement began to wane during the late 1960's and early 1970's. There are indications that as the movement became more militant, whites were hard pressed to find common ground with some organizations. There are also indications that the Vietnam "antiwar" movement became the focus of attention, detracting from the civil rights effort. Still others suggest that the death of Martin Luther King, Jr., in 1968 deprived the movement of its most influential leader, causing disarray and abandonment by liberal whites. Others maintain that the Civil Rights movement never ended, but that it has experienced only moderate support from liberals and outright hostility from conservatives.

Despite the ups and downs of the struggle, the civil rights of all citizens have been enhanced by the efforts of African Americans and their supporters. Women have gained tremendously, as have other minority groups, such as Hispanics, Native Americans, Asian Americans, and gays and lesbians. The tactics and strategies employed by African Americans during the 1950's and 1960's became standard operating procedure for many activist groups.

SIGNIFICANT ORGANIZATIONS

The NAACP, founded in 1909 by African Americans and white liberals, assumed leadership in the civil rights struggle during the first half of the twentieth century. From its inception, the NAACP began the struggle to achieve legal redress in judicial systems around the country on behalf of African Americans. Throughout most of the twentieth century, the NAACP has fought for antilynching legislation, the fair administration of justice, voting rights for African Americans in the South, equal educational opportunity, and the ending of discriminatory practices in the workplace.

The NUL was founded in 1911. Although it is considered a proactive civil rights organization, it stood on the periphery of the civil rights struggle until about 1960. Prior to the 1960's, the Urban League concentrated almost exclusively on improving employment opportunities for African Americans migrating from the South.

CORE, founded in 1942, did not become actively involved in the Civil Rights movement until about 1961. It was one of the first civil rights organizations to employ the strategy of nonviolent direct action. It began utilizing the sit-in as a protest strategy following the initiation of the Journey of Reconciliation (freedom rides).

The SCLC was founded in 1957, under the leadership of the Reverend Martin Luther King, Jr., and often worked hand in hand with the NAACP. It grew out of an effort to consolidate and coordinate the activities of ministers and other civil rights activists in southern cities.

SNCC was organized by the SCLC and African American student leaders in 1960 to help guide antisegregation activities in the South. It broke away from Martin Luther King, Jr., and the SCLC within a year, arguing that its tactics for achieving integration were too conservative. Over the years, as the leadership of SNCC became more militant, it began to exclude whites from the decision-making process. This militant posture culminated in the call for "Black Power" by SNCC in 1966.

Charles C. Jackson

FURTHER READING

Blumberg, Rhoda L. *Civil Rights: The 1960s Freedom Struggle.* Rev. ed. Boston: Twayne, 1991.
Bosmajian, Haig A., and Hamida Bosmajian. *The*

Rhetoric of the Civil-Rights Movement. New York: Random House, 1969.

D'Angelo, Raymond, comp. *The American Civil Rights Movement: Readings and Interpretations.* Guilford, Conn.: McGraw-Hill/Dushkin, 2001.

D'Emilio, John. *The Civil Rights Struggle: Leaders in Profile.* New York: Facts On File, 1979.

Price, Steven D., comp. *Civil Rights, 1967-68.* Vol. 2. New York: Facts On File, 1973.

Sobel, Lester A., ed. *Civil Rights, 1960-66.* New York: Facts On File, 1967.

SEE ALSO: *Brown v. Board of Education*; Civil disobedience; Civil Rights Act of 1964; Civil rights and liberties; Commission on Civil Rights, U.S.; Congress of Racial Equality; Du Bois, W. E. B.; Jackson, Jesse; King, Martin Luther, Jr.; National Association for the Advancement of Colored People; Segregation.

Class struggle

DEFINITION: Belief that all societies are divided into social classes based on their relation to the economy and that these classes have fundamentally different interests which cause them to struggle against one another

TYPE OF ETHICS: Politico-economic ethics

SIGNIFICANCE: Since the model of class struggle necessarily precludes belief that all members of a society can share common interests, it has profound implications for political philosophy, public policy, and social practice.

The ethical concept of class struggle revolves around the notion that more or less clearly defined classes exist in every society. These classes are defined by their relationships to the predominant means of production, with one class dominant in its ownership or control of society's assets. Since different policies will affect various classes in diverse manners, each class inherently has its own set of interests. Since resources are limited, each class will struggle, albeit at times unconsciously, against others to attempt to gain benefits.

While social conflict has doubtlessly existed since the formation of social classes, "class struggle" as a concept dates back to the French Revolution of 1789. Before this time, awareness of social classes was certainly widespread, but conflict was seen as primarily being between different groups or peoples. First articulated by Gracchus Babeuf within his small "Conspiracy of Equals," the concept of class struggle was fully developed in the nineteenth century by Karl Marx and Friedrich Engels.

Marx denied that he had discovered class struggles, pointing to various historians before him who "had described the historical development of this struggle between classes." Yet it remained for Marx and Engels to take these empirical observations and transform them into a theory. They came to the conclusion that at the root of all conflicts was a struggle between different social classes, no matter in which arena a conflict might occur: religious, political, or ideological. That the participants themselves did not see the conflict in explicit class terms was immaterial. What counted was that there was always an underlying class interest that motivated various social groups, even if the conflict was expressed in nonclass language.

Therefore, even an event such as the Reformation, which appears at first glance to be almost wholly religious in nature, is in the final analysis the disguised expression of class conflict. This struggle is not solely an economic one. For Marx, the struggle between competing classes has taken many forms. Its expression is constrained by the ideology of the day. For example, class struggles during medieval times naturally cloaked themselves in the language of Christianity because that was the common shared culture of all contending classes.

The cause and intensity of class struggles in different areas and at diverse times vary widely in terms of specifics. Still, they all share a root communality. Whenever a portion of society has ascendancy in terms of the means of production, that dominant class will exploit the common people. This exploitation may be open and direct as in the case of slavery or less obvious as is the situation with modern workers. All the same, the antagonism generated by the opposed interests of owners and workers will result in class conflict.

MODERN CLASS STRUGGLE

In the modern era, the main protagonists of class struggle were the capitalists on one side and workers on the other. Put crudely, employers desire high profits and workers want high wages. This is the source of struggle between the classes. This conflict is not simply between the opposing classes; the governmental apparatus or the state is always a major player.

For Marx and Engels, no government or state is really above, or neutral in, the class struggle. Far from being impartial, the state is itself the historical product of class society. That is, the state was established (and later its power expanded) because of the need the dominant class had for protection from the exploited. Thus, in ancient Rome, slave revolts led to battles not so much between slaves and their owners per se as between slaves and the Roman state.

Although the state was seen by Engels "in the final analysis as nothing more than a body of armed men," governmental apparatuses function as more than repressive institutions. They can mediate class conflicts with an eye to reducing their intensity. In addition, governments serve an ideological function in that they legitimize the dominant system of wealth and power.

Although Marx hoped that class struggle would lead to a consciousness among workers that would lead them to overthrow capitalism, he realized that this was far from automatic or assured. Further, he argued that the only solution to the history of class conflict would be the establishment of a classless society that was free of exploitation. With the abolition of private property, the basis for classes and class struggle would disappear.

Karl Kautsky argued that social conflicts need not always be between classes, saying that struggles have often taken place between status groups. By contrast, V. I. Lenin and the Russian Bolsheviks took a more strict interpretation of the primacy of class struggle. Subsequent socialist thinkers have often stressed that classes are by no means homogeneous and that gender, racial, and occupational divisions are a counterweight to general class cohesion.

In the final analysis, the significance of the concept of class struggle goes beyond nuances of interpretation. As an ethical formulation, it suggests a view of the world that seeks to go beyond platitudes of common interest. Moreover, it is an ethical tool for a certain type of understanding of the world.

William A. Pelz

FURTHER READING

Beer, Max. *The General History of Socialism and Social Struggles.* 2 vols. New York: Russell & Russell, 1957.

Berberoglu, Berch. *Globalization of Capital and the Nation-State: Imperialism, Class Struggle, and the State in the Age of Global Capitalism.* Lanham, Md.: Rowman & Littlefiled, 2003.

Callinicos, Alex, ed. *Marxist Theory.* New York: Oxford University Press, 1989.

Kautsky, Karl. *The Class Struggle.* Chicago: C. H. Kerr, 1910.

Marx, Karl, and Friedrich Engels. *The Marx-Engels Reader.* Edited by Robert C. Tucker. 2d ed. New York: W. W. Norton, 1978.

Milliband, Ralph. *Divided Societies: Class Struggle in Contemporary Capitalism.* Oxford, England: Oxford University Press, 1991.

Poulantzas, Nikos. *Classes in Contemporary Capitalism.* London: Verso, 1978.

SEE ALSO: Communism; *Communist Manifesto, The*; Lenin, Vladimir Ilich; Marx, Karl; Marxism; Poverty and wealth; Revolution; Socialism.

Clean Air Act

IDENTIFICATION: Federal law that directs the states to take action to control and prevent air pollution, on the premise that air pollution is essentially a state or local problem

DATE: Enacted in 1963

TYPE OF ETHICS: Environmental ethics

SIGNIFICANCE: The Clean Air Act acknowledged that air pollution was a problem of the commons rather than an individual problem, requiring action by the community to protect the health of the public.

The federal Clean Air Act of 1963 superceded the Air Pollution Act of 1955, which had authorized studies of air pollution and recognized air pollution as an emerging national problem. The 1963 Act was passed as a result of a report by the U.S. surgeon general that found that motor vehicle exhaust can be dangerous to human health. The 1963 Act, however, did not permit action by the federal government; instead, grants were made available to state and local governments to undertake initiatives to control pollution in their areas.

The act was amended in 1970 and again in 1977, both times to set or change national standards for air quality in response to state and local government inaction. In 1990, significant changes were made to the 1963 Act to deal with remaining lower atmosphere pollution and, particularly, to act against upper atmosphere problems such as acid rain and the thinning of the ozone layer, which could damage forests, animal life, and the ability of humans to live a healthy life.

Sandra L. Christensen

SEE ALSO: Biodiversity; Clean Water Act; Ecology; Environmental ethics; Environmental Protection Agency; Global warming; Greenhouse effect; Pollution; Pollution permits.

Clean Water Act

IDENTIFICATION: Federal law enabling broad federal and state campaigns to prevent, reduce, and eliminate water pollution
DATE: Enacted in 1972
TYPE OF ETHICS: Environmental ethics
SIGNIFICANCE: The Clean Water Act recognized the nation's waters as a part of the commons, of benefit to all. With its passage, the federal government accepted the responsibility for ensuring the safety of those waters for human health, and for maintaining the biological diversity of the waters.

The Federal Water Pollution Control Act (FWPCA) of 1972 (known as the Clean Water Act) was an amendment to the FWPCA of 1956. It continued a line of federal legislation of water pollution that began with the Rivers and Harbors Act of 1899, which required a permit to discharge pollutants. In the FWPCA of 1972, responsibility was generally left to the states to control pollution, with the federal government providing grants for local construction of sewage treatment plants.

Other acts, such as the Water Pollution Control Act of 1956 and the Clean Water Restoration Act of 1966, set federal standards for water quality and imposed fines on source point polluters. The goals of the Clean Water Act were to achieve waters clean enough for recreation use by 1983 where such uses had been discontinued because of pollution, and, by 1985, to have no discharge of pollutants into the nation's waters. The act established a National Pollutant Discharge Elimination System that required permits for all source points of pollution, focusing attention on specific polluters rather than on specific bodies of water. The Clean Water Act criminalizes the act of pollution by imposing fines and prison terms for persons found guilty of polluting the waters.

Sandra L. Christensen

SEE ALSO: Biodiversity; Clean Air Act; Ecology; Environmental ethics; Environmental Protection Agency; Pollution; Pollution permits.

Clinton, Bill

IDENTIFICATION: President of the United States, 1993-2001
BORN: August 19, 1946, Hope, Arkansas
TYPE OF ETHICS: Politico-economic ethics
SIGNIFICANCE: Clinton was the first elected U.S. president to be impeached—on charges of perjury and obstruction of justice relating to his affair with the White House intern Monica Lewinsky. Publicity over the incident led to public ethical debate over the extent to which a president's private life should be used as a criterion to judge his public performance.

Bill Clinton faced attacks—including allegations of wrongdoing—from political opponents almost from the first day after he elected president in 1992. However, no allegations were proved against him, other than those associated with his sexual relationship with Monica Lewinsky. Since Clinton and Lewinsky were both legally adults, their adulterous relationship would probably have been a private matter, of concern mainly to Clinton's wife, Hillary Rodham Clinton, were it not for Clinton's status as president of the United States.

Allegations of sexual improprieties were made against earlier presidents, such as Thomas Jefferson, Andrew Jackson, and Grover Cleveland, during their election campaigns. All three survived the attacks, largely because members of the voting public appeared to make distinctions between public accomplishments and private peccadilloes. Indeed, public opinion polls, even at the height of the Clinton impeachment effort, continued to show broad support for Clinton's presidency and reflected the continuation of that attitude.

Clinton's situation was complicated by his denial of the Lewinsky relationship in sworn testimony during a civil lawsuit over sexual harassment charges brought by another woman. While the exact wording of Clinton's deposition questioning left some room for him later to deny he perjured himself in a narrow legal sense, his answers and other public statements he made were obvious attempts to avoid telling the truth. Given a president's constitutional obligation to enforce the law, Clinton's avoidance of the truth until it was forced on him in a grand jury proceeding raised serious questions about whether the distinction between public and private wrongdoing could be maintained in Clinton's case. Beyond Clinton, the in-

President Bill Clinton reads an apology to the nation for his conduct in the Monica Lewinsky affair, at a White House press conference on December 11, 1998. (AP/Wide World Photos)

cident may well force a reexamination of this distinction in the future.

Richard L. Wilson

FURTHER READING

Anderson, Christopher P. *Bill and Hillary: The Marriage.* New York: Morrow, 1999.

Clinton, Bill. *My Life.* New York: Alfred A. Knopf, 2004.

Clinton, Hillary Rodham. *Living History.* New York: Simon & Schuster, 2003.

Morris, Dick. *Behind the Oval Office.* New York: Random House, 1997.

Sheehy, Gail, *Hillary's Choice.* New York: Random House, 1999.

Stephanopoulos, George. *All Too Human: A Political Education.* Boston: Little Brown, 1999.

SEE ALSO: Adultery; Character; Leadership; Morality; Perjury; Politics; Prisoner's dilemma; Sexuality and sexual ethics.

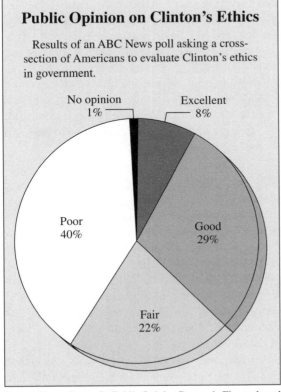

Public Opinion on Clinton's Ethics

Results of an ABC News poll asking a cross-section of Americans to evaluate Clinton's ethics in government.

No opinion 1%
Excellent 8%
Good 29%
Fair 22%
Poor 40%

Source: Roper Center for Public Opinion Research. Figures based on responses of 515 adults surveyed in January, 2000.

Cloning

DEFINITION: Artificial production of identical copies of genes, at the molecular level, or production of genetically identical organisms at the macroscopic level

DATE: First attempted in 1952

TYPE OF ETHICS: Bioethics

SIGNIFICANCE: In theory, any living organism can be cloned, resulting in genetically identical copies of the original organism. However, the concept of cloning human beings has raised both medical and philosophical questions as to the desirability of the procedure.

The basis for cloning dates to the early twentieth century, when German zoologist Hans Spemann found that individual embryonic cells from salamanders each contained the hereditary information necessary to create identical organisms. He later performed nuclear transfer experiments using amphibians and was eventually honored with the Nobel Prize in Physiology or Medicine for his work in 1935. Similar experiments were attempted by Robert Briggs and T. J. King in 1952 using tadpoles. Though initially unsuccessful, they were eventually able to clone tadpoles.

The first successful cloning of large life-forms occurred in 1984, when Danish scientist Steen Willadsen demonstrated the cloning of a lamb from embryonic sheep cells. Using similar techniques, others were subsequently able to clone a variety of other animals. Although categorized as "twinnings," none of these experimental procedures involved the transfer of hereditary material from one cell to another.

The first actual case of cloning a mammal using nuclear transfer techniques was reported in February, 1997. Ian Wilmut at the Roslin Institute in Scotland reported the cloning of an adult sheep by transplanting the nucleus obtained from cells of the sheep's udder into an enucleated egg cell. The cloned animal, nicknamed "Dolly," quickly became world famous. However, it soon became apparent that the procedure

Cloned cows with nearly identical markings on an Iowa farm. (AP/Wide World Photos)

was not as straightforward as first claimed. More than 250 separate attempts had been made prior to the successful experiment. By 2003, animals as diverse as cattle, mules, mice, and cats had reportedly been cloned, but no primates had been successfully cloned.

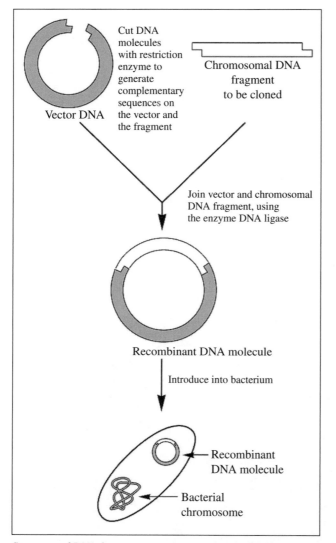

Segments of DNA from any organism can be cloned by inserting the DNA segment into a plasmid—a small, self-replicating circular molecule of DNA separate from chromosomal DNA. The plasmid can then act as a "cloning vector" when it is introduced into bacterial cells, which replicate the plasmid and its foreign DNA. This diagram from the Deparment of Energy's Human Genome Program site illustrates the process. (U.S. Department of Energy Human Genome Program, http://www.ornl.gov/hgmis.)

CLONING HUMANS

The question of whether it is desirable, or even possible, to clone humans has engendered two schools of thought. First is the question of reproductive cloning. In theory, this would involve the production of genetically identical individuals using either individual cells, or isolated nuclei in transfer experiments, their implantation into a female, and subsequent development. It is difficult to justify such a procedure, especially given the high rate of failure. Simply put, the creation of genetically identical offspring is arguably more in the realm of egotism than simple desire for children.

Given the early twenty-first century state of understanding how embryonic cells are regulated, as well as the limited technology that exists, it is questionable whether reproductive cloning of humans is even possible. Even when attempting the procedure with less evolved animals, the process is highly inefficient and subject to large numbers of chromosomal changes. Successful nuclear transplantation requires both the inactivation of genes normally expressed in the donor cell, as well as activation, in the proper sequence, of genes necessary for proper embryonic development. The result has been that most animal clones do not survive implantation; those that do grow to term often have a variety of defects. Among such defects is the problem of premature aging that probably results from changes in the telomeres, the repeat sequences on the ends of chromosomes that shorten as cell division occurs. Even the famous Dolly was physically an old sheep in a young body.

A different school of thought addresses a second application of the procedure: therapeutic cloning. The difference between the two cloning procedures is that the first, reproductive cloning, is to generate an identical embryo. Therapeutic cloning is performed for the purpose of producing cells identical to those of the donor, not to produce embryos. Nuclear transfer experiments can therefore be applied to the understanding of regulation of both embryonic and adult genes.

In addition, the procedure would result in creation of embryonic stem cells genetically

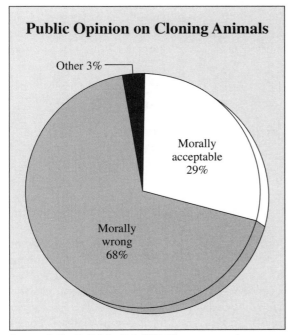

Public Opinion on Cloning Animals

Other 3%

Morally
acceptable
29%

Morally
wrong
68%

Source: Gallup Poll, May 5-7, 2003. Figures summarize responses of 1,005 adults throughout the United States.

identical to that of the donor. Being identical, such cells could be transplanted back into the donor to serve as "seeds" or replacement cells for those which have died or undergone pathological changes. For example, such cells might replace brain or heart cells that had been damaged without the need of immune suppression, or dependency on not identical donors. Cell transplantation using cloned embryonic cells would thus not require immunosuppressive drugs to prevent rejection.

Since the fetus does not develop as a result of therapeutic cloning, those genes that are necessary for fetal differentiation are unnecessary. The embryonic cells that do develop are multipotential in that, in theory, they could be programmed to develop into any type of body cell. In effect, these can be considered as forms of embryonic stem cells. In the year 2003, science was still unable to program these cells into the desired differentiation pathway; however, it appeared to remain only a matter of time until this problem would be solved.

It is of interest that while most established churches object to the use of cloning procedures for the purpose of reproduction, most have expressed a willingness to accept therapeutic cloning as long as

there are proper guidelines. For example, aborted embryos should not be a source of cells. Even Orrin Hatch, a conservative Republican senator from Utah and a man considered observant within the Mormon Church, introduced legislation to support research in the technique of therapeutic cloning in early 2003.

Richard Adler

FURTHER READING

Gould, Stephen Jay, et al. *Flesh of My Flesh: The Ethics of Cloning Humans.* Lanham, Md.: Rowman & Littlefield, 1998.

Hochedlinger, K., and R. Jaenisch. "Nuclear Transplantation, Embryonic Stem Cells and the Potential for Cell Therapy." *New England Journal of Medicine* 349, no. 3 (2003): 275-286.

Kass, Leon R., ed. *Human Cloning and Human Dignity: The Report of the President's Council on Bioethics.* New York: Public Affairs, 2002.

Kass, Leon, and James Wilson. *Ethics of Human Cloning.* Washington, D.C.: American Enterprise Institute, 1998.

Silver, Lee. *Remaking Eden: How Genetic Engineering and Cloning Will Transform the American Family.* New York: Avon Books, 1998.

Snedden, Robert. *DNA and Genetic Engineering.* Chicago: Heinemann Library, 2003.

SEE ALSO: Bioethics; Biotechnology; Genetic engineering; Human Genome Project; Medical research; Stem cell research; Technology.

Code of Professional Responsibility

IDENTIFICATION: Code of professional ethics established by the American Bar Association

DATE: Adopted in 1970

TYPE OF ETHICS: Legal and judicial ethics

SIGNIFICANCE: Originally created to improve ethical standards throughout the law profession, the Code of Professional Responsibility was quickly adopted by every state but soon proved inadequate to the complex needs of the profession.

In the early years of the twentieth century, the American Bar Association (ABA) took the lead in developing standards of legal ethics for practicing lawyers. The nation's largest association of lawyers, the ABA first proposed rules of legal ethics in 1908. During the second half of the twentieth century, however, the ABA attempted to revise those rules and ultimately adopted, in 1970, the Code of Professional Responsibility. This code addressed a broad assortment of ethical issues relating to the practice of law, from the fees charged by lawyers to the confidences they obtained from clients. Although the ABA does not itself have authority to regulate the conduct of lawyers, it proposed that states adopt its code as the basis for their own regulation of lawyers. Within a few years of its creation by the ABA, every state had adopted some version of the code.

The Code of Professional Responsibility gave lawyers attempting to practice ethically a common set of rules to guide their conduct. It also gave authorities with responsibility for disciplining lawyers a basis for evaluating attorney conduct and for punishing wayward lawyers. In most states the state supreme courts, generally assisted by the state bars, have authority to discipline lawyers who act unethically. Crucial to this disciplinary oversight are rules that give attorneys advance warning of the kinds of conduct for which they can be punished. These punishments vary from private or public reprimands to suspension from the practice of law or even disbarment.

The Code of Professional Responsibility soon proved to be too ambiguous and not sufficiently comprehensive in its scope to guide legal practice in the late twentieth and early twenty-first century. In 1977, just seven years after approving the code, the ABA launched the Kutak commission—named after its original chairman, Robert J. Kutak—to draft a new set of ethics rules for the profession. Over the next five years the Kutak commission labored to devise what ultimately became known as the Model Rules of Professional Conduct, officially adopted by the ABA in 1983. Again, the ABA proposed that states adopt the Model Rules as the new basis for ethical guidance and discipline of attorneys. By the early years of the twenty-first century, a large majority of states had abandoned the Code of Professional Responsibility and replaced it with the new Model Rules. A few states, however, continued to rely on the 1970 Code of Professional Responsibility.

Timothy L. Hall

SEE ALSO: American Inns of Court; Attorney-client privilege; Attorney misconduct; Codes of civility; Jurisprudence; Law; Legal ethics; Professional ethics.

Codes of civility

DEFINITION: Informal standards of etiquette observed by members of the legal professions
TYPE OF ETHICS: Legal and judicial ethics
SIGNIFICANCE: Courts and legal organizations have attempted to curb excessive rancor among lawyers by adopting codes of civility.

Toward the end of the twentieth century, many observers were noticing a decline in civility among lawyers, especially among trial lawyers. Lawyers, according to a common lament, too often resort to win-at-all-costs, scorched-earth practices characterized by rudeness and uncooperativeness. Although lawyers must comply with the rules of professional ethics, established rules such as the American Bar Association's Model Rules of Professional Conduct seem to be insufficient to restrain the aggressive tendencies of many lawyers. As a result, judges and professional legal organizations have increasingly turned to codes of civility as blueprints for less rancorous professional conduct.

The codes are relatively informal exhortations for lawyers to treat one another—and other participants in the judicial process—with greater politeness and typically suggest how politeness might express itself in particular contexts. For examples, lawyers are encouraged to refrain from engaging in disparaging comments toward other attorneys, parties, or witnesses; to refrain from scheduling hearings and other court matters at times calculated to pose scheduling conflicts for other lawyers; and to avoid delaying procedures as a tactical device.

Timothy L. Hall

SEE ALSO: American Inns of Court; Attorney-client privilege; Attorney misconduct; Code of Professional Responsibility; Etiquette; Jurisprudence; Law; Legal ethics; Professional ethics.

Coercion

DEFINITION: Manipulation of other persons, groups, or entities by force or by threat

TYPE OF ETHICS: Personal and social ethics

SIGNIFICANCE: In addition to being an ethical transgression on the part of the perpetrators, the fact of coercion may mitigate one's moral and legal responsibility for acts one was coerced into performing.

Reinhold Niebuhr, the most politically influential American theologian of the twentieth century, wrote in *Moral Man and Immoral Society* (1932) that "all social co-operation on a larger scale than the most intimate social group requires a measure of coercion." Modern ethicists agree that coercion is present, if not necessary, in every area of social life. The task of ethicists is to lead in critical discussions that will help to identify the nature of coercion, assess responsibility for coerced acts, determine if and when coercion can be appropriately employed, and control coercion.

THE NATURE OF COERCION

Although coercion is sometimes considered to be synonymous with force, they are in fact distinct. When force is used, the person is acted upon; the forced person does not act. In the case of a forced deed, the victim has no freedom to act otherwise. The victim of force is a medium of another person or power. Personal physical force (for example, being manacled or shot) and natural forces (for example, hurricanes, gravity, or illness) can override or remove an agent's ability to act.

If someone pushes another person out of the way of an oncoming car, the first person forces the other person to move but does not coerce that person. Coercive threats are, however, obstacles to self-determination. They limit one's freedom to act, but they are not overwhelming or insuperable. Some choice remains. A coerced person still acts. Although autonomy is diminished, a measure of autonomy remains.

A coercive threat is intended to motivate a person to act by stimulating in the person an irresistible desire to avoid a penalty although the act is also contrary to the person's will. Offers also intend to motivate a person to act by stimulating in the person an irresistible desire, though here the similarity stops.

Scholars agree that threats and offers are different types of proposals. Threats can coerce; offers cannot.

Even so, threats and offers (also incentives, rewards, bribes, and so forth) can be linguistically structured in terms of one another. A merchant could threaten a customer, saying, "Give me your money or I will deprive you of the merchandise." One could also construe a mugger's proposal, "your money or your life," not as a threat but as an offer to preserve one's life for a fee, but such machinations obscure the issues. The meaning of a proposal, not its linguistic structure, determines whether it is an offer or a coercive threat.

Coercive threats can be further understood and distinguished from offers by means of other characteristics. First, and most fundamental, is that victims of coercion perceive coercive threats as dangers, penalties, or some kind of loss. An offer is considered a beneficial opportunity. Second, a coercive threat cannot be refused without unwanted consequences. Moreover, the consequences of acting in accordance with a coercive threat are also undesired. Regardless of a coerced person's actions, an unwanted consequence is unavoidable. The recipient of an offer, however, can refuse without the recipient's life conditions being altered. Third, a coercive threat requires an imbalance of power, while an offer is usually proposed in a more egalitarian relationship. Fourth, with coercion, the will of the coercer predominates. The threat's recipient submits reluctantly

---

When Coercion Can Be Beneficial

Some acts of coercion are considered beneficial when they are directed toward the coerced persons' well-being and are compatible with the latters' autonomy. Some theologians have even written that coercion may be an act of love if it leaves the beloved one with more freedom than would have been secured otherwise.

If a child, for example, were riding his bike in the middle of the street as a car approached and the child refused to move despite parental warnings, a loving parent could coerce him, shouting, "Nathan! If you don't get out of the street this minute, I'll ground you until you're twenty-one!"

---

with mitigated freedom. With an offer, the will of the recipient dominates, is freer, and more readily accepts or rejects the proposal.

RESPONSIBILITY

To be responsible for one's acts is to be accountable for their impact on oneself and on others. If a person were forced to perform certain actions, that person would be relieved of moral responsibility for those actions. Neither praise nor blame would apply. By contrast, when persons freely act, they are responsible for their behavior. Between these two poles is the moral territory of responsibility for coerced acts.

Not forced, but not wholly free, coerced persons are only partially accountable for their actions. Coerced persons act with less freedom than normal, contrary to their will, and subject to the influence—not control—of a coercer. All apparent options are rendered morally undesirable. A coerced person's responsibility is therefore limited. The degree of this limitation depends upon the cultural context, the historic background, the immediate situation, and the moral framework.

LIMITING COERCION

Because coercion can be personally beneficial and socially necessary, efforts must be made to control it, not eliminate it. To restrain coercion, regardless of the coercer's claim to benevolence, it must be subject to an impartial, third-party evaluation. Human beings are simply too self-interested to weigh their own acts of coercion impartially. Reducing the number of incidents of unjust coercion, however, is more fundamental than is controlling coercion. Unjust coercion can be limited by redressing the inequality from which it grows. History has shown that egalitarian social institutions such as democracy, income redistribution, and public education enhance equality and thereby reduce coercion.

Paul Plenge Parker

FURTHER READING

Colvin, Mark. *Crime and Coercion: An Integrated Theory of Chronic Criminality.* New York: St. Martin's Press, 2000.
Frankfurt, Harry G. "Coercion and Moral Responsibility." In *Essays on Freedom of Action*, edited by Ted Honderich. Boston: Routledge & Kegan Paul, 1973.
King, Martin Luther, Jr. *Why We Can't Wait.* New York: Harper & Row, 1964.
McCloskey, H. J. "Coercion: Its Nature and Significance." *Southern Journal of Philosophy* 18 (Fall, 1980): 335-352.
Nozick, Robert. "Coercion." In *Philosophy, Science, and Method.* Edited by Sidney Morgenbesser, Patrick Suppes, and Morton White. New York: St. Martin's Press, 1969.
Wertheimer, Alan. *Coercion.* Princeton, N.J.: Princeton University Press, 1987.
Williams, Daniel Day. *The Spirit and the Forms of Love.* New York: Harper & Row, 1968.

SEE ALSO: Autonomy; Consent; *Nicomachean Ethics*; Niebuhr, Reinhold; Power; Responsibility; Violence; Will.

Cognitivism

DEFINITION: View that moral statements make judgments of fact that are either true or false
TYPE OF ETHICS: Theory of ethics
SIGNIFICANCE: The possibility of any sort of normative ethics depends upon moral statements having truth value. Failing that, ethics becomes a merely descriptive discipline.

Distinctions between cognitivism noncognitivism arises within twentieth century metaethics as a result of disagreements about whether moral statements have truth values. Indeed, if moral statements are neither true nor false, as noncognitivists believe, then they are not really statements at all. That is, moral expressions of the form "X is right" or "X is wrong," though they have the grammatical appearance of making factual claims, really do not make factual claims. Noncognitivists are divided over how such expressions actually do function. There are relatively few noncognitivist metaethical theories.

All other moral theories are cognitivist theories. They have in common the view that locutions of the form "X is right" and "X is wrong" are either true or false. Cognitivist theories differ at two levels. At the most general level, there is a distinction between objectivist theories and subjectivist theories. Each of these categories of moral theory can be further subdivided according to what a given theory says makes an action right or wrong, or an agent good or bad.

SOME COGNITIVIST THEORIES

Cognitivists hold that a statement of the form "is right" is just what it appears to be: a statement that some action exemplifies an important and desirable moral property. The statement is true if the property in question is exemplified by the action and false if it is not. A statement of the form "is wrong" is a statement that some action fails to exemplify a moral property that should be exemplified, or that it exemplifies a property that it should not exemplify. It too is either true or false. In any case, there is a class of actions whose members have moral properties.

Cognitivists differ about what makes an action right or wrong. If one believes that the feelings of some person or persons determine whether an action has the relevant moral property, then one is a subjectivist. Private subjectivists would hold that "is right" means "I (the speaker) approve of, and that is what makes right." Social subjectivists hold that the moral quality of an action is relativized to the feelings of approval or disapproval of a group or society of persons rather than some individual.

If one denies that the moral quality of an action depends upon the feelings of some person or persons, then one is an objectivist. There are many different types of objectivist theories of ethics. Again, they can be distinguished in terms of what makes an action right or wrong. Thus, for the hedonistic utilitarian, "is right" can be translated as "Among all alternative courses of action, will produce the most happiness for the largest number of people." A divine command theorist would hold that "is right" means "God wills." The ethical egoist takes "is right" to mean that "is in my own best interests." Each of these theories looks like an attempt to define what is right or good in terms of something else.

The English philosopher G. E. Moore repudiated any attempt to define the good in terms of some other property, but he was still a cognitivist and an objectivist. He held that "is right" means something like "Among all alternative actions, will be most productive of the nonnatural property goodness." Thus, while good is a property, it cannot be analyzed in terms of something else.

SOME NONCOGNITIVIST THEORIES

Noncognitivists agree with Moore that goodness cannot be analyzed in terms of something else. They explain that this is because moral terms (such as "good," "evil," "right," and "wrong") are not genuine predicates that stand for independently existing properties of any kind. For this reason, noncognitivists have sometimes been called subjectivists. This form of subjectivism is quite radical, however, for according to the noncognitivist, moral terms do not refer to anything. There is no question of the ultimate source of the property of goodness, since goodness is not a property of any kind. Obviously, the noncognitivist offers a very different analysis of moral statements and of the moral terms embedded in them.

The best-known type of noncognitivist theory is the emotivist theory of ethics, which was developed by A. J. Ayer, Charles L. Stevenson, and others. According to emotivism, moral utterances merely express the feelings of their speakers. Thus, an expression of the form "is right" can be translated as "Hurrah for !" There is nothing more to the meaning of the utterance than that.

Prescriptivists have argued that moral utterances do more than simply express the feelings of the speakers. They also prescribe or commend behavior. Thus, "is right" means "Do!" and "is wrong" means "Avoid doing !" Yet to say that X is right is not to say that X has a certain property.

R. Douglas Geivett

FURTHER READING

Alston, William P. "Moral Attitudes and Moral Judgments," *Nous* 2 (February, 1968): 1-23.

Ayer, A. J. "On the Analysis of Moral Judgments." In *Philosophical Essays*. London: Macmillan, 1954. Reprint. Westport, Conn.: Greenwood Press, 1980.

Dancy, Jonathan, ed. *Normativity*. Malden, Mass.: Blackwell, 2000.

Hare, R. M. *Freedom and Reason*. Oxford, England: Clarendon Press, 1963.

_____. *The Language of Morals*. Oxford, England: Clarendon Press, 1952.

Moore, G. E. *Principia Ethica*. Rev. ed. New York: Cambridge University Press, 1996.

Snare, Francis. *The Nature of Moral Thinking*. London: Routledge, 1992.

Stevenson, Charles L. *Ethics and Language*. New Haven, Conn.: Yale University Press, 1960.

Taylor, Paul W., ed. *The Moral Judgment: Readings in Contemporary Meta-ethics.* Englewood Cliffs, N.J.: Prentice-Hall, 1963.

Urmson, J. O. *The Emotive Theory of Ethics.* New York: Oxford University Press, 1969.

SEE ALSO: Ayer, A. J.; Emotivist ethics; Hare, R. M.; Metaethics; Moore, G. E.; Normative vs. descriptive ethics; Objectivism; Prescriptivism; Subjectivism.

Cohen, Randy

IDENTIFICATION: Author of a syndicated weekly column on applied ethics

BORN: July 12, 1948, Charleston, South Carolina

TYPE OF ETHICS: Personal and social ethics

SIGNIFICANCE: Cohen's column, *The Ethicist*, uses engaging prose and wit to draw public attention to applied ethics, thereby promoting the cultivation of civic virtue in a diverse democracy.

Randy Cohen, who previously published fiction and essays and has written for popular television shows, approaches ethics as an ordinary, thoughtful citizen. He writes with care and wit, but has no formal training in philosophical ethics and brings no formal ethical system to his work. His approach is a kind of rational problem-solving, derived from several working principles that he develops as he applies them to concrete cases. As Cohen explains in his book about his column, *The Good, the Bad, and the Difference: How to Tell Right from Wrong in Everyday Situations* (2002), he admires those virtues that allow human beings to live together in a diverse society: honesty, kindness, compassion, generosity, and fairness. He endorses actions that increase human happiness and do not contribute to human suffering, and that are consonant with American values of egalitarianism and human freedom.

Cohen's column, which he launched in *The New York Times Magazine* in 1999, treats ordinary but specific moral questions posed by his readers. Typical of the issues raised are questions such as these: Should bosses read employee email? Should a woman tell his best friend that she saw her husband with another woman? Is it ethical to drive a gas-guzzling SUV? Cohen's answers to such questions

The Burden of Being an Ethicist

After Randy Cohen's book *The Good, the Bad, and the Difference* came out in 2002, he was asked how it felt to have millions of people depend upon his ethical decisions. In his reply, he said

I'm not sure that anyone actually does anything I suggest. On a good day, however, I hope I've helped the readers reach their own conclusions. My job is to make the discussion illuminating, the analysis thoughtful, and the prose lively. At least, that's what I try to do, and if I can present the questions in a way that lets the reader see them fresh, I'm pleased.

respect the conflicting interests of the people involved, but at the same time train a steady eye on how individual actions influence social institutions at large. He argues that ethical choices affect not only the people directly involved but also contribute to the tenor of the entire community.

Cohen's column regularly considers broader issues about what constitutes a just and decent society. For example, he worries that commercial exchanges increasingly dominate human interactions in the public sphere and thus erode a sense of civic life, that property rights are too readily permitted to eclipse human rights, and that strident individualism ignores the many ways in which citizens shape, and are shaped by, their communities.

Maria Heim

SEE ALSO: Advice columnists; Applied ethics; Journalistic ethics; Personal relationships; Political correctness.

Cold War

THE EVENT: Nonviolent rivalry between the United States, representing the West, and the Soviet Union, representing the communist East, after the end of World War II

DATE: 1946-1989

TYPE OF ETHICS: International relations

President John F. Kennedy (right) confers with Air Force officers during the crisis precipitated by the installation of Soviet missiles in Cuba in October, 1962. (National Archives)

SIGNIFICANCE: The Cold War posed the problem of how foreign and domestic policy ought to be pursued in the age of the atom bomb and of the national security state.

As John Lewis Gaddis stated in *The Origins of the Cold War*, President Harry S. Truman and his advisers decided by early 1946 that the Soviet Union threatened the security of the United States. The reasons for this decision have been debated intensely by historians, who have argued about the extent to which a Cold War was necessary and about the motivations of both superpowers. How the Cold War is viewed depends upon how historians have assessed the moral validity of each side's arguments, policies, and actions.

HISTORY

Traditionalist historians posit an aggressive, totalitarian Soviet Union, as revealed in events such as the Berlin Blockade (1948-1949), in which the Soviet Union closed down all routes to West Berlin, so that the United States and its allies had to airlift sup-

plies to the city; the institution of Soviet-dominated governments in Poland (1944), Romania (1945), Yugoslavia (1945), and East Germany (1945); the rapid communist takeover of Albania (1946), Bulgaria (1947), Czechoslovakia (1948), and Hungary (1949); communist insurgency in Greece (1946-1949); the later victories of communists in China (1949), Cuba (1959), and Vietnam (1975); and several Marxist-inspired governments in Africa.

Traditionalists also contend that the United States was justified in opposing communist subversion of governments throughout the world—not only by producing weapons of mass destruction but also by establishing security organizations, such as the Central Intelligence Agency (CIA), to monitor and to thwart the "communist conspiracy" in secret operations conducted by spies.

Revisionist historians hold that the United States, beginning with the Truman administration, overreacted to the Soviet Union's drive to secure its borders and to maintain a sphere of influence guaranteeing that it would never again be invaded by a militaristic Germany, which had attacked the Soviet Union in both world wars. Similarly, the development of Soviet atom bombs and missiles is regarded as a defensive measure, necessitated by the fact that the United States did not share its knowledge of atomic energy with the Soviet Union, its wartime ally, and that, indeed, the dropping of two atom bombs on Japan was, in part, an effort to intimidate the Soviets, who had agreed to invade Japan after the conclusion of the war in Europe.

Revisionists also contend that, for reasons of domestic politics, the Truman and subsequent administrations inflated the Soviet threat, inventing a witch-hunt at home for communist subversives in government, in the schools, in Hollywood, and in other institutions, in order to maintain a huge defense establishment and to exercise conservative policies that strengthened the U.S. grip on the global economy. Even the Marshall Plan (1948-1951), which successfully helped Western European economies rebuild after World War II, is viewed by revisionists as an effort to isolate the Soviet Union's economy and the socialist economies of Eastern Europe and the Third World.

ETHICAL INTERPRETATIONS AND ISSUES

Other historians do not fit into either category. They draw away from both the traditionalist and revisionist interpretations in order to raise ethical and moral questions about the tactics of both sides during the Cold War. Was it necessary, for example, for the CIA to participate in the overthrow of the Guatemalan government in 1954 because of that government's supposed communist ties? Historians have also questioned the CIA-inspired efforts to embarrass and even to assassinate Fidel Castro. By the same token, Soviet premier Nikita Khrushchev's introduction of missiles into Cuba in 1962, the Soviet invasion of Afghanistan in 1979, and the Soviet Union's supplying of arms to various regimes around the world have been roundly attacked by historians who do not fit into any single ideological camp.

Time Line of the Cold War

Time	Event
1949	The Soviet Union tests its first atomic bomb.
1953	The Soviet Union tests a hydrogen bomb.
1957	The Soviet Union successfully tests an intercontinental ballistic missile.
1962	The Cuban Missile Crisis brings the United States and the Soviet Union closer than ever before to the brink of nuclear war.
1968	The Soviet Union invades Czechoslovakia, establishing the Brezhnev Doctrine of Soviet military domination over Warsaw Pact states.
1970-1979	During an era of détente, more stable relations prevail between the Soviet Union and the United States and their respective allies.
1985	Mikhail Gorbachev is chosen as the new general secretary of the Soviet Communist Party, and his reforms initiate a thaw in relations between the Soviet Union and the United States.
1987	U.S. president Ronald Reagan and Soviet general secretary Gorbachev sign the INF Treaty governing intermediate nuclear forces (INF) and calling for the destruction of U.S. and Soviet missiles and nuclear weapons.
1989	Gorbachev is elected state president in the first pluralist elections since 1917, and by the end of the year all Warsaw Pact nations had overthrown their communist leadership.
1991	After the Baltic States of Estonia, Latvia, and Lithuania are granted independence and other former soviets join the Commonwealth of Independent States, Gorbachev resigns as president and the Soviet Union is officially dissolved.

No matter how responsibility for the Cold War is distributed, it seems undeniable that neither the United States nor the Soviet Union achieved what they undertook to guarantee in the establishment of the United Nations: a respect for human rights everywhere and the establishment of a concept of collective security that would govern the world and prevent nations from acting unilaterally in war.

ETHICAL QUESTIONS

With the fall of the Berlin Wall in 1989 and the dissolution of communist governments in Eastern Europe and of the Soviet Union itself, historians will continue to debate the extent to which each party was culpable in the Cold War. Was the Cold War necessary? If so, did it have to last as long as it did? Did the arms race itself bankrupt the Soviet Union and lead to its breakup? Did the actions of the Federal Bureau of Investigation (FBI) during the Cold War period, when it kept lists of so-called subversives, undermine individual liberties? Does a massive security state itself represent a threat to freedom at home and abroad? Is there a justification for the abrogation of certain human rights in the quest to combat what some regard as the absolute evil of communism? Did the United States and its allies "win" the Cold War, and if so, can it be deemed a moral victory?

Carl Rollyson

FURTHER READING

Dudley, William, ed. *The Cold War: Opposing Viewpoints.* San Diego, Calif.: Greenhaven Press, 1992.

Gaddis, John Lewis. *The Long Peace: Inquiries into the History of the Cold War.* New York: Oxford University Press, 1987.

_____. *The United States and the Origins of the Cold War, 1941-1947.* New York: Columbia University Press, 1972.

Kolko, Joyce, and Gabriel Kolko. *The Limits of Power: The World and United States Foreign Policy, 1945-1954.* New York: Harper & Row, 1972.

Leebaert, Derek. *The Fifty-Year Wound: The True Price of America's Cold War Victory.* Boston: Little, Brown, 2002.

Lynn-Jones, Sean M., ed. *The Cold War and After: Prospects for Peace.* Cambridge, Mass.: MIT Press, 1991.

McMahon, Robert. *The Cold War: A Very Short Introduction.* New York: Oxford University Press, 2003.

Maddox, Robert James. *The New Left and the Origins of the Cold War.* Princeton, N.J.: Princeton University Press, 1973.

Maier, Charles S. *The Cold War in Europe.* New York: M. Wiener, 1991.

Naylor, Thomas H. *The Cold War Legacy.* Lexington, Mass.: Lexington Books, 1991.

SEE ALSO: Limited war; McCarthy, Joseph R.; Marshall Plan; Mutually Assured Destruction; North Atlantic Treaty Organization; Nuclear arms race; Potsdam Conference; Realpolitik; SALT treaties; Stalin, Joseph; Truman Doctrine.

Collective guilt

DEFINITION: Corporate culpability that obtains when a collective or group causes harm to others

TYPE OF ETHICS: Beliefs and practices

SIGNIFICANCE: The debate over the nature of collective guilt has refined human notions of collective responsibility and has legitimized international efforts to seek reparations for grievous harms inflicted by groups.

When groups cause harm, the injured parties may seek restitution of liberty, social status, and property. They may also seek reparations in the form of money, public apologies, or revised histories. However, a difficulty arises in answering such questions as who is blameworthy and for how long. For example, is an entire group guilty or merely some of its members? After the Holocaust of World War II, survivors wondered if it were fair to hold all of Germany accountable for the atrocities committed by its Nazi rulers. If not all of Germany, who among the Germans *were* guilty: the nation's political leaders, members of the Gestapo police force, or the ordinary soldiers of the German army? Who among the millions of German citizens knew about their government's systematic efforts to exterminate other human beings and did nothing to prevent it? Another question is whether the guilt of the actual perpetrators of the Holocaust can be inherited.

Hannah Arendt, a political philosopher who had escaped Nazi Germany, wrote that collective guilt is not possible since true remorse must always be personal. Moreover, the harmful acts inflicted by groups are ultimately carried out by individual persons. On the other hand, all human beings, by virtue of their humanity, are collectively responsible for all harms inflicted upon other people. Arendt argued that shame, rather than guilt, is an appropriate response to human evil. Arendt's views regarding collective responsibility are similar to the Dalai Lama's belief in universal responsibility—although the Dalai Lama believes responsibility originates in universal consciousness.

At the other extreme, some people believe that *all* members of groups that harm others should be regarded as collectively guilty of the wrongdoing. For example, Christians who accept the doctrine of original sin believe that all humans are guilty because of the biblical Adam's disobedience to God. According to this view, even people living today—people who could not have contributed to Adam and Eve's expulsion from the Garden of Eden—are somehow guilty for being the descendants of Adam.

A related issue concerns involuntary membership. For example, one belongs to a family and an ethnic group not by choice but by birth. Should a person nevertheless be held accountable for harms inflicted by groups one cannot leave? Some thinkers, such as Karl Jaspers and Larry May, discuss the problem in terms of identity and choice. Personal identity is shaped by sharing beliefs and values with members of groups to which one belongs. Although one may not be personally guilty of harms committed by one's group, one may still feel shame or moral taint because of one's solidarity with the group. However, one can escape shame or taint by choosing to distance oneself. In the case of involuntary group membership, one can disavow the group publicly or privately. In failing to remove oneself either physically or symbolically, one chooses to share guilt and responsibility for harms committed by one's group.

Tanja Bekhuis

FURTHER READING

Amato, Joseph A. *Guilt and Gratitude.* Westport, Conn.: Greenwood Press, 1982.

Branscombe, Nyla R., et al., eds. *Collective Guilt: International Perspectives.* New York: Cambridge University Press, 2004.

May, Larry, and Stacey Hoffman, eds. *Collective Responsibility: Five Decades of Debate in Theoretical and Applied Ethics.* Savage, Md.: Rowman & Littlefield, 1991.

Tangney, June Price, and Rhonda L. Dearing. *Shame and Guilt.* New York: Guilford Press, 2002.

SEE ALSO: Anti-Semitism; Apologizing for past wrongs; Dalai Lama; Gratitude; Guilt and shame; Mercy; Reparations for past social wrongs; Sin; South Africa's Truth and Reconciliation Commission.

College applications

DEFINITION: Information that students seeking admission to institutions of higher learning provide so that their qualifications can be evaluated

TYPE OF ETHICS: Personal and social ethics.

SIGNIFICANCE: Obtaining a good college education is such a critically important matter to young people that many ethical issues arise from the process of applying—from the standpoint of both the applicants' honesty and the care and fairness with which colleges and universities treat their applications.

Formal applications are a standard feature of the admissions processes used by four-year American colleges that do not have "open admissions" policies that allow any high school graduate to enter simply by supplying a high school transcript. Most competitive four-year colleges require applicants to take national standardized tests, such as the Scholastic Aptitude Test (SAT) or the American College Test (ACT) and also require applicants to submit original essays on selected subjects to test their writing and thinking abilities. High school transcripts and national test results are considered to be so objective that they do not usually generate ethical issues, unless there is evidence of outright fraud.

Evaluations of application essays, by contrast, are more subjective and open the door to ethical issues, from the standpoint of both applicants and the institutions. Because most applicants to highly competitive colleges have strong transcripts and impressive national test scores, their essays may be the best opportunities they have to separate themselves from other candidates. To enhance their chances of admission, many applicants turn to Internet services that promise—for a price—to help them write "winning" essays. Is it ethical, however, for applicants to have others write their application essays or to give them so much help that the essays they submit will misrepresent their true writing abilities?

Students who gain admission to competitive colleges under false pretenses may find themselves in academic environments whose challenges go beyond their own capabilities, thus ensuring their chances of failure. It would seem to be clearly unethical for such students to take admission spots that would otherwise go to more capable students who have not paid others to write their application essays for them.

Members of college application evaluation committees should be, and often are, aware of the availability of essay-writing services and may discount essays they judge to have been written by people other than the actual applicants. The possibility of making incorrect judgments increases the chances of unfairly rejecting qualified candidates. In fact, the process itself becomes an imperfect guessing game in which the essay-writing services look for ever more clever deceptions to fool admissions boards, such as giving the essays they provide a less polished look.

The entire process of college admissions raises serious ethical questions that can affect applicants' entire futures. In their efforts to seek objective standards for admission or for finding new ways to evaluate applicants, colleges will continue to grapple with these serious issues.

Richard L. Wilson

FURTHER READING

Allen, Andrew. *College Admissions Trade Secrets: A Top Private College Counselor Reveals the Secrets, Lies, and Tricks of the College Admissions Process.* New York: Writer's Press Club, 2001.

Fiske, Edward B., and Bruce G. Hammond. *The Fiske Guide to Getting into the Right College.* Napierville, Ill.: Sourcebooks, 2004.

Steinberg, Laurence. *Beyond the Classroom.* New York: Simon & Schuster, 1997.

SEE ALSO: Academic freedom; Cheating; Hiring practices; Honesty; Honor systems and codes; Resumes; Title IX.

Colonialism and imperialism

DEFINITION: Conquest and imposition of a nation's rule over a foreign territory

TYPE OF ETHICS: International relations

SIGNIFICANCE: Colonialism and imperialism involve political domination by alien powers, economic exploitation, and cultural and racial inequalities. The practice has often been defended in moral terms, however, as involving the "civilization" or "enlightenment" of "primitive" or "savage" peoples.

Colonialism and imperialism are two of the major forces that have shaped and influenced the modern world. Yet the two regions of the world that have been largely involved in colonialism and imperialism—the West and the "Third World"—have been affected differently by the two phenomena. The Western world has generally been the colonizer and beneficiary, whereas the "Third World" has been the colonized and the exploited.

Colonialism and imperialism are interrelated systems; both involve the conquest, settlement, and imposition of rule over a foreign territory. Hence, colonialism is not only often associated with imperialism but also typically results from a policy of imperialism. Whereas imperialism often involves the political and economic integration of the subordinate territories into the dominant nation to create a single imperial system, colonialism entails the territorial separation of colonies from the mother countries.

Historically, colonialism as a political-economic phenomenon was associated with Europe from the time of the so-called Age of Discovery in the fifteenth and sixteenth centuries. Various European nations explored, conquered or settled, and exploited other parts of the world. The major colonial powers were Spain, Portugal, England, France, and the Netherlands. In the nineteenth century, Belgium, Germany, Italy, the United States, Russia, and Japan also became colonial powers. The regions of colonial exploitation were the Americas, Africa, Asia, Australia, and the South Pacific.

Theoretical distinctions can sometimes be made between two broad types of colonialism: colonies of settlement and colonies of exploitation. In practice, however, these are distinctions of degree rather than of kind, since most colonial structures involved both immigrant settlement and political control. Furthermore, colonial systems everywhere were essentially identical. They were headed by a representative of the sovereign nation, usually a governor or viceroy; their governments were nonrepresentative because legislative power was monopolized by colonialists to the exclusion of the native populations; and their underlying philosophies sought to pattern the colonies after the mother countries and assimilate the subordinate populations into the culture, language, and values of the metropolitan nations. In consequence, colonialism and imperialism entail not only political control but also economic and cultural domination.

Although the concept of empire and its practice have a long history going back to ancient times, it was not until about the 1870's that the ideology of imperialism was formulated and came into common usage. Among the earliest theoretical formulations was A. J. Hobson's *Imperialism* (1902), which established that imperialism served the needs of capitalism, such as the provision of raw materials, cheap labor, and markets. This thesis was further advanced by V. I. Lenin's *Imperialism: The Highest Stage of Capitalism* (1917), which held that capitalist expansion would lead to imperialist wars that would in turn destroy capitalism itself and pave the way for socialism. Critics have pointed out the weakness of this thesis in that imperialist expansion long preceded the rise of capitalism. Nevertheless, Marxist interpretations of imperialism inspired underdevelopment theorists such as André Gundar Frank to emphasize capitalist expansion as the root cause of "Third World" underdevelopment. To modern African nationalists such as Ghana's Kwame Nkrumah, imperialism was a powerful political slogan that fueled independence movements. What is clear is that imperialism has a variety of meanings.

Three phases in imperialism can be identified. The first is the early period from ancient times to the end of the fifteenth century. Early imperialism was characterized by the despotic rule of emperors. Examples of early empires included Egypt, Babylonia, Assyria, and the Greek, Roman, Ottoman, and Mongolian empires. The second phase of imperialist expansion spanned the period from the fifteenth to the early nineteenth centuries. It was ushered in by the European exploration of Africa and Asia and Christopher Columbus's voyages to the Americas, and it resulted in the colonization of the entire Western Hemisphere and much of Asia by various European nations.

A number of motivations inspired imperial expansion. There was a strong drive to obtain gold and other precious metals as well as the desire for cheap colonial products such as spices, sugar, cotton, and tobacco. In some cases, imperialism was spurred on by appeals to religious zeal. Above all, however, the possession of colonies was linked to European political rivalries and prevailing economic doctrines, especially mercantilism. In this respect, chartered companies that received trading monopolies and the protection of the mother country became prime instruments in colonial expansion and exploitation.

The third phase, "New Imperialism," covers the period from about 1880 to 1914 and is marked by the subjugation of virtually all of Africa and parts of the Far East by Europe. As before, motivations were varied. Not only were colonies considered indispensable to national glory, but imperialism was fed by an atmosphere of jealousy in which one European nation grabbed overseas colonies in fear that another might do so first. Additional justification was found in racist theories regarding the presumed inferiority of some races and the belief in colonies as markets for the sale of surplus manufactured goods produced through the Industrial Revolution. At the same time, strategic considerations, missionary activities, and advances in European military technology were all linked to imperialist expansion.

In the decades immediately following World War II, the proliferation of democratic ideas around the world, the rise of self-determination in Africa and Asia, and United Nations condemnations did much to undermine imperialist concepts. With the advance of nationalism in Africa and Asia, most of the imperial regimes in these regions crumbled. Some manifestations of colonialism, however, persist. One of these is the phenomenon of internal colonialism, whereby one segment of the state that is politically and economically powerful dominates another segment in a subordinate, peripheral relationship; one example of internal colonialism is the system of apartheid in South Africa. Another is neocolonialism, the continued domination and exploitation of postcolonial independent states by the technologically advanced world, often through foreign investment capital, the provision of technical skills, and trade expansion, which tends to lead to an increase in influence without actual political domination. A further legacy of colonialism, especially in Africa, is the artificially created political boundaries that do not conform to indigenous ethnic patterns, an issue that continues to undermine political integration.

Joseph K. Adjaye

FURTHER READING

Amin, Samir. *Imperialism and Unequal Development.* New York: Monthly Review Press, 1977.

Larrain, Jorge. *Theories of Development: Capitalism, Colonialism, and Dependency.* Cambridge, Mass.: Basil Blackwell, 1989.

Mommsen, W. J. *Theories of Imperialism.* Translated by P. S. Falla. London: Weidenfield & Nicolson, 1981.

Robinson, Ronald E., and John Gallagher. *Africa and the Victorians: The Official Mind of Imperialism.* London: Macmillan, 1961.

Said, Edward. *Orientalism.* New York: Vintage Books, 1994.

Warren, Bill. *Imperialism: Pioneer of Capitalism.* Edited by John Sender. London: NLB, 1980.

Weil, Simone. *Simone Weil on Colonialism: An Ethic of the Other.* Edited and translated by J. P. Little. Lanham, Md.: Rowman & Littlefield, 2003.

SEE ALSO: Capitalism; Communism; Developing world; Slavery; Social Darwinism; Sovereignty; *Wretched of the Earth, The.*

Commission on Civil Rights, U.S.

IDENTIFICATION: Federal body formed to investigate charges that citizens have been deprived of their civil rights

DATE: Established in 1957

TYPE OF ETHICS: Civil rights

SIGNIFICANCE: The establishment of the Civil Rights

President Dwight D. Eisenhower (second from right) oversees the swearing in of the Commission on Civil Rights that was authorized by passage of the Civil Rights Act of 1957. (Library of Congress)

Commission in 1957 was the first federal civil rights action taken in eighty-two years in the United States.

The U.S. Commission on Civil Rights was formed as part of the demands of the Civil Rights Act of 1957. President Dwight D. Eisenhower had called for such a commission in 1956, and previous president Harry S. Truman's Committee on Civil Rights had called for a formal congressional committee as early as 1947. Southern senators and congressmen, however, blocked establishment of the commission until 1957.

The commission was initially charged with investigating allegations that American citizens had been denied equal treatment because of their color, race, religion, or national origin. In 1972, it also began investigating discrimination based on sex. It also acts as a national clearinghouse for information about discrimination. The commission does not prosecute offenders or pass laws protecting those who are discriminated against. It simply gathers information, investigates charges, and reports its findings to the Congress and the president. Still, recommendations made by the commission are often enacted. The commission played a major role in the passage of the 1965 Voting Rights Act. Important protections for minorities in the areas of education, housing, and economic opportunity have been signed into law because of its reports and recommendations.

Cynthia A. Bily

SEE ALSO: Civil Rights Act of 1964; Civil rights and liberties; Civil Rights movement; Discrimination.

Common good

DEFINITION: Benefit to all members of society, or a good which is in the interests of everyone

TYPE OF ETHICS: Personal and social ethics

SIGNIFICANCE: Belief in and commitment to the common good underpins some systems of ethics that encourage individuals to be less selfish and more concerned with the community or with humanity as a whole than with their own personal values and desires. It is anathema to systems which deny that there is a single set of values that is of benefit to all people.

The common good is, simply, a holistic, humanistic philosophy that considers the good of the whole or the good of all. It should be the first virtue of the state and its institutions, as well as the first virtue of society and of society's individuals. Its greatest manifestation would likely be worldwide "voluntary" socialism wherein people would abandon selfishness and act for the good of all humanity. For the common good, when personal goals collide with communal needs, sometimes personal goals must be sacrificed for the good of all. For example, when monopolistic corporations have a "stranglehold" on consumers, government regulations are necessary (and, depending on the amount of abuse, corporations may well need to be nationalized).

During the 1990's, after the collapse of the Soviet Union, socialism appeared to be waning, while capitalism was in the ascendancy. Ironically, the economic philosophy that apparently "won" is the only one worldwide that is based entirely on human greed. Many thinkers view the capitalistic "victory" as especially heinous because capitalism is completely unconcerned about the justice of its means and ends and, indeed, is unconcerned about the ends of human life, as well.

As opposed to selfishness, the common good is nothing less than the realization of the social, economic, and spiritual qualities inherent in the word "civilization." It is nothing less than the "goodness" of a community and goodness for the sake of all community members. The concept asks that individual liberalism as well as individual conservatism be laid aside; in their places come the common good and a form of communitarianism.

In small social groups, action that emphasizes the common good might well be simple friendship and fellowship, whereas on the political level that action might be the passage of reform laws that seem to help and protect all people; on the worldwide level, that action could involve the United Nations or another international agency that, for example, seeks to end war, which condones the practice of mass murder. A national or international group dedicated to saving the world's environment would also be working for the common good.

Another way to examine the common good is to consider its antithesis. For example, gender discrimination (degradation of women) is not the common good, nor is discrimination based on race or ethnicity.

Forever fouling the environment is not the common good, nor is insensitivity to world hunger and poverty; international terrorism, wars, and strife in general are not; anything that hurts human beings physically or mentally is not. Allowing older people to die because they cannot afford health care not only is not the common good but also is a disgrace.

Albert Camus, a noted twentieth century French philosopher and a Nobel Prize winner, seldom used the phrase "common good," but he captured the essence of the term when he held that the worth of individuals could be measured by observing what they will allow other people to suffer. Likewise, Camus believed that the worth of a society could be measured by observing how that society treats its most unfortunate people. One might also add that the worth of any international agency, movement, or institution can be gauged by observing what that agency, movement, or institution allows any world citizen to suffer. Many other philosophers, past and present, have agreed with Camus.

INDIVIDUALS, SOCIETY, AND THE COMMON GOOD

To achieve the common good, individuals naturally must respect the rights of all others; however, individuals must also "put away" egotism and create a just society wherein all people have their basic needs—economic, social, political, and spiritual—met. Society must also examine itself and remove contradictions between what it professes and what it actually does—in other words, society should remove the contradictions between appearance and reality. So long as a society reproduces patterns of living that harm some of its members (poverty and discrimination, for example), the common good cannot be realized; instead, continuing alienation will take place until even the "in" group or the affluent are hurt.

As one example, in the United States of the 1990's, 20 to 25 percent of the people lived in self-esteem-crushing poverty (with racial, ethnic, and gender minorities suffering disproportionately). Given such suffering, American society could not call itself just and certainly cannot say that the common good is being realized. Likewise, as the world entered the next century, the United States—while bespeaking world peace—manufactured 50 percent of the world's armaments, which were used to kill and maim human beings.

CONCLUSIONS

It is remotely possible that in the indefinite future American society might promote the common good. To do so, however, people must release selfishness and personal greed, because when people hurt others they eventually ruin their own society as well.

James Smallwood

FURTHER READING

Amoia, Alba della Fazia. *Albert Camus.* New York: Continuum, 1989.

Diggs, Bernard James. *The State, Justice, and the Common Good: An Introduction to Social and Political Philosophy.* Glenview, Ill.: Scott, Foresman, 1974.

Hamilton, Lawrence. *The Political Philosophy of Needs.* New York: Cambridge University Press, 2003.

Held, Virginia. *The Public Interest and Individual Interests.* New York: Basic Books, 1970.

Leys, Wayne A. R., and Charner M. Perry. *Philosophy and the Public Interest.* Chicago: Committee to Advance Original Work in Philosophy, 1959.

Meyer, William J. *Public Good and Political Authority: A Pragmatic Proposal.* Port Washington, N.Y.: Kennikat Press, 1975.

Phenix, Philip H. *Education and the Common Good.* New York: Harper, 1961.

Sturm, Douglas. *Community and Alienation: Essays on Process Thought and Public Life.* Notre Dame, Ind.: University of Notre Dame Press, 1988.

Vallentyne, Peter, ed. *Equality and Justice.* New York: Routledge, 2003.

Wallach, Michael A., and Lise Wallach. *Rethinking Goodness.* Albany: State University of New York Press, 1990.

SEE ALSO: Capitalism; Class struggle; Communism; Communitarianism; Distributive justice; Good, the; Nietzsche, Friedrich; Pluralism; Public interest; *Utopia.*

Communism

DEFINITION: Theoretically classless society of equality and freedom in which private property has been abolished and replaced with communal ownership of material possessions, or, an actual society modeled to a greater or lesser extent upon the ideal of communism

TYPE OF ETHICS: Politico-economic ethics

SIGNIFICANCE: Classical communist theory envisions a society of perfect freedom and perfect justice in which all people live fundamentally ethical lives, free from social strife and oppression, within a community based on mutual human interdependence. Communist ideology, however, has been used to create and defend several repressive regimes.

The idea of a society based on communal rather than private property, communism was advanced long before the birth of Jesus Christ. There were elements of this idea present in some of the writings of ancient Greek philosophers. Plato, for example, argued in his *Republic* that ruling Guardians should be prohibited from owning property. Further, communism was raised by some radical critics of the status quo in the days of the Roman Republic. There is evidence that some of the slave insurgents involved in the slave rebellion led by Spartacus in 73 B.C.E. wanted their future "Sun Republic" to be without private ownership.

During the early years of Christianity, the followers of Christ practiced a type of communism based on communal ownership of material possessions. For the first Christians, private property was to be forsaken as a sign of their faith. Any number of Christ's teachings appear to argue that private property was, at best, a dangerous distraction from the process of earning salvation and, at worst, a sin. When the son of God said, "It is easier for a camel to walk through the eye of a needle than for a rich man to enter the kingdom of heaven," the early Christians took him at his word.

By the time of the collapse of the Western Roman Empire, the Christian Church had adapted itself to a world based on social classes and private property. Still, the ethical belief in communism as the truly Christian way of living persisted in various forms. During the era of feudalism, monasteries were based on a vow of poverty with monks held up as examples of Christian rejection of material wealth. Within the monastery, the members were to practice a type of communism in the communal sharing of all possessions.

Toward the end of the feudal period, this tradition asserted itself in the sixteenth century in the work of Saint Thomas More. More wrote his famous *Utopia* (1516) to show an ideal society based on a common community of possessions. More's views were in no way unique, since during the Reformation a number of religious rebels, such as the Taborites in Bohemia, came to the conclusion that God had meant the earth to be shared equally by all.

During the Reformation, a German priest named Thomas Münzer helped to lead a revolt of thousands of peasants. In 1525, Münzer formed the Eternal League of God, which was not only a revolutionary organization but also fought for a radically egalitarian Christian society. Basing his views on his interpretation of the Bible, Münzer preached that a classless society was God's will and the princes should be replaced with democratically elected leaders.

Communism appeared again as an important idea during the French Revolution, which began in 1789. Some radical republicans believed that the revolution would not be complete until political freedom was complemented by social equality. The revolutionary Gracchus Babeuf organized a "Conspiracy of Equals" that sought unsuccessfully to establish a society in which all land would be held in common and all would receive equal diet and education.

With the Industrial Revolution, earlier theories of communism that had stressed common ownership of the land became updated to accommodate the new mode of production. During the 1840's, the term "communism" became fairly well known as a result of the writings of Étienne Cabet, who favored the use of machinery on collectivized land as well as large communal factories. Despite such innovations, Cabet considered his theory of communism to be based on "true Christianity."

With Karl Marx, the concept of communism was further modernized. Marx argued against what he deemed the primitive communism of past thinkers who would merely extend ownership of land to the entire population. Marx argued that a classless society had to be based on a cooperative economy, not merely a diffusion of private property. This future communist society would unleash the forces of production to maximize efficiency and reduce the amount of labor necessary. In addition, it would eliminate the rigid division of labor so that people would be free to do both mental and physical work and rotate jobs. With the end of private property, humanity would no longer be alienated from work. Labor would be cooperative and technology would allow people to avoid unpleasant tasks. Therefore, people would be able to take pride in labor and the resulting self-fulfillment would increase the general happiness.

Marx saw these changes as creating a world in which authentic, moral relationships between people would exist. Moreover, humanity would be able to work with nature rather than being intent on conquering the environment. Freedom would be the basis of this new society, in which "the free development of each is the prerequisite for the free development of all."

Marx's vision was taken up by numerous later socialists, including V. I. Lenin, who outlined his views in State and Revolution. Following the Russian Revolution, Lenin attempted to implement some of these ideas, but the material conditions for the construction of a communist society were absent. By the late 1920's, with the isolation of Soviet Russia, communism became an empty political slogan under the dictatorship of Joseph Stalin. Despite its popular association with the Russian dictatorship, the concept of communism remains appealing as an ethical concept that promises to free humanity from exploitation, poverty and oppression.

William A. Pelz

FURTHER READING

Beer, Max. *The General History of Socialism and Social Struggles.* 2 vols. New York: Russell & Russell, 1957.

Cole, G. D. H. *Socialist Thought: The Forerunners of 1789-1850.* Vol. 1 in *A History of Socialist Thought.* London: Macmillan, 1953.

Engels, Friedrich. *The Peasant War in Germany.* Translated by Moissaye J. Olgin. 3d ed. New York: International, 2000.

Lenin, Vladimir I. *The State and Revolution.* Translated by Robert Service. London: Penguin, 1992.

Levine, Andrew. *A Future for Marxism? Althusser, the Analytical Turn, and the Revival of Socialist Theory.* London: Pluto, 2003.

Marx, Karl, and Friedrich Engels. *The Marx-Engels Reader.* Edited by Robert C. Tucker. 2d ed. New York: W. W. Norton, 1978.

More, Thomas. *Utopia: A Revised Translation, Backgrounds, Criticism.* 2d ed. New York: Norton, 1992.

Renton, David. *Classical Marxism: Socialist Theory and the Second International.* Cheltenham, Gloucestershire, England: New Clarion, 2002.

SEE ALSO: Anarchy; Capitalism; Class struggle; *Communist Manifesto, The*; Lenin, Vladimir Ilich; McCarthy, Joseph R.; Marx, Karl; Marxism; Orwell, George; Revolution; Socialism; Stalin, Joseph; Truman Doctrine.

The Communist Manifesto

IDENTIFICATION: Political tract by Karl Marx (1818-1883) and Friedrich Engels (1820-1895)

DATE: Published in 1848

TYPE OF ETHICS: Modern history

SIGNIFICANCE: *The Communist Manifesto* rejected private property and argued that class conflict would ultimately lead to a just and equal society for all.

Written by Karl Marx and Friedrich Engels for the Communist League, *The Communist Manifesto* has become a classic formulation of socialist political ethics. The authors based their work on the ethical belief that all people should live in a condition of equality and democracy. They contend that all previous societies have been marked by class struggle. This conflict between different social classes is rooted in the classes' economic relationships to the means of production. Classes themselves are seen as an inherent result of the institution of private property. Thus, for Marx and Engels, some people have always owned property while forcing those without to work for them. Although the form of this exploitative relationship has changed over time from master/slave to lord/serf and then bourgeois/worker, the inequality has remained present. This injustice has led world history to be the history of class struggle.

With the rise of capitalism, the new ruling class (the bourgeoisie) constantly revolutionizes the way things are produced and exchanged. As capitalism

Marxist Tenets in *The Communist Manifesto*

1. All societies since early communal times have been inequitable class societies.

2. All history has been the history of class struggle.

3. The institution of private property has exploited and oppressed the majority of people.

4. Capitalist societies, like other class societies, do not allow people to develop freely.

5. To create a just and ethical world, the institution of private property should be eliminated. Bourgeois society uses labor to increase capital, whereas the future society will use capital to benefit workers.

6. Individuals should be free to choose their social relationships, free of outside interference. Therefore, the family in its present form should be abolished.

7. Workers have no nation, and as exploitation ceases, so will the need for nationalities.

8. All instruments of production should be centralized in the workers' state.

9. Because workers are in the majority, they must rule themselves democratically.

10. Because no one should possess unearned wealth, there should be no right of inheritance.

11. Credit, communications, and transportation should be placed in the hands of the people.

12. Factories should be government owned, and the government should protect the environment.

13. All able-bodied persons should work.

14. The differences between cities and rural areas should be eliminated gradually by means of population redistribution.

15. Free public education should be provided for all children.

means a smooth process and is constantly beset with crisis. Since workers as a whole produce more in value than they are paid in wages, there are periodic periods of overproduction. These crises of overproduction take the form of business downturns or depressions that the bourgeoisie can overcome only by mass destruction of productive property (such as war) or by conquest of new markets (imperialism). Even when a crisis has been surmounted, the seeds of a future disaster remain within the very nature of capitalist society.

Further, the workings of the capitalist economy exploit the vast majority of people who increasingly have only their labor to sell to the capitalists. Labor is a component of production, so it becomes a commodity that is bought and sold like any other on the market. Thus, the worker becomes subject to the whims of the market and may fall from employment and relative comfort into unemployment and poverty without warning. As labor becomes simplified by machines, there are more workers who are capable of any one job; therefore, the oversupply of labor causes a decline in demand and thereby a decrease in real wages. In addition, the ever-increasing reliance on machines means that work loses its individual character for the worker, who becomes a mere appendage to the machine. This is profoundly unjust, unfair, and undemocratic, according to Marx and Engels.

Even for small businesspersons and professionals, capitalism ultimately spells disaster, since they find themselves unable to compete with the always-growing big bourgeoisie. As these new social layers are forced into the working class, many people will help fight against this unjust system. Because the entire capitalist society is based on exploitation and oppression and promotes the values of greed and inequality, the increasingly large working class will

grows, the need for a constantly expanding market causes the bourgeoisie to expand borders until capitalism has engulfed the world. In the process of this ever-growing expansion, there is, of necessity, more economic and political centralization. This centralization of economic and political power further reduces the actual power of the majority of the population.

Marx and Engels note that this expansion is by no

fight to destroy the dictatorship of the bourgeoisie. For Marx and Engels, this fight is historically unique because it is a movement of the vast majority against an ever-decreasing minority. Thus, only a workers revolution will allow true democracy to prevail.

ACHIEVING A JUST SOCIETY

To achieve this just and democratic society, Marx and Engels believe, the most conscious workers should band together and fight for the interests of the world's people, regardless of nationality. While struggling against the bourgeoisie, these "communists" must always consider the interests of the working-class movement as a whole. The first step is to make the working class, which is a class in itself, a class for itself. Then, the now-united workers must combat the bourgeois control of society. Moreover, when fighting against any form of injustice, communists must always raise the property question, since private property is at the root of all oppression. Ultimately, workers will need to take power themselves, since the bourgeoisie will manipulate any system of government, even a parliamentary one, to maintain class rule. Thus, the abolition of capitalism and the establishment of workers' rule is the only ethical path according to Marx and Engels.

William A. Pelz

FURTHER READING

Draper, Hal. *Karl Marx's Theory of Revolution.* 4 vols. New York: Monthly Review Press, 1977-1990.

Drennen, D. A. *Karl Marx's Communist Manifesto.* Woodbury, N.Y.: Barron's Educational Series, 1972.

Fischer, Ernst. *Marx in His Own Words.* Translated by Anna Bostock. New York: Penguin, 1984.

Hodges, Donald Clark. *The Literate Communist: One Hundred Fifty Years of the Communist Manifesto.* New York: P. Lang, 1999.

Mandel, Ernest. *From Class Society to Communism: An Introduction to Marxism.* London: Ink Links, 1977.

Marx, Karl, and Friedrich Engels. *The Marx-Engels Reader.* Edited by Robert C. Tucker. 2d ed. New York: W. W. Norton, 1978.

SEE ALSO: Capitalism; Class struggle; Communism; Freedom and liberty; Marx, Karl; Marxism; Socialism.

Communitarianism

DEFINITION: Ethical system that insists that the good of the community must not be subordinated to that of the individual

TYPE OF ETHICS: Theory of ethics

SIGNIFICANCE: Communitarianism rejects Western culture's traditionally one-sided emphasis on individual rights and seeks to balance rights with responsibilities. As such, it may represent the most powerful ethical challenge to individualism since the Enlightenment.

Communitarianism carries with it a sense of profound urgency. As one leader of the movement, Robert Bellah, has declared, society is no longer merely in crisis: It is in a state of emergency. The social fabric has deteriorated to the extent that morality has become a virtual impossibility. The communities, institutions, and social relationships that make morality possible are quickly succumbing to a pervasive individualism. Although this social deterioration may be most visible in poverty-stricken urban areas where gangs, violence, and homelessness are commonplace and children must attend school in fear for their lives, it is nevertheless rampant throughout American society. Important social institutions such as families, churches, community groups, and even towns and cities have been drastically weakened, leaving society as a mere collection of individuals who have nothing in common but self-interest and the fear of death. Ironically, these developments threaten individualism itself, for community is the very basis of individuality. Because of this emergency, communitarians believe that it is necessary to nurture and foster constructive communities wherever they can still be found.

Although communitarianism has roots that extend deep into the past, it has existed as a self-conscious school of thought and moral theory only since the 1980's. Two important books published in that decade, *After Virtue* (1984), by the philosopher Alasdair MacIntyre, and *Habits of the Heart* (1985), by the sociologist Robert Bellah, signaled the appearance of a new ethic that repudiated both modern individualist liberalism and the rejuvenated conservatism of the Reagan era.

A former Marxist who became a Roman Catholic, MacIntyre argued that moral discourse in the modern West has become incoherent and meaningless. He traced this incoherence to the Enlightenment, which tried to develop a morality that was based entirely on individuality and reason. The attempt was bound to fail, MacIntyre argued, because morality requires the very things that the Enlightenment took away: community, tradition, and narrative. That is why Immanuel Kant, Søren Kierkegaard, and John Stuart Mill all failed to develop a genuine morality, and why all attempts that do not repudiate the Enlightenment concept will fail.

MacIntyre's book ends on a pessimistic note, concluding that there is little to do except to wait for a new Saint Benedict (the founder of Catholic monasticism) to lead society out of its predicament. *Habits of the Heart*, though influenced by MacIntyre, is more hopeful in tone. Robert Bellah gathered a team of researchers to investigate "individualism and commitment in American life." After interviewing numerous people about their lives and commitments, the researchers concluded that, while many forms of community were being undermined in American life, there were still signs of a remarkable resilience. The research focused in particular on "voluntary associations," or nonprofit institutions that embody various forms of community: churches and synagogues, community service organizations, youth organizations, activist organizations, charities, and the like (but not including political parties). This "third sector" of American society (as distinguished from the governmental sector and the for-profit business sector), according to Bellah and his researchers, is essential to democracy and human flourishing, and must be encouraged.

Communitarianism rejects ordinary political liberalism, which emphasizes personal freedom at the expense of community, but it also rejects political conservatism, which emphasizes personal property and wealth at the expense of community. Bellah and his coauthors issued a powerful call to reaffirm the importance of community in American life, to form anew a "culture of coherence." Similar calls have been issued by the religious historian Martin E. Marty and the political scientist Amitai Etzioni. (One of the most impressive things about communitarianism is its broad interdisciplinary base.)

SPECIFIC ISSUES

Communitarianism as a self-conscious movement is in its infancy. Some communitarian posi-

tions, however, are readily apparent. In the realm of economics, communitarians are less interested in maximizing individual personal income and more interested in how economic production can foster and support human communities and relationships. With respect to children and the family, communitarians are less interested in the abstract "rights" of children and parents, and more interested in improving the human ecology of the family—including discouraging divorce. Communitarians point with alarm to the fact that, since the 1950's, all measurable indices of child welfare in America have declined—even during periods of economic growth. Similarly, with respect to women's issues, communitarians are less interested in simply maximizing women's freedom and more concerned with advancing women's well-being in the context of community and relationships, including relationships with men and children.

With respect to diversity and multiculturalism, communitarians support measures that would enable diverse communities to flourish, but they reject those measures that seek to divide society into separate cultural fiefdoms. A communitarian approach to the environment might likewise be skeptical of animal or species "rights" but would strongly emphasize the community of nature and humankind's important and dangerous part in it. With respect to the health care crisis, communitarians would recognize the impossibility of obtaining the "best" health care for every individual and would ask what types of health care would foster human flourishing in the midst of the natural trajectory from life to death. Communitarians generally also have more sympathy for a public role for religion in our common culture.

CHALLENGES

Like any other movement, communitarianism faces numerous challenges and dangers as it works out its implications. Perhaps its greatest peril is nostalgia for a past that never was, or worse, for a past that embodied specific evils. Many communities embody racist and sexist practices and traditions that are morally outrageous. Communitarians who strongly reject the Enlightenment also run the risk of disregarding the Enlightenment's great achievements—abolition of slavery, establishment of civil liberties, freedom of the press, popular elections, religious tolerance, emancipation of women, human rights.

Much of the communitarian movement, too, has a strongly American focus, and needs to develop a broader international perspective. The collapse of Soviet-style communism may offer an opportunity to internationalize communitarianism; voluntary associations may be just the thing to fill the vacuum left by the collapse of communist parties.

Despite these challenges, however, communitarianism remains one of the most promising modern moral philosophies.

Garrett E. Paul

FURTHER READING

Bellah, Robert N., et al. *Habits of the Heart: Individualism and Commitment in American Life.* Updated ed. Berkeley: University of California Press, 1996.

Elshtain, Jean Bethke, Enola Aird, and Amitai Etzioni. "A Communitarian Position of the Family." *National Civic Review* 82 (Winter, 1993): 25-36.

Etzioni, Amitai. "Communitarian Solutions/What Communitarians Think." *Journal of State Government* 65 (January/March, 1992): 9-11.

_____. *The Spirit of Community: Rights, Responsibilities, and the Communitarian Agenda.* New York: Crown, 1993.

Hauerwas, Stanley. *Naming the Silences.* Grand Rapids, Mich.: Eerdmans, 1990.

Little, Adrian. *The Politics of Community: Theory and Practice.* Edinburgh: Edinburgh University Press, 2002.

MacIntyre, Alasdair. *After Virtue: A Study in Moral Theory.* 2d ed. Notre Dame, Ind.: University of Notre Dame Press, 1984.

Marty, Martin E. *The Public Church: Mainline, Evangelical, Catholic.* New York: Crossroad, 1981.

Soule, Edward. *Morality and Markets: The Ethics of Government Regulation.* Lanham, Md.: Rowman & Littlefield, 2003.

SEE ALSO: Common good; Drug testing; Human nature; Individualism; Kierkegaard, Søren; MacIntyre, Alasdair.

Comparative ethics

DEFINITION: Discipline that studies the various ways in which human morality and conduct are defined and practiced in different communities

TYPE OF ETHICS: Theory of ethics

SIGNIFICANCE: Comparative ethics can provide evidence to support almost any ethical system: Those who believe in human nature, the common good, or universal moral law will find fundamental similarities among different cultures. Those who believe in situational ethics, pluralism, relativism, and other nontotalizing systems will find irreducible differences between those same cultures.

Ethics incorporates the scope and purport of morality and associated conduct. Ideas of morality may be determined by rational judgments or by inspired transhuman monistic notions. When the moral worth of an action or a person is determined according to a conscious ideal in any society, rationally determined moral laws guide and define well-being, order, harmony, and security. Both the explicit formulation of and implicit obedience to normative laws, codes, and decrees ensure the maintenance of individual and community well-being. Thus, socially useful regulations, juxtaposed with morally right rationalistic ideals, become the operative ethical norm of the community. When morality and virtue are contextualized in the orderly harmony of the universe, however, and when human life and actions are recognized as factors of that order, the monistic element rather than the rational is given primary cognizance in the definition of ethics.

Generally, in societies that are not avowedly theocratic, ethical ideals are defined according to a rationally determined context. By contrast, in myriad religious communities, the essential ethical directives that govern religious adherents are both defined and enforced on the basis of a monistic ideal of its intrinsic worth. As a survey of various traditions will portray, ethics at a comparative level is essentially a construct of a society or culture or religion that defines and formulates particular moral norms and values. Evaluations of morality thus depend on the estimation of conduct or norms according to specific values and notions—hence the importance of comparative ethics.

ANCIENT GREECE AND EGYPT

Although the ethics (both theoretical and practical) of ancient Greece has many trends and representatives, Plato, Socrates, and Aristotle may be regarded as thinkers who exemplify the norms, conduct, and values of their society. According to Plato, Socrates regarded moral obligation as a construct of rational insight. Plato himself identified morality and virtue as normative conduct that reflected heavenly prototypes or the eternal ideas of the good. In contrast, ethical norms for Aristotle were bound by the social and empirical character of people.

In ancient Egypt, the theory of the soul and its divisions dictated ethics and conduct. The norms for different strata of the society were varied; for example, priests, kings, and shepherds had specific criteria for their own ethical conduct.

MONOTHEISTIC TRADITIONS

In diverse religious traditions, the ethical code that dictates the conduct of a moral agent and the compulsion that ensures its maintenance are regulated by injunctions that are presumed to originate not from rationality or societal utilitarianism but from a monistic or suprahuman transcendent source. Thus, in the monotheistic religious traditions, ethics is dominated by a theocentric ideology. The authority of divine law or God is both the source and the aim of the moral realm.

In the Judaic tradition, for example, the authority of the Torah as moral law is based on divine proclamation. The ought of actions is primarily associated with the appeasement of God, and individual or collective pleasure is incidental. Virtue and ethics become aspects of the nexus between God and humanity as embodied in the notion of a covenant. Although many detailed regulations have been codified and accepted over the centuries, in the main the Ten Commandments form the salient ethical grid for all other injunctions. To be conscious of the identity of God, to be aware of obligations to parents, to maintain the Sabbath, and to refrain from bearing false witness or being adulterous or covetous are some of the moral imperatives contained in the Ten Commandments. Over the centuries, prayer, neighborliness, generosity, dietary regulations, learning, and purity became the essential ethos that governed the lives of the adherents of Judaism.

In Christianity, the person of Jesus Christ is the governing inspiration of all ethical norms. According to general Christian theology, Christ's descent and crucifixion represents love—God's love for humanity and the redemption of souls. The account of Christ, his passion and resurrection, become the standards for normative ethics. Thus, to imitate Jesus Christ is the moral goal and destination of devout Christians. Ideas of Christian fellowship, altruism, and humility are derived from the idea of the sacrifice of Christ in order to redeem humanity.

In Islam, the relationship of the human soul to God—to submit to God's command and gain peace—is the governing ethos of normative ethics. The Qurʾān situates the divine-human connection in a primordial covenant between God and human souls. Ethical imperatives (both practical conduct and moral intent) hence revolve around a transcendent authority that ought to be complied with by the core of one's being. Ethical obligations and responsibilities extend toward a transcendent power, the individual self, society, and nature, and they include personal qualities such as generosity, humility, and kindness. Sectarian differences aside, the five essential "pillars of faith" of Islam are testimony of acceptance of God's being and the prophecy of Muḥammad, prayer, charity, fasting, and pilgrimage, or *hajj*, to the Kaʾba (the Abrahamic shrine in Mecca).

EASTERN TRADITIONS

In Hinduism, India's main religious tradition, the ideals of ethics are incorporated in the salient notions of dharma and karma that are mandated by a transcendent monist predicate. On an individual level, one's dharma, or sacred duty, is determined as a factor of birth by one's place in society. Accordingly, karma, actions and consequences, are evaluated according to individual dharma. Society is divided into four groups, each with a differentiated dharma—*Brāhmins* as priests, *Kṣatriyas* as warrior/rulers, *vaiśya* as traders or farmers, and *Śūdras* as performers of menial tasks. Merit was accrued to karma by fulfilling the moral imperatives of personal dharma. On a cosmic level, maintenance of individual dharma precludes chaos and causes harmonious balance.

The focal notion of Buddhist ethics is the "middle way," a way of conduct and morals that will enable the adherent to attain transcendent enlightenment, represented by the term *nirvāṇa*. These norms are monist in form, since their avowed purpose is a self-ennobling conduct that maintains and designates the cosmic value of human existence per se, though, in content, the norms are apparently rationalistic. The suffering (*dukkha*) of life is presented as a given, and the purpose of conduct and ethics is to transcend it. One may achieve this transcendence by following the "eightfold path," which includes right understanding, thought, speech, action, livelihood, effort, mindfulness, and concentration. Both monks and laypeople are to follow these general precepts, though the requirements are more stringent for the former.

In China, Confucian evaluations of morality and conduct are essentially governed by the ideals associated with the "sage." The perfected virtues or ethics of the sage include benevolence, righteousness, propriety, sincerity, loyalty, reciprocity, wisdom, and filial piety. When inculcated and adhered to, these ethics of the sage lead to harmony and well-being. These virtues are evidently rationalistic, since the notion of a revealed transcendent source is not a basis for the ethical imperatives; however, millennia of traditional acceptance have conferred upon them a sacred monistic value.

TRANSTRADITIONAL WESTERN ETHICS

In modern secularistic communities, especially in the West, a humane rationalistic idiom provides the essential grid for normative ethics. For example, Ethical Culture is a movement that is dedicated to the ethical growth of the individual. The nondenominational New York Society for Ethical Culture was founded in May, 1876, by Felix Adler, son of rabbi Samuel Adler of New York's Temple Emanu-El. He espoused the necessity of using morality and ethical regulation to address issues of societal malaise, such as inner city crime, education, welfare, health, and housing. In such a context, values and morals are generally based on a sense of the responsibilities of being human.

At the end of the twentieth century, issues such as abortion, euthanasia, capital punishment, race relationships, and gender relationships (in and out of wedlock) have ethical nuances which require resolutions. The solutions are proffered both by the monistically oriented religious traditions and by diverse forms of rationalistic secular thought. The normative moral resolutions so proffered are sometimes convergent but are frequently antithetical.

Habibeh Rahim

FURTHER READING

Bujo, Bénézet. *Foundations of an African Ethic: Beyond the Universal Claims of Western Morality.* Translated by Brian McNeil. New York: Crossroad, 2001.

Crawford, S. Cromwell, ed. *World Religions and Global Ethics.* New York: Paragon House, 1989.

Madsen, Richard, and Tracy B. Strong, eds. *The Many and the One: Religious and Secular Perspectives on Ethical Pluralism in the Modern World.* Princeton, N.J.: Princeton University Press, 2003.

Navia, Luis E., and Eugene Kelly, eds. *Ethics and the Search for Values.* New York: Prometheus Books, 1980.

Robertson, Archibald. *Morals in World History.* Reprint. New York: Haskell House, 1974.

Singer, Peter, ed. *A Companion to Ethics.* Cambridge, Mass.: Blackwell Reference, 1993.

Smart, John Jamieson C. *Ethics, Persuasion, and Truth.* Boston: Routledge & Kegan Paul, 1984.

Smurl, James F. *Religious Ethics: A Systems Approach.* Englewood Cliffs, N.J.: Prentice-Hall, 1972.

Sterba, James P., ed. *Ethics: Classical Western Texts in Feminist and Multicultural Perspectives.* New York: Oxford University Press, 2000.

SEE ALSO: Absolutism; African ethics; Buddhist ethics; Christian ethics; Confucian ethics; Feminist ethics; Karma; Multiculturalism; Native American ethics; Pluralism.

Compassion

DEFINITION: Emotion involving the feeling of others' troubles or sorrows combined with a disposition to alleviate or, at least, share in them

TYPE OF ETHICS: Personal and social ethics

SIGNIFICANCE: Compassion is generally taken to be a morally admirable trait, although an excess of compassion may lead to moral paralysis in the face of extreme suffering.

Compassion is a combination of emotional and volitional elements that are also referred to by such words as "care," "sympathy," "pity," and "empathy." Compassion refers not only to the emotional ability to enter into another's feelings but also to an active will to alleviate and/or share in the other's plight.

The emotional element plays a large role in compassion. Theorists who, like Plato, Aristotle, and Immanuel Kant, argue that reason must rule over emotion in ethics give compassion at best a secondary role in their systems. Others, such as Joseph Butler, David Hume, and many utilitarians, argue that ethics is rooted in human emotion. They give compassion a larger role. Feminist theorists such as Carol Gilligan and Nel Noddings have argued that care and compassion should be at the center of moral reasoning.

Persons working in applied ethics have also often suggested that human emotions deserve focused attention in ethical decision making. Those who seek to apply ethical theories in everyday settings, such as clinical medicine, have often urged that the common human experience of compassion for others deserves a larger place in decision making. They suggest that without a focus on compassion, ethical theorizing is in danger of neglecting what is most human in favor of satisfying abstract rational standards.

Emotions such as compassion must nevertheless also be served by rational assessment of situations. Compassionate persons employ reason to assess the source and significance of the troubles that are to be confronted, to weigh alternative ways of alleviating those troubles, and to relate projected actions to other ethical considerations, such as those concerning justice and/or self-interest.

Compassion includes not only the feeling of others' troubles and sorrows but also an active will to alleviate and/or share in them. Thus, compassion also includes a volitional element.

THE ORIGIN OF COMPASSION

Joseph Butler and David Hume both thought that compassion is a feature of human life that arises naturally. Using the word "compassion" as a verb, Butler wrote during the 1720's that human beings "naturally compassionate all . . . whom they see in distress." He also argued that concern for others is not motivated by self-interest. During the 1980's, Nel Nodding spoke of a foundational experience of "natural caring."

Sociobiologists, such as E. O. Wilson and Richard Dawkins, have argued that evolutionary natural selection may favor other-directed dispositions such as compassion. Behavior that is not in an individual's

self-interest can nevertheless be favorable to the survival of the species. Thus, an individual bird risks its own survival as it cries out to warn others.

Others suggest that, whatever natural basis there may be, compassion and concern for others must be nurtured. For example, health care professionals are advised to play the role of patient from time to time in order to develop compassion for patients' suffering. Some Christian thinkers claim that genuine compassion goes "against the grain." They assert that "compassion is not . . . the outcome of our hard work but the fruit of God's grace."

ETHICAL SIGNIFICANCE OF COMPASSION

Human beings experience many different emotions, including anger, envy, and lust. Why should compassion be ranked as a primary human virtue and thus cultivated?

Plato, Aristotle, and Kant worried that the emotions generally are too unsteady and nonrational to be given first rank. Friedrich Nietzsche rejected the priority of compassion on the grounds that concern for others is often based upon a retreat from the higher discipline required to live a fully human life. He worried that compassion is too often expressed as concern for "the 'creature in man,' for what must be formed, broken, forged, torn, burnt, made incandescent, and purified—that which *necessarily* must and should suffer."

Other thinkers, such as Butler, Hume, Wilson, Dawkins, and Noddings, have based the ethical priority of compassion and care upon one or another type of appeal to nature. Alternatively, some religious thinkers appeal to what is revealed in the life of a person such as Jesus Christ or in God's revelation and gift of this virtue. While they may all agree with critics that reason is needed to guide one to effective compassion, they all also say that reason must be informed by compassion. They would agree with Nietzsche that compassion ought not to be a retreat from fully human living, but they assert that genuine human compassion arises from a positive sense of the meaning and purpose of one's own and others' lives.

THE OBJECTS OF COMPASSION

Should compassion follow a path of care for those near at hand only or should it express itself equally in care for the far removed and unfamiliar? Some see a general and impartial compassion as the highest good, while others argue that compassion is inherently partial and best focused on particular individuals. The word "object" itself suggests a difficulty. Many worry lest compassion reduce the individual being helped to the status of an object to be manipulated without concern for the individual's dignity or autonomy.

Who are the appropriate others upon whom compassion should focus? Many discussions presume that the objects of compassion are fellow human beings. Some argue, however, that compassion should extend to animals and/or to the entire environment.

James V. Bachman

FURTHER READING

Butler, Joseph. *Fifteen Sermons Preached at the Rolls Chapel and A Dissertation upon the Nature of Virtue*. London: G. Bell, 1964.

Hume, David. *A Treatise of Human Nature*. London: Everyman, 2003.

Kreiglstein, Werner J. *Compassion: A New Philosophy of the Other*. Amsterdam: Rodopi, 2002.

McNeill, Donald, Douglas A. Morrison, and Henri N. M. Nouwen. *Compassion: A Reflection on the Christian Life*. Garden City, N.Y.: Doubleday, 1982.

Midgley, Mary. *Beast and Man: Roots of Human Nature*. Ithaca, N.Y.: Cornell University Press, 1978.

Noddings, Nel. *Caring: A Feminine Approach to Ethics and Moral Education*. Berkeley: University of California Press, 1984.

Schopenhauer, Arthur. *On the Basis of Morality*. Translated by E. F. J. Payne. Providence, R.I.: Berghahn Books, 1995.

SEE ALSO: Benevolence; Butler, Joseph; Cruelty to animals; Hume, David; Love; Mercy; Passions and emotions; Personal relationships; Physician-patient relationship; Schopenhauer, Arthur.

Compromise

DEFINITION: Arrangement for settlement of a dispute by mutual concession

TYPE OF ETHICS: Personal and social ethics

SIGNIFICANCE: Negotiation by mutual concession may be based on recognition of the moral legitimacy of an opponent's interests. Compromising

on matters of principle, however, may be seen as a moral fault rather than a virtue.

Negotiation is the process used by parties or groups to come to terms or reach agreement regarding issues about which they are in conflict. Compromise is a subprocess of negotiating that involves making mutual concessions to reach an acceptable agreement. Compromise implies conflict—either an open disagreement or a difference leading to a disagreement that must be resolved. Compromise requires all parties to alter their claims or positions in order to reach an accommodation. If only one party or group alters its position, the result is not compromise but capitulation; even if one of the parties eventually agrees with the other, it may constitute appeasement. Compromisable conflicts exist when there is a partial coincidence of interests resulting in a setting of both competition and cooperation between parties. Such a situation can occur only when there is a recognizable and relatively stable social order in which there are explicit rules about compromising that are known and accepted by the parties involved in the negotiations.

Compromising to resolve conflicts is not the same as bargaining, although both processes involve each party's agreeing to give up something in order to get the other to give up something. At each stage of the negotiating process in both compromising and bargaining, one party proposes a resolution and argues for it. There is, however, a marked difference between bargaining and compromising that revolves around the attitude of the negotiating parties. In bargaining, each side assumes that the other will try to get the best for itself, and each knows that the other knows this, so the situation is mostly strategic.

In a compromise, the parties have a certain level of respect for each other and therefore are willing to agree to an accommodation rather than make the best deal for themselves that they can. The distinction between bargaining and compromise can be seen clearly where one negotiating party is more powerful than the other. If the more powerful party is able to impose on its opponent a solution that is favorable to itself and uses its power to do so, the two parties are bargaining. Also, the fact that a negotiation's outcome may be equally favorable to both parties does not indicate that a compromise was reached; it merely demonstrates that the two parties shared relatively equal bargaining power during the negotiations.

Compromise involves acknowledging the moral legitimacy of the interests of one's opponent. To reach a compromise, each party must give its opponent's interests due consideration during negotiation. If a party has no ground for assuming that its opponent is morally inferior, then compromise is morally possible. If both parties' interests are similar, neither party has grounds for not recognizing the moral legitimacy of the other. When opponents' interests are at odds, compromise is possible only if a plurality of interests can be recognized or some level of tolerance can be exhibited. Fanatics do not recognize a plurality of interests or an environment of toleration, and although fanatics may bargain and make deals, they do not compromise. By the same token, idealists, while not rejecting the existence of mutual interests, invariably regard some negotiating points as illegitimate and also are unable to compromise.

NEGOTIATING COMPROMISE

Negotiating a compromise is more difficult when principles, rather than specific interests, of the opposing parties are in conflict. A compromise involving a conflict of interests means giving an opponent's interests due consideration in attempting to negotiate a resolution. When principles are in conflict, however, neither party can give due consideration to the other's principles, because at least one of the parties is presumed to be fundamentally wrong in its stance and hence entitled to no consideration. When a conflict of principles exists, there is no requirement to consider the opposition's principles as being as important as one's own in negotiating toward compromise. In many instances, cultural or philosophical principles may present insurmountable barriers to compromise. For example, a society's principles of right and wrong may limit what can be legitimately compromised; from a philosophical and moral standpoint, some points are thus nonnegotiable. It is usually the conflict of principles that limits the ability to negotiate compromises, but compromises can be achieved if the parties believe that their opponents are sincere and earnest about the principles they present to defend their negotiating position.

Negotiating in the spirit of compromise requires both parties to consider the legitimate interests of the opposition as morally equal to their own, and this may depend either on the recognition of a plurality of interests or on simple toleration. Reaching a compromise also involves understanding the principles that formulate an opponent's negotiating position and trusting the sincerity of an opponent's stance regarding principles governing the ability to reach a compromise. If during a negotiation of compromise either party fails to acknowledge the legitimacy of the opponent's interest or fails to understand the basis for the opponent's commitment to guiding principles, the parties are not negotiating a compromise, but engaging in a morally questionable palaver.

Randall L. Milstein

FURTHER READING

Bellamy, Richard. *Liberalism and Pluralism: Towards a Politics of Compromise*. New York: Routledge, 1999.

Benjamin, Martin. *Splitting the Difference: Compromise and Integrity in Ethics and Politics*. Lawrence: University of Kansas Press, 1990.

Hall, Lavinia, ed. *Negotiation: Strategies for Mutual Gain*. Newbury Park, Calif.: Sage, 1993.

Pennock, J. R., and J. W. Chapman, eds. *Compromise in Ethics, Law, and Politics*. New York: New York University Press, 1979.

Strauss, Anselm. *Negotiations: Varieties, Contexts, Processes, and Social Order*. San Francisco: Jossey-Bass, 1978.

SEE ALSO: Conflict of interest; Conflict resolution; Self-interest.

Computer crime

DEFINITION: Direct or indirect use of computer technology to break the law
TYPE OF ETHICS: Scientific ethics
SIGNIFICANCE: Computer technology has provided both new tools and new targets of opportunity for criminals, spies, and vandals.

Computer crimes typically involve breaches of well-defined ethical issues, but one aspect of the nature of computers raises the possibility of new interpretations of these issues. This is true because computers represent and exchange information in the form of digital electronic signals rather than as tangible objects. This distinction raises the question of whether copying programs or information from computers is really theft if the original programs and data remain in place after the illegal copies are made. Also, are people really trespassing if they remain thousands of miles away from the computer system on which they intrude?

MOTIVES

The psychological motives of persons and groups who engage in computer abuse fall into three categories. The first set of motives include personal gain of money, goods, services, or valuable information. The second is revenge against another person, company, institution, government, or society at large. A variation on the motive of revenge is political motivation. The third type of motivation is to gain stature in one's own mind or those of one's peers by demonstrating mastery over complex technology.

These motivations serve as the bases for several types of activity, which include theft, fraud, espionage, vandalism, malicious mischief, and trespassing.

THEFT AND FRAUD

Theft in computer crime takes many forms. Embezzlement is one of the most publicized. One type of scheme involves the transfer of small amounts of money from bank accounts over a period of time into accounts established by the thieves. One of the most notorious forms of computer crime in the early years of the twenty-first century was the so-called "Nigerian scam," through which con artists in developing countries had bilked citizens of wealthy countries out of millions of dollars. Thieves use e-mail to canvas millions of prospects at minimal cost. Offers of low-priced merchandise that buyers never receive, fraudulent investment opportunities, and false charitable solicitations, abound. Computers make unauthorized use of credit cards particularly easy. Criminals need only the card numbers, expiration dates, and names of the cardholders to order merchandise over the Internet. Such information is often available on discarded credit card receipts or may be procured from the victims through trickery.

Another common and well-known form of theft is software piracy, which is the unauthorized copying of proprietary programs. The scope of piracy is broad. Well-organized groups mass-produce "bootleg copies" of popular personal computer programs. These are then sold to unsuspecting people as legitimate copies. At the other end of the piracy spectrum are isolated individuals who make copies of computer games for friends without even realizing that they are breaking any law.

Sometimes computers themselves are the targets of theft, either for their intrinsic value or for information they may contain. One celebrated case involved the theft of a staff officer's portable computer from his car in the Middle East late in 1990. The computer contained strategic plans for the impending U.S. Operation Desert Storm. The thief was evidently unaware of the computer's sensitive contents, however, and the act did not result in a serious breach of security.

VANDALISM AND MALICIOUS MISCHIEF

Computer systems are often the targets of vandalism, either by disgruntled individuals or by organized groups. Some of the most serious cases of vandalism against computers were committed in France and Italy by the radical Red Brigades during the late 1970's. One of their attacks resulted in the loss of all computer records of automobiles and drivers' licenses in Italy.

Commercial sites on the World Wide Web have been vandalized and their contents altered. In August, 2000, for example, a British supermarket site was defaced with a hoax message announcing price increases and urging viewers to shop elsewhere.

Perpetrators of malicious mischief on computer systems have come to be known as "hackers." Hackers are motivated by a desire to demonstrate mastery over computer technology, especially among their peers. One of their methods is to write programs that, when executed, cause damage to other programs and data files or even cause other computers to crash. These programs vary widely in their nature and are variously known as Trojan horses, worms, and viruses.

Worms and viruses are usually programmed to replicate themselves on every computer system with which they come into contact. One of the most notorious was the Internet Worm, the work of a young computer scientist who placed it on the world's largest computer network in 1988. Within a matter of hours it spread to thousands of computer installa-

The "Nigerian Scam"

During the 1990's a new form of computer crime began sweeping the world—the so-called "Nigerian scam." It takes its name from the West African nation of Nigeria, where it appears to have originated. However, similar scams are practiced in almost every country with lax banking laws. Whatever a scam's form or origin, its essence is always the same: The perpetrators ask correspondents in wealthy nations for help in extracting large sums of money from bank accounts. The correspondents are to keep part of the money in return for their help; however, they must supply confidential information on their own bank accounts, with predicatable unhappy results. Patently fraudulent though these pitches are, many people have taken the bait and lost fortunes for their trouble. The scams succeed because of the power of the Internet. They are, in effect, a form of spam. Messages go to so many millions of people, that a few people are likely to take the bait. By 2004, the frauds had become so prolific that numerous Web sites had been established to help combat the Nigerian scam. The sample below is remarkable only in its writer's honest description of the scam's negative effect on Nigeria's international reputation.

From: The Desk of DR. Ibrahim Coker
Attn: MD/CEO
Sir,
REQUEST FOR URGENT BUSINESS PROPOSAL

I am DR. Ibrahim Coker 58 years old and a engineer contacting you based on the recommendation given to me by my international business associates. I was the chairman of the Nigeria Railway Co-operations contracts review committee (NRC CRC) of the Federal Republic of Nigeria. We were mandated to review all the contracts awarded by the defunct Nigeria Railway Trust Fund (NRTF) to Foreign Firms since the last five years. On completion of our job, we discovered that most of the contracts were grossly over-invoiced to the tune of One Hundred and Seventy-Seven Million United States Dollars (US$177,000,000.00). In our report we arranged, recommended, and subsequently returned only the sum of US$140,000,000.00 to the government leaving out the balance of US$37,000,000.00 for our own use.

However, I feel highly inhibited to contact anybody for this type of transaction because of what we read in the daily newspapers about the incessant involvement of some undesirable Nigerians in the different kinds of scams and fraudulent practices. These acts have not only battered and tarnished the image of Nigeria, but have also drastically reduced the number of intending foreign investors in our country. Considering my international position and status and that of my colleagues involved in this particular transaction, please I would like you to give this transaction utmost confidentiality and sincerity it deserves. The said money (US$37,000,000.00) is already in a security company abroad. Therefore all we require from you are your bank particulars so that we can file and facilitate the application process in your name, at Federal Ministry of Finance. Adequate arrangements are already on ground to give this project full substantial legal backing. So you have nothing to worry about. All the documents that will authenticate our claims are available. Our code of conduct forbids civil servants from owning or operating foreign accounts. This is exactly what informed my decision to contact you. We have agreed to give you the sum of US$11,100,000.00 (Eleven million, one hundred thousand United States Dollars) which represents 30% of the total sum, the balance of 70% will be for us members of the committee.

If you are interested in the transaction, please reply immediately through my e-mail address: so that I can give you the particulars of the security company abroad. I will join you at the security company to assist you to receive the funds.

Best regards
DR. Ibrahim Coker

tions, including those of the U.S. Defense Department and many universities, causing tens of millions of dollars in damage.

Later attempts have been even more disruptive. The Melissa virus in 1999 multiplied by e-mailing copies of itself to all names in recipients' Internet address books, thus reaching computers throughout the world at an astonishing speed. In the United States the Melissa virus disabled more than one million computers and caused damaged that cost hundreds of millions of dollars to correct. The Love Bug worm of May, 2000, shut down e-mail servers in a majority of American corporations, reportedly doing several billion dollars worth of damage.

In February 2000, a "Denial of Service" attack launched by a fifteen-year old Canadian high school student identified only as "Mafiaboy," rendered Web sites of major American corporations inoperable. Using automated tools and scripts easily available on the Internet, Mafiaboy planted Trojan horses within many innocent computers, using them to send a flood of simultaneous messages that overwhelmed service at such computer-savvy online companies as Amazon.com, eBay, CNN News, and Yahoo!.

TRESPASSING

In the context of computer crime, trespassing is unauthorized access to a computer system. The most common form of trespassing is committed by hackers, who often have no intention of causing damage to the systems they break into but are lured by the challenge of overcoming another system's security measures. Once inside a system, they are often content to view its contents and exit without damaging anything. Some hackers, however, have been prosecuted for such acts as breaking into telephone company installations and circulating private access codes.

Spyware programs, which track the buying habits of computer users, are often installed on the computers of user who are downloading free music and game programs. Criminals try to sneak in less benign spyware as e-mail attachments that permit them to control other people's computer from a distance. The intruders can then read files and discover passwords, and Social Security and other account numbers. The acquisition of such information makes theft of the computer owners' identities easy.

Another form of trespassing is committed by per-

sons engaging in espionage. Companies engage in industrial espionage by breaking into rival companies' systems to look for trade secrets and other proprietary information. A rarer variation of espionage occurs when agents of one country break into the computer systems of another government. This occurred during the late 1980's, when West German hackers were discovered using the Internet to access classified information from the U.S. Defense Department.

ONLINE HARASSMENT AND PREVENTION

Internet stalking may appear less threatening than physical harassment, but the emotional impact, and sometimes the tangible results, can be equally damaging. Stalking can include sending continual abusive, obscene, or threatening e-mail messages; placing victims' names on mailing lists so they will receive hundreds of unwanted messages every day; or impersonating the targets and sending fraudulent or abusive mail in their names. In one case a stalker posted a message purporting to come from a woman having unfulfilled fantasies of being raped, including her name, address, and telephone number. Her phone rang endlessly and six men came to her apartment.

Computer crime has become so widespread that most Western industrialized countries have enacted laws against it. In the United States, much of this legislation has been enacted at the state level. Most U.S. states had computer crime laws on their books by the late 1970's or early 1980's. Federal statutes on computer crime are printed in Title 18 of the United States Code, especially sections 1029 and 1030.

The rapidly developing countries of eastern Asia have lagged behind in efforts to police computer crime, and in many of those countries software piracy has become a flourishing business.

Attention to security by programmers, systems managers, corporate management, and government agencies is the single most effective method of computer crime prevention. Many recorded cases of computer crime have been committed by previously honest individuals who spotted opportunities created by lax security methods and succumbed to temptation. The trend of replacing large mainframe computer systems with networks of personal computers raises further problems, because networks and personal computer operating systems do not have security features as effective as those designed for large systems.

Personal computers are also the most vulnerable to attacks by viruses. Virus detection and "disinfection" programs are available from a variety of vendors, sometimes on a free trial basis. Firewalls have also become vital equipment for Internet users having broadband connections, either through cable or via telephone company dedicated subscriber lines (DSL). Because these connections are always open, they present tempting targets for criminals who continually test them to see if they can enter and take control of other computers.

It is generally recognized that if the ethics of computer use were routinely incorporated into computer science and vocational training, people would have a better understanding of responsible behavior. They should know it is wrong to duplicate copyrighted programs and that it is wrong to access other computer systems without proper authorization.

Charles E. Sutphen
Updated by Milton Berman

FURTHER READING

Betts, Mitch. "What About Ethics?" *Computerworld* 27 (June 7, 1993): 84.

Furnell, Steven. *Cybercrime: Vandalizing the Information Society*. Boston: Addison-Wesley, 2002.

Harley, David, Robert Slade, and Urs Gattiker. *Viruses Revealed*. Berkeley, Calif.: Osborne/McGraw-Hill, 2001.

Hunter, Richard. *World Without Secrets: Business, Crime, and Privacy in the Age of Ubiquitous Computing*. New York: J. Wiley, 2002.

Jewkes, Yvonne, ed. *Dot.cons: Crime, Deviance, and Identity on the Internet*. Cullompton, Devon, England: Willan, 2002.

Kizza, Joseph Migga. *Computer Network Security and Cyber Ethics*. Jefferson, N.C.: McFarland, 2002.

Parker, Donn B. *Fighting Computer Crime: A New Framework for Protecting Information*. New York: J. Wiley, 1998.

SEE ALSO: Computer databases; Computer misuse; Computer technology; Fraud; Identity theft; Internet piracy; Napster.

Computer databases

DEFINITION: Collections of information electronically stored on computers and organized in systematic ways designed to facilitate information retrieval

TYPE OF ETHICS: Legal and judicial ethics

SIGNIFICANCE: Rapid advances in computer technology have made it necessary for courts to set forth legal standards governing the use of the information contained in databases. In addition to the legal principles governing database information, general ethical imperatives also govern the use of this data.

In a modern computerized and technologically oriented society, information and the ability to rapidly and accurately retrieve data are of paramount importance. Names, addresses, medical and credit card information are among the kinds of sensitive data being stored for retrieval in computer databases. As technology progresses, the sophistication, size, and relative invisibility of information-gathering activities increases.

Among the general ethical principles that govern computer databases are the needs to respect the privacy rights and confidentiality of individual persons and groups. Ownership rights in data must be respected by the users of information contained in databases, regardless of whether the data are protected by copyright, patent, trade secret or other intellectual property law provisions. Another ethical principle, avoiding harm to others, is also important in this connection.

PRIVACY AND CONFIDENTIALITY

Many types of data in computer databases are inherently sensitive in nature. In order to obtain many goods and services, such as credit cards, mortgages, insurance, and even medical attention, much personal information must be provided. Compilers of such information are responsible for ensuring that its accuracy and privacy are maintained. When databases are integrated, information from various sources may become available to unintended recipients. When that happens, the unintended recipients of the data should be mindful of their ethical obligation to safeguard the privacy rights of others.

Related to the issue of privacy is the question of

maintaining confidentiality of information contained in a database. When information provided to a database is subject to promises to safeguard it from disclosure, it is the ethical obligation of the database maintainers to protect that information. From time to time, individuals or organizations, including the government, may demand access to the information contained in databases. The moral right to access to database information should certainly presuppose a need to know on the part of the requestor. If requests for information are granted, the recipients should be subject to responsibilities similar to those of the database maintainers.

AVOIDING HARM

Enormous amounts of information are contained in databases, and those amounts were increasing exponentially at the beginning of the twenty-first century. Since information can become obsolete quickly, constant updating and revising are essential. In the rush to update and revise data, errors are inevitable. Database maintainers should be required to ensure that the information contained in their databases is as error-free as possible. In the event that erroneous data find their way into databases, and innocent persons suffer harm as a result, the injured parties should have recourse to remedies.

Gloria A. Whittico

FURTHER READING

Mackall, Joseph. *Information Management.* Chicago: Ferguson, 1998.

Mason, Richard O. "Four Ethical Issues of the Information Age." *Management Information Systems Quarterly* 10, no. 1 (March, 1986).

Wessells, Michael G. "The Challenge to Privacy." In *Computer, Self, and Society.* Englewood Cliffs, N.J.: Prentice Hall, 1990.

SEE ALSO: Computer crime; Computer misuse; Computer technology; Electronic mail; Electronic surveillance; Espionage; Identity theft; Information access; Inside information; Privacy.

Computer misuse

DEFINITION: Unauthorized use of computer hardware or software that may cause damage, regardless of intent, to persons, property, or services

TYPE OF ETHICS: Business and labor ethics

SIGNIFICANCE: The presence of computers in the workplace, libraries and other locations is almost universal. Therefore, businesses may face loss of productivity as a result of the misuse of the equipment and their digital resources. Ethical issues arise when the misuse is not the direct or indirect cause of damage, such as unauthorized remote examination of records or files.

Because of the rapid pace of technological innovation in computer technology and use in the late twentieth and early twenty-first centuries, many activities have become commonplace that several decades earlier would have seemed impossible. As the technology continues to develop, handling ethical questions relating to computer use have become increasingly important.

In *Computers, Ethics, and Society* (1990), M. David Ermann, Mary B. Williams, and Claudio Gutierrez offered a theoretical framework for discussions about which behaviors may be considered as blameworthy. For example, should it be considered as unethical simply to gain access to the computer files of other persons, without their permission and knowledge, even if there is no intention to destroy or alter those files? The authors suggest that utilitarian theorists might conclude that such acts are neither morally wrong nor morally right. No measurable harm actually results from the unauthorized access. An alternative approach would involve analysis of the act from the perspective of Immanuel Kant. The Kantian categorical imperative, that people must always treat other persons as ends in themselves and never merely as means to an end, might suggest the act of gaining unauthorized access to the files of another is morally wrong. By committing such an act, the actor fails to take into account the right of privacy of the person whose files have been accessed.

WORKPLACES, LIBRARIES, AND ACADEMIC SETTINGS

Many activities in the workplace create opportunities for computer abuse. For example, an employee may have access to a computer with an Internet connection that enables the employee to perform tasks as assigned by the employer. The employer's expectation is that the computer will be used solely within the course or scope of employment. From time to time, however, this is not the case. Instances of computer misuse present ethical questions regarding the moral implications of those misuses.

Computer misuses in the workplace fall into at least three broad categories. First, there are misuses of a relatively benign, personal nature. Misuses in this category might involve online shopping, downloading files or trading stock in personal brokerage accounts, sending non-business-related electronic mail to relatives and friends, and so on. A second category might include such activities as downloading copyrighted material such as music or software, thereby potentially exposing the employer to copyright infringement liability. A third, and most severe, category of misuse would include forwarding or receiving pornography, producing and disseminating computer viruses, threatening or harassing others, committing fraud, hacking, or mishandling confidential information of the business itself or of its clients.

The misuses in the second two categories, while certainly posing serious ethical issues, may additionally expose the perpetrator to legal liability, either civil or criminal in nature. The activities in the first category, while not of a strictly illegal nature, nevertheless present questions of ethical import. While employees are involved in personal activities, they are not performing tasks assigned by their employers and may also be tying up limited office resources. One ethical question arising from such behavior is how the blameworthiness of such activities be determined. Some might argue that these misuses should not be evaluated any differently than any other actions that decrease workplace productivity, such as arriving late to work, leaving early, and taking overly long lunch breaks. Others would suggest that because of the public nature of the latter forms of misbehavior, they are easier for employers to guard against. By contrast, computer misuse activities typically occur in the relative privacy of individual employee offices and cubicles, leaving much if not all of the policing of such activities to the individual employees. For this reason, questions of ethics and individual choice are of paramount importance.

In addition to the types of computer misuses that arise in the workplace, libraries and academic setting such as high schools, colleges and universities face additional potential for misuse. Computer users in such environments are frequently children or teenagers. The free access to the Internet afforded by library and school computers presents risks in the form of sites on the World Wide Web dedicated to pornography and pedophilia. As a result, librarians face ethical questions of whether access to such sites should be blocked completely, thereby protecting younger patrons. This action would also serve to deny access to older patrons, who might not feel that the library was receptive to their information needs.

In response to computer misuse, many companies, libraries, and academic institutions have developed written policies containing lists of authorized and unauthorized uses. These policies also set forth penalties for failure to comply with their requirements.

Gloria A. Whittico

FURTHER READING

Baird, Robert M., Reagan Ramsower, and Stuart E. Rosenbaum, eds. *Cyberethics: Social and Moral Issues in the Computer Age.* Amherst, N.Y.: Prometheus Books, 200.

Ermann, M. David, Mary B. Williams, and Claudio Gutierrez, eds. *Computers, Ethics, and Society.* New York: Oxford University Press, 1990.

Ermann, David, and Michele S. Shauf, eds. *Computers, Ethics, and Society.* 3d ed. New York: Oxford University Press, 2002.

Forester, Tom, and Perry Morrison. *Computer Ethics: Cautionary Tales and Ethical Dilemmas in Computing.* 2d ed. Cambridge, Mass.: MIT Press, 1994.

Hafner, Katie, and John Markoff. *Cyberpunk: Outlaws and Hackers on the Computer Frontier.* New York: Simon & Schuster, 1991.

Iannone, A. Pablo. *Contemporary Moral Controversies in Technology.* New York: Oxford University Press, 1987.

Weckert, John, and Douglas Adeney. *Computer and Information Ethics.* Westport, Conn.: Greenwood Press, 1997.

SEE ALSO: Artificial intelligence; Computer crime; Computer technology; Electronic mail; Identity theft; Internet chat rooms; Napster; Plagiarism.

Computer technology

DEFINITION: Electronic devices for storing, manipulating, and retrieving data.

TYPE OF ETHICS: Scientific ethics

SIGNIFICANCE: The advent of the Information Age and the proliferation of computers creates a wide range of ethical issues, from the personal conduct of individuals using computers to public policy questions involving the equitable distribution of technological resources.

Many computer professionals face ethical dilemmas in their work. These dilemmas relate to protecting people's privacy by guarding against unauthorized access to confidential data and preventing the misuse of personal data. Computer professionals are obligated to design and program systems that ensure the accuracy of data, since critical decisions are made based on the output of their systems. Inaccurate information can have grave economic consequences and in some situations can even place people's lives in danger.

Computer professionals have opportunities to enrich people's lives. Conversely, through the improper application of their knowledge and talents, they can have devastating effects on large segments of society. This reality makes clear the necessity of an ethics for computer technology.

BACKGROUND

Traditionally, computers and their use were looked upon as value-neutral. By the late 1960's, however, some ethicists and computer professionals were questioning this assumption. By the late 1980's, computer ethics was being recognized as a legitimate academic pursuit and a professional necessity. As a field between science and moral studies, computer ethics has attempted to define the values inherent in computer technology. Pioneers in this field include Walter Maner, Donn Parker, Deborah G. Johnson, James H. Moor, and Terrell Ward Bynum.

PRIVACY ISSUES AND SURVEILLANCE

Computers are used to store massive amounts of information, much of which is personal and the subjects of which are deserving of protection against misuse of these data. Computer networking over various communication facilities, including ordinary telephone lines, allows electronic access to this confidential information. This environment requires a heightened awareness of the potential for political abuses of personal liberties and commercial exploitation through insensitive misuse and inappropriate manipulation of personal information.

Computers can and are used to monitor activities in the workplace. They track work done on computer terminals, monitor phone calls, and browse electronic mail without the individual's knowledge of this activity. While some of these activities may be historically grounded in efficient business management practices (Fred Taylor introduced time and motion studies at the beginning of the twentieth century), the intensity of monitoring activities with computers raises ethical issues. Awareness of monitoring produces stress and contributes to health problems; employees who know that they are monitored feel that they are in an electronic straitjacket.

The invasion of privacy threat posed by computer monitoring is real. Improperly applied, monitoring is nothing short of eavesdropping on individuals' private lives. Employers may argue that every act by an employee while "on the clock" is their concern. This ethical dilemma needs to be evaluated on the basis of principles of fairness and quality of life in the workplace.

POOR SYSTEM DESIGN AND ASSIGNING RESPONSIBILITY

One of the greatest obstacles to the ethical uses of computers is caused by incompetent system designers, however well intentioned, who develop and program systems that do not accomplish the required tasks, create frustration and aggravation for the users of the systems, and even generate erroneous information. In terms of their cumulative cost to organizations, individuals, and society, poorly designed systems that fail to utilize properly the power of the technology create the greatest and most persistent ethical quandaries. Error-prone, inflexible, unimaginative, and insensitive systems are an ethical issue because of the toll they take on human well-being.

Computers themselves do not have values: They do not make independent decisions, they do not make mistakes, and they can do only what they are programmed to do. The utilization of computer technology, however, is not a value-neutral activity. Faulty programs, invalid data, or lack of proper controls creates computer errors. It is unethical for computer professionals and users to attempt to transfer blame for errors away from themselves. This constitutes denying responsibility and lying.

Also key to this issue is that ethical norms must be applied to situations in which the computer is essentially involved, not passively involved; that is, where computer technology is used, or misused, in the actual perpetration of moral wrongdoing. For example, using a computer to gain unauthorized access to company secrets essentially involves the computer; stealing computer equipment, wrong though it may be, only passively involves the computer.

Using computers to do dull, repetitive, noncreative tasks is useful. Using them to replace workers simply for the purpose of reducing payrolls raises serious ethical questions of fairness and obligation. Computer technology ought to be applied in the workplace in ways that allow time for and actually encourage the pursuit of more creative activities.

INTELLECTUAL PROPERTY

Computer technology focuses attention on the whole issue of intellectual property because computer software is often viewed as such. Some people argue that programmers who write software create in much the same way that an author or an artist creates. Others argue that programming is simply stringing together series of instructions and algorithms that are in the public domain. Therefore, programming is not truly creative, and the end product is not someone's intellectual property.

For those who subscribe to the argument that software is intellectual property, the question of ownership must be answered. Does the programmer, as creator, own the software? Does her employer, who is paying her to create the software, own it? Should those who work to develop software or pay others to develop it expect to be reimbursed by those who use it? Still others argue that all software is in the public domain, since it is nothing more than ideas and thoughts, actualized on a computer, and therefore is not intellectual property at all. Proponents of this latter view oppose exclusive "ownership" of any software.

If the ownership of software can be established, however, then unauthorized use of the software raises serious ethical questions.

Edwin R. Davis

FURTHER READING

Edgar, Stacey L. *Morality and Machines: Perspectives on Computer Ethics*. 2d ed. Sudbury, Mass.: Jones and Bartlett, 2003.

Forester, Tom, and Perry Morrison. *Computer Ethics*. 2d ed. Cambridge, Mass.: MIT Press, 1994.

Hunter, Richard. *World Without Secrets: Business, Crime, and Privacy in the Age of Ubiquitous Computing*. New York: J. Wiley, 2002.

Johnson, Deborah G. *Computer Ethics*. 3d ed. Upper Saddle River, N.J.: Prentice Hall, 2001.

Kling, Rob, ed. *Computerization and Controversy: Value Conflicts and Social Choices*. San Diego, Calif.: Academic Press, 1996.

Langford, Duncan. *Internet Ethics*. New York: St. Martin's Press, 2000.

Mossberger, Karen, Caroline J. Tolbert, and Mary Stansbury, eds. *Virtual Inequality: Beyond the Digital Divide*. Washington, D.C.: Georgetown University Press, 2003.

Parker, Donn B., Susan Swope, and Bruce N. Baker. *Ethical Conflicts in Information and Computer Science, Technology, and Business*. Wellesley, Mass.: QED Information Sciences, 1990.

Spinello, Richard A. *CyberEthics: Morality and Law in Cyberspace*. 2d ed. Boston: Jones and Bartlett, 2003.

SEE ALSO: Artificial intelligence; Computer crime; Computer databases; Computer misuse; Internet piracy; Robotics; Technology; Virtual reality.

Comte, Auguste

IDENTIFICATION: French philosopher
BORN: January 19, 1798, Montpellier, France
DIED: September 5, 1857, Paris, France
TYPE OF ETHICS: Modern history
SIGNIFICANCE: Comte was a founder of the philosophical school of positivism, which he laid out in a six-volume course on positive philosophy (1830-1842). He also helped to create the nascent discipline of sociology, from which viewpoint he argued that "moral progress" was a fundamentally social phenomenon and a crucial societal responsibility.

A social theorist as well as a philosopher, Auguste Comte believed that the history of humankind passed through three distinct stages: a theological phase, a transitional metaphysical period, and finally the modern age. The primary focus of this historical evolution, and indeed of all human activity, was "moral progress." Despite his broad societal framework, however, Comte was deeply concerned with the fate of the individual within modern society.

Comte recognized the problems associated with modern society and the impact of science and the industrial order. He searched for elements of a good and ethical society that could command a consensus in the midst of varying individuals' beliefs. Further, he looked for a common ground for agreement on values in spite of the turbulent alterations in the structures of modern society. Finally, although Comte advanced the concept of a communal or societal order, he recognized the need for personal fulfillment in this ethical society. Comte has been criticized for his pro-Catholic and anti-Protestant statements and sentiments.

William T. Walker

SEE ALSO: Ayer, A. J.; Hart, H. L. A.; Humanism; Language; Morality; Santayana, George.

Concentration camps

DEFINITION: Places in which groups of people are confined, tortured and killed by recognized governments advancing authoritarian, totalitarian, or racial supremacist policies

TYPE OF ETHICS: Human rights

SIGNIFICANCE: During the twentieth century concentration camps were used by nation-states to deny human, civil and political rights to individuals who were viewed as enemies or potential dangers to the states because they held dissenting political views or were members of racial or ethnic groups that were viewed as dangerous or undesirable.

Prisoner-of-war camps have been a part of history from antiquity; however, the use of concentration camps to confine political prisoners or "enemies of the state" has been largely an invention of the late nineteenth and twentieth centuries. From the arbitrary confinement of Native American tribes in "reservations" by the United States government during the nineteenth century and the British treatment of enemy civilians by the British during the South African (Boer) War, through the death camps of Nazi Germany, the internment of Japanese Americans in the United States during World War II, the gulag camps of the Soviet Union, and the ethnic cleansing of the 1990's in the former Yugoslavia, these concentration camps have violated basic human rights and freedoms with the sanction of the state.

Governments and societies that tolerate concentration camps usually are experiencing periods in which the prevailing political sentiment supports a cultural view that is based on the dominant interests of the group, not those of the individual. The fascist ideology that succeeded in Nazi Germany, Benito Mussolini's Italy, Francisco Franco's Spain, and Juan Peron's Argentina, was based on a corporate philosophy of society in which the state's interest was paramount and there were no individual human rights that were sacred.

FASCIST STATES

Fascism has historically been characterized by authoritarianism, totalitarianism, militarism, organic views of the state as a "living" reality, and ethical systems that have been the antithesis to Western liberal democracy, which is predicated on liberty and the recognition of the value of the individual. During the 1930's and 1940's Adolf Hitler's fascist regime in Germany used concentration camps to confine political and religious opponents—Jews, Roman Catholic clergy, Gypsies, homosexuals, prostitutes, and others. The victims were treated in inhumane ways; substandard housing and food were provided, little or no health care was available, forced labor was excessive, and torture and arbitrary executions were used.

Through fascist ideology and Nazi anti-Semitism more than eleven million people, including six million Jews, were killed during the Holocaust. The most notorious of the Nazi concentration camps were Auschwitz, Bergen-Belsen, and Lublin-Majdanek.

Joseph Stalin's communist regime in the Soviet Union also maintained concentration camps before, during, and after World War II. These "corrective labor camps" imprisoned dissenters, farm leaders, edu-

Bodies carted from a liberated Nazi concentration camp at the conclusion of the European sector of World War II. (National Archives)

OTHER STATES

Concentration camps have also appeared in societies that were not fundamentally authoritarian. For example, the U.S. government established concentration camp-like devices in handling Native American tribes, including the Sioux, Apache, and Cherokee peoples. The federal government also established internment camps for Japanese Americans during World War II. In early 1942, President Franklin D. Roosevelt signed an executive order that authorized interning Japanese Americans in camps for the duration of the war against Japan. Fearing that the large number of Japanese Americans living along the Pacific Coast would betray the United States and contribute to its defeat, Roosevelt's administration set up camps in remote regions of the western part of the country. Internees lost much of their property and virtually all their legal rights during the period from 1942-1945. Nearly a half-century later, the federal government formally apologized and paid cash settlements for the hardships experienced and the abrogation of the rights of the Japanese Americans.

After the late 1980's and early 1990's political revolutions in Eastern Europe and the collapse of the Soviet Union, concentration camps appeared in the former Yugoslavia when the Serbs introduced a policy of ethnic cleansing in order to gain control of Kosovo and expel non-Serbs. These camps resulted in the deaths of hundreds of Albanians and others. The United Nations intervened and the Serb nationalist leader Slobodan Milošević was removed from power in 2000 and was later tried as a war criminal.

The United Nations issued the Universal Declaration of Human Rights in 1948 as a reaction to the horrors of concentration camps and the denial of human and political rights. While it is hoped that concentration camps will never again reappear, Human Rights Watch, Amnesty International, and other groups remain vigilant in the defense of individual rights.

William T. Walker

cators, intellectuals, and others who were viewed as threats to the Soviet state. While the systematic executions that occurred in Nazi camps were not replicated in the Soviet Union, millions of Russians and others died because of Soviet mistreatment. The system of Soviet camps has been called the gulag and included five major camp clusters. The Soviet rationale for these concentration camps and the terrors that they witnessed was based upon the Marxist view of history in which the state viewed individual human rights as expendable. As was the case in fascist ideology, Soviet communism was fundamentally focused on a group or collective view of history; individualism, and therefore individual human rights, was not of value.

FURTHER READING

Applebaum, Anne. *Gulag: A History*. New York: Doubleday, 2003.

Arendt, Hannah. *The Origins of Totalitarianism*. New York: Harvest Books, 1973.

Aroneanu, Eugene, and Thomas Whissen. *Inside the Concentration Camps*. New York: Praeger, 1996.

Evans, Richard J. *The Coming of the Third Reich*. London: Allen Lane, 2004.

Feig, Konnilyn G. *Hitler's Death Camps: The Sanity of Madness*. New York: Holmes & Meier, 1981.

Laquer, Walter, and Judith Tydor Baumel, eds. *The Holocaust Encyclopedia*. New Haven: Yale University Press, 2001.

Paxton, Robert O. *The Anatomy of Fascism*. New York: Knopf, 2004.

Solzhenitsyn, Aleksandr I. *The Gulag Archipelago, 1918-1956: An Experiment in Literary Investigation*. Translated by Thomas P. Whitney. 3 vols. New York: Harper & Row, 1974-1978.

Zakaria, Fareed. *The Future of Freedom: Illiberal Democracy at Home and Abroad*. New York: W. W. Norton, 2003.

SEE ALSO: Bosnia; Choiceless choices; Ethnic cleansing; Fascism; Genocide and democide; *Gulag Archipelago*; Holocaust; Japanese American internment; Nazi science; Nazism; Nuremberg Trials; Wiesel, Elie.

Confidentiality

DEFINITION: Expectation that disclosures made in certain relationships will remain private

TYPE OF ETHICS: Personal and social ethics

SIGNIFICANCE: The confidentiality of communications between lawyers and clients, doctors and patients, and those in similar relationships, is generally deemed to be necessary for the good of society, but there are times when adherence to that principle can pose ethical and legal dilemmas.

Many professions have ethical rules requiring their members not to disclose confidential communications—roughly the same thing as keeping a secret—under most circumstances. A secret is information that is told to someone else with the reasonable ex-

pectancy that it will be private. Anything disclosed when other people can overhear it is not confidential. The ethical rules do not attempt to control general gossip. They cover only secrets revealed to professionals during professional work. Some laws (privileges) protect professional confidences. Other laws (exceptions to privilege and reporting statutes) permit or force the betrayal of confidentiality. These laws create new ethical dilemmas.

The concept of professionals having an ethical obligation to maintain confidentiality dates back to writings known as the *Corpus Hippocraticum*, attributed to the Greek physician Hippocrates about 400 B.C.E. Hippocrates is credited with stating: "Whatever I shall see or hear in the course of my profession . . . if it be what should not be published abroad, I will never divulge, holding such things to be holy secrets." This rule of confidentiality became a core concept in the medical ethics of the sixteenth century, when physicians discovered that infectious diseases were being spread by diseased persons who feared that disclosure of their condition would cause them to be punished by social isolation.

Physicians continued to apply the rule of confidentiality and, with time, the ethical codes of all mental health-related professions incorporated it. In the twenty-first century, it is a universal ethical concept in the helping professions and is seen as vital to promoting the full client disclosure necessary for effective treatment.

CONFIDENTIALITY AND THE PROFESSIONS

Psychotherapy is assumed to require the honest communication of clients' secret private feelings and the subsequent treatment of clients' symptoms. Clients will not reveal such matters if they do not trust the professional to keep them secret. Such trust, which is assumed to be essential for effective treatment, requires firm rules requiring that things that are said in confidence be kept confidential. Violating the client's expectations of privacy violates professional ethical rules, the client's constitutionally based civil rights, and most state laws that govern professional conduct. Violations can give rise to lawsuits.

Hippocrates' basic insight that physicians can best perform their duties if their clients trust them enough to reveal sensitive information also applies to other nonmedical professions. Legal clients will not discuss sensitive details of their cases if they do not trust their attorneys. Penitents will not bare their souls to clerics if they fear gossip about their confessions. News sources will not speak to reporters if they fear that their lives will be disrupted by disclosure of their identities. Business clients are reluctant to allow accountants access to sensitive business data without assurances of privacy. Therefore, all these professions have also developed ethical traditions of confidentiality to reassure clients that it is safe to speak freely with members of these professions.

LEGAL PRIVILEGE AND ITS EXCEPTIONS

All traditions of confidentiality in the ethics of professions thus arise out of utilitarian considerations. Many of these considerations are considered so important that laws have been passed creating legal rights (privileges) for some professions to protect some types of confidences even against court orders. The attorney-client privilege, the oldest such privilege, is universal in the Anglo-American legal tradition. Most U.S. states also recognize the physician-patient, cleric-penitent, and psychotherapist-client privileges. The psychotherapist-client privilege does not apply to all mental health professions in all states. Communications with other professionals, such as divorce mediators and accountants, are privileged in some states. Members of professions having a privilege are ethically required to assert that privilege to protect confidential information when they are served with subpoenas. Communications in certain nonprofessional relationships, such as marriage, may also be privileged.

In recent years, courts and legislatures have decided that the social benefits of privileges are not as important as access to information in some types of situations, and they have created exceptions to privilege (preventing protection of information) and reporting statutes (requiring disclosures). Examples of exceptions to privilege include a therapist's duty to disclose threats made by a client against another person. Further, both medical and mental health professionals are legally required by reporting statutes to violate confidentiality when the subject matter is child abuse.

These exceptions to privilege and reporting statutes create new ethical dilemmas for professionals and for professions. Jail terms and fines have been used to punish the defiant. Obeying has put professionals in opposition to the ethical standards of their professions. The professional associations have retreated after fierce opposition. Today, the ethical codes of most professional groups say that the professional must protect confidentiality to the extent allowed by laws and legal duties. The Principles of the American Psychological Association (APA) state that confidentiality should be maintained unless to do so would clearly increase danger to the client or to another person or unless the client or the client's legal representative has given consent to disclose. The American Counseling Association (formerly the AACD) requires members to take reasonable personal action or to inform responsible authorities when they are faced with clear and imminent danger to the client or others.

Areas of Professional Confidentiality

Professional field	Confidential subject matter	Exceptions
Physicians	Patients' medical information	Signs of child abuse and information about certain contagious diseases
Lawyers	Almost all client information	Information regarding future crimes
Journalists	Identities of news sources	
Mental-health professionals	Almost all patient information	Information regarding potential dangers to patients or others or to child abuse
Clerics	All parishioner information	
Accountants	Clients' business data	Blatantly fraudulent tax information

Although the new flexibility in the ethical rules solves one set of problems, it also creates another set. Clients may feel betrayed when a professional discloses confidential information for legal reasons. Required disclosures can violate professional ethical duties to help clients (beneficence) and not to harm them (nonmaleficence). Revealing a client's past child abuse because of a reporting statute may betray that client's trust and make further therapy impossible. One solution is to have the professional explain to the client, in advance of any professional services, what is confidential and what is not. Many professionals reject this approach because they believe that prior warnings make the therapy process seem too legalistic and inhibit client trust.

Another approach is to keep required disclosures as limited as possible. Ethical guidelines for school counselors call for reporting information disclosed by pupil clients that reveals circumstances that are likely to have negative effects on others without revealing the identity of the student.

Leland C. Swenson

FURTHER READING

American Association of Counseling and Development. *Ethical Standards of the American Association of Counseling and Development.* 3d ed. Alexandria, Virginia: AACD Governing Council, 1988.

American Psychological Association. "Ethical Principles for Psychologists." *American Psychologist* 45 (March, 1990): 390-395.

Denkowski, Kathryn, and George Denkowski. "Client-Counselor Confidentiality: An Update of Rationale, Legal Status and Implications." *Personnel and Guidance Journal* 60 (February, 1982): 371-375.

Feldman, James H. "Testimonial Privilege: Between Priest and Penitent, Doctor and Patient, Lawyer and Client . . . Which Confidences Are Protected?" *Family Advocate* 14, no. 2 (Fall, 1991): 20-24.

Petronio, Sandra, ed. *Balancing the Secrets of Private Disclosures.* Mahwah, N.J.: Lawrence Erlbaum Associates, 2000.

Slovenko, Ralph. *Psychiatry and Law.* Boston: Little, Brown, 1973.

Swenson, Leland C. *Psychology and Law for the Helping Professions.* Pacific Grove, Calif.: Brooks/Cole, 1993.

Taylor, Linda, and H. S. Adelman. "Reframing the Confidentiality Dilemma to Work in Children's Best Interests." *Professional Psychology: Research and Practice* 20 (April, 1989): 79-83.

Welfel, Elizabeth Reynolds. *Ethics in Counseling and Psychotherapy: Standards, Research, and Emerging Issues.* 2d ed. Pacific Grove, Calif.: Brooks/Cole-Thomson Learning, 2002.

SEE ALSO: Gossip; Hippocrates; Identity theft; Marriage; Medical ethics; Personal relationships; Physician-patient relationship; Professional ethics; Therapist-patient relationship.

Conflict of interest

DEFINITION: Situation in which two or more interests are not mutually realizable

TYPE OF ETHICS: Personal and social ethics

SIGNIFICANCE: The irreducible conflict of different kinds of interests, between people and especially within a single person, is often resolved by recourse to morality as a "trump value." In the absence of any other principle for deciding between competing interests, the most moral choice is usually assumed to be the appropriate one.

In pursuing their lives, individuals must establish goals and put into practice plans to achieve them. A goal to which an individual is committed is commonly called an "interest" of that individual.

Not all goals can be achieved. Many people set impossible goals, goals that conflict with the nature of reality—for example, the goal of discovering the secret of instantaneous interplanetary travel. Individuals can also set goals that conflict with each other—for example, a student of below-average intelligence setting the goals of getting A's in all of his courses while working a full-time job and playing a sport. Individuals can set goals that conflict with the goals of other individuals—for example, a burglar's goal of stealing a television conflicts with the owner's goal of keeping it.

Conflicts of interest can also arise in professional agent/client relationships. An agent can be hired by two clients with conflicting interests or can have a personal interest arise that conflicts with his or her professional role. An example of the former is a corporate director who is offered a job in a government agency that regulates her corporation. An example of the latter is an attorney who is hired by the plaintiff in a case in which the defendant turns out to be an old school friend.

Professional agent conflicts of interest raise moral concerns because such conflicts make it more difficult for the agent to be objective in evaluating the interests of both sides; thus, the clients are less certain that the agent will act in their best interests.

The above cases present no intractable moral problems, since all of them arise either because of ignorance (instantaneous travel), unrealistic expectations (the student), illegitimate goals (the burglar), or happenstance that makes objectivity more difficult but not impossible (the attorney and the director). Throughout most of the history of philosophy, however, the standard view has been that conflicts of interest must necessarily exist. This thesis is a conclusion derived from premises about human nature and the creation of values.

HUMAN NATURE

In dualist theories of human nature (such as those of Plato, Christianity, and Sigmund Freud, to take three influential examples), one part of the self (for example, the appetites, body, or id) is said to have innate interests that are absolutely opposed to those of another part of the self (for example, reason, the soul, or the superego). International conflicts of interest are thus built into human nature.

Reductive materialist theories tend to necessitate conflicts of interest among individuals. In Thomas Hobbes's theory, for example, human nature is constituted by drives for gain, safety, and glory that can be satisfied only at the expense of others. In the absence of social mechanisms created to mediate these conflicts of interest, life is "solitary, poor, nasty, brutish, and short."

In economics, the premise that someone's gain is always balanced by someone else's loss is called the "zero-sum" premise. Competitive games are often offered as zero-sum metaphors for life. Someone wins and someone loses; both parties want to win, but a conflict of interest exists since only one can.

ETHICAL IMPLICATIONS

If conflicts of interest are fundamental to human social relationships, then ethics is about resolving conflicts. Since such fundamental conflicts of interest can be settled only by someone's interests being sacrificed, however, it follows that ethics is about deciding whose interests must be sacrificed.

Against the standard view is the position that all conflicts of interest are a result of error, not of human nature or zero-sum theory. The harmonious thesis holds that human nature is at birth a set of integrated capacities rather than an aggregation of innate, conflicting parts. The capacities exist to be developed so as to be able to satisfy one's needs, and it is by reference to one's needs that one's interests are defined. Since one's ultimate need is to maintain one's life, one's interests are defined by reference to maintaining one's life. Because life is a long-term endeavor, it follows that one must adopt long-range principles by which to guide one's actions.

Many principles are involved, but of special relevance to the question of conflicts of interest are the principles that life requires individual effort and that each individual's life is an end in itself. If these principles are true, then since other individuals are not one's property, one's interests must be specified by what one can do by one's individual effort. In a society based on the division of labor, this means that one must produce goods for trade. Since trade is a voluntary exchange, the long-range social principle is to interact with others on a mutually voluntary basis. If this broad, long-range context is established as the framework for defining interests, then social cooperation rather than conflict is a consequence of pursuing one's interests.

WIN-WIN

The zero-sum account of production and distribution can also be challenged. If one purchases gasoline, the exchange is win-win for oneself and the gas station owner. Michelangelo's sculptures and Thomas Edison's inventions were not produced at the expense of those who did not create them; therefore, the sculptures and inventions are a net gain for everyone.

If legitimate interests are not in conflict, then it follows that personal and social harmony are possible without the sacrifice of legitimate interests. Accordingly, the task of ethics will not be to decide who must be sacrificed, but rather how to identify and fulfill legitimate interests.

Stephen R. C. Hicks

FURTHER READING

Freud, Sigmund. *Civilization and Its Discontents*. Translated by David McLintock. 1930. Reprint. Introduction by Leo Bersani. London: Penguin, 2002.

Hobbes, Thomas. *Leviathan*. Edited by Richard Tuck. Rev. student ed. New York: Cambridge University Press, 1996.

Kane, Robert, ed. *The Oxford Handbook of Free Will*. New York: Oxford University Press, 2002.

Nietzsche, Friedrich. *Beyond Good and Evil*. Translated by Walter Kaufmann. New York: Vintage, 1989.

Plato. *The Republic*. Translated by Desmond Lee. 2d ed. New York: Penguin Books, 2003.

Rand, Ayn. "The 'Conflicts' of Men's Interests." In *The Virtue of Selfishness: A New Concept of Egoism*. New York: New American Library, 1964.

SEE ALSO: Compromise; Ethics in Government Act; Hobbes, Thomas; *Leviathan*; Nietzsche, Friedrich.

Conflict resolution

DEFINITION: Set of nonadversarial techniques for the satisfactory adjudication or mediation of struggles and disputes

TYPE OF ETHICS: Personal and social ethics

SIGNIFICANCE: Conflict resolution embraces an egalitarian ethic which rejects zero-sum models of competition and seeks a conclusion which will benefit all parties in a dispute.

Arguments, yielding, yelling, stalling, threats, coercion—these are all images of conflict. It is understandable that some people try to avoid dealing with any conflict. Yet there are techniques for resolving conflict productively and ethically. Many people are familiar with the concept of "win-win" negotiation, but few actually practice it. It seems, however, that "principled conflict management," as some call win-win negotiation, is finally moving into the mainstream. Universities are granting advanced degrees in conflict management and creating advanced centers of study such as the Harvard Negotiation Project. Nonadversarial, alternative dispute resolution methods, such as mediation, are now required in many contracts. Empowerment management styles such as Total Quality Management and Self-Directed Work Teams require win-win conflict management to be successful.

Authors Joyce L. Hocker and William W. Wilmot, in their book *Interpersonal Conflict*, find that "One of the most dysfunctional teachings about conflict is that *harmony is normal and conflict is abnormal.*" Some people think of conflict as the result of "personality clashes." In fact, however, conflict is a natural process that is inherent in all important relationships. Conflict is here to stay. No one can change that, but people can change their perceptions of conflict and the ways in which they manage it.

AVOIDANCE AND COMPETITIVE NEGOTIATION

There are three basic styles of conflict management: avoidance, competitive negotiation, and principled negotiation. Many people use more than one style, depending on the situation. Avoidance is very common when people perceive conflict as a negative and conflict resolution as an unpleasant problem. Avoidance can be useful when open communication is not possible, when the issue or relationship is not important to one—something one regards as trivial and not worth the energy required to reach a mutually agreeable solution—and when the costs of confrontation are too high. Continual avoidance of conflict, however, can be highly destructive.

Competitive negotiation is the familiar win-lose style. In this approach, each party pressures the other to change. Control, coercion, threats, walkouts, and lying are techniques that are employed. One pursues one's own concerns at the expense of another. Competitive negotiations work with set positions or predetermined solutions. Each party comes to the negotiations with a "solution" to the conflict and attempts to get the other to change or give up something. With this style someone always loses. Someone is disappointed. Someone may leave angry and wish to "get even" the next time. Competitive negotiation can be useful if the external goal is more important than the relationship or if the other party really has one's detriment at heart; for example, when there has been physical abuse in a divorce case. Relationships are rarely enhanced by competitive negotiation. The goal has to be so important that one is willing to sacrifice the relationship.

301

Guidelines for Principled Negotiation

1. Attack problems, not people.

2. Build trust.

3. Start discussion and analysis of the interests, concerns, needs, and whys of each party—the essence of principled negotiation. Begin with interests, not positions or solutions.

4. Listen.

5. Brainstorm. Suggesting an idea does not mean you agree with it. Solve problems. Develop multiple options.

6. Use objective criteria whenever possible. Agree on how something will be measured.

PRINCIPLED NEGOTIATION

Principled negotiation, also called collaborative negotiation, is the win-win style. With this model, one strives for a mutually favorable resolution to the conflict by inducing or persuading the other party to cooperate. While competitive negotiations start with positions or solutions, in principled negotiations the parties do not come with predetermined solutions. Instead, they come with interests, specific needs, or underlying concerns that may be met in several ways. The parties may have ideas about solutions, but they are not attached to them. They are open to different solutions, provided that their key interests, concerns, and needs are met. Principled negotiation takes the approach that the parties have both diverse and common interests and that, in the end, both parties will have their interests satisfied. The needs of each party are revealed, and both work to find mutually agreeable, and often new, solutions.

Although principled negotiation can be empowering for both parties and can lead to a long-term solution to the conflict, it has some disadvantages. It requires keen perception, good communication skills, and creativity. It also takes time and requires trust.

COMMUNICATING EFFECTIVELY

Conflict is more often than not a product of communication behavior. Therefore, resolving conflict starts with improving communication skills. For most people, listening is "waiting to talk" rather than listening and validating (not necessarily agreeing with, but acknowledging) what the person is saying. Listening is more effective when the listener demonstrates that he or she understands by using phrases such as "I hear you saying that . . ." It is also effective to ask questions and to speak from the "I" position, saying what he or she thinks, rather than attacking the other party. It is more effective to say "I feel discriminated against" than it is to say "You are a racist." When one party takes a stance and "attacks" from a positional view, it is wise for the other party to break the cycle by refusing to participate in that destructive style of conflict management. In such a case, it is often effective for the party who is being attacked to express his or her own interests, to ask why the other party has this view, and to listen to the response. Often, when people are "heard," they soften their positional stands. Understanding need not imply agreement. When one party understands the other, then that party can calmly explain his or her concerns, needs, and interests, inviting the other party to cooperate to find a solution. It should be kept in mind that the two parties have a relationship and that it is better for both parties to resolve the conflict in an agreeable manner.

Principled negotiation is not appropriate for all conflicts, but it is a technique that deserves to be used more widely. It is the only style of conflict management that gets results and maintains and even enhances relationships.

Kathleen D. Purdy

FURTHER READING

Fisher, Roger, and Scott Brown. *Getting Together: Building Relationships as We Negotiate*. New York: Penguin Books, 1989.

Fisher, Roger, and William Ury. *Getting to Yes: Negotiating Agreements Without Giving In*. Boston: Houghton Mifflin, 1981.

Hocker, Joyce L., and William M. Wilmot. *Interpersonal Conflict*. 5th ed. Boston: McGraw-Hill, 1998.

Kremenyuk, Victor A., ed. *International Negotiation: Analysis, Approaches, Issues*. 2d ed. San Francisco: Jossey-Bass, 2002.

Masters, Marik F., and Robert R. Albright. *The Com-

plete Guide to Conflict Resolution in the Workplace. New York: AMACOM/American Management Association, 2002

Raiffa, H. *The Art and Science of Negotiation.* Cambridge, Mass.: Harvard University Press, 1982.

SEE ALSO: Business ethics; Compromise; International justice; League of Nations; Peace studies; United Nations.

Confucian ethics

DEFINITION: Maxims and prescriptions for social and political behavior based on writings by Confucian philosophers

TYPE OF ETHICS: Classical history

SIGNIFICANCE: In addition to their continuing relevance to modern ethics, Confucian moral principles have influenced Asian and world history, serving as guidelines for personal and professional conduct for rulers, officials, and the upper classes in China, Korea, Vietnam, and Japan.

First postulated during the feudal period in China (771-221 B.C.E.), Confucian ethics sought to effect peace and harmony in Chinese society. Starting with simple maxims, the school gradually developed into a comprehensive system of ethics that was primarily political but also emphasized social and religious conduct. Never a popular religion, its rites and ethical dictates were practiced by elites in several East Asian countries.

HISTORY

The first thinker in China to address the problem of the wars and uncertainty that characterized the breakdown of the feudal system was Confucius (Kongfuzi), who lived from 551 B.C.E. to 479 B.C.E. His solution to the problem of societal breakdown was to return to an idealized form of feudalism. Such a system would be based on the family; the king would act as father and role model for his subjects, who in turn would behave like filial children. While emphasizing hereditary rights, Confucius also called upon kings to act in a kingly fashion and upon noblemen to act with noble integrity. If this were done, laws would be unnecessary.

The next major Confucian, Mencius (371-289 B.C.E.), in response to the accelerated decline of feudalism, added to the responsibilities of the king welfare projects and the requirement to hire officials on the basis of merit and education rather than birthright. Mencius stipulated that those who worked with their minds were entitled to be the ruling class, thus creating the idea of a literocracy rather than a hereditary aristocracy. A ruler who did not provide for his people should be replaced by another member of his family.

The next major Confucian, Xunzi (298-238 B.C.E.) expanded on Confucian themes, but unlike Confucius and Mencius, who either implied or asserted that human nature was good, Xunzi argued that human beings were born evil. It was human nature to seek to be good in order to protect oneself, thereby engaging in a form of social contract with the state. All three philosophers considered that human beings could be good. To Confucius, the ruler and the nobility had to provide the proper role models. Mencius added the obligation to provide education and welfare to the weak and needy. Xunzi's ideal ruler, however, could also mete out rewards and punishments in order to weed out incorrigibles and promote social harmony.

During China's Eastern Zhou and Qin Dynasties (771-210 B.C.E.), the Confucian school was neither large nor powerful. In fact, the prime minister of the Qin (221-210 B.C.E.) persecuted Confucians despite the fact that he had been Xunzi's student. During the Han Dynasty (206 B.C.E. to 9 C.E.), Emperor Han Wudi (140-86 B.C.E.) made Confucianism the official school of China. This action was primarily the result of efforts of the emperor's minister Dong Zhongshu (179-104 B.C.E.), who combined Confucianism with other schools and also suggested that a ruler was a cosmic figure who coalesced the forces of Heaven, Earth, and Humanity. No doubt the prospect of having well-behaved citizens who were loyal to the throne also contributed to the emperor's decision.

By the end of the seventh century C.E., there was a regularized examination system that required prospective officials to know the Confucian canon by memory. In this way, the imperial throne sought to ensure that its officials would all adhere to the high moral standards of Confucianism. Subsequent neo-Confucian thinkers cemented the symbiotic relationship between the absolute throne and the Confucian literocracy by assuming responsibility for many of the failures of any given monarch or dynasty. Confucians accepted the displacement of one dynasty by another, ascribing such changes to the moral deficiencies of dynastic family. They did, however, fight tenaciously against any efforts to alter the system itself.

In 1911, when the last dynasty fell, an already weakened Confucian literocracy fell as well, although the religious and social practices of Confucianism have survived to some degree in many places in Asia.

ETHICAL PRINCIPLES

In addition to requiring a monarch to set a proper moral example for his subjects, Confucius stressed that all humans should strive to be *ren*, which generally means "humane." Expressed by the character combining the meanings "man" and "two," this concept called for people to be considerate and compassionate toward one another. One method of developing one's *ren* was to observe the proper rituals and ceremonies. It was essential that people be obedient and loving toward their parents and superiors, who, in turn, should be kind and nurturing. Other concepts presented by Confucius and developed by his disciples included *li* ("principle") and *yi* (righteousness), both of which connoted acting in accordance with ancient precedents.

Mencius and Xunzi further developed the concept of the five cardinal human relationships. These involved affection between father and son, respect between husband and wife, hierarchy between the old and the young, propriety between ruler and minister, and loyalty between friend and friend. All three of the Eastern Zhou philosophers stressed ritualistic behavior in order to achieve discipline and nurture moral principles.

With the syncretism of Dong Zhongshu and of later neo-Confucians, other concepts of ethical behavior were incorporated from Daoism and Buddhism into Confucianism. Concepts such as *qi* ("inner spirit") crept into Confucian theory and practice. Nevertheless, the basic principles of Confucian morality were evident by 250 B.C.E. and have remained fairly consistent to this day.

Hilel B. Salomon

FURTHER READING

Creel, Herrlee Glessner. *Confucius and The Chinese Way.* New York: Harper, 1960.

Ivanhoe, Philip J. *Confucian Moral Self Cultivation.* 2d ed. Indianapolis: Hackett, 2000.

_____. *Ethics in the Confucian Tradition: The Thought of Mengzi and Wang Yangming.* 2d ed. Indianapolis, Hackett, 2002.

Legge, James, trans. *The Four Books: Confucian Analects, The Great Learning, The Doctrine of the Mean, and the Works of Mencius.* Shanghai: Chinese Book, 1933.

Li Chenyang, ed. *The Sage and the Second Sex: Confucianism, Ethics, and Gender.* Foreword by Patricia Ebrey. Chicago: Open Court, 2000.

Shryock, John Knight. *The Origin and Development of the State Cult of Confucius: An Introductory Study.* New York: Century Press, 1932. Reprint. New York: Paragon, 1966.

Taylor, Rodney Leon. *The Religious Dimensions of Confucianism.* Albany: State University of New York Press, 1990.

Tu, Wei-ming. *Humanity and Self-Cultivation: Essays in Confucian Thought.* Berkeley: Asian Humanities Press, 1979.

SEE ALSO: Buddhist ethics; Christian ethics; Confucius; Daoist ethics; Laozi; Mencius; Mozi; Wang Yangming; Zhu Xi; Zhuangzi.

Confucius

IDENTIFICATION: Ancient Chinese philosopher
BORN: Kongfuzi or Kongzi; 551 B.C.E., state of Lu (now in Shandong Province), China
DIED: 479 B.C.E., Qufu, state of Lu (now in Shandong Province), China
TYPE OF ETHICS: Classical history
SIGNIFICANCE: The founder of one of the world's most influential systems of philosophy, Confucius integrated governing with the teaching of morality. He developed the moral category of the "elite scholar," the moral principles of *ren* (humanity) and *li* (rites), and advocated basic virtues such as "filial piety."

Confucius lived at a time when the ancient empire of China was being broken up into numerous feudal states, whose struggles for power or survival created an urgent need for able state officials. For the first time in Chinese history, it became possible for a commoner to attain high court position and to effect political changes. A new class of literati was thus formed in Chinese society. As one of the forerunners of that class, Confucius was greatly distressed by the chaotic situation of his time, which was characterized by corruption, conspiracy, and usurpation in courts; harsh measures of oppression carried out against the people; and aggressive wars between states. He believed that this was a result of the moral degeneration of the rulers and that the only way to correct it was to teach and to practice morality.

Unable to persuade the rulers of his time to listen to his morally oriented political advice, Confucius devoted his life to teaching a large number of private students, in order to foster a special group of elite scholars (*junzi*, or superior people) who would serve the needs of the time and realize his political ideals. His teaching was made authoritative by the Han emperors in the second century B.C.E. and became the official Chinese ideology until the beginning of the twentieth century. The earliest biography of Confucius was written by Sima Qian in his *Records of the Historian (Shiji)* at the beginning of the first century B.C.E.

The *Analects* (*Lunyu*, late sixth or early fifth century B.C.E.)is a collection that consists mainly of Confucius's teachings, comments, and advice, along with some contributions from his main disciples. Also included are short records and descriptions of issues that concerned Confucius. The work was compiled and edited by the students of Confucius's disciples a century or so after his death. It was beautifully written, and many of the sayings contained in it became proverbs and everyday maxims. It is one of the most reliable texts among the Chinese classics, and it provides the most accurate information about Confucius and his teachings. The primary text of Confucianism, the *Analects* was the most influential book in China until the early twentieth century.

JUNZI AND SELF-CULTIVATION

Junzi originally meant the son of a nobleman. Confucius used the term to mean a person with a noble character. It means an elite, superior man in a moral sense. The way to be a *junzi* is not by birth but

Confucius. (Library of Congress)

by self-cultivation, which for Confucius is a synonym for learning. A *junzi* is a true scholar—that is, an elite scholar.

Confucius was famous for not discriminating on the basis of the social origins of his students. Anyone could choose to engage in learning, and thus to cultivate himself and become an elite scholar. It was not Confucius's aim, however, to turn everybody into *junzi*. He was characteristically practical and accepted the fact that his society was a hierarchical one. The majority belonged in the category of the inferior man, who was not required to espouse the high morals of the *junzi*. In fact, to be a *junzi* means to sacrifice one's own interests for the benefit of others. It is only natural to allow the majority to concentrate on their own interests instead of asking them to sacrifice themselves for morality's sake, given the social condition that the majority was governed by the rulers through the hands of elite scholars.

REN AND LI

Ren (humanity or benevolence) is the leading principle for self-cultivation. To be *ren* is to love others, though one should still differentiate in the degree of love among different social relationships. The love that is advocated is ultimately, however, and in its highest sense, directed toward the majority. In other words, one should never do to others what is undesirable to oneself.

Li is the principle of acting in accordance with custom, of preserving a special code of ceremony, and of performing the rites appropriate to one's social status. The emphasis on *li* is not only a way of guiding one's moral behavior for self-cultivation but also plays an important role in integrating governing with the teaching of morality.

GOVERNING BY MORALS RATHER THAN BY LAW

For Confucius, the ideal government is a moral government. It does not govern by rules, regulations, or laws, but by taking care of people's interests and teaching people to be moral. The rulers themselves must act morally, in order to set a good example for the people to follow. *Li* dictates the norm of proper social behavior for both rulers and the people. Observing *li* keeps all people in their social positions and thus makes the society stable. Confucius believed that a stable society would naturally become prosperous.

Weihang Chen

FURTHER READING

Bell, Daniel A., and Hahm Chaibong, eds. *Confucianism for the Modern World*. New York: Cambridge University Press, 2003.

Confucius. *The Analects*. Translated by Raymond Dawson. New York: Oxford University Press, 2000.

Dawson, Raymond. *Confucius*. Oxford, England: Oxford University Press, 1981.

Fung Yu-lan. *A History of Chinese Philosophy*. Vol. 1. Translated by Derk Bodde. Princeton, N.J.: Princeton University Press, 1983.

_____. *The Spirit of Chinese Philosophy*. Translated by E. R. Hughes. Boston: Boston Press, 1967.

Ivanhoe, Philip J. *Confucian Moral Self Cultivation*. 2d ed. Indianapolis: Hackett, 2000.

Lin Yutang, ed. and trans. *The Wisdom of Confucius*. New York: The Modern Library, 1966.

Liu Wu-chi. *Confucius: His Life and Time*. Reprint. Westport, Conn.: Greenwood Press, 1972.

_____. *A Short History of Confucian Philosophy*. Westport, Conn.: Hyperion Press, 1979.

SEE ALSO: Confucian ethics; Daoist ethics; Mencius; Mozi; Wang Yangming; Zhuangzi.

Congress

IDENTIFICATION: Legislative branch of the U.S. federal government that comprises the House of Representatives and the Senate

TYPE OF ETHICS: Politico-economic ethics

SIGNIFICANCE: Throughout their histories, both houses of Congress have struggled to codify and implement ethics rules for their members.

The U.S. Constitution gives each house of Congress the authority to discipline its own members. Consequently, each house has established an ethics committee. These committees have equal numbers of members from each major party, for a total number of four members in the Senate Select Committee on Ethics and ten in the House Committee on Standards of Official Conduct.

Upon committee recommendations, a two-thirds vote of the House of Representatives can expel a member. It takes but a simple majority vote to censure a member as well as to reprimand a member, a lesser penalty. In some cases the committee itself simply sends an offending member a letter of reproval. However, the committees may also fine members, order restitution in appropriate cases, suspend a member's voting rights, or inflict other penalties. On some occasions, no penalties are imposed.

A CASE OF EXPULSION

In 2002, Representative James A. Traficant of Ohio was expelled from the House of Representatives for bribery, racketeering, and tax evasion. His offenses were matters of individual ethics, not institutional ethics. (While he was still in the House, his daily one-minute speech before the House usually ended with "Beam me up, Scotty, there's no intelligent life down here.") His case could have been treated as a breach of institutional ethics, as his behavior appeared to cast aspersions on Congress, thereby lowering the public's confidence in the body. However, institutional ethics are rarely seen as a problem in Congress, although the House rules, for example, stress the institutional. Personal ethics are almost always the focus in ethics cases, even though institutional ethics tend to be more serious. Misbehavior such as taking a bribe is more concrete and thus easier to deal with.

Traficant's case was not typical of either kind of ethics. It was only the second time that the House voted to expel a member since the Civil War. The expulsion was voted only after Traficant had been convicted of the same charges in a court of law. Membership in an ethics committee is not something that congresspersons typically seek. It is difficult to sit in judgment on colleagues with whom one has worked closely and still remain objective. When does one's party affiliation play a legitimate role? In Traficant's case, it was a matter of a Democrat who usually voted with the Republicans. It simplified things for the committee when a court earlier found him guilty of criminal acts, leaving the committee to recommend expulsion by an unanimous vote prior to the vote of the whole House.

Is it a good idea to let the courts decide ethics cases? Some believe it is. Others hold that ethical and legal matters should be decided separately as the criteria are different. Besides, court cases are not likely to deal with institutional corruption, such as the short-circuiting of the democratic process or aiding in bringing Congress into disrepute, even if only giving the appearance of doing so. The appearance factor is taken seriously in Congress.

PERSONAL CORRUPTION

The practice of accepting cash payments (honoraria) has been common among senators and representatives. The abuse of this practice became public information in the cases of Minnesota's Republican senator David Durenberger and Speaker of the House Jim Wright during the 1990's. Both men also sold their own books at their speaking engagements. Other charges were leveled as well. Durenberger, for example, was using public funds to maintain a residence in Minneapolis. This was technically legal; however, he owned the residence himself and was thus paying rent to himself. In July, 1990, he was unanimously denounced by the Senate but retained

his seat there until 1995. In May, 1989, Wright resigned from his House speakership, and a month later he resigned from Congress. Congress has since banned its members from accepting honoraria for public speeches. It has also set out in detail rules about what is legal and what is not in the writing and selling of books and articles.

OTHER CASES

During the early 1990's, five U.S. senators from different states were involved in aiding financier Charles H. Keating, Jr., in his attempt to bail out Lincoln Savings and Loan Association of Irvine, California. A Senate investigation found that the most culpable senator involved in the scheme was California's Alan Cranston, who had received campaign donations from Keating while pressuring an independent regulatory commission on Keating's behalf. That Cranston gave most of the money to charity did not save him from a reprimand. The other four senators were given lesser penalties.

In 1991, Senator Alphonse D'Amato was rebuked for allowing his brother to use his office to lobby the Department of the Navy. In 1983, two representatives were censured for sexual misconduct with House pages. Several members of Congress have been cited for drug use with none censured. The franking (free postage) privilege has been abused by some. Taking illegal campaign contributions that were really bribes happens now and again. The point of all this is that it is difficult to deal with ethical infractions in Congress and ethics committees are reluctant to do so. That there must be a better way is a common comment. However, Congress seems to want to keep it this way.

PUBLIC MISUNDERSTANDING

Not all congressional scandals are actually scandals. The so-call House Bank scandal of the early 1990's is a case in point. The public did not understand that it was not a bank in the usual sense of the term. Some representatives wrote checks on the bank while not having deposited sufficient funds to cover them. However, that in itself was not an offense. The members paid back the money when it was convenient to do so. The institution had been established for that purpose. However, the media did not make it clear that such was the case. Many House members lost their seats due to the consequent misunderstanding—a case of outrage fueled by uninformed opinion. It can be viewed as a case of institutional corruption by the entire House for failing to consider the possible appearance of corruption and not remedying it.

Robert W. Small

FURTHER READING

Congressional Quarterly. *Congressional Ethics.* Washington, D.C.: Author, 1980.

_____. *Congressional Ethics: History, Facts, and Controversy.* Author, 1994.

Thompson, Dennis F. *Ethics in Congress: From Individual to Institutional Corruption.* Washington, D.C.: Brookings Institution, 1995.

Tolchin, Martin, and Susan J. Tolchin. *Glass Houses: Congressional Ethics and the Politics of Venom.* Boulder, Colo.: Westview Press, 2001.

SEE ALSO: Civil Rights Act of 1964; Equal Rights Amendment; Ethics in Government Act; Lobbying; National Labor Relations Act; Politics.

Congress of Racial Equality

IDENTIFICATION: Organization that, looking to Africa for inspiration, seeks the right of African Americans to govern and educate themselves

DATE: Founded in 1942

TYPE OF ETHICS: Civil rights

SIGNIFICANCE: From its origin as a broad-based organization with white and black membership, Congress of Racial Equality (CORE) evolved into one of America's first important black separatist groups.

CORE was founded in 1942 by James Farmer and a group of University of Chicago students. Its membership included African Americans and whites, and its primary purpose was to combat segregation. CORE used various peaceful but confrontational techniques to achieve its aims. In 1943, its members began sitting in at segregated lunch counters, demanding to be served and willing to face arrest. CORE moved into the national spotlight in 1963, when the freedom rides challenged southern segregated bus stations. Freedom riders rode public buses to southern cities,

where white riders entered the "coloreds only" waiting areas and black riders entered "whites only" rooms. Although they sat quietly and peacefully, the demonstrators were met with mob violence time after time.

CORE also worked for voter registration in the South through the early 1960's. In 1966, CORE leadership adopted the new slogan "black power" and began a shift toward black separatism that alienated many of its members, both white and black. The organization struggled through the next decades but during the early twenty-first century was still operating a national office and several local groups, with a budget of over one million dollars.

Cynthia A. Bily

SEE ALSO: Civil disobedience; Civil rights and liberties; Civil Rights movement; National Association for the Advancement of Colored People; Segregation.

Conscience

DEFINITION: Subjective awareness of the moral quality of one's own actions as indicated by the moral values to which one subscribes

TYPE OF ETHICS: Personal and social ethics

SIGNIFICANCE: Since a person always chooses either against or in accord with the dictates of conscience, such dictates may form the immediate basis for the moral evaluation of intentional human actions.

Although they may not be explicitly aware of doing so, human beings everywhere and always have evaluated their own actions in the light of their own moral values. The earliest attempt at a philosophical analysis of this type of self-assessment—that is, of conscience—is found in the *Tusculan Disputations* of the Roman orator Cicero (first century B.C.E.). The most famous early casuistical employment of this notion is found in the letters of the apostle Paul (first century C.E.). It was not until the Middle Ages, however, that the understanding of conscience that is still employed was articulated.

In their commentaries on St. Jerome's exegesis of scripture, Philip the Chancellor, St. Bonaventure, and St. Thomas Aquinas developed an analysis of conscience that made explicit several crucial distinctions. Awareness of the moral quality of one's own actions involves two aspects: first, the awareness of an act, and second, the awareness of one's values as exemplified (or not) by the act. This general knowledge of one's own values was distinguished by medieval moral theologians from conscience proper. "Conscience" itself was regarded as the activity of one's mind in bringing those values to bear upon one's own individual actions. It is thus a species of self-consciousness or a way of being aware of oneself.

DEVELOPMENT OF CONSCIENCE

A person's disposition to engage in this type of self-reflection develops as part of his or her general moral upbringing. People are taught how to identify their acts as examples of types and are taught that certain types of acts are good, bad, or morally indifferent. After a certain point in the person's development (the precise age varying greatly from culture to culture and from individual to individual) the individual becomes aware of this labeling process and of the good, bad, and other types in terms of which the labeling is carried out. From this point on, the person's general values are reflected upon and either endorsed or rejected. In this developmental sequence, the conscience of the person becomes a mental activity that is distinct from the functioning of the "superego" (which contains unreflected-upon and repressed prohibitions, injunctions, and so forth). The mature conscience of an adult involves applying values of which the individual is fully aware.

People differ greatly, however, with regard to the degree and extent of their awareness of the moral qualities of their own actions, just as people differ with regard to the degree and extent to which they are self-aware in general. Someone who is "hyperaware" of the moral quality of all of his or her actions is said to be "scrupulous." Such a condition can become very problematic if the person becomes incapable of acting without severe apprehension that he or she is doing something wrong or scrutinizes the most trivial action for its possible moral significance. The opposite condition is exemplified by the "lax" person. Such an individual consistently fails to concern himself or herself with the morality of his or her own actions. The point at which scrupulosity or laxity be-

comes immoral in itself depends upon the moral values to which the particular individual subscribes: Some moralities demand strict solicitousness, while others allow for much greater lack of moral concern.

ACTS OF CONSCIENCE

The acts of a person's conscience have traditionally been divided into four types. First is the mental act of "command," whereby one senses that an act is "to be done." Second is the act of "forbidding," whereby one senses that an act is "not to be done." Third is the act of "permitting," in which one regards an act as "allowed" by one's own moral values. Fourth is the activity of "advising," in which one is aware that an act is either probably better to do or probably worse to do (the act is not sensed as being strictly required or strictly forbidden). Furthermore, the specific actions of the person to which these states of mind are directed can be in the future (in which case the act of conscience is referred to as "antecedent conscience"), in the past ("consequent conscience"), or in the present ("occurrent conscience"). If the past or current action is in accord with the dictates of conscience, the person is said to be in "good conscience" (or "to have a good conscience" or to be "acting in good conscience"). This state of mind is characterized phenomenologically as one of peace, quiet, self-contentment, and ease. If the past or current action is not in accord with the dictates of conscience, then the person has a "bad conscience." This condition is characterized subjectively as apprehensive, conflicted, anxious, and ashamed.

Two points are crucial with regard to these various activities of the mind. First, in all these acts, the dictate of conscience pertains only to one's own actions: "Conscience" does not refer to evaluations of other people's acts. Second, the "voice of conscience" must be distinguished from other ways of evaluating one's own actions (other "voices," as it were). Conscience is most often confused with self-admonitions of a merely prudential nature. For example, people may admonish themselves for stealing simply because they are in trouble after being caught. A sure indication that it is not their conscience that is bothering them is that if they were not caught, they would not admonish themselves. In effect, they are berating themselves for being caught, not for stealing.

In these various acts of moral self-reflection, the individual may be either "certain" or "doubtful" concerning the moral quality of the deed at issue. Since a person only performs a deed on the basis of her awareness of what she is doing, if the individual is assured that the act she is contemplating has a particular moral quality, then she is morally required to act on that assuredness. If what is truly or objectively wrong appears to be the right thing to do, one must do it. In such a case, assuming that one does the deed, the act is objectively wrong but subjectively right (one performed in "good conscience"). A primary and purely formal rule of all morality, then, is to "do what conscience demands." This rule is the only guarantee that people will choose rightly when their beliefs about right and wrong are accurate. All people are under an obligation to ensure that the evaluation of their own actions is accurate. Hence, an even more important purely formal rule of morality is to "ensure that conscience is accurate."

THE DOUBTFUL CONSCIENCE

If one is in doubt about the accuracy of the dictates of one's own conscience, then it is morally imperative to eliminate the doubt before acting. If one acts although uncertain of the morality of one's own act according to the values to which one subscribes, one thereby expresses a lack of concern for those values. Acting while in doubt is tantamount to disdain for those values even if one happens to do what those values demand. The problem is how to move from doubt to certainty about the morality of a contemplated act.

When one is uncertain about the moral value of an anticipated act, one must first attempt to remove the doubt directly, perhaps by pausing to think about what one is doing, by consulting "experts" (people of practical wisdom), or by reading about similar cases. Often, such attempts fail or are not possible because of time constraints. In order to resolve remaining doubts about the right thing to do, people employ what moralists refer to as "reflex principles" of conscience, which stipulate what is required of one in such a condition. Although there is disagreement among moralists about the degree of probability required to ground the shift from doubt to certainty, most people in Western culture adhere to principles of roughly the following nature. If not doing something would result in grievous harm to oneself or to others or would result in failing to fulfill some other important moral obligation, then it is certain that one

must do the deed regardless of how improbable the outcome might appear to be (this improbability is the source of the doubt about the morality of the action).

A traditional example of this is the pharmacist who thinks it is possible that a deadly poison has been accidentally mixed in with some medicines. Most people in such a situation would regard themselves as bound to refrain from dispensing the medicines. Another such principle is that if not doing something would *not* result in harm, then it is certain that one must do the deed only if there is an overwhelming probability that so acting is morally required (in other words, only an overwhelming probability is sufficient grounds for acting).

Finally, if the moral reasons for doing something are as good as the reasons for not doing it and no grievous harm is involved either way, then it is certain that either course of action is morally acceptable. What is to be avoided through the use of such guidelines for becoming certain of acting correctly while under conditions of uncertainty are the extremes of "laxism" and "rigorism." Laxism results from adopting the attitude that if there is any doubt about the morality of the matter at hand, then moral considerations may be completely ignored. Rigorism results from adopting the attitude that if there is the slightest chance that one's morality demands that one act in a particular way, then it is certain that one must act in that way. The problem with rigorism is that there is always a possibility, however slight, that one is required to do something in any situation. This attitude leads immediately to extreme scrupulosity.

THE ERRONEOUS CONSCIENCE

The distinction between a certain and doubting conscience is different from the distinction between a "correct" and an "erroneous" conscience. An erroneous or false conscience is the state of mind of someone who believes an action to have a moral quality that in fact it does not have. If such an error is culpable, then the person can and should "know better" and is held accountable for whatever wrong is committed (because the person is held accountable for being in error about the act's morality). For example, the person could have easily found out that the item taken belonged to someone else. If the error is inculpable, then the person cannot know better and is not held accountable for whatever wrong is done. These errors, which lead the person into wrongdoing, are either factual or moral. Factual errors concern simply the facts of the situation or action. For example, the person is unaware that the suitcase taken from the conveyor belt at the airport belongs to someone else. Moral error is about morality itself—that is, the moral rules that apply to the situation (about which there may be no factual misunderstanding). For example, one knows that the suitcase belongs to another, but taking other people's belongings is not something the individual regards as wrong. People tend to regard inculpable error about basic principles of morality as being simply impossible (assuming no mental abnormality). For example, no adult is regarded as being ignorant of the immorality of killing people for utterly no reason. With regard to the application of principles in specific situations and with regard to less-general principles, however, inculpable error is quite possible. In other words, people can in good conscience disagree about the morality of certain types of actions or about the morality of a particular act in a specific situation even if they are in complete accord concerning the basic principles of morality.

If the "other" party to a moral dispute is regarded as *not* acting in "good conscience," then he or she is taken to be either acting in culpable moral error or acting unconscientiously. In the former case, the other person's difference of opinion is regarded as being caused by negligent ignorance for which he or she is held accountable. If the dissenter is regarded as being unconscientious, then in effect the person is held to be a moral fraud who is merely using the profession of conscience as a rationalization for acting out of sheer self-interest. Hence, in conditions of moral dispute, the virtue of conscientiousness becomes of paramount importance. These disagreements are about issues of vital moral importance, and the sincerity of others' moral allegiances determines the response to their dissension. If those with whom I disagree are not being sincere—that is, if they do not really believe in the morals in terms of which they justify their opposing point of view—then I have no reason to respect their merely apparent moral stand on the issue. In fact, if they are unconscientious, then their morals may not really differ from mine: They might "really" agree with my moral evaluation of the issue and merely invoke (in bad faith) different "morals" in order to justify their self-interest.

CONSCIENTIOUSNESS

If the possibility of disagreement in good faith is accepted, then it becomes vitally important to clarify the distinguishing marks of being in good conscience. How can one tell that someone else is sincere when he or she takes a moral stand on an issue that differs from one's own? A common instance of this problem is that of the "conscientious objector" to military conscription. Insincerity of an objector's moral appeal to exemption from military service means that the individual does not really "believe in" the moral values in terms of which the exemption is being demanded.

Two general characteristics of sincerity (or conscientiousness or "really believing") are a willingness to make sacrifices for the sake of adherence to one's values and a willingness to make an effort to abide by the values professed. If no effort is forthcoming or no sacrifice is willingly undergone, then that counts as evidence that the person is not acting in good faith. Someone who is willing to face a firing squad rather than serve in the military is most certainly quite sincere in his or her moral dissension from conscription. Another individual who would rather serve in the military than be forced to spend the same amount of time in prison is probably not dissenting in "good conscience." Therefore, the general virtue of conscientiousness involves a disposition to do what one judges ought to be done regardless of the sacrifice of other interests that may be entailed by so acting.

What must be kept in mind, however, is that this virtue is compatible with at least occasional failure to live by one's moral ideals. It is true that if one is not conscientious then one will fail to abide by one's own moral convictions. It is *not* true that if one has the habit of abiding by the dictates of conscience one will never fail to do so. The difference between conscientious failure and unconscientious failure to act according to the dictates of one's conscience is that the former is followed by repentance and a renewed effort to abide by those dictates, whereas the latter is not followed by such acts. Failure to live according to one's moral convictions may be the result of the fact that the person has established moral ideals that are too "high" for any human to achieve. Furthermore, consistent success in living according to the dictates of one's conscience may be indicative of establishing moral standards for oneself that are too "low."

CONSCIENTIOUS DISSENT

These distinctions plus the formal principles of conscience previously noted create an intractable dilemma. Since one must act in accord with the dictates of an assured conscience, it is wrong for others to coerce someone into acting against the dictates of his or her conscience. In order to test the moral sincerity of dissenters, however, it is necessary to observe how they respond when prompted to act in a way that is contrary to the dictates of their conscience. The assumption in this situation is that if the person caves in to very little pressure, then his or her moral conviction is insincere. Thus, to ensure that a person's moral objection to conscription is conscientious, society must, in effect, prompt the individual to act against the dictates of conscience. Because of increasing sensitivity to the fact that coercing people in this manner is actually a species of scandal, conscientious objection is no longer severely punished in most countries.

Nevertheless, there are limits to what can be tolerated in the name of respecting conscientious action. If an individual's conscience dictates that he harms the innocent, then others are justified in protecting the innocent by forcing that person to act against the dictates of his conscience. The classic historical example of this is the outlawing of the practice of *thuggee* by the British colonialists in India during the nineteenth century. The Thugs believed that they had a moral obligation to waylay and murder travelers. The general principle in terms of which the British occupying force justified punishing the Thugs was (roughly) that "it is wrong to coerce someone to act against sincere moral conviction unless allowing the person to act according to the dictates of conscience would result in harm to the innocent."

Mark Stephen Pestana

FURTHER READING

D'Arcy, Eric. *Conscience and Its Right to Freedom.* London: Sheed & Ward, 1979. Contains an excellent presentation of the history of the concept of conscience and the defense of the right to religious freedom.

Davis, Henry. *Moral and Pastoral Theology.* New York: Sheed & Ward, 1952. A good source for the standard Catholic teachings on conscience and the methods of casuistry. Contains a lengthy discussion of probabilism, probabiliorism, and equiprobabilism.

Donagan, Alan. *The Theory of Morality.* Chicago: University of Chicago Press, 1977. Most of chapter 4 is devoted to the problems of the erroneous conscience and the corruption of conscience. A superb updating of the traditional conceptions.

Donnelly, John, and Leonard Lyons, eds. *Conscience.* Staten Island, N.Y.: Alba House, 1973. A collection of articles on the nature, existence, meaning, and authority of conscience by analytic philosophers. Fairly advanced material.

Freud, Sigmund. *Civilization and Its Discontents.* Translated by David McLintock. 1930. Reprint. Introduction by Leo Bersani. London: Penguin, 2002. Includes a significant and very influential discussion of the conscience on a collective, social level. Covers both its genesis and function within civilization.

_____. "The Dissolution of the Oedipus Complex" and "On Some Psychical Consequences of the Anatomical Distinction Between the Sexes." In *The Standard Edition of the Complete Psychological Works of Sigmund Freud*, edited by James Strachey. Vol. 19. London: Hogarth, 1953-1974. These are the most important works for understanding Freud's theory of the individual's conscience, which he believes forms as a direct result of identification with the father and the repression of oedipal desire.

Kirk, Kenneth. *Conscience and Its Problems: An Introduction to Casuistry.* London: Longmans, Green, 1948. A twentieth century classic in the study of "cases of conscience" by the Anglican Bishop of Oxford. Contains chapters on doubt, error, loyalty, and moral perplexity.

Langston, Douglas C. *Conscience and Other Virtues: From Bonaventure to MacIntyre.* University Park: Pennsylvania State University Press, 2001. Traces the history of the concept of conscience within moral philosophy. Explains why that concept has fallen out of favor, and why it needs to be recovered, then goes on to produce a new, useful, and defensible modern theory of conscience.

Nelson, C. Ellis, ed. *Conscience: Theological and Psychological Perspectives.* New York: Newman Press, 1973. A large collection of articles, many of which are devoted to the development of conscience in childhood and the distinction between conscience and superego.

Wallace, James D. *Virtues and Vices.* Ithaca, N.Y.:

Cornell University Press, 1978. Chapter 4 of this work is an outstanding analysis of the meaning of conscientiousness and the reason for its preeminence as a virtue in pluralistic societies.

SEE ALSO: Bad faith; Casuistry; Conscientious objection; "Everyone does it"; Guilt and shame; Intention; Moral education; Motivation; Responsibility; Self-deception.

Conscientious objection

DEFINITION: Refusal on moral or religious grounds to perform an action (usually military service or participation in warfare) demanded or required by an external authority

TYPE OF ETHICS: Politico-economic ethics

SIGNIFICANCE: Recognition by the state of the right to conscientious objection constitutes a decision that citizens should not be compelled to act contrary to deeply held personal beliefs, nor punished for refusing to act in such a fashion.

Conscientious objection establishes a moral relationship between the individual and external authority. The key element of the relationship is the claim that authority is not absolute; it cannot demand total obedience, especially when obedience would violate the individual's conscience. Conscientious objection, then, stands as a limit to the extent of the power of the state. In claiming conscientious objection, an individual seeks to justify opposition to an action or demand that the state deems necessary and may require of others.

HISTORY AND SOURCES

One of the major concerns of the ancient Greek philosophers Plato and Aristotle was that of the relationship of the individual to the state. They noted that human life was fundamentally social, which entailed duties to the state. It was possible, however, for the demands of the state to come into conflict with an individual's own moral values. The source of the conflict was the assertion that the state did not totally control the conscience of an individual. Conscience was a person's moral self-understanding, the combination of values and ideals that provided the individual with a sense of ethical self-definition that also demanded loyalty. Violating an individual's moral integrity could lead to a crisis of conscience. A person might want to serve the state, but in this particular case could not without violating the sense of self.

The play *Antigone* (c. 441 B.C.E.), by Sophocles, offers an explicit example of the conflict between the individual and the state. Antigone follows her conscience and refuses to obey King Creon's orders concerning the burial of her brother. In moral terms, the tension between the individual and the state rests on whether the state should recognize the demands of conscience when an individual cannot in good conscience obey the state's demands. In order to avoid breaking the law, the conscientious objector often seeks an exemption from obedience. The exemption would grant legal recognition to the disobedience, and the individual would escape punishment. For Antigone, escape was not an option, and the play serves as a stark reminder of the tension between individual conscience and the demands of the state.

The question of loyalty and obedience to the state became more acute with the rise of Christianity. Given the pacifist views of some early Christians and the resulting opposition to war, many refused to serve in the military. The refusal to participate in war on moral grounds rested on the teachings of Jesus. The conscience of the Christian, formed by the values associated with Jesus and out of loyalty to those values, would not permit military service or participation in war. Yet not all Christians were pacifists or conscientious objectors, and military service became more likely as Christianity became the dominant religion in the West. Still some Christians steadfastly refused to serve in the military. During the Protestant Reformation, the Anabaptists held to a pacifist view and sought exemption from the state's demands to participate in war. These exemptions, when granted, were only at the pleasure of the prince or ruler in whose territory the exemption seekers resided.

AMERICAN DIMENSIONS

There have been examples of conscientious objection throughout American history. People fled Europe during the colonial period to escape persecution, and many were pacifists. As a result, conscientious objection entered into American wars and politics. James Madison wanted to add recognition of conscientious objection to his version of what was to become the Second Amendment to the U.S. Constitution. He wanted to allow persons with religious and moral objections to bearing arms the freedom not to serve in the military. Madison's suggestion was not approved in later debates, but it did serve to provide a basis for the legal recognition of conscientious objection in U.S. law.

The Selective Service Act of 1917 established guidelines for conscientious objection; specifically, the requirement that an applicant needed to show membership within a religious tradition that upheld conscientious objection as part of its teachings. This rule made it difficult, if not impossible, for those outside the pacifist church tradition to be granted conscientious objector status. Although the guidelines were more flexible during World War II, the insistence on a religious basis for conscientious objection remained. The refusal of military service was not recognized unless an applicant equated moral and religious reasons. Two U.S. Supreme Court decisions, handed down during the Vietnam War, changed the basis for asserting conscientious objection. In *United States v. Seeger* (1965) and *United States v. Welch* (1970), the Court ruled that sincere and strongly held moral beliefs were a sufficient basis for granting an individual status as a conscientious objector to military service. While the requirement for opposition to all wars remained, there was no longer a religious test for conscientious objection.

TYPES OF CONSCIENTIOUS OBJECTION

There are two major types of conscientious objection with reference to the opposition to war. The first is absolute or universal conscientious objection (ACO or UCO). Usually based on a pacifist perspective, it leads to the moral conclusion that all wars are wrong. The ethical argument centers on the immorality of war and killing. The nature and purpose of the war are irrelevant to the moral opposition to the war.

A second type is selective conscientious objection (SCO). The focus of selective conscientious objection is on the particular war, hence the notion of selection. An individual may not be morally opposed to all wars as such, but to a specific war. The moral basis for selective conscientious objection is just war theory, which is designed to differentiate between wars that are just and those that are unjust. This selection equates just with moral and unjust with immoral.

An individual would hold that it is wrong to fight in an unjust war. Selective conscientious objection rarely, if ever, receives legal recognition. It is possible for both absolute conscientious objectors and selective conscientious objectors to accept military service as noncombatants such as medics. The moral opposition would center on the refusal to bear arms, not on military service itself.

Ron Large

FURTHER READING

Childress, James. *Moral Responsibility in Conflicts: Essays on Nonviolence, War, and Conscience.* Baton Rouge: Louisiana State University Press, 1982.

Finn, James, ed. *A Conflict of Loyalties.* New York: Pegasus, 1968.

Flynn, Eileen. *My Country Right or Wrong? Selective Conscientious Objection in the Nuclear Age.* Chicago: Loyola University Press, 1985.

Gioglio, Gerald. *Days of Decision: An Oral History of Conscientious Objectors in the Military During the Vietnam War.* Trenton, N.J.: Broken Rifle Press, 1989.

Levi, Margaret. *Consent, Dissent, and Patriotism.* New York: Cambridge University Press, 1997.

Zahn, Gordon. *War, Conscience, and Dissent.* New York: Hawthorn Books, 1967.

SEE ALSO: Civil disobedience; Conscience; Pacifism; Private vs. public morality; Thoreau, Henry David; Vietnam War; War.

Consent

DEFINITION: Agreement, freely given, by one party in response to a proposal by another party

TYPE OF ETHICS: Theory of ethics

SIGNIFICANCE: Consent is fundamental to the concept of autonomy; in giving consent, a party exercises free choice and should be accorded due respect in the bargaining.

Consent is one means by which social arrangements are regulated. Through consent, persons agree to conform their actions to the expectations of others. Following consent, individuals can act cooperatively as wife and husband, teammates, club members, or parties to a contract.

Consent obtained through coercion is no consent at all. What constitutes coercion, however, may be difficult to define. On the one extreme, a highwayman's demand of "Your money or your life!" is coercive. By contrast, if a man lost in the desert meets a shepherd who offers to lead him to safety for a thousand dollars, the man's only alternative is to wander off on his own and eventually die. To him the shepherd's proposal seems coercive—much like the highwayman's demand. However, to the shepherd, who did not cause the man's predicament, the proposal is merely an offer for a voluntary exchange.

Political philosophers such as John Locke and John Rawls have suggest that consent of the governed is the basis of all legitimate government. That consent is theoretical, however, as individual citizens are never truly allowed to choose, point by point, the scope of any government's full powers. Libertarians, including Robert Nozick, therefore have concluded that all governments are coercive and illegitimate, except those of extremely limited powers. In contrast to the libertarians, communitarian philosophers contend that humans are not single-minded, autonomous decision-makers but are bound by shared values to the community at large. The libertarian idea of consent, with its focus on free choice and rights, flies in the face of this web of shared values.

Many social scientists tend to avoid bright-line distinctions between consensual and coerced acts. To such theorists, cultural norms can impose such pressure to conform that choice is effectively eliminated. So, it is argued, cultural pressures cause women routinely to make workplace decisions that elevate their families above their careers. These women neither wholly "consent" to trading career for family, nor are they "coerced" as that term is traditionally used.

Concern over the relationship between consent and coercion is not new. In the early Greek philosopher Plato's *Prōtagoras*, Socrates and Protagoras debate whether virtue is teachable or such teaching amounts to inappropriate coercion of the will of the pupil. That debate is largely theoretical, but the difference between consent and coercion does have important practical significance, especially in the law. If the shepherd leads the lost man from the desert, he will expect payment of the thousand dollars. Modern courts of law have tended to find such agreements co-

ercive and unenforceable. Eventually, however, the pendulum may swing back in response to cultural trends that promote personal responsibility.

Robert L. Palmer

FURTHER READING
Cudd, Ann. "Oppression by Choice." *Journal of Social Philosophy* 25 (June, 1994): 22-44.
Hetherington, Andrew. "The Real Distinction Between Threats and Offers." *Social Theory and Practice* 25, no. 2 (1999): 211-242.
Nozick, Robert. *Anarchy, State, and Utopia*. New York: Basic Books, 1974.
Rawls, John. *A Theory of Justice*. Cambridge, Mass.: Harvard University Press, 1971.

SEE ALSO: Coercion; Constitutional government; Diagnosis; Electroshock therapy; Experimentation; Institutionalization of patients; Libertarianism; Physician-patient relationship; Rights and obligations; Therapist-patient relationship.

Consequentialism

DEFINITION: Belief that the rightness or wrongness of an action is determined by the goodness or badness of its result

TYPE OF ETHICS: Theory of ethics

SIGNIFICANCE: Consequentialism constitutes a moral standard in which the end justifies the means, while rejecting intention- or virtue-centered ethical systems.

As a moral standard, consequentialism can be divided into two varieties: In the first, the desired end is the long-term self-interest of the individual; In the second, the desired end is the greatest happiness of the greatest number. The first variety is called the theory of ethical egoism, and Thomas Hobbes and Ayn Rand are associated with it. The second is called utilitarianism, and it is associated with Jeremy Bentham and John Stuart Mill. Ethical egoism claims that before making a moral decision, one should consider the end of long-term self-interest, and if by using a reasonably moral means the long-term self-interest can be achieved, then that action should be performed. This means that short-term self-interest should be sacrificed for the sake of long-term self-interest. Utilitarianism, however, considers the desired end to be the greatest happiness of the greatest number of people; an action that achieves this end by using a reasonably moral means should be performed.

Krishna Mallick

SEE ALSO: Bentham, Jeremy; Biodiversity; Dominion over nature, human; Environmental movement; Hobbes, Thomas; Mill, John Stuart; Rand, Ayn.

Conservation

DEFINITION: Prudent use of natural resources
TYPE OF ETHICS: Environmental ethics
SIGNIFICANCE: As increasing amounts of the earth's resources are used up, conservation for many people ceases to be merely a prudent course of action and acquires the status of an ethical imperative. At the same time, the involuntary imposition of strategies of conservation upon individuals, corporations, or governments may be seen as an ethical violation of their rights or freedoms.

The conservation ethic has its American roots in colonial times with the imposition of game limits at Newport, Rhode Island, in 1639, the limitation of timbering in Pennsylvania in 1681, and many other similar regulations that were intended to protect resources for the future. Later, authors such as Henry David Thoreau and Ralph Waldo Emerson emphasized the ethical interrelationship of humankind and nature.

At the beginning of the twentieth century, Theodore Roosevelt and Gifford Pinchot wrote extensively on the conservation ethic; they are widely considered as the founders of modern conservationism. Their programs, such as the Reclamation Act of 1902, the Inland Waterways Commission of 1907, and the massive expansion of National Forest lands, reflect their emphasis on wise use of resources. They also were concerned with the preservation of natural and cultural assets, as in passage of the Antiquities Act of 1906. Harold Ickes, Henry Wallace, and their associates continued the advocacy of the wise consumption ethic during the 1930's, emphasizing land planning and soil management. Again, wise use was

the principal concern. Preservation of unique natural entities, however, continued to be part of the mainstream conservation ethic. Preservationism as a part of conservation, however, has been more heavily promoted since World War II, leading to the vigorous reevaluation of many conservation-for-use programs.

Ralph L. Langenheim, Jr.

SEE ALSO: Deforestation; Ecology; Environmental ethics; Leopold, Aldo; Muir, John; National Park System, U.S.; Sierra Club; Sustainability of resources; Thoreau, Henry David.

Conservatism

DEFINITION: Approach to politics and society that emphasizes continuity and change.
TYPE OF ETHICS: Politico-economic ethics
SIGNIFICANCE: Skeptical that humanity has the moral or rational capacity to rule itself, conservatives argue that one's duty is to conform to natural law by dutifully following time-honored practices based on the wisdom accrued through the ages

American conservatism takes a variety of forms. Neoconservatives, for example, tend to be former liberals who, after World War II, saw most liberals as crossing the line from liberalism to a form of socialism that held equality, rather than liberty, as its major motivating principle. Neoconservatives also held that liberals failed to appreciate the dangers of communism. Libertarians too, have often been viewed as conservatives, whereas their roots are in classical liberalism. Many classical liberals do see themselves as conservatives. Some scholars see conservatism as an ideology; others hold that it is not an ideology at all, but rather a reaction to liberalism and radicalism. It appears, however, to contain elements of both.

ORIGINS

Traditionalist conservatism, according to most observers, began with Edmund Burke, who reacted vigorously to the very earliest stage of the French Revolution, and, in 1790, in his *Reflections on the Revolution in France*, quite accurately predicted the consequences of what was then a quite mild event. He predicted tyranny if the French continued to throw away their past and begin anew. He also, in fact, laid down the basic tenets of conservatism.

Burke saw the state as divinely ordained and worthy of reverence. He believed that the law of God reigned and that natural law, which emanated from it, was superior to manmade law, taking precedence if the two conflicted, still a principle of conservatism. Consequently the tenets of conservatism are its ethical norms.

The role of the state is important, unlike the libertarian view, which borders on anarchism. Its major function is to preserve order and oversee orderly change in accordance with tradition. Change is necessary if society is to be preserved. Conservatism, therefore, is not a status quo ideology as is often maintained.

ETHICAL NORMS

Conservatism holds to the belief that there is a contract between the present generation, those of the past, and those not yet born. Attempting to put abstract theories into practice contrary to the wisdom of the ages leads to disaster. Revolution is thus to be avoided, unless its aim is to regain lost rights, as with the American Revolution. Fostering too much dependence on the state through unnecessary governmental programs is also wrong.

A hierarchical society is natural. Attempts to impose equality on this earth means leveling down to the lowest common denominator. At the same time, one should never look down on those who do lowly jobs. It takes all kinds to maintain a society. A harmonious society, with its varied parts acting in unison is the best attainable. Moreover, private property is a natural right and the state has no right to appropriate one's property unless society would be harmed by not doing so. The good of society takes priority over that of the individual, even though the individual has natural rights, including the rights to life, liberty, and property. This is tied in with an organic concept of society. Some scholars hold that Burke did not hold to this notion. He did, indeed, sound as if he did. However, whether he did or not is not the point; the point being that organicism became embedded in traditionalist conservative thought.

Loyalty to family, friends, and institutions is basic to conservatism. Moral absolutism, not liberal moral relativism, is also fundamental; some values do not change with the times. Cooperation between church and state is welcome; a strict separation of the two, as liberalism demands, is seen as detrimental to society.

Subsidiarity also belongs in this list. Issues should be settled on the lowest level possible. In other words, people should not try to make "federal cases" out of everything. Within the United States, this literally means that if an issue can be addressed on the state level, the state, not the federal government, should deal with it. Moreover, if an issue can be addressed on an even lower level, that is where it should be resolved

AMERICAN CONSERVATISM

One might argue that American conservatism antedates Burke by several years by noting that John Adams published *A Defense of the Constitutions of the United States of America* in 1787-1788. Adams himself was little read, but his ideas were influential. Adams was much like Burke in that both saw religion as necessary for upholding a society. They were also alike in citing the flaws of human nature, thus denying the validity of the French *philosophes* of the Enlightenment, who held to the perfectibility of human beings and the related idea that an ideal society was capable of being constructed. In other words, they favored common sense over abstract theory. Moreover, both men put society above the individual. Burke and Adams laid the foundations of modern or traditionalist conservatism. Although there have been numerous offshoots and variations down through the years to conservative thought and practice, their foundations have endured.

PRACTICAL APPLICATION

It would be incorrect to view all twenty-first century Republicans as conservatives and all Democrats as egalitarian liberals. Family, local tradition and political advantage are also important in determining one's political orientation. It would appear that in the modern United States classical liberalism tends to overshadow the traditionalist factor in most conservatives. Government involvement in the economy and excessive regulation of society are rejected by conservatives of all sorts.

Robert W. Small

FURTHER READING

Burke, Edmund. *Reflections on the Revolution in France*. Amherst, N.Y.: Prometheus Books, 1987.

Covell, Charles. *Redefinition of Conservatism: Politics and Doctrine*. New York: St. Martin's Press, 1986.

Divigne, Robert. *Recasting Conservatism: Michael Oakeshott, Leo Straus and Conservative Political Thought's Response to Postmodernism*. New Haven: Yale University Press, 1994.

Kirk, Russell. *The Conservative Mind: From Burke to Eliot*. 7th ed. Chicago: Regnery Books, 1986.

Nisbet, Robert A. *Conservatism: Dream and Reality*. Somerset, N.J.: Transaction Publishers, 2001.

Sowell, Thomas. *A Conflict of Visions*. New York: William Morrow, 1987.

Will, George F. *Statecraft as Soulcraft: What Government Does*. New York: Simon & Schuster, 1983.

SEE ALSO: Accuracy in Media; Burke, Edmund; Communitarianism; Liberalism; Libertarianism; Politics; Progressivism.

Consistency

DEFINITION: Coherence and non-contradiction of the various rules and principles of an ethical system
TYPE OF ETHICS: Theory of ethics
SIGNIFICANCE: Consistency is a necessary component of any rationally based ethics, but is irrelevant to nonrational approaches to morality.

Given that the discipline of ethics involves reasoned reflection upon moral issues and that consistency is a necessary condition of any system, theory, or activity that is governed by reason, consistency must play an important role in the development of ethical theories. The two most important respects in which reason's commitment to consistency manifests itself in the development of an ethical theory are systematic consistency and nomothetic consistency.

SYSTEMATIC CONSISTENCY

Systematic consistency is a characteristic of any ethical system whose fundamental principles may all be true. Put negatively, systematic consistency does not apply to a system that has two or more principles that are contradictory. The reason that ethical systems must exhibit this property is that one can prove absolutely anything from an inconsistent set of pre-

mises. An inconsistent set of ethical principles would therefore counsel both for and against every action and thus offer no guidance to the morally perplexed.

NOMOTHETIC CONSISTENCY

If a particular course of action is said to be morally permissible, it would be arbitrary and irrational to claim that the action would not be permissible on a distinct occasion when all the relevant factors were the same. In this way, reasoned reflection on morality implies a commitment to general rules that specify classes of morally correct and morally incorrect behavior. The presupposition that moral judgments apply universally gives rise to the requirement of nomothetic consistency, the demand that a specific moral judgment can be coherently transformed into a general law.

The importance of nomothetic consistency to ethical theory is seen in the fact that one of the oldest and most prevalent of moral principles, the "golden rule," demands that one treat others as one wants to be treated, a requirement that imposes a certain degree of generality on one's moral judgments. Although concern with nomothetic consistency thus goes back at least as far as the sixth century B.C.E. Confucian formulation of the golden rule, it was in the eighteenth century that German philosopher Immanuel Kant focused attention on it to an unprecedented level by arguing that it alone is sufficient to generate an entire moral code.

The primacy of nomothetic consistency to Kant's ethics is clearly expressed in that version of his fundamental ethical principle (the "categorical imperative"), which commands that one should act only according to that plan of action that one can will at the same time to be a universal law. According to Kant, a sufficient test of the moral permissibility of a specific action is found in the attempt to will that the action be universalized. If willing such universality can be consistently achieved, then one knows that the action is morally permissible. If the attempt to will the universality of some plan of action leads to an inconsistency, however, then one knows that the action is impermissible.

To grasp the full force and scope of this version of the categorical imperative, it is important to note that there are two ways in which a plan of action can fail the test of universalizability. The first occurs when the content of the law that results from the attempted universalization is internally inconsistent. A standard Kantian example to illustrate this kind of inconsistency is found in the attempt to universalize the activity of promise-breaking. When one wills that all promises be entered into with the intent that they be broken, one also wills that there can be no promises insofar as one wills the impossibility of trust, a necessary condition for the practice of promising. In this way, willing that promise-breaking be a universal law entails both the existence and the nonexistence of promises.

The second way in which some proposed plan of action can fail the universalizability test does not involve an inconsistency within the content of the universal law that is willed. Instead of the conflict being internal to the universalized plan of action, the conflict in these cases obtains between the universalized plan of action and the very activity of willing. The possibility of this second kind of inconsistency depends upon Kant's conviction that willing is an inherently rational activity and his acceptance of the fact that it would be irrational to will certain universal laws even though these universal laws are not internally inconsistent. A standard Kantian example used to illustrate this second type of inconsistency involves the intention to neglect the development of all of one's talents. It is, says Kant, possible to conceive that all human beings neglect the development of their talents without contradiction; however, it is not possible to *will* that this be the case, for willing is an activity that affirms one's rationality, an affirmation that conflicts with the fact that the universal law being willed is one that it is irrational to will.

James Petrik

FURTHER READING

Ashmore, Robert B. *Building a Moral System.* Englewood Cliffs, N.J.: Prentice-Hall, 1987.
Donagan, Alan. *The Theory of Morality.* Chicago: University of Chicago Press, 1977.
Feezell, Randolph M., and Curtis L. Hancock. *How Should I Live?* New York: Paragon House, 1991.
Haack, Susan. *Philosophy of Logics.* New York: Cambridge University Press, 1978.
Kant, Immanuel. *Groundwork for the Metaphysics of Morals.* Edited and translated by Allen W. Wood. New Haven, Conn.: Yale University Press, 2002.
McNaughton, David. *Moral Vision: An Introduction to Ethics.* New York: Basil Blackwell, 1988.
O'Neill, Onora. "Consistency in Action." In *Kant's "Groundwork of the Metaphysics of Morals": Critical Essays*, edited by Paul Guyer. Lanham, Md.: Rowman and Littlefield, 1998.
Rawls, John. *A Theory of Justice.* Rev. ed. Cambridge, Mass.: Belknap Press of Harvard University Press, 1999.
Rost, H. T. D. *The Golden Rule.* Oxford, England: George Ronald, 1986.

SEE ALSO: Gewirth, Alan; Golden rule; Impartiality; Kant, Immanuel; Truth; Universalizability.

Constitution, U.S.

IDENTIFICATION: Foundation document that established and regulates the national governing system of the United States
DATE: Written in 1787, ratified in 1788
TYPE OF ETHICS: Civil rights
SIGNIFICANCE: The U.S. Constitution was framed to ensure political and economic liberty for American citizens by defining and limiting the powers of a resilient democratic republic.

The design of governments depends on the political values and interests of the people who hold power. Individuals' desires for political liberty, civil rights, and democratic elections within a country may be thwarted by the will of militarily powerful dictators or by ethnic, religious, or geographic conflicts that divide a nation. The Founders of the nation sought to avoid both divisive conflicts and the risk of dictatorship by drafting the Constitution in 1787. By electing officials to a government of limited powers and by guaranteeing representation to each geographic subdivision within the nation, the founders sought to create a governing system that would ensure political liberty and social stability for years to come.

HISTORY

After the North American colonists' Declaration of Independence from Great Britain in 1776 and the concomitant revolutionary war, the newly independent American states attempted to govern themselves through a document called the Articles of Confederation. The Articles of Confederation established a weak national government that depended on the cooperation of the various states for economic and military matters. Because each state retained the primary power to govern itself, there were frequent disagreements between the states. Their failure to fully cooperate with one another made the new nation economically and militarily vulnerable.

The failure of the Articles of Confederation led representatives from each state to meet in Philadelphia, Pennsylvania, during 1787 to draft a new document that would provide a fundamental structure of government for a cohesive nation. The Constitution, produced in Philadelphia, was the product of extensive debate and compromise among men who feared the prospect of granting too much power to government. They had fought a war of independence against Great Britain because they believed that the British king had trampled on their civil rights and prevented them from effectively participating in democratic decision making concerning taxation, tariffs, and other policies. They sought to diminish the risk that any individual or branch of government would accumulate too much power and thereby behave in a tyrannical fashion.

The Constitution provides the basis for the governing system of the United States. Although specific aspects of the Constitution have been changed through the enactment of amendments, the basic words and principles of the Constitution remain the same. As American society changed over the years, the U.S. Supreme Court interpreted the words of the Constitution to give them applicability to new and changing social circumstances.

ETHICAL PRINCIPLES

The Constitution seeks to avoid the risk of governmental tyranny through the principle of separation of powers. The legislative, executive, and judicial branches of government are separate from one another, and each possesses specific powers that enable it to prevent excessive actions by the other branches of government.

Political liberty and democratic decision making are guaranteed through the Constitution's provisions mandating elections for representatives in the legislative branch (Congress) and for the president and vice-president in the executive branch. The Constitution also grants the broadest list of specific powers to the legislative branch so that representatives from

throughout the nation can enact laws rather than having one person be responsible for authoritative decision making. The legislative branch is divided into two chambers, one providing representation according to each state's population (House of Representatives) and the other providing equal representation to each state (Senate) in order to prevent the largest states from dominating all decisions.

The Constitution sets specific terms in office for elected officials in the legislative and executive branches. The voters have the opportunity to select new officials every two years for the House of Representatives, every four years for the president and vice-president, and every six years for the Senate. This mechanism helps to preserve political liberty by holding individuals accountable to the citizens.

ETHICAL ISSUES

As it was drafted in 1787, the Constitution did not specifically address several important ethical issues. Some of these issues were addressed later through amendments added to the Constitution. For example, the Constitution did not address the issue of slavery except to say that any congressional decisions on that issue must wait until twenty years after the document first went into effect. Slavery was eventually abolished through the Thirteenth Amendment in 1868 after a bloody civil war was fought over this unresolved issue. The original Constitution also did not guarantee specific civil rights for citizens. Freedom of speech, freedom of religion, criminal defendants' rights, and other civil rights were guaranteed in 1791 when the first ten amendments to the Constitution, known as the Bill of Rights, were ratified.

Although the Constitution's design for a representative democracy was intended to protect citizens' political liberty, several aspects of the Constitution are undemocratic. Because the drafters of the Constitution feared that the voters could be swayed by a charismatic demagogue, citizens do not elect the president directly. They vote instead for electors, known as the Electoral College, who can select someone other than the leading vote getter as president if they believe that the people have made an unwise choice.

In addition, because representation in Congress is determined by state, people who live in the District of Columbia, although they outnumber the populations of several small states, do not have voting representation in Congress. The citizens residing in the nation's capital city lack the basic political liberty to elect representatives to the national legislature. Thus, although the Constitution has been effective in creating a stable democratic governing system, it remains imperfect as a document seeking to guarantee political liberty and participation in decision making for all citizens.

Christopher E. Smith

FURTHER READING

Ackerman, Bruce. *We the People.* Cambridge, Mass.: Harvard University Press, 1991.

Edling, Max M. *A Revolution in Favor of Government: Origins of the U.S. Constitution and the Making of the American State.* New York: Oxford University Press, 2003.

Levinson, Sanford. *Constitutional Faith.* Princeton, N.J.: Princeton University Press, 1988.

Levy, Leonard W., Kenneth L. Karst, and Dennis J. Mahoney, eds. *American Constitutional History: Selections from the Encyclopedia of the American Constitution.* New York: Macmillan, 1989.

Mead, Walter B. *The United States Constitution: Personalities, Principles, and Issues.* Columbia: University of South Carolina Press, 1987.

Urofsky, Melvin I. *A March of Liberty: A Constitutional History of the United States.* New York: Knopf, 1988.

SEE ALSO: Bill of Rights, U.S.; Civil rights and liberties; Constitutional government; Declaration of Independence; Democracy; Geneva conventions; Political liberty; Supreme Court, U.S.

Constitutional government

DEFINITION: Political system regulated by a formal contract between the governors and the governed which explicitly apportions and limits political power

TYPE OF ETHICS: Politico-economic ethics

SIGNIFICANCE: Constitutional government is based on the principles that government must be limited and that leaders and citizens alike are governed by the rule of law.

The idea of constitutional government is that the social contract, or that system of social relationships that constitutes the origin of any community, is given concrete manifestation in a constitution. In sum, the legitimacy of a constitutional regime is based on formal agreement between the rulers and the ruled. Government accepts limitations based on citizen consent and the rule of law will govern all. In modern politics, few governments maintain legitimacy without a constitutional foundation. A constitution guarantees that the government rules in the name of the many (not the few or the one, as in dynastic or despotic regimes) and is limited in scope by agreement on the rules and structure of governance. Nevertheless, in practice a constitution is only as valid and effective as the citizens and leaders believe it to be and make it.

HISTORY OF THE CONCEPT

Constitutions can be considered power maps that give form to the distribution of power within a political system. Although this conception emphasizes institutions, these power maps also reflect the political culture and the ideologies that undergird a society. In ethical terms, the constitutional idea expresses an ideological principle itself—that of government limited by law, government that emanates from the culture, customs, and mores of a community.

The principle of government founded on code and law can be traced back to antiquity. The covenant of the Hebrew people was one expression of this idea. The legal codes of Hammurabi (1792-1750 B.C.E.), the Athenian laws of Draco (c. 621 B.C.E.) and Solon (594 B.C.E.), and the Byzantine Roman emperor Justinian's legal code (529-533 C.E.) were also forerunners of the constitutional principle. In fact, the Greek concept of the polis lies at the heart of the ethical ideal of constitutionalism. From the experience of ancient Athens in particular, Western culture had inherited the ethical value of the rule of law, the ideal of the polis, and the immanent legitimacy of the state that governs in the name and by the consent of the citizens.

THE GREEKS

The concept of the polis as a spiritual identification of the individual with the community was the hallmark of Greek civilization. Most important, in the evolution of Athenian democracy, the Greeks emphasized the superiority of the rule of law as opposed to the "rule of men" in the forms of monarchs and tyrants. Law and constitution create a sphere of political discourse, freedom, and dignity for the citizen that is absent in the rule of another human being, no matter how benevolent a despot.

Freedom under the law became the highest moral principle for the Greek polis, and in the Greek mind it distinguished Greek civilization from barbarian civilizations. This idea was the point of departure between Aristotle's *Politics* (335-322 B.C.E.) and Plato's *Republic* (386-367 B.C.E.). Plato presented a constitution in the *Republic* that was based on the governance of picked individuals whose legitimacy was based on knowledge. Aristotle preferred constitutional rule founded on law, which preserved human dignity and participation. Only later in life did Plato rediscover the importance of this principle, as can be seen in *Laws* (360-347 B.C.E.). The connection of constitutional government to rule of law is the most significant political inheritance from the Greek experience.

THE SOCIAL CONTRACT

After the sixteenth century in Europe, through the age of Enlightenment, there emerged a movement for democracy and constitutionalism that was associated with the ideas of the social contract. This movement, which presaged the rise of the modern secular state, is descended from the ideas of Thomas Hobbes, John Locke, Jean-Jacques Rousseau, David Hume, and many others.

Although there are many differences in the ideas of these authors, at their core was agreement about certain principles concerning constitutional government. In essence, they argued that a social contract preexists the contract of government. An original community must exist, and grounded upon established social relations, a contract of government may be created. This contract is the formal agreement of all within the community to accept laws and limitations on government, and hence government is legitimated by consent. Ultimately, no government is legitimate unless it governs in the name of the people.

THE MODERN STATE

Modern states rule in the name of their people. Most modern states do not rest their legitimacy on rule by a person, a dynastic family, or a theocracy. Even the most authoritarian regimes of the twentieth century claimed to rule in the name of the people. In this sense, modern states are constitutional governments. In fact, most modern states perceive themselves as "founded nations" and thus have required a founding document. Because most modern nation-states are large and complex, and require participation by masses of citizens in their projects, constitutional government and consent evolved as the fundamental form of legitimization. The ideological basis of the secular state is supported by constitutionalism and law, and constitutions perform many functions.

Constitutions express the ideology of founded nations in their rules and structures. For example, the Constitution of the United States not only preserved private property and a free market but also reflected a desire for limited government in its separation of powers. Constitutions embody basic laws and rights of the people. These vary with the culture and experience of a people, and are influenced by the ideological origins of the state. Formally recognized rights and liberties are a major reason for establishing constitutional government. Constitutions define the organization of government and the distribution of powers. Herein lies the specific way in which governments submit to limitation. They must abide by the contract or be overthrown. Finally, constitutions hold the promise that people may change them as necessity requires. Because a constitution reflects the consent of the governed, the ability to amend a constitution may safeguard liberty and regime longevity.

Ultimately, these functions require qualification. This is how constitutions should function. Perhaps the greatest ethical problems in constitutional government are the importance of belief and the fact that it requires the participation of human beings, citizens and leaders, to make constitutions work on behalf of the people. Many authoritarian regimes have constitutions that espouse the values of consent, guarantees of rights, and rule of law. In fact, the rule of law is the ethical core of constitutional government. The essential promise of constitutional government is that no person, institution, or party may be above the law.

Anthony R. Brunello

FURTHER READING

Duchacek, Ivo. *Power Maps: Comparative Politics of Constitutions*. Santa Barbara, Calif.: ABC-Clio Press, 1973.

Gordon, Scott. *Controlling the State: Constitution-*

alism from Ancient Athens to Today. Cambridge, Mass.: Harvard University Press, 1999.

Hamilton, Alexander, James Madison, and John Jay. *The Federalist Papers.* New York: Washington Square Press, 1976.

Locke, John. *Two Treatises of Government.* Edited by Peter Laslett. New York: Cambridge University Press, 1988.

Plato. *The Republic.* Translated by Desmond Lee. 2d ed. New York: Penguin Books, 2003.

Rousseau, Jean-Jacques. *"The Social Contract" and "The First and Second Discourses,"* edited by Susan Dunn. New Haven, Conn.: Yale University Press, 2002.

SEE ALSO: Constitution, U.S.; Hammurabi's code; Jefferson, Thomas; Law; Locke, John; Rousseau, Jean-Jacques; Supreme Court, U.S.

Warning Label on Alcoholic Beverages

In response to public concerns, the federal government began requiring manufacturers of alcoholic beverages to put this warning on their products in 1989:

Government warning: (1) According to the Surgeon General, women should not drink alcoholic beverages during pregnancy because of the risk of birth defects. (2) Consumption of alcoholic beverages impairs your ability to drive a car or operate machinery, and may cause health problems.

Consumerism

DEFINITION: Movement aimed at improving the status and power of the consumer relative to the seller in the marketplace

DATE: Began during the late 1960's

TYPE OF ETHICS: Business and labor ethics

SIGNIFICANCE: Consumerism is strongly associated with the introduction of morality into the otherwise amoral marketplace, since it emphasizes the responsibilities of manufacturers to consumers in such areas as product safety, fair pricing, and honest advertising.

The publication in 1965 of Ralph Nader's book *Unsafe at Any Speed,* which criticized the dangerous design features of the Chevrolet Corvair, is often viewed as the birth of modern-day consumerism. Since that time, Nader and others have founded such consumer organizations as the Center for Auto Safety, Public Citizen, the Health Research Group, and various buyers' cooperatives to promote safer products, lower prices, and full and honest disclosure in advertising.

Two important trends have encouraged the growth of consumerism: the fact that sellers (manufacturers and retailers) increasingly tend to be giant corporations with whom individual buyers have little influence; and the growing complexity of many consumer products, which prevents buyers from making informed judgments. Consumerism has led to the passage of such legislation at the federal level as the Child Protection and Safety Act, the Hazardous Substances Act, and the Fair Credit Reporting Act, as well as the creation of the Consumer Product Safety Commission. The movement has been unsuccessful, however, in lobbying for the establishment of a federal cabinet-level consumer protection agency.

D. Kirk Davidson

SEE ALSO: Advertising; Boycotts; Business ethics; Infomercials; Nader, Ralph; Price fixing; Product safety and liability; Sales ethics; Warranties and guarantees.

Conversion of one's system of beliefs

DEFINITION: Comprehensive change in one's understanding of the world and one's place in it

TYPE OF ETHICS: Beliefs and practices

SIGNIFICANCE: Exemplifying the complexity and drama of human thought, individual conversions have left a major legacy in every system of beliefs.

Conversions represent a long-standing and memorable drama in the intellectual and spiritual history of humankind. All major systems of belief have, to a greater or lesser extent, sought and obtained converts, although Christianity perhaps places the most emphasis on the individual conversion experience, as most famously illustrated by the apostle Paul's being knocked off his horse while on the road to Damascus.

Conversion of one's system of beliefs generally entails a complete change of one's life. The values and perspectives of the individual experiencing the conversion undergo major shifts, often resulting in dramatic changes in the person's way of life. Old relationships may be severed, while new ones are created; allegiances may be transferred from one community to another; career, home, friendships, family ties, all may hang in the balance.

The conversion experience has been much studied, particularly from a psychological point of view. A notable example can be found in psychologist William James's book *The Varieties of Religious Experience* (1902). Other similar studies typically fall into the danger of simplifying and subjectivizing complex ideas and ideologies by reducing all conversion experiences to matters of psychology. Entire peoples and communities have been converted, although distinctions must be made between true individual conversions of beliefs and the changing tributes paid to external rulers.

History and literature are filled with famous conversions, from Saint Augustine's late fourth century *Confessions* to the Buddha's awakening under the Bodhi tree to V. I. Lenin's adoption of revolutionary Marxism after the czarist execution of his brother. A modern narrative of a conversion experience is *Turning* (1982), by Emilie Griffin, whose chapter titles—"Turning," "Desire," "Dialectic," "Struggle," "Surrender," and "Afterward"—manifest some of the stages, both turbulent and peaceful, that are typical in the conversion of one's system of beliefs.

Howard Bromberg

SEE ALSO: Augustine, Saint; Bodhisattva ideal; Buddha; Calvin, John; Edwards, Jonathan; Holy war.

Copyright

DEFINITION: Legal protection of intellectual property giving the copyright holder exclusive right to publish, reproduce, and sell or lease the property for a set period of time

TYPE OF ETHICS: Legal and judicial ethics

SIGNIFICANCE: Finding a satisfactory ethics of copyright requires striking a balance between the rights of copyright owners and the rights of the public.

Throughout American history, copyright law has protected the rights of authors to control their own works. The Framers of the U.S. Constitution included a passage in the very first article of the document expressing the wish to encourage creativity by promoting "the progress of science and the useful arts." The original U.S. copyright law gave authors fourteen years of protection, followed by an additional fourteen years if the authors were still alive. After copyright of a work lapsed, the work fell into the public domain and could be freely used by anyone without payment to the authors or their estates. By limiting the duration of copyright protection, American law avoided the kind of hereditary monopolies that had stifled the creativity of other nations.

Over the years, the U.S. Congress gradually extended the duration of copyright protection. The copyright law enacted in 1976 significantly lengthened ownership duration but also introduced new fair-use guidelines that exempted nonprofit organizations from having to secure permission to use reasonable portions of copyright-protected material.

CHANGES IN COPYRIGHT LAW

Modern digital technology has made it easier than ever before to reproduce materials. In the modern digital environment, the original intent of the U.S. Constitution still serves as a basis for ethical debate on copyright. Among the new questions being asked in the twenty-first century is whether authors and other creative persons need added protections of their works to guard against digital piracy. Additions to U.S. copyright law in 1976 and 1998 were designed to support copyright owners for much longer periods than original constitutional guidelines allowed.

Before 1976, the burden of securing copyright protection for work was on the owners of the copyrightable material who had to take steps themselves to register individual items to ensure protection. After 1976, all original materials that exist in tangible form are automatically protected by U.S. copyright and do not require individual registration. Amendments to the federal copyright law enacted in 1998 criminalized the unauthorized use of all Web resources. A 2002 amendment to copyright law limited nonprofit organizations to use copyrighted materials only under very stringent limitations, with heavy fines and jail sentences for infringements. The implicit philosophical shift from predigital interpretation of the law to the postdigital world view is from a philosophy that assumed central importance for protection of the public domain to a philosophy that centers its main focus on protection of owned property.

Copyright Holders' Perspectives

Owners of copyright-protected material maintain that piracy of their material is simply a form of property theft. Owners point out that the Constitution's Framers could not have anticipated modern digital environments, which make piracy of exact reproductions easy. Among the methods that copyright owners employ to enforce their rights in a digital environment include pay-per-play and licensing agreements, expanding duration of protection, making it a crime

to circumvent software protection, campaigns targeting illegal file sharing and pressuring schools and other institutions that provide Internet service to detect and punish infringing users.

Some copyright owners view a commitment toward a good faith compliance with the law on the part of users as a firm basis on which to balance needs of private enterprise with society's need to have access to a public domain that supports further invention and creativity. Such corporations return good faith by becoming partners with scholars and by backing initiatives to create rich public domain resources that will contribute to national security and prosperity.

Public Perspectives

Some people argue that the delicate balance between public interest and private good has been compromised by corporate pursuit of short-sighted efforts that shrink the public domain, threatening education

Japanese music fans using camera phones at a music awards event near Tokyo in May, 2003. (AP/Wide World Photos)

Camera Phones and Copyright

In 2003, Japan led the world in camera cell phones, with an estimated 25 million instruments in private hands. With no traditions in ethical behavior to guide them in the use of this new technology, many camera phone owners were using them to do such things as copy pages from books and magazines in shops, thereby obtaining copyrighted material free of charge. Bookstore owners claimed that this form of theft was cutting into their sales, and a magazine publishers association urged consumers to buy their magazines and not use camera phones to photograph the magazine pages.

In an ironic twist, Samsung, a leading manufacturer of cell phones, was evidently afraid of the camera phones itself. It required its own employees and visitors to its research facilities to cover their camera phone lenses with tape to protect trade secrets from being photographed.

and the cultural heritage by making many cultural indicators unavailable for reinterpretations except through owner approval, which may carry prohibitively expensive use fees or restrictions on how the work is to be reinterpreted. In the view of public domain advocates, intellectual property is not ordinary property; it is the basis of intellectual freedom and prosperity due to recycling of cultural wealth. On this side of the debate are many representatives of educational and nonprofit institutions, who feel that instead of being rewarded for safeguarding the nation's cultural commons, they have been financially, legally and politically penalized.

There is also a rationale among some users, especially among computer hackers, that their circumvention activities strengthen society in the digital age by exposing weaknesses in security systems. However, in the view of many nonprofit advocates of public domain, good faith should be to be able to report weaknesses in the system without fear of reprisal from overly zealous owners on one hand and without attempting to cause economic strain or chaos on the other hand.

A practical ethics responds in a balanced manner to these issues, helping to preserve the cultural heritage and supporting long-term prosperity. Groups such as NINCH (The National Initiative for a Networked Cultural Heritage), SPARC (The Scholarly Publishing and Academic Resources Coalition), Open Source, and also freeware offerings by private citizens and corporations all seek equitable compensation for scholars and artists, helping to retain a shared cultural heritage through approaches that remain within the law.

Suzanne Araas Vesely

FURTHER READING

Crews, Kenneth. *Copyright Essentials for Librarians and Educators*. Chicago: American Library Association, 2000.

Hoffman, Gretchen McCord. "What Every Librarian Should Know About Copyright." *Texas Library Journal* 78 (2002): 56-59, 108-111, 148-151; 79 (2003): 12-15.

Minow, Mary, and Thomas A. Lipinski. *The Library's Legal Answer Book*. Chicago: American Library Association, 2002.

Patterson, L. Ray. *The Nature of Copyright: A Law of User's Rights*. Athens: University of Georgia Press, 1991.

Vaidhyanathan, Siva. *Copyrights and Copywrongs: The Rise of Intellectual Property and How It Threatens Creativity*. New York: New York University Press, 2003.

Wherry, Timothy Lee. *The Librarian's Guide to Intellectual Property in the Digital Age: Copyright, Patents, Trademarks*. Chicago: American Library Association, 2002.

SEE ALSO: Art; Computer misuse; Intellectual property; Internet piracy; Napster; Plagiarism; Property.

Corporate compensation

DEFINITION: Salaries, stock options, bonuses, and other benefits received by top corporate officers

TYPE OF ETHICS: Business and labor ethics

SIGNIFICANCE: Many people think it unethical that chief executive officers (CEOs) and other high officers of many American corporations receive immense salaries, huge bonuses, the right to purchase company stock below market prices, and extravagant perquisites ("perks"); however, there are arguments on both sides of the issue.

Many people believe that huge gaps in income levels between corporate CEOs and their employees are unethical. An early twenty-first century analysis of corporate compensation found that the average CEO received slightly more than 280 times the amount earned by the average worker. In 2002, the highest-paid executives among Standard and Poor's five hundred top firms received compensation worth as much as $20 million apiece.

In addition to their salaries, many CEOs receive "golden parachute" packages at retirement or exit-compensation packages that enable them to land safely in the event they get fired from their companies, or their companies are taken over or fail. CEOs also usually have unusually strong job security through multiyear contracts and the close relationships they enjoy with members of their boards of directors. By contrast, most employees work under "employment-at-will" conditions and can be dismissed at any time and for any reason. The ethics of these distinctions can be considered from the perspectives to contrasting philosophical theories: libertarianism and distributive justice.

Libertarian philosopher Robert Nozick holds the view that since Americans live in a free market society, they should be willing to compensate people for goods and services they provide based on supply and demand, thereby maximizing individual rights. Inequalities in incomes are natural products of differing natural abilities and should not be subjected to moral or ethical judgments. It is natural that large and complex corporations are willing to offer CEOs high salaries and extravagant compensation packages in return for the rare and valuable skills that CEOs bring to their positions. Corporations must compensate their CEOs with extraordinary financial and other inducements if they expect to hire and retain them. In most cases corporate compensation is pegged to overall organizational performance and corporate organizational health, and serves as a baseline in calculating compensation for other employees.

Philosopher John Rawls, a proponent of the theory of distributive justice, represents a contrasting school of thought. He asks whether it is ethical for CEOs to receive high salaries and other corporate compensation schemes, while their employees face

Disney Chief Michael Eisner

Michael Eisner, who became chief executive officer of the Disney Company in 1984, has long ranked among the highest-paid corporate executives in the world. During the five years leading up to 2001, he received, in salary and benefits, approximately $737 million—a sum that *Forbes* magazine estimated was nineteen times greater than the average chief executive officer's income. While Eisner's income was widely criticized for its sheer magnitude, the steady income increases that he was receiving confounded laissez-faire economic theories because the net income of the Disney Company itself declined through the same period by an average of 3.1 percent per year. To compensate for this decline in early 2001, Eisner laid off four thousand employees— 3.3 percent of the company's total full-time work force. The amount of money the layoffs saved the company each year was estimated to be less than the compensation Eisner alone had received over the previous five years.

(AP/Wide World Photos)

the possibility of losing their jobs through corporate downsizing. Huge disparities in income levels between management and ordinary employees make the lower-level employees cynical, foster morale problems, and cultivate feelings of inequality.

Joseph C. Santora

FURTHER READING

Brancato, Carolyn Kay, and Christian A. Plath. *Corporate Governance Best Practices: A Blueprint for the Post-Enron Era*. New York: Conference Board, 2003.

Nozick, R. *Anarchy, State and Utopia*. New York: Basic Books, 1974.

Rawls, John. *A Theory of Justice*. Cambridge, Mass.: Harvard University Press, 1971.

SEE ALSO: Business ethics; Corporate responsibility; Corporate scandal; Distributive justice; Downsizing; Greed; Income distribution; Minimum-wage laws; Professional athlete incomes.

Corporate responsibility

DEFINITION: Moral accountability of corporations for their actions, including but not limited to their duty to conform to the laws of the state

TYPE OF ETHICS: Business and labor ethics

SIGNIFICANCE: Corporate responsibility raises important issues for ethics in regard to the nature of collective action and the division between personal and group morality. The disjunction between the ethical responsibilities and the legal accountability of large corporations may lead some to question the level of social justice available within late capitalist society.

Business corporations are collectivities of persons that are granted legal personhood and limited liability by the state for the purpose of carrying on commerce. The purposes for which a general corporation is created—primarily to make profit from commerce for its shareholders—raise questions about whether corporations ought to undertake supererogatory actions for the public good. This issue is further complicated by the issue of minority stockholders' rights, since there are few noncontroversial issues of public

policy and the unanimous agreement of stockholders is scarcely to be anticipated in large, publicly traded corporations.

Nobel laureate Milton Friedman has argued eloquently for restricting the moral obligation of corporations to obeying the laws of their respective nations. In this view, minority stockholders' rights are a prime consideration, but the economic efficiency of the market is another desired aim of this policy. The purely economic arrangement of the market, this theory argues, would be damaged by the noneconomic behavior of altruistic corporations. The lessening of the profitability of some enterprises, the potential for boycott, counter-boycott, and so forth, threaten the normal functioning of the capitalistic market economy, in this view.

The contrary view would hold that it is absurd to separate financial profitability from questions of the general quality of life: Would it make sense for a businessman to indulge in some as-yet legal form of polluting if that pollution would significantly shorten his life and/or that of his family? Would it be "profitable" for one to make money by legally selling weaponry to a potential enemy who might be expected to use those weapons to conquer or to destroy one's nation?

Patrick M. O'Neil

SEE ALSO: Accountability; Boycotts; Business ethics; Consumerism; Corporate scandal; Duty; Employee safety and treatment; Leadership; Sales ethics; Self-regulation.

Corporate scandal

DEFINITION: Highly publicized legal and ethical misconduct of corporate leaders

TYPE OF ETHICS: Business and labor ethics

SIGNIFICANCE: During the first years of the twenty-first century, a long string of financial frauds in public American corporations cast public doubt on the ethics of even untarnished corporations. Such trust, once lost, is slow to return. The immediate measure result was a slow down in the financial markets.

President Theodore Roosevelt is credited with saying that to "educate a person in mind and not in morals is to educate a menace to society." Rarely has the truth of that observation been more apparent than in the early years of the twenty-first century, when numerous corporate scandals, perpetrated by highly educated and highly paid corporate officers, dominated the news media.

Corporate financial scandals are not new; they have been around since the dawn of the corporate form of business in the late nineteenth century. They have been called the "agency problem." As agents of their companies' stockholders, corporate officers utilize corporation assets on behalf of the stockholders. At the same time, the officers have a vested interest in maximizing their own well-being. The result is that stockholders need some form of governance over the officers of the corporations. Such governance is supposed to be provided by corporate boards of directors, audit committees, and internal auditors who oversee the activities of management. However, during the early years of the twenty-first century, several corporations, including Enron, WorldCom, Global Crossing, HealthSouth, Tyco, and others, were driven into bankruptcy or other financial embarrassments due to the overly greedy activities of their high-level executives.

In some cases, corporate stock options—the right to purchase shares of stock at a certain price—were the cause of the financial fraud. In other cases, opportunities to receive year-end salary bonuses were the incentive. After exercising their options to buy stock at low prices, corporate officers could then manipulate their companies' financial reports to make reported income appear to be higher than it actually was, thus raising the value of their own stock. The result was that many corporate officers benefitted at the expense of stockholders. In instances in which employees were offered bonuses for achieving specific income goals for their companies, officers used various methods to report greater revenues or lower expenses, or both. These actions were clearly unethical acts on the part of the officers, but the practice was widespread enough to dampen all stock market activity severely.

Former Enron chief executive officer Jeffrey Skilling (right) listening to his defense attorney after pleading innocent to three dozen federal charges in February, 2004. Skilling resigned from his job a few months before the giant communications company was shattered by revelations of insider trading and other scandals. (AP/Wide World Photos)

ENRON AND WORLDCOM

In most cases of corporate scandal, external auditors were blamed, either for agreeing to the questionable practices of the corporate officers, or for failing to uncover the illegal activities. One of the most highly publicized scandals, which affected the Enron Corporation, was uncovered in late 2001. After Andersen & Company (formerly Arthur Andersen & Company), the external auditor that had approved some questionable Enron transactions, was discovered to have shredded thousands of documents related to its audit of Enron, that venerable auditing firm was destroyed. By the spring of 2002, Andersen essentially ceased to exist—not merely because it had failed in conducting an audit, but because it attempted to hide its audit coverage by shredding key documents.

As the news coverage of the Enron scandal waned, a new fraud was uncovered at WorldCom, a major telecommunications firm in Clinton, Mississippi. Internal auditors at WorldCom discovered that the company's chief financial officer, controller, and other accounting employees had recorded expenses as assets, which resulted in ostensibly higher income and the consequent awarding of huge bonuses to top-level employees. The WorldCom scandal was essentially the straw that broke the camel's back. Investors prevailed upon Congress to do something about the unethical acts of corporate executives. The result was the passage on July 31, 2002, of the Sarbanes-Oxley Act, which limited the types of nonaudit work that external auditors are allowed to perform for their clients. The law also required corporate executives to certify to the accuracy of their company's financial statements.

INTERNAL AUDITORS

One of the reasons that the Sarbanes-Oxley Act limited the types of work done by external auditors was that large audit firms were selling consulting services to their clients as well as conducting audits. Since auditors are supposed to be independent of their clients, their providing consulting services was regarded as a conflict of interest that inhibited their independence. This practice was particularly noted at Enron, where Andersen had either designed or approved the use of subsidiary organizations that would absorb losses that would otherwise have appeared on Enron's books.

Internal auditors are considered the first line of defense against questionable corporate ethics, but at Enron there were no internal auditors. Andersen had convinced Enron's board of directors that it could also handle the company's internal auditing duties. This concept of outsourcing the internal audit function to the external auditor had become a common American business practice during the late 1990's. However, the breakdown at Enron led to the prohibition against the practice in the Sarbanes-Oxley Act.

CORPORATE FRAUD IN HISTORY

The perpetration of fraud by corporate insiders is not a new phenomenon. During the 1870's, half of the railroads in the United States were in receivership, many because of the immoral acts of insiders. In 1932, the bankruptcy of the Swedish financier Ivar Kreuger's scandal-ridden empire following his suicide led to a national outcry that resulted in Congress's passage of the 1933 Securities Act. During the 1980's, hundreds of financial institutions failed because of insider fraud, leading to a congressional investigation.

In many respects, Enron, WorldCom, and their ilk are merely extensions of the nineteenth century railroads and the Kreuger debacle. In every case, the governance system broke down or did not exist, and unethical individuals succumbed to greed. Laws cannot make individuals ethical, but by reducing opportunities for personal enrichment through the use of internal auditors, audit committees, and other forms of governance, unethical persons will have fewer opportunities for gain.

Dale L. Flesher

FURTHER READING

Brancato, Carolyn Kay, and Christian A. Plath. *Corporate Governance Best Practices: A Blueprint for the Post-Enron Era*. New York: Conference Board, 2003.

Bryce, Robert. *Pipe Dreams: Greed, Ego, and the Death of Enron*. New York: Public Affairs, 2002.

Cruver, Brian. *Anatomy of Greed: The Unshredded Truth from an Enron Insider*. New York: Carroll & Graf, 2002.

Fox, Loren. *Enron: The Rise and Fall*. Hoboken, N.J.: Wiley & Sons, 2003.

Jeter, Lynne. *Disconnected: Deceit and Betrayal at WorldCom*. Hoboken, N.J.: Wiley & Sons, 2003.

Swartz, Mimi, and Sherron Watkins. *Power Failure: The Inside Story of the Collapse of Enron*. New York: Doubleday, 2003.

SEE ALSO: Business ethics; Corporate compensation; Corporate responsibility; Corruption; Ethical codes of organizations; "Everyone does it"; Insider trading; Private vs. public morality; Stewart, Martha; Whistle-blowing; White-collar crime.

Corruption

DEFINITION: Impairment or dissolution of integrity, virtue, and moral principles
TYPE OF ETHICS: Personal and social ethics
SIGNIFICANCE: Corruption generally denotes a pervasive or potentially pervasive weakening of moral principles throughout a given institution or segment of society.

While a number of factors account for individual corruption, one important factor is contempt for humanity. A threshold of corruption has been crossed when a person comes to despise other people. Furthermore, most corrupt individuals share an overwhelming desire for power (control and domination) over others and a lust for wealth, and they will try to corrupt or ruin all those who stand in their way. Such a corrupt individual adapts easily. He or she can "move" and change stratagems quickly. Having an immoral or amoral approach to life (and ethics), such a person becomes a liar as needed, manipulates others as needed, uses the law as needed, and finds loopholes in laws and uses them to advantage as needed. Many corrupt people also exploit and hide behind religion.

Because of their contempt for others, corrupt persons become unscrupulous in addition to being utterly ruthless, while also becoming consciously and deeply aware of their ruthlessness. Other traits include their absorption with their own affairs to the exclusion of all else, as well as secretiveness and extreme sensitivity to real or imagined insults. Such persons become conspirators who are "positive" that others are conspiring against them. They then develop rationales for their actions, which include "punishment" of others. The truly corrupted eventually become criminals. For example, the Watergate scandal and U.S. president Richard M. Nixon's White House tapes revealed that Nixon and many of his aides had become corrupt and committed criminal acts.

CORRUPT SOCIETIES

Just as individuals become corrupt, so, too, do societies. Corrupt societies are usually ruled by dictators or by cliques of lawless and ruthless people. However, government under such rulers is mediocre at best. The cliques and the people they rule become intolerant and develop contempt for foreign peoples. The leaders become something of father-figures and near worship of them develops. Rights—such as those found in the U.S. Constitution's Bill of Rights—are curtailed, and censorship becomes the order of the day. In the economy, extremes develop between fabulously wealthy people and the poverty stricken, with much of the wealth being amassed by the ruling clique. Furthermore, social mobility of any kind is restricted to certain elite groups.

Corrupt societies also exhibit decisiveness, instability, and senseless murders that devalue life, but turn cynical when such wrongs are committed. Furthermore, the state gives only minimal assistance to the needful young, old, and sick. Corrupt societies use religion as a type of "window-dressing," with most people who appear to be "saints" on their day of worship reverting to cold-blooded ruthlessness on the other days of the week. As a consequence, ethics are ignored, immorality replaces morality, sexual mores change for the worse, and families become weak to the point of almost ceasing to exist. Additionally, if the state has a heritage of "multiculturalism," the "in" groups eventually persecute and suppress the "out" groups, as was the case in Nazi Germany.

THE UNITED STATES

Many signs of corruption became evident in the United States, as the nation moved into the twenty-first century. Everywhere, it seemed, were signs that elites expected and demanded too much. In the savings and loan scandals of the late 1980's and early 1990's, when bankers took billions of dollars, there was corruption. When defense contractors cheated on their government contracts from the 1940's to the present, again there was corruption.

When college football coaches or their "boosters" bribe the impressionable young, all parties become corrupted. When ministers commit immoral and perhaps illegal acts while continuing to beg for money, they become corrupt and may well corrupt all those around them, including their own congregations. When college students cheat on examinations, they become corrupt and may influence others to cheat, thereby spreading their corruption.

People who abuse relatives violently, sexually, or psychologically, become corrupt and may also "warp" the beliefs of the persons so abused. When the friendly neighborhood policeman takes his first bribe, the policeman becomes corrupt. When physicians treat the poor and charge them more than they can pay, the physicians become corrupt. Perhaps worst of all, corrupted individuals and societies have no sense of shame when such wrongs are committed.

It thus appears that the United States—like many other countries—may not measure up to the standards set by the French Nobel Prize winner Albert Camus, a philosopher who held that the worth of an individual could be measured by observing what that individual would allow others to suffer and that a society's worth could be measured by observing how it treated its most unfortunate people.

James Smallwood

FURTHER READING

Benson, George C. S. *Political Corruption in America.* Lexington, Mass.: Lexington Books, 1978.

Bull, Martin J., and James L. Newell, eds. *Corruption in Contemporary Politics.* New York: Palgrave Macmillan, 2003.

Harris, Godfrey. *Corruption: How to Deal with Its Impact on Business and Society.* Los Angeles: Americas Group, 2003.

Payne, Robert. *The Corrupt Society: From Ancient Greece to Present-Day America.* New York: Praeger, 1975.

Schweitzer, Albert. *The Decay and Restoration of Civilization.* Translated by C. T. Campion. New York: Macmillan, 1953.

Spengler, Oswald. *The Decline of the West.* Translated by Charles F. Atkinson. New York: Knopf, 1957.

Sykes, Charles J. *The Hollow Men: Politics and Corruption in Higher Education.* Washington, D.C.: Regnery Gateway, 1990.

Wise, David. *The Politics of Lying.* New York: Random House, 1973.

SEE ALSO: Cheating; Corporate scandal; Dirty hands; Ethics in Government Act; "Everyone does it"; Honesty; Lobbying; Lying; Morality; White-collar crime.

Cost-benefit analysis

DEFINITION: Method of deciding between alternative courses of action that weighs economic costs and benefits in order to ensure that net benefits outweigh net costs

TYPE OF ETHICS: Environmental ethics

SIGNIFICANCE: Cost-benefit analysis is a tool especially valued by environmental and regulatory agencies that must make choices in proposals for public land use. The ethical challenge is determining whether the assumption that preferences for such issues as wilderness and clean air protection can be measured in economic terms is valid.

Cost-benefit analysis was developed by economists in the early 1950's as a test for the desirability of government policies and projects. Just as a corporation maximizes profits, good government should maximize the benefits for society. Cost-benefit analysis is a procedure for decision making that emphasizes consequences. The procedure is simple: Given alternative courses of action, policy makers should choose the course that maximizes public benefits after subtracting associated costs, which are expressed in dollars.

Economists have touted cost-benefit analysis as an especially useful and rigorous way of thinking about issues such as health care and environmental and regulatory policies. Common sense seems to dictate a preference for choices that maximize benefits and minimize costs. However, cost-benefit analysis is not without its critics, notably environmentalists and philosophers who are concerned about the ethical implications of this thinking.

ESTIMATING VALUE

Preferences for health care, clean water, environmental beauty, and safe consumer products, can be affected by regulation and policies. Cost-benefit analysis requires that such preferences be expressed in dollar amounts. For example, in a case in which the installation of pollution control equipment will result in the savings of human life, it should be easy to estimate the equipment costs. However, it is notoriously difficult to assign dollar values to the benefit of saving human lives. How can such costs be measured? For example, should the baseline be the annual salaries of the people whose lives are saved?

Critics also argue that cost-benefit analysis raises

serious fairness issues by implying that people with higher incomes are more important than those with lower incomes. If society thinks of workers in terms of their incomes, because low-income workers cost less than higher income workers, they might consequently be afforded less protection because they are cheaper to replace.

MAKING DECISIONS

Cost-benefit analysis offers a procedure for resolving disputes between competing interests to everyone's benefit. An example might be one in which two parties disagree over the use of a piece of land—one party wishes to develop it, and the other to preserve it. To resolve the dispute one could ask what the parties are willing to pay to develop or to preserve the land. Analysts claim that the party willing to pay more money is the party that desires the property more and consequently will benefit more from its acquisition.

That line of reasoning seems to be intuitive—if one party is willing to pay more for something, then one must want it more. The "losers" in the bidding war could then be compensated for their losses, and no one would be worse off. However, this result is also controversial. If willingness to pay is equated to what a party can actually pay on demand, then the losing bidder must desire the outcome less. However, what if one party just has fewer financial resources than the other? It does not follow that that party wants the property less. Furthermore, financial compensation for "losers" may be irrelevant if their interest in the land is noneconomic and cannot be measured in dollar amounts.

Edward W. Maine

FURTHER READING

Hausman, Daniel, Michael S. McPherson. *Economic Analysis and Moral Philosophy.* Cambridge, England: Cambridge University Press, 1998.

Kelman, Stephen. "Cost-Benefit Analysis: An Ethical Critique." *Regulation* (1981): 74-82.

VanDeVeer, Donald, and Christine Pierce. *The Environmental Ethics and Policy Book.* Belmont, Calif.: Wadsworth, 1998.

SEE ALSO: Choice; Economic analysis; Free-riding; Future-oriented ethics; Health care allocation; Incommensurability; Medical insurance; Outsourcing; Pollution permits; Utilitarianism.

Courage

DEFINITION: Mental or moral strength to stand firm in the face of difficulty or danger
TYPE OF ETHICS: Personal and social ethics
SIGNIFICANCE: Courage is one of the cardinal virtues, a trait indicative of strong moral character.

Courage, along with prudence, justice, and temperance, is one of the four cardinal virtues (states of character) of ancient Greek moral philosophy. Some authors and translators call it "fortitude" or "bravery."

In book 4 of his *Republic* (c. 390 B.C.E.), Plato describes what he believes would be the ideal city-state. It would include courageous soldiers who would go to war on its behalf. These soldiers would be taught what to fear and what not to fear. Furthermore, they would be trained to act in accordance with this knowledge when on the battlefield. Plato compares the courageous soldier to fabric that is dyed in such a manner that it retains its color when it is washed. The courageous soldier's "dye" must withstand the "lye" of pleasure, fear, and pain.

Plato's student Aristotle discusses the virtue of courage in book 3 of his *Nicomachean Ethics* (c. 330 B.C.E.). For Aristotle, many of the virtues are states of character that fall between opposing vices. Courage is a virtuous mean between the vicious extremes of cowardice on one side and rashness and excessive fearlessness on the other. The courageous person stands firm in the face of what is frightening. Although many things are frightening, courageous persons distinguish themselves most clearly from those who lack the virtue of courage by standing firm in the face of death, and it is in standing firm and fighting with confidence in the face of death on the battlefield that the virtue of courage is exercised to the fullest degree.

Aristotle's account of courage is more complicated than are his accounts of many other virtues, because it is a mean of two feelings: fear and confidence. Of the two, fear is the more important. The coward, who is both excessively fearful and deficiently confident, is distinguished most clearly by excessive fear of frightening things and fear of things that should not be frightening at all. There is no name (or was not in the Greek of Aristotle's day) for persons who have too little fear, because they are so rare. They are, he says, like madmen. Persons who are excessively confident about frightening things are rash, and they sometimes prove themselves to be cowards. Genuinely courageous persons do not seek danger. Rash persons, in attempting to imitate the courageous, wish for dangers but often retreat when they arrive.

While many of the Aristotelian virtues are means between extremes, they are not necessarily midpoints. Courage lies closer to excessive fearlessness and rashness than to cowardice. In other words, cowardice is the vice that is most directly opposed to the virtue of courage.

Aristotle identifies five states of character that are distinct from genuine courage but are often called "courage." The "courage" of the citizen-soldier is really desire for praise and honor, combined with fear of reproaches and legal penalties. Also included in this category are citizen-soldiers who stand firm and fight only because they are less afraid of their enemy than of their own officers. Experienced soldiers sometimes appear to be courageous when, in fact, they are standing firm only because their experience tells them they are not in great danger. When they learn that they actually are in great danger, they turn and run. Emotion is sometimes called "courage" but is not genuine courage. For Aristotle, persons act virtuously only when their rational faculties govern their emotions. Courageous soldiers fight with passion, but not all passionate soldiers are courageous. In addition, those soldiers who are optimistic only because they have been victorious many times in the past are not courageous. When they learn that their lives are in danger, they are no longer confident. Finally, soldiers who give the appearance of courage only because they are ignorant of their situation do not possess the virtue of courage.

Among the most significant developments in the history of courage between Aristotle's day and the twenty-first century is that in the medieval synthesis of the classical and Christian traditions, while courage was still understood to be chiefly about death on the battlefield, martyrdom also came to be understood as an act of courage. Josef Pieper's *The Four Cardinal Virtues: Prudence, Justice, Fortitude, Temperance* (1965) provides a concise introduction to courage in the Christian tradition.

In early twenty-first century ethics, justice receives far more emphasis than do the other cardinal virtues. One area in which this imbalance of emphasis is most striking is that of the ethics of war and peace. Many writers address the questions of whether there can be just wars and, if so, what criteria should be used to distinguish just from unjust wars. Relatively little, however, is written about the courage of soldiers fighting in just wars. There is far more interest in the ethics of killing than in the ethics of dying.

David Lutz

FURTHER READING

Aristotle. *Nicomachean Ethics*. Translated and edited by Roger Crisp. New York: Cambridge University Press, 2000.

Darling-Smith, Barbara, ed. *Courage*. Notre Dame, Ind.: University of Notre Dame Press, 2002

Miller, William Ian. *The Mystery of Courage*. Cambridge, Mass.: Harvard University Press, 2000.

Nisters, Thomas. *Aristotle on Courage*. New York: Peter Lang, 2000.

Pieper, Josef. *The Four Cardinal Virtues: Prudence, Justice, Fortitude, Temperance*. Translated by Richard Winston, Clara Winston, et al. Notre Dame, Ind.: University of Notre Dame Press, 1966.

Plato. *"Laches" and "Charmides."* Translated by Rosamond Kent Sprague. Indianapolis: Hacket, 1992.

_____. *The Republic*. Translated by Desmond Lee. 2d ed. New York: Penguin Books, 2003.

Pybus, Elizabeth. *Human Goodness: Generosity and Courage*. London: Harvester Wheatsheaf, 1991.

Rachman, S. J. *Fear and Courage*. 2d ed. New York: W. H. Freeman, 1990.

Tillich, Paul. *The Courage to Be*. 2d ed. Introduction by Peter J. Gomes. New Haven, Conn.: Yale University Press, 2000.

Walton, Douglas N. *Courage: A Philosophical Investigation*. Berkeley: University of California Press, 1986.

SEE ALSO: Aristotelian ethics; Character; Heroism; Military ethics; *Nicomachean Ethics*; Platonic ethics; *Republic*; Socrates; Virtue ethics.

Covert action

DEFINITION: Gathering of proprietary information or the taking of physical action by clandestine means

TYPE OF ETHICS: Politico-economic ethics

SIGNIFICANCE: Covert actions are generally secret not merely from their target but also from most members of the corporation or government undertaking them. This raises important ethical concerns involving the limits of political or business leaders' rights to undertake actions in the name of their constituents without the knowledge or consent of those constituents.

In democratic, free, and open societies, the use of clandestine methods to achieve political, military, or industrial gains is the focus of argument. The argument is based on the question of whether it is moral and ethical to spy and engage in clandestine operations for the safety of the nation and its way of life or to obtain commercial advantage over a competitor. If it is decided to use secretive methods, what lengths and means are justified in pursuing particular goals? To what extent must the public be informed regarding the success or failure of the actions taken?

In totalitarian states, the morality of the governing power is the morality of the dictator or ruling group. In such states, the use of covert action is dictated by the goals and agenda of a single person or a small group of empowered individuals, without the consent or knowledge of the citizenry. In a democracy, a consensus is usually formed through elections, and national agendas reflect the morality and ethics of the majority of the population. As a result, government, military, and law-enforcement agencies must not violate the morality of the citizens, as understood by their elected representatives, in the pursuit of goals or information. This is an idealistic view. The perceived morality of a nation's people may vary greatly, depending on the extent of the governing mandate and the judgment of those who interpret the prevailing moral trends, and these trends may quickly shift direction depending on the public's views of and responses to perceived national threats, outrages, and insults, or to changes in elected officials.

In the case of industrial covert actions, the morality and ethics of engaging in secretive methods in business are clearly linked to financial gain and competitive survivability, and as in totalitarian governments, the decision to use covert methods reflects the ethics and morality of corporate leaders. Most industrial covert action involves theft or sabotage. Government-sanctioned covert action is more complicated.

DANGERS OF COVERT ACTION

Societies of all types are most vulnerable to threats that are held in secret from them. For this reason, it is vital to be able to detect, identify, evaluate, and react to secret threats. To this end intelligence-gathering agencies exist. Collected intelligence data can be assessed to determine whether and how secret threats should be met, preferably by overt means if feasible, but when necessary and appropriate, by covert action. Covert actions are usually undertaken by one government to influence the affairs or policies of other nations by secret and unattributable means. The rationale for such actions is dictated by national interest, and national interest is defined by the moral and ethical values of totalitarian leaders or by a majority of a democratic nation's population.

It is important to remember that when a democratic government takes covert action in the national interest, it does so under the umbrella of public consent. In either instance, covert actions are intended, at least in concept, to support broader national policy goals and to advance national interests. To this effect, covert actions are methods that support a nation's foreign policies and intent and that provide options located somewhere between diplomacy and military force. Whether in a totalitarian state or a free society, covert actions are ultimately "official" government-sponsored activities, despite being planned and conducted in a manner that hides or disguises their official sanctioning.

NATIONS AND COVERT ACTION

Covert actions are not a modern phenomenon. They have existed as long as groups of people have found points of disagreement and wish to influence the actions of others in a manner more favorable to themselves. As a result, the ethics of covert actions are reflective of the society that initiates them. If a nation can justify covert actions as a means to ensure its security or to further its national interests, or if a corporation can justify covert actions to ensure its commercial viability, then there is little posed in the way of a moral or ethical dilemma. When covert actions take place, they express the goals adopted by a nation and the values excepted, or tolerated, by its society. Covert actions reflect national behavior in the same manner as do other external actions, such as trade agreements, foreign aid, and military posturing. Because of their clandestine nature and their danger for those directly involved, covert actions are hidden from direct public knowledge and involvement.

In many societies in which an open flow of information on government activities is available for public scrutiny, however, certain elements of society often express open disagreement over principles and beliefs that are related to both the ends and the means of their government's covert activities. Some democratic nations go so far as to define "covert actions" legislatively, in effect defining, or attempting to define, their national attitude toward the ethics of clandestine operations. In any case, the role and the extent of covert actions used as an instrument of a society's governmental or industrial policies reflect the ethics and morals of that society.

Randall L. Milstein

FURTHER READING

Ameringer, Charles D. *U.S. Foreign Intelligence: The Secret Side of American History.* Lexington, Mass.: Lexington Books, 1990.

Blackstock, Paul W. *The Strategy of Subversion: Manipulating the Politics of Other Nations.* Chicago: Quadrangle Books, 1964.

Carter, John J. *Covert Operations and the Emergence of the Modern American Presidency, 1920-1960.* Lewiston, N.Y.: Edwin Mellen Press, 2002.

Dobson, Christopher, and Ronald Payne. *The Dictionary of Espionage.* London: Harrap, 1984.

Johnson, Loch K. *America's Secret Power: The CIA in a Democratic Society.* New York: Oxford University Press, 1989.

Kurland, Michael. *The Spymaster's Handbook.* New York: Facts On File, 1988.

Nutter, John Jacob. *The CIA's Black Ops: Covert Action, Foreign Policy, and Democracy.* Amherst, N.Y.: Prometheus Books, 2000.

Oseth, John M. *Regulating U.S. Intelligence Operations: A Study in Definition of the National Interest.* Lexington: University Press of Kentucky, 1985.

SEE ALSO: Assassination; Corporate responsibility; Democracy; Dictatorship; Electronic surveillance; Espionage; International Monetary Fund.

Criminal punishment

DEFINITION: Unpleasant consequence, such as a fine, imprisonment, or death, that a state imposes on an individual for violation of a legal rule

TYPE OF ETHICS: Legal and judicial ethics

SIGNIFICANCE: Moral philosophy has traditionally been closely concerned with the justifications and purposes of criminal punishment in general, as well as the principles for determining which punishments are appropriate for particular crimes.

Each society is ordered through various laws, which represent that society's understanding of what is important for the general welfare and what is right and wrong. When laws are violated, the society must take measures to minimize the violations in order to preserve itself and its values. This minimization is usually achieved by means of punishment.

Early human societies often viewed crimes as offenses against deities or ancestral spirits. They believed that the community would experience adversity if the violators were not punished. Death was a widely used form of punishment. One of the oldest codes of laws in existence, the Code of Hammurabi (Babylonia, c. 1700 B.C.E.), prescribed death for about thirty different offenses, including incest, swearing, casting a spell, burglary, and (for women) drinking in public.

JUSTIFICATIONS FOR CRIMINAL PUNISHMENT

Some people argue that punishment promotes social solidarity by reinforcing foundational social values, while others argue that punishment is usually imposed by the ruling economic and political class on the lower class to maintain the status quo. Still others reject punishment entirely, arguing that crime is a disease and should not be treated by inflicting pain upon criminals.

Attempts to address the issue of the moral justification of punishment have mainly fallen into two broadly opposed groups: utilitarian and retributive theories of punishment. The retributivist stresses guilt and desert, looking back to the crime to justify punishment. The basic characteristic of the utilitarian theory of punishment is that it is oriented toward the future, insisting that punishment can be justified only if it has beneficial consequences that outweigh the intrinsic evil of inflicting suffering. Retributivism holds that the justification for punishment is found in the fact that a rule has been broken—punishment is properly inflicted because, and only because, a person deserves it. The offender's desert, and not the beneficial consequences of punishment, is what justifies punishment. This is the "eye-for-an-eye" view, according to which a wrongdoer deserves to be punished in proportion to his or her crime.

The history of retributive punishment, which begins with biblical and Talmudic ethical and legal ideas, has been the most prevalent form of punishment. The most important and influential classical retributivist is Immanuel Kant. The classical form of retributivism holds not only that the guilty should be punished but also that there is a duty to punish the guilty. In knowingly breaking the law, the criminal declares, for example, that he or she has a license to steal, thus putting those who respect property rights at a disadvantage. The criminal weakens the fabric of justice and must be punished to vindicate justice. Failure to punish not only condones the wrongful act but also is unfair to those who practice self-restraint and respect the rights of others. Thus, punishment is imposed for the sake of justice.

Retributivists hold that wrongful acts and harms can be ranked in order of their moral gravity and that the proper amount of punishment is proportionate to the moral gravity of the offense. In its most complete form, the retributive theory of punishment contains the following tenets: The moral right to punish is based solely on the offense committed; the moral duty to punish is grounded solely on the offense committed; punishment should be proportionate to the offense; punishment annuls the offense; and punishment is a right of the offender.

In September, 1971, the bloodiest prison revolt in U.S. history occurred at New York's maximum security prison at Attica, where twelve hundred inmates rose up to protest the facility's harsh conditions by taking hostage thirty-nine guards and civilian employees. After forty-three lives were lost in the brutal suppression of the uprising, a need for prison reform throughout the United States was widely recognized. (AP/Wide World Photos)

UTILITARIAN THEORY

The utilitarian theory of punishment also has had a long history, beginning with Plato (c. 428-348 B.C.E.) The most comprehensive formulation of the theory is found in the writings of Jeremy Bentham. The utilitarian theory justifies punishment solely in terms of the good consequences that it produces. For a punishment to be justified, it should have at least some of the following good effects. First, the punishment should act as a deterrent to crime. It should sway the offender not to commit similar offenses in the future and serve as an example to potential offenders. Second, the punishment should be a means of reforming or rehabilitating the offender. The offender is reformed in the sense that the effect of the punishment is to change the offender's values so that he or she will not commit similar offenses in the future because he or she believes them to be wrong. A third good consequence should be the incapacitative effect of the punishment. When an offender is in prison, he or she is out of the general social circulation and thus does not have the opportunity to commit offenses. Finally, the punishment should act as a means of moral education in the community. It should demonstrate the moral wrongness and unacceptability of an offense and strengthen moral beliefs that curb criminal inclinations.

The utilitarian theory of punishment can be summarized in the following propositions: Social utility is a necessary condition for justified punishment; social utility is a sufficient condition for justified punishment; and the proper amount of punishment is that amount that will do the most good or the least harm to those who are affected by it.

Attempts have been made to mix the utilitarian and retributive theories in order to combine the positive elements of each. One such attempt maintains that the aim of punishment is to prevent or reduce crime, a utilitarian idea, but insists that only those who have voluntarily broken the law be punished and that the punishment be proportionate to the offense, which are retributive ideas.

Cheri Vail Fisk

FURTHER READING

Baird, Robert M., and Stuart E. Rosenbaum, eds. *Philosophy of Punishment.* Buffalo, N.Y.: Prometheus Books, 1988.

Coyle, Andrew, Allison Campbell, and Rodney Neufeld, eds. *Capitalist Punishment: Prison Privatization and Human Rights.* Atlanta: Clarity Press, 2003.

Foucault, Michel. *Discipline and Punish: The Birth of the Prison.* Translated by Alan Sheridan. New York: Vintage Books, 1979.

Moberly, Walter. *The Ethics of Punishment.* Hamden, Conn.: Archon Books, 1968.

Murphy, Jeffrie G., ed. *Punishment and Rehabilitation.* 2d ed. Belmont, Calif.: Wadsworth, 1985.

Norrie, Alan. *Punishment, Responsibility, and Justice: A Relational Critique.* New York: Oxford University Press, 2000.

Primoratz, Igor. *Justifying Legal Punishment.* Atlantic Highlands, N.J.: Humanities Press, 1989.

Ten, C. L. *Crime, Guilt, and Punishment: A Philosophical Introduction.* New York: Oxford University Press, 1987.

SEE ALSO: Bentham, Jeremy; Capital punishment; Consequentialism; Foucault, Michel; Hammurabi's code; Kantian ethics; Moral responsibility; Nietzsche, Friedrich; Parole of convicted prisoners; Punishment.

Critical theory

DEFINITION: Fundamentally interdisciplinary approach to the study and critique of culture and society

TYPE OF ETHICS: Theory of ethics

SIGNIFICANCE: Although the various practitioners of critical theory hold radically different beliefs on almost every subject, most of them would agree that there is a primary ethical imperative to understand one's own culture, the power structures operative within that culture, and one's relationship to those structures.

"Critical theory" is an umbrella term that is used to define a range of social theories that surfaced in the nineteenth century and continued through the latter part of the twentieth century. A critical theory is characterized by strong opposition to the traditions of all disciplines. These traditions have existed for the purpose of articulating and advancing "timeless" truths, "objective" facts, singular interpretations of texts, and so on. A critical theory posits that these universal truths, objective facts, and singular interpretations in all disciplines lack any sort of philosophical or theoretical grounding that could not be effectively challenged, and that to present them as if they are objective is a politically destructive act.

Theories are usually removed from political practice, interpreting the world rather than prescribing a solution to whatever ills are discovered. Critical theory differentiates itself from other theories on this point; it has a very different view of the relationship between theory and practice. Striving to do more than define how society is unfair, critical theory attempts to turn the status quo upside down and offer a solution. This connection between social theory and political practice is critical theory's distinguishing characteristic.

Those who espouse critical theory believe that the traditional disciplines must attempt to change the world in a way that gives those who have been "marginalized," or placed on the fringes of society, the insights and intellectual understanding they need in order to empower and eventually free themselves. In his book *Critical Theory in Political Practice*, Stephen T. Leonard articulates three criteria that must be met if critical theory is to bring about self-emancipation. A critical theory must first of all provide a coherent explanation of how the self-conceptions of the marginalized are largely responsible for the reality of the situations of those people. Second, critical theory must provide a completely different perspective of social relations that the oppressed can adopt for their own vision. The third criterion is that the first two actions will be successful only if critical theory manifests a sufficiently deep understanding of itself that in the end, it can translate its theory into a language that is comprehensible to the very people it wants to empower.

JUDGING CRITICAL THEORY

Unlike other theories, critical theory is not judged simply by its ability to give an account of the world; instead, it is judged by its ability to show the oppressed how their institutionalized beliefs and conceptions of themselves help sustain their marginalization. Critical theory is successful when the oppressed act in their own interest to free themselves from their dependence upon the mainstream.

There have been several influential attempts at developing a critical theory, the first of which was the work of Karl Marx. Marx argued from a philosophical perspective that the point is to change the world, not simply to interpret it, and because of this view, Marx is considered by many to be the founding father of critical theory. Marxism has presented many prob-

lems in the twentieth century, however, so even though Marx has had a tremendous influence upon defining critical theory, critical theory has not easily identified with Marx. His critique of nineteenth century capitalism has been difficult to apply to the capitalism of the twentieth century. Consequently, Marxist theorists have reinterpreted his theory, and those reinterpretations have been even more problematic. The most widely known of these interpretations has been orthodox Marxism, which has been used to support authoritarian regimes.

Other theorists have attempted to learn from the mistakes of the orthodox Marxists and have chosen to concentrate on the antiauthoritarian elements of Marx's theory. The most influential of these has been the Frankfurt School, which includes Max Horkheimer, Theodore Adorno, and Herbert Marcuse, as well as Jürgen Habermas. The Frankfurt School was interested in Marxism's insights but wanted to use them in a way that would be relevant to the twentieth century, without falling into a dogmatic theory of authoritarian social structures and political institutions.

"Western" Marxism, the Frankfurt School's theory, agrees with Marx that it is possible for modern society to overcome oppressive domination. It disagrees with both Marx and traditional Marxists, however, regarding the traditional Marxist theory that overcoming this domination can only be achieved through a revolution by the working class.

Marx, the Frankfurt School, and Jürgen Habermas are considered part of the modernist movement of critical theory, of which Western Marxism has been the most influential element thus far. Modernist theorists are characterized by their belief that the current forms of thought and action in society are neither critical nor reflective. They believe that critical theory is possible only if serious critical thought can be recaptured, which they believe is entirely possible.

Modernist critical theory has been followed by "postmodernist" critical theory. Most influential postmodernist thinkers have been French, and the historian Michel Foucault has been the most prominent postmodernist. Postmodernist critical theory shares with modernist critical theory a commitment to a social theory that is politically engaged and is opposed to domination as a political solution. Both schools of thought have been opposed to orthodox Marxism. What is distinctly different between the two is the postmodernist assertion that the recovery of critical reason in the modern world is not possible; therefore, emancipation cannot be achieved through the recovery of critical reason. Foucault argues that the recovery of reason is impossible because of the limitations of language.

Modernist and postmodernist theory have had an enormous influence in shaping critical theory. United on many fronts, these schools of thought have established good reasons for the necessity of a theory that incorporates both social and political theory. Much of the discourse between the two in the latter part of the twentieth century, however, has centered on their essential difference—the question of whether modern society holds the possibility of reason and critical thought—and little of it has concentrated upon articulating the theory to the oppressed for their empowerment.

Jill S. Marts

FURTHER READING

Dewey, John. *Outlines of a Critical Theory of Ethics.* Westport, Conn.: Greenwood Press, 1969.

Eagleton, Terry. *Literary Theory: An Introduction.* 2d ed. Minneapolis: University of Minnesota Press, 1996.

Leonard, Stephen T. *Critical Theory in Political Practice.* Princeton, N.J.: Princeton University Press, 1990.

MacKenzie, Ian, and Shane O'Neill, eds. *Reconstituting Social Criticism: Political Morality in an Age of Scepticism.* New York: St. Martin's Press, 1999.

Merod, Jim. *The Political Responsibility of the Critic.* Ithaca, N.Y.: Cornell University Press, 1987.

Nealon, Jeffrey T., and Caren Irr, eds. *Rethinking the Frankfurt School: Alternative Legacies of Cultural Critique.* Albany: State University of New York Press, 2002.

Norris, Christopher. *Uncritical Theory: Postmodernism, Intellectuals, and the Gulf War.* London: Lawrence & Wishart, 1992.

SEE ALSO: Deconstruction; Derrida, Jacques; Foucault, Michel; Freud, Sigmund; Marx, Karl; Marxism; Postmodernism; Theory and practice.

Cruelty

DEFINITION: Intentional, malicious infliction of physical and/or psychological injury on another person or animal

TYPE OF ETHICS: Personal and social ethics

SIGNIFICANCE: Cruelty is often taken to be the greatest moral transgression: Those crimes committed out of cruelty are usually deemed the most evil and the least forgivable.

Although cruelty has existed at virtually all stages of civilization, philosophical interest in cruelty began in the nineteenth century. Earlier thinkers usually considered cruelty within the context of another concern. Niccolò Machiavelli, in *The Prince*, advocates the quick, expeditious use of cruelty by a prince to maintain unity, loyalty, and order in his state, since criminal behavior is encouraged when a ruler is too merciful to his subjects. Judicious cruelty creates fear, and if a prince cannot be both loved and feared, it is better to be feared than to be loved.

French essayist Michel de Montaigne condemns cruelty as being so repulsive that he approves of nothing harsher for criminals than quick execution, believing that anything "beyond plain death" is pointlessly wanton. He also condemns cruelty to animals, with whom humans share mutual obligations.

Although he is remembered more for his depravity than for his contribution to historiography and literature, the Marquis de Sade is an important figure in the history and literature of cruelty. Sade provides, through his life and writing, extensive depictions of physical and mental cruelty as a prelude to sexual gratification. His justification of sexual cruelty is rooted in his belief that natural sexual pleasure is always preceded by an erotic desire to suffer and inflict pain, behavior that should not be censured, since it is the fulfillment of natural human instinct.

PHILOSOPHICAL CONSIDERATIONS OF CRUELTY

The earliest philosophical interest in cruelty is shown by Arthur Schopenhauer. Schopenhauer abhors cruelty, also censuring the insensitive treatment of animals, which stems from the erroneous belief that they cannot suffer. He sees in Christianity the root of this insensitivity because of the Christian emphasis on the unique and exclusive value of human life. In Asian cultures, animals are better treated and more highly valued. Human cruelty springs from the suffering of the individual will in its struggle to satisfy its desires. A frustrated individual who believes that his own suffering is greater than that of others becomes envious. When envy and frustration become so great that the individual delights in the infliction of suffering, the individual has crossed the threshold from the moral frailty natural in everyone to a fiendish, diabolical cruelty. The only preventative for such deeply depraved acts is an equally deep compassion.

Friedrich Nietzsche considers human cruelty from both a historical and a philosophical perspective. In *On the Genealogy of Morals*, he recognizes its powerful influence on human culture, attributing to cruelty a central role in the generation of historical memory: "Man could never do without blood, torture, and sacrifices when he felt the need to create a memory for himself; . . . all this has its origin in the instinct that realized that pain is the most powerful aid to mnemonics."

Modern moral concepts are rooted in ancient legal obligations, in which justice was obtained through violent personal revenge as compensation for an injury—creditors having the right to "inflict every kind of torture and indignity upon the body of the debtor . . . as much as seemed commensurate with the debt." As communities become confident of their power, however, they become lenient toward those who injure them, there being a direct relationship between strength and humaneness, just as there is between vulnerability and the capacity for cruelty. In Nietzsche's view, in a strong, confident community, as in a strong, confident individual, cruelty evolves into mercy. The fact that cruelty provided pleasure for "more primitive men" explains the prevalence of violent atrocity, a feature of its past that modern humanity hypocritically denies. The tragedy of modern humanity, however, is that it has replaced primitive, blood-seeking cruelty toward transgressors with "psychical cruelty" against itself: it has abased itself before God, in whose eyes it deserves only punishment for its unworthiness.

The philosophical interest in cruelty that was initiated by Schopenhauer and Nietzsche has been maintained by American philosopher Philip Hallie, who gives it deliberate, intense philosophical attention. Hallie distinguishes "episodic cruelty" (unrelated, occasional acts of cruelty) from "institutionalized cruelty," which consists of using the fundamental institutions of society—government, education, and so forth—to execute and perpetuate both blatant and subtle acts of cruelty. He identifies the imbalance of power as a defining feature of cruelty and searches for its opposite, which he initially determines to be freedom. Freedom must be consummated by "hospitality," however, meaning the carrying out of a positive ethic of beneficence, often at significant risk to the benefactor, in addition to negative injunctions against doing harm.

Hallie contrasts the Nazi Holocaust with the quiet, heroic goodness of the villagers of Le Chambon-sur-Lignon in southern France, whose goodness resulted in the saving of thousands of Jewish refugees during the Occupation, despite grave danger to themselves. Throughout Hallie's treatment of cruelty runs an exhortation against forgetting the presence and identity of the victim in every act of cruelty, an oversight that resulted in the systematic inhumanity of the Holocaust; it was the recognition of the victims that produced the "riskful, strenuous nobility" of the Chambonnais.

Barbara Forrest

FURTHER READING

Baraz, Daniel. *Medieval Cruelty: Changing Perceptions, Late Antiquity to the Early Modern Period.* Ithaca, N.Y.: Cornell University Press, 2003.

Foucault, Michel. *Discipline and Punish: The Birth of the Prison.* Translated by Alan Sheridan. New York: Vintage Books, 1979.

Hallie, Philip. *Cruelty.* Rev. ed. Middletown, Conn.: Wesleyan University Press, 1982.

Hood, Stuart, and Graham Crowley. *Introducing the Marquis de Sade.* New York: Totem Books, 1999.

Machiavelli, Niccolò. *The Prince.* Edited and translated by Angelo M. Codevilla. New Haven, Conn.: Yale University Press, 1997.

Miller, James. "Carnivals of Atrocity: Foucault, Nietzsche, Cruelty." *Political Theory* 18 (August, 1990): 470-491.

Montaigne, Michel de. "Of Cruelty." Translated by Donald M. Frame. In *The Complete Works: Essays, Travel Journal, Letters.* New York: Alfred A. Knopf, 2003.

Nietzsche, Friedrich. *On the Genealogy of Morals.* Edited and translated by Walter Kaufmann. New York: Vintage Books, 1967.

Schopenhauer, Arthur. *On the Basis of Morality.*

Translated by E. F. J. Payne. Providence, R.I.: Berghahn Books, 1995.

_____. *The World as Will and Representation.* Translated by E. F. J. Payne. 2 vols. 1958. Reprint. New York: Dover, 1969.

SEE ALSO: *Being and Nothingness*; Cruelty to animals; Hate; Nietzsche, Friedrich; Rape; Schopenhauer, Arthur; Torture; Violence; Wickedness.

Cruelty to animals

DEFINITION: Intentional or wanton infliction of suffering upon living creatures, or indifference to their suffering

TYPE OF ETHICS: Animal rights

SIGNIFICANCE: To take pleasure in the suffering of animals is considered immoral by most world religions and ethical philosophies.

The keenly perceptive twentieth century dramatist George Bernard Shaw observed that when a man kills a lion he is praised as being a sportsman, while when a lion kills a man he is condemned as vicious. Mohandas K. Gandhi, the charismatic moral and spiritual leader, once lamented that the terrible thing about the British was not only that they did terrible things to his people but also that they were not even aware of it.

It is often the case that humans are cruel to animals without being aware they are. It has been widely accepted, as was maintained by British philosopher John Locke, that feeling pleasure in the suffering of others is the main ingredient in cruelty, but there are some who feel nothing. Thus, Tom Regan, animal rights philosopher, distinguishes between what he calls *sadistic cruelty*, which occurs when people *enjoy* causing suffering, and *brutal cruelty*, which involves *indifference* to suffering.

René Descartes, the father of modern philosophy, was so indifferent to cruelty to animals that he in-

A volunteer at an Arkansas Humane Society center walks an injured dog that was brought to the center for help. (AP/Wide World Photos)

sisted that because animals do not reason, they cannot even feel pain. This meant that one could torture animals and still not be considered cruel. Indeed, as recently as the mid-nineteenth century, it was common for horses to be beaten to death in Great Britain. Cattle, sheep, and pigs were slowly bled to death, and there was no moral outcry against such cruelty.

PREVENTIVE LEGISLATION

The first time any legal effort was made to address the problem of cruelty to animals was 1800, when a bill was sponsored in Britain to outlaw bullfighting. Even so small an effort as that, however, was ridiculed by the *Times* of London. Finally, after years of indifference, in 1822 Parliament passed an act outlawing cruel treatment to cattle.

Against a historical background of ethical indifference toward animals, in the eighteenth and nineteenth centuries some Christian leaders and free thinkers took a stand against cruelty to animals. The philosopher Lord Shaftesbury (Anthony Ashley Cooper) condemned the act of taking pleasure in the suffering of animals, calling it unnatural. A protest group known as the Clapham Sect denounced bullfighting as barbarous. Queen Victoria herself believed that there was something wrong with a civilization that would condone cruelty to animals or deny charity and mercy for them.

In 1824 in England, the Society for the Prevention of Cruelty to Animals (SPCA) was founded. In 1832, there appeared a Christian declaration that cruelty to animals was against the Christian faith. The drive to oppose cruelty to animals and to seek ethical treatment for them was gaining momentum. In answer to the charge that there should be no ethical concern for creatures who cannot reason, the nineteenth century British philosopher Jeremy Bentham declared that the question is not whether animals can reason or talk, but whether they can suffer.

As ethical concern for animals expanded, the very definition of cruelty to them also had to be expanded. Thus, Andrew Linzey, a distinguished theologian and advocate of animal rights, enlarged the concept of cruelty to make it identical with wantonness, meaning any act that is not morally justifiable. In such terms, cruelty regardless of intention would include the use of animals for sport, recreation, pleasure, and entertainment, as well as negligence and lack of care toward them. Linzey ethically condemns

Indications That Animals Are Being Treated Cruelly

- untreated tick or flea infestations
- body wounds
- patches of missing hair
- extreme thinness—a sign of starvation
- limping
- persons in the act of striking or otherwise physically abusing animals
- dogs that are frequently left alone without food or water, often chained up in yards
- dogs that are kept outside without shelters in extreme weather conditions
- animals that cower in fear or behave aggressively when approached by their owners

Source: American Society for the Prevention of Cruelty to Animals (http://www.aspca.org/site).

as cruel "hunting," bull or cock fighting, and the use of performing animals in films, television, or the circus. For Linzey, both animals and humans are God's creations, and thus to be cruel to any of them is to offend God.

PHILOSOPHICAL CONCERNS

As philosophers came to believe that cruelty to animals was unethical, they also came to see that it was not possible to isolate cruelty to animals from cruelty to humans. The great eighteenth century Prussian philosopher Immanuel Kant observed that if people were indifferent to cruelty to animals, that would desensitize them, and they would become indifferent to cruelty to humans. The celebrated playwright George Bernard Shaw insisted that it would be impossible to be cruel to animals without damaging one's own character.

The famous medieval Roman Catholic philosopher Saint Thomas Aquinas maintained that it is not that cruelty could dehumanize people but that it necessarily does. Thus, Andrew Linzey stated that cruelty to animals leads to moral meanness of life. C. S. Lewis, the celebrated twentieth century novelist and theologian, used the argument that if people can justify cruelty on the grounds of a difference in species, they can justify it on racial grounds, or on the grounds of advanced people against backward people, and the culmination of this kind of thinking is the behavior of the Nazis during World War II.

Following the lead of Britain in opposing cruelty to animals, in 1866 the American Society for the Prevention of Cruelty to Animals (ASPCA) was founded, and in the twentieth century many humane organizations have been formed that do not merely oppose cruelty to animals but also aggressively promote a general program of animal rights.

T. E. Katen

FURTHER READING

Linzey, Andrew. *Christianity and the Rights of Animals.* New York: Crossroad, 1987.

Regan, Tom, and Peter Singer, eds. *Animal Rights and Human Obligations.* 2d ed. Englewood Cliffs, N.J.: Prentice-Hall, 1989.

Ruesch, Hans. *Slaughter of the Innocent.* New York: Civitas, 1983.

Sharpe, Robert. *The Cruel Deception.* Wellingborough, England: Thorsons, 1988.

Singer, Peter. *Animal Liberation.* New York: Ecco, 2002.

Spiegel, Marjorie. *The Dreaded Comparison.* Philadelphia: New Society, 1988.

SEE ALSO: Animal consciousness; Animal research; Animal rights; Cruelty; Dominion over nature, human; Humane Society of the United States; People for the Ethical Treatment of Animals; Sentience; Singer, Peter; Society for the Prevention of Cruelty to Animals.

Custom

DEFINITION: Practices and beliefs common to a particular region or class of people

TYPE OF ETHICS: Beliefs and practices

SIGNIFICANCE: If ethical views are formed in significant part by local custom, then the quest for universal ethical principles may be unsuccessful.

At the highest level of generality, perhaps every human culture subscribes to the same ethical rule: Do good and avoid evil. At lower levels of generality, however, ethical rules vary widely from one culture to another, and definitions of what constitute good and evil are not uniform among different cultures. Whether something is good is a question that is influenced or determined by the customs of the culture in which the issue arises. For example, in some cultures custom dictates that no work be done on the Sabbath day. In some cultures custom dictates that men should work out of their homes, and women should work within their homes. Many cultures have taboos on what people may eat, but these taboos differ widely among cultures.

Ethical rules or propositions can be thought of as either universal or parochial. A universal ethical rule is one that is valid and applicable in all cultures, among all humankind. Such rules are ordinarily associated with natural law. Just as the laws of physics are true everywhere on Earth, certain ethical laws, according to proponents of natural law, are valid in all human cultures. An example would be universal proscriptions on killing one's parents.

In contrast, parochial rules depend on the customs of a given culture. Because customs vary, parochial ethical rules vary as well. Thus, parochial ethical rules are present in some, but not all, human cultures. As an empirical proposition, parochial rules are far more common than universal ones. Tax rates vary, as do the definitions of crimes such as murder and rape. Indeed, over the course of human history, ethical norms have varied dramatically, whereas the laws of physics have not. The second law of thermodynamics, for example, has always been valid, yet slavery, which has come to be regarded as unethical in most of the world, was widely accepted for centuries as an ethical practice.

Even at a given moment in history, rules vary significantly among cultures. Certain cultures, for example, regard capital punishment as unethical and therefore forbid it, while other cultures put many people to death.

Similarly, most industrialized cultures forbid polygamous marriages, whereas most cultures in the nonindustrialized world permit them. In certain cultures, abortion is categorically forbidden; in others, it is freely available.

The fact that ethical outlooks vary from one culture to another, not only over time but also at any given time, suggests either that proponents of natural law are mistaken and that there are few universal moral rules, or that ethicists have not succeeded in identifying specific ethical rules that are universal.

Classical proponents of natural law were confident that universal ethical principles existed. The Roman statesman Cicero observed that true law in Rome is the same as true law in Athens. Cicero was confident that jurists would discover and articulate eternal ethical laws that would be valid at all times and in all places. More than two millennia later, however, with such norms yet to be identified at a low enough level of generality to be useful as laws, even modern proponents of natural law acknowledge the role of custom in shaping ethical outlooks.

David R. Dow

FURTHER READING

Chow, Rey. *Ethics After Idealism: Theory-Culture-Ethnicity-Reading.* Bloomington: Indiana University Press, 1998.

Geertz, Clifford. *The Interpretation of Culture.* New York: Basic Books, 1973.

Inglis, Fred. *Clifford Geertz: Culture, Custom and Ethics.* Cambridge, England: Polity Press, 2000.

Leiser, Burton. *Custom, Law, and Morality.* Garden City, N.Y.: Anchor Books, 1969.

SEE ALSO: Anthropological ethics; Cicero; Genocide, cultural; Good, the; Infanticide; Marriage; Relativism; Rights and obligations; Taboos.

Cynicism

DEFINITION: Philosophical and ethical movement originating in ancient Greece

DATE: Developed between the fourth century B.C.E. and the sixth century C.E.

TYPE OF ETHICS: Classical history

SIGNIFICANCE: Cynicism denounced established convention and inhibition and advocated asceticism, self-sufficiency, intellectual freedom, virtuous action, and self-realization.

The movement that came to be known as Cynicism, the "dog philosophy," cannot be characterized by reference to a systematic philosophical doctrine or a rigorously organized school. Instead, it was formed by individual thinkers who embraced slightly varying sets of ethical tenets that were concerned primarily with practical ethics and who adopted ways of life that suited what they taught. Few members of the Cynic movement can be directly connected with their predecessors in terms of a master-pupil relationship. There is considerable chronological continuity of Cynics, however, who cover, in a fairly uninterrupted manner, a span of about ten centuries.

GREEK ORIGINS

The origins of Cynic ideas can be traced to the end of the fifth or the beginning of the fourth century B.C.E., to the doctrine of Antisthenes, who was one of the closest companions of Socrates. The archetypical figure of the Cynic, however, is Diogenes of Sinope, a contemporary of Aristotle, Demosthenes, and Alexander the Great. Diogenes was an influential thinker whose death in 323 B.C.E. marked the beginning of a period of development and popularity for the Cynic movement.

During the last decades of the fourth century and during the third century B.C.E., the Cynics Monimus of Syracuse, Onesicritus, Crates of Thebes and his wife Hipparchia, Metrocles of Maronea, Menippus of Gadara, Menedemus, Bion of Borysthenes, and Cercidas of Megalopolis extended the pure ethical core of the doctrine of Diogenes into domains such as literature and politics, making it known not only in Athens but also throughout the Hellenistic world. Cynicism lost its prominence during the next two centuries because of the growing influence of Epicureanism and Stoicism as well as the absence of charismatic Cynics.

The movement revived during the mid-first century C.E. in the form of an almost anarchist reaction to Roman leaders such as Caligula, Nero, and Vespasian. The influence of the Cynics of the Roman period reached its peak during the late first century and early second century with Dio Chrysostom and Favorinus. Other well-known figures were Demonax of Cyprus and Oenomaus of Gadara. The reputation of Cynicism suffered, however, as a result of the activities of various charlatans who carried the staff and knapsack and wore the cloak of the Cynics without bearing any resemblance to the Cynics. The satirist Lucian (second century) and the emperor Julian (fourth century) spoke of a noisy crowd that imitated the mannerisms of Diogenes and Crates but was ignorant of Cynic philosophy and was socially worthless.

PHILOSOPHICAL BASES

Although the various individual exponents of Cynicism adopted different tones in their teaching and stressed different things, there is a core of practical attitudes and ethical tenets that they all share.

A key notion of ancient Cynicism lies in the metaphor of devaluation—or, rather, defacing or falsifying—the currency of human standards. The Cynics set out to undermine and reverse all the values, practices, and institutions on which conventional society was based. This "falsifying of the coin" is necessitated by the fact that the pleasures, attachments, and obligations nurtured by conventional society are impediments to happiness. Society burdens humans with a set of artificial values and corrupts them by means of self-indulgence, ignorance, and confusion. It is an active source of unhappiness in that it gives rise to unsatisfied desires for physical goods and to irrational fears about the gods, the turns of fortune, malady, and death.

The Cynic's aim is to free people from the fetters of passion and convention, to make them observe the demands of nature and to guide them toward a natural life. In order to obtain this result, humans must, first, eradicate the desire and quest for pleasure, and, second, acquire both the physical and the mental strength to arm themselves against the difficulties that fortune may bring. This strength (*ischys*) can be obtained only by means of constant training (*askesis*) involving significant toil (*ponos*) of both body and mind. The Cynics consider toil as an instrumental good, since it leads to the realization of a double ideal: the reduction of one's needs and desires to a bare minimum comparable to the minimal needs of animals, leading to self-sufficiency (*autarkeia*) and the achievement of spiritual freedom, independence, and impassibility (*apatheia*), which are truly godlike.

In line with the Socratic tradition, the Cynics believed that virtue was sufficient for happiness, and they partly analyzed it in intellectual terms. To them, virtue is based on "unlearning what is bad" and on developing a rational account of the distinction between natural and conventional values; it can be taught, and it probably depends heavily upon memory. The Cynic conception of virtue deviates from Socraticism, however, in that it has strong anti-intellectualist traits: Knowledge is not sufficient for virtue but must be complemented by training and strength. The two kinds of *askesis* (hardening of the body and exercising of the mind) are complementary, and the *askesis* of the body can establish virtue in the soul.

The reversal of values affects the Cynic attitude toward religion and politics, two particularly conspicuous domains of ordinary activity. In religion, the Cynics denounced superstition in all forms, criticized the providentialist conception of the gods as well as any notion of divine interference in human affairs, and contrasted the intentions and practices of traditional believers with the pious behavior of morally pure men. Although the most important Cynics were not acknowledged atheists but only professed ignorance about the nature of the divine, their "falsification of the coin" in religious matters extended to the very roots of traditional religion. Their agnosticism was a springboard for attacks on both the content and the practices of Greco-Roman religion, and it left little room for an active belief in the existence of divinities. Their criticisms of traditional mythology should also be seen in the light of this radical defacement of religious values.

POLITICS

In politics, the Cynics were among the first philosophers to defy citizenship and its obligations in a coherent and radical way. The Cynic has no attachment to the vestiges of the city-state and expresses no regret for the fall of the *polis*. Instead, the Cynic takes pride in being without a city (*apolis*) and professes to be a citizen of the world (*kosmopolites*). The Cynic's cosmopolitanism entails ignoring all civic rules and obeying the only law that ought to be obeyed; namely, the natural law. Its ideal implementation in Diogenes' utopian *Republic* embarrassed Cynic sympathizers: Incest, cannibalism, the abolition of coinage and arms, the dissolution of the family, and a limitless sexual freedom are some of the implications of substituting natural law for the laws of society.

Cynic ethics is both individualistic and philanthropic. The individualistic features of the movement are found primarily in the image of the self-sufficient, self-fulfilled, self-controlled sage, a solitary man detached from society and free from its bonds, a wandering, homeless (*aoikos*) beggar, a dog barking at those who approach him. The Cynic is also, however, "the watchdog of humankind," showing by example and through his own actions what people should do to liberate themselves from the illusions and fears that make them miserable and leave them defenseless in an unpredictably changing world. His sharp tongue and shameless behavior are pedagogic strategies rather than exhibitionistic devices: They convey the radicalism of the Cynic reform by stressing the extent to which the adherents of the movement must violate the conventional codes of society in order to function as "the heralds of God."

Voula Tsouna McKirahan

FURTHER READING

Attridge, Harold W. *First-Century Cynicism in the Epistles of Heraclitus.* Missoula, Mont.: Scholars Press for the Harvard Theological Review, 1976.

Downing, Francis Gerald. *Christ and the Cynics: Jesus and Other Radical Preachers in First-Century Tradition.* Sheffield, England: JSOT, 1988.

Dudley, Donald Reynolds. *A History of Cynicism from Diogenes to the Sixth Century A.D.* 1937. Reprint. New York: Gordon Press, 1974.

Malherbe, Abraham J., ed. *The Cynic Epistles: A Study Edition.* Missoula, Mont.: Scholars Press for the Society of Biblical Literature, 1977.

Navia, Luis E. *Classical Cynicism: A Critical Study.* Westport, Conn.: Greenwood Press, 1996.

_____. *Diogenes of Sinope: The Man in the Tub.* Westport, Conn.: Greenwood Press, 1998.

Sloterdijk, Peter. *Critique of Cynical Reason.* Translated by Michael Eldred. New York: Verso, 1988.

SEE ALSO: Asceticism; Autonomy; Cyrenaics; Platonic ethics; Socrates; Stoic ethics.

Cyrenaics

DEFINITION: Practitioners of a school of ancient Greek philosophy that taught that pleasure is the goal of life

DATE: Fourth to third centuries B.C.E.

TYPE OF ETHICS: Classical history

SIGNIFICANCE: The Cyrenaics advocated a form of hedonism that deemphasized abstract studies and stressed practical ethics.

Aristippus of Cyrene, the founder of Cyrenaicism, was an associate of the philosopher Socrates, and Cyrenaicism—along with Cynicism and Megarianism—was one of three diverging philosophical schools that sprang from Socrates' emphasis on rational control and ethical self-consciousness. Aristippus taught that, since humans can know only their own sensations, no universal standards of pleasure can be discovered, and all pleasures are thus equally valuable; in this view, any act has value only in its usefulness to the one who controls it. This notion, influenced by the Sophists' belief that knowledge comes only through direct experience, was amplified by Aristippus's grandson (also named Aristippus) and later modified by Hegesias, Annikeris, and Theodorus—thinkers whose names are associated with their own sects.

Socrates had taught that moral action should lead to happiness, so Aristippus concluded that life's meaning lay in pleasure. This attitude, called hedonism (from the Greek *hedone*, "pleasure"), explains one sense of the familiar Latin motto *carpe diem*, "seize the day."

CYRENAIC ETHICS

In deducing their philosophy, Cyrenaics ignored physics and mathematics, concentrating instead on practical ethics under various headings: things to pursue and avoid, sensations, actions, causes, and proofs. They believed that all action should aim at pleasure; this meant not merely avoiding pain but also seeking palpable sensation. They devalued both memory and the anticipation of future happiness, and they emphasized physical pleasures over mental activities.

Cyrenaics aimed for rational control that would manipulate people and circumstances to their own pleasurable ends. They defined right and wrong in terms of personal pleasure and pain. Rather than abstinence, which contemporary Cynics urged, Aristippus favored the prudent "use" and control of pleasure.

THE LAST PHASE

Early in the third century B.C.E., followers who tried to distinguish among higher and lower pleasures blurred the Cyrenaics' focus on self-interest, their central philosophical principle: Hegesias (the death-persuader) stressed avoiding pain (rather than pursuing pleasure) and actively encouraged suicide; Annikeris promoted social relationships, altruism, and patriotism; and Theodorus the Atheist urged a quest for enduring inner joy, not momentary physical pleasures. These disagreements seemed to splinter Cyrenaicism, which died out by 275, while another hedonistic school, Epicureanism, advanced.

Roy Neil Graves

FURTHER READING

Edwards, Paul, ed. *The Encyclopedia of Philosophy.* New York: Macmillan, 1967.

Hicks, Robert D. *Stoic and Epicurean.* New York: Russell & Russell, 1962.

Long, A. A. *Hellenistic Philosophy: Stoics, Epicureans, Sceptics.* 2d ed. Berkeley: University of California Press, 1986.

Owens, Joseph. *A History of Ancient Western Philosophy.* Englewood Cliffs, N.J.: Prentice-Hall, 1959.

Reese, William L. *Dictionary of Philosophy and Religion: Eastern and Western Thought.* Atlantic Highlands, N.J.: Humanities Press, 1980.

Tsouna, Voula. *The Epistemology of the Cyrenaic School.* New York: Cambridge University Press, 1998.

SEE ALSO: Epicurus; Hedonism; Socrates.

D

Dalai Lama

IDENTIFICATION: Tibetan religious leader

BORN: Lhamo Dhondrub, later renamed Tenzin Gyatso; July 6, 1935, Taktser, Amdo, Tibet

TYPE OF ETHICS: Religious ethics

SIGNIFICANCE: The Dalai Lama is the spiritual and temporal head of the traditional Buddhist community of Tibet, which has been under Chinese occupation since the 1950's. Tenzin Gyatso's leadership of Tibet's government in exile has made him a symbol of religious and ethical opposition to oppression. In 1989 he was awarded the Nobel Peace Prize.

Perhaps no other modern figure from Asia, except Mohandas K. Gandhi, has gained such worldwide recognition for his ethical teachings as has the fourteenth Dalai Lama. The writings and actions of Tenzin Gyatso, like those of Gandhi, reflect a concern for combining ancient religious traditions with a contemporary political cause. Also, the Dalai Lama's cause, like that of Gandhi, is not limited to the political affairs of his own country but extends to the arena of international politics and human relations generally. To understand how the fourteenth Dalai Lama came to represent the principles that won him the Nobel Peace Prize in 1989, one must investigate the traditional origins of the position that he holds in the Tibetan Buddhist world.

THE FIRST DALAI LAMA AND HIS SUCCESSORS

Properly speaking, the spiritual role of all Dalai Lamas since the life of the first (Gendun Drub, born in 1391, died in 1474) belongs within the broader religious framework of Buddhism, a religion that has various "schools." In somewhat narrower spiritual and temporal terms, the Dalai Lamas belong to the long national tradition of Tibet, a country nestled in the Himalayan mountain range between China and India.

It was Gendun Drub who, after studying both at the Padma Chöling Monastery, where his teacher called him "Omniscient One," and at the Evam Monastery, went on to found a monastery called Tashi Lhunpo in southern Tibet. There he compiled many spiritual works that have remained seminal Buddhist texts. Gendun Drub did not carry the formal title of Dalai Lama (a tradition initiated with the third in the lineage) but preferred a title given by his teacher: Tamche Khyenpa, "Omniscient One," a term still used by devout Tibetans when referring to the fourteenth Dalai Lama, Tenzin Gyatso.

Tashi Lhunpo remained the seat of the successors to Tamche Khyenpa until 1642 when the fifth Dalai Lama left the monastery under the keeping of his own tutor, Panchen Chökyi Gyaltsen. The latter was the first Panchen Lama, whose spiritual lineage is recognized in Tibet as second in importance only to the lineage of the Dalai Lamas.

Successors to the ultimate Tibetan spiritual and temporal post of Dalai Lama by the beginning of the twenty-first century number thirteen. Each of these successors has been assumed to be an incarnation of his predecessor. The process of succession thus involves the discovery of the new Dalai Lama among the newborn of the Tibetan population in every generation. There is a rich tradition describing the importance of symbols that may serve to guide the devout Tibetan religious hierarchy in the search for a new Dalai Lama.

DALAI LAMA'S KEY ETHICAL PRINCIPLES

A number of key spiritual concepts appear in the writings and sermons of the Dalai Lamas over the centuries. One of these is associated with the tradition called *lo-jong*, which is reflected in the teachings of Tenzin Gyatso, the Dalai Lama during the first part of the twenty-first century. Briefly stated, *lo-jong* involves spiritual discipline as a prerequisite for "training" the mind and imbuing it with the values of prior generations of Buddhist masters. Key to the *lo-jong* tradition (among other spiritual practices of Buddhism) is the importance of meditation based on the guidance of spiritual texts to help the individual escape the influences of the external world, which impede full spiritual realization. Such realization is believed to give rise to the fullest forms of love and kindness, which, ideally, should establish themselves in human interrelationships.

THE FOURTEENTH DALAI LAMA'S DILEMMA

Two years after his birth in 1935 in the small farming village of Taktser in the Tibetan province of Amdo, Tenzin Gyatso was identified as the incarnation of the deceased thirteenth Dalai Lama. Already during the period of the search for the new Dalai Lama, peculiarities of the traditional guiding signs that appeared, including curious cloud formations and the growth of a giant fungus in the northeast corner of the room in which the deceased Dalai Lama lay, were thought to be harbingers of change. The discovery of Tenzin Gyatso far to the northeast of Lhasa, not to the south (traditionally deemed the most auspicious direction) was taken to be confirmation of the significance of the celestial signs.

When he reached the age of four and one-half years, the child came to Lhasa and, upon mounting the Lion Throne, assumed his responsibilities as Tibet's highest leader. For more than a decade, the young Dalai Lama's educational progress, both in traditional religious and modern subjects, seemed to prepare him for normal passage to full responsibility for his people's spiritual and temporal welfare. The events of October, 1950, however, were destined to affect this passage. The Chinese communist invasion of Tibet forced the Dalai Lama first to attempt to maintain the basic rights of his people even under occupation, and then—in the wake of violent uprisings (1956-1959) following unsuccessful attempts to negotiate Tibet's freedom—to flee to exile in neighboring India. Following Tenzin Gyatso's departure, the Chinese regime attempted to assign religious legitimacy to his immediate subordinate in the Tibetan Buddhist hierarchy, the Panchen Lama.

A particular role was thus cast for the fourteenth Dalai Lama, who assumed a much expanded symbolic function as a world-renowned spiritual and temporal leader beginning in the troubled second half of the twentieth century. In a sense, Tibet's plight became part of the shared cause of those who defend

justice wherever individual or group repression exists. This fateful calling not only affected the Dalai Lama's writings and actions but also brought recognition of the importance of his work in the form of the 1989 Nobel Peace Prize.

PRINCIPLES IN TENZIN GYATSO'S LIFE

As a spiritual leader in exile, the fourteenth Dalai Lama found himself in a position to bring the troubled case of his country to the attention of the world as a whole. His writings and speeches tend to reflect his concern that Tibet's particular problem should serve to incite awareness of the human costs of oppression of body and spirit wherever they occur. Thus, his origins as a Buddhist leader in a particular area of the world provided a frame of reference for his focus on much wider considerations. Paramount among these is the importance of cooperation, not competition or hostility, among world religions. A secondary feature is recognition that all peoples living in the modern world need to find a path that can combine spiritual values with the possibilities presented by the application of reason and scientific knowledge. It was the Dalai Lama's emphasis on such principles and the importance of using them to develop happiness and kindness that built his reputation for supporting the cause of world peace.

THE NOBEL PEACE PRIZE

The Nobel Prize committee's selection of the Dalai Lama to receive its 1989 Peace Prize provided an additional framework for this extraordinary religious leader to try to emphasize the importance of combining ethical values and the development of humanitarian politics in the world. Although his Nobel lecture reflected specific political concerns in Tibetan-Chinese relations (including a compromise plan for resolution of the state of foreign occupation of his country), the Dalai Lama drew attention to a number of other "trouble spots" around the globe. Here, his diagnosis of the origins of political conflicts, as well as his prognosis of the best means of resolving them, mirrored the content of his spiritual writings: the idea that living with an attitude of love and kindness toward other individuals is the way to connect the inner sphere of existence with the external world of different peoples and nations.

Byron D. Cannon

FURTHER READING

Avedon, John F. *An Interview with the Dalai Lama*. New York: Littlebird, 1980.

Hicks, Roger, and Ngakpa Chögyam. *Great Ocean: An Authorized Biography of the Buddhist Monk Tenzin Gyatso, His Holiness the Fourteenth Dalai Lama*. London: Penguin Books, 1990.

Gyatso, Tenzin [Fourteenth Dalai Lama]. *Freedom in Exile*. New York: HarperCollins, 1990.

Mullin, Glenn H., ed. *Selected Works of the Dalai Lama I*. 2 vols. Ithaca, N.Y.: Snow Lion, 1985.

Piburn, Sidney, ed. *The Dalai Lama: A Policy of Kindness*. 2d ed. Ithaca, N.Y.: Snow Lion, 1993.

Willis, Clint, ed. *A Lifetime of Wisdom: Essential Writings by and About the Dalai Lama*. New York: Marlowe, 2002.

SEE ALSO: Bodhisattva ideal; Buddha; Buddhist ethics; Four noble truths; Nobel Peace Prizes.

Dallaire, Roméo

IDENTIFICATION: Canadian commander of the U.N. peacekeeping force in Rwanda during that nation's 1994 genocide

BORN: June 25, 1946

TYPE OF ETHICS: Human rights

SIGNIFICANCE: Dallaire called attention to the world community's failure to prevent the genocide that killed 800,000 people.

In 1993 Canadian brigadier general Roméo Dallaire was appointed to command the U.N. peacekeeping force sent to the central African nation of Rwanda, which had a long history of bloody ethnic rivalry between the majority Hutu population and the Tutsi minority. In April of 1994, an airplane carrying Rwanda's Hutu president was shot down, killing the president. The Hutu-dominated government—which

Roméo Dallaire at a Paris press conference in early 2004. (AP/Wide World Photos)

Dallaire's Assumption of Guilt

After returning home from Rwanda, Roméo Dallaire blamed himself for not having done more to stop the massacres. He fell into a deep despair and tried to kill himself. Diagnosed with post-traumatic stress disorder, he was told that he was not responding to treatment and was medically dismissed from the Canadian army. While on a regimen of strong antidepressant drugs in 2000, he ignored physicians' warnings by drinking alcohol and went into a coma while sitting on a park bench. After being hospitalized, he decided to expiate his feelings of guilt by writing a book about Rwanda. Over the next three years he relived his nightmare experience while composing *Shake Hands with the Devil: The Failure of Humanity in Rwanda* (2003). Writing about Rwanda relieved some of Dallaire's stress, but he remained pessimistic about the future. Had the major powers intervened in Rwanda, he said, "we could have saved millions from this calamity. But I'm afraid that we haven't learned, and the same thing could happen again. How do you live with that?"

may have been responsible for downing the plane—then blamed the Tutsi for the president's death and began a long-planned campaign to exterminate the Tutsis.

Dallaire pleaded for reinforcements and supplies for his peacekeeping force, but the United States urged withdrawal of the force, and the United Nations reduced Dallaire's troops from 2,500 to 270 men. In an apparent violation of his orders, Dallaire used what was left of his ill-supplied and largely untrained force to save the lives of approximately 20,000 Rwandans but was unable to halt the general violence. By the time the wave of genocide finally ended in July, as many as 800,000 people had been killed.

After Dallaire requested a reassignment, the United Nations sent him back to Canada, where he was promoted to major general and deputy commander of the Canadian army. Some U.N. diplomats blamed Dallaire for failing to keep peace in Rwanda, but others leaked memos proving he had warned his superiors of the genocide and had been ordered not to

intervene. After retiring from the army in 2000, Dallaire suffered from depression, apparently blaming himself for the mass killings in Rwanda and attempted to analyze and publicize what went wrong in that African nation. In 2003 he published *Shake Hands with the Devil: The Failure of Humanity in Rwanda*.

Recalling the world outrage that biologist Dian Fossey evoked when she had brought to the world's attention the slaughter of Rwanda's gorillas in the 1970's, Dallaire said of the 1994 genocide: "I always wondered if the international community would have done more if 800,000 mountain gorillas were being slaughtered."

William V. Dunlap

SEE ALSO: Genocide and democide; Peacekeeping missions; Rwanda genocide; United Nations; United Nations Convention on the Prevention and Punishment of the Crime of Genocide.

Daoist ethics

DEFINITION: Moral philosophy developed in ancient China that rejects conventional moral codes in favor of a natural, simple, spontaneous life

TYPE OF ETHICS: Classical history

SIGNIFICANCE: An important branch of Eastern asceticism, Daoism has traditionally functioned as a major rival to Confucianism in Chinese philosophy. It has had a strong influence on the development of both Zen Buddhist ethics and neo-Confucian ethics.

Daoism is one of the great classical philosophies of China. It is named after its central concept, *Dao*, which literally means "path" in Chinese. The philosophy is mainly represented by the books of Laozi (the author of *Dao De Jing*) and Zhuangzi (the author of *Zhuangzi*).

MORALITY AND DECLINE OF THE DAO

Daoists use the concept Dao to name both the way of the natural world of reality and the proper way of life, including the way of government and the way of the right social order. To the Daoist, the best way of life is to live in harmony with nature. It is a life of simplicity and spontaneity. According to the Daoists, this is how ancient people used to live. As skill and conventional knowledge developed, however, people came to have more and more desires; the increase of desires led to conflicts among people and conflicts between humans and their natural environment, which made life more difficult. Morality was introduced to cope with the problems, but morality does not remove the causes of these problems; it creates new problems because it imposes rules on people, thus making them constrained and mentally crippled. Morality should therefore be cast away in favor of a better solution. Thus, Laozi wrote:

> Banish wisdom, discard knowledge,
> And the people will be benefitted a hundredfold.
> Banish kindness, discard morality,
> And the people will be dutiful and compassionate.
> Banish skill, discard profit,
> And thieves and robbers will disappear.
> As these three touch the externals and are inadequate,
> The people have need of what they can depend upon:
> To see the simplicity,
> To embrace one's uncarved nature,
> To cast off selfishness,
> And to have few desires.

SUPERIOR DE AND INFERIOR DE

In saying "discard morality," the Daoist is not encouraging immoral acts. As Chuang Chou puts it, it is better for fish to live in water and be able to forget about each other than to be on a dry road and have to moisten each other with their spit. The *De* (virtue) of helping each other with spit is inferior to the *De* of living in accordance with the Dao. Daoist ethics contains teachings that resemble those of other normative ethics. For example, from the *Dao De Jing*: "In dealing with others, be gentle and kind. In speech, be true. In ruling, get peace. In business, be capable. In action, watch the timing." "I am good to people who are good. I am also good to people who are not good. Virtue is goodness. I have faith in people who are faithful. I also have faith in people who are not faithful. Virtue is faithfulness." Here, however, virtue (*De*) is not to be understood as moral virtue. The Daoist uses *De* in the sense of the power or proper function of something. Thus, for example, mercy is considered virtue, because it brings courage, strength, and victory.

DAO OF GOING FORWARD RESEMBLES RETREAT

"The superior *De* let go of (the inferior, moral) *De*, and therefore has (the superior) *De*." Daoism values freedom, but freedom is to be achieved by having no "self" (desires and expectations) rather than by fighting against restrictions. "Only if you do not fight, no one can fight against you." "This is known as the virtue of not striving." Daoism values happiness, but "the highest happiness has no happiness." It does not come from active searching for happiness. Daoism values true wisdom, but true wisdom does not mean the wisdom of obtaining profits. It is the wisdom of seeing the value of simplicity and spontaneity. To the Daoist, a truly mature person is like a little child who has few desires and less knowledge. Such a person is simple-minded and even looks like a fool, because great knowledge is like ignorance. The Daoist teaches being calm, soft, female-like, desireless, nonaggressive, and content. The Daoist likes the image of water: It is soft, yet there is nothing it cannot penetrate.

ETHICS OF RELIGIOUS DAOISM

Philosophical Daoism (*Dao jia*) is the origin of, yet must not be confused with, religious Daoism (*Dao jiao*). Religious Daoism turned respect for nature into the worship of numerous deities, such as the gods of wealth, war, and longevity. It turned the De of living a simple and spontaneous life into the principles of serenity and calmness in therapeutic techniques and martial arts that could be used to achieve personal advantages (mainly immortality). Misfortunes were no longer considered the result of having excessive desires, but instead were considered mainly the result of magic trespasses.

Peimin Ni

FURTHER READING

Chan, Wing-tsit. *A Source Book in Chinese Philosophy.* Princeton, N.J.: Princeton University Press, 1963.

Chuang Tzu. *Basic Writings.* Translated by Burton Watson. New York: Columbia University Press, 1964.

Fung Yu-lan. *A History of Chinese Philosophy.* Vol. 1. Translated by Derk Bodde. Princeton, N.J.: Princeton University Press, 1983.

Graham, Angus C. *Disputers of the Tao.* La Salle, Ill.: Open Court, 1989.

Hansen, Chad. *A Daoist Theory of Chinese Thought: A Philosophical Interpretation.* New York: Oxford University Press, 2000.

Lao Tzu. *Tao Te Ching: A Book About the Way and the Power of the Way.* Translated by Ursula K. Le Guin and J. P. Seaton. Boston: Shambhala, 1997.

_____. *The Way and Its Power: A Study of Tao Te Ching and Its Place in Chinese Thought.* Edited and translated by Arthur Waley. New York: Grove Press, 1958.

Welch, Holmes. *Taoism: The Parting of the Way.* Rev. ed. Boston: Beacon Press, 1966.

SEE ALSO: Asceticism; Buddhist ethics; Confucian ethics; Confucius; Laozi; Manichaeanism; Shinto ethics; Zen; Zhuangzi.

Darwin, Charles

IDENTIFICATION: English naturalist

BORN: February 12, 1809, Shrewsbury, Shropshire, England

DIED: April 19, 1882, Downe, Kent, England

TYPE OF ETHICS: Modern history

SIGNIFICANCE: Since it was first advanced in *On the Origin of Species by Means of Natural Selection* (1859), Darwin's theory of evolution has had a profound impact on almost every aspect of intellectual thought. It has been the basis of at least two movements within ethics: Social Darwinism in the nineteenth century and evolutionary ethics in the twentieth.

Charles Darwin's lifelong concern was with the natural origins of animals and plants. He knew that animal and plant breeders had modified domestic species by selecting desired variants as breeding stock. Nature, he argued, was always doing the same thing, practicing natural selection by allowing certain individuals to leave more offspring than others. Each species constantly produces more eggs, seeds, or offspring than can possibly survive; most individuals face an early death. Any heritable traits that confer some advantage in this "struggle for existence" are passed on to future generations; injurious traits are destroyed.

In his writings, Darwin did not address the ethical implications of his theories, leaving such speculations to others. Herbert Spencer, who coined the phrase "survival of the fittest," founded an ethic of unbridled competition known as Social Darwinism. American Social Darwinists favored a ruthless competition in which only the strongest would survive; several industrialists used these ideas to justify cutthroat competition, the suppression of labor unions, and a lack of concern for the welfare of workers.

Socialists and other political dissidents drew exactly the opposite conclusion from Darwin's works. They saw evolution as a theory of "progress," of merit triumphant over established privilege, and of science triumphant over religious superstition.

Social Darwinism, like its socialist response, was a normative ethical system: It argued that people *should* act in accordance with the principle of survival of the fittest, by refraining from acts of charity, for example. Evolutionary ethics, a branch of sociobiology, is more descriptive than normative: It argues that humanity as a whole already *does* act in accordance with its evolutionary interests, and those interests can therefore be used to explain human behavior. From this point of view, morality is itself a product of evolution, and the fact that people have come over time to engage in acts of charity, for example, is an indication that such acts are of benefit to the survival of the species.

Evolutionary ethics has been highly influential as a social science because of its descriptive and explanatory power. It has largely failed to produce a convincing normative theory. This is because, while natural selection is a useful lens for *understanding* human conduct, it is not necessarily a *guide* for human conduct. What is natural is not necessarily good, and what is good for a species over the course of millions of years is not necessarily good for individuals, groups, or nations over the smaller spans of time that make up lived human experience.

Eli C. Minkoff
Updated by the editors

SEE ALSO: Eugenics; Evolutionary theory; Naturalistic fallacy; Normative vs. descriptive ethics; Science; Social Darwinism; Sociobiology.

Death and dying

DEFINITION: Cessation of human physiological, psychological, and possibly spiritual existence
TYPE OF ETHICS: Beliefs and practices
SIGNIFICANCE: Defining death precisely has become crucial to such medical and moral issues as euthanasia, living wills, quality of life, abortion, organ transplantation, and cryonics.

The modern study of death and dying, thanatology (named for the Greek god of death, Thanatos), could be said to have begun in 1956, when the American Psychological Association held a symposium on death at its annual convention. This resulted in the publication in 1959 of an anthology of essays on death written by scholars from a wide range of disciplines. Popular attention focused on death and dying with the publication of Elisabeth Kübler-Ross's *On Death and Dying* (1969), a study of the stages of dying.

BIOLOGICAL DEFINITIONS

Historically, definitions of death have undergone a number of revisions. The earliest medical determination of death was the cessation of heart activity, respiration, and all functions consequent thereon (now commonly referred to as "clinical death"). With the advancement of respirators and other sophisticated medical equipment, however, it became possible for a patient with no brain activity to be artificially kept "alive." In 1970, Kansas became the first state to adopt a brain-based criterion for determining death in addition to the cessation-of-vital-functions definition.

A number of states followed that definition, while others eliminated the traditional definition altogether and focused solely on a "brain death" model. The term "brain death" in these legal documents referred to the total and irreversible cessation of the functions of the entire brain, including both the "higher brain," which is regarded as the seat of conscious mental processes, and the "brain stem," which controls cardiopulmonary activity. This usually takes place from three to five minutes after clinical death, although the process can take much longer in cases of death by freezing or barbiturate overdose.

In 1981, a presidential commission proposed a "Uniform Determination of Death Act," which de-fined death as either "irreversible cessation of circulatory and respiratory functions" or "irreversible cessation of all functions of the entire brain, including the brain stem." Such a determination, it added, must be made "in accordance with accepted medical standards." This legal definition was adopted by more than half the states within the first decade after its formulation. As is evident from this formulation, rather than viewing death as an "event," it is more accurate to define death as a process encompassing at least three different types of death: clinical death (the cessation of vital signs), biological death (including the cessation of brain activity), and cellular death (including the deterioration of all of the body's cells).

PROPOSED CHANGES

While state legislations have employed a "whole-brain" definition of death, there have been attempts made by some states to define death in terms of the cessation of cerebral activity in the upper portion of the brain. Proponents of this position argue that an individual's "personhood" relies upon the cognitive faculties of the "higher brain." According to this definition, an individual in a "persistent vegetative state" in which only the brain stem, controlling heartbeat and respiration, is functioning would not be considered a living "person." Since no consensus can be reached regarding the proper definition of "person," however, and since reliance on cognitive awareness would exclude severely senile, mentally deficient, and anencephalic individuals from the category of "persons," a "higher-brain" definition of death has been almost universally rejected by the medical community and general public.

AUTONOMY OVER ONE'S DEATH

The American Medical Association's position that one need not use "extraordinary means" to keep a person alive is almost universally accepted. This is commonly referred to as "passive euthanasia." ("Euthanasia" comes from the Greek phrase meaning "good death.") This position has led to the development of a "living will," which states that the individual does not want life-sustaining devices and extraordinary medical procedures used to prolong his or her life. Although the "living will" is not a binding legal document in all states, it is considered by most courts of law to be a valid expression of the signer's wishes.

A more extreme example of belief in the authority

of the individual to determine his or her death can be seen in the practice of "active euthanasia." Defined as the act of directly bringing about a person's death by a means unrelated to the illness itself (for example, injection, anesthesia without oxygen, and so forth), active euthanasia is illegal in virtually all parts of the world. The practice became widespread during the 1980's in Holland, however, where one out of every five deaths of older patients was caused by active euthanasia.

Although the usual argument for active euthanasia cites extreme physical suffering as an acceptable reason, other justifications, including psychological distress, old age, limited mental capacity, and an unacceptable "quality of life," also have been advanced. In fact, in the latter half of the 1980's, Holland extended the practice to include Down syndrome infants and anorexic young adults. Those ethicists opposed to active euthanasia point to the danger that more and more categories of candidates would become acceptable, were it to be allowed.

OTHER BIOETHICAL ISSUES

For many people, the debate over abortion hinges on how the fetus is to be categorized. If the fetus can be considered a human being at a particular point in its prenatal development, abortion after that point would be regarded as the unlawful taking of a human life. A precise definition of both life and death is, therefore, crucial to the issue. Some people argue that the determination of where human life begins should employ the same criteria that are used to define the absence of life, or death.

Even though the first organ transplant in the United States took place in 1954, early transplants did not meet with a great deal of success, because cadaveric organs were not widely available during the 1950's and 1960's as a result of the difficulty of defining death. With the establishment of brain-based criteria for determining death and with the discovery of the immunosuppresive drug cyclosporine, organ transplantation increased dramatically during the 1980's.

In order for organs from cadavers to remain viable for transplantation, heart and respiratory functions must be sustained artificially until the procedure can be performed. This necessitates a definition of death that would allow for the artificial maintenance of vital functions.

CRYONICS

During the late 1960's, the procedure called "cryonic suspension" was first attempted. The procedure involves freezing the human body immediately after clinical death in the hope that it can be thawed and resuscitated at a later date when a cure for the illness causing the death is available. Since the procedure depends upon freezing the body before deterioration of the brain and other organs takes place, it is crucial that death be pronounced immediately so that the procedure can begin. An additional ethical issue arose when, during the 1980's, a prominent mathematician who had been diagnosed with brain cancer was denied permission from a U.S. court to have his head removed prior to his clinical death. He had requested that his head be placed in cryonic suspension in order to halt the deterioration of his cerebral functions.

Mara Kelly Zukowski

FURTHER READING

Brennan, Herbie. *Death: The Great Mystery of Life.* New York: Carroll & Graf, 2002.

Choron, Jacques. *Death and Western Thought.* New York: Collier, 1973.

Kübler-Ross, Elisabeth. *On Death and Dying.* New York: Macmillan, 1969.

Ladd, John, ed. *Ethical Issues Relating to Life and Death.* New York: Oxford University Press, 1979.

President's Commission for the Study of Ethical Problems in Medicine and Biomedical and Behavioral Research. *Defining Death: A Report on the Medical, Legal, and Ethical Issues in the Determination of Death.* Washington, D.C.: Government Printing Office, 1981.

Veatch, Robert M. *Death, Dying, and the Biological Revolution: Our Last Quest for Responsibility.* Rev. ed. New Haven, Conn.: Yale University Press, 1989.

SEE ALSO: Abortion; Bioethics; Brain death; Euthanasia; Homicide; Immortality; Infanticide; Life and death; Quinlan, Karen Ann; Right to die; Suicide.

Declaration of Independence

IDENTIFICATION: Document in which colonial American leaders declared themselves independent of British rule

DATE: Signed on July 4, 1776

TYPE OF ETHICS: Politico-economic ethics

SIGNIFICANCE: America's Declaration of Independence spread arguments around the world justifying a right to revolution against rulers found to deny their subjects fundamental rights and has remained widely influential to the present day.

On July 4, 1776, the Second Continental Congress of the thirteen original American states, which only a few days before had been the "United Colonies," passed a unanimous declaration announcing to the world that it had unilaterally taken the decision to end its status as a group of British colonies and giving reasons justifying the decision. The document announced that the "one people" of America's former colonies had decided to become—and henceforth proclaimed themselves to be—free and independent states.

Important questions of political ethics arise in the course of the arguments found in the Continental Congress's document, now long since regarded as one of the most significant legislative acts in human history. According to Ralph Waldo Emerson, the declaration was "the shot heard 'round the world"—a judgment fully justified by its subsequent history. However, it might be asked whether the declaration was ethically justified, how the colonists justified themselves, and whether they were correct in their justification.

ETHICAL ISSUES

The primary ethical issue of the Declaration of Independence was its justification of violent revolution—the suggestion that every people have a right by "the Laws of Nature and of Nature's God" to be independent and to gain their independence, if necessary, through violent means. In this case, a government was being overthrown that, formally at least, had ruled the colonies for well over a century, and in some cases, for more than a century and a half.

The Declaration of Independence makes several key arguments. It states that all people ("all Men" in the document) have a God-given right, inherent in human nature, to political liberty. This includes the right to decide how they will be politically ruled. The declaration see this as an individual right that devolves onto a collectivity of people who freely join together for the purpose of forming a polity. The declaration further states that political power over persons can be justified only by their consent. In forming government, people consent only to have their God-given rights protected by government, thus limiting the legitimate powers of government. When government attacks rather than protects those rights, the people's obligation to obey their government ceases, and they have a right—using force, if necessary—to rid themselves of that government and to establish a new government in its place.

Although the "unalienable Rights" identified by the declaration are undoubtedly possessed by individuals, the declaration itself is careful to say that it is "the Right of the People" to overthrow oppressive government. The declaration follows the argument of John Locke in his *Second Treatise of Civil Government* (1690) that history shows that long-established governments are not overthrown for "light and transient causes," and it identifies "prudence" as a limit on hasty action. Nonetheless, the declaration's claim of a right to revolution evokes powerful ethical issues. Even if the right to violent revolution is accepted, the question of who is entitled to make this decision arises. If individuals have inalienable rights that are trampled upon, may an "oppressed" individual lay his own assault upon government? The fact that lone individuals took 168 lives in the April, 1995, bombing of the Oklahoma City federal building illustrates the serious ethical issues involved.

The declaration deals with this problem implicitly by placing the right to resist tyranny in the collective hands of "the people." It also implicitly answers that it is representatives of the people who can make this decision. However, that still leaves the question of whether these representatives must represent a majority of the people. The Continental Congress conveniently skirted this issue, as few of its members could have seriously believed that a majority of the people in their colonies would support a war of independence from Great Britain. John Adams opined that perhaps a third of the colonists favored independence, while another third opposed it, and the rest were undecided.

The declaration raises the question of whether it is

ever ethical for a minority to act on behalf of a majority. For example, Russian revolutionary leader Vladimir Ilich Lenin insisted on organizing his revolutionary Bolshevik Party as a conspiratorial minority and cared little for the views of the majority, believing that the party alone possessed the wisdom and historical insight required to take decisive action. However, the consequences of Lenin's 1917 Russian Revolution were catastrophic for the world, eventuating in the deaths of tens of millions of people and the political enslavement of hundreds of millions.

JUSTIFYING VIOLENT REVOLUTION

Another ethical question is whether the Declaration of Independence should be condemned for its defense of violent revolution. Few serious moralists—outside eighteenth century Britain—have thought so. How could it be that people are morally obliged to endure tyrannical government? What might be said is that the "right to revolution" championed by the declaration is itself morally dangerous. Like the right to possess guns for self-defense, the right to overthrow government can lead to consequences that run the gamut of the completely defensible to the morally catastrophic.

Nevertheless, leaving aside controversy over possession of arms by individuals, few believe that nations—peoples—should be denied the means to self-defense. The fact that arms may be misused is hardly an argument for denying a people the right to defend their fundamental rights. Thus the central ethical issue raised by the declaration must necessarily remain unresolved. Like any moral weapon, the right to revolution may be put to good use or ill, depending upon who decides whether it shall be invoked as well as how and when it is to be used. If the ethics of making revolution are not taken seriously, further tragedy is inevitable.

Charles F. Bahmueller

FURTHER READING

Becker, Carl L. *The Declaration of Independence: A Study in the History of Political Ideas.* New York: Vintage Books, 1958.

Jayne, Russell. *Jefferson's Declaration of Independence: Origins, Philosophy and Theology.* Lexington: University Press of Kentucky Press, 2000.

Kirk, Russell. *The Roots of American Order.* 3d ed. Washington, D.C.: Regnery Gateway, 1991.

Machan, Tibor R. ed. *Individual Rights Reconsidered: Are the Truths of the U.S. Declaration of Independence Lasting?* Stanford, Calif.: Hoover Institution Press, 2001.

Maier, Pauline. *American Scripture: Making the Declaration of Independence.* New York: Alfred A. Knopf, 1997.

SEE ALSO: Bill of Rights, U.S.; Constitution, U.S.; Democracy; Egalitarianism; Emerson, Ralph Waldo; English Bill of Rights; Jefferson, Thomas; Liberalism; Natural rights; Revolution.

Deconstruction

DEFINITION: Strategy of interpretation that reduces a text to its fundamental elements, which, when unraveled, reveal that no single essence or meaning can be determined

DATE: Concept developed during the late 1960's

TYPE OF ETHICS: Modern history

SIGNIFICANCE: Deconstruction holds both that no single meaning or interpretation of a text is correct and that any given text will privilege some meanings and attempt to hide other possible meanings from its readers. Which meanings are privileged and which meanings are hidden or denigrated is largely determined by the power structures operative in a given society. There is therefore a fundamental ethical imperative within deconstruction to reveal hidden meanings in order to reveal unequal power relations and resist dominant ideologies. The central ideology that all deconstruction is meant to attack is most commonly referred to as Western metaphysics or the "metaphysics of presence."

The structuralism conference at Johns Hopkins University in 1966 was intended to introduce into the United States structuralist theory, an approach to reading in which a poem or novel is viewed as a closed entity that has specific meanings. When Jacques Derrida read his paper, "Structure, Sign, and Play in the Discourse of the Human Sciences," the demise of structuralism and the arrival of a new theory, deconstruction, was unexpectedly announced.

POSTSTRUCTURALISM

Deconstruction has since become the main philosophical tenet of poststructuralism, an intellectual movement that is largely a reaction to structuralism. Poststructuralism includes not only the deconstructive analyses of Derrida, who has had an enormous influence on the development of literary theory, but also the work of other French intellectuals, including the historian Michel Foucault, the feminist philosopher and critic Julia Kristeva, and the psychoanalyst Jacques Lacan.

Ferdinand Saussure, the founder of modern structuralist linguistics, saw language as a closed, stable system of signs, and this view forms much of the foundation of structuralist thought. These signs helped structuralists to arrive at a better understanding of a text, because it was thought that they offered consistent, logical representations of the order of things, or what Foucault called "a principle of unity."

Rather than attempting to understand the logical structure of things, poststructuralism, and deconstruction in particular, attempts to do much more: It attempts to understand the limits of understanding. Deconstruction is an extraordinarily complex strategy of reading that is based primarily on two presuppositions.

The first presupposition relies heavily on Saussure's notion of signs; however, Derrida argues that rather than representing the order of things, signs represent disorder, because they can never be nailed down to a single meaning. He posits that because meaning is irreducibly plural, language can never be a closed and stable system.

The second presupposition involves Derrida's observation of Western modes of thought. He noticed that "universal truths" have gone unquestioned in terms of their "rightness," and that these concepts are defined by what they exclude, their binary opposites (for example, man is defined as the opposite of the identity that constitutes woman). Derrida's strategy is to reveal the hierarchy that is inherent in these binary oppositions and to show that by meticulously examining what are believed to be the distinctions between them, in each instance the privileged term of the hierarchy is found to be dependent upon the subordinate term for its meaning and existence. Thus both meaning and value are created through the hierarchical organization of language, an organization that is only perpetuated by the history of its acceptance but is logically untenable.

CRITICISMS OF DECONSTRUCTION

Although some people see Derrida as a brilliant theorist who instigated a radical reassessment of the basic concepts of Western thought, critics have argued that deconstruction's main presupposition—that one must always be resigned to the impossibility of objective truth because meaning is irreducibly plural—makes Derrida's theory nihilistic at worst and an elitist, bourgeois game at best.

Derrida defends deconstruction against the charge of nihilism by pointing out that he is not attacking truth—indeed every word he writes constantly produces more truth or "truth effects" whether he wants it to or not. Rather, he is revealing where truth comes from, how it works, and why there is a fundamental conflict between truth and ethics. He therefore posits that it is necessary to suspend ethics in order to arrive at ethical understanding. He claims that ethics has emerged as a defense against violence; however, the binary oppositions established by ethics to bring about order are also a form of violence because they force one kind of truth to be accepted by destroying other contradictory truths through imposed hierarchies. He believes that the problem of ethics involves being able to move from one term in the pair to the other while maintaining the co-valence of the two rather than their inequality.

While Derrida and other theorists were defending deconstruction, revelations surfaced that Paul de Man—a member of the "Yale School," a group of deconstructionists at Yale who helped to introduce Derrida to America—had written more than one hundred articles for an anti-Semitic, pro-Nazi newspaper in Belgium during World War II. After the discovery of de Man's collaboration, a great deal of comment was generated both against deconstruction and against de Man, who died in 1984, having successfully concealed his past from his colleagues and students.

In response, Derrida stated that de Man's acts were unforgivable; however, he believed that it must be realized that these acts were committed more than half a century earlier, when de Man was in his early twenties. That argument helped ameliorate to some extent the moral problems caused by de Man's wartime activities, but it did nothing to resolve the more serious problem that occurred after the war—his lifelong secrecy about the collaboration, a serious moral contradiction for a practitioner of a theory that has as its main goal the revelation of what is excluded, or kept secret, in a text. Thus, the idea that deconstruction is nihilistic was strengthened by the revelation of de Man's collaboration. Other theorists defended deconstruction by asserting that those who adopt deconstructionist positions have various agendas, including radical feminism and other progressive movements, so that any attempt to invalidate all deconstruction because of de Man's past is unfair.

Derrida has also had numerous well-publicized disagreements about deconstruction with Michel Foucault. Their conflict centered on Derrida's efforts to deconstruct texts in order to set free hidden possibilities and Foucault's attempts to experience history to reveal its latent structures. It is in these public disagreements that Foucault, whose writings centered on history and language and had nothing to do with deconstruction, has dramatically influenced poststructuralist theory. Much has been written about the disagreements, and most of these writings attempt either to reconcile or to choose between the writings of these two intellectuals.

Both opponents and proponents of deconstruction agree that while Derrida is radically subversive, his attack on Western notions of truth and reason does not lead to utter meaninglessness. Because of Derrida's influence, deconstruction has expanded the range of literary theory and has led to a much deeper questioning of the assumed naturalness of structure in systems of thought. Derrida's work shows that by unraveling key binary oppositions of the Western tradition, one may eventually uncover more important things that are just beyond the limits of ordinary understanding.

Jill S. Marts
Updated by the editors

FURTHER READING

Boyne, Roy. *Foucault and Derrida: The Other Side of Reason.* London: Unwin Hyman, 1990.

Critchley, Simon. *The Ethics of Deconstruction: Derrida and Levinas.* 2d ed. West Lafayette, Ind.: Purdue University Press, 1999.

Culler, Jonathan, ed. *Deconstruction: Critical Concepts in Literary and Cultural Studies.* 4 vols. New York: Routledge, 2003.

De Man, Paul. *Blindness and Insight: Essays in the Rhetoric of Contemporary Criticism.* 2d ed., rev. Minneapolis: University of Minnesota Press, 1983.

Derrida, Jacques. *Ethics, Institutions, and the Right to Philosophy.* Edited and translated by Peter Pericles Trifonas. Lanham, Md.: Rowman & Littlefield, 2002.

_____. *Margins of Philosophy.* Translated by Alan Bass. Chicago: University of Chicago Press, 1982.

Dronsfield, Jonathon, and Nick Midgley, eds. *Responsibilities of Deconstruction.* Coventry, Warwickshire, England: University of Warwick, 1997.

Eagleton, Terry. *Literary Theory: An Introduction.* 2d ed. Minneapolis: University of Minnesota Press, 1996.

Johnson, Barbara. *A World of Difference.* Baltimore: Johns Hopkins University Press, 1987.

Sallis, John, ed. *Deconstruction and Philosophy: The Texts of Jacques Derrida.* Chicago: University of Chicago Press, 1987.

Srajek, Martin C. *In the Margins of Deconstruction: Jewish Conceptions of Ethics in Emmanuel Levinas and Jacques Derrida.* Pittsburgh: Duquesne University Press, 2000.

SEE ALSO: Critical theory; Derrida, Jacques; Foucault, Michel; Language; Postmodernism.

Deep ecology

DEFINITION: Branch of environmental ethics asserting that all creatures and ecosystems have inherent rights that exist independently of the needs and judgments of humans

DATE: Concept formulated in 1949; term coined in 1972

TYPE OF ETHICS: Environmental ethics

SIGNIFICANCE: As the world's human population expands and exerts greater demand on the planet's resources, deep ecology provides an ethical guide to how humans may coexist with other life-forms. Critics see deep ecology as a misguided attempt to thwart the satisfaction of important human needs.

Although the world of nature has long commanded the attention of philosophers, it was not until the late twentieth century that they began exploring whether humans had ethical duties to the natural world. Like so many others, modern ethicists were shocked and dismayed by the persistent destruction of natural habitat, the extinction of wildlife, the pollution of air and water, and the depletion of natural resources. The causes of these destructive forces were an ever-expanding industrialism and a growing human population. In fact, many thinkers predicted an ecological catastrophe was fast approaching. Out of this anguish came several "ecophilosophies" that came to frame an ongoing debate about environmental ethics. Among the most prominent and controversial of them is deep ecology.

BASICS OF A NEW ENVIRONMENTAL ETHIC

More of an intellectual movement than a specific philosophy, deep ecology is nonetheless based on a few core principles. Among them is a rejection of the "human-centered" view of nature that assumes human beings alone have ethical value and are superior to other life-forms. Deep ecology also spurns the Judeo-Christian assertion that the Bible gives human beings a divine right to hold dominion over nature. To deep ecologists these beliefs form the foundation for many of the attitudes in the West that are morally indefensible because they breed arrogance and indifference to the natural world and lead to the destruction and despoliation of living things.

Deep ecologists also argue that any opposition to environmental destruction merely because it is detrimental to human beings is morally shallow. Instead, they advocate a deeper ethic—one that holds that all living creatures and biological systems also have a right to exist. Moreover, this intrinsic value does not depend on how much pleasure or usefulness it provides human beings. Every life-form is unique and exists as an end onto itself. Deep ecology holds that it is morally wrong to assume that nature exists primarily to serve as raw material for human exploitation, consumption, and overproduction. No one, deep ecologists argue, has the moral right to jeopardize the richness and variety of life on Earth, unless to meet basic survival needs.

ORIGINS OF DEEP ECOLOGY

A Sand County Almanac (1949), a book by American forester and professor Aldo Leopold, heralded the deep ecology movement with his "land ethic."

According to Leopold, humans have a moral duty to preserve the biological integrity of living things and ecosystems. Humans, says Leopold, share a biotic-community, or ecosystem, with other living creatures. Drawing upon the thinking of Ezekiel and Isaiah in the Old Testament of the Bible that says despoliation of nature is wrong, Leopold concludes that humans must not act as conquerors of nature. Instead, they should respect fellow living things and biotic-communities and work to preserve them.

Other thinkers found common ground with Leopold. One of them was Norwegian philosopher Arne Naess, who coined the expression "deep ecology" in 1972. According to Naess, an appreciation for deep ecology develops when human beings undergo a transformation of consciousness that creates within them new "ecological selves" that provide deeper and clearer perspectives of interconnected relationships among all living things, including human beings. This consciousness, it is suggested, spawns an ethical conscience concerning the natural world.

For many deep ecologists, this realization often accompanies a transcendental experience in nature. Others seek enlightenment in various religious and philosophies found in Asia, such as Buddhism and Daoism, and among the cultures of certain indigenous peoples in North America and in some nonindustrialized countries. However, some deep ecology philosophers also believe it is possible to re-interpret Judeo-Christian scripture and discover a case for revering nature, rather than exploiting it.

ETHICS BY WHICH TO LIVE

Deep ecology offers more than a critique of Western culture; it also offers ethical principles by which people may live. Among these principles is a call to oppose immoral acts of destruction against nature. Deep ecology also admonishes human beings to turn away from materialism and consumerism, and instead use alternative "soft" energy sources, such as those produced by solar and wind power. Such actions are ethical, suggest deep ecologists, because they help reduce human demands on nature. Deep ecology also instructs humans to live by personal codes of conduct that are more spiritual and natural than those generally demonstrated in industrialized society. Finally, it demands that elected leaders discard economic systems that measure the quality of human life solely in terms of production and consumption. In its place should come new economic systems that consider preservation of the natural world as their highest priority.

CRITICS OF DEEP ECOLOGY

Despite its growing influence, deep ecology faces an array of critics. For example, some environmentalists point out that concentrating on the preservation of the integrity of ecosystems at all costs is misguided. They argue that ethical concern should focus on dynamics in nature, not ecosystems. For example, these critics point out that the violent destruction of an ecosystem, as by a hurricane or a forest fire, is part of a larger interplay of natural forces that relentlessly restructures ecosystems and is often essential to the survival of some species. Others argue that human intervention is often morally good, because it can, at times, preserve and conserve nature using methods that exceed the restorative power of nature. Some opponents also claim that deep ecology itself is ethically flawed because it is "antihuman." Moreover, they argue that a "human-centered" approach to nature is ethical because it meets the needs of human beings. Ecofeminists, on the other hand, insist that not all humans are responsible for the current environment crisis—that only those with power and money are—elite, white men.

In response, many advocates of deep ecology steadfastly insist that humans have no inalienable right willfully to destroy the natural world for their own selfish interests. Deep ecologists also deny their ideas are antihuman. Rather, they say, they are rooted in an ethical creed that commands humans to treasure all living things—including members of their own species. They suggest that if all humanity lived by deep ecology ethics, the natural world, including human beings, might be spared from annihilation.

John M. Dunn

FURTHER READING

Barnhill, David Landis, and Roger S. Gottlieb, eds. *Deep Ecology and World Religions: New Essays on Sacred Ground*. Albany: State University of New York Press, 2001.

Devall, Bill, and George Sessions. *Deep Ecology*. Salt Lake City: Peregrine Smith Books, 1985.

Katz, Eric, Andrew Light, and David Rothenberg, eds. *Beneath the Surface, Critical Essays in the Philosophy of Deep Ecology*. Cambridge, Mass.: MIT Press, 2000.

Leopold, Aldo. *A Sand County Almanac: With Essays on Conservation from Round River*. New York: Ballantine Books, 1970.

Rolston, Homes, III. *Environmental Ethics: Duties to and Values in the Natural World*. Philadelphia: Temple University Press, 1988.

SEE ALSO: Biodiversity; Conservation; Deforestation; Earth and humanity; Ecofeminism; Ecology; Endangered species; Environmental ethics; Environmental movement; Nature, rights of; Rain forests.

Deforestation

DEFINITION: Destruction of forest cover and forest ecosystems by agriculture, urbanization, and the direct exploitation of timber, ores, and other forest resources in ways that prevent forests from being restored

TYPE OF ETHICS: Environmental ethics

SIGNIFICANCE: Forests are important to human society for food, energy supplies, building materials, natural medicines, and recreation and as spiritual sites. They are also important to global ecology for atmospheric cleansing, climate control, soil and water conservation, and biodiversity. Deforestation thus threatens the future of human society and the sustainability of the global ecology.

Ethical issues posed by deforestation transcend cultures, human generations, geographic locations, and species. Throughout history, advancing human societies both increased forest resource exploitation and increased efforts to sculpture forests to meet human ideals of beauty and utility. Hunter-gatherers, slash-and-burn farmers, timber-frame builders, charcoal manufacturers, pulp and plywood producers, and royal and wealthy estate owners all have used forests in their own ways and limited use by others. Many forests are eventually destroyed by overuse. The modern developed world's demand for timber and pulp is especially devastating. By the early twenty-first century, European forests were virtually extinct, and tropical forests had been reduced by one-half from their pre-exploitation states.

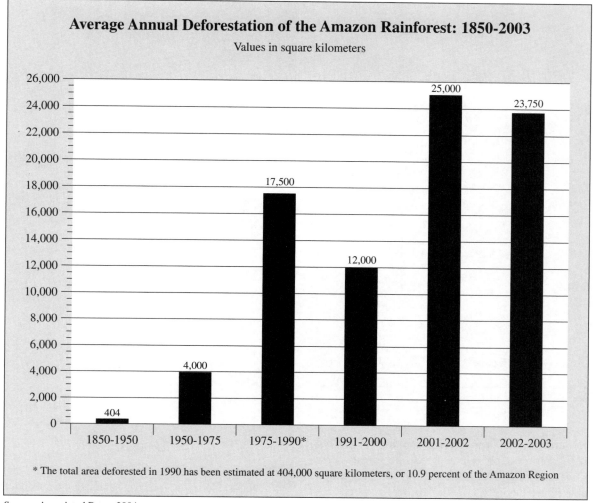

Average Annual Deforestation of the Amazon Rainforest: 1850-2003

Values in square kilometers

* The total area deforested in 1990 has been estimated at 404,000 square kilometers, or 10.9 percent of the Amazon Region

Source: Associated Press, 2004.

Deforestation creates social inequalities. The modern developed society's demand for timber and pulpwood in manufacturing limits the availability of wood for homes and fuel in the developing world and the availability of forests for subsistence and indigenous societies. Excessive exploitation by a single human generation of forest resources that required many centuries to grow leaves future human generations poorer. While the sale of forest resources is often necessary to raise capital in the developing world, such sales leave developing nations poorer in resources.

Deforestation in one location also creates social problems in adjacent and distant regions by damaging shared soil, surface water, and biodiversity resources; allowing desertification to destroy agricultural and grazing lands; altering rainfall patterns and agricultural production; impacting economically important migratory species; and allowing greenhouse gasses and other pollutants to accumulate. Deforestation by humans thus has global and ecological significance for all species and for the survival of the earth itself.

Well-intentioned efforts at forest management, conservation and husbandry, as alternatives to deforestation, often promote species extinction or species dominance and increase threats of natural disasters such as floods, fires, and insect infestations. The results may negatively affect innumerable unmanaged forest resources and place management demands and

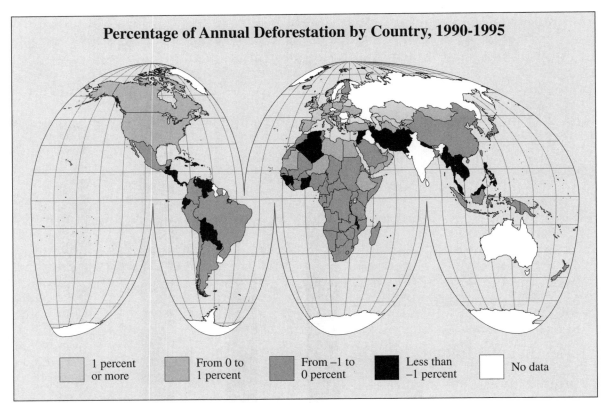

Percentage of Annual Deforestation by Country, 1990-1995

1 percent or more | From 0 to 1 percent | From −1 to 0 percent | Less than −1 percent | No data

Source: United Nations Food and Agriculture Organization.

resource-use limits on future generations. While outright deforestation is prevented, the forests themselves may be left in degraded states with questionable future viability.

Gordon Neal Diem

FURTHER READING

Des Jardins, Joseph R. *Environmental Ethics: An Invitation to Environmental Philosophy.* Belmont, Calif.: Wadsworth, 2001.

Eisenberg, Evan. *The Ecology of Eden.* New York: Alfred A. Knopf, 1998.

Orr, David W. *Earth in Mind.* Washington, D.C.: Island Press, 1994.

Sandler, Todd. *Global Challenges: An Approach to Environmental, Political and Economic Problems.* New York: Cambridge University Press, 1997.

SEE ALSO: Biodiversity; Bioethics; Deep ecology; Ecofeminism; Ecology; Environmental ethics; Land mines; Rain forests; Sustainability of resources.

Deism

DEFINITION: Belief that on the basis of reason and "natural religion," one can establish the existence of an intelligent and ethical Supreme Being, the creator and preserver of the universe

DATE: Concept developed during the sixteenth century

TYPE OF ETHICS: Beliefs and practices

SIGNIFICANCE: Deism represents the deliberate attempt in the sixteenth, seventeenth, and eighteenth centuries to establish a nonsectarian basis for a theistic, rational morality.

In the wake of the sectarian strife that swept Europe in the seventeenth century, there was a desire to find a rational and theistic basis for moral behavior that did not rest on the particular confession of any organized religious tradition, be it Protestant, Roman Catholic, Orthodox, Jewish, Muslim, Buddhist, Hindu, Confucian, or Daoist. The founder of Deism was Lord Herbert of Cherbury, an English statesman and philosopher who had observed the horrors of religious war both in Britain and on the Continent.

Because of the failure to arrive at a consensus regarding Christian ethics, Lord Herbert believed that a natural rather than a revealed religion could furnish the basis of civilized behavior. Taking the word "Deism" (from *deus*, Latin for "god"), a term already in use, Lord Herbert taught, in such books as *On Truth* (1624), *On the Religion of Laymen* (1645), and *On the Religion of Gentiles* (1663), that such "self-evident truths" as the existence of a Supreme Being, who merits human worship and who is best served by moral action, should be sufficient religion for a modern person. In doing so, he forged a spiritual and theistic foundation for morality.

C. George Fry

SEE ALSO: Anti-Semitism; Christian ethics; Enlightenment ethics; God; Humanism; Religion; Voltaire.

Democracy

DEFINITION: Rule by the people
TYPE OF ETHICS: Politico-economic ethics
SIGNIFICANCE: Democracy is rooted in a fundamentally egalitarian ethic, encapsulated in the phrase "one person, one vote," which values self-determination as the primary principle of government. Pure democracy, however, has also been labeled a "tyranny of the majority," and modern democratic nations have universally instituted safeguards to ensure that persons in the minority retain basic civil rights despite the will of the majority.

The ideal of democracy is perhaps the most powerful force in politics since the seventeenth century. In fact, democracy can be traced all the way to the sixth century B.C.E., although the question of the efficiency and legitimacy of democracy has primarily been a modern issue. The irony of democracy has always been its elusiveness. Democracy means rule by the people, but that phrase has meant many different things and has been used as both a force for liberation and a cloak to legitimize tyranny. Ironically, few modern authoritarian regimes have neglected to claim that they rule in the name of the people.

HISTORY

The word "democracy" comes from the Greek word *dīmokratia*, meaning "rule by the people." The Greek ideal, originating with the polis of Athens, was that only democracy and rule of law preserved human dignity. Athenians believed that citizens had both the responsibility and the ability to govern themselves. Self-governance preserved human agency and creativity in a way that was impossible for monarchy and dictatorship. Only when engaged in politics could a citizen be free from necessity and self-interest. Democracy and political action freed one to pursue the common good. As citizens within the polis, all were inherently equal. These core beliefs of responsibility, creativity, equality, and dignity are the foundation of democratic ethics.

Greek democracy is often criticized for being exclusive, yet after 500 B.C.E., citizenship in Athens was extended to all adult male citizens. Participation in the assembly was open and membership in the Council of Five Hundred was chosen annually by lot, as were many positions in public service. Citizen participation was high, and the decision rules emphasized direct democracy. Wealth was no bar to citizen participation. In this environment, the values of democracy and of participation as the source of human dignity were established for the millennia.

MODERN DEVELOPMENTS

Much that had been taken from the Greeks was preserved in the Roman Republic. From the Romans, the world inherited a great legacy according to which law and human rights are inextricably linked by natural law. This idea was repeated in the American Declaration of Independence (1776) and in the French Declaration of the Rights of Man and the Citizen (1789). These documents demonstrated an evolving sense that citizen self-government is a right of all people that provides the greatest opportunity for human dignity. The source of this ideal is the belief in human equality.

Modern democracy is born of the democratic revolutions against European feudalism in the eighteenth century. The ideas of the social contract, found in the works of John Locke, Jean-Jacques Rousseau, and others, were lashed together with liberalism to ignite a democratic explosion in America and beyond. The consistent theme in these democratic revolutions was the belief in a natural human equality. This ideal did not originally include women and

The Failure of Democracy in Latin America

Over nearly two centuries, the forces of democracy and authoritarianism have struggled for control of Latin America's many governments. The failure of democracy to grow deep roots in the Spanish- and Portuguese-speaking nations south of Canada and the United States was dramatized when the findings of a three-year study conducted by the United Nations Development Program were released in April, 2004.

Drawing on polls conducted among 18,600 Latin Americans and interviews with political leaders in eighteen countries (all the Spanish- and Portuguese-speaking nations except Cuba, which has the most authoritarian government in the Western Hemisphere), the survey found growing popular support for authoritarian government. Proauthoritarian sentiment was especially strong among the poor—who constitute the majority in most Latin American countries. Among the specific findings of the survey:

- 58.1 percent of all people polled believed that presidents should be allowed to act outside the law

- 56.3 percent believe that economic development is more important than democracy

- 54.7 percent would support authoritarian regimes if they solved economic problems

- 43.9 percent do not believe that democracy can solve their nations' problems

- 38.2 percent believe that democracy can exist without national legislatures

- 37.2 percent believe that presidents should use force to establish order

- 37.2 percent believe that presidents should control the news media

Source: Los Angeles Times, April 22, 2004, drawing on United Nations Development Program.

consent of the governed. This denied the legitimacy of theocratic or personalist regimes. Liberalism, with its link to free-market capitalism, argued that all people were inherently equal and must have the opportunity to participate without regard to birthright. This attack on the prerogatives of feudalism hinged on the notion that freedom of choice and competition would make for social progress.

In liberal capitalism, equality is based on human value and requires only an equal opportunity to participate. Included herein were the ideas of inalienable rights, civil liberties, and freedoms espoused by modern democracies. It was not long before critics of the the liberal paradigm, in the wake of the pain of the Industrial Revolution, argued that this idea of equality was false. Competiton is not "equal" if those who are born poor and excluded do not enjoy either equality or the fruits of democracy. Associated with the ideas of socialism and Karl Marx, this critique of liberal capitalism argued that all societies in history are dominated by economic classes. According to this critique, capitalist democracy is only another form of class domination, and the liberal façade only masks the dictatorship of the capitalists.

Several streams of thought concerning democratic values and equality emerged. In the liberal capitalist idea, democracy was a direct outgrowth of the capitalist free market. For the socialist, democracy could be obtained only in a classless society that guaranteed not only equal opportunity but also material equality. All states rule in the name of a dominant class. Until social classes vanished, true democracy could not exist. To this may be added the anarchist vision that argued that all forms of government create hierarchies of power. For the anarchist, the only meaningful democracy is one founded in small communities based on direct democracy.

slaves or those without property, but the idea had a momentum that gradually expanded the rights and powers of citizen participation.

CONFLICTS AND PRINCIPLES

The ideas of liberal philosophy and the social contract theory of the Enlightenment imparted several themes. Social contract theory argued that the only legitimate government was one that was based on the

GENERAL OUTLINE

Modern democracy has several key elements. In it, citizen participation in decision making always exists in some form. This usually includes a system of representation, which is necessary in large, complex nation-states. Representation must be the result of an open contest and pluralist setting. Democracies accept the rule of law, at least in the sense that the rule of a despot or a dictatorship is unacceptable. Governors and governed must submit to the same laws. An electoral system based on majority rule is usually present, and universal suffrage of all citizens is strongly featured. Some form of citizen equality must be present, and liberties and freedoms, recognized as rights and granted by the state, must exist to allow open participation, association, and expression. Significantly, there will be some kind of political education about democratic principles and responsibilities. Democratic polities must be educated polities if democracy is to be meaningful. To participate, citizens must understand rules, issues, and their own responsibility to the common good.

The ethics of democracy go beyond the structure of governments. Equality, creativity, dignity, and the free space for political discourse that allows human beings to be free from self-interest and to make a lasting imprint on history—these are the immutable and elusive values of democracy.

Anthony R. Brunello

FURTHER READING

Almond, Gabriel A., and Sidney Verba. *The Civic Culture: Political Attitudes and Democracy in Five Nations.* Newbury Park, Calif.: Sage, 1989.

Anderson, Charles W. *A Deeper Freedom: Liberal Democracy as an Everyday Morality.* Madison: University of Wisconsin Press, 2002.

Arendt, Hannah. *The Human Condition.* 2d ed. Introduction by Margaret Canovan. Chicago: Chicago University Press, 1998.

Aristotle. *The Politics.* Translated by Ernest Barker. Rev. ed. Introduction by R. F. Stalley. New York: Oxford University Press, 1995.

Churchill, Robert Paul, ed. *The Ethics of Liberal Democracy: Morality and Democracy in Theory and Practice.* Providence, R.I.: Berg, 1994.

Lincoln, Abraham. *The Gettysburg Address.* Los Angeles: G. Dawson, 1961.

Mill, John Stuart. *On Liberty, and Other Essays.* Edited by John Gray. New York: Oxford University Press, 1998.

Stripling, Scott R. *Capitalism, Democracy, and Morality.* Acton, Mass.: Copley, 1994.

Ziarek, Ewa Płonowska. *An Ethics of Dissensus: Postmodernity, Feminism, and the Politics of Radical Democracy.* Stanford, Calif.: Stanford University Press, 2001.

SEE ALSO: Aristotle; Constitution, U.S.; Constitutional government; Declaration of Independence; *On Liberty*; Political liberty; Rousseau, Jean-Jacques.

Deontological ethics

DEFINITION: School of ethics that considers actions to be intrinsically right or wrong, regardless of their consequences
TYPE OF ETHICS: Theory of ethics
SIGNIFICANCE: Deontological ethics is one of the two major categories of modern ethical theory.

Modern ethical theories can be divided into two broad categories: deontological and teleological, the ethics of duty and obligation versus the ethics of ends and consequences. In order to understand properly the nature of deontological theories, it is necessary to understand the essential features of teleological theories. A teleological theory gives the good priority over the right. The good is defined as the end or purpose of human actions; for example, "the greatest happiness for the greatest number." These theories evaluate moral actions in terms of whether they contribute to the good. For example, does one's action maximize happiness for the greatest number? If so, it is the right thing to do. In other words, the right is adjectival to the good and completely dependent upon it. Thus, according to teleological theories such as consequentialism, consequences or results determine the rightness or wrongness of moral actions.

Deontological theories, however, argue for the priority of the right over the good or the independence of the right from the good. Actions are intrinsically right or wrong, regardless of the consequences that they produce. The right or ethically appropriate action might be deduced from a duty or a basic human right, but it is never contingent upon the outcome or consequences of an action. In short, according to this perspective, actions do have intrinsic moral value.

PHILOSOPHICAL ORIGINS

The term "deontological" is derived from the Greek word *deon*, which means obligation or duty. Hence, deontological approaches to morality stress what is obligatory, what one ought to do, but with no reference at all to value or a conception of goodness.

An important distinction is generally made between act-deontological and rule-deontological theories. Act deontologists claim that moral judgments expressing obligations must be specific; for example, "In this situation I must not break my promise." They do not accept general obligations or rules such as "we must always keep promises." According to the act deontologist, one cannot generalize about obligations but must derive and formulate them in the context of particular circumstances. This view of ethics is expressed in the writings of the ethicist Edgar F. Carritt, such as his *Theory of Morals* (1928).

A more common approach is known as rule deontology. Rule deontologists maintain that morality consists of general rules that are usually expressed as duties or obligations. Such duties are fundamental and do not depend on the concrete circumstances of a particular situation. According to this viewpoint, one deduces one's particular obligation from a general rule or duty. The divine command theory, contractarianism or rights-based ethics, ethical intuitionism, and Kantianism represent some examples of rule deontology. The divine command theory, for example, argues that whatever God commands is right or obligatory. Thus, the rules of ethics might be the Ten Commandments or other divine commands revealed by God. Despite the appeal of this theory, it is considered problematic by ethicists for one basic reason: To interpret morality as something that depends on the will of another, including an infinite God, seems to undermine the autonomy of morality.

IMMANUEL KANT

The most prominent deontological thinker is undoubtedly Immanuel Kant. According to Kant, an action's moral worth is not found in what it tries to accomplish but in the agent's intention and the summoning of one's energies to carry out that intention.

Results, purposes, and consequences are excluded from Kant's moral philosophy, and this is obviously in direct contrast to consequentialism and teleological approaches to ethics. The moral person must perform actions for the sake of duty regardless of the consequences, but what is the duty of the rational moral agent? According to Kant, one's moral duty is simple and singular: to follow the moral law that is expressed in the categorical imperative—always act according to a maxim that is at the same time valid as a universal moral law. In other words, can the action in question (such as breaking a promise) pass the test of universalization? If not, the action is immoral and one has a duty to avoid it.

Ethical intuitionism is a related deontological theory developed by William D. Ross. Ross claims that through reflection on ordinary moral beliefs, people can *intuit* the rules of morality. These rules are duties such as "one ought to keep promises and tell the truth." They are prima facie obligations, which means that they do allow for exceptions; however, one of these basic duties can be superseded only by a more important, higher obligation, usually only under very exceptional circumstances. Thus, a moral principle or prima facie duty can be sacrificed, but only for another moral principle. As with Kant, so with Ross; one is obliged to follow one's moral duty regardless of the consequences.

Finally, contractarianism (rights-based ethical theories) represents another species of deontological ethical reasoning. For example, in *A Theory of Justice* (1971), the modern philosopher John Rawls contends that the principle of justice as fairness is prior to the conception of goodness and must also limit that conception. According to Rawls's framework, a just society is one that requires "equality in the assignment of basic rights and duties." It is important to appreciate that in Rawls's view, it is the fairness of society's norms or rules, not their consequences, that gives those norms any genuine moral force.

Despite their differences, all these theories have in common the basic premise that the right is prior to the good and that beneficial results do not determine one's moral duty. They emphasize fidelity to principle and the independence of rightness, which is the main focus of the moral life.

Richard A. Spinello

FURTHER READING

Brandt, Richard B. *A Theory of the Good and the Right.* Foreword by Peter Singer. Rev. ed. Amherst, N.Y.: Prometheus Books, 1998.

Darwall, Stephen, ed. *Deontology.* Malden, Mass.: Blackwell, 2003.

Frankena, William K. *Ethics.* 2d ed. Englewood Cliffs, N.J.: Prentice-Hall, 1973.

Kant, Immanuel. *Groundwork for the Metaphysics of Morals.* Edited and translated by Allen W. Wood. New Haven, Conn.: Yale University Press, 2002.

Rawls, John. *A Theory of Justice.* Rev. ed. Cambridge, Mass.: Belknap Press of Harvard University Press, 1999.

Ross, William D. *The Right and the Good.* New ed. New York: Oxford University Press, 2002.

SEE ALSO: Divine command theory; Duty; Justice; Kant, Immanuel; Kantian ethics; Rawls, John; Teleological ethics; *Theory of Justice, A.*

Derrida, Jacques

IDENTIFICATION: French philosopher
BORN: July 15, 1930, El Biar, Algeria
DIED: October 8, 2004, Paris, France
TYPE OF ETHICS: Modern history
SIGNIFICANCE: Derrida is most noted as an originator of a school of philosophy and literary criticism known as deconstruction. His best-known works, including *Speech and Phenomena* (*La Voix et le phénomène*, 1967), *Writing and Difference* (*L'Écriture et la différence*, 1967), and *Margins of Philosophy* (*Marges de la philosophie*, 1972), engage in extended critiques of the metaphysical model underlying all of traditional Western philosophy. This critique has forced philosophers to reconsider the very nature, methodology, and boundaries of the field of ethics.

Although Jacques Derrida's philosophy has an implicit ethical component, he pointedly refrains from proposing an ethics of his own in any straightforward sense. The closest he comes is to offer something like a metacritique, a critical analysis of the concept of ethics, or what one might call an ethics of ethics. This is radically different, however, from metaethics,

which is a philosophical attempt objectively to ground the practice of ethics. Derrida's most sustained critiques have been leveled against precisely the notion that such objective philosophical grounding is either possible or desirable.

DECONSTRUCTION

Derrida's larger philosophical project, often succinctly described by others as deconstruction, is one that seeks to undermine Western philosophy's pretension to totality, as a foundational, closed system of explanation. Ethics, together with metaphysics and epistemology, forms one of three branches of Western philosophy. As such, Derrida's deconstruction of ethics does not offer an ethics, but rather makes ethics an object of critical analysis. As part of the pretension of Western metaphysics to totality, he works to show ethics' own conceptual limitations. In fact, Derrida regards his project less as a critical analysis of ethics than one in which ethics unravels under its own weight: It deconstructs itself.

LEVINAS, VIOLENCE AND METAPHYSICS

Derrida's own meditation on ethics takes place in large part through a critical analysis of the work of another contemporary French philosopher, Emmanuel Levinas. Levinas affirms that ethics, rather than knowledge (epistemology or metaphysics) is first philosophy. Ethics is logically primary. This is so because one's first considered or self-conscious human encounter with the world is an encounter with the Other, with other people whose minds and desires are fundamentally different from one's own. This encounter remains at the center of the philosophical project, because it raises what for both Levinas and Derrida is the fundamental philosophical question: How is it possible to respect the otherness of the Other? How is it possible to avoid the violence inherent in comprehension, to refrain from understanding the Other solely in terms of one's own values, and instead to preserve radical otherness in a pure ethical relationship?

Derrida affirms his proximity to Levinas's project and the notion of ethics as first philosophy, all while radicalizing Levinas's work by questioning whether the so-called purity of the ethical relation to the other is not itself a form of violence. He works with two hands. What he gives with one hand, he takes away with the other. What Derrida suggests in this critical confrontation with the concept of ethics is that the ethical is always already contaminated by the non-ethical, so that ethics may be a desirable first philosophy, but first philosophy itself remains impossible. His argument is perhaps best thought of in terms of the lesser violence of a vaccine: One acknowledges and suffers a minor contamination at the outset of an inoculation in order to avoid the disease itself. This perversion then, the admixture of nonethical concerns with the supposedly pure ethical relationship, is the positive condition of possibility of all ethical values (justice, virtue, the Good).

Derrida's approach to ethics situates itself as a hinge, as a moment in the willful ambivalence between the articulation of an ethical relation and its own impossibility. As a critical, destabilizing gesture, he consistently situates himself between two philosophical poles. For instance, he places himself between Levinas's claim of ethics as first philosophy and the phenomenological critique of the traditional divisions of philosophy, and thus of ethics itself as a distinct field. Also, he affirms Levinas's critique of the autonomous Western subject through his insight into alterity (that is, the radically alien as the place where one comes to know one's own values) as the site of the ethical, all while seeking to question the concept of alterity itself.

It is through this analysis of an absolute alterity that Derrida hopes to articulate a sense of responsibility that finds its source neither in a form of sheer alterity (the responsibility to refrain from violating the otherness of the Other), nor in the expression of a voluntaristic subjective will (the responsibility to choose correctly, free from all constraint and outside influence). As a riposte, Derrida seems to confront Levinas's work with a form of decisionism: a singular decision, beyond any concept or universal rule, made in the face of singular events.

However, Derrida's call for decisionism also outstrips the conceptual resources of the Western subject. As a consequence, between these mutually insufficient poles of the autonomous subject (activity) and alterity (passivity), Derrida begins to articulate a form of responsibility as a decisionism that nevertheless is not the mere voluntaristic expression of the subjective will. If the idea of a singular decision without a deciding subject seems difficult to grasp conceptually, then Derrida has succeeded in forcing others to reconsider traditionally received accounts of ethics.

One of Derrida's central contributions to ethics is his destabilization of the very concept of ethics, and it is his call for the constant rethinking of the ethical that should itself be understood as an ethical act.

F. Scott Scribner
Updated by the Editors

FURTHER READING

Bennington, Geoffrey. *Interrupting Derrida*. London: Routledge/Taylor and Francis Group, 2000.

Critchley, Simon. *The Ethics of Deconstruction: Derrida and Levinas*. 2d ed. West Lafayette, Ind.: Purdue University Press, 1999.

Culler, Jonathan, ed. *Deconstruction: Critical Concepts in Literary and Cultural Studies*. 4 vols. New York: Routledge, 2003.

Derrida, Jacques. *Ethics, Institutions, and the Right to Philosophy*. Edited and translated by Peter Pericles Trifonas. Lanham, Md.: Rowman & Littlefield, 2002.

Dronsfield, Jonathon, and Nick Midgley, eds. *Responsibilities of Deconstruction*. Coventry, Warwickshire, England: University of Warwick, 1997.

Duncan, Diane Moira. *The Pre-Text of Ethics: On Derrida and Levinas*. New York: P. Lang, 2001.

Srajek, Martin C. *In the Margins of Deconstruction: Jewish Conceptions of Ethics in Emmanuel Levinas and Jacques Derrida*. Pittsburgh, Pa.: Duquesne University Press, 2000.

SEE ALSO: Critical theory; Deconstruction; Epistemological ethics; Foucault, Michel; Language; Levinas, Emmanuel; Metaethics; Nietzsche, Friedrich; Other, the; Postmodernism.

Descartes, René

IDENTIFICATION: French mathematician and philosopher

BORN: March 31, 1596, La Haye, Touraine, France

DIED: February 11, 1650, Stockholm, Sweden

TYPE OF ETHICS: Renaissance and Restoration history

SIGNIFICANCE: Descartes shifted the focus of philosophy from metaphysics toward the human self, preparing the way for the increased interest in ethics and human behavior that is typical of modern thought.

René Descartes. (Library of Congress)

René Descartes was educated at the Jesuit College of La Flèche. In his influential works *Discourse on Method* (*Discours de la méthode*, 1637) and *Meditations on First Philosophy* (*Meditationes de Prima Philosophia*, 1641), Descartes moved toward epistemology, questioning what a person can know. This move was accompanied by a particular method that proceeded by systematically doubting everything that could be doubted. Only an "unshakable foundation" that was absolutely impregnable to doubt could serve as a reliable basis for a system of knowledge.

Descartes believed that he had found this foundation in the formulation *cogito ergo sum*—"I think, therefore I am." Consciousness of one's own existence appeared to be a certainty that could not be doubted. The rest of his system proceeds from this initial certainty.

The Cartesian method, which aims to take nothing for granted and assumes that truth is to be defined in terms of certainty and mathematical clarity, presented ground rules of scientific inquiry that are still used.

Descartes's dualism, which divides reality into two categories of things—human consciousness, defined as "thinking things" (*res cogitans*), and all matter, defined as "place-filling things" (*res extensa*)—played a central role in founding the modern perception of human beings as "subjects" and things as "objects."

Ted William Dreier

SEE ALSO: Christian ethics; Epistemological ethics; Locke, John; Spinoza, Baruch; Stoic ethics; Will.

Desire

DEFINITION: Positive psychological inclination toward possession of an object or achievement of a state of affairs

TYPE OF ETHICS: Personal and social ethics

SIGNIFICANCE: Desire motivates action, so it is a crucial factor in theories of moral responsibility that focus on intention. For some philosophers, having particular desires or even the strength of one's desires can be morally praiseworthy or blameworthy.

To desire something is to want it. Desire motivates action and directs an agent toward an intended object or state of affairs that the agent wishes to possess or bring about. It provides a reason to act and a structure by means of which a connected series of actions can be ordered in means-ends relations to explain and sometimes justify why an agent behaves in a certain way. The desires that move persons to act are often essential to the moral evaluation of their actions.

HISTORY

The history of desire begins with prehuman animal wants and motivations. Desire features in the explanation of action from the time of the earliest Greek philosophy. Eros and Aphrodite (Venus), gods of love and desire, epitomize the inclination to possess or achieve desired objects. In ancient poetry and philosophy, Aphrodite in particular is frequently appealed to as the force that moves the cosmos.

In Plato's *Symposium*, Socrates presents the view that the search for knowledge and moral perfection begins with an attraction to and desire for physical beauty that leads to more intellectual desires. Philosophy itself is love of or desire for knowledge, from which Socrates concludes that the gods are not philosophers, since they already possess complete knowledge and cannot desire what they already have. In the *Nicomachean Ethics*, Aristotle maintains that all persons act out of the desire to achieve happiness, by which he means a good life in fulfillment of human purpose. This idea provides a foundational theory of moral action, according to which all actions are undertaken for the sake of accomplishing an end and all ends can be ordered in a hierarchy of ends, each of which contributes as a means to another end, terminating finally in the desire for happiness as the ultimate end.

Modern philosophy in the intentionalist tradition similarly emphasizes wants and desires in understanding what an agent intends to do, in order to explain and morally justify or condemn the agent's actions. Robert Audi, Roderick M. Chisholm, Donald Davidson, Joseph Margolis, and Richard Taylor are among philosophers who have developed theories of morally responsible action based on the intentional concepts of wanting or desire. They hold that desire is the intentional component of action in the same way that belief is the intentional component of knowledge.

EXPLANATION AND MORAL EVALUATION

An action is undertaken to satisfy a desire. Desires determine action goals, motivate, and give agents a reason to act. The agent wants to do something and may be aware of the desire that motivates the act. To explain a particular action according to this theory, it is necessary to identify the desire an agent tries to satisfy. Psychoanalysis presupposes that persons act out of subconscious as well as conscious desires, so that even seemingly meaningless actions for which the agent can give no explanation may also be driven by hidden desires or wants. Even if that assumption is not true, it is plausible to characterize all action as being motivated by desire. The simplest action of moving a finger for no other purpose is at least the result of a desire to move a finger. The fact that actions appear to be unexplained unless or until a desire is identified as an end for which action is the means of satisfaction supports the intentionalist theory that desire motivates action.

Desires can be good, bad, or indifferent, according to various moral outlooks and theories. Moral philosophies can often be distinguished and categorized on the basis of their attitudes toward desires and the kinds of desires they encourage, permit, or forbid. Ordinarily, it is regarded as wrong or morally blameworthy to desire that innocent persons suffer or that evil triumph over good, while it may be right or morally praiseworthy to desire the greatest possible happiness for all persons. Particular moral systems postulate that certain kinds of desires are intrinsically ethically right or wrong. Sometimes the desire for worldly things, especially when it involves the appetites, is considered wrong. The extreme form of this moral attitude is asceticism, in which ethical conduct is made synonymous with resisting temptations, exercising self-control, and renouncing bodily desires. More abstract or universal desires that are in accord with preferred moral principles, such as the desire for peace and mutual respect of persons, are usually judged to be intrinsically good.

CONFLICTING DESIRES

If Aristotle is right about the common hierarchy of purposes that has happiness as its ultimate end, then all other desires, even as proximate ends or purposes of other actions, are related as means to that single end. This idea implies that desires are in some sense mutually consistent and compatible. Yet there appear to be conflicts of desires that cannot be jointly satisfied, as is the case when a conscientious objector desires to obey both conscience and the law. Conflicts of this kind are often interpreted as moral dilemmas. Intentionalist action theory is divided over the question of whether Aristotle's foundational hierarchy of means and ends terminating in a single end is correct or whether the more appropriate model of desires involves many different shorter chains of actions as means to desires as ends that do not contribute to a single purpose but may either cohere or conflict with one another.

Dale Jacquette

FURTHER READING

Blackburn, Simon. *Lust.* New York: Oxford University Press, 2004.

Brecher, Bob. *Getting What You Want? A Critique of Liberal Morality.* New York: Routledge, 1998.

Chisholm, Roderick M. *Person and Object: A Metaphysical Study.* London: Allen & Unwin, 1976.

Davidson, Donald. *Essays on Actions and Events.* Oxford, England: Clarendon Press, 1980.

Loar, Brian. *Mind and Meaning*. Cambridge, England: Cambridge University Press, 1981.

McGinn, Colin. *Mental Content*. Oxford, England: Basil Blackwell, 1989.

Margolis, Joseph. *Philosophy of Psychology*. Englewood Cliffs, N.J.: Prentice Hall, 1984.

Schueler, G. F. *Desire: Its Role in Practical Reason and the Explanation of Action*. Cambridge, Mass.: MIT Press, 1995.

Taylor, Richard. *Action and Purpose*. Englewood Cliffs: N.J.: Prentice Hall, 1966.

Thorndike, Edward Lee, et al. *The Psychology of Wants, Interests, and Attitudes*. New York: Appleton-Century, 1935. Reprint. New York: Johnson, 1970.

SEE ALSO: Aristotle; Asceticism; Dilemmas, moral; Intention; Intrinsic good; Needs and wants; Passions and emotions; Plato; Responsibility; Self-control.

Determinism and freedom

DEFINITION: Determinism is the view that everything including human thought and action has a cause; freedom is the ability to govern one's own actions

TYPE OF ETHICS: Theory of ethics

SIGNIFICANCE: Some philosophers believe that determinism would rule out freedom and that without freedom people could not be morally responsible—that is, blameworthy or praiseworthy—for their actions. Others believe that only actions that are determined—that is, that result necessarily from the fundamental character of the actor—can be the object of moral judgments.

Compatibilism is the view that determinism is compatible with freedom and moral responsibility. Incompatibilism is the view that determinism is incompatible with freedom and moral responsibility. Libertarianism and hard determinism are the major varieties of incompatibilism. Libertarians claim that determinism is false and that people are free and morally responsible. In contrast, hard determinists claim that because determinism is true, people are neither free nor morally responsible.

A major argument for hard determinism goes as follows. "Everything one does is causally determined, and therefore no one can ever act otherwise than he or she does. That being the case, no one ever acts freely, and without freedom, no one is ever morally responsible for what he or she does."

It may be tempting to reject hard determinism because it is a socially dangerous view, providing as it does a wholesale excuse for any wrongdoing. This response, however, is irrelevant, since it is clear that a view can be socially dangerous and can still be true.

Agreeing that determinism would rule out freedom, libertarians reject the hard determinist argument by claiming that there is good introspective evidence for freedom and against determinism. They argue that the belief in freedom is justified by a feeling of freedom, a feeling of not being causally determined, when making moral decisions. While all people may have a feeling of some kind of freedom in these cases, for many it is not a feeling of libertarian "contracausal" freedom. Instead, one has a feeling of being able to choose as one wants, not a feeling of not being caused. Moreover, even if one does have a feeling of libertarian freedom, such feelings can be misleading. A person acting under posthypnotic suggestion may also have such a feeling. The feeling of being contracausally free does not seem to be a reliable basis for rejecting the hard determinist argument.

Even if libertarians can provide good evidence that people are contracausally free, they still need to explain why contracausal choices are not merely matters of pure chance. Libertarians try to account for contracausal choices by appealing to reasons that do not cause people to choose as they do. The view that reasons are not causes, however, seems less plausible than the view that reasons are causes. The latter view makes better sense of the relationship between reasons and actions and makes it clear how to distinguish one's real reason for acting from other reasons for acting. If neither noncausing reasons nor causes explain contracausal choices, such choices would seem to be pure matters of chance. If that is the case, it is difficult to see how people could be morally responsible for their choices.

THE COMPATIBILIST VIEW

Compatibilists maintain that the hard determinist argument is based on misunderstandings of key terms and phrases, such as "freely," "caused," and "could have done otherwise." Many compatibilists claim that acting freely is a matter of acting as one pleases, instead of acting without being caused to do so. They point out that acting as one pleases does not conflict with one's being causally determined to act as one does. Believing that freedom also requires the capacity to do otherwise, they attack the hard determinist argument by claiming that determinism would not rule out this capacity.

Many compatibilists claim that hard determinists are misled by a faulty theory of causality. Hard determinists think of causality in terms of necessitation, when in fact causality is nothing more than one type of event being regularly followed by another type of event. In this regularity view, causal laws do not prescribe what must happen; they describe only what does happen. Compatibilists maintain that since causes do not necessitate, being causally determined to act in a certain way does not rule out the capacity to act otherwise; therefore, the hard determinist argument fails.

The regularity theory is itself problematic. According to it, there are causal relations between types of events only because people live in a world in which these types of events happen to be constantly conjoined. Causal relations seem, however, to involve more than this. It seems incredible that arm wrestling is nothing more than one person's exertion that simply is followed by another person's arm going down. If one's arm goes down because of the force exerted against it, the regularity theory seems implausible.

Without relying on the regularity theory, other compatibilists still maintain that determinism would not rule out one's capacity to do otherwise. They analyze the phrase "He could have done otherwise" as "He would have done otherwise had he so chosen" and then point out that one's being causally determined to do something does not mean that one would not have done something else if one had so chosen.

This hypothetical sense of "could have," however, does not seem to be the one that is important for freedom. Consider a man who has no control over his choices, since he has been drugged and hypnotized. The reason that he does not act freely in this case is that he could not do anything else. He could have done otherwise, however, in the sense that he would have done otherwise if he had so chosen.

Compatibilist senses of "could have," such as "not having a dispositional property that rules out alternatives," may fare better. In any case, compatibilist accounts of freedom should take into account not only the ability to do otherwise but also the ability to choose otherwise.

Gregory P. Rich

FURTHER READING

Berofsky, Bernard, ed. *Free Will and Determinism*. New York: Harper & Row, 1966.

Hook, Sidney, ed. *Determinism and Freedom in the Age of Modern Science*. New York: Collier Books, 1961.

Hume, David. *Enquiries Concerning Human Understanding and Concerning the Principles of Morals*. 3d ed. Oxford, England: Clarendon Press, 1975.

Kane, Robert, ed. *The Oxford Handbook of Free Will*. New York: Oxford University Press, 2002.

Mackenzie, Patrick T. *Mind, Body, and Freedom*. Amherst, N.Y.: Humanity Books, 2003.

Morgenbesser, Sidney, and James Walsh, ed. *Free Will*. Englewood Cliffs, N.J.: Prentice-Hall, 1962.

Van Inwagen, Peter. *An Essay on Free Will*. New York: Oxford University Press, 1983.

Watson, Gary, ed. *Free Will*. New York: Oxford University Press, 1982.

SEE ALSO: Aristotle; Augustine, Saint; Fatalism; Freedom and liberty; Hobbes, Thomas; Hume, David; Locke, John; Moral responsibility; Will.

Deterrence

DEFINITION: Prevention of an undesirable action through the threat of retaliation

TYPE OF ETHICS: Military ethics; legal and judicial ethics

SIGNIFICANCE: The use of deterrence in criminal law and international relations raises the moral question of whether the means (capital punishment, the possibility of massive destruction) justifies the end (prevention of crimes, the maintenance of international peace).

The need to deter people from committing violent crimes has frequently been used to justify capital punishment. The argument has been made that stronger punishments are more frightening than weaker punishments, and the ultimate punishment is therefore the one most likely to deter potential murderers. Those who disagree with this argument have countered that extreme crimes such as murder are generally not committed by rational agents who weigh all the pros and cons before deciding whether to act. They are crimes of passion, committed without thought to the consequences. If this point of view is correct, the very model of deterrence would seem to be misapplied by states that seek to use capital punishment, or any punishment, as a deterrent to murder.

Nuclear deterrence was conceived as preventing the use of nuclear weapons by others by assuring a second-strike capability that was capable of inflicting considerable damage on the aggressor. This concept replaced the traditional balance-of-power system of the conventional arms age, ushering in the balance-of-terror age of nuclear technology. While some argued that it was instrumental in avoiding nuclear war during the Cold War and therefore helped to maintain international peace, others saw the persistent threat of nuclear retaliation as a morally bankrupt policy. In a deterrence scenario, each party is constrained to see the other as a potential inflicter of harm, a scenario that encourages a mutual permanent state of distrust.

Although there is a consensus regarding the moral importance of defending oneself against external aggression, where nuclear deterrence is concerned, there is more skepticism regarding the moral character of the means by which this is to be achieved. Perhaps what makes this concept so ethically controversial is the paradox it embodies: As one informed observer put it, people threaten evil in order not to do it, and the doing of it will be so terrible that the threat seems in comparison to be morally defensible.

Olusoji A. Akomolafe

SEE ALSO: Capital punishment; Cold War; Mutually Assured Destruction; Sanctions; Weapons research.

Developing world

DEFINITION: Comprehensive term for nations that are undeveloped or in various stages of industrial development, such nations are also often called "Third World" nations

TYPE OF ETHICS: International relations

SIGNIFICANCE: Because virtually all the world's developing nations were formerly under direct colonial rule or subject to economic exploitation by European nations and the United States, questions arise as to what moral and ethical responsibilities developed nations have toward the nations facing great problems of poverty, disease, and political instability.

The term "developing world" emerged from ethical debates over the propriety of using such expressions as "undeveloped" or "underdeveloped"—both judgmental words based upon Western assumptions about standards of economic or political progress. In an effort to minimize the negative connotations of such assessments, the United Nations (U.N.) allows each country to decide for itself whether it should be designated "undeveloped" or "developing." Since the 1960's, the euphemism "developing" has been used to ease the prejudicial connotations of the older terms, but ethical questions concerning responsibility for the lack of development in such countries remain controversial.

THE POSTCOLONIAL WORLD

Vast inequities in the standards of living between developed and developing nations raise fundamental questions of global justice. According to early twenty-first century U.N. statistics, 826 million people in the developing world lack adequate nutrition, more than 850 million are illiterate, and one in five children die from preventable causes. At the same time, the 15 percent of the world's population living in the richest nations enjoy almost 80 percent of the world's wealth, while the poorest 46 percent of the world's population have only 1.25 percent of global wealth. Inequity alone would raise ethical questions, but there is also the question of blame for these inequities.

Some political theorists argue that the West has a large responsibility for the lack of economic development in developing nations that is the result of

Western imperialism or economic exploitation, and in the case of Africa, the enslavement of millions of people. Focusing particularly on the destructive consequences of slavery, critics argue that since the industrial and economic development of Europe and the United States benefited from the exploitation of colonial peoples, the developed world owes reparations to the developing world as compensation for such damage. Some economists deny that either imperialism or slavery were crucial in the capital accumulation leading to the industrialization and subsequent prosperity of European nations and the United States, attributing the success of economic development to growth factors internal to their domestic markets.

There is, however, much less debate that imperialism had deleterious effects upon the socioeconomic development of most colonies and there is no disagreement over the horrendous consequences of slavery upon the Africa. In a seminal conceptual reformulation of the concept of "underdevelopment,"

the historian André Gundar Frank observed that what was meant by "underdevelopment" was not some original or primitive precolonial condition, but the actual results of the destructive process of imperial exploitation. Moral responsibility toward the developing world thus arises both from obligations to ease the suffering of nations that are the worst off as well as obligations to rectify wrongs committed by former colonial powers.

NATION-STATE BUILDING

Recognizing that there are moral obligations to the least fortunate across the globe does not determine what remedy should be pursued to relieve their suffering. Modern ethicists and political theorists agree that individuals should collectively decide what is in their own best interests, but there is great debate about what should be the mechanism of collective decision making. During the Cold War era, both democratic and communist powers articulated their foreign policy agenda in ethical terms of pro-

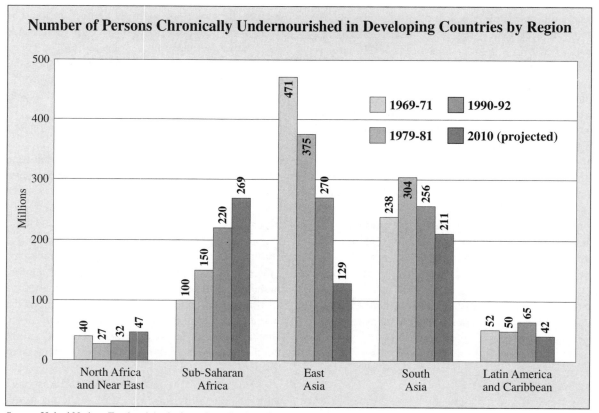

Source: United Nations Food and Agriculture Organization (FAOSTAT Database, 2000).

moting freedom and self-determination among their client states in the developing world. Nobel Prize-winning economist Amartya Sen has pointed out that freedom must be measured not only in terms of political liberties but also in terms of socioeconomic opportunities and that each area is dependent on the other. Initiatives by industrial powers to promote state development in poor nations, which are to some degree self-serving, raise other ethical questions.

International law, providing ethical guidelines for dealings between the developed and developing world, clearly prohibits the violation of national sovereignty, except in cases of self-defense, but some experts argue that crimes against humanity, particularly genocide, can also legitimate such intervention. In the developing world, ethical issues thus arise around competing principles of national sovereignty and other values, such as human rights or democracy. Further, the nature of the intervention, particularly when it entails military force, raises additional questions. Ethically, measures taken to remedy a wrong should be adequate to the task, but where it is legitimate to use force, the extent of that force cannot exceed what is necessary to accomplish the desired good.

ETHICAL ISSUES IN THE DEVELOPING WORLD

A variety of ethical issues arise depending on the nature of the problem. For instance, if a poor nation faces famine because insects are destroying its crops, should it be held to the environmental standards governing use of pesticides established by well-fed rich nations? Or, what obligations do developed nations have to recognize and to compensate indigenous peoples for folk medicines used for centuries but never protected by modern patent laws? Where is the line that establishes a violation of a universal human right, if such can be shown to exist, from the unusual but legitimate practices of a different culture, for instance, stoning adulterers or female genital circumcision?

Differences in values between the modern industrial world and the developing world in many cases lead some ethicists to conclude that the only morally acceptable action is that agreed to by both worlds. Others argue that on certain restricted issues, a universal moral standard applies to all humanity, and ethical decision making is a matter of how such decisions should be determined by the world. Because of

this moral complexity, even well-intentioned acts of humanitarianism must be pursued with great caution and reflection.

Bland Addison

FURTHER READING

Bello, Walden, Shea Cunningham, and Bill Rau. *Dark Victory: The United States, Structural Adjustment, and Global Poverty.* London: Pluto Press, 1994.

Boucher, Douglas M. *The Paradox of Plenty: Hunger in a Bountiful World.* Oakland, Calif.: Institute for Food & Development Policy, 1999.

Handelman, Howard. *The Challenge of Third World Development.* 2d ed. Upper Saddle River, N.J.: Prentice Hall, 2000.

Marglin, Stephen M., and Frederique Appfel Marglin, eds. *Dominating Knowledge.* Oxford, England: Clarendon Press, 1993.

Rau, Bill. *From Feast to Famine: Official Cures and Grassroots Remedies to Africa's Food Crisis.* London: Zed Books, 1991.

Rieff, David. *A Bed for the Night: Humanitarianism in Crisis.* New York: Simon & Schuster, 2002.

Sen, Amartya. *Development as Freedom.* New York: Alfred A. Knopf, 2001.

Singer, Peter. *One World: The Ethics of Globalization.* New Haven, Conn.: Yale University Press, 2002.

SEE ALSO: Agribusiness; Colonialism and imperialism; Famine; Globalization; Peace Corps; Poverty; Poverty and wealth; World Trade Organization.

Dewey, John

IDENTIFICATION: American philosopher
BORN: October 20, 1859, Burlington, Vermont
DIED: June 1, 1952, New York, New York
TYPE OF ETHICS: Modern history
SIGNIFICANCE: The leading progressive ethicist of the twentieth century, Dewey developed a theory of ethics in which human moral development resulted from active engagement with a fluid environment. His most famous works include *Human Nature and Conduct* (1922) and *Theory of Valuation* (1939).

John Dewey. (Library of Congress)

John Dewey attacked traditional ethical theories. His objection to these theories (absolute idealism's categorical imperative and "will of the absolute," Herbert Spencer's Social Darwinism, and Jeremy Bentham's utilitarianism) was that they posited the existence of an absolute moral code independent from and knowable in advance of human interaction with an ever-changing environment. Dewey's ethical theory, "instrumentalism," was grounded in a progressivist prescription for participatory democratic decision making. His views on the normative and prescriptive requirements of ethical theory remain strongly influential.

THE REFLEX ARC CONCEPT

Dewey came to believe that human experience was not shaped by the dualisms of traditional philosophy: mind and body, idea and sensation. Experience, Dewey wrote in "The Reflex Arc Concept in Psychology" (1896), was not "a patchwork of disjointed parts"; it was a "comprehensive, organic unity." The reflex arc concept, Dewey reasoned, required a model

of stimulus and response in which both were "divisions of labor, functioning factors within the single concrete whole" rather than "disconnected existences." Humans functioned in this "unity of activity," or experience, unconsciously. Only with an interruption of coordinated, continuous experiencing, Dewey argued, did individuals need to become mindful of the reflex arc of stimulus, response, and intervening psychical event in order to resolve interrupted experiencing. Dewey's view of experience was to shape profoundly his theory of ethics.

For Dewey, components of the reflex arc, or circuit, did not consist of disassociated separate categories of stimulus and response in which sensory input (stimulus) is viewed as occurring chronologically prior to the event of muscular discharge (motor response), for example, with attention, awareness, or idea emerging as a central activity or intervening psychical event. Rather than being considered as distinctive partitions of experience, reminiscent of earlier formulations of body-mind dualism, the stimulus and response components of the reflex arc of human behavior required a conceptual shift in Dewey's view.

Dewey argued that stimulus and response are not distinctive entities, categories of human behavior used to describe sequential neural or physical events; they are integrative divisions of labor that are interrelated with the psychical component of the reflex arc to form an inclusive holism of human behavior. The psychical event, the attention given to maintenance or restoration of ongoing experiencing or human activity, Dewey described as mediation in *The Study of Ethics: A Syllabus* (1894), as intelligence in *Human Nature and Conduct* (1922), and as exploration for reasonable decision in the *Theory of Valuation* (1939).

THEORY OF THE MORAL LIFE

While Dewey noted his discontent with absolutist moral codes in *Outlines of a Critical Theory of Ethics* (1891) and utilized *The Study of Ethics: A Syllabus* (1894) to discuss "psychological ethics"—that is, the individual's conduct and its relation to moral experience—his theory of the moral life appeared originally with the publication of *Ethics* (1908), which included "Theory of the Moral Life." Stipulating that moral action was voluntary conduct, "activity called forth and directed by ideas of value or worth," Dewey argued that the moral life consisted of the individual's pursuit of self-realization through development of a democratic character. For Dewey, the challenge of moral life was, as he put it, "the formation, out of the body of original instinctive impulses which compose the natural self, of a voluntary self in which socialized desires and affections are dominant." For Dewey, humans were preeminently social beings; the moral person was one who transformed desires of the self into sympathetic regard for the common good. This view of a constructed rather than a received moral life permeates Dewey's later writing on ethical theory.

HUMAN NATURE AND CONDUCT

Human Nature and Conduct (1922), subtitled *An Introduction to Social Psychology*, was Dewey's critique of behaviorist and psychoanalytic explanations of human behavior. Both explanations were reductionist, Dewey assumed: Freudian psychoanalysis restricted causation of human behavior to sexual impulses, a term Dewey preferred to "instincts"; behaviorists, to a simplistic map of stimulus and response. Defining "habit" as "special sensitiveness or accessibility to certain classes of stimuli, standing predilections and adversions," not mere recurring actions, Dewey reasoned that in a democratic society such as the United States ethical decisions should result only from the practice of habitual deliberation, not from "routine, unintelligent habit." This accent on deliberative intelligence, reflective thought, which assumed a special importance in Dewey's theory of ethics, given his claim of contingency and predictability as coexistent in the world, is manifest in Dewey's last major work on ethical theory, *Theory of Valuation*.

THEORY OF VALUATION

Written to contest British philosopher A. J. Ayer's assertion in *Language, Truth, and Logic* (1936) that ethical statements were merely emotive, irrational statements of preference and, as such, inexplicable by scientific canons of veracity, Dewey's *Theory of Valuation* highlights experiential contexts of value judgments. Given his conception of the importance to ethical theory of reflective thought responding to a "precarious and perilous" world, a view discussed in arguably his most philosophically comprehensive work of the 1920's, *Experience and Nature* (1925),

Dewey eschewed any attempt to rank values hierarchically in *Theory of Valuation*.

Dewey believed that value judgments depended for their veracity on an experiential context and thus were subject to empirical testing. "Valuation," Dewey wrote, "involved desiring." Dewey insisted that desires be scrutinized carefully. Investigation, he averred, of the experiential conditions for human preferences and consideration of consequences resulting from acting on these desires would yield the efficacy of ethical judgments. Efficacy depended on the abolition of the experiential cause for desiring: "some 'trouble' in an existing situation."

IMPLICATIONS FOR ETHICAL CONDUCT

Dewey's philosophy challenges people to derive their morality from their everyday experiential world rather than from some predetermined cosmological order. In Dewey's view, the individual actively constructs morality through conscious and deliberate implementation of actions designed to achieve the most beneficial consequences. For Dewey, ethical conduct is a dimension of human behavior that the individual creates rather than passively receives from some external source of "goodness."

Malcolm B. Campbell

FURTHER READING

Bernstein, Richard J. *John Dewey.* New York: Washington Square Press, 1966.

Boydston, Jo Ann, ed. *Guide to the Works of John Dewey.* Carbondale: Southern Illinois University Press, 1970.

Dewey, John. *The Collected Works: The Early Works, The Middle Works, The Later Works.* 37 vols. Edited by Jo Ann Boydston. Carbondale: Southern Illinois University Press, 1967-1992.

Edel, Abraham. *Ethical Theory and Social Change: The Evolution of John Dewey's Ethics, 1908-1932.* New Brunswick, N.J.: Transaction, 2001.

Gouinlock, James. *John Dewey's Philosophy of Value.* New York: Humanities Press, 1972.

McDermott, John, ed. *Philosophy of John Dewey.* Chicago: University of Chicago Press, 1981.

Morgenbesser, Sidney, ed. *Dewey and His Critics.* New York: Journal of Philosophy, 1977.

Sleeper, R. W. *The Necessity of Pragmatism: John Dewey's Conception of Philosophy.* New Haven, Conn.: Yale University Press, 1986.

Talisse, Robert B. *On Dewey: The Reconstruction of Philosophy.* Belmont, Calif.: Wadsworth, 2000.

Westbrook, Robert B. *John Dewey and American Democracy.* Ithaca, N.Y.: Cornell University Press, 1991.

SEE ALSO: Good samaritan laws; *Human Nature and Conduct*; Humanism; James, William; Peirce, Charles Sanders; Pragmatism; Progressivism.

Diagnosis

DEFINITION: Investigation of a problem, especially a medical problem, to determine its cause

TYPE OF ETHICS: Bioethics

SIGNIFICANCE: Successful diagnoses and care of patients may require physicians to make ethical judgments about their duty to disclose information to their patients and the confidentiality of information that must be shared with others in order to make their diagnoses.

For many physicians, the principle of confidentiality tends to produce a kind of knee-jerk reflex. The popular belief is that confidentiality is essential to the physician-patient relationship and must be safeguarded at all costs. Contrary to popular belief, however, it is not an absolute principle. In many cases, health care is now a product of teamwork, so that the physician is forced to pool information to some degree. The advent of computers makes it far easier for the physician's duty of confidentiality to be abused. Thus, there is confusion among professionals and administrators about what should be and what should not be revealed. Attitudes among physicians have departed from absolute certainties to a confusion of views between those who would have no difficulty divulging information and those who feel that divulging information violates various ethical codes.

It is generally accepted that information gained by a professional in the course of a relationship with a client is the property of the client. Instances do occur, however, in which medical professionals must weigh their ethical duty against their secondary duty as citizens to prevent harm from befalling others. For example, physicians have a statutory obligation to disclose the existence of infectious diseases. In some way, however, disclosure should hinge around patient consent, whenever it is practicable.

There is a general consensus that physicians have an obligation to tell the truth. Some doctors assume that they also have a right, which they sometimes exercise, to withhold information from a patient about a condition. Many physicians find it difficult to tell their patients that they are terminally ill. Some believe that a failure to tell a patient the truth is a type of dishonesty. Various arguments for truthfulness apply in medical ethics in diagnosis. Medicine is practiced on the assumption that the patient consents to treatment, but consent becomes meaningless unless it is informed. Thus, truth telling is vital to medical practice and medical diagnosis. The right to be adequately informed is based upon patients' freedom of choice, which becomes compromised if they are not given adequate data about their conditions. Reaction to the truth (of a terminal diagnosis, for example) is varied and unpredictable, and physicians are aware of this, as are pastors. In fact, "privileged communication" between patient and physician is one of the priestly aspects of the doctor's role that have been left over from ancient times.

A sensitive person can sympathize with one physician who showed, in a plaintive remark, the duty to tell the truth, yet his dislike of it. "Devotion to the truth does not always require the physician to voice his fears or tell the patient all he knows. But, after he has decided that the process of dying has begun, only in exceptional circumstances would a physician be justified in keeping the opinion to himself."

No one can better guard the ideal of absolute respect for the human person than the medical profession.

Jane A. Slezak

SEE ALSO: Confidentiality; Consent; Genetic testing; Illness; Medical ethics; Physician-patient relationship; Psychopharmacology; Therapist-patient relationship.

Dictatorship

DEFINITION: System of government in which one person has absolute authority

TYPE OF ETHICS: Politico-economic ethics

SIGNIFICANCE: Dictators create their own systems of law and order. The ethical status of a dictator's society is therefore determined solely by the dictator's own values and level of benevolence toward the people.

Dictatorships have existed in all times and all places. In ancient Greece, "tyrants" were given temporary authority by the populace to rule during times of war and invasion. When the crisis passed, power was returned to the legitimate authorities and the tyrant stepped down. That custom continued in Roman society when absolute power was given to military rulers until order was restored. In ancient China, the emperor became a dictator during critical times and ruled with an iron hand. One of the bloodiest dictators in Chinese history, Qin Shi Huangdi, killed thousands of his countrymen between 221 and 210 B.C.E. in an effort to put down peasant rebellions and opponents to his rule.

According to the Chinese Legalists, proponents of a school of philosophy that stressed the wickedness of human nature, severe punishments and frequent use of the death penalty were necessary to keep order in society. Human beings obeyed only laws that were strictly and savagely enforced; without fear and terror, society would fall apart. Thus, Chinese Legalist philosophers presented the major ethical defense of absolute rule, a view echoed later by Thomas Hobbes, an English political theorist, in his book *Leviathan* (1651). Both the Chinese and Hobbes argued that most humans preferred order to freedom and that order became possible only with strict enforcement of laws. Only absolute authority could reduce criminal activity and create an orderly society.

MODERN DICTATORS

During the twentieth century, dictatorships were created principally to create a utopian vision of a perfect society. Whether in Joseph Stalin's Soviet Union, Adolf Hitler's Germany, or Mao Zedong's China, modern dictators have assumed absolute power, killed millions of people, and imposed horrifying levels of terror on their populations in the name of creating a better world.

Joseph Stalin, ruler of the Soviet Union from 1927 to 1953, achieved more absolute power than perhaps any other modern dictator. He summarized his ethical philosophy in a comment he made to Communist Party leaders in 1932 when he was advised that Ukrainian farmers were causing problems by refusing to move to giant collective farms run by the Soviet government. In reply Stalin reportedly said, "No people, no problem." To carry out this policy, the Soviet dictator ordered all food to be taken out of Ukraine until his orders were obeyed. Within two years more than 8 million Ukrainians had starved to death and the resistance to authority was crushed.

One rule of modern dictatorship is that the leader is the law. During the 1930's in the Soviet Union, Stalin came close to achieving this goal. Between 16 million and 20 million Russians died in prisons and slave labor camps established to maintain order and control over the Soviet people. Stalin's secret police, a key ingredient in any successful dictatorship, had spies in every village, classroom, and office in the country. Spies informed on other spies, and children were rewarded for turning in their parents for disloyal conduct. Disloyalty was defined as any questioning of Stalin's authority. Under such conditions, a severe dictatorship emerged, though Stalin fell far short of his goal of turning the Soviet Union into a self-sufficient, economically successful worker's paradise. Terror and death were defended, for as true communists believed, the killing of millions was necessary in order to create a class-free, perfect society. Would not the deaths of millions be justified if one could produce a perfect society on Earth? That Stalin and his supporters failed to come close to their goal makes his dictatorship even more horrifying.

ADOLF HITLER

Adolf Hitler, German dictator from 1933 to 1945, justified his mass murders with the phrase "life unfit for life." The German leader promoted biological warfare in his attempt to create a master race. Unlike most other modern dictators, Hitler did not seize power but took over the German government by constitutional means. Once in charge, however, he followed the same methods as other dictators, eliminating all opposition and imposing a violent reign of terror upon his nation. Soon there were no limits on

381

Notable Dictators in History

Date	Dictator	Nation
221-210 B.C.E.	Ch'in Shih Huang Ti	China
54-68 C.E.	Nero	Rome
1241-1279	Genghis Khan	Mongolia
1370-1405	Tamerlane	Central Asia
1547-1584	Ivan the Terrible	Russia
1799-1815	Napoleon Bonaparte	France
c. 1818-1828	Shaka Zulu	South Africa
1876-1911	Porfirio Díaz	Mexico
1923-1943	Benito Mussolini	Italy
1927-1953	Joseph Stalin	Soviet Union
1930-1945, 1950-1954	Getúlio Vargas	Brazil
1930-1961	Rafael Trujillo	Dominican Republic
1932-1968	António de Oliveira Salazar	Portugal
1933-1945	Adolf Hitler	Germany
1937-1956	Anastasio Somoza García	Nicaragua
1949-1975	Francisco Franco	Spain
1948-1994	Kim Il Sung	North Korea
1949-1975	Mao Zedong	China
1954-1989	Alfredo Stroessner	Paraguay
1957-1971	François Duvalier	Haiti
1959-	Fidel Castro	Cuba
1965-1997	Mobutu Sese Seko	Congo/Zaire
1967-1989	Nicolae Ceausescu	Romania
1971-1979	Idi Amin	Uganda
1976-1978	Pol Pot	Cambodia
1979-2003	Saddam Hussein	Iraq
1990-2000	Alberto Fujimori	Peru

physically and mentally handicapped people were murdered on Hitler's command. Hitler used his immense power to benefit one group, the "pure-blooded Aryans," while all others were to be destroyed. Absolute power was used to perform absolute evil, and Hitler's empire was brought to judgment only by the bloodiest war in human history. "Life unfit for life" became the ethical standard for one of the most destructive régimes in human history.

The third example of modern dictators, Mao Zedong, who ruled China with total power from 1949 to 1975, also killed millions of people (the exact number is still subject to dispute) in his pursuit of a perfect society. Mao tried to destroy China's past totally and to create a new world order based on economic and political equality. He seized power in 1949 after a long civil war and declared a campaign of terror against his, and hence China's, enemies. He, like many dictators, saw himself as the voice of the people and someone who was supremely interested in their welfare and prosperity. If millions had to die, it was ethically correct because "the people" demanded it and because the deaths of traitors would help bring about a heaven on Earth. Executions of landlords, massacres of Buddhist monks and nuns, and rigid obedience to the teachings of the leader were all expected, encouraged, and accomplished during Mao's brutal reign of terror, which lasted for most of his tenure as Chinese ruler. Only his own death brought an end to his campaign against the people of China.

During the late twentieth and early twenty-first centuries, relatively small-time dictators such as Kim Il Sung in North Korea (1948-1994), Pol Pot in Cambodia (1976-1979), and Saddam Hussein in Iraq (1979-2003), continued the tradition of murdering opponents and creating secret police forces to terrorize their people. Dictatorships continue to exist, and dictators continue to impose suffering upon their people. This form of government has existed for thousands of years and is unlikely to

Hitler's authority, and laws were passed that attempted to create a strict racial state. To build a master race, millions of "inferiors" were persecuted and eventually eliminated. Along with six million Jews, thousands of Gypsies, Slavs, homosexuals, and disappear as long as dictators are able to command obedience through fear, terror, and promises of perfection.

Leslie V. Tischauser

FURTHER READING

Arendt, Hannah. *The Origins of Totalitarianism.* New ed. San Diego, Calif.: Harcourt Brace, 1979.

Bullock, Alan. *Hitler and Stalin: Parallel Lives.* New York: Alfred A. Knopf, 1992.

Friedrich, Carl J., and Zbigniew K. Brzezinski. *Totalitarian Dictatorship and Autocracy.* 2nd ed. Cambridge, Mass.: Harvard University Press, 1965.

Halberstam, Michael. *Totalitarianism and the Modern Conception of Politics.* New Haven, Conn.: Yale University Press, 1999.

Linz, Juan J. *Totalitarian and Authoritarian Regimes.* Boulder, Colo.: Lynne Rienner, 2000.

Plato. *The Republic.* Translated by Desmond Lee. 2d ed. New York: Penguin Books, 2003.

Talmon, Jacob L. *The Origins of Totalitarian Democracy.* New York: Praeger, 1968.

Wittfogel, Karl A. *Oriental Despotism: A Comparative Study of Total Power.* New Haven, Conn.: Yale University Press, 1963.

Žižek, Slavoj. *Did Somebody Say Totalitarianism? Five Interventions in the (Mis)Use of a Notion.* New York: Verso, 2002.

SEE ALSO: Arendt, Hannah; Fascism; Hitler, Adolf; Hobbes, Thomas; Hussein, Saddam; Orwell, George; Stalin, Joseph; Tyranny.

Dignity

DEFINITION: Innate worthiness of each person to be respected and to enjoy fundamental human rights.
TYPE OF ETHICS: Religious ethics
SIGNIFICANCE: The belief that all people have an innate and inviolable dignity is the foundation of a belief in human rights that transcend any particular society and that no government or person can legitimately take away.

The concept of the dignity of humankind was originally based on the theological belief that all men and women possess God-given rights because they are formed in the image of God. Foremost among these divine gifts are freedom and immortality. Unlike other animals, humans are not dominated purely by physical instincts. People can use their freedom to create works of great beauty and to improve the quality of life for themselves and others. Freedom may, of course, be abused if one chooses to limit the rights of others.

In his influential book *The City of God* (413-427), the Christian writer Saint Augustine argued persuasively that practices such as slavery, which demeaned individuals, were incompatible with Christian beliefs. Since God freely granted immortality to all men and women, it is absolutely essential that human beings respect the dignity and freedom of each individual.

To Saint Augustine, Earth is a "city of God" in which all men and women enjoy the same basic rights and privileges. A North African bishop who lived on the outskirts of the Roman Empire, Saint Augustine specifically rejected the belief that any government had the right to invade or dominate another country. Those who accept the basic tenet that all men and women possess freedom and immortality must ask themselves if certain forms of behavior are morally compatible with God's teachings on the dignity of all people. If there is a conflict between social practices and religious beliefs, a Christian is required to obey the higher divine law. Saint Augustine argued that Christians are always responsible for their decisions. It is unacceptable to claim that one must simply obey all laws, since certain laws may be morally reprehensible if they fail to respect the dignity and rights of all men and women.

Saint Augustine's comments on the dignity of humankind had a profound influence on Christian ethics. In his 1580 essay "On the Cannibals," Michel de Montaigne stated that it was morally wrong for Europeans to colonize the New World. European political leaders had developed the specious argument that it was permissible for them to exploit Native Americans because they were superior to them. Montaigne denounced this position as racist. Like Saint Augustine, Montaigne recognized the dignity of each man and woman. Although Montaigne was both the mayor of Bordeaux and an adviser to French kings, his condemnation of the conquest of the New World was ignored by French government officials because an acceptance of his position would have put an end to French imperialism in the Americas.

HUMAN RIGHTS

Over the centuries, people have recognized that certain human rights are so important that they must be enumerated. A mere declaration of human rights is not sufficient. A mechanism must be created to protect these inalienable rights. In democracies, independent judges have the power to require even recalcitrant government officials to respect constitutionally protected rights. Famous declarations of human rights include the 1689 English Bill of Rights; the 1791 U.S. Bill of Rights; the Universal Declaration of Human Rights, which the United Nations approved in 1948; and the 1969 Human Rights American Convention of the Organization of American States.

The Founders of the American democracy felt that certain rights, such as freedom of religion, freedom of speech, and the right to a jury trial, were essential to the quality of life and that the American government should be permanently prevented from restricting these inalienable rights. Although it was admirable, the U.S. Bill of Rights was imperfect because it failed to recognize the rights of women and African Americans. The U.S. Constitution may, however, be amended, and it was, in fact, amended in order to end slavery and to grant African Americans and women the right to vote.

The concept of the dignity of humankind has continued to evolve. In her famous 1949 book *The Second Sex*, Simone de Beauvoir argued persuasively that a failure to recognize the dignity and equality of women was morally unacceptable. Both the Universal Declaration of Human Rights and the Human Rights American Convention denounced torture and racism and also stressed the need to respect the rights of people from indigenous and minority cultures so that all citizens might enjoy the same rights and privileges.

The right of citizens to use their native language has also been recognized as a basic human right. Canada, for example, is a bilingual country, and the Canadian Parliament has specifically declared that any Canadian may use either French or English in all public and private matters. Although the official languages of Canada are French and English, the Canadian Parliament also took specific action to recognize the linguistic rights of native peoples living in Canada. The ancient concept of the dignity of humankind is based on certain inalienable rights. Although numerous totalitarian governments have sought to limit personal freedoms, such efforts have consistently been resisted by those who respect the dignity and freedom of each man and woman.

Edmund J. Campion

FURTHER READING

Augustine, Saint. *The City of God Against the Pagans.* Edited and translated by R. W. Dyson. New York: Cambridge University Press, 1998.

Baker, Herschel. *The Dignity of Man: Studies in the Persistence of an Idea.* Cambridge, Mass.: Harvard University Press, 1947.

Beauvoir, Simone de. *The Second Sex.* Edited and translated by H. M. Parshley. 1953. Reprint. New York: Alfred A. Knopf, 1993.

Kamali, Mohammad Hashim. *The Dignity of Man: An Islamic Perspective.* Cambridge, England: Islamic Texts Society, 2002.

Lawson, Edward, comp. *Encyclopedia of Human Rights.* Edited by Mary Lou Bertucci. 2d ed. Washington, D.C.: Taylor & Francis, 1996.

Montaigne, Michel de. *The Complete Works: Essays, Travel Journal, Letters.* Translated by Donald M. Frame. Introduction by Stuart Hampshire. New York: Alfred A. Knopf, 2003.

Osmanczyk, Edmund Jan. *Encyclopedia of the United Nations and International Relations.* New York: Taylor and Francis, 1990.

SEE ALSO: Augustine, Saint; Character; Civil rights and liberties; Equality; Freedom and liberty; Honor; Human nature; Human rights; Self-respect.

Dilemmas, moral

DEFINITION: Moral choices—usually forced—that, no matter how they are decided, have negative consequences

TYPE OF ETHICS: Theory of ethics

SIGNIFICANCE: Moral dilemmas present great difficulties for people who are striving to think and to behave rationally and ethically.

Moral dilemmas represent some of the hardest choices that people must make in the course of their lifetimes. The core of a moral dilemma is the fact that, no mat-

A Simple Moral Dilemma

If you make a promise to meet a friend for lunch tomorrow, you have a moral duty to keep that promise. However, if your father suddenly has a heart attack and is hospitalized, your duty to be at his side far outweighs your promise to your friend. After using your power of reason and deciding that you have just cause for following the other course of action, you should not not keep your lunch date with your friend.

ter what course is chosen by the person who is facing the dilemma, making the choice involves deciding on a course of action that will have negative moral consequences. The following are typical examples of situations that involve moral dilemmas: A sea captain on an overloaded life raft must select a small number of people to throw overboard if most of the people aboard the life raft are to be saved; a general who has been ordered to direct a suicide mission for the good of his country must decide which soldiers will be sent to a certain death; a German resistance leader can save only one of two Jewish families from death in a concentration camp at the hands of the Nazis. Such scenarios involve attempting to identify and choose the lesser of two evils.

BABY JANE DOE

In New York state in 1983, a moral dilemma arose regarding the fate of "Baby Jane Doe." She suffered from multiple difficulties, including a broken and protruding spine (spina bifida) and fluid on her brain (hydrocephaly). Worse, she had a brain that was abnormally small (microencephaly). She needed surgery immediately after her birth, but her parents refused to allow it. Without the surgery, Jane would live for two years at most, but the surgery would still leave her in a hopeless situation. A "right to life" group intervened and demanded that the surgery be done. The New York Supreme Court ruled in the group's favor, but a higher court immediately overturned the decision. Next, the federal Justice Department intervened, launching an investigation to determine whether a "handicapped" person was being discriminated against, but a judge dismissed that suit

also. Baby Jane did not receive the operations, went home with her parents, and soon died.

Were the parents right or wrong? A few more details might help the reader decide. If Jane had received the complicated surgeries, she would have had a 50 percent chance of living into her twenties, but her life never would have been anything approaching an existence that most people would want to experience. She would have been paralyzed, epileptic, and extremely vulnerable to various diseases, such as meningitis. She would never even have recognized her parents. It was these facts on which the parents based their decision.

FACING THE DILEMMA

The Baby Jane tragedy illustrates two typical elements of moral dilemmas. The first is the fact that human rights are involved. The second is that, as in Jane's case, two rights come into conflict: in that case, Jane's right to life and the parental right of choice. In a more ordinary case, most people would no doubt hold that Jane's right to life was paramount. The mitigating circumstances in Baby Jane's case, however, swayed various judges and many people in the general public to support the parents, who based their moral judgment on specific information and had good reasons for making that judgment. Most true moral dilemmas must be solved in the same way. Usually, two "wrongs" or two "rights" will be involved, and decision makers must weigh the facts of each case with impartiality (if that is possible) and then develop good reasons for their decisions. In other words, in a dilemma, one must weigh *prima facie* duties and good reasons for making a specific decision. Reason, self-examination, and internal argument pro and con—these factors help in solving moral dilemmas. People who are searching for moral answers to dilemmas must remember that moral "truth" is the truth of reason and logical thinking and that dilemmas can be solved satisfactorily only if an individual's decision is based on the best reasons that are available. Conclusions backed by reason are the key element in solving moral dilemmas.

CONCLUSIONS

Certainly, people as members of society need all their powers of reason in facing the many moral dilemmas that arise in modern life. Is abortion absolutely right? Is it absolutely wrong? Can mitigating circumstances in individual abortion cases "tip" the answer one way or the other? Is euthanasia ever justified? Should society condone or oppose capital punishment? The list of modern moral dilemmas is endless, and many people believe it is the duty of all reasonable people to try to resolve them.

James Smallwood

Further Reading

Arthur, John, ed. *Morality and Moral Controversies: Readings in Moral, Social, and Political Philosophy.* 6th ed. Upper Saddle River, N.J.: Prentice Hall, 2002.

Cohen, Martin. *101 Ethical Dilemmas.* New York: Routledge, 2003.

Cook, Fred J. *The Corrupted Land: The Social Morality of Modern America.* New York: Macmillan, 1966.

Dworkin, Ronald. *Taking Rights Seriously.* Cambridge, Mass.: Harvard University Press, 1977.

Gewirth, Alan. *Reason and Morality.* Chicago: University of Chicago Press, 1978.

Rachels, James. *The Elements of Moral Philosophy.* 3d ed. Boston: McGraw-Hill, 1999.

_____, ed. *Moral Problems: A Collection of Philosophical Essays.* 3d ed. New York: Harper & Row, 1979.

Ross, William D. *The Right and the Good.* New ed. New York: Oxford University Press, 2002.

Singer, Peter. *Rich and Poor.* Cambridge, England: Cambridge University Press, 1979.

White, James E. *Contemporary Moral Problems.* 7th ed. Belmont, Calif.: Wadsworth, 2003.

SEE ALSO: Casuistry; Choice; Choiceless choices; Duty; Kohlberg, Lawrence; Moral education; Prisoner's dilemma; Right and wrong.

are performed. Typically, dirty hands considerations are used to judge politicians.

Cynics hold the empirical view that all politicians are corrupt. According to common interpretations of the sixteen century Italian political philosopher Niccolò Machiavelli's *The Prince* (1532), adds the normative position that all politicians are morally obligated to perform wrong actions and, thus, to act with dirty hands.

Many ethicists endorse the normative claim. Michael Walzer, for example, argues that a political leader in the midst of a war crisis may be morally required to order the torture of prisoners for the sake of gaining information needed to save innocent lives from a hidden rebel bomb. In Walzer's view, the politician would be responsible both for a wrong act (torturing) and for a right act (saving innocent people). Moreover, a truly moral person would feel guilty after ordering that the prisoners be tortured.

Opposing ethicists respond, first, that it misleads to describe dirty acts as simultaneously right and wrong, since acts with those contrary properties are logically impossible. Also, it is better to characterize dirty acts as exceptional right acts that are wrong in normal circumstances. For this reason, individuals with dirty hands should not feel guilty because they have, in fact, done nothing wrong. Finally, politicians should rarely, if ever, have dirty hands since political morality is not distinct from private morality.

F. Scott McElreath

SEE ALSO: Apologizing for past wrongs; Corruption; Machiavelli, Niccolò; Power; Private vs. public morality; Responsibility; South Africa's Truth and Reconciliation Commission.

Dirty hands

DEFINITION: Trait that individuals possess when they perform morally tainted actions

TYPE OF ETHICS: Politico-economic ethics

SIGNIFICANCE: Morally evaluating a person necessitates determining when, if ever, it is moral to act with "dirty hands" and determining what emotions, if any, are morally required after dirty acts

Disability rights

DEFINITION: Legal formulations of the rights of disabled persons to have access to the same benefits and opportunities as nondisabled persons

TYPE OF ETHICS: Civil rights

SIGNIFICANCE: The passage of laws formally codifying the rights of the disabled places a new, positive ethical responsibility upon both public and private institutions to strive not to exclude or marginalize disabled persons. The recognition of this responsibility represents a significant change in cultural values.

Recognition of the special needs and requirements of the disabled and the emergence of legislation guaranteeing their civil rights have evolved slowly. Following other civil rights movements, disability rights laws were merely symbolic, and did not include strategies to guide policy implementation. With the enactment of the Rehabilitation Act of 1973 and the Americans with Disabilities Act of 1990, the rights of the disabled became legally enforceable.

A neglected minority constituting 20 percent to 25 percent of Americans differing in extent of impairment and range of ability, the disabled are not a homogenous group. The disabled historically have been stigmatized, viewed as "different" and therefore not equal to other members of society. Through prejudices and misunderstandings, personal fears and anxieties, reactions of pity, helplessness, uneasiness, and sometimes inaccurate media and literary representations, society has erected barriers that have kept the disabled from participating in various areas of American life. The needs of the disabled were ignored in the design of public buildings and facilities and the delivery of public services; educational programs and employment practices resulted in discrimination and exclusion of disabled persons.

Vocational rehabilitation programs following World War I were initiated in favor of veterans with combat injuries and later expanded first to all physically disabled persons and then to mental rehabilitation. Programs to provide income to persons whose disabilities prevented their employment—Social Security Disability Insurance and Supplemental Security Income—began during the mid-1950's and expanded during the 1970's. The Architectural Barriers Act of 1968 brought about such modifications as specially designated parking places for the disabled near commercial establishments and public buildings, special entrance ramps and doors, curb cuts, elevators with Braille floor designations, and specially equipped restrooms.

LEGISLATION

Called a "bill of rights" for the disabled, the Rehabilitation Act of 1973 ensures that federally funded programs can be used by all disabled persons. It requires the institution of affirmative action programs to actively recruit, hire, train, accommodate, and promote "qualified disabled persons." The act prohibits discrimination in the recruitment, testing, or hiring of the disabled, as well as special or different treatment that would tend to stigmatize or set apart handicapped people from the nonhandicapped. The act also aims to grant to the disabled equal opportunity to participate or benefit in the services of federally funded government agency programs.

Considered landmark civil rights legislation for all persons with disabilities, the Americans with Disabilities Act (ADA) provides for disabled persons legal protection in employment, access to state and local government, public transportation, public accommodation, and telecommunications. From July, 1992, until July 26, 1994, the ADA covered employers with twenty-five or more employees. After that date, it encompassed employers with fifteen or more employees. Agencies, unions, and joint labor/management committees are included; the U.S. government, Indian tribes, and tax-exempt private membership clubs are excluded.

Title I of the ADA and its Equal Employment Opportunity Commission (EEOC) regulations prohibit

---

Politically Incorrect Terms and Their Preferred Alternatives

Incorrect	*Correct*
Handicapped or disabled person	Person with a disability
Impairment	Disablement
Deaf	Hearing impaired
Mute or dumb	Speech-impaired
Blind	Visually impaired
Insane or crazy	Emotionally impaired
Normal	Able-bodied person
Crippled or spastic	Mobility-impaired
Fit or spell	Seizure
Mongolism	Down syndrome
Harelip	Cleft palate

an employer from discriminating against a "qualified individual with a disability" in job application procedures, including recruitment and advertising, hiring, promotion, awarding tenure, demotion, transfer, layoff, termination, right of return from layoff, rehiring, compensation, job assignments, classifications, seniority, leaves of absence, sick leave, fringe benefits, training, employer-sponsored activities, and any other terms and conditions of employment.

Under the ADA, it is unlawful for an employer to use selection criteria or tests that tend to screen out persons with disabilities. Preemployment medical examinations are unlawful, but employment may be contingent on the results of a postemployment examination if required of all entering employees and if records remain confidential. The disabled have the same legal remedies that are available to other minorities under the Civil Rights Act of 1964, amended in 1991 to include compensatory and punitive damages for intentional discrimination.

Effective January 26, 1992, title II requires that all state and local government agencies, and public transportation agencies make all of their services accessible to the disabled. It also includes school systems, parks and recreation programs, jails, libraries, public hospitals and clinics, state and local courts and legislatures, and government activities carried out by private contractors.

Title III requires equal access to public accommodations in a variety of places, such as hotels, theaters, restaurants, parks, libraries, museums, and banks. Auxiliary aids and services to ensure effective communication with the hearing impaired and visually impaired must be provided.

Title IV requires that local and long distance telephone companies provide telecommunication relay services across the nation to permit persons using TDD's (telecommunication devices for the deaf) or text telephones to have conversations with persons using conventional telephones. All television public service announcements produced or funded by the federal government are required to include closed captioning.

OTHER RIGHTS

Public school systems must provide a free, appropriate education to handicapped children. Federal money is available to states for special education. To the extent possible, handicapped children are to be educated with those who are not handicapped (a practice called "mainstreaming"). Disabled students at federally funded colleges must also be treated equally with nondisabled students. Health and social service agencies receiving federal assistance cannot discriminate against the disabled, and auxiliary aids must be provided. Discrimination in housing and access to air transportation is also prohibited.

Marcia J. Weiss

FURTHER READING

Albrecht, Gary L. _The Disability Business: Rehabilitation in America._ Newbury Park, Calif.: Sage, 1992.

Frierson, James G. _Employer's Guide to the Americans with Disabilities Act._ Washington, D.C.: BNA Books, 1992.

National Association of the Deaf. _Legal Rights: The Guide for Deaf and Hard of Hearing People._ 5th ed., completely rev. Washington, D.C.: Gallaudet University Press, 2000.

Percy, Stephen L. _Disability, Civil Rights, and Public Policy: The Politics of Implementation._ Tuscaloosa, Ala.: University of Alabama Press, 1989.

Stroman, Duane F. _The Disability Rights Movement: From Deinstitutionalization to Self-Determination._ Lanham, Md.: University Press of America, 2003.

Switzer, Jacqueline Vaughn. _Disabled Rights: American Disability Policy and the Fight for Equality._ Washington, D.C.: Georgetown University Press, 2003.

SEE ALSO: Affirmative action; Americans with Disabilities Act; Discrimination; Keller, Helen; United Nations Declaration on the Rights of Disabled Persons; Veterans' rights.

The Disappeared

IDENTIFICATION: Group of roughly ten thousand people who were imprisoned or killed as part of a campaign of clandestine terror carried out by the military regime in Argentina

DATE: 1975-1980

TYPE OF ETHICS: Modern history

SIGNIFICANCE: The "disappearance" of thousands of Argentinian citizens constituted the most serious

Picture of an Argentine army torture-training camp taken in 1986 and released in early 2004, when the government ordered an investigation into charges that its army had continued to teach torture techniques after the 1983 fall of the military dictatorship. (AP/Wide World Photos)

mass violation of civil and human rights in Argentine history. The Mothers of the Plaza de Mayo, often referred to abroad as Mothers of the Disappeared, became an international symbol of the desperate need for, and frustrating impotence of, protest in the face of unspeakable injustice.

After the fall of Argentine president Juan Perón in 1955, a struggle over political control and economic policy ensued between left-wing and right-wing civilian factions and between moderates and hard liners in the military. Except for the period from 1973 to 1976, the military controlled Argentina until 1983. In 1970, guerrilla war, waged by leftists, began and was countered by rightist groups. In 1975, the military intensified the war against subversion that it had begun in 1971.

Between 1975 and 1980, the "dirty war" carried on by the Argentine military attempted to eliminate members of leftist organizations, the Peronista Party, and any group that was opposed to the military administration. This phase of guerrilla warfare was the most terrifying and bloody in Argentine history. Due process was ignored, systematic torture became routine, and at least ten thousand people "disappeared" and were assumed to have been tortured and killed. Repression was deliberately arbitrary, uncoordinated, and indiscriminate; military power was used to intimidate anyone who opposed it.

By 1980, the repression declined, and it finally ended in 1982. One of the main groups that opposed the military terrorism was the Mothers of the Plaza de Mayo, who assembled weekly in silent protest in the Plaza de Mayo in front of the Casa Rosada, the Argentine White House. In 1985, the civilian government tried the top military leaders and sentenced them to life in prison for their crimes during the "dirty war."

Robert D. Talbott

SEE ALSO: Oppression; Tyranny.

Discrimination

DEFINITION: Differential treatment based on physical characteristics or social affiliation or identity

TYPE OF ETHICS: Civil rights

SIGNIFICANCE: Discrimination is generally thought to be a fundamentally unjust practice, although arguments continue to proliferate within almost all modern societies justifying specific forms of discrimination on both practical and moral grounds.

Discrimination in one form or another appears to be endemic to all societies. In the United States, various groups have experienced various forms of discrimination, including racial discrimination, sexual discrimination (denial of certain rights to women), religious discrimination, discrimination against certain cultural groups (for example, Appalachians, the Amish, and so forth), discrimination against the disabled (both physically and mentally), discrimination against the aged, and discrimination against homosexuals. Many whites immigrating from Europe have at one time or another experienced discrimination.

Discrimination, according to Joan Ferrante in *Sociology: A Global Perspective* (1992), is the unequal treatment, whether intentional or unintentional, of individuals or groups on the basis of group membership that is unrelated to merit, ability, or past performance. Discrimination is not limited to individuals. In fact, the two most pervasive types of discrimination are legal discrimination and institutional discrimination. Legal discrimination is unequal treatment that is sustained by law. Institutional discrimination (or racism), according to Stokely Carmichael and Charles V. Hamilton's *Black Power* (1967), is a subtle form of unequal treatment based on race that is entrenched in social custom (that is, social institutions).

Institutional discrimination may include segregated housing patterns, redlining by financial institutions, and the practice of minority group members being forced continually into low-paying jobs. Prejudice, which is often confused with discrimination, is the prejudgment of people, objects, or even situations on the basis of stereotypes or generalizations that persist even when facts demonstrate otherwise (for example, the majority of women on welfare are white, yet the stereotype of a female welfare recipient is that of a black woman with a brood of children).

RACIAL DISCRIMINATION

The most pernicious acts of prejudice and discrimination in the United States have been directed against racial minorities. The history of race relations in the United States demonstrates that differential treatment has been accorded to all minority groups. A minority group, according to John E. Farley in *Sociology* (1990), is any group in a disadvantaged or subordinate position. In this sense, a minority may actually constitute a numerical majority, such as black South Africas under the former apartheid system. Minority populations have experienced the entire range of race relations, including assimilation, pluralism, legal protection, population transfer, continued subjugation, and extermination. While all minority populations have experienced some degree of discrimination, perhaps the most cruel and enduring discrimination has been experienced by those of African descent.

Africans were first brought to North America as slaves in 1619, one year after the Mayflower landed. They proved to be an excellent source of inexpensive labor for the developing European colonies. In its early development, slavery was not justified by attitudes of racial inferiority, but simply by the need for cheap labor. Racial justification for slavery came later as a strategy for maintaining the continued subjugation of blacks. Depicting blacks as subhuman, irresponsible, promiscuous, and lazy helped to stave off, for many years, groups (for example, abolitionists) bent upon ending slavery. The development of racist ideology during slavery has—over the years—continued to influence the relationship between blacks and whites in the United States.

Until the latter part of the eighteenth century, when the slave trade began to become a profitable business, there was very little prejudice based on race. Justification for slavery had to be found by the Christian slave traders who professed to believe in the brotherhood of all men and the ideals of democracy, which established the equality of all men before the law.

The end of slavery in the United States did not, and could not, bring an end to discrimination. Discrimination had become institutionalized—embedded in social custom and in the very institutions of society. Initially, the Thirteenth, Fourteenth, and Fifteenth Amendments to the Constitution, along with the Civil Rights Acts of 1866 and 1867, did much to eliminate legal discrimination against the newly freed slaves. Yet many of those gains were abrogated by state legislatures in the South following the abrupt end of Reconstruction in 1877. The states of the Old Confederacy were able to circumvent much of the legislation passed during the Reconstruction period. They were able to sanction discrimination and deny civil rights by means of a set of laws called the "black codes."

The black codes virtually reintroduced many of conditions that existed during slavery. Although the Fourteenth and Fifteenth Amendments guaranteed citizenship and the right to vote, these rights were abridged through intimidation, the poll tax, the "grandfather" clause, and through literacy tests. Beginning during the 1880's, a more comprehensive set of laws—referred to as "Jim Crow"—gave rise to a system of legal segregation in South. This system of legal segregation was sanctioned by the "separate but equal" philosophy established in the *Plessy v. Ferguson* decision of 1896.

Substantial progress against Jim Crow did not occur until fifty-eight years later, with the *Brown v. Board of Education* decision (1954). In the *Brown* decision, the Supreme Court overturned *Plessy*, arguing that the concept of "separate but equal" was "inherently unequal" and had no place in a society that professes to treat all its citizens equally. The *Brown* decision helped to give rise to a determination on the part of African Americans to exercise the rights and

---

Delivery Refused

Is it unethical for restaurants that offer delivery service to refuse to make deliveries to public housing projects? in 2003, this question was submitted to Randy Cohen, author of the syndicated column *The Ethicist*. Cohen replied that while a restaurant might legally refuse to deliver in a neighborhood that might pose dangers to its employees, it would be unethical for it to refuse to deliver to neighborhoods offering no threats of danger. Moreover, it would be unethical for a restaurant to practice racial discrimination under the guise of employee safety. To avoid misunderstandings, Cohen suggested that restaurants should state "delivery available to selected areas" on their menus.

---

privileges guaranteed to all citizens under the Constitution. Beginning during the 1960's, the underlying legal, political, and economic context of race relations changed in the United States.

RESISTING DISCRIMINATION

Demonstrations, sit-ins, and marches by African Americans and their supporters caused the United States to wake up and begin addressing the second-class citizenship of minority groups. As a consequence, epoch-making legislation was passed in the form of the 1964 Civil Rights Act, affirmative action (in employment and education) was introduced, and governmental agencies (for example, the Equal Employment Opportunities Commission, the U.S. Civil Rights Commission, the Office of Federal Contract Compliance Programs, and so forth) actively tried to stamp out much of the discrimination against minorities.

Despite these changes, riot after riot erupted across the nation during the 1960's. A combination of economic frustration, police brutality, resistance to desegregation (both in housing and schooling), and the assassination of the civil rights leader the Reverend Martin Luther King, Jr., contributed to the eruptions. The Kerner Commission, which was commissioned to study the conditions leading up to the riots, concluded that "white racism" and discrimination were responsible for the outbreak of violence.

Joseph S. Hines suggests in *Politics of Race* (1975) that African Americans have operated in a castelike racial structure in the United States that has relegated them to inferior status, relative powerlessness, material deprivation, and socio-psychic resentment. Segregation and discrimination have been used as mechanisms for maintaining the sociopolitical structure (status quo). Within this structure, African Americans are members of a racial category for life; they are generally consigned to marry within their group; they are often avoided, both as ritual and as custom; and they experience limited opportunities.

Although African Americans and other minorities have made substantial gains since 1954, they still have not experienced a society that judges them based upon merit and ability. They also have not experienced a society that does not prejudge them based upon physical characteristics and stereotypes. It could be said that discrimination continues to be embedded in the social, political, and economic fabric of the United States. Employment and promotional opportunities are still strongly influenced by race. Consequently, minorities typically earn only a fraction of what white males earn, they tend to hold political office far less often than their numbers in the general population should warrant, and they are still excluded from membership in certain elite clubs because of their race.

Charles C. Jackson

FURTHER READING

Cruz, Hernan S. *Racial Discrimination*. Rev. ed. New York: United Nations, 1977.

Feagin, Joe R., and Clairece Booher Feagin. *Discrimination American Style*. Englewood Cliffs, N.J.: Prentice-Hall, 1978.

Fuller, Robert W. *Somebodies and Nobodies: Overcoming the Abuse of Rank*. Gabriola Island, B.C.: New Society, 2003.

Kluger, Richard. *Simple Justice: The History of "Brown v. Board of Education" and Black America's Struggle for Equality*. New York: Alfred A. Knopf, 1976.

Van Dyke, Vernon. *Human Rights, Ethnicity, and Discrimination*. Westport, Conn.: Greenwood Press, 1985.

Williams, Mary E., ed. *Discrimination: Opposing Viewpoints*. San Diego, Calif.: Greenhaven Press, 2003.

SEE ALSO: Affirmative action; Ageism; Apartheid; Bigotry; Civil Rights movement; Gray Panthers; Inequality; Oppression; Racial prejudice.

Distributive justice

DEFINITION: Ethical concept pertaining to how resources and opportunities should be distributed among people within a given population

TYPE OF ETHICS: Politico-economic ethics

SIGNIFICANCE: Questions about how resources and opportunities should be distributed within a society are among the fundamental ethical problems that arise in social and political philosophy.

Resources that society distributes include goods that people own, such as income, property, and assets,

and goods and services that people may enjoy, such as education and health care. The central issues in ideas about justice in distribution are concerned with issues of the equality and inequality in the distribution of limited resources. Among the questions that must be addressed are these: Should all people be treated equally or unequally, and in what ways should they be treated equally or unequally? Most premodern concepts of the just society tended to portray human beings as divided into different and unequal stations (such as nobles and peasants) and to suggest that people should receive and enjoy standards of life appropriate to their stations.

The ancient Greek philosopher Aristotle made one of the earliest attempts systematically to address justice in distribution. In the fifth book of his *Nicomachean Ethics*, Aristotle stated that "injustice arises when equals are treated unequally and also when unequals are treated equally." The growth of industrial economies over the past three to four centuries of the second millennium tended to increase social mobility and undermine beliefs that human beings occupy social positions as a result of nature or divine will. One of the most influential social philosophies that developed in response to the modern condition was utilitarianism, a line of thinking associated with the early nineteenth century British philosopher Jeremy Bentham. As Bentham expressed it, the utilitarian view was that any society should seek the greatest good for the greatest number of its citizens. From this perspective, a society that is just in distribution will divide its resources and opportunities in a manner that provides the greatest overall well-being.

The German economic philosopher Karl Marx viewed absolute equality in distribution as the chief characteristic of the ideally just society. In 1875, he expressed this in his famous formulation "from each according to his ability; to each according to his need." This may be criticized because it apparently punishes abilities by insisting that those with greater abilities contribute more than others, and because it pays no attention to the utilitarian question of general well-being.

Even many of those who have seen problems with absolute equality have taken equality as a goal of distributive justice. The contemporary political philosopher Will Kymlicka has argued that every reasonable political and social theory should take equality as its ultimate value. The most influential theory of distributive justice in the past half-century, that of John Rawls, attempted to balance the goal of equality of individuals with that of the well-being of individuals.

THE THEORY OF JOHN RAWLS

In *A Theory of Justice* (1971), John Rawls defined a just society as the kind of society rational people would choose if they did not know what their own positions in that society would be. He maintained that this would be a society that provided the greatest possible resources to its least fortunate members. The ethical implication of this argument was that inequality among people could be taken as just only to the extent that it was in the interest of those at the bottom. Perhaps the most serious problem with this view of distributive justice is that it treats people as anonymous units, without regard to their virtues, vices, interests, or energies. Some writers have suggested that only a very strange version of justice can ignore what people deserve.

A colleague of John Rawls at Harvard University, Robert Nozick wrote *Anarchy, State, and Utopia* (1974) partly as a response to *A Theory of Justice*. Nozick maintained that justice requires respect for individuals, which means recognition of the rights of individuals to self-ownership and to ownership of the products of their own labor. Resources are created by the things that individuals do and they are exchanged among individuals. As long as people have acquired the objects that they own through work and exchange, they have just and ethical claims to their property. Redistribution involves taking from some individuals and giving to others. Unless it is redistribution of goods acquired unjustly, through force, this is equivalent to making some people work unwillingly for other people, taking away the right to self-ownership.

The principle of self-ownership may be a problem as a basis for social ethics. If people belong to communities, then it may be argued that their ownership of themselves is limited. In addition, although goods are created by individuals, they are almost always created by individuals cooperating in a society, so that one might see property as at least partly belonging to the whole society. Some forms of property, such as land and other natural resources, exist before people have claimed them and are not produced by individual efforts.

WELFARE EQUALITY AND RESOURCE EQUALITY

Ronald Dworkin, the most prominent theorist of distributive justice to follow Nozick, turned away from Nozick's hands-off approach and suggested that equal treatment of individual citizens is the fundamental premise of any idea of justice. According to Dworkin, equal treatment can take different forms. It may be equality of welfare or equality of resources. Dworkin argued against equality of welfare, pointing out that people can define well-being in various ways. Even if resources are equalized, people may make different uses of their resources. Therefore Dworkin argued that in the just society, all individuals are enabled to start out with equal resources, but that they may end up with unequal economic and social benefits because of their choices.

Advocates of egalitarian distribution, such as Rawls and Dworkin, tend to dominate philosophical debate about social justice. However, they generally fail to deal adequately with the political implications of their theories. If welfare or resources or other sets of desirable things are to be distributed, someone must be distributing them. This raises the question of what forms of government will be created by attempting to put ideas of distributive justice into practice. There is always the danger that the pursuit of social justice can lead to political dictatorship.

Carl L. Bankston III

FURTHER READING

Nozick, Robert. *Anarchy, State, and Utopia.* New York: Basic Books, 1974.

Rawls, John. *A Theory of Justice.* Cambridge, Mass.: Harvard University Press, 1971.

Rescher, Nicholas. *Fairness: Theory and Practice of Distributive Justice.* New Brunswick, N.J.: Transaction Publishers, 2002.

Roemer, John E. *Theories of Distributive Justice.* Cambridge, Mass.: Harvard University Press, 1996.

Sen, Amartya. *Inequality Reexamined.* Cambridge, Mass.: Harvard University Press, 1992.

SEE ALSO: Capitalism; Common good; Good, the; Income distribution; Inequality; Lifeboat ethics; Marx, Karl; Mean/ends distinction; Poverty and wealth; *Theory of Justice, A*; Utilitarianism.

Diversity

DEFINITION: Racial, cultural, and gender differences among human groups

TYPE OF ETHICS: Race and ethnicity

SIGNIFICANCE: Globalizing trends that favor social mobility and transnational migration have served to intensify cultural diversity, which in turn highlights contrasts between individual and group rights, often defined along racial, ethnic, or gender lines.

Human beings vary biologically, psychologically, and along a vast spectrum of sociocultural dimensions, ranging from language to religion, and from subsistence patterns to political organization. Throughout history, some of these dimensions have become markers of group membership, often precipitating intergroup conflict and systematic discrimination. Race, ethnicity, and gender are the three types of human diversity that have created the most complex ethical issues since the nineteenth century. In fact, in the context of cultural diversity in general, these issues have challenged the very foundations of ethical theory.

HUMAN EVOLUTION AND CULTURAL RELATIVISM

Charles Darwin's theory of human evolution, combined with the growing awareness of cultural differences catalyzed by colonial expansion, tested many of the most entrenched beliefs held by Westerners on matters of social hierarchy and intergroup relations. These challenges led to the emergence of two opposed sets of views: cultural relativism and "scientific racialism."

Cultural relativism—the belief that culture is the adaptive mechanism of human species and that therefore all human behavior can only be understood in the context of its culture-specific adaptive function—became the founding principle of a new discipline, cultural anthropology,. However, it did not have a major public impact until the last quarter of the nineteenth century. On the other hand, racialism—the belief that human species are divided into biologically discrete racial groups, endowed by inherited characteristics that make each groups "naturally" superior or inferior—rapidly became influential and was translated into racist policies, leading to systematic discrimination against, and even the attempted genocide of, various groups.

RACE AND ETHNICITY

As biologists amassed information about the characteristics of human species, it rapidly became clear that the concept of race—originally developed simply on the basis of observation of gross physical characteristics, such as skin color, hair type, eye shape, skull dimensions, and bodily form—did not have scientific relevance. In fact, especially as genetics provided ever more refined information about human characteristics, it was discovered that there is at last as much biological variation within so-called racial groups as there is among different groups.

This information, combined with a general recoiling from the consequences of racism, has contributed to the growing influence of cultural relativism since the 1970's. In fact, the end of the twentieth century was characterized by a so-called "cultural turn" in the humanities and social sciences, and by "cultural identity politics" as an influential popular trend. Nevertheless, neither racism nor racial pride have disappeared. This is because so-called racial characteristics often define ethnic membership, and ethnic diversity is constantly growing because of the migratory trends encouraged by globalization.

MULTICULTURALISM AND GENDER ISSUES

While ethnic differences are overwhelmingly cultural, rather than biological, and cultural relativism should therefore assuage any intergroup conflict they may trigger, the ethical issues involved with the protection of both individual and group rights remain difficult. Multiculturalism has emerged as the perspective attempting to constructively address these issues within liberal democratic states. It has had a particularly strong impact on education, business, and international relations. The objective of multiculturalism is to encourage cross-cultural understanding so that relations between different nation-states on one hand, and ethnic groups and mainstream populations on the other, are facilitated and human rights protected.

The ethics of multiculturalism, however, are challenged by the fact that some of its basic principles have been attacked as expressions of Western cultural imperialism. This often emerges in reference to issues related to age, sexual orientation, and, especially, gender. These issues are particularly sensitive because, while they have biological components, they are also influenced by culture. As a consequence, behaviors that some may consider discriminatory—such as child labor, polygamy, or female circumcision—may be considered perfectly acceptable within a different cultural tradition.

UNIVERSAL HUMAN RIGHTS

To address these challenges, attempts have been made by various international organizations to promulgate a set of universal human rights that would provide ethical guidelines for addressing major diversity issues. However, the application of such principles often meets the resistance of even their supposed beneficiaries. Diversity puts in question the very foundations of ethical theory.

On the other hand, there is widespread consensus on the need to distinguish between cultural and moral relativism. On this basis it is generally recognized that while cultural differences may lead to behavior that can only be understood within the context in which it originates, they do not provide individuals with a carapace protecting them from moral, or indeed legal judgment. In the application of such judgment ethical distinctions must be made, but these must be based on truly universal principles. In turn, this requires further exploration of the characteristics of the human species. The ethical challenge of diversity demands a honing of society's very understanding of what it means to be human.

E. L. Cerroni-Long

FURTHER READING

Cooper, David E. *Ethics for Professionals in a Multicultural World.* Upper Saddle River, N.J.: Pearson/Prentice Hall, 2004.

Gutmann, Amy, ed. *Multiculturalism: Examining the Politics of Recognition.* Princeton, N.J.: Princeton University Press, 1994.

Hutchinson, John, and Anthony D. Smith, eds. *Ethnicity.* Oxford, England: Oxford University Press, 1996.

Lukes, Steven. *Liberals and Cannibals: The Implications of Diversity.* New York: Verso, 2003.

Monges, Miriam Ma'at-Ka-Re. "Beyond the Melting Pot: A Values Clarification Exercise for Teachers and Human Service Professionals." In *Teaching About Culture, Ethnicity, and Diversity: Exercises and Planned Activities*, edited by Theodore M. Singelis. Thousand Oaks, Calif.: Sage, 1998.

Montagu, Ashley. *Man's Most Dangerous Myth: The Fallacy of Race.* Walnut Creek, Calif.: AltaMira Press, 1997.

Nussbaum, Martha C. *Sex and Social Justice.* New York: Oxford University Press, 1999.

Okin, Susan Moller, ed. *Is Multiculturalism Bad for Women?* Princeton, N.J.: Princeton University Press, 1999.

Shanklin, Eugenia. *Anthropology and Race.* Belmont, Calif.: Wadsworth, 1994.

Shweder, Richard A., Martha Minow, and Hazel Rose Markus, eds. *Engaging Cultural Differences: The Multicultural Challenge in Liberal Democracies.* New York: Russell Sage Foundation, 2002.

SEE ALSO: Absolutism; Bilingual education; Feminist ethics; Globalization; Immigration; Multiculturalism; Political correctness; Racism; Relativism; Tolerance.

Divine command theory

DEFINITION: Theory maintaining that the ethical values and principles binding upon human beings depend only on the commands of a god or gods

TYPE OF ETHICS: Religious ethics

SIGNIFICANCE: Divine command theory constitutes one attempt to provide an objective foundation for moral judgment.

The attempt to evaluate human behavior in terms of moral laws often leads to questions concerning the origin and authority of such laws. Advocates of divine command theories of morality have attempted to answer these questions by maintaining that human ethical values and principles are as they are merely because a god has willed or commanded that they be so. According to this theory, the ultimate explanation for the rightness or wrongness of any action is that some divinity has willed that the action be either good or evil.

It is important to distinguish divine command theories of morality from other theistically oriented ethical theories that relate human morality to the will of some deity. Many philosophers and theologians maintain that God is connected to human morality insofar as God's freely bestowed grace is necessary for the possibility of human beings living lives of moral rectitude. It has also been maintained that God's will is necessary for the possibility of human morality insofar as God must somehow promulgate or make known those laws that humans are obliged to observe. In addition, the conviction that an individual's degree of happiness ought to correspond to his or her moral desert is sometimes reconciled with instances of good people suffering by appealing to God's commitment to see that the demands of justice are met in an afterlife.

While all three of these points have accompanied divine command theories, none of them is a necessary component of a divine command theory. What is distinctive about divine command theories is their insistence on the following three points: the entire content of human moral principles is derived solely from the free choices of some god, the god in question is under no constraint to will a given set of moral principles, and the god could have willed the opposite of the set of moral principles that was, in fact, chosen.

The appeal of divine command theories is twofold. First, they offer an unqualified foundation for human morality. Second, they emphasize that God's freedom and power are unlimited by insisting that there are no moral principles that are independent of and binding upon the will of God. Despite these advantages, divine command theories have been attacked from a number of different directions. It has, for example, been pointed out that divine command theories lead to the conclusion that God could have decided to make moral atrocities (such as child abuse, rape, murder, and genocide) morally praiseworthy. Insofar as it is well-nigh impossible to reconcile the possibility of a world in which child molestation would be truly good with one's deepest moral intuitions, the implication that a good god could bring about such a world is taken to show the absurdity of divine command theories. Although this is a troubling consequence of divine command theories, it is important to note that some divine command theorists have openly embraced this aspect of their theory.

OBJECTIONS TO DIVINE COMMAND THEORY

A somewhat different objection points out that if the divine command theory were true, then it would not make sense to wonder whether God's commands were morally good. Because the divine command theorist maintains that God's commanding an action is a necessary and sufficient condition for the action's moral goodness, it follows that it would be contradictory to suppose that a divine command was evil. This point is thought to be problematic because it implies that speculation concerning the moral status of divine commands is actually as pointless as speculation about the triangularity of a triangle. To see that speculation about the moral status of God's commands is meaningful, however, one may think of the moral uneasiness that most readers of the Old Testament experience upon encountering God's command that Abraham sacrifice Isaac, his son. (Indeed, it is comforting to read that an angel stays Abraham's hand at the last instant.) The moral qualms that naturally arise over God's command to Abraham show that people do, meaningfully, evaluate divine commands in moral terms, a practice that would be pointless if the divine command theory were true.

This objection, however, is not decisive, for most divine command theories are not, at bottom, theories purporting to describe human conventions of moral discourse; rather, they are theories concerning the origin of those moral laws that are truly binding upon human beings. It is thus open to the divine command theorist to argue that conventions of moral discourse have developed in the absence of a clear awareness of the connection between divine commands and moral laws, and thus explain the fact that linguistic conventions have led people to question, however inappropriately, the goodness of God's commands.

Perhaps the strongest objection of divine command theories points out that they undermine the possibility of upholding divine goodness. Since divine command theories take God's power to be primary and maintain that moral goodness is wholly consequent to this power, it follows that God transcends, and thus cannot be characterized by, moral goodness. For this reason, divine command theories are accused of reducing the worship of God to a mere power worship and of maximizing God's power only at the price of forfeiting God's goodness.

James Petrik

FURTHER READING

Burch, Robert. "Objective Values and the Divine Command Theory of Morality." *New Scholasticism* 54 (Summer, 1980): 279-304.

Chandler, J. H. "Is the Divine Command Theory Defensible?" *Religious Studies* 20 (September, 1984): 443-452.

Hare, John E. *God's Call: Moral Realism, God's Commands, and Human Autonomy.* Grand Rapids, Mich.: W. B. Eerdmans, 2001.

Helm, Paul, ed. *Divine Commands and Morality.* New York: Oxford University Press, 1981.

Quinn, Philip L. *Divine Commands and Moral Requirements.* Oxford, England: Clarendon Press, 1978.

Rooney, Paul. *Divine Command Morality.* Brookfield, Vt.: Avebury, 1996.

Wierenga, Edward. "A Defensible Divine Command Theory." *Nous* 17 (September, 1983): 387-408.

SEE ALSO: Anthropomorphism of the divine; Descartes, René; God; Jesus Christ; Obedience; Religion; Revelation; Ten Commandments.

Divorce

DEFINITION: Dissolution of marriage

TYPE OF ETHICS: Beliefs and practices

SIGNIFICANCE: On the level of individual practice, divorce has variously been seen as a moral right, since it provides a means for individuals to seek happiness by ending destructive or inappropriate marriages, and as a moral transgression, since it is a violation of the vow to stay together forever. On a social level, the high rate of divorce in modern society is often interpreted as a sign of the moral decline of that society.

Divorce is related to two sets of ethical problems. The first has to do with the ethics of sexual behavior in societies in which the Judeo-Christian-Islamic tradition is dominant. Because only sex within a marriage is approved and marriage is supposed to last until one partner dies, divorce may both properly punish an adulterous partner and free the adulterer to form new sexual and marriage bonds. Freeing the adulterer has been viewed as encouraging immoral conduct in restrictive societies. As recently as the middle of the twentieth century, some predominantly Roman Catholic countries—notably Italy and Ireland—did not permit divorce.

The second set of ethical issues involves distributive justice issues having to do with the terms of division of marital assets and children upon divorce. Until the 1970's, more property was usually awarded to an innocent spouse at divorce; this unequal division was intended to punish the other spouse for engaging in unethical conduct. The dominant pattern at the start of the twenty-first century was to place more emphasis on equal divisions of property, or divisions based on contributions, and less emphasis on division based on the immoral conduct of one spouse.

HISTORY OF DIVORCE

In most ancient societies, husbands treated wives and children as property. Some commentators have suggested that the golden ring of marriage is a relic of a slave collar used to restrain the wife, or perhaps of her chains, the literal "marriage bonds." In some primitive societies (for example, the Tiwi of Melville Island), husbands still purchase wives from fathers. In most of these societies, divorce is mainly an economic affair; usually it involves returning the payments made at the time of the marriage. In traditional Eskimo society, the family simply divided into two households.

Written rules about marriage and divorce in the Western world can be traced to ancient Hebrew and Roman laws and customs. The Old Testament of the Bible relates that a Jewish wife at that time did not have the right to divorce her husband, but she did have the right to remarry if her husband divorced her: "When a man takes a wife and marries her, if then she finds no favor in his eyes because he has found some indecency in her . . . he writes her a bill of divorce and puts it in her hand and sends her out of his house, and she departs out of his house, and if she goes and becomes another man's wife . . ." (Deuteronomy 24:1).

Roman law did not make marriage a legal formality, and religious ceremonies were not required. Parental consent was the main formal prerequisite. Both husband and wife could possess their own property and end the marriage by a sign, such as a formal letter, of a clear intent to divorce. This secular, economic, and amoral approach to marriage and divorce is common today in most cultures in which the Judeo-Christian-Islamic tradition was never dominant and is reappearing in Western cultures.

CHRISTIANITY AND DIVORCE

When the emperors of Rome became Christians, they worked to bring marriage and divorce under legal and religious authority. Emperor Justinian I, the lawgiver of the sixth century, sought to impose the church's view opposing divorce, but an outraged public successfully defended its traditional liberties. In the Christian church's view, marriage was for life. The Roman Catholic canon law of the Middle Ages became the family law of most of Europe. Even after the Protestant Reformation, the Roman Catholic Church continued to permit only a partial divorce from bed and board that did not permit remarriage in the case of sexual misconduct or if a spouse left the church. Priests could annul some marriages if a partner violated the marriage-related complex and arbitrary rules of canon law, providing a potential escape from at least some miserable marriages. Annulment meant that no marriage had existed, so it made remarriage possible.

The phrase from the marriage ceremony "What therefore God has joined together, let not man put asunder" (Matthew 19:6) states the canon law position on divorce. Martin Luther and other Protestants who successfully rebelled against the Roman Catholic Church in the sixteenth century also rebelled against the theory that the ethical authority of the church permitted the religious regulation of marriage. Luther called marriage "an external worldly thing, subject to secular jurisdiction, just like dress and food, home and field." Most of the new Protestant religions sanctioned complete divorces for certain reasons, including unethical conduct such as adultery, cruelty, or abandonment.

In England, the Roman Catholic Church refused to allow Henry VIII to divorce a wife after she failed to provide him with a son. Arguing that the needs of England took precedence over church control of marriage, Henry VIII broke away from the Roman Catholic Church and formed what became the Church of England. Regulation of divorce was transferred from church to Parliament. Parties had to lobby to obtain a special act of the House of Lords in Parliament to obtain a divorce. These legislative divorces were too expensive for most people. In 1857, the British Parliament established the Court for Divorce and Matrimonial Causes and initiated divorce by judge. The new civil courts had jurisdiction of divorces and made civil divorces available, but only when the party seeking the divorce was mainly blameless.

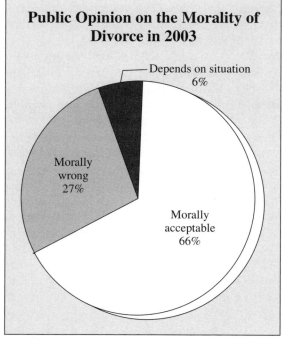

Public Opinion on the Morality of Divorce in 2003

Depends on situation 6%

Morally wrong 27%

Morally acceptable 66%

Note: Figures are rounded to nearest whole number.
Source: Gallup Poll, May 7, 2003.

DIVORCE AND CIVIL LAW

With the shift toward civil regulation of marriage came the adoption of many other civil law concepts into the relationship of marriage. Among these concepts were principles from the law of contracts, and marriage became a contractual relationship. The ethical basis of marriage and divorce shifted from religiously based concepts to concepts derived from the morality of contracts or commercial ethics.

In most places in the world where the courts regulated marriage, marriage was viewed as a status entered into by contract and the marriage vows as oral contracts. Therefore, grounds for divorce were those related to breaking the terms of the contract: fraud, breach of promise, inability to perform, and coercion. In divorce, fraud took the form of false representations prior to marriage. Adultery, desertion, and willful neglect were breaches of promise. An inability to perform took the form of impotence, homosexuality, habitual intemperance, conviction of a felony, and physical and mental cruelty. Only injured parties could initiate divorces, and courts considered the other parties "at fault." This fault doctrine justified giving property and support payments to the injured party as a sort of fine against the wrongdoer. Under the fault rules, family law was much like tort or contract law, with plaintiffs suing defendants and courts deciding who was wrong and who was right. The "innocent" spouse received an award in the same way that a successful plaintiff received an award in a personal injury lawsuit.

The economic and social consequences of the fault doctrine were good and bad and depended largely upon fault. If a woman wanted to end a marriage and could not prove that her husband was at fault, she received no share of property acquired during the marriage and usually no alimony. If the husband wanted to leave or the wife could prove adultery or other grounds, however, then she could bargain. Property and alimony were the wages of sin and the price of freedom. The result was that economic necessity kept many people in failed marriages. There were few children living in single-parent households and few divorced adults.

MOVING TO NO-FAULT DIVORCE

Love without marriage for those in loveless marriages often took the form of adultery. As Benjamin Franklin put it, "Where there's marriage without love, there will be love without marriage." Adultery was the primary cause of action for divorce suits under the fault doctrine rules. In the United States, this doctrine was a casualty of social upheaval during the 1960's. The first change was to permit divorce if both parties gave evidence of their intentions by voluntarily separating and living apart for a specified time.

In 1967, New York State abandoned its rule that the only grounds for divorce were fault grounds such as adultery and allowed divorce for couples legally separated for two years. In 1969, the California legislature commissioned leading judges, family lawyers, law professors, and behavioral scientists to carry out extensive research on the fault system. Based on the research results, the California legislature passed, in January, 1970, the California Family Law Act, which abolished the fault doctrine requiring "grounds" for a divorce. The legislature replaced the traditional ethical-moral grounds for divorce (adultery, abuse, and so forth) with no-fault grounds of "irreconcilable differences leading to an irremediable breakup of the marriage."

"Irreconcilable differences" means that one of the

parties does not want to remain married. "Irremediable breakup" means that the partners will not changes their minds.

The significance of the California Family Law Act was that it was the first law in the Western world to abolish a showing of fault as a requirement of divorce and to permit divorce upon demand. Gradually, all other American jurisdictions followed California. Today, people can obtain no-fault divorces in all states, although twenty states also retain the traditional fault grounds. The modern trend is not to allow evidence of fault in court except for financial misconduct related to property and support awards.

Gone with the fault doctrine was the tort cause of action of "alienation of affection." This tort had allowed an innocent spouse to sue an adulterous spouse's lover for loss of affection and consortium—a legal remedy for moral outrage. Gone also in most states were all defenses against the divorce. The traditional defenses allowed a nonconsenting partner to block divorce proceedings by disproving the stated grounds for the divorce. Gone was the rule preventing the "at-fault" party from initiating the proceedings. Only a few jurisdictions retained the traditional defenses.

Although the new laws abolished most of the traditional adversary trappings of divorce, fault was still important in custody disputes. As no-fault divorces became the norm and the new rules reduced or eliminated the power of one partner to stop the divorce proceedings, the divorce rate increased.

NO-FAULT DIVORCE AND ETHICAL ISSUES

Criticism of the no-fault doctrine also increased. Judge R. Michael Redman, in *Coming Down Hard on No-Fault* (1987), comments that no-fault divorce has shifted the focus of marriage from a cornerstone of society, a moral statement, to a relationship of convenience, an "I'll love you until you get ugly" idea. He suggests that the legal system, with its adversary traditions, is best suited to determining fault and allocating property and support accordingly. He bemoans the trend away from viewing marriage as a protected relationship.

Some family law experts object that no-fault is contrary to established ideas of morality, which hold that those who do wrong should suffer the consequences. Under a no-fault system, a marital partner who is blameless may still lose much property and may have to support an adulterous or brutal former spouse. Fault may protect an innocent spouse, and many no-fault states still apply fault considerations in some circumstances. Fault preserves the idea of individual accountability. Even when fault is no longer a legal issue, the fault of a partner may influence judges to be more generous to the innocent spouse. It is not coincidental that many of the sharpest critics of no-fault divorce have been women. Women are more likely to file for divorce because of alleged misconduct by their husbands, and alimony awards to women have decreased in the no-fault era.

Clients who want to have fault adjudicated in a divorce and be compensated will often abuse and manipulate the legal system to make a statement about the marriage. Couples denied expression of resentment in no-fault hearings dividing property may seek other avenues for their anger. It has been noted that in California, where fault is relevant only in custody disputes, couples tend to release their pent-up rage in those disputes, harming their children. Many divorcing people believe that ethical concerns and their view of justice should still dominate divorce.

Lawyers rarely see the long-term psychological damage done by a full-blown adversary process. Mental health professionals who do, however, have collected data showing long-term adjustment to be superior in parents who mediate rather than litigate their custody disputes. While advocates of a fault-based adversary system base the desirability of this system on moral grounds, the resulting harm to children violates other ethical values.

Many legal authors, trained to be advocates for a particular client, see the loss of fault grounds for divorce as promoting injustice. Rarely is either party in divorce completely innocent. The bitterness created by the adversary process usually causes harm outweighing the benefits arising out of the cathartic process of litigating disputes. The concept of justice in interpersonal relationships is more elusive than the legal-ethical concept of justice. It may be better for society and the involved parties to deal with the emotional issues of blame and anger with the help of therapists. Less adversarial divorce has made it easier to get divorced, however, and that development correlates with more frequent divorce.

Reducing the importance of fault does not eliminate the stress and pain of divorce. Data from the U.S. Bureau of the Census and the National Center for Health Statistics show that in 1988 the divorce rate was three times higher than the 1979 rate. The United States has the highest divorce rate in the world—twice that of England and Wales. The blended family is the new reality, and stepchildren are now 20 percent of all American children. Stepfamilies are created by loss and do not re-create nuclear families. The situation is not likely to improve soon. The U.S. Census Bureau estimates that close to two-thirds of children of married couples will experience their parents' divorce before they reach legal adulthood.

DISTRIBUTIVE JUSTICE ISSUES AND NO-FAULT DIVORCE

Legislatures based no-fault laws on the assumption that men and women are equals and should be treated equally. Judges assumed that spousal support for young healthy women, except on a short-term basis, was not needed, since women had equal opportunities to work. For numerous reasons, women are not usually the economic equals of men, and the equality assumption can lead to distributive injustices. One consequence of no-fault divorce has been a large increase in the number of women and children living in poverty, which violates ethical norms to protect children. This feminization of poverty has no simple solution. Working mothers tend to work fewer hours for lower wages than men in jobs that offer some flexibility in scheduling. Childcare expenses further reduce available funds. Child support payments, if collected at all, rarely fill the gap. Ethically, who is responsible for the harmful consequences of divorce on demand? Should divorced men without custody rights be impoverished to prevent the impoverishment of their former wives and children?

STATE CONTROL OF DIVORCE AND MARRIAGE

Marriage is not only a religious or civil act; it is also a legal status entered into by means of a contract. Because marriage is a legal status, the state has clear and legitimate interests in it. Because lawmakers and judges consider it a matter of local state interest, state legislatures pass most marriage and divorce laws. Case law has established marriage and divorce as fundamental civil freedoms. Because the right to marry is a basic right, states can significantly interfere with this right only when the state interest is "compelling."

The U.S. Supreme Court has made it clear that a

father's failure to pay support to his former family after divorce is not cause for a state to prevent him from remarrying. Divorce is no longer seen as a pariah status created by moral failure, and the state creates no special disabilities for the divorced. By the 1990's, the change from conceptualizing divorce in religious-ethical terms to seeing it as a pragmatic, legal, and secular process seemed complete.

Leland C. Swenson

FURTHER READING

Allison, Susan. *Conscious Divorce—Ending a Marriage with Integrity: A Practical and Spiritual Guide for Moving On.* New York: Three Rivers Press, 2001. Combines logistical advice for dealing with lawyers, friends, and family with a more value-oriented discussion of the personal meaning of divorce and its emotional toll. Attempts to delineate the most ethically responsible way to handle divorce by advocating respect and compassion for all involved.

Kitson, Gay C., and William M. Holmes. *Portrait of Divorce: Adjustment to Marital Breakdown.* New York: Guilford Press, 1992. An analysis of research into the reasons for, and the consequences of, divorce.

Macoby, Eleanor E., and Robert H. Mnookin. *Dividing the Child: Social and Legal Dilemmas of Custody.* Cambridge, Mass.: Harvard University Press, 1992. Discusses the effects of divorce and custody issues on children, paying special attention to the importance of workable relationships between divorced parents.

Schwitzgebel, Robert L., and R. Kirkland Schwitzgebel. *Law and Psychological Practice.* New York: Wiley, 1980. An excellent guide to the interaction of law and counseling. The chapter on divorce and family law contains interesting historical material.

Seichter, Marilyn P. "Alienation of Affection." *Family Advocate* 10, no. 2 (1987). A discussion of the use of the legal system to enforce social morality during the era of fault.

Simon, Rita J., and Howard Alstein. *Global Perspectives on Social Issues: Marriage and Divorce.* Lanham, Md.: Lexington Books, 2003. A sociological and anthropological analysis of current marriage and divorce practices in twenty-five nations around the world. Includes a brief survey of marriage and divorce from the beginnings of recorded history and employs both cultural analysis and hard statistical data to paint a picture of the current situation.

Swenson, Leland C. *Psychology and Law for the Helping Professions.* Pacific Grove, Calif.: Brooks/Cole, 1993. A guide intended to help those who are not attorneys understand the workings of the legal system. Approximately one-third of the book deals with family law, marriage, and divorce.

Tiemann, Adrian R., et al., eds. *Divorce Shock: Perspectives on Counseling and Therapy.* Philadelphia: Charles Press, 1992. This collection of articles addresses the issue of the effects of divorce on divorced spouses.

SEE ALSO: Adultery; Adversary system; Child support; Children; Children's rights; Family therapy; Family values; Marriage.

Dōgen

IDENTIFICATION: Japanese Zen master
BORN: January 19, 1200, Kyōto, Japan
DIED: September 22, 1253, Kyōto, Japan
TYPE OF ETHICS: Religious ethics
SIGNIFICANCE: The founder of the Sōtō school of Japanese Zen Buddhism and one of the finest prose stylists in the Japanese language, Dōgen taught no formal system of ethics as such. Instead, his *Shōbōgenzō* (1244; treasury of the eye of the true dharma) emphasized the practice of meditation in the belief that truly ethical action arises out of the direct experience of reality in each moment.

Buddhism originated before 500 B.C.E. in India, where the historical Buddha Śākyamuni experienced an awakening, or enlightenment, and taught others that they too could experience such an awakening and be free from the suffering caused by ignorance of the true nature of reality. A thousand years later, Buddhism spread to China, where it combined with the native Daoist tradition and evolved into Chan Buddhism. Chan Buddhism then spread to Japan, where it became known as Zen Buddhism.

In 1227, Dōgen Kigen, a liberally educated Japanese Buddhist from an aristocratic family, traveled to China in search of an enlightened Chan master. Dōgen studied there for four years under Tiantong Rujing, who transmitted to him the seal of confirmation of the Chan lineage whose approach ultimately became that of the Sōtō school of Japanese Zen.

Dōgen brought the teachings to Japan, where much of Buddhism had come to rely too heavily on theory and ritual, neglecting the meditative practice that is the heart of Buddhism. Dōgen brought the focus of Japanese Zen back to *zazen*, or sitting meditation practice, revitalizing the Zen tradition in Japan.

There are two major schools of Zen: Rinzai and Sōtō. Both schools emphasize sitting meditation (*zazen*), but Rinzai Zen also utilizes *kōan* study, in which a practitioner examines an apparently paradoxical phrase (for example, "What was your original face before you were born?") that poses a problem that cannot be solved by means of logic, thus forcing the practitioner to bypass conceptual understanding. Dōgen's Sōtō Zen, however, emphasizes the practice of *shikan taza* ("simply sitting"), which involves cultivating awareness without striving for enlightenment.

ETHICAL IMPLICATIONS

Dōgen's fullest discussion of Zen ethics comes in "Shoakumakusa," part of his *Shōbōgenzō*. Dōgen denies any absolute distinction between good and evil—while still affirming traditional moral teachings—by interpreting an important classical Chinese scripture as a description of an ideal rather than a command. "The nonproduction of evil,/ The performance of good,/ The purification of one's own intentions:/ This is the teaching of all Buddhas." *Shōbōgenzō* also stresses experiencing the present moment and not wasting time. Dōgen's Sōtō Zen, like other schools of Buddhism, teaches the importance of compassion for all beings. In Buddhism, however, compassion is not a mode of behavior to which one strives to adhere; instead, compassion arises spontaneously when one experiences the true reality of each moment of existence.

Roy Neil Graves

FURTHER READING

Dōgen. *Moon in a Dewdrop: Writings of Zen Master Dōgen*. Edited by Kazuaki Tanahashi. San Francisco: North Point Press, 1985.

Kasulis, T. P. *Zen Action/Zen Person*. Honolulu: University Press of Hawaii, 1981.

Katagiri, Dainin. *You Have to Say Something: Manifesting Zen Insight*. Boston: Shambhala, 1998.

Kim, Hee-Jin. *Dōgen Kigen: Mystical Realist*. Tucson: University of Arizona Press, 1975.

Kodera, Takashi James. *Dōgen's Formative Years in China: An Historical Study and Annotated Translation of the Hōkyō-ki*. Boulder, Colo.: Prajñā Press, 1980.

Kopf, Gereon. *Beyond Personal Idenity: Dōgen, Nishida, and a Phenomenology of No-Self*. Richmond, Surrey, England: Curzon, 2001.

Loori, John Daido, ed. *The Art of Just Sitting: Essential Writings on the Zen Practice of Shikantaza*. Boston: Wisdom, 2002.

Ross, Nancy Wilson. *Three Ways of Asian Wisdom: Hinduism, Buddhism, Zen, and Their Significance for the West*. New York: Simon & Schuster, 1966.

Yokoi, Yūhō, with Daizen Victoria. *Zen Master Dōgen: An Introduction with Selected Writings*. 4th ed. New York: Weatherhill, 1987.

SEE ALSO: Bodhidharma; Bodhisattva ideal; Buddha; Buddhist ethics; Four noble truths; Zen.

Dominion over nature, human

DEFINITION: Idea that humanity has the right to use nature to further its own ends

TYPE OF ETHICS: Environmental ethics

SIGNIFICANCE: Some ethical systems hold that nature has been given to humanity to dispose of as it sees fit, while others claim that humans have an obligation to the natural world. Moreover, human dominion over nature has increased to such an extent that humanity may place its own future existence and happiness in jeopardy, which raises practical ethical concerns regardless of one's theoretical value system.

Human beings have always exploited natural resources for their own well-being. Early in human history, people learned how to domesticate plants and animals—to collect or capture them, to breed them selectively, and to harvest them for human use. People also learned how to "capture," "tame," and "harvest" many inanimate resources, such as fire, water, minerals, and fossil fuels.

In most societies, it was either assumed or explicitly taught that human dominion over nature was a natural, or even God-given, right, and as long as human populations were small, this philosophy posed no major problems. As the human population increased and technology made it increasingly easy to harvest natural resources, however, many natural resources began to disappear. Many people are now questioning the idea of the human right of dominion over nature, on both practical and ethical grounds.

Linda Mealey

SEE ALSO: Animal rights; Biodiversity; Conservation; Deep ecology; Earth and humanity; Ecology; Endangered species; Environmental ethics; Exploitation; Future generations.

Dostoevski, Fyodor

IDENTIFICATION: Russian novelist
BORN: November 11, 1821, Moscow, Russia
DIED: February 9, 1881, St. Petersburg, Russia
TYPE OF ETHICS: Modern history
SIGNIFICANCE: Dostoevski, one of the greatest novelists in any language, was profoundly concerned with the personal experience and practice of morality and its relationship to Christianity. Dostoevski's most famous characters transgress, suffer, and achieve redemption, all the while fighting tooth and nail against the very religious system that gives meaning to those terms. His works include *The Double* (*Dvoynik*, 1946), *Notes from the Underground* (*Zapiski iz podpolya*, 1864), *Crime and Punishment* (*Prestupleniye i nakazaniye*, 1866), *The Idiot* (*Idiot*, 1868), *The Possessed* (*Besy*, 1871-1872), and *The Brothers Karamazov* (*Bratya Karamazovy*, 1879-1880).

Inherent in Fyodor Dostoevski's literary canon is the primacy of the freedom of the individual. He argued in *The Double* and other works that the problems of society were caused by the absence of freedom; humankind had been "overcome" by the impact of human institutions—the church, the state, and economic structures—and by the assumed beliefs in

God and in economic and social values. Dostoevski advanced a radical philosophy in which he condemned encumbrances to freedom.

Dostoevski maintained that the so-called "laws of nature" did not exist; sustaining a belief in these laws would inevitably result in the restriction of freedom. It was only through unbridled and anarchical freedom that the individual would be totally free and thus recognize his or her own identity. This condition would preclude all forms of ethics except for a hedonistic ethics based on the interests of the self. Dostoevski recognized the anarchical ramifications of his argument and attempted unsuccessfully to address them in *Crime and Punishment* and *The Brothers Karamazov*. If truth does not exist, there is no basis for ethical principles.

William T. Walker

SEE ALSO: Anarchy; Freedom and liberty; Gratitude; Life, meaning of; Nihilism; Secular ethics.

Downsizing

DEFINITION: Reduction of a company's size through employee layoffs
TYPE OF ETHICS: Business and labor ethics
SIGNIFICANCE: Downsizing is a management decision that has ethical implications for managers, who must consider their responsibilities to maintain the financial health of their firms for shareholders and to honor the rights of their employees.

According to the federal Bureau of Labor Statistics, 11,947 mass layoff actions were implemented during the first half of 2003 alone, prompting 1,183,045 unemployment insurance benefits filings. Such downsizing decisions are management choices that have different ethical implications and perceptions depending on whether the affected people are managers formulating and implementing downsizing plans or employees losing their jobs.

It is generally believed that company managers have an ethical obligation to make sound business decisions that maintain the financial integrity of their firms and that are in the best interests of their firms' owners. Beyond the bottom-line impact of downsizing decisions, managers must consider, in varying degrees, the ethical implications that impact their employees in formulating and implementing downsizing decisions. At one extreme are managers who believe that any downsizing decisions are correct in light of their responsibilities to their firms' owners and that they have little or no ethical responsibility to employees in whatever subsequent actions result from their decisions.

At the other extreme are managers who factor in ethical considerations at every step of the downsizing process by exhausting every other alternative for maintaining the financial health of their organizations and choosing downsizing as their last alternative. Then, as they formulate and implement their decisions, they remain conscious of the ethical obligations they have to the employees who are affected by their decisions. For example, in addition to providing severance pay for employees who lose their jobs, the manages may also provide benefits packages that include outplacement assistance; personal, financial, and career counseling; and assistance with medical insurance coverage.

Studies have shown that employees believe that their employers violate their ethical responsibilities when management denies their rights on any of three aspects of downsizing. The first aspect is poor timing. Employers should not implement their downsizing decisions on dates near major holidays, and they should give their employees ample advance notice. Sixty days' notice is a standard used by many and is the law in some situations.

The second aspect is the method of communication through which the news is conveyed to employees. No person losing a job wants to learn the bad news while reading the morning newspaper. Finally, employees who lose their jobs want to know there are valid reasons for their firms' layoff decisions. When management provides adequate notice, communicates through appropriate channels, and provides cogent reasons for downsizing, employees are likely to believe they have received ethical treatment during the difficult downsizing process.

Stephen D. Livesay
Corinne R. Livesay

FURTHER READING

De Meuse, Kenneth, and Mitchell Lee Marks. *Resizing the Organization*. San Francisco: Jossey-Bass, 2003.

Radin, Tara, et al. *Employment and Employee Rights*. Malden, Mass.: Blackwell Publishing, 2004.

SEE ALSO: Business ethics; Corporate compensation; Corporate responsibility; Cost-benefit analysis; Employee safety and treatment; Hiring practices; Multinational corporations; Outsourcing.

Dresden firebombing

THE EVENT: Destruction of a historic German city by Allied bombers during World War II that killed thousands of civilians and left thousands of others homeless

DATE: February 13-14, 1945

TYPE OF ETHICS: Military ethics

SIGNIFICANCE: Because Dresden was not a significant military target and because so many civilians were harmed in the attacks, the British Royal Air Force's saturation bombing campaign has been labeled by some as at best morally questionable and at worst a serious war crime.

On February 8, 1945, late in World War II, the Allied Combined Strategic Targets Committee reported to the Supreme Headquarters Allied Expeditionary Force (SHAEF), headed by American General Dwight D. Eisenhower, that the German city of Dresden had been made a target. Dresden reputedly was a center for German military movements toward the eastern front against the advancing Russians. Allied military officials conceded later, however, that one of their basic purposes in targeting Dresden was to demoralize the Germans in an attempt to shorten the war. The code name for such massive air operations against Germany, which had included thousand-plane raids on Berlin and Hamburg, was Clarion.

On the afternoon of February 13, Royal Air Force (RAF) bombers struck Dresden in waves, exhausting anti-aircraft and fighter-plane resistance while smothering the city with incendiary bombs. These bombs drove 600,000 civilians and refugees out of shelters just as a more devastating attack began. The intensity of the fires caused a colossal "firestorm." Ultimately, losses were calculated at 18,375 dead, 2,212 seriously wounded, and 13,918 slightly wounded. Some 350,000 people were made homeless.

Dresden shortly after the Allied firebombings of February, 1945. (AP/Wide World Photos)

Outrage at the raids was expressed in the British press and in the British Parliament. Critics of the raids charged that Dresden was an ancient, beautiful, culturally rich city that had little military value. In spite of the criticism, however, the Allied military leaders continued to conduct massive bombing raids against enemy cities. Dresden and the Japanese cities of Hiroshima and Nagasaki, which became targets of atomic-bomb attacks conducted by the U.S. military, became symbols of Allied brutality. The primary ethical issue involved was whether it is possible to justify morally the bombing of targets that consist primarily of civilians. Historians continue to debate the military value of the attacks on Dresden, Hiroshima, and Nagasaki.

Clifton K. Yearley

SEE ALSO: *Art of War, The*; Hiroshima and Nagasaki bombings; Just war theory; Limited war; Military ethics; *On War*; War crimes trials.

Dress codes

DEFINITION: Explicit or implicit rules about what clothing may be worn and what may not be worn in schools or workplaces

TYPE OF ETHICS: Personal and social ethics

SIGNIFICANCE: Dress codes for workplaces or schools often create tension between the supposed good of the employers or schools and the individual freedoms of employees or students.

405

Most American employers have dress codes that are either stated or implied. Both public and private primary and secondary schools generally have written dress codes, some more specific than others. Public and secular private colleges and universities rarely have dress codes, but even the most liberal of campuses have boundaries for dress, as the suspension of a student dubbed the "Naked Guy" at the University of California at Berkeley in 1992 showed.

In the workplace, attention is ordinarily focused not on uniforms but on individually selected civilian clothing. When disputes arise, they often involve differences of opinion about where the controls exercised by employer for safety, sanitation, security, identification, teamwork, and image ought to end and the rights of individual employees to govern their own appearances begin.

Trends toward casualness and away from supposedly arbitrary rules have combined with individualism and defiance of authority to create disagreements between supervisors and the supervised. With the

*Dress codes took on an international flavor in early 2004, when the French government announced a ban on the wearing of Muslim head scarves (*hijab*) and other religious apparel in public schools. Here, Muslim students protest outside the French embassy in Jakarta, Indonesia.* (AP/Wide World Photos)

Dressing "Down" on Casual Friday

During the 1990's a new custom spread rapidly through American workplaces: "Casual Friday." With the explicit or tacit consent of employers, growing numbers of office workers began dressing in jeans, T-shirts, and other articles of casual apparel, rather than their normal suits and ties, on Fridays. The custom appears to have originated in high-tech firms in California's Silicon Valley during the late 1980's and then spread to other industries. By the turn of the twenty-first century, it was estimated that Casual Friday was being observed in more than two-thirds of American companies. While the popularity of the custom reflected a clear willingness of employers to be more permissive in matters of dress codes, many employers still set limits on what was permissible. For example, when IBM permitted its executives to adopt Casual Friday attire in 1995, its chief executive officer, Louis Gerstner, Jr., issued a memo to employees stating that "business casual attire at the office is acceptable as long as employees dress appropriately for meetings with customers and business partners."

---

consent of their employers, men who work in offices often dispense with neckties and jackets, as well as white shirts. Leaving their skirts in the closet, women might wear T-shirts and blue jeans in their office jobs, or even shorts, with employer approval. However, sometimes overly relaxed or daring employees overstep their employers' notions of casual propriety in what they wear, and the range of disputes about workplace clothing expands.

In schools, disagreements about clothing between administrators and teachers, on the one hand, and students, on the other, have also been abundant, even as the trend toward greater casualness in attire has spread. In many public schools, shorts and T-shirts, for instance, have become acceptable for girls and boys, but some students, like workers, still wish to assert through their clothing their sense of individual liberty. Their motivations are usually for reasons of fashion but are occasionally for religious or even political purposes. In *Tinker v. Des Moines* (1969), the U.S. Supreme Court upheld the plaintiffs' right to wear black armbands to protest the Vietnam War.

Students who deliberately break what they consider unreasonable rules about clothes collide with administrators who believe that even public schools should exert some degree of control over students' clothing for the sake of safety, decency, and, in general, a proper environment for learning. That control can range from vague rules about appropriate dress to specific requirements for uniforms, which, supporters say, reduce violence and social competition among students, while instilling a school pride that improves student behavior and academic performance.

Victor Lindsey

FURTHER READING

Cruz, Barbara C. *School Dress Codes: A Pro/Con Issue*. Hot Pro/Con Issues. Berkeley Heights, N.J.: Enslow Publishers, 2001.

Maysonave, Sherry. *Casual Power: How to Power Up Your Nonverbal Communication and Dress Down for Success*. Austin, Tex.: Bright Books, 1999.

SEE ALSO: Employee safety and treatment; Ethical codes of organizations; Fear in the workplace; Honor systems and codes; Islamic ethics; Nation of Islam; Sexuality and sexual ethics.

Dronenburg v. Zech

THE EVENT: Federal appellate court decision holding that a U.S. Navy regulation requiring mandatory discharge for homosexual conduct did not violate the constitutional right of privacy or the equal protection clause

DATE: Ruling made on August 17, 1984

TYPE OF ETHICS: Civil rights

SIGNIFICANCE: Robert Bork's opinion in *Dronenburg* denied that the right to privacy extends to the sexual conduct of military personnel and endorsed the Navy's assertion that homosexuality posed a threat to military morale and discipline.

James Dronenburg, a twenty-seven-year-old U.S. Navy petty officer, was found to have engaged regu-

larly in homosexual conduct. The Navy discharged him involuntarily, as its regulations required. Dronenburg admitted the allegations but appealed on the ground that there is a constitutional right of privacy that protects consensual homosexual conduct and that his discharge consequently deprived him of the equal protection of the laws.

The U.S. Court of Appeals for the District of Columbia held against Dronenburg, 3-0. Judge Robert Bork's opinion argued that the constitutional right of privacy established by the Supreme Court is not as well delineated as are certain other constitutional rights. Moreover, it had never been held to cover homosexual conduct. Bork suggested that any change in these regulations should be determined by "moral choices of the people and the elected representatives" rather than by the courts.

Robert Jacobs

SEE ALSO: Gay rights; *Griswold v. Connecticut*; Homosexuality; Privacy; Supreme Court, U.S.

Drug abuse

DEFINITION: Practice of using a substance, for nonmedical reasons, that adversely affects the user's physical, mental, or emotional condition

TYPE OF ETHICS: Personal and social ethics

SIGNIFICANCE: The abuse of drugs can lead to personal harm and have devastating social consequences. Its moral status is largely dependent upon whether one believes that drug abuse is a personal failing or a form of mental illness.

One of modern industrial society's most challenging problems is drug abuse. The cost in terms of personal health problems, destabilizing families, crime, and accidents brought on by abusing drugs has been staggering. Drug abuse, often referred to as "substance abuse," includes any deliberate use of illegal or legal drugs that leads to physical, emotional, or mental problems.

EXTENT OF DRUG ABUSE

The National Institute on Drug Abuse reported that in 1990, approximately 27 million people (13.3 percent of the population) in the United States had used some form of illegal drug during the previous year. In addition, one must add to this number the roughly 14.5 million Americans who were believed to be problem drinkers or alcoholics. Alcohol, although a legal substance, has a long-standing record for being the most frequently abused drug. Marijuana, cocaine, hallucinogens, and stimulants were the most frequently used illegal substances.

POTENTIAL HARM TO SELF OR SOCIETY

Ethical questions abound when an individual contemplates the decision to use an illegal drug. Is it wrong to take this drug? What will be the legal, emotional, or personal health consequences of taking this drug? Will the decision to take the drug have an im-

pact on other people? Disregarding the fact that purchasing and using an illegal substance violates social norms and breaks the law, the morality of a particular behavior can be judged, in part, by its personal and social outcomes. Drug abuse involving a psychoactive drug (a drug that affects how a person thinks or feels) can lead to horrendous consequences. The National Highway Traffic Safety Administration reported in 1991 that there were nearly twenty thousand alcohol-related fatalities in the United States. This number represents only deaths, not the additional tens of thousands of people who suffer severe head injuries in alcohol-related accidents.

Substance abuse can cut short the goals and aspirations of a person. It can lead to personal health

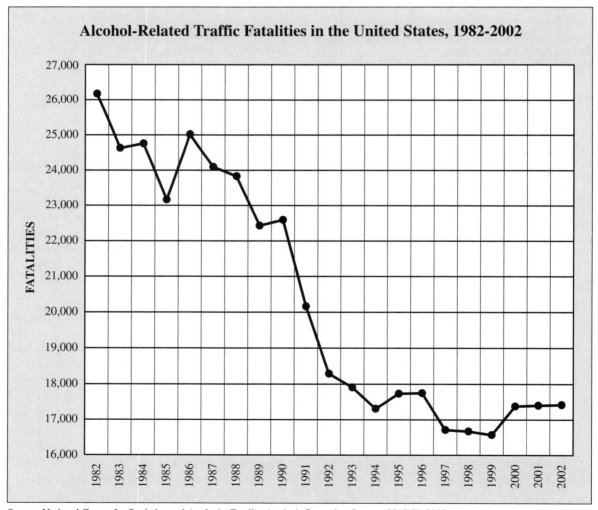

Source: National Center for Statistics and Analysis. Fatality Analysis Reporting System (NARS), 2002.

problems and death (for example, cirrhosis of the liver, overdose). It can interfere with a person's desire to pursue an education or hold down a job.

What might originally begin as a personal (free) decision to explore drugs and alcohol may eventually lead to both physiological and psychological dependency. This process of drug abuse turned drug addiction strips the individual of many of the personal freedoms he or she once enjoyed. The free choice to use or not to use drugs, when someone is addicted, is no longer present. Drug dependency leads to drug craving, which is difficult to overcome without intensive treatment. The control that a drug can exert on a person's life has profound ethical consequences for an individual's personal liberties.

Drug abuse can also do harm to society. People have a right to live in neighborhoods that are safe for raising families, working, and recreation. Social scientist Ronald Akers, in his book *Drugs, Alcohol, and Society* (1992), reports that substance abuse is significantly correlated with crime and juvenile delinquency. Society diverts billions of dollars each year that could go toward important social services in combating the violence and crime associated with drugs. Organized drug cartels and youth gangs pose formidable threats to community safety because of their involvement in drug trafficking.

Not only does society have to bear the cost of additional crime and law enforcement, but also billions are spent each year for drug treatment and rehabilitation. The National Institute on Alcohol Abuse and Alcoholism estimates that the cost to society, for alcohol alone, is about $117 billion each year for treatment, reduced work productivity, prevention efforts, law enforcement, and so forth. Another social problem that is exacerbated by drug abuse involves the use of drugs that are administered parenterally, which have contributed to the transmission of the AIDS virus. It could easily be argued that the harm caused by drug abuse for both individuals and society is not only unjust but also immoral.

LEGALIZATION

Efforts have been put forth to either decriminalize or legalize a number of psychoactive substances that are frequently abused. Decriminalization of marijuana by reducing the penalty of possession to less than a misdemeanor offense has come into law in a few states. The legalization of drugs such as marijuana has not, however, received state or national support. Advocates for the legalization of drugs argue that it is an individual right to be able to use drugs and that governments should stop interfering with them. In addition, advocates argue that many of the problems brought on by drug abuse (such as crime and violence) have been caused by the oppressive enforcement tactics of the government. They also state that monies that are used for drug interdiction and enforcement could be better spent on social programs.

Arguments against legalization include the prediction that the greater availability of drugs would increase the number of chemically dependent people—not decrease them as many advocates argue—thus posing even more of a threat to society. Furthermore, since the drugs influence the mind and behavior, the right-to-privacy principle does not apply because of the consequences incurred by those individuals in contact with the drug user.

Bryan C. Auday

FURTHER READING

Akers, Ronald L. *Drugs, Alcohol, and Society: Social Structure, Process, and Policy.* Belmont, Calif.: Wadsworth, 1992.

Carroll, Charles R. *Drugs in Modern Society.* 5th ed. Boston: McGraw-Hill, 2000.

Doweiko, Harold E. *Concepts of Chemical Dependency.* Pacific Grove, Calif.: Brooks/Cole, 1990.

Egendorf, Laura K, ed. *Chemical Dependency: Opposing Viewpoints.* San Diego, Calif.: Greenhaven Press, 2003.

Goode, Erich. *Drugs in American Society.* 5th ed. Boston: McGraw-Hill, 1999.

SEE ALSO: Lifestyles; Moral education; Permissible acts; Psychopharmacology; Public interest; Self-interest; Tobacco industry; Vice.

Drug testing

DEFINITION: Chemical analysis of the hair, bodily fluids, or breath of individuals to detect or rule out their recent consumption of illegal substances

TYPE OF ETHICS: Personal and social ethics

SIGNIFICANCE: Increases in the availability and use of drug testing methods have placed concerns about public safety and employers' rights at odds with principles of individual liberty, privacy, and dignity.

Methods of drug testing were available prior to the 1980's, but their use was generally limited to situations involving special circumstances, such as testing athletes for performance-enhancing drugs or determining whether vehicle drivers might be drunk. By the end of the 1980's, however, growing public concerns about drug use in society combined with decreased costs and increased availability of drug testing stimulated a dramatic upsurge in substance-use screening in both the public and private sectors. A series of court rulings set clear guidelines for the testing of government employees that limited testing to employees in positions involving public safety and national security. However, courts were reluctant to restrict drug testing in the private sector, and private employers continued to make increasing use of drug-testing procedures.

SAFETY VS. LIBERTY

Ethical questions about drug testing often focus on conflicts between public health and safety and personal liberty. Most arguments in favor of drug testing rest on commonly held beliefs that illicit-drug use is immoral, unhealthy, and destructive to society. Many proponents of testing cite the presence of illegal drug use as justification in itself for widespread testing. These arguments are sometimes rooted in the paternalistic belief that government, private employers, and other authority figures have both the right and the responsibility to protect people from their own and others' misbehavior. Civil libertarians, however, argue that the negative effects of drug testing upon personal liberty and privacy outweigh its potential positive effects on the community, and summarily reject the notion that government has a responsibility to protect people from themselves by regulating private behavior that does not directly harm others.

Many proponents of drug testing adhere to a communitarian social philosophy that prioritizes community health and welfare over the rights of individuals. This philosophy holds that ordinary citizens should be compelled to endure "minor" intrusions upon their liberty and privacy for the good of the community. Many communitarians also reject the notion that drug use is a "victimless crime," citing evidence of drug-related crime, accidents, and increased costs of health care and law enforcement as sufficient reason for utilizing testing to reduce both the harm associated with drug use and drug use itself. Civil libertarians respond that the alleged societal costs of drug use cannot be accurately measured, and that many of the purported consequences of drug use are the results of public policy and societal attitudes that encourage criminal behavior associated with drug use and discourage persons with drug problems from seeking treatment—issues that drug testing does not directly address.

EMPLOYEE VS. EMPLOYER RIGHTS

Employers often approach the issue of drug testing from both paternalistic and communitarian perspectives. Public employers, for example, may justify drug testing as a necessary means of ensuring public health and safety and may also claim the authority to safeguard the health and morals of their subordinates for their own and for the public good. Private employers often cite the need to ensure safe and orderly workplaces as a rationale for drug testing; however, many also claim the "right" to healthy, productive, and law-abiding workforces as justification to police employee drug use both on and off the job. Employer rationales for drug testing are often utilitarian in nature; some employ drug testing programs in response to pressure from insurance companies, to reap tax breaks and other financial incentives, or as a means of boosting consumer confidence.

Other ethical considerations connected with drug testing concern relationships between employers and employees. Civil libertarians point out that few drug tests distinguish between drug use on the job and drug use off the job; therefore, employees might be punished for off-the-job behaviors that have little or no bearing on their fitness to perform their jobs. This possibility again poses the question of whether and to what extent employers have the right to regulate the off-the-job behavior of their employees—a right that many insist must be restricted to ensure equitable relationships between employers and employees.

Civil libertarians believe that employees' rights should take priority over the rights of employers, who typically possess more money, power, and resources than their employees and are not subject to the same constitutional standards that government officials must follow when enacting drug-testing policies. Therefore, employers enjoy a large degree of authority to invade the privacy of employees, who have little recourse if they are falsely accused of drug use. Indeed, many opponents of drug testing cite the inaccuracies of drug tests as a rationale to limit their use. Other questions involve the potential for humiliation that drug testing poses; many urine testing programs, for example, require the subjects' urination to be witnessed to minimize the possibility of deception.

ALTERNATIVES AND COMPROMISES

Although improvements in drug testing procedures have lessened the possibility that subjects might be falsely implicated or falsely cleared, inaccuracies in testing still exist. Although the employment of less intrusive measures such as testing of hair samples could eliminate overt humiliation, many still argue that the process of collecting one's bodily fluids and tissues to detect drug use is in itself intrusive, humiliating, and ethically indefensible. Finally, many would argue that employers have other means of evaluating the job fitness of employees and applicants, such as background checks and impairment-testing procedures that test actual decision-making skills, reaction times, and other indicators of job fitness that are less intrusive and equally accurate methods of evaluation and screening.

Opponents and advocates of drug testing have often found middle ground; for example, most civil libertarians do not oppose limited drug testing of drug felons on probation or in treatment programs, while many paternalists and communitarians do not support random testing of licensed drivers or welfare recipients.

Michael H. Burchett

FURTHER READING

Coombs, Robert H., and Louis J. West, eds. *Drug Testing: Issues and Options*. New York: Oxford University Press, 1991.

Gottfried, Ted. *Privacy: Individual Rights v. Social Needs*. New York: Millbrook Press, 1994.

Jussim, Daniel. *Drug Tests and Polygraphs: Essential Tools or Violations of Privacy?* New York: Julian Messner, 1988.

Murphy, Kevin R. *Honesty in the Workplace*. New York: Brooks/Cole, 1992.

Newton, David E. *Drug Testing: An Issue for School, Sports, and Work*. Springfield, N.J.: Enslow Publishers, 1999.

SEE ALSO: Biometrics; Drug abuse; Hiring practices; Invasion of privacy; Loyalty oaths; Privacy; Psychopharmacology; Whistleblowing.

Du Bois, W. E. B.

IDENTIFICATION: American writer and social activist
BORN: February 23, 1868, Great Barrington, Massachusetts
DIED: August 27, 1963, Accra, Ghana
TYPE OF ETHICS: Modern history
SIGNIFICANCE: Du Bois worked both to understand and to rectify the ethical effects of racial divisions. He wrote *The Souls of Black Folk* (1903) and edited the journal *The Crisis* (1910-1932).

W. E. B. Du Bois. (Library of Congress)

After a successful early career as a publishing scholar, W. E. B. Du Bois recognized that the resolution of American racial problems could not be accomplished solely by revealing the truth; therefore, he became an activist. His famous statement, "The problem of the twentieth century is the problem of the color line," demonstrates the focus of his ethical inquiries. Well-read in history, Du Bois argued that the premature end of the Reconstruction left not only practical problems but also ethical ones. He believed that it was unethical for the United States to blame the freed slaves for the vices that had been instilled in them during generations of enslavement. Slavery, followed by a system of strict racial segregation, had left African Americans economically and psychologically vulnerable. Economically, slavery was replaced by peonage, a system in which indebted African American sharecroppers were forced to work in the fields or face starvation or imprisonment. Psychologically, black "double consciousness" caused a divided and vitiated purpose.

Du Bois saw the solutions to the problems as economic independence and the creation of an environment that would be free of racism and in which "true self-consciousness" could be attained. Du Bois is most famous for his disagreements with Booker T. Washington, the most prominent African American of the early 1900's. Du Bois believed that Washington, in his efforts to secure industrial training and a prosperous economic future for the masses of blacks, had depreciated the need for political rights, higher education, and acquaintance with the higher values of civilization. The promise of prosperity, Du Bois believed, could not substitute for civil rights and liberal learning.

William L. Howard

SEE ALSO: Civil rights and liberties; Civil Rights movement; National Association for the Advancement of Colored People; Pan-Africanism; Washington, Booker T.

Due process

DEFINITION: Fair procedure of law to which all persons are constitutionally entitled should the government attempt to deprive them of life, liberty, or property

TYPE OF ETHICS: Legal and judicial ethics

SIGNIFICANCE: The due process clauses of the Fifth and Fourteenth Amendments to the U.S. Constitution and similar provisions in all state constitutions stand as barriers to arbitrary or tyrannical treatment of individuals by the government.

The historical roots of due process go back at least as far as the Magna Carta (1215), by which King John of England was forced to eschew arbitrary power over the lives and estates of his barons. Although "due process" case law has become technically complex in the United States, its fundamental elements continue to be notice of the charges against one, an opportunity to defend oneself before a fair tribunal, and the benefit of general laws rather than any made for the particular case. The due process clause of the Fifth Amendment protects against the federal government, while a nearly identical clause of the Fourteenth Amendment protects against arbitrary state government action. These clauses promise that no person will "be deprived of life, liberty, or property without due process of law."

Robert Jacobs

SEE ALSO: Adversary system; Bill of Rights, U.S.; Constitution, U.S.; English Bill of Rights; *Gault, In re*; *Gideon v. Wainwright*; *Goss v. Lopez*; Jury system; Law; Scottsboro case.

Durkheim, Émile

IDENTIFICATION: French social scientist

BORN: April 15, 1858, Épinal, France

DIED: November 15, 1917, Paris, France

TYPE OF ETHICS: Modern history

SIGNIFICANCE: The founder of the French school of sociology, Durkheim suggested in such works as *The Division of Labor in Society* (*De la division du travail social*, 1893), *Suicide: A Study in Sociology* (*Le Suicide: Étude de sociologie*, 1897), and *The Elementary Forms of the Religious Life*

(*Les Formes élémentaires de la vie réligieuse*, 1912) that the new industrial, urban order created a condition of "anomie" that undermined ethical and social structures. He maintained that reforms could be introduced to correct this problem through changes in education.

Émile Durkheim expressed anxiety about the impact of modern society on the ethical basis of society. He argued that the advance of science and technology was not necessarily progressive; indeed, it resulted in creating a condition of "anomie" that was characterized by ethical and social isolation. Anomie resulted in a disconnected, rootless society in which ethical structures collapsed or were rendered meaningless. Durkheim's experiences as a youth during the Franco-Prussian War and the high expectations of his parents contributed to his naturally somber personality and his rather pessimistic sense of "reality."

In *The Division of Labor in Society*, Durkheim identified the alienation of workers with the separation of work; in *Suicide*, he noted that suicides occur less frequently in societies that are ethically and culturally integrated. Durkheim maintained that a genuinely progressive, ethical, and enlightened society could be realized through education and religion.

William T. Walker

SEE ALSO: Alienation; Anthropological ethics; Moral education; Politics; Socialism.

Duty

DEFINITION: Positive moral obligation
TYPE OF ETHICS: Theory of ethics
SIGNIFICANCE: Since one is morally required to perform one's duty by definition, one of the central projects of ethics is to determine what that duty is and how to recognize it. Only ethical systems that deny that morality is a trump value deny that performing one's moral duty is the most important activity one can undertake.

The concept of duty is familiar to people from a very early age. Already in early childhood, there is an acute awareness that there are certain requirements regarding one's behavior. Usually, these are require-ments to omit or refrain from certain types of forbidden behavior, and one quickly learns the types of behavior that one is expected to avoid.

Not all of one's duties are moral duties. Some duties are job related; for example, one has a duty to report for work at a certain time. Some duties arise because of one's role as a spouse or parent. Some duties are prescribed by the laws of the land. There are even duties that arise in the context of games, such as the duty of a pitcher to cover first base under certain circumstances. Some of these duties might also turn out to be moral duties, but in general they are not moral duties.

Moral duties are duties generated by morality itself; therefore, the failure to carry out these duties is a moral failure. In ethics, the failure to fulfill duty is referred to as action or inaction that is morally forbidden. More specifically, if one has a duty to perform a certain action, then it is forbidden to fail to perform the action. If one has a duty to refrain from a certain action, then it is forbidden to perform the action.

Ethicists are in agreement that people must obey their duties, but there is a great deal of disagreement regarding what these duties are and how people can come to know what they are. Some philosophers have followed the lead of Plato by believing that there is a fixed, eternal, unchanging standard of what is good, holding that through serene contemplation of the Good or the Absolute Good, one can come to know how to conduct one's life in accord with the requirements of morality. The contemplative tradition does not currently hold much appeal, however, at least in the moral tradition of Western culture, and modern moralists have looked elsewhere to find the sources or grounds of moral duty.

Many moralists have concluded that moral duty is grounded in religious truth. Here, the idea is that deities of one sort or another have decided or established how human moral agents ought to conduct their lives. The divine command theory, which states that moral duties are grounded in God's eternal decrees, is a version of this type of approach that is currently held by a relatively large number of philosophical and theological moralists.

DEONTOLOGICAL AND CONSEQUENTIALIST TRADITIONS

The two dominant traditions in modern ethical thinking are the deontological and the consequentialist traditions, each of which provides an account of how moral duties are generated. The deontological tradition seeks to generate duty from a basic and fundamental principle that is seen as an unqualified good, dependent neither upon its results nor upon people's currently held ethical beliefs. Some people have proposed that principles of justice are fundamental to morality. Kantian ethics regards the categorical imperative as such a fundamental principle; roughly speaking, it asserts that people should act from a rule or maxim only if they are willing that this rule govern everyone's actions.

Consequentialist ethics seeks to ground duty in the good results that are produced by people's actions. For example, a simple version of act utilitarianism states that one has a duty to act in such a way as to bring about the greatest benefits for the greatest number of people. One's duty is not to obey some fundamental principle; it is to look to the future and do what is necessary to maximize utility.

Some moralists have shown a preference for returning to older ways of thinking about morality in which the concept of duty is assigned a less important role. There has been a resurgence of interest among modern philosophers in Aristotelian ethics, which places a greater emphasis upon the development of virtue and the avoidance of vice. Although it makes sense to talk about duty in the context of a virtue-based ethic, its role in such an ethic is much less significant than is the case in other systems currently in fashion.

There is also much disagreement about whether duties have an absolute standing. Some hold the view handed down from the tradition of Plato that duties rest upon standards that are absolute, eternal, and unchanging. In this view, there are moral standards that do not vary from culture to culture or from one period of history to another. Thus, one might argue that people have a duty to refrain from murder or from incest, and anyone who grows up in a culture that teaches otherwise and believes that these acts are permissible is simply mistaken. In this view, certain things are morally forbidden, regardless of what is believed by the people of one's culture or period of history.

Others, known as relativists, hold that there are no moral absolutes and that people's moral duties are generated by moral systems that are essentially human constructs. For example, a given culture might find that prohibitions against adultery or premarital sex lead to greater societal stability, and hence it becomes a moral duty to refrain from these activities in this culture. In this view, what counts as a person's duty is relative to the culture or time period in which one is reared. There are no duties that apply to everyone.

Gregory F. Mellema

FURTHER READING

Chisholm, Roderick. "The Ethics of Requirement." *American Philosophical Quarterly* (April, 1964): 147-153.

Darwall, Stephen, ed. *Deontology*. Malden, Mass.: Blackwell, 2003.

Fishkin, James S. *The Limits of Obligation*. New Haven, Conn.: Yale University Press, 1982.

Gewirth, Alan. *Reason and Morality*. Chicago: University of Chicago Press, 1978.

Prichard, H. A. *Moral Writings*. Edited by Jim MacAdam. New York: Oxford University Press, 2002.

Selborne, David. *The Principle of Duty: An Essay on the Foundations of the Civic Order*. Notre Dame, Ind.: University of Notre Dame Press, 2001.

Singer, Marcus. *Generalization in Ethics*. New York: Russell & Russell, 1971.

SEE ALSO: Accountability; Bribery; Cicero; Citizenship; Deontological ethics; Dilemmas, moral; Kant, Immanuel; Maximal vs. minimal ethics; Permissible acts; Responsibility; Supererogation.

E

Earth and humanity

DEFINITION: Human beings' attitudes and behavior toward Earth and its ecosystems

TYPE OF ETHICS: Environmental ethics

SIGNIFICANCE: The relationship of humankind to the earth has ethical significance within the context of many religious traditions, including Native American religions which require respect of the land and the Judeo-Christian belief that nature is the dominion of humanity. In more recent times, the need to preserve dwindling resources and the plight of endangered species have created new ethical dilemmas.

Human beings have a combination of qualities that are unique among other forms of life on Earth: the capacity for symbolic thought and communication, hands with opposable thumbs, and a predilection to accumulate goods. Their impact on Earth's ecosystems has been significant and distinctive.

HISTORY

Earth's origin is dated at 4.5 billion years ago. Humankind's earliest humanoid ancestors appeared approximately five million years ago. The span of human existence, then, has been limited to a mere one-tenth of one percent of the earth's existence. Human evolution has not been strictly linear. There were both extinctions and overlappings among the variety of human species that existed between *Australopithecus*, the earliest-known human ancestor, and the modern species, *Homo sapiens*. The most anatomically modern human appeared 100,000 years ago.

Despite the seeming antiquity of the human presence on Earth, for most of that time, the species survived by gathering vegetation and scavenging meat until successful hunting methods were established; throughout all this time, the species had very little impact on Earth and its ecosystems. It was not until humankind began to domesticate animals and plants and had learned how to generate fire that the human species could begin making notable changes in the course of its future and in the future of the earth's ecosystems. This power was acquired between nine thousand and twelve thousand years ago.

Humankind's psychosocial awareness—the basis for the development of an ethical system—emerged very gradually. In the earliest years, there was no recognition of being distinct as a species or as individuals. Life was a series of instinctive responses to the environment and to physical needs. Jean Gebser describes it as "a time of complete nondifferentiation of man and the universe."

With humankind's growing awareness of its separateness from the rest of the ecosystem came a sense of insecurity about its relationship to the external world. As human societies began to experiment with their potential autonomy, they developed rituals to support their systems of magical beliefs in order to maintain an amicable relationship with the all-powerful outer world and to avoid any punishment for their "defection." Killing animals for food, for example, was no longer an instinctive behavior. It involved asking permission from some life-sustaining force. When disaster struck—or perhaps to forestall it—sacrificial rituals were offered to appease the force. Using rituals based on magical beliefs is evidence of perceiving an adversarial position between the human and outer worlds.

When human beings began to understand Earth's rhythms, some fears were resolved. The Earth-human relationship changed. Myth systems were developed to record and pass on the body of knowledge that humankind had been accumulating. It became possible to predict future occurrences based on past experiences and observations. This development, then, made it possible to begin taking advantage of predictable beneficial conditions and to try avoiding harmful ones. Agriculture made permanent settlements possible. The resultant increase in the size and density of human populations began overtaxing the environment. Cheryl Simon Silver reports that as early as eight thousand years ago, areas around the Mediterranean showed that wild animal populations were being replaced by domesticated ones. Plant communities there have been disrupted so badly and for so long that it is now difficult to determine what constituted the indigenous vegetation.

When humans turned their vision of the life-giving force from being Earth centered to being heaven centered, humankind assumed dominion over the rest of Earth's life-forms and its nonliving "resources." Based on this concept, the most aggressive human societies have exercised their presumed rights through activities such as strip mining, clear-cut logging, growing monocultures, using nuclear power, damming or channelizing rivers, forbidding human contraception, and causing the deliberate extinction of other species.

MODERN ENVIRONMENTAL CONCERNS

Because humanity's ethical systems have evolved along with humanity's awareness of its uniqueness on Earth, it might seem that these models exist along a continuum. In fact, they exist as diffuse elements within a mosaic design. They all still survive throughout the world and guide human behavior.

It does not seem likely or practical that individually any of these paradigms will or can solve the problems of environmental damage. The range of proposed solutions, however, is a reflection of each of them. Totally opposite conclusions, both of them based on faith, exist within the dominion-of-humankind paradigm. In humanistic ethical systems there is the belief that progress in technology will find solutions to overturn ecological damage. In religion-based systems, there is the belief that humanity should continue to take advantage of the provided resources and not be concerned about Earth's future, because a transcendent god will rescue at least a portion of humankind in times of mortal danger. Elements of the magical and mythical systems are expressed by groups such as the Nature Conservancy and Releaf, which advocate the preservation or rehabilitation of the environment. The first model, in which there was no differentiation between humankind and its environment, is expressed in groups such as Earth First! or those that represent the deep ecology movement. They define their views as "ecoethics," because they hold that all other approaches to the environment are arrogantly egocentric, based entirely on human self-interest, and have little to do with the reality of humankind's minuscule time span in the total scheme of Earth's existence.

Because there has been evolution in ethical systems, however, there is reason to assume that humankind may evolve some other ethical system that might solve the problems that now threaten both Earth and human beings. Indeed, Daniel Kealey and Gebser believe that the new paradigm is emerging and that it is based on an integration of all the previous ethical systems.

Marcella T. Joy

FURTHER READING

Allsopp, Bruce. *Ecological Morality.* London: Frederick Muller, 1972.

Attfield, Robin. *Environmental Ethics: An Overview for the Twenty-First Century.* Malden, Mass.: Blackwell, 2003.

Gebser, Jean. *The Ever-Present Origin.* Translated by Noel Barstad and Algis Mickunas. Athens: Ohio University Press, 1985.

Kealey, Daniel. *Revisioning Environmental Ethics.* Albany: State University of New York Press, 1990.

Light, Andrew, and Holmes Rolston III, eds. *Environmental Ethics: An Anthology.* Malden, Mass.: Blackwell, 2003.

Maguire, Daniel. *The Moral Choice.* Garden City, N.Y.: Doubleday, 1978.

Miller, Alan. *Gaia Connections: An Introduction to Ecology, Ecoethics, and Economics.* Savage, Md.: Rowman & Littlefield, 1991.

Regan, Tom, ed. *Earthbound: New Introductory Essays in Environmental Ethics.* New York: Random House, 1984.

Silver, Cheryl Simon, with Ruth DeFries. *One Earth, One Future: Our Changing Global Environment.* Washington, D.C.: National Academy Press, 1990.

SEE ALSO: Biodiversity; Conservation; Deep ecology; Dominion over nature, human; Earth Day; Ecology; Environmental ethics; Environmental movement; Global warming; Nature, rights of; *Silent Spring*.

Earth Day

THE EVENT: Day set aside to celebrate the earth and focus attention on the relationship of people to Earth

DATE: Begun on April 22, 1970

TYPE OF ETHICS: Environmental ethics

SIGNIFICANCE: Earth Day was the first nationwide event to focus on the environment; it emphasized individual and consumer responsibility for environmental quality.

Earth Day was first organized by Senator Gaylord Nelson of Wisconsin as an opportunity for "teach-ins" on the environment and on the effects of human actions on the environment. Many teach-ins focused on air and water pollution, the relationship between environmental quality and human health, and the individual consumer's responsibility for environmental quality. Grassroots activities included picking up litter along roads and streams. Colleges, universities, and public schools were the locales of many of the first Earth Day activities and continued to be the centers for organized Earth Days in subsequent years.

In 1970, a reported twenty-five million Americans participated in Earth Day activities. Through intensive media coverage of Earth Day, information about the environment reached millions more. Following Earth Day, public opinion polls reflected increased awareness of environmental problems and increased support for maintaining environmental quality. Earth Day both reflected and increased public, media, and official interest in environmental quality and in individual responsibility for the environment. The media continue to present stories on environmental trends and issues on Earth Day each year.

Marguerite McKnight

SEE ALSO: Conservation; Earth and humanity; Ecology; Environmental ethics; Environmental movement; Environmental Protection Agency; Nature, rights of; Pollution.

Ecofeminism

DEFINITION: Plurality of positions and perspectives emerging from a common assumption that the patriarchal domination of women and other social groups is also manifest in human exploitation of nature

TYPE OF ETHICS: Sex and gender issues

SIGNIFICANCE: Ecofeminist positions have evolved from various fields of feminist inquiry and activism, relating to such ethical issues as peace, labor, women's health care, antinuclear activity, the environment, and animal liberation.

Influential forms of ecofeminism tend to be multicultural in nature and to include in their analyses of women-nature connections the inextricable interconnections among all social systems of domination. A basic assumption within the various perspectives is that no attempt to liberate women or any other oppressed group will be successful without a simultaneous attempt to liberate nature in its myriad forms. Ecofeminism thus emphasizes the concurrence of oppression based on gender, race, class, and nature. Writings on the subject include critiques of racism, classism, ageism, ethnocentrism, imperialism, colonialism, androcentrism, heterosexism, and sexism.

The term "ecofeminism" was coined by the French feminist Francois d'Eaubonne in 1974, before there was a body of ecofeminist theory. Since that time, theoretical strands of ecofeminism have emerged that unmask traditional Western philosophical and religious dependence upon what has been cited in feminist literature as a philosophical logic of dualism. With varying degrees of radicalism, ecofeminists such as Rosemary Ruether, Val Plumwood, Karen Warren, Carol Adams, Carolyn Merchant, and Elizabeth Dodson Gray have shown that the characteristic logical structure of dualism in Euro-American philosophical and theological traditions is based upon an alienated form of differentiation and a problematic representation of otherness.

As indicated by the proliferation of writings ecofeminism has produced, it describes how the diverse forms of oppression are a result of a dominant ideology whose fundamental self/other distinction is based on an influential "modern" view of self that is separate and atomistic. Thus, an emphasis in many ecofeminist writings is that varied conceptions of self promote different ethical systems: The view of a separate self often operates on the basis of rights and justice, while the notion of an interconnected self makes moral decisions on the basis of an ethic of responsibilities or care. As an academic discourse, ecofeminism has also been associated with environmental ethics and with such theories and movements as deep ecology and social ecology, and it has promoted ethical commitments to valuing and preserving ecosystems understood as organisms, individuals, populations, communities, and their interactions.

Various strands of ecofeminism postulate ethical theories that provide as fully as possible inclusive and global analyses of intersectional oppression. Further, ecofeminists often argue that ethical solutions to global problems cannot be found if contemporaries ignore the interconnectedness of all life—humans, and the creatures and plants with whom human beings share the earth. However, ecofeminism is pluralistic in rejecting any one right way or answer in addressing human social and ecological problems.

Many ecofeminists envision ethical practices involving creative interchange among activists, public policy makers, academics, scientists, ecologists, and ethicists. Ecofeminism currently has a significant academic and activist presence in the United States, Canada, Northwest Europe, India, and Australia.

Carol Wayne White

FURTHER READING

Adams, Carol J., ed. *Ecofeminism and the Sacred.* New York: Continuum, 1993.

Bigwood, Carol. *Earth Muse: Feminism, Nature, and Art.* Philadelphia: Temple University Press, 1993.

Cuomo, C. J. *Feminism and Ecological Communities: An Ethic of Flourishing.* London: Routledge, 1998.

Plumwood, Val. *Feminism and the Mastery of Nature.* London: Routledge, 1993.

Ruether, Rosemary Radford. *Gaia and God: An Ecofeminist Theology of Earth Healing.* San Francisco: Harper & Row, 1992.

_____. *Women Healing Earth: Third World Women on Ecology, Feminism, and Religion.* Maryknoll, N.Y.: Orbis Books, 1996.

Sturgeon, N. *Eco-Feminist Natures: Race, Gender, Feminist Theory, and Political Action.* London: Routledge, 1997.

Warren, Karen J., ed. *Ecological Feminism.* New York: Routledge, 1994.

_____. *Ecological Feminist Philosophies.* Bloomington: Indiana University Press, 1996.

SEE ALSO: Ecology; Feminist ethics; Women's ethics; Women's liberation movement.

Ecology

DEFINITION: Study of relationships among organisms and between organisms and the environment
TYPE OF ETHICS: Environmental ethics
SIGNIFICANCE: The discipline of ecology forms the scientific basis for an ethic of environmental conservation and preservation.

Ecology is broadly divided into "autecology," pertaining to individual organisms or species, and "synecology," or the ecology of communities of organisms. Synecology places humankind in organic "communities," or ecosystems, thus positing a human ethical responsibility to the environment as broadly defined. Since World War II, an "ecological movement" has advocated programs designed to ensure that humankind will live within the limitations of the earth's resources. By means of these programs, communities modify their environments, thus causing successional replacement and moving toward stable, organic "climax communities" that are adapted to current environmental conditions. Short-term changes in community character, especially retreat from "climax," is a practical measure of humankind's effect on the ecosystem.

Biogeography refers to community distribution, while paleobiogeography considers succession over geologic time. Ecology arose from Alexander von Humboldt's approach to natural history and from Carolus Linnaeus's studies of plant life histories. Plant ecology in America became well established during the early twentieth century in Nebraska, where Frederic Clements established the community concept and coined an overabundance of technical terms. Victor Shelford of the University of Chicago contemporaneously developed the fundamentals of animal ecology. Among subdivisions of ecology are limnology, oceanography, plant ecology, animal ecology, phenology, biogeography, and paleobiogeography.

Ralph L. Langenheim, Jr.

SEE ALSO: Biodiversity; Conservation; Deforestation; Earth and humanity; Endangered species; Environmental ethics; Environmental Protection Agency; Greenpeace; Sierra Club; Sustainability of resources; Wilderness Act of 1964.

Economic analysis

DEFINITION: Method of evaluating the desirability of actions by determining the relationship of cost to benefit or of finding the least costly way to achieve a goal

TYPE OF ETHICS: Politico-economic ethics

SIGNIFICANCE: Economic analysis provides a conceptual framework within which to make ethical decisions. Some thinkers have condemned this form of analysis, however, because it can dehumanize people by reducing them to mere statistics or by overlooking the importance of emotion and treating choice as a purely rational process.

Economic analysis involves discovering how to meet desires at the lowest cost. Although most commonly applied to business and budgeting problems, economic analysis can be applied to virtually any decision involving expenditures of resources such as money, time, or even emotional energy.

The problems that economics addresses apply to all individuals and societies, even to the animal kingdom. Formal analysis of these problems began in earnest in the eighteenth century. Pioneers of what was called "political economy," including Adam Smith, David Ricardo, and Thomas Malthus, wrote about such topics as division of labor, international trade, and population control. Economists quickly refined their tools of analysis and extended the range of topics under consideration. Gary Becker, winner of the 1992 Nobel Prize in Economics, has extended economic analysis to the study of marriage, the family, and discrimination, among many other topics.

THE SCIENCE OF ECONOMICS

Economics as a discipline is designed to provide objective answers to questions. It is not intended to be a normative discipline (one that answers questions concerning values) and therefore is not itself a theory of ethics. The distinction often becomes blurred.

Economics accepts value judgments and tells people how they can achieve what they want; it does not tell people what they should want. In practice, however, many economists promote their own values, trying to convince others that their goals are desirable.

One basic tool of economics is cost-benefit analysis, which weighs the costs of alternative actions against the benefits that will result from them. This tool allows identification of the least costly way of achieving a certain goal. The goal and the alternative actions are presented to the economic analyst, who is not supposed to pass judgment on the "correctness" of the goal. Economic analysis applies to any question involving a choice among alternatives but is most commonly used to address personal questions of budgeting and finance and societal questions of distribution and market behavior.

DISTRIBUTION

Government policymakers face many issues of distribution of various services. Many of the issues involve questions of perceived fairness. The most basic questions facing policymakers are what will be provided, how it will be distributed, and who will pay for it.

Economic analysis cannot answer any of these questions directly. It can, however, provide information that is helpful in making the decisions. For example, policymakers might consider spending money on education. Once policymakers have identified the different educational programs that could be provided, economists can determine the likely effects of each, giving some idea of the costs and benefits. They can also determine the benefits that would be derived by various individuals or groups, information that will help policymakers decide how to allocate the educational programs.

Economists also examine the ways of financing programs. Income taxes can be designed so that one income group pays a higher proportion of the cost than does another. Sales taxes do not affect everyone equally, because people spend and save different proportions of their income, thus paying the tax at different times in their lives. In addition, most sales taxes do not affect all products, so those buying more of the taxed products pay more in taxes. Typically, for example, taxes on gasoline, other forms of energy, liquor, and tobacco products place a heavier burden, proportional to income, on poor people. A fixed amount of tax on each person may appear to be fair, but it would represent a higher proportion of income for people who earn less. Issues of financing government programs thus become complicated. The normative questions of which programs should be provided, who should receive benefits, or how it would be fair to finance the programs can better be answered by policymakers once economists have provided their analysis.

MARKETS

Economic analysis applies to all types of behavior and all market systems. Costs and benefits are easier to identify in capitalist systems, in which virtually everything has a price that is determined by the market. Socialist systems also rely on economic analysis, however, with costs and benefits determined more abstractly by policymakers. Socialist policymakers sometimes have to make somewhat arbitrary decisions concerning the value or cost of a program, since there may not be prices to measure values. In societies in which medical care is provided free or at subsidized prices, for example, policymakers have a more difficult time deciding how to allocate that care, since no true price shows how much people value medical care. People tend to say that they value any service that is offered and to complain when any service is cut off. The question for economic analysis is to determine how much people would be willing to pay in an unsubsidized market.

Economic analysis can be used to help determine what types of markets will exist, even as broadly as analyzing the effects of establishing a communist versus a capitalist market. Branches of economics concern the behavior of various types of firms, such as monopolies, and how regulation affects them. It can provide information that is useful in determining government policy concerning such topics as population control, medical research, health insurance, education, the environment, use of nonrenewable resources, immigration, employment and unemployment, and foreign aid. Provision of benefits in any one of these areas may mean that money cannot be spent on benefits in another. Economic analysis can help in determining such trade-offs among vastly different projects. It cannot determine which projects should be chosen but can help to identify the benefits of money spent on each one.

A. J. Sobczak

FURTHER READING

Blinder, Alan S. *Hard Heads, Soft Hearts: Tough-Minded Economics for a Just Society.* Reading, Mass.: Addison-Wesley, 1987.

Brockway, George P. *Economics: What Went Wrong, and Why, and Some Things to Do About It.* New York: Harper & Row, 1985.

Cameron, Samuel. *The Economics of Sin: Rational Choice or No Choice at All?* Northampton, Mass.: Edward Elgar, 2002.

Gabor, Dennis. *The Mature Society.* New York: Praeger, 1972.

Hodgson, Bernard. *Economics as Moral Science.* New York: Springer, 2001.

Pearce, Joseph. *Small Is Still Beautiful.* Foreword by Barbara Schumacher Wood. London: HarperCollins, 2001.

Rosenbaum, Robert A. *The Public Issues Handbook: A Guide for the Concerned Citizen.* Westport, Conn.: Greenwood Press, 1983.

Schumacher, Ernst Friedrich. *Small Is Beautiful.* New York: Harper & Row, 1973.

SEE ALSO: Antitrust legislation; Business ethics; Capitalism; Communism; Cost-benefit analysis; Economics; Monopoly; Poverty and wealth; Profit economy; Taxes.

Economics

DEFINITION: Study of the production, distribution, and consumption of goods and services

TYPE OF ETHICS: Politico-economic ethics

SIGNIFICANCE: The question of the production and distribution of wealth or value is an important component of any socially or politically oriented moral philosophy. Economics, as a science designed to analyze those processes, is both useful for, and itself subject to, ethical evaluation.

The primary concern of economics is the production, distribution, and consumption of goods and services. One conventional view that has generated perennial debate is that economics is value-free or ethically neutral. This view rests primarily on what is called the "naturalistic fallacy" (identified, but not so named, by David Hume), according to which it is a mistake to attempt to deduce a conclusion concerning what ought to be the case from premises that state exclusively what is the case. In other words, it is impossible to derive an "ought" from an "is." Furthermore, precisely because economics is a social science, it is concerned only with descriptive statements and not at all with ethical considerations (including value judgments); descriptive statements, by definition, can imply nothing of an ethical nature whatsoever. Consequently, it does seem reasonable that, methodologically, economics can be said to be ethically neutral.

Even if a particular discipline, such as economics, is ethically neutral in its methodology, however, it is still an open question whether that same discipline is subject to ethical implications or associations either in its theoretical aspects or in its practical application. In fact, there is a vast array of ethical implications and associations in both the theoretical aspects and the practical applications of economics. Even on the theoretical level, the relationship between economics and ethics takes various forms. For example, an economist who specializes in economic systems—that is, the principles and technical methods by which both the ownership and the allocation of a society's resources are determined by that society—might engage in several different types of analysis, including the ethical evaluation of the diverse systems under consideration for comparison purposes. Such an evaluation would involve an intricate network of economic and ethical concepts.

The Wealth of Nations

The premier argument for the profit motive is to be found in Adam Smith's *The Wealth of Nations* (1776). According to Smith, the development of a full-blown economy depends on the existence of various individuals in the society who possess a greater quantity of either raw materials or goods that have been produced than they themselves need. Such a phenomenon encourages the development of a system of bartering, which presents the opportunity for the various members of the society to devote their time, energy, and individual talents to a single economic endeavor. This "division of labor" benefits both the individual members of the society and the society as a whole. The individual members of the society derive benefit from this new opportunity to determine what particular economic activities they are,

individually, suited for and interested in pursuing, and that can profit them the most.

Important, too, is the expectation that to the extent that one is engaged in a particular economic activity, one should, over time, become quite adept at it. This skill should lead to an increase in both the quantity and the quality of individual production in such a way as to also increase the economic compensation of the individual worker. Moreover, such an improvement in the efficiency of production should result in higher-quality products at lower costs in the marketplace. Ultimately, the society as a whole is improved to the extent that this process represents an enhancement of the entire economy as well as an increase in the standard of living for all.

So it is, then, that, in the final analysis, the individual's pursuit of the profit motive is advantageous to the society as a whole. According to Smith, one neither does nor should pursue a particular economic activity in order to promote either the interests of others in the society or the interest of the society as a whole. Rather, one should pursue a chosen economic activity solely out of self-interest, because the economic relationship between the interests of the individual and the interest of the society as a whole is such that "an invisible hand" translates the former into the latter.

Marxist Views

With the advent of the Industrial Revolution came harsh criticism of the type of competitive free-market economy that Smith had championed. The primary critic of the free-market type of economic system was Karl Marx. In various works, including *The Communist Manifesto* (1848; a collaborative effort with Friedrich Engels) and *Economic and Philosophic Manuscripts of 1844*, Marx argues at length against both the profit motive and private property acquisition.

The classical argument for private property acquisition and property rights is the fifth chapter of John Locke's *Second Treatise of Government* (1690), in which he maintains that even in a "state of nature"—that is, a social environment prior to the institution of any governmental authority—one is free and possesses oneself, which includes one's own body and, by extension, one's own labor. Furthermore, the earth's natural resources are owned by no one in particular but are held in common by all of humankind.

The question becomes how one may legitimately appropriate to oneself some of the fruits of the earth in order to sustain one's own existence. Locke's answer is that upon "mixing one's labor" with some portion of the fruits of the earth in order to take it out of the state in which nature has left it and render it usable for human sustenance, one may, as a natural right, lay claim to it as one's own private property. Locke proceeds to add some practical limitations and to flesh out the details of this moral argument for private property acquisition and property rights.

Against both the profit motive and private property acquisition, Marx argues that, taken in conjunction, these two economic rights inevitably result in inordinate accumulation of wealth for the bourgeoisie (the owners of the means of production) and only subsistence wages for the proletariat (the working class). Workers in a capitalistic free-market economic system are actually selling their labor in order to sustain themselves, and thereby they become mere commodities to be bought by the bourgeoisie at the lowest possible wages. The profit motive is such that any profit that is realized from the sale of manufactured goods either is reinvested in the production process or merely becomes additional wealth for the bourgeoisie. The right to private property is such that the bourgeoisie, as the owners of literally all of the means of production, make the proletariat subservient not only to themselves but also to the means of production. All of this, together with numerous types of alienation that are experienced by the proletariat because of the menial and dehumanizing nature of their work, leads, by the nature of the case, to a class struggle in which the proletariat constantly fights to overcome its exploitation by the bourgeoisie.

It should be clear from only these two examples that even theoretical economic concepts and the arguments for their implementation engender an array of both ethical implications and moral disagreements.

Stephen C. Taylor

FURTHER READING

Little, I. M. D. *Ethics, Economics, and Politics: Principles of Public Policy.* New York: Oxford University Press, 2002.

Locke, John. *Two Treatises of Government.* Edited by Peter Laslett. New York: Cambridge University Press, 1988.

Marx, Karl, and Friedrich Engels. *The Marx-Engels Reader.* Edited by Robert C. Tucker. 2d ed. New York: W. W. Norton, 1978.

Myers, Milton L. *The Soul of Modern Economic Man: Ideas of Self-Interest, Thomas Hobbes to Adam Smith.* Chicago: University of Chicago Press, 1983.

Schultz, Walter J. *The Moral Conditions of Economic Efficiency.* New York: Cambridge University Press, 2001.

Sen, Amartya. *On Ethics and Economics.* Oxford, England: Blackwell, 1987.

Smith, Adam. *An Inquiry into the Nature and Causes of the Wealth of Nations: A Selected Edition.* Edited by Kathryn Sutherland. New York: Oxford University Press, 1998.

SEE ALSO: Capitalism; Class struggle; Communism; Cost-benefit analysis; Economic analysis; Free enterprise; Marx, Karl; Poverty and wealth; Smith, Adam; Zero-base ethics.

Edwards, Jonathan

IDENTIFICATION: American cleric, theologian, and philosopher
BORN: October 5, 1703, East Windsor, Connecticut
DIED: March 22, 1758, Princeton, New Jersey
TYPE OF ETHICS: Religious ethics
SIGNIFICANCE: In *Freedom of Will* (1754) and "Sinners in the Hands of an Angry God" (1741), Edwards reiterated the strict Calvinistic doctrine of communion only for the elect—those predestined to salvation—while simultaneously stressing the individual emotional conversion experience.

Arguably one of America's keenest intellectuals, Edwards was a commanding Puritan minister who emphasized traditional Calvinist doctrines of humanity's utter depravity and total dependence upon God. His *Great Christian Doctrine of Original Sin Defended* (1758) added a cornerstone to the debate regarding the fundamental depravity of human nature and provided a strenuous defense of Calvinism against the increasingly secularized Enlightenment. By combining Puritan intellectualism with a unique

Jonathan Edwards. (Library of Congress)

thereafter, he preached among Native Americans. Suggesting that the "great tribulations" of the Christian faith had passed, in his pioneer sermon "Humble Attempt to Promote Explicit Agreement and Visible Union of Gods People . . ." (1747), Edwards had earlier cleared his way by lessening theological inhibitions against missionizing.

Mary E. Virginia

SEE ALSO: Benevolence; Calvin, John; Christian ethics; Human nature.

Egalitarianism

DEFINITION: Belief in human equality and the need to eliminate social inequities
TYPE OF ETHICS: Theory of ethics
SIGNIFICANCE: Egalitarianism in different forms underpins moral and political systems which advocate equal protection of law, civil rights, human rights, universal justice, social justice, economic equality, the right to property, and the abolishment of property.

emotionalism, Edwards became a singularly dynamic preacher and theologian.

After assuming leadership of the Northampton, Massachusetts, parish in 1728 from his famous grandfather, Solomon Stoddard, Edwards became immediately controversial with his repudiation of Stoddard's Half-Way Covenant, the agency by which children of the predestined—themselves not necessarily of the elect—were entitled to receive communion. Edwards preached a peculiarly complex blend emphasizing the apparently antagonistic tenets of predestination and conversion experience. Although the development of evangelical religion was antithetical to traditional Calvinism, Edwards's emotionally charged yet intellectually compelling sermons inaugurated in New England the religious revival known as the Great Awakening.

Amid controversy regarding his insistence on emotional conversion as proof of election, Edwards was dismissed from his Northampton post in 1751;

Egalitarian principles in Western thought originated in ancient Greece. Athenian citizens were chosen for political office by lot, since all were thought to be capable of fulfilling the functions of public office. All Spartan men served equally as soldiers. Christian thought has stressed egalitarian concepts, both the notion that all human beings are equal in the sight of God, and that faith, not position or social status, determines one's worthiness for salvation.

In a more secular approach, both Thomas Hobbes and John Locke, sixteenth century English thinkers, stressed that society was created by humans through mutual consent. Egalitarian ideas formed the basis for the American Declaration of Independence and the Rights of Man and the Citizen in the French Revolution, despite the persistence of slavery in America and the fact that women were not accorded equal rights as citizens in France. The goal of equality was valued by the leaders of these revolutions and has profoundly influenced those societies in which they occurred. In the twentieth century, egalitarianism has influenced movements for civil rights, women's rights, and equal opportunities for the disabled, and has promoted the idea that equality is an important moral principle.

James A. Baer

SEE ALSO: Civil rights and liberties; Elitism; Equal pay for equal work; Equality; Minimum-wage laws; Natural rights; Social justice and responsibility.

Egoism

DEFINITION: Doctrine that each person ought to maximize his or her own self-interest and that no one should ever sacrifice his or her self-interest

TYPE OF ETHICS: Theory of ethics

SIGNIFICANCE: Egoism is a challenge to every altruistic or other-regarding ethics, since egoism maintains that one has no unconditional obligation to others and that altruistic behavior is justified only as a means to self-interest and never for its own sake.

Egoism is a normative guide to action and an outlook on life. It draws its inspiration from diverse traditions and sources, from the discussions of justice and advantage in Plato's *Republic* to the egocentric account of human nature in the writings of Thomas Hobbes. It both influences and is influenced by cost-benefit analysis in economics, the theory of practical reasoning, and libertarian political theory.

According to egoism, each person ought to do all and only those acts that maximize his or her self-interest. (The theory may also be formulated in terms of rules, or even virtues, but so-called "act" egoism is the most common variety.) Furthermore, according to egoism, one has no basic or unconditional obligations to others. Any obligations one might have to others are derived from one's interest in or use of them. Thus, egoism implies that one should be prepared to take advantage of others when this is in one's own interest.

Egoists maintain that maximizing self-interest is the most rational thing to do. Therefore, if rationality and moral rightness are equivalent, egoism will be a theory of moral rightness. If the two can conflict, however, egoism will be a nonmoral theory of ratio-

nal action, and in cases of conflict between the rational and the right, egoism will give rise to the question "Why be moral?"

SELF-INTEREST

Egoists have offered different accounts of self-interest. Some egoists have been hedonists, maintaining that only one's own pleasure is worth seeking for its own sake. Others have emphasized power, and still others have stressed wealth or honor. It has even been argued that virtue or good character is intrinsically good and is as much a part of a person's self-interest as pleasure, wealth, or power. Obviously, those who defend egoism must provide some specification of "self-interest" in order to convey fully the content and practical implications of their theory. Many philosophers use "self-interest" in a generic sense to refer to "happiness" or "well-being." In this respect, defenders of egoism emphasize that one's obligations and decisions are grounded in one's long-term enlightened self-interest, not simply in the satisfaction of desire.

SELF AND OTHERS

For egoism, self-interest is the criterion of overriding value. When one's interests come into irreconcilable conflict with others, egoism authorizes one to seek one's self-interest at their expense—not only when the other person is an enemy or stranger, but even when that person is a spouse, child, parent, or friend. This follows from the fact that one has no unconditional obligation to serve the interests of others. Of course, if helping others or refraining from harming them would help oneself, one ought to do so. Thus, according to egoism, one ought to keep promises, tell the truth, and give the appearance of being generally fair-minded and cooperative as long as these acts are in one's own self-interest. Yet egoists have no principled reasons to place constraints on self-interested behavior that might harm others.

CRITICISMS

Three distinct, if partially overlapping, criticisms have been raised against egoism. First, it has been argued that egoism is inconsistent, since in conflict-of-interest situations, egoism requires or authorizes that everyone come out on top. Defenders of egoism respond to this criticism by pointing out that egoism advocates that a certain state of affairs be brought about in which each person tries to maximize his or her self-interest. Moreover, conflicts can be resolved within a system of rules that it is in one's self-interest to adopt as long as others do so as well.

A second criticism is that since it would not be in one's self-interest for one's egoism to be widely known, egoists cannot participate in public activities and practices such as teaching, advocacy, and advising, which are characteristic of morality. Egoists argue that since acts of teaching, advocating, and advising are not, according to this criticism, to be justified in terms of self-interest, the criticism begs the question against egoism. In addition, egoists point out that where there are no conflicts, egoists can engage in sincere moral teaching, advocacy, and advising, and where conflicts do arise, egoists can keep their silence.

A third criticism is that egoism is simply an immoral doctrine. By maintaining that any act is justified if and only if it promotes self-interest, egoism is said to sanction acts of lying, theft, blackmail, and murder. Some defenders of egoism have responded to this criticism by denying that egoism, when properly formulated, would authorize acts of this kind. Others have conceded the theoretical possibility that such acts would be egoistically justified but have argued that it is very unlikely that immoral acts would in fact promote one's self-interest.

Criticisms such as these have led defenders of egoism to numerous reformulations and refinements of the doctrine. Rule-based, rights-based, and virtue-based forms of egoism are developments in the project of making egoism a coherent, consistent, and morally defensible action-guide and outlook on life.

Steven M. Sanders

FURTHER READING

Baier, Kurt. *The Moral Point of View.* Ithaca, N.Y.: Cornell University Press, 1958.

Hospers, John. *Human Conduct.* 3d ed. Fort Worth, Tex.: Harcourt Brace College, 1996.

Kalin, Jesse. "In Defense of Egoism." In *Morality and Rational Self-Interest*, edited by David P. Gauthier. Englewood Cliffs, N.J.: Prentice-Hall, 1970.

Machan, Tibor R. *Individuals and Their Rights.* La Salle, Ill.: Open Court, 1989.

Pojman, Louis P. "Egoism, Self-Interest, and Altruism." In *The Moral Life: An Introductory Reader in Ethics and Literature*, edited by Louis P. Pojman. 2d ed. New York: Oxford University Press, 2003.

Rachels, James. "Ethical Egoism." In *The Moral Life: An Introductory Reader in Ethics and Literature*, edited by Louis P. Pojman. 2d ed. New York: Oxford University Press, 2003.

Regis, Edward, Jr. "What Is Ethical Egoism?" *Ethics* 91 (October, 1980): 50-62.

Sanders, Steven M. "Is Egoism Morally Defensible?" *Philosophia* 18 (July, 1988): 191-209.

Shaver, Robert. *Rational Egoism: A Selective and Critical History.* New York: Cambridge University Press, 1999.

Williams, Bernard. "Egoism and Altruism." In *Problems of the Self.* Cambridge, England: Cambridge University Press, 1973.

SEE ALSO: Altruism; Egotist; Hobbes, Thomas; Impartiality; Individualism; Narcissism; Rand, Ayn; Self-interest; Selfishness; Self-love.

Egotist

DEFINITION: One who seeks to promote one's own interests and goals at all times

TYPE OF ETHICS: Theory of ethics

SIGNIFICANCE: Sometimes mistaken for the moral theory of egoism, egotism is widely regarded as a moral failing.

An egotist adopts the general policy of acting selfishly. In common parlance, the term "egotist" is used to label those people who have exaggerated opinions of themselves. Egotism, which is not a moral theory, must not be equated with egoism, which is the moral theory that one ought always to act to promote one's own interests. It might be thought that egotism is at least compatible with egoism.

The two concepts are indeed compatible if acting selfishly is always in one's own best interests, but egoists have been known to argue that egotism is not in one's best interests. In any case, egotists do not usually have moral reasons for their policy of action. Also, to the extent that egotism reveals anything about the egotist's beliefs, it reveals that the egotist believes himself or herself to be superior to others in some general sense. The egoist is not necessarily committed to such a belief in personal superiority. Thus, while egoism is a moral theory whose merit must be investigated philosophically, egotism is a form of behavior whose causes and cure are a matter of psychological interest. Egotism certainly is incompatible with altruism and thus is incompatible with most normative ethical theories.

R. Douglas Geivett

SEE ALSO: Altruism; Egoism; Gewirth, Alan; Self-interest; Selfishness; Self-love.

Either/Or

IDENTIFICATION: Book by Søren Kierkegaard (1813-1855)

DATE: *Enten-Eller*, 1843 (English translation, 1944)

TYPE OF ETHICS: Modern history

SIGNIFICANCE: *Either/Or* represents two radically different forms of existence, the aesthetic and the ethical, in the writings of two fictional characters who typify those forms of existence, thereby challenging readers to choose between them.

In the two volumes of *Either/Or*, the Danish philosopher Søren Kierkegaard confronts readers with a sharp choice between two forms of existence, the aesthetic, which regards enjoyment and pleasure as the highest values, and the ethical, which views the world in terms of right and wrong. Rather than describing these two forms of existence, Kierkegaard brings them to life in the writings of two fictional characters. An unnamed sophisticated young man, designated "A," is credited with the widely varied essays and aphorisms that make up volume 1; Judge William, a family man and minor court official, writes the two long letters to "A" that make up volume 2. A third fictional character, Victor Eremita, claims to have found the papers of "A" and Judge William in an old desk and to have arranged for their publication.

VOLUME I

After a preface in which Victor Eremita describes finding the papers that make up *Either/Or*, volume 1 is composed of the papers of "A." The first section is a group of aphorisms that "A" calls "Diapsalmata." These aphorisms set the tone for volume 1 by vividly conveying the cynical and world-weary but also sensitive and enthusiastic character of "A." These aphorisms further show "A's" strong interest in literary and musical art, an interest that is amply demonstrated in the five substantial essays on art and artistic themes that follow the Diapsalmata. The first and longest of these, "The Immediate Stages of the Erotic or the Musical Erotic," is an impassioned celebration of Wolfgang Amadeus Mozart's opera *Don Giovanni*.

Don Juan is significant to "A" because he represents a distinctive form of aesthetic existence: the immediate. An immediate aesthete, such as Don Juan, seeks pleasure in a wholly spontaneous, unselfconscious manner. His consciousness is confined to the here and now, and no thought of guilt for his many seductions ever clouds his enjoyments. While "A" enthuses over Don Juan, his self-consciousness, or reflectivity, separates his form of aesthetic existence decisively from the Don's. "A's" mode of aesthetic existence is best illustrated in the essay "The Rotation of Crops," in which "A" humorously states his strategy for finding enjoyment and avoiding boredom. To seek pleasure directly, like Don Juan, eventually jades the self; overused enjoyments grow stale. So "A" constantly varies his amusements just as farmers rotate crops so as not to exhaust their fields.

Despite the witty, jesting tone of "The Rotation of Crops," this and other entries in volume 1 show "A" to be afflicted by a deep and dark melancholy. He even cultivates this melancholy as a source of enjoyment, calling sorrow his castle and naming hopelessness as the precondition of the aesthetic life. "A" is also profoundly interested in the sorrow of others. Many of his essays are analyses of tragic figures from literature that he presented to a ghoulish club, the Symparanekromenoi, "the society of the already dead."

The final section of volume 1, "Diary of a Seducer," is both the longest section of the volume and the most chilling picture of aesthetic existence. "A" claims to have copied a large section of the journal of an acquaintance named Johannes, which chronicles the devious seduction and callous abandonment of an innocent young girl. In his introductory remarks to the copied journal entries, "A" shudders at Johannes's calculating coldness and worries that Johannes reveals the demoniac character of aesthetic existence by carrying it through to its logical extreme.

VOLUME 2

Kierkegaard brings the ethical form of existence to life in three letters, two very long and one short, from Judge William to "A." Judge William tries to convert "A" from aesthetic existence to ethical existence by analyzing and criticizing aesthetic existence and depicting ethical existence in a highly positive light. It is significant that Judge William writes letters rather than essays: He is not interested in a disinterested, impersonal, theoretical analysis of aesthetic and ethical existence. Rather, he speaks as a concrete, existing, concerned individual to another such individual.

Like "A," Judge William is especially concerned with the romantic dimension of human life. Whereas "A" focuses on brief and usually tragic romantic liaisons, Judge William is an enthusiastic advocate of marriage. Marriage represents for him the ideal example of ethical existence. It represents an open-ended, infinite commitment rather than a short-term, fulfillable task. Furthermore, Judge William uses the example of marriage to show that a life of duty is not less but more enjoyable than an aesthetic life, even though the aesthetic life makes enjoyment its highest end. The first of his letters to "A" is accordingly titled "The Aesthetic Validity of Marriage." Here, Judge William argues at great length that duty, the obligation entered into with the wedding vows, preserves, nurtures, and strengthens spontaneous love rather than banishes it as "A" asserts. The second letter, "The Balance Between the Aesthetic and the Ethical in the Development of the Personality," makes the same essential point: The choice is not between a life of enjoyment and a life of duty; in living responsibly and ethically, the person can have a much better time and enjoy himself or herself much more thoroughly than if he or she is always focused on getting enjoyment.

Volume 2 ends as did volume 1: with a copied text by someone else. Judge William sends to "A" a copy of a sermon written by an old university friend entitled "The Upbuilding That Lies in the Thought That in Relation to God We Are Always in the Wrong." The sermon emphasizes the infinity of the ethical demand and the impossibility of actually fulfilling it. Although Judge William writes that the sermon makes the same point he had been making in his two letters, it seems to call into question Judge William's whole project of existing as a morally righteous person. This ending of *Either/Or* points ahead to later works by Kierkegaard in which religious modes of existence are contrasted with both the aesthetic and the ethical.

George Connell

FURTHER READING

Kierkegaard, Søren. *Either/Or*. Translated by Edna Hong and Howard Hong. Princeton, N.J.: Princeton University Press, 1987.

Lowrie, Walter. *A Short Life of Kierkegaard*. Princeton, N.J.: Princeton University Press, 1942.

Mackey, Louis. *Kierkegaard: A Kind of Poet*. Philadelphia: University of Pennsylvania Press, 1971.

Malantschuk, Gregor. *Kierkegaard's Thought*. Translated by Edna Hong and Howard Hong. Princeton, N.J.: Princeton University Press, 1971.

Perkins, Robert L., ed. *Either/Or*. 2 vols. International Kierkegaard Commentary 3-4. Macon, Ga.: Mercer University Press, 1995.

Taylor, Mark. *Kierkegaard's Pseudonymous Authorship*. Princeton, N.J.: Princeton University Press, 1975.

SEE ALSO: Choice; Choiceless choices; Dilemmas, moral; Hedonism; Kierkegaard, Søren.

Electronic mail

DEFINITION: Communications medium that allows individuals, at home and in the workplace, to exchange messages and information electronically

TYPE OF ETHICS: Personal and social ethics

SIGNIFICANCE: Certain personal and business uses of electronic mail raise ethical issues that will likely attract continued public attention as the use of electronic mail increases.

In 2002, computer users in the United States sent an average of approximately eight billion messages by electronic mail (e-mail) every day. As e-mail has become more popular, its use in the home and in the workplace has increasingly become a subject of debate among government leaders and others concerned with the potential for its abuse.

E-mail has features of both conventional, pen-and-ink correspondence and telephonic communication. Like the former, its content is generally expressed in the form of text or images, as opposed to purely aural communication. Like the latter, e-mail communication requires an electronic interface—a computer or other device that provides access to the Internet. In addition to substantive content, e-mail messages contain coded information about who is sending the e-mail and its destination. When an e-mail message is sent, its content is broken down into digital packets, which are transmitted via different Internet routes and reassembled at the message's destination. Copies of the message may be stored in several different locations—on the sender's computer, on the recipient's computer, or on the various Internet servers that facilitate transmission. Because of the digital nature of e-mail, its use raises ethical issues associated with storage and dissemination.

Storage of e-mail is an issue because digital information can be difficult to destroy. Even after an e-mail message has been deleted from a computer, its content may remain accessible until it is overwritten, or "wiped" from a computer's memory. Thus, messages that contain potentially inappropriate, offensive, or defamatory content, or that reveal confidential personal or business information, may be made public in ways that comparable pen-and-ink letters could not. This aspect of e-mail may aid those who seek such improper ends as harassing particular individuals in the workplace or trading on confidential information.

DISSEMINATION

E-mail messages are susceptible to widespread dissemination in ways that nondigital forms of communication are not. For example, messages may be quickly and easily distributed to individuals for whom they are not intended. In a well-publicized incident that occurred in 2003, a young lawyer at a large New York City law firm inadvertently sent an e-mail message containing offensive language to every lawyer at his firm. His e-mail was subsequently forwarded to scores of people across the United States.

The ease with which e-mail messages can be sent in bulk has been the subject of efforts to regulate the distribution of unsolicited e-mail, commonly known as "spam." Any governmental regulation, however, must address the First Amendment rights of spammers. Moreover, individuals who seek to control spammers through civil suits must contend with the California Supreme Court's decision in *Intel Corporation v. Hamidi* (2003) holding that spammers cannot be sued for trespass to computer systems unless recipients can show they have suffered damage.

Lawrence Friedman

FURTHER READING

Doubilet, David M., Vincent I. Polley, and John R. Sapp, eds. *Employee Use of the Internet and E-Mail: A Model Corporate Policy—With Commentary on Its Use in the U.S. and Other Countries.* Chicago: American Bar Association, 2002.

Macdonald, Lynda. *Managing E-mail and Internet Use: A Practical Guide to Employers' Obligations and Employees' Rights.* Croydon, Surrey, England: Tolley, 2001.

Rooksby, Emma. *E-mail and Ethics: Style and Ethical Relations in Computer-Mediated Communications.* New York: Routledge, 2002.

SEE ALSO: Advertising; Cell-phone etiquette; Computer misuse; Computer technology; Electronic surveillance; Internet chat rooms; Technology.

Electronic surveillance

DEFINITION: Use of audio, visual, and computerized devices to monitor people, places, and communications

TYPE OF ETHICS: Legal and judicial ethics

SIGNIFICANCE: Proponents of widespread electronic surveillance generally approach the ethics of surveillance from either utilitarian or egoistic perspectives. Opponents generally advocate surveillance ethics grounded in individual rights or in a Kantian respect for personhood.

Electronic surveillance has existed since the invention of the telegraph in the mid-nineteenth century, when Union and Confederate agents tapped telegraph wires during the Civil War. However, its use began growing exponentially only after the mid-twentieth century. Advances in computer and communications technology not only created new electronic surveillance tools but also increased society's reliance on media that are vulnerable to electronic surveillance.

Electronic surveillance was once solely the government's domain. The U.S. Supreme Court in 1928 refused to treat wiretapping as a "seizure" restricted by the Fourth Amendment, and prompted Congress to enact limits on wiretapping. During World War II, both Allied and Axis military forces intercepted enemy radio communications. The Cold War thrust electronic surveillance into the space age, in the form of satellite-based photography and signal interception. In later decades, as electronic surveillance devices became more widely available, private enterprises and even private individuals joined the fray.

USERS OF ELECTRONIC SURVEILLANCE

Governments use electronic surveillance far more during the twenty-first century than ever before. Law enforcement, counterterrorism, espionage and counterespionage are the most prominent government applications for electronic surveillance. Government agencies have a host of electronic surveillance tools at their disposal. Common surveillance techniques include planting hidden microphones and cameras, tapping telephone lines, monitoring wireless telephone communications, and monitoring Internet communications.

The world's most extensive electronic surveillance network is Echelon, a project directed by the United States in cooperation with Canada, the United Kingdom, Australia, and New Zealand. Its global network monitors satellite transmissions, radio transmissions, telephone conversations, and Internet traffic, and it uses computer programs to sift through the collected data. According to some estimates, up to 90 percent of the world's Internet traffic passes through Echelon. Although the United States government neither confirms nor denies its own role in Echelon, other governments have admitted its existence, and the European Parliament and the U.S. Congress have launched inquiries into Echelon's activities.

Businesses have also become pervasive users of electronic surveillance. Businesses conduct substantial electronic surveillance on their own employees. Justifications for employee surveillance include monitoring productivity, protecting confidential business information, deterring theft and vandalism, and deterring employee misconduct that might give rise to employer liability. Surveillance techniques used on employees include the use of video and telephone monitoring devices, as well as software applications designed to monitor employees' computer, Internet, and e-mail use.

Businesses also use electronic surveillance to monitor their customers. For many years, the primary form of customer surveillance was video monitoring. With the advent of Internet commerce, however, customer surveillance exploded, allowing businesses to monitor online shoppers' preferences through the use of cookies, Web bugs, and other data-collection tools.

The journalism media also make substantial use of electronic surveillance, particularly although not exclusively the tabloids and paparazzi. Telephoto lenses capture revealing or embarrassing moments in celebrities' or politicians' lives, and hidden cameras and microphones have become mainstays in investigative reporting.

Finally, private citizens are increasingly turning to electronic surveillance. Some use video or audio monitoring in their homes for security reasons. Others may have voyeuristic motivations, as they spy on neighbors or acquaintances with video cameras or microphones, or monitor their children's or spouses' computer use with surveillance software. With constantly evolving technologies, the potential applications of electronic surveillance will only increase.

ETHICAL JUSTIFICATIONS

Utilitarianism is a common justification for government use of electronic surveillance. Under this view, the benefits of preventing terrorism and other crimes outweigh the individual harms that widespread surveillance may cause. Additionally, the media argue that their information collection techniques help promote the free flow of information and knowledge about public figures. Moreover, businesses suggest that greater knowledge about customer preferences helps deliver goods to consumers more efficiently, thereby helping maximize society's overall wealth.

Egoism, a second justification for electronic surveillance, is most apparent in surveillance by private persons who disclaim any obligation to consider the interests of others. Egoism is also a likely justification for business surveillance, if one sees corporate officers' highest duty as maximizing the shareholders' return on their investment. In the case of business surveillance, egoism and utilitarianism may actually overlap, in light of the free-market argument that the rational pursuit of self-interest by all players in a given market will produce the optimal allocation of resources in that market.

ETHICAL OPPOSITION

Much of the antisurveillance rhetoric in the United States is rights-based and draws on a variety of legal authorities. In the United States, surveillance opponents often rely on Supreme Court decisions finding a constitutionally protected right to privacy. Some state constitutions explicitly protect the right to privacy, as does Article 12 of the United Nations Universal Declaration of Human Rights. Additionally, some state and federal statutes in the United States limit electronic surveillance by the government as well as by private parties, and most states protect individuals against intrusions on their reasonable expectation of privacy.

A second strain of opposition to surveillance embodies the Kantian ethic of respect for personhood. This approach rejects treating people as mere means to an end, and challenges electronic surveillance for intruding on individual autonomy and dignity. Pervasive electronic surveillance diminishes autonomy by treating people as if they are not to be trusted and are therefore unworthy of autonomy.

Individual dignity also suffers when surveillance data are used to limit individuals' opportunities to gain such essentials as employment, credit, and health or life insurance, and to discriminate against particular classes of people.

Shaun B. Spencer

FURTHER READING

Gandy, Oscar H., Jr. *The Panoptic Sort: A Political Economy of Personal Information.* Boulder, Colo.: Westview Press, 1993.

Garfinkel, Simson. *Database Nation: The Death of Privacy in the Twenty-first Century.* Cambridge, Mass.: O'Reilly 2000.

Henderson, Harry. *Privacy in the Information Age.* New York: Facts On File, 1999.

Lyon, David. *Surveillance Society: Monitoring Everyday Life.* Philadelphia: Open University, 2001.

Rosen, Jeffrey. *The Unwanted Gaze: The Destruction of Privacy in America.* New York: Vintage Books, 2001.

Schoeman, Ferdinand David, ed. *Philosophical Dimensions of Privacy: An Anthology.* New York: Cambridge University Press 1984.

SEE ALSO: Computer technology; Covert action; Electronic mail; Espionage; Homeland defense; Internet chat rooms; Photojournalism.

Electroshock therapy

DEFINITION: Induction by electric current of convulsions in patients in order to alleviate severe depression and suicidal ideation

DATE: 1938 to present

TYPE OF ETHICS: Psychological ethics

SIGNIFICANCE: Electroshock therapy intentionally causes pain and suffering in order to help patients with mental problems. This raises two fundamental ethical issues: First, is it ever acceptable to inflict pain, not as a by-product of treatment, but as a method of treatment, even if that pain brings about the desired benefits? Second, are patients with depression and other mental illnesses competent to consent to or refuse this type of treatment?

Depression is one of the most prevalent and most treatable life-threatening illnesses. As many as 5 percent of Americans are likely to experience at least one episode of clinical depression during their lifetimes. The most probable cause of death from depression is suicide: Indeed, approximately 15 percent of patients with major depression eventually take their own lives.

Electroshock therapy, or, more properly, electroconvulsive therapy (ECT), is used to treat severe depression that does not respond to drug therapy or that occurs in patients who cannot tolerate antidepressant drugs.

HISTORY

ECT was introduced in 1938 by two psychiatrists, U. Cerletti and L. Bini, who devised a means of inducing a convulsion in a patient by using an electric current delivered via electrodes fastened to one or both of the patient's temples. It had long been observed that some mental patients had temporary relief from their symptoms following a spontaneous seizure. Prior to Cerletti and Bini's work, seizures had been induced by the inhalation of various substances.

ECT enjoyed a peak of popular use during the 1950's and 1960's, when it was considered a virtual panacea for mental illness. It had the additional benefit of making otherwise "difficult" patients more manageable, causing it to be used in some cases for behavior control. Partly because of its misuse and its negative depiction in the popular media (such as in Ken Kesey's 1962 novel *One Flew Over the Cuckoo's Nest*), ECT has earned a reputation as a high-risk treatment with an enormous capacity for abuse and severe long-term side effects. This is not, in fact, the case.

INDICATIONS AND EFFECTS

ECT is extremely effective in the treatment of severe depression and the depressive phase of bipolar disorder. Patients with atypical depression, however, which includes features such as acute anxiety or vegetative symptoms, tend not to respond as well to ECT. The treatment is strongly indicated in cases in which suicide seems imminent. ECT is used primarily for patients who have not responded to, or who cannot tolerate, drug therapy. Studies have shown that between 50 percent and 80 percent of patients in this category respond positively to ECT.

There are no absolute contraindicators in the use of ECT. The treatment does raise blood and intracranial pressure, however, and therefore it must be used with caution in patients who already have high readings in these areas. ECT is often administered under anesthesia, and muscle relaxants are used to reduce the risk of bone fractures, so patients who have problems with these treatments need to be assessed carefully. Also, patients with cardiovascular problems are only rarely given ECT, because of reported complications. In studies to date, however, the highest mortality rate associated with ECT has been 0.8 percent.

The major side effect of ECT is memory loss. The loss is primarily short-term. Studies indicate that there is little, if any, observable difference six months after treatment between the memory abilities of pa-tients who have had ECT and those who have not. Since memory impairment is associated with depression in general, it is difficult to assess what loss is attributable to ECT.

ETHICAL ISSUES

The ethical issues involved with the administration of ECT revolve around the determination of what constitutes informed consent and competency to give consent or refuse treatment. In all psychiatric treatments, the question of the competency of a patient who suffers from some form of mental illness to give consent is raised. Other issues include the use of ECT for behavior control and decision making for patients considered not competent.

INFORMED CONSENT

The ethical issue of informed consent may be divided into two areas: consent by a competent adult and consent for an incompetent patient.

The question of competency is raised in all cases of mental illness. Can a person in the depths of severe depression, with its accompanying hindrances of judgment, be considered competent under any circumstances? Legally, yes. Legal competency is judged on the basis of observable behavior rather than on the basis of the patient's mental status, which can only be inferred. If a patient can make what is considered to be a rational decision, shows no signs of delusions, and is able to understand the risks and benefits of a treatment, that person is considered competent. The common negative societal view of ECT, however, often causes legally competent patients to refuse the treatment. Can their biased view of ECT, which is based on fictional portrayals, be considered delusional? Furthermore, consistency of consent becomes an issue because of the indecisiveness inherent in depression.

If a patient is judged to be incompetent, determining who will make treatment decisions becomes an issue. Most commonly these decisions are made by a close relative. It must be ascertained that the best interests and values of the patient have primacy in the decision, rather than such issues as ease of management by caretakers or punitive measures by other parties.

In the case of the hospitalized patient, the aspect of voluntariness of consent must be considered. A patient does not automatically relinquish the right to

431

refuse treatment upon hospitalization. If consent is sought, it must be clear that it is in no way coerced; for example, by telling a patient that release from the hospital will occur sooner if ECT is used.

RISKS AND BENEFITS

One of the important aspects of informed consent is the patient's ability to comprehend and evaluate the risks and benefits inherent in a given procedure. In the case of ECT, the risks of the procedure must be evaluated in the light of the continued risk of suicide in depressed individuals. A competent patient has the right to refuse ECT, however, if he or she considers that the risk of memory loss or other brain damage outweighs the possible benefits.

Margaret Hawthorne

FURTHER READING

Abrams, Richard. *Electroconvulsive Therapy.* 4th ed. New York: Oxford University Press, 2002.

"American Psychiatric Association Practice Guidelines for Major Depressive Disorder in Adults." *American Journal of Psychiatry*, supp. 150 (April, 1993): 4.

Baldwin, Steve, and Melissa Oxlad. *Electroshock and Minors: A Fifty-Year Review.* Westport, Conn.: Greenwood Press, 2000.

Bloch, Sidney, and Paul Chodoff, eds. *Psychiatric Ethics.* New York: Oxford University Press, 1981.

Childress, James F. *Who Should Decide? Paternalism in Health Care.* New York: Oxford University Press, 1982.

Edwards, Rem B., ed. *Psychiatry and Ethics.* Buffalo, N.Y.: Prometheus Books, 1982.

Keller, Martin B. "The Difficult Depressed Patient in Perspective." *Journal of Clinical Psychiatry*, supp. 54 (February, 1993): 4-8.

Kneeland, Timothy W., and Carol A. B. Warren. *Pushbutton Psychiatry: A History of Electroshock in America.* Westport, Conn.: Praeger, 2002.

Schoen, Robert E. "Is Electroconvulsive Therapy Safe?" *Postgraduate Medicine* 87 (May 1, 1990): 236-239.

SEE ALSO: Consent; Mental illness; Psychology; Psychopharmacology; Suicide; Therapist-patient relationship; Torture.

Elitism

DEFINITION: Doctrine that some people are superior to others because of a special knowledge, ability, or characteristic that they possess

TYPE OF ETHICS: Personal and social ethics; beliefs and practices

SIGNIFICANCE: Elitism can provide a basis for arguments against the ethics of equality as well as arguments in favor of some forms of ethical paternalism.

There have been many different types of elitism, such as those based on race, religion, sex, social class, or physical beauty. Racism, sexism, religious elitism, and so forth are generally condemned as unethical practices, if for no other reason than that the criteria used to sort out and rank people are seen as arbitrary. This view does not dismiss elitism completely, however, but only those forms that base it on irrelevant differences among people. More serious elitist arguments are a natural outgrowth of any doctrine that claims that human beings have a potential for excellence. Those who work toward realizing this essence will often view themselves as superior to those who do not. Two types of human potential stand out within elitist arguments—the potential to develop the intellect and the potential to become a unique individual.

INTELLECTUAL ELITISM

As early as 600 B.C.E., the Greeks spoke about the differences between human beings based on the development of a virtuous or unvirtuous character. For the Greeks, differences in character served as a natural basis for ranking people. The aristocracy saw this division as a sound justification for an unequal distribution of power and privilege as well as for the practice of slavery.

Socrates and Plato developed Greek elitism into a sophisticated philosophical doctrine. Socrates, after arguing for a strong dualism of soul and body, claimed that the soul constituted human essence and that the body was a mere vehicle, even a prison, for the soul. In the Socratic view, the perfectibility of the human soul and the avoidance of bodily temptations thus became the single most important task of life. Those who sacrificed their souls for the sake of their bodies became the objects of harsh criticism, as people who turned their backs on their own essential nature. The familiar image of Socrates testing the knowledge of others through his questioning can be understood as his effort to determine the true elite of Greek society.

Plato took the Socratic teaching and developed it further with complex metaphysical and epistemological theories. Plato argued that the soul was positioned between a world of shadows generated by the opinions of mass society and a world of absolute truth accessible only to the trained human intellect. Plato took it as obvious that the person who disciplined his mind to seek truth was better than the person who gave himself over to the world of opinion. He argued that justice could be obtained only if all political power was handed over to the wise elite of society, holding that the ignorant masses should not be allowed to participate in the political process. Intellectual elitism of this sort has been prevalent throughout the history of philosophy and is still easy to find.

INDIVIDUALIST ELITISM

In the nineteenth century, Friedrich Nietzsche argued for a different type of elitism based on a human being's capacity for development as a singular, unique, and powerful individual. In works such as *Thus Spoke Zarathustra* and *Beyond Good and Evil*, Nietzsche argued that all reality consists fundamentally of assertions of power. Thus, he asserted that humans could be divided up into two basic groups: those who embrace and assert their power, and those who fear and repress their power.

Nietzsche's elitism considers the powerful ones to be masters and the repressed ones to be slaves. The master is the true individualist, a free spirit, a creator and a warrior. He or she is "beyond" the social conventions, taboos, mores, and moral imperatives that slaves create to hold themselves and others back. The slaves, however, try to subordinate individuality and uniqueness to generalized rules for appropriate thought and behavior. While the master creates rules by means of an individual act of will, the slaves subordinate themselves to the community will and follow the orders of others.

ETHICAL PRINCIPLES

Despite their obvious differences, both these forms of elitism share important similarities: Both

advocate that it is an ethical duty for humans to develop that potential which will make them superior people—the intellect or the will. Both advocate the duty to avoid that which will corrupt—the world of shadows or the commonplace. Each offers a definition of the highest good in terms of that which will perfect a human being—truth or power.

Both forms of elitism are faced also with the ethical problem of what attitude and/or behavior the elite few should take toward the nonelite majority. While intellectual elitists will have a tendency to avoid the ignorant masses, they do not shun community life itself. Rather, they seek associations within an elite community founded on the books, music, plays, films, and so forth that serve to improve the mind and provide rational insight into truth. Moreover, the intellectual elitist often feels a certain duty to protect the ignorant from their own degradation and to persuade them to partake in their own self-improvement. This attitude, however, creates a moral dilemma. Socrates was tried and executed as a "corrupter" of the youth by the people he claimed he was trying to help. Today, as well, the well-intentioned social reformer is often accused of both elitism and paternalism by those persons whom the reformer seeks to help.

Nietzschean individualists draw a different lesson from the trial and death of Socrates. They feel no moral duty to help the nonelite to do better and will try to avoid them entirely. The master does not desire a community of masters but is instead driven more toward a reclusive and solitary life. The Nietzschean hero Zarathustra lives alone like a god, high in the mountains, with only powerful animals such as lions and snakes as his companions.

Daniel Baker

FURTHER READING

Arendt, Hannah. *The Human Condition*. 2d ed. Introduction by Margaret Canovan. Chicago: Chicago University Press, 1998.

Nehamas, Alexander. *Nietzsche: Life as Literature*. Cambridge, Mass.: Harvard University Press, 1985.

Nietzsche, Friedrich. *On the Genealogy of Morals*. Edited and translated by Walter Kaufmann. New York: Vintage Books, 1967.

_____. *Thus Spoke Zarathustra: A Book for All and None*. Translated by Walter Kaufmann. New York: Penguin Books, 1983.

Pareto, Vilfredo. *The Rise and Fall of the Elites*. Totowa, N.J.: Bedminster Press, 1968.

Pina-Cabral, João de, and Antónia Pedroso de Lima, eds. *Elites: Choice, Leadership, and Succession*. New York: Berg, 2000.

SEE ALSO: *Beyond Good and Evil*; Egalitarianism; Existentialism; Individualism; Nietzsche, Friedrich; Paternalism; Plato.

Emancipation Proclamation

IDENTIFICATION: Proclamation by President Abraham Lincoln freeing all slaves held in rebel portions of the United States

DATE: Issued on January 1, 1863

TYPE OF ETHICS: Civil rights

SIGNIFICANCE: The Emancipation Proclamation extended the legal state of freedom to most American slaves but actually freed few of them at first because the Union government had no power to enforce its provisions in rebel-held territories.

Although the American Civil War was the result of sectional conflict that involved the issue of slavery, both the Union and the Confederate governments initially denied that slavery was a war issue. The Confederate government claimed that it was fighting only to defend the principle of states' rights. The Union government claimed that it was fighting to preserve the Union of states against Confederate efforts to destroy it.

LINCOLN'S CAUTIOUS APPROACH TO EMANCIPATION

From the very beginning of the war, abolitionists, radical Republicans, and black activists urged President Abraham Lincoln to use the war as an opportunity to strike down slavery. Lincoln, though, acted in a cautious manner during the early months of the war. Until September, 1862, Lincoln refused to include the abolition of slavery as one of the Union's war aims. Furthermore, when radical commanders in the Union Army ordered the emancipation of slaves in parts of the occupied South in 1861-1862, Lincoln countermanded the orders.

These actions caused reformers to question the depth of Lincoln's own commitment to ending slavery. In Lincoln's defense, it must be noted that Lincoln both publicly and privately often expressed a heartfelt abhorrence of slavery. Yet Lincoln knew that a premature effort to turn the war into a crusade for emancipation would be counterproductive to the cause of freedom. An early act of emancipation would prompt loyal slave states such as Kentucky, Maryland, and Missouri to join the Confederacy and probably cause the defeat of the Union. From a practical point of view, the Union government could not abolish slavery in the South if it lost the war.

ORIGINS OF LINCOLN'S EMANCIPATION POLICY

Lincoln was finally encouraged to seek emancipation because of the actions of the slaves themselves. During the war, some 600,000 slaves—about 15 percent of the total—escaped from their masters. Slaves understood that the advance of the Union Army through the South presented them with an unprecedented opportunity for escape. Most escaped slaves sought shelter with the Union Army.

The presence of large numbers of slaves within Union Army lines presented Union commanders with the question of whether the slaves should be returned to their rebellious masters or allowed to stay with the Army and consume its limited resources. Most Union commanders allowed the slaves to remain with the army, justifying this decision out of military necessity. Pointing to the right of armies under international law to seize or destroy enemy property being used to sustain the war effort, Union commanders claimed the right to seize the Confederacy's slave laborers as contraband of war.

The actions of Union commanders shifted the focus of emancipation from human rights to military necessity, thereby encouraging Lincoln to adopt a general policy of emancipation and giving Lincoln an argument with which to win public support for this policy.

THE PROCLAMATION AND ITS LIMITS

Lincoln's Emancipation Proclamation, which was issued January 1, 1863, declared that slaves in areas in rebellion against the United States were free. Slaves in the loyal slave states and slaves in areas of the Confederacy already under Union control were

Time Line of Legal Emancipation Outside the United States

Year	Country	Year	Country
1775	Madeira	1863	Dutch colonies
1793	Ontario	1873	Portuguese colonies
1804	Haiti		Puerto Rico
1813	Argentina		Spanish colonies
1814	Colombia	1874	Gold Coast
1819	Tunisia	1875	Angola
1823	Chile	1877	Madagascar
1824	Central America	1886	Cuba
1829	Mexico	1888	Brazil
1831	Bolivia	1890	Belgian colonies
1833	British colonies	1897	Zanzibar and
1836	Portugal		Pemba
1843	India	1907	Kenya
	Uruguay	1910	China
1847	Swedish colonies	1923	Rwanda
1848	Virgin Islands	1928	Sierra Leone
1851	Ecuador	1930	Ethiopia
1854	Peru	1962	Saudi Arabia
	Venezuela	1970	Muscat and Oman

Confederacy previously captured were not currently being used to support the enemy's war effort. In making this argument, Lincoln was not being evasive or cautious in seeking the emancipation of all American slaves. One month before he issued the Emancipation Proclamation, Lincoln proposed to Congress the passage of a constitutional amendment that would have freed all slaves living in the loyal border states and in currently occupied portions of the Confederacy.

EFFECTS OF THE PROCLAMATION

Eventually, perhaps two-thirds of American slaves were freed by the Emancipation Proclamation. The remainder of American slaves were freed by the laws of state governments in loyal slave states and by the Thirteenth Amendment (1865), which abolished slavery in the United States.

Harold D. Tallant

not freed by the Proclamation. Because of this fact, some commentators have criticized the Proclamation, claiming that the Proclamation had little impact because it sought to free the Confederate slaves who were beyond Lincoln's control and neglected to free the slaves within his control. This criticism ignores several facts regarding Lincoln's action. The Emancipation Proclamation amounted to an announcement that henceforward, the Union Army would become an army of liberation. Whenever the Union Army captured an area of the Confederacy, it would automatically free the slaves in that region.

Additionally, the limited scope of Lincoln's Proclamation was prompted by the limited powers of the president under the Constitution. Lincoln pointed out that, as president, his only constitutional power to emancipate slaves was derived from his power as commander-in-chief to order the military destruction of property that supported the enemy's war effort. Slaves belonging to masters in states loyal to the Union and slaves belonging to masters in areas of the

FURTHER READING

Berlin, Ira, et al. *Slaves No More: Three Essays on Emancipation and the Civil War.* Cambridge, England: Cambridge University Press, 1992.

Cox, LaWanda. *Lincoln and Black Freedom: A Study in Presidential Leadership.* Columbia: University of South Carolina Press, 1981.

Foner, Eric. *Nothing But Freedom: Emancipation and Its Legacy.* Baton Rouge: Louisiana State University Press, 1983.

Franklin, John Hope. *The Emancipation Proclamation.* Garden City, N.Y.: Doubleday, 1963.

McPherson, James M. *Ordeal by Fire: The Civil War and Reconstruction.* 2d ed. New York: McGraw-Hill, 1992.

Perman, Michael. *Emancipation and Reconstruction.* 2d ed. Wheeling, Ill.: Harlan Davidson, 2003.

SEE ALSO: Abolition; Alienation; Civil rights and liberties; Lincoln, Abraham; Slavery.

Emerson, Ralph Waldo

IDENTIFICATION: American theologian, essayist, and poet

BORN: May 25, 1803, Boston, Massachusetts

DIED: April 27, 1882, Concord, Massachusetts

TYPE OF ETHICS: Modern history

SIGNIFICANCE: The leading proponent of New England Transcendentalism, Emerson inspired individuals to develop their spiritual selves in such works as *Nature* (1836), "The American Scholar" (1837), "Divinity School Address" (1838), and "Self-Reliance" (1841).

The catalyst for most of Emerson's finest writings was his search for a liberating personal philosophy. Ordained a Protestant minister, Emerson resigned his pastorate at a Boston Unitarian church because he believed that conventional religions told their parishioners what to think and how to act rather than instructing them how to use their own divinely inspired

Ralph Waldo Emerson. (Library of Congress)

"moral sentiments." He believed that only through this innate moral sense could one adequately meet one's most important ethical responsibility: self-reliance.

Failure to follow one's conscience was to live in a mind-numbing conformity that was, at bottom, spiritually suicidal. In a controversial address, he urged a graduating class of Harvard divinity students to "cast behind you all conformity, and acquaint men at first-hand with Deity." He attributed Americans' over-reliance on material things to a lack of self-reliance: Citizens "measure their esteem of each other, by what each has and not by what each is." His solution was for each person to find in the expansive American natural setting an "original relationship to the universe."

Emerson believed that nature itself embodied ethical principles; thus, it could be used as a kind of holy sanctuary in which the individual, without the aid of irrelevant intermediaries such as dogmas, rituals, and ministers, could "transcend" material considerations and achieve a spiritual union with the deity. Despite the affirmative tone of his essays, Emerson, like Thoreau, sometimes despaired of finding a vocation. In a materialistic society, Transcendentalists were neither allotted a place of respect nor afforded the kind of meaningful work they were eager to perform. Not considered "good citizens," they believed that most of the ordinary work of humanity, even that devoted to the best causes, required conformity rather than originality and therefore precluded the original use of one's own spirit.

William L. Howard

SEE ALSO: Conservation; Declaration of Independence; Idealist ethics; Thoreau, Henry David; Transcendentalism.

Emotivist ethics

DEFINITION: System of moral philosophy based on the notion that the purpose of ethical language is to prescribe behavior by stirring one's emotions and influencing one's attitude

TYPE OF ETHICS: Theory of ethics

SIGNIFICANCE: Emotivist ethics is an important development in the evolution of ethical theory because it represents a departure from the dominant cognitive ethical theory. In its extreme form, emotivism denies that ethical judgments can be rationally justified.

To a certain extent, emotivist ethics has its roots in the philosophy of David Hume. In the second book of the *Treatise of Human Nature* (1739), Hume argues that reason is subordinate to the emotions and that moral judgments are "sentiments." These sentiments are feelings of approval or disapproval toward an action. The bottom line for Hume is that morality is derived from and based on feeling. As he observes in the *Treatise*, "Morality is more properly felt than judged of."

The real impetus for this well-known movement in ethics came from logical positivism, which could not accept intuition as a means of verifying propositions. Since moral judgments cannot be verified, they could not be meaningful or significant propositions. Positivism stresses that propositions must be verifiable, and since this is not possible with ethical propositions, they must be treated very differently. Thus, according to A. J. Ayer, echoing David Hume, moral judgments serve only to express the feelings or sentiments of the speaker.

Emotivism as a full-fledged ethical theory was developed primarily by the American philosopher Charles L. Stevenson. Stevenson wrote *Ethics and Language* (1944), which has become one of the most significant and influential ethical works of the twentieth century.

PREMISE OF EMOTIVISM

The fundamental premise of emotivist ethics is that language has different functions. One function or purpose of language is to state facts or to describe some aspect of reality. For example, "It's quite cold outside—the temperature is 23 degrees Fahrenheit." This statement can be easily verified. When language is used in this fashion it is considered to be descriptive. According to the emotivist theory of ethics, however, moral discourse is definitely not descriptive, since it does not convey any such factual information.

What, then is the purpose and import of moral language? According to Stevenson, moral discourse has two key features. In order to explain the first feature, Stevenson drew a sharp distinction between beliefs and attitudes. In making a moral judgment, it is possible to distinguish between the facts that are the subject of judgment and the positive or negative evaluation of those facts. Hence, if someone makes the judgment that "euthanasia is wrong," euthanasia is the state of affairs under scrutiny and a negative evaluation is being advanced. This negative evaluation represents one's attitude about euthanasia. In moral disputes, there is a divergence or disagreement in attitude. For example, some people may disagree with opponents of euthanasia: They may believe that euthanasia is permissible, which means that they have a different attitude toward euthanasia.

The second feature of moral discourse is its dynamic character, or magnetic power. Hence, according to Stevenson, besides expressing an attitude, moral judgments "create an influence," since they seek to provoke a response in those to whom the judgment is addressed. With regard to this second feature of moral discourse, Ayer and Stevenson would agree that ethical terms such as "good," "right," and so forth are emotionally provocative. In his seminal work *Language, Truth, and Logic* (1936), Ayer points out that ethical terms such as "good" and "evil" are similar to aesthetic words such as "beautiful." Such words do not describe or state facts; instead, they express feelings and seek to evoke a response.

In short, then, ethical language and judgment has a dual function. Its first purpose is to express the belief as well as the attitude of the speaker, and its second purpose is to change the attitude of those to whom this language is addressed. Hence, when someone utters the moral judgment that euthanasia is a grave moral error, that person is expressing a feeling and an attitude about this controversial topic. The speaker is also trying to persuade others to adopt this same attitude if they have not already done so. Thus, moral discourse is clearly influential: It seeks to influence others and change attitudes.

RATIONAL ARGUMENTS

In its extreme form, emotivism does not recognize the validity of rational arguments that might support one's ethical attitude or feelings. This appears to be Ayer's position. Stevenson, however, does not go so far; he admits the possibility of such rational justification. Thus, Stevenson concedes that the attitudes that are expressed in ethical judgments are based on beliefs, and people can offer reasons and justifications for those beliefs. For Stevenson, however, it is unclear whether the most fundamental ethical attitudes are grounded in any rational beliefs; if this is so, these attitudes would be irrational, since they could not be swayed by reason.

Philosophers recognize that there is considerable merit to the line of reasoning put forward by emotivists such as Stevenson, but they also point out some problems. To begin with, it is not clear that the purpose of influencing attitudes is distinctive of moral discourse. Also, there is nothing necessarily emotional about rendering a moral judgment—after all, is it not possible to articulate a judgment in an unemotional and dispassionate way? Finally, emotivism stresses that moral discourse is used primarily to produce an effect—to change the attitude of others. If one evaluates moral judgments in terms of their effectiveness, however, one looks away from the reasons and arguments underlying that judgment, and this is somewhat problematic. Simply because a moral judgment is effective does not mean that it is valid.

Richard A. Spinello

FURTHER READING

Ayer, A. J. *Language, Truth, and Logic*. London: V. Gollancz, 1936. Reprint. Introduction by Ben Rogers. London: Penguin, 2001.

Stevenson, Charles L. *Ethics and Language.* New Haven, Conn.: Yale University Press, 1960.

Urmson, J. O. *The Emotive Theory of Ethics.* New York: Oxford University Press, 1969.

Werkmeister, W. H. *Theories of Ethics: A Study in Moral Obligation.* Lincoln, Nebr.: Johnsen, 1961.

Wilks, Colin. *Emotion, Truth, and Meaning: In Defense of Ayer and Stevenson.* Library of Ethics and Applied Philosophy 12. Boston: Kluwer Academic, 2002.

SEE ALSO: Ayer, A. J.; Cognitivism; Fact/value distinction; Good, the; Hare, R. M.; Language; Moore, G. E.; Normative vs. descriptive ethics; Perry, R. B.; Reason and rationality; Skepticism; Subjectivism.

Employee safety and treatment

DEFINITION: Policies and procedures used by employers to protect the on-the-job safety and welfare of their workers

TYPE OF ETHICS: Business and labor ethics

SIGNIFICANCE: Employers have an ethical responsibility for the general workplace health and safety because they—and not their workers—control the facilities and equipment used. To place responsibility on workers would be to create a gap between responsibility and authority.

Worker treatment is generally seen as falling into two basic categories: the physical safety of employees in the workplace and the rights of workers to fairness and dignity with respect to hiring, compensation, promotions, job security, and discrimination.

PHYSICAL SAFETY

As approximately 10,000 workers are killed each year in American workplaces, and another 2.8 million workers are injured (these numbers do not include workers who suffer from occupational diseases, which can take decades to develop), safety is a critical issue in business. Ensuring physical safety requires the elimination of workplace hazards and implementation of safety standards. Although many hazards have been eliminated, many dangerous conditions still exist. Among these dangers are textile fibers that can cause brown lung disease, paint vapors that cause emphysema, excessive noise that may cause hearing loss, and debilitating carpal tunnel syndrome from computer keyboard operation.

To improve worker safety and to establish forums in which employees may seek remuneration, individual states began enacting legislation to guarantee payment for workplace injuries as early as 1920. This legislation, known as worker's compensation, or "worker's comp," compensated workers only for existing injuries and did not eliminate the conditions that caused injuries. To reduce workplace injuries, the federal government enacted the Occupational Safety and Health Act, which established the Occupational Safety and Health Administration (OSHA) in 1970.

With the creation of OSHA, employers had a new legal duty to maintain a safe working environment, provide proper supervision, and educate their employees about their products and their workplace. OSHA required all employers to conform to certain minimum safety standards and sought to reduce hazards in the workplace by establishing corporate responsibilities for improving worker safety and health. OSHA sometimes disciplines employers who think that compensating injured workers is cheaper than implementing costly safety standards to prevent accidents. OSHA may impose criminal penalties upon individuals within the corporate structure—rather than only upon the corporation itself—if it finds that corporate managers understood the risks to workers and ignored them.

One famous example of how disastrous it can be for a company to fail to provide for employee safety is Johns Manville, formerly the leading manufacturer of asbestos products. During the 1930's the company discovered that exposure to asbestos fibers could result in serious, even fatal, disabilities. However, the company kept this information private and did not inform its thousands of workers about the hazards of asbestos exposure. When the dangers of asbestos finally became known to the public in the early 1980's, thousands of lawsuits were filed by former employees of Manville and other companies that used asbestos products supplied by Manville. As a result, Manville declared bankruptcy, established a fund to help pay for injuries, and became widely vilified for its failure to warn workers. The result of Manville's negligence was catastrophe—for the injured workers and their families, and for the company, which was nearly destroyed. More even than OSHA, the common law character of American courts makes employers liable for negligent or malicious behavior on their part.

By the early twenty-first century, one of the important twentieth century assumptions about worker's compensation legislation had come under widespread attack. As American labor costs—including insurance premiums to pay for worker's compensation claims—rose, businesses increasingly found it cheaper to export jobs to low-wage environments in countries abroad. In an effort to save American jobs, business have pressured many state governments to reduce the benefits awarded under their worker's compensation laws or face the loss of jobs to other less protective American states or to overseas locations.

This growing trend raised new ethical issues, and not only for workers who may find themselves with reduced protection. If workers are injured in facilities controlled by irresponsible employers and the new worker's compensation laws do not provide adequately for medical costs or permanent disabilities, the injured workers will be forced into some form of state financed welfare. This is an ethical issue not only for the workers but also for responsible employers. Caring employers who attempt to maintain safe working environments for their employees will pay twice: once for the safety measures they provide and again when they pay increased taxes to cover the losses foisted on the taxpayers by less responsible employers.

Safety in the workplace is of paramount importance to all ethical employers, and ideas about what

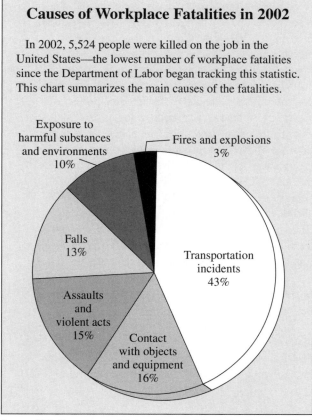

Causes of Workplace Fatalities in 2002

In 2002, 5,524 people were killed on the job in the United States—the lowest number of workplace fatalities since the Department of Labor began tracking this statistic. This chart summarizes the main causes of the fatalities.

Exposure to harmful substances and environments
10%

Fires and explosions
3%

Falls
13%

Transportation incidents
43%

Assaults and violent acts
15%

Contact with objects and equipment
16%

Source: U.S. Department of Labor, Bureau of Statistics, Census of Fatal Occupational Injuries, 2002.

constitutes safety have evolved as new knowledge has become available. A classic example of how opinions can change regarding what constitutes a safe workplace is the issue of secondhand smoke. During the early 1980's, few employers saw a need to protect their employees from coworkers' secondhand smoke. By the early twenty-first century, however, secondhand smoke was recognized as a serious workplace concern. Although there is no doubt that the workplace has become safer and that employers' concern for the safety of workers has increased, the issue of safety merits continued close attention.

WORKERS' RIGHTS AND FAIRNESS

All workers have the right to expect fairness from their employers and to be treated with respect and dignity. Fairness is especially important in the areas of hiring practices, compensation, promotions, privacy, discrimination, job security, and sexual harassment.

The federal government has enacted legislation to protect employees from discrimination in the workplace based on race, religion, sex, color, and national origin. Title VII of the Civil Rights Act of 1964 specifically protects women, African Americans, Hispanics, Native Americans, Asian Americans, and Pacific Islanders. In addition, some states and local communities have added to the list more protections, such as those relating to marital status, veteran status, and sexual orientation. The Pregnancy Discrimination Act of 1978 protects pregnant women from discrimination, and the Age Discrimination in Employment Act of 1975 extends protection to workers forty years of age or older. The 1990 Americans with Disabilities Act requires all companies with more than fifteen employees to provide reasonable accommodations for workers with disabilities. The goal of all this legislation is to incorporate fairness into the workplace so that ability will be the primary criterion in decisions that involve hiring, promotions, compensation, discipline, and firing.

Another twenty-first century issue in the workplace is sexual harassment, which is a form of gender discrimination. While a precise definition of sexual harassment is not always clear to employers, employees, or even lower courts, the U.S. Supreme Court has moved in the direction of greater clarity in successive cases. Sexual harassment is an ethical issue because it unfairly focuses job advancement or retention on a factor other than the ability to do a job. As a result of legislation and well-publicized lawsuits, many companies have adopted guidelines for dealing with sexual harassment as well as training programs to educate employees about the dangers of harassment and discrimination.

Jonathan Hugh Mann
Updated by Richard L. Wilson

FURTHER READING

Broadhurst, Arlene Idol, and Grant Ledgerwood. *Environmental Ethics and the Corporation*. Houndmills, England: Macmillan, 2000.

Buchholz, Rogene A., and Sandra B. Rosenthal. *Rethinking Business Ethics*. New York: Oxford University Press, 2000.

Collins, Larry R., and Thomas D. Schneid. *Physical Hazards of the Workplace*. Boca Raton, Fla.: Lewis, 2001.

Des Jardins, Joseph R., and John J. McCall, eds. *Contemporary Issues in Business Ethics*. 4th ed. Belmont, Calif.: Wadsworth, 1999.

Hofmann, David A., and Lois E. Tetrick, eds. *Health and Safety in Organizations: A Multilevel Perspective*. San Francisco, Calif.: Jossey-Bass, 2003.

Nielsen, Richard P. *The Politics of Ethics: Methods for Acting, Learning, and Sometimes Fighting with Others in Addressing Ethics Problems in Organizational Life*. New York: Oxford University Press, 1996.

Pava, Moses L. *The Search for Meaning in Organizations*. New York: Quorum Books, 1999.

Solomon, Robert C. *A Better Way to Think About Business*. New York: Oxford University Press, 1999.

SEE ALSO: Ageism; Biometrics; Business ethics; Downsizing; Dress codes; Fairness; Fear in the workplace; Medical ethics; Medical insurance; Product safety and liability; Sexual abuse and harassment.

Endangered species

DEFINITION: Living creatures that are threatened with extinction in all or part of their geographical range

TYPE OF ETHICS: Environmental ethics

SIGNIFICANCE: Advocates of environmental ethics believe that it is morally wrong for humans to cause the extinction of a species, while more anthropocentric arguments are made on the basis of the potential utility of existing species for humanity and the inadvertent self-destruction which may result from the destruction of other members of an ecosystem. As a result, endangered species are recognized and protected by law.

An endangered species is one that has so few individual survivors that it could soon become extinct in all or part of its range. Examples include animals such as the California condor and plants such as orchids and cacti. Those species classified as threatened are presently abundant in their range but likely to become endangered within the near future because of a decline in numbers. Examples include the grizzly bear and the bald eagle.

WILDLIFE PROTECTION

There are three general methods to prevent wildlife from becoming endangered. These methods are to establish treaties and laws to protect a particular species from being killed and to preserve its habitat; to use gene banks, zoos, botanical gardens, and research centers to preserve species and possibly breed individuals of a critically endangered species to reintroduce them to the wild; and to preserve a variety of unique and representative ecosystems, which tends to save a variety of species rather than an individual species.

The U.S. Congress has passed a variety of laws for the protection of endangered species. Legislation to prohibit the illegal collection of species began in 1900 with the Lacey Act. In 1966, the Endangered Species Preservation Act made an official list of endangered species and authorized the expenditure of funds to acquire their habitats. The Endangered Species Conservation Act of 1969 banned the importation and sale of wildlife threatened with worldwide extinction. These legislative acts applied only to vertebrate animals; they did not protect species that were threatened, and they provided no absolute protection against major federal projects that could exterminate a species.

Numbers of Endangered and Threatened Species in 1996

As Listed by U.S. Government

	Mammals	Birds	Reptiles	Amphibians	Fishes	Snails	Clams	Crustaceans	Insects	Arachnids	Plants
Total listings	335	274	112	21	116	23	59	17	33	5	496
Endangered species,											
total	307	252	79	15	76	16	53	14	24	5	406
United States	55	74	14	7	65	15	51	14	20	5	405
Foreign	252	178	65	8	11	1	2	—	4	—	1
Threatened species,											
total	28	22	33	6	40	7	6	3	9	—	90
United States	9	16	19	5	40	7	6	3	9	—	90
Foreign	19	6	14	1	—	—	—	—	—	—	—

Source: U.S. Department of Commerce, *Statistical Abstract of the United States, 1996*, 1996. Primary source, U.S. Fish and Wildlife Service.
Note: Numbers reflect species officially listed by U.S. government; actual worldwide totals of species that could be considered threatened or endangered are unknown but are believed to be much higher.

Notable Species Endangered in the Early Twenty-first Century

Species	Locales	Approximate number	Reason for endangerment
Asian elephant	South and Southeast Asia	50,000	Habitat loss
Black rhinoceros	Eastern and Southern Africa	2,400	Poaching (for horns)
Black-footed ferret	U.S. and Canadian plains	100	Habitat loss, disease
California condor	Western North America	less than 100	Habitat loss, poaching, pollution
Florida manatee	Florida	2,000	Habitat loss, boat collisions
Gorilla	Central Africa	700	Habitat loss, disease
Marine turtle	tropical and subtropical seas	unknown	Hunting, habitat loss, pollution
Panda	China	1,000	Habitat loss, hunting
Pika	North America alpine regions	unknown	Habitat loss
Polar bear	Arctic regions	unknown	Habitat loss
Snow leopard	Central Asia and Himalayas	3,000-5,000	Habitat loss, hunting
South China tiger	China	20-30	Hunting, habitat loss
Sumatran tiger	Indonesia	less than 500	Hunting

Source: World Wildlife Fund; Sea World

The 1973 Endangered Species Act protected endangered and threatened species and provided a program for the recovery of those species. The 1973 act included all plants and animals except a few that had been determined to be pests. The act recognized the relationship between a species and its environment by requiring the Department of the Interior to determine the critical habitat of endangered and threatened species. The act authorizes the National Marine Fisheries Service of the Department of Commerce to identify and list marine species, and the Department of the Interior's Fish and Wildlife Service to identify all other plant and animal species threatened in the United States or abroad. Any decision by either agency to add or remove a species from the list must be based solely on biological grounds without economic consideration.

The 1973 Endangered Species Act also prohibits interstate and international commercial trade involving endangered plant or animal species. Section 7 directs federal agencies not to carry out, fund, or authorize projects that would jeopardize endangered species or destroy habitats critical to their survival. This section was challenged in 1975 when conservationists filed suit against the Tennessee Valley Authority to stop construction on the $137 million Tellico Dam on the Little Tennessee River because the river would flood the only known breeding ground of the tiny snail darter, an endangered species. Courts stopped construction on the dam, though the dam was 90 percent complete. In 1979, Congress passed special legislation exempting the project from the Endangered Species Act. The case of the Tellico Dam raises the ethical problem that if one interprets the 1973 act as favoring species over development in all cases, then the value of the species would be so high that it could not be exceeded by the benefits of development.

The ethical principle of saving endangered species is a high one, but it is not absolute. In some cases, there are higher values that must take precedence over endangered species preservation. Although environmentalists understand this principle, they have argued that the Endangered Species Act is not being carried out as directed by Congress because of budget cuts and administrative rules.

ETHICAL PRINCIPLES

The ethical principle of preserving all plant and animal species often entails practical costs that are extremely high. There will continue to be situations in which a development project that is truly necessary for human well-being will come into conflict with the existence of one or more species. With only limited resources, a priority system must be devised so that the maximum number of species is saved. The ecological value of a species is the value of the species in question to its native habitat or what the impact of its extinction will be on the ecosystem. The uniqueness of a species places greater value on a species if it is the only existing member of a family rather than one of many members of a given family. Those species with a current or promising biological, medical, or chemical utility have a high preservation effort. Those species with a commercial value should not be allowed to be harvested to extinction.

In some cases, extinctions may be ethically justifiable. The following reasons may apply in such cases: benefits accrue to large numbers of people and not merely a chosen few; the beneficial action is related to genuine human needs, not luxuries; the preservation costs are too great to be borne by society; the species is not unique and has no known medical value; or alternate habitats are not available. Justifiable extinctions include those of the smallpox virus and of some nonharmful animals in East Africa.

By saving endangered species and preserving Earth's genetic pool, options are kept open for nature and science to maintain a healthy environment in the future. There is a growing understanding that all life-forms are part of one interdependent ecosystem and that the declining health of one species signals danger for all species, including humans.

David R. Teske

FURTHER READING

Allen, Thomas B. *Vanishing Wildlife of North America*. Washington, D.C.: National Geographic Society, 1974.

Attfield, Robin. *Environmental Ethics: An Overview for the Twenty-first Century*. Malden, Mass.: Blackwell, 2003.

Fritsch, Albert J., et al. *Environmental Ethics: Choices for Concerned Citizens*. Garden City, N.Y.: Anchor Press, 1980.

Kohm, Kathryn, ed. *Balancing on the Brink of Extinction: The Endangered Species Act and Lessons for the Future*. Washington, D.C.: Island Press, 1991.

Korn, Peter. "The Case for Preservation." *The Nation* 254 (March 30, 1992): 414-417.

Miller, G. Tyler, Jr. *Environmental Science: Working with the Earth*. 9th ed. Pacific Grove, Calif.: Brooks/Cole, 2003.

Wilson, Edward O. *The Future of Life*. New York: Alfred A. Knopf, 2002.

SEE ALSO: Animal rights; Biodiversity; Darwin, Charles; Deep ecology; Deforestation; Earth and humanity; Ecology; Environmental ethics; Evolutionary theory; Nature, rights of; Rain forests.

English Bill of Rights

IDENTIFICATION: English law that established fundamental rights of citizens by specifying limits of governmental power
DATE: Enacted in December, 1689
TYPE OF ETHICS: Civil rights
SIGNIFICANCE: The enactment of the English Bill of Rights was an important landmark in the development of the concept of inalienable human rights and political freedoms.

Originally proposed as the Declaration of Right, the English Bill of Rights was adopted under the title "An Act Declaring the Rights and Liberties of the Subject, and Settling the Succession of the Crown." Most of its provisions limiting monarchical power had long been supported as established liberties under English common law. By effectively limiting governmental power, it dealt a death blow to the monarchical concept of divine right. It limited monarchical action by forbidding the suspension of established laws, the formation of ecclesiastical courts, and the levying of taxes without parliamentary approval. It also required parliamentary approval for a standing army. As further enhancements of parliamentary power, it upheld freedom of elections and freedom of speech, and it specified regular meetings of parliament.

For all English subjects, the bill guaranteed the right of petition, the right of trial by jury, and the right of reasonable bail. It prohibited fines and forfeitures of property prior to conviction. It forbade cruel and unusual punishments and granted Protestant subjects the right to bear arms. By enshrining in law rights that are central to a concept of human rights, the Bill became important in the development of freedoms throughout the Western world.

Stanley Archer

SEE ALSO: Bill of Rights, U.S.; Civil rights and liberties; Constitution, U.S.; Declaration of Independence; Freedom and liberty; Jury system; Magna Carta.

Enlightenment ethics

DEFINITION: Set of rationalist ethical systems developed in the seventeenth and eighteenth centuries by various philosophers and social and political theorists.

DATE: c. 1688-1789

TYPE OF ETHICS: Enlightenment history

SIGNIFICANCE: The moral, social, and political philosophies developed during the Enlightenment shaped the later course of Western history. They are the basis for the liberal individualism which dominates modern moral and political theory and practice, including the principles of natural civil rights, the sovereign individual, government as a contract between the governing and the governed, and the primacy of reason in determining what is good and how to achieve it.

During the Enlightenment, the hundred-year period from 1688 to 1789, a diffuse group of political and philosophical leaders shared dynamic key ideas that reshaped the political and religious institutions of European culture, culminating in the establishment of the United States of America and the French Revolution. These ideas were in open conflict with the established beliefs of Christian churches and of the monarchical governments of that time.

The ideas of Enlightenment writers developed from two primary sources: the ancient classics of Greece and Rome and the Protestant movement within Christian Europe. Beginning with the Renaissance, when many "lost" works of ancient Greek and Roman writers were reintroduced into Europe, European students and scholars mastered Latin and Greek in order to know and appreciate these classics. Students studied, along with traditional religious works, many pre-Christian Latin and Greek texts, such as Plato's *Republic*. These pagan texts reintroduced ancient philosophical ideas to Europeans and sanctioned ethical views that contradicted Christian teachings, such as the idea that the power of reason, instead of faith, could lead humans to perform good actions.

The ancient Greek spirit of scientific inquiry also inspired this period. From the Renaissance on, well-educated men such as Francis Bacon and Isaac Newton applied principles of rational inquiry to the study of the natural world, and in doing so they established the scientific method of investigation as a powerful means of gaining new knowledge of the physical world. This mode of inquiry turned away from pious Christian thinking and toward empirical experience in the search for objective universal law. The practitioners of scientific investigation were tough-minded, worldly, and philosophical.

As a result of the Protestant religious movements of the previous centuries, education had become more widely available in northern European countries. This occurred because literacy was a necessary prerequisite for reading and interpreting the Bible as part of religious worship. This practice developed close critical reading and thinking skills, confidence in working with written texts, and tolerance for diverse views of religious topics. The tragic psychological and economic effects of religious persecution of Europe also had brought about a greater appreciation of religious tolerance.

In 1688, a change in England from absolute monarchy to constitutional government signaled the opening of the new age of the Enlightenment. The so-called Glorious Revolution, which banished the autocratic Roman Catholic king James II and substituted the Protestant king William with legally curtailed royal powers, was accomplished without war. This revolution successfully applied the idea that legitimate government was established by a legal contract between the people and their monarch, instead of by a divine right given to the monarch by God. This transformation of England's government and the surge of economic prosperity that followed it marked the beginning of radical social changes that culminated in the French Revolution in 1789.

ETHICAL PRINCIPLES

Tolerance for new ideas and confidence in the human power of reason as a means to achieve the good life characterize the core ethical views of Enlightenment thinkers. The human mind rather than sacred teachings and values became the focus of intellectual life as humankind's quest for life, liberty, and the pursuit of happiness on Earth gradually overshadowed a lifestyle of Christian values lived for rewards that would be received in a spiritual life after death. Although the vast majority of Europeans remained Christian, the leading thinkers, such as John Locke, Voltaire, David Hume, Immanuel Kant, and Jean-Jacques Rousseau, were often atheists, agnostics, or Deists. They regarded God's place in the world as remote or even nonexistent.

NATURAL MORALITY

The secular morality developed during the period conceives of humans using reason, not faith, to find the good life. Their well-developed faculty of reasoning and common sense, together with their natural desire for pleasure, can lead people to shun evil and pursue good. This process makes it possible for people to enjoy happiness, the goal and reward of living well, on Earth.

Concerning the basic nature of human beings, some leading thinkers claimed that people are inherently good and that their desire for pleasure, if guided by reason, can lead them to the good life. Other Enlightenment thinkers, however, asserted that humans are inherently neither good nor evil but are made good or evil by the environment in which they live.

Natural morality recognizes that an egoistic desire for pleasure and aesthetic enjoyment motivates human action and thought; thus, according to this idea, virtue is defined as creating the greatest happiness and pleasure for the greatest number of people. Therefore, a virtuous person expresses self-interest and self-love in a way that not only avoids causing pain in others, since all people have an equal right to experience pleasure and happiness, but also increases happiness for others.

HUMANISM

The natural morality of the Enlightenment emphasizes the fraternity of humankind in the shared innate faculty of reason, the shared innate desire for pleasure, and the universal power of education to bring happiness to all people. In theory, all people may pursue and find happiness by cultivating their reasoning powers, so fraternity may minimize political, economic, racial, and religious inequities. In fact, however, the political and social institutions of the time did not create equal opportunities for all to become educated and pursue the good life. Enlightenment ideas did promote a cosmopolitan spirit in Europe, since those accepting the idea of humanism acknowledged a bond of commonality stronger than those of nationalism and patriotism. The philosopher Rousseau declared, "There are no longer Frenchmen or Germans . . . there are only Europeans."

SCIENTIFIC INQUIRY

Scientific thinking developed and gained enormous credibility during the Enlightenment for several reasons. Science serves as an excellent means of exercising and developing the ability to reason, a faculty necessary to achieving happiness. It also promotes discussion and criticism and thus furthers more general education in society. Publications of experimental studies and meetings of scientific societies play an essential role in the growth of scientific thinking and are key components of scientific inquiry. During the Enlightenment, leading philosophers envisioned scientific inquiry and its fruits of inventions and discoveries about the natural world as the sure path to an ideal future life. Thus, the idea of progress through science to a perfect life sparked the imaginations of Enlightenment thinkers.

The qualities of reasonableness came to be regarded as those of good manners during the Enlightenment; it became fashionable to show in one's behavior rationality, tolerance, self-control, cordiality, partiality, and modesty. Good manners were not only an expression of humanity but also a humanizing way of behavior. Women also became more influential in public life, in part because of new ideas about manners and in part because women came to be regarded as reasonable beings instead of only as caretakers of the home, or as property.

RELIGION AND THE ENLIGHTENMENT

The role of religion in natural morality was a key issue during this period. Other significant issues were the roles of laws, education, and government in leading humankind to live the happy life.

With respect to religion, a powerful group of atheist thinkers, including David Hume and Denis Diderot, envisioned society totally without religion, with reason alone being able to guide people to a good life. Another group, including the brilliant and influential Voltaire, called themselves Deists and argued that humankind should recognize the role of the higher power of God in forming and sustaining the world.

All members of these groups agreed that European Christianity had failed to prepare humankind for a happy life and had instead destroyed its happiness. These groups allied themselves in passionate rejection of all Christian doctrines and rituals. Some asserted that Christianity was a disease that made society sick and therefore should be destroyed. "Crush the infamy!" (*Écrasez l'infame!*) became the slogan of Enlightenment philosophers as they endeavored to annihilate both the doctrines and the customs of the Roman Catholic and Protestant churches.

These philosophers wanted to replace religion with education and the development of reason to guide people to the good life. To accomplish their objective, a group of French Enlightenment thinkers prepared and published, in 1751, an impressive thirty-seven volume *Encylopédie*, a collection of all knowledge in a great scheme of education through reading. They also argued for separating schools, universities, and libraries from the control and influence of churches, the traditional custodians and guardians of educational institutions of Europe. Even though they, the enlightened ones, were the products of church-influenced education, they advocated a sharp break with tradition.

Supporters of Enlightenment ideas also expanded the scope of education to include decreasing crime through the education of criminals and delinquents; they assumed that wrong ideas and antisocial behavior could be changed by education. Enlightenment thinkers rejected the traditional basis of government, the divine right of kings as God's representatives on Earth to carry out a divine plan. Instead, they claimed, governments should be negotiated contracts between the governed subjects and the representatives of government. The role and responsibility of such governments should be to assist the people by promoting their happiness. Only those governments constituted by legal contract were believed to serve the best interests of the people they ruled. Thus, the Enlightenment thinkers dismissed traditional forms of government and the wisdom gained through centuries of trial and error. One issue related to the role of government and the governed is the right of people to reject a government that does not serve them well. Enlightenment philosophers defended this right and therefore supported the American Revolution and the French Revolution.

THE INFLUENCE OF ENLIGHTENMENT ETHICS

The ideas and ideals of the Enlightenment have had profound and lasting effects on government, education, and religion. Other social institutions, such as the family and marriage, have also been shaped by Enlightenment ideas.

The primary influence of the Enlightenment has been increased tolerance of diverse ideas and opinions, together with a shift away from orthodoxy. The modern ideals of open-mindedness and acceptance of diversity stem from the Enlightenment. The traditions of a free press with clearly limited government censorship and of a literate population that participates in a free exchange of ideas also are legacies of the period.

In the realm of government, one famous creation derived directly from Enlightenment ideas is the government of the United States. Established during the Enlightenment partly as a philosophical experiment, the U.S. government has remained a successful democracy for more than two hundred years. The Declaration of Independence, the first policy statement made in formulating that government, is regarded as a preeminent Enlightenment document of civil liberty. The United States government's humanistic ideals and policies have been relevant and flexible enough to have adapted to changing social and economic conditions for two centuries; also, it has served as a model for incorporating democratic elements into government institutions.

Regarding education, the tradition of humanistic learning as a means to becoming a well-rounded person continues to be valued today. In many colleges and universities, certain courses are labeled humanities or liberal arts subjects, in accordance with the Enlightenment concept of reason leading the individual to become a humane and liberal person.

Another related Enlightenment notion that survives in education today is the separation of church and school. The goals of education are perceived as distinct from, although related to, the goals of religion; as a result, the path of inquiry and knowledge need not conform to church doctrines, a key factor in the development of scientific thought.

The position of Christianity with reference to science was influenced dramatically by Enlightenment ideas. Before the Enlightenment, scientists had been imprisoned as heretics or agents of Satan, sometimes to be tortured and executed for holding forbidden ideas that had been censored by religious authorities; after this period, however, scientists were relatively free to pursue their investigations and experiments. In fact, the doctrines of Christian churches were attacked virulently by Enlightenment philosophers, and church leaders were forced into defensive positions on scientific issues such as the accuracy of biblical accounts of historical events.

Patricia H. Fulbright

FURTHER READING

Durant, Will, and Ariel Durant. *The Age of Voltaire: A History of Civilization in Western Europe from 1715 to 1756, with Special Emphasis on the Conflict Between Religion and Philosophy*. New York: Simon & Schuster, 1965. An excellent historical discussion of the period that refers to writings of key philosophers and philosophical works. This is a fine first text for a student of this topic, since it is readable and well organized.

Gay, Peter. *The Rise of Modern Paganism*. Vol. 1 in *The Enlightenment: An Interpretation*. New York: Alfred Knopf, 1967. Reprint. New York: Norton, 1977. A detailed scholarly discussion of ancient Greek and Roman texts and thinkers that influenced Enlightenment philosophers. This work traces the legacy of the classics and the conflict between pagan and Christian ideas.

_____. *The Science of Freedom*. Vol. 2 in *The Enlightenment: An Interpretation*. New York: Alfred Knopf, 1969. Reprint. New York: Norton, 1977. An excellent scholarly presentation of political issues related to Enlightenment philosophy. Includes a comprehensive bibliography and extensive notes.

Hazard, Paul. *European Thought in the Eighteenth Century from Montesquieu to Lessing*. Translated by J. Lewis May. Cleveland, Ohio: World, 1963. A criticism of major Enlightenment philosophers that focuses on their major ideas and works.

Horkheimer, Max, and Theodor W. Adorno. *Dialectic of Enlightenment: Philosophical Fragments*. Translated by Edmund Jephcott. Edited by Gunzelin Schmid Noerr. Stanford, Calif.: Stanford University Press, 2002. The most famous and influential of the Frankfurt School critiques of the Enlightenment and its legacy. Details the failures of reason in the West and relates Enlightenment rationality directly to the rise of fascism.

Hyland, Paul, Olga Gomez, and Francesca Greensides, eds. *The Enlightenment: A Sourcebook and Reader*. New York: Routledge, 2003. Anthology collecting both important source texts by Enlightenment thinkers and contemporary criticism on the subject. The source texts are organized by topic; sections include "Moral Principles and Punishments," "Political Rights and Responsibilities," and "The Development of Civil Society."

Kant, Immanuel. *Critique of Practical Reason*. Edited and translated by Lewis W. Beck. 3d ed. New York: Maxwell Macmillan, 1993.

_____. *Critique of Pure Reason*. Translated by Norman Kemp Smith. Introduction by Howard Caygill. Rev. 2d ed. New York: Palgrave Macmillan, 2003.

_____. *Critique of the Power of Judgment*. Edited by Paul Guyer. Translated by Paul Guyer and Eric Matthews. New York: Cambridge University Press, 2000. Kant's work is generally taken to be the culmination of all Enlightenment thought. In his Three Critiques, he synthesizes all the major philosophical schools of the period into a single, overarching system. The Second Critique, that of "practical reason," or reason based upon empirical experience, is the one which deals most directly with ethics.

SEE ALSO: Bacon, Francis; Deism; Hume, David; Kant, Immanuel; Kantian ethics; Leibniz, Gottfried Wilhelm; Locke, John; Montesquieu; Patriotism; Post-Enlightenment ethics; Rousseau, Jean-Jacques; Voltaire.

An Enquiry Concerning the Principles of Morals

IDENTIFICATION: Book by David Hume (1711-1776)
DATE: Published in 1751
TYPE OF ETHICS: Enlightenment history
SIGNIFICANCE: Hume's *Enquiry* represents the classic statement of British skeptical empiricism concerning moral and ethical issues.

Perhaps Great Britain's greatest philosopher, David Hume considered *An Enquiry Concerning the Principles of Morals* to be his finest work, a judgment shared by many of his contemporaries and later readers who admire the clarity and objectivity of his examination of a complex and complicated subject.

The *Enquiry* is in large part a revision and extension of book 3 of Hume's masterpiece *A Treatise of Human Nature*, in which he surveyed the full range of human psychology, but it is a much more concentrated review of the topic. In the *Enquiry*, Hume has two basic purposes. The first is to establish a method of writing about human ethical behavior; the second, to describe that behavior and explain its workings. In neither case, however, does Hume explicitly prescribe specific moral or ethical activities or values as "good," "bad," or even "indifferent." Instead, he objectively describes what actions and beliefs human beings have characteristically labeled "good" and "evil" and explains why those judgments have been rendered. In this sense, the *Enquiry* is a study of how human ethics operate rather than an argument for or against any particular ethical theory or system.

BENEVOLENCE AND JUSTICE

Seeking to build in the realm of philosophy upon the scientific achievements of Sir Isaac Newton, Hume attempted to discover the ultimate principles of human morality and ethics. In the *Enquiry*, Hume first examined what he considered the two most fundamental human and social virtues, benevolence and justice, which he viewed as the basis of both individual and communal happiness and progress.

In Hume's view, actions are accounted ethical or good by human beings for one or both of two reasons: either because they appeal to human sympathy or because they serve the purpose of social utility. In other words, actions appear to be good or worthwhile either in themselves or because they make human intercourse not only possible but also enjoyable and profitable.

Benevolence is valued because it appeals instinctively to human sympathy, in large part because almost every individual can appreciate how personally beneficial benevolence can be. In addition, Hume notes, human beings connect benevolence with social good. When a benevolent person is praised, there is always mention, and therefore recognition, of the good or satisfaction that he or she brings to the general community, because the inherent appeal to human sympathy is reinforced by the call of social utility.

Justice, however, is viewed by Hume as having a purely utilitarian function, primarily because he has defined the word in rather narrow terms and is concerned with property relationships rather than human or social affairs. These Hume discusses under the heading of impartiality as an aspect of fully moral judgment. In the usual run of human experience, Hume states, justice is a matter of what best serves the individual or society in terms of the overall situation. For example, nations habitually suspend traditional rules of international law during warfare because to adhere to them would impose obvious and, in Hume's and humanity's view, unwarranted disadvantages. In the largest sense, then, human law and justice are nothing more than agreed-upon conventions that advance the common good of all human beings.

Hume provides a variety of examples to demonstrate that justice is valued for its utility to human society and that it is defined by that utility. For example, respect for property is universally acknowledged as an element of justice, but if an honest man is captured by outlaws, he acts in accordance with justice if he seizes his captors' weapons and uses them against them. Practical utility, rather than abstract idealism, is the determining factor of human considerations of justice.

UTILITY IS THE BASIS OF VIRTUES

Hume's intellectual background made him the successor of philosophers John Locke and Bishop George Berkeley. Locke had rejected the concept of innate ideas in his famous concept of the mind as a *tabula rasa*, or blank slate, upon which outside impressions were engraved, while Berkeley argued that abstract ideas did not exist and that only sense perception confirmed, and perhaps even established, the reality of objects outside the mind. Building upon these precepts, Hume established a rigorous skepticism that sought to replace abstruse metaphysical reasoning with practical logic.

Hume argued that the real basis of all human virtues was utility, or how well these particular beliefs and actions served to advance and preserve human society. He rejected the view proposed by Thomas Hobbes that all human beings acted primarily out of selfish interests; instead, he stated that there was a natural sympathy among human beings that recognized and appreciated virtues such as humanity, friendship, truthfulness, and courage. Hume further proposed that these virtues were judged according to a universal standard of utility, which in the moral sphere corresponded to the physical laws discovered and enunciated by Newton.

MORAL JUDGMENT AND SENTIMENT

Finally, Hume made a distinction between judgments based on reason and those based on sentiment. The first kind of decision plays but a relatively small part in moral life. Rationality is primarily used in determining objective truths, such as those of mathematics, which are independent of human beings. Situations calling for a moral or ethical response, however, incite a response that is emotional rather than strictly rational. Reason may be necessary to determine the complexities of a certain situation, but once the essence has been established, sentiment determines how one will act. As Hume puts it, the moral response "cannot be the work of the judgment, but of the heart."

In Hume's view, then, human morals are subjective in that they depend upon the internal, emotional response of the individual. Since there is a universal bond among human beings that creates a single standard for moral actions, however, this subjectivity is tempered by a common unity that can be discovered by empirical study.

Michael Witkoski

FURTHER READING

Ayer, A. J. *Hume.* 1980. Reprint. Very Short Introductions 33. New York: Oxford University Press, 2000.

Baillie, James. *Routledge Philosophy Guidebook to Hume on Morality.* New York: Routledge, 2000.

Flew, Antony. *David Hume: Philosopher of Moral Science.* New York: Basil Blackwell, 1986.

Mackie, John Leslie. *Hume's Moral Theory.* Boston: Routledge & Kegan Paul, 1980.

MacNabb, D. G. C. "David Hume." In *The Encyclopedia of Philosophy,* edited by Paul Edwards. Vol. 4. New York: Macmillan, 1972.

Morice, G. P., ed. *David Hume: Bicentenary Papers.* Austin: University of Texas Press, 1977.

Russell, Paul. *Freedom and Moral Sentiment: Hume's Way of Naturalizing Responsibility.* New York: Oxford University Press, 2002.

SEE ALSO: Hobbes, Thomas; Hume, David; Locke, John; Morality; Utilitarianism.

Entitlements

DEFINITION: Rights, usually in the form of benefits, conferred by law or contract
TYPE OF ETHICS: Politico-economic ethics
SIGNIFICANCE: The nature of entitlements—particularly so-called welfare entitlements in the United States and under international law—has been a flash point for political debate as to what an ethical society can or should be.

Legal entitlements may arise either from legislative acts or from some more fundamental sources, such as the U.S. Constitution. While virtually any nondiscretionary government benefit, whatever its purpose, may be characterized as an "entitlement," discussions of the ethics of entitlements usually focus on programs designed to support basic human needs for individuals living in poverty. Such so-called welfare rights or welfare entitlements have been the subject of intensive political and legal debate.

In the 1970 case of *Goldberg v. Kelly*, the U.S. Supreme Court found welfare benefits to be a matter of "statutory entitlement" for those persons qualified to receive them. Characterizing these benefits as "entitlements" generates procedural requirements to which government must adhere when determining eligibility to benefits or terminating benefits. The notion of "welfare" itself as an entitlement, however, underwent a sea change in the United States with the passage by Congress of the Personal Responsibility and Work Opportunity Reconciliation Act of 1996. Among things, the act explicitly stated that it should not be interpreted as an entitlement to welfare assistance.

Debates about welfare entitlements tend to focus on cash assistance. Legal entitlements to "subsistence"—apart from cash assistance, such as to food, shelter, and medical care—have yet to be recognized, at least at the national level in the United States. Some commentators have noted, however, that the exercise of well-established rights, such as the right to free speech, necessarily presupposes adequate levels of food, shelter, and medical care, for a speaker could not engage in expressive speech without them.

At bottom, legal, political, and philosophical debates about legal entitlements are often generated by divergent views on the responsibility of government to ensure minimal standards of living and on the role that personal responsibility plays in generating poverty.

THE INTERNATIONAL DEBATE

Apart from the domestic debates, considerable attention has been paid to welfare entitlements and subsistence rights in international law. The International Covenant on Economic, Social and Cultural Rights of 1966 proclaims a right to "adequate food, clothing, and housing." Through 2003, however, the United States had failed to ratify this covenant, and the economic privations of some countries that have ratified it ensure that its language will not translate into a meaningful and enforceable entitlement. In the international sphere, as in the domestic sphere, in order for the status of legal entitlements to rise above rhetoric, they must be viewed in the context of the distribution of wealth and the eradication of poverty.

Robert Rubinson

FURTHER READING

Cimini, Christine A. "Welfare Entitlements in the Age of Devolution." *Geographical Journal on Poverty Law and Policy* 89 (2002).

Chemerinsky, Erwin. *Constitutional Law: Principles and Policies.* 2d ed. New York: Aspen Law & Business, 2002.

Trattner, Walter I. *From Poor Law to Welfare State: A History of Social Welfare in America.* 6th ed. New York: Free Press, 1999.

Tribe, Laurence. *American Constitutional Law.* 3d ed. New York: Foundation Press, 2000.

SEE ALSO: Gratitude; Homeless care; Poverty; Rights and obligations; Social justice and responsibility; Welfare programs; Welfare rights.

Environmental ethics

DEFINITION: Standard of conduct which treats the preservation of the integrity of the environment as a moral good and the needless destruction of any part of nature as a moral evil

TYPE OF ETHICS: Environmental ethics

SIGNIFICANCE: In contrast to many other branches of moral thought, environmental ethics is based primarily upon the concept of obligation—recognizing obligations to the natural world, future generations, and one another—rather than upon virtues, rights, or freedoms.

Humans have long exploited nature in the belief that their planet was so vast and enduring that people could never inflict devastating harm on it. Events since the 1980's have called this perception into question. Half the biospheric change caused by humans has taken place since World War II. Humans have transformed or manipulated half the ice-free ecosystems on the planet and have made a significant impact on most of the rest. People have steadily reduced the number of other species in the world through pollution, hunting, and the destruction of natural habitat.

Projections vary. Some argue that if human activity continues at the present rate, within a few decades humans will "overshoot" the carrying capacity of the biosphere and precipitate a collapse. Other scientists say that the earth itself is in no danger at the hands of humans. Still others acknowledge harm to the biosphere but justify it because of the benefits received from growth, development, and technology. They assert that some degree of harm to the biosphere is a cost of the Western lifestyle. Increasingly, complex problems are reduced to a "jobs or owls" choice.

Is it possible to prevent broad damage to the biosphere while accommodating the economic needs of a growing population? The answer is no, unless the world adopts a new model for environmental ethics—one based on common values. Once people agree at a values level, they can begin to communicate and develop solutions to perhaps the greatest challenge faced by humanity.

DO NO HARM—UNLESS . . .

Much of the debate about business and the environment has involved harm versus benefits. Industrial accidents happen, factories shut down, the stock market takes a plunge, pollutants are released into the atmosphere; in all cases, some people suffer harm. The benefits of economic activity are weighed against the harm they cause. In this model of environmental ethics, decisions are based on whether the harm is offset to a significant extent by a corresponding benefit. For example, clear-cutting tropical rain forests causes long-term ecological harm. That harm may outweigh any immediate economic concerns, but the argument is that stopping the activity would deprive many people of their only means of livelihood and further impoverish developing countries. If one can prove that its benefits outweigh its harmful effects, then a destructive activity is permitted. Few people disagree with this trade-off, provided it protects existing human beings. The controversy occurs when people consider the harm done to future generations of humans, animals, plants, or the planet itself.

Costs and profits guide corporate behavior in this ethical model. If an incident's long-term damage is small, it pays to adopt a strategy of reaction or defense. If the long-term damage is perceived to be high, the strategy should be one of proaction or accommodation.

Introduced during the 1960's, this management model, called the mechanistic school, entails an anthropocentric view in which humanity perceives itself to be the center and ultimate goal of the universe, viewing the environment as existing for its convenience. Nature is viewed as a mere storehouse of raw materials for human use. The environment is seen as relatively stable, unlimited, and well understood. Although many businesses now embrace newer models of environmental decision making, many large, hierarchical, rigid corporations are stuck at this level.

During the 1970's came the organic school. In this more adaptive model of decision making, the goal is the exploitation of rapid changes through innovations and the exploration of new opportunities. It views the environment as highly unpredictable, turbulent, dangerous, and presenting unlimited new market opportunities.

Organizations embracing this model look for opportunities in the environmental movement. Consumers and investors are voting with their dollars, and businesses see the opportunities. Sacha Millstone and Ferris Baker Watts, in *The Greening of American Business* (1992), cite surveys indicating that 77 percent of Americans say that a company's environmental reputation affects what they buy. Too often, however, businesses operating in this management model exploit the trend rather than integrate and fully embrace environmental responsibility.

One example of this type of thinking is explored in David Chittick's writings in *The Greening of American Business*. Chittick makes a strong financial case for proactive environmental programs. By being en-

vironmentally responsible, a corporation can save millions of dollars by avoiding costs of waste disposal, costs of penalties and fines for noncompliance, costs of handling hazardous materials (insurance, protective equipment), costs of negative publicity, and costs of decreased employee morale and community confidence. The emphasis, however, is on taking advantage of the opportunity presented by environmental programs.

SHIFT TO BIOCENTRISM

By the late 1980's, more and more individuals and businesses began shifting to a model of environmental ethics that embraces biocentrism, viewing the planet Earth as a living system of interdependent species. This approach's "do no harm" principle provides an adaptive model of decision making. It takes a holistic view in which ethical and environmental considerations enter into all decisions. A balance is sought between organizational goals and environmentally based values. The environment is viewed as fragile, limited in resources, and vulnerable to organizational actions. The approach sees the planet as a community of life-forms in which each contributes to and depends upon all the others.

Every act of pollution and resource depletion is viewed not as an isolated event, but as a contributing factor to a collective impact of increasingly accelerating global proportions. As Brian Edwards Brown, an attorney and professor at Iona College, explains: "Nature is not merely an object of anthropocentric concern, an environment that, if contaminated or otherwise damaged, interferes with human use and enjoyment. . . . Nature is a subject in its own right, a totality of diverse, unique, interdependent life-forms, of which the human is but one and without which the human would not be possible."

A DIFFERENCE OF VALUES

The difference in values prohibits the development of workable solutions. The anthropocentric view is the older one. The biocentric view reflects strides that the science of ecology has made in discovering and understanding the intricate interdependence of species, as well as the interconnectedness of their habitats. It reflects an increased understanding of the environment and its problems. It is an ethically based view. These value differences contribute to difficulties in communication between holders of the two views. They lead to mistrust and misinterpretation of the other's arguments and proposals.

Both groups have an obligation to seek to understand the other's views and arguments. Candid, honest, and respectful communication can lead to the creation of shared values. Communication should include education. The anthropocentrics should un-

dertake to know and understand the workings and interdependencies of the biosphere. The biocentrics should seek to understand the concerns of business. A holistic view considers all the parts of the problem. It is not realistic to attempt to eliminate all business, to retreat to a lifestyle of a prior century, or to prevent growth in developing countries. People must, how-

The Valdez Principles

Protection of the biosphere	"Minimize and strive to eliminate the release of any pollutant that may cause environmental damage to the air, water, or earth or its inhabitants."
Sustainable use of natural resources	"Make sustainable use of renewable natural resources, such as water, soils and forests . . . conserve nonrenewable resources through efficient use and careful planning . . . protect wildlife habitat, open spaces, and wilderness, while preserving biodiversity."
Reduction and disposal of waste	"Minimize the creation of waste, especially hazardous waste, and wherever possible recycle materials . . . dispose of all waste through safe and responsible methods."
Wise use of energy	"Make every effort to use environmentally safe and sustainable energy sources . . . invest in improved energy efficiency and conservation . . . maximize the energy efficiency of products" produced or sold.
Risk reduction	"Minimize the environmental, health and safety risks to . . . employees and the communities . . . by employing safe technologies and operating procedures and by being constantly prepared for emergencies."
Marketing of safe products and services	"Sell products or services that minimize adverse environmental impacts and that are safe as consumers commonly use them. Inform consumers of the environmental impacts" of products and services.
Damage compensation	"Take responsibility for any harm . . . caused to the environment by making every effort to fully restore the environment and to compensate those persons who are adversely affected."
Disclosure	Disclose to employees and to the public incidents or potential harm caused by the operation relating to environmental harm or that pose health or safety hazards. Take no action "against employees who report any condition that creates a danger to the environment or poses health and safety hazards."
Environmental directors and managers	Put on the board of directors at least one member "qualified to represent environmental interests." Demonstrate the commitment to these principles by funding an "office of vice president for environmental affairs or an equivalent position, reporting directly to the CEO, to monitor and report" the implementation efforts.
Assessment and annual audit	Conduct and make public an annual self-evaluation of progress in implementing these principles and complying with all applicable laws and regulations throughout worldwide operations.

ever, evaluate the ways in which they live and make appropriate changes. People must consider ethics and the environment in all of their decision making.

WE ARE ALL RESPONSIBLE

If, for example, one asks who is responsible for the pollution caused by automobiles, the answer is the auto manufacturers, the gasoline manufacturers, the auto users, and perhaps even the members of the community that do not provide mass transportation. Everyone shares the responsibility, and everyone must work together for solutions.

Environmental problems are ethical dilemmas. People begin to solve any ethical dilemma with an acknowledgment of facts and perceptions. Next, with a new model, people change their perception of the biosphere and their relationship to it. Then, as in solving all ethical dilemmas, it is necessary to begin with an analysis of the alternatives and their various effects on each stakeholder. A new model of environmental ethics broadens the stakeholder concept. The old model did not include all components of the biosphere, or future generations, as stakeholders. It is not surprising that the solutions put forth have been less than adequate. With the stakeholder analysis complete, it is possible to proceed to synthesis, choice, action, and communication.

This new model creates a permanent shift in the way business operates. With an environmental ethics view, the mission of a corporation is to "manage in an ethical and effective manner in order to maximize shareholder value," replacing the less restrictive, "maximize shareholder value."

In 1989, the Coalition for Environmentally Responsible Economies (CERES) adopted the Valdez Principles, which define guidelines for responsible corporate behavior regarding the environment. Although the Valdez Principles are a good start, they are noticeably general. They do not identify specific standards of conduct. There are also loopholes, in that these principles are expressed in terms of "take every effort" or "minimize." Still, they set the stage for a new look at environmental ethics.

Collaboration is a key word in successful environmental programs. For example, a joint effort of the Environmental Defense Fund and McDonald's Corporation sought solutions to McDonald's environmental problems. The organizations jointly commissioned four scientists to examine ways in which

McDonald's could reduce and recycle waste. The result was a set of sound proposals, including the phasing out of bleached paper; the testing of reusable cups, coffee filters, and shipping containers; the use of recycled materials; and continuing experimentation.

More and more companies are looking at what consultant Joel S. Hirschhorn calls taking a total approach to environmental ethics. In this approach, the company culture is permanently changed to include environmental values. Since culture can be broadly defined as the collection of the individual values of the people in the organization, a total approach must begin with individuals. It recognizes the importance of having every person in the organization passionately interested in environmental responsibility.

In this new model, a company does not look at regulatory compliance, which concentrates on better management of wastes and control of pollutants. It looks instead at the beginning of the process—at what the company produces, how it produces it, and how it markets its products and services.

An example of this new type of company is The Body Shop, which not only uses posters, pamphlets, and window displays in the shop to promote environmental messages but also starts with the product. The Body Shop manufactures and markets naturally based skin and hair products. It actively seeks out suppliers in remote parts of the world, including many developing countries. It has an ambitious recycling program and does not test cosmetics on animals. Its marketing programs do not promote idealized notions of beauty or claim that the company's products will perform cosmetic miracles. Practicing what it preaches, The Body Shop encourages its employees to devote time and energy to volunteer projects in their communities.

FIRST STEPS

Hirschhorn calls for setting three priorities in redefining the corporate culture: First, focus on people and the corporate culture to develop and deepen the commitment to corporate environmental responsibility. Second, focus on technology, manufacturing facilities, and products to improve environmental performance. Third, focus on products and customers to incorporate effective "green marketing" into the strategic planning of the firm.

A significant first step was taken in June, 1992,

when most of the world's top political, spiritual, and business leaders gathered with leading environmentalists in Rio de Janeiro for the historic United Nations Conference on Environment and Development—the Earth Summit. The purpose of the Summit was to reconcile the conflicting demands of the environment and development into global strategies that will ensure a viable future. Among the Summit's accomplishments were the following:

Establishing the environment as an international issue—a point of transition on how to deal with global issues.

An agreement on the concept that human development and protection of the earth's environment are inextricably intertwined.

A legally binding treaty that recommends curbing emissions of carbon dioxide, methane, and other "greenhouse" gases thought to warm the climate by trapping the sun's heat close to Earth.

A legally binding treaty that requires making inventories of plants and wildlife and planning to protect endangered species.

A realization of the difficulties of negotiating worldwide solutions to worldwide problems.

Gathering together the greatest number of world leaders ever assembled with a single aim.

The creation of a Sustainable Development Commission to monitor compliance with the promises made at Rio. The commission will rely on evidence gathered by private environmental groups and will use peer pressure and public opinion to shame countries into following the policies agreed to at the Summit.

The realization that there is no common model for environmental ethics. There is a gap between those who say that humans are at the center of concerns and those who say that by putting humans at the center of things, with the implied right to dominate and exploit the rest of nature, humans perpetuate existing problems and create new ones.

The Earth Summit, by its very purpose, was a major step toward adopting a new model for environmental ethics. The human species now ranks with grand natural forces such as volcanoes as a transformer of the earth's life-support system. The model that people will embrace to solve environment and

development conflicts will determine not only the very survival of the human race but also the quality of life for future generations.

Kathleen D. Purdy

FURTHER READING

Attfield, Robin. *Environmental Ethics: An Overview for the Twenty-First Century.* Malden, Mass.: Blackwell, 2003. Surveys the field through both theoretical discussion and practical case studies; argues in favor of consequentialist and objectivist ethics.

Gore, Albert. *Earth in the Balance: Ecology and the Human Spirit.* Boston: Houghton Mifflin, 1992. Embracing the new model in environmental ethics, Gore argues that only a radical rethinking of the human/Earth relationship can save Earth's ecology for future generations. The book presents a comprehensive plan for action.

Hargrove, Eugene. *Foundations of Environmental Ethics.* Englewood Cliffs, N.J.: Prentice-Hall, 1989. Presents a justification for protecting nature using an argument called "ecocentric holism."

Light, Andrew, and Holmes Rolston III, eds. *Environmental Ethics: An Anthology.* Malden, Mass.: Blackwell, 2003. A comprehensive collection of essays, representing both traditional work and more innovative points of view. Both mainstream and alternative approaches to the field are included.

National Conference on Business Ethics. *Business, Ethics, and the Environment: The Public Policy Debate.* Edited by W. Michael Hoffman, Robert Frederick, and Edward S. Petry, Jr. New York: Quorum Books, 1990. A collection of essays addressing the public policy questions of how and whether to regulate corporations to deal with important environmental issues.

_____. *The Corporation, Ethics, and the Environment.* Edited by W. Michael Hoffman, Robert Frederick, and Edward S. Petry, Jr. New York: Quorum Books, 1990. A companion book to *Business, Ethics, and the Environment.* This collection addresses the role of business in protecting the environment. Presents a series of cases and analyses, corporate strategies, and suggestions.

Scherer, Donald, and Thomas Attig, eds. *Ethics and the Environment.* Englewood Cliffs, N.J.: Prentice-

Hall, 1983. A basic book that puts forth a range of ecocentric approaches to environmental issues.

Sullivan, Thomas F. P., ed. *The Greening of American Business*. Rockville, Md.: Government Institute, 1992. Readings on the impact of the green movement on business. Topics include labeling, liability, market opportunities, and investing.

SEE ALSO: Clean Air Act; Clean Water Act; Deep ecology; Dominion over nature, human; Ecology; Environmental movement; Environmental Protection Agency; Gaia hypothesis; Muir, John; Nature, rights of.

Environmental movement

IDENTIFICATION: Cooperative effort of individuals, organizations, and governments to make others aware of environmental issues and attempt to solve environmental problems

DATE: Began during the 1960's

TYPE OF ETHICS: Environmental ethics

SIGNIFICANCE: The environmental movement has successfully changed the ways in which many people in industrial societies understand their relationship to the environment. It has also created controversy in the business world, where it is sometimes perceived as an obstacle to maximizing profits.

The environmental movement—if it can properly be called a "movement"—is a loose, shifting, often sharply divided coalition of individuals and organizations concerned about environmental degradation. The modern movement began during the early 1960's, prompted by Rachel Carson's book *Silent Spring* (1962) and by concern over nuclear war and weapons testing, overpopulation, and the damage caused by postwar growth and technology.

Silent Spring was a widely read account of how pesticides damaged the environment. In 1963, in the face of industry attacks on Carson and her book, President Kennedy's Science Advisory Committee reviewed pesticide use, confirmed Carson's conclusions, and issued a call for legislative measures to safeguard the land and its people against pesticides and industrial toxins. In 1970, the Environmental

Protection Agency (EPA) was established, and in 1972 it banned production and use of DDT in the United States. Within fifteen years of *Silent Spring*'s publication, Congress enacted the Endangered Species Act (1972), the Pesticide Control Act (1972), the Clean Air Act (1977), and other landmark environmental legislation. Carson's poetics were thus transformed into public policy.

GOVERNMENT INVOLVEMENT

Since its founding, the EPA has grown to more than thirty times its original size. Moreover, dozens of other federal agencies and hundreds of state agencies, bureaus, and services deal with the environment. Around the turn of the twenty-first century, however, successful efforts were made in Congress and the executive branch to repeal or loosen laws and regulations in the name of economic efficiency.

Internationally, the United Nations Environment Programme has been called upon to coordinate the environmental efforts of numerous U.N. bodies with diverse international and regional organizations, both governmental and private sector. The Regional Seas Programme, for example, fosters cooperation among 140 nations to improve environmental quality in thirteen regional seas, including the Mediterranean, Caribbean, Red, and Black Seas.

DIVERSE APPROACHES

The environmental movement in the United States is diverse and fragmented. Constituents differ not only in their approaches to environmental action but also in their philosophies. Most of the movement—mirroring American society—is from the Western anthropocentric tradition holding that, to one degree or another, the environment is here for the benefit of humankind and that the purpose of the environmental movement, whether through preservation or conservation or development of new resources or efficiencies, is to benefit people. This is exemplified historically by Theodore Roosevelt and Gifford Pinchot's efforts to create a National Park System and by twenty-first century environmentalists who would open the national forests to logging and recreation. At the other end of the spectrum are the ecophilosophers who view human beings and their culture as part of the seamless web of nature. They trace their roots to sources as varied as St. Francis of Assisi, Zen Buddhism, Baruch Spinoza, and Daoism.

Represented by deep ecologists and the Gaia movement, their emphasis is on the necessity of adapting human behavior to nature's terms, rather than controlling nature for the benefit of human beings.

This broad range is reflected in the variety of organizations in the United States. Conservationist organizations constitute the largest category; these broad-based membership groups, such as the Sierra Club, are typically moderate in their positions. Legalist organizations, such as the Environmental Defense Fund and the Natural Resources Defense Council, were founded to litigate environmental issues and are fighting to build a body of case law establishing a right to a clean environment. Other groups have a strong grassroots presence, professing citizen empowerment—getting ordinary people involved in local environmental problems. They may not have significant technical expertise, but they are experts on local conditions.

Outside the mainstream, organizations such as Earth First!, the Earth Liberation Front, and People for the Ethical Treatment of Animals (PETA) have opted for direct, often illegal, action aimed at halting or delaying projects they deem environmentally unsound. The nature of their activities—heavily inspired by Edward Abbey's novel *The Monkey-Wrench Gang* (1975)—makes reliable data difficult to obtain, but destruction of sport utility vehicles (SUVs), sabotage of earth-moving equipment, release of laboratory animals, and arson at construction sites in environmentally sensitive areas make occasional headlines. The Sea Shepherds carry out similar, sometimes illegal, operations against whaling and other controversial maritime activities, but do so openly.

Influence

Environmental groups that were on the political fringes as 1960's activists were integral parts of the political process by the twenty-first century. The Green Party, though never gaining more than a few percent of votes nationally, has won local offices and may have altered the course of the 2000 presidential election, in which its candidate, Ralph Nader, may have taken away votes that would have given Democrat Al Gore the election. Some organizations have acquired economic clout similar to that of large industrial concerns. Greenpeace's worldwide revenues, for example, amounted to $175 million in 2000. If the annual revenues of all the conservation groups in the United States were collected together, the sum would exceed $1 billion. This political and economic success has spawned countermovements and even sham environmental organizations, set up by industries to advance their positions under the guise of environmentalism. One influential countermovement is the Wise Use Movement, which borrowed its name from Gifford Pinchot but fights environmental preservation and regulation.

Religious Concerns

Environmental movements began to take root in the religious community simultaneously with the birth of the popular movement. Early evangelical thinking suggested that the chief value of creation was to fuel human industry, but in 1961, at the World Council of Churches Assembly in New Delhi, Lutheran theologian Joseph Sittler pointed out the declining health of the world's environment, sparking widespread Christian concern over environmental issues. In 1967, *Science* published an address by Lynn White, "Historic Roots of Our Ecologic Crisis." It asserted that through such ideas as human dominion, the desacralizing of nature, and the belief that ultimate human destiny is with God and not with Earth, Christendom has encouraged a destructive use of creation. Christian missions and relief organizations have come to recognize that environmental and developmental needs are not only compatible but also inseparable. During the 1990's, a significant environmental movement began developing within evangelical and Pentecostal Christianity.

The Islamic concept of *khalifa* rejects the Judeo-Christian doctrine of human dominion over creation, holding stewardship of the earth to be humankind's sacred duty, a concept also long held in several strains of Judaic theology. Care for the natural environment and the rights of animals and natural resources play a fundamental role in *sharīʿa*, Muslim religious law. In stark contrast to James Watt, a fundamentalist Christian and former U.S. secretary of the interior who denied the importance of environmental stewardship in light of the impending destruction of the earth on doomsday, the Prophet Muḥammad said: "When doomsday comes, if someone has a palm shoot in his hand, he should plant it."

The aboriginal religions of the Americas and Australasia have inspired considerable activism with their emphases on the interrelatedness of land, knowledge, and human identity. A common theme is reverence for the land and the incomprehensibility of treating it as a commodity, to be bought and sold.

CRITICAL ISSUES

Many view overpopulation as the most serious environmental problem in the twenty-first century and the root of most other problems. Modern Malthusians, such as Paul Ehrlich and Garrett Hardin, predict that population will eventually outstrip resources and cause widespread poverty, starvation, and general disaster. Some governments have tried to encourage or mandate small families, with some success, but most leave this to individual families. In U.S. constitutional law, family-planning decisions constitute a fundamental right, subject only to narrow governmental interference under the most compelling circumstances. The population issue is vexing for religious groups concerned about the environment, as many oppose certain birth-control methods such as contraception and especially abortion.

Another concern of the environmental movement, spanning national boundaries, is that of nuclear weapons and energy. The threat of nuclear weapons proliferation appears not to have ended with the Cold War, as many had hoped. "Rogue states" and terrorists have replaced the Soviet Union as the West's primary concern. Even peaceful uses of nuclear energy pose serious threats. The 1979 accident at the Three Mile Island nuclear power plant, which called the American public's attention to the dangers of nuclear energy, paled in comparison to Soviet-era incidents at Chernobyl and the lesser-known but far more serious accidents at Chelyabinsk during the 1950's and 1960's. Since then, people of the Chelyabinsk region have become the core of the young but growing environmental movement in Russia.

A dilemma facing modern environmentalists is that nuclear technology promises cheap energy without depleting nonrenewable fossil fuels or polluting the atmosphere with burned hydrocarbons—on its face an environmentalist's dream. Opponents reply that "cheap" does not include the price of health and environmental threats or the yet-unknown costs of long-term disposal of nuclear waste, which has a half-life of up to fifty thousand years. On the whole, the environmental movement favors replacing nuclear energy with solar energy and renewable organic sources such as ethanol made from grain.

The U.S. government's announcement in 2004 that it intends to put astronauts on Mars by the year 2030 was certain to ignite another environmental debate, over the ethics of militarization, colonization, and exploitation of the resources of outer space.

David R. Teske
Updated by William V. Dunlap

FURTHER READING

Desjardins, Joseph R. *Environmental Ethics: An Introduction to Environmental Philosophy.* Belmont, Calif.: Wadsworth, 1993.

Dobson, Andrew, ed. *Green Political Thought.* 3d ed. New York: Routledge, 2000.

Jamieson, Dale. *A Companion to Environmental Philosophy.* Oxford: Blackwell, 2003.

Marietta, Don E., and Lester Enbree, eds. *Environmental Philosophy and Environmental Activism.* Lanham, Md.: Rowman & Littlefield, 1995.

Miller, G. Tyler, Jr. *Environmental Science: Working with the Earth.* Belmont, Calif.: Wadsworth, 1997.

Sessions, George, ed. *Deep Ecology for the Twenty-first Century.* Boston: Shambhala, 1995.

Stone, Christopher D. *Should Trees Have Standing? And Other Essays on Law, Morals, and the Environment.* Dobbs Ferry, N.Y.: Oceana, 1996.

Walker, Melissa. *Reading the Environment.* New York: W. W. Norton, 1994.

SEE ALSO: Conservation; Earth and humanity; Earth Day; Ecology; Endangered species; Environmental ethics; Environmental Protection Agency; Green parties; Greenpeace; Sierra Club; *Silent Spring.*

Environmental Protection Agency

IDENTIFICATION: Independent federal government agency responsible for the development, implementation, and direction of all federal environmental management programs in the United States

DATE: Established on December 2, 1970

TYPE OF ETHICS: Environmental ethics

SIGNIFICANCE: The Environmental Protection Agency (EPA) monitors and regulates industrial activity in order to protect the well-being of the nation's environment and the health of its citizens.

President Richard M. Nixon created the EPA by Executive Order, as Reorganization Plan 3 of 1970 (dated July 9, 1970) to be effective December 2, 1970. The Reorganization Plan brought fifteen separate components of five executive departments and agencies with programs related to the environment under one independent executive agency that reported directly to the president.

The EPA took responsibility for the control of pollution in seven environmental areas: air, water, solid and hazardous waste, pesticides, toxic substances, radiation, and noise. The EPA was created in response to rising public concerns about the increasing degradation of the environment in those areas. The job given to the EPA was to set and enforce standards that would adequately protect the environment, which constituted an acknowledgment of the seriousness of the problems of pollution and a recognition of the interrelated nature of environmental problems. The role of the EPA grew over time as the U.S. Congress passed more environmental protection legislation, although the issues upon which the EPA focuses shift from public health to the ecological depending on political and social concerns of the times.

Sandra L. Christensen

SEE ALSO: Clean Air Act; Clean Water Act; Congress; Environmental ethics; Environmental movement; Pollution permits; Toxic waste; Wilderness Act of 1964.

Envy

DEFINITION: Ill-will toward those who have what one lacks

TYPE OF ETHICS: Personal and social ethics

SIGNIFICANCE: Traditionally listed among the "seven deadly sins," envy can motivate immoral actions as well as damage the relationships or happiness of the person feeling it.

Envy is precipitated by occasions in which another person enjoys something that, though valued greatly, is lacked by the person who is subject to the envy. The other's enjoyment and the person's lack are not by themselves sufficient to result in the experience of envy; the lack of the good thing must be regarded by the individual as evil, and must be so regarded simply because the other person possesses that good. A salient feature of this vice is that the envious individual's actual deprivation of the good at issue need not be caused by the envied person's possession of that good (as if there was "not enough to go around").

The envious response in such circumstances is felt as a gnawing, resentful anguish over the other person's possession or achievement of a good. Less frequently, joy may be felt when evils befall the envied person. Several types of desires typically arise in the envious person. First is the impulse to deny (to oneself and others) that one lacks the good at issue. Second is the urge to deny (to oneself and others) that the person who is envied really does possess the good for which he or she is envied. Third is the urge to deny that the envied one really does enjoy the good possessed or achieved. Finally, and most common, is the drive to disparage and denigrate the good that the other is acknowledged to possess and enjoy. The actions that all these desires prompt the envious person to choose may be manifested either in thought or in word and deed. If the envy is strong enough, the person may be prompted actually to destroy the good possessed by the one who is envied ("If I can't have it, no one can!"). This result of extreme envy is one reason why the vice is especially deadly; the other reason concerns the effect of the vice on the one who is envious.

Most vices appear to bring good at least to their practitioners; for example, a glutton derives pleasure from overindulgence, a slothful person enjoys chronic relaxation, and so forth. Envy, however, essentially involves a painful experience of deficiency or privation and accordingly is both agonizing to experience and difficult to acknowledge to oneself. Furthermore, the vice wreaks havoc with the envier's own system of values. As noted above, envy naturally leads to the urge to denigrate a good thing enjoyed by someone else. If this urge is acted upon, then the pain caused by the experience of deficiency (in the light of the other's enjoyment) is assuaged, since the object of envy no longer appears to be so good. The envious desire has prompted one to act, however, in a way that negates (at least in thought) precisely what one values.

MANIFESTATIONS OF ENVY

This most deadly vice has manifestations at the level of society; the object of envy can be the types of goods enjoyed by a whole class of people, in addition to a specific good enjoyed by a specific person. The "have-nots" may envy the "haves" for the great goods they enjoy. Because of this possibility, the haves may accuse the have-nots of merely acting out of envy when they (the have-nots) demand, in the name of justice, changes in society. This correlates with the accusation against the haves by the have-nots of merely acting out of avarice when they (the haves) demand, in the name of justice, maintenance of the status quo. The desire to *be* envied and the counter-tending *fear* of being envied must also be considered among the social aspects of this vice. A desire to be the object of others' envy leads some people to engage in conspicuous displays of good fortune. The fear of being envied (based on anticipated efforts by enviers to deprive one of goods enjoyed) leads other people to engage in the reclusive and protected enjoyment of good fortune. An awareness of and commitment to what is truly good and just appears to be the only way to avoid these social manifestations of envy.

Envy is, however, an extremely difficult vice to overcome (in part, because it is so difficult to become aware of in oneself). The most rational response to an occasion of envy is to attempt to possess or achieve the good at issue for oneself. If this is not possible, one must try to admire or appreciate the fact that someone is enjoying something highly valued. Such a response, though very difficult, is consonant with one's values. If this effort is too demanding, then simply trying to be content with the goods one does enjoy is the only reasonable remaining response. The difficulty arising in each of these rational reactions to what precipitates envy stems from the general principle operative in the vice; the primary cause of one's lack of a good, being evil, is regarded as the mere fact that someone else enjoys that good. Thus, the surest remedy for envy is to rid oneself of this idea.

Mark Stephen Pestana

FURTHER READING

Kant, Immanuel. "Jealousy and Its Offspring—Envy and Grudge." In *Lectures on Ethics*, edited by Peter Heath and J. B. Schneewind. Translated by Peter Heath. New York: Cambridge University Press, 2001.

Moldoveanu, Mihnea, and Nitin Nohria. *Master Passions: Emotion, Narrative, and the Development of Culture*. Cambridge, Mass.: MIT Press, 2002.

Nozick, Robert. *Anarchy, State, and Utopia*. New York: Basic Books, 1974.

Rawls, John. *A Theory of Justice*. Rev. ed. Cambridge, Mass.: Belknap Press of Harvard University Press, 1999.

Taylor, Gabriele. "Envy and Jealousy: Emotions and Vices." *Midwest Studies in Philosophy* 13 (1988): 233-249.

SEE ALSO: Buddhist ethics; Compassion; Evil; Greed; Impartiality; Jealousy; Pride; Self-respect; Sin; Vice.

Epictetus

IDENTIFICATION: Stoic philosopher
BORN: c. 55, Hierapolis, Phrygia (now Pamukkale, Turkey)
DIED: c. 135, Nicopolis, Epirus (now in Greece)
TYPE OF ETHICS: Classical history
SIGNIFICANCE: Epictetus founded a school in which he taught Stoic philosophy. His teachings, preserved in the *Encheiridion* (c. 138) and *Discourses* (*Diatribai*, second century), advocated leading a disciplined life in accordance with natural law and influenced later religious and philosophical movements.

Epictetus's ethical system identified areas in which personal freedom and individual responsibility coexist with a deterministic universe. His approach resembled that of earlier Stoics: The purpose of life is happiness, which is reached through conformity with a pantheistic natural order. Reason makes the good life possible by disclosing those things that are beyond human power and those that are not. Environmental forces such as health and status belong to Providence; freedom and responsibility operate in matters of opinion, aim, and desire. Attempts to dominate outside forces produce frustration and unhappiness. Disciplined impulses directed toward proper ends bring liberation, establish a proper relationship between the self and the cosmos, allow the exercise of responsibility toward others, and benefit society.

Much of Epictetus's work consisted of practical advice on controlling and directing impulses. His school at Nicopolis, in Epirus, presented Stoicism as a way of life as well as a set of general principles. Epictetus's austere, subjectivist ethics inspired later Roman stoics and reinforced stoic elements in Christianity. His approach to the problems of freedom and dependence also influenced later systems of natural religion and rationalistic philosophical movements such as Kantian idealism.

Michael J. Fontenot

SEE ALSO: Altruism; *Foundations of the Metaphysics of Morals*; Marcus Aurelius; Self-control; Stoic ethics.

Epicurus

IDENTIFICATION: Greek philosopher
BORN: 341 B.C.E., Greek island of Samos
DIED: 270 B.C.E., Athens, Greece
TYPE OF ETHICS: Classical history
SIGNIFICANCE: Epicurus developed the ethical theory that personal pleasure is the greatest good and founded the Garden, a community which put that theory into practice.

The only writings of Epicurus that have survived are various fragments and three letters presented in Diogenes Laertius's *Life of Epicurus*. From these writings and from the writings of his disciples, however, one may obtain a reliable description of Epicurus's ethical theory. In an uncertain world, the immediate experiences of the senses are the most certain knowledge available. The senses respond to pleasure and pain. Thus, Epicurus equates pleasure with good and pain with evil. Practical wisdom is necessary if one is to weigh pleasures and pains. According to Epicurus, the duration of pleasure is more important than its intensity; thus, mental pleasures are preferred to physical ones. It is better to strive for the absence of pain than for the high peaks of pleasure.

Epicurus's theory of atomism, that everything is composed of material atoms, allows him to banish the two fears that bring so much pain to human beings: the fear of God and the fear of death. Epicurus sees philosophy as the medicine of the soul. If one de-

Epicurus. (Library of Congress)

sires little and is able to distinguish natural and necessary desires from those that are artificial, then one will be able to attain *ataraxia*, or serenity. This state involves peace of mind and bodily health. The best life is that lived with friends, engaged in moderation of the passions.

Rita C. Hinton

SEE ALSO: Altruism; Egoism; Evil; Friendship; Good, the; Hedonism; Human nature; Subjectivism.

Epistemological ethics

DEFINITION: Branch of ethics that deals with the truth or falsity of ethical judgments and the basis for knowledge about right and wrong
TYPE OF ETHICS: Theory of ethics
SIGNIFICANCE: In the post-Enlightenment philosophical tradition, epistemology is a necessary metadiscipline for all other branches of philosophy, including ethics, because it is the discipline that

grounds the judgments reached by the other disciplines. It is eschewed by antifoundational philosophies, which believe that grounding such judgments a priori is neither necessary nor possible.

When one makes a specific ethical claim, one presupposes that one knows what one is talking about. Epistemology deals with how one knows, what one knows, and the source of one's knowledge. If, for epistemological reasons, one must be skeptical about one's knowledge, then one must be skeptical about one's ethical claims. Thus, one might claim, "Not paying a worker a living wage is wrong." Someone might ask "How do you know that is true?" A complete answer to the question would involve an analysis of the terms used in the statement itself. Ethics is involved in making the claim of right and wrong, good or bad. Epistemology is involved in ensuring that the claim in this case is in contact with reality, that it is true or false.

When one moves from individual ethical and epistemological analysis to examine in general the relationship of ethical claims and reality, one is involved in metaethics and metaepistemology. One is also involved in a possible discussion of the relativity, subjectivity, and objectivity of ethics. The reason is that one is discussing whether what one ought to do is or is not reflected in the world outside one's conscience and in one's consciousness. Is ethics a mind game that has no contact with reality?

ETHICS AND REALITY

Many people believe that what one ought to do or ought not do is not made up by one's imagination or desires. Some people believe that the way one thinks and what one thinks about puts one in contact with the world outside one—reality. That is why, they suggest, the human development of mathematics and the hard sciences has made it possible, through technology, to change the world. Ethical decisions are the same as scientific decisions. When one sees what a situation is and decides what is the right way to act in the situation, one is dealing with reality both in analyzing the situation and in deciding how to act. Ethical values are like scientific facts: They hold true no matter what the circumstances, everywhere in the world. There is an ethical order beyond human wishes, knowledge, and desires. One can know that order, and when one disagrees with it, one acts at one's own peril.

Those who obtain their ethical order from the revelation of a God also believe in the human ability to know what God reveals and, with God's help, to follow God's commands. God created an ordered world. God reveals how humans fit into that order, and humans must follow God's will or suffer the consequences.

Many modern ethicists have difficulties with the seemingly naive realism of the previous position. Empirically, they observe the variety of ethical systems throughout the world. There is no single system in today's world. Human values are, from this perspective, more like opinions than like facts. Facts can be proved by the scientific method. Values cannot be proved; they exist only within human beings and are expressed in their actions. Psychological, sociological, and cultural circumstances do make a difference in what is held to be right and wrong. To say that there is some objective norm that can be known with certainty is to make a claim that is contrary to experience and also to claim that ethics can never change because of circumstances.

CONTACT WITH A REAL WORLD

If one stops thinking of humanity and reality as separate and begins to realize that one's thoughts both express and influence reality, one can begin to see that the ethical as well as the epistemological endeavor is an involvement with an ever-changing reality, which means that when one does the good that one claims one must do, one has already changed the reality that motivated that claim. When one swims in the ocean, one can do so only because of the water (reality), and every stroke (doing good) places one in a different part of the ocean, providing one with courage to continue to swim to shore and the necessity to swim differently in order to get there. The waves one makes change the ocean in which one swims. One's thoughts as well as one's ethical actions happen only because one is part of the reality in which one wishes to become better. Each person swims in the reality of an ever-changing ethical sea.

While the sea changes, however, one must realize that there are constants—one is in the sea, one is swimming, and there is a shore toward which to strive. Most modern ethicists agree that ethical statements are action guiding. If one says that it is immoral to lie, one's actions will be guided by this principle. Most would also agree that when one uses words such as "right," "wrong," "good," and "bad," one is, at the very least, saying that actions that coincide with these judgments should be judged accordingly. Thus, when someone tells a lie in a situation that is nearly identical to one in which it is judged wrong to tell a lie, that person has not acted ethically.

Although there are many ethical theories and systems of lived ethics, as the world becomes more homogeneous and its languages similar, the desire for universal moral judgments will increase. The fact of language and the fact of the human ability to communicate with those of vastly different cultures and languages suggest that a common sense of right and wrong will grow as the ability to communicate in this ever-shrinking world increases. If people cannot communicate about general principles of right and wrong, there is little hope of any significant communication taking place.

Nathan R. Kollar

FURTHER READING

Audi, Robert. *Belief, Justification, and Knowledge.* Belmont, Calif.: Wadsworth, 1988.

Brandt, Richard B. "Epistemology and Ethics, Parallel Between." In *The Encyclopedia of Philosophy*, edited by Paul Edwards. New York: Macmillan, 1972.

Chisholm, Roderick. *Theory of Knowledge.* 3d ed. Englewood Cliffs, N.J.: Prentice-Hall, 1989.

McCloskey, Henry John. *Meta-ethics and Normative Ethics.* The Hague: Martinus Nijhoff, 1969.

Miller, Alexander. *An Introduction to Contemporary Metaethics.* Cambridge, England: Polity Press, 2003.

SEE ALSO: Derrida, Jacques; Descartes, René; Ethics; Gewirth, Alan; Ideal observer; Language; Locke, John; Metaethics; Subjectivism; Truth.

Equal pay for equal work

DEFINITION: Principle that persons who perform the same tasks in the workplace must be paid the same regardless of racial, ethnic, or gender differences

DATE: Codified in law in 1964

TYPE OF ETHICS: Sex and gender issues

SIGNIFICANCE: The concept of equal pay for equal work presupposes that the value of labor is determined by the labor itself regardless of who performs it, and that justice demands all laborers be paid what their labor is worth, rather than taking into account the relative needs of different laborers or the extraneous value judgments of the employer or society.

The principle of equal pay for equal work was formally established in United States federal law by the Civil Rights Act of 1964. The principle was long contended for by the labor, civil rights, and feminist movements in the United States. Throughout most of the twentieth century, there was great workplace discrimination against women and nonwhites. At the time of the passage of the Civil Rights Act, women who were doing the same jobs as men were being paid salaries that were about two-thirds the amounts of those that were being paid to men. People of color were similarly disadvantaged. The Civil Rights Act of 1964 makes these practices unlawful, though it does not address the greater problem of the relegation of minorities to inferior jobs.

Robert Jacobs

SEE ALSO: Americans with Disabilities Act; Civil Rights Act of 1964; Egalitarianism; Equality; Gender bias; Hiring practices; Inequality; Minimum-wage laws; Wage discrimination; Women's ethics.

Equal Rights Amendment

IDENTIFICATION: Failed constitutional amendment that would have mandated that both sexes be treated equally under U.S. law

DATE: First proposed in 1923

TYPE OF ETHICS: Sex and gender issues

SIGNIFICANCE: If passed, the Equal Rights Amendment (ERA) would abrogate legal distinctions between the sexes.

In 1921, the National Woman's Party, fresh from its battles for woman suffrage, decided to push for passage of an Equal Rights Amendment. The party thought that the equal protection clause of the Four-

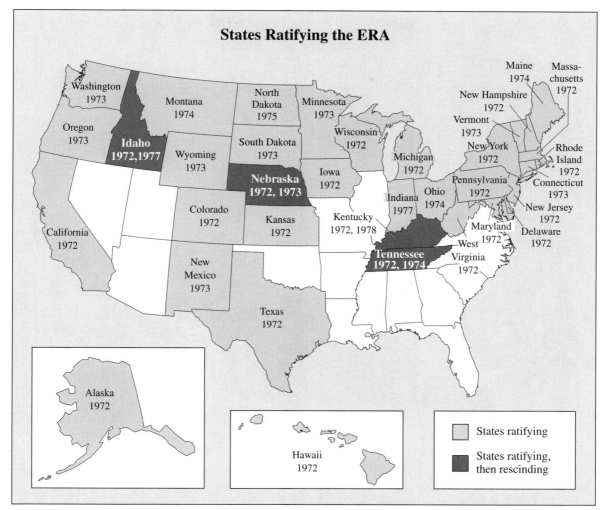

States Ratifying the ERA

Washington 1973
Oregon 1973
California 1972
Idaho 1972, 1977
Montana 1974
Wyoming 1973
Nevada
Utah
Arizona
New Mexico 1973
North Dakota 1975
South Dakota 1973
Nebraska 1972, 1973
Colorado 1972
Kansas 1972
Oklahoma
Texas 1972
Minnesota 1973
Wisconsin 1972
Iowa 1972
Missouri
Arkansas
Louisiana
Michigan 1972
Indiana 1977
Kentucky 1972, 1978
Tennessee 1972, 1974
Mississippi
Alabama
Georgia
Florida
South Carolina
North Carolina
Ohio 1974
West Virginia 1972
Maine 1974
New Hampshire 1972
Vermont 1973
New York 1972
Pennsylvania 1972
Massachusetts 1972
Rhode Island 1972
Connecticut 1973
New Jersey 1972
Delaware 1972
Maryland 1972

Alaska 1972

Hawaii 1972

States ratifying

States ratifying, then rescinding

Source: Data are from Janet K. Boles, *The Politics of the Equal Rights Amendment*. New York: Longman, 1979.

teenth Amendment did little to address those areas of discrimination against women that still remained. Under the leadership of Alice Paul, the ERA was first introduced to Congress in 1923.

Resolutions proposing the ERA were introduced in every succeeding Congress until 1971. Several times the ERA almost passed the Houses, but with riders attached that effectively nullified the resolution. In 1971, Representative Martha Griffiths introduced it again. This time, the ERA passed both Houses and was sent out to the states for ratification. Originally, the time limit for ratification was seven years. President Jimmy Carter extended the deadline for an additional thirty-nine months. At the end of that period, the ERA had still failed to achieve ratifi-

cation by a margin of three states. Seventeen months later, in 1983, when it was introduced in Congress again, it failed to pass. Afterward, public interest in the ERA waned.

The success and failure in passage of the ERA in both the Congress and the states have had much to do with changing conditions and circumstances in the country. For example, opponents have always feared that legislation that protected women's rights in the workplace would be negated by passage of the ERA. This fear was undercut when Title VII of the Civil Rights Act of 1964 included women as a protected class. Opponents have also feared that if the ERA passed, women would be drafted into the military. The ERA passed Congress when the Vietnam War

Women marching in support of the Equal Rights Amendment in 1970. (Library of Congress)

was coming to an end and the fear of women being drafted was diminished; it did not command enough of the states' votes when the war in Afghanistan was starting and the fear had returned.

At the time that the ERA passed Congress, there had been no gender discrimination cases that the Supreme Court had decided in favor of women. After the ERA passed Congress, the Supreme Court began deciding cases under the equal protection clause of the Fourteenth Amendment favorably to women, thus diminishing the need for an ERA.

Jennifer Eastman

SEE ALSO: Civil Rights Act of 1964; Egalitarianism; Equal pay for equal work; Equality; Gender bias; Sexual stereotypes; Title IX; Wage discrimination; Women's ethics; Women's liberation movement.

Equality

DEFINITION: Moral entitlement of all people to the same legal, civil, economic, and social rights
TYPE OF ETHICS: Theory of ethics
SIGNIFICANCE: The belief in a fundamental equality of all people, and the enactment of laws to ensure equal protection and equal treatment, is based upon the belief that all people have the same innate value as moral agents and that they are entitled to the same levels of opportunity and respect.

Most analyses of human life find that individuals are unequal in many respects—in intelligence, talents, wealth, lifestyles, and so forth. Further, equality is difficult to define precisely and is, indeed, ambiguous, unless qualifiers are added. Equality can be expressed as an equation. What is on the right side must be exactly equal to what is on the left side; for example: $4 + 4 = 7 + 1$. To express this equation in relation to human equality, one must specify which entities are under consideration and in what dimension those entities exist.

Although opinions vary as to the exact nature of equality, most people would agree that human beings share many characteristics. All are members of one species and are the same "class" of objects (*Homo sapiens*). All have basic needs to sustain their lives (food, for example), all can feel pleasure and pain, and all are thinking creatures and have some capacity for reason and "common sense" logic. It follows, then, that all should be of equal dignity and worth. It follows, next, that all people are entitled to be treated equally because they all have the same moral and natural rights to life. Likewise, in a just society, all people deserve legal equality. In this view, equality simply seems to be the norm and inequality a deviation. Equality should never be abandoned unless there are strong reasons to do so—as when equality as a basic value collides with another value, in the case, for example, of wartime hoarders of food who leave others to starve. The hoarders demand equal treatment in terms of property rights, but because the starving have a right to live, the hoarders' excess food might be confiscated.

Perhaps the "idea" of basic equality could be expressed thus: If I have a pizza party with four friends and I split the pizza into five equal parts, I will have no critics and need make no justification. Alternatively, if I give one-half of the pizza to one friend and split the other half into four very small but equal pieces, I will be expected to give an explanation for my action.

Given the general belief that in many ways humans are equal, it is not surprising that almost all literature that depicts humankind's societal dreams depicts an egalitarian society. Many fictional paradises may not be democratic and may be ruled by a benevolent despot, but virtually all stress equality of people.

EQUALITY AND RELIGION

Modern religious thinkers often assert that all people are equal but then talk and act as if all are unequal. The sixteenth century Protestant reformer Martin Luther believed that all people were equal in possessing capacity for spiritual understanding, but his contemporary John Calvin turned that notion on its head, arguing that, yes, people were equal— equally depraved and sinful.

Jacob Viner argued that it was an error to see egalitarianism in religion, for the rich do not usually voluntarily share with their poor brothers—except to put a little money in the weekly collection plate. Further, he maintained that such equality as did exist in churches was equality in the next world—"pie in the sky when you die"—not in this world. Viner added that in "Heaven" egalitarianism may be practiced, but only in that all must accept common subordination to God's authority.

HISTORY

Plato believed in the political equality of men and women, and Aristotle thought that all free citizens were equal, but the ancient Greek Stoics were the first philosophers to assert that all humans were rational beings who had an equal capacity for virtue. The religious expression of a similar idea is found in the New Testament, which recognizes the equality of all souls.

Although the Lollards and Hussites of the late Middle Ages also espoused a doctrine of equality, they were not influential, because they were trapped in a world where hierarchy and antiegalitarianism ruled. The modern concept of egalitarianism arose in the seventeenth century. In a limited way, Calvinists advanced the cause by stressing the equality of the "elect." Some of the Parliamentarians in the English civil war gave secular expression to the same idea when they spoke of natural rights and the social contract. Such ideas became so popular during Thomas Hobbes's times that he took it for granted that humans were equal in the state of nature.

Some later philosophers supported Hobbes's assumption. They agreed with critics who still scorned egalitarianism and who still pointed to the obvious inequalities they saw all about them; they argued that among humans differences of intelligence and talents did indeed exist, but that they existed because people lived in different environments and had different life experiences. At birth, they believed, all people have similar, virtually unlimited, potentialities. Even Jean-Jacques Rousseau granted this argument, while holding that the world's "sophisticated" societies bred social inequalities. Indeed, Rousseau tried to square natural equality with the political authority of the one or the few who ruled the many.

The doctrine of equality saw its greatest manifestation near the close of the eighteenth century in both the American and the French Revolutions, revolutions wherein leaders made explicit the freedoms that human beings should have. The revolutionaries focused on political and social rights, however, while ignoring economics and the great chasm between the rich and the poor.

Nineteenth and twentieth century socialists emerged to champion the cause of economic equality, but they found followers in only a few areas. Indeed, the collapse of the Soviet Union during the 1990's probably ended the last hope of those who favored worldwide socialism. The world might, however, one day evolve into a moderate socialist society such as Sweden's. Still, it is ironic that the world appeared to be "captured" by the capitalistic system, which revels in human avarice and which allows the exploitation of many humans by the few who control the means of production. Workers actually produce the profit that the rich reap, but the workers receive few rewards. Unequal capitalistic exploitation is also unconcerned about "means and ends." Whatever makes money counts, and profits remain the measure of all things. The fate of human beings in the capitalistic systems matters not, as long as they are consumers who put money on the table.

Even within the capitalistic system, reformers still try to ensure some elements of equality. Various welfare programs in the United States, for example, provide aid to the poor, programs including outright monetary payments, food stamps, free or partially subsidized medical aid, and so forth. Mothers with dependent children also receive assistance, as do the physically or mentally disabled. Likewise, the unemployed at any age qualify for temporary assistance. In addition, the poorest students qualify for aid and receive a subsidized education. All the above examples work to "level the playing field" in that they all relate to equal opportunity and are intended to allow industrious people to "work" their way out of dangerous poverty.

CHARACTERISTICS OF EGALITARIANISM

The traditional definition of the term "egalitarianism" included impartiality, a view that required equal responsibilities and equal rewards for all who performed similar jobs. Other related values include equal justice instead of justice according to rank, wealth, other personal consideration, and so on; and equal economic opportunity rather than discrimination based on race, ethnic group, gender, age, sexual preference, and so forth. Further, humans are thought to deserve the equal satisfaction of basic needs such as food, housing, and personal freedoms.

In many cases, cries for equality have been directed at specific inequalities. Patrician misrule of the Roman Empire led plebeians to revolt on many occasions, demanding a greater voice in the empire's affairs (political equality). The American Civil Rights movement of the 1950's and 1960's attacked racial inequality. The women's movement, from the 1960's to the present, demanded that gender inequality cease. The modern senior citizen movement sought to end discrimination based on age. Even the modern environmental movement embraces the concept of equality by holding that small minorities (big business, for example) should not be allowed to forever foul the environment that all people need to share for their ultimate survival. Reformers who advocated change such as that mentioned above are pursuing a secular version of a religious doctrine that held that God created the world and wanted it to be a vast treasure trove that all people would share equally.

EQUALITY AND PROBLEMATIC ISSUES

Typical dictionary definitions of equality, while leaving much to be desired, nevertheless include the condition of having equal dignity and rank as others, the condition of being equal in power, and society operating with fairness and equity. Applying these definitions has sometimes led to contradictions. Critics of the equality doctrine pointed out that if humans (in the real world) are unequal in talents, skills, and excellence, then adherence to definition 3 will violate definition 1. Likewise, adherence to definition 1 will violate definition 3.

After observing the above contradictions, some thinkers have held that, because humans operating in the real world are not all equal in terms of ability and excellence, elevating those people who have inferior ability and intelligence would be an injustice to the former group. A degree of inequality, therefore, seemed to be the natural result of equity and fairness. To continue arguing for maximum equality in an unequal world, some thinkers developed the concept of "equal shares to equals"—equal pay for equal work in an economic world in which differing levels of talent and skills supposedly justify some inequalities.

In reference to economic issues, critics of the equality doctrine threw yet one more dart: Equality of opportunity, through time, usually produces inequalities of wealth, given people's differing intelligence, motivation, and career choices. Further, some critics question the equality doctrine by referring to the concept of justice, which demands that each person be given his or her due but that only equal people receive equal rewards, given differences in intelligence and drive—in other words, to each according to personal merit. Additionally, some philosophers pointed out that if all work rewards were equal, rational people would probably minimize their work as much as possible, a pattern that would lead to gross inefficiency. Thus, equality, critics contended, would work only in a perfect world in which work was not necessary or in which work was a pleasure.

Some philosophers asserted further that, at times, egalitarian rules sometimes conflict not only with each other (equal opportunity and welfare, for example) but also with important social goals. Critics contended that tension will always exist between equal welfare and equal freedom. In pursuing equal welfare, government necessarily imposed more restrictions on economically dominant groups. Yet it was freedom of opportunity that created the unequal situation in the first place. Likewise, political freedom for all citizens might lead to a situation wherein the dominant majority suppresses a certain minority (slavery is the best example). Worse, critics argued that egalitarianism could lead to a decline of civilization, for it might bring a downward leveling of society, wherein cultural excellence, great diversity, and individuality would be stifled.

REFORMS LEADING TO GREATER EGALITARIANISM

In modern America, President Franklin D. Roosevelt in 1941 signed Executive Order 8802, which banned racial discrimination in the defense industry. By 1945, at least two million African Americans were working in that industry. In 1948, President Harry S. Truman, campaigning for another term, advocated national health insurance. Although Truman did not have enough congressional support to accomplish the goal, he made the effort. On that issue, he proved to be a progressive egalitarian who was more than half a century ahead of his time.

Truman also campaigned against racism and later set up the Civil Rights Commission; its investigations led to a well-researched report condemning racial segregation and discrimination. Success in resolving the civil rights question would have to wait more than fifteen years. Nevertheless, President Lyndon B. Johnson signed the historic Civil Rights Act of 1964, and that act, enforced over time, changed the social and political face of the United States. Johnson also shared Truman's concern for health insurance and older people. When he signed his Medicare legislation, Johnson flew to Truman's home in Independence, Missouri, to allow the former president to witness the signing.

The Medicare Act of 1965 was only one of a host of reforms that Johnson advocated in his Great Society program. Although his program affected many different groups in society (notably the poor), to show the egalitarian intent, one need mention only the massive financial aid that the federal government poured into education—education being one avenue that could provide equal opportunity for millions of people and allow them to rise both economically and socially.

EQUALITY IN MODERN AMERICA

From the 1970's to the early twenty-first century, there has been an apparent retreat from equality. American society appears to have become more inegalitarian. In American economic life, the rich added much to their coffers at the expense of the poor. When President Johnson began his "Great Society" during the mid-1960's, approximately 25 percent of all Americans fell below the government's definition of the "poverty line." When Johnson left office, that definition fit only 11 percent of the people. At the threshold of the twenty-first century, the figure was again rising above 25 percent.

Economic gloom aside, the inegalitarian trend was also seen in social life. Now, more than ever, the "underclass" (people who live in soul-crushing poverty) is further away from the middle and upper classes. Likewise, the gap is growing between the middle and upper classes, with the latter engaging in vulgar conspicuous consumption and the former trying desperately to keep up. In many other aspects of life, inequality can be seen. In the health care field, for example, despite some modern reforms, the rich continue to get the best care, while the poor do without care because they cannot pay the price. In law, modern America said that all were equal, for justice was blind and knew no prejudice. In fact, however, the wealthy hire the best lawyers while the poor settle for public defenders or abandon their rights and stay out of court altogether.

Although there have been more inegalitarian setbacks, such as the failure to ratify the Equal Rights Amendment and the institution of unfair taxation policies (regressive taxes that unfairly hurt the poor and the aged), general trends suggest that the country is still moving slowly in the direction of greater egalitarianism. During the 1990's, reformers began gaining more support and therefore exercised more power to bring change.

CONCLUSIONS

The simplest ethical or moral argument in favor of continuing to extend the doctrine of equality is an appeal to reason. A person should grant equalities to others that he or she would demand for himself or herself; one should grant equalities that no rational human would be willing to give up voluntarily. No human should be so morally deficient as to withhold from others in similar circumstances benefits that he or she has demanded for himself or herself. In other words, one's equality may well be conditional; for a person to maintain and protect his or her own equality, it may be necessary to grant equality to all.

There are remedies for inequalities in American life, but a new "Great Society" program or another "New Deal" likely will be necessary. Further, the elite (economic and social) must stop taking more than its share and must remember that others must live, too.

James Smallwood

FURTHER READING

Cecil, Andrew R. *Equality, Tolerance, and Loyalty: Virtues Serving the Common Purpose of Democracy.* Dallas: University of Texas at Dallas Press, 1990. Cecil makes a strong case for the virtues he names in the hope that Americans will turn away from intolerance and selfishness; otherwise, the country will likely not survive.

Cook, Fred J. *The Corrupted Land: The Social Morality of Modern America.* New York: Macmillan, 1966. Although he wrote more than two decades before the country's savings and loan fiasco and the major Wall Street scandals, Cook exposed the corruption of everyday "ethics" in the business world and found that those ethics were, indeed, unethical.

Coons, John E., and Patrick M. Brennan. *By Nature Equal: The Anatomy of a Western Insight.* Princeton, N.J.: Princeton University Press, 1999. Argues that people are inherently equal in the sense that they share a common capacity and desire for moral self-perfection. Surveys the history of thinking on equality and ethics along the way.

Kaus, Mickey. *The End of Equality.* New York: Basic Books, 1992. Kaus examines the modern United States as it approached the twenty-first century. He focuses on liberalism and social classes, and, true to his title, he finds much inequality among different racial, ethnic, and income classes.

Rousseau, Jean-Jacques. "Discourse on the Origin and Foundations of Inequality Among Mankind." In *"The Social Contract" and "The First and Second Discourses,"* edited by Susan Dunn. New Haven, Conn.: Yale University Press, 2002. Rousseau is a good starting point on the subject of equality, for he argued that equality was most "unnatural." His ideas must be addressed.

Ryan, William. *Equality.* New York: Pantheon Books, 1981. With his focus on the modern United States, Ryan discusses in depth the following topics: equal pay for equal work, sexual discrimination in employment, equality before the law, and American social policy. Like other researchers, he finds much inequality.

Slote, Michael A. *From Morality to Virtue.* New York: Oxford University Press, 1992. Reexamining the philosophy of Immanuel Kant, Slote surveys many topics, including ethics, virtue, "common sense," and utilitarianism.

SEE ALSO: Dignity; Egalitarianism; Equal Rights Amendment; Fairness; Human rights; Inequality; Natural rights; Taxes; Women's liberation movement.

Erroneous convictions

DEFINITION: Cases in which legally convicted persons are later found to be innocent

TYPE OF ETHICS: Legal and judicial ethics

SIGNIFICANCE: Establishing one's innocence after one has been convicted is difficult in the American legal system, and getting an innocent person to be released from prison following an erroneous conviction is even more difficult.

The difficulty of overturning erroneous convictions of innocent persons can be traced to the idea that although a criminal defendants are presumed innocent until proven guilty in trials, once they are convicted by juries, the presumption of innocence is no longer applicable. Indeed, the opposite presumption now applies: that the convicted defendants are, in fact, guilty. That presumption is actually stronger than the original presumption of innocence.

In *Herrera v. Collins* (1993), the U.S. Supreme Court considered a claim raised by a death row inmate in Texas who argued that he was actually innocent of the crime of which he had been convicted and that it would therefore be unconstitutional for the state to carry out his execution. In an opinion by Chief Justice William Rehnquist, the Court conceded that the proposition that the U.S. Constitution forbids the execution of someone who is innocent has an "elemental appeal," but the Court nonetheless held that a mere claim of innocence (that is, a claim of innocence unaccompanied by the identification of any other constitutional violation) does not permit a federal court to grant relief and order that the inmate be released from custody. As a result, inmates seeking to overturn a conviction on the grounds that they are innocent must seek relief through either state court systems or the states' clemency processes.

In *Ohio Adult Parole Authority v. Woodard* (1998), the Supreme Court ruled that states are not constitutionally required to have clemency systems. However, if the states do have such programs, the systems must be fair. Fairness in this context means that the inmate must have the opportunity to have the decision maker receive and give effect to his or her evidence of innocence. Since inmates have had opportunities to present evidence of their innocence to juries, evidence adduced in clemency procedures typically consists of at least some new material that was unavailable during the original trials.

The standard for having wrongful convictions overturned in clemency proceedings varies widely from state to state. In general, such decisions lie within the discretion of the states' governors. If governors believe that inmates have demonstrated their innocence, then the appropriate relief will be granted.

In addition, inmates may seek relief in state courts by filing *habeas corpus* petitions raising their claims of actual innocence. Unlike the federal court system, which does not view mere innocence as a sufficient ground for overturning a conviction, most states do permit a pure claim of innocence to be raised as a challenge to the conviction. The precise legal standard for obtaining such relief varies somewhat from state to state. In general, however, inmates are required to establish that, in light of the newly discovered evidence, no reasonable juror could have voted to convict them. Evidence other than DNA evidence rarely satisfies this standard. However, DNA evidence alone had led to more than 130 exonerations throughout the United States by the end of 2003.

David R. Dow

FURTHER READING

Amnesty International. *Fatal Flaws: Innocence and the Death Penalty.* London: Amnesty International Report, 1999.

Dwyer, Jim, Peter Neufeld, and Barry Sheck. *Actual Innocence: When Justice Goes Wrong and How to Make It Right.* New York: New American Library, 2003.

Leipold, Andrew D. "The Problem of the Innocent, Acquitted Defendant." *Northwestern University Law Review* 94 (2000): 1297-1356.

SEE ALSO: Accused, rights of; Arrest records; Capital punishment; Parole of convicted prisoners; Peltier conviction; Punishment; Scottsboro case; Three-strikes laws; Victims' rights.

Espionage

DEFINITION: Attempting to discover, through clandestine means, the secrets of others

TYPE OF ETHICS: Politico-economic ethics

SIGNIFICANCE: Political espionage traditionally has an unusual moral status, since the citizens of a given nation often believe that it is morally wrong for others to spy upon them but morally permissible and even necessary for their agents to spy upon others. Industrial espionage is less justifiable but is also considered a less extreme transgression.

Secrecy exists, and is maintained, for the advantage of one entity over another. Keeping information secret has always been recognized as a highly effective means of ensuring success in military operations, diplomatic negotiations, private enterprise, and even many personal interactions. The fact that secrets exist and are maintained for one entity's advantage over another makes it imperative that the opposition acquire the secrets of rivals. The acquisition of secrets is the fundamental task of espionage.

The element of secrecy is responsible for the distinction between standard intelligence gathering and espionage. Most electronic and human intelligence gathering, despite its elaborate secrecy, is carried out overtly. Espionage, however, is carried out entirely in a covert manner: Espionage is the effort to discover by clandestine methods the secrets of others. It must be made clear that espionage is the secret act of information gathering and should not be confused with other covert activities such as sabotage, misinformation campaigns, the placement of agents of influence or agents provocateurs, and assassination.

In all forms of espionage, the act of secretly gathering information is carried out by espionage agents, or spies. Usually highly trained and motivated individuals dedicated to their information-gathering mission, spies are sent from one entity to secretly gather information about another entity. People from one entity who sell information to another entity are not spies, but traitors. This is an important and often overlooked distinction. A spy is required to conceal his or her true identity by assuming a false one; to hide the nature of his or her mission and lines of communication, operate under a cloak of secrecy, and if captured deny organizational affiliation. Because the ultimate goal of any spy is to steal secrets, spies must often employ tactics that are perceived as immoral to fulfill their information-gathering missions; for example, blackmail, bribery, coercion, deception, burglary, and subterfuge. As a result, no matter how noble the cause, spies are commonly regarded as criminals and outcasts even by their own organizations.

IMAGES OF SPIES

Historically, the portrayal of the spy as a criminal has been reinforced by propaganda and popular entertainment venues. Because of the spy's cultural image and the amoral or even immoral aspects of espionage operations, the organizations initiating them camouflage or deny their existence. Most governments and businesses publicly disavow use of espionage agents and, when a spy is captured, deny any association with that person. Those who employ spies to gather information, however, do so believing that their spies are noble, self-sacrificing individuals, while the opposition's spies are evil interlopers.

Despite many negative societal attitudes regarding the secret nature of espionage, it is a legitimate and essential function of every government and many large corporations that are aware of their responsibilities to either citizens or shareholders. The practice of espionage is justified by the knowledge that all nations, and most competitive businesses, conceal important phases of their activities from rivals. With this understanding, it then becomes a necessity to acquire knowledge about the disposition of concealed information that may influence or threaten a nation's peace and security or a corporation's competitive standing in the marketplace. Espionage gathers this important information and places it in the hands of authorities who use it to build a database of intelligence from which they can plan future decisions and actions.

By this definition, espionage is an important activity that is separate from any moral view of the act of spying. Because of the clandestine nature of espionage and the fact that its ultimate goal is to steal secrets, it is perceived as the most unethical and lawless activity in which a government or corporation may engage, short of unwarranted hostilities. Using clandestine means to obtain secret information is ethically justifiable, however, if the end use of the gathered intelligence meets the goals and objectives of the society or organization that initiates the espionage activity. The setting of goals and objectives for espionage operations is reflective of the culture initiating the espionage activity. In totalitarian states and many private corporations, espionage operations are initiated by individuals or small groups whose objectives and actions are not answerable to the remainder of society.

In open societies, representative governments and publicly owned corporations who use espionage are often obliged to defend their decisions before the public if the activities are disclosed.

Randall L. Milstein

FURTHER READING

Bergier, Jacques. *Secret Armies: The Growth of Corporate and Industrial Espionage.* Translated by Harold J. Salemson. Indianapolis: Bobbs-Merrill, 1975.

Dobson, Christopher, and Ronald Payne. *The Dictionary of Espionage.* London: Harrap, 1984.

Farago, Ladislas. *War of Wits: The Anatomy of Espionage and Intelligence.* New York: Funk & Wagnalls, 1954.

Fleisher, Craig S., and David L. Blenkhorn, eds. *Controversies in Competitive Intelligence: The Enduring Issues.* Westport, Conn.: Praeger, 2003.

Kurland, Michael. *The Spymaster's Handbook.* New York: Facts On File, 1988.

Powers, Thomas. *Intelligence Wars: American Secret History from Hitler to al-Qaeda.* New York: New York Review Books, 2002.

Turner, Stansfield. *Secrecy and Democracy: The CIA in Transition.* Boston: Houghton Mifflin, 1985.

SEE ALSO: Computer crime; Computer databases; Covert action; Electronic surveillance; Industrial research; Treason.

Ethical codes of organizations

DEFINITION: Guidelines adopted by professional organizations and businesses that seek to impose or encourage ethical conduct through either mandatory or permissive rules

TYPE OF ETHICS: Business and labor ethics

SIGNIFICANCE: Numerous organizations of all sorts have adopted or are adopting ethical codes. How-

ever, whether such codes have a meaningful impact or are designed merely to project positive images to the public continues to be debated.

Ethical codes for organizations have both a long history and a recent resurgence of interest in light of the corporate scandals of the early twenty-first century. Such codes can be broken down into codes adopted by trade or professional associations to guide the conduct of members and codes adopted by businesses, typically corporations.

The first category has a long and established history. There are, for example, long-standing codes governing the conduct of lawyers, psychologists, accountants, doctors, journalists, engineers, and many others. Some of these efforts, such as the famous Hippocratic oath taken by physicians, are of ancient vintage, while others began early in the twentieth century. The first attempt to institute an ethical code by the American Bar Association, for example, was in 1908.

The second category tends to be of more recent vintage and has become increasingly common. A prime reason for this movement is that companies that want to be perceived as good corporate citizens adopt codes of ethics, particularly in the wake of publicity surrounding corporate scandals involving WorldCom, Enron, and others. Moreover, the Sarbanes-Oxley Act, passed by the U.S. Congress as a response to corporate scandals, requires, among other things, that public companies adopt codes of ethics for their senior financial officers, and that their codes be made publicly available. In a similar vein, many stock exchanges mandate that the companies they list adopt codes of ethics for all their corporate employees. In light of these trends, the vast majority of Fortune 500 companies had codes of ethics by 2003.

THE CONTENT OF ETHICAL CODES

Given the variety of organizations and issues ethical codes can address, on one code is typical. Many, perhaps most, address issues such as conflicts of interest, confidentiality of information, labor relations, and political contributions. Other codes cover such matters as business goals and aspirations and social responsibility.

A critical issue involving such codes has to do with how and when they are enforced. Some codes permit or mandate discharging employees or other disciplinary action if they are violated. Others, however, contain provisions allowing appropriate authorities within the organizations to waive the codes' prohibitions. With the passage of the Sarbanes-Oxley Act, such waivers may need to be publicly disclosed—an attempt by Congress to discourage corporate boards of directors from rubber-stamping unethical behavior, such as self-dealing among corporate senior executives.

RATIONALES AND CRITIQUES

Drafters of ethical codes justify them as a means of embodying best practices and ideals for a group. In a similar vein, codes raise group consciousness so that members of organizations are sensitized to ethical issues that may not be immediately obvious, such as subtle conflicts of interest. This is seen as especially important in light of what some perceive as a moral decline in culture generally. Moreover, in some instances, violations of a code can serve as the basis for discipline within or expulsion from a professional organization, thus maintaining the organization's integrity and reputation.

Ethical codes are not without their critics. Some people argue that ethics are, by definition, deliberative and collaborative—something that no code of ethics can be. Others question the ability of a code either to encourage ethical behavior or to discourage unethical behavior. Another critique is that such codes may foster a misleading sense of complacency; the very existence of such a code may be taken to mean that an organization and, by extension, its members take ethics seriously. An infamous example is that the Enron Corporation had its own code of ethics. That code, like many similar ones, had a conflict-of-interest provision that prohibited Enron employees from participating in both sides of any transaction taking place between Enron and other entities with which it did business. However, such forbidden practices were later found to have been done repeatedly within the organization.

Some people have argued that an organization's "culture"—the "way things are done" and the types of behavior that garner recognition and advancement within an organization—influences the behavior of its members far more than a written code of ethics ever could.

A major influence and perhaps disincentive in the adoption of codes of ethics is the looming threat of litigation. Many companies fear that their adoption of codes will enable litigants to sue them privately for violations of codes. As a matter of public policy, some argue that this is a good way to impose account-

---

Finding Ethical Codes on the Web

The full texts of many organizations' ethical codes are posted on the World Wide Web. Those codes may be found by searching on the names of the individual organizations. An overview of the range and variety of codes, as well as a shortcut to their texts, is available at the Web site of the Center for the Study of Ethics in the Professions of the Illinois Institute of Technology (www.iit.edu/departments/csep/PublicWWW/codes/index.html). The institute's Web site offers the texts of nearly one thousand different organizations' ethical codes (most as of 1996), organized under these headings:

- Agriculture
- Animal Breeding and Care
- Arts
- Business
- Communications
- Computing and Information Systems
- Construction Trades
- Education and Academia

- Engineering
- Finance
- Fraternal and Social Organizations
- Government and Military
- Health Care
- Industrial
- Law and Legal
- Management

- Media
- Other Professions
- Real Estate
- Religion
- Service Organizations
- Science
- Sports and Athletics
- Travel and Transportation

ability on corporate behavior. Others, however, argue that such litigation will simply increase the cost of doing business, which is in the interest of neither the company nor the public.

Robert Rubinson

FURTHER READING

Davies, Peter W. F. *Current Issues in Business Ethics*. London: Routledge, 1997.

Di Norcia, Vincent. *Hard Like Water: Ethics in Business*. Oxford, England: Oxford University Press, 1998.

Gorlin, Rena A. *Codes of Professional Responsibility: Ethics Standards in Business, Health, and Law*. 4th ed. Washington, D.C.: Bureau of National Affairs, 1999.

Manley, Walter W., II. *Executive's Handbook of Model Business Conduct Codes*. Englewood Cliffs, N.J.: Prentice-Hall, 1991.

SEE ALSO: Applied ethics; Code of Professional Responsibility; Codes of civility; Corporate scandal; Dress codes; Ethical Principles of Psychologists; Honor systems and codes; Judicial conduct code; Medical bills of rights; *Principles of Medical Ethics*; Professional ethics.

Ethical monotheism

DEFINITION: Belief in a single personal and transcendent God who requires strict moral conduct and metes out rewards or punishments

TYPE OF ETHICS: Religious ethics

SIGNIFICANCE: All three of the world's dominant monotheistic religions—Christianity, Islam, and Judaism—have strong ethical components, which are observed and respected to a greater or lesser extent by individual practitioners.

The world's major monotheistic religions generally suppose that ethical monotheism was the original religion revealed to the first human parents (Adam and Eve) but was quickly corrupted through error and transgression. Judaism maintains that ethical monotheism was reconfirmed to the patriarch Abraham, who battled against the widespread belief in the many, often capricious and amoral, gods of the an-

cient Near East. He taught that God is ethical and demands the same from all adherents to true religions.

Islam validates the role of Abraham while claiming him as their progenitor and proclaiming Muḥammad to be the last and greatest of a long line of prophets to teach ethical monotheism. It has sometimes been asserted that Christianity does not profess pure monotheism because of its dogma of the Holy Trinity. Critical, scholarly, nineteenth century theories saw monotheism as an evolutionary step emerging from polytheism. More modern views have argued that ethical monotheism developed as a response in opposition to polytheism. Scholars see ethical monotheism as a remarkable achievement of Hebrew history, though they disagree about the period in which the explicit worship of "the one true God" began. There is no question, however, that ethical monotheism has been a major world force in determining the behavior of nations and civilizations, and that it formed the foundation for such codes as the Ten Commandments.

Andrew C. Skinner

SEE ALSO: Anthropomorphism of the divine; Christian ethics; God; Hammurabi's code; Islamic ethics; Jewish ethics; Muḥammad; Pantheism; Ten Commandments.

Ethical Principles of Psychologists

IDENTIFICATION: Professional ethical code required of psychologists and enforceable through sanctions from various bodies

DATE: First enacted in December, 1992; revised on June 1, 2003

TYPE OF ETHICS: Psychological ethics

SIGNIFICANCE: Health care professionals who deal with the mind and mental health face special ethical dilemmas over and above those common to all providers of care. The Ethical Principles set out by the American Psychological Association seek to aid practitioners in negotiating those issues, as well as reassuring the public that psychologists will not be permitted to abuse their position.

The Ethical Principles are primarily based on the potential for harming others through incompetence, improper emotional coercion, or misinformation that curtails free and informed thought and behavior. Freedom of inquiry and expression is central to psychology, but discriminating against others or allowing the misuse of research is unethical. Psychologists have a particular responsibility to be self-aware, to be honest, and to use the methods of science, scientific explanation, and critique, rather than expressing mere personal opinion and authority. They must be aware of the basic and unique needs of other people and groups. Supervision, instruction, advisement, and treatment have considerable intellectual and emotional power.

Psychologists must avoid potential harm or exploitation by being candid about their services and fees, qualifications, confidentiality, allegiances, the requests they make of research volunteers (informed consent specifying risks and benefits, providing feedback, and minimizing deception), and avoiding potentially harmful multiple relationships. Psychologists do not engage in sexual relationships with students, supervisees, and patients because of the potential for biased judgment or exploitation through lack of interpersonal reciprocity. Tests, diagnoses, evaluations, and interventions must be based on scientific competence and avoidance of harm.

John Santelli

SEE ALSO: Animal research; Bioethics; Medical research; Metaethics; *Principles of Medical Ethics with Annotations Especially Applicable to Psychiatry*; Professional ethics; Psychology; Therapist-patient relationship.

Ethics

DEFINITION: Philosophical science that deals with the rightness and wrongness of human actions
TYPE OF ETHICS: Theory of ethics
SIGNIFICANCE: The formal practice of moral philosophy has profoundly influenced, and been influenced by, the course of social, political, intellectual, and religious history.

Ethics has been in many ways the most general study of human behavior, since every other form of analysis of human action, whether economic, psychological, sociological, anthropological, or historical, can be subjected to an ethical analysis.

In Plato, the subordination of ethics to ontology and epistemology was manifest, and it was not until Aristotle that ethics achieved full status as an independent branch of the philosophical sciences. In the *Nicomachean Ethics* especially, Aristotle was at pains to distinguish ethical knowledge from other forms of human knowledge—as when he contrasted the exactitude to be anticipated in mathematics from that attainable in ethical reasoning.

Ethics is the name now given to that most general study of the rightness and wrongness of human actions, including not only the determination of whether particular acts are morally permissible but also the derivation of those theories by which such a determination may be made, as well as an analysis of the meaning of the language that is peculiar to such determinations and derivations.

Modern ethics is divided into normative ethics, on one hand, which involves both standard ethical theory and its application to particular actions and classes of actions, and metaethics, on the other hand, which examines the meaning of ethical language. From its beginnings, ethics—the more general term—has concerned itself with the human "mechanism" of morality: the faculties of the human soul and the needs, passions, and desires of the human mind and body.

Plato and Aristotle did not neglect the theoretical side of ethics, and Aristotle especially presented a rather systematic theoretical framework throughout his exposition of natural eudaimonism. In Plato, much of the emphasis on human character and motivations does not remain restricted to the words of the philosophical disputations but is embedded in the action/drama of the dialogues themselves. In the *Republic*, one sees Thrasymachus storm away from the discussion, driven by the angry passion that drove his lawless philosophy of unrestrained power. In the *Euthyphro*, the eponymous character fled from Socrates, motivated by the senseless pride that had imprisoned him in the darkness of ignorance. In the *Philebus*, Protarchus had to bear the burden of the argument for hedonism because Philebus, the archvoluptuary, could not be bothered to defend his ethical position or to leave his pleasures to indulge in philosophical disputations.

Instead of considering the virtuous man in the abstract, Plato related incidents from the life of Socrates. Socrates remained sober and articulate into the dawn in the *Symposium*, in which dialogue he is also shown resisting the sexual blandishments of Alcibiades. At his trial, Socrates (in the *Apologia*) was unmoved by the danger he faced and displayed compassion toward his accusers, whom he did not blame for their machinations. In the *Phaedo*, awaiting execution, Socrates calmly speaks with friends on the immortality of the soul, and in the *Crito*, he refuses to contemplate flight or any other stratagem to save his life. Thus, Socrates served as a kind of *spoudaios*—the wise, virtuous man whom Aristotle counsels the young to observe and imitate.

THE MIDDLE AGES AND LATER

In the Middle Ages, patristic and Scholastic writers continued to explore the boundaries of ethics, but with a heavy concern for theological ethics. Saint Thomas Aquinas's ethics, for example, which are directly descended from Aristotle's natural eudaimonism, are designated supernatural, or theological, eudaimonism on account of the regard that his ethical system gives to the attainment of beatitude in the afterlife. This concentration upon theological concerns led to an emphasis upon free will for theodic purposes—making evil the product of the human will and the human will the necessary source of virtue, as well as the cause of evil.

From the coming of the Renaissance well into the latter half of the eighteenth century, ethical philosophy returned to its classical roots and once again emphasized the passions and sentiments in humanity that conflict and that drive those behaviors that support the institutions of society, from friendship and the family to cooperative activities and the nation-state.

In the latter half of the eighteenth century, Immanuel Kant returned ethics to a theoretical orientation with his development of the categorical imperative. Kant's deontology—or science of duty, as he called it—contained many complex aspects, such as the autonomous and heteronomous wills and the hypothetical and categorical imperatives, thus giving priority again to abstract, theoretical models of ethical thought. Indeed, Kantian formalism temporarily eclipsed the firm concretization that necessarily accompanies consequentialistic analysis.

Although the nineteenth century saw a step back

from the degree of formalistic abstraction inherent in Kantian ethics, Hegelian and other forms of idealist ethics, utilitarianism (of both the Benthamite and Millian variety), and the variegated Darwinistic ethical systems failed to return to the classical model of virtue analysis.

In the twentieth century, the proliferation of academic publications and university-based scholars was instrumental in the resurrection, if not the reinvigoration, of virtually every philosophical tradition in ethics. Nevertheless, virtue- and sentiment-based ethical theories enjoyed a rather desiccated existence, except in somewhat altered form under the various phenomenological approaches.

In general, metaethical investigations predominated throughout the discipline in the last years of the twentieth century, undoubtedly stimulated by G. E. Moore's discovery of the naturalistic fallacy and the renewed interest in the Humean is/ought dilemma that Moore caused. Contributing to the same effect was the dominance of logical positivism and its offshoots, which have insisted upon the analysis of language as the key methodological operation in philosophy.

Finally, the central role of commerce and the professions in modern life has led to a significant compartmentalization of normative ethics: Legal ethics, business ethics, biomedical ethics, ethics of engineering, and so forth, each with its specialized vocabulary and subject matter, have threatened to replace the general overview of the duties of person and citizen (the classical model) as the primary focus of normative ethical inquiry.

Patrick M. O'Neil

FURTHER READING

Aristotle. *Nicomachean Ethics*. Translated and edited by Roger Crisp. New York: Cambridge University Press, 2000.

Kant, Immanuel. *Groundwork for the Metaphysics of Morals*. Edited and translated by Allen W. Wood. New Haven, Conn.: Yale University Press, 2002.

Mill, John Stuart. *Utilitarianism*. Edited by George Sher. 2d ed. Indianapolis: Hackett, 2001.

Nietzsche, Friedrich. *On the Genealogy of Morals*. Edited and translated by Walter Kaufmann. New York: Vintage Books, 1967.

Plato. *The Republic*. Translated by Desmond Lee. 2d ed. New York: Penguin Books, 2003.

Wyschogrod, Edith, and Gerald P. McKenny, eds. *The Ethical*. Malden, Mass.: Blackwell, 2003.

SEE ALSO: Applied ethics; Ethics/morality distinction; Feminist ethics; Metaethics; Morality; *Nicomachean Ethics*; Normative vs. descriptive ethics; Situational ethics; Theory and practice; Virtue ethics.

Ethics

IDENTIFICATION: Book by Baruch Spinoza (1632-1677)
DATE: *Ethica*, 1677 (English translation, 1870)
TYPE OF ETHICS: Renaissance and Restoration history
SIGNIFICANCE: Spinoza's *Ethics* argues that the knowledge of the systematic unity of all things, and of God as their source and essence, is humankind's greatest good and blessedness.

In Baruch Spinoza's chief work, the *Ethics*, he attempted to deduce his results from certain fundamental conceptions by using the geometric method. He even adopted the external form of Euclidean geometry, beginning each of the five parts into which the work is divided with definitions, axioms, and postulates, and advancing by formally demonstrating a series of definite propositions. Spinoza, like René Descartes before him, believed that mathematics furnished the universal type of true science, and he assumed that absolute certainty, which was then generally regarded as essential to science, could be attained only by following the same method. It has been pointed out that what is most valuable in Spinoza's system is not the result of his formal deductions, however, but the genius evident in his speculative intuition and keen psychological analysis.

In the *Ethics*, Spinoza is most directly concerned with the problem of humanity's place in nature—its relation to God or the total system of things—and the possibility of freedom. He demonstrates the possibility that human freedom depends upon first recognizing that one is part of nature and that one's mind, like everything else, is subject to uniform natural laws. It is not contingency or some peculiar power of free will that governs mental experiences; here as well as elsewhere, all takes place according to law and

necessity. Nature's laws, he argues, are always and everywhere the same. Thus, there should be one method of understanding the nature of all things: through nature's universal laws and rules.

THE EMOTIONS

Spinoza goes on to consider human actions and desires in the same way that he considers lines, planes, and solids. From this standpoint, he gives a scientific account of the origin and nature of the emotions, showing how they necessarily arise from certain assignable causes and how their intensity depends on definite natural conditions. The emotions are all found to be variations of the primary states: desire, pleasure, or joy, which is the passage of the organism to a higher state of perfection; and pain, or sorrow, which is the passage to a lower state. To pass to a higher or lower state is not to become better or worse in the moral sense, but to become more or less active. The man of inadequate ideas is passive in that what he does depends on what happens to him rather than what he does or who he is.

This reduction of the emotions to law, however, is only a preliminary step in Spinoza's treatment. To attain freedom, it is first necessary to recognize the bondage of humanity, the fixed determination of the emotions through natural laws. Just as knowledge is power with regard to external nature, however, so one can free oneself from the emotions by understanding their laws. In Spinoza's view, the mind is something more than a series of passive states. Its essence consists in an effort to preserve its own being to promote its own good. In carrying out this purpose, it finds that nothing is so helpful as knowledge.

KNOWLEDGE AND INTUITION

Through knowledge, it is possible to free humanity from the bondage of emotions. An emotion, when understood, becomes transformed and ceases to be a mere state of passivity. Moreover, when the conditions of an emotion are understood, it is possible to arrange and associate the various emotions in such a way as to strengthen and promote the occurrence of those that are desirable and to weaken and repress those that are harmful. The highest kind of knowledge for Spinoza is not scientific reason, but intuition, the direct insight that all things follow necessarily from the nature of God and hence form one system. To see all things not as a series of events in time but in their necessary logical relation to God is what Spinoza calls viewing the world under the form of eternity. Spinoza's conception of God is very different from the ordinary theological one. For Spinoza, God is not transcendent, existing apart from nature, but nature itself as an active self-determining process.

HUMANITY'S HIGHEST GOOD

This highest knowledge gives rise to the intellectual love of God, which is the highest good, or blessedness, for humanity. It is through the strength of this emotion, which is not a passion but the highest activity of mind, that the other emotions are most successfully governed and transformed. This intellectual love of God enables the mind to renounce entirely all finite or personal desires, as well as all envy and jealousy. Spinoza argues that he who loves God does not demand that God should love him in return. He demands nothing for himself; instead, he acquiesces completely in the order of the universe. Moreover, Spinoza maintains that since this knowledge and the intellectual love to which it gives rise are eternal, the mind that experiences these must have something in it that is eternal and that cannot be destroyed with the body. An interesting feature of Spinoza's philosophy is the close relationship between the individual and society. It is not merely the individual good that he sought but one that as many as possible would share. In many passages in the *Ethics*, Spinoza approaches the modern conception of the individual as standing in an organic relation to society.

Genevieve Slomski

FURTHER READING

Bennett, Jonathan. *A Study of Spinoza's Ethics*. Indianapolis: Hackett, 1984.

Garrett, Aaron V. *Meaning in Spinoza's Method*. New York: Cambridge University Press, 2003.

Grene, Marjorie, ed. *Spinoza: A Collection of Critical Essays*. Notre Dame, Ind.: University of Notre Dame Press, 1979.

Hampshire, Stuart. *Spinoza*. New York: Penguin Books, 1987.

Joachim, Harold H. *A Study of the "Ethics" of Spinoza*. New York: Russell & Russell, 1964.

Lloyd, Genevieve. *Routledge Philosophy Guidebook to Spinoza and the "Ethics."* New York: Routledge, 1996.

Scruton, Roger. *Spinoza*. New York: Routledge, 1999.

Smith, Steven B. *Spinoza's Book of Life: Freedom and Redemption in the "Ethics."* New Haven, Conn.: Yale University Press, 2003.

Strauss, Leo. *Spinoza's Critique of Religion*. Translated by E. M. Sinclair. New York: Schocken Books, 1965.

SEE ALSO: Freedom and liberty; Hate; Intuitionist ethics; Perry, R. B.; Spinoza, Baruch.

Ethics in Government Act

IDENTIFICATION: U.S. federal law setting standards for appointments of government officials

DATE: Became law October 26, 1978

TYPE OF ETHICS: Legal and judicial ethics

SIGNIFICANCE: This law requires nominees for positions requiring Senate confirmation to make financial disclosure reports; it also established the Office of Government Ethics to oversee the administration of ethics policies in the executive branch of the federal government.

The Ethics in Government Act was passed in the aftermath of the scandals during the Nixon administration to lessen the likelihood that future presidential nominees for government positions would have conflicts of interest that might result in personal or financial gain. The law requires presidential nominees for positions requiring Senate confirmation to file financial disclosure reports. Their reports should list sources of income, assets and liabilities, and affiliations with organizations that may lead to conflicts of interest. The act also created the Office of Government Ethics, which reviews the disclosure reports of presidential nominees and issues opinion letters concerning possible conflicts of interest.

POSSIBLE CONFLICTS OF INTEREST

The principal concerns that guide the reviews of financial disclosure reports are the potentials for officials to (1) participate in matters in which they have personal financial interests, (2) receive income from nongovernment sources for government service, (3) participate in outside activities that may involve the government, and (4) experience conflicts following their government employment because of restrictions on dealings with former agencies. The latter issue primarily affects former officials, but it is frequently a concern for officials entering government service because it can affect their future employment prospects.

THE REVIEW PROCESS

The Office of Counsel to the President typically solicits complete financial records to anticipate problems before nominations are announced and explains reporting requirements to potential nominees. The Office of Counsel provides forms to potential nominees and gives the completed reports to designated agency ethics officials and to the Office of Government Ethics. Agency heads are responsible for compliance with the ethics program, and they appoint the agency's ethics official. The financial disclosure reports are also reviewed by the employing agency's representative, and the agency's evaluation is included in the Office of Government Ethics's opinion letter. The opinion letters are reviewed by the president before the nomination is sent forward. The members of the Senate involved in the confirmation process review the letters and generally include their own assessment of possible conflicts of interest.

Identification of possible conflicts may result in nominees being asked to disqualify or recuse themselves from participation in decisions regarding firms or industries in which they may have personal or financial interests, divest themselves of financial interests in particular firms or industries which may cause conflicts of interest, or put their financial holdings into "blind trusts" so that they will have no knowledge of their financial interests in particular firms or industries. A waiver may also be granted if it is determined that a nominee's interests in a particular firm or industry are so slight or peripheral as to assure that any conflict of interest will be very minor.

RESTRICTIONS ON FUTURE EMPLOYMENT

In 1989, President George Bush appointed a Commission on Federal Ethics Law Reform that recommended strengthening the provisions dealing with "influence peddling" as well as broadening the provisions dealing with conflicts of interest when officials may gain personally or financially. Subsequent amendment of the Ethics in Government Act expanded its scope to include influence peddling by former officials. The act restricts what former government officials may do upon leaving office, principally in terms of a two-year prohibition against representing private interests before their former agencies. These provisions were designed to lessen conflicts of interest that may arise during an official's tenure with an agency, when he or she may be anticipating future employment outside government, and to help stop the "revolving door" pattern of employment in which individuals move from government agencies to the industries they were responsible for regulating and vice versa. The provisions also include a one-year prohibition on former officials representing private interests before their former government employer when the individual had no responsibilities relating to his or her current employer.

IMPACT OF THE ACT

Critics of the Ethics in Government Act have charged that it makes it difficult to recruit potential officials from the private sector. This criticism was expressed numerous times during the Reagan administration. At issue are whether the financial disclosure requirements themselves are impediments to recruitment because individuals do not want to make their finances public or whether other restrictions on employment discourage individuals from accepting nominations. In addition to financial disclosure and limitations on relationships with former and future employers, the act restricts the freedom of officials to manage their own financial affairs.

Supporters of the act argue that it focuses attention on the issue of ethics and, in particular, reinforces the principle that even the appearance of impropriety is to be avoided in public-sector employment. The Ethics in Government Act also reaffirms the principles that government officials should not use their positions for personal gain and that government business should be conducted "in the sunshine." Moreover, the act serves to protect appointing officials from inadvertently selecting someone who might be motivated to seek public employment for personal gain or who might later be charged with bias in making decisions.

The standards set in the Ethics in Government Act have had a broad impact in government. States and municipalities are increasingly requiring financial disclosure by political appointees and elected officials to lessen the potential for conflicts of interest. Conflicts that may arise because of dual employment, financial interests in businesses that deal with government agencies, and the use of public positions to benefit private interests are examined closely. Conflicts arising from the employment of law enforcement officers in private security during their off-duty hours are cases in point.

William L. Waugh, Jr.

FURTHER READING

Bull, Martin J., and James L. Newell, eds. *Corruption in Contemporary Politics.* New York: Palgrave Macmillan, 2003.

Richter, William L., Frances Burke, and Jameson Doig, eds. *Combating Corruption: Encouraging Ethics, a Sourcebook for Public Service Ethics.* 2d ed. Washington, D.C.: American Society for Public Administration, 1995.

Denhardt, Robert B. *Public Administration: An Action Orientation.* 2d ed. Belmont, Calif.: Wadsworth, 1995.

SEE ALSO: Apologizing for past wrongs; Campaign finance reform; Conflict of interest; Constitutional government; Corruption; Lobbying; Politics; Private vs. public morality; Public's right to know; Realpolitik.

Ethics/morality distinction

DEFINITION: Distinction drawn by moral philosophers between the study of moral judgments and choices (ethics) and the systems of rules and values governing those choices (morality)

TYPE OF ETHICS: Theory of ethics

SIGNIFICANCE: Ethics is the study of morality, but almost every system of ethics also attempts to create, formulate, or advocate its own moral principles, thus blurring the distinction.

Ethics refers to the most important values and beliefs of an individual or a society. These beliefs help shape the character of the people in that society, teaching them what is good and bad. Ethics implies knowledge of these basic principles and the responsibility to make the appropriate choice when necessary. The strong bond between ethics and a society's customs raises the issue of relativism. Moral philosophers argue that ethics implies values that are universal and are not tied to one society or time period.

The particular rules implementing ethical beliefs in a specific society may change, but not the fundamental principles. In a society composed of subcultures, the specific laws or customs of each may be expressed differently. The distinction between ethics and morality becomes important when the rules used by different groups are not understood or accepted. Unacceptable behavior may be assumed to mean unacceptable values. In that case, the ethos, or unifying characteristics, of a society is weakened and individuals within that society must justify their actions, because morality cannot be assumed.

James A. Baer

SEE ALSO: Applied ethics; Choice; Ethics; Moral education; Morality; Multiculturalism; Normative vs. descriptive ethics; Pluralism; Relativism; Theory and practice.

Ethnic cleansing

DEFINITION: Forced expulsion of a specific population from a territory

TYPE OF ETHICS: Race and ethnicity

SIGNIFICANCE: Ethnic cleansing is predicated either upon a judgment that the presence of a specific ethnic group in an area is harmful, or upon a judgment that the cleansing group has a moral right or imperative to create a homogeneous culture for itself. Either judgment will activate ethical concerns about violence, warfare, prejudice, human rights, minority rights, and the rights to self-determination of both groups.

"Ethnic cleansing" is a euphemism for murder and land theft that is sanctioned by a state government. It usually refers to the expulsion of an "undesirable" population from a given territory for political, strategic, or ideological reasons, or because of religious or ethnic discrimination. Forced emigration and population exchange are elements of ethnic cleansing. Forced population removal or transfers have occurred repeatedly throughout history, most often to create or secure an ethnically homogeneous home-land or state.

The Assyrian king Tiglath-Pileser III (745-727 B.C.E.) carried out one of the earlier recorded cases of ethnic cleansing. One-half of the population of any land that he conquered was forcefully removed and replaced by settlers from other regions who were loyal to him. Many centuries later, European settlers in North America slowly "cleansed" the land of most Native Americans with the tacit consent of the state. By expelling the entire East Indian community from Uganda during the early 1970's, Idi Amin of Uganda "cleansed" that country of East Indians so that indigenous Africans could take over their land and businesses. During the 1990's, Serbians in the former Yugoslavia tried to "cleanse" territory that they claimed for Serbian Christians by driving out Muslim citizens. They used murder, rape, starvation, and a variety of other deplorable techniques to achieve their goal.

There is no moral justification for ethnic cleansing. It is carried out by those who hope that if they occupy the land long enough, their right to it will not be challenged. Yet history has shown that time neither heals every wound nor justifies every action. Ethnic cleansing is and has always been criminal. It should not be sanctioned by any self-respecting government, because it is ethically unjust.

Dallas L. Browne

SEE ALSO: Bosnia; Concentration camps; Genocide, cultural; Genocide and democide; Kosovo; Land mines; Refugees and stateless people.

Ethnocentrism

DEFINITION: Attitude according to which one's own race or society is the central criterion for evaluating other groups or cultures

TYPE OF ETHICS: Race and ethnicity

SIGNIFICANCE: Ethnocentrism promotes loyalty to the group, sacrifice for it, and hatred and contempt for those outside it.

Ethnocentrism is the emotional attitude that places a high value on one's own customs and traditions and belittles all others, rating as least valuable those who differ most. One's own group is the center of everything, and all others are scaled with reference to it. Each group nourishes its own pride and vanity, believes itself to be superior, exalts its own divinities, and looks with contempt on outsiders.

Sociologists and anthropologists have found that people everywhere seem to believe that the groups to which they belong are the best and that their ways and morals are superior. Others outside their group are something else—perhaps not defined—but not real people: the Jews divided all mankind into themselves and the Gentiles, the Greeks and Romans called outsiders "barbarians," the Arabs referred to others as "infidels," and the whites in South Africa called the blacks "kaffirs." Although ethnocentrism serves a useful purpose in that it performs the function of discipline and social control within the group, it can be very irritating and disruptive, and when it gets out of hand, it may be dangerous and even fatal.

Olusoji A. Akomolafe

SEE ALSO: Anthropological ethics; Bigotry; Multiculturalism; Oppression; Post-Enlightenment ethics; Racism; Social Darwinism.

Etiquette

DEFINITION: Code of manners governing social behavior and interactions

TYPE OF ETHICS: Personal and social ethics

SIGNIFICANCE: Disagreement exists as to whether etiquette should be considered a branch of ethics. The answer depends on the extent to which politeness and manners are judged to be moral requirements.

Normative ethics and etiquette are alike in that each offers prescriptions concerning how people ought to behave. Ethics tells people to avoid certain forms of conduct because they are morally reprehensible and recommends that they engage in others because they are morally admirable. Etiquette, in contrast, prohibits certain forms of conduct because they are discourteous or vulgar and recommends others as polite or elegant. Ethics and etiquette are separate at least to the extent that ethical violations can be committed without violating etiquette, and to violate at least some aspects of etiquette, it is not necessary to violate ethics.

Etiquette, unlike ethics, is much concerned with characterizing the social meanings of forms of behavior, determining what behavior expresses respect, contempt, gratitude, aggression, and so forth. Different societies have very different conventions about these matters. For example, in Turkey, the normal way in which men greet one another with respect is by kissing, while in English-speaking lands, kissing is deemed improper and a handshake is preferred. Since these conventions vary so widely, the prescriptions of etiquette are far more socially relative than are those of ethics. The maxim "When in Rome do as the Romans do" generally applies to etiquette, though it is less sound as a maxim of ethics.

The *Instructions of Ptah Hotep*, an Egyptian text dating from about 2500 B.C.E., provides the earliest known account of polite behavior. Later Western notions of etiquette are rooted in medieval chivalry, according to which the knight should be not only a powerful warrior but also honorable and well mannered. In particular, he is to display gentle, sincere devotion toward ladies, and they, in turn, are to be delicately refined and of absolute purity. The Renaissance writer Baldassare Castiglione expresses these ideals in *The Courtier* (1528). Later, the term "etiquette" entered English with the publication of Lord Chesterfield's *Letters to His Son* (1774), in which the author expounded gentlemanly deportment.

ETIQUETTE AND CLASS

These codes of manners were aristocratic. Persons of lower-class birth did not understand or conform to them and therefore were marked off from the upper class. In the nineteenth and twentieth centuries, however, class divisions weakened and an expanding circle of people sought to advance themselves socially by cultivating good manners. Books on etiquette multiplied. In the United States, the writings of arbiters such as Emily Post, Amy Vanderbilt, and Miss Manners (Judith Martin) have enjoyed

---

Categories of Personal Etiquette

Behavior	Examples of prescriptions
Eating	Style and self-restraint in table manners, table settings, and service.
Dressing	Modesty and elegance according to sex, age, and occasion—formal or informal.
Communicating	Tact and skill in handling introductions, polite conversation, writing letters, telephoning, use of calling cards.
Socializing	Graciousness in giving and attending parties and other entertainments, having and being houseguests, making and receiving social visits.
Celebrating	Appropriate degrees of ostentatious formality in private celebrations of weddings, engagements, births, graduations, and anniversaries.
Rituals	Propriety in observing formalities of official diplomatic, religious, military, or governmental ceremonies.

---

wide circulation. These authors have sought to present etiquette not class-consciously but democratically, offering guidance in civility for everyone. They consider not only everyday personal etiquette but also special areas of etiquette; for example, in business, in the professions, in diplomacy, and so on.

Iconoclastic persons often view etiquette with contempt, because they condemn class-conscious snobbishness and artificial conventions and because they suppose that the ethical virtues of sincerity and truthfulness are all that are needed in life. They are right, of course, that arbiters of etiquette sometimes have defended frivolous rules and sometimes have done so for blameworthy reasons. They are wrong, however, to suppose that egalitarian society has no need of etiquette and that social interactions could successfully proceed were manners guided by sincerity and truthfulness alone. The point that they miss is that human beings in their everyday contacts readily generate antagonisms that can become destructive unless they are covered by the cloak of tactfulness and smoothed by the oil of polite formalities. A society that is polite, at least to a judicious degree, can function more efficiently and more happily than can a sincerely truthful but uncivil society.

ETIQUETTE VS. ETHICS

Do ethics and etiquette sometimes conflict? It might seem so, since ethics is thought to prescribe that people not engage in lying or deception, while etiquette encourages the use of white lies. ("I'm so sorry, but I'm busy that night," one is supposed to say, instead of the more truthful "I don't like you and don't want to come.") This supposed conflict between ethics and etiquette is not deep-seated, however, since the white lies of etiquette can be justified in terms of the ethical principle of nonmaleficence (avoiding hurting the feelings of others). Moreover, the saying of something not literally true is scarcely a lie when everyone knows that it is prescribed by social custom.

Etiquette enjoins people always to be polite. In rare cases, when there are strongly countervailing ethical considerations, one ought to abandon politeness in order to do what is morally right (for example, a firefighter, in order to extinguish a fire, may have to intrude violently on someone's privacy). Usually, however, etiquette conflicts very little with ethics, and violations of etiquette commonly are violations of ethics also, because they tend to injure others, at least mildly.

A controversial question that philosophers have not discussed extensively is whether politeness itself should be classified as a moral virtue, along with honesty, fidelity, modesty, and the like. If by "moral virtues" are meant those admirable human qualities that enhance a person's capacity for contributing to the well-being of society, then politeness can be a virtue in this sense. Notice, however, that being polite is not the same thing as being favorably disposed toward everyone else. Someone possessing the virtue of politeness knows ways of politely expressing negative reactions toward others, and especially toward those who are out of line.

Stephen F. Barker

FURTHER READING

Caldwell, Mark. *A Short History of Rudeness: Manners, Morals, and Misbehavior in Modern America.* New York: Picador USA, 1999.

Castiglione, Baldassare. *The Book of the Courtier.* Translated by George Bull. Harmondsworth, England: Penguin Books, 1976.

Chesterfield, Philip, earl of. *Lord Chesterfield's Letters to His Son and Others.* London: Dent, 1963.

Post, Emily. *Emily Post's Etiquette.* 16th ed. New York: HarperCollins, 1997.

Singer, Peter, ed. *A Companion to Ethics.* Cambridge, Mass.: Blackwell Reference, 1993.

Tuckerman, Nancy, and Nancy Dunnan. *The Amy Vanderbilt Complete Book of Etiquette.* New York: Doubleday, 1995.

SEE ALSO: Cell-phone etiquette; Chivalry; Codes of civility; Gossip; Internet chat rooms; Legal ethics; Scientology.

Eugenics

DEFINITION: Attempt to alter human evolution through selection
TYPE OF ETHICS: Bioethics
SIGNIFICANCE: Even in its most benign form, eugenics raises serious ethical questions, since it almost unavoidably involves some people making reproductive choices for others, and making decisions about which genetic traits should be preserved, strengthened, and eliminated from the human race. The darker forms of the science entail much clearer and more heinous transgressions, up to and including involuntary sterilization and genocide.

Although the idea of selective breeding dates back to antiquity, the first detailed exposition of eugenics founded in genetic and evolutionary science was produced by Sir Francis Galton in *Hereditary Genius* (1869). Two main strategies of eugenics are possible: increasing the gene contributions of those who have desirable traits (positive eugenics) and decreasing the gene contributions of those who have undesired traits (negative eugenics). Genetic testing must first determine what traits people have and to what extent each trait is heritable. Supporters of eugenics claim that intelligence is genetically determined, but most data concerning this claim are suspect, and the true heritability of intelligence is still hotly debated.

Positive eugenics encourages people with desirable traits to produce more numerous offspring. Encouragement may take the form of monetary rewards, paying the educational expenses for children, and so forth. Sperm of desirable men could be collected and stored for the future artificial insemination of selected women, but this suggestion has rarely been followed because of the expense of the procedure.

Negative eugenics applications may mean that individuals carrying undesired traits might be killed or sterilized. Advocates of eugenics say that this cruelty is for the greater good of humanity, but opponents strongly object. Beyond this issue, other ethical questions arise: Which traits are desired? Who will make the decisions? Since many traits vary by race, negative eugenics raises questions of racism and brings humanity close to the dangers of genocide. (The only nationwide eugenics laws in history were used in Nazi Germany to exterminate Jews and other non-"Aryans.") Geneticists have also determined that negative eugenics is very limited in its ability to change gene frequencies. Most genetic defects are rare, and selection against rare traits is very ineffective. Selection is especially ineffective if a trait is influenced by environment or education, as intelligence scores are. Also, if negative eugenics could succeed, it would reduce the genetic variability of the population, and variability may itself be desirable, especially if future environments change.

Eli C. Minkoff

FURTHER READING

Black, Edwin. *War Against the Weak: Eugenics and America's Campaign to Create a Master Race.* New York: Four Walls Eight Windows, 2003.

Kevles, Daniel J. *In the Name of Eugenics: Genetics and the Uses of Human Heredity.* Cambridge, Mass.: Harvard University Press 1995.

Kline, Wendy. *Building a Better Race.* Los Angeles: University of California Press, 2001.

SEE ALSO: Bioethics; Cloning; Evolutionary theory; Future-oriented ethics; Genetic counseling; Genetic engineering; Genetic testing; Genocide and democide; Intelligence testing; Nazi science; Social Darwinism; Sterilization of women.

Euthanasia

DEFINITION: Active or passive encouragement of the death of a person to prevent further suffering

TYPE OF ETHICS: Bioethics

SIGNIFICANCE: Euthanasia continues to be an extremely controversial issue, since it engages one of the most fundamental moral questions: Under what circumstances, if any, is it ethical to cause the death of another person?

The term "euthanasia" is derived from the Greek phrase that means a pleasant or easy death. Relieving suffering was part of the Hippocratic oath, dating from the fourth century B.C.E., when Greek physicians were sworn to preserve life and never willingly to take it. This sanctity-of-life principle was not, however, honored always and in all places. The Greeks and Romans, for example, ruled that slaves and "barbarians" had no right to life. In Sparta, the law required the death of deformed infants. The philosophers Plato and Aristotle regarded infanticide and abortion as acceptable, and Plato himself was a victim of compulsory suicide.

Before and during World War II, Nazi Germany practiced euthanasia on those viewed as socially unproductive: Jews, older people, the deformed, the chronically ill. Memories of these compulsory deaths have caused many people to resist the idea and practice of euthanasia, even by what would be considered humane methods. In 1969, however, Great Britain's House of Lords passed a voluntary euthanasia law; earlier bills had been defeated in 1938 and 1950. The main purpose of the British law was to authorize physicians to give euthanasia to a patient thought to be suffering from an incurable physical condition and who has made a declaration requesting euthanasia. A clause provides that a declaration may be revoked at any time. Passive euthanasia had been generally accepted, but Parliament by this act legalized active euthanasia.

Euthanasia is divided into two types: active and passive. Active euthanasia is direct intervention to bring about the death of one suffering from a terminal illness, while passive euthanasia is letting nature take its course. The intent to bring about death requires ethical analysis to find a moral consensus, since the rights of an individual and those of society come into play.

CHRISTIANITY AND EUTHANASIA

Throughout the twentieth century, Western churches—the Roman Catholic Church in particular—took strong stands against both types of euthanasia. During the medieval era, Saint Augustine of Hippo and Saint Thomas Aquinas affirmed that only God is the arbiter of life and death. They taught that pain and suffering have purpose in God's sight. In 1940, the Catholic Church officially condemned the administration of euthanasia for any reason as contrary to natural and divine law. In late 1957, however, Pope Pius XII, speaking to an International Congress of Anaesthesiologists, stated that "morally one is held to use only ordinary means" to sustain life and that in cases of terminal illness, there is no obligation to continue lifesaving measures. Differences exist, however, regarding what constitutes ordinary versus extraordinary means and who should decide when death is preferable to treatment.

Ordinary means of treating a sick or dying person are means that are in common use, while extraordinary means involve nonstandard treatment, the new and the rare. Scientific and technological advances have transformed the extraordinary into the ordinary. This development complicates the issue, since such factors as scarce funds and facilities also come into play, introducing another ethical problem: the acceptability of utilitarianism.

The sanctity-of-life principle holds that it is absolutely prohibited either intentionally to kill a patient or intentionally to let a patient die and to base decisions for the prolongation or shortening of human life on considerations of the quality of that life. Under no circumstances is there a "right to die." This is true irrespective of the competency or noncompetency of a person to decide for himself or herself whether to choose euthanasia.

Patients, doctors, and the patients' families are generally the decision makers in cases of possible euthanasia, whether active or passive. By 2004, virtually all states accepted living wills whereby competent adults give directions for the health care they want if they become terminally ill and cannot direct their own care. Those who believe in the sanctity of life fear that these living wills are a wedge that will allow nonvoluntary euthanasia to become acceptable.

While staunchly opposed to euthanasia, some churches and courts accept the "double-effect" principle. This principle holds that an action whose primary effect is to relieve suffering may be ethically justified, although a secondary effect may be death. Physicians, they argue, have a duty to relieve pain as well as to preserve life—although doing so may shorten the person's life.

THE QUALITY-OF-LIFE ETHIC

Much debate centers on the quality-of-life ethic. Some argue that if there is little hope that a given treatment prolonging a person's life will allow that person to live a beneficial, satisfactory life, then euthanasia is justified. In such cases, the sanctity-of-life principle is set against the quality-of-life approach. How can a proper quality of life be guaranteed to all citizens and an equitable distribution of medical care be ensured? Using utilitarianism as a guideline, providing high-quality life for a majority takes priority over prolonging the lives of a few. Cost-effectiveness becomes a major factor in the decision to choose or not to choose euthanasia. This is unacceptable to many persons, since it places an economic value on people.

The counterargument is made that while every person is equal to all others, not every life is of equal value. The case of Karen Ann Quinlan is cited as an example of the quality-of-life and sanctity-of-life dilemma. The victim of an accident, Quinlan went into a coma in 1975 and was kept on a respirator for several years. After repeated requests from her guardian, a court decision allowed discontinuance of the respirator. Quinlan's life was not benefiting her and was burdening her parents unduly. The quality-of-life judgment prevailed in that case.

In 1990, the U.S. Supreme Court ruled that patients have a constitutional right to discontinue unwanted life-sustaining medical treatment. In 1992, the Netherlands's parliament approved liberal rules on euthanasia and doctor-assisted suicide. The guidelines require, however, that the patient must be mentally competent, be suffering unbearable pain, and request euthanasia repeatedly; and the doctor must consult a second physician before proceeding.

The right to die with dignity, free of terminal agony, is a concept that enjoys strong public support. Most of this support, however, is for passive euthanasia; support for active euthanasia is more moderate. The notion of a right to die is still very controversial, making moral standards of judgment ever more imperative. Whether supporting the sanctity-of-life doctrine or the quality-of-life argument, there is general agreement among those most engaged with this issue that not every patient's life ought to be prolonged. The moral debate is over how this life should be ended. Individuals, families, courts, and ethics committees struggle over euthanasia, striving for justice for both patient and society.

S. Carol Berg

FURTHER READING

Bernards, Neal, ed. *Euthanasia: Opposing Viewpoints.* San Diego, Calif.: Greenhaven Press, 1989.

Churchill, Larry R. *Rationing Health Care in America: Perspectives and Principles of Justice.* Notre Dame, Ind.: University of Notre Dame Press, 1987.

Kluge, Eike-Henner W. *The Ethics of Deliberative Death.* Port Washington, N.Y.: Kennikat Press, 1981.

Lammers, Stephen E., and Allen Verhey, eds. *On Moral Medicine: Theological Perspectives in Medical Ethics.* Grand Rapids, Mich.: William B. Eerdmans, 1987.

Van Zyl, Liezl. *Death and Compassion: A Virtue-Based Approach to Euthanasia.* Burlington, Vt.: Ashgate, 2000.

Weir, Robert F., ed. *Ethical Issues in Death and Dying.* 2d ed. New York: Columbia University Press, 1986.

SEE ALSO: Health care allocation; Hippocrates; Homicide; Infanticide; Kevorkian, Jack; Medical bills of rights; Quinlan, Karen Ann; Right to die; Suicide; Suicide assistance.

Medgar Evers during a television interview in 1962. (Library of Congress)

Evers, Medgar

IDENTIFICATION: Martyred American civil rights activist

BORN: July 2, 1925, Decatur, Mississippi

DIED: June 12, 1963, Jackson, Mississippi

TYPE OF ETHICS: Race and ethnicity

SIGNIFICANCE: The National Association for the Advancement of Colored People's (NAACP) first field secretary in Mississippi, Evers was an important civil rights activist and organizer. His assassination received widespread news coverage and was a source of national outrage that helped to galvanize the Civil Rights movement.

After growing up and attending segregated high schools in Decatur and Newton, Mississippi, Evers served in the army, seeing action in the European theater of World War II. Afterward, he attended the all-black Alcorn Agricultural and Mechanical College, graduating in 1950. He became an insurance salesman but devoted much spare time to his work for the NAACP. Trying to organize local affiliates for the NAACP, he visited most areas of the state and began building a wide-ranging base of support. By 1954, he had moved to Jackson to become field secretary for the entire state.

In relocating to Jackson, Evers had moved to a city that had rigid segregation. To bring change, in 1963 Evers organized a massive nonviolent protest movement. Day in, day out, Evers challenged segregation and discrimination by personally leading the protests. The protests and Evers's life were cut short when, on June 12, 1963, Evers was assassinated by Byron de La Beckwith. De La Beckwith was tried twice for the crime in 1964, but both trials resulted in hung juries. He was finally retried and convicted in 1994 and spent over six years in prison before dying of heart problems on January 21, 2001.

In the twelve weeks after Evers's death, 758 racial demonstrations occurred in the United States. Such pressures convinced President John F. Kennedy to send a civil rights bill to Congress, a bill that eventually became the Civil Rights Act of 1964, a law that gave minorities more justice than they had ever had before.

James Smallwood
Updated by the editors

SEE ALSO: Assassination; Civil Rights Act of 1964; Civil Rights movement; King, Martin Luther, Jr.; National Association for the Advancement of Colored People; Racism.

"Everyone does it"

DEFINITION: Rationalization invoked to excuse, justify, or otherwise neutralize the moral bind of law, freeing one to commit acts deemed morally, legally, and socially undesirable
TYPE OF ETHICS: Personal and social ethics
SIGNIFICANCE: Originally thought to explain delinquency among delinquent youth, the idea that "everyone does it" has been shown to explain why white-collar offenders commit crime and simultaneously maintain their sense of being upright citizens.

In his 1994 book "*Everybody Does It!*," criminologist Thomas Gabor describes how people justify their involvement in dishonest, unethical, or immoral behavior, using phrases that "normalize" their actions to themselves and others. Phrases such as "everyone's doing it" were first identified by sociologists

David Matza and Gresham Sykes during the late 1950's as techniques of "neutralization" for questionable behavior.

Neutralizations are words and phrases that negate the moral and ethical binds of law. Those who use them draw on the explicit exceptions to law such as "I was not myself at the time" or "I was acting in self-defense." Embezzlers commonly describe their stealing as "borrowing." Dishonest employees typically blame their excessive expense-account claims, time thefts, or thefts of company property on their companies or unscrupulous supervisors, claiming that their companies have treated them badly, their bosses have cheated them out of vacation days, or their managers have prevented them from receiving deserved raises or promotions.

LANGUAGE OF NEUTRALIZATION

Similarly, corporations themselves use neutralizing words and phrases to explain that their fraudulent actions are necessary for them to remain competitive. Government agencies may explain their abuses of power as necessary to "protect the public." The use of such phrases is self-serving, in that they reduce the sense of moral culpability of wrongdoers, while also freeing them to commit further offenses, especially if they sense that their excuses will be accepted by judging audiences.

Neutralizations may be excuses that people use to acknowledge committing misdeeds, while denying responsibility for them; an example is "I was ordered to do it." Alternatively, neutralizations may be justifications offered to accept responsibility for misdeeds or to assert the rightfulness of the actions, such as "no one got hurt."

Most people use such "claims to normality" in varying degrees to excuse or justify their deviant behavior; some to negate serious deviant, and even criminal, behavior. As a claim of normality, saying that "everyone does it" promotes the commonality of the action over any principle of ethics or law.

A crucial issue of neutralizations is their timing. When they occur after the acts, neutralizations are seen merely as rationalizations seeking to minimize the culpability or consequences for questionable behavior. When they occur prior to the acts, they can motivate misbehavior by freeing potential wrongdoers from the moral and ethical bind of law.

Criminologists argue that to counteract the effect

Examples of Neutralizing Accounts

Claim of normality	"Everyone cheats on their taxes."
Denial of responsibility	"It's not *my* fault."
Denial of injury	"No one got hurt."
Denial of victim	"They had it coming!"
Condemning the condemners	"The police are corrupt." "Judges are biased." "Our priests are immoral."
Appeal to higher loyalties	"I did it for the good of my family."
Metaphor of the ledger	"If you weigh all the good things I've done against all the bad things, I must come out on the good side."

of neutralization that undermines morality and ethics, it is necessary continuously to point out the harm caused by the misdeeds—through the media, meetings, and interpersonal relations. It is also important to be clear that words and phrases used to neutralize are nothing less than self-deception, designed at best to minimize the consequences for the offenders, and at worst, to justify doing harm to others because of harm others have done in the past. An example of the latter would be to justify any action that undermines corporate power because of the damage corporations have done to the environment in the past.

Stuart Henry

FURTHER READING

Gabor, Thomas. *"Everybody Does It!": Crime by the Public.* Toronto: University of Toronto Press, 1994.

Katz, Leo. *Bad Acts and Guilty Minds: Conundrums of the Criminal Law.* Chicago: University of Chicago Press, 1987.

SEE ALSO: Bystanders; Choice; Conscience; Corruption; Hypocrisy; Role models; White-collar crime.

Evil

DEFINITION: Morally reprehensible behavior or force

TYPE OF ETHICS: Religious ethics

SIGNIFICANCE: The existence of evil poses a problem for any religious system that posits a benevolent, omnipotent deity or for any secular system that represents human history as fundamentally meaningful. Indeed, many such systems seems to have been created precisely in order to explain or to mitigate evil's presence in the world.

The contradiction within the problem cited above can be solved logically only by denying any one of the three propositions. One must hold that God is not all powerful or that God is not all good. Alternately, theists such as Saint Augustine denied that evil exists; instead, there is only privation caused by humankind's distance from God. Modern Christian Scientists and Stoics generally follow the thought of Augustine. Some philosophers, however, such as William James, tried to solve the contradiction by denying the omnipotence of God, arguing instead that God had much, but limited, power.

All monotheistic religions that stress the omnipotence and goodness of God develop a system of ethics that defines what is right, what is wrong, what is good, and what is bad. The presence of evil in the world, however, threatened to destroy belief in God and thereby destroy absolute ethical values. In God's defense, theodicy developed. Theodicy, in its classical form, is the philosophical and/or theological attempt to justify the righteousness of God.

The Greek philosopher Epicurus (341-270 B.C.E.) was apparently the first to articulate the dilemma that the "question of evil" raises. The ancient Hebrews also grappled with the problem, as did early Christian theorists such as Saint Irenaeus, Saint Augustine, and Saint Thomas Aquinas. In the modern era, scholars who have examined the problem include Immanuel Kant, David Hume, John Stuart Mill, and Albert Camus.

DEFINITIONS

Several kinds of evil exist. The first is moral "radical" evil that occurs when an intelligent person knowingly and willingly inflicts suffering upon and harms another being, human or animal. The second type is natural evil, which is self-explanatory and which includes all manner of natural calamities such as earthquakes, tornadoes, tidal waves, cancer, heart disease, and so forth. The third is metaphysical evil, an abstract concept that "wonders" why a perfect, all-powerful God did not create a perfect universe.

Within the definitions above, the magnitude of evil varies. Some evil is personal, as is the case when an individual beats, robs, or murders another person. Evil can be "transpersonal," as is the case when one group (German Nazis, for example) tries to murder millions of other people. Evil can be "transgeneric"; that is, if imperfect beings exist on other planets, evil goes beyond humanity as we know it. Finally, evil can be cosmic, as is the case when nuclear powers threaten to blow up the world or when greed-driven corporations foul the world's environment beyond repair.

Genocide, terrorism, threats of nuclear war, individual callousness, and cruelty—all are evil. In a Texas town during the early 1990's, eight adults were charged with multiple counts of sexual assault on children who were related to the perpetrators—this is radical evil. In another state, four teenagers were found guilty of the murder of a twelve-year-old girl who was beaten, whipped, sodomized with a tire iron, raped, and—finally—doused with gasoline and burned alive; this is radical evil. Such evils, multiplied thousands of times are, according to nonbelievers, what the "silent" God must explain.

THE PROBLEM'S COMPLEXITY

Within the framework of monotheism, the existence of evil suggests that God does not exist. If God does exist amid flourishing evil, then He is either not all-powerful or is not all good. To paraphrase philosopher David Hume: Is God willing but not able to stop evil? Then he is impotent. Can he stop evil but is not willing to do so? Then he is not all good, and is probably malevolent. If he is willing and able, how does evil survive?

Looking at the problem another way, one might formulate the following set of ideas: Individuals are aware of the world around them; they see the world's evil, which causes death and suffering; they then have *prima facie* evidence that either there is no God or God is not all-benevolent; if God is not all-benevolent, if he allows innocents to suffer, he is capricious and cannot be trusted. Some critics say that it would be better to have no God than to have one who is capricious enough to allow evil.

Philosophically and theologically, the problem can be solved only through "belief" in the unknown, only with some rapid mental "footwork," with a mental "leap" of logic. For example, various scholars, including Saint Augustine, the historic defender of the faith, advance the "free will" concept, which blames humankind for most evils, beginning with the original "sin" of Adam and Eve (either literally or symbolically). Critics reply, however, that a good God would have made the pair incapable of sin, would have given them such basic values that they would always choose not to do wrong.

One nineteenth century German critic, Friedrich Schleiermacher, argued that God, being perfectly good, could only have created a perfectly good Adam and Eve. They would have been free to sin, but they would never have to do so. To cite them as the authors of a willful evil crime is to assert a major contradiction—it is, in effect, to assert that evil has created itself *ex nihilo* (out of nothing).

OTHER ASPECTS OF THE DEBATE

Another rationalization hinges on the process of "soul-making," which incorporates ideas that imperfect humans who created evil must, with God's help, evolve into better beings and that evil and suffering are a part of the evolutionary process. Critics charge, again, that a perfect God could have created better beings in the first place. Furthermore, they point out that part of the "soul-making" has to do with developing virtues, but why should this be necessary if everything is perfect in Heaven?

Another aspect of the debate is the Augustinian and Calvinist doctrine of predestination. Indeed, predestination sets up another dilemma. If God wants to "save" all humans but cannot do so, he has limited power. If, on the other hand, he chooses to "save" some and eternally damn all others to eons of torture, then he is not perfectly good and, indeed, has a streak of sadism. Sadism is a form of evil. Therefore, is God himself evil?

The concept of "hell" also raises problems. Hell

as laypeople understand it is a place of torment to which "bad" people go to be punished forever through eternity. How could a good God create such a place or allow it to exist? Why would a good God create such a place or allow it to exist? Is God, then, not good? Is he again playing the role of a sadist who enjoys watching people suffer? Many fundamentalist televangelists would gleefully tell one so.

Associated with Hell is Satan, or the "Devil," a supposed fallen angel that, many Christians, Jews, and Muslims believe, causes moral and natural evil. The concept of Satan probably had its origins in "extreme" religious dualism, one way that some people tried to rationalize about the existence of evil in a good world. One such dualistic religion was founded by Zarathustra (Zoroaster) about 1200 B.C.E. Zoroastrianism (or Mazdaism) taught that God—called Ohrmazd—was perfectly good but not all-powerful. Ohrmazd had a powerful antagonist, Ahriman, the personification of evil, destruction, and death.

Zoroastrianism also had its Adam and Eve, whose names were Mashye and Mashyane. Ahriman tempted them with lies, and they believed him—thus committing their first "sin." Then they offered an ox as a sacrifice—their second "sin." Zoroastrianism has various concepts in common with Christianity; for example, the fighting between God and the Devil (Ahriman) generally follows the Christian pattern.

Another example of dualism—a good being fighting a bad being, with the two having almost equal power—is found in Manichaeanism, a movement that was contemporary with early Christianity; indeed, Manichaeanism attracted Saint Augustine for a time.

Other philosophers turn to natural evils and explain them on the basis of the natural scientific laws of the universe. God, they argue, will never change those laws, because humankind needs their stability; without them, each new day would bring chaos to the natural world. Detractors again point out that an all-powerful God could intervene when necessary to modify natural laws (in the interest of saving human lives, for example).

ZOROASTRIANISM

As if they have taken a "lesson" from Zoroastrianism and Manichaeanism, some lay Christians have "promoted" Satan to the post of junior god; they believe that this world is ruled by Satan and has been

since he was cast down from Heaven. True, demonology does not have the following that it did in the medieval era, but even so, many laypersons, especially fundamentalist Protestants, still believe that the Devil exists and has power over this world. Even if the Devil is directly responsible for evil, a philosophical problem still exists, because God is responsible for everything in the universe, including Satan. If Satan is responsible for evil, why does a perfectly good all-powerful God allow "him" to exist?

Just as some modern theists and believers deny that real radical evil exists, many also deny that Satan exists. Again, such a view is problematic; it contradicts what is found in the Bible. Specifically, belief in the Devil permeates the New Testament. The Gospels show that Jesus knew that Satan and demons really existed, because he was forever speaking of them and trying to cast them out of people. It appears that, dogma aside, Christianity has developed a type of dualism within monotheism. The dualism is represented by the struggle between the good God and the Devil; hence, evil results.

Some philosophers, such as Friedrich Nietzsche, did not grapple with the above questions, but instead rejected God on other grounds. Nietzsche argued that the very definitions of the words "good" and "evil" had become corrupted. Christian good led to meekness, humility, and cowardliness. Conversely, Christians labeled as evil such traits as creativity, passion, self-assertion, and the willingness to fight for ideals. Nietzsche then proclaimed that "God is dead" and said that people should go beyond "good and evil"; Nietzsche stressed moral pluralism rather than moral absolutism. Christianity had only mired people in guilt and made them escapists who would settle for rewards in Heaven because, surely, they would get no rewards in this world. Nietzsche argued that the strong, with a "will to power," were the right people to lead a civilization; they could lead without guilt or regret.

Twentieth century horrors such as the death and destruction of two world wars—the last of which witnessed the killing of approximately six million Jews and at least that many Slavs—convinced many intellectuals that God did not exist, since he would have stopped such evil. The optimistic progressivism that characterized philosophical theism before 1914 gave way when mass destruction and death forced many thinkers to confront evil directly.

After living to see such evil, the existentialist Jean-Paul Sartre stressed the apparent powerlessness of God and went on to present a unique criticism. Sartre held that of the many people who try to believe in one God, a good number suffer overwhelming anxiety and puzzlement; they try to believe but are torn by doubt. After referring to the anxiety, the puzzlement, and the doubt, Sartre added simply that an all-powerful and all-good God would never allow his "children" to have such negative and perhaps destructive thoughts and feelings. Sartre's contemporary and countryman Albert Camus developed the concept of the absurd—that is, the nonexistence of God, the meaningless of human life, and the existence of evil all around. Camus believed that the appropriate response was to face the meaninglessness, to create personal meaning by making a commitment to something larger than oneself, and to work to make life as meaningful as possible.

THEODICY

Other writers have attacked theodicy in more specific ways. For example, some scholars have studied the testimony given at the Nuremberg Trials after World War II. One particularly unsettling type of murder at Auschwitz was committed by Nazi guards who isolated children who were too young or too sick to work. Those children would then be thrown directly into crematorium furnaces or into blazing pits. Some witnesses noted that the children were thrown in while still alive and that their screams could be heard all over the camp. No witnesses knew just how many children were viciously murdered in this way.

After he had studied the appropriate trial transcripts and had learned of the burning children, Irving Greenberg attacked theists with a vengeance. In making their defense of theodicy, Greenberg demanded that they should propose no argument, theological or otherwise, that would not be credible in the presence of the burning children. Greenberg submitted that no attempted justification of God was possible, that anyone who attempted it—with the burning children in mind—was guilty of something even worse than blasphemy.

Elie Wiesel, a victim who managed to stay alive in a Nazi death camp, added his own testimony about the problem of evil. He saw babies burned alive, yet the death by hanging of a small fifteen-year-old boy seemed to trouble him the most—perhaps because

the boy was so slight that the hanging did not immediately kill him. Instead, hanging by the rope, the boy struggled in the air, and twisted and turned; he suffered for at least an hour before he died. Just then, someone asked Wiesel "Where is God now?" Wiesel pointed at the boy on the gallows and spit out the word: "There!"

Animal pain is another aspect of evil. In the animal "kingdom," one species preys on and devours another. Still-conscious animals are literally eaten alive by their predators. Painful accidents and diseases are also common. Indeed, nature is "red in tooth and claw." How can nature's struggle of survival be reconciled with an omnipotent and perfectly good Creator? Scholarly attempts to answer such a question fall short of the mark. Some argue that animals live totally in the present and lack the human abilities of memory and anticipation that give rise to suffering; even though an animal's life may be violently terminated, the animal's life is most likely active and pleasurable up to the point of death. Such arguments about animal suffering are morally bankrupt, and such rationalizations may well be part of the evil world that no one can adequately explain.

Another answer to nature's brutal ways was advanced by such philosophers as C. S. Lewis, who, in *The Problem of Pain*, argued that Satan's premundane fall has had cosmic consequences, one of which was the perversion of the entire evolutionary process to create a savage world. Again, however, such statements can be criticized because the all-powerful God allows Satan to exist.

James Smallwood

FURTHER READING

Haybron, Daniel M., ed. *Earth's Abominations: Philosophical Studies of Evil*. New York: Rodopi, 2002. An anthology of essays by a wide range of secular philosophers discussing the nature of evil.

Hick, John. *Evil and the God of Love*. London: Collins, 1970. Advances the "soul-making" theodicy that holds that humans are finite and fallible beings who, in this world, need to be "schooled" in the ways of perfection, and that evil plays an important role in building the "character" of humans, who will eventually grow into the "likeness" of their Creator.

Midgley, Mary. *Wickedness: A Philosophical Essay*. Boston: Routledge & Kegan Paul, 1984. Midgley takes on all philosophers, past and present, who have ever investigated God's supposed role in the problem of evil. Blaming God, Midgley holds, is an intellectual exercise that is beside the point; instead, she looks at the human role in the creation of the problems of the world.

Parkin, David, ed. *The Anthropology of Evil.* New York: Basil Blackwell, 1985. A collection of fourteen essays written by outstanding anthropologists. Parkin's introduction is especially noteworthy because it helps readers understand the problem of evil.

Peterson, Michael L., ed. *The Problem of Evil: Selected Readings.* Notre Dame, Ind.: University of Notre Dame Press, 1992. A book that covers its topic from many viewpoints, including classical statements on the problem, modern statements, and essays on logic, existentialism, theodicy, and the nature of the perfectly good God.

Pinn, Anthony B., ed. *Moral Evil and Redemptive Suffering: A History of Theodicy in African-American Religious Thought.* Gainesville: University Press of Florida, 2002. A collection of essays by African American theologians, scholars, and political leaders, which put forward, examine, and critique the notion that suffering is redemptive and the evils faced by African Americans are therefore part of a greater good.

Plantinga, Alvin. *God, Freedom, and Evil.* New York: Harper & Row, 1974. A classic statement of the free-will defense and the minimalist defense in answering how a good God and evil can exist side by side.

Rowe, William L., ed. *God and the Problem of Evil.* Malden, Mass.: Blackwell, 2001. A collection of essays on evil and theodicy. Includes essays by Enlightenment thinkers as well as contemporary philosophers.

Russell, Jeffrey Burton. *The Prince of Darkness: Radical Evil and the Power of Good in History.* Ithaca, N.Y.: Cornell University Press, 1988. An outstanding volume that "follows" the Devil through a many-sided philosophical maze. Among the chapters are "The Good Lord and the Devil," "Dualism in the Desert," "The Classical Christian View," "Auschwitz and Hiroshima," and "The Meaning of Evil."

Surin, Kenneth. *Theology and the Problem of Evil.* New York: Basil Blackwell, 1986. A well-written volume that analyzes theodicy, the philosophical and/or theological method that tries to justify the righteousness of God—an exercise that must also attempt to reconcile the existence of evil with a morally perfect deity.

Zweig, Connie, and Jeremiah Abrams, eds. *Meeting the Shadow: The Hidden Power of the Dark Side of Human Nature.* Los Angeles: J. P. Tarcher, 1991. A reader that includes work by Carl Jung. Unlike many philosophical treatises, this volume delves into the "common" life of ordinary people and shows what harm radical evil can do; topics are covered from many points of view—religious, psychological, and sociological.

SEE ALSO: Augustine, Saint; *Beyond Good and Evil;* Epicurus; God; Hitler, Adolf; Moral principles, rules, and imperatives; Morality; Religion; Right and wrong; Wickedness.

Evolutionary theory

DEFINITION: Theory that living species change over time due to a process of natural selection of genetic traits by the environment

DATE: Articulated by Charles Darwin in 1859

TYPE OF ETHICS: Modern history

SIGNIFICANCE: Darwin's theory of evolution challenged the authority of revealed religion, strengthened biologically deterministic arguments, and encouraged an ethical outlook based on processes at work in the natural world.

In his seminal work *On the Origin of Species* (1859), Charles Darwin advanced a convincing explanation for the changes that occurred in life-forms throughout geological time. His conclusions, based partly on insights gleaned from prevailing economic theory and new geological discoveries and largely on his own extensive investigations, contradicted the biblical view of creation. It also challenged the previously dominant eighteenth century Deistic view of a benign, carefully designed cosmos. In place of a master watchmaker harmonizing creation, Darwin posited a violent, indifferent natural order in which advances occurred as the more fit vanquished the less fit. In the

Darwinian universe, values were placed at the service of natural selection.

HISTORY

The idea of evolution gradually gained momentum throughout the eighteenth and nineteenth centuries. This was largely the result of significant advances in several specific areas: classification, which placed living beings in logical relationships with one another; comparative anatomy and embryology, which allowed comparisons between simpler and more complicated organisms; and paleontology, which increasingly revealed a progressive fossil record. Pre-Darwinian evolutionary theories, however, were overspeculative, lacked sufficient evidence, and had weak theoretical underpinnings. Darwin's work profited from Sir George Lyell's geological analyses, which greatly extended the known age of the earth, and the economic writings of David Ricardo and Thomas Malthus, which introduced the allied concepts of population pressure on scarce resources and the struggle for existence. Darwin's theory of evolution through natural selection intertwined a massive volume of evidence with those leading ideas. The re-

Charles Darwin and the *Beagle*

In 1831, a twenty-two-year-old Charles Darwin, who had been studying for the ministry at Cambridge, by luck was offered a position as naturalist on the ship HMS *Beagle*, which was about to embark on a round-the-world voyage of exploration. His domineering father was against the trip at first, but he finally relented. The expedition would turn the young man into a scientist. Over the next five years, Darwin recorded hundreds of details about plants and animals and began to notice some consistent patterns. His work led him to develop new ideas about what causes variations in different plant and animal species:

> [The] preservation of favourable individual differences and variations, and the destruction of those which are injurious, I have called Natural Selection, or the Survival of the Fittest. . . . slight modifications, which in any way favoured the individuals of any species, by better adapting them to their altered conditions, would tend to be preserved. . . .
> —*On the Origin of Species by Means of Natural Selection*, 1859

Until Darwin and such colleagues as Alfred Russel Wallace, the "fixity" or unchangingness of species had been accepted as fact, and the appearance over time of new species remained a mystery. Darwin's lucky trip laid the foundation for today's understanding of life and its diversity.

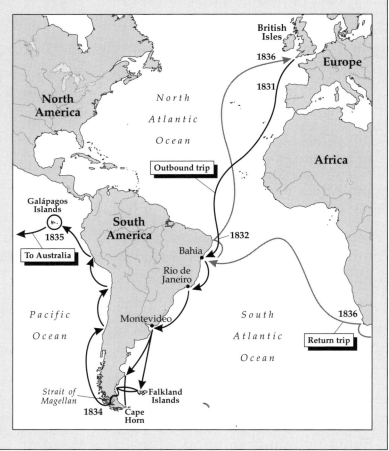

492

sult was a methodologically convincing tour de force; criticism of Darwinian evolutionism was generally based on its religious and ethical implications rather than on any pronounced scientific deficiencies.

ETHICAL IMPLICATIONS

The theory of evolution advanced the view of an amoral universe in which change occurred blindly and was perpetuated through impersonal mechanistic processes. Random mutations made a given organism more or less able to cope with its environment and more or less able to propagate itself. Its relative success in the struggle for existence defined its value. In the intense interspecies and intraspecies competition for scarce resources, the rule was survival of the fittest. Individuals and species were naturally selected; that is, harsh environmental factors determined survivability. Favorable changes accumulating through time produced more fit, and therefore more highly evolved, individuals and species. Darwin did not always present the selection process as a direct function of an unforgiving environment, since he discussed the possible impact of variables such as accidents and sexual selection.

In a later work, *The Descent of Man* (1871), Darwin also praised the value of cooperation, altruism, and self-sacrifice. Even then, however, perpetual strife remained the motor of evolutionary change. Sexual selection was competitive, accidents were chance outcomes issuing from a violent context, and the value of traits such as cooperation and altruism lay in their contribution to the survival of one group that was engaged in competition with others. Darwin's dour deterministic theory impartially challenged beliefs in a benign universe, a personal savior, the biblical view of special creation, and ethical systems derived from revealed religion.

SOCIAL DARWINISM

Darwin noted that humans were less subject to evolutionary pressure than lower organisms were because societies modified their environments. Social theorists such as Herbert Spencer, Benjamin Kidd, and Lewis H. Morgan, however, were less exacting; known as Social Darwinists, they applied Darwin's ideas to human behavior in a wholesale fashion. Adopting concepts such as variation and natural selection, they placed social and cultural differences in an evolutionary context and justified existing power

relationships as examples of survival of the fittest. During the late nineteenth century and early twentieth century, Social Darwinists promoted unrestricted competition, laissez-faire economics, and neocolonialism in the belief that survival of the fittest invariably produced advances in civilization. The movement declined as it became apparent that human societies could not easily be classified as more or less primitive, that evolutionary change did not automatically mean progress, and that the notion of survival of the fittest provided cover for the unequal treatment of individuals and groups.

NATURE VS. NURTURE

The theory of evolution perpetuated, in secularized form, traditional disputes regarding free will and predestination. That issue was exacerbated in the second half of the twentieth century by two important developments: breakthroughs in genetics that further underscored the characteristic biological determinism of Darwinism, and advances in the study of animal behavior (ethology), which had immediate sociological implications. The activities of ethologists such as Nikolaas Tinbergen, Konrad Lorenz, and E. O. Wilson were particularly significant because they related human behavior to the wider context of ethology. By rigorously examining evolutionary antecedents, parallels, and alternatives to human behavior, they reopened the nature/nurture controversy in the sharpest possible way. In one way or another, their investigations touched upon numerous ethical issues. Was aggression learned or biologically dictated? What was the evolutionary value of aggression? Were gender roles social constructs or did they reflect natural, necessary biological relationships? By placing such issues into an evolutionary context, they revisited an investigative path followed cautiously by Darwin and much less carefully by the Social Darwinists—that is, the attempt to align human behavior with the physical laws of nature.

Michael J. Fontenot

FURTHER READING

Archer, John. *The Behavioural Biology of Aggression*. Cambridge, England: Cambridge University Press, 1988.

Cameron, Donald. *The Purpose of Life: Human Purpose and Morality from an Evolutionary Perspective*. Bristol, England: Woodhill, 2001.

Casebeer, William D. *Natural Ethical Facts: Evolution, Connectionism, and Moral Cognition.* Cambridge, Mass.: MIT Press, 2003.

Darwin, Charles. *The Origin of Species by Means of Natural Selection: Or, The Preservation of Favored Races in the Struggle for Life.* New York: Modern Library, 1998.

Dawkins, Richard. *The Blind Watchmaker: Why the Evidence of Evolution Reveals a Universe Without Design.* New York: W. W. Norton, 1987.

Ruse, Michael. *The Darwinian Revolution: Science Red in Tooth and Claw.* Chicago: University of Chicago Press, 1979.

Thompson, Paul, ed. *Issues in Evolutionary Ethics.* Albany: State University of New York Press, 1995.

Wilson, E. O. *Sociobiology: The New Synthesis.* Cambridge, Mass.: Harvard University Press, 1975.

SEE ALSO: Aggression; Darwin, Charles; Endangered species; Eugenics; Human nature; Racism; Social Darwinism; Sociobiology.

Excellence

DEFINITION: Superiority at performing a given practice or function

TYPE OF ETHICS: Theory of ethics

SIGNIFICANCE: While innate excellence is of no particular moral significance, excellence as an ideal toward which one strives is an important value for many ethical systems.

Although "excellence" is prominently associated with the ethical thought of Plato and Aristotle, the concept dates back at least as far as Homeric Greece (eighth century B.C.E.), when it designated not strictly the virtues of personal character but the uniquely Greek *aretê*, the skillful performance of any function, be it running, fighting, or even thinking. It applied also to certain masculine and feminine virtues necessary for the protection of countrymen and family.

The masculine and feminine excellences may be viewed as "competitive" and "cooperative" excellences, respectively, denoting the proper fulfillment by men and women of the obligations entailed by their social and cultural roles. The competitive excellences of men were indispensable to the defense of countrymen, family, guests, and friends. To be virtuous, a man had to be well-armed, strong, swift on his feet, and skilled in the strategy and techniques of warfare, qualities that explain why courage was a centrally important virtue in Homeric Greece. He also had to possess wealth, which implied high social status. A man in whom all these conditions were met was the epitome of Homeric excellence. Women, who had no need for the competitive excellences and were not permitted to demonstrate them, were designated as excellent by virtue of the cooperative or "quiet" excellences—beauty, skillful weaving, housekeeping, chastity, and fidelity, the latter being the central feminine virtue. Hence, whereas men protected society and family by acquiring largely military virtues, women offered protection of a different sort to home and family by cultivating the domestic virtues.

Homeric excellence was modified by fifth-century Athenians to include additional virtues. *Sōphrosynī*, self-control, had greater importance as a virtue for both men and women, indicating that men were judged in the fifth century according to a "quiet" virtue that had once been considered a criterion of feminine excellence. In addition, social status was less a determinant of excellence than it had been during the Homeric period. This evolution of the understanding of "aretê" culminated in the sense that the term ultimately acquired in the moral theory of Plato and Aristotle, although it was Aristotle who, in his *Nicomachean Ethics*, conferred upon this concept its most prominent philosophical status.

CLASSICAL VIEWS

In the classical view epitomized by the thinkers of fifth and fourth century B.C.E. Athens, excellence was determined by one's generic role as a human being in addition to one's particular societal role. There were now as many excellences as there were functions for an individual to perform. One could be an excellent father, physician, and citizen, and therefore an excellent human being. The latter excellence, however, denoting the quality of intellect as well as character, both encompassed and eclipsed in importance the virtues derived from more specialized (and therefore secondary) roles. The cooperative virtues played a more prominent role in classical excellence. In addition to the competitive Homeric virtue of courage, there were the virtues of friendship, self-control, wisdom, and justice, all contributing to the civic virtue of citizenship, without which one could not be good. There was general agreement that these virtues were proper to humanity even while there was disagreement about their definition, as in Plato's *Republic*, in which the point of contention was the nature of justice.

The *Republic* was the culmination of Plato's earlier dialogues in which the nature of virtue was a common theme. Plato depicted virtue as highly personalized, attainable by the individual who controlled his passions and made constructive use of his ambition through the exercise of disciplined intelligence. Platonic excellence, therefore, consisted of the harmonious interaction of the virtues of self-control, courage, and wisdom, which together constituted the civic virtue of justice. It was achieved only by the most intellectually gifted—Plato's "philosopher-kings"—who, after an educational process marked by rigorous intellectual discipline, were endowed with intuitive insight into genuine moral goodness. In a larger context, the excellence of the state was an extension of this personal excellence, constituted by the wise, disciplined governance by the philosopher-kings of their fellow citizens, whose natural capabilities relegated them to the more mundane activities of society.

ARISTOTLE

Whereas for Plato true excellence was confined to the philosopher-kings, Aristotle believed that excellence was achievable in various degrees by anyone with sufficient experience and rational judgment. While Aristotelian excellence was to some extent compatible with the common wisdom of ordinary men, it was, however, refined and most prominently exemplified in the intellectually accomplished. This reflected Aristotle's division of excellence into intellectual and moral excellence, intellectual excellence being attained through education, and moral excellence through virtuous habits. Genuine human excellence, therefore, consisted of being intelligent enough to judge correctly how to do the right thing at the right time in the right place and in the right manner, and to do so consistently and deliberately, thus fulfilling the proper function of a human being.

Although for Aristotle excellence was essentially a "mean"—a point of equilibrium between extremes—it was, paradoxically, an extreme as well:

It was the mean, or perfect moderation, between two vices, while also the extreme, or highest degree of what is right and good, with respect to feeling and action. Successfully ascertaining the mean and avoiding extremes of feeling and action required the keenest exercise of the powers of rational judgment. For Aristotle, as for Plato, excellence was highly personalized but also inextricably linked to citizenship; the exercise of personal virtue could not be comprehended apart from the political context.

The idea of excellence as virtue is found in the ethical theory of modern thinkers. Alasdair MacIntyre, in *After Virtue: A Study in Moral Theory*, retains the understanding of excellence as virtue in essentially its original Aristotelian form. John Rawls, in *A Theory of Justice* (1971), regards the "excellences" as natural talents and assets such as wit and beauty, as well as personal virtues such as courage and self-control. For both thinkers, excellence as the rational exercise of the virtues acquires significance only within a social and political context.

Barbara Forrest

FURTHER READING

Adams, Robert Merrihew. *Finite and Infinite Goods: A Framework for Ethics*. New York: Oxford University Press, 1999.

Adkins, Arthur W. H. *Merit and Responsibility: A Study in Greek Values*. New York: Oxford University Press, 1960. Reprint. Chicago: University of Chicago Press, 1975.

Aristotle. *Nicomachean Ethics*. Translated and edited by Roger Crisp. New York: Cambridge University Press, 2000.

Gardner, Howard, Mihaly Csikszentmihalyi, and William Damon. *Good Work: When Excellence and Ethics Meet*. New York: Basic Books, 2001.

Homer. *The Iliad*. Translated by Robert Fitzgerald. Garden City, N.Y.: Anchor Press, 1975.

MacIntyre, Alasdair. *After Virtue: A Study in Moral Theory*. 2d ed. Notre Dame, Ind.: University of Notre Dame Press, 1984.

Plato. *The Collected Dialogues of Plato*. Edited by Edith Hamilton and Huntington Cairns. 1961. Reprint. Princeton, N.J.: Princeton University Press, 1984.

Rawls, John. *A Theory of Justice*. Rev. ed. Cambridge, Mass.: Belknap Press of Harvard University Press, 1999.

495

SEE ALSO: Aristotelian ethics; Golden mean; Justice; MacIntyre, Alasdair; *Nicomachean Ethics*; Platonic ethics; Rawls, John; *Republic*.

Executive Order 10988

IDENTIFICATION: Federal executive order that gave federal employees the right to collective bargaining

DATE: Signed on January 17, 1962

TYPE OF ETHICS: Business and labor ethics

SIGNIFICANCE: Executive Order 10988 made the labor policies of federal offices and agencies consistent throughout the country and influenced the labor policies of state and local agencies.

Before the 1960's, federal agencies dealt with organized labor unions individually; some agencies recognized unions, and some refused to negotiate with them. The administration of President John F. Kennedy took a more favorable attitude toward unions. On January 17, 1962, Kennedy signed Federal Executive Order (EO) 10988, giving federal employees the right to form unions and to bargain collectively through them. Under the terms of the order, employees had the right to form a union but could not be forced to join one. Federal agencies were required to bargain with properly elected unions. These unions were forbidden to strike.

Once the order was signed, there was a tremendous increase in the number of federal employees represented by unions, especially among white-collar workers. Some groups, including postal workers, are represented by unions for all of their contract negotiations. The rights of federal employees were amended several times during the late 1960's and the 1970's. In 1978, the Civil Service Reform Act became the first unified code of federal sector labor relations, formalizing the bargaining rights first endorsed by the executive order.

Cynthia A. Bily

SEE ALSO: American Federation of Labor; Fair Labor Standards Act; Hasidism; Knights of Labor; Labor-Management Relations Act; National Labor Relations Act; Work.

Existentialism

DEFINITION: School of philosophy that emphasizes individual subjectivity, freedom and responsibility, and the irrational as primary features of the human condition

TYPE OF ETHICS: Theory of ethics

SIGNIFICANCE: On one hand, existentialism denies that the individual is beholden to or constrained by any traditional system of morality. On the other hand, it asserts that the individual is morally obligated not merely to create and abide by his or her own moral values, but to create and abide by a worldview which will make sense of an otherwise meaningless cosmos.

The history of systematic ethics started with the ancient Greek philosopher Socrates' question "Is the unexamined life worth living?" Socrates, like most Western philosophers since, believed that the intellect was the key to answering this question. Moreover, prior to existentialism, most ethicists had assumed that humankind's essential nature was rational. Consistent with these views, Western ethical tradition has generally assumed that the rational individual pursuing the rational life is the essence of "the good life."

In contrast, existentialism—a broad movement in philosophy and literature—boldly challenges these basic assumptions of the Western tradition. Existential ethics refuses to understand the good as a norm or a law. Existentialists contend that Western thought has been obsessed by the idea of regulating the life of the world by reason. Hence, unlike previous ethics, existentialism emphasizes the tragic and absurd facets of life rather than the empirical and rational facets.

THE TERM "EXISTENTIALISM"

It is impossible to discuss an existential theory of ethics without briefly considering the existential movement as such. The term "existentialism" may be properly used in at least two senses. The first is a narrow one referring to a movement in philosophy and literature that emerged in the nineteenth and twentieth centuries. The second and broader sense refers to a much earlier trend in Western thought dating back to the Old Testament book of Ecclesiastes (300 B.C.E.) and including such diverse works as *The Confessions* (c. 400) of Saint Augustine, the *Pensées*

(1670) of Blaise Pascal, and the works of William Shakespeare and Fyodor Dostoevski.

In the broader sense, the existential movement is seen in the tendency of some Western religious and literary writers to dwell upon the sense of paradox and tragedy in the human condition. Even within the narrow sense of the term, however, there is little substantive agreement among existentialists on specific ethical precepts; thus, easy generalizations about existential ethics cannot be drawn.

A partial list of existentialists will help readers appreciate the diversity of ideas and viewpoints that constitute this "school." Søren Kierkegaard, an early nineteenth century Danish existentialist, was a fanatical Christian. Friedrich Nietzsche, another nineteenth century existentialist, was a militant atheist. In twentieth century existentialism, there is an equal degree of heterogeneity. Martin Heidegger was a Nazi, Martin Buber a Jew, Albert Camus a humanist, Jean-Paul Sartre a communist, and Gabriel Marcel a Roman Catholic. The list could go on with further diversifications. It is sufficient to note, however, that there is no common denominator of substantive agreement within the existential movement. Existentialism does not predefine any substantive moral program. Many philosophers have described existentialism as more of a "mood" or "attitude" than a doctrine of thought.

SOME COMMON EXISTENTIAL THEMES

In spite of all this diversity, there do appear to be several elements upon which most existentialists agree. For example, existentialists generally regard freedom, responsibility, suffering, and commitment as the highest of human values. They tend to have a pessimistic or despairing view of the human condition. The religious existentialists, however, balance this with a great hope. Although existentialists generally reject such a thing as human nature, they agree that it is meaningful to speak of the human condition. The existential approach to ethics emphasizes the freedom and responsibility of the existing individual as the wellspring of all ethical considerations. Several other common themes appear to run through most, if not all, existentialist ethics: People are free to choose how they will live and no system can guide them, and the highest good is in the struggle to be one's authentic self. Existentialists endlessly contrast the "authentic" with the "inauthentic" and agree that any philosophy that is not actually lived is worth-

less. Any appeal to a transcendent rule or utilitarian principle would constitute "bad faith"—that is, self-deception.

By looking at the historical situation in which existentialism arose and the systems against which existential thought protested, one may see some of the common core of existential thought. Historically, existentialism arose as a reaction against idealism, materialism, and empirical science. The existentialists have staunchly protested any "ism" that would encapsulate humanity. A review of several historical examples may sift out several of the unique qualities that are associated with existential ethics.

SOME HISTORICAL EXAMPLES

Søren Kierkegaard's writings were an attack upon the work of Georg Wilhelm Friedrich Hegel, who was an idealist philosopher of the metaphysical system-building variety. Hegel proposed that the individual was a subordinate cell in the organic whole of the cosmos. Kierkegaard rebelled fiercely against what he believed was the excess rationalism and collectivism of Hegel. In this sense, Kierkegaard was antirational and opposed to any system that made society greater than any existing individual member.

In existential ethics, the question "What ought I do?" can never be answered by appeals to logic or society's norms. For Kierkegaard, the ethical act is unique and unrepeatable—in other words, existential. Only the existing individual in the crucible of his or her own inner life can answer the question. Here no elder, no rule book, no formula can apply. Consequently, authentic ethical behavior has no ultimate court of appeal except the individual. There is only the existing individual, with his or her freedom and responsibility. Sartre puts it unequivocally: "Man is the undisputed author of his own behavior."

Nietzsche, the militant atheistic existentialist, proclaimed that "God is dead!" The God who was the basis for all ethical and moral values underpinning the old rules for guiding conduct has become obsolete. Nietzsche notes that this strange and awful event of God's death, which at first seemed so terrible, is actually a great gift, for now humankind is truly free to create its own values. The only criterion for ethical conduct becomes the quality of life. Is the quality of life enhanced or ennobled by this action? Nietzsche does not refer to the maximum quantity of life; the quality of life that he hoped would guide people's actions has more to do with human nobility and the individual overcoming his or her all-too-human weaknesses.

ETHICAL KNOWLEDGE

Existential ethical knowledge attempts to give a concrete presentation of human life—its meaning, aims, and values. The basis of existential ethics is concrete moral experience. A dialectic that does not rest upon any moral experience is only an intellectual game. Ethics cannot be a merely theoretical discipline; it is also a moral and existential activity. Existential ethics attempts to turn to reality itself, to actual life, and to overcome the duality that undermines the value of academic or traditional philosophy.

According to Nikolay Berdyayev, a Russian Christian existentialist, the dilemma of ethical knowledge is that existence is irrational and individual, but people can know only the general and universal. Consequently, existential ethics moves from the epistemological subject of traditional philosophy to the concrete individual. Existential writers believe that what is essential about ethics is not that people should have ideas about what authenticity is, but that they should live authentically. Ethical knowledge is communion with truth and existence. Ethical objects cannot be described in a formal scientific way at all. They are revealed only to the person who performs creative acts of valuation and commitment.

Abstract a priori systems of ethics have minimal value. Sartre's often quoted existential dictum "Existence precedes essence" points to the irrelevance of any a priori system. One's identity and values emerge from one's choices, not from some essence of human nature that was given to one at birth. The individual, in struggle and anguish, must wrest his or her essence from existence by means of concrete moral choices. Humankind cannot rely on animal instinct, and people do not have some prepackaged morality that will serve to guide their choices. Nothing is authoritative. Thus, Sartre notes that people are "condemned to freedom." Moral life presupposes freedom in evil as well as good. Yet for Sartre it is unclear how it is possible to escape the no-win scenario of "bad faith" that he depicted. Sartre appeared to believe that it was impossible for humans to escape one form or another of "self-deception," no matter how hard or what they tried.

EXISTENTIALISM AND PLEASURE

Hedonistic ethics, whether it be heavenly or earthly, ultimately rests on fear. A hedonistic individual is bound to fear for his or her happiness and the happiness of others. Happiness is threatened with danger on all sides and bought at the cost of opportunism in actions and judgments. Berdyayev notes, "If I make happiness my aim I am doomed to fear all the time." Thus, the existentialists univocally renounce pleasure or happiness as a criterion of action. This renunciation takes resolve and courage. For Heidegger, the resolve of the authentic life alone liberates one from fear. For Paul Tillich, a Christian existentialist, the "courage to be" triumphs over fear.

Existentialists often recognize a dual nature of human beings and an ensuing inherent tension between these contradictory natures. Although humans are endowed with reason, they are irrational beings. The human being is a wounded creature. For the Christian existentialist, human beings aspire to the loftiest values and divine reality. Kierkegaard, discovering in human nature fathomless darkness, conflict, and pain, also recognized that the human being is a creator of values in the image and likeness of God. For Christian existentialists, human beings do not exist apart from the divine element in them. Thus, the authentic person is a bearer of the divine image. The soul is afraid of emptiness: Without *commitment*, it has no positive creative content and becomes filled with false illusions and fictions. At the same time, each person is a sick being, divided within and influenced by a dark subconscious. Sartre, taking a consistently atheistic position, defines each individual as a "useless passion."

The cognitive and optimistic psychology of either humanism or behaviorism, according to which people seek bliss and positive reinforcement, is erroneous. Humans are irrational beings who may long for suffering rather than happiness. "Happiness" is a meaningless and empty human word. Existential ethics, far from seeking happiness, may call people to the line of greatest resistance to the world, demanding heroic efforts.

SUFFERING AND AUTHENTICITY

Kierkegaard notes there are two kinds of suffering: the redeeming suffering that leads to life and the dark suffering that leads to death. Suffering may raise and purify people or crush and humiliate them. An individual may go through life suffering serenely and graciously and be born into a new life as a result of it. All the suffering sent to humankind—the death of nearest and dearest, illness, poverty, humiliation, and disappointments—may serve to purify and regenerate an individual depending on the attitude that the individual takes toward them.

Victor Frankl, a twentieth century existential psychiatrist, points out that individuals can endure tremendous suffering if they see meaning in it. Attempts to avoid suffering only create more suffering; such an escape is one of the greatest delusions of life. Paradoxically, suffering is tied to alienation and despair, but it is also the way to light and renewal.

Existential ethics may be contrasted with Eastern thought. Unlike Hinduism, for example, existentialism stresses the individual's separateness from the world as a positive value. There is no *tat twam asi* (That art thou) in existentialism. The "other" is seen as truly "other," which serves to enrich the individual self through communion rather than merger. For the existentialist, the highest expression of selfhood does not entail the drop of water returning to the ocean; instead, it is an affirmation of the individual self and its higher destiny, which is, in some inescapable sense, separate from the world and from others.

THE PRIMACY OF THE INDIVIDUAL

The history of ethics is complicated by the opposing rights of the individual and those of society. As early as the time of Socrates, Greek thought tried to free itself from the power of law and society and penetrate to the individual authentic conscience. The moral conscience of Socrates came into conflict with the Athenian democracy. As a consequence, Socrates was martyred by the mob. Socrates proclaimed the principle that "God ought to be obeyed more than men." This means that God, conscience, truth, or the inner light ought to be obeyed more than society or any formal law. Radical reliance on truth alone provides authenticity. Thus, Socrates made a tremendous advance toward the liberation of personality and the discovery of the individual conscience. Existentialists go further than Socrates, saying, "You must always act individually, and everyone must act differently." Authentic existential behavior is truly original, not determined by social influences.

Existentialists have been outspoken in declaring the tyranny of the social unit. The power of society over the individual has been found everywhere in history. Because of Western society's conditioning, the individual is not aware of living in a madness that is only superficially concealed. R. D. Laing, an existential psychiatrist, argues that the "fleet" is off course; hence, the individual "deviating" ship may represent the true course. Thus, society's norms are useless. The task of existential ethics is to distinguish between the authentic and the social in moral life and to reveal the pure conscience. In its essence, the authentic moral life is independent of social life. Christian existentialists urge people to remember the eternal principle in the human soul that is independent of historical changes, which in this sense is not social. Existential ethics places the individual above the law. A person *is* a value. A living human being is of higher value than any abstract idea—even the idea of the good.

In the work of Nietzsche, ethics cannot depend upon the herd morality, since it represents a slavish image of humankind, an image based upon resentment and cowardice. Nietzsche's noble individual, who is a yea-sayer to life, embodies the highest good and the supreme value. Everything that increases life is good, and everything that decreases life, leading to death and nonbeing, is evil. Such an ethic rejects any form of hedonism. A rich, full life is good and valuable even if it brings with it suffering rather than happiness. Thus, Nietzsche's championing of the noble life led to his being a bitter enemy of hedonism and utilitarianism. The supreme value and good is not life as such, but the authenticity with which it is lived.

DEATH, FREEDOM, AND EXISTENTIAL ETHICS

Existentialists, whether atheistic or religious, agree that one's attitude will be more authentic if one regards all people as though they were dying and determines one's relationships with them in the light of death—both their death and one's own. Berdyayev writes, "Every man is dying, I too am dying, I must never forget about death."

For Frankl, death is a message of hope, not doom. The imminence of death provides the impetus that is needed to live life authentically, above the petty cares that would otherwise fetter human fulfillment. The ever-present possibility of death, while terrifying, gives a sense of preciousness to the "now" that would otherwise be missing.

Ethics would be meaningless without freedom,

since "ought" implies "can." Humans are free, creative beings who prefer freedom to happiness. Existential analysis details the insidious assaults upon human freedom. The mass media pose a number of false images of happiness as supreme values. These misrepresentations of "happiness" as the supreme good and final end have been instilled in people to keep them in slavery. Human freedom and dignity forbid the individual from regarding popular images of happiness and satisfaction as the primary goals of existence.

Any person—even a slave—can be inwardly free. Frankl's experience in a Nazi concentration camp proved that acceptance of circumstances that have fallen to one's lot can be interpreted as mastery over the external world. It is an existential victory. This does not mean that one must not try to improve one's circumstances or strive for social reform. One must, however, remain spiritually free even in prison.

The point of fundamental importance for existential ethics is that one must strive first and foremost to free oneself from slavery. Because every state that is incompatible with existential freedom is evil, the inner conquest of slavery is the fundamental task of moral life. Every kind of slavery is meant here: slavery to the pull of the past and the future, slavery to the external world and one's self, and slavery to one's lower self. One's existential task in life is to radiate creative energy that brings with it light, strength, and transfiguration.

Paul August Rentz

FURTHER READING

Barnes, Hazel. *An Existentialist Ethics*. New York: Alfred A. Knopf, 1967. An exciting book dealing with an existential approach to liberating the individual that is based on the groundwork of Jean-Paul Sartre. Barnes, unlike Sartre, finds alternatives to bad faith. Especially useful for those interested in how existentialism relates to Eastern philosophy; seventy pages of the text explicitly compare the two. A good reference for those already familiar with the basics of existential ethics.

Barrett, William. *Irrational Man: A Study in Existential Philosophy*. Garden City, N.Y.: Doubleday, 1962. A superb introductory reference to existential philosophy. This work is widely recognized as the finest discussion of existentialism written by an American. This book addresses the literary and religious approaches to existentialism as well as the rigorously philosophical approach. Strongly recommended.

Berdyayev, Nikolai. *The Destiny of Man*. Translated by Natalie Duddington. New York: Harper & Row, 1960. A somewhat advanced work in existential ethics written by a former Russian communist who converted to Christianity after the Russian Revolution. In "Concrete Problems of Ethics," Berdyayev deals with sex, love, family, technical progress, and other topics from a rigorously existential viewpoint. An excellent reference for the serious student.

Frankl, Viktor. *Man's Search for Meaning: An Introduction to Logotherapy*. 4th ed. Boston: Beacon Press, 1992. Millions of copies of this book have been sold to both laypersons and mental health professionals who wish to understand how existential ethics were lived in a Nazi concentration camp. The original title of this work was *From Death Camp to Existentialism*. An excellent reference for those interested in psychology, ethics, and existentialism.

Golomb, Jacob. *In Search of Authenticity: Existentialism from Kierkegaard to Camus*. New York: Routledge, 1995. An analysis of existentialist ethics in terms of the existentialist's drive for authenticity. Golomb embraces authenticity as a way out of postmodern scepticism and detachment, and he reads classic existentialist texts for clues as to how to live today.

Kaufmann, Walter. *Existentialism from Dostoevsky to Sartre*. Rev. ed. New York: New American Library, 1975. An extremely rich anthology of readings from ten leading representatives of the existential movement. Kaufmann's introduction tells the reader how to approach the specific texts. An excellent collection of primary sources in existentialism for the beginning student who would like to read what the existentialists actually said. Accessible and widely available.

SEE ALSO: Atheism; Beauvoir, Simone de; Berdyayev, Nikolay; Buber, Martin; Camus, Albert; Hare, R. M.; Hegel, Georg Wilhelm Friedrich; Heidegger, Martin; Kierkegaard, Søren; Life, meaning of; Nietzsche, Friedrich; Sartre, Jean-Paul.

Experimentation

DEFINITION: Conduct of practical scientific or medical research

TYPE OF ETHICS: Scientific ethics

SIGNIFICANCE: Experiments conducted on humans and animals are governed by formal and informal codes of ethics designed to protect the rights and welfare of the subjects, to ensure that the experiments serve a legitimate public interest, and to regulate the use of the information obtained as a result of the experiments.

What are the moral principles to be considered in evaluating the rightness or wrongness of using humans as research subjects? In *The Patient as Partner* (1987), Robert M. Veatch summarized the ethical principles and issues involved in research: The principle of beneficence, which has its roots in the ethics of medical treatment, states that research with humans is justified only when some good can come from it; this is the minimum justification for human research.

Research may do good (therefore meeting the criterion of beneficence) but may also cause harm. Research that causes harm is morally wrong; that is, it does not meet the principle of nonmaleficence. When research causes both good and harm, which principle, beneficence or nonmaleficence, takes priority? If avoiding harm takes priority, then a vast amount of research with human subjects with the potential for doing much good would be considered unethical. Therefore, the ratio of benefit to harm is a more reasonable criterion for justifying human experimentation.

If benefit/harm is adopted as the moral principle, a new problem emerges, because this principle would justify inhumane experimental procedures such as those employed by the Nazis as long as it could be shown that severe harm or death to a few human subjects was of benefit to large numbers of people.

Benefit/harm, a form of beneficence, is therefore a necessary but insufficient justification for research with human subjects. Additional principles are required.

The principle of autonomy recognizes that among the inalienable rights of persons is the right to liberty. The principle of autonomy implies a right to self-determination, including the right, when informed of the benefits and harms, to consent to participate in research that may entail certain risks to the subject. Therefore, autonomy is the basis for the use of informed consent in research with human subjects; informed consent helps to mitigate some of the problems posed by sole reliance on beneficence as a moral criterion.

Still another principle involves considerations of justice (fairness) in the conduct of human research. According to one theory of justice, distributive justice, fairness involves attempting to equalize the benefits and harms among the members of society. This principle has implications for the selection of subjects for research in the sense that disadvantaged subjects—for example, members of minority groups—should not be chosen as subjects, since this would add another burden to an already unduly burdened group. This principle would not apply when minority status was a variable under study in the research.

The principles of beneficence, autonomy, and justice form the basis for some of the criteria set by the U.S. Department of Health and Human Services (DHHS) and used by institutional review boards (IRBs) for judging whether proposed research involving human subjects is ethically sound. These criteria are (1) risks to subjects are minimized, (2) risks are reasonable relative to anticipated benefits, (3) prior informed consent will be obtained from subjects or their legal representatives, (4) informed consent will be documented, and (5) selection of subjects will be equitable. Two additional criteria are that (6) subjects' privacy and confidentiality will be maintained and that (7) the research plan involves monitoring the data, when applicable, so as to ensure subject safety.

The application of ethical principles to particular instances of research with human subjects highlights the complexities involved in the use of these principles. One question that arises concerns the obligations of a scientist when the nature of the research precludes informed consent, as in psychological research that involves the use of deception. While many people believe that deception is permissible under certain limited conditions—for example, when there is little or no risk to subjects and there are no alternative ways of gathering the data—others feel that deception is intrinsically harmful to subjects and is never justified.

Another question has to do with the issue of informed consent with subjects who may not be competent to give informed consent; for example, in cases involving children or individuals who were formerly competent but are no longer so (such as individuals who have some form of dementia). When risks are minimal, informed consent by parents of children and informed consent by guardians of the formerly competent have been employed as criteria.

In circumstances in which the subject is competent but informed consent may be obtained under potentially coercive conditions, as in the case of prisoners or clinic patients, complex ethical questions are raised.

The ethics of experimentation also extend into such other areas as issues of animal care and rights, and the ethical obligations of scientists with regard to the integrity of the research process.

Sanford Golin

FURTHER READING

Caplan, A. L. *When Medicine Went Mad: Bioethics and the Holocaust.* Totowa, N.J.: Humana Press, 1992.

Cothran, Helen, ed. *Animal Experimentation: Opposing Viewpoints.* San Diego, Calif.: Greenhaven Press, 2002.

Foster, Claire. *The Ethics of Medical Research on Humans.* New York: Cambridge University Press, 2001.

Garattini, Silvio, and D. W. van Bekkum, eds. *The Importance of Animal Experimentation for Safety and Biomedical Research.* Boston: Kluwer Academic, 1990.

Group for the Advancement of Psychiatry. *A Casebook in Psychiatric Ethics.* New York: Brunner/Mazel, 1990.

Institute of Medicine Committee on Assessing the System for Protecting Human Research Participants. *Responsible Research: A Systems Approach to Protecting Research Participants.* Edited by Daniel D. Federman, Kathi E. Hanna, and Laura Lyman Rodriguez. Washington, D.C.: National Academies Press, 2003.

Sieber, J. E., ed. *Fieldwork, Regulation, and Publication.* Vol. 2 in *The Ethics of Social Research.* New York: Springer-Verlag, 1982.

Veatch, R. M. *The Patient as Partner: A Theory of Human-Experimentation Ethics.* Bloomington: Indiana University Press, 1987.

SEE ALSO: Animal research; Animal rights; Bioethics; Consent; Medical research; Milgram experiment; National Commission for the Protection of Human Subjects of Biomedical and Behavioral Research; Nazi science; Science.

Exploitation

DEFINITIONS: The indecent or illegitimate use of others for one's own advantage or profit

TYPE OF ETHICS: Beliefs and practices

SIGNIFICANCE: Exploitation of individuals violates the post-Kantian ethical principle that people should be treated as ends in themselves, or subjects, and not as means to ends, or objects. The systematic exploitation of groups or classes by other groups or classes may be cause for the moral condemnation of an entire social structure or society.

Many ethicists find that the definition of what exploitation is and what can be effected by it are inextricably linked. By examining the categories of existence that are understood to be capable of being exploited, however, a clearer, broader view of the definition can be seen.

What is considered as decent or legitimate must be sorted out in the context of what is merely socially acceptable and what is ethical, correct conduct. According to Peter Singer, "Ethics takes a universal point of view. This does not mean that a particular ethical judgment must be universally applicable. . . . What it does mean is that in making ethical judgments we go beyond our own likes and dislikes."

EXPLOITATION OF HUMAN BEINGS

The area in which exploitation has been studied most is the ethical treatment of human beings. Even so, there are many unanswered questions, and new ones arise as technology advances. Yet human behavior has still not even caught up with ethical standards that are already well established in nearly every society. For example, slavery is no longer deemed acceptable in most cultures, but near-slavery conditions continue to exist in many of these cultures. To provide for the wealthy minority in the technologically developed industrialized world, millions of people live in desperate poverty. These people earn lower than subsistence wages by performing hazardous and strenuous jobs, live in unsanitary and unsafe housing, eat a diet that does not provide adequate nutrition, receive insufficient medical care, and are unable to obtain enough education to be informed citizens. Surely these pitiable people are being exploited.

How can such an unethical situation exist? There are at least three possible explanations. First, perhaps not many people are aware of the situation. Second, perhaps there are not sufficient numbers of aware people with both enough political power and enough ethical strength to stop the situation. Third, perhaps humanity has ceased to care. As Elizabeth Pybus states, "If it is possible to turn a blind eye to suffering, it may also be possible to direct a steady seeing eye towards it."

The situation of near slavery, however, is an old problem. Other human problems that have arisen in more recent times have to do with dilemmas such as the mass marketing of untested medical devices, double-blind drug tests, the whole range of uses of the information obtained from the human genome study, the use of prison labor for commercial enterprises, and informed consent in medical testing and treatments.

EXPLOITATION OF ANIMALS

Exploitation does not always involve humans as its objects. Various people are working on the problems of animal rights and the humane treatment of animals. One of the first philosophers to formalize a system of proposals for the ethical treatment of animals was Jeremy Bentham. He believed that the basis for human behavior toward animals is in exploitation's definition of "other." He maintained that the point is not whether animals can reason or speak, but whether they can suffer. Their capacity to feel is called sentience. Peter Singer believes that what will determine ethical treatment of animals is for humans to give them "equal consideration" of their interests. Ethicists such as Singer believe that people will come to realize that the use of animals for food, to test cosmetics and drugs, or as pets constitutes animal exploitation and that understanding this concept will guide people to treat animals more humanely.

Most philosophers have maintained that only sentient, living creatures can be exploited, because those that are not in this category have no interests that

need to be considered. Yet the concept that even plant species can be exploited has crept into the human consciousness and vocabulary. Consider trees in an old-growth forest that are exploited for their timber or patches of tasty wild mushrooms that are harvested to extinction. Are these truly cases of exploitation? The answer lies in the definition of the concept. Are these human uses indecent or illegitimate? Yes, because people have planned poorly in using forest products and have wasted vast amounts of forest "resources." Yes, because the mushrooms are not essential for human sustenance.

In these examples concerning plants, two conditions in the definition of exploitation—indecent or illegitimate use for advantage or profit—have been met. The problem lies with the third condition: that in these situations, a nonsentient "other" has been so used. Singer asks that humans do not practice "speciesism" in their treatment of animals, yet even he maintains that only sentient creatures need be given this consideration. It is when ethicists push past animal rights into the area of ecoethics that equal consideration for plants comes into question.

Ecoethics has existed throughout the ages, manifesting itself in such systems as Jainism and Native American belief systems. Since the nineteenth century, there has been a growing formalized understanding of what ecoethics involves. The study has become much more intense since about 1950, with Aldo Leopold's discussions of a "land ethic," and the early 1960's, with Rachel Carson's revelations in *Silent Spring* about pesticides accumulating in the environment.

The concept of ecoethics allows that it is possible for humankind to exploit any of the environment's manifestations, capacities, or systems. Each of these elements has been recognized as one of the "others" from the definition of exploitation. Therefore, it is possible to exploit not only plants but also mineral deposits or other geologic formations. It is possible to exploit a water table or an oil deposit. Wetlands and whole forests are potential victims of exploitation. So are the oceans and the atmosphere.

Terms that have been used with increasing frequency in discussing the environment are the biosphere and the Gaia concept. Using this expanded vocabulary, humankind is beginning to understand its potential for damaging, through exploitation, all that sustains human life.

As human technology progresses, people are beginning to discuss whether it will be necessary to apply ethical standards to any potential "rights" of artificial intelligence systems and robots.

Since organized human behavior seems to lag far behind the establishment of ethical injunctions, it might seem unlikely that humankind will ever stop its practice of exploiting all that it encounters. Yet it is in an increasing awareness of these universal views and in self-examination that the possibility of the human practice of exploitation coming to an end exists.

Marcella T. Joy

FURTHER READING

Allsopp, Bruce. *Ecological Morality.* London: Frederick Muller, 1972.

Attfield, Robin. *A Theory of Value and Obligation.* New York: Croom Helm, 1987.

Maguire, Daniel. *The Moral Choice.* Garden City, N.Y.: Doubleday, 1978.

Marx, Karl. *Capital.* Vol. 1. Translated by Ben Fowkes. New York: Penguin Books, 1990.

Miller, Alan. *Gaia Connections: An Introduction to Ecology, Ecoethics, and Economics.* Savage, Md.: Rowman & Littlefield, 1991.

Pybus, Elizabeth. *Human Goodness: Generosity and Courage.* London: Harvester Wheatsheaf, 1991.

Sample, Ruth J. *Exploitation: What It Is and Why It's Wrong.* Lanham, Md.: Rowman & Littlefield, 2003.

Singer, Peter. *Practical Ethics.* 2d ed. New York: Cambridge University Press, 1993.

Wertheimer, Alan. *Exploitation.* Princeton, N.J.: Princeton University Press, 1999.

SEE ALSO: Abuse; Animal rights; Child labor legislation; Human rights; Ideal observer; Medical research; Nature, rights of; Personal injury attorneys; Robotics; Therapist-patient relationship.

F

Fact/value distinction

DEFINITION: Distinction between that which is either true or false and that which can be neither true nor false

TYPE OF ETHICS: Theory of ethics

SIGNIFICANCE: Because it is so difficult to justify placing normative judgment within the domain of fact, the fact/value distinction suggests that normative ethics is ultimately a subjective discipline that cannot be evaluated in terms of truth or falsity. Postmodern and some other late-twentieth-century ethics hold that it is morally wrong to treat values as facts, or to obscure the value-laden nature of purportedly factual statements and judgments.

The fact/value distinction is based upon the intuition that there is an important difference between sentences whose truth-value can and sentences whose truth-value cannot be determined empirically (with one or more of the five senses) or mathematically (by thinking about logical, numerical, or spatial relationships). Among the sentences whose truth-value cannot be determined empirically or mathematically are those of normative ethics: sentences about what is ethically obligatory, permissible, and forbidden, good and evil, right and wrong. Few would deny that there is such a difference and that it is important, but there is profound disagreement concerning the nature of the difference. In one camp are those who maintain that even though it is not possible to determine the truth-value of normative-ethical language by empirical observation or mathematical reflection, it is just as true, or just as false, as the language of physics and biology, geometry, and logic.

Just as there is a real, material world and a real world of mathematics, so there is moral reality. Normative ethical statements are true when they conform to that moral reality and false when they do not. In the opposing camp are those who say that since the truth-value of normative ethical sentences cannot be deter- mined by empirical or mathematical means, they are neither true nor false. (This is an oversimplification, because there is disagreement within each camp, and some ethical theorists attempt to stake out intermediate positions, but seeing the disagreement between the extremes is the best way to understand the importance of determining whether the domains of fact and value are mutually exclusive.)

HISTORY OF THE CONCEPT

Like most concepts in ethical theory, the fact/value distinction has a long history. While its roots can be found in ancient ethical theory, its rapid growth began with the Enlightenment. In English-language ethical theory, "fact" was contrasted with "right" before being opposed to "value." In *Leviathan* (1651), Thomas Hobbes distinguishes "matters of fact" and "matters of right," and the third earl of Shaftesbury draws a distinction between a "mistake of fact" and a "mistake of right" in his *Inquiry Concerning Virtue, or Merit* (1711). The meaning of the English word "value," as used in phrases such as "fact/value distinction" and "value judgment," owes its origin in part to the influence of nineteenth century German writers, especially theologian Albrecht Ritschl and philosopher Friedrich Nietzsche.

Perhaps the clearest explicit distinction between statements of fact and judgments of value is found in British philosopher A. J. Ayer's *Language, Truth, and Logic* (1936; 1946). Many philosophers observe a distinction between sentences and propositions, in order to account for both the fact that different sentences, in different languages or different contexts, for example, can have the same meaning, and the fact that a single sentence can have different meanings, for example, when written by or about different persons. Given this distinction, propositions are either true or false; it is possible, however, for a sentence to be neither true nor false, because not all sentences express propositions. With this distinction in mind, Ayer writes: "Since the expression of a value judgement is not a proposition, the question of truth or falsehood does not here arise." At another point he adds: "In saying that a certain type of action is right or wrong, I am not making any factual statement."

Ayer did not claim that to say that a certain type of action is right or wrong is to do nothing. He argued that sentences of normative ethics express emotions rather than propositions and are sometimes calculated to change other persons' behavior by arousing their emotions. Thus, the metaethical theory that normative ethical language does not express propositions is called "emotivism."

While ethical subjectivism, relativism, and emotivism are clearly distinct from one another at the level of metaethical theorizing, they frequently have the same cash value for those whose life's work is not the study of ethical theory. According to both subjectivism and emotivism, the meaning of normative ethical language is to be understood in terms of emotions. The difference is that according to subjectivism such language states propositions about the speaker's emotions, while emotivism says that such language expresses the speaker's emotions. According to both relativism and emotivism, there is no absolute truth in normative ethics. The difference is that according to relativism there is only relative truth in normative ethics, while emotivism says there is no truth at all. For someone wondering whether, for example, abortion is immoral, these distinctions have little relevance and often tend to blur.

Although the question of whether the domains of fact and value are mutually exclusive cannot be answered by empirical observation or mathematical reflection, simple logic does reveal the magnitude of the bullet one must bite in order to maintain that they are. If only one sentence about the immorality of child abuse, torture, rape, murder, cannibalism, or genocide both makes a value judgment and states a fact, then no line can be drawn between facts and values.

David Lutz

FURTHER READING

Arkes, Hadley. *First Things: An Inquiry into the First Principles of Morals and Justice*. Princeton, N.J.: Princeton University Press, 1986.

Ayer, A. J. *Language, Truth, and Logic*. London: V. Gollancz, 1936. Reprint. Introduction by Ben Rogers. London: Penguin, 2001.

Holmes, Arthur F. *Fact, Value, and God*. Grand Rapids, Mich.: W. B. Eerdmans, 1997.

Nietzsche, Friedrich. *On the Genealogy of Morals*. Edited and translated by Walter Kaufmann. New York: Vintage Books, 1967.

Putnam, Hilary. *The Collapse of the Fact/Value Dichotomy, and Other Essays*. Cambridge, Mass.: Harvard University Press, 2002.

Ritschl, Albrecht. *The Christian Doctrine of Justification and Reconciliation*. 2d ed. Edinburgh: T & T Clark, 1902.

Stevenson, Charles L. *Facts and Values: Studies in Ethical Analysis*. New Haven, Conn.: Yale University Press, 1963.

SEE ALSO: Cognitivism; Deconstruction; Emotivist ethics; Epistemological ethics; Foucault, Michel; Is/ought distinction; Normative vs. descriptive ethics; Objectivism; Postmodernism; Subjectivism.

Fair Labor Standards Act

IDENTIFICATION: Labor legislation regulating wages, hours of labor, and the use of child labor

DATE: October 24, 1938

TYPE OF ETHICS: Business and labor ethics

SIGNIFICANCE: The Fair Labor Standards Act arose out of a progressive ideal that holds government responsible for protecting the economic and social welfare of laboring people by regulating business.

The Supreme Court ruled unconstitutional attempts such as the National Industrial Recovery Act of 1933 by the Roosevelt administration to regulate prices, wages, hours, and other labor conditions. In 1938, however, Congress passed wages and hours legislation as an omnibus bill, and the Supreme Court upheld it in 1941. The Fair Labor Standards Act regulated minimum wages, overtime pay, child labor, and the production of goods for interstate commerce.

Beginning with the third year after its effective date, the act raised the minimum wage to forty cents per hour, made it subject thereafter to review by a congressional committee, and required overtime pay of one and one-half times the employees' regular pay above forty hours work per week. The act eliminated child labor (by children under age sixteen) with certain exceptions. One of the most significant amend-

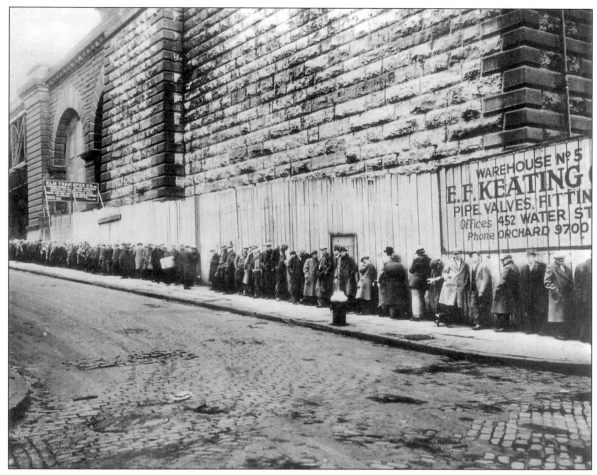

Unemployed men form a long breadline during the depression. New Deal legislation such as the Fair Labor Standards Act was designed to reduce the need for such services. (Library of Congress)

ments to the act, which came in 1963, required equal pay for equal work without regard to sex. Although more than forty exemptions to the act exist, including the regulation of professional employees and outside salespersons, the act is a milestone for labor, since in it Congress and the president recognized their responsibility to be the guardians of economic and social justice for labor.

Stephen D. Livesay

SEE ALSO: Child labor legislation; Congress; International Labour Organisation; Minimum-wage laws; National Labor Relations Act.

Fairness

DEFINITION: Moral principle used to judge procedures for distributing benefits and burdens justly and equally among parties

TYPE OF ETHICS: Beliefs and practices

SIGNIFICANCE: As an ethical principle, fairness regulates an exceptionally wide range of activities, from the conduct of games and other frivolous pastimes, to hiring and employment practices, to equal protection of the law and other fundamental civil rights.

Fairness is one of several ethical concepts, along with justice and equity, that are concerned with the distribution of benefits and burdens among individuals and groups. It is sometimes used in a broad sense, connoting attitudes and features characteristic of much wrongdoing, including putting one's own interests ahead of others and favoring oneself or one's own at the expense of others. In this broad sense, fairness is a central component of the moral point of view, in contrast to a purely egoistic or self-interested standpoint. The individual adopting the moral point of view is fair-minded, looking at claims in a balanced, impartial, and reasonable way.

The ancient Greek philosopher Aristotle, in his classic discussion of justice in book 5 of the *Nicomachean Ethics*, observed that justice is used in a narrow sense as well as a broad sense. Fairness, like justice, seems to have a narrower sense as well. In fact, it might be more accurate to say it has several narrower senses or uses. One of these senses is exemplified in cases of the differential treatment of individuals on arbitrary or irrelevant grounds. The awarding of a job on the basis of political favoritism or nepotism is usually condemned as unfair. Another related sense is that used in connection with procedures; for example, when people speak of a fair trial or a fair contest. In these cases, fairness is a matter of there being rules or guidelines that are closely followed. Additionally, the rules or guidelines shaping the procedure should not give an undue advantage to certain parties. Sometimes these notions are referred to as "procedural fairness" and "background fairness."

A third sense involves profiting at another's expense; if such advantage-taking is not allowed by the rules of some competition, it is deemed unfair. Oddly, however, allowing another to gain at one's own expense is not regarded as unfair. A fourth sense of fairness and unfairness is found in situations of blame and punishment: Punishing an innocent person ("scapegoating") and blaming or punishing an individual more than is deserved are seen as unfair. While several elements of unfairness are present in such cases, the main offense to fairness seems to be the singling out of the individual for disfavor, the sacrificing of that individual even if he or she is not totally innocent and even if some greater good will come of it.

"FAIRNESS" VS. "JUSTNESS"

While the concepts of justice and fairness are closely related and are used interchangeably in some contexts, they are not identical. The terms "just" and "unjust" often carry a stronger tone of condemnation than do "fair" and "unfair." At times, there is a readiness to admit that something is unfair but to tolerate it nevertheless, perhaps with an observation that "life is not fair." By contrast, the idea of tolerable or justifiable injustices is not countenanced. John Stuart Mill, in his discussion of justice in *Utilitarianism* (1861), made note of the avoidance of the idea that there can be "laudable injustice" by accommodating language so that "we usually say, not that justice must give way to some other moral principle, but that what is just in the ordinary case is, by reason of that other principle, not just in the particular case." Furthermore, fairness seems more appropriately applied to procedures and processes, while justice is often used for outcomes. Familiar examples of this are references to fair trials and just verdicts.

In *A Theory of Justice* (1971), philosopher John Rawls develops a theory of social justice that he calls "justice as fairness." He makes use of this association of the idea of fairness with procedures to extract principles of a just society as ones that would be the outcome of a bargaining process among parties under conditions marked by background fairness. One notion of fairness discussed by Rawls is identified with pure procedural justice. Pure procedural justice is characterized by the existence of a correct or fair procedure without an independent criterion of a correct or right result. In such a situation, provided the procedure has been followed, the result is correct or fair, whatever it happens to be. The fairness of the procedure transfers to the result.

In *A Theory of Justice*, Rawls attempts to develop a theory of a just society by treating social justice as a type of fairness or pure procedural justice. Pure procedural justice is contrasted with perfect procedural justice, in which there is an independent criterion of a correct result and the possibility of devising a procedure to arrive at that result, and imperfect procedural justice, in which there is an independent criterion of a correct outcome but no possibility of devising a procedure to consistently achieve that outcome.

Rawls also provides an extensive discussion of the principle of fairness or fair play. This is a principle of duty or right action, which relates to the sense of fairness in not taking advantage of others. If people enjoy the benefits of cooperative activities, benefits made possible by the contributions of others, then they have a duty to contribute their share or to do their part. Otherwise they are "free-riding." The tax evader who benefits from tax-supported programs is an example of a person unfairly benefiting from the efforts of others.

Mario F. Morelli

FURTHER READING

Aristotle. *Nicomachean Ethics.* Translated and edited by Roger Crisp. New York: Cambridge University Press, 2000.

Barry, Brian. *Political Argument.* London: Routledge & Kegan Paul, 1965.

Mendus, Susan. *Impartiality in Moral and Political Philosophy.* New York: Oxford University Press, 2002.

Mill, John Stuart. *Utilitarianism.* Edited by George Sher. 2d ed. Indianapolis: Hackett, 2001.

Rawls, John. *Justice as Fairness: A Restatement.* Edited by Erin Kelly. Cambridge, Mass.: Belknap Press, 2001.

_____. *A Theory of Justice.* Rev. ed. Cambridge, Mass.: Belknap Press of Harvard University Press, 1999.

Shklar, Judith N. *The Faces of Injustice.* New Haven, Conn.: Yale University Press, 1990.

SEE ALSO: Equality; Free-riding; Justice; Mill, John Stuart; Rawls, John; Social contract theory; Social justice and responsibility; *Theory of Justice, A*; Utilitarianism.

Fairness and Accuracy in Reporting

IDENTIFICATION: Left-leaning watchdog group that encourages the news media to report the diverse concerns and opinions of the American public rather than privileging mainstream conservative voices.

DATE: Founded in 1986

TYPE OF ETHICS: Media ethics

SIGNIFICANCE: FAIR works to correct what it perceives as a conservative bias in news reporting.

FAIR believes that the national and local news media are increasingly influenced by political and economic powers—that instead of independently challenging and criticizing government and big business, the news media tend to accept and pass along official versions of events. For example, FAIR examined news coverage of the 1991 Gulf War and found that most news stories and editorials echoed official government press releases and statements, and reflected little or no attempt to confirm or refine government versions of events. When some official statements turned out to be exaggerated or false, corrections were given minimal attention. FAIR also found that on talk shows and other analysis programs, only a small range of views was presented, and the views of those opposed to the war were seldom heard.

In 1989, FAIR published an important report showing that the guest analysts on two of the most widely watched television news programs were overwhelmingly white males from large institutions. Representatives of labor, social movements, minority groups, and local civic groups were very rarely featured on these programs. FAIR maintains contact with the public through a magazine that is published eight times a year and through a weekly radio program.

Cynthia A. Bily

SEE ALSO: Accuracy in Media; Journalistic ethics; Media ownership; News sources; Photojournalism.

Faith healers

DEFINITION: People who use prayer, religious faith, the power of suggestion, and touch to promote healing.

TYPE OF ETHICS: Religious ethics

SIGNIFICANCE: The cures ostensibly effected by faith healers have never been adequately or scientifically proven and may keep patients from pursuing more beneficial medical care and advice and may cause the patient serious financial loss or difficulty.

Faith healers see themselves as instruments empowered by God to heal. They attract clients or "patients," who seek relief from often serious medical or personal problems for which they have not found help and who seek assistance in divine intervention through faith healing.

Faith healers are also sometimes known as "spiritual healers." Spiritual healing, however, has a broader significance that encompasses cultural relationships and spiritual dimensions of the personality. Research has shown that spiritual perspectives and religious beliefs do influence personal values, attitudes and behaviors, and therefore biochemistry. For example, beliefs in healing powers of magical objects, people, and places have always been known. Faith healers, on the other hand, have generally been associated with evangelical and fundamentalist religions based on literal biblical interpretations and Christian healing traditions. A common theme in the various types of spiritual and faith healing is an appeal to God or gods to change for the better a person's physical or mental condition.

Some faith healers, such as those in the Pentecostal Church who use divine healing as part of their denominational dogma, do not prohibit use of professional medical care. They see professional physicians as receiving their healing skills from God. Some religious groups, notably Christian Scientists, however, reject the use of professional medical care in treating illness. They use Christian Science practitioners to help encourage faith directed to healing through God, teaching that illness is an illusion.

Spiritual healing has ancient origins. However, James Randi, an investigator of paranormal claims, has shown that the modern day faith-healing movement, which is fueled by claims of nineteenth century European and American evangelists, may have originated in the 1940's with the Reverend William Branham. A Jefferson, Indiana, resident, Branham conducted charismatic sermons and healings and acquired a huge following. Similar healers quickly multiplied, conducting sessions in the homes of clients and in their own churches, or traveling around the country holding healing tent "revivals."

EFFICACY OF FAITH HEALING

Various investigators have tried to determine the validity of faith healing by attempting to follow up on cases of numerous well-known faith healers including Oral Roberts, Pat Robertson, Father DiOrio, and Kathryn Kuhlman. Similar outcomes were obtained in all cases, with no criteria offered for failure and no cooperation or success in obtaining provable results through thorough pre- and post-healing medical examinations. Where some follow-up was possible, the

healings were not substantiated. William Nolen, a Minnesota physician who attempted to approach investigation of healing miracles with an open mind, was unable to confirm a single case. He did find that many people who thought themselves healed had relapses of their medical conditions within one to two weeks. Although physicians point out that around 80 percent of human illnesses will heal themselves without medical or spiritual intervention, successful cures are often credited to faith healers. Nolen concluded that people with disorders having psychological components may have benefited on a psychological level but others, who were not "healed," perceived themselves as unworthy or undeserving in God's eyes and therefore suffered heavy burdens of guilt and despair.

There are other problems with proving the results of faith healing. Since healers claim that an absolute and unquestioning faith is required from the client in order to be healed, failure can be blamed on insufficient faith or on personal transgressions and shortcomings of the client. Randi and other investigators point out that many techniques used by faith healers are identical to, or adaptations of, techniques used by magicians and mentalists, including use of memory techniques in calling out names and afflictions based upon data collected by associates before the service. Psychological conditioning sets up behavioral expectations for hands-on healing when a strike on the forehead causes the recipient to fall backward into the hands of assistants. Speaking in tongues relates to a psychological phenomenon called glossolalia, which was described by Plato long before the Christian manifestation and was noted in pronouncements by Greek and Roman oracles. These techniques, even when understood and exposed, do not lessen the beliefs or faith of many followers.

ETHICAL ISSUES

Modern scandals involving popular television evangelists, in addition to unproven results of their healings, have added to the concern of highly questionable ethics on the part of practitioners. Divinity appears to reside in the interpretation of the healer. There are no codes of ethics or any unifying organization. In fact, there is often intense competition for the minds and dollars of the clientele. It also seems that healing applies only to those clients who have afflictions that can be exploited before an audience. A lost leg or body part never reappears, there is no way to prove the removal of a tumor without medical tests, and visible skin diseases, disfigurements, or afflictions always require days or weeks for a cure after the healers and audience are long gone. Television and radio add to the illusion and can be manipulated as required.

Commercialism is most certainly an issue, since faith healing generates millions of dollars. Many cases investigated by James Randi would, by law, constitute fraud. On the other hand, complaints were not forthcoming, and cases are difficult or impossible to prove without cooperation. Individuals who can least afford it may be defrauded of their limited resources and savings.

Where issues of consent are concerned, adults may make their own decisions regarding beliefs and practices. However, the courts have generally held that freedom of religion does not include the right to withhold medical care from a child. Faith healers do use children in their healing services, and if a child has afflictions that are not medically addressed, as in cases of Christian Science, this would constitute child abuse.

Martha O. Loustaunau

FURTHER READING

Fraser, Caroline. *God's Perfect Child: Living and Dying in the Christian Science Church*. New York: Metropolitan Books/Henry Holt, 1999.

Frazier, Claude A. *Faith Healing*. New York: Thomas Nelson, 1973.

Nolen, William A. *Healing: Doctor in Search of a Miracle*. New York: Random House, 1974.

Pullum, Stephen J. *"Foul Demons, Come Out!": The Rhetoric of Twentieth Century American Faith Healing*. Westport, Conn.: Praeger Publishers, 1999.

Randi, James. *The Faith Healers*. Buffalo, N.Y.: Prometheus Books, 1989.

SEE ALSO: Holistic medicine; Hypocrisy; Medical ethics; Televangelists.

Family

DEFINITION: Fundamental social group, often consisting of a man, a woman, and their offspring
TYPE OF ETHICS: Personal and social ethics
SIGNIFICANCE: Families are the basic social units that make up larger societies. They also constitute one of the core institutions that educate and inculcate children with ethical values.

All known societies value the family. In American society, the family is customarily defined as a social group based on a heterosexual partnership of procreation that creates a community of parents and children.

FAMILY TYPES

The concepts of household and family should not be confused. A household is a group of people who live together and share cooking and toilet facilities. Households may include unrelated boarders who rent rooms from a family, as is the case with many college students. "Household" is a descriptive term, whereas the term "family" is prescriptive. A family consists of people who are related to one another by blood or marriage and who thus ought to care for one another and share life's joys and sorrows. Duty and obligation bind family members as much as rights and privileges do. Family and household often overlap but do not necessarily do so. Members of a family may live in scattered households.

There are many types of family, each of which has evolved in response to different circumstances. In the United States, the term "family" commonly refers to the "nuclear family": a husband, a wife, and their children, all of whom share a home, often cook and eat together, and offer one another support. The word "family" also encompasses a person's ancestors and other relatives, such as aunts, uncles, and cousins. Most families are based on kinship, which simply means that the family members are related to one another by blood, marriage, or recognized forms of adoption. "Foster families" are an exception, because the children are neither adopted nor related to their foster parents by blood or marriage. Despite this fact, the members of such families live together and treat one another as family members.

Anthropologists, sociologists, and psychologists believe that nuclear families were well adapted to the demands of industrial America. Their small size made it easy for industrial workers to relocate when employment demanded that they move. From the 1840's until the 1940's, the nuclear family was considered the norm in the United States and in the industrialized sections of Europe.

In the postindustrial United States, many other types of families are emerging. Skyrocketing housing costs have forced many parents with children to move in with grandparents, forming three- or even four-generational "extended families" made up of two or more nuclear families. Like the nuclear family, such a family is a "conjugal family," because some of its members are related by blood and others are related by marriage. Because many husbands and wives work, grandparents often provide no-cost child care for young couples. An extended family might also include aunts, uncles, and cousins. Many immigrant families form "joint extended families" composed of several related families that live together, pool their earnings, and share most expenses. Many of these families are headed by an old patriarch and his wife. Usually, married sons and their wives and children, as well as unmarried children, attach themselves to a grandfather's household to form a joint family. Such families are more common among families that own property or businesses than they are among the working class. Family type represents adaptation to circumstances, not moral imperatives. Ethics develop to justify and reinforce family structures.

Extended families can accumulate capital rapidly, which encourages early entry into small businesses. Family members often work in these businesses without pay in return for total support for themselves and their children. Since family members feel obligated to work for relatives, even without pay, some sociologists are critical of these families. They believe that this arrangement amounts to little more than slavery and exploitation. Sometimes, children are forced to work and, as a result, miss school to help maintain the family business.

These families raise many moral issues. Do obligations to extended family members limit an individual's freedom and stifle personal growth? If so, is a person justified in ignoring these demands? What duty do people owe their grandparents and relatives who are not within their immediate families? If one inherits financial benefits from distant relatives, es-

pecially as a result of heinous institutions, such as slavery, does one also inherit a moral obligation to right those persons' wrongs? Should those who prosper under a system work to change that system if they know that it is morally wrong? History has often provided examples of families that chose practicality and personal gain over morality; for example, slave-owning families.

Chinese immigrants to the United States provide an example of a type of extended family that is known as the "stem family." Betty Lee Sung's book *Mountain of Gold: The Story of the Chinese in America* (1967) notes that filial piety and a display of absolute loyalty to and respect for parents obligate one married son to live with his aging parents and become their caretaker. Other sons and daughters are free to marry and leave the family unit without being condemned for abandoning or neglecting the parents. This social obligation would make it both unethical and unthinkable for first-generation Chinese Americans to place their aging parents in homes for older people or allow them to struggle to maintain a household alone. Although caring for aging parents is a burden and may create economic hardships, moral imperatives take precedence in this situation. This tradition often changes in the second and third generation.

DECLINE OF THE NUCLEAR FAMILY

Some social scientists argue that the American family is doomed because "single-parent families" are a growing phenomenon. Rising levels of education make it possible for many women to support children without help from a father. Welfare creates similar options for less-well-educated poor women.

The conservative view of female-headed households implies that they are not ethical. Bearing children out of wedlock is considered immoral. Also important to conservatives is the fact that children born out of wedlock cost the government billions of dollars annually. Conservatives often assert that women who develop what conservatives like to think of as irresponsible sex lives contribute to the growing feminization of poverty. People who think in this way believe that character flaws, bad values, and personal weakness on the part of such women create "matrifocal families." These are "consanguineal families" in which the members are related by blood ties only. This view ignores the possibility that the man may have abandoned the woman or that a woman may be widowed or divorced. Conservatives also believe that matrifocal families unfairly condemn millions of children to live as welfare wards and dependents of the state, plagued by persistent poverty.

WELFARE

Most families on welfare are matrifocal. Some observers believe that welfare is debilitating because it undermines the work ethic, which values work rather than leisure. To many Americans, work is a moral duty and an obligation to the family, the community, and the state. As early as 1898, Jacob Riis's book *How the Other Half Lives* (1898) argued that poor families should be given jobs, not charity. Riis believed that work restored a moral environment, which was the key to reducing poverty, strengthening nuclear families, and restoring people's self-respect and dignity. Conservative supporters of welfare reform echo Riis's views. They want to tie welfare eligibility to moral norms. Workfare programs are built on this assumption, and some of them allow nuclear families to receive aid if parents assume responsibility for the family and seek work or self-improvement through education in preparation for future jobs.

When investigating how female-headed families form, a different picture emerges. In slum neighborhoods, many single mothers have that status thrust upon them by high levels of male unemployment. *The Truly Disadvantaged* (1990), by sociologist William Julius Wilson, notes that in 1950, 80 of every 100 ghetto men were gainfully employed; by 1980, however, the number had dropped to 17 of every 100. The result was that few ghetto men were able to support wives and children. Wilson believes that economics is largely responsible for this disaster. Fathers without families feel guilty because they accept society's dictate that they should care for their children. Such shame is dysfunctional, and many males seek to escape from it by means of alcohol, drug abuse, or crime. Consequently, 25 percent of African American males between the ages of 17 and 35 are caught up in the criminal justice system, and many others are in the armed forces. In either case, they are not in their communities.

The absence of these endangered men from slum communities creates a void. Many men contract AIDS while they are in prison because they engage in homosexual affairs or become intravenous drug users and share dirty needles. Once the infected person is released from prison, the disease is transmitted to his female lovers. For this reason, epidemics and drug abuse threaten to destroy urban low-income families.

As medical science increases longevity, society strives to offer all its members that benefit, but often only wealthy families benefit. This problem is most evident in figures calculating life expectancy in terms of race. Whites can expect to live ten years longer than African Americans may expect to live, because many whites can afford better nutrition and medical care for their families. This fact creates an ethical dilemma. Are rich families entitled to live longer than poor families? Is access to adequate health care a privilege or a right?

INFANT MORTALITY

Another cause of matrifocal families is the falling infant mortality rate, which is reflected in the increased number of adolescent girls who give birth. In *When Children Want Children* (1989), Leon Dash points out that although the overall rate of adolescent births has declined since 1970, the number of infants born to unwed mothers has increased threefold, from 91,700 in 1960 to 270,076 in 1983. Add to this the fact that 23 percent of these mothers said that they intentionally became pregnant and the moral crisis becomes clear. Early unmarried parenthood is closely tied to reduced education, marginal income-earning capacity, and welfare dependence. Teenage mothers also tend to have larger-than-average families, and married teenage couples have the highest divorce rate in the United States.

Children of teenage mothers have poorer-than-average health, lower-than-average IQ scores, low cognitive scores, and a better-than-average chance of living in a disruptive home during their high school years, and these children are more likely to become sexually active before marriage and repeat this tragic cycle than are other teenagers. The ethical crisis is clear, but the remedy is far from clear, despite the fact that Peter Laslett's book *Family Life and Illicit Love in Past Times* argues that this dilemma has faced Americans since the frontier era. In the past, high infant mortality rates and forced marriages covered up moral lapses. Decreasing infant death rates and greater freedom in mate selection are bringing old dilemmas into sharp focus, according to Laslett. Is

513

technology revealing a conflict between family ideals and reality?

POWER RELATIONSHIPS WITHIN FAMILIES

Practical matters dictate that there are vast differences in power within families. Traditionally, American men were expected to be monarchs within the family and to wield great power. The father's word was final. It has become clear that, in an alarming number of cases, the intimacy of the family conceals abuses of this power involving incest and beatings of wives, children, and older relatives. Family members may engage in denial and hide such abuse even from themselves. The rights of women, children, and older people within families need to be made clear and public in order to protect these people. The abuse of power becomes institutionalized when fathers are also the sole judges of injustice and their victims are delegated roles as custodians of patience, forgiveness, and forbearance. Lord Acton noted that power corrupts and that absolute power corrupts absolutely. This seems to be true within families; relations should be democratized by distributing power within the family to minimize abuses of all kinds.

Plato charged that families were bad because they made people acquisitive and thus subverted devotion to the good of the community. In his ideal republic, the guardian class would live and reproduce in communal groups, thus creating one huge extended family based on group marriage. This would reduce psychological and material divisions. The practice was tried in Israel and Russia, with little success. Thomas Jefferson wanted to allow private households and nuclear families but limit inheritance as a method of reducing the advantages that family wealth would give one American over another. Inheritance is an element of the issues of family favoritism and nepotism, which are banned for those who hold public office because they give family members unfair opportunities to secure jobs, political office, income, and other benefits.

DIVORCE

In 1930, American schoolchildren would have been shocked if any of their peers admitted to having divorced parents. By the early twenty-first century, such information was commonplace. Although this fact gives rise to fear that the family is breaking down, such fear is unrealistic. The highest divorce rate of the twentieth century occurred in 1945, following World War II. This occurred because many couples married hurriedly, without knowing each other. The men went off to war, and the stress of separation caused both men and women to develop other relationships, leading to divorce after the war. The divorce rate dropped sharply after 1945 but began to rise steadily again between 1950 and 1980. Although the current rate is high, it is not nearly as high as the 1945 rate.

Divorce alone is not responsible for the increase in single-parent families, as some people have suggested. Drastic reductions in death rates mean that fewer parents are widowed and fewer children are orphans than was the case earlier in the century. These statistics offset the increase in single-parent households caused by divorce. Moreover, record numbers of parents remarry shortly after a divorce and form "blended families." Although stepparents assume responsibility for the children of their new spouses, remarriage raises questions. What are the best interests of the children? Who should have custody?

Children who have been given up for adoption can now use their rights to divorce their biological parents if there is an attempt to reunite them. Children who have done so have argued that they do not know their biological parents and are happy with their adopted social parents. Adopted parents choose these children out of love. In such cases, the genitor, or social parent, supersedes the biological parent. The courts have upheld the right of children to remain with adopted parents despite the wishes of the biological parents who put them up for adoption earlier in life. Is it ethical for the state to uphold individual rights at the expense of group rights?

CONCLUSIONS

Although some people have predicted the demise of the American family, the evidence suggests that this is not a likely scenario. The family is undoubtedly changing in response to new social environments and new challenges, but it remains basically healthy. In fact, families may be stronger than ever. Lesbian and gay couples, for example, do not wish to destroy the family; instead, they view it as an institution that is so desirable that they want its definition expanded to include same-sex couples who wish to make lifelong commitments. In the years ahead, society will be challenged to redefine the family, its mission, and the ethics of relationships within it as it becomes possible to reproduce asexually through cloning and as other developments take place. Future families are likely to be more democratic and to avoid abusive sexism. Families may even drift away from privatism and favoritism toward close relatives, but changes in this area should be expected to occur slowly. Since families play pivotal roles in shaping the morality of the nation, business is likely to become more involved in family issues in order to ensure a steady supply of trustworthy and reliable workers. The declining roles of churches and schools as shapers of values may force business to play such a role. Finally, as families become more democratic, children will acquire more power within them, and those children must be taught how to use that power appropriately. The future of the family holds many problems and many ethical challenges.

Dallas Browne

FURTHER READING

Aiken, William, and Hugh LaFollette, eds. *Whose Child? Children's Rights, Parental Authority, and State Power.* Totowa, N.J.: Rowman & Littlefield, 1980.

Blustein, Jeffrey. *Parents and Children: The Ethics of the Family.* New York: Oxford University Press, 1982.

Ditzion, Sidney. *Marriage, Morals, and Sex in America: A History of Ideas.* New York: Bookman Associates, 1953.

Laslett, Peter. *Household and Family in Past Times.* Cambridge, England: Cambridge University Press, 1972.

Okin, Susan Moller. *Justice, Gender, and the Family.* New York: Basic Books, 1989.

Scarre, Geoffrey, ed. *Children, Parents, and Politics.* New York: Cambridge University Press, 1989.

Shapiro, Michael J. *For Moral Ambiguity: National Culture and the Politics of the Family.* Minneapolis: University of Minnesota Press, 2001.

Teichman, Jenny. *Illegitimacy: An Examination of Bastardy.* Ithaca, N.Y.: Cornell University Press, 1982.

Ulanowsky, Carole. *The Family in the Age of Biotechnology.* Brookfield, Vt.: Avebury, 1995.

Wilson, William J. *The Truly Disadvantaged: The Inner City, the Underclass, and Public Policy.* Chicago: University of Chicago Press, 1990.

SEE ALSO: Birth control; Child abuse; Children; Divorce; Family therapy; Family values; Incest; Marriage; Parenting; Personal relationships.

Family therapy

DEFINITION: Type of group psychotherapy that seeks to address the needs of families or individuals within families by analyzing and modifying relationships and dynamics within the family

TYPE OF ETHICS: Psychological ethics

SIGNIFICANCE: Family therapy raises all the ethical issues raised by individual psychotherapy, but it also raises special ethical concerns involving the need for evenhandedness in the relationship of the therapist to each member of the family group, the need for patients to balance honest work in therapy with the feelings of the other family members, and the confidentiality of information revealed between family members in therapy sessions.

Family therapy is guided by systems theory, which believes that psychological problems of the individual must be approached as a dysfunction of life within the family. Rather than attempting to promote behavioral and cognitive changes in the dysfunctional individual alone, the family therapist views the family unit as the agent or system for achieving change. It is through the family that understanding of individual behavior is achieved. Actions by any single family member have an effect on all other family members. Family therapists may work with individuals, couples, parents and children, siblings, the nuclear family, the family of origin, and social networks in order to understand their clients' problems and to formulate strategies for change.

ETHICAL STANDARDS IN FAMILY THERAPY

Gayla Margolin observed that the ethical questions facing the family therapist are even more different, numerous, and complicated than those faced by therapists who do individual therapy. In an attempt to provide guidance on how to deal with these ethical issues, the American Association of Marriage and Family Therapists published a code of ethics in 1991. The code addresses eight areas: (1) responsibility to clients; (2) confidentiality; (3) professional competence and integrity; (4) responsibility to students, employees, and supervisees; (5) responsibility to research participants; (6) responsibility to the profession; (7) fees; and (8) advertising.

Most of these areas (areas 3 through 8) are essentially the same for individual and family therapists because they focus on only the therapist: his or her qualifications and training, behavior, and income. It is in the first two areas of responsibility to clients and confidentiality that unique ethical issues confront the family therapist. These unique ethical concerns have been summarized by Gerald Corey, Marianne Schneider Corey, and Patrick Callanan (1993) in four general areas:

1. Treating the entire family. Most family therapists believe that it is crucial for all members of the family to participate. Ethical questions arise when a family member or members refuse to participate. Coercing militant members to participate is unethical. Some therapists may withhold therapy until all members participate, but this strategy is controversial. Besides resembling coercion, it can be argued that this tactic denies therapy to the willing participants.

Conversely, Rachel T. Hare-Mustin contends that involving the whole family may not always be in the best interests of a particular member. Giving priority to the good of the entire family may jeopardize the legitimate goals or desires of that member. Ethical considerations require the therapist to minimize risks for any family member.

2. Value system of the therapist. The therapist's value system crucially influences the course of family therapy in two ways: first, when the therapist has values that are different from those of a member or members of the family, problems can arise; second, value systems influence the formulation and definition of the problems that are presented, the goals and plans for therapy, and the course the therapy takes. For example, Irene Goldenberg and Herbert Goldenberg contend that family therapists generally believe in maintaining the family way of life. Such a belief could, however, be harmful or inappropriate under some circumstances.

Ethical considerations demand that the therapist make known his or her attitudes and commitments to each family member. Gerald Corey et al. further state that it is not the function of the therapist to make decisions for clients or dictate how they should change.

The therapist's role is to provide insight into family dynamics and to help and encourage the family to make necessary changes. The therapist must be aware of how his or her values can influence the course of therapy.

3. The ethics of consulting. This issue arises if one of the family members terminates joint sessions and begins therapy with another therapist. To complicate the situation further, Corey et al. pose a situation in which a person might persuade other family members to also consult with his or her therapist while still seeing their original therapist. Is this new therapist ethically obligated to consult with the original therapist? Are the two therapists ethically obligated to receive permission of their clients before talking with each other? Would it be ethical for the two therapists to ignore each other? These are difficult questions to answer.

4. The issue of confidentiality. In the course of family therapy, the therapist will see the family as a group and also individually. During individual sessions, of course, the client may divulge information that is not known to other family members. What is the ethically correct approach regarding the confidentiality of information revealed during these one-to-one sessions? Some therapists will not reveal such information. Other therapists believe that it is appropriate to reveal such information under appropriate circumstances that would benefit the rest of the family. Again, this is a difficult issue to resolve.

The implications of revealing confidences can be serious. Revealing confidences may, however, facilitate resolution of the family's problems. Corey et al. suggest a middle position. The therapist is ethically obligated to inform the family that information revealed during private sessions may be divulged, if in the therapist's opinion that shared information would benefit the family. This position allows the therapist maximum flexibility and options to act in the family's best interests.

In conclusion, the increasing popularity and usefulness of family therapy require sensitivity to and understanding of the unique ethical issues it can present to the family therapist.

Laurence Miller

FURTHER READING

Corey, Gerald, Marianne Schneider Corey, and Patrick Callanan. *Issues and Ethics in the Helping*

Professions. Pacific Grove, Calif.: Brooks-Cole, 1993.

Goldenberg, Irene, and Herbert Goldenberg. *Family Therapy: An Overview.* 6th ed. Pacific Grove, Calif.: Thomson, Brooks/Cole, 2004.

Margolin, Gayla. "Ethical and Legal Considerations in Marital and Family Therapy." *American Psychologist* 37 (July, 1982): 788-801.

Nichols, Michael P., and Richard C. Schwartz. *Family Therapy: Concepts and Methods.* 2d ed. Boston: Allyn & Bacon, 1991.

Patten, Christi, Therese Barnett, and Daniel Houlihan. "Ethics in Marital and Family Therapy: A Review of the Literature." *Professional Psychology: Research and Practice* 22 (April, 1991): 171-175.

Walsh, Froma, ed. *Normal Family Processes: Growing Diversity and Complexity.* 3d ed. New York: Guilford Press, 2003.

SEE ALSO: Behavior therapy; Divorce; Ethical Principles of Psychologists; Family; Group therapy; Therapist-patient relationship.

Family values

DEFINITION: Qualities of life that are necessary for the preservation of, or arise out of the practice of, the family as a social institution

TYPE OF ETHICS: Personal and social ethics

SIGNIFICANCE: The family is one of the most important and powerful institutions for the creation, perpetuation, and inculcation of values. The precise meaning of the phrase "family values," however, is a source of controversy. The phrase has been used, beginning during the 1980's, to refer only to those values preserved within morally and politically conservative families. More recently, leftist political and moral leaders have attempted to reclaim the phrase to refer to their own value systems.

"Family values" is a complex concept, and such terms as "family," "family life," and "moral development" appear as frequently as does the term "family values." No one word or idea adequately expresses all that is involved; however, the two words in the phrase suggest two vital elements: a family unit and values that hold the family unit together so that both social and personal needs are met.

"Family values" means, first of all, the existence of a family. In biblical thought (Gen. 1-2), the idea of family was integral to the creative activity of God. The beginning of humankind was cast in the form of family; namely, Adam and Eve and their children. Thus, values associated with the family are religious values or have religious connotations.

This religious idea of family carries through to the New Testament. When presenting a family code of behavior (Eph. 5-6), the apostle Paul specifically drew on Old Testament concepts. Ephesians 5.31 refers to Genesis 2.24, and Ephesians 6.2-3 refers to the Ten Commandments. Paul gave the family code as an example of walking (living) the Christian life (Eph. 4.1, 17; 5.1, 8, 15). Then he placed the code within the context of mutual submission of family members to one another (Eph. 5.21). The code itself (5.22-6.9) further emphasized these mutually beneficial relationships with a literary framework that may have roots in Aristotle (Politics, book 1, chapters 3, 12, 13). Thus, Paul Christianized the code and raised the status of every family member by emphasizing genuine care and concern of the members for one another—care based on Christian principles. Finally, the passage on walking the Christian life concluded with a call for Christians to overcome evil, not only in the home but everywhere, by means of all the defensive and offensive armor provided by God (Eph. 6.10-20).

With this as its background, the Christian concept of family takes on an aura of religious commitment. A man leaves his father and mother and cleaves to his wife. A woman leaves her father and mother and cleaves to her husband.

LOVE

This commitment and the mutual care and concern of the members provide enough glue to hold the family together for its own sake and against all assaults from outside. Without the glue, the unit dissolves. Whatever the reasons for joining together in the first place, there is a sense of mutual responsibility and commitment. At the heart of the idea of "values" in "family values" is love.

For this reason, child abuse, for example, is regarded as a heinous crime, not only because an indi-

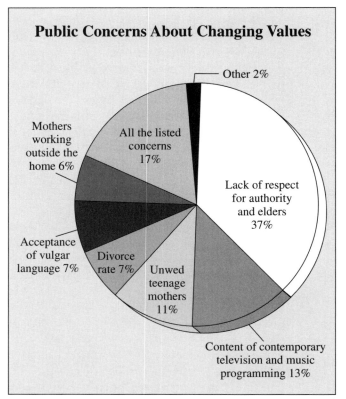

Public Concerns About Changing Values

Other 2%

Mothers working outside the home 6%

All the listed concerns 17%

Lack of respect for authority and elders 37%

Acceptance of vulgar language 7%

Divorce rate 7%

Unwed teenage mothers 11%

Content of contemporary television and music programming 13%

Source: NBC News/*Wall Street Journal* Poll, June 16-19, 1999. Figures based on poll of 2,011 adult Americans.

vidual is hurt but also because the whole concept of a caring family unit is endangered. Similarly, divorce is also regarded as the antithesis of family because it dissolves the unit. Because of these views, many religious groups reach out to embrace and care for these splintered families. The individuals are valued for themselves, and this caring also helps to preserve the picture of the ideal family by showing that splintering is not the ideal.

IDEAL FAMILY

In "family values," the ideal family is one with at least two essential poles: mother and father. Children are usually included in the ideal. This traditional concept is generally consistent with both philosophical commentary on the family and Christian views. In Christian thought, however, the ideal family is considered to be an instrument of God and the best means of fulfilling human needs and development.

Alternative family concepts challenge this ideal. Some of these alternatives result from necessity. Oth-

ers exist because of choices people have made. For example, there are single-parent families with female or male parents, couples without children, and families with divorced or separated parents. The list can go on and on. According to traditional ideals of family values, however, these alternatives are not the ideal and are therefore deficient to some degree.

"Family values" are about the family, not about business or religion or politics, even though "family values" intersect other sets of values. For example, one set of "family values" may include belief in God as integral to the family itself. Obviously, this value intersects specifically religious values. Beliefs that prohibit family members from lying and stealing and cheating also affect other values. Economic, educational, and other social values interact with "family values." A family does not live in an ivory tower. Nevertheless, "family values" are usually given preference.

RESPONSIBILITY

For there to be a family and "family values," someone must take responsibility for choosing and enforcing values. Someone must say, "We do this. We do not do that." Enforcing values usually has two aspects. On one hand, someone must exercise discipline to enforce the values. On the other hand, someone must say, "I love you" and hold out a comforting embrace when the values are not met. Choosing and enforcing values in autonomous families is traditionally the task of parents, not that of state or social agencies.

S. M. Mayo

FURTHER READING

Blustein, Jeffrey. *Parents and Children: The Ethics of the Family.* New York: Oxford University Press, 1982.

D'Antonio, William V., and Joan Aldous, eds. *Families and Religions: Conflict and Change in Modern Society.* Beverly Hills, Calif.: Sage, 1983.

Herlihy, David. "Family." *American Historical Review* 96 (February, 1991): 1-16.

Scudder, C. W. *The Family in Christian Perspective.* Nashville, Tenn.: Broadman, 1962.

Smith, George P. II. *Family Values and the New Society: Dilemmas of the Twenty-first Century.* Westport, Conn.: Praeger, 1998.

Stacey, Judith. *Brave New Families: Stories of Domestic Upheaval in Late Twentieth Century America.* New York: Basic Books, 1990.

Trueblood, Elton, and Pauline Trueblood. *The Recovery of Family Life.* New York: Harper, 1953.

Winfield, Richard Dien. *The Just Family.* Albany: State University of New York Press, 1998.

SEE ALSO: Children; Children's television; Christian ethics; Family; Individualism; Love; Marriage; Motion picture ratings systems; Personal relationships.

Famine

DEFINITION: Extreme and protracted food shortages, causing widespread and persistent hunger and malnutrition, with associated health problems and substantial increases in death rates

TYPE OF ETHICS: Human rights

SIGNIFICANCE: Throughout history governments have used famine to oppress citizens who oppose their policies or coerce them into participating in programs of the state.

Famines have occurred in many parts of the world throughout history. The earliest written reference to a

Time Line of Major World Droughts and Famines

Date	Place	Event and estimated casualties
3500 B.C.E.	Egypt	Earliest recorded famine.
1700 B.C.E.	India	Indus Valley civilization collapses because of drought.
436 B.C.E.	Rome	Thousands are said to drown themselves in the Tiber River to avoid starvation.
450 C.E.	Italy (Dufresnoy)	Parents said to eat their own children to survive.
1300	Southwestern U.S.A.	Cliff Dwellers vanish after drought.
1769-1770	India	Drought kills 3-10 million.
1790-1792	India	Doji Bara, or skull famine—so named because skulls of the dead were too numerous to count.
1846-1851	Ireland	Potato famine kills more than 1 million and spurs emigration of 1 million people to America.
1876-1878	India	5 million die.
1876-1879	China	9-13 million die.
1921-1922	Soviet Union	5 million die.
1932-1934	Soviet Union	5 million die in failed collectivization scheme.
1943-1944	India	More than 1.5 million die.
1960-1980	Sahel (West Africa)	More than 1 million die.
1967-1970	Biafra (Nigeria)	More than 1.5 million starve to death during civil war.
1975-1979	Cambodia	More than 1 million die during civil war.
1984-1994	Ethiopia and Somalia	Wars and droughts lead to starvation of more than 1 million.
1990's-	North Korea	More than 1 million have died
2000-	Ethiopia	Unknown

famine was in Egypt in 3500 B.C.E. Famines develop in situations in which there are too many people and insufficient food to feed them. The many causes of famines usually can be broken down into natural and human categories. Natural causes spring from unfavorable weather conditions, such as drought, heavy rains and flooding, plant diseases, and insect and vermin infestations. Human causes are primarily political and cultural in nature and are indicative of underlying problems in food production, distribution, earning capacity, medical care, and levels of development.

Some social scientists see famines as products of power relations, of the use of violence by states that leads to mass starvation. Famines occurred in early Roman times because of Rome's inability or unwillingness to transport food to regions experiencing shortages. It was a common practice for the Roman emperors to hoard grain in the center of the empire, while famines gripped other regions of the empire. The violence of warfare by both attacking and defending forces has caused famines not only by deliberately destroying crops and food supplies but also by disrupting distribution by sieges and blockades. Scorched-earth policies used by retreating troops to deprive their attackers of food have also starved local peoples who are dependent on their land.

In famine-stricken areas, populations generally turn to their governments for relief but do not always receive the help they seek. Government authorities may not admit the severity of famine conditions for fear that they will be held responsible for them. Rulers may ignore or conceal famine conditions in order to maintain their international prestige. The greatest mortality from famine in the twentieth century resulted from communist regimes withholding food supplies in order to coerce unwilling citizens into collectivization. During the 1930's, peasants in the Ukraine who resisted the Soviet government's proscription against private ownership of property burned their own grain and slaughtered their livestock rather than turn them over to the government.

Communist authorities confiscated what remained and prevented other food from entering the area. The result was Joseph Stalin's greatest atrocity, the Great Famine of 1932-1933, in which six million people died. In a similar way, Chairman Mao Zedong's Great Leap Forward program in the People's Repub-

lic of China in the late 1950's resulted in twenty million to thirty million fatalities through malnutrition and famine. In both the Soviet Union and China, the communist parties exported grain while the famines raged.

The prevalence of widespread famines has continued in parts of Africa, Southeast Asia, and Latin America, but the ability of countries to import food and the efforts of international relief organizations have lessened the effects of modern famines. Developed nations face the difficult ethical choice of either helping oppressive regimes develop their countries' agricultural productivity in order to avoid famines or waiting until famine conditions require the shipment of food aid.

Theodore M. Vestal

FURTHER READING

Arnold, David. *Famine: Social Crisis and Historical Change.* Oxford, England: Blackwell, 1988.

Bello, Walden F., et al. *Dark Victory: The United States and Global Poverty.* 2d ed. Oakland, Calif.: Food First, 1999.

Edkins, Jenny. *Whose Hunger?* Minneapolis: University of Minnesota Press, 2000.

Rau, Bill. *From Feast to Famine: Official Cures and Grassroots Remedies to Africa's Food Crisis.* Highlands, N.J.: Zed Books, 1991.

SEE ALSO: Agribusiness; Developing world; Future-oriented ethics; Genocide and democide; Hunger; Lifeboat ethics; Malthus, Thomas; Outsourcing; Poverty and wealth; Power; Vegetarianism.

al-Fārābī

IDENTIFICATION: Muslim philosopher
BORN: 870, Farab, north of Tashkent, Turkistan (now in Kazakhstan)
DIED: 950, Damascus, Syria
TYPE OF ETHICS: Religious ethics
SIGNIFICANCE: Influential in Islamic ethics and in medieval European thought, al-Fārābī's *The Agreement of Plato and Aristotle* (tenth century) attempted a reconciliation of Plato, Aristotle, and Neoplatonic philosophy.

Al-Fārābī's ethical thought is intimately intertwined with his Neoplatonic emanation scheme, in which the One generates a hierarchy of concentric spheres. The intellect of the lunar sphere (the active intellect) emanates pure intelligibles to the human realm. In *The Opinions of the Inhabitants of the Virtuous City* (tenth century), al-Fārābī argued that the immortality of the soul was dependent on its actualization in apprehension of that Intellect. The virtuous city is well-led, so that its citizens are reminded of a life beyond this one. Its citizens achieve moral virtue, which allows reason to govern appetites and passions, and they turn their attention to the gifts of the Active Intellect. Such souls find bliss in the afterlife. Less-actualized souls simply cease to exist (if they were ignorant of the Active Intellect) or, if they were excessively attached to bodily pleasures, endure a limited series of transmigrations or torment caused by separation from the body after death.

Al-Fārābī had an important place in the philosophy of Avicenna, Albertus Magnus, and, through them, Saint Thomas Aquinas.

Thomas Gaskill

SEE ALSO: Avicenna; Ghazālī, al-; Kindī, al-.

Farrakhan, Louis

IDENTIFICATION: African American religious leader and minister of the Nation of Islam
BORN: May 11, 1933, New York, New York
TYPE OF ETHICS: Religious ethics
SIGNIFICANCE: Louis Farrakhan filled an important leadership void in the Nation of Islam left by the death of Elijah Muhammad but became a controversial public figure.

Born with the name of Louis Eugene Walcott, Farrakhan changed his name to Louis X after joining the Nation of Islam. He later changed it again to Louis Farrakhan. Farrakhan was at one time the right-hand man of Malcolm X. Malcolm often referred to Farrakhan as his "little brother" when the latter was head minister of the Boston mosque and

Malcolm was the head minister of the Harlem, New York, mosque during the early 1960's.

After Malcolm was expelled from the Nation of Islam in 1964 for making disrespectful statements about the assassination of President John F. Kennedy, Farrakhan grew critical of Malcolm's attacks on the ethical behavior and sexual immorality of Elijah Muhammad. Farrakhan said that Malcolm deserved to die and that Malcolm would not get away because of his criticisms of the Nation of Islam and Elijah Muhammad. Although Farrakhan has never denied making such statements, he has steadfastly denied having anything to do with Malcolm X's assassination in 1965. Similarly, when Jesse Jackson ran in the democratic presidential primaries in 1984, Farrakhan threatened that harm would come to anyone who attempted bodily harm to Jackson.

In 1975, Farrakhan succeeded Elijah Muhammad as the head of the Nation of Islam after Muhammad's death. Questions related to Farrakhan's ethical conduct were raised in connection with his relationships with both Malcolm X and Jesse Jackson. In the first case, Farrakhan had implied (but later denied) that he would be associated with the death of Malcolm X. In the second case, he tacitly asserted that injury would come to anyone who harmed Jackson. Both cases raise the issue of ethical or unethical behavior related to threats outside the normal boundaries of morality in the political system.

Mfanya D. Tryman

FURTHER READING
Goldman, Peter. *The Death and Life of Malcolm X.* 2d ed. Urbana: University of Illinois Press, 1979.
Jenkins, Robert L., and Mfanya Donald Tryman. *The Malcolm X Encyclopedia.* Westport, Conn.: Greenwood Press, 2002.
Magida, Arthur J. *Prophet of Rage: A Life of Louis Farrakhan and His Nation.* New York: Basic Books, 1996.
Tryman, Mfanya Donald, ed. *Institutional Racism and Black America.* Lexington, Ky.: Ginn Press, 1985.

SEE ALSO: Islamic ethics; Jackson, Jesse; Malcolm X; Nation of Islam; Reverse racism.

Fascism

DEFINITION: Governmental system of, or political belief advocating, autocratic rule by a charismatic leader and subordination of the individual to the nation or race

DATE: Term coined in 1919

TYPE OF ETHICS: Politico-economic ethics

SIGNIFICANCE: Fascism severely restricts or eliminates personal liberty; punishes opponents by imprisonment, torture, or death; and regards all peoples not of the officially decreed nationality as inferior.

Like communism, fascism is a type of totalitarian system that attempts to control every aspect of life (political, economic, and personal), usually through a secret police force. Unlike communism, however, fascism allows private ownership of industry as long as the government or its authorities are served. Fascism also promotes extreme patriotism ("state over self"), militarism, and the organized persecution of minorities. A fascist government controls newspapers, radio, and other means of communication in order to issue propaganda supporting its policies and to silence all opposing views.

Some historians trace the origins of modern fascism to the dictatorship of Napoleon Bonaparte of France, who controlled his country through some fascist means. Later dictators adopted many of his methods, as well as harsher ones. Benito Mussolini, who first used the term "fascism," controlled Italy from 1922 to 1943.

In Germany (where fascism reached its zenith) Adolf Hitler and his fascist Nazi Party began in 1933 to wipe out all opposition and systematically destroy the Jewish race, Slavs, Gypsies, the mentally ill, and other "inferior" groups. During the 1930's, fascist

In speech to the White House Correspondents' Association in early 1941, before the United States entered World War II, President Franklin D. Roosevelt denounced Europe's fascist regimes in words that were later inscribed in this Washington Mall memorial. (Noelle Penna)

parties gained much support in Hungary, Japan, Romania, and Spain. Fascists usually come to power after some national disaster by promising to revive the economy and to restore national pride.

Andrew C. Skinner

SEE ALSO: Communism; Dictatorship; Hitler, Adolf; Holocaust; Nationalism; Natural rights; Nazism; Oppression; Orwell, George; Tyranny.

Fatalism

DEFINITION: Belief that all events are predetermined by forces beyond human control, and hence that one's destiny cannot be altered
TYPE OF ETHICS: Beliefs and practices
SIGNIFICANCE: Fatalism is a species of determinism that connotes resignation to one's destined end and a lack of resistance to the forces governing that end. It holds submission to one's fate to be the ultimate ethical wisdom.

Fatalism is a concept as ancient as civilization and as widespread as the human race. The English word "fate" is from the Latin root *fatum*, meaning "oracle" or "prophecy." Both the Greeks and the Romans were persuaded that three goddesses, the Fates—Atropos, Clotho, and Lachesis—determined one's destiny.

Similar beliefs, however, were evidenced in Celtic, Germanic, and other mythologies, in which "norms" or "powers" overruled human desires and initiative. Fatalism is apparent in the Hindu concept of karma (the factor that binds one to cycles of rebirth), the Muslim teaching of *kismet* ("one's allotted role"), and certain types of Christian predestinationism. Modern philosophies and psychologies have offered "fatalism" in "secular garb," viewing history or personality as being controlled by impersonal and amoral forces.

C. George Fry

SEE ALSO: Accountability; Determinism and freedom; Karma; Mozi.

Fāṭima

IDENTIFICATION: Daughter of Muḥammad
BORN: c. 606, Mecca, Arabia (now Saudi Arabia)
DIED: 632, Medina, Arabia (now Saudi Arabia)
TYPE OF ETHICS: Religious ethics
SIGNIFICANCE: Revered throughout the Islamic world as the matriarch of the house of ʿAlī, Fāṭima stands as an exemplar of piety, spiritual purity, and spiritual power.

The daughter of Khadīja and the Prophet Muḥammad, Fāṭima was married (in August, 623, or June, 624) to the Prophet's cousin, ʿAlī ibn Abī Ṭālib, and was the mother of Ḥusayn and Ḥasan. She and Khadīja were the women most beloved by the Prophet, and the tragedies that befell her husband and sons contribute to the pathos of her story. Reverence for Fāṭima, whose father is the Prophet, is so deep that she is often referred to as *umm abīhā* ("her father's mother"). The Qurʾan refers to God's wish "to remove uncleanness far from" the "Folk of the Household" of the Prophet (*sūra* 33:33).

Fāṭima is often included in that Household, which has contributed to her popular image as a model of purity (much as Mary the mother of Jesus is also revered in Islam). Such spiritual purity brings with it spiritual power (*barakat*), and Fāṭima is often asked to intercede on behalf of the faithful. Fāṭima, ʿAlī, and their descendants are still specially honored as *sādāt* (singular, *sayyid*) or *ashrāf* (singular, *sharīf*), and widely believed to participate still in the residual *barakat* of Muḥammad.

Thomas Gaskill

SEE ALSO: Ḥusayn; Islamic ethics; Muḥammad.

Fear in the workplace

DEFINITION: Emotion experienced in the face of job-related threats
TYPE OF ETHICS: Business and labor ethics
SIGNIFICANCE: Fear can be both a cause and a result of unethical behavior.

Fear is fuel for unethical behavior, and unethical actions are fuel for fear. Fear is therefore both a cause of and a result of unethical behavior. When people manage ethically, they do not operate in an environment of fear. Fear is an emotion experienced in the face of threats or danger that one feels unable to control. It has two components: the presence or perception of a danger or threat and a lack of control over the danger or threat. Kathleen Ryan and Daniel Oestreich, in their book *Driving Fear Out of the Workplace* (1991), observe, "We see fear as a background phenomenon that undermines the commitment, motivation, and confidence of people at work. It is most easily observed as a reluctance to speak up about needed changes, improvements, or other important work issues."

EFFECTS OF FEAR

Managers often do not see the impact of fear because it is hidden in the process of how the work gets done. The cost of having fear in the workplace can be figured out by examining the influence of negative emotions on people's work. Ryan and Oestreich's research indicates that the two greatest impacts fear has on an organization are negative feelings about the organization and decreased quality and productivity. Fear translates into a loss of trust and pride, and employees often react to fear by increasing self-protective behavior. Negative feelings about the organization also result in sabotage (theft, fraud, and the destruction of company property). Fear translates into a lasting resentment, the making and hiding of mistakes, or failure to meet deadlines and budgets. W. Edwards Deming has said that quality is impossible to achieve when people are afraid to tell the truth. They fear being ethical. Scrap and breakage are hidden, numbers and schedules are misrepresented, and bad products are shipped to customers because someone is afraid to stop the production line.

Fear shows up in "falsifying" reports and over-promising customers. Employees may not ask for personal time off for fear that their supervisors will not understand and their requests will be denied, so they lie and call in sick. Falsifying reports, over-promising customers, and calling in sick when one is not soon become the norm. Employees become used to behaving unethically. There is an old saying, "It is easy to tell a lie, but difficult to tell only one." Negative feelings about the organization make unethical behavior easier to live with.

Fear is often at the center of "whistle-blowing." The employee fears the results of the improper activity (harm to employees, customers, or the community) and also management's reaction. He or she feels pushed to go outside to have the injustice resolved. The employee does not trust management to handle the problem.

WHAT CREATES FEAR

The employee's relationship with his or her immediate supervisor has the most impact on creating fear. Ambiguous or abusive behavior destroys trust. Other behaviors contributing to fear are blaming, insulting, and ignoring. A manager who is not fair, who plays favorites, or who takes credit for an employee's idea invites mistrust from subordinates and executives. Unethical actions such as asking employees to mislead and lie to customers send a signal that perhaps the employees are being misled and lied to as well. Ethical management is at the center of efforts to create an atmosphere in which fear cannot survive. A good relationship with one's manager is a start.

The systems, procedures, and culture of the organization also contribute to fear. Will the company support the employee or not? The employee asks, "My manager is okay, but if I complain to the human resources department about a sexual harassment incident, will I be labeled a troublemaker and laid off in the next round of cutbacks? Is top management really concerned about people, customers, and employees? Is the leadership honest and does it convey a sense of integrity? Is management honestly communicating to employees about the health of the company?" The prevalence of rumors signals a culture of fear.

In an atmosphere of fear, managers and employees do not trust one another. Managers believe that employees are manipulative and operate only on the basis of self-interest. Employees worry that their managers will put their own self-interest ahead of the needs of employees and customers. Each group fears the other and reacts out of fear. It becomes a self-propagating behavior. If I fear that you will act first in your self-interest, I will interpret all your actions in the light of that fear, and react accordingly with self-preserving behavior and retaliation. It is not difficult to imagine the unethical actions that permeate such an environment.

FEAR AND UNETHICAL BEHAVIOR

Laura Nash says, in *Good Intentions Aside* (1990), "I cannot think of a single ethical problem in business that does not rest on a . . . betrayal of trust." Which comes first, lack of trust and fear or unethical behavior? Fear is not the only cause of unethical behavior. Another cause is the lack of awareness of the ethical implications of decision making. Unethical behavior is not fear's only result. Good employees often leave a company in which there is an environment of fear. Fear is both a cause of and a result of unethical behavior. It is a red flag, a signal that the health of the organization needs attention. If company employees and managers look for the effects of fear and take action to develop an atmosphere of trust, the ethical pulse of the organization will improve accordingly.

Howard Putnam, in *The Winds of Turbulence* (1991), summarizes fear's effect: "Fear is the most imposing barrier to transformation. Fear flows from the feelings of instability caused by dealing with the unknown, and it can strangle creative thinking."

Kathleen D. Purdy

FURTHER READING

Covey, Stephen R. *Principle-Centered Leadership.* New York: Simon & Schuster, 1992.

De George, Richard T. "Whistle-Blowing." In *Business Ethics.* 5th ed. Upper Saddle River, N.J.: Prentice Hall, 1999.

Dozier, Rush W., Jr. *Fear Itself: The Origin and Nature of the Powerful Emotion That Shapes Our Lives and Our World.* New York: St. Martin's Press, 1998.

Nash, Laura L. *Good Intentions Aside.* Boston: Harvard Business School Press, 1990.

Putnam, Howard D. *The Winds of Turbulence.* New York: Harper Business, 1991.

Ryan, Kathleen D., and Daniel K. Oestreich. *Driving Fear Out of the Workplace: Creating the High-Trust, High-Performance Organization.* 2d ed. San Francisco: Jossey-Bass, 1998.

SEE ALSO: Business ethics; Corporate responsibility; Dress codes; Electronic mail; Employee safety and treatment; Equal pay for equal work; Hiring practices; Merit; Sexual abuse and harassment; Wage discrimination; White-collar crime.

The Feminine Mystique

IDENTIFICATION: Book by Betty Friedan (1921-   )
DATE: Published in 1963
TYPE OF ETHICS: Sex and gender issues
SIGNIFICANCE: *The Feminine Mystique* challenged the then-prevalent view that women should be completely (and only) fulfilled by their roles as wives, mothers, and homemakers.

Friedan defined the feminine mystique as the myth of female fulfillment based on domestic labor and proposed that the myth is based on a vision of woman not as a whole person but only in terms of her sexual role. This limiting view of woman, which further suggested that a woman's value could be expressed only through her potential as wife and mother, discouraged women from pursuing educations or professions, thus effectively trapping them within the myth.

According to Friedan, post-World War II economic and social factors combined to force American women to confine their interests and energies solely to serving their husbands and children through their roles as housewives, a situation that led women to devalue themselves and their contributions to soci-

Betty Friedan, author of The Feminine Mystique.

ety. She based this assessment in part on extensive interviews with women, many of whom were highly educated and were plagued with feelings of frustration, guilt, and inadequacy because they were not completely satisfied by the rewards of homemaking. These women felt isolated from one another and alienated from society by their failure to conform to the myth. Friedan asserted that women must look outside the narrow role assigned to them by the feminine mystique in order to discover identity and fulfillment.

Mary Johnson

SEE ALSO: Feminist ethics; National Organization for Women; Sexual stereotypes; Women's ethics; Women's liberation movement.

Feminist ethics

DEFINITION: Ethics that are grounded in a feminist perspective and that are characterized by a feminist commitment that calls into question traditional ethical assumptions and seeks to construct ethics that are more inclusive of women's lived experiences

DATE: Emerged during the 1960's

TYPE OF ETHICS: Sex and gender issues

SIGNIFICANCE: Emerging as a reaction against the traditional, male-dominated modes of doing ethics, feminist ethics both critiques traditional ethics and seeks to redefine the field and its methods.

Feminist ethics developed out of the feminist movement of the mid-twentieth century. Feminist ethical theories reflect the diversity of feminist theories. Liberal, socialist, radical, social constructionist, and postmodern feminism have all influenced feminist ethics. It is neither simply defined nor monolithic in perspective. However, feminist ethics can be defined as ethics with gender issues as its main organizing principle, characterized by a commitment to the general feminist goal of gender equality, the critique of Western traditional ethics, and the reconstruction of traditional ethics to include women's lives and experiences.

CRITIQUING TRADITIONAL ETHICS

Feminist ethics criticizes the notion of the moral agent as dispassionate and disengaged for its failure to recognize the social foundation of self. Following on Carol Gilligan's critique of Lawrence Kohlberg's work on moral dilemmas and moral decision making, feminists reject what they see as an androcentric, or male-dominated, notion of the moral agent who stands outside a social context. The construction of an idealized human moral agent has been shown to actually mean "man" in its particular sense and not the so-called inclusive sense that male ethicists, theologians and philosophers maintain is what they "really mean." The detached moral agent ignores, hides, and makes invisible the inequality between men and women. The emphasis on justice as an abstract principle unrelated to social life made women's lives and their concerns invisible in most traditional ethical theories.

CONSTRUCTING A FEMINIST ETHICS

Early feminist attempts at moral theorizing claimed not only that women's issues were being ignored but also that women and men define and interpret moral problems differently. Carol Gilligan characterized women's morality as an "ethic of responsibility." Nel Noddings calls women's morality an "ethic of caring." Sara Ruddick ties ethics more specifically to women's lives by using the term "maternal thinking" for understanding women's ethical and moral behavior. However, as other feminists and critics point out, this kind of feminist ethical theorizing tends to valorize "feminine" traits or characteristics in ways that make it seem as if women "naturally" think in these ways.

Later feminist ethicists have tried to avoid such essentialist notions by reconstructing ethics based on women's lived experiences. They understand women's moral thinking and choices as contextualized in a particular community: family, neighborhood, or workplace. These choices are the result of living in particular social circumstances rather than tied to biological characteristics. Therefore, feminist ethics are seen to be constructed out of the diversity of women's experiences. Ignoring social context and relations within a family, community, or workplace limits women's moral agency.

Alison Jagger and others have brought together the traditional ethical concern for justice with these so-called feminine concerns. A feminist approach to ethics must offer a guide to action that will tend to subvert rather than reinforce the systematic subordination of women. Jagger also sees feminist ethics as an extension of politics handling moral issues in both the so-called public and private domains, providing guidance on issues of intimate relations, such as affection and sexuality, which, until quite recently, were largely ignored by modern moral theory. Feminist ethicists are developing ways of dealing with actual problems through consideration of both justice and care.

FEMINIST ETHICS, DIVERSITY, AND CHOICE

Analyses of women's experiences bring to light a crucial component of how feminist ethics are socially constructed. Women's lives are different—not only from men's lives but also from one another. If feminist ethics are to be based on the experiences of all women and avoid the problem of false universalization, then such differences in women's experiences must be acknowledged and incorporated into feminist theory. This inclusive relationality takes into account the economic as well as the social and cultural dimension in moral decision making and understanding how it often constrains women's choices. The economic dependency of women in the family, the inequality of pay and promotion in the labor force tied to women's role as child-bearer and child-rearer, the possibility of sexual harassment or physical abuse from a stranger or an intimate, and further, in psychological terms, the tendency toward lack of ego differentiation in women's personality formation are all factors impinging upon women's sense of a self that can be autonomous in confronting or defining ethical situations.

A framework for feminist ethics starts with reflection upon concrete situations. Challenging abstract models of ethical theorizing, Carol Robb has argued that morality and ethics cannot be tested via prefabricated dilemmas based on an androcentric viewpoint. "Doing ethics" means that ethicists must gather data about the historical situation and context: They must analyze the roots of oppression, uncover loyalties and community ties as well as political ones, and eventually clarify a theory of values rooted in women's lived experiences. Feminist ethics, then, are transdisciplinary, using perspectives from philosophy, sociology, psychology, education, medicine, theology, business, and the natural sciences.

Feminist ethicists have expanded traditional ethical theorizing by exploring the moral dimension of all aspects of women's and men's lives, breaking down distinctions between the public and the private. From procreative choice, abortion, and new reproductive technologies to gendered work and the economy, issues of peace and war, and the environment, social analysis is inherent in almost all feminist ethics. How do social institutions work? How do they shape the ways in which people structure their lives, their moral development, and their ethics? Feminist ethics are socially constructed within the context of culture and society, history, and geography. Rather than a complete theory and method, feminist ethics are a process based on the ongoing experiences of women's and men's lives.

Susan A. Farrell

FURTHER READING

Allen, Amy. *The Power of Feminist Theory: Domination, Resistance, Solidarity.* Boulder, Colo.: Westview Press, 1999.

Allen, Anita L. *Why Privacy Isn't Everything: Feminist Reflections on Personal Accountability.* Lanham, Md.: Rowman & Littlefield, 2003.

Brennan, Samantha, ed. *Feminist Moral Philosophy.* Calgary: University of Calgary Press, 2002.

Cole, Eve Browning, and Susan Coultrap-McQuin, eds. *Explorations in Feminist Ethics: Theory and Practice.* Bloomington: Indiana University Press, 1992.

Gilligan, Carol. *In a Different Voice: Psychological Theory and Women's Development.* Cambridge, Mass.: Harvard University Press, 1982.

Held, Virginia, ed. *Justice and Care: Essential Readings in Feminist Ethics.* Boulder, Colo.: Westview Press, 1995.

Hirschmann, Nancy J. *The Subject of Liberty: Toward a Feminist Theory of Freedom.* Princeton, N.J.: Princeton University Press, 2003.

Jagger, Alison M., ed. *Living with Contradictions: Controversies in Feminist Social Ethics.* Boulder, Colo.: Westview Press, 1994.

Noddings, Nell. *Caring: An Ethical Approach to Ethics and Moral Education.* Berkeley: University of California Press, 1984.

Ruddick, Sara. *Maternal Thinking: Toward a Politics of Peace.* New York: Ballantine Books, 1990.

SEE ALSO: Ecofeminism; *Feminine Mystique, The*; Inequality; National Organization for Women; Women's ethics; Women's liberation movement.

First Amendment

IDENTIFICATION: Amendment to the U.S. Constitution providing that government may not establish a religion, interfere with an individual's religious liberty, or abridge freedom of speech, press, or assembly or the right to petition the government for a redress of grievances

DATE: Adopted on December 15, 1791

TYPE OF ETHICS: Civil liberties

SIGNIFICANCE: The First Amendment guarantees various aspects of the freedom of conscience: It ensures that citizens of the United States may hold any beliefs, may express those beliefs, may worship in accordance with those beliefs, and may gather to discuss those beliefs, without government interference. It also protects the rights of the people to watch over, and respond to transgres-

First Amendment Controversies

Issue	*Reasons to Limit*	*Reasons Not to Limit*
Does the First Amendment protect the right of members of the Native American Church to use peyote as part of their religious rituals?	Peyote is a controlled substance. To permit its use might endanger the lives of the user and others.	The free exercise of religion by the Native American Church requires the use of peyote. Freedom of religion should not be infringed.
Does the First Amendment protect the right of art galleries to display publicly artworks that may be considered obscene or offensive?	The First Amendment does not protect pornography or obscenity. If a work is considered offensive by people in the community, it should not be displayed.	Freedom of speech and freedom of the press imply free expression. Art is in the eye of the beholder.
Does the First Amendment protect those who burn the American flag in violation of state laws?	The flag is the country's most important symbol. State governments ought to be allowed to protect it.	Burning the flag is as legitimate an act of protest as speaking out against a government policy. Preventing flag-burning would be banning a form of political expression.
Should schools and public libraries ban books that contain racially offensive terms?	Use of some racial terms is offensive and may lower the self-esteem of minority students.	Censorship restricts the flow of ideas. Students would be prevented from reading literature that was written in a time when such terms were considered more acceptable.
Should the press be allowed to print any government documents?	The press's freedom should be restricted to ensure national security.	Government decisions should be exposed to the will of the people.
Should newspapers and the media be allowed access to participants in a trial before a verdict has been delivered?	Unlimited discussion of trial-related matters in a public forum may infringe upon Fifth Amendment rights to due process.	All matters of public concern should be open for discussion.

sions by, the government, whether through the press, through public acts of political dissent, or through direct governmental petitions.

For the framers of the U.S. Bill of Rights, the freedoms of religion and speech were the most important substantive liberties. Years of struggle, often violent, between Protestants and Catholics in England persuaded Americans that the government should have no role in promoting religion or in controlling religious observances. Three additional themes provide the most common justifications for considering these the "first" liberties: The first stresses the value of liberty of conscience in promoting individual self-realization and self-expression, the second emphasizes the importance of free communication and discussion for informing the citizenry in a representative democracy, and the last emphasizes the value of free discussion in establishing truth in the "marketplace of ideas."

First Amendment questions often arise in the United States, and many Supreme Court cases have been devoted to settling such issues as subversive advocacy, obscenity, school prayer, and flag burning.

Robert Jacobs

SEE ALSO: Bill of Rights, U.S.; Censorship; Constitution, U.S.; Freedom of expression; Mill, John Stuart; Sedition Act of 1798.

Five precepts of Buddhism

DEFINITION: Buddhist vows to abstain from taking life, stealing, sexual misconduct, lying, and using intoxicants

TYPE OF ETHICS: Religious ethics

SIGNIFICANCE: The five precepts, which are incumbent upon all Buddhists, both laity and priests, are the basic ethical tenets of Buddhism.

Traditionally associated with the Buddha (Siddhārtha Gautama, c. 563-c. 483 B.C.E.) but generally taught in older Hinduism as well, the five precepts are roughly equivalent to the ethical rules in the Ten Commandments.

The first, the precept to abstain from taking life, includes any intention to use either direct or indirect

means to cause death. It refers not only to human but also to other animal life. As a consequence, most Buddhists are vegetarians.

The second precept requires abstinence from taking what is not given and includes trickery and gambling as well as outright stealing. The blameworthiness of an offense depends partly on the value of whatever is stolen and partly on the worth of its owner.

The third precept, to abstain from sexual misconduct, precludes homosexual sexual relations as well as heterosexual relations with family members, married persons, concubines, slaves, and others. For monks, the precept requires celibacy.

The fourth precept, to abstain from false speech, refers to words and actions that are intended to deceive others. It also prohibits deliberately concealing the truth.

The final precept, to abstain from intoxicants, prohibits both alcohol and other drugs that dull the mind. These precepts are supplemented by as many as five more for monks or serious lay practitioners.

Paul L. Redditt

SEE ALSO: Ahiṁsā; Bodhisattva ideal; Buddha; Buddhist ethics; Four noble truths; Lying; Mādhyamaka; Zen.

Forgiveness

DEFINITION: Act of giving up one's resentment toward a person who has morally wronged or seriously disappointed one

TYPE OF ETHICS: Personal and social ethics

SIGNIFICANCE: Forgiveness is a defining characteristic of God in portions of the Judeo-Christian tradition and a central human virtue in Christian ethics, but it is a questionable virtue in modern secular ethics.

The concept of forgiveness occurred first as a revealed characteristic of God: God announced to Moses that God forgives creatures' sin (Exodus 34:6-7). Early Judaism (c. 250 B.C.E. to 200 C.E.) taught that forgiveness was a personal virtue for humans. The New Testament commands people always to forgive one another, because they all have enjoyed

God's forgiveness (Matthew 5:7, 6:12, 14-15, 18:21-35; Ephesians 4:32; Colossians 3:13; and the book of Philemon).

Outside this Judeo-Christian context, a forgiving spirit has been called a vice rather than a virtue. Moral philosophers since the 1970's have examined in the context of secular ethics both the definition of forgiveness and the ethics of forgiveness (Is a readiness to forgive always a virtue for humans? Is forgiveness a duty?). Here are some highlights of this rich debate.

DEFINING FORGIVENESS

What is forgiveness? The occasion for forgiveness entails one (or someone one identifies with—as a parent identifies with her child, for example) being mistreated by someone. This offense may be moral wrongdoing, but it is also possible to forgive close friends when they do nothing morally wrong but deeply disappoint one. Forgiveness is not an emotion itself, but it involves letting go of negative emotions such as hatred, contempt, or deep disappointment toward the offender.

Forgiveness may be a decision, but often it is a difficult process of construing in a new way the mistreatment and the offender, and this process is only partially under one's control. Either way, forgiveness must be deliberate and directed toward mistreatment. Simply forgetting about it, coming to see it as not mistreatment after all, and engaging a therapist to focus one's attention away from it are ways of curbing negative emotions caused by the injury, but they do not count as forgiving the offender. Also, the reason for forgiving must be concern for the offender's welfare or some other concern for others. Letting go of negative emotions only because one is tired of dealing with them might be advisable sometimes, but it is not forgiveness, because it is self-absorbed.

A forgiving spirit has seemed to many to be a virtue because forgiveness appears to be a morally acceptable, healthy way of dealing with negative emotions. Hatred or disappointment, when harbored, begin to distort one's moral sensitivity and sense of fairness toward others. Releasing these emotions helps one to see and to act morally. In the context of a personal relationship, forgiveness enables us to reestablish the intimacy and caring we enjoyed.

Is forgiveness always morally acceptable? Consider a tough case. Suppose a person motivated by cruelty hurts one in a serious way. Self-respect and respect for the moral law (which includes condemnation of all malicious wrongdoing) causes one to be angry at this cruel offense. Why should one ever give up one's righteous indignation and forgive the offender? If one forgives, will one not either ignore wrongdoing or cease to condemn it? Either way (by willful ignorance of or lack of concern for moral offense) one will endorse cruel treatment of others and fail to respect oneself as a person valued by the moral community. In this case, is not forgiveness morally wrong?

Granted, if one's ultimate loyalty is to an abstract moral order, forgiveness in this and other such cases would be unacceptable. The order must be preserved, and one must do one's part to preserve it by harboring righteous hatred for serious moral offenders. We cannot afford to "hate the sin but love the sinner." In the context of a secular ethic, a generous, forgiving spirit would be a vice.

However, in the Judeo-Christian worldview from which the concept of personal forgiveness originated, one's ultimate loyalty is to a generous God who desires the moral growth and flourishing of each created person. The moral order is important in this perspective, but human loyalty to it is part of one's fundamental commitment to God. When one is cruelly treated, one naturally responds with anger first. Yet one prays to see the situation from God's point of view. As one deeply enters God's perspective, one continues to see the offense honestly, in all of its cruelty, and the offender as malicious. One also sees the offender in a more complex way, however, as a person with problems, hurting others, and yet a person deeply loved by a God who can reform and correct the offender. A Christian must leave to God the role of judge and executioner, and accept a role as a coworker with God in caring for the offender. This perspective enables one to love the offender, while maintaining self-respect and respect for the moral order.

Modern debates on forgiveness highlight key differences between secular and Judeo-Christian ethics. These differing moral evaluations of forgiveness remind one that ethical theories cannot be fully understood or evaluated apart from the worldviews that they presuppose.

Robert B. Kruschwitz

FURTHER READING

Adams, Marilyn McCord. "Forgiveness: A Christian Model." *Faith and Philosophy* 8, no. 3 (July, 1991): 277-304.

Haber, Joram Graf. *Forgiveness.* Savage, Md.: Rowman & Littlefield, 1991.

Kselman, John, James H. Charlesworth, and Gary S. Shogren. "Forgiveness." In *The Anchor Bible Dictionary*, edited by David N. Freedman. Vol. 2. New York: Doubleday, 1992.

Murphy, Jeffrie G. *Getting Even: Forgiveness and Its Limits.* New York: Oxford University Press, 2003.

Murphy, Jeffrie G., and Jean Hampton. *Forgiveness and Mercy.* New York: Cambridge University Press, 1988.

Richards, Norvin. "Forgiveness." *Ethics* 99, No. 1 (October, 1988): 77-97.

Schimmel, Solomon. *Wounds Not Healed by Time: The Power of Repentance and Forgiveness.* New York: Oxford University Press, 2002.

SEE ALSO: Christian ethics; Guilt and shame; Jewish ethics; Justice; Karma; Mercy; Parole of convicted prisoners; Reconciliation; Revenge; Sin; Virtue.

Foucault, Michel

IDENTIFICATION: French philosopher
BORN: October 15, 1926, Poitiers, France
DIED: June 25, 1984, Paris, France
TYPE OF ETHICS: Modern history
SIGNIFICANCE: A philosopher and activist whose *Discipline and Punish: The Birth of the Prison* (*Surveiller et punir: Naissance de la prison*, 1975) helped bring about significant prison reforms in France, Foucault believed that societal norms and morality are revealed in studies of those individuals who are excluded from society. His other works include *Madness and Civilization: A History of Insanity in the Age of Reason* (*Folie et déraison: Histoire de la folie à l'âge classique*, 1961), *The Order of Things: An Archaeology of the Human Sciences* (*Les Mots et les choses: Une Archéologie des sciences humaines*, 1966), and *The History of Sexuality* (*Histoire de la sexualité*, 1976-1984).

Foucault and Genealogy

In many ways Michel Foucault is the philosophical descendant of German philosopher Friedrich Nietzsche, author of the 1887 work *On the Genealogy of Morals*. Foucault's lifelong project is best understood as an extended "genealogy of morals," in which he examines the history of fundamental moral categories such as guilt and innocence. The purpose of genealogy, for both Foucault and Nietzsche, is to demonstrate that these categories *have* a history. They are not immutable, eternal, self-evident aspects of human nature but are rather constructed in different ways by different societies at different historical moments.

The entity at the center of both Nietzsche and Foucault's genealogical projects is what they refer to as the "modern soul." Foucault understands this soul to be the creation of specific nineteenth century disciplinary institutions such as the asylum, the prison, and the school. These institutions teach their inmates to discipline themselves by placing their inner identities under ethical scrutiny. In so doing, they create a new object of study and repression (the soul), as well as new techniques and sciences for understanding and manipulating people (such as psychology, behaviorism, statistics, and criminology). For this reason, Foucault proclaims, "the soul is the prison of the body."

Michel Foucault was a twentieth century French philosopher who studied the concept of "principles of exclusion." His career at the University of Paris-Vincennes and the College de France expressed two broad themes. The first, which was represented in Foucault's 1961 book *Madness and Civilization*, focused on mental illness and society's response through the institution of the insane asylum.

Later, Foucault began to expand the concept of exclusion to include the penal system and prisons, and in 1975 he published *Discipline and Punish: The Birth of the Prison*. In this book, Foucault described the societal changes that led to the move from castigating the body by means of torture to imprisoning both the body and the spirit. Capitalist society, said Foucault, is a carceral society of control and domination. Later in his life, Foucault focused on the evolution of human self-mastery. In *The Order of Things: An Archaeology of the Human Sciences*, he surveyed the history of ideas and categories of thought in order to understand societies' self-definitions. His *History of Sexuality* was an attempt to determine the relationships of individual and social attitudes with human sexuality.

Perhaps Foucault's most lasting contribution to philosophy and social theory was the concept of "power/knowledge." Foucault believed that all social practices, all knowledge, and indeed all things in the world are created through, express, and perpetuate relationships of power. This notion has several profound ethical consequences. First, it means that every action, every thought, and every belief of every person either supports or resists the current configuration of power, so that people have a moral responsibility to understand their relationship to power and to act only in ways which will increase human freedom and reduce dominance. Second, however, Foucault is often read to believe that attempts to increase freedom or resist dominance are inherently doomed, since power is in operation at all times and in all places. Finally, the doctrine of power/knowledge constitutes as assertion that the fact/value distinction is a myth, since all facts are actually the product of power, and there can be no disinterested or objective truth.

James A. Baer
Updated by the editors

SEE ALSO: Criminal punishment; Critical theory; Derrida, Jacques; Fact/value distinction; Institutionalization of patients; Nietzsche, Friedrich; Punishment.

SIGNIFICANCE: *Foundations of the Metaphysics of Morals* is the clearest and most concise statement by Kant of his basic approach to ethics, an approach that is now regarded as the model of rationalist, deontological ethics.

Foundations of the Metaphysics of Morals is a preliminary sketch of the fundamental metaphysical laws governing moral experience. These laws are metaphysical in that they can be discerned a priori—that is, by the exercise of pure reason and without reference to psychology. Kant's goal is to set forth the supreme principle of morality. The attempt is organized into three sections. In the first section, he argues that only a will may be good in any unqualified sense. For Kant, a good will is one that acts not only in accordance with duty but also from a sense of duty. The standard of a morally good action, then, is that it is performed simply because it is right. This conception of duty (as the condition of a will that is good in itself) leads Kant to formulate the principle that governs the good will. He calls this principle the categorical imperative: Act only according to that maxim that you can at the same time will that it should become a universal law. In section 2, Kant offers a closer analysis of the nature of the categorical imperative and of derivative (and thus, he thinks, equivalent) formulations of it. Finally, he defends the autonomy or freedom of the will in section 3.

R. Douglas Geivett

SEE ALSO: Deontological ethics; Kant, Immanuel; Kantian ethics; Morality; Motivation; Reason and rationality; Will.

Foundations of the Metaphysics of Morals

IDENTIFICATION: Book by Immanuel Kant (1724-1804)
DATE: *Grundlegung zur Metaphysik der Sitten*, 1785 (*Fundamental Principles of the Metaphysics of Ethics*, 1895; better known as *Foundations of the Metaphysics of Morals*, 1950)
TYPE OF ETHICS: Enlightenment history

Four noble truths

DEFINITION: Buddhist doctrine asserting that existence is marked by suffering, that suffering is caused by desire, that desire can be overcome, and that there is a specific way to overcome desire
DATE: Formulated in the sixth century B.C.E.
TYPE OF ETHICS: Religious ethics
SIGNIFICANCE: The doctrine of the four noble truths, which is perhaps the most basic tenet of Buddhism, provides the foundation of Buddhist ethics.

The Four Noble Truths

1. All existence is characterized by suffering.

2. Suffering is caused by desire.

3. Desire, and therefore suffering, can be overcome.

4. The way to overcome desire and suffering is to follow the eightfold noble path.

The first of the four noble truths states that life entails suffering. There is no way to escape this facet of existence. The fact that existence is characterized by suffering should not, however, be taken to mean that suffering is all that is experienced in life. It is also possible to feel happiness, joy, comfort, and many other positive and neutral emotions and sensations. The problem is that no sensation lasts. When an individual experiences joy, it is inevitable that that joy will end. It is also true that negative emotions and sensations do not last, but that is not where the problem lies. It is the transitory nature of happiness and satisfaction that causes problems for people.

The second noble truth states that the cause of suffering is desire. People typically seek experiences that they believe will make them happy and shun experiences that they think will make them unhappy. This process is, however, extremely problematical. Often, the process of striving for happiness does not give rise to happiness. People's positive expectations about their lives may remain unrealized. Unexpected problems may arise or things simply may not happen in the way that was intended. In such cases, it is all too easy for people to attempt to block out negative experiences and continue to strive for happiness. This attempt is easy to understand, but it can lead to an unwillingness to accept the unpleasant experiences that are an inescapable part of human existence, and when people attempt to reject the unpleasant parts of their lives, they can begin to live in a world of fantasy, divorcing themselves from their own experiences and creating further suffering for themselves by refusing to see things as they are. When people do not face up to the truth of their situations, they are hampered in their attempts to put things right.

The third noble truth states that there is a solution to the problem of suffering. It is not necessary to live in a world of wishes that will never be fulfilled. There is a definite method by which the problems of suffering can be overcome. This does not mean, however, that following this path will mean that one experiences no more suffering in life. What it does mean is that it is possible to accept all situations as they are, without magnifying or minimizing them. The real problem is not so much one's experiences as it is the way in which one reacts to one's experiences.

The fourth noble truth states that the solution to the problem of suffering is to follow the comprehensive method set forth in the eightfold noble path. The eight aspects of the path are (1) *samyag-dṛṣṭi*, right understanding; (2) *samyak-saṁkalpa*, right aspiration; (3) *samyag-vācā*, right speech; (4) *samyak-karmanta*, right action; (5) *samyag-ājīva*, right livelihood; (6) *samyag-vyāyāma*, right effort; (7) *samyak-smṛti*, right mindfulness; and (8) *samyak-samādhi*, right concentration.

APPLYING THE FOUR NOBLE TRUTHS

Right understanding involves, first, knowing and understanding the basic concepts of Buddhism. After one understands them rationally, one must work to test those concepts and, if one finds that they are sound, one comes to understand them on an experiential level.

Right aspiration means not only aspiring to understand and to practice Buddhism but also aspiring

---

The Eightfold Noble Path

	English	*Sanskrit*
1.	Right understanding	*samyag-dṛṣṭi*
2.	Right aspiration	*samyak-saṁkalpa*
3.	Right speech	*samyag-vācā*
4.	Right action	*samyak-karmanta*
5.	Right livelihood	*samyag-ājīva*
6.	Right effort	*samyag-vyāyāma*
7.	Right mindfulness	*samyak-smṛti*
8.	Right concentration	*samyak-samādhi*

---

to do so for the right reasons. Basically, this means that one should not be practicing to benefit oneself. Right aspiration means working toward living in a more selfless way.

In order to practice right speech, one must refrain from lying or deceiving in any way. In addition, one should not indulge in harsh language toward others or engage in slander or backbiting. Instead, one's speech should serve to promote harmony among people.

Right action involves refraining from killing sentient beings, from stealing (or taking what is not given in any way), and from engaging in unlawful sexual intercourse, such as adultery or incest.

Right livelihood means not earning one's living by means of deception or trickery, not trading in arms, not trading in living beings of any kind, not selling flesh of any kind, not selling intoxicants or poisons, and not engaging in any kind of livelihood that involves killing beings, such as being a soldier, a hunter, or a fisherman.

Right effort means preventing evil thoughts, suppressing those evil thoughts that have arisen, cultivating good thoughts, and maintaining good thoughts after they have arisen.

Right mindfulness and right concentration refer to the practice of meditation, which can take many forms. It particularly involves the cultivation of awareness and the direct perception of reality as it is, including particularly the truth that all things that apparently exist are in fact empty. There is no self, although people cling to the idea that the individual self exists.

By exerting oneself in these eight areas, according to Buddhist doctrine, it is possible to rid oneself of the desire that causes suffering, thereby solving the primary problem of existence by cutting it off at the root.

Shawn Woodyard

FURTHER READING

Bstan-dzin Rgya-mtsho [Fourteenth Dalai Lama]. *Buddha Heart, Buddha Mind: Living the Four Noble Truths*. Translated by Robert R. Barr. New York: Crossland, 2000.

_____. *The Four Noble Truths: Fundamentals of Buddhist Teachings*. Translated by Geshe Thupten Jinpa. Edited by Dominique Side. London: Thorsons, 1997.

Conze, Edward. *Buddhism: Its Essence and Development*. Preface by Arthur Waley. New York: Harper & Row, 1975.

_____. *Buddhist Thought in India: Three Phases of Buddhist Philosophy*. 1962. Reprint with corrections. London: Allen & Unwin, 1983.

Dharmasiri, Gunapala. *Fundamentals of Buddhist Ethics*. Antioch, Calif.: Golden Leaves, 1989.

Sangharakshita. *A Survey of Buddhism: Its Doctrines and Methods Through the Ages*. 6th rev. ed. London: Tharpa, 1987.

Snelling, John. *The Buddhist Handbook: A Complete Guide to Buddhist Schools, Teaching, Practice, and History*. Rochester, Vt.: Inner Traditions, 1991.

SEE ALSO: Bodhisattva ideal; Buddha; Buddhist ethics; Dōgen; Five precepts of Buddhism; Kūkai; Mādhyamaka; Nirvana.

Fraud

DEFINITION: Deliberate deception intended to give one an advantage in a transaction
TYPE OF ETHICS: Legal and judicial ethics
SIGNIFICANCE: Fraud is one of the fundamental kinds of unethical acts.

The long history of ethical condemnation of deception helps to show fraud's significance to ethics; in the Judeo-Christian tradition, for example, one of the Ten Commandments is "Thou shalt not bear false witness." This commandment is broad enough to cover fraud.

The famous English Statute of Frauds, which was passed in 1677 and has now been adopted in one form or another in almost every part of the United States, requires that one must "get it in writing" before one can sue to recover more than a specific monetary amount (for example, $500) or to enforce a contract that extends beyond a certain period of time (for example, one year). The statute's point was to reduce the number of claims regarding purported fraud. Leaving important matters to memories of oral statements resulted too often in cases that pitted one person's word against another's.

Good faith precludes fraud even when honest mistakes are made. The classic slogan defining good faith is "white heart and empty head," which refers to having good intentions but being stupid. Stupid mistakes are not fraud.

Deceptive advertising is a matter of degree, but at some point, exaggeration becomes fraud. This is especially true of intentionally false quantitative claims. Qualitative claims are difficult to classify as fraud, since quality is characteristically a matter of opinion rather than fact. Therefore, U.S. law recognizes "puffing" as nonfraudulent falsehood. Puffing is, essentially, an overstatement of the quality of something that is being sold. An example of puffing is a cologne maker's claim that Cologne *X* makes one as "mysterious as the wind." Furthermore, if the falsehood is so obvious that no reasonable person would be deceived by it, then stating that falsehood does not constitute fraud. (For example, one brand of toothpaste was sold with the claim that it would straighten teeth!)

Fraud can be committed by either commission or omission. A fraud of commission involves lying or making some other type of material misrepresentation. A fraud of omission involves the failure to disclose some significant fact that the law requires to be disclosed. Libertarianism, an ethical principle that has been politically influential, endorses the idea of *caveat emptor* ("Let the buyer beware") rather than the idea that some bureaucracy should interfere with the free market by legally requiring disclosures. Libertarianism supports laissez-faire capitalism with only minimal government and opposes the welfare state that began with President Franklin Delano Roosevelt's New Deal. Libertarianism condemns fraud but defines it narrowly, requiring that a lie be committed for fraud to exist.

Egalitarianism, by contrast, is an ethical principle that allows the mere withholding of information to be considered fraud. Egalitarians condemn exploitation, which involves taking advantage of an innocent person's predicament. Therefore, egalitarians support laws defining fraud so as to include the failure to disclose key facts. Libertarians do not recognize the applicability of the concept of exploitation in its ethi-

cally pejorative sense. They view charging whatever the market will bear, for example, not as exploitation but as entrepreneurship, which they see as a virtue. The two approaches of libertarianism and egalitarianism correspond at least roughly to actual fraud and constructive fraud, respectively. Actual fraud involves some active deception or lie. Constructive fraud includes any act of commission or omission that is contrary to law or fair play.

Sterling Harwood

FURTHER READING

Bok, Sissela. *Lying: Moral Choice in Public and Private Life*. 2d ed. New York: Vintage Books, 1999.

Broad, William, and Nicholas Wade. *Betrayers of the Truth*. New York: Simon & Schuster, 1982.

Cahn, Steven M. *Saints and Scamps: Ethics in Academia*. Totowa, N.J.: Rowman & Littlefield, 1986.

Gould, Stephen Jay. *The Mismeasure of Man*. New York: W. W. Norton, 1981.

Kant, Immanuel. *Critique of Practical Reason*. Edited and translated by Lewis W. Beck. 3d ed. New York: Maxwell Macmillan, 1993.

Levi, Michael, ed. *Fraud: Organization, Motivation, and Control*. 2 vols. Brookfield, Vt.: Ashgate, 1999.

Magnuson, Warren G., and Jean Carper. *The Dark Side of the Marketplace: The Plight of the American Consumer*. Englewood Cliffs, N.J.: Prentice-Hall, 1968.

Newman, John Henry. *Apologia Pro Vita Sua: Being a History of His Religious Opinions*. New York: Modern Library, 1950.

Plato. *The Republic*. Translated by Desmond Lee. 2d ed. New York: Penguin Books, 2003.

Schneider, Friedrich, and Dominik H. Enste. *The Shadow Economy: An International Survey*. New York: Cambridge University Press, 2002.

Stuart, Iris, and Bruce Stuart. *Ethics in the Post-Enron Age*. Mason, Ohio: Southwestern/Thomson, 2004.

SEE ALSO: Cheating; Computer crime; Corporate scandal; Identity theft; Lying; Science; Voting fraud.

Free enterprise

DEFINITION: Economic practice based on the principle that businesses should be allowed to organize themselves and compete in the marketplace free from excessive government regulation

TYPE OF ETHICS: Politico-economic ethics

SIGNIFICANCE: Free enterprise is the economic embodiment of the general principle that government should interfere in the affairs of its citizens as little as possible, and that self-regulation and mutual regulation are preferable to legal controls and standards.

Free enterprise is an economic system characterized by private property and private investment decisions, the profit motive, supply and demand as the regulator of prices, and limited government involvement. The economic systems of most Western European nations, the United States, Canada, Australia, and Japan are to varying degrees free enterprise systems.

Advocates of free enterprise fall into two categories. Members of the first category hold that free enterprise is morally neutral and that it is justified on practical grounds as the most efficient system known for producing wealth. Members of the second category agree that free enterprise is practical, but they argue that it is justified primarily on moral grounds.

MORAL JUSTIFICATION

Free enterprise is advocated as the only system that is, in principle, compatible with the requirements of human survival. To survive, individuals need values such as food and shelter. These values must be created by individual initiative and effort. (Cooperative ventures depend for their success on individual initiative and effort.) Therefore, human survival depends on individual initiative and effort.

In a social context, however, individuals run the risk of coercion by other individuals. Coercion is a danger to human life because it undermines individual initiative and effort: Coercion can end an individual's life (murder) or remove to some degree an individual's control over his or her life (slavery, assault, or theft). Coercion, accordingly, is wrong in principle, and all social arrangements should be based on the principle that only voluntary interactions are moral.

The rejection of coercion is spelled out in terms of rights. If murder, slavery, and theft are, broadly speaking, the fundamental social wrongs, then life, liberty, and property are the fundamental social rights.

ROLE OF GOVERNMENT

Since some individuals will resort to coercion in order to benefit from the productive efforts of other individuals, and since the primary social need of individuals is freedom from such coercion, it follows that there is a need for an institution with the power to protect individuals' rights: government.

The moral task of government is to ensure that individuals are at liberty to use their property as they see fit to sustain and enhance their lives. Governments thus are given the power to use coercion in defense of individuals' rights.

A government can use coercion against individuals, however, so individuals also need protection from their government. In a free enterprise system, this protection is provided by a constitution that limits the coercive power of government to defensive purposes. Since the political power of government is a coercive power and free enterprise requires that all economic transactions be voluntary, the constitution of a free enterprise system will require a separation of economics and politics. Governments will not be able to use political power to subsidize one business at the expense of another or, more generally, to redistribute wealth from one individual or group of individuals to another.

PRACTICALITY

If individuals thus have a reasonable guarantee of freedom from both other individuals and the government, they will invest, produce, and reap as much profit as their skills, dedication, and ingenuity allow them. They will be free to reinvest or consume their profits. They will be free to form voluntary associations (such as partnerships, corporations, and stock markets) to enhance their production and hence their profits. They will be free to pursue specializations, since specialization generally yields higher production, and to exchange their products in a market in which rates of exchange (prices) are governed by the forces of supply and demand.

The practicality of free enterprise is a consequence of individual effort. The freedom to pursue profit releases enormous amounts of human productive energy, and this explains the historical success of free enterprise systems.

CRITICISMS

Free enterprise is sometimes criticized for being harsh, since it provides no guarantee of success for all individuals. Since some individuals will fail, the critics continue, the government should use its coercive power to redistribute some wealth from the successful to the needy. Advocates of free enterprise respond that using coercive means to redistribute wealth is not only impractical—since coercion undermines the conditions of wealth production in the first place—but also immoral, since it involves coercively using individuals as a means to the ends of others. There is nothing to prevent the establishment of voluntary charitable associations to assist those in need, and in a free enterprise system the only moral way to solve problems is through voluntary associations.

Free enterprise is also criticized for encouraging the profit motive. Advocates of free enterprise respond that the profit motive is moral. It is moral that individuals take charge of their lives, and profit is necessary for life. To stay alive, an individual must consume at least as much energy as he or she expended in producing the value to be consumed, and to grow, an individual must consume more energy than he or she expended in producing the value. In economic terms, this means he or she must achieve a net return on the investment—that is, profit.

Finally, free enterprise is sometimes criticized for leading to inequalities in wealth. Advocates of free enterprise respond that the only relevant sense of equality in this context is equality before the law. As long as the government ensures that everyone plays by the same rules, the fact that individuals of differing natural endowments, acquired skills, and moral characters will acquire different amounts of wealth is perfectly just.

Stephen R. C. Hicks

FURTHER READING

Bandow, Doug, and David L. Schindler, eds. *Wealth, Poverty, and Human Destiny.* Wilmington, Del.: ISI Books, 2003.

Hayek, Friedrich. *The Road to Serfdom.* 50th anniversary ed. Introduction by Milton Friedman. Chicago: University of Chicago Press, 1994.

Hazlitt, Henry. *Economics in One Lesson.* New Rochelle, N.Y.: Arlington House, 1979.

Rand, Ayn. *Capitalism: The Unknown Ideal.* New York: New American Library, 1966.

Reisman, George. *The Government Against the Economy.* Ottawa, Ill.: Caroline House, 1979.

Roth, Timothy P. *The Ethics and the Economics of Minimalist Government.* Northampton, Mass.: Edward Elgar, 2002.

Smith, Adam. *An Inquiry into the Nature and Causes of the Wealth of Nations: A Selected Edition.* Edited by Kathryn Sutherland. New York: Oxford University Press, 1998.

Von Mises, Ludwig. *Liberalism: A Socio-Economic Exposition.* Translated by Ralph Raico. Edited by Arthur Goddard. Mission, Kans.: Sheed Andrews and McMeel, 1978.

Younkins, Edward W. *Capitalism and Commerce: Conceptual Foundations of Free Enterprise.* Lanham, Md.: Lexington Books, 2002.

SEE ALSO: Capitalism; Communism; Economics; Marxism; Profit economy; Smith, Adam; Socialism.

Free-riding

DEFINITION: Enjoying a benefit produced by the efforts of others without contributing a fair share oneself

TYPE OF ETHICS: Beliefs and practices

SIGNIFICANCE: Free-riding is generally considered unfair behavior that threatens the success of cooperative endeavors among people.

Free-riding, as the expression suggests, involves gaining a benefit, such as a ride, at no cost to the one enjoying the benefit. Free-riding activity is seen as unfair, at least where the provision of the benefit involves costs borne by some and there is an expectation that those enjoying the benefit share in the cost.

One of the more common uses of the idea in ordinary contexts is in connection with union membership. Typically, in labor relations in the United States, one union or agent is authorized to serve as the exclusive representative of workers in a bargaining unit. Under such exclusivity, the union can speak for all the employees, but all the employees in turn have a right to be fairly represented by the union as their agent. Each employee is thought to have a duty to pay a fair or proportionate share of the cost of such representation; those not paying their share are accused of free-riding.

Samuel Gompers, an early leader in the American labor movement, stated the point as follows: "Non-unionists who reap the rewards of union efforts, without contributing a dollar or risking the loss of a day, are parasites. They are reaping the benefits from the union spirit, while they themselves are debasing genuine manhood."

Two points are illustrated in the labor example. The first is the moral condemnation of free-riding as unfair. The other is the more general issue about the provision of certain types of benefits or goods from cooperative activities: Benefits made possible by the cooperative efforts of some are available to all. Some goods or benefits are not easily divisible; therefore, it is not feasible to exclude noncontributors from enjoying them. In the case of such goods, it may seem rational in a sense to free-ride, since one can obtain the benefits at no cost to oneself. Cooperative ventures producing goods available to all need to provide some way of discouraging such free-riding. In the organized labor arena, unions have sought closed-shop or union-shop arrangements to prevent free-riding of the sort decried by Gompers. Under these arrangements, employers either must hire only union members or may hire anyone, with the proviso that all employees hired and retained must join and remain in the union.

HOBBES'S LEVIATHAN

Thomas Hobbes's classic work *Leviathan* (1651) is seen as the earliest treatment of the free-rider issue, posing it in the context of self-interested individuals in a state of nature using reason to find a way out of the miserable condition of life stemming from the absence of a sovereign power "to keep men in awe." While mutual restraint is the reasonable way out, it is not a sound choice for an individual who has no assurance that others will restrain themselves. The famous Hobbesian solution is the creation of an enforcement mechanism, the sovereign or "great Leviathan," who will lay down rules of conduct to secure peace and order and will enforce the rules against any lawbreakers or free-riders.

One of the points about free-riding behavior that is illustrated in Hobbes's discussion is the problematic connection with rational choice. From the narrow view of the individual intent on maximizing personal satisfaction, free-riding seems like the reasonable course of action, so long as enough others are willing to cooperate and contribute to a sufficient extent to make the cooperative venture a success. From a more general standpoint, however, when cooperation with others offers substantial mutual benefits, then it seems reasonable for each individual to cooperate and thus not free-ride. The free-rider seems to threaten the establishment of a cooperative endeavor or the stability of an endeavor that is already underway.

Many cooperative ventures can get started and remain going concerns even when there are some free-riders, since the benefits of cooperation are great enough that many persons are willing to contribute regardless of free-riding. In welfare economics and public finance, the often-used example of a public or collective good susceptible to free-riding is that of the lighthouse. Some shipowners may find it worth their while to build and maintain a lighthouse for use by their vessels, even though other ships will be able to use the lighthouse for navigation. The owners of these other ships will be free-riding—that is, benefiting without paying any share of the cost—if they make no contribution to the building or maintenance of the lighthouse. The free-riding owners are not, however, adding to the costs of those supporting the lighthouse. Despite the free-riders, building the lighthouse may be a rational choice for the contributing shipowners because the benefits of the lighthouse outweigh the cost of construction and maintenance.

In ethics, the unfairness of much free-riding poses a difficulty for utilitarian theories that seek to equate wrongdoing with doing harm, since free-riding often does not harm contributors to a cooperative scheme. It does not always harm them in the sense of adding to their costs, although it may engender feelings of resentment toward the free-riders and lessen the morale of contributors, who believe that they are being made "suckers." Other ethical theories emphasizing the role of consent and contract also find it difficult to account for the wrongness of free-riding, since free-riders are typically not breaking any contract. The unfairness of such conduct, the act of taking advantage of others, seems to provide the most plausible and direct explanation for its wrongness.

Mario F. Morelli

FURTHER READING

De Jasay, Anthony. *Social Contract, Free Ride: A Study of the Public Goods Problem.* New York: Oxford University Press, 1989.

Dunbar, Robin. "Culture, Honesty, and the Freerider Problem." In *The Evolution of Culture: An Interdisciplinary View*, edited by Robin Dunbar, Chris Knight, and Camilla Power. New Brunswick, N.J.: Rutgers University Press, 1999.

Gauthier, David P. *Morals by Agreement.* New York: Oxford University Press, 1986.

Hobbes, Thomas. *Leviathan.* Edited by Richard Tuck. Rev. student ed. New York: Cambridge University Press, 1996.

Klosko, George. *The Principle of Fairness and Political Obligation.* Lanham, Md.: Rowman & Littlefield, 1992.

Olson, Mancur. *The Logic of Collective Action.* Cambridge, Mass.: Harvard University Press, 1965.

SEE ALSO: Cheating; Cost-benefit analysis; Economics; Fairness; Hobbes, Thomas; *Leviathan*; Reason and rationality; Responsibility.

Freedom and liberty

DEFINITION: Psychologically, the capacity to choose; socially, the ability to act without interference from others

TYPE OF ETHICS: Personal and social ethics

SIGNIFICANCE: The nature of freedom is a central question in moral, social, and political philosophy. Some philosophers define freedom only negatively as a lack of constraint, while others think of it as the positive ability to live an ethical and fulfilling life. Moreover, while some thinkers hold freedom to be a characteristic of individuals, others assert that only an entire society can be judged to be free or not free.

Freedom of the will, sometimes referred to as "free will" or "volition," makes ethics possible and necessary. Free will is the capacity to control the direction one's thoughts and actions take, and even whether one thinks or acts at all. Because humans do not think or act automatically, their thinking and acting can go in a variety of directions, some of which are benefi-

cial and some of which are not. Since whether a beneficial or a harmful direction is taken is within one's control, one is responsible for the direction taken. Accordingly, moral praise is warranted for using one's volitional capacity to select beneficial thoughts and actions, while moral blame is warranted either for not exercising one's volitional capacity or for using it to select harmful thoughts and actions.

"Freedom" and "liberty," then, designate fundamentally a capacity of human nature. Freedom of the will is the capacity to choose between alternatives; by extension, social freedom is the ability to act upon one's choices without interference from others. In parallel, the term "libertarianism" is sometimes used to name the position that holds that freedom of the will exists, as well as the social philosophy that holds that respect for individual freedom is the fundamental social principle.

FREEDOM THROUGH HISTORY

Freedom is a fragile thing. Throughout most of human history, it has existed only in brief, isolated instances. The city-states of classical Greece experimented successfully with democratic social institutions, and classical Rome derived much of its strength from its republican social institutions. Yet Rome's decline marked the West's return for a thousand years to the historical norm of human social arrangements: tribal and feudal versions of authoritarian social arrangements. Not until the end of the Middle Ages did freedom begin to become an increasingly normal part of some humans' existence.

During the Renaissance and the Enlightenment, a number of major, related institutional changes brought about a gradual decentralization of intellectual, economic, and political power, and a corresponding increase in the powers and freedoms enjoyed by individuals. Intellectually, the rapid growth of science contributed to the increasing secularization of society and gave rise to a greater diversity of opinions; and in northern Europe, the impact of the Reformation and Protestantism's emphasis upon each individual's being able to read and interpret the Bible was partly responsible for the rapid increase in the number of literate individuals. Politically, the decline of the European monarchies gave rise to a variety of democratic and republican forms of government. Economically, the rapid increase in wealth made possible by increasing international trade and new forms of finance and production, culminating in the Industrial Revolution, gave increasing numbers of individuals unprecedented economic control over their lives.

The rise of liberal social arrangements in economics, politics, and the quest for knowledge often occurred prior to an explicit, theoretical understanding of their political, economic, and intellectual value. While the practical value of liberty became obvious to many, it was also obvious that liberty conflicted with many traditional theories of morality. Accordingly, an explicit theoretical understanding of freedom's moral standing became crucial. Indeed, most opposition to individual economic and political freedom stems fundamentally from moral disagreements with freedom's individualist ethical foundations.

THE MORALITY OF FREEDOM

The morality of freedom is based on its being a requirement of human survival. To survive, individuals need values such as food and shelter. These values must be produced by individual initiative and effort. Production, however, depends upon the individual's having acquired the requisite knowledge, and the acquisition of knowledge in turn depends upon the individual's exercise of free will to control his or her mind's operations. Human survival, therefore, depends ultimately upon freely directed individual initiative and effort. Individuals need to choose to think, in order to acquire knowledge, in order to put their knowledge into practice, and in order to produce the values they need to consume in order to survive and flourish. At each step of the process—thinking, production, and consumption—the individual's freely chosen initiatives determine the degree of his or her self-determination.

Humans live in social groups. Although social arrangements can yield great benefits to individuals, social living also raises the risk of the use of coercion by some individuals against other individuals. Coercion, which can take many forms—killing, slavery, kidnapping, assault, theft—is a danger to human life because it removes to some degree an individual's control over his or her life. Coercion, accordingly, is wrong in principle, and all social arrangements should be based on the principle that only freely chosen interactions are moral; that is, respect for individual freedom is the fundamental social principle.

The rejection of coercion and the protection of freedom are often spelled out in terms of rights. Rights specify spheres of autonomy that leave individuals free to think and act as they deem necessary to sustain their lives. An individual's right to control his or her own life is the fundamental social principle in terms of which all other rights are defined. Since the process of life involves three subprocesses—thinking, producing, and consuming—the right to life is specified in greater detail to make explicit the protection individuals need in each subprocess. Individuals need to think independently in order to acquire knowledge; therefore, people recognize the right to freedom of conscience. Individuals need to act upon their beliefs, so people recognize the right to liberty; and since the actions that individuals believe are necessary often involve communicating and acting cooperatively with other individuals, people recognize the rights to freedom of speech and freedom of association. Since individuals need to consume the values they have produced, they need to be able to control the fruits of their production; therefore, people recognize the right to property. Overriding an individual's rights in any area means undermining that individual's freedom, which in turn means undermining that person's self-control.

THE ROLE OF GOVERNMENT

Since some individuals will resort to coercion in order to benefit from the productive efforts of other individuals, and since the primary social need of individuals is freedom from such coercion, government is established as the institution charged with protecting individuals' rights. The moral task of government, then, is to ensure that individuals are at liberty to use their property as they see fit to sustain and enhance their lives. A government thus is given the power to use coercion defensively, in protecting individuals' rights.

Since a government too can use coercion against individuals, however, individuals also need protection from government. In liberal social systems, this protection is usually provided by a constitution that explicitly limits the coercive power of a government to defensive purposes in the service of individuals' rights. As a further safeguard, the power given to a government to do its job is broken up and spread among the various branches of government so that each branch can serve as a check upon possible abuses by the others.

Such liberal political arrangements have economic consequences. If individuals have a reasonable political guarantee of freedom from both other individuals and government, they will invest, produce, and reap as much profit as their skills, dedication, and ingenuity allow them. They will be free to reinvest or consume their profits. They will be free to form voluntary associations (such as partnerships, corporations, and stock markets) to enhance their production and hence their profits. They will be free to specialize, since specialization generally yields higher production, and to exchange their products in a market in which rates of exchange (prices) are governed by the forces of supply and demand.

The practicality of free enterprise is a consequence: The freedom to pursue profit releases enormous amounts of human productive energy, and this explains the historical success of liberal social systems.

CRITICISMS OF LIBERTY

Neither such moral justifications of individual liberty nor the historical success of liberal social institutions has won over the advocates of the many doctrines that are opposed to freedom. Opposition to and attacks upon individual freedom generally stem from opposing fundamental premises about morality. In most such attacks, the common theme is that the individual's life and freedoms have less moral significance than does the individual's duty to sacrifice himself or herself for the benefit of some higher being. Opponents of freedom disagree among themselves about what or who that higher being is, although religion, monarchism, and collectivism have been the three historically dominant sources of candidates for beings for whom individuals should be willing to sacrifice their lives and liberties.

RELIGION AND LIBERTY

The history of the relationship between religion and liberty has been long and varied. Some religious theorists conclude that secular liberty and independence are compatible with religious obedience and subservience to a higher being—God—by arguing, first, that God created humankind to be his stewards of the natural world and charging them with the task of using the world's resources efficiently and fruitfully, and second, that politically and economically free social systems are more efficient and fruitful

than are authoritarian systems. The central thrust of most religions, however, has been to exalt God's power and, correspondingly, to diminish humans' power. Instead of individuals volitionally selecting their lives' goals and the methods to achieve them, the ends and means of human life are held to be established by God.

The range of valid options open to individuals is thus limited severely by God's decrees, and moral virtue, it follows, consists not in liberty in thought and action, but rather in strict obedience to God's commands. Although many religions grant that one has the volitional capacity to think independently and freely, such self-indulgence is held to be immoral; to be moral, one must choose to recognize one's dependence and be obedient. To the extent that religion is translated into political doctrine, theocracy is the result: God's agents on Earth are charged with the authority to enforce God's commands, so they should have the political power to enforce obedience on the part of the rest of society.

MONARCHY AND SECULAR AUTHORITARIANISM

Structurally, monarchy is a secular form of theocracy. Individuals are held to exist to serve and glorify a higher being—in this case, the king or queen, rather than God. The ends and means of individuals' lives are established by the monarch, and the monarch's decrees serve to limit the range of options open to individuals. Moral virtue again does not consist fundamentally in independence in thought and liberty in action, but rather in obedience to the monarch's commands. Individual liberties exist only by default; that is, to the extent that the monarch fails to prescribe the course of his or her subjects' lives or is politically unable to enforce his or her decrees.

Historically, some advocates of secular monarchies have used religious appeals to justify the concentration of political power in the hands of a monarch who is not also a duly constituted religious authority. According to the doctrine of the divine right of kings, the monarch's possession of great power is justified not merely by the fact that he or she has succeeded in acquiring it or by the fact that he or she is the biological descendant of the previous monarch, or by the claim that the concentration of political power in the monarch's hands is the most efficient means of realizing political aims in the best interests of the subjects, but rather by his or her selection by God to carry out part of God's plan on Earth.

Another general form of secular authoritarianism is based on collectivist ethical principles. According to collectivism, individual human beings are of less moral value than is some larger group to which they belong; therefore, individuals are expected to devote their lives to serving the larger group. Different versions of collectivism define the larger group differently; some hold that the appropriate group is the nation, while others hold that it is the race, the culture, one's economic class, or, more vaguely, society as a whole. Collectivists argue that individuals are not morally free to pursue their own ends, but rather that they have a duty to sacrifice and to serve the ends of the collective, as determined by the collective's leaders.

The twentieth century saw the rise of several versions of collectivism, with a corresponding diminution of individual freedoms to the extent that collectivist doctrines were practiced.

Marxism, for example, holds that the dictatorship of the proletariat (the working class) is a necessary step in the transition between capitalism and international socialism. During the dictatorship of the proletariat, the leaders of the Communist Party will hold absolute power and will determine what is necessary, while individuals will sacrifice themselves, voluntarily or not, to bring about a new collective entity— the international socialist state.

Fascism, to take another prominent example, holds that dictatorship is a necessary step toward realizing a national or racial version of socialism. Again, the leaders of the party will hold absolute power and will determine what is necessary, while individuals will sacrifice themselves, voluntarily or not, to bring about a new collective entity—the national socialist state.

Some versions of radical environmentalism, to take a final example, hold that the ecosystem is the collective entity that is the unit of value, and that humans exist to serve the ecosystem as a whole. While humans have a duty to serve the ecosystem, however, most of them seem shortsighted and have abused their freedoms (by causing pollution and overpopulation). Accordingly, the freedoms of individuals to produce and reproduce should be overridden by enlightened leaders who have the best interests of the ecosystem as a whole at heart.

PESSIMISM VS. FREEDOM

In addition to religious, monarchic, and collectivist attacks on individual freedom, certain positions on the status of human nature have also led directly to attacks on freedom. To the extent that a pessimistic evaluation of human nature is accepted, there is a tendency to reject political and economic freedom in favor of some version of paternalism. Paternalists typically hold that humans are too evil or too incompetent to be left free to determine their own affairs. Accordingly, rather than conceiving of the state as a servant whose job it is to protect individuals' freedoms while they pursue their lives, paternalists urge the state to take control of individuals' lives, either as a strong and stern authority suppressing the natural tendencies of humans to do evil, or as a wise and benevolent leader organizing individuals' lives so as to protect them from their own incompetencies.

THE SCOPE OF FREEDOM

Individual freedom is at stake in scores of major practical moral controversies. People continue to debate, for example, abortion, censorship, free trade, taxation, the use of alcohol and drugs, the military draft, and homosexuality. Each practical issue focuses on whether individuals should be free to act as they judge best or should be forced to act as some other individual or group judges best. In each debate, the acceptance or denial of the legitimacy of individual freedom is a conclusion derived from more fundamental premises about metaphysics, human nature, and ethics. If, for example, God has all the power, then humans have none; therefore, freedom is not an issue. If humans are not intellectually competent enough to run their own lives, then intellectual control should be given to someone who is, so censorship is a practical option. If humans are basically evil, then freedom is folly, and so is allowing humans access to alcohol and drugs. If individual humans are merely servants of a larger collective, then freedom is unnecessary; therefore, a draft is justifiable. A full defense of freedom and liberal social institutions, then, depends on a full philosophical system of premises demonstrating that human beings are by nature none of the above—that, instead, they are competent individuals who are morally ends in themselves.

Stephen R. C. Hicks

FURTHER READING

Flathman, Richard E. *Freedom and Its Conditions: Discipline, Autonomy, and Resistance.* New York: Routledge, 2003. A Nietzschean/Foucauldian analysis of resistance and discipline in democracy, with an emphasis upon the types of resistance necessary to ensure continued liberty and the nature of the self in a free society.

Hayek, Friedrich. *The Road to Serfdom.* 50th anniversary ed. Introduction by Milton Friedman. Chicago: University of Chicago Press, 1994. A critical analysis of some of the twentieth century's major collectivist attacks on freedom.

Hegel, Georg Wilhelm Friedrich. *The Phenomenology of Spirit.* Translated by A. V. Miller. Oxford, England: Oxford University Press, 1977. Contains a famous and influential argument that freedom is a property of societies and not of individuals, so that no single person can ever be free or not free.

Locke, John. *Two Treatises of Government.* Edited by Peter Laslett. New York: Cambridge University Press, 1988. Locke's second treatise defends individual freedom from a natural rights perspective.

Mill, John Stuart. *On Liberty, and Other Essays.* Edited by John Gray. New York: Oxford University Press, 1998. Particularly influential in its defense of freedom of speech, Mill's work gives a utilitarian defense of liberty.

Novak, Michael. *Free Persons and the Common Good.* Lanham, Md.: Madison Books, 1989. Argues that Catholicism, a traditionally hierarchical religion, is compatible with the capitalist system of economic liberty.

Plato. *The Republic.* Translated by Desmond Lee. 2d ed. New York: Penguin Books, 2003. A classic argument against liberty and in favor of communal authoritarianism, based explicitly upon argued metaphysical, epistemological, and ethical premises.

Rand, Ayn. *Atlas Shrugged.* 35th anniversary ed. New York: Dutton, 1992. A twentieth century classic of fiction and a philosophical defense of intellectual independence and laissez-faire capitalism.

Rosenberg, Nathan, and L. E. Birdzell, Jr. *How the West Grew Rich.* New York: Basic Books, 1986. An economic history of the role of liberalism and pluralism in making possible the West's great increases in wealth.

SEE ALSO: Determinism and freedom; Egoism; First Amendment; Freedom of expression; Libertarianism; Locke, John; Mill, John Stuart; *On Liberty*; Platonic ethics.

Freedom of expression

DEFINITION: Right to speak and otherwise communicate without interference or fear of government reprisal.

TYPE OF ETHICS: Civil liberties

SIGNIFICANCE: Free expression is considered one of the most fundamental rights in democratic societies. It is founded upon two ethical ideas: first, that freedom of conscience (the right to one's own beliefs) is meaningless unless one is also free to express those beliefs to others; and second, that society as a whole benefits from a free "marketplace of ideas" in which all points of view may be heard and considered.

The modern belief in freedom of speech is assumed to include all other forms of free expression. These forms include the right to speak freely in political assemblies, the right to petition those assemblies, the right to relate and publish debates of the assemblies, and freedoms of correspondence, of teaching, of worship, of publishing newspapers and books, and of expression in the arts. Freedom of expression is all-inclusive, but it is epitomized in freedom of speech. It is from freedom of speech that all other individual expressions take their distinctive forms. Understood to accompany the freedom of expression are freedom of thought (spiritual freedom) and the right to criticize—to inquire or to research old dogmas.

ANCIENT GREECE

The language, theory, and practice of freedom of expression in the modern, Westernized world are linked to Greek and Latin ideas and institutions. Freedom of expression was born in Athens in the archaic period (c. 800-600 B.C.E.), when the aristocratic rulers allowed certain classes to voice their opinions without fear of reprisal. This freedom was increased under the reforms of Solon (c. 594 B.C.E.), and it reached a high point in the golden age of Pericles (c. 507 B.C.E.) and Cleisthenes (c. 443-429 B.C.E.). The citizens of Athens were granted freedom of expression in the political arena, including the council, the assembly, the courts, and in society at large, and also in the areas of philosophy and the arts. Freedom of speech is excellently illustrated by the dramatist Aristophanes' criticism of Cleonymus, an Athenian politician of considerable power, as a "glutton," a "perjurer," and one who throws away his shield in battle (a coward).

Despite the broad latitude permitted in Athens for freedom of expression, such freedom was by no means absolute. Restrictions were placed upon the speakers, the content of the speech, and the time and place of utterance. The leaders of the assembly restricted freedom of speech to the citizen class; those individuals who were considered "unworthy" or "dishonorable" were punished by having their right to speak taken away.

ANCIENT ROME

In Republican Rome, freedom of expression differed markedly from the variety found in Athens. The representative democracy of Rome was established on the basis of the idea that all political authority came from the people. The notions of liberty (*libertas*) and of the political process (*civitas*) were considered inseparable. Therefore, there was no basic clash between the individual and the state, for the free and responsible citizen had certain rights that the state could legitimately support so long as they furthered *civitas*.

Roman law did not support legal guarantees for freedom of expression, but a tradition of tolerance evolved in Rome that permitted and encouraged freedom of expression. Both orators and writers freely criticized public and private figures by name. Some controls were exercised regarding who could speak and what could be said. The government also established theaters and exercised censorship over them.

The right to speak and speech content in the assembly were controlled by procedures. The republican constitution provided that the assembly serve as the principal legislature and as the supreme court. The ordinary citizen who participated in the assembly did not have a right to speak but did have a right to listen to debates by magistrates, senators, and

juriconsults (lawyers). They also had the right to vote. The right to speak was controlled by the governing class.

The Twelve Tablets, Rome's first written law, which was codified in 451 B.C.E., provided for the punishment of seditious libel or defamation. Nevertheless, orators often engaged in defamation and invective. Cicero attacked his opponent Piso, calling him a "beast," "funeral pyre of the state," "mud," "donkey," "hog," and a "piece of rotten flesh." Libelous expression was constrained, although the record is not clear about the existence or enforcement of specific laws governing sedition or defamation in the assembly and the senate. Defamation, however, was actionable if it occurred on the stage or in the courts.

In the Roman Empire, government control mutated from democratic institutions to one-man rule. Free expression was commonly tolerated on an ad hoc basis, depending on the emperor. Augustus was moderately tolerant of dissent, Tiberius allowed a considerable degree of freedom of expression, and Caligula started with a policy of leniency but soon turned toward brutal repression that included having one writer burned alive in the amphitheater. Claudius suspended the law of treason, but his successor, Nero, reinstated it; Vespasian and Domitian applied the law of high treason vigorously, including having the historian Hermogenes Tarsus put to death and his secretaries crucified.

THE WESTERN TRADITION

The late classical world's pattern of constraints on freedom of expression formed the basis for the emergent practices in the West for more than seventeen centuries. During this lengthy period, no Western nation extended to its citizens a legal guarantee of freedom of expression. The Christian Church fervently persecuted those whom it thought unorthodox or heretical. Inquisitions of various kinds were carried out by the Church from the thirteenth century through the eighteenth century.

During this dark period for human liberty, England moved quietly but unquestionably toward establishing a tradition of civil liberty. In June, 1215, King John, a tyrant, was forced to sign the Magna Carta, which is now recognized as the foundation of constitutional liberty for both England and the United States. This charter did not mention freedom of expression, but it did claim that no free man could be deprived of life or property except by peer judgment and by the law of the land. The word "liberty" appears several times in the document.

The regal Magna Carta gave support, through its transformation, to political liberty, including freedom of expression. While there is no direct line of descent from antiquity to Western Europe and England of freedom of expression, the West had to learn the principles and practice of freedom of expression reflexively and by intentional emulation. Once the idea of freedom of expression took hold, its growth was assured by an increasingly mobile and rational society that was beginning to debate and test everything.

The Renaissance, the Scientific Revolution, the Reformation, the Enlightenment, and the two great revolutions of the eighteenth century imbued views of freedom of expression with much of their modern implications and tone. The debate and testing of worldviews blossomed in the United States in 1791 with the ratification of the Bill of Rights. In the meantime, following King John's signing of the Magna Carta, church and state in England continued for centuries to restrain the development of liberty of speech by controlling the content of speech and the medium of speech—the printing press.

THE EARLY MODERN ERA

John Milton was the first to decry prior restraint of the press. Milton published his argument in *Areopagitica* (1644). Milton's essay states in cautious prose four arguments against prior restraint or press censorship by Parliament. First, prior restraint was conceived and used by the Roman Catholic Church to suppress the Protestant Reformation. Second, prior restraint, according to Milton, weakens character, since individuals do not have the chance to determine the truth for themselves. Third, prior restraint does not work; the censored ideas will inevitably become known. Fourth, prior censorship discourages learning and the search for truth (it replaces the pursuit of truth with unquestioned authority), which injures society. Milton had many reservations about extending freedom of expression to everyone (for example, Milton did not believe that freedom of expression should be extended to Catholics). Nevertheless, his work was a milestone in the development of civil liberties in the West and Westernized societies.

John Stuart Mill, an English philosopher and economist, went much further than Milton in his argument in support of freedom of expression. In his work *On Liberty*, Mill asserts three basic reasons for government to permit freedom of expression. First, the "hated ideas" may be true and the orthodox ideas may be false. Second, truth is powerful enough to triumph over falsehood without the artificial protection of government, and the continual challenging of truth prevents it from becoming dead dogma. Third, there is probably some degree of truth in all ideas or opinions; therefore, to suppress any idea is to endanger possible truth. Mill's argument for freedom of expression is that it is socially useful. Freedom of expression must have purpose beyond itself. Mill maintains that "absolute certainty" is not available to human beings, and therefore the suppression of any idea "is an assumption of infallibility"; such an assumption is unwarranted. Mill's espousal of freedom of expression is best exemplified in one of his quotations: "If all mankind minus one, were of one opinion, and only one person were of the contrary opinion, mankind would be no more justified in silencing that one person, than he, if he had the power, would be justified in silencing mankind."

THE AMERICAN SYNTHESIS

The next leap forward in the progression of human rights occurred in America. It took its most complete development in the First Amendment to the U.S. Constitution. The framers of the Constitution placed freedom of conscience first, and then freedom of speech and the press. James Madison, Thomas Jefferson, and the others who inspired the First Amendment were inheritors of the Enlightenment and its antecedents. They believed in the power of reason, in the search for truth, in progress, and in the inevitable perfectibility of humankind. Freedom of expression was considered essential to the discovery and advancement of truth, for only by constant testing in a public forum could falsehood be uncovered.

The twentieth century, especially its last third, was a high point for freedom of expression. Alexander Meiklejohn, a foremost constitutional scholar, maintained that a teacher's freedom to pursue knowledge (academic freedom) may be curtailed in certain circumstances; political speech, however, enjoys "an absolute, preferred position" in the Constitution. James Madison, author of the First Amendment, said, "If we *examine* the nature of Republican Government, we shall find the censorial power is in the people over the Government, and not in the Government over the people." It is only by freedom of expression that the people can voice their grievances and aspire to redress them. It is principally by exercising free speech that people can build without molestation political power that can counter recurrence of excesses by government.

THE JUDICIARY

The Supreme Court, as the final decipherer of the Constitution, has acted as the guardian of freedom of expression. In *Garrison v. Louisiana* (1964), Justice Joseph Brennan declared: "Speech concerning public affairs is more than self-expression; it is the essence of self-government."

The primacy of freedom of expression has never been absolute in the United States, and it has been even more circumscribed in Western Europe. In times of war or similar crisis, for example, some publications that may threaten national security are prohibited. Other forms of expression are restrained on certain occasions by the courts, since they may unfairly assail the communal interest in public morality. Picketing, parades, and even words, if permitted at a particular time and place, may threaten public safety or order despite the constitutionality of the information or ideas.

The Court employed the bad-tendency test, or the "nip it in the bud" approach, to judging expression. This approach stops or punishes speech that the Court believes has a tendency to create a serious danger at some point in the future if it is allowed to continue. The principal statement of this position was in *Gitlow v. United States* (1925), in which the Supreme Court upheld the sedition conviction of Benjamin Gitlow: "A single revolutionary spark may kindle a fire that, smoldering for a time may burst into a sweeping and destructive conflagration"; therefore, it is reasonable and expected for the state to seek to extinguish the spark to protect the public peace and safety.

The Supreme Court began to inquire into the limits of freedom of expression only in 1919. The first landmark case decided by the Court was *Schenck v. United States* (1919). In more than seven decades, the Court assembled a body of constitutional law, but it did not formulate a theoretical basis for interpreting the First Amendment. The Court has consistently held that freedom of expression, especially of speech

and of the press, ensures the survival of the American political system. The chief purpose of the First Amendment, in the eyes of the Court, is to serve the political needs of an open and democratic society. Such political needs also include the right of the people to alter by lawful means the political process itself. Justice Felix Frankfurter's famed pronouncement reflects the Court's consistent opinion that freedom of expression is a means to better the political system: "Winds of doctrine should freely blow for the promotion of good and the correction of evil." Justices Hugo Black and William O. Douglas reiterated the contention that freedom of expression exists to preserve American democracy: "It is the purpose of the First Amendment to preserve an uninhibited marketplace of ideas in which truth will ultimately win."

TWENTIETH AND TWENTY-FIRST CENTURIES

Before the mid-twentieth century, the Court and political philosophers argued for freedom of expression in general terms. Zechariah Chafee, Jr., writing during the 1940's, discussed problems of preserving the peace, defamation, and obscenity. His emphasis was on political expression and seditious libel. Chafee's theory recognizes two types of expression: that which serves an individual interest and that which serves a more broad social interest. Chafee tries to balance freedom of expression in searching for truth against public safety. Every effort, Chafee says, should be made to maintain both interests unimpaired. Free expression should be sacrificed only when the interest in public safety is really imperiled, not when it is narrowly affected. Chafee espoused the doctrine of a clear and present danger test. Profanity and defamation, to Chafee, were socially "worthless" activities that were unprotected by the First Amendment.

Thomas Emerson, another constitutional scholar, wrote during the 1960's. Emerson argued that freedom of expression includes the right to form and hold beliefs on any subject and to communicate those beliefs to others by whatever medium one chooses—whether through speech or by other means, including art or music. Freedom of expression, according to Emerson, includes the right to hear the opinions of others, the right to inquire, reasonable access to information, and the rights of assembly and association. Freedom of expression, Emerson declares, operates in four ways: first, individual self-fulfillment; second, discovering truth; third, democratic decision making, and fourth, finding a balance between healthy strife and necessary consensus. Emerson tried to fashion a theory that would determine where the line should be drawn between expression and action in the many cases involving freedom of expression. Speech, ideally, should not be punishable at all; however, in certain situations, actions, if they are pernicious and unlawful, can and must be punishable.

Franklyn Haiman wrote during the 1980's and argued for a free marketplace of ideas. The law is an inappropriate tool for dealing with "hated" speech. The remedy for such speech is more speech, never (or nearly never) the repression of speech. Even in cases of defamation, the remedy is a right of reply, except when the alleged defamer refuses to provide for such a reply or when time is inadequate to permit a reply. Haiman is even tolerant of speech that incites unlawful actions. Haiman insists that those who allegedly incite others to illegal conduct should not be held accountable themselves for the actions of their listeners, unless the audience is deceived, is coerced, or is mentally impaired. Haiman also argues for a wide dissemination of all ideas. The law should be used to enrich and expand communications and to ensure that the marketplace of ideas remains free. Even the views of nonconformists should be distributed, Haiman concludes. Also, the scheduling of the time and place of speech should be done in a content-neutral way. Owners and managers of quasi-public private property (such as shopping centers and airports) should make provisions for nondisruptive communications with the public by any individual. Haiman further emphasizes that government in a free society is the servant and should not inhibit, distort, or dominate public discourse.

Most constitutional scholars agree that the freedom of American citizens to participate in governing themselves is best protected by the First Amendment. Free people, who govern themselves, must not be shielded from any idea that is considered unwise, or unfair, or dangerous; it is they, the American people, who must judge any idea. Freedom of expression is not a law of nature or a principle of abstract reason, but a basic American agreement that public issues shall be decided by the people. A general theory may be stated in the following way: The people's suffrage in a democracy must always be couched broadly in terms of freedom of expression in the political process; however, government interference in personal conduct must be permitted rarely or not permitted at all.

Claude Hargrove

FURTHER READING

Beatson, Jack, and Yvonne Cripps, eds. *Freedom of Expression and Freedom of Information: Essays in Honor of Sir David Williams*. New York: Oxford University Press, 2000. An anthology of essays about the freedoms guaranteed by the First Amendment, as well as freedom of information and the issues raised by informational technologies in the twenty-first century.

Bonner, Robert J. *Aspects of Athenian Democracy*. New York: Russell & Russell, 1967. A lucidly written work on various aspects of freedom of expression. The author examines the constraint of free expression and the procedures that those in power use to control public speech.

Chafee, Zechariah, Jr. *Free Speech in the United States*. Cambridge, Mass.: Harvard University Press, 1942. An important work by a constitutional scholar who has had a major influence on American constitutional law and the theory of balancing free speech against unlawful conduct.

Cohen-Almagor, Raphael. *Speech, Media, and Ethics—The Limits of Free Expression: Critical Studies on Freedom of Expression, Freedom of the Press, and the Public's Right to Know*. New York: Palgrave, 2001. Attempts to outline the limits of free expression, when that right comes into conflict with other civil and human rights.

Emerson, Thomas I. *The System of Freedom of Expression*. New York: Random House, 1970. A solid work that attempts to establish a theory that differentiates speech from action. Holds that the speaker is not responsible for the unlawful action of his or her audience.

Haiman, Franklyn S. *Speech and Law in a Free Society*. Chicago: University of Chicago Press, 1981. Endorses the wide dissemination of ideas in quasi-public places; he holds that even slanderous speech should be tolerated.

Meiklejohn, Alexander. *Political Freedom: The Constitutional Powers of the People*. New York: Oxford University Press, 1965. The author is a constitutional scholar who helped to give direction to constitutional theory. He argues that speech should hold a preferred position with reference to other considerations, such as public morality.

Mill, John Stuart. *On Liberty, and Other Essays.* Edited by John Gray. New York: Oxford University Press, 1998. Mill's absolutist views were very modern and were nearly a definitive position of absolutism.

Schauer, Frederick. *Free Speech: A Philosophical Enquiry.* New York: Cambridge University Press, 1982. A composite work that surveys the theoretical basis of the freedom of expression.

SEE ALSO: Censorship; Civil Rights Act of 1964; English Bill of Rights; First Amendment; *Griswold v. Connecticut*; Library Bill of Rights; Mill, John Stuart; Song lyrics.

Freedom of Information Act

IDENTIFICATION: U.S. law mandating that records possessed by federal agencies must be made available to the public upon request

DATES: Effective July 4, 1967; amended in 1974, 1976, and 1986

TYPE OF ETHICS: Politico-economic ethics

SIGNIFICANCE: The Freedom of Information Act strengthened the American public's right to know, reaffirming the view that an informed citizenry is vital to the functioning of a democratic society.

Before the enactment of the U.S. Freedom of Information Act (FOIA) in pre-Watergate 1967, the public's "right to know" was merely a slogan coined by journalists, not a legal right. The press led the fight for "open government" and cited numerous instances of random and unexplained denials of access to information about crucial governmental decisions. Claims of executive privilege without any requirement of justification shielded the nondisclosure of materials to Congress for legislation and supervision. Government records were required to be revealed only to persons properly and directly concerned with them. Any records could be kept secret if such policy was in the public interest or if the records related solely to the internal management of an agency.

THE ACT

The rights conferred on the people by the FOIA are not specifically protected in the Constitution. Its goals, however—the elimination of secrecy and preservation of government accountability—were familiar even to the nation's founding fathers (James Madison, Alexander Hamilton, and Thomas Jefferson), who viewed excesses of power in the seat of big government with alarm.

Under the FOIA, all individuals have an equal right of access to information. The act provides that "any person" (citizen or noncitizen, partnership, corporation, association, foreign or domestic government) may file a request for an agency record for any reason. The requester does not have to be a party in an agency proceeding, and no showing of relevancy or involvement in litigation is required. The purpose for which the request is made has no bearing on its merits. The FOIA specifies only that requests must reasonably describe the documents sought and must comply with agencies' published procedural regulations. The agency must provide the document unless it falls within one of the nine exemptions contained in the act. If the agency refuses to produce the record, the requester may go to court, where the agency must prove that the documents in question are exempt under the law and that its refusal to produce them is justified. Courts determine the propriety of agency action without deference to agency opinion and expertise, unlike the course of action followed in other matters.

The FOIA establishes two categories of information that must be disclosed. The first requires publication in the Federal Register of basic information regarding the transaction of agency business; descriptions of the organization, including its functions, procedures, and rules; and policy statements of the agency. The second requires the availability for inspection and copying of so-called "reading room" materials: final adjudicatory opinions, specific policy statements, and administrative staff manuals. These materials must be indexed to facilitate public access, to help any citizen involved in a controversy with an agency, and to guard against the development of internal agency secrets. Records covered by the foregoing are subject to disclosure upon an agency's receipt of a request by any person.

The FOIA applies only to "records" maintained by "agencies" within the federal government. Not included are records maintained by state and municipal governments, courts, Congress, or private citizens. Many states have counterparts to the FOIA. The Supreme Court has developed a basic two-pronged test for determining what constitutes an "agency record" under the FOIA: documents that must be either created or obtained by an agency and be under agency control at the time of the request.

EXEMPTIONS

Release of information contained in nine categories of exemptions is not required. These include national security and foreign policy matters, internal personnel rules and practices, exemptions specified by other federal statutes, privileged or confidential trade secrets and commercial or financial information, interagency or intraagency memoranda, personnel and medical files constituting an unwarranted invasion of privacy, investigatory records compiled for law enforcement purposes (including protecting the identity of confidential sources and information furnished to authorities), financial institution reports, and geological and geophysical information and data. It should be noted, however, that the exemptions are discretionary rather than mandatory. When challenged, therefore, their application to particular records and situations must be determined on a case-by-case basis and may be subject to varying interpretations by the courts.

SIGNIFICANT AMENDMENTS

As a reaction to the abuses of Watergate and widespread concern over excessive government secrecy, the FOIA was substantially amended in 1974. The overall scope of the act's law enforcement and national security exemptions was narrowed and its procedural aspects broadened. The 1974 amendments included a provision whereby a court could conduct an *in camera* (behind closed doors) inspection of withheld information in order to determine the propriety of nondisclosure and classification and whether certain portions of otherwise withheld records could be segregated and released. A time limit of ten working days for agency response to a request was also established, as was a provision for the disciplining of persons responsible for arbitrary and capricious withholding of information, and the awarding of court costs and attorney's fees to a plaintiff who prevails in an FOIA case.

As part of the Anti-Drug Abuse Act of 1986, the FOIA was amended to provide broader exemption protection for law enforcement information, special law enforcement record exclusions, and new fee and fee waiver provisions. The 1990's brought discussions about the need to implement refinements to the FOIA to accommodate technological advances such as electronic record-keeping. Numerous treatises and legal journal articles contain references to the Freedom of Information Act.

Marcia J. Weiss

FURTHER READING

Botterman, Maarten. *Public Information Provision in the Digital Age: Implementation and Effects of the U.S. Freedom of Information Act.* Santa Monica, Calif.: RAND, 2001.
Citizen's Guide to the Freedom of Information Act. Chicago: Commerce Clearing House, 1987.
Foerstel, Herbert N. *Freedom of Information and the Right to Know: The Origins and Applications of the Freedom of Information Act.* Westport, Conn.: Greenwood Press, 1999.
Sherick, L. G. *How to Use the Freedom of Information Act.* New York: Arco, 1978.
United States Department of Justice, Office of Information and Privacy. *Freedom of Information Act Guide and Privacy Act Overview.* Washington, D.C.: Government Printing Office, 1992.

SEE ALSO: Confidentiality; Constitutional government; Democracy; Information access; Inside information; Journalistic ethics; Privacy; Public's right to know; Watergate scandal.

Freud, Sigmund

IDENTIFICATION: Austrian pioneer in psychoanalytic theory
BORN: May 6, 1856, Freiburg, Moravia, Austrian Empire (now Příbor, Czech Republic)
DIED: September 23, 1939, London, England
TYPE OF ETHICS: Psychological ethics
SIGNIFICANCE: Freud founded the theoretical and clinical discipline of psychoanalysis, providing the twentieth century with one of its most power-

ful and influential models of psychological development, the formation of one's moral character, and the relationship between desire and culture. His many works include *The Interpretation of Dreams* (*Die Traumdeutung*, 1900) and *Civilization and Its Discontents* (*Das Unbehagen in der Kultur*, 1930).

Although Sigmund Freud has had a powerful impact on the field of ethics, he did not initially set out to study moral questions. Freud's original interest was medical research, and he was trained in Vienna as a physician. Financial constraints, however, forced him to abandon his chief interest in pure research, and he began to practice during the 1880's as a neurologist. In 1884, Freud was introduced to Josef Breuer, a Viennese physician, who had developed a "cathartic" method for the treatment of hysterical

symptoms. This method involved encouraging patients to talk in a completely free and unencumbered manner about the development of their symptoms. The talking alone seemed to produce a surprising improvement in patients' conditions. This discovery was the starting point of what later became the field of psychoanalysis. Freud and Breuer collaborated on *Studies in Hysteria* (1895), in which they described their groundbreaking work in this area.

RISE OF PSYCHOANALYSIS

Freud continued this work alone, publishing such seminal volumes as *The Interpretation of Dreams* (1900), *Three Essays on the Theory of Sexuality* (1905), and *The Origin and Development of Psychoanalysis* (1910). In all these works, Freud developed a new way of examining the structure, nature, and diseases of the human mind. Freud's original focus

Sigmund Freud. (Library of Congress)

was on the understanding and treatment of emotional disorders, but as the field of psychoanalysis rapidly progressed, Freud's ideas gradually took a broader perspective. Freud eventually left his followers with a theory of the human psyche, a therapy for the relief of its ills, and a method for the interpretation of culture and society. It was in his later works, such as *Totem and Taboo* (1913), *The Future of an Illusion* (1927), and *Civilization and Its Discontents* (1930), that Freud spoke most directly to ethical and social issues.

ETHICAL IMPLICATIONS

In many ways, Freud rejected the conventional ethics of his era. His focus on the egoistic, narcissistic, and aggressive roots of human behavior led some readers to conclude that Freudian psychoanalysis was an amoral discipline that left no room for either a philosophical or a practical theory of morality. It is true that Freud rejected many traditional religious values. He believed that a number of central religious beliefs were merely a misguided human effort to overcome infantile feelings of helplessness and dependence. In *The Future of an Illusion*, Freud argued that the belief in God is a mythic attempt to overcome the human sense of powerlessness. Like an idealized parent, the concept of God is, for Freud, the projection of childish wishes for an omnipotent protector. In *Civilization and Its Discontents*, Freud again argued that religious phenomena were merely the reflection of unresolved psychological needs from the early years of life. In the opening chapter of the book, Freud described the oceanic feeling, or sense of indissoluble oneness with the universe, which mystics have often celebrated as the most fundamental of all religious experiences. Freud believed that the origin of this feeling was the desire to re-create the undifferentiated infant's profound sense of fusion with its mother. By attempting to debunk such central aspects of religious belief, Freud called into question many religious notions of moral right and wrong.

In addition to his rejection of religious morality, Freud also disagreed with Immanuel Kant's position that reason and duty should be the central grounds for morality. While Freud believed that reason must play a part in the development of ethical guidelines, he also saw a place in ethics for the promotion of human happiness and welfare. Freud advocated a practical form of ethics that was designed to promote the general welfare of society while simultaneously allowing individuals a sufficient degree of instinctual gratification.

FREUD'S VIEW OF HUMAN NATURE

For Freud, this position grew logically from his rather mixed view of human nature. Freud believed that most individuals possessed powerful aggressive and egoistic tendencies, along with a capacity for self-observation and altruistic behavior. Freud consistently maintained that theorists who saw human nature as inherently good were seriously deluded. For this reason, Freud believed that the golden rule—to love one's neighbor as oneself—was a destructive and unrealistic goal. Freud also suggested that utopian schemes such as communism were destined to failure, because they called for humans to give more than they were capable of giving.

According to Freud, the best course for humanity was to establish civilizations in which the more destructive elements of instinctual drives were prohibited, in order to promote the common social good. People will be able to tolerate the rules of such social organizations if nondestructive outlets for aggressive and narcissistic wishes can be developed. This will not be an easy task, and Freud believed that individual and group needs will generally be in conflict. Freud's hope was that society would adopt a realistic view of human nature and gradually learn more effective ways to manage the individual's need for instinctual gratification.

Steven C. Abell

FURTHER READING

Deigh, John. *The Sources of Moral Agency: Essays in Moral Psychology and Freudian Theory.* New York: Cambridge University Press, 1996.

Freud, Sigmund. *Letters.* Edited by Ernst L. Freud. Translated by Tania Stern and James Stern. New York: Basic Books, 1960.

_____. *The Standard Edition of the Complete Psychological Works of Sigmund Freud.* Translated by James Strachey. London: Hogarth Press, 1953-1974.

Hartmann, Heinz. *Psychoanalysis and Moral Values.* New York: International Universities Press, 1960.

Marcuse, Herbert. *Eros and Civilization: A Philosophical Inquiry into Freud.* Boston: Beacon, 1974.

Meissner, W. W. *The Ethical Dimension of Psycho-analysis: A Dialogue.* Albany: State University of New York Press, 2003.

Ricoeur, Paul. *Freud and Philosophy: An Essay on Interpretation.* Translated by Denis Savage. New Haven, Conn.: Yale University Press, 1970.

Rieff, Philip. *Freud: The Mind of the Moralist.* Garden City, N.Y.: Doubleday, 1961.

Roazen, Paul. *Freud: Political and Social Thought.* New York: Knopf, 1968.

Wallwork, Ernest. *Psychoanalysis and Ethics.* New Haven, Conn.: Yale University Press, 1991.

SEE ALSO: Aggression; Alienation; Hypnosis; Jung, Carl; Motivation; Narcissism; Psychology; Psychopharmacology; Therapist-patient relationship; Violence.

Friendship

DEFINITION: Attachment to another person, characterized by mutual affection, esteem, and goodwill

TYPE OF ETHICS: Personal and social ethics

SIGNIFICANCE: Friendship is seen by some as a moral good in itself, and the ability to be a good friend is often a morally admirable quality. Friendship may also create new moral obligations for friends, especially obligations to be loyal to one another.

Friendship became a topic of Western philosophical discussion in Plato's early dialogue *Lysis* (early fourth century B.C.E.). Because this work belongs to a type of inquiry called aporetic, meaning that the author was interested in raising difficult questions about the topic, it is irritatingly inconclusive, but the questions Plato raises are ones that later Greek and Roman philosophers energetically set about discussing. He also touches upon friendship in many of his later works; in the *Laws* (middle fourth century B.C.E.), for example, he describes love as a "vehement" form of friendship, and love, one of Plato's favorite topics, is the subject of his celebrated *Symposium* (early fourth century B.C.E.).

Not surprisingly, Aristotle, who defined man as a "political animal" (the adjective carries the wider meaning of "social"), devotes the eighth and ninth books of his *Nicomachean Ethics* (c. 330 B.C.E.) to friendship. He allows that friendship may be based on the relatively selfish motives of utility and pleasure but finds that the highest and most permanent form of friendship derives from a perception of goodness. All friends wish one another well, but a good person will value a friend not for a mere advantage but also for the friend's sake, and for the sake of the goodness in that friend.

Aristotle is one of many thinkers who point out that friendship does not, on the surface, appear to be necessary. It is neither a preliminary to the creation of new life, like erotic love, nor a condition of civil order. People cannot exist without water or food or shelter from the elements, and they normally crave human companionship, but they can and do exist without friends. To the question of why the happy person, presumably in possession of the good and essential things, would need friends, Aristotle applies another of his basic ideas, that of happiness as virtuous *activity*. The virtuous actions of one's own friend will be a delight, even a need, in one's own pursuit of happiness.

CICERO'S PRACTICAL ETHIC OF FRIENDSHIP

Of all the treatises on friendship from the ancient world, Marcus Tullius Cicero's *Laelius on Friendship* (44 B.C.E.) has had the most pervasive influence. From its composition through the Middle Ages and into the Renaissance, Cicero's was by far the discussion most often cited and reiterated. His philosophy is eclectic and unsystematic, drawing upon Platonic, Aristotelian, Stoic, and Epicurean thought. An accessible authority as well as a practical one, Cicero offered the medieval and Renaissance eras guidance on such questions as How far should the love of a friend extend? Cicero's answer: As far as is honorable. Accepting the common Greek idea that virtue induces friendship, he argues that virtue cannot be forsaken for the sake of friendship. For Cicero, the obligations of friendship include the avoidance of hypocrisy and suspicion, but he acknowledges that even good friends can go wrong. Therefore, it is one's duty not only to advise but also to rebuke one's friend if necessary.

CHRISTIANITY AND FRIENDSHIP

If friendship is a type or degree of love, as several of these ancient philosophers have claimed, Christianity has tended to see friendship as one of the manifestations of charity—or love for the sake of God. Thus argued Saint Thomas Aquinas, the greatest of the medieval Scholastics, who also incorporated much Aristotelian thought into his *Summa Theologica* (1266-1272). It is difficult to reconcile the disinterestedness of charity with the exclusiveness of friendship (for the Greco-Roman philosophers had pointed out that one's circle of true friends cannot be large), but Christianity has generally held that all true love is divine at its core.

MODERN VIEWS OF FRIENDSHIP

Modern philosophers have concerned themselves little with friendship, and Freudian psychology, which argues that expressed motives are often not the real underlying ones, has complicated later discussions of friendship. One modern advocate of classical and Christian thought, C. S. Lewis, in his *The Four Loves* (1960), deplores the modern habit of equating friendship with the nonethical concept of companionship. Lewis also vigorously rejects the tendency to regard friendships between those of the same sex as homoerotic. He recognizes that friendships can, and frequently do, turn into erotic love; his strong disapproval of homosexual love, however, detracts somewhat from his noteworthy attempt to reaffirm traditional moral dimensions of friendship.

It remains unclear whether friendship should be regarded as distinct in kind or only different in degree from erotic love. While exclusive, it does not nearly so often foment the jealousies that afflict the latter. A friendship of two can grow into a circle. For Cicero, the fact that *amicitia* derives from *amor* proves that friendship is a version of love, but in many other languages, English among them, the characteristic terms for the two concepts are etymologically distinct.

It is also not clear to what extent friendship is a human need. Although it is obviously a need for some people, it now seems presumptuous to argue, as does Aristotle, that those who feel the greatest need for it are the *best* people; that is, the people most desirous of cultivating goodness. The great moral philosophers agree, however, that the motivation for friendship cannot be *merely* satisfaction of a need. If friendship were primarily a need, Cicero remarks, then the weakest and most deficient people would make the best friends.

Robert P. Ellis

FURTHER READING

Aristotle. *Nicomachean Ethics*. Translated and edited by Roger Crisp. New York: Cambridge University Press, 2000.

Bloom, Allan. *Love and Friendship*. New York: Simon & Schuster, 1993.

Cates, Diana Fritz. *Choosing to Feel: Virtue, Friendship, and Compassion for Friends*. Notre Dame, Ind.: University of Notre Dame Press, 1997.

Cicero, Marcus Tullius. *"Laelius, on Friendship (Laelius de Amicitia)" and "The Dream of Scipio (Somnium Scipionis)."* Edited and translated by J. G. F. Powell. Warminster, England: Aris & Phillips, 1990.

Friedman, Marilyn. *What Are Friends For? Feminist Perspectives on Personal Relationships and Moral Theory*. Ithaca, N.Y.: Cornell University Press, 1993.

Grunebaum, James O. *Friendship: Liberty, Equality, and Utility*. Albany: State University of New York Press, 2003.

Lewis, C. S. *The Four Loves*. New York: Harcourt Brace Jovanovich, 1991.

Plato. *Lysis*. Translated by W. R. M. Lamb. Cambridge, Mass.: Harvard University Press, 1975.

SEE ALSO: *I and Thou*; Love; Loyalty; Personal relationships; Platonic ethics; Self-love; Trustworthiness.

Future generations

DEFINITION: Descendants of the people currently making environmental and other ethical decisions, and of the decision makers' constituents

TYPE OF ETHICS: Beliefs and practices

SIGNIFICANCE: The happiness and well-being of future generations is one of the central ethical concerns raised whenever nonrenewable resources are allocated, expended, used, or destroyed.

Since the time of the Stoics, most mainstream Western philosophers have agreed that people have some ethical obligations toward human beings in general, simply because they are human. Thus, Immanuel Kant wrote that the moral law commands one to "treat humanity, whether in one's own person or that of another, always as an end, and never as a means only"; and John Stuart Mill prescribed that one ought to maximize the happiness of all who will be affected by what one does.

These traditional philosophers did not specify, however, whether unborn future generations are to be included in this mandate. It did not occur to them to confront this issue, because the ethical problems with which they were preoccupied concerned transactions among contemporaries only.

The environmental movement has alerted people to the possibility that the profligate treatment of nature may leave to future generations a despoiled planet much less suited to human life. In the economic sphere, lavish public spending may saddle future generations with a crushing burden of debt. Here, the theoretical question of whether individuals have ethical obligations to those who do not yet exist becomes linked with large practical questions of public policy relating to intergenerational equity.

CENTRAL THEORETICAL QUESTION

There are three ways of answering the central theoretical question. The narrowest answer holds that people can have obligations only toward persons who are now in existence. Those advocating this answer seek to justify it by arguing that analysis of locutions of the form "*x* has an obligation toward *y*" shows that these cannot be true unless *y* exists at the time of utterance. Such reasoning is sophistical, however, and the conclusion drawn is morally repugnant in its selfishness.

The broadest answer is that people ought to give equal consideration to all human beings who may be affected by their actions, regardless of when they exist. This answer is troublingly radical, because it goes so far in imposing obligations to promote the wellbeing of merely potential persons who are very remote in time.

An in-between answer would say that the interests of those as yet unborn ought not to be disregarded, yet that what consideration they are given should be less, other things being equal, the greater their distance in time from the present. Those favoring this answer presumably see temporal distance as generating a type of moral distance that diminishes obligations. They might mention that one's obligations toward contemporary persons vary, depending on how close one's genetic and social links with these

persons are (for example, one has stronger obligations toward close relatives than toward strangers). The idea would be that separation in time tends to generate moral distance; hence, the amount of ethical consideration one owes to future persons will tend to be less, the more remote in time they are from one.

In modern times, birth rates have been declining sharply in most advanced nations and family lines have been dying out at an increasing rate. As a result, individuals of each successive generation have had less and less reason to suppose that distant generations will include direct descendants of theirs. Many people regard direct biological descent as a particularly important tie creating ethical obligations. If they are right, the dwindling of that tie will tend to diminish ethical obligations. It would seem to follow that in modern times the ethical obligations of people of a given generation toward unborn future generations have been decreasing.

When one tries to decide which of the three theoretical answers concerning obligations to future generations to accept, one's reflection tends to be severely obstructed by the uncertainty of predictions about the future. No one knows with certainty what the needs and abilities of future people will be, how well they will be able to adapt to a changing environment, how much need they will have of natural resources that the present population contemplates exhausting, or even whether human life will endure into future centuries. Moreover, one not only cannot be sure that any human successors will be one's biological descendants but also cannot be sure that any such descendants will be persons whom one would wish to benefit.

People usually believe, for example, that ingratitude on the part of others lessens their obligations toward them; and if it should be that the persons of the future are not going to feel gratitude for any consideration that the present population shows them, then the present population perhaps owes them considerably less than would otherwise be the case. Thus, in trying to assess specific obligations to future generations, it is easy to become lost in a fog of speculations. Uncertainty concerning the theoretical issue about how much, in principle, the living owe to the unborn tends to be smothered by myriad other uncertainties concerning what sort of future lies ahead, and decisive answers become difficult to reach.

Stephen F. Barker

FURTHER READING

Attfield, Robin. *Environmental Ethics: An Overview for the Twenty-first Century.* Malden, Mass.: Blackwell, 2003.

Cooper, David E., and Jay A. Palmer, eds. *The Environment in Question: Ethics and Global Issues.* New York: Routledge, 1992.

De George, Richard T. "The Environment, Rights, and Future Generations." In *Ethics and Problems of the Twenty-first Century*, edited by K. E. Goodpaster and K. M. Sayre. Notre Dame, Ind.: Notre Dame University Press, 1979.

Dobson, Andrew, ed. *Fairness and Futurity: Essays on Sustainability and Social Justice.* New York: Oxford University Press, 1999.

Dower, Nigel, ed. *Ethics and the Environmental Responsibility.* Brookfield, Vt.: Avebury, 1989.

Griffith, William B. "Trusteeship: A Practical Option for Realizing Our Obligations to Future Generations?" In *Moral and Political Reasoning in Environmental Practice*, edited by Andrew Light and Avner de-Shalit. Cambridge, Mass.: MIT Press, 2003.

Regan, Tom, ed. *Earthbound: New Introductory Essays in Environmental Ethics.* New York: Random House, 1984.

Scherer, Donald, ed. *Upstream/Downstream: Issues in Environmental Ethics.* Philadelphia: Temple University Press, 1990.

SEE ALSO: Deep ecology; Dominion over nature, human; Environmental ethics; Environmental movement; Future-oriented ethics; Global warming.

Future-oriented ethics

DEFINITION: Discipline devoted to understanding the ethical import of the effects of current actions on future conditions and future generations

TYPE OF ETHICS: Politico-economic ethics

SIGNIFICANCE: Future-oriented ethics asserts that current generations have a positive moral responsibility to improve the lives of those not yet born, or at the very least, to refrain from worsening their lives.

Future-oriented ethics concerns the influence of current decisions on the future. Some decisions affect people who are not yet living and who therefore have no voice in the decisions. Some choices, in fact, will influence which people will be alive in the future.

In some senses, future-oriented ethics began when humans first acquired the ability to reason and choose. Many religions discuss the possibility of an afterlife, with behavior during this life determining an individual's fate in the afterworld. Development of future-oriented ethics as a guide to political and social policy in addition to individual action developed slowly. During the eighteenth century, philosophers such as Adam Smith and Thomas Robert Malthus began to explore formally the implications of various types of social, political, and economic behavior. Malthus is famous for his theories of population, which state that human populations are destined to experience cycles of prosperity and famine because population will grow more rapidly than will food supplies until there is insufficient food and people starve.

POPULATION CONTROL

Malthus's theories, based on agricultural economies, in general have proved to be overly pessimistic. The Industrial Revolution allowed production to increase more rapidly than did population, allowing rising standards of living.

Many less-industrialized countries, however, face Malthusian cycles of poverty. In these countries, agricultural production serves as a check on population: If there is not enough food produced, possibly because the population has grown too rapidly, people do starve to death. Nature thus controls population if people do not do so consciously.

Ethical issues of population control concern whether policy planners are willing to let nature take its course. Many of the wealthier countries step in, providing food and other supplies, when famine or other disasters threaten populations. Some population theorists argue that this type of aid perpetuates the problem, allowing populations to survive and grow even though the natural environment cannot support them.

Wealthier nations face similar, though less desperate, questions. Welfare programs of various sorts provide a better standard of living, or perhaps even survival itself, for those less able to support themselves. These programs may create a cycle of poverty in which parents who are unable to support themselves have children who in turn are unable to support themselves.

MEDICINE

Population also can be controlled through various medical means. Birth control is one example. Some countries—China is a prominent example—actively promote birth control as a means of keeping their populations at sustainable levels. Many religions, however, prohibit artificial means of birth control, ruling out that option of poverty alleviation for some countries.

As life extension through medical technology becomes possible, societies must decide the value of a human life. The fact that it is possible to prolong or save a life does not mean that it is beneficial or ethical to do so. Medical care costs money that could be spent on something or someone else. Saving one life could mean failing to save (or improve) others. Furthermore, money spent on research to delay or even prevent future deaths could be spent on care for current populations.

Medicine also has increasing power to determine and control life chances of infants and even fetuses. The theory of eugenics proposes that people should be bred so as to improve the genetic pool, creating "better" children. Medical technology can determine some characteristics of fetuses and can abort those fetuses found to be "undesirable." Ethical questions surround the choices of which characteristics should be promoted and the circumstances under which such abortions should be performed. Medical technology literally has the ability to determine the characteristics of future generations. That ability will increase as scientists learn better how to manipulate genes.

EDUCATION AND INVESTMENT

Education provides a nonmedical means of ending the cycle of poverty. Through education, people can learn how better to provide for themselves. Education, however, has real costs. The starkest cases again are in poorer nations. A day spent in school can mean a day not spent out in the fields producing food. Even in wealthier countries, money spent on education, which will benefit people in the future, must be taken away from programs that benefit people today.

A basic problem of future-oriented ethics is the trade-off, illustrated by education, of present versus future. People can improve their abilities to produce and earn a living through investment in education; similarly, a society can increase its ability to produce through investment in various types of infrastructure and through research and development. A power supply system, a railroad network, or a factory, for example, can significantly increase future productive capacity. Building or purchasing these things, however, takes money. Poorer nations may be unable to pay the cost without endangering current populations.

The development of financial markets offered one solution to this dilemma. Nations (or individuals) can borrow to pay for the means to improve their productivity; these loans can be repaid through higher earnings now possible in the future. Such borrowing is rational for loans that will be repaid within an individual's lifetime by his or her own earnings; ethical questions come up, however, concerning loans of longer duration. Policymakers today must decide whether to borrow money to invest in projects that will have benefits for generations to come.

The debt incurred may have to be repaid by future generations. The question is whether it is ethical to force generations of the future to pay the debts incurred in the present. The issue is less troublesome if the debt is incurred for the benefit of those who will repay it; for example, in the case of research that benefits future generations. It is more troublesome if the debt is incurred to increase standards of living for those currently alive. Borrowing is a way of forcing one's children to finance one's own well-being.

TECHNOLOGY AND THE ENVIRONMENT

Investment in technology poses other questions. The type of investment made will determine the types of jobs available in the future. Increasing sophistication of technology creates the possibility of a small number of skilled, high-paying jobs existing alongside a large number of unskilled, low-paying jobs. Technological advance thus presents the possibility of creating a technological elite at the expense of the majority of workers.

Many methods of producing goods involve the exhaustion of nonrenewable resources such as oil and metals. Any of these resources used today simply will not be available for the people of the future. In addition, production processes often involve pollution of the environment. There is a clear trade-off between producing more today (possibly by producing through processes that are cheaper in dollar terms but use more resources or pollute more) and being able to produce more tomorrow.

A. J. Sobczak

FURTHER READING

Chapman, Audrey R., and Mark S. Frankel, eds. *Designing Our Descendants: The Promises and Perils of Genetic Modifications*. Baltimore: Johns Hopkins University Press, 2003.

Dobson, Andrew, ed. *Fairness and Futurity: Essays on Sustainability and Social Justice*. New York: Oxford University Press, 1999.

Gabor, Dennis. *The Mature Society*. New York: Praeger, 1972.

Griffith, William B. "Trusteeship: A Practical Option for Realizing Our Obligations to Future Generations?" In *Moral and Political Reasoning in Environmental Practice*, edited by Andrew Light and Avner de-Shalit. Cambridge, Mass.: MIT Press, 2003.

Hine, Thomas. *Facing Tomorrow: What the Future Has Been, What the Future Can Be*. New York: Alfred A. Knopf, 1991.

Inayatullah, Sohail, and Susan Leggett, eds. *Transforming Communication: Technology, Sustainability, and Future Generations*. Westport, Conn.: Praeger, 2002.

Jungk, Robert. *The Everyman Project: Resources for a Humane Future*. New York: Liveright, 1976.

Rosenbaum, Robert A. *The Public Issues Handbook: A Guide for the Concerned Citizen*. Westport, Conn.: Greenwood Press, 1983.

Schumacher, Ernst Friedrich. *Small Is Beautiful*. New York: Harper & Row, 1973.

SEE ALSO: Environmental ethics; Famine; Future generations; Genetic engineering; Lifeboat ethics; Politics; Public interest; Technology.

G

Gaia hypothesis

DEFINITION: Theory holding that the earth is a living entity whose biosphere is self-regulating and is able to maintain planetary health by controlling its chemical and physical environment

DATE: Developed between 1969 and 1979

TYPE OF ETHICS: Environmental ethics

SIGNIFICANCE: The Gaia hypothesis creates a model of earthly existence that is fundamentally biocentric rather than anthropocentric. Such a model might be seen ethically to require the maintenance of balanced relationships between humans and other forms of life. It might also be seen, however, as an indication that humans are no more responsible for their environmental effects than are any other organisms, since the system as a whole actively maintains itself independently of its individual living components.

While working on a project that would send a space probe to determine whether life exists on Mars, British geochemist and inventor James Lovelock theorized that one could answer the question by observing the activity in the planet's lower atmosphere. Lovelock developed his idea and came to recognize its implications through discussions with U.S. biologist Lynn Margulis. His thinking culminated in the book *Gaia: A New Look at Life on Earth* (1979), which presented his hypothesis that life and its natural environment have coevolved and that the lower atmosphere provides the raw materials for life to exist on the planet. The original title of the theory was the Biocybernetic Universal System Tendency (BUST), but novelist William Golding suggested that the theory be named for Gaia, the Greek Earth goddess who is also called Ge (from which root the words "geography" and "geology" are derived).

Although the Gaia hypothesis did not generate much scientific activity until the late 1980's, it was supported by both industrialists (who believed that it supplied a justification for pollution, since the earth could theoretically counteract any harmful effects) and some environmentalists. Other environmentalists, however, believe that the theory argues against any attempt by humans to try to correct environmental degradation.

Sandra L. Christensen

SEE ALSO: Biodiversity; Deep ecology; Dominion over nature, human; Environmental ethics; Exploitation.

Gandhi, Mohandas K.

IDENTIFICATION: Indian nationalist and spiritual leader

BORN: October 2, 1869, Porbandar, India

DIED: January 30, 1948, New Delhi, India

TYPE OF ETHICS: Modern history

SIGNIFICANCE: Gandhi lead the ultimately successful resistance to British colonial rule in India. His nonviolent methods and unwavering commitment, in accordance with the ethics of the *Bhagavadgītā*, inspired millions of people around the world, including Martin Luther King, Jr., and many other practitioners of nonviolence.

Gandhi incorporated the teachings of the *Bhagavadgītā*, a Hindu scripture, and the Sermon on the Mount of the Christian New Testament into a philosophy of nonviolence that he used as an ethical standard. Gandhi's message to the world was that nonviolence is truth and love in action. The ethics of the *Bhagavadgītā*, which Gandhi followed and which he urged others to follow, held that one has a duty to fight against evil or injustice by persuading one's opponents to do good. One should not hate a person who does evil, because human beings are basically good. One should hate the action that the person performs and, through noncooperation, resist that ac-

Mohandas K. Gandhi (right) with fellow nationalist leader and future prime minister Jawaharlal Nehru in 1946, the year before India became independent. (AP/Wide World Photos)

tion. If one is ready to experience suffering, eventually the evildoer will realize the injustice and make an attempt to change it. One must hold on to truth no matter what. Gandhi's way of life is a discipline that must be practiced. Gandhi used the term *satyagraha*, or truth-force, which is sometimes translated as passive resistance, for this method of nonviolence.

Krishna Mallick

SEE ALSO: *Bhagavadgītā*; Civil disobedience; Hindu ethics; King, Martin Luther, Jr.; Nonviolence; Pacifism; Poona Pact.

Gangs

DEFINITION: Structured subcultures of individuals organized primarily by socioeconomic and ethnic status and promoting actions that deviate from the laws and morality of the culture

TYPE OF ETHICS: Personal and social ethics

SIGNIFICANCE: Gangs openly advocate and commit moral transgressions up to and including rape and murder. These acts, however, often take place within the context of a positive moral code that values traits such as loyalty, commitment, responsibility, and self-sacrifice for the good of the group.

In the eyes of many, the violence and drug-related activities of many late-twentieth century gangs appear to be anything but ethical; however, as Plato pointed out in *Republic*, even the individuals in a gang of thieves must cooperate and be just among themselves if they are to achieve their ends. Many researchers on twentieth century gangs have made this same point. For example, Frederic Thrasher, in his landmark study *The Gang: A Study of 1,313 Gangs in Chicago* (1927), claims that the members of gangs are highly committed to protecting each other, and James Vigil, in his article "Group Processes and Street Identity: Adolescent Chicano Gang Members" (1988), argues that gang members' sense of self is motivated and affirmed by their commitment to the gang.

The nature of this commitment and the way in which it is motivated have received much attention, but there are two primary interpretations. Some scholars argue that people join gangs on the basis of rational self-interest. They join in order to achieve goals that they believe they would not otherwise be able to accomplish, such as acquiring money, sex, friends, and a sense of power and security. Others argue that individuals join gangs primarily as a means of securing a sense of self, or as a way of expressing who they are. Despite these differences, most scholars agree that gangs develop and emerge on the margins of traditional mainstream culture and that they often mimic and mock that culture. The reason for this, as Thrasher has argued, is that gangs generally appear in what he calls a "zone in transition." That is, gangs usually surface in communities that are removed from the stability of both urban central business districts and working-class neighborhoods.

More recent research, however, has shown that gangs do thrive in some neighborhoods or places that are stable; as Vigil argues, however, it is true that individuals are more likely to join gangs when they come from an environment that suffers what he calls "multiple marginality." Vigil claims that family, school, work, the ethnic majority of the culture, and other mainstream institutions and values are each elements with which an individual gang member, like a geographical "zone in transition" that is only marginally assimilated by stable urban centers and suburban neighborhoods, may be only marginally associated. The more an individual is marginally related to one or more of these elements, the more "multiple" is that person's marginality and the more "stressors" that person will experience. It is as a response to these stressors that the values and ethics of a gang, and the marginal and deviant nature of these values and ethics, are to be understood.

As a response to the stressors of "multiple marginality," individuals who join a gang attempt to compensate for these marginal attachments. The result is that these individuals tend to overcompensate. For example, adolescents who join gangs often have had little or no caretaking from their parents, the father in particular, and these juveniles overcompensate for this lack by adopting stereotyped and oversimplified masculine values that honor being tough and violent. In addition, individuals who join gangs also attempt to compensate for the ambiguous and weak sense of self that results from being marginally attached to those institutions that can give them a sense of who they are. By joining gangs, they overcompensate for this weak sense of self by identifying solely with the gang. Sigmund Freud discussed this phenomenon in *Group Psychology and the Analysis of the Ego* (1921), arguing that a result of this phenomenon is that other groups appear as threats not only to gang members' territory but also to their very sense of self. This explains why gang members often say that "you're either with the group or against it"; this, in turn, explains why real or imagined enemies are such an extremely important focal point for gangs.

Gangs and Self-Identity

Since a gang member's self-identity is defined in terms of the group and other groups are seen as a threat to this identity, it is not surprising that most of what is valued and honored by gang members concerns the ability to defend, violently if necessary, the

gang and its territory. Being and acting tough, Vigil argues, is the "focal value" of most gangs of the late twentieth century. One must be able to protect and defend the gang and its members. In return, one will also be protected, but only, as many researchers have noted, if one proves that one is dependable and loyal to the gang.

The morality of the gang, therefore, although in many respects deviating greatly from mainstream society, is nevertheless a morality—a morality that can be most clearly understood if placed in the context of the group. To this extent, the morality of gangs could be given a relativistic interpretation: That is, as Ruth Benedict argued in "Anthropology and the Abnormal" (1934) and Gilbert Harman later argued in "Moral Relativism Defended" (1975), moral claims are about the practices of the sociocultural group (for example, a gang) and nothing else. The moral claims of gangs, likewise, such as those that value violence, commitment, dependability, and the development of a "tough" character, are themselves expressive of the group dynamics and processes of the gang and its members' "marginal" relationship to traditional culture and morality.

Jeff Bell

Further Reading

Benedict, Ruth. "Anthropology and the Abnormal." *Journal of General Psychology* 10 (January, 1934): 58-82.

Freud, Sigmund. *Group Psychology and the Analysis of the Ego*. Translated by James Strachey. New York: W. W. Norton, 1959.

Harman, Gilbert. "Moral Relativism Defended." *Philosophical Review* 84 (January, 1975): 3-22.

Roleff, Tamara L., ed. *What Encourages Gang Behavior?* San Diego, Calif.: Greenhaven Press, 2002.

Thrasher, Frederic M. *The Gang: A Study of 1,313 Gangs in Chicago*. 1927. 2d rev. ed. Chicago: University of Chicago Press, 1960.

Vigil, James. "Group Processes and Street Identity: Adolescent Chicano Gang Members." *Ethos* 16, no. 4 (December, 1988): 421-445.

See also: Anthropological ethics; Character; Ethnocentrism; Loyalty.

Gault, In re

THE EVENT: U.S. Supreme Court decision holding that juvenile defendants have a right in criminal proceedings to due process of law

DATE: Ruling made on May 15, 1967

TYPE OF ETHICS: Children's rights

SIGNIFICANCE: The majority opinion in *Gault* supports the proposition that juveniles are as entitled as adults to a fair hearing guaranteed by basic procedural guarantees and evidentiary rules.

In re Gault was the result of the arrest of Gerald Gault in 1965 for making a lewd telephone call to a neighbor. Gault, who was then fifteen years old, was on probation for an earlier minor offense. On the basis of police rumor about Gault as well as statements elicited from him in the absence of his parents or his lawyer, and without evidence or hearing, the juvenile judge found Gault to be delinquent. He was committed to a state industrial school until his eighteenth birthday. Gault's appeal to the Arizona Supreme Court was unsuccessful, and he brought the case to the U.S. Supreme Court. The Court decided by a 7-2 vote that juveniles are entitled to notice of charges, right to counsel, right to confrontation and cross-examination of witnesses, privilege against self-incrimination, a transcript of the proceedings, and appellate review. The majority argued that these minimal guarantees assure fairness without unduly interfering with any of the benefits of less formal procedures for juveniles.

Robert Jacobs

SEE ALSO: Bill of Rights, U.S.; Children's rights; Due process; *Goss v. Lopez*; Supreme Court, U.S.

Gay rights

DEFINITION: Rights of homosexuals to enjoy the same constitutional protections as other members of society

TYPE OF ETHICS: Sex and gender issues

SIGNIFICANCE: As American society has become more tolerant of diversity, members of the gay minority have gradually received legal redress to the various forms of discrimination that they have long endured.

Throughout American history, and indeed throughout most of world history, homophobia, the fear and hatred of homosexuals, forced gay people to suppress their natural feelings and engage in deceptions to mask their homosexuality. Attempts by gays to become heterosexuals generally proved futile. The American Psychiatric Association has established that people do not choose their sexual orientation.

Societal pressures that gay people "straighten up" have forced many homosexuals to suppress their natural sexual orientation to the point of attempting to use heterosexual marriage as a smoke screen for their own sexuality. This practice raises significant ethical questions because it often brings suffering to both the marriage partners of gay people and their children. Smoke screen marriages frequently encounter insuperable problems that lead to their collapse, raising ethical questions about the damage done to all concerned.

THE CIVIL RIGHTS ACT OF 1964

The U.S. Congress passed the Civil Rights Act of 1964 largely to ensure that members of racial minorities would receive equal treatment under the law. At the same time, however, it also prohibited discrimination in employment, housing, and public accommodations against all American citizens based on their gender, ethnic background, or religious affiliation. Since the law's passage, many conservatives and their legislators have attempted to exclude sexual orientation from the protections of the Civil Rights Act. Commenting on the scope of the Civil Rights Act, ethicist Richard Mohr has demolished most of the arguments against extending to gay people the same equal protections that members of other minorities have received under the Civil Rights Act. Such exclusion, he argues, is ethically unconscionable on two grounds. First, if homosexuality is something one cannot control because its base is genetic or psychological, being homosexual is comparable to being a member of a disadvantaged racial, gender, or ethnic minority. On the other hand, if, as others have contended, being homosexual is a matter of choice, then being homosexual is analogous to choosing to belong to a certain religion—which is also constitutionally protected.

Legal decisions affecting the civil rights of homosexual Americans have gradually concluded that the constitutional protections accorded to all Americans must, on logical and ethical grounds, be accorded to gays. If gay Americans are, as a class, denied their constitutional rights, then similar rights granted to other Americans are seriously compromised. Laws—federal, state, or local—that abridge these guarantees undermine the equal protection clause of the U.S. Constitution.

STONEWALL INN RIOTS

A turning point in the movement for gay rights occurred in New York City on June 27, 1969. On that date, New York City police officers raided the Stonewall Inn, a gay bar in Greenwich Village. At that time, gay bars were routinely raided but only small numbers of people were arrested. Most arrestees were quickly released on bond and had the morals charges made against them dismissed. However, the police kept records of these charges, and those records were sources of serious concern to the people who were arrested. Both the arrests and the police records seemed to be unethical violations of the right of all citizens to enjoy freedom of association without having to fear being arrested and face the possibility of embarrassing and possibly damaging future public exposure.

When the police arrived at the Stonewall Inn on that 1969 date, gay people at the bar resisted arrest and brawls broke out. The ensuing riots focused national attention on the right of homosexuals to enjoy equal treatment under the law and became an enduring symbol of the struggle for equal rights.

EMPLOYMENT ISSUES

Before passage of the Civil Rights Act of 1964 and subsequent federal rights laws, the status of homosexuals in the workplace was tenuous. Employees suspected of being gay were often fired without cause. Many people were denied employment merely because they appeared to be gay. The federal government did not hire known homosexuals on the rationale that gay employees might be subjected to blackmail that could compromise national security. Gays passing as straight had limited job security.

Gays were also barred from serving in the armed forces of the United States until 1994, when a policy nicknamed "Don't ask, don't tell" was instituted in the military as a compromise measure intended to afford gays equal protection while placating irate conservative groups similar to those who had protested

loudly in the late 1940's and early 1950's when the armed forces were racially desegregated.

The argument that gay employees might be subjected to blackmail is circular and illogical. If it is unnecessary for people to hide their natural sexual orientations, the danger of their being blackmailed would be eliminated. Arguments that morale in the armed forces would decline if openly gay people were to serve in the military were as unconvincing as the anti-integration arguments advanced four decades earlier, during the Civil Rights movement. Like all employees, gays are expected to behave ethically and circumspectly in the workplace. The removal of employment barriers to gays has not led to moral disintegration within the workplace, so there is no reason to suppose that allowing openly gay people in the military would lead to moral disintegration there.

LANDMARK COURT DECISIONS

In 1986, the case of *Bowers v. Hardwick* reached the U.S. Supreme Court. The case stemmed from the arrest in Atlanta of a man named Michael Hardwick by a police officer who went to his home to serve a warrant. When the officer arrived, he found Hardwick engaged in oral sex with another man in the privacy of his own bedroom. The officer arrested both men under an 1816 law prohibiting oral sex between two people regardless of gender. In a 5-4 decision, the Supreme Court ruled that Georgia had the right to prohibit private sexual acts that were construed as contrary to community standards of morality. Ten years earlier, the Court had ruled that the state of Virginia had the right to make sodomy between consenting adults a felony.

The Court had historically supported even ethically questionable state laws depriving groups of citizens of their right to equal treatment under the law. However, seventeen years after *Bowers v. Hardwick*, the Court heard the similar case of *Lawrence v. Texas*, which arose from the arrest of two men in Texas under an antisodomy law. When this case reached the Supreme Court in 2003, the Court voted six to three to uphold the right of consenting adults to have sex in private, thereby overriding the Texas law. This decision marked a victory for gay rights.

GAY MARRIAGE

In his dissenting opinion in *Lawrence v. Texas*, Justice Antonin Scalia warned that the decision might lead to gay marriage. Court actions in several states indicated that such a movement was already underway. In 1993, Hawaii's supreme court had reversed a lower court ban on gay marriage; however, in 1999, the state's legislature passed a law banning same-sex marriage. Vermont began recognizing same-sex unions in 2000 but stopped short of calling such unions "marriages." In 2003, the Massachusetts supreme court, by a narrow vote, declared the state's refusal to grant marriage licenses to gay couples a violation of its constitution. The court ordered marriage licenses to be granted to gay couples applying for them at the expiration of a 180-day waiting period, during which the state assembly would have an opportunity to enact legislation regarding gay marriage.

The issue of gay marriage is highly controversial. Gay advocates contend that gay people should have the legal and ethical right to choose the partners with whom they wish to make lifelong commitments. Indeed, gay marriage might bring to gay relationships a desirable stability. The legal ramifications of legaliz-ing gay marriage are important. Legally sanctioned marriages would enable gay partners to have access to and make decisions for seriously ill partners, adopt children, and enjoy other legal benefits that heterosexual married couples enjoy. The ethical issue involved in this controversy is whether governments can contravene the rights of adults to select their own marriage partners.

The public outcry against gay marriage has been strong. For example, Senate majority leader Bill Frist vowed to support a constitutional amendment that would define marriage as a union only between a man and a woman. Concurring with Frist's statement, in 2003, President George W. Bush announced that his administration was exploring legal means to block gay marriage.

Almost simultaneous with Bush's statement was a Vatican edict declaring gay marriage unacceptable to Roman Catholics on scriptural grounds. The edict also called the adoption of children by gays a form of child abuse. In a nation such as the United States in

---

Arguments for and Against Same-Sex Marriage

Arguments for	*Arguments against*
Banning same-sex marriage discriminates against gays and lesbians.	Homosexual acts are immoral, and same-sex relationships are open to greater health risks.
Same-sex marriages would benefit societies and individuals in the same ways that heterosexual marriages do.	Marriage is a fundamental and unchangeable institution that is traditionally between persons of opposite sex.
Legalizing same-sex marriage does not hurt heterosexuals.	Allowing same-sex marriages will damage the institution of traditional heterosexual marriage.
Allowing same-sex marriages may benefit the institution of marriage.	Same-sex relationships are less stable and less faithful than opposite-sex relationships.
Banning same-sex marriage restricts freedom of choice and labels homosexuals as second-class citizens.	Society has an interest in promoting marriage for procreation and child-rearing, and same-sex couples cannot have children.
Same-sex marriage would benefit the children involved.	Same-sex parenting is not as good for children as traditional family parenting and may influence children to adopt homosexual lifestyles.
Banning same-sex marriage mixes church and state in an illegitimate way.	Marriage is defined by scripture and tradition as involving one man and one woman and is a religious sacrament

which church and state are separate, religious arguments against gay marriage, although widespread, are considered irrelevant by many people who interpret the law more liberally than religious conservatives do.

THE CONTINUING STRUGGLE

With every advance made to ensure equal rights for gays, a backlash develops that questions the wisdom and ethics of enacting and enforcing legislation to protect a minority that has traditionally been reviled by large numbers of mainstream Americans. A major ethical issue is one of minority rights, which have generally been protected by law.

Homophobic attitudes have, however, begun to moderate. Meanwhile, society is being forced to address the basic question of whether legally and ethically any segment of American society can be accorded unequal treatment under the law simply on the basis of who or what its members happen to be.

R. Baird Shuman

FURTHER READING

Andryszewski, Tricia. *Gay Rights*. Brookfield, Conn.: Twenty-First Century Books, 2000. Directed at adolescent readers, this book considers such issues as gays in the military, same-sex marriage, and religion.

Bull, Chris. "Justice Served." *The Advocate* (August 19, 2003): 35-38. Brief but thorough discussion of the Supreme Court's decision in *Lawrence v. Texas*.

Durham, Martin. *The Christian Right, the Far Right, and the Boundaries of American Conservatism*. Manchester, England: Manchester University Press, 2000. A comprehensive presentation of conservative antihomosexual arguments.

Feldblum, Chai. "Gay Rights." In *The Rehnquist Court: Judicial Activism on the Right*. Edited by Herman Schwartz. New York: Hill & Wang, 2002. Study tracing the conservative Rehnquist court's gradual shift toward support of gay rights.

Galas, Judith C. *Gay Rights*. San Diego, Calif.: Lucent Books, 1996. Directed at adolescent readers, this book considers family rights, discrimination in the workplace, and legislation affecting gays.

Kranz, Rachel, and Tim Cusick. *Gay Rights*. New York: Facts On File, 2000. Overview of the gay rights movement through the years.

Mohr, Richard. "Gay Rights." In *Contemporary Moral Issues: Diversity and Consensus*. Edited by Lawrence M. Hinman. Upper Saddle River, N.J.: Prentice Hall, 1996. Perhaps the most closely reasoned argument questioning the ethics of gay discrimination.

SEE ALSO: Civil rights and liberties; *Dronenburg v. Zech*; Hate crime and hate speech; Homophobia; Homosexuality; Men's movement; National Gay and Lesbian Task Force; Stonewall Inn riots.

Gender bias

DEFINITION: Discrimination in thought or action based on cultural demarcation of gender or sex

TYPE OF ETHICS: Sex and gender issues

SIGNIFICANCE: Discrimination based on sex or gender is an expression of ethical values. Many actions that may appear value-neutral with regard to gender may actually be found to contain implicit biases that are based on assumptions of gender inequality within philosophical foundations.

"Gender bias" may describe discrimination against either men or women. In practice, however, it is mostly a prejudice against women, typically because of implicit philosophical assumptions. Gender bias is also not merely a "battle of the sexes," that is, men discriminating against women, although such discrimination does occur. Rather it is a structural phenomenon of a patriarchal hegemony that empowers men and the masculine in which both men and women participate and help to perpetuate.

ORIGINS OF GENDER BIAS

Gender bias has its roots in sexual differences. Distinctions between "sex" and "gender" originate within feminist thought as a way to indicate that cultural values are overlaid upon sex, which is often seen as natural. In this way, some feminist thought argues that patriarchy is based upon prejudicial views of women, rather than upon any essential nature of the female sex. Taking this argument a step further, Judith Butler famously argued, in *Gender Trouble* (1990), that the many ways in which people can conceptualize sex—such as anatomy, hormones, chemicals, or genes—speak to the cultural determination of even the very concept of sex. As a cultural determination, there is an essential valuing attached to differences, conceived of in terms of sex and/or gender, such that sexual difference is never without an ethical determination, though this determination is often hidden by the implicit ethico-political valuing within metaphysical foundations.

Sexual difference has been depicted throughout Western philosophy in an oppositional manner, beginning with the Pythagorean table of opposites. Along with the setting out of difference, which in itself is not necessarily biased, the Pythagorean table aligned male with "good" and female with "bad," thereby affixing ethical values upon sexual differences. Throughout the course of Western thought this correlation has been taken up in various extensions of this dichotomy, including the alignment of maleness with form, reason, subject, mind, rationality, culture, public, freedom, justice, and the universal. Conversely, femaleness has been associated with matter, emotion, object, body, intuition, nature, private, subjection, love, and the particular. The alignment here is not a description of the behavior of men and women, but rather a description of the essences of femaleness, that is, what it means to be a woman. In its description, then, the pronouncement becomes a prescription, or how one ought to act in accordance with one's essence.

Reviewing the metaphysical categories reveals the cultural bias against women, as the values associated with femaleness are subordinate in importance and even denigrated. These ethically weighted dichotomies are present in the philosophy of nearly every thinker of the traditional Western philosophical canon, including Aristotle, Saint Augustine, Thomas Aquinas, René Descartes, David Hume, Jean-Jacques Rousseau, and Immanuel Kant. These philosophers have integrated this bias into the ethical and political systems that act to structure both past and present societies such that the patriarchal hegemony that marks contemporary life has its roots so firmly entrenched that the bias appears "natural." For example, the idea that women's place and work is in the home is an expression of the metaphysical alignment of femaleness with a lack of reason, with which to engage in the public affairs of the civic world. This is one instance of gender bias that manifests in the inequity of women in the public workforce, including the far

lesser number of women in public office than of men.

Similarly, contemporary sexual objectification of women finds its origin in the alignment of femaleness with bodies and objects, despite the fact that men too have bodies. However, set in opposition to the mind—the source of knowledge and judgment—the body takes on a denigrated status, an object to be captured by the mind; that is, by men. One consequence of this type of thinking can be found in the modern global sex industry that enslaves more women and girls than were enslaved throughout the earlier history of world slavery, including slavery in the United States. The lack of political action taken to remedy this situation is at least in part another indication of gender bias; the status of women and girls is given little import. These examples help to demonstrate that the ethical phenomena of gender bias rest in the value-laden appointment of metaphysical categories.

VIOLENCE

The concrete ethical ramifications of gender bias are both deeply imbedded and ubiquitous. Worldwide, women and girls are subject to disproportionately greater incidents of violence, including rape, physical and sexual abuse, female genital mutilation, female infanticide, and dowry murder. Violence is also enacted against lesbians, the transgendered, and those who fail to exhibit traditional gender roles.

Violence perpetrated against men because of their homosexuality or their failure to act according to traditional masculine roles is a form of gender bias that discriminates against men. However, it also acts to maintain gender bias against women: Men are punished for exhibiting womanly—thus demeaning—qualities, while women are punished not only for exhibiting masculine qualities but also because this is an indication of a failure to serve the needs of men in some way. Globally, women lack power over their sexuality, as seen in forced marriages and forced sexual servitude in the sex industry, absence of resources, and access to fertility options and to health and medical aid. Economic inequity is manifest in women's lower wages, unpaid work, hostile work environments stemming from sexual harassment, and lower literacy rates. Politically, women's particular needs are not represented to a full degree of legality, nor are women represented in political institutions in proportion to the female populace.

While these facts of gender bias are known, the subject is rarely discussed as a philosophical and ethical concern. Rather, the problem often is taken either as belonging to the private realm—thus re-inscribing the very metaphysical origin of gender bias—or as a problem of cultural difference when analyzing global discrimination of women. In both cases, the ethical import of gender bias is not addressed at the structural level; thus, discrimination against women solely because of the very fact that they are women continues. Ethical systems are designed to address the treatment of humanity on both the individual and societal levels, making gender bias an indispensable component to any ethical discussion.

Maria Cimitile

FURTHER READING

Beauvoir, Simone de. *The Second Sex*. Translated by H. M. Parshley. New York: Vintage Books, 1952.

Butler, Judith. *Gender Trouble: Feminism and the Subversion of Identity*. New York: Routledge, 1990.

Irigaray, Luce. *Speculum of the Other Woman*. Translated by Gillian Gill. Ithaca, N.Y.: Cornell University Press, 1985.

Lloyd, Genevieve. *The Man of Reason: "Male" and "Female" in Western Philosophy*. Minneapolis: University of Minnesota Press, 1986.

Rooney, Phyllis. "Gendered Reason: Sex Metaphor and Conceptions of Reason." *Hypatia* 6, no. 2 (Summer, 1991): 77-103.

SEE ALSO: Equal pay for equal work; Equal Rights Amendment; Feminist ethics; Inequality; Title IX; Women's ethics; Women's liberation movement.

Generosity

DEFINITION: Magnanimity; freedom in giving
TYPE OF ETHICS: Personal and social ethics
SIGNIFICANCE: Generosity is thought of as a virtue, but one that can be self-destructive if taken to extremes.

A virtue can be briefly defined as a form of moral excellence, goodness, or righteousness. Generosity clearly fits into this definition. The term "generosity" is often used interchangeably with benevolence, altruism, charity, or kindness, and it is linked to the concepts of sympathy and forgiveness. All these virtues are associated with giving, but each is distinct.

There are four prerequisite conditions that distinguish generosity from the other virtues that are associated with giving. Generosity must arise from an awareness of circumstances, it must be based on a desire to benefit the recipient and be free of any other underlying motive, what is given must be of value to the giver, and what is given must be more than would be considered necessary under the circumstances.

In addressing the issue of awareness, Elizabeth Pybus states, "Being aware of the world around us is necessary for us to exercise our agency well and helpfully towards other people." In other words, those people (agents) who lack awareness of the needs of others cannot be generous.

Lack of awareness takes different forms. There is simple want of information, which, once it is provided, promotes generous behavior. Charitable organizations base their appeals on educating the public about the needs of others in order to stimulate contributions. There may be a lack of awareness because of a high degree of self-interest. Very young children exhibit such a lack of awareness. So do people with sociopathic personalities. Regardless of the cause, the result is the same. Without awareness of the circumstances of others, the agent cannot express generosity. This, then, lends a certain weight of moral obligation to awareness.

It is true that one cannot know everything. Individuals and societies are morally obligated, however, to try to be informed about the circumstances that others are experiencing. It can be very difficult to obtain information about some topics, especially when there is an organized effort to suppress truth or to spread disinformation. In these cases, it is even more important than usual to be aggressive in searching out the facts. Lack of awareness allows Holocausts to happen. While most situations that people face are not that extreme, the premise is the same: People are morally obligated to be as aware as possible.

Generosity is an other-oriented behavior. It flows freely from goodwill without the weight of other obligations. It must not be linked with motives such as reciprocity or duty. The only motive that can be involved is the desire to benefit the recipient. This does not mean, however, that all self-interest must be disregarded. To value the other above the self in a benevolent act is not generosity but altruism.

Generosity requires that there be no motive of personal gain. That is, one who gives must not expect anything in return. Generosity precludes even a minimal degree of the attitude, "You scratch my back, and I'll scratch yours." Likewise, there must not be any expectation on the part of the agent of gratitude or recognition from the recipient for generous acts. While the agent may derive pleasure from giving, the anticipation of that pleasure cannot be the motive for the act, or it will not be generosity.

To give because one feels obligated is not generosity but charity. Generosity involves free choice, and the decision can be based on rationality or emotion. The campaign presented by a charitable organization is factual, but its appeal is emotional. Some people respond out of duty, because it is morally correct to give to those in need, and they will feel guilty if they do not give. Others give out of generosity because they decide that they want to, because they are persuaded by the facts or are moved by sympathy.

What a person gives is an important factor in generosity. It does not necessarily have to be anything material. It must, however, be something of value to the giver. Time is quite valuable to most people, and those who are given the gift of someone's time have often been given a treasure. There are those, however, who feel that they have much spare time, and therefore to give it may not mean very much. They may choose to use that time to share their particular talents. This, then, could be an act of generosity, if they did it purely for the benefit of the recipient and not just to fill up their hours with activity. Although it is usually so, what is given does not necessarily have to be valuable to the recipient. Its value in terms of generosity is in the intent of the giver.

In order for an act to be considered generosity, what is given should exceed what might be considered reasonable under the circumstances. This factor can be viewed from the context of either the giver or the situation. If two people—one wealthy and one earning minimum wage—each decided to donate a day's wages to some cause, the one with low income might be considered to be giving more than was required by his financial circumstances, and that contribution would be considered truly generous. In another situation, if a person's shoes were worn out and

someone gave him three new pairs, that also would be an act of generosity.

James Wallace states that a virtue such as generosity tends "to foster good feelings based on mutual good will." In some cases, however, the recipient may not appreciate a generous act in his behalf and may even be harmed rather than benefited. These results may not be possible to anticipate. If the agent is acting in the recipient's best interest and with compassionate awareness, however, the generosity that is offered is authentic.

Marcella T. Joy

FURTHER READING

Attfield, Robin. *A Theory of Value and Obligation.* New York: Croom Helm, 1987.

Berking, Helmuth. *Sociology of Giving.* Translated by Patrick Camiller. Thousand Oaks, Calif.: Sage, 1999.

Butler, Joseph. *"Fifteen Sermons Preached at the Rolls Chapel" and "A Dissertation upon the Nature of Virtue."* London: G. Bell, 1964.

Pybus, Elizabeth. *Human Goodness: Generosity and Courage.* London: Harvester Wheatsheaf, 1991.

Spaemann, Robert. *Basic Moral Concepts.* Translated by T. J. Armstrong. New York: Routledge, 1989.

Wallace, James. *Virtues and Vices.* Ithaca, N.Y.: Cornell University Press, 1978.

SEE ALSO: Altruism; Benevolence; Charity; Duty; Integrity; Moral responsibility; Social justice and responsibility; Supererogation.

Genetic counseling

DEFINITION: Identification, explanation, and discussion of deleterious genes in potential parents

DATE: Practiced began around 1960; formally defined in 1975

TYPE OF ETHICS: Bioethics

SIGNIFICANCE: Genetic counseling raises serious ethical questions in clinical practice, since reproductive decisions are central to conventional morality and the identification of inherited defects carries the possibility of discrimination.

Although it has roots in the eugenics movements of the early twentieth century, which have been justly criticized as being hampered by imperfect understanding of inheritance and tainted by racial and class prejudice, genetic counseling relies on landmark genetic discoveries of the 1950's—the elucidation of the structure of DNA and of the specific biochemical bases for a number of inherited disorders, including Tay-Sachs syndrome, sickle-cell anemia, and hemophilia. Beginning in 1960, specialists in medical centers began advising couples who had already had a child with such a disorder or had close relatives who were affected. In 1975, the American Society of Human Genetics published a formal definition and guidelines on genetic counseling. The availability of these services and the number of conditions amenable to testing have risen steadily, although access is not universal even in the developed world. Most severe genetic diseases are recessive; carriers with one defective gene may or may not be identifiable. Gross chromosomal abnormalities and some metabolic disorders can be diagnosed *in utero* through amniocentesis.

U.S. government guidelines for genetic testing and counseling caution against using the process for perceived societal good and stress that the impetus for testing and reproductive decisions must come from the affected individuals, without outside compulsion. Nevertheless, many people perceive that a genetically abnormal individual places a burden on society and believe that it is immoral to bear a defective child; this attitude is seen by others as providing a justification for abandoning the handicapped. Voluntarily abstaining from conceiving children is morally acceptable to most people in Western society, but objections to abortion are widespread. Some heritable abnormalities are commonest among small, inbred ethnic minorities, in which case refraining from having children and marrying outside the group, the most prudent courses of action from a medical standpoint, have genocidal overtones. Not all genetic disorders are equally debilitating, and it is uncertain whether genetic counseling is appropriate for less-severe conditions. Finally, there are many disorders (alcoholism, for example) that may be at least partially heritable, whose genetic basis is unknown, and for which the scientific basis for genetic counseling is tenuous.

Tests exist for some genetically transmitted con-

ditions (for example, certain cancers) that manifest themselves late in life, and more are continually being developed. Although knowing of their existence is helpful to medical professionals, there is real concern that this information could be used to deny employment or insurance coverage to those who are affected. Maintaining confidentiality and respecting the rights of individuals are paramount in genetic counseling.

Martha Sherwood-Pike

SEE ALSO: Abortion; Bioethics; Birth defects; Eugenics; Genetic engineering; Genetic testing; Genocide and democide; Intelligence testing.

Genetic engineering

DEFINITION: Branch of genetics that manipulates genetic material in living organisms, animal or vegetable

TYPE OF ETHICS: Bioethics

SIGNIFICANCE: As genetic engineering rushes toward eliminating genetic ills, it has produced such substances as industrial enzymes, the human growth hormone, and insulin and made possible the cloning of vertebrates and other sophisticated but ethically controversial procedures.

Long practiced by animal breeders and botanists, genetic engineering entered a new phase in the late 1950's when Francis Crick, James Watson, and Maurice Wilkins unraveled the mystery of the double-helix structure of deoxyribonucleic acid, commonly called DNA, paving the way for research that seems almost a product of science fiction. The adult human genome contains approximately three billion chemical bases and some one hundred thousand genes, each with its function yet each containing the same DNA. The DNA from a single cell found in a person's saliva on the lip of a glass can identify with almost absolute certainty the person to whom it belongs. Every cell in a person's body possesses identical DNA. Every living organism has unique DNA except for identical organisms—in humans, identical twins. As the mysteries of DNA have continued to unfold, they have generated myriad ethical questions about the uses of genetic engineering.

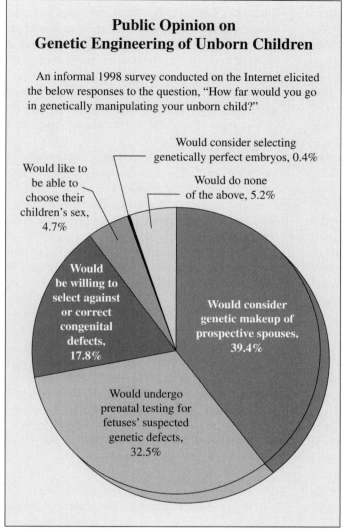

Public Opinion on Genetic Engineering of Unborn Children

An informal 1998 survey conducted on the Internet elicited the below responses to the question, "How far would you go in genetically manipulating your unborn child?"

Would consider selecting genetically perfect embryos, 0.4%

Would like to be able to choose their children's sex, 4.7%

Would do none of the above, 5.2%

Would be willing to select against or correct congenital defects, 17.8%

Would consider genetic makeup of prospective spouses, 39.4%

Would undergo prenatal testing for fetuses' suspected genetic defects, 32.5%

Source: Moms Online.

FUNDAMENTAL CONCERNS

Many religious organizations and their members actively resist supporting research in genetics and have expressed alarm that genetic engineering tampers with nature in indefensible ways. Contradictions underlie many such arguments. For example, if farmers turn rocky woodlands into cultivated fields in which crops can grow, are they not meddling with nature? Few would contest farmers' rights to cultivate land on a basis analogous to arguments objecting to genetic engineering.

Nevertheless, considerable controversy surrounds such matters as the use of stem cells in genetic re-search. Stem cells are harvested from human embryos, most of which have the potential of developing into humans but that exist unused in the freezers of fertility clinics. When a woman wishing to become pregnant receives fertility treatments, several of her egg cells are fertilized. The fertilized eggs that are not used to impregnate her are frozen and eventually discarded.

Stem cells are essential for research purposes because, as undifferentiated cells—that is, cells that have not yet assumed the specialized functions that distinguish more developed cells—they can adopt the characteristics of cellular material introduced into them and can reproduce rapidly. Animal experiments have revealed that neural or nerve stem cells not only replicate themselves but also, when placed in bone marrow, can produce several types of blood cells. These experiments provide hope that paraplegics may eventually have their spinal injuries repaired to the point of regaining the use of their paralyzed limbs and that genetic diseases may be contained or even cured.

Stem cell research offers hope that Parkinson's and Alzheimer's disease, diabetes, and heart trouble, as well as some cancers, will ultimately be controlled or wholly eliminated through the genetic engineering that such research makes possible. However, the question looms of whether it is ethically acceptable to use human embryos as sources of stem cells, inasmuch as the embryos that produce such cells have the potential to become human beings.

The stem cell controversy has become heated and fraught with political, religious, and moral implications. In 2001, President George W. Bush signed a bill permitting federal funds to be spent on stem cell research only on a limited basis. The bill restricts such research to the small number of stem cells currently available in a limited number of laboratories, but forbids any continuation of government-supported research once this supply has been exhausted.

569

Ironically, one of Bush's predecessors, President Ronald Reagan, opposed stem cell research during his administration, and such research might have provided a means of controlling the Alzheimer's disease that severely disabled him through the last years of his life after he left office. Very much aware of this fact, his wife, Nancy Reagan, publicly called for continuation of stem cell research in early 2004. Meanwhile, despite a lack of federal support, privately financed research organizations like the Howard Hughes Medical Institute continued crucial stem cell research.

THE HUMAN GENOME PROJECT

The systematic study of genetics, initiated in the mid-nineteenth century by Gregor Johann Mendel, an Augustinian monk, advanced greatly when, around 1869, a Swiss physician, Friedrich Miescher, discovered deoxyribonucleic acid, commonly called DNA, in pus from the wounds of German soldiers he was attending. Interest in the study of inherited traits increased steadily in the late nineteenth and early twentieth centuries.

A major breakthrough occurred in 1953 when Francis Crick and James Watson published a landmark article on the double-helix configuration of DNA in *Nature*, a well-respected scientific journal. Their work and that of Maurice Wilkins led to further DNA research for which this trio shared the Nobel Prize in Physiology or Medicine in 1962. In 1975, the first decoding of a gene from the DNA of a virus was accomplished. In 1977, the human gene that manufactures a blood protein was isolated.

In 1990, the Human Genome Project was launched with the expectation that it would, within fifteen years, map completely the human genome, the so-called blueprint of life. The project advanced with remarkable speed. By mid-2000, about 95 percent of the human genome had been sequenced using accelerated sequencing methods developed in the preceding decade and considered 99 percent accurate.

This research enabled scientists to uncover genetic problems in the cells of organisms and either correct them immediately or work toward discovering ways to culture antidotes or messenger cells that would, once introduced into the organism, eliminate defective cells. The implications of such work are enormous for the control and treatment of all sorts of genetic diseases as well as for such conditions as paraplegia resulting from accidents.

PRENATAL GENETIC MANIPULATION

Some of the ethical implications of advanced genetic research are daunting. Through assessment of the condition of cells in pregnant women, various genetic predispositions can be identified. Potential parents presently can learn of genetic abnormalities that are correctable in the unborn fetus. Prenatal microscopic surgery has already corrected serious genetic defects in fetuses.

Before the twenty-first century ends, it should be technologically possible for parents to select characteristics they consider desirable in their offspring. They may be able to choose sex, hair and eye color, height, and body structure as well as such characteristics as intelligence, disposition, athletic ability, and manual deftness. Although to do so would require expensive procedures not covered by health insurance, it would enable parents willing to bear the expenses to tailor to their own tastes the children they want.

One must inevitably address the ethical considerations this sort of genetic manipulation presents. For example, the creation of made-to-order children would be affordable only by the affluent. Class distinctions would surely arise from it. A genetically manufactured ruling class with which the rest of society would be unable to compete could result from such genetic meddling, spawning serious ethical dilemmas.

CLONING

Significant reservations accompany cloning, which genetic engineering has brought far beyond the simple cloning done by farmers taking slips of plants and rooting them to create genetically identical plants. Complex vertebrates, notably sheep and cows, have been cloned, and the technology exists to clone humans, although most industrialized countries prohibit human cloning.

Through genetic engineering, it should soon be possible to clone individual body parts—kidneys, livers, hearts, and other vital organs—that will be created from the donors' own DNA and, when sufficiently developed, be transplanted into donors without fear of rejection. Although few people have ethical reservations about this use of cloning, many view with alarm the possibility that some people might have identical whole selves cloned to provide spare parts when the organs of the original donors fail.

Selling DNA on eBay

In May, 2004, an unlikely story made world headlines when the giant online auction site eBay shut down an auction for violating its rule against selling human body parts. The "body part" in question was the DNA of California governor Arnold Schwarzenegger. What the seller was actually offering was a partly consumed cough drop that had been retrieved from the trash can into which the governor—according to the anonymous seller—had discarded it. The auction invited bids with the come-on, "Own a piece of DNA from the man himself." After the auction was closed, the seller relisted the item as "Arnold Schwarzenegger's 'Infamous' cough-drop, 'The Gov'mint,'" dropping all references to DNA. The new auction quickly drew bids exceeding ten thousand dollars.

Among the interesting ethical questions that auctioning the cough drop raised was what anyone buying the drop would do with it. The buyer would have no way of knowing whether the cough drop actually contained Schwarzenegger's DNA without having a known sample against which to compare it; however, anyone possessing such a sample should have no need for the cough drop.

The U.S. Supreme Court ruled that a cloned human cannot be patented, although in 1980, in its *Diamond v. Chakrabarty* ruling, it affirmed the right of an inventor to patent a genetically altered life-form. The Court has forbidden patenting cloned humans because such patents would, in the Court's judgment, enable one person to own another person, constituting slavery.

GENETIC PRIVACY

Genetic engineering can reveal potential physical and mental problems. Such revelations can result in finding ways to control and possibly overcome these problems, but a threat accompanies the use of information gained from this sort of genetic investigation. If genetic information is not considered sacrosanct and strenuously protected, it could conceivably be made available to insurance companies, courts of law, potential employers, and others who might penalize people for their genetic predispositions even though there is no guarantee that such predispositions would eventuate in illness or disability.

Although uncovering genetic information can be extremely valuable in meeting potential problems, the irresponsible dissemination of such information might destroy people's lives. What is sacrosanct today may not be considered sacrosanct tomorrow. A case in point concerns a disease such as Huntington's disease, a disabling and potentially fatal condition that is likely to afflict about half the offspring of parents suffering from it. At present, genetic testing can determine whether the children of people with Huntington's will develop the disease, whose onset typically occurs in middle age.

Many children of Huntington's disease victims decline to be tested. They resist knowing that they might eventually develop the disease. They are faced with an array of ethical dilemmas. Should they marry? Should they have children? Should they inform prospective mates or employers of their predisposition? How should they plan for their futures? How should they answer probing questions about their medical histories on insurance and employment applications?

INCREASED LIFE EXPECTANCY

Life expectancy in the United States increased dramatically during the twentieth century. In 1900, the average man could anticipate living 44.3 years, the average woman 48.3 years. By 1950, those figures had grown to 65.6 years for men and 71.1 years for women. The figures for 1997 increased to 73.6 and 79.2 respectively.

Reliable sources indicate that genetic engineering and other technological advances may, by the year 2100, extend the life expectancy in the United States and Canada to as much as two hundred years. The thought that people may reach or surpass such an age poses thorny ethical questions, chief among them the question of how the elderly will survive economically. Will they be forced to work well into their second centuries? At present, the average American works from the age of about twenty to seventy. Given a theoretical life expectancy of eighty, they thus work for about two-thirds of their lives. If such a proportion is applied to a life span of two hundred years, people beginning to work at twenty would have to work until they are at least 160 years old. Even then, their least productive period, some of it probably involving costly disability and illness, would extend to forty years, whereas for most people currently it is between fifteen and twenty years.

It might be expected that social upheavals would be loosed by such increases in life expectancy as younger members of society question the ethics of saddling them with the socioeconomic responsibilities that are bound to ensue from such an extended life spans. The national economy in the early twenty-first century is already under severe pressure from a Social Security Administration faced with overwhelming economic problems and a health care system threatened by insolvency within two decades. Caring for the aged is costly.

In the brave new world that genetic engineering and other technological advances make possible, a major concern is a population explosion that exceeds the ability of society to support it. Questions of right and wrong arise as people ponder whether it is ethical to burden upcoming generations with decades of supporting, directly or indirectly, the elderly while, with increasing life expectancy, the economic security of their own futures remain in doubt.

R. Baird Shuman

FURTHER READING

Boon, Kevin Alexander. *The Human Genome Project: What Does Decoding DNA Mean for Us?* Berkeley Heights, N.J.: Enslow Publishers, 2002.

Espejo, Roman, ed. *Biomedical Ethics: Opposing Views*. San Diego: Greenhaven Press, 2000.

Snedden, Robert. *DNA and Genetic Engineering*. Chicago: Heinemann Library, 2003.

Tagliaferro, Linda. *Genetic Engineering: Progress or Peril?* Minneapolis: Lerner Publications, 1997.

Toriello, James. *The Human Genome Project*. New York: Rosen Publishing, 2003.

VanDeVeer, Donald. *The Environmental Ethics and Policy Book: Philosophy, Ecology, Economics*. Belmont, Calif.: Thomson/Wadsworth, 2003.

Walker, Mark, and David McKay. *Understanding Genes: A Layperson's Guide to Genetic Engineering*. St. Leonards, New South Wales, Australia: Allen and Unwin, 2000.

SEE ALSO: Bioethics; Cloning; Genetic counseling; Genetic testing; Genetically modified foods; Human Genome Project; In vitro fertilization; Stem cell research; Sustainability of resources; UNESCO Declaration on the Human Genome and Human Rights.

Genetic testing

DEFINITION: Laboratory analyses of genetic materials designed to determine if subjects are carrying certain diseases, are likely to contract the diseases, or have other genetic disorders

TYPE OF ETHICS: Bioethics

SIGNIFICANCE: Genetic testing is a potentially powerful tool for the prevention, early detection, and improved treatment of diseases that have known genetic characteristics. However, such testing carries with it serious concerns about the ethical, social, legal, and psychological implications of how the information collected is used.

With the completion of the mapping work of the Human Genome Project, genetic information is rapidly moving into mainstream clinical medicine. Genetic testing is a powerful method of establishing diagnoses, and in some areas of medicine it is becoming a routine part of diagnostic testing.

GENETIC TESTING VS. GENETIC SCREENING

Genetic testing that is used to predict risks of disease and influence individual clinical care should be distinguished from population-based genetic screening. An example of genetic screening is state-mandated newborn screening programs that are aimed at detecting genetic diseases for which early diagnosis and treatment are available. Population-based genetic screening is ethically justifiable when the benefits of screening outweigh the potential harms. Any such screening tests should provide clear diagnoses, and accurate information on risks and effective treatments for the conditions should be available. Screening is justifiable when the prevalence of the disease is high in the population screened, and when screening is acceptable to the population screened.

Population-based genetic screening is becoming increasingly common for adult-onset disorders for which known and accepted treatments are available. Population-based genetic screening to reduce the incidence of a disease, however, may sacrifice the values of individuals for the sake of social goals. Individuals may feel pressure to undergo genetic screening tests they would not otherwise have chosen.

THE PRIVACY OF GENETIC INFORMATION

Maintaining the privacy of medical information is a concern that is not limited to genetic information. Privacy has instrumental value through the control that it affords individuals in providing protection from harm. For example, giving individuals absolute control over their own genetic information helps protect them from insurance or employment discrimination. Laws that guarantee the privacy of genetic information are instrumental in allowing every individual to control who has access to potentially damaging genetic information.

As the number of genetic tests clinically available has increased there has been greater public concern about genetic privacy. One of the ironies of advances in human genetic research is that the very people who stand to gain most from this information may not seek genetic testing out of fear of discrimination. In a national telephone survey, 63 percent of participants said they probably would not or definitely would not take genetic tests for diseases if health insurers or employers were to have access to the test results. Such concerns about the potential for insurance and employment discrimination are at the heart of a national effort to accord genetic information special privacy protections.

By mid-2003, forty-two states had enacted legislation designed to protect against genetic discrimination in health insurance, and thirty-two states had legislated protection against genetic discrimination in employment. However, the specific provisions of these laws varied greatly from state to state.

On the federal level, President Bill Clinton signed an executive order prohibiting discrimination in federal employment based on genetic information. In addition, a new set of federal privacy regulations, issued pursuant to the Health Insurance Portability and Accountability Act of 1996 (HIPAA), created a minimum set of general privacy protections that preempt state law. Although multiple bills have been introduced into Congress, no federal legislation has been passed specifically relating to genetic discrimination in individual insurance coverage or to genetic discrimination in the workplace.

Efforts to enact legislation to ensure the privacy of genetic information stem from concerns that health insurers might use such information to deny, limit, or cancel insurance policies. There are also reasons for concern that employers might use genetic information to discriminate against their workers or to screen applicants for jobs. The use of genetic testing in the workplace presents employers with challenging decisions related to promoting health in the workplace while avoiding the potential misuse of genetic information. However, concerns about genetic discrimination may actually be out of proportion to the actual incidence of documented instances of information misuse.

Types of Genetic Testing and Screening

Category	Subjects	Purpose
Carrier identification	Prospective parents	Identification of recessive gene disorders that may give future offspring such diseases as cystic fibrosis, Tay-Sachs disease, or sickle-cell anemia
Prenatal diagnosis	Fetuses	Determination of possibility of babies being born with such disorders as Down syndrome
Newborn screening	Newborn babies	Determination of whether newborns carry such treatable conditions as phenylketonuria and congenital hypothyroidism
Late-onset disorders	Adults	Determination of whether subjects have such adult diseases as cancer, heart disease, and Huntington's disease

DISCLOSURE OF FAMILIAL GENETIC INFORMATION

Genetic test results of individuals have implications for other blood relatives. This feature of genetic information raises difficult ethical questions about the obligation of family members to share their genetic information with relatives, who may share the same genetic disorders, and the obligations of physicians to disclose information about disease risks with the relatives of patients who refuse to share the information themselves.

Studies of patients' attitudes toward disclosure of genetic information to at-risk family have documented varied attitudes toward disclosure of genetic information within families. Genetic information carries the potential for economic, psychological, and relational harm. For example, individuals who carry genetic alterations may see themselves as defective and feel guilty about the possibility of their transmitting genetic alterations to their offspring. There is an underlying fear that society will view those with genetic alterations as defective. Some perceive the identification of individuals with altered genes as the first step toward eugenics, or attempts to limit procreative freedom based on genotype.

Genetic testing should always be accompanied by the subjects' written informed consent to prevent misunderstanding and to minimize anxiety. The ethical, legal, social, and psychological implications of genetic testing are so complex that genetic counselors should be involved before, during, and after patients agree to undergo testing. Genetic counseling is a process of evaluating family histories to identify and interpret the risks of inherited disorders.

The mere fact that genetic tests are available does not mean that they should necessarily be ordered. Decisions to conduct tests should consider not only the possible benefits but also the potential social and psychological risks. Genetic counselors can be invaluable in helping individuals decide which tests are appropriate, deciphering complex test results, and helping individuals understand and reach decisions about what to do with the results of their tests.

PRE-IMPLANTATION AND PREDISPOSITION GENETIC TESTING

Pre-implantation genetic diagnosis (PGD) has raised many ethical concerns. It is an alternative to prenatal diagnosis for individuals undergoing in vitro fertilization. PGD allows scientists to screen embryos for chromosome abnormalities and select unaffected embryos for implantation with the goal of reducing the transmission of genetic diseases. The process has been used for sex-linked disease and human leukocyte antigen matching. The ethical boundaries of employing this procedure are unresolved. It raises a variety of questions. For example, should parents be allowed to use the process to select the sexes of their offspring when no evidence of genetic diseases is present? Who should decide how this technology should be used?

Many of the earliest forms of genetic tests were designed to detect or confirm rare genetic diseases. Information obtained from single-gene disorders with high penetrance was relatively easy to interpret. However, later advances in genetics led to the discovery of gene alterations that contribute to common, complex diseases that develop later in life. These so-called predisposition tests determine the probabilities of healthy individuals developing the diseases. When unaffected family members are found to have genetic alterations that increase their risks of developing diseases, they may take measures to reduce their risk of developing the diseases. Such situations may also affect reproductive decisions and result in targeted medical diagnostics and therapeutics.

Appropriate uses of predisposition testing have been challenged. Predisposition genetic tests can identify alterations within genes, but they cannot always predict how severely the altered genes will affect the people who carry them. For example, finding an alteration on chromosome number 7 does not necessarily predict whether a child will have serious lung problems or milder respiratory symptoms.

Many ethical questions arise from predisposition testing. For example, should children undergo genetic testing for adult-onset disorders? Should predisposition testing be allowed prior to adoption decisions? Generally speaking the best interests of the children should guide decisions about genetic testing. When no immediate benefit to a child is evident, inessential testing should be avoided.

Genetic testing carries the promise of disease prevention, risk modification, and directed therapy. These benefits, however, are accompanied by the potential for discrimination and stigmatization. Informed consent and genetic counseling are essential to ensuring that genetic testing is appropriate and that the risks to individuals and social groups are minimized. The greatest benefits of the Human Genome Project are yet to be realized, and as new genetic tests emerge new questions will certainly arise.

Lisa Soleymani Lehmann

FURTHER READING

Andrews L. B., et al., eds. *Social, Legal and Ethical Implications of Genetic Testing: Assessing Genetic Risks.* Washington, D.C.: National Academy Press; 1994.

Kevles, Daniel J. *In the Name of Eugenics: Genetics and the Uses of Human Heredity.* Cambridge, Mass.: Harvard University Press, 1995.

Kristol, William, and Eric Cohen, eds. *The Future Is Now: America Confronts the New Genetics.* Lanham, Md.: Rowman and Littlefield, 2002.

Krumm, J. "Genetic Discrimination: Why Congress Must Ban Genetic Testing in the Workplace." *Journal of Legal Medicine* 23, no. 4 (2002): 491-521.

Lehmann, L. S., et al. "Disclosure of Familial Genetic Information: Perceptions of the Duty to Inform." *American Journal of Medicine* 109, no. 9 (2000): 705-711.

Otlowski, Margaret F., Sandra D. Taylor, and Kristine K. Barlow-Stewart. "Genetic Discrimination: Too Few Data." *European Journal of Human Genetics* 11 (2002): 1-2.

SEE ALSO: Bioethics; Biotechnology; Diagnosis; Eugenics; Genetic counseling; Genetic engineering; Human Genome Project; Intelligence testing; Surrogate motherhood.

Genetically modified foods

DEFINITION: Foods artificially created by manipulating living organisms using methods involving the transfer of genetic information (DNA) from one source to another

DATE: Began in the late twentieth century

TYPE OF ETHICS: Bioethics

SIGNIFICANCE: The emergence of genetically modified foods at the end of the twentieth century led to wide public debate regarding food safety and quality, consumer rights, environmental impact, the value of small-scale farming, and the potential need to regulate certain technological applications.

Human beings have been manipulating living organisms for food for thousands of years. Early examples were wine and bread production and the domestication of the ancestor to the modern corn plant. As scientists learned more about plant and animal biology, selective breeding practices became more efficient. Later, methods developed to alter DNA led to new traits important for commercial growing practices or that enhanced the quality of the food. With the development of genetic engineering, new ways to modify plant and animal food sources became possible. In 1990, the U.S. federal Food and Drug Administration gave approval for the first food ingredient produced through recombinant DNA technology: chymosin or rennet, which is used in the production of cheese and other dairy products. Shortly afterward, Calgene, Inc. introduced the Flavr Savr tomato—the first genetically modified whole food approved for market.

By the early years of the twenty-first century, genetically modified (GM) foods had been altered for a variety of reasons including improving plant resistance to pests, disease, and such environmental stresses such as drought and frost. Other goals of genetically modifying foods have been to improve taste, quality, or nutritional value; to improve ability to transport or store the product; and to use plants to produce novel products for industry, medicine, and consumer use.

Animals used as food sources have also been modified—most commonly by treating them with hormones produced through genetic engineering to increase their milk production or their muscle mass. Hormone-treated dairy cows and the appearance of herbicide-resistant crops were particularly important in leading to public outcry against genetically modified foods. As a result, a new field of food and agriculture ethics emerged in which ethical principles related to general welfare, justice, and people's rights are applied. Environmental ethics and questions regarding what is considered "natural" enter into the assessment of this technology.

A UTILITARIAN APPROACH

One way to assess any new technology is to consider its potential benefits and harms. This approach,

Symbolic of a growing world backlash against the uncertain hazards of genetic engineering, Greenpeace activists staged a protest against genetically altered foods in the capital of Brazil in January, 2004. Their Portuguese-language banner reads, "Seven of ten Brazilians do not want genetically modified foods." (AP/Wide World Photos)

however, can lead to major dilemmas when considering genetically modified foods. Food is essential for survival of all animals, and thus has value. The Food and Agricultural Organization (FAO) of the United Nations has pointed out that access to safe, sufficient, and nutritious food is a universal right that impacts other values of enhanced well-being and human health. Proponents of genetically modified foods argue that they can contribute to sustainable agricultural systems and food of high nutritional quality—both of which are critical to support the expanding world population.

Opponents of genetically modified foods argue that genetic manipulation damages food quality by decreasing its nutritional value and increasing risk for the presence of dangerous chemicals in food that might cause allergic reactions or even cancer. Although regulatory agencies and scientists have deemed these foods safe, insufficient scientific data exist to conclusively address public concerns.

Genetically modified foods indirectly impact other aspects of human well-being including quality of life (the aesthetic value of rural settings and the natural environment) and satisfactory income and working conditions. Concerns about genetically modified food technology range from fears and uncertainties about the environmental and ecological impact of genetically engineered crops to the demise of small-scale farmers or possible disrespect for local customs and traditions. Given the ever-decreasing space available to grow food and the long history of environmental disturbances resulting from other agricultural practices, ethical analyses should compare the relative benefits and risks of both genetic modification technology and traditional practices.

ISSUES OF JUSTICE AND FAIRNESS

The world human population doubled between 1960 and 2000 and is expected to increase by an additional 50 percent by 2050. This increase, coupled with the growing gap between wealthy and less developed nations, forces consideration of new technologies and policies for food production and distribution. The value of enhanced well-being for all is intimately linked to the need for practical rural infrastructure and sustainable agriculture on a global basis.

Proponents of genetically modified foods argue that the technology may be the only way to address growing global food shortages and malnutrition. Opponents argue that other sound practices should be considered, that potentially unsafe food is being touted as a solution to world hunger, and that wealthy nations are forcing developing countries into abiding by patent rules and trade agreements to get the food supplies they need.

Certain business practices associated with genetically modified food production have been controversial. Widely differing public views on genetically modified foods in Europe versus the United States have led to international debates on fair trade laws and practices. Other concerns arise from patenting issues, the costs of genetically modified seed, and industry-imposed limitations on how farmers can use these products.

Interestingly, patent and intellectual property legal complications might actually lead to the underdevelopment and underutilization of genetically modified foods that could be applied for the greater public good. An example of this is "golden rice," a form of rice that was genetically modified to contain extra vitamin A in order to address nutritional deficiencies among Asian societies. The public views the intentions of businesses associated with genetically modified foods with skepticism, since many believe that corporate profit is valued more than either the condition of humankind or the long-term health and sustainability of the global environment.

Environmental ethicists question what is fair to the natural world. Will the technology that produces genetically modified organisms, including those used as food, negatively impact biodiversity—perhaps through the production of genetic pollution, "superweeds," or new pathogens—or will the technology actually enable scientists to help preserve biological diversity or perhaps even restore populations of en-

dangered or extinct species? During the first years of the twenty-first century, genetically modified food technology was still too new to know whether there were unforeseen risks or to assess its impact on ecosystem balance and natural selection.

OTHER ISSUES

Another controversial issue surrounding genetically modified foods is whether the products should be labeled as such. Regulatory agencies in the United States have ruled that because such foods are essentially the same as natural and traditionally grown foods, they do not require special labeling. Companies producing genetically modified foods argue that given misperceptions and a lack of public understanding of the technology, such labeling would unfairly skew market competition. Consumer rights advocates argue the importance of the public's right to know and the need for freedom of informed choice in a democratic society.

As with the broader issue of genetically modified organisms, genetically modified food technology leads to concerns that science may have gone too far in intervening with nature. An underlying fear is that if humans continue to reduce living organisms to the status of manufactured goods, the standards set for genetically manipulating any organism, including humans, will also be relaxed. Traditional ethical principles and commonly used risk-benefit analyses do not readily apply to situations in which genetically modified crops begin to impact biodiversity, irreversibly change the concept of natural selection, or alter human activities involving basic needs and long-valued human interactions with the land.

Diane White Husic

FURTHER READING

Doyle, Jack. *Altered Harvest: Agriculture, Genetics, and the Fate of the World's Food Supply.* New York: Penguin Books, 1986.

Lambrecht, Bill. *Dinner at the New Gene Cafe: How Genetic Engineering Is Changing What We Eat, How We Live, and the Global Politics of Food.* New York: St. Martin's Press, 2001.

Pinstrup-Anderson, Per, and Ebbe Schioler. *Seeds of Contention: World Hunger and the Global Controversy Over Genetically Modified Crops.* Baltimore: International Food Policy Research Institute, 2001.

Pringle, Peter. *Food, Inc.: Mendel to Monsanto—The Promises and Perils of the Biotech Harvest.* New York: Simon & Schuster, 2003.

Rissler, Jane, and Margaret Mellon. *The Ecological Risks of Engineered Crops.* Boston: MIT Press, 1996.

SEE ALSO: Agribusiness; Bioethics; Biotechnology; Famine; Genetic engineering; Hunger.

Geneva conventions

THE EVENTS: Series of international meetings that codified the rules of warfare

DATES: 1863-1977

TYPE OF ETHICS: Modern history

SIGNIFICANCE: The Geneva conventions encourage the humanitarian treatment of civilians and enemy combatants. They arise in part from the idealist moral belief that human worth and dignity transcend nationalist concerns even in wartime, and in part from each nation's practical desire to protect its own citizens by joining a collective agreement which will protect all people.

The background for the Geneva conventions can be found in European diplomatic and military development since the sixteenth century. The breakup of the medieval Christian outlook during the Reformation era and the devastating religious and dynastic wars that resulted led to the growth of international law. During the eighteenth century Enlightenment, several philosophers applied these rules with some success to the conduct of war.

The French Revolution and the wars of national liberation that resulted broke the comparative calm of the Age of Reason and introduced a new note of savagery into armed conflict. Writing in the wake of the revolutionary age, Carl von Clausewitz advocated the concept of total war—that is, the necessity to push conflict to the utmost bounds of violence in order to crush the enemy. These teachings were widely accepted in the Western world, and the nineteenth century Industrial Revolution made it possible to produce the various weapon systems that could carry out Clausewitz's dictum.

The new attitude of "efficiency" and ferocity in warfare led to a strong humanitarian reaction. During the Crimean War, Florence Nightingale and her colleagues worked with the wounded and drew public attention to the scandalously inadequate arrangements made for them by the armies. A few years later a Genevan businessman, Jean Henri Dunant, was traveling in north Italy and happened upon the battlefield at Solferino (1859). Encouraged by the example of hospital work in the Crimea and moved by the tragic plight of the wounded and dying, he organized groups to help the unfortunate soldiers. For Dunant, this was such a traumatic experience that he dedicated his life to helping soldiers, a category of poor who seemed to be neglected by their employers. In 1862, he published a moving account of his reminiscences of the Italian experience which, along with his personal contacts, aroused the sympathy of the rulers of Europe and led to the Geneva Conference of 1863.

ACCOMPLISHMENTS

The meeting had two results; a decision to create Red Cross societies and a decision to provide a set of rules for the humane treatment of those who were incapacitated. The second of these decisions led to the Geneva Convention of 1864. Attended by representatives from sixteen states, it did not give official recognition to the Red Cross societies as such but did lay down a series of rules that were to be followed in time of war. These rules provided for the care of sick and wounded soldiers, the neutrality of the medical corps, the humane treatment of prisoners, and the display of a distinctive emblem, such as the Red Cross, by persons and places involved in medical work. The conventions were signed by twelve states and were open to acceptance by others whenever they wished. By the early twentieth century, they were ratified by forty-eight nations, including even the non-Western powers of China, Japan, Siam, and the Ottoman Empire.

The International Red Cross movement flourished more or less under the direction of the entirely Swiss leadership of an international committee yet was made up of a series of nationally controlled societies. The articles of 1864 were extended in a series of meetings held at The Hague in 1899 and 1907 and at Geneva in 1906, 1929, 1949, and 1977.

The Hague meeting of 1899, called at the suggestion of Czar Nicholas II of Russia, was attended by

Geneva and Hague Conventions

Summary of the treaties concluded in Geneva, Switzerland, and at The Hague, Netherlands, for the purpose of ameliorating the effects of war on soldiers and civilians

Year	Convention	Significant provisions
1864	Convention for the Amelioration of the Wounded in Time of War	Initiated by Henri Dunant. Provided for (1) immunity from capture and destruction of all establishments for treating wounded and sick soldiers and their personnel; (2) impartial reception and treatment of all combatants; (3) protection of civilians rendering aid to the wounded; (4) recognition of the Red Cross symbol to identify persons and equipment covered by the agreement.
1899	First Hague Conference	Convened at the invitation of Count Mikhail Nikolayevich Muravyov, minister of foreign affairs of Czar Nicholas II of Russia. Twenty-six nations were represented. The conference defined the conditions of a state of belligerency and other customs relating to war on land and sea. Declarations prohibited: (1) the use of asphyxiating gases; (2) the use of expanding bullets (dumdums); (3) discharging of projectiles or explosives from balloons. Also adopted the Convention for the Pacific Settlement of International Disputes, which created the Permanent Court of Arbitration.
1906	Second Geneva Convention	Amended and extended the provisions of the first convention.
1907	Second Hague Conference	Proposed by U.S. president Theodore Roosevelt, convened by Czar Nicholas II. Forty-four nations attended. Conventions adopted re-employment of force for recovery of contract debts; rights and duties of neutral powers and persons in war on land and sea; laying of automatic submarine contact mines; status of enemy merchant ships; bombardment by naval forces in wartime; establishment of an international prize court. Renewed declaration prohibiting discharge of projectiles from balloons. Did not reaffirm declarations prohibiting asphyxiating gas and expanding bullets.
1929	Third Geneva Convention	Amended and extended the provisions of the first two conventions. Introduced the convention relating to the treatment of prisoners of war. Provisions included: Belligerents must (1) treat prisoners humanely; (2) supply information about them; (3) permit visits to prison camps by representatives of neutral states.
1949	Fourth Geneva Convention	More than 150 nations party to this agreement. Following the horrors of World War II, this was the most complete of the treaties and included these provisions: (1) provision for care of the wounded and sick in land warfare; (2) rules for the care of those injured or shipwrecked at sea; (3) laws guaranteeing the just treatment of prisoners of war; (4) provisions protecting citizens of occupied territories by condemning such practices as deportation, hostage taking, torture, collective reprisals, wanton destruction of property, and discrimination based on race, religion or nationality.
1977	Fifth Geneva Convention	Only slightly more than half of the nations who signed the Fourth Convention signed the 1977 protocols. Supplemented the provisions of the previous conventions with two additional protocols that extended international law protections to wars of liberation and civil wars.

delegates from twenty-six nations. The Geneva rules commanded such respect that there was a strong desire among the major powers to extend them to naval conflict and to limit the use of new, more horrible weapons. At The Hague conference, conditions regulating a state of war were defined and the use of asphyxiating gases, expanding bullets (dumdums), and aerial bombardment (dropping projectiles from balloons) was forbidden. The conference also established a permanent court of arbitration to encourage the peaceful settlement of disputes between nations.

The second Geneva Conference (1906) revised the decisions of the first meeting, based upon the war experiences of the intervening years. It provided for the policing of battlefields, the identification of the dead, the protection of the name and sign of the Red Cross, and the dissemination and enforcement of the Convention's decisions through military penal codes.

A second meeting (1907) was suggested by President Theodore Roosevelt and called by the czar. Attended by delegates from forty-four nations, it passed a series of acts that provided for the enforcement of contracts, the recognition of rights of neutrality, the prohibition of submarine contact mines, the limitation of bombardment by naval forces, and restriction on aerial warfare. Ominously, when one looks back on the meeting after the experience of World War I, it did not renew the 1899 prohibitions against the use of gas or dumdum bullets. The third Geneva Convention's (1929) most original contributions concerned prisoners of war. They were to be dealt with in a humane manner, information about them was to be supplied to their governments, and their treatment was to be monitored by neutral observers.

Probably the most important of the Geneva meetings was held in 1949 in response to the horror of World War II. It drew up the most complete of the Geneva Conventions, including provision for care of the wounded and sick in land warfare; rules for the care of those who were injured or shipwrecked at sea; laws guaranteeing the just treatment of prisoners of war; and provisions that protected citizens of occupied territories by condemning such practices as deportation, the taking of hostages, torture, collective reprisals, wanton destruction of property, and discrimination based on race, religion, or nationality.

In 1977, another conference supplemented these provisions with two additional protocols that extended the protection of international law to wars of liberation and civil wars. More than 150 nations have signed the 1949 conventions, but far fewer have agreed to the 1977 protocols.

Robert G. Clouse

FURTHER READING

Best, Geoffrey. *Humanity in Warfare.* New York: Columbia University Press, 1980.

Bordwell, Percy. *The Law of War Between Belligerents: A History and a Commentary.* Chicago: Callaghan, 1908.

Davis, Calvin D. *The United States and the Second Hague Peace Conference.* Durham, N.C.: Duke University Press, 1976.

Forsythe, David P. *Humanitarian Politics: The International Committee of the Red Cross.* Baltimore: Johns Hopkins University Press, 1977.

Kalshoven, Frits, and Liesbeth Zegveld. *Constraints on the Waging of War: An Introduction to International Humanitarian Law.* 3d ed. Geneva: International Committee of the Red Cross, 2001.

Roberts, Adam, and Guelff Richard, eds. *Documents on the Laws of War.* New York: Oxford University Press, 1982.

SEE ALSO: Chemical warfare; International Criminal Court; International law; International Red Cross; League of Nations; Military ethics; Scorched-earth policies; United Nations Convention on the Prevention and Punishment of the Crime of Genocide; War; War crimes trials.

Genocide, cultural

DEFINITION: Deliberate and systematic destruction of a particular culture

TYPE OF ETHICS: Race and ethnicity

SIGNIFICANCE: Cultural genocide is a violation of egalitarian moral principles such as inalienable human rights and the right to self-determination. It has been justified by recourse to other moral principles, such as the responsibility of a sovereign nation to watch over or educate members of ethnic subcultures or colonial subjects.

Cultural genocide is the deliberate and systematic destruction of a culture. Absent harm, it is not ethical to destroy the culture of another group of human beings or change it without their consent. Each culture should be judged by its own standards of excellence and morality, unless its cultural practices threaten to harm others physically or mentally.

A dramatic example of cultural genocide is the Canadian government's attempts to outlaw many indigenous customs of the Kwakiutl Indians of the Northwest Coast of Canada in an effort to convert them into imitations of Europeans. The Kwakiutl were renowned for a unique custom that they called the potlatch. Kwakiutl chiefs competed with one another for status and power through this custom. It involved accumulating vast wealth in the form of artistic items known as "coppers," blankets, and food. After accumulating a fortune, a chief would invite his rival and the rival's followers to a feast. During this feast, the host would wine and dine all of his guests lavishly. Dancers would entertain them. At a prearranged time, the host would conspicuously destroy the valuable coppers and other treasures to demonstrate that he could afford to do so. He would challenge his guest to top this feat or accept inferior status. Upon leaving the feast, guests were given many blankets and foodstuffs to take home with them. The Canadian government viewed this practice as a wanton and savage destruction of valuable property and a waste of labor, so they outlawed the potlatch.

Anthropologists have argued that, in addition to serving the overt function of leveling individuals, the potlatch served a covert or hidden function by redistributing wealth from areas that had accumulated a surplus to areas that had experienced shortages during bad years. The destruction of this and other pivotal institutions caused the Kwakiutl culture to collapse, leaving in its wake a vacuum that was soon filled by alcoholism, dysfunctional families, and other social problems.

Another example of cultural genocide comes from Africa. In 1884, at the Berlin Conference, European powers unilaterally carved up the African continent into territories that they claimed for themselves. Africans were not invited to this meeting. These European powers pledged to support the "civilizing" of Africans by Christian missionaries, which was "calculated to educate the natives and to teach them to understand and appreciate the benefits of civilization."

The missionaries immediately declared traditional religions "devil worship." They collected all indigenous statues, relics, and artifacts and destroyed them. They fought to outlaw clitoridectomy, polygyny, and other native customs that they found "repugnant." These acts led to a clash of cultures and to an identity crisis for many Africans.

The classic example of cultural genocide in North America grew out of slavery. Plantation owners feared that allowing African slaves to speak their own languages, use African names to identify themselves, or practice African culture would encourage slave revolts. Consequently, every effort was made to stamp out African culture in the United States. The people survived, but much of their culture was destroyed. Today, African Americans are culturally more like other Americans than they are like Africans, despite strong physical similarities and a common ancestry.

The assumption that one's own culture is better for others than theirs is constitutes the ultimate cultural arrogance. It assumes that one's own culture is superior and that one has the right to impose one's values on others. This imposition is unfair and unethical. Cultures, like individuals, have a right to life unless their customs threaten the lives of others, as in the case of head-hunting and cannibalism.

Dallas L. Browne

SEE ALSO: Bigotry; Ethnic cleansing; Genocide and democide; Genocide, frustration-aggression theory of; Native American genocide; Racial prejudice; Racism.

Genocide, frustration-aggression theory of

DEFINITION: Theory of Neal Miller and John Dollard that genocidal behavior is the result of hostility and frustration caused by the blockage or interruption of goal-directed behavior

DATE: Formulated during the late 1930's

TYPE OF ETHICS: Theory of ethics

SIGNIFICANCE: The frustration-aggression theory of genocide attempts to adduce a mechanistic psychological cause which would explain the most horrific forms of collective behavior.

John Dollard and Neal Miller's frustration-aggression theory asserts that the blockage or interruption of goal-directed behavior can cause frustration and hostile feelings. Often, these cannot be directed at the source of the frustration, which may be either unknown or too powerful to confront. Consequently, a person may displace this hostility onto an unrelated scapegoat.

After World War I, the Allied nations imposed harsh economic conditions upon Germany for "causing" the war. As a result, Germans experienced severe hardships. Defeated and too weak to lash out at the Allied powers, Germany turned against its Jewish population. According to the frustration-aggression theory, between 1920 and 1945 Germans scapegoated the Jewish population and persecuted them instead of hitting back at Britain and France, who were causing their suffering. The Jews were too weak to fight back. When a German bought a loaf of bread, he paid a Jewish merchant, not a French capitalist, so the Jewish merchant became the target for his anger.

Adolf Hitler took advantage of this popular anti-Jewish resentment, which was widespread in Poland, Russia, France, and England as well as in Germany and Austria, to help him rise to power. Hitler accused the German Jews of subversion and of making deliberate attempts to sabotage the German people in order to further selfish Jewish economic interests. Nazi propaganda films compared Jews to rats and suggested that the only true means of ridding Germany of either pest was extermination.

The Nazi Party wanted to deport all German Jews to Madagascar, but this plan proved to be impractical because Allied submarines were sinking many German ships, and the Vichy regime in France, which controlled Madagascar, did not relish the idea. Therefore, soon after the German conquest of Poland in 1939, the Nazis ordered the extermination of all known Jews. More than six million Jews were exterminated between 1939 and 1945. This horrific act did not, however, relieve the German sense of frustration. Instead, it created a false consciousness, because Britain, France, and a weak economy—not the Jews—were the real sources of Germany's problems.

The Jews had been treated as scapegoats for centuries throughout Europe and elsewhere before Hitler and the Nazi Party attempted to exterminate them. They were herded into segregated ghettos and became the target of frequent pogroms in Russia and elsewhere. Because the frustration-aggression theory of genocide fails to account for this long history of abuse prior to the rise of Hitler and the Nazi Party, the theory has limited explanatory value.

SCAPEGOATING

Despite the fact that scapegoating is based on misconceptions, aggression aimed at a scapegoat has been alleged to have a cathartic effect because it temporarily relieves frustrations. Regrettably, this temporary effect only reinforces negative behavior. In theory, the release of such tension onto a third party should promote mental health. Thus, games such as football have been thought to be cathartic and actually to help to reduce the probability of war. In fact, however, such games may increase the likelihood of aggression by reinforcing antisocial violent behavior. Once set in motion, a vicious self-perpetuating cycle can be created. A wiser course of action is to teach people to control negative thoughts and behavior rather than vent them.

The frustration-aggression model and the accompanying scapegoating and oppression of another group produce behavior that is ethically deplorable. Members of the persecuted group receive prejudicial treatment and may become targets of genocide. Flawed and rigid thinking encourages people to adopt this model of behavior. Insecurity feeds it. Once such attitudes are formed, they are difficult to change unless society can force prolonged contact with members of the other group on a frequent basis, under conditions in which neither group is superior to the other and competition is minimal. Under such conditions, people find that it is easier to abandon prejudices and to adopt healthier attitudes that view others as equals deserving of whatever rewards their talents earn them. Ethically, society has a social and moral obligation to create the sustained contact and minimal competition that will be required to reduce or stamp out the prejudice, bigotry, stereotyping, racism, and discrimination that breed the human tragedy of genocide.

Dallas L. Browne

SEE ALSO: Aggression; Anti-Semitism; Apartheid; Behaviorism; Bigotry; Genocide and democide; Genocide, cultural; Hate; Hate crime and hate speech; Holocaust; Racial prejudice.